Sport and the Law

SPORT AND THE LAW
SECOND EDITION

LAURA DONNELLAN

CLARUS PRESS

Published by
Clarus Press Ltd,
Griffith Campus,
South Circular Road,
Dublin 8.
www.claruspress.ie

Typeset by
Gough Typesetting Services
Dublin

Printed by
CPI Anthony Rowe,
Wiltshire

ISBN
978-1-911611-19-6

A catalogue record for this book is available from the British Library

In memory of my father,
Michael Donnellan (1936-2022)

FOREWORD

It is my great pleasure to write the foreword for the 2nd edition of Dr Laura Donnellan's seminal Irish book *Sport and the Law*. The publication of this comprehensive and scholarly, yet eminently readable, book is particularly timely in an Irish context. It will no doubt deservedly attract a large audience of academic and practising lawyers, not only in the fast growing area of sports law but also in all areas of the law which intersect with sport, including the criminal law, the law of torts, the law of contract, employment law and commercial and intellectual property law. Much of this excellent book will also be essential reading for those involved in sporting bodies and in the governance of sport.

The book contains chapters which discuss highly topical issues including drugs in sport (very much in the news at the time of writing this foreword in the context of the case brought by the International Tennis Integrity Agency (ITIA) against men's tennis world number one, Jannik Sinner (a case in which a number of top Irish lawyers are involved) and hyperandrogenism (where the leading case of the South African athlete, Caster Semenya is discussed in detail) and the approaches taken by different international sporting bodies to this issue and that of gender testing and the involvement of transgender athletes. These highly topical and complex issues are addressed by Dr Donnellan in a characteristically clear and considered manner and should be of great interest to all those interested in sport and the law.

There is also a very relevant chapter on Alternative Dispute Resolution (ADR) which outlines the advantages and disadvantages of ADR in the context of sports disputes and explains the role of the Court of Arbitration for Sport (CAS) (a tribunal on which a number of leading Irish lawyers sit and before which several others regularly appear). The discussion on CAS is particularly timely in light of the rules recently adopted by UEFA (UEFA Authorisation Rules governing International Club Competitions – Edition 2024) which provide for an option to select Dublin as the seat of the arbitration in the case of a dispute related to the new rules (which govern UEFA's international club competitions) instead of Lausanne and, in the event of that choice being made, provide that any challenge to an award made by the CAS in respect of such dispute would be made to the Irish Courts. Such a challenge would, under the Arbitration Act 2010, have to be made to the President of the High Court or to a judge designated by the

President to deal with such cases. These new UEFA rules may well provide significant opportunities for those interested in this area of work in Ireland.

The book contains an important chapter on European Union law and sport. That chapter was completed before the landmark judgment delivered by the Court of Justice of the European Union (CJEU) on 4th October 2024, involving the former Chelsea and Real Madrid player, Lassana Diarra, in which the CJEU held that certain provisions of FIFA's Regulations on the Status and Transfer of Players were in breach of EU law, being those relating to the free movement of workers (Article 45 TFEU) and competition (Article 101 TFEU). This important judgment will, no doubt, feature in the next edition of Dr Donnellan's book which, having regard to the rapidly evolving changes taking place the area of sports law and sport and the law, will be no doubt be required sooner rather than later.

I cannot conclude this foreword without referring to perhaps one of the best written judgments of the Irish courts which discusses sport and the law, that of O'Donnell J in *O'Connell v The Turf Club* [2015] IESC 57. Although the case involved a judicial review of a decision of the Turf Club, O'Donnell J's judgment contains a wonderful description of the importance of sport and of the need for sport to have rules, while also considering the significant commercial aspects of sport. O'Donnell J referred to the 'paradox of modern sport that occupies so much of our time and attention, and generates so much business [as being] that at the heart of even the biggest sporting enterprise is a game' (para 7). He continued:

> All the modern sports are related to games played from time immemorial, whether of throwing or kicking a ball of different dimensions, striking it with a stick, running the fastest, or in this case, attempting to see who can ensure that an animal runs the fastest. It is the essence however of any game that it requires some rules. Otherwise it will not be possible to measure sporting excellence or demonstrate sporting skill. It is also the case that many of those rules are somewhat arbitrary, but sanctified by tradition. Why a team of 11, 13, 15 (or as was once the case in Gaelic sports, 17) players? Why a game of 70, 80 or 90 minutes? Why should some games end at the expiry of the time and others only when the ball goes dead? Why is a pass forward by player in rugby an occasion for loss of possession and accompanying groans, but one of the glories of American football? Why, as some have had reason to ruefully observe, is a second serve

> permitted in tennis but not in golf? There is no good answer to any of these questions. They are so because they are so. These rules are peculiarly inapt for judicial consideration, as Carroll J. and Hogan J., among others, have had occasion to observe. There must be rules for the organisation of any game, and accordingly there must a rule-making, and rule-enforcing, body. To some extent at least, the idiosyncrasies of the rules become part of the tradition valued by the game's participants and spectators. (para 8)

With reference to traditions in sport, O'Donnell J said:

> 'Traditions are important in general because they preserve what is valued beyond any single generation, and can be of particular importance in the field of sport. Games may be intrinsically trivial activities–the placing of a ball by action of foot or head across the line between two posts and under a third–but they capture the imagination not only because they showcase the athleticism of the human body and of animals but also because they distil so much of the human condition: courage; fortitude and grace under pressure; cowardice; mean-spiritedness and cynicism; the emergence of youthful talent; the slow decline of age resisted by determination; skill and experience;, the value of discipline; the excitement of unpredictable flamboyance; the collective strength of a team and the joy of irrepressible individualism; the fine line between triumph and tragedy; and the significant role of luck. Sport involves measurement, not just against the best of contemporary standards, but also against the inspirational stories of the past. It unquestionably matters when sportsman or woman walk for the first time on the Centre Court in Wimbledon, or onto the field of play at Croke Park or Semple stadium, approaches the first tee in a major championship or enter the parade ring at the Curragh, Cheltenham or Epsom Downs. These are the fields of dreams and memories. They follow in the footsteps of heroes, tragic victims and occasional villains.'

We should, I think, bear in mind these words when we delve into the substantive content of Dr Donnellan's brilliant book. I urge everyone interested in sport and in the law to read this book.

16 October 2024
Mr Justice David Barniville
President of the High Court

PREFACE

Sport and the Law, Second Edition has been fully revised, expanded and updated since its first publication in 2010. The book explores the intersection between sport and the law by applying established branches of law, including tort law, contract law, human rights law, criminal law and European Union law, to sport. In the 14 years since the First Edition, the sports ecosystem has changed immensely. While the book draws on the experiences of other jurisdictions, Ireland's position in the world of sporting disputes has recently been bolstered by the decision of the Union des Associations Européennes de Football (UEFA) to designate Dublin as an alternative seat of arbitration to Court of Arbitration for Sport (CAS) hearings in matters relating to UEFA's Authorisation Rules. Arbitration in Ireland is governed by the Arbitration Act 2010 as amended by the Courts and Civil Law (Miscellaneous Provisions) Act 2023 which by virtue of s 124 inserted s 5A into the 2010 Act. Section 5A permits, subject to prescribed criteria, third-party litigation funding in dispute resolution disputes. UEFA did not elaborate on why Ireland was chosen, however, as a member state of the European Union (EU) and an English-speaking common law jurisdiction with an established reputation for international arbitration, it means that arbitral awards involving UEFA's Authorisation Rules can be appealed in the Irish courts and a preliminary reference under Article 267 of the Treaty on the Functioning of the European Union (TFEU) can be made to the Court of Justice of the European Union (CJEU). The CJEU considered the compatibility with EU law of the authorisation rules of the International Skiing Union (ISU, as discussed in Chapter 13) where it questioned the severity and disproportionality of sanctions imposed on the skiers under the governing body's eligibility rules in the absence of objective and verifiable authoritarisation criteria. The CAS and the Swiss Federal Tribunal (SFT), the CJEU acknowledged, were not bound by EU law. Although UEFA was not party to the ISU proceedings, the observations of the CJEU were influential in the decision to choose Ireland as an alternative seat of arbitration. It was party, however, to two seminal CJEU preliminary references involving the proposed Superleague and the *Royal Antwerp* case concerning home-grown players.

Sport and the Law is intended for use by sports governing bodies, sports persons, coaches, referees, lawyers, and those studying sports or law related courses. It is also a useful source for those who have an interest in the interaction between sport and the law.

This book addresses a wide range of topics including criminal and civil liability for on-field violence; doping; employment law, contract law and animals in sport. Chapters on governance, judicial review and child protection have been added to the second edition. The book does not address all topics pertaining to sport and the law, for example taxation and sportspersons and sports bodies, nor does it discuss hooliganism, the control and safety of spectators and match-fixing. Hooliganism is not a notable feature of Irish sport; the legal protections surrounding spectators are obliquely covered in the discussion of the law of tort and its application to sport, and the taxation system is regularly updated and thus information becomes quickly obsolete. Match-fixing is a complex topic that encompasses a wide range of societal issues including organised crime, it is international and an area that has been the subject of academic discourse.

While every effort has been made to ensure that this book reflects the most recent developments relating to the law and its application to sport, the law stated in this book is as it stood in October 2024.

I would like to thank David McCartney and the staff at Clarus Press for their patience and guidance. To my family, friends and my colleagues in the School of Law who would always ask me how I was getting on and provided me with invaluable advice.

To Bubbles with whom I started this journey in the First Edition, to Wilberforce who became my second lagomorph housemate following Bubbles' passing, to Sheldon and Penny who got me through the first couple of chapters and to Paddington, Erskine, Tuppence and Murla whose unconditional love got me through to the end. They endured hours of me not admiring them, being latch-key cats and whose invaluable insight greatly 'helped' with the chapter on Animals in Sport!

Dr Laura Donnellan
12 November 2024

TABLE OF CONTENTS

TABLE OF CASES

IRELAND

UNITED KINGDOM

UNITED STATES

AUSTRALIA

CANADA

GERMANY

SWITZERLAND

EU CASES

COURT OF ARBITRATION FOR SPORT AWARDS

DISPUTE RESOLUTION AUTHORITY

DRA06/2023 Patrician Academy Mallow v Munster Council and Munster Council Hearings Committee and Abbey CBS Tipperary Town 12–27

ECHR CASES

EMPLOYMENT TRIBUNAL DECISIONS: IRELAND AND UNITED KINGDOM

TABLE OF LEGISLATION

IRELAND STATUTES

IRELAND STATUTORY INSTRUMENTS

UNITED KINGDOM

UNITED KINGDOM STATUTORY INSTRUMENTS

UNITED STATES

CANADA

AUSTRALIA

NEW ZEALAND

SWITZERLAND

IRELAND CONSTITUTIONAL PROVISIONS

INTERNATIONAL TREATIES AND CONVENTIONS

EUROPEAN LEGISLATION

Directives

Regulations

CHAPTER 1

HISTORICAL EVOLUTION OF SPORT: FROM PAST TO PRESENT

Introduction

This book provides a detailed examination of the intersection between law and sport. Professionalisation and commercialisation are 'structural properties' of modern sport.[1] While the commercialisation, professionalisation and regulation of sport began in the mid–19th century, a more recent development is the intervention and application of the public law to what was primarily considered an activity governed by private law. The professionalisation and commercialisation of sport has evolved and matured from simpler times when it concerned the payment of player wages to multi-million complex media deals involving the use of digital platforms as well as long term broadcasting contracts with streaming media companies such as Paramount+ and Amazon (Prime Video).[2] **1–01**

Irish sport is largely amateur (with the exception of rugby and horseracing) and thus much of the discussion in this book will relate to other jurisdictions, namely England and Wales, Canada, Australia and the United States (US). However, the developments in these other jurisdictions will be of importance to Ireland in the future. The nature of Irish sport has changed over the years.[3] As more and more sports become professionalised in Ireland, the issues raised in this book will become increasingly pertinent. In addition, although sport may be classified as a pastime or recreational activity, this does not mean that it is immune from judicial scrutiny. On-field violence should be equally dissuaded in a local Gaelic Athletic Association (GAA) match as much as it is in a professional match.[4] While Ireland has limited case law and legislation **1–02**

---

1 Eric Dunning and Kenneth Sheard, *Barbarians, Gentlemen and Players* (2nd edn, Routledge 2005) 30.

2 Brad Adgate, 'More Live Sports Are Joining The Streaming Wars' *Forbes* (Jersey City, 7 June 2021) <https://www.forbes.com/sites/bradadgate/2021/06/07/more-sports-are-joining-the-streaming-wars/?sh=4ca2256a52bc/> accessed 19 April 2024.

3 On 26 August 1995, the International Rugby Football Board (IRFB) announced Rugby Union was an 'open game', which paved the way for the professionalisation of rugby.

4 As will be discussed in ch 4, there is reluctance on the part of players and clubs to pursue on-field violence cases through the courts. The adage 'what happens on the field, stays on the field' seems to deter players bringing cases to the

on sport, the comparative analysis of the law in other countries will provide a template from which Irish sporting bodies and the courts can develop a body of sporting jurisprudence.

1–03 Sport is an industry. It accounts for around 2% of the European Union's (EU) Gross Domestic Product (GDP).[5] The EU uses the Vilnius definition of sport, which includes 'all upstream industries producing goods and services needed for sport, and downstream industries for which sport is an important input – media, tourism, advertising'.[6] The Vilnius definition is broad and, in relation to goods and services, it includes sports shoes and clothing, horse breeding, watches and clocks, sports cars, education, sports arenas and stadiums, swimming pools, skiing and skating facilities and sports clubs.[7] In relation to the downstream industries, this includes television broadcasts, betting, hotels and restaurants, dietary supplements, health services and veterinary services.[8]

1–04 In 2022, according to Eurostat, '1.51 million people were employed in the sports sector in the EU, representing 0.8% of total employment'.[9] This was an increase of 10.9% on the 2021 figures and demonstrated a recovery in the sports sector following the COVID–19 pandemic, when 1.31 million people were working in the industry in 2020.[10] The sports

courts. Players feel that it is unsportspersonlike to do so and may feel that they are 'letting the team down' by pursuing a case. In contrast, there are many cases where the determinations of governing bodies have been challenged. There have been numerous doping cases where the sportsperson has argued that their right to fair procedures has been breached, or a lengthy suspension has resulted in an unreasonable restraint of trade. This is discussed in ch 9.

5 European Commission, 'Sport in the EU', <http://ec.europa.eu/assets/eac/sport/library/documents/eu-sport-factsheet_en.pdf> accessed 19 April 2024. More recent figures are not available. A study published in 2018 related to the base year of 2012. The report states that sports-related GDP in the EU amounted to €279.7bn or 2.12% of the total GDP, European Commission, Directorate-General for Education, Youth, Sport and Culture, *Study on the Economic Impact of Sport through Sport Satellite Accounts* (Publications Office of the European Union 2018) 15 <https://data.europa.eu/doi/10.2766/156532> accessed 23 April 2024.

6 European Commission, 'Memo: Sport Keeps Not Only You, But Also Industry Fit' MEMO/14/35 (Brussels, 21 January 2014) <http://europa.eu/rapid/press-release_MEMO–14–35_en.htm> accessed 23 April 2024. See also European Commission, 'Definition of Sport – Version 2.0 (Vilnius Definition 2.0) According to CPA 2008' (*Eurostat*, 19 September 2013) <http://ec.europa.eu/eurostat/documents/6921402/0/Vilnius+Definition+Sport+CPA2008+official+2013_09_19.pdf/30838d11-01ea–431f–8112–50786e187c1c> accessed 23 April 2024.

7 Memo (n 6).

8 ibid.

9 European Commission, '10.9% Increase in Employment in Sport in 2022 in the EU' (*Eurostat*, 23 July 2023) <https://ec.europa.eu/eurostat/web/products-eurostat-news/w/ddn–20230728–1> accessed 23 April 2024.

10 The 2019 statistics recorded 1.37 million people working in the sports sector: European Commission, 'Employment in Sport in the EU' (*Eurostat*, 23 September 2022) <https://ec.europa.eu/eurostat/web/products-eurostat-news/-/edn–20220923–1> accessed 23 April 2024. For a recent report on the impact of COVID–19 and sport in the EU, see European Commission, Directorate-General

sector is a broad category that includes those working with teams and clubs, as trainers, as athletes, fitness centres and those involved in the promotion and management of sports events.[11] In Ireland, 0.9% of people work in a sports-related activity; Sweden recorded the highest percentage of 1.4%, while Romania had the lowest percentage of 0.2%.[12] The 2022 statistics reveal that 35% of those working in the sports sector are aged 15 to 29.[13]

According to a financial review carried out by Deloitte in 2023, the European football market is worth €29.5bn.[14] The 'Big Five'-Premier League, Bundesliga, Serie A, La Liga, and Ligue 1-generated a revenue of €17.2bn in 2021/2022, a €1.6bn increase from 2020/2021.[15] It exceeded the pre-pandemic benchmark of €17bn.[16] Following the return of fans to the stadia, match-day revenues improved in relation to the 'Big Five', amounting to 12% of revenue in 2021/2022.[17] Interestingly, there was a 12% decline in broadcast revenues; however, this was explained by the inflated revenues in 2020/2021 due to match 'deferrals from the previous, COVID–19 impacted season'.[18] **1–05**

The English Premier League's revenue was largely generated by broadcasting arrangements (54%), match-day (14%) and sponsorship/ commercial deals (32%).[19] The average wages-to-revenue ratio of the 'Big Five' in 2021/2022 were as follows: Premier League 67%, La Liga 73%, Bundesliga 59%, Serie A 83% and Ligue 1 87%.[20] **1–06**

In the Premier League, Manchester City recorded the highest pre-tax profit of £42m in 2021/2022, an increase of £37m from 2020/2021,[21] **1–07**

for Education, Youth, Sport and Culture, European Commission Expert Group on 'Strengthening the Recovery and the Crisis Resilience of the Sport Sector During and in the Aftermath of the COVID–19 Pandemic' – Final report (Publications Office of the European Union 2024) <https://data.europa.eu/doi/10.2766/045032> accessed 23 April 2024.

11 Memo (n 6).

12 European Commission, 'Eurostat Statistics Explained: Employment in Sport' (*Eurostat*, May 2023) <https://ec.europa.eu/eurostat/statistics-explained/index.php?title=Employment_in_sport> accessed 23 April 2024.

13 ibid.

14 Deloitte, 'A Balancing Act: Annual Review of Football Finance 2023' (Deloitte's Sports Business Group June 2023) 3 <https://www2.deloitte.com/content/dam/Deloitte/uk/Documents/sports-business-group/deloitte-uk-annual-review-of-football-finance-2023.pdf> accessed 23 April 2024.

15 ibid.

16 ibid 6.

17 ibid.

18 ibid. The broadcast revenue for 2021/2022 was €8.9bn.

19 ibid 14. The projected percentages for 2023/2024 are broadcasting arrangements (56%), match day (13%), and sponsorship/commercial deals (31%).

20 ibid 9.

21 ibid 18.

whereas Manchester United incurred the largest pre-tax loss of £150m, an increase of £126m from 2019/2020.[22]

1–08 However, Deloitte explains that the increase 'was largely driven by an unfavourable change in foreign exchange rates resulting in an increase in finance costs on US dollar-denominated borrowings'.[23]

1–09 The above figures demonstrate that sport is an industry, and, like any other industry, it needs to be regulated, held accountable, be transparent, and subject to scrutiny, both internal and external. As a commercial activity, its economic viability changes from one financial year to the next. Chapter 2 on 'Sports Governance' will explore these issues in detail. To put Chapter 2 and the following chapters into context, it is important to look at the origins of sport and the emergence of governing bodies, with a focus on the GAA.

Historical Evolution of Sport

1–10 The word 'sport' is a shortened version of the word 'disport', meaning a diversion, merriment or to amuse oneself. For early humans, sport was not a mere diversion but a necessity. Sport provided an outlet for primitive humans to release aggression and tension through play, which 'served as an innocuous outlet for otherwise harmful urges'.[24] Sport gave early humans a sense of achievement and served to further their innate desires to compete and dominate others; it also created muscular strength and skill, while in colder climes it helped with blood circulation.[25] Sport was a medium through which early humans could establish victory over their foes.[26] Perhaps most importantly, sport provided humans with the necessary training to defend their family and property and to escape danger.[27] Even ball sports, including football and baseball, were created as a means of battle between tribes.[28] Sport aroused a sense of mysticism as early humans regarded it as gift from the gods.[29] Children used play as a form of training in order to learn the hunting and gathering skills needed to ensure survival. Over time, sport changed from being seen as having a function that reflected the realities of life to one reflecting pleasure and distraction.

1–11 The early modern period (1500–1800) saw the emergence of organised sport. Sport was given a very wide definition to include activities as

---

22 ibid.
23 ibid.
24 Rudolph Brasch, *How Did Sports Begin? A Look into the Origins of Man at Play* (Longman 1972) 1.
25 ibid 2.
26 ibid 1.
27 ibid.
28 ibid 2.
29 ibid.

diverse as stone throwing, pantomime and ballet. In Ireland, dancing was considered the most popular physical activity in the later part of the early modern period.[30] Animals amused crowds by performing tricks, while other animals were trained for baiting. Bear baiting, bull baiting, hurling and quoits were popular pastimes.[31] In the 16th and early 17th centuries, these activities were banned as they were viewed as 'unproductive or culturally disagreeable'.[32] A similar view was proffered in regard to cockfighting and cock throwing.[33] Kelly notes that during the period from 1600 to 1800, the only recreational activities that 'enjoyed official favour' were hunting, horseracing and bowling.[34] That is not to say that these pastimes remained immune from state intervention as there were attempts during this period to restrict them.[35] This was not the only opposition, as 'public opinion became ever-more critical'.[36]

Societal attitudes changed in relation to animals in the later part of the 18th century. The catalyst for change was not the result of a single factor, but rather several causal factors which were interlinked. Elite claims-makers placed animal cruelty in the same rubric as racism and slavery and the protection of the vulnerable, the oppressed and marginalised.[37] Similarly, the feminist movement identified with animals from the point of view of oppression and dominion of the patriarchy.[38] Equally, the French Revolution had highlighted the inequalities that existed within society, and this too drew parallels with the animal welfare movement.[39] Some animal welfare groups espoused a broader remit of reform, most notably the reform of the working-class.[40] Developments **1–12**

---

30 James Kelly, *Sport in Ireland 1600–1840* (Four Courts Press 2014) 15.

31 ibid. Quoits involves throwing a rubber or metal ring that is aimed at a pen or a peg stuck in the ground. It was banned in England in 1388 as it was seen as disrupting archery practice and other military preparations during the war between England and France: see Alan Tomlinson, *Dictionary of Sports Studies* (Oxford University Press 2010) 376–77. Another factor for the ban was that of gambling, which also covered football, tennis and dice: Trevor Dean, *Crime in Medieval Europe: 1200–1550* (Routledge 2001) 54. Quoits remained a popular sport despite the ban.

32 Kelly (n 30) 16.

33 Animals in sport is discussed in ch 15.

34 Kelly (n 30) 16.

35 ibid.

36 ibid.

37 The elite claims-makers exemplified an internal pacification and restraint on instinctive drives. They were members of the middle-class and several of them, including William Wilberforce, Richard Martin and Thomas Erskine were members of Parliament.

38 Katie Whitaker, *Mad Madge Margaret Cavendish, Duchess of Newcastle, Royalist, Writer and Romantic* (Vintage 2003); Mary Wollstonecraft, *A Vindication of the Rights of Women with Strictures on Political and Moral Subjects* (3rd edn, J Johnson 1796).

39 John Oswald, *The Cry of Nature, Or, An Appeal to Mercy and to Justice on Behalf of the Persecuted Animals* (E Mellen Press 2000) 42; Justin Killian 'Végetarian Radicaux: John Oswald and the Trope of Sympathy in Revolutionary Paris' in Simon Boerboom (ed), *The Political Language of Food* (Lexington Books 2015).

40 For example, the Proclamation Society, which subsequently became known as the

in science highlighted the similarities between humans and animals, the previous fear of the unknown was replaced with a more moderate view of animals, and one of the results of this change was the emergence of pet-keeping, animals that had no function other than human companionship.[41] Religion was also an influential factor as it encouraged benevolence and charity towards animals for the betterment of the human soul. While anthropocentric in its view, it nevertheless called for the humane treatment of animals. Rational recreation saw a change in the leisure pursuits of the masses, as society became more urbanised and space was limited, the introduction of regulated holidays and the emergence of middle-class evangelicalism resulted in the waning of several animal sports.[42]

The Civilising Process

1–13 Nobert Elias's *Civilizing Process* examined the transformation of human behaviour from the middle ages to the 18th century.[43] At its core, the *Civilizing Process* charts 'modes of behaviour centrally ... considered typical of people who are civilized in a western way'.[44] By drawing on etiquette books from that time period, Elias documented how sensibilities over the centuries had drastically changed in relation to bodily functions and social character. This transformation resulted in the gradual introduction of rules and norms which governed human behaviour and conduct. Standards of social behaviour, conduct and sentiment began to change drastically. Elias observed that the 'ruling of conduct and sentiment became stricter, more differentiated and all embracing, but also even, more temperate, banishing excesses as well as of self-indulgence'.[45] Erasmus of Rotterdam had coined the word 'civility' in reference to the change in social behaviour.[46] The state had become more involved in the regulation of the behaviour of its citizens and with that came a stricter control of the warrior classes, and the nobles.[47] Leisure pursuits and sport also experienced a change in conduct and sentiment. The modern regulation of football in England

---

Society for the Suppression of Vice, was concerned about raising the standard of public morality. This included concerns about blasphemy, brothels, illegal lotteries and cruelty to animals. See MJD Roberts, 'The Society for the Suppression of Vice and Its Early Critics, 1802–1812' (1983) 26 (1) The Historical Journal 156.

41 Harriet Ritvo, 'The Emergence of Modern Pet Keeping' (1987) 3(1) Anthrozoös 158.

42 Rachel Vorspan, 'Rational Recreation and the Law: The Transformation of Popular Urban Leisure in Victorian England' (2000) 45 McGill Law Journal 891.

43 Norbert Elias, *The Civilizing Process: Sociogenetic and Psychogenetic Investigations* (Basil Blackwell 2000).

44 ibid ix.

45 Norbert Elias, 'An Essay on Sport and Violence' in Norbert Elias and Eric Dunning (eds), *Quest for Excitement: Sport and Leisure in the Civilising Process* (Blackwell Publishers 1993) 21.

46 ibid.

47 ibid.

can be traced back to the 19th century when the Football Association was formed in 1863. In earlier centuries violence was often associated with games but a new sensitivity towards violence was to emerge in the 19th century. A similar development occurred with boxing. Prize fighting and bare-knuckle fighting were not devoid of rules but lacked a uniform set of principles.[48] In 1743 the Broughton Rules were introduced, which became the sport's first uniform set of rules.[49] The Broughton Rules, while welcomed at first, proved to be inadequate.[50] In 1865 the Queensberry Rules were introduced by the eighth Marquis of Queensberry.[51] The introduction of rules and regulations into English boxing attracted the attention of other countries, most notably France, who adopted the English rules as a blueprint.[52] This global export of English sporting rules, or 'sportisation', was not just confined to boxing but also included horseracing, tennis, and athletics.[53]

By the 1850s sports and pastimes noted for their brutality, disorganisation and rowdiness, among them street games, blood sports and local festivals, had waned in popularity.[54] These sports gave way to more 'morally respectable' pastimes, namely seaside vacations and spectator sports.[55] Vorspan identifies five contributing factors that caused this change in pastimes: regulated holidays; middle-class evangelicalism; limited urban spaces; association of undisciplined public recreation with disorder and crime; and the emergence of capitalism.[56] The literature has traditionally overlooked the contribution made by the courts in this period.[57] The judiciary, coming from an affluent and respectable background, looked on blood sports, prize fighting, horseracing, music halls and professional team sports with much disdain and hostility.[58] However, they held amateur athleticism and the theatre in high esteem.[59] Judicial decisions from England during this period show the courts' willingness to use the criminal law to reflect its moral sensibilities, most **1–14**

48 Jack Anderson, *The Legality of Boxing: A Punch Drunk Love* (Birkbridge Law Press 2007) 15.
49 ibid 14.
50 ibid 25.
51 ibid 28.
52 Elias (n 45) 21.
53 ibid 21–22.
54 Vorspan (n 42) 894.
55 ibid.
56 ibid 897–98.
57 ibid 894.
58 ibid 895.
59 ibid.

notably in the cases of *R v Coney*,[60] *R v Perkins*,[61] *R v Bradshaw*,[62] and *R v Billingham, Savage and Skinner*.[63]

1–15 In the mid–19th century, modern organised rules for sport emerged. The industrial revolution and subsequent automation gave people more time to engage in leisurely pursuits.[64] Sporting associations were established and organised rules of sport were created. The primary function of these newly created governing bodies was to draw up and enforce rules in the sport.[65] The governing body would organise national competitions and select national teams to play against teams from other countries.[66]

1–16 The functions of modern governing bodies are more onerous. Nowadays, sporting bodies range from local teams to international level. The national body, which is responsible for regulating sport at local and national level, is also affiliated with the European body, which in turn is affiliated with the international body. In the mid-19th century, governing bodies had little interaction with governmental policy.[67]

1–17 As discussed in Chapter 2, governments are not directly involved in sport but have assigned the regulation of sport to sports councils. In Ireland, the Sport Ireland Act 2015 established Sport Ireland. Sport Ireland's predecessor, the Irish Sports Council, was created under the Irish Sports Council Act 1999, which was repealed by the Sport Ireland Act 2015. Sports councils provide funding, grants, advice, and draft

---

60 (1882) 8 QBD 534. It was held that the fight was a prize fight and not a sparring match and as a prize fight it caused a breach of the peace. Coney, Gilliam, and Tully as spectators were found guilty of aiding and abetting even though they had no active role in the fight. The Court did not hold boxing or sparring legal but declared prize fighting illegal. Their conviction was subsequently overruled by an 8–3 majority. This case is discussed in detail in ch 4 paras 4–94—4–101.

61 (1831) 4 0 & P 537. Patterson J held that all those that attend a prize fight, spectators and pugilists and everyone else connected with the fight, are guilty of a breach of the peace and it was immaterial which of the combatants struck the first blow.

62 (1878) 14 Cox 83. The accused jumped in the air and struck an opponent in the stomach with his knee during a football match. The injury caused the death of the victim. Bramwell LJ (at 85), in his direction to the jury, outlined the criminal law's involvement in sport. The judge directed the jury to find the accused guilty of manslaughter if they were satisfied that the accused intentionally or recklessly caused serious harm to the deceased. The accused was acquitted after testimony from the referee showed that there had been no unfair play.

63 (1825) 2 C & P 234. This case involved the assault of a magistrate who, in the course of his duty, attempted to prevent a prize fight taking place. At trial the combatants, Billingham, and Savage, were convicted of assault on the grounds that consent was immaterial, and that the assembly was unlawful. Skinner was convicted of assaulting the magistrate. All three were found guilty of causing a riot as the crowd of over 1000 that had come to see the fight descend into tumult.

64 David Thorpe and others, *Sports Law* (Oxford University Press 2009) 3.

65 Barrie Houlihan and Anita White, *The Politics of Sports Development: Development of Sport or Development through Sport?* (Routledge 2002) 164.

66 ibid.

67 ibid.

policies on various issues, including anti-doping, participation and non-discrimination, and child protection.

The Emergence and Evolution of the Gaelic Athletic Association

Resistance to British Sports

When tracing the history of sport in Ireland, two interesting points emerge. While there are several unique aspects in relation to sport in Ireland, in many ways the evolution of sport in Ireland mirrors that of other countries.[68] Rouse contends: **1–18**

> This is partly a reflection of the universal instincts that draw humans to the idea of play, partly a reflection of the history of Ireland within what was once the British Empire, and partly, also, a reflection of an international cultural exchange where political and geographic borders are permeable.[69]

Resistance to British sports emerged in the 1880s. The GAA was founded in 1884 and, while not exclusively a nationalist organisation in the early years, it soon emerged as an organisation which brought together different strands of nationalism.[70] The GAA viewed itself as a Christian, amateur and character-building organisation.[71] While it endeavoured to act as a bulwark against British sports, the ideals it espoused were in fact the core tenets of British sport.[72] Cronin notes: **1–19**

> the GAA championed the values of muscular Christianity and manliness in the same way as the rest of British sport. Although the inspiration was different and hedged in Irish terms, it does appear that the founders and supporters of the GAA adopted values originally championed in British public schools.[73]

In a similar vein Mandel observes: **1–20**

> While adopting hostility to all England, and particularly English sport ... the Association was forced, unconsciously as it may be, to imitate the features of Victorian sport – its emphasis on morality, health, on organization, codification and competition. Much of what the GAA

---

68 Paul Rouse, *Sport in Ireland – A History* (Oxford University Press 2015) 1.
69 ibid.
70 John Bairner, 'Irish Sport' in Joe Cleary and Claire Connelly (eds), *The Companion to Modern Irish Culture* (Cambridge University Press 2005) 194.
71 ibid 195.
72 ibid. Bairner adds that the organisation of the GAA along Catholic parish lines and competition between counties was a bastion of British administration under colonial rule. See also Mike Cronin, 'Fighting for Ireland, Playing for England? The Nationalist History of the Gaelic Athletic Association and the English influence on Irish Sport' (1998) 15 The International Journal of the History of Sport 36. Cronin (at 50) argues that 'the inspiration for the codification of Gaelic Games was undoubtedly British'.
73 Cronin (n 72) 52.

> regarded as distinctive about the meaning of its games was merely the result of the substitution of the word 'Ireland' for 'Britain' or 'England'.[74]

1–21 While there is merit in the above observations, the GAA still carved out a niche 'within broader hegemony of an imperial power'.[75] The GAA was established at a time when it was feared that the Irish identity was becoming increasingly diluted.[76] Irish sport also became synonymous with the fight for independence. Thus, 'there was an urgent need to revitalise Irish sports and pastimes and to ally these to a broad cultural nationalist movement'.[77] Some historians have placed the creation of the GAA in a broader international context of the 'Victorian Sports Revolution', which allowed it to use British sport as a template but incorporated inherently Irish characteristics.[78] However, McAnallen disagrees as the amateur nature of the GAA was very different to the 'gentleman amateur ethos of Victorian English sporting bodies' as the GAA provided for the reimbursement of travel expenses.[79] Thus, the amateur status of the GAA was not a bastion of the English Victorian sporting revolution, it was a based on a prudent financial strategy which embraced 'Irish Catholic/Christian communalism and fraternal solidarity'.[80]

1–22 In the early days, the 'nationalist pretensions' of the GAA manifested

---

74 William Frederick Mandle, *The Gaelic Athletic Association and Irish Nationalist Politics, 1884–1924* (Christopher Helm 1987) 14.

75 Barrie Houlihan, 'Homogenization, Americanization and Creolization of Sport: Varieties of Globalization' (1994) 11 Sociology of Sport Journal 356, 368.

76 For an interesting discussion on national identity and sport, see Barrie Houlihan, 'Sport, National Identity and Public Policy' (1997) 3 Nations & Nationalism 113.

77 Bairner (n 70) 62. See Andrew McGuire and David Hassan, 'Cultural Nationalism, Gaelic Sunday and the Gaelic Athletic Association in Early Twentieth Century Ireland' (2012) 29(6) The International Journal of the History of Sport 912. The writers contend that the GAA was more a representation of cultural nationalism than political nationalism.

78 Richard McElligott, 'Contesting the Fields of Play: The Gaelic Athletic Association and the Battle for Popular Sport in Ireland, 1890–1906' (2016) 19(1) Sport in Society 3, 4.

79 Dónal McAnallen, '"The Greatest Amateur Association in the World"? The GAA and Amateurism' in Mike Cronin, William Murphy, and Paul Rouse (eds), *The Gaelic Athletic Association 1884–2009* (Irish Academic Press 2009) 158. McAnallen adds that the early rule books did not expressly state that hurling and Gaelic football were amateur sports. Initially, it was only stated that athletics was amateur and subsequently cycling. It was 'understood', however, that team sports were amateur. The rules were drafted in such a way that made certain that the games developed with amateurism at its core: for example, there were no transfer fees and residency requirements which provided that players could only play for their parish club, the parish rule.

80 ibid 181. Richard Holt places the GAA within a wider international context and notes that the GAA was part of 'the creation of modern sport'. Emerging governing bodies had written rules and were organised in contrast to the traditional village sports, which were in decline. The introduction of rules and regulations were characteristics of modern sport: Richard Holt, 'Ireland and the Birthday of Modern Sport' in Mike Cronin, William Murphy, and Paul Rouse (eds), *The Gaelic Athletic Association 1884–2009* (Irish Academic Press 2009) 33.

in a number of ways with the inclusion of its three patrons: the political Archbishop Croke of Cashel, Charles Stewart Parnell, the leader of the Irish Parliamentary Party that was calling for home rule and Michael Davitt, the founder of the Land League and former Fenian prisoner and 'radical nationalist'.[81] The Irish Republican Brotherhood (IRB), an organisation fighting for a democratic and independent republic, were members of the GAA's administration from the beginning.[82]

In the later part of the 19th century, British sport had been transformed from unregulated games to being codified through the auspices of governing bodies. The origins of modern sport emanate from this period. Sport has existed for centuries; however, this period is the starting point in most discussions that surround sport. Bairner observes, 'In the long period from the collapse of the Roman Empire to the nineteenth century, however, sport was largely archaic in Ireland as elsewhere.'[83] The influence of British sport in Ireland was attributed to two factors, namely educational institutions and the army. The sons of Anglo-Irish elite were sent to English public schools and at these schools they were exposed to rugby and cricket.[84] These young men returned to Ireland and introduced rugby and cricket to Trinity College Dublin (TCD).[85] The presence of British army garrisons throughout Ireland saw the emergence of popular British sports. As these British sports began to reach outside the confines of TCD and the army garrisons, there was a corresponding decline in hurling, an indigenous sport which had all but faded into obscurity by the 1830s.[86] When British sports were introduced to Ireland, there was very little resistance at first. British sports were not just the preserve of the Anglo-Irish elite; Catholic schools began to embrace rugby and cricket. However, these sports remained very much the sports of the middle- and upper-classes except for association football, which attracted a working-class following.[87] **1–23**

Origins and Development of Hurling and Gaelic Football

The GAA covers the following sports: football, hurling, ladies' football, camogie, handball, and rounders.[88] Hurling and football were popular **1–24**

81 Neal Garnham, 'Accounting for the Early Success of the Gaelic Athletic Association' (May 2004) 34 (113) Irish Historical Studies 65, 65.

82 ibid. Grenfell Morton, *Home Rule and the Irish Question* (Routledge 2014) 49. Morton (at 49) notes that despite early attempts by the IRB to control the GAA Councils being thwarted, the IRB, however, successfully infiltrated the administration of the GAA and over time ensured that it reflected a 'narrow and exclusive nationalism'.

83 Bairner (n 70) 192.

84 Alan Bairner, 'Ireland, Sport and Empire' in Keith Jeffrey (ed), *An Irish Empire? Aspects of Ireland and the British* (Manchester University Press 1996) 62.

85 ibid.

86 ibid 64.

87 Bairner (n 70) 192.

88 Liam Delaney and Tony Fahey, *Social and Economic Value of Sport* (Econ & Soc Research Inst 2005) 11 <https://www.esri.ie/system/files/media/file-uploads/2015-08/BKMNINT180.pdf> accessed 23 April 2024.

sports in Ireland prior to the founding of the GAA in 1884. Hurling, a ball and stick game, is an ancient sport that dates back centuries.[89] The Statutes of Kilkenny in the 14th century refer to 'horlinge'; the purpose of the 35 acts was to restrict or prohibit '"native" Irish behaviour and tendencies'.[90] Hurling was also referred to in a number of early legends, most notably, Cuchulain, an Irish folklore hero, who was said to be a champion hurler.[91] Hurling has been cited as the precursor to hockey.[92] Hurling was banned by the Galway Corporation Statutes of 1527. The Statutes did not ban football but banned hurling and handball: 'at no tyme the use ne ocupye the horlinge of the litill balle with hockie stickes or staves, nor use no hande ball to playe without the walles, but onely the great foote balle, on payn of the paynis above lymittid (a fine of 8 pence)'.[93] One of the earliest references to Gaelic football dates back to 1308 where a man was accidentally stabbed while 'playing at ball' in County Dublin.[94]

1–25 By the end of the 18th century, Gaelic football was in decline as Republican fervour culminated in the Irish Rebellion of 1798, an uprising against British rule in Ireland. The authorities opposed the gathering of large groups of young men, thus sports including Gaelic football were restricted.[95] In the early 1800s, churches of all denominations were at the forefront of encouraging more morally respectable pastimes, as football was often accompanied by drinking and gambling.[96] Economic depression and the Great Famine in the 1840s resulted in depopulation

---

89 AB Gleason, 'Hurling in Medieval Ireland' in Mike Cronin, William Murphy, and Paul Rouse (eds), *The Gaelic Athletic Association 1884–2009* (Irish Academic Press 2009) 1–13. Ireland seemed to have its own version of the Olympic Games, the Tailteann Games, which dates to 1169: see Bairner (n 70) 60. It was Maurice Davin, the first president of the GAA, who developed rules for hurling: Paul Rouse, 'Journalists and the Making of the Gaelic Athletic Association, 1884–1887' (2011) 17(2) Media History 117, 124.

90 Gleason (n 89) 2. While there is disagreement over whether 'horlinge' or 'hockie' as described under the Galway Corporation Statutes were native sports and thus hurling, Gleason (at 3) contends that the objective of the Kilkenny and Galway Statutes was to restrict or ban native games, therefore it follows that 'horlinge' and 'hockie' were native games.

91 Brasch (n 24) 106.

92 Thomas Reilly and Kieran Collins, 'Science and the Gaelic Sport: Gaelic Football and Hurling' (2008) 8 European Journal of Sport Science 231, 233 and Rudolph Brasch (n 24) 106–07.

93 Taken from the National University of Ireland (NUI) Galway Archives, *A Ban on Ye Small Ball: Hurling Banned in Galway City in 1527* <http://nuigarchives.blogspot.com/2012/10/a-ban-on-ye-small-ball.html> accessed 23 April 2024. The modern English translation is as follows: 'at no time the use nor occupy the hurling of the little ball with hockey sticks or staves, nor use a handball to play outside the walls, but only the great football on pain of the pains above limited'.

94 RM Peters and Neal Garnham, *The Origins and Development of Football in Ireland: Being a Reprint of RM Peter's 'Irish Football Annual' of 1880* (Ulster Historical Foundation 1999) 1; for a summary on the origins of the GAA, see Gemma Hussey, *Ireland Today: Anatomy of a Changing State* (Townhouse 1993) 448–54.

95 Peters and Garnham (n 94) 1–2.

96 ibid 2.

and as a result the numbers playing traditional sports waned.[97] In Britain, sports such as rugby and football became popular during this period in the public schools. Ireland, being in such proximity to Britain, began to absorb these popular sports as former public-school pupils enrolled at university in TCD. The world's second-oldest rugby club, which is still in existence, was established in TCD in 1854.[98]

On 14 December 1874, the Irish Football Union was founded. The Irish Football Union had clubs affiliated to it and only three of the clubs were from Ulster. There were no Belfast teams, so in response the Northern Football Union of Ireland was established in 1875. The Belfast clubs had not been excluded from the Irish Football Union. They had failed to attend meetings when the plans to create a football union were discussed. When it came to selecting players for the national team, both Unions were involved.[99] A merging of the two unions was discussed in 1875; however, it was deemed inconvenient and thus the creation of one union to represent all of Ireland was postponed. In 1877, the idea of merging the two unions was mooted once again; however, relations were strained between the two unions and the plans were shelved.[100] The amalgamation was finally agreed upon in 1878. The Northern Football Union, who had disagreed with the terms of the proposed merger in 1877, was more amenable in 1878. It was believed that the Munster teams under the Irish Football Union were contemplating establishing their own union and, fearing the dilution of the Northern Football Union in light of two Southern unions, the Northern Union agreed to the amalgamation in 1879.[101] In 1880, the Irish Rugby Football Union (IRFU) was established and held its first meeting in February of that year.[102] In November 1880, the Irish Football Association (IFA) was established. The IFA governed football in both Southern and Northern Ireland. **1–26**

By 1880, the rules of both football and rugby in Ireland had been codified. The indigenous game of Gaelic football was the third form of football to be regulated.[103] The GAA, as noted, was established in 1884 to preserve **1–27**

[97] ibid.

[98] Bairner (n 70) 62. It may be the oldest rugby club as Guy's Hospital FC was established in 1843; however, this club lay in a state of latency for some period during the 19th century.

[99] Peters and Garnham (n 94) 6.

[100] ibid.

[101] ibid 7.

[102] ibid. The two unions merged under the following terms: (1) A Union to be known as the Irish Rugby Football Union was to be formed for the whole country, (2) Branches were to be formed in Leinster, Munster, and Ulster, (3) The Union was to be run by a Council of 18, made up of six from each province. This information was sourced from Nigel Trueman, 'History of the IRFU' <https://www.rugbyfootballhistory.com/ireland.html> accessed 23 April 2024. The Connacht branch was founded on 8 December 1885: Connaught Rugby, 'Our History' <https://www.connachtrugby.ie/about-us/history/272/> accessed 23 April 2024.

[103] Peters and Garnham (n 94) 9.

and cultivate national pastimes. The first meeting at Hayes Hotel, Thurles, in November 1884 'was the harbinger for the democratisation of modern, codified and competitive sport on the island'.[104] Within five years of its inception, there were 777 affiliated clubs and over 41,000 members from the entire island.[105]

1–28 In the first decade of the GAA, Gaelic football was considered a minority sport. The unique game of hurling and the sport of athletics (with hurling being the more popular spectator sport in Ireland) were the main focus for the GAA.[106] Testament to this was the GAA's promotion of Irish sports (and funding expedition) in the US in 1888, where most of Ireland's leading athletes and two hurling teams were in attendance; however, no Gaelic football team was represented.[107] The rules of Gaelic football were first published in 1885 and, instead of codifying the game, the rules actually proved to be more a hindrance as they provided that a team could be between 15 and 21 players, the pitch was to be at least 120 yards in length, the only specific rule related to scoring a point when the ball went under the cross bar.[108] To some, Gaelic football closely resembled rugby. Hurling was seen as the sport of the Irish hero.[109] In the latter part of 1886, rule changes were implemented to distinguish Gaelic football from rugby. Wrestling and lifting the ball with the hand from the ground were banned. The distinctive hand pass began to emerge at this time.[110] Gaelic games' popularity grew as games were held on Sundays; the day most working-class people would be free. It may have alienated the Protestant population; it meant that rural workers and the urban working-class could participate in the game and attend the Sunday matches.[111] In order to distinguish Gaelic football from its rugby and football counterparts, matches became cultural and political events. Poetry recitals and Irish dancing would entertain the crowds.[112] A single entrance fee was paid and often three matches would be held consecutively. Beer tents and bookmakers were present, neither of which would have been acceptable at a rugby or football match.[113] Despite

---

[104] McElligott (n 78) 3.
[105] ibid.
[106] Peters and Garnham (n 94) 10.
[107] ibid. See also Paul Darby, 'Gaelic Sport and the Irish Diaspora in Boston, 1879–90' (2003) 33(132) Irish Historical Studies 387, 396. It was hoped that £5,000 would be raised to fund the Tailteann Games, which were planned to take place in the summer of 1889. However, the necessary funds were not raised, and the expedition was deemed a financial failure. Darby notes that there were mitigating factors for the low turnout at events. It was the year of the US presidential election, and as a result publicity was directed towards that and not the GAA tour. The tour was important and a success in one respect as it raised the profile of Gaelic games in the US, in particular hurling, which had been codified.
[108] Peters and Garnham (n 94) 10. A Gaelic football team has 15 players.
[109] ibid.
[110] ibid 11.
[111] ibid.
[112] ibid.
[113] ibid.

the attempts to increase the popularity of Gaelic football, it remained a minority sport at the end of the 19th century. By 1890, there were 777 GAA clubs in the country; however, only six counties had entered the previous year's football championships.[114] Macro-level politics impacted at a micro level within the GAA, and between the years of 1892 and 1896 the GAA almost ceased to operate.[115] Its membership was in great decline owing to a number of factors, including economic depression and the resulting emigration of young rural men, many of whom would have played and supported the GAA; also the political landscape had changed as Charles Stewart Parnell, one of the three original patrons of the GAA and leader of the Home Rule movement, was defeated in the bi-election in 1891 following a fall-out among his supporters over his involvement with a married woman.[116] During this time, membership had to fallen to 118 affiliated clubs and membership had decreased to just over 5,000.[117] Within the GAA's organisational structure, there were a number of deficiencies, namely the lack of clearly defined rules, the ad hoc nature of most of the affiliated clubs and the lack of patronage from wealthy landlords and gentry who avoided being associated with the GAA due to its nationalist undertones.[118] Instead, rugby and cricket benefitted from their association with the landed elite.[119] In the 1890s cricket flourished as membership of the GAA waned; similarly, rugby experienced a surge in membership in Munster.[120]

The GAA's Decline and Subsequent Revival

In the 1890s, the GAA 'came close to total disintegration'.[121] However, its continuation into the 20th century was largely attributed to Richard Blake, the General Secretary of the GAA from 1895–98.[122] Blake had been actively involved in the GAA since the late 1880s and by 1894 he had become a prominent match official as well as being elected as the Meath official on the GAA's Central Council.[123] Blake was very vocal in **1–29**

[114] ibid 12.
[115] ibid 13.
[116] ibid 4.
[117] ibid 5.
[118] ibid.
[119] ibid.
[120] McElligott (n 78) 6–7. The Irish press was instrumental in helping the fledging GAA in the early years as a number of GAA journalists campaigned against cricket and rugby, which resulted in many young men returning as members of the GAA. Hunt contends that those who took part in British sports were 'stigmatised as West Britons'. He cites the Midland Reporter as the 'vanguard of promoting Irish–Ireland and attacking the West Briton': Tom Hunt, *Sport and Society in Victorian Ireland: The Case of Westmeath* (Cork University Press 2007) 193–94. Cusack's weekly column in the *United Ireland* was used as forum for answering queries about the rules: see Rouse (n 89) 124.
[121] Richard McElligott, 'Richard Blake and the Resurrection of the GAA, 1890–98' (2013) XXIV In Ríocht na Midhe, Records of the Meath Archaeological and History Society 226, 256.
[122] ibid.
[123] ibid.

his opposition to the continued association of the GAA with the IRB.[124] On being appointed to the Central Council, Blake declared the GAA non-political and non-sectarian.[125] Blake was instrumental in introducing reforms to the way the game was played as Gaelic football failed to keep spectators' interests. This was attributed to the low-scoring nature of the game, playing fields of inferior quality, players' lack of skill, the overcrowded field of 42 men (21 aside), the use of everyday footwear and the design of the football, which was both cumbersome and water-absorbing, among other reasons.[126] In 1892, new Gaelic football rules were introduced which restricted the number of players to between 14 and 17. In 1893 Blake suggested that the number be reduced to 14 to increase scoring opportunities.[127]

1–30 Blake refereed the All-Ireland hurling and football finals in 1894.[128] He was acutely aware of the indiscipline that permeated both codes. Players did not seem to respect the referee or his decisions and disputes frequently took place during the game and teams would oftentimes walk off the pitch.[129] When the rules for both hurling and Gaelic were codified in 1884, there were only 10 rules for football and 12 for hurling, very few of which dealt with the actual playing of the game.[130] The rules of hurling and Gaelic football were revised in 1888.[131] In order to dissuade breaches of the rules in Gaelic football, the free kick was introduced under the revised rules.[132] By 1896 there were 27 rules governing Gaelic

---

[124] ibid. For a discussion on the IRB and GAA, see William Frederick Mandel, 'The IRB and the Beginnings of the Gaelic Athletic Association' (1977) 20(80) Irish Historical Studies 418.

[125] McElligott (n 121) 261.

[126] ibid 262.

[127] ibid 263.

[128] In the All-Ireland Senior Football Final of Dublin v Cork in March 1895, the score was 1–1 and 0–6. At the time a goal was worth five points, so the two teams were level. Blake mandated that a further 30 minutes be played, however, Cork refused to play the extra time. Blake deemed Dublin the winners of the game. Cork appealed the decision on the grounds that Blake had played a 40-minute second half instead of 35 and had no authority to declare Dublin the victors. At the GAA Annual Convention on 7 April 1895 the matter was discussed, and it was decided that a replay would take place on 21 April 1895. In the replay, Cork was leading 1–2 to 0–5, however, Cork supporters began to attack several Dublin players, with the players refusing to finish the game with 10 minutes remaining. Blake refereed the replay. The Central Council awarded Dublin the match. Cork appealed this decision and several Central Council meetings followed; a second replay was scheduled for 12 May 1895 in Limerick, however, if Limerick was not available it would take place in Thurles. Cork would not agree to the replay on the grounds that the title was rightfully theirs. A motion was passed on 1 June 1885 with Dublin declared as the All-Ireland Senior Football Champions. See TM Mhic Chonbhui, *Cork: A History In the All Ireland Senior Hurling Championship Volume One 1887–1949* (Lulu Press 2017).

[129] McElligott (n 121) 262.

[130] ibid. McElligott (at 263) notes that only four of the 10 rules on Gaelic football dealt with the playing of the game.

[131] ibid.

[132] John Connolly and Paddy Dolan, 'The Civilizing and Sportization of Gaelic

football,[133] including the rule that players who threatened or abused a referee now faced 12 months' suspension.[134] Once elected as Secretary in 1895, Blake introduced further changes, including the use of a whistle by the referee.[135] In 1896, the points for a goal were reduced from five to three points.[136] McElligott contends, 'The changes pioneered by Blake led to a faster, more open and higher scoring game which could at least compete with its more illustrious, international rival sporting codes for public interest.'[137]

Developments in the 20th Century

Further rule changes to Gaelic football helped create a more distinctive game from that of rugby and football.[138] For example, the ball could not be carried or thrown, with carrying constituting more than four steps with the ball.[139] From 1901 onwards, the popularity of Gaelic football soared as a younger, more dynamic administrative team took over the management of the GAA.[140] In 1910 the H-shaped goals were introduced, players began to wear specialised footwear and lighter footballs replaced the old heavier balls.[141] More of an emphasis was placed on skills and players were training more in order to compete in this faster and more adroit game.[142] **1–31**

Changes to the rules continued and the establishment of Provincial Councils helped the sport gain more followers.[143] School competitions were established and, by 1913, a team was limited to 15 players. By 1914, Gaelic football was the most widely played of the three sports, the other two being rugby and football.[144] Gaelic football attracted followers in **1–32**

Football in Ireland: 1884–2009' (2010) 23(4) Journal of Historical Sociology 570, 577.

133 ibid.

134 ibid. Connolly and Dolan note that violence continued to erupt on the pitch despite the introduction of such a rule.

135 McElligott (n 121) 264.

136 ibid.

137 ibid. Blake's tenure as Secretary ended in 1898. The President of the GAA, Frank Dineen, was involved in the IRB and Blake was quite vocal about his disdain for such an association. Blake was blamed for the mismanagement of finances and was dismissed in 1898.

138 It is outside the remit of this chapter to go through the entire history of Gaelic sports; for a more detailed discussion, see Eoghan Corry, *The History of Gaelic Football* (Gill & MacMillan 2009); and Peters and Garnham (n 94).

139 The Playing Rules of Gaelic Football: Rules of Fair Play, r 1.7 of the Gaelic Athletic Association, *Official Guide – Part 2* (Central Council of the Association 2024) 40 <https://www.gaa.ie/article/gaa-official-guides-codes> accessed 24 April 2024.

140 Peters and Garnham (n 94) 19. There had been retirements and deaths among the previous administration.

141 McElligott (n 121) 266.

142 ibid.

143 Peters and Garnham (n 94) 19. McElligott (n 78) 10 refers to the new class of well-educated young men joining the GAA.

144 Peters and Garnham (n 94) 23.

the US as Irish emigrants established clubs there.[145] Hurling was not as easily translated abroad as football due to the fact that there was a shortage of ash trees needed to make the hurling sticks.[146]

1–33 In the early part of the 20th century, a number of political events affected the GAA, the Easter Rising of 1916 being the most notable.[147] The British authorities restricted the movement of people throughout Ireland including Croke Park, the headquarters of the GAA.[148] World War II also affected the GAA as travel and fuel restrictions severely inhibited the playing of hurling and football. The post-War period saw the GAA continue its funding and promotion of indigenous games in the US as the 1947 All-Ireland Senior Football Final took place at the Polo Grounds in New York.[149] GAA exhibition games were also played in Wembley Stadium from the late 1950s to 1975.[150]

Rule 27

1–34 Since its inception, there have been a few controversial rules that were introduced to preserve and cultivate Irish pastimes and insulate them from 'imported sport'. Following the adverse publicity in the aftermath of the 'Parnell Split', the GAA endeavoured to distance itself from politics.[151] Within this new vista, the ban on members of the Royal Irish Constabulary (RIC) joining the GAA was removed in 1893.[152] As discussed above, while the GAA had encountered a number of difficult years, the election of Blake as its National Secretary in 1895 heralded a number of reforms, including the declaration that the GAA was a non-political and non-sectarian organisation.[153] In 1896 the ban on foreign games was removed, much to the chagrin of Michael Cusack, the founder of the GAA.[154] At the Annual Convention in 1901, T.F O'Sullivan put forward the following motion:

---

145 Darby (n 107). Darby (at 392) refers to the creation of the Irish Athletic Club of Boston (IACB) in September 1879. This club preceded the creation of the GAA.

146 Reilly and Collins (n 92) 232.

147 In the early part of the 20th century, the GAA had close ties with nationalist political parties. This is no longer the case as its Rules explicitly forbid any political affiliations; see Chapter 1 Aims & Ethos, Rule 1.9 of the Gaelic Athletic Association, *Official Guide – Part 1* (Central Council of the Association 2024) 4 <https://www.gaa.ie/article/gaa-official-guides-codes> accessed 24 April 2024. Any breach of this provision may result in a suspension of up to 24 weeks.

148 The stadium was purchased in 1913. It has a capacity of 82,300.

149 Reilly and Collins (n 92) 232.

150 See <http://www.gaa.ie/the-gaa/history/1945–2015> accessed 9 July 2018.

151 Cormac Moore, *The GAA v Douglas Hyde: The Removal of Ireland's First President as GAA Patron* (Collins Press 2012) 31.

152 The ban was introduced in 1887. The ban did not extend to the army nor the navy. At the time, the inclusion of such a rule highlighted the control the IRB had over the GAA: see Moore (n 151) 20.

153 ibid 31. Blake was a supporter of rugby and cricket.

154 The ban on foreign games was first introduced in January 1885. For an interesting discussion on the life of Michael Cusack, see Marcus de Búrca, *Michael Cusack and the GAA* (Anvil Books 1989).

> That we the Representatives of the Gaels of Ireland in convention assembled hereby pledge ourselves to resist by every means in our power the extension of English pastimes to this country as a means of preventing the Anglicisation of our people: that County Committees be empowered to disqualify and suspend members of the Association who countenance sports which are calculated to interfere with the preservation and cultivation of our own national pastimes: that we call on the young men of Ireland not to identify themselves with rugby or Association football or any other form of imported sport which is likely to injuriously affect the national pastimes which the GAA provides for self-respected Irishmen who have no desire to ape foreign manners and customs.[155]

In 1901, the ban on foreign games was voluntary in nature, it was up to the county boards whether the ban was enforced. It was 'more of a plea than a demand'.[156] One year later, Rule 27 was to be given a more solid basis at the Annual Convention in 1902. Vigilance committees were created: it was their role to monitor the activities of its members and they would attend foreign games to see if members of the GAA were in attendance.[157] The ban was removed in 1903 with discretion given to the county boards whether it was to be enforced or not. At the Annual Convention of 1904, which was held in 1905, the ban was re-introduced and was to remain in the rule book until 1971. The 1905 ban was politically motivated and seen as a mechanism through which Irish nationalism could be promoted.[158] In 1938 the President of Ireland, Dr Douglas Hyde, had his patronage of the GAA removed after he attended an international soccer match between Ireland and Poland at Dalymount Park in Dublin. Hyde had become the sixth patron of the GAA at its Annual Convention in 1902. President Hyde had attended the match in his capacity as head of state; his arrival at the match was announced in both Irish and English.[159] The President's patronage was not reinstated prior to his death in 1949. **1–35**

In the late 1960s, the ban was compared to the Berlin Wall and apartheid in South Africa.[160] Protests outside Croke Park ensued; however, the GAA remained beholden to the ban. By 1970, the GAA could not ignore the wishes of the county boards and clubs. Thirty counties supported the removal of the ban.[161] It was finally removed on Easter Sunday, 11 April 1971. **1–36**

---

155 Cited by John Connolly and Paddy Dolan, *Gaelic Games in Society: Civilising Processes, Players, Administrators and Spectators* (Palgrave Macmillan 2019) 141.

156 Moore (n 151) 35.

157 ibid.

158 ibid.

159 ibid 87. He was accompanied by several Irish politicians, including Taoiseach Éamon de Valera, who would later become the President of Ireland.

160 ibid 202.

161 ibid 204. Sligo and Antrim were the only two counties to object.

The GAA in the 21st Century

1–37 In 2001, Rule 21 was removed from the Rule Book, which had prevented members of the Northern Ireland British Security Forces from joining the GAA.[162] The Report of the Independent Commission for Policing in Northern Ireland in 1999 (also known as the Patten Report) recommended that the GAA remove the ban.[163] The Independent Commission was tasked with the role of creating a new police force 'capable of attracting and sustaining support from the community as a whole'.[164] Paragraph 15.2 of the report stated:

> We specifically recommend that the Gaelic Athletic Association should repeal its rule 21, which prohibits members of the police in Northern Ireland from being members of the Association. The continued existence of this rule in the light of our recommendations can only be a deterrent to the recruitment of Catholics, or a factor in separating those Catholics who do join the police from an important part of their culture.[165]

1–38 At a specially convened congress meeting in November 2001, every delegate from the south of Ireland voted in favour of repealing Rule 21, however, the only delegate to do so in Northern Ireland was County Down.[166] County Down was considered to be the most liberal of the six counties in the North due to a number of factors, including the presence of young professionals who commuted to Belfast for work but resided in commuter towns in County Down; these young professionals were wealthier and more outward-looking than those from the other counties.[167] In addition, it was hoped that the removal of the ban would result in the cessation of arson attacks of clubs and murders of members by loyalist paramilitaries if 'one potential source of persecution' was removed.[168] Before the special congress convened on 17 November 2001, the decision had been made to remove Rule 21. At the one-agenda meeting on that day, the rule was deleted from the rulebook.

1–39 In 2005, Rule 42, which banned the playing of non-GAA sports at GAA

---

[162] For an interesting discussion on Rule 21 see David Hassan, 'The Gaelic Athletic Association, Rule 21, and Police Reform in Northern Ireland' (2005) 29(1) Journal of Sport and Social Issues 60.

[163] The Independent Commission was established under the terms of the Good Friday Agreement of 10 April 1998. See Independent Commission for Policing in Northern Ireland, 'A New Beginning: Policing in Northern Ireland' (HM Stationery Office September 1999) <http://cain.ulst.ac.uk/issues/police/patten/patten99.pdf> accessed 24 April 2024. The Royal Ulster Constabulary (RUC) was replaced by the Police Service of Northern Ireland (PSNI). The RUC replaced the RIC in Northern Ireland following the partition of Ireland in 1921.

[164] ibid 1.

[165] ibid 86.

[166] Down passed a resolution in 1995 to remove the ban, however, the resolution was withdrawn and internal discussions surrounding the withdrawal of the motion were not made public. There was another attempt to remove the rule in 1998 at the GAA's annual congress: see Hassan (n 162) 68–70.

[167] ibid 72.

[168] ibid.

venues, was temporarily lifted to allow the Irish rugby team and the Republic of Ireland football team play at Croke Park while Lansdowne Road, now known as the Aviva Stadium, was being redeveloped.[169] According to Rule 5.1 (b) of the Official Guide – Part 1, the

> Central Council has the power, in exceptional circumstances, to authorise the use of Association Property held by a County Committee, Provincial Council or Central Council for activities other than those controlled by the Association in accordance with policy adopted by Central Council.[170]

In 2010, Congress voted to allow the Central Council to approve the use of Croke Park by other sports on a case-by-case basis.[171] Congress in 2012 extended this to allow the Central Council to consider applications for use of Croke Park and other grounds for the Rugby World Cup in 2023 and 2027, if those tournaments were to be staged in Ireland.[172] A further decision was voted on in 2018, which permits the Central Council to consider applications for use of GAA grounds outside Ireland by other sports on a case-by-case basis. In 2019 Congress voted to allow the Central Council to decide, on a case-by-case basis, applications for use of county grounds by other sports.[173] According to its use of property policy: **1–40**

> Apart from the specific exceptions provided for in the case of Croke Park, only American Football, Australian Rules Football and Soccer have in the past received the sanction of Central Council to be played on GAA facilities, and all on the basis that they were not considered to be contrary to the objectives of the GAA.[174]

Any club, County Committee or Provincial Council that contravenes Rule 5.1 may be fined or suspended.[175] **1–41**

At the GAA Annual Congress in 2005, the GAA adopted an Arbitration Rule and a Disputes Resolution Code. A Disputes Resolution Authority (DRA) was established to implement the Code. The DRA is independent of the GAA and bound only by the provisions of the Code.[176] Disputes can be referred to the DRA once 'all available avenues of Appeal under the Rules of the Association have been exhausted'.[177] **1–42**

---

169 In 2009, the GAA received rental income of €13 million from the IRFU and the FAI. See Brendan O'Brien, '€600m Full Cost of Croker Exit' *Irish Examiner* (Cork, 12 March 2010) <https://www.irishexaminer.com/sport/gaa/euro600m-full-cost-of-croker-exit–114315.html> accessed 24 April 2024.

170 (n 147) 38.

171 Gaelic Athletic Association, 'Use of GAA Property 2019' (Approved by Ard Chomhairle 23ú Marta 2019) 1 <https://www.gaa.ie/api/pdfs/image/upload/ya4iokndnrmvidi2vdll.pdf> accessed 26 April 2024.

172 ibid.

173 ibid.

174 ibid 5.

175 ibid 6.

176 *Official Guide – Part 1* (n 147) Appendix 5, Disputes Resolution Code 90–102.

177 ibid r 7.7 (d). The Disputes Resolution Authority publishes decisions on its

1–43 In 2001, it was decided that senior Inter-County players would be tested for prohibited substances.[178] Now, all Inter-County GAA players are subject to the anti-doping rules and are subject to drug testing. The Medical, Scientific and Welfare Committee of the GAA in partnership with the Central Council has adopted the Sport Ireland Anti-Doping Rules as the Anti-Doping Rules of the GAA.[179] GAA players may only be tested at training or at games. In January 2016, the testing methods were extended to include blood testing. In 2023, Dried Blood Spot (DBS) Testing, as discussed in Chapter 6, was introduced by Sport Ireland.[180] This less-invasive method requires only a few drops of blood and is used in conjunction with urine and venous blood samples.[181]

1–44 Despite its amateur status, the GAA has used sponsorship as a valuable revenue stream. The sponsorship of jerseys began in 1991. Currently, the Football All-Ireland Championship is officially sponsored by Allianz, AIB and SuperValu, while the official sponsors of the Hurling All-Ireland Championship are Bord Gáis Energy, Centra and Eir.[182] The GAA passed a motion in February 2018 with a 93% majority voting to ban gambling sponsorship.[183]

---

website: <http://www.sportsdra.ie/the-code/> accessed 26 April 2024. The DRA is discussed in more detail in ch 12.

[178] Inter-County is defined as matches or competitions between two GAA counties. There are 32 GAA counties as the GAA encompasses both Northern and Southern Ireland. *Official Guide – Part 1* (n 147) r 1.13 refers to the Anti-Doping Rules. As the ingredients of medicinal products can vary between the North and the South, players are advised to consult the recently launched Sport Ireland's medicine checker website <https://medcheck.sportireland.ie/> to check for medicines obtained in the 26 counties and for medicines purchased in the six counties should consult <https://www.globaldro.com/Home> accessed 22 October 2024.

[179] The Medical, Scientific and Welfare Committee is comprised of medical personnel, players, and administrators. Its role is to advise the GAA of issues pertaining to the health and welfare of the players. For example, since 1 January 2014, Gaelic footballers in all age grades must wear a mouth guard. The requirement prior to January 2014 applied to underage players but now it applies to all players. Mouthguards are required for all levels of Ladies' Gaelic football since 1 January 2017, Ladies Gaelic Football Association, 'Mouthguards' <https://ladiesgaelic.ie/lgfa-hub/players/mouthguards/> accessed 26 April 2024. It is the responsibility of players to wear a mouthguard and failure to do so will exclude them from the GAA Player Injury Scheme: Gaelic Athletic Association, 'GAA Mouthguard Information' <https://learning.gaa.ie/sites/default/files/GAA-Mouthguard-Information%202016.pdf> accessed 26 April 2024.

[180] Sport Ireland, 'Dried Blood Spots' <https://www.sportireland.ie/dried-blood-spots> accessed 26 April 2024.

[181] Gaelic Football Association, 'GAA Anti-Doping Information' <https://learning.gaa.ie/antidopinginfo> accessed 26 April 2024.

[182] See <https://www.gaa.ie/the-gaa/partnerships> accessed 26 April 2024. Sponsorship is discussed in detail in ch 11.

[183] Martin Brehony, 'Betting Companies Booted Out of Sponsorship in the GAA' *Irish Independent* (Dublin, 24 February 2018) <https://www.independent.ie/sport/gaelic-games/betting-companies-booted-out-of-sponsorship-in-the-gaa/36639062.html> accessed 26 April 2024. See also Gaelic Football Association, 'GAA Gambling Awareness' <https://www.gaa.ie/my-gaa/community-and-health/substance-use-gambling-awareness/gambling-awareness> accessed 26 April 2024.

Revival of the Olympics

A significant revival of the ancient Olympics took place in Athens in 1896.[184] Baron Pierre de Coubertin, a French aristocrat, had voiced his concerns about the lack of physical education in French schools and attributed this to French military defeats.[185] He lamented: **1–45**

> How well one understands that France should go and play dominoes instead of exercising its tired muscles. Sated with victory, France gradually fell asleep while its black, total, horrible defeat had awakened energies which laboured grimly at the undertaking that you know: the German Empire. It was thus that military athletics was born in Berlin.[186]

De Coubertin contended that French schools were too academic and intellectual and that there was not enough physical training and sports. He travelled to the US and Britain to observe the administration of athletes.[187] The public schools in England greatly influenced de Coubertin, he was fascinated by books including *Tom Brown's School Day* and Taine's *Notes on England*.[188] As his attempts to overhaul the French education system never materialised, he instead turned his focus to a larger scale plan. Initially de Coubertin was motivated by a desire to avenge his country's military defeat at the hands of the Prussians. However, modern technology in the form of the advent of the steamships, railroads, the telephone and telegraphs resulted in the world becoming smaller, a 'global village'.[189] Travel had helped de Coubertin adopt a more humane philosophy, whereby he 'shed some of the xenophobia that had always hindered the development of international cooperation'.[190] The French Government commissioned de Coubertin to hold athletic congresses and in 1892, at a jubilee of the French Union of Athletic Sports Societies, de Coubertin spoke of his intention to revive the Olympic Games.[191] At this time, the idea was very **1–46**

---

[184] The ancient Olympics had ended in 393 AD as Emperor Theodosius I banned the Games due to their alleged affiliation with pagan rituals. Theodosius wished to eradicate from Greek society any non-Christian activities and festivals: see International Olympic Committee, 'The End of the Ancient Games' <https://olympics.com/ioc/ioc-overview/ioc-history/ancient-olympics/the-end-of-the-ancient-games> accessed 28 April 2024.

[185] France had suffered defeat in the Franco-Prussian War. See Ingomar Weiler, 'The Predecessors of the Olympic Movement, and Pierre de Coubertin' (2004) 12(3) European Review 427, 435–36. See also Allen Guttmann, *The Olympics: A History of the Modern Games* (University of Illinois 2002) 8.

[186] Pierre de Coubertin and Norbert Müller, *Olympism: Selected Writings* (Comité Internationnal Olympique 2000) 288.

[187] The influence of English and American educators on de Coubertin was not greeted with universal approval from some of his fellow 'anglophobic countrymen': see Guttmann (n 185) 10.

[188] MI Finley and HW Pleket, *The Olympic Games: The First Thousand Years* (Chatto & Windus 1976) 2.

[189] ibid 10–11.

[190] ibid 11.

[191] De Coubertin is often referred to as the father or inventor of the modern Olympics. However, some commentators disagree. Before the War of Independence

much in its infancy, however, in 1894 de Coubertin convened a meeting at the Sorbonne in Paris, which was attended by 79 delegates from 12 countries.[192] At this meeting, the International Olympic Committee (IOC) was formed. It was agreed that the Games would be held every four years, beginning in 1896 in Athens.[193] The Games opened on 6 April and ended on 15 April.[194] Finley and Pleket note that the 1896 Games were 'genuinely Olympic', with 42 events in 10 sports with 285 male competitors.[195] Gymnastics was the only team sport event.[196]

The Move from Amateur to Professional

1–47 The Olympic Games remained amateur until the 1984 Summer Games. At the Los Angeles Games in 1984 the rules relating to the admittance of professional athletes were changed to reflect economic realities.[197] Until 2016, boxing remained the only amateur sport at the Olympic Games for safety reasons. In 2013, the International Boxing Association (IBA) announced that male boxers at the Olympics would no longer wear headgear. Rio 2016 saw the male boxers compete without headgear. Female boxers continue to wear the protective headgear, as women's

---

(1821–29), the Greeks, drawing their inspiration from the Romantic poets, endeavoured to revive the Olympics. However, their attempts never came to fruition. Thirteen Olympic Games are said to have taken place before the revival in 1896, the first being the Cotswold Games in 1612; see Weiler (n 185) 428–29. Weiler (at 435) questions de Coubertin's knowledge of Ancient Greece and argues that de Coubertin's 'chief contribution should primarily be seen in the fact that he emphasised certain pedagogical and philosophical views, created the ideology of Olympism, the internationalism of the Olympics (of course, in the background of the international sports movement) and helped to organise the so-called Olympic movement'.

192 The site in Greece where the ancient Olympics took place was, ironically, excavated by the Germans. Originally, an English antiquary, Richard Chandler, discovered the site in 1766. In 1829 a group of French archaeologists spent six weeks excavating the site, however, it was a German team led by Professor Ernst Curtius with the financial backing of the German government that uncovered the site between 1875 and 1881: Finley and Pleket (n 188) 2–3.

193 A new stadium was built which had the capacity for almost 50,000 spectators: ibid 4.

194 Fourteen countries took part with the largest group of competitors coming from Greece, Germany, France, and Great Britain. See International Olympic Committee, 'Olympic Games Athens 1896' <http://www.olympic.org/en/content/Olympic-Games/All-Past-Olympic-Games/Summer/Athens–1896/> accessed 28 April 2024. Women did not compete until 1900. De Coubertin did not wish for women to compete as he stated: 'the true Olympic hero, in my view, is the individual adult male'. He was not against women participating in sport *per se*, 'provided that they do not make a public spectacle of themselves. In the Olympic Games, as in the contests of former times, their primary role should be to crown the victors,' as cited by Weiler (n 185) 435.

195 Finley and Pleket (n 188) 4.

196 ibid.

197 Many of the Eastern-bloc states were funding full-time amateur athletes. The Western athletes were self-financing amateurs. From the 1970s onwards, there were requests to change the criteria as Western athletes argued that they were at a disadvantage.

boxing is a relatively recent addition to the Games. It was at the London 2012 Olympics that female boxers competed for the first time. The IBA removed the headgear requirement for male boxers as studies had shown that the boxer was more likely to suffer a head injury due to foam padding around their faces. On 3 March 2024, the IBA Board of Directors at a meeting in Sochi, Russia, decided to remove the headguard requirements for female boxers in IBA-championships and sanctioned events.[198]

Structure of the Book

With this chapter providing context for the following chapters, Chapter 2 examines 'Sports Governance'. The term sports governance came to the fore in 1998 following the resignation or expulsion of 10 IOC members in what was dubbed the 'Salt Lake City scandal'.[199] It was alleged that members had accepted bribes from the Salt Lake Organising Committee (SLOC) to secure the 2002 Winter Games. While the behaviour of IOC members was deemed unethical, it was not illegal.[200] In response, the IOC revised its structures. Sports governance has been an important policy consideration for the EU. In 2013, the EU Expert Group on Good Governance drafted a list of principles of good governance in sport.[201] Notwithstanding the developments in promoting good governance, a number of recent scandals have highlighted the lack of accountability and responsibility among international governing bodies, for example, World Athletics, formerly known as the International Association of Athletics Federations (IAAF) and the Fédération Internationale de Football Association (FIFA). A feature of this chapter is the examination of state-sponsored doping and Russia. **1–48**

The discussion on governance will highlight several key principles that sports governing bodies should embrace, namely accountability, responsibility, and transparency. The chapter provides a comprehensive **1–49**

[198] International Boxing Association, 'Removal of Women's Headguards, Brazil Boxing Confederation Gaining Provisional Membership, and Belgrade Being Awarded the Women's World Championships amongst Pivotal Decisions Taken by the IBA Board of Directors' <https://www.iba.sport/news/removal-of-womens-headguards-brazil-boxing-confederation-gaining-provisional-membership-and-belgrade-being-awarded-the-womens-world-championships-amongst-pivotal-decisions-taken-by/> accessed 28 April 2024. IBA rule changes in 2016 allowed for professional boxers to compete in the Olympics for the first time.

[199] Jean-Loup Chappelet, 'Beyond Governance: The Need to Improve the Regulation of International Sport' (2018) 21(5) Sport in Society 724, 727.

[200] Jean-Loup Chappelet, 'Towards Better Olympic Accountability' (2011) 14(3) Sport in Society 319.

[201] The group was established by a Resolution of the Council and of the Representatives of the Governments of the Member States, meeting within the Council, on a European Union Work Plan for Sport for 2011–2014, OJ C 162 (1 June 2011) 1–5. The principles are available at <http://ec.europa.eu/assets/eac/sport/library/policy_documents/xg-gg–201307-dlvrbl2-sept2013.pdf> accessed 28 April 2024.

analysis of the direct and indirect involvement of the state with a focus on the role of Sport Ireland.

1–50 Chapter 3 places in context the social, political, and cultural importance of sport in society. Sport, although considered an industry, is treated differently from other industries. For instance, men and women are segregated in sporting events. Such segregation would not be tolerated in other sectors. However, sport occupies a very special position in society. The intervention of the law into the sporting realm has caused much debate. Some academic commentators favour the interference of the law and see such intervention as a positive step; others are of the view that sport is a private matter that should be exempt from the intrusion of the law except in the most exceptional of circumstances. It is not just the application of the law of the land to sport that has caused much debate, the actual term for such a branch of law has caused a rift between academic writers. Some purist lawyers argue that there is no such area as *Sport and the Law* or *Sports Law*, others argue that *Sport and the Law* or *Sports Law* is not a discrete area of law but rather borrows its content from the more established areas of law, including contract, tort, and criminal law. There also exists an academic debate whether the appropriate term is *Sport and the Law* or *Sports Law*. *Sports Law* implies that there is a distinct body of law that pertains to sport. *Sport and the Law* is a more moderate term, while recognising the application of the law to sport, it posits that there is currently no distinct body of law relating to sport, however, with time it should develop into a specific branch of law. As an analogy, areas such as family law and labour law were initially not discrete areas, but over time came to be accepted as distinct branches of law. This chapter will also examine the characteristics of a sport and will analyse the Court of Justice of the European Union's (CJEU) decision in the case of *The English Bridge Union Limited v Commissioners for Her Majesty's Revenue & Customs*.[202] The emerging area of esports will also be discussed. While not considered a sport, current trends suggest that it might be in the future.

1–51 Chapter 4 on 'Participator Violence in Sport' examines the role of the criminal law in dealing with participator violence on the field of play. The use of the criminal law in sport in both Ireland and in England and Wales is quite rare. However, there have been a few high-profile cases involving the GAA, including the recent Court of Appeal case, *Director of Public Prosecutions (DPP) v Prendergast*.[203] While sports participants enjoy immunity from suit for most injuries sustained during a game, the criminal law will only involve itself in cases whether there is the intentional, deliberate, or reckless infliction of harm. However, in fast-paced games where tensions are high, it may be very difficult to ascribe the necessary *mens rea* (mental element). It becomes even more difficult in cases involving an 'on-the-ball' incident. The analysis suggests

[202] Case C–90/16 [2017] ECLI:EU:C:2017:814.
[203] [2015] IECA 318.

that the internal disciplinary mechanisms should be able to deal with most incidents. Only acts of egregious violence should attract criminal prosecution. In general, a person may not consent to the infliction of actual bodily harm or serious harm. However, contact sport is given an exemption. There is a public interest or benefit derived from the playing of contact sports. Sportspersons consent to harm that is within the rules of the game or incidental to the playing of the game or within the playing culture.

'Civil Liability in Sport' is examined in Chapter 5. This chapter looks at the application of the law of tort to sport. The law of tort covers a wide range of issues, including personal injuries, defective products, defamation, and nuisance both public and private. Some of the issues are relevant to sport, particularly the liability of participators, referees, coaches, instructors, and governing bodies. Regarding participants, a player is under a duty to take all reasonable care taking account of the circumstances. The standard is objective; it is based on the reasonable person rather than the individual defendant. Liability will not attach in situations where there is an error or lapse of judgement. Something more serious is required for the defendant to be held liable, as the recent case of *Fulham FC v Jones* demonstrates.[204] The threshold for liability is high and thus very difficult to reach. The issue of concussion in rugby and the legal implications will be assessed in relation to clubs, and governing bodies. **1–52**

Chapter 6 deals with 'Drugs in Sport'. The chapter defines what is meant by doping, the methods of doping, the Irish Sport Anti-Doping Rules, and the Irish Sport Anti-Doping Disciplinary Panel (ISADDP). It examines the World Anti-Doping Code (WADC). It will look at the methods of testing. The chapter ends with a discussion on the fundamental rights of athletes when it comes to drug testing with a focus on the right to privacy, the right to fair trial, and the prohibition of discrimination under the European Convention on Human Rights (ECHR). References are also made to case law from domestic courts which have countenanced doping cases, including the right to earn livelihood, fair procedures, and the presumption of innocence. **1–53**

Chapter 7 discusses 'Athletes with Differences of Sex Development and Transgender Athletes'. World Athletics introduced the Hyperandrogenism Regulations in 2011. The regulations were challenged by Dutee Chand and were provisionally suspended by the Court of Arbitration for Sport (CAS).[205] Following the publication of a study that linked athletic performance and higher levels of testosterone in female athletes, the regulations were modified and were challenged by Caster Semenya with the Swiss Federal Supreme Court upholding **1–54**

---

[204] [2022] EWHC 1108 (QB).

[205] CAS 2014/A/3759 *Chand v AFI & IAAF* award of 24 July 2015.

the decision of the CAS.[206] Semenya lodged a case against Switzerland in the European Court of Human Rights in 2021. By a 4–3 majority, it found there to be a violation of Article 14 taken together with Article 8 and a violation of Article 13 in relation to Article 14 taken together with Article 8 of the ECHR.[207] On 6 November 2023, Switzerland lodged an appeal which was accepted by the Grand Chamber of 17 judges. The appeal was heard on 15 May 2024. On 23 March 2023, the Council of World Athletics agreed to update the eligibility regulations for transgender and Differences of Sex Development (DSD) athletes to compete in the female category. The new rules came into effect on 31 March 2023. The Council agreed to exclude male-to-female transgender athletes who have been through male puberty from female World Rankings competition from 31 March 2023.

1–55 Gender testing is another issue that affects female athletes. While no longer mandatory, the IOC and World Athletics retain the right to gender-test athletes in situations where there are suspicions raised to the athlete's femininity. This chapter examines the background to gender testing in the 1960s and its evolution from the nude parades to more scientific methods.

1–56 The eligibility of transgender athletes will be examined. The IOC relaxed the rules to allow female-to-male transgender athletes compete without any restriction and male-to-female transgender athletes to compete subject to certain restrictions regarding testosterone levels that had to be below a cut-off level one year prior to participation. Previous rules (from 2004) had requirements in relation to pre-pubescent gender reassignment and post-pubescent gender reassignment. A change to the rules in 2015 removed the requirement of surgery and permitted female transgender athletes to compete in female events once their testosterone levels were reduced to what was considered within the average female range. However, since March 2022, the IOC has permitted each sport to determine its own policies regarding transgender athletes. Examples of the rules in relation to eligibility of transgender athletes of a few sports will be discussed, including the British Triathlon Federation, World Rugby, World Athletics and World Aquatics.

1–57 Chapter 8 on 'The Law of Contract and Sport' examines the application of the law of contract to sport, including the elements of a contract, contractual relationships in sport and contract disputes. It discusses the capacity of athletes under the age of 18 to enter contractual relations. It

---

[206] CAS 2018/O/5794 *Mokgadi Caster Semenya v International Association of Athletics Federations* & CAS 2018/O/5798 *Athletics South Africa v International Association of Athletics Federations* award of 18 June 2018.

[207] *Semenya v Switzerland* App no 10934/21 (ECtHR, 17 May 2021) <https://hudoc.echr.coe.int/eng#{%22itemid%22:[%22001-226011%22]}> accessed 3 September 2024.

concludes by looking at how a contract is discharged and the available remedies for breach of contract.

Chapter 9 on 'Employment Law and Sport' deals with sportspersons as employees and the distinction between employees and independent contractors. It examines the doctrine of restraint of trade, Collective Bargaining Agreements (CBAs), termination of the employment relationship, FIFA's Regulations and the Status and Transfer of Players and breach of contract, and morals clauses in sponsorship contracts. **1–58**

While the commercialisation of sport is not a recent development, the ways in which sport became commodified changed. As the law has a role to play in sport, the nature of relationships between those involved in sport has changed and this is reflected in the selected areas of commercial law and its impact on sport. Chapter 10 on 'Commercial Issues in Sport' assesses the role of sponsorship, broadcasting rights, image rights, merchandising and the law of agency. **1–59**

Chapter 11 focuses on 'Judicial Review and Sporting Bodies'. In the past decade there have been several judicial review cases involving sports governing bodies in Ireland. While the courts have been willing to hear such cases, it has been repeatedly emphasised that judicial intervention in the decisions of sporting organisations should not occur lightly and recourse to the courts should only happen in the most exceptional of circumstances. The Irish courts have referred to the need for sports bodies to submit their dispute to arbitration or mediation. **1–60**

Chapter 12 leads on from Chapter 11 and looks at 'Alternative Dispute Resolution'. The advantages and disadvantages of arbitration will be considered. The role of Sport Dispute Solutions Ireland (SDSI) and the GAA's DRA will be discussed. This chapter will also examine origins, structure, and jurisdiction of the CAS. **1–61**

Chapter 13, 'European Union Law and Sport', observes the initial reluctance of the then European Economic Community (EEC) to involve itself in sporting matters. This chapter traces Treaty and other developments relating to sport up until the Treaty of Lisbon. It will examine the 'specificity of sport' and situations where the EU courts and the European Commission do not get involved namely in matters that are of 'purely sporting interest'. The chapter analyses seminal sport-related cases and looks at some recent referrals to the CJEU. **1–62**

Given the increasing awareness of the need to protect children from abuse and exploitation, especially in the wake of child sex abuse scandals involving the clergy in Ireland, vetting of coaches and mentors is now an important feature of the public regulation of sport. Ireland has had its controversies in relation to sex abuse of children and young people in the sporting context. The most notable of these involved **1–63** sexual abuse of children by swimming coaches which emerged in the 1990s. Two coaches within the Irish Amateur Swimming Association (IASA) were found to have abused several children. The scandals led to a parliamentary inquiry, and the IASA was reformed and renamed Swim Ireland. Chapter 14 on 'Child Protection in Sport' details the legislative protections for children in sport, including the National Vetting Bureau (Children and Vulnerable Persons) Act 2012–2016, the Criminal Justice (Withholding of Information on Offences against Children and Vulnerable Persons) Act 2012, the Children First Act 2015, the Protections for Persons Reporting Child Abuse Act 1998 and the Criminal Law (Sexual Offences) Act 2006 as amended by the Criminal Law (Sexual Offences) Act 2017. It also documents the non-legislative protections for children in sport, including the *Code of Ethics and Good Practice for Children's Sport.*

1–64 Finally, Chapter 15, 'Animals in Sport', focuses on the current regulation of animal sports in Ireland and other jurisdictions. It examines fox hunting, horseracing, equestrianism, and greyhound racing. Beginning with fox hunting, the chapter discusses its legal status in Ireland, Northern Ireland, England and Wales and Scotland. The chapter documents the legislative framework of horseracing and how horseracing is governed in Ireland. Against the backdrop of an Independent Review, the Irish Horseracing Regulatory Board's (IHRB) equine anti-doping programme will be examined. Animal welfare issues, namely jumps racing and the use of the whip, will be explored. The roles of Horse Sport Ireland (HSI) and the Fédération Equestre Internationale (FEI) will be noted. The regulations relating to doping at national and international level are examined through the lens of the FEI's equine anti-doping programme and by reference to seminal arbitral awards of the CAS. The chapter concludes with a brief discussion of greyhound racing's legislative framework.

CHAPTER 2

SPORTS GOVERNANCE

Introduction

2–01 The traditional approach to sports governing bodies has been to view them as autonomous and private associations.[1] By defining sports governing bodies as private entities irrespective of whether they are local, national or international, 'non-profit' or 'non-governmental organisations' has facilitated them in operating, to a large extent, with impunity.[2] A number of recent scandals at international level include World Athletics, formerly the International Association of Athletics Federations (IAAF) and corruption and extortion in the wake of widespread doping of Russian athletes; and the Fédération Internationale de Football Association (FIFA) and the indictment of a number of officials on charges of racketeering and money-laundering. At a national level, the Olympic Federation of Ireland (OFI, formerly the Olympic Council of Ireland, OCI) and its former President were the subject of a non-statutory inquiry following his incarceration in a Rio prison for allegedly touting Irish allocation tickets. The Irish Athletic Boxing Association (IABA) and the resignation of its head coach of the high performance unit culminated in a meeting of the Joint Committee on Transport and Communications.[3] As sport has become increasingly commercialised and professionalised, there is a need for sports governing bodies to 'blend' characteristics of corporate governance from the business world and democratic governance from the public sector.[4]

2–02 This chapter begins with a discussion on sports governance and endeavours to highlight a few key principles that sports governing bodies should embrace – namely accountability, responsibility, and transparency. A detailed discussion of the Salt Lake City Olympic scandal will demonstrate how international sports bodies have dealt with allegations of corruption and misfeasance. While the Salt Lake

---

1 Gareth Sweeney, 'Executive Summary' in Gareth Sweeney and Kelly McCarthy (eds), *Global Corruption Report: Sport* (Routledge 2016) IX.

2 ibid.

3 See Laura Donnellan, 'Sports Governance in Ireland: The Irish Amateur Boxing Association and its Fraught Relationship with Sport Ireland' (2016) 7(1) Global Sports Law and Taxation Reports 44.

4 Jean-Loup Chappelet, 'Beyond Governance: The Need to Improve the Regulation of International Sport' (2018) 21(5) Sport in Society 724, 725–26. Chappelet (at 732) concludes that in order to have an international legal framework an intergovernmental treaty would be needed, and he suggests calling such an agreement the Lausanne Convention, which would 'combat the "dark side of sport" and promote its "bright side"'.

City scandal emerged in late 1998, more recent examples of FIFA and doping in Russian sport demonstrate that international sports 'provide a fertile ground for corruption'.[5] As global sports organisations are mainly non-governmental and often categorised as non-profit organisations, what distinguishes international sports bodies from other non-profit organisations is their 'enormous abilities to generate income via global sporting events ... In turn these revenues are the incentive for corruption'.[6]

2–03 As sport in Ireland becomes increasingly professionalised and commercialised, the governance of sports bodies becomes even more pertinent. Beginning with an analysis of the direct and indirect involvement of the state with a focus on the Department of Tourism, Culture, Arts, Gaeltacht, Sport and Media, and Sport Ireland, the governance and reform of the Football Association of Ireland (FAI) provides an interesting discussion on the importance of good governance at a domestic level. Similarly, the OFI was restructured following the Rio ticket scandal. The chapter will conclude by looking at recent developments in World Athletics.

What is Sports Governance?

2–04 There is no universally accepted definition of sports governance; numerous attempts have been made to define it.[7] Sport Ireland acknowledges that there is 'no single and exhaustive definition', however, it states that

> it is generally accepted that good governance means that policies and procedures are in place to ensure an organisation is run well. Good governance is not all about rules and regulations. It is an attitude of mind. It is about the ethical culture of the organisation and the behaviour of the people on the governing body. An organisation with good governance should demonstrate transparency, responsibility, accountability and participation with all their stakeholders.[8]

2–05 The benefits of an organisation that is 'governed to a high standard' are that it 'promotes confidence amongst the organisations [*sic*] stakeholders, it leads to better and more ethical decision making and it also helps organisations meet their legislative responsibilities'.[9] The

---

5 Brigida Benitez and John London, 'Has the International Olympic Committee Risen Above Corruption?' (2017) 32 Maryland Journal of International Law 160, 160.

6 John Forster, 'Global Sports Governance and Corruption' (2016) 2(15048) Palgrave Communications 1.

7 Russell Hoye and Graham Cuskelly, *Sport Governance* (Taylor & Francis Group 2015) 9.

8 Sport Ireland, 'What Is Good Governance', 21 May 2014 <https://www.sportireland.ie/news/what-is-good-governance> accessed 29 April 2024.

9 ibid.

National Sports Policy 2018–2027 states that 'good governance is the foundation on which NGBs can thrive'.[10] However, the Policy recognises that a one-size-fits-all approach does not work in a sport system that has a diverse range of sporting organisations.[11] It concedes that

> there is a degree of convergence internationally around what constitute good principles of governance for sport; principles which are adequately captured in Ireland's Governance Code for the Community, Voluntary and Charity (CVC) sector which has been adopted by Sport Ireland. The Code provides a framework against which to assess the progress of NGBs, LSPs and clubs in developing stronger governance.[12]

All funded sports bodies are encouraged to adhere to the Governance Code.[13] The Code applies to community, voluntary and charitable organisations in Ireland. It is hoped that by using the Code, which is on a voluntary basis, sports bodies will be run more responsibly, and thus result in a more efficient and effective organisation that will see its reputation flourish among all stakeholders, including the public.[14] The benefits of good governance are summarised as follows: **2–06**

- Reassure funders that finances are being managed by a well-run organisation.
- Increase transparency.
- Help avoid serious risks.
- Help your organisation achieve its goals faster.
- Reduce costs.[15]

---

[10] Department of Tourism, Culture, Arts, Gaeltacht, Sport and Media, 'National Sports Policy 2018–2027' (Dublin 2018) 55 <http://www.dttas.ie/sites/default/files/publications/sport/english/national-sports-policy-2018-2027/national-sports-policy-2018.pdf>. See also Sport Ireland, 'Sport Ireland Statement of Strategy 2023–2027' <https://www.sportireland.ie/sites/default/files/media/document/2023-09/strategy_FINAL.pdf> accessed 30 April 2024.

[11] National Sports Policy 2018–2027 (n 10) 69.

[12] ibid. NGBs stands for National Governing Bodies. LSP is the abbreviation for Local Sports Partnerships. Governing bodies had to adopt the Governance Code for Sport by the end of 2021. On 6 June 2019 it was announced that Sport Ireland had taken over the Governance Code for Community, Voluntary and Charitable Organisations as a Governance Code for Sport. The Governance Code for Community, Voluntary and Charitable Organisations was adopted in 2012 and was the 'de-facto standard for excellent practice in corporate governance for non-profit organisations': see Sport Ireland, 'Sport Ireland Takes Over Governance Code for Sporting Organisations' (6 June 2019) <https://www.sportireland.ie/news/sport-ireland-takes-over-governance-code-for-sporting-organisations> accessed 29 April 2024.

[13] It was introduced in 2012 and was last updated in October 2016 and rebranded by Sport Ireland in 2020: Sport Ireland, 'The Governance Code – Organisational Types' <https://www.sportireland.ie/governance-code/organisational-types> accessed 29 April 2024. The full code can be accessed here: <https://www.sportireland.ie/sites/default/files/media/document/2020–12/the-governance-code-for-sport-a-guide.pdf> accessed 29 April 2024.

[14] ibid 4.

[15] ibid.

2–07 The Code of Governance applies to sports clubs run by volunteers. It is based on five principles:

- Principle 1: Providing Leadership
- Principle 2: Exercising Control Over the Organisation
- Principle 3: Being Transparent and Accountable
- Principle 4: Working Effectively
- Principle 5: Behaving with Integrity.[16]

2–08 The Gaelic Athletic Association (GAA) has its own Governance Guide, which was written and published by the National Oversight and Audit Committee (NOAC) in 2016.[17] The NOAC is a statutory body created under the Local Government Reform Act 2014, which amended the principal act, the Local Government Act 2001. It incorporates the five principles of Leadership, Control, Transparency and Accountability, Operating Effectively and Integrity.[18]

2–09 In recent years, there have been several independent reports in relation to governing bodies in Britain. These reports have highlighted 'weak governance' and the effect it has on not only the sport but public confidence. A thread that weaves throughout is that of sports governing bodies as 'holders of public trust':

> Public funding is a privilege, not an entitlement, and carries a responsibility to uphold the highest standards of integrity, creating a trustworthy, safe and inclusive environment not only for those wishing to take part but also for those investing or donating time and money.[19]

2–10 The British Equestrian Federation (BEF) in 2017 commissioned an Independent Review Panel Report following the resignation of its Chief Executive Officer (CEO) Clare Salmon amid allegations of bullying, elitism, self-interest, and corruption.[20] The Review and subsequent report, while commissioned by the BEF, was administered by Sport Resolutions UK. Sport Resolutions UK was tasked with appointing the

---

[16] ibid 7.

[17] Gaelic Athletic Association, 'GAA Governance Guide' <https://learning.gaa.ie/sites/default/files/GovernanceGuidelr_English.pdf> accessed 29 April 2024.

[18] ibid 10–19. The Australian Sports Commission has identified nine principles of governance in sport: see 'Sport Governance Principles' (Australian Government March 2020) <https://www.sportaus.gov.au/__data/assets/pdf_file/0006/912705/Sport-Governance-Framework.pdf> accessed 29 April 2024. Several governance theories have emerged, for a summary see Hoye and Cuskelly (n 7) 11–15.

[19] UK Sport, 'A Charter for Sports Governance in the United Kingdom' <https://sportengland-production-files.s3.eu-west–2.amazonaws.com/s3fs-public/a-charter-for-sports-governance-in-the-uk.pdf> accessed 29 April 2024.

[20] The BEF was established in 1972 and is an umbrella organisation for member bodies of which there are 19, with 15 members and four associates. The Independent Review Panel Report into the BEF was published in March 2018. The report is no longer available online. For more details, see Laura Donnellan, 'Equestrianism: Allegations of Misgovernance at the British Equestrian Federation' (2018) 9(1) Global Sports Law and Taxation Reports 49.

three individuals to the independent review.[21] The terms of reference explicitly excluded the three-panel review team from taking any disciplinary actions against the BEF. If there were any matters outside the terms of the investigation, then these were to be reported back to the BEF who, in turn, would decide what action, if any, was appropriate in accordance with its rules and regulations.[22]

The Panel Report, which was published in March 2018, unanimously **2–11**
found that the relationship between the CEO of the BEF and certain member bodies 'had irretrievably broken down by July 2017', and the relationship between the BEF and member bodies was dysfunctional for a number of years.[23] While Salmon 'was of strong character and was a protagonist of change', she had been undermined by senior figures within the BEF and from certain member bodies.[24] It was the objective opinion of the Panel that the conduct of certain member bodies amounted to bullying, elitism and self-interest.[25] On the evidence provided, the Panel concluded that the actions of the member bodies could not be said to constitute corruption.[26]

The report recommended that three key areas of concern should be **2–12**
'closely considered by all relevant stakeholders':

1. identification of the role and responsibilities of the BEF;
2. establishment of strong leadership within the BEF; and
3. maintenance of good governance.

In relation to the maintenance of good governance, the Panel Report **2–13**
noted the inappropriateness of the conduct of certain bodies which was unacceptable for a 'publicly funded sport'. It emphasised the importance of the new BEF Constitution being followed and the reiterated the role of UK Sport and Sport England in suspending funding and/or other reasonable measures for such breaches. It acknowledged that while the member bodies and the BEF may have appeared to have shown a united front, the Founding members, more specifically the Olympic Disciplines of British Dressage, British Eventing and British Show jumping 'wielded real power of the BEF' and this 'imbalance of power' could not continue as a publicly funded sport. Fear of suspension, it surmised, would incentivise the member bodies to redress the balance.

---

21 Sports Resolutions UK was formerly known as the Sports Dispute Resolution Panel (SDRP), which was created in 1997 after the British Athletic Federation (BAF) went into administration due to the lengthy litigation involving Diane Modahl. In 2008, it became known as Sports Resolutions UK.

22 Terms of Reference of the Independent Investigation, <https://www.sportresolutions.com/assets/documents/Scoping_Paper_BEF_Independent_Review_FINAL.pdf> accessed 29 April 2024.

23 Independent Review BEF (n 20) para 2.1.

24 ibid.

25 ibid.

26 ibid.

The Panel welcomed the BEF's amended Articles of Association, the result of consultation with the member bodies. The new Articles of Association reduced the power of the BEF Council and transferred some powers to the BEF Board.[27]

2–14 The BEF is not the only governing body to be subject to an independent review in recent years. In 2016, an investigation regarding the welfare of British cyclists was conducted. The report found 'failings in British cycling governance and leadership, monitoring and supervision of the World Class Programme'.[28]

2–15 Just before the Sochi Winter Games, in 2014, the British Bobsleigh and Skeleton Association (BBSA) informed competitors that they would lose their place in the team if they publicly discussed allegations of bullying, sexism and racism within the sport.[29] Competitors were warned, via an email from the performance director, about 'bringing the sport into disrepute'. The 'culture of fear' was likened to the situation in British cycling.[30]

2–16 Sport UK was very slow to intervene which, in turn, raised questions as to its system of governance.[31] A few months before the 2018 Winter Olympics, the BBSA announced that it did not have the money to fund a women's team, even though it was in receipt of £5m in state funding.[32] It was alleged that the BBSA had 'mismanaged' £50,000 in funding.[33] The BBSA had funds to cover the three men's teams, leading some

---

27 ibid para 8.12.

28 UK Sport, 'UK Sport Set to Drive a More Sustainable Winning Culture Across High Performance System in Response to Independent Review' (14 June 2017) <https://www.uksport.gov.uk/-/media/files/resources/cycling-independent-review-panel-report.ashx?la=en&hash=855A19D710CED75D2EF48C0EDC57570A> accessed 29 April 2024.

29 Sean Ingle, 'British Bobsleigh Team Told: Keep Quiet about Bullying or Miss Olympics' *The Guardian* (London, 17 June 2017) <https://www.theguardian.com/sport/2017/jun/17/british-bobsleigh-team-told-be-quiet-about-bullying-or-miss-olympics> accessed 29 April 2024.

30 Independent Review in Cycling (n 28) 4. The BBSA issued a statement refuting the claims on 13 June 2017: see <https://www.thebbsa.co.uk/2016/bbsa-statement/> accessed 29 April 2024.

31 Sean Ingle, 'Inside British Bobsleigh's "Toxic" Culture: The Latest Olympic Sport in the Dock' *The Guardian* (London, 9 October 2017) <https://www.theguardian.com/sport/2017/oct/09/british-bobsleigh-toxic-culture-uk-sport-winter-olympics–2018> accessed 29 April 2024.

32 Bobsleighing had £5m in funding taken away from it following a poor performance at the Winter Games in PyeongChang: Ben Bloom, 'GB Bobsleigh Faces Huge Funding Cuts After Woeful Performances at Winter Olympics to Round Off Year of Turmoil' *The Telegraph* (London, 25 February 2018) <https://www.telegraph.co.uk/winter-olympics/2018/02/25/gb-bobsleigh-faces-huge-funding-cuts-woeful-performances-winter/> accessed 29 April 2024.

33 Martha Kelner, 'British Bobsleigh Driver Attacks Decision to Cut Funding for Women's Team' *The Guardian* (London, 25 September 2017) <https://www.theguardian.com/sport/2017/sep/25/british-bobsleigh-driver-attacks-decision-to-cut-funding-for-womens-team> accessed 29 April 2024.

female competitors to question if the decision not to fund a women's team was 'sexist'.[34] One of the drivers, Mica McNeill, was prompted to use crowdfunding to cover the cost of a team travelling and competing in PyeongChang.[35] The BBSA subsequently reversed its decision not to fund the women's team. One of the reasons cited for the issues within the BBSA is that it is 'overly hierarchical' owing to its historic links with the military.[36] According to Ingle:

> Many of the squad are still in the army but take what is called paid training to compete in bobsleigh. Yet whether they were from the army or not, senior coaches often gave the impression that independent thought was not welcome.[37]

The BBSA was again subject to allegations of misconduct by its Board, which had been reconstituted in the aftermath of the issues raised in 2018. In the summer of 2020, allegations of bullying, discrimination and harassment were raised by Colin Rattigan, the only black member of the Board of the BBSA.[38] UK Sport commissioned an independent inquiry carried out by Quest; however, it was concluded that none of the claims made by Rattigan could be substantiated.[39] **2–17**

UK Sport allocates funding to elite athletes who are competing at Olympic and Paralympic level.[40] Sport England funds non-Olympic sports, including riding clubs, to encourage public participation in equestrian sports. Sport England is the national sports council for England and an investor of public money. Sport England and UK Sport's Code for Sports Governance imposes mandatory requirements on bodies seeking public funding.[41] However, it allows flexibility using **2–18**

---

[34] ibid.

[35] ibid.

[36] Ingle (n 31).

[37] ibid.

[38] Rattigan was a former Olympian who competed in the 1988 and 1992 Winter Games.

[39] UK Sport, 'UK Sport Statement on Outcome of Independent Investigation into British Bobsleigh and Skeleton Association' (2 June 2021) <https://www.uksport.gov.uk/news/2021/06/02/bbsa-statement> accessed 29 April 2024. Rattigan responded to the findings as 'a hit job': see Patrick Nathanson, 'Bobsleigh: Ex-BBSA Director Colin Rattigan Calls UK Sport Investigation "a hit job"' (BBC Sport, 26 March 2021) <https://www.bbc.com/sport/winter-sports/56541626> accessed 29 April 2024.

[40] UK Sport, 'FAQs' <http://www.uksport.gov.uk/about-us/faqs> accessed 29 April 2024. Both UK Sport and Sport England are funded via the lottery and the Exchequer. UK Sport and Sport England are answerable to the Department for Culture, Media and Sport. For more details on the Department, see <https://www.gov.uk/government/organisations/department-for-culture-media-and-sport> accessed 30 April 2024.

[41] Sport England and UK Sport, 'A Code for Sports Governance' (December 2021) <https://sportengland-production-files.s3.eu-west–2.amazonaws.com/s3fs-public/2021–12/A%20Code%20for%20Sports%20Governance.pdf?VersionId=Q0JD6BVXB.VgwbGEacG0zWsNPiWcGDHh> accessed 29 April 2024.

tiers. Tier 1 prescribes minimum mandatory requirements which 'seek to ensure the protection of public funding through good governance processes, without being unreasonably onerous'.[42] It contains eight principles under the headings of Structure, People, Communication, Standards and Conduct, and Policies and Processes.[43] Under the heading of People, it requires the regular election of committee members and a term of no more than nine years.[44] A separate code for Tier 1 provides more details and explains that it is aimed at those who receive funding for a specific project with a fixed end date and the total amount of funding is between £10,000 and £250,000.[45] If further investment is made and the relationship between the sporting body and Sport England and UK Sport goes beyond the initial project, the Tier 1 organisation may progress to Tier 2 or Tier 3 and as a corollary it will be subject to additional mandatory requirements.[46]

2–19 Tier 2 provides that 'Organisations receiving an investment categorised as Tier 2 are expected to meet all of the mandatory requirements in Tier 1 and some additional mandatory requirements from Tier 3'.[47] Tier 3 Principle 1 details the requirements of Boards which must be 'properly constituted and operating effectively'.[48] It imposes term limits, rules relating to the size and composition of Boards, and requirements relating to meetings.[49] Tier 3 Principle 2 requires diversity and inclusion.[50] The principles of Tier 1 are reiterated – Structure, People, Communication, Standards and Conduct, and Policies and Processes – however, they are detailed and require more formalities, for example, the publication of annual accounts.[51]

2–20 Governance in English football has been placed on a statutory footing. On 18 March 2024, the Football Governance Bill was introduced in the House of Commons.[52] It had reached the Committee Stage in the House of Commons, however, the General Election of May 2024 meant

---

42 ibid 14.
43 ibid.
44 ibid.
45 Sport England, 'A Code for Sports Governance Tier 1' October 2021 <https://sportengland-production-files.s3.eu-west-2.amazonaws.com/s3fs-public/2021-11/A%20Code%20for%20Sports%20Governance%20-%20Tier%201.pdf?VersionId=BqmsD9EEBJALDdi1njTgx058syoWBXXn> accessed 29 April 2024.
46 ibid 6.
47 ibid 9.
48 ibid 16.
49 ibid 16–17.
50 ibid 18.
51 ibid 16–22.
52 Its long title is 'A Bill to establish the Independent Football Regulator; to make provision for the licensing of football clubs; to make provision about the distribution of revenue received by organisers of football competitions; and for connected purposes'. The full text of the Bill is available at <https://publications.parliament.uk/pa/bills/cbill/58-04/0187/230187.pdf> accessed 29 April 2024.

that it did not progress any further. The Prime Minister, Keir Starmer, announced Labour's plan to reintroduce the Bill as part of its legislative programme during the King's Speech on 17 July 2024.[53] Its main purpose is 'to protect and promote the sustainability of English football'.[54] In order to achieve that purpose, it provides for the establishment of a body corporate called the Independent Football Regulator (IFR). Section 6 states the objectives of the IFR are:

> (a) to protect and promote the financial soundness of regulated clubs (referred to in this Act as 'the club financial soundness objective')
> (b) to protect and promote the financial resilience of English football (referred to in this Act as 'the systemic financial resilience objective') and
> (c) to safeguard the heritage of English football (referred to in this Act as 'the heritage objective').

Misgovernance can have serious consequences for a governing body. **2–21**
In June 2023, the IOC under Rule 3.7 of the Olympic Charter removed recognition of the International Boxing Association (IBA) for the 2028 Games.[55] Following the Tokyo Olympics in 2021, in December of that year, the IOC raised continued concerns regarding the governance, finance, and referees and judges involved in the sport.[56] The IOC Inquiry Committee in May 2019 recommended the withdrawal of the recognition of the IOC of the then AIBA; however, it was 'concerned with the protection of boxing athletes and with the maintenance of boxing as a sport in the Olympic Games Tokyo 2020'.[57] The IBA sought to annul

---

[53] It had been referred to a Public Bill Committee and a report was expected by 6 June 2024: Parliamentary Bills, 'Football Governance Bill' <https://bills.parliament.uk/bills/3701> accessed 8 August 2024.

[54] Football Governance Bill (n 44) s 1.

[55] International Olympic Committee, 'IOC Executive Board Recommends to IOC Session to Withdraw Recognition of International Boxing Association' 7 June 2023 <https://olympics.com/ioc/news/ioc-executive-board-recommends-to-ioc-session-to-withdraw-recognition-of-international-boxing-association> accessed 28 April 2024. As of 19 March 2024, 188 boxers had qualified for the Paris 2024 Games: see International Olympic Games, '188 Athletes Already Qualified for the Paris 2024 Boxing Tournament' 19 March 2014 <https://olympics.com/ioc/news/188-athletes-already-qualified-for-the-paris–2024-boxing-tournament> accessed 28 April 2024.

[56] International Olympic Committee, 'IOC EB Maintains Suspension of AIBA's Recognition; Expresses Serious Concerns with Regard to IWF' 9 December 2021 <https://olympics.com/ioc/news/ioc-eb-maintains-suspension-of-aiba-s-recognition-expresses-serious-concerns-with-regard-to-iwf> accessed 28 April 2024. The IBA was named the AIBA, Association Internationale de Boxe Amateur until 2007. It was renamed the International Boxing Association yet retained the abbreviation of IABA. In December 2021, it changed the abbreviated name to IBA to distance itself from its previous administration. For more information see, International Boxing Association, 'AIBA Becomes IBA as Extraordinary Congress Embraces Widespread Reform' <https://www.iba.sport/news/aiba-becomes-iba-as-extraordinary-congress-embraces-widespread-reform/> accessed 28 April 2024.

[57] International Olympic Committee, 'IOC Comprehensive Report on the Situation of the International Boxing Association (IBA – formerly known as AIBA' (Lausanne, 2 June 2023) [5] <https://stillmed.olympics.com/media/Documents/

the decision of the IOC and appealed it to the Court of Arbitration for Sport (CAS).[58] In April 2024, the CAS confirmed the decision of the IOC Session of 22 June 2023, in which the IOC withdrew recognition of the IBA.[59] In a press release following the publication of the decision, the IBA voiced its 'strong' disagreement with the CAS's failure to uphold its appeal.[60] In referring to the roadmap of reforms recommended by the IOC, the IBA contended that its 'diligent efforts' and 'extensive reforms' were overlooked by both the IOC and CAS.[61] On 2 July 2024, the IBA announced that it had filed an appeal to the Swiss Federal Tribunal (SFT).[62] World Boxing has expressed an interest in being recognised as the International Federation (IF) for boxing. On a statement published on its website, it stated:

> The comments made by the IOC send a clear message to Boxing National Federations that they must join and support a new International Federation immediately if boxing is to remain on the Olympic Programme, or the sport will not be part of future editions of the Olympic Games after Paris 2024, which will have devastating consequences for young boxers, at all levels, across the world.[63]

2–22 World Boxing is a not-for-profit, international sports federation consisting of members from national federations which was launched in April 2023.[64] It 'aims to be the new International Federation and has

News/2023/06/2023-06-IOC-Comprehensive-Report-IBA.pdf> accessed 28 April 2024.

58 CAS 2023/A/9757 *International Boxing Association v International Olympic Committee* award of 2 April 2024 <https://www.tas-cas.org/fileadmin/user_upload/Award_Final_9757__for_publ._.pdf> accessed 28 April 2024.

59 International Olympic Committee, 'IOC Session Withdraws Recognition of International Boxing Association' (22 June 2023) <https://olympics.com/ioc/news/ioc-session-withdraws-recognition-of-international-boxing-association> accessed 28 April 2024.

60 International Boxing Association, 'IBA to Fully Scrutinize CAS Award Prior to Considering Necessity of Swiss Federal Tribunal appeal' (3 April 2024) <https://www.iba.sport/news/iba-to-fully-scrutinize-cas-award-prior-to-considering-necessity-of-swiss-federal-tribunal-appeal/> accessed 28 April 2024.

61 ibid.

62 Chapter 12 discusses in detail the CAS and appeals to the SFT.

63 International Boxing Association, 'IBA appeals to Swiss Federal Tribunal over IOC's threat to the future of boxing' (2 July 2024) <https://www.iba.sport/news/iba-appeals-to-swiss-federal-tribunal-over-iocs-threat-to-the-future-of-boxing/> accessed 13 August 2024. The statement refers to the IOC Press Conference dated 19 March 2019. It is available on YouTube: <https://www.youtube.com/live/HsH1RKAksLo?si=Jimv2Ey8qkGFxb8Y> accessed 28 April 2024. See World Boxing, 'Statement from World Boxing Following the IOC Executive Board Meeting' (20 March 2024) <https://worldboxing.org/statement-from-world-boxing-following-the-ioc-executive-board-meeting/> accessed 28 April 2024.

64 World Boxing, 'Strategic Plan 2024 to 2028' (Renens, Switzerland, 2024) 3 <https://worldboxing.org/wp-content/uploads/2024/03/WORLDBOXING_Strategic-Plan_6.pdf> accessed 28 April 2024.

been established with the primary aim of ensuring that boxing remains at the heart of the Olympic Movement'.[65]

The above examples demonstrate the importance of national and international sports governing bodies adopting good governance practices; the discussion on the Salt Lake City Scandal, Russia and state-sponsored doping in track and field athletics, and FIFA and bribery, document the impact of corruption allegations on a global scale. Governance must be interpreted in a more holistic manner that includes the regulation of sport at an international level.[66] **2–23**

Salt Lake City Scandal

In November 1998, the IOC became embroiled in a scandal after it emerged that the daughter of an IOC member received a scholarship to attend a United States (US) university which was funded by the Salt Lake Organising Committee (SLOC) for the Winter Olympic Games of 2002.[67] While it may have appeared somewhat innocuous, the reporting of the scholarship was just the beginning. It soon transpired that a number of irregularities had occurred that 'threatened the entire existence of the International Olympic Committee'.[68] The IOC's 'operational autonomy and financial foundation' were both threatened by the intense media coverage of the events that followed a television report by KTVX, a Salt Lake City station, on 24 November 1998.[69] A number of investigations were carried out by the IOC, the United States Olympic Committee (USOC), the SLOC, the Sydney Organising Committee for the Olympic Games (SOCOG), the House Commerce Subcommittee on Oversight and Investigations and the US Department of Justice.[70] Twenty-four IOC members were implicated in the gift and cash payment scandal, with 20 receiving some form of sanction, of which four resigned and six were expelled from the IOC, three were exonerated and one, René Essomba, who would most likely have been expelled, passing away in 1998.[71] It was Essomba's daughter, Sonia, that was the subject of the **2–24**

---

65 ibid.

66 Chappelet (n 4) 725.

67 Bill Mallon, 'The Olympic Bribery Scandal' (2000) 8(2) Journal of Olympic History 11. In June 1995, Salt Lake City was awarded the 2002 Winter Olympic Games.

68 ibid 11.

69 Stephen R Wenn, and Robert Knight Barney, and Scott G Martyn, *Tarnished Rings: The International Olympic Committee and the Salt Lake City Bid Scandal* (Syracuse University Press 2011) xv.

70 ibid xv–xvi.

71 ibid xvi. Several allegations arose in relation to other cities that had bid to host the Olympics. Amsterdam lost out in its 1986 bid to host the 1992 Summer Olympics, however, it was alleged that to influence the decision, prostitutes, jewellery, and video cassette recorders (VCRs) were offered to IOC members. The 1992 Summer Olympic Games were held in Barcelona. In 1991, Nagano, Japan, was selected as host for the Winter Olympics of 1998 and it was reported that $33,000 was spent on 62 IOC member visits. Salt Lake City had come second to Nagano as host city. Atlanta won the vote in 1990 to hold the 1996 Summer Games. It was claimed

report by KTVX. After losing the bid to host the 1998 Winter Games in Salt Lake City in 1991, 13 scholarships amounting to $400,000 were paid to 13 individuals, with at least six of them being closely related to IOC members.[72] The televised report was the start of a sequence of events which culminated in the IOC introducing 50 reform measures to its Olympic Charter, beginning with the creation of an ad hoc Commission headed by Richard Pound, the then IOC Vice-President and Marketing Commission Chairman.

The IOC ad hoc Commission

2–25 In advance of the IOC Executive Board meeting in Lausanne in January 1999, the then President of the IOC, Juan Antonio Samaranch, wrote to the IOC Juridical Commission (now the Legal Affairs Commission) to investigate the scholarship awarded to Essomba.[73] In response, an ad hoc Commission was established to investigate the allegations of bribery, corruption and impropriety.[74] The terms of reference of the ad hoc Commission were to investigate the allegations of bribery and impropriety surrounding the candidacy of Salt Lake City for the 2002 Winter Games, on foot of this investigation to make recommendations in relation to the IOC members involved and the process around candidate cities becoming host cities for the Olympic Games.[75]

---

that it had given some IOC members golf clubs that cost $475, when the gift limit was $200. Some IOC members were furnished with tickets to Disneyland and several members were supplied with extra first-class airline tickets, more than the two tickets allocated per member and their spouse.

[72] Before the televised report, one of the 40-member SLOC, Ken Bullock, received the letter outlining the details of the Essomba scholarship from an anonymous source and passed the letter to the SLOC vice-president, Dave Johnson, at a board meeting on 8 October 1998. By all accounts, Bullock was very much in favour of transparency. It was not until the KTVX report that the allegations were made public: see Helen Lenskyj, *Inside the Olympic Industry: Power, Politics, and Activism* (Suny Press 2000) 10–11. More information on this letter can be found in the Report of the IOC ad hoc Commission to Investigate the Conduct of Certain IOC Members and to Consider Possible Changes in the Procedures for the Allocation of the Games of the Olympiad and Olympic Winter Games, Presented to the IOC Executive Board (Lausanne, 24 January 1999) <https://www.jensweinreich.de/wp-content/uploads/2009/03/1-pound-report–2411999.pdf> accessed 30 April 2024. The letter was addressed to Sonia Essomba and was purporting to come from the SLOC. It stated that the amount specified in the letter was the final payment that would be addressed to Sonia Essomba. The report raised questions as to the authenticity of the letter as there was no record of it coming from the SLOC, nor was there any evidence that a cheque for the specified amount had come from the SLOC. According to the Washington Post, the final cheque amounted to $10,114.99: Marc Fisher, 'Salt Lake's Tarnished Olympic Ring' *The Washington Post* (Washington DC, 17 January 1999) <https://www.washingtonpost.com/archive/politics/1999/01/17/salt-lakes-tarnished-olympic-ring/da36aeac-10e6-4670-a0e2-587a092f04b5/?utm_term=.8632fc2d23ba> accessed 30 April 2024.

[73] ibid.

[74] Report of the IOC ad hoc Commission (n 72).

[75] The Legal Affairs Commission advises the IOC Session, the IOC Executive Board and the IOC President on legal matters and has both a consultative and operational role: see <https://www.olympic.org/legal-affairs> accessed 30 April 2024. The

The IOC Executive Board met on 12 December 1998 and the ad hoc Commission met the following day.[76] Following the Executive Board meeting, Swiss IOC member Marc Hodler informed the press that approximately 5–7% of IOC members had requested money in return for votes.[77] Hodler added: 'To my knowledge, a certain part of the votes always have been given through corruption.'[78] In the wake of Hodler's comments, a media crisis ensued.[79] The ad hoc Commission worked on its investigation throughout December and January and presented its findings to the IOC in late January 1999. While the IOC faced increased media scrutiny, by launching its own investigation, engaging with the media, its sponsors and television partners, it managed to survive the negative publicity with its autonomy intact.[80] **2–26**

On 24 January 1999, the ad hoc Commission and the IOC Executive Board met in Lausanne, Switzerland. The investigation found that the bid committee of the SLOC had created a financial assistance programme **2–27**

IOC Executive Board was founded in 1921 and consists of the President of the IOC, four Vice-Presidents and 10 other members. It is responsible for the overall administration of the IOC and ensures that the Olympic Charter is adhered to by its members: see <https://www.olympic.org/executive-board> accessed 30 April 2024.

[76] It comprised of Pound (lawyer, first President of the World Anti-Doping Agency from 1999–2007 and current Chairman of the Olympic Broadcasting Services), Thomas Bach (ninth President of the IOC 2013-present, Kéba Mbaye (former member of the IOC, former President of the CAS and former Vice-President of the International Court of Justice), Jacques Rogge (eighth President of the IOC 2001–13), and Pál Schmitt (former Chief of Protocol of the IOC and President of Hungary from 2010–12), and was coordinated by François Carrard, the then IOC Director General (term of office from 1989–2003).

[77] Christopher Clarey, 'OLYMPICS; Senior IOC Official Says Votes on Sites Were Sold' *The New York Times* (New York, 13 December 1998) <https://www.nytimes.com/1998/12/13/sports/olympics-senior-ioc-official-says-votes-on-sites-were-sold.html> accessed 30 April 2024.

[78] ibid. Hodler indicated that the bidding process for both Atlanta (1996 Summer Games) and Nagano, Japan (1998 Winter Games) involved bribes.

[79] Stephen R Wenn and Scott G Martyn, '"Tough Love": Richard Pound, David D'Alessandro, and the Salt Lake City Olympics Bid Scandal' (2006) 26(1) History in Sport 64, 66. Hodler raised his concerns about bribes for bid cities in 1986. While no investigation was carried out at the time, the Executive Committee asked Hodler to draft regulations in relation to IOC member visits to bid cities. The regulations became known as the Hodler Rules and were adopted in 1992; however, the authors (at 69) note that '[i]nstitutional indifference to compliance with the Hodler Rules festered'.

[80] ibid. Wenn and Martyn discuss the relationship between Pound, the Chairman of the ad hoc Commission, and David D'Alessandro, the CEO of John Hancock, a major sponsor of the Olympics. John Hancock continued its relationship with the IOC until the 2008 Olympics in Beijing. D'Alessandro, unlike the other major sponsors, spoke directly for John Hancock and did not delegate the duty to a spokesperson like UPS and Coca-Cola. D'Alessandro used the media to convey his discontent at the slow pace of the investigation; he was most vociferous in his calls for major reforms within the IOC. Pound's handling of the scandal and his endeavours to introduce more transparency and accountability were instrumental in 'saving the Games': see James Deacon, 'Saving the Games' (8 February 1999) 112(6) Macleans 16.

in late 1991 or early 1992 after Salt Lake City had lost out to Nagano in the bid for the 1998 Winter Olympics.[81] The SLOC characterised the scholarships as being part of the National Olympic Committee (NOC) Assistance Programme, a form of humanitarian aid that benefitted athletes from poorer nations, however, the public and media were not convinced.[82] While the investigation could not conclusively find if the entire bid committee was aware of the programme, two individuals were named in the report. These individuals were: Thomas Welch, who was president of the bid committee and subsequently the president of the SLOC and David Johnson, the then Executive Vice-President of the SLOC.[83] Both Welch and Johnson were aware of the programme and were actively involved in its implementation.[84] The IOC Executive Board met with SLOC representatives following the meeting of 13 December and in return for full disclosure and cooperation, the Executive Board expressed its 'confidence in SLOC'.[85]

2–28 The ad hoc Commission referred to the comments of Hodler and after meeting with him, it was found 'that he had no personal knowledge of any inappropriate action on the part of any member of the IOC'; all the information he had heard was from secondary sources.[86] The ad hoc Commission recommended the expulsion of six members of the IOC and that further investigations be made in relation to three other members. The IOC Executive Board accepted the recommendations of the ad hoc Commission.

SLOC Board of Ethics

2–29 The SLOC Board of Ethics was established on 10 April 1997. In early February 1999, the SLOC Board of Ethics published a detailed report on the allegations following the request of the SLOC Executive Committee to carry out 'an independent and thorough investigation'.[87] The Board of Ethics Panel was established in response to the issues raised by the media. The five-member panel found that up to one-fifth of IOC delegates received 'money and other material benefits' to induce them to vote for Salt Lake City to host the 2002 Winter Games.[88] The Board of Ethics investigation uncovered the payment of medical bills for Jean-

---

[81] Report of the IOC ad hoc Commission (n 72) 2.
[82] Lenskyj (n 72) 11.
[83] Report of the IOC ad hoc Commission (n 72) 2. Welch resigned in 1997 and Johnson was one of the few bid committee members who made it onto the Organising Committee of the Olympic Games (OCOG).
[84] ibid.
[85] ibid.
[86] ibid 4.
[87] Bill Mallon, 'The Olympic Bribery Scandal' (2000) 8 Journal of Olympic History 11, 13 <http://isoh.org/wp-content/uploads/JOH-Archives/johv8n2f.pdf> accessed 30 April 2024.
[88] The information is taken from the case of *United States of America v Thomas K Welch and David R Johnson*, 327 F3d 1081, 1085 (10th Cir 2003) as the original report is not available electronically.

Claude Ganga, the Congolese IOC member. During visits to Salt Lake City, Ganga's wife had cosmetic surgery while his mother-in-law had a knee replacement, all covered by the Bid Committee.[89] The report found that there was 'no personal relationship between a Bid Committee official and an IOC member that appears more improper than the business dealings between Mr Welch and Mr Ganga'.[90]

The SLOC Ethics Panel documented 57 pages of 'revelations and various indiscretions' and concluded with nine recommendations, including more robust filing of reports with details of all expenditures and a prohibition on bid cities from taking part in NOC assistance or Olympic Solidarity programmes during the bid process.[91] **2–30**

Special Bid Oversight Commission of the United States Olympic Committee

The USOC established a special inquiry with five members, including former Democrat Senator George Mitchell as chair. The 'Mitchell Commission', as it became known, published its report on 1 March 1999. While not referring to any names, it criticised the bidding process, the structure of the IOC and deficiencies in the USOC.[92] It was a lengthy report which took a more holistic view by examining the IOC, the USOC and the bidding process. The Mitchell Report called for reforms at every level of the IOC, with Mitchell stating at a press conference at the launch of the report: 'If all the IOC top members and president (Juan Antonio) Samaranch resign now and nothing else is done, nothing will change.'[93] It put forward a number of recommendations, including the prohibition on bid cities from giving members of the IOC and the USOC financial assistance above a nominal value and from directly paying travel and other expenses of IOC and USOC members.[94] In order to bring about more transparency and accountability, the Mitchell Report advocated **2–31**

---

[89] Jere Longman, 'OLYMPICS: African Expelled from IOC Lobbies for His Reinstatement' *The New York Times* (New York, 16 March 1999) <https://www.nytimes.com/1999/03/16/sports/olympics-african-expelled-from-ioc-lobbies-for-his-reinstatement.html> accessed 30 April 2024. His mother-in-law had been flown from Paris to Salt Lake City and her travel was paid by the Salt Lake City Bid Committee. It was reported to have cost $27,675: see Wenn and others (n 69) 23.

[90] Cited by Mallon (n 87) 14. Welch and Ganga had set up a partnership called 'Claudet Investments' in 1994.

[91] ibid 15.

[92] Bill Mallon, Jeroen Heijmans, *Historical Dictionary of the Olympic Movement* (Scarecrow Press 2011) 249. The Mitchell Commission did not interview any of the IOC members involved. It relied on information from the SLOC, the USOC and media sources.

[93] 'Mitchell Calls for IOC to Face Radical Reform', *The Irish Times* (Dublin, 2 March 1999) <https://www.irishtimes.com/sport/mitchell-calls-for-ioc-to-face-radical-reform–1.158516 > accessed 30 April 2024.

[94] This is taken from the Mallon article (n 87) 15 as the report is no longer available electronically.

a more central approach to travel and other expenses in relation to bid and candidate cities that would be administered respectively by the USOC and the IOC.[95] It called for a prohibition on bid and candidate cities from being involved in international assistance programmes.[96]

2–32 While the Mitchell Commission carried some weight as George Mitchell was an internationally renowned figure given his involvement in the Northern Ireland peace process, it had little power and operated in a consultative role only.[97] The Mitchell Report called for the Recommendations of Bribery in International Business Transactions of the Organisation of Economic Co-operation and Development (OECD) and the Foreign Corrupt Practices Act to apply to the IOC.[98] However, the IOC was deemed not to constitute a foreign public official under the definition provided for in Article 1(4)(a) of the Convention on Bribery in International Business Transactions.[99]

2–33 Simultaneously, the US Department of Justice carried out an investigation into the allegations of bribery and corruption surrounding the SLOC whether any federal law could be invoked, including the Foreign Corrupt Practices Act 1977.[100] Fifteen criminal charges were brought against Johnson and Welch, including bribery, conspiracy, and fraud. Both were acquitted with US Federal Court Judge Sam holding:

---

95 ibid.

96 ibid. For details of the current bidding process see International Olympic Committee, 'Becoming an Olympic Games Host: From Vision to Election' <https://olympics.com/ioc/becoming-an-olympic-games-host> accessed 30 April 2024.

97 ibid. See also Maurice Roche, *Megaevents and Modernity: Olympics and Expos in the Growth of Global Culture* (Routledge 2002) 207.

98 These recommendations were introduced in 1994 and added to in 1995. The proposals were adopted by way of convention signed in Paris on 17 December 1997 by 34 countries accounting for 70% of world trade. The Convention entered into force on 15 February 1999: see Flavio M Menezes, 'The Microeconomics of Corruption' in Peter Larmour and Nick Wolanin (eds), *Corruption and Anti-corruption* (ANU E Press 2013) 139. The signatories are required to incorporate the Convention into domestic law providing for criminal penalties on businesses who offer bribes to foreign officials in order to gain an unfair business advantage: see Angela Saloufakos-Parsons, 'Going for the "Gold": An Application of the OECD Bribery Convention to the Olympic Games Scandal' (2001) 31(2) California Western International Law Journal 297, 302 <https://scholarlycommons.law.cwsl.edu/cwilj/vol31/iss2/6> accessed 30 April 2024. See also Mark Dodds, 'Revisiting the Salt Lake City Olympic Scandal: Would the Outcome Be any Different Today?' (2015) 12(1) Sport Management International Journal 1.

99 The definition of foreign public official is as follows: 'any person holding a legislative, administrative or judicial office of a foreign country, whether appointed or elected; any person exercising a public function for a foreign country, including for a public agency or public enterprise; and any official or agent of a public international organisation': see Convention on Combating Bribery of Foreign Public Officials in International Business Transactions and related documents (OECD 2011) <https://olympics.com/ioc/becoming-an-olympic-games-host> accessed 30 April 2024.

100 The question arose whether an IOC member constituted a foreign official for the purposes of the 1977 Act.

> In my 40 years' experience with the criminal justice system, as a defence and prosecuting attorney, and as a Utah state judge and a United States District Court Judge, I have never seen a criminal case brought to trial that was so devoid of … criminal intent or evil purpose.[101]

This was the second time Sam J had presided over the trial of Welch and **2–34**
Johnson.[102] Citing the allegations as 'ambiguous and unconstitutionally vague', Sam J dismissed the case.[103] The case was appealed with the 10th Circuit Court of Appeals in Denver deciding to re-open the case in 2003 and the case being returned to Sam J.[104] Pound was the final witness in the five-week trial – he contended that the actions of Welch and Johnson did not amount to bribery but rather 'payments to encourage good feelings about Salt Lake'.[105]

Second Report of the ad hoc Commission

The Second Report of the ad hoc Commission was presented to the IOC **2–35**
Executive Board on 11 March 1999.[106] The Second Report referred to the SLOC Board of Ethics Report and noted that information relating to accounts of the SLOC provided to the ad hoc Commission were not necessarily accurate and that reimbursement cheques were often signed by the person being reimbursed.[107] It was critical of the naming in the Board of Ethics Report of IOC members, none of whom were given the opportunity to respond to the allegations prior to its publication.[108]

---

[101] Cited by Lex Hemphill, 'OLYMPICS; Acquittals End Bid Scandal that Dogged Winter Games' *The New York Times* (New York, 6 December 2003) <https://www.nytimes.com/2003/12/06/sports/olympics-acquittals-end-bid-scandal-that-dogged-winter-games.html> accessed 28 June 2024. The charges were as follows: one count of conspiracy, five counts of wire fraud, five counts of mail fraud, and four violations of the United States Immigration and Travel Act laws. Welch and Johnson were facing a maximum five-year prison sentence per offence and/or a fine of $250,000, see Wenn and others (n 69) 139.

[102] Jo Thomas, 'OLYMPICS; 4 Salt Lake City Charges Dismissed' *The New York TImes* (New York, 17 July 2001) <https://www.nytimes.com/2001/07/17/sports/olympics-4-salt-lake-city-charges-dismissed.html> accessed 28 June 2024.

[103] ibid. See also Lex Hemphill, 'Judge Dismisses IOC Bribery Case' *The New York Times* (New York, 5 December 2003) <https://www.nytimes.com/2003/12/05/sports/othersports/judge-dismisses-ioc-bribery-case.html> accessed 28 June 2024.

[104] *United States of America* (n 88).

[105] Cited by Wenn and others (n 69) 139. Prosecutor Richard Wiedis of the Justice Department pleaded with Sam J to allow the case to go before a jury. He stated, 'To dismiss this case now is to deprive the jury of its right to make a statement that Olympic corruption must be stopped': cited by Alan Abrahamson, 'Judge Drops Olympic Bid Case', *LA Times* (Los Angeles, 6 December 2003) <https://www.latimes.com/archives/la-xpm–2003-dec-06-sp-saltlakecity6-story.html> accessed 30 April 2024.

[106] Second Report of the ad hoc Commission to Investigate the Conduct of Certain IOC Members and to Consider possible changes in the Procedures for the Allocation the Games of the Olympiad and Olympic Winter Games, Presented to the IOC Executive Board, 11 March 1999 <https://www.jensweinreich.de/wp-content/uploads/2009/03/2-pound-report–1131999.pdf> accessed 30 April 2024.

[107] ibid 1–2 (fn 1).

[108] ibid 3.

However, the ad hoc Commission acknowledged that several of the suggestions put forward by the Board of Ethics were useful and supported by the Commission.[109] In regard to the Report of the Special Bid Oversight Commission of the USOC, the ad hoc Commission gave cognisance to some of the 'valuable suggestions' that the IOC Executive Board could consider relating to its structure.[110] The ad hoc Commission proffered that the NOCs should have a 'considerably more active role, supervisory, and otherwise ... in future bid processes'.[111] The ad hoc Commission iterated that it was making recommendations based on the information supplied to it; it had no power to compel third parties to provide information.[112] If more facts about IOC member impropriety came to light in the future then it would be up to the IOC to fully review the situation and take appropriate action.[113] While insisting that it was in no way absolving the IOC from blame, the ad hoc Commission contended that the Salt Lake Bid Committee had been persistent in its efforts to entice IOC members with gifts and other benefits in exchange for votes.[114] There were instances where the IOC member had refused the gift or benefit, including a Romanian IOC member who refused the offer of his living expenses being paid while he was a visiting scholar in the US.[115] The Olympic Charter provided for only one type of sanction – expulsion – however, there were some IOC members that deserved a warning as their conduct was not 'sufficiently egregious to justify a recommendation for expulsion'.[116]

2–36 The ad hoc Commission recommended the expulsion of five IOC members (including Ganga).[117] Another member, Paul Wallwork, was expelled following the discovery of a $30,000 loan made by Welch to Wallwork's wife.[118] While the loan had been subsequently paid and

---

109 ibid.

110 ibid. The ad hoc Commission was not in favour of some of the more 'extreme characterisations' contained in the report. This is discussed in detail on page 10 of the report. The report acknowledged that some members exercised poor judgement and as such did not warrant expulsion. It highlighted the uniqueness of IOC membership and its diversity. Its independence and freedom have been instrumental in resisting 'political pressures in extreme situations'. It also noted that cultural differences should be recognised and what is considered an improper gift in some parts of the world might be acceptable in other parts of the world. Added to this is the personal friendships between IOC members and bid committees, the report at page 11 contends that some IOC members believed that the gifts they received from the Salt Lake Bid Committee were personal and refusal could amount to offence in some cultures.

111 ibid 4.

112 ibid 5. The SLOC Board of Ethics and Special Bid Oversight Commission were similarly constrained.

113 ibid 6.

114 ibid.

115 ibid 7.

116 ibid.

117 ibid 7–8. There was a sixth member, Charles Mukora; however, he had resigned since the first ad hoc Commission Report.

118 ibid 50–52. The Welch and Wallwork families had developed a friendship in the

Wallwork and his wife were separated at the time, the ad hoc Commission considered the conduct of Wallwork to amount to impropriety and a conflict of interest that warranted expulsion from the IOC.[119] A further nine IOC members, the ad hoc Commission advised, should be issued with warnings.[120] The ad hoc Commission recommended that three members be exonerated on grounds that their conduct fell within IOC guidelines in relation to travel to candidate cities.[121]

The report concluded that structural reforms within the IOC were needed to prevent another Salt Lake City scandal from occurring.[122] While contending that the IOC should have done more, the report recognised that the IOC was focussed on other areas of the Olympic Movement and consequently 'gave this problem less attention that it deserved'.[123] The IOC guidelines relating to travel and gifts needed 'stricter rules and better enforcement', however, the ad hoc Commission refuted the claims that the IOC 'actively fostered or encouraged a "climate of corruption"'.[124] The report asserted: '[s]uch allegations are neither fair nor true'.[125] It defended the position of the IOC in relation to the bidding process, pointing to the introduction of guidelines in 1988 concerning travel and gifts in order to reduce the costs of the bidding city [126] The IOC encountered hostility from bidding cities who showed distain for the 'paternalistic' approach of the IOC.[127] The report noted that the IOC, on hearing the allegations following the KTVX televised report, took immediate action.[128] **2–37**

The ad hoc Commission recommended the following: **2–38**

- Reforms to the host city selection process.
- Limitations on travel by IOC members to bid cities.
- Establishment of a permanent and independent Ethics Commission tasked with creating a Code of Ethics comprised of senior officials from around the world, the majority of whom would be independent, non-IOC members.[129]

The report concluded that the IOC should not dwell on what occurred in **2–39**

late 1980s.

119 ibid 51.

120 ibid 8.

121 ibid 12–14, 34–6 and 42–43.

122 ibid 8.

123 ibid 9.

124 ibid.

125 ibid.

126 ibid. The guidelines had been subject to refinement and elaboration over the 10 years since they were introduced.

127 ibid.

128 ibid.

129 ibid 10.

Salt Lake City but to look to structural reforms to prevent such conduct occurring again in the bidding process.[130]

108th Extraordinary IOC Session

2–40 The first Report of the ad hoc Commission recommended that IOC President Samaranch hold an Extraordinary Session at his earliest convenience.[131] The IOC Extraordinary Session took place over two days in March 1999 in Lausanne. The IOC was under immense pressure to show how seriously it was taking the fallout from the Salt Lake City scandal. Wenn notes that there was a lot of work to be done to improve the IOC's image and brand and

> the peak level of media's agitation had been reached and a sense of measured optimism soon flowed through the IOC's headquarters where only grim faces, blank stares, and furrowed brows had been seen over the last few months.[132]

2–41 The 108th Extraordinary Session was a 'critical juncture', as it was hoped that the proposed reforms along with the expulsion of six members would endear the IOC to the media.[133] Samaranch assured sponsors that the IOC was dealing with the issues and that reforms were imminent.[134] The IOC president was fearful of a 'palace revolt' as it was claimed that some IOC members were calling for his resignation.[135]

2–42 On the first day of the Extraordinary Session, 17 March 1999, Samaranch spoke of the need to 'act quickly, decisively and unanimously'.[136] He put forward a number of reforms, including a change in the bid process for cities and the creation of an Ethics Commission.[137] He also advocated the creation of a group called the IOC 2000 Commission which would comprise of IOC members and 'prominent outside individuals'.[138] This

---

[130] ibid 11.

[131] Report of the ad hoc Commission (n 72) 17

[132] Stephen R Wenn, 'Two Days Lausanne Stood Still: The 108th Extraordinary IOC Session, March, 1999' in Robert K Barney and others (eds), *Pathways: Critiques and Discourse in Olympic Research: Proceedings of the Ninth International Symposium for Olympic Research* (University of Western Ontario 2008) 180.

[133] ibid.

[134] ibid 181.

[135] Duncan Mackay, '2002 Winter Olympic Bid Scandal: Palace Revolt Rocks Samaranch' *The Guardian* (London, 4 February 1999) <https://www.theguardian.com/sport/1999/feb/04/ioc-samaranch-olympic-venue-selection-process> accessed 30 April 2024. Samaranch was not only recommending changes to the bidding process but also the voting system.

[136] The minutes of this meeting are no longer available on the IOC Archives webpage; the secondary account of Wenn (n 132) 182 is being used to summarise the main points raised during the two-day meeting. The six members who were facing expulsion appeared and attempted to defend their actions, the most vocal of all being Jean-Claude Ganga, see 183–84.

[137] ibid.

[138] ibid.

group would be entrusted with the task of making recommendations for the reform of the Olympic Charter.[139]

The IOC members voted by secret ballot to expel the six members with Ganga receiving 88 votes in favour of his expulsion and two against. Some IOC members took issue with Wallwork being expelled and Un Yong Kim, the South Korean member, merely receiving a warning. Kim's son had secured a job in America and at least half his salary was paid by the Salt Lake Bidding Committee, however, his father denied any knowledge of this.[140] Kim was tipped to succeed Samaranch as IOC President, however, was unsuccessful in 2001 and was subsequently imprisoned for embezzlement.[141] **2–43**

On day two, 18 March, Samaranch's motion for a modification of the bidding selection for host cities was accepted with only one abstention and no votes against.[142] While the members disagreed over the ratio of non-members to IOC members being appointed to the Ethics Commission, Samaranch suggested a four (non-IOC) to three (IOC) member balance with the logistics to be discussed in more detail at the IOC's June Session.[143] The members voted unanimously in favour of the motion. The President suggested that the IOC 2000 Commission consist of 20–24 members with IOC members being in the majority.[144] The IOC 2000 Commission would be tasked with preparing a preliminary report and submitting it to the June Session and a final one in advance of the December Session.[145] **2–44**

It was at the 108th Extraordinary Session that the proposed establishment of the World Anti-Doping Agency (WADA) was accepted. In February 1999, the World Conference on Doping in Sport was held in Lausanne following several high-profile doping scandals in cycling.[146] The importance of WADA was 'overshadowed by expulsion and reform initiatives', however: **2–45**

> it signalled that the IOC was prepared to play a more significant role in tackling the modern-day scourge of international sport, and gave IOC

[139] ibid. Samaranch also called for a secret ballot on a vote of confidence for his continued leadership with 86–2 voting in favour and one spoiled vote.

[140] Duncan Mackay, 'Top Korean Caught in Bribery Row' *The Guardian* (London, 10 January 2004) <https://www.theguardian.com/sport/2004/jan/10/athletics.duncanmackay> accessed 30 April 2024.

[141] Wenn (n 132) 184.

[142] ibid 185.

[143] ibid.

[144] ibid.

[145] ibid.

[146] The Lausanne Declaration on Doping in Sport, 4 February 1999 <https://www.wada-ama.org/sites/default/files/resources/files/lausanne_declaration_on_doping_in_sport.pdf> accessed 30 April 2024.

officials another talking point in their efforts to convince reporters that the IOC had followed through on its promise to confront its problems.[147]

IOC 2000 Commission

2–46 Samaranch was appointed as Chair of the IOC 2000 Commission. The IOC 2000 Commission's role was to enquire into reforming the IOC structures and the bidding process for candidate cities. It consisted of 82 members, less than half of which were IOC members, and an Executive Board of 26, with 13 IOC members and 13 non-IOC members.[148] An interim report was produced in June 1999 and the final report containing 50 recommendations was approved by the Executive Committee of the IOC 2000 Commission, albeit with 'slight modifications' on 30 October 1999.[149] At the 110th IOC Session on 11 and 12 December 1999, the 50 recommendations were approved, leading to a major overhaul of the Olympic Charter. The final report noted that the main objective of the IOC 2000 Commission was to examine three areas:

1. Composition, structure, and organisation of the IOC.[150]
2. Role of the IOC.[151]

---

[147] Wenn (n 132) 186.

[148] John Grasso, and Bill Mallon, and Jeroen Heijmans, *Historical Dictionary of the Olympic Movement* (5th edn, Rowman & Littlefield 2015) 271.

[149] The IOC 2000 Commission operated on three levels: Plenary Commission, Executive Committee and Three Working Groups with each of the working groups responsible for one of the three areas. Report by the IOC 2000 Commission to the 110th IOC Session, Lausanne, 11 and 12 December 1999: <https://stillmed.olympic.org/media/Document%20Library/OlympicOrg/IOC/Who-We-Are/Commissions/IOC–2000-Reform-Follow-up/EN–110th-IOC-Session-Report-by-the-IOC–2000-Commission-December–1999.pdf> accessed 30 April 2024.

[150] ibid 3–6, Recommendations 1–12.The recommendations included setting the maximum number of members at 115 (Recommendation 1), an age limit of 70 for all members (Recommendation 5), an increase in the number of members of the Executive Board from 11 to 15 (Recommendation 8), an eight-year term for the President with two options: one non-renewable term; possibility of one re-election for a second term of four or eight years (Recommendation 9). Recommendation 12 proposed that the new rules come into force on 1 January 2000 with one year for implementation. John J MacAloon contends the reform regarding member selection was of utmost importance as previously Samaranch had too much personal control resulting in some members not being properly screened: 'Scandal and Governance: Inside and Outside the IOC 2000 Commission' (2011) 14(3) Sport in Society 292, 296–97. Under the new system, potential members would be nominated by IOC Members, IFs, NOCs, the Athletes Commission and Continental Olympic Associations, thus meaning the nominees were 'more likely to be established sport world persons'.

[151] Report by the IOC 2000 Commission (n 149) 7–26. Eight areas were dealt with under this: The Olympic Games, Athletes, Solidarity, Education and Culture, Doping, Relations with Governmental and Non-governmental organisations, Communication and Transparency. These are contained in Recommendations 13–49. In relation to doping, the IOC 2000 Commission stated that it fully supported the the World Anti-Doping Code (WADC) and strongly supported the creation of the Olympic Movement Anti-Doping Code. It reiterated that the WADC would be in force from 1 January 2000.

3. Designation of Olympic Games Host Cities.[152]

Of particular importance were the recommendations regarding the bid process.[153] Recommendation 49 proposed the strengthening of the role of the NOC in the bid process. It also called for a new candidature procedure whereby a city nominated by its NOC should not be considered a candidate city until the IOC Executive Board examined and approved the city so that only cities that were adequately equipped and in compliance with IOC procedures would be permitted to proceed to the full bid process. Recommendation 50.3 purposed the drafting of a code of conduct and sanctions for breaches in the form of a contract between the IOC, the candidature committee, and the NOC. Recommendation 50.7 stated that it was 'not considered necessary for IOC members to visit the candidate cities nor for the representatives or candidate cities, or third parties acting on their behalf not considered necessary for representatives of candidate cities, or third parties acting on their behalf, to visit IOC members'.[154] However, the IOC 2000 Commission added that if visits to a candidate city were considered necessary by IOC members in order 'to be in a position to make an objective assessment of the city concerned' then a request to the IOC Executive Board should be made. If the request was granted, the IOC Executive Board would decide the conditions under which the visits could be made, and the IOC Administration would organise and cover the costs of such visits. The 50 recommendations were accepted 'most unanimously' by the IOC members at the 110th Session.[155] **2–47**

Ethics Commission

The Ethics Commission, as noted above, was created during the 108th Extraordinary IOC Session. Its role is to examine the responsibilities of the IOC and supervise the selection process of bid cities.[156] It has nine members, four of which are IOC members, one of whom must be an Athletes' Commission member, and five independent members.[157] The IOC Ethics Commission is referred to as the 'Guardian of the Ethical Principles' and its role is stated in Rule 22 of the Olympic Charter: **2–48**

> The IOC Ethics Commission is charged with defining and updating a framework of ethical principles, including a Code of Ethics, based upon the values and principles enshrined in the Olympic Charter of which the

---

152 ibid 27–28, Recommendations 49–50.
153 ibid.
154 ibid.
155 MacAloon (n 150) 296.
156 Mallon (n 87) 18.
157 International Olympic Committee, 'Ethics Commission' <https://olympics.com/ioc/ethics-commission> accessed 30 April 2024. There is also a Chief Ethics and compliance officer, a position which was created in 2015.

said Code forms an integral part. In addition, it investigates complaints raised in relation to the non-respect of such ethical principles, including breaches of the Code of Ethics and, if necessary, proposes sanctions to the IOC Executive Board.[158]

2–49 The Ethics Commission authored a Code of Ethics in spring of 1999 which included provisions on dignity, integrity, and confidentiality. The IOC Ethics Commission is still in existence and its role is to maintain the Code of Ethics and investigate complaints and issue sanctions.[159] Allegations of breaches of the Code of Ethics can be referred to the Ethics Commission via an 'Integrity and Compliance Hotline'.[160] In September 2017, the former United Nations' Secretary General Ban Ki-moon was elected as chair of the IOC Ethics Commission.[161] The IOC, in its efforts to be transparent and embrace reform, published the host city contract on its website in July 2018.[162]

United States Congress

2–50 The conduct of IOC officials reached the United States Congress, although its jurisdiction was questionable given that the IOC is an international sports organisation based in Switzerland.[163] The House Commerce Subcommittee on Oversight and Investigations requested that the bid for the Atlanta Olympics be examined following a report (the 'Bell Report') from former US Attorney General Griffin B Bell, a lawyer with the firm King & Spaulding.[164] Bell stated: 'This is not a corrupt system, but it is subject to abuse.'[165] In a similar vein, the then

---

[158] The most recent version of the Olympic Charter is in force from 15 October 2023 <https://stillmed.olympics.com/media/Document%20Library/OlympicOrg/General/EN-Olympic-Charter.pdf> accessed 30 April 2024. The IOC Ethics Commission has a Code of Ethics: see International Olympic Committee, 'Ethics' (Lausanne, 2024) 113–27 <https://stillmed.olympics.com/media/Document%20Library/OlympicOrg/Documents/Code-of-Ethics/Code-of-Ethics-ENG.pdf> accessed 30 April 2024.

[159] Ethics Commission (n 157).

[160] International Olympic Committee, 'Welcome to the International Olympic Committee's Integrity and Compliance Hotline' <https://ioc.integrityline.org/#_ga=2.240913866.83253739.1538145139–1611282452.1538145139> accessed 30 April 2024.

[161] International Olympic Committee, 'IOC Elects Former United Nations Secretary General Ban Ki-moon to Head its Ethics Commission', 17 September 2017 <https://www.olympic.org/news/ioc-elects-former-united-nations-secretary-general-ban-ki-moon-to-head-its-ethics-commission> accessed 30 April 2024. Ki-moon remains in the post as of April 2024.

[162] International Olympic Committee, 'IOC Reinforces its Commitment to Transparency and Reform by Publishing Host City Contract', 2 July 2018 <https://www.olympic.org/news/ioc-reinforces-its-commitment-to-transparency-and-reform-by-publishing-host-city-contract> accessed 30 April 2024.

[163] Mallon (n 87) 20.

[164] Grasso and others (n 148) 415.

[165] The Associated Press, 'PLUS: OLYMPICS — 1996 ATLANTA GAMES; Officials Deny Bidding "Excesses"' *The New York Times* (New York, 17 September 1999)

IOC Director General, François Carrard, in his testimony before the United States House of Representatives on 14 October 1999, stated:

> unfortunately, while the Games evolved, our organizational structure did not keep up with pace of change. In effect, we did not realize we were going through a growth crisis. The result of an old-fashioned structure managing modern Games was not corruption, but a situation in which some of the less responsible members – a small minority – showed poor judgment and abused the system. Our problems were caused by weak people, structures and procedures.[166]

Current Bidding System

The bidding process for host cities continues to feature in the reforms **2–51** of the IOC. A recent development is that of the creation of the Future Contests Commission for the Games of the Olympiad. There is a Future Contests Commission for the Summer Games and another Future Contests Commission for the Winter Games. The role of the Future Contests Commission is 'to oversee interest in hosting future Olympic Games and Youth Olympic Games' and report back to the IOC's Executive Board.[167] The Executive Board accepted the changes in May 2019, and it was at the IOC's 134th Session in Lausanne in late June 2019 that the Future Contests Commission was approved.[168] It defines 'host' broadly to include multiple cities/regions/countries and not just a single city.[169]

The current candidature process is outlined on the IOC website, referred **2–52** to as the 'new norm', and it explains how the Olympic Games are run and cities seeking to host the games will be provided with more support from the IOC.[170]

While the IOC has endeavoured to tighten up its system of governance, **2–53**

<https://www.nytimes.com/1999/09/17/sports/plus-olympics–1996-atlanta-games-officials-deny-bidding-excesses.html> accessed 1 July 2024

[166] Grasso and others (n 148) 416. See Mallon (n 87) 24–25 for a detailed discussion of the testimonies provided.

[167] International Olympic Committee, 'Future Olympic Games Elections to Be More Flexible', 22 May 2019 <https://olympics.com/ioc/news/future-olympic-games-elections-to-be-more-flexible> accessed 30 April 2024.

[168] International Olympic Committee, 'Evolution of the Revolution: IOC Transforms Future Olympic Games elections', 26 June 2019 <https://olympics.com/ioc/news/evolution-of-the-revolution-ioc-transforms-future-olympic-games-elections> accessed 1 May 2024.

[169] ibid.

[170] International Olympic Committee, '2026 Host City Election' <https://olympics.com/ioc/2026-host-city-election> accessed 1 May 2024. More details on the new norm can be found in this infographic: International Olympic Committee, 'The New Norm: Candidature ⊚ Delivery ⊚ Legacy' <https://stillmed.olympic.org/media/Document%20Library/OlympicOrg/News/2018/02/Infographic-New-Norm.pdf#_ga=2.73312083.1160181653.1518251830–1585815676.1518251830> accessed 1 May 2024.

controversy still pervades the organisation, as the IOC was accused of taking a 'weak stand' against the Russian Anti-Doping Agency (RUSADA), to which the chapter now turns.

Sport Governance and Doping: Russia

State-Sponsored Doping

2–54 On 3 December 2014, a documentary called *Top Secret Doping: How Russia makes its Winners* premiered on German television. It made a number of serious allegations in relation to state-sponsored doping within the All Russia Athletics Federation (ARAF), the governing body for track and field athletics in Russia and recognised by the then IAAF now World Athletics.[171] The documentary centred on allegations made by a former RUSADA employee, Vitaly Stepanov, and his wife, Yuliya.[172] It was claimed that doping was widespread and included athletes, coaches, national and international sport federations including ARAF and the IAAF, RUSADA and the WADA-accredited laboratory in Moscow. In response, on 16 December 2014, the President of WADA commissioned an investigation with Pound as President. The Independent Commission Report #1, a 335-page report, was published on 9 November 2015.[173] It was entrusted with conducting

> an independent investigation into doping practices; corrupt practices around sample collection and results management; and, other ineffective administration of anti-doping processes that implicate Russia, the International Association of Athletics Federations (IAAF), athletes, coaches, trainers, doctors and other members of athletes' entourages; as well as, the accredited laboratory based in Moscow and the Russian Anti-Doping Agency (RUSADA).[174]

---

171 AFAR has been renamed the Russian Athletics Federation (RAF). It is also known as RusAF.

172 They both are living in the US and fear for their safety if they return to Russia. Yuliya is a middle-distance runner who was banned following a doping infraction: Juliet Macur, 'The Whistle-Blowers Next Door' *The New York Times* (New York, 26 December 2019) <https://www.nytimes.com/2019/12/26/sports/olympics/yuliya-stepanova-russia-doping.html> accessed 1 May 2024.

173 World Anti-Doping Agency, 'The Independent Commission Report #1: Final Report, 9 November 2015' <https://www.wadaama.org/sites/default/files/resources/files/wada_independent_commission_report_1_en.pdf> accessed 1 May 2024.

174 World Anti-Doping Agency, 'Independent Commission Terms of Reference' <https://www.wada-ama.org/sites/default/files/wada-independent-commission-terms-of-reference–2015-jan-en.pdf> accessed 1 May 2024. The terms of reference were extended in August 2015 following the transmission of another documentary by ARD ('Doping-Top Secret: The Shadowy World of Athletics') that questioned the IAAF's follow-up of 'suspicious indications of doping' between 2001 and 2012. The documentary also made allegations against Kenyan distance runners and doping: see World Anti-Doping Agency, 'Independent Commission Terms of Reference – Addendum' 20 August 2015 <https://www.wada-ama.org/en/resources/legal/independent-commission-terms-of-reference-addendum> accessed 1 May 2024. See also: World Anti-Doping Agency, 'Statement Regarding

Independent Commission Report #1

2–55

The Independent Commission (IC) found there to be 'a deeply rooted culture of cheating'.[175] It handed over a vast amount of data and information to Interpol owing to the alleged criminal nature of the behaviour of certain individuals and organisations.[176] The report 'identified systemic failures within the IAAF and Russia that prevent or diminish the possibility of an effective anti-doping program, to the extent that neither ARAF, RUSADA, nor the Russian Federation can be considered Code-compliant'.[177] It described Dr Grigory Rodchenkov, the Director of the Moscow laboratory and a key figure in the concealment of positive doping tests, 'as an aider and abettor of the doping activities'.[178] The concealment of positive tests was facilitated by the swapping of clean samples for known dirty 'A' samples.[179] In return, athletes paid both Rodchenkov and the President of the ARAF, Valentin Balakhnichev, for the service.[180] Balakhnichev was the IAAF Treasurer from 2011 until his resignation following the ARD documentary.[181] The IC recommended that WADA deem ARAF and RUSADA to be World Anti-Doping Code (WADC) non-complaint.[182] It questioned the independence of the Moscow laboratory and found a 'direct interference into the laboratory's operations by the Russian State' and also questioned the reliability of testing methods used by the laboratory.[183] The IC advised that WADA withdraw its accreditation of the Moscow

Extended Mandate of Independent Commission', 14 August 2015 <https://www.wada-ama.org/en/media/news/2015-08/statement-regarding-extended-mandate-of-independent-commission> accessed 1 May 2024.

175 Independent Commission Report #1 (n 173) 10.

176 ibid 9.

177 ibid. It opined that there was no reason to believe that athletics was the only sport in Russia that imbued a culture of doping (at 48).

178 ibid 12. It was recommended that he be permanently removed from his post (at 37).

179 ibid 212.

180 ibid.

181 He received a lifetime ban from the IAAF Ethics Commission which he, along with Papa Massata Diack and Alexei Melnikov, the Russian national team coach, challenged before the CAS; however, the CAS dismissed the appeal in August 2017 and confirmed the decision of the IAAF Ethics Commission: see CAS 2016/A/4417 *Balakhnichev v International Association of Athletics Federations (IAAF)* & CAS 2016/A/4419 *Melnikov v IAAF* & CAS 2016/A/4420 *Massata Diack v IAAF & Ethics Commission of the IAAF* award of 21 August 2017 <https://jurisprudence.tas-cas.org/Shared%20Documents/4417,%204419,%204420.pdf> accessed 1 May 2024. A press release outlining the IAAF Ethics Commission decision in Balakhnichev can be found on its website, World Athletics, 'IAAF Response to Ethics Board Decision Concerning Four Former Officials' 7 January 2016 <https://worldathletics.org/news/press-release/ethics-board-diack-balakhnichev-dolle-melniko> accessed 1 May 2024.

182 Independent Commission Report #1 (n 173) 38 and 40. It added that the IOC should not accept any entries from Russia for the 2016 Summer Olympics in Rio until the ARAF complied with the WADC.

183 ibid 197.

laboratory and for its Director to be 'permanently removed from his position'.[184]

2–56 The IC examined the influence of the Federal Security Services (FSB) into the workings of the Moscow laboratory.[185] A Moscow laboratory employee informed the IC of an FSB agent frequenting the laboratory and questioning staff and that some staff suspected the wiretapping or bugging of telephones.[186] While the IC could not independently verify the veracity of these allegations, it acknowledged that

> the reported statements demonstrate the perceptions of laboratory officials, who believe they are under constant state surveillance. For example, the IC learned that staff members were routinely questioned by FSB upon their return from global laboratory and WADA seminars. Following the airing of the ARD documentary, select laboratory staff members were directed by the FSB not to cooperate with the WADA investigation.[187]

Reaction to the Independent Commission Report

2–57 The IC Report #1 was welcomed by several sports councils, including Sport Ireland, who issued a statement on its website:

> The evidence released demonstrates a shocking level of corruption and exposes serious concerns around governance and leadership. The Independent Commission's findings highlight that the international playing field has not been level. Our athletes deserve better and we will fight on behalf of Irish athletes to ensure that they compete on the world stage, on a level playing field.[188]

2–58 WADA also welcomed the report with President Sir Craig Reedie admitting that 'the contents of the Report are deeply disturbing', however, the report was 'hugely positive for the clean athlete as it contains significant recommendations for how WADA and its partners in the anti-doping community can, and must, take swift corrective action to ensure anti-doping programs of the highest order are in place across the board'.[189]

2–59 The IAAF President Sebastien Coe stated that the findings were

---

184 ibid 37.

185 ibid 196–97.

186 ibid. Another employee spoke of their belief that some of the offices in the laboratory were bugged.

187 ibid 197.

188 Sport Ireland, 'Sport Ireland Response to WADA Independent Commission' (10 November 2015) <https://www.sportireland.ie/news/sport-ireland-response-to-wada-independent-commission> accessed 1 May 2024.

189 World Anti-Doping Agency, 'WADA Welcomes Independent Commission's Report into Widespread Doping in Sport' (9 November 2015) <https://www.wada-ama.org/en/news/wada-welcomes-independent-commissions-report-widespread-doping-sport> accessed 1 May 2024.

'alarming' and that time was needed to 'properly digest and understand the details' provided for in the IC Report.[190] In referring the matter to the IAAF Council to consider the sanctions against the ARAF, Coe noted that 'athletes, partners and fans have my total assurance that where there are failures in our governance or our anti-doping programmes we will fix them'.[191] The IAAF Council had to consider the following:

- whether to proceed with a potential sanctions' process against the ARAF;
- to seek a response from the ARAF in relation to the allegations and proposed sanctions; and
- on receiving a response from the ARAF, to decide on the next steps.[192]

On foot of the recommendations of the IC Report #1, on 10 November 2015, WADA, with immediate effect, suspended the Moscow laboratory resulting in the laboratory not being permitted to carry out any WADA-related anti-doping activities, including the testing of blood and urine samples.[193] In April 2016, WADA revoked the accreditation of the Moscow laboratory due to non-compliance with the International Standard for Laboratories (ISL).[194] **2–60**

On 13 November 2015, the IAAF Council voted 22–1 in favour of provisionally suspending, with immediate effect, the ARAF as an IAAF member.[195] This meant that Russian athletes and support personnel were banned from competing in international competitions, including the World Athletics Series and the Olympics.[196] Athletes were, however, **2–61**

[190] World Athletics, 'IAAF Statement – WADA's Independent Commission Report' (9 November 2015) <https://worldathletics.org/news/press-release/statement-wada-independent-commission-report> accessed 1 May 2024.

[191] ibid.

[192] ibid.

[193] Under Art 4.6.4.3 of the ISL. The latest edition of the ISL, in force since 1 January 2021, can be accessed on the WADA website <https://www.wada-ama.org/en/resources/world-anti-doping-code-and-international-standards/international-standard-laboratories#resource-download> accessed 1 May 2024. An appeal to the CAS of the decision to revoke or suspend accreditation can be made within 21 days of receipt of the decision of WADA: see Art 4.6.4.7 of the ISL.

[194] WADA revoked the accreditation of the Moscow laboratory again in 2021: World Anti-Doping Agency, 'WADA revokes approval of Moscow Laboratory' 9 October 2021 <https://www.wada-ama.org/en/news/wada-revokes-approval-moscow-laboratory> accessed 1 May 2024. The laboratory was provisionally suspended on 21 January 2020, World Anti-Doping Agency, 'WADA Provisionally Suspends Approved Status of Moscow Laboratory' 22 January 2020 <https://www.wada-ama.org/en/news/wada-provisionally-suspends-approved-status-moscow-laboratory> accessed 1 May 2024.

[195] World Athletics, 'IAAF Provisionally Suspends Russian Member Federation ARAF' 13 November 2015 <https://worldathletics.org/news/press-release/iaaf-araf-suspended> accessed 1 May 2024. There were 24 members of the Council and 23 voted as Russia was precluded from voting. The decision was taken under Arts 6.11(b) and 14.7 of the 2015 IAAF Constitution.

[196] ibid.

permitted to take part in domestic competitions.[197] The IAAF anti-doping rules, such as out-of-competition testing, still applied to international-level athletes in Russia.[198] The IAAF Council decision also stipulated that ARAF refer to the CAS all outstanding doping cases.[199]

2–62 In referring to the next steps, the Press Release specified several conditions. In the event of the ARAF not voluntarily accepting a full suspension, the IAAF would be empowered to hold a full hearing to decide whether the provisional suspension should be commuted to a full suspension.[200] In order to be recognised as a member of the IAAF once again, the new federation would be subject to a number of criteria. The ARAF did not contest the IAAF decision and did not request a hearing.

2–63 On 18 November 2015, RUSADA was declared Code non-compliant by WADA.[201] Sir Reedie commented: 'The world is watching and we have acted.'[202] The WADA Board called for increased protection for whistle-blowers, however, it acknowledged the need for resources in order for WADA to enhance its 'investigative and whistleblowing efforts'.[203]

2–64 There was a criminal aspect to the Russian doping scandal as former IAAF President Lamine Diack became the focus of a police investigation in France following allegations that he had been given €1m by ARAF for covering up positive drug tests.[204] In June of 2015 WADA searched the IAAF headquarters in Monaco and handed over to Interpol a number of incriminating documents.[205] In 2020, Diack was convicted by a French

---

197 ibid.

198 ibid.

199 ibid.

200 ibid.

201 World Anti-Doping Agency, 'Foundation Board Media Release: WADA Strengthens Anti-Doping Worldwide', 18 November 2015 <https://www.wada-ama.org/en/news/foundation-board-media-release-wada-strengthens-anti-doping-worldwide> accessed 1 May 2024. Five other signatories to the code were deemed to be non-compliant: the National Anti-Doping Organizations (NADOs) of Andorra and Israel. Argentina, Bolivia, and Ukraine were found to have non-accredited laboratories.

202 ibid.

203 ibid.

204 Sean Ingle, 'Lamine Diack, Former IAAF Head, Under Investigation in Corruption and Doping Inquiry' *The Guardian* (London, 4 November 2015) <https://www.theguardian.com/sport/2015/nov/04/lamine-diack-investigation-iaaf-corruption-doping> accessed 1 May 2024.

205 ibid. Dr Gabriel Dollé, the former director of the IAAF's medical and anti-doping department, was taken into custody in Nice. Dollé had resigned following an interview with the IAAF's Ethics Commission: see Sean Ingle and Owen Gibson, 'IAAF's Most Senior Anti-doping Official, Dr Gabriel Dollé, Leaves Job' *The Guardian* (London, 11 December 2014 <https://www.theguardian.com/sport/2014/dec/11/iaafs-most-senior-anti-doping-official-dr-gabriel-dolle-leaves-job> accessed 1 May 2024. In 2020, Dollé was handed down a two-year suspended sentence and a €144,000 fine. Balakhnichev and Melnikov were tried and convicted in absentia with Balakhnichev sentenced to three years in prison and a fine of €22m and Melnikov was handed down a two-year custodial sentence.

court after he was found guilty of corruption and sentenced to four years in prison with two suspended and a fine of €500,000.[206]

Independent Commission Report #2

Due to the ongoing criminal investigation, the IC Report #1 could only refer to the investigation by the French authorities, it could not discuss any of the evidence pertaining to the criminal investigation. A second report by the IC was written and submitted on 14 January 2016 and this was incorporated into the first report, thus consolidating the two reports.[207] The second IC Report was divided into three parts.[208] Part I examined the criminal investigation, Part II documented the leaked email, dated 19 July 2013, sent by the IAAF Deputy Secretary General Nick Davies to Papa Massata Diack, the son of Lamine Diack who was accused of fixing the bidding for the Tokyo 2020 Summer Olympics.[209] Part III examined allegations made by ARD and other media, including the *Sunday Times* that questioned the competency of the IAAF's anti-doping procedures, in particular blood doping.[210] The IC Report #2 was highly critical of the IAAF's governance structures which facilitated nepotism during Diack's term of office, as he had appointed relatives and friends to positions within the IAAF.[211] Diack appointed two of his sons as consultants, Papa Massata Diack as a marketing consultant and Khalil Diack as an independent consultant.[212] Diack also appointed Habib Cissé as his legal advisor and in November 2011 tasked him with managing Russian athletes' Athlete Biological Passport (ABP) cases within the Medical and Anti-Doping Department (MADept).[213] The IC Report #2 noted how unorthodox this was – not only had Cissé no experience of **2–65**

Jonathan J Rusch, 'French Court Sentences Diacks to Prison in IAAF Corruption Case' (*International Enforcement Law Reporter Blog*, 24 September 2020) <https://ielrblog.com/index.php/2020/09/24/french-court-sentences-diacks-to-prison-in-iaaf-corruption-case/> accessed 1 May 2024.

206 Sean Ingle, 'From Head of the IAAF to a Jail-Term: The Unmasking of Lamine Diack' *The Irish Times* (Dublin, 17 September 2020) <https://www.irishtimes.com/sport/other-sports/from-head-of-the-iaaf-to-a-jail-term-the-unmasking-of-lamine-diack–1.4357419> accessed 1 May 2024. His son was convicted in absentia as Senegal refused to extradite him to France. He was sentenced to five years in prison. Cissé received a three-year custodial sentence and a fine of €100,000.

207 World Anti-Doping Agency, 'Independent Commission Report #2' <https://www.wada-ama.org/sites/default/files/resources/files/wada_independent_commission_report_2_2016_en_rev.pdf> accessed 1 July 2024.

208 ibid 1.

209 Sean Ingle, 'Papa Massata Diack "Tried to Lock African Votes" to Take 2020 Olympics to Tokyo' *The Guardian* (London, 20 October 2017) <https://www.theguardian.com/sport/2017/oct/20/2020-tokyo-olympics-papa-massata-diack-lock-african-votes> accessed 1 July 2024

210 Independent Commission #2 (n 207) 1.

211 ibid 4. Diack served as a President from 1999 to 2015, four consecutive terms.

212 ibid. See (n 206).

213 Independent Commission Report #2 (n 207) 6. In 2017, the Medical & Anti-Doping Department was reconfigured as two bodies, the Health & Science Department, and the Athletics Integrity Unit. The Athletics Integrity Unit is discussed later in this chapter. See (n 206) about Cissé.

any doping or ABP cases in general, but he was 'inserted' by Diack 'into the day-to-day operations of the department only as it applied to Russian athletes. The IC was not aware of any other IAAF member federations that had senior management (internally or externally) assigned for the management of their cases.'[214]

2–66 The leaked database concerned blood test results of over 12,000 athletes from the period of 2001 to 2012. It was a personal database in Excel format held by an IAAF delegate.[215] The database was leaked to Seppelt, a German journalist with ARD.[216] Seppelt did not disclose the source of the leak; it was clear that neither the IAAF nor WADA had any involvement in the leak.[217] Seppelt shared the database with the *Sunday Times*, who in turn contacted two scientists, Dr Ashenden and Dr Parisotto.[218] The scientists prepared independent reports, however, they later contacted each other about their findings prior to the publication of a number of articles based on the two reports.[219] Both scientists refused to make public the reports, as did the *Sunday Times*. Although the IC was furnished with a copy of the reports, it made assurances that its confidentiality would be preserved and it would only be shared with WADA experts who were assisting the IC.[220] The IC concluded: 'Expert opinion evidence is not necessarily correct … no one has challenged the methodology applied in reaching their conclusions.'[221] The WADA expert group was of the opinion that the IAAF targeting system was 'fit for purpose' and since 2005 the IAAF had significantly increased blood testing.[222] The IAAF, in response to the two scientific reports, issued a rebuttal on 6 November 2015 which the WADA experts deemed to be 'scientifically sound'.[223] The IAAF was one of a few Anti-Doping Organisations (ADOs) that started collecting blood samples in the 2000s

---

[214] ibid 6.

[215] ibid 54. It was put together by Dr Fischetto for the purpose of targeting athletes for EPO testing. Erythropoietin has only been detectable since 2000 when testing began at the Sydney Olympic Games. EPO is a hormone produced in the kidneys; however, it can also be created in a laboratory using cell cultures. It regulates how many red blood cells one's body produces and is mainly used in endurance sports, including cycling. While it has been detectable only since 2000, the first clinical reports were published in 1987 and EPO was attributed to the deaths of 18 Belgian and Dutch cyclists in the late 1980s, David J Armstrong, 'Enhanced Oxygen Transfer' in David R Mottram (ed), *Drugs in Sport* (5th edn, Routledge 2011) 138–39.

[216] Independent Commission #2 (n 207) 52.

[217] ibid.

[218] ibid.

[219] ibid 52–53.

[220] ibid 54.

[221] ibid 55.

[222] ibid 60. It commended the IAAF on the number and frequency of its response to atypical blood samples, ibid 62. The WADA experts referred to some delays on the part of the IAAF regarding ABP; however, since January 2015, 'it had one of the most reactive ABP programmes': ibid 70.

[223] ibid 73.

when the WADC did not require such samples.[224] The leaked database given to the scientists was 'incomplete' and its purpose 'was to gather information for improved intelligent target testing, while ADAMs (Anti-Doping Administration & Management System) was the "official" IAAF database for the use of blood profiles to prosecute an athlete'.[225]

In referring to the nepotism involving the appointment of Diack's sons and Cissé, the IC Report #2 stated: 'All three of these individuals operated outside the formal hierarchical structure of the IAAF taking on organizational functions within the day-to-day operations of the IAAF, all the while being compensated by the IAAF.'[226] 2–67

The IC Report #2 was highly critical of the IAAF and its 'lack of political appetite' to 'confront Russia with the full extent of its known and suspected doping activities', especially as the actions of senior officials entailed 'questionable or criminal conduct' which brought into question the reputation of the IAAF.[227] WADA President Reedie found it 'hugely disturbing that individuals at the highest level of the IAAF were abetting and covering up doping for their own financial gain'.[228] 2–68

Independent Person Reports 1 and 2: McLaren Reports

As noted above, the IC Report #1 referred to Dr Rodchenkov, the Director of the Moscow laboratory, as a key figure in the concealment of positive doping tests. In May 2016, Rodchenkov informed the New York Times of his involvement in the covering-up of positive test results for several years before the Sochi Olympics in 2014.[229] At least 15 Russian medallists from Sochi were said to be involved. Rodchenkov claimed 2–69

---

224 ibid.

225 The ADAMs system was hacked by hackers called 'Fancy Bear'. The group published information relating to Therapeutic Use Exemptions (TUEs) of high-profile athletes: World Anti-Doping Agency, 'Cyber Security Update: WADA's Incident Response' 5 October 2016 <https://www.wada-ama.org/en/news/cyber-security-update-wadas-incident-response> accessed 1 May 2024.

226 Independent Commission #2 (n 207) 4.

227 ibid 47–48.

228 World Anti-Doping Agency, 'WADA Welcomes Conclusion of Independent Commission into Doping in International Athletics' 16 January 2016 <https://www.wada-ama.org/en/news/wada-welcomes-conclusion-independent-commission-doping-international-athletics> accessed 1 May 2024.

229 Rebecca R Ruiz and Michael Schwirtz, 'Russian Insider Says State-Run Doping Fuelled Olympic Gold' *The New York Times* (New York, 12 May 2016) <https://www.nytimes.com/2016/05/13/sports/russia-doping-sochi-olympics-2014.html> accessed 1 May 2024. Rodchenkov had fled Russia and moved to the US as he feared for his life following the suspicious deaths of two of his former colleagues. Rodchenkov had also given an interview to CBS's 60 Minutes in February 2016. See CBS, 'Running from Putin after Helping Him Cheat' 8 February 2018 <https://www.cbsnews.com/news/running-from-putin-after-helping-him-cheat/> accessed 1 May 2024. Rodchenkov is under the Federal Witness Protection Programme in the US: see Murad Ahmed, 'Whistleblower Grigory Rodchenkov: "Sport won't be clean. Never"' *The Financial Times* (London, 31 July 2020) <https://

he developed a 'three-drug cocktail of banned substances' that were mixed with alcohol.[230] The covert operation involved several Russian anti-doping experts and members of the intelligence service replacing samples containing prohibited substances with 'clean urine' which had been collected a few months previously.[231] Tamper-proof bottles containing the 'dirty' urine samples were penetrated and replaced with the clean urine. The personnel involved worked through the night 'in a shadow laboratory lit by a single lamp, passing bottles of urine through a hand-size hole in the wall, to be ready for testing the next day'.[232] Around 100 athletes are believed to have had their samples replaced and thus evaded detection.[233] Russia won the highest number of medals at the Sochi Games, surpassing its nearest rival, the US.[234]

2–70 The IAAF Council in June 2016 unanimously voted not to reinstate the Russian Athletics Federation (RusAF).[235] This decision meant that Russian athletes could not compete in International Competitions, including the European Championships and the Rio 2016 Olympic Games.[236] RusAF officials and athlete support personnel also remained suspended. The IAAF made a provision for athletes training outside of Russian to compete as neutrals if they 'clearly and convincingly show that they are not tainted by the Russian system because they have been outside the country, and subject to other, effective anti-doping systems, including effective drug-testing'.[237]

2–71 In the wake of Rodchenkov allegations, WADA established an Independent Person (IP) Report presented in two parts by Professor Richard H McLaren.[238] Part I of the IP Report was published two

www.ft.com/content/0630521e-37d3-4a44-a7ea-b2dc82f8bad9> accessed 1 July 2024

230 Ruiz and Schwirtz ibid.

231 ibid.

232 ibid.

233 ibid.

234 ibid.

235 World Athletics, '"RusAF Has Not Met Reinstatement Conditions" – IAAF Council Meeting, Vienna' 16 June 2016 <https://worldathletics.org/news/press-release/iaaf-council-meeting-vienna> accessed 1 May 2024. RusAF replaced the ARAF.

236 ibid.

237 ibid. The IAAF also decided that any individual who had made 'an extraordinary contribution to the fight against doping in sport' could apply for permission to compete as a neutral athlete. The IAAF Council explicitly referred to Yuliya Stepanova, who it contended should be 'considered favourably'.

238 World Anti-Doping Agency, 'WADA Investigation of Sochi Allegations' (Part I: Richard H McLaren, Independent Person) 16 July 2016 <https://www.wada-ama.org/sites/default/files/resources/files/20160718_ip_report_newfinal.pdf> accessed 1 May 2024. World Anti-Doping Agency, 'Independent Person, WADA Investigation of Sochi Allegations (Part II: Richard H McLaren, Independent Person) 9 December 2016 <https://www.wada-ama.org/sites/default/files/resources/files/mclaren_report_part_ii_2.pdf> accessed 1 May 2024. For the Terms of Reference, see: World Anti-Doping Agency, 'Independent Investigation into the Sochi Allegations Made by Grigory Rodchenkov: Terms of Reference' 20 May 2016 <https://www.wada-ama.org/sites/default/files/resources/files/wada-

weeks before the start of the Rio Summer Olympics.[239] It found 'beyond a reasonable doubt' that between 2011 and 2015 that there was 'institutionalised manipulation and cover up of the doping control process in Russia. The conspiracy and cover up involved Russian athletes in virtually all of the Olympic sports.'[240] The Moscow laboratory was found to have 'operated, for the protection of doped Russian athletes, within a State-dictated failsafe system'.[241] McLaren referred to this as the 'Disappearing Positive Methodology'.[242] It found that the Sochi laboratory engaged in a 'unique sample swapping methodology' which facilitated the participation of doped Russian athletes.[243] McLaren also found that the Ministry of Sport 'controlled and oversaw the manipulation' of samples and was aided by the FSB, the Centre of Sports Preparation of National Teams of Russia and the Moscow and Sochi laboratories.[244]

The McLaren Report did not make any recommendations as this was not within the Terms of Reference.[245] As WADA is not empowered to make decisions regarding entries to competitions, its Executive Committee recommended that the relevant organisations make decisions based on their rules and regulations.[246] It directed the relevant bodies as follows: **2–72**

1. The IOC and the International Paralympic Committee (IPC) to consider, under their respective Charters, to decline entries, for Rio 2016, of all athletes submitted by the Russian Olympic Committee (ROC) and the Russian Paralympic Committee.[247]
2. The IFs from sports implicated in the McLaren Report to consider

independent-investigation-of-g-rodchenkov-allegations-tor-en_0.pdf> accessed 1 May 2024.

239 The Independent Person was given 57 days to investigate and publish the report.

240 McLaren Part I (n 238) 35.

241 ibid 86.

242 ibid.

243 ibid.

244 ibid. McLaren did not know the method used by the FSB to open the Sochi sample bottles but stated that 'IP experts conclusively established that the caps can be removed and reused later': ibid 89.

245 Terms of Reference (n 238) 1. The Terms of Reference required McLaren to establish that there had been sample manipulation and identify the modus operandi of those involved in the cover-up and to identify any athlete who may have benefitted from the swapping of samples. It was also asked to identify if there was any further information held by Rodchenkov.

246 World Anti-Doping Agency, 'WADA Statement: Independent Investigation Confirms Russian State Manipulation of the Doping Control Process', 18 July 2016 <https://www.wada-ama.org/en/media/news/2016-07/wada-statement-independent-investigation-confirms-russian-state-manipulation-of> accessed 1 July 2024

247 International Olympic Committee, 'Statement of the Executive Board of the International Olympic Committee on the WADA Independent Person Report' 19 July 2016 <https://olympics.com/ioc/news/statement-of-the-executive-board-of-the-international-olympic-committee-on-the-wada-independent-person-report> accessed 1 May 2024.

their responsibilities under the WADC as far as their Russian National Federations (NFs) are concerned.

3. Russian government officials to be denied access to international competitions, including Rio 2016.
4. RUSADA to remain non-compliant under the Code and its staffing and independence to be further reviewed by WADA.
5. The accreditation process of the WADA-accredited laboratory in Moscow to be stopped.
6. The FIFA Ethics Committee to investigate allegations concerning football and the role played by a member of its Executive Committee, Minister Vitaly Mutko.
7. Professor McLaren and his team to complete their mandate provided WADA can secure the funding that would be required.[248]

2–73 The Executive Committee of WADA spoke of its 'great disappointment' that the issues highlighted in the IC Report #1, despite 'public undertakings' on the part of the Russian government, were still occurring by the time of the WADA IP Report.[249] Accordingly, it demonstrated a 'total disregard for the international community' and 'urgent need for true and demonstrable commitment by the Russian authorities for a culture of change'.[250]

2–74 As recommended by WADA, the IOC and the IPC adopted their respective positions on the eligibility of Russian athletes to compete in the upcoming Summer Games. The IOC decided to leave it to the IFs to decide whether Russian athletes could compete in the Rio 2016 Olympics subject to several criteria, and the absence of a positive national anti-doping test could not 'be considered sufficient'.[251] It further required that IFs engage in 'individual analysis of each athlete's anti-doping record, taking into account only reliable adequate international tests, and the specificities of the athlete's sport and its rules, in order to ensure a level playing field'.[252] The ROC was prevented from entering any athlete who had been sanctioned for a doping infraction even if the athlete had served a period of ineligibility.[253] Any Russian athlete permitted to compete at Rio 2016 would be subject to additional out-of-competition testing.[254] The ROC and 68 athletes challenged the decision of the IAAF/World Athletics before the CAS.[255] The ROC and complainant athletes

---

248 ibid.

249 ibid.

250 ibid.

251 International Olympic Committee, 'Decision of the IOC Executive Board concerning the participation of Russian athletes in the Olympic Games Rio 2016' 24 July 2016 <https://olympics.com/ioc/news/decision-of-the-ioc-executive-board-concerning-the-participation-of-russian-athletes-in-the-olympic-games-rio–2016> accessed 1 May 2024.

252 ibid.

253 ibid.

254 ibid.

255 CAS 2016/O/4684 *The Russian Olympic Committee (ROC) et al v IAAF* award of 21 July 2016/10 October 2016 <https://jurisprudence.tas-cas.org/Shared%20Documents/4684.pdf> accessed 1 May 2024. The operative part of the award was

sought clarification from the CAS in relation to the IAAF's Competition Rules on 'neutral athletes' who were not tainted by the Russian system and had been subject to effective testing outside of Russia. Rule 6.1.1 of World Athletics' Eligibility Rules (the current rules) provides that athletes and other personnel that are members of a suspended national federation are ineligible to compete in international competition.[256] Rule 6.1.3 also provides that athletes who are currently serving a period of ineligibility due to a doping infraction or other disciplinary offences are precluded from competing internationally. Rule 6.2 states that Rule 6.1.1 may be waived by the World Athletics' Council (or delegate) in exceptional circumstances where the athlete can demonstrate to the satisfaction of the Council (or delegate) that the suspension of the national federation was due to a lack of 'adequate systems to protect and promote clean athletics, fair play, and the integrity and authenticity of the sport'[257] and the athlete was not directly implicated either knowingly or unknowingly and the athlete has been subject to effective testing for a sufficiently long period of time.[258] If the athlete cannot satisfy these conditions, they may rely on Rule 6.2.3, which provides that the Council (or delegate) may allow an athlete compete if they have 'made a truly exceptional protection and promotion of clean athletics, fair play, and the integrity and authenticity of the sport'.[259] The then IAAF Doping Review Board (DRB), as a delegate of the IAAF Council, made the decision not to allow any of the 68 claimants compete as authorised neutral athletes as defined in the IAAF Competition Rules (2015–2016) which included track and field events at the 2016 Olympic Games.[260] The CAS found that

published on 21 July 2016 given the urgency of the matter: see Media Release, 'The Court of Arbitration for Sport (CAS) rejects claims/appeal of the Russian Olympic Committee (ROC) and of 68 Russian Athletes, 16 July 2016 <http://www.tas-cas.org/fileadmin/user_upload/Media_Release_4684_210716.pdf> accessed 1 May 2024. The full decision was published on 10 October 2016.

256 World Athletics, 'Book C – C3.3: Eligibility Rules' (Approved by Council on 13 July 2022 and effective from 15 August 2022) <https://worldathletics.org/about-iaaf/documents/book-of-rules> accessed 1 May 2024.

257 ibid r 6.2.1.

258 ibid r 6.2.2 (a) and (b). Rule 6.3 refers to a national federation which has been suspended through no failure on its part 'to protect and promote clean athletics, fair play, and the integrity and authenticity of the sport'. This was not applicable in the case of the ROC. In the CAS, the DRB considered the term 'sufficiently long period' to mean 'from 1 January 2014 to date', CAS 2016/O/4684 (n 255) [36].

259 Rule 6.3 further provides that the 'more important the International Competition in question, the more corroborating evidence the Athlete must provide in order to be granted special eligibility under r 6.2 of these Rules'.

260 In 2022, World Athletics' Doping Review Board renewed and revised the rules relating to authorised neutral athletes: World Athletics, 'Doping Review Board Approves Process and Guidelines for Authorised Neutral Athletes in 2022' 21 December 2021 <https://worldathletics.org/news/press-releases/process-guidelines-authorised-neutral-athletes–2022> accessed 1 May 2024. For details on the 2022 rules see World Athletics, 'Authorised Neutral Athletes Guidelines for Applications under Eligibility Rule 3.2' <https://worldathletics.org/download/download?filename=5e362225-eec5–49cc-bea6–9ff03d39a517.pdf&urlslug=ANA%20Guidelines%202022> accessed 1 May 2024.

the appellants were ineligible to compete in the 2016 Olympic Games and thus affirmed the decisions of the DRB.

2–75 The IPC Governing Board, in contrast to the IOC, unanimously decided to suspend the Russian Paralympic Committee (RPC) resulting in no Russian Athletes competing at the Rio 2016 Paralympic Games.[261] The IPC Governing Board allowed the RPC to make written submissions and present in person.[262] The RPC had 21 days to appeal the decision of the IPC Governing Board.[263] The RPC appealed the decision to the CAS with the CAS dismissing the appeal and upholding its suspension.[264] The ROC appealed the decision to the SFT, however, the appeal was dismissed and an order of costs made against the ROC.[265]

2–76 The second part of the McLaren Report was published on 9 December 2016.[266] Given the time constraints imposed on McLaren in producing the first report, the second part fully analysed the data that was condensed in Part I.[267] The report reiterated the findings of the first report and referred to 'institutionalised' doping and cover ups that occurred between 2011 and 2015. It noted how the 'systematic and centralised cover up' became increasingly refined from London 2012 up to Sochi in 2014. The swapping of tainted samples with clean urine continued after the Sochi Winter Games. It found that over 1000 athletes and not 643 identified in Part I competing in Summer and Winter Games were involved or benefitted 'from manipulations to conceal positive doping tests'.[268]

Reaction to the McLaren Report

2–77 Part II noted that Part I of the report had not been criticised or contested and the world's media, including Russian media, the ad hoc Division of the CAS at the Rio Games, federations, and organisations involved

261 Media Centre, 'The IPC Suspends the Russian Paralympic Committee with Immediate Effect', 7 August 2016 <https://www.paralympic.org/news/ipc-suspends-russian-paralympic-committee-immediate-effect> accessed 1 July 2024.
262 ibid.
263 ibid. The McLaren Report found 35 Disappearing Positive Test Results in Paralympic sport from the 2014 Sochi Paralympics, McLaren Part II (n 238) 41.
264 CAS 2016/A/4745 *Russian Paralympic Committee v International Paralympic Committee* award of 30 August 2016 <https://www.paralympic.org/sites/default/files/document/161005070210720_RPC+vs+IPC_CAS+4745_English.pdf > accessed 1 May 2024.
265 Decision of the Swiss Federal Tribunal 4A–470/2016, Judgment of 3 April 2017 <https://jusmundi.com/en/document/decision/en-russian-paralympic-committee-rpc-v-international-paralympic-committee-ipc-decision-of-the-swiss-federal-tribunal–4a–470–2016-monday–3rd-april–2017#decision_46042> accessed 1 May 2024.
266 McLaren Part II (n 238).
267 ibid 7. Part II documents the work carried out by the investigative team between July and November 2016. It provided a link, on page 4, to non-confidential evidence it had relied on, Evidence Disclosure Package (EDP), however, this link is no longer accessible.
268 ibid 2 and 57.

accepted the findings of Part I. However, the McLaren Report has been the subject of academic discourse.[269] Girginov and Parry assert that there is a lack of consistency in the language used in the two reports. The use of the phrase of 'state-sponsored doping' in the first report, was replaced by 'institutionalised' doping conspiracy in the second part of the report.[270] The writers also contend that there was 'a lack of consistency between its stated objectives and main findings', for example, the involvement of the Russian state was not within the IP's mandate.[271] The standard of beyond reasonable doubt, the writers conclude, was not proved, and considering that the IOC holds itself out as an apolitical organisation, this was undermined by the fact that an entire state and not just individual athletes were held responsible.[272]

An internal report from WADA was leaked to the *New York Times* which found that 95 out of 96 athletes who had been implicated in the McLaren Reports were found to have no Anti-Doping Rule Violation (ADRV).[273] **2–78**
The IP Report made all of its documents available online through the Evidence Disclosure Package (EDP).[274] It meant that ADOs could access the documents to see if any of their athletes had benefitted from the manipulation of samples. Governing bodies were required to examine the results of their athletes and sanction where appropriate and this was subject to a review by WADA, who in turn would either approve or challenge the finding. The English translation of documents was finalised in early May 2017. WADA received decisions concerning 96 athletes: one sample was sent for re-analysis by WADA, resulting in an Adverse Analytical Finding (AAF).[275] The leaked WADA report noted that Dr Rodchenkov was unable to testify due to circumstances beyond WADA's or the IP Team's control. As only one of the athletes was found to have committed an ADRV, it raises a number of considerations, namely the superior execution of Russia's doping system that it managed to destroy evidence and thus making it impossible to sanction a number

[269] See Vassil Girginov and Jim Parry, 'Protecting or Undermining the Integrity of Sport? The Science and Politics of the McLaren Report' (2018) 10(2) *International Journal of Sport Policy and Politics* 393.

[270] ibid 395.

[271] ibid 398.

[272] ibid 403.

[273] This was due to a lack of sufficient evidence. See 'An Excerpt from the World Anti-Doping Agency's Internal Report Related to the Russian Doping Scandal' *The New York Times* (New York, 12 September 2017) <https://www.nytimes.com/interactive/2017/09/12/sports/olympics/WADA-russian-doping-report.html> accessed 1 May 2024.

[274] McLaren did not name any athletes in the report, athletes were assigned an alpha-numeric code. A summary on each athlete was provided for the relevant organisations who would then review the evidence in each case to see if a ADRV had occurred: see Press Release, 'WADA Statement Regarding Conclusion of McLaren Investigation' 9 December 2016. It is no longer available on the WADA website; however, Sports Integrity Initiative published it on its website: <https://www.sportsintegrityinitiative.com/wada-statement-regarding-conclusion-mclaren-investigation/> accessed 1 May 2024.

[275] ibid.

of athletes.[276] Equally, it raises questions as to 'whether officials have taken a soft approach to punishments'.[277] McLaren identified 714 athletes in Part II of the report, yet only 96 decisions were referred from the IFs to WADA.[278] WADA explained that accessing samples at the Moscow laboratory was impossible as it was under the protection of Russian authorities.[279] Rodchenkov's inability to testify was challenged in a letter from his lawyer to WADA as Rodchenkov, who is under the Witness Protection Program in the US, stated that he was willing to cooperate but had only been contacted by one IOC investigator.[280] Some anti-doping officials questioned the impartiality of their respective governing bodies who had a vested interest in not sanctioning some of their athletes.[281] In a telephone interview, WADA's Director General, Olivier Niggli, defended the McLaren Report on the ground that its 'purpose was to prove a system, not individual violations'.[282] The exoneration of 95 athletes may have signalled to Russia a 'partial vindication', who consistently disputed that there was state-sponsored doping.[283]

IOC Disciplinary Commission's Report to the IOC Executive Board: Schmid Report

2–79 The IOC welcomed the IP Report #1 and praised McLaren and offered its continued support to him in carrying out further investigations.[284] In response, the IOC Executive Board established two Disciplinary Commissions (DCs). One Disciplinary Commission, under the chairmanship of Samuel Schmid (the Schmidt Commission), was tasked with examining the involvement of officials within the Russian Ministry of Sports and other individuals referred to in the report for breaches of both the Olympic Charter and the WADC.[285] The IOC Executive Board

---

276 Rebecca R Ruiz, 'World Anti-Doping Agency Clears 95 Russian Athletes' *The New York Times* (New York, 12 September 2017 <https://www.nytimes.com/2017/09/12/sports/olympics/russian-doping-wada.html?mcubz=3> accessed 1 May 2024.

277 ibid.

278 Andy Brown, 'Analysis: Just One ADRV to Date from McLaren Reports' (*Sports Integrity Initiative*, 13 September 2017) <http://www.sportsintegrityinitiative.com/analysis-just-one-adrv-date-mclaren-reports> accessed 1 May 2024.

279 ibid, WADA in a statement to *Sports Integrity Initiative*. Brown questions this explanation. Brown contends that WADA is culpable as it announced a 'surprise' visit to the Moscow laboratory on 7 December 2014, 10 days before the 17 December visit giving ample time for the destruction of samples.

280 Ruiz (n 276). Rodchenkov was charged by the Investigative Commission of the Russian Federation with abuse of power under the Russian Criminal Code, Brown (n 278).

281 Ruiz (n 276).

282 ibid.

283 ibid.

284 International Olympic Committee, 'Statement of the Executive Board of the International Olympic Committee on the WADA Independent Person Report' 19 July 2016 <https://olympics.com/ioc/news/statement-of-the-executive-board-of-the-international-olympic-committee-on-the-wada-independent-person-report> accessed 1 May 2024.

285 ibid. Guy Canivet, Vice-Chair of the IOC Ethics Commission and former member

adopted a number of provisional measures including that it would not give patronage or organise any sports event or meeting in Russia and accreditation for the 2016 Summer Olympics would not be given to any official in the Russian Ministry of Sports or any other person mentioned in the McLaren Report.[286]

The second DC, under the direction of Denis Oswald (the Oswald Commission), was established to 'initiate reanalysis' of samples and to conduct a full inquiry into all Russian athletes who participated in the Olympic Winter Games Sochi 2014 and their coaches, officials and support staff.[287] Thirty-nine athletes appealed decisions of the Oswald Commission with the CAS upholding 28 appeals and partially upholding the remaining 11.[288] Matthieu Reeb, the General Secretary of the CAS, stated: 'This does not mean that these 28 athletes are declared innocent, but in their case, due to insufficient evidence, the appeals are upheld, the sanctions annulled and their individual results achieved in Sochi are reinstated.'[289] **2–80**

The Schmid Commission's role 'was not to assess the value of the IP Reports but to establish the facts on the basis of documented independent and impartial evidence'.[290] It concluded that there was a Disappearing Positive Methodology and that samples had been tampered with; it confirmed 'the seriousness of the facts, the unprecedented nature of the cheating scheme and, as a consequence, the exceptional damage to **2–81**

---

of the French Constitutional Court, was initially appointed as chair but had to stand down due to personal reasons. See Associated Press, 'IOC Extends Doping Sanctions on Russia as Richard McLaren's Report Looms' *The Guardian* (London, 8 December 2016) <https://www.theguardian.com/sport/2016/dec/07/ioc-extends-doping-sanctions-on-russia> accessed 1 May 2024.

286 IOC Statement (n 284).

287 International Olympic Committee, 'IOC Sanctions Four Russian Athletes as Part of Oswald Commission Findings' 24 November 2017 <https://www.olympic.org/news/ioc-sanctions-four-russian-athletes-as-part-of-oswald-commission-findings–2017–11–24> accessed 1 May 2024.

288 Media Release, 'The Court of Arbitration for Sport (CAS) delivers its decisions in the matter of 39 Russian athletes v the IOC: 28 appeals upheld, 11 partially upheld' 1 February 2018 <https://www.tas-cas.org/fileadmin/user_upload/Media_Release__decision_RUS_IOC_.pdf> accessed 1 May 2024. See also CAS 2017/A/5379 *Alexander Legkov v International Olympic Committee (IOC)* award of 23 April 2018 (operative part) of 1 February 2018 <https://jurisprudence.tas-cas.org/Shared%20Documents/5379.pdf> accessed 1 May 2024. The CAS set aside the decision of the IOC Disciplinary Commission that had placed a lifetime ban on Legkov, a cross-country skier. Legkov's case was heard jointly with the appeals of the 38 other Sochi athletes.

289 'IOC: CAS Decision to Overturn Russian Doping Bans "May Have Serious Impact on Fight Against Doping' *Irish Examiner* (Cork, 1 February 2018) <https://www.irishexaminer.com/sport/othersport/arid–30825896.html> accessed 1 May 2024.

290 International Olympic Committee, 'IOC Disciplinary Commission's Report to the IOC Executive Board' 2 December 2017 <https://stillmed.olympic.org/media/Document%20Library/OlympicOrg/IOC/Who-We-Are/Commissions/Disciplinary-Commission/IOC-DC-Schmid/IOC-Disciplinary-Commission-Schmid-Report.pdf> accessed 1 May 2024.

the integrity of the IOC, the Olympic Games and the entire Olympic Movement'.[291] However, it could not find 'any documented, independent and impartial evidence confirming the support or the knowledge of this system by the highest State authority'.[292] While it acknowledged that there were 'some similarities' between the doping systems of the former German Democratic Republic (GDR) and that of Russia, the Schmid Commission considered the system in the GDR as being different to the one detailed in the Pound and McLaren Reports.[293] In contrast to the Pound and McLaren Reports, the Schmid Commission referred to the role of the ROC in the doping system.[294] It observed that the function of the ROC during the Sochi Olympics was to ensure that the WADA Code was respected, in addition to 'its various legal obligations', consequently, it should 'held legally responsible for the breach of its legal and contractual obligations'.[295]

2–82 The Schmid Commission made the following recommendations to the IOC Executive Board:

- to take the appropriate measures that should be strong enough to effectively sanction the existence of a systemic manipulation of the anti-doping rules and system in Russia, as well as the legal responsibility of the various entities involved (ie including uniform, flag and anthem);
- while protecting the rights of the individual Russian clean athletes; and
- to take into consideration the multiple costs incurred by the two IOC DCs, those linked to the investigations, the various expertise and the re-analysis of the samples of the Olympic Games.[296]

2–83 The IOC Executive Board suspended the ROC with immediate effect and invited individual Russian athletes to compete under 'strict conditions' in the Olympic Winter Games PyeongChang 2018.[297] Such athletes were permitted to compete under the title of Olympic Athlete from Russia (OAR).[298] At the Winter Games 2018, 168 OAR competed, with two athletes testing positive for a prohibited substance.[299] As a result, the ROC was reinstated even though the IOC had planned to lift

[291] ibid 24.
[292] ibid.
[293] ibid 25.
[294] ibid 26.
[295] ibid 27.
[296] ibid 28. IOC DCs referred to the IOC Disciplinary Commission chaired by Schmid and the IOC Disciplinary Commission chaired by Oswald.
[297] International Olympic Committee, 'IOC Suspends Russian NOC and Creates a Path for Clean Individual Athletes to Compete in PyeongChang 2018 under the Olympic Flag' 5 December 2017 <https://olympics.com/ioc/news/ioc-suspends-russian-noc-and-creates-a-path-for-clean-individual-athletes-to-compete-in-pyeongchang–2018-under-the-olympic-flag> accessed 1 May 2024.
[298] ibid. These athletes competed under the Olympic flag and Olympic Anthem.
[299] International Olympic Committee, 'IOC Statement' 28 February 2018 <https://olympics.com/ioc/news/ioc-statement–2018-02–28> accessed 2 May 2024.

the suspension after the Winter Games if there were no positive tests. The reinstatement attracted criticism from the international sporting community.[300]

Roadmap to Compliance

Following the IC Report #1, RUSADA was declared non-complaint with the WADC. WADA began working with RUSADA from November 2015 and the terms of a 'Roadmap to Compliance' were agreed upon and published in August 2017.[301] WADA established an independent Compliance Review Committee (CRC) in 2015 to monitor the ADO's compliance with the 2015 WADC.[302] In May 2017, WADA's Foundation Board, the 'highest decision-making body', accepted the CRC's recommendation, that subject to the fulfilment of certain conditions, RUSADA could again become Code complaint.[303] The Roadmap of Compliance contained two parts; Part I outlined the criteria that RUSADA had fulfilled, for example, that RUSADA used the services of UK Anti-Doping (UKAD) to carry out testing during its period of non-compliance.[304] UKAD was employed to provide training and upskilling of RUSADA's anti-doping programme.[305] RUSADA was also required to recruit new Doping Control Officers (DCOs) who were vetted by international experts and who would be trained by the experts and **2–84**

300 Martha Kelner, 'Russia's Olympic Membership Restored by IOC after Doping Ban' *The Guardian* (London, 28 February 2018 <https://www.theguardian.com/sport/2018/feb/28/russia-says-ioc-reinstated-membership-after-doping-allegations> accessed 2 May 2024.

301 World Anti-Doping Agency, 'WADA Publishes RUSADA Roadmap to Code Compliance' 2 August 2017 <https://www.wada-ama.org/en/news/wada-publishes-rusada-roadmap-code-compliance> accessed 2 May 2024.

302 The Compliance Review Committee was initially established as an expert group but was made a WADA Standing Committee in November 2016: see World Anti-Doping Agency, 'Compliance Review Committee' <https://www.wada-ama.org/en/who-we-are/governance/compliance-review-committee> accessed 2 May 2024. Since 2022 following governance reforms, it was reclassified as a Permanent Special Committee. For more information on these reforms, see World Anti-Doping Agency, 'WADA Foundation Board Unanimously Approves Final Round of Governance Reforms' 19 May 2022 <https://www.wada-ama.org/en/news/wada-foundation-board-unanimously-approves-final-round-governance-reforms> accessed 2 May 2024.

303 The WADA Foundation consists of 42 members comprising equally of representatives from Olympic organisations and public authorities. World Anti-Doping Agency, 'Foundation Board' <https://www.wada-ama.org/en/who-we-are/governance/foundation-board> accessed 2 May 2024. UKAD was established in 2009 to ensure that sports bodies in the UK were WADC compliant; it is referred to as a Non-Departmental Public Body (NDPB) and is accountable to the Parliament through the Department for Culture, Media and Sport, UK Anti-Doping, 'What We Do' <https://www.ukad.org.uk/what-we-do> accessed 2 May 2024.

304 World Anti-Doping Agency, 'RUSADA: Roadmap to Compliance' <https://www.wada-ama.org/sites/default/files/2017-08-02_rusada_roadmaptocompliance_en.pdf > accessed 2 May 2024.

305 ibid. There were 19 criteria listed in Part I.

UKAD.[306] RUSADA introduced changes to its Supervisory Board statutes to provide for an independent chair and developed a Code of Ethics and Anti-Corruption.[307] Government funding would no longer be allocated to national federations that failed to comply with anti-doping rules.[308]

2–85 Part II listed the criteria that RUSADA had not yet fulfilled, including the public acceptance of the McLaren Report, the provision of access by the Russian government to officials to the stored urine samples in the Moscow laboratory, which was sealed off due to a Federal Investigation.[309] These two criteria were subsequently fulfilled, the public acknowledgment through the auspices of a letter from the Russian Ministry of Sport and the acceptance by the WADA Executive Board of the appointment of an independent expert to access the Moscow laboratory subject to a clear timeline being imposed by the Executive Board.[310]

2–86 On 20 September 2018, WADA announced that it was reinstating RUSADA subject to 'strict conditions'.[311] The decision was condemned by anti-doping organisations and athletes, with the chief executive of UKAD contending that WADA had cast 'aside its responsibilities to clean athletes, sports fans and those who work tirelessly for clean sport'.[312] The US Anti-Doping Agency (USADA) issued a statement urging WADA to postpone the reinstatement on the grounds

> that the two remaining conditions – regarding Russian acceptance of the McLaren Report and access for WADA to the Moscow laboratory – remain unfulfilled, and yet WADA's leading compliance body is recommending

---

306 ibid.
307 ibid.
308 ibid.
309 ibid. Part II contained 12 criteria that RUSADA had yet to fulfil.
310 World Anti-Doping Agency, 'WADA's Executive Committee to Discuss Updated Recommendation from independent Compliance Review Committee in Relation to RUSADA Roadmap to Compliance' 14 September 2018 <https://www.sportsintegrityinitiative.com/wadas-executive-committee-to-discuss-updated-recommendation-from-independent-compliance-review-committee-in-relation-to-rusada-roadmap-to-compliance/> accessed 2 May 2024. The original media release from the WADA website is no longer available.
311 World Anti-Doping Agency, 'WADA Executive Committee Decides to Reinstate RUSADA Subject to Strict Conditions' 20 September 2018 <https://www.wada-ama.org/en/media/news/2018-09/wada-executive-committee-decides-to-reinstate-rusada-subject-to-strict-conditions> accessed 2 May 2024.
312 Sean Ingle, 'Wada Lifts Russia's Three-Year Doping Suspension and Faces its Biggest Crisis' *The Guardian* (London, 20 September 2018) <https://www.theguardian.com/sport/2018/sep/20/wada-crisis-lifts-russia-suspension-anti-doping> accessed 2 May 2024. Sport Ireland was critical of the decision to reinstate RUSADA without all the criteria fulfilled: see Sport Ireland, 'Sport Ireland Statement on WADA Recommendation to Reinstate Russia' 18 September 2018 <https://www.sportireland.ie/news/sport-ireland-statement-on-wada-recommendation-to-reinstate-russia> accessed 1 May 2024.

> the reinstatement of a country that perpetrated the worst doping system ever seen in international sport.[313]

The statement was made on behalf of a number of anti-doping leaders from the following countries: Australia, Austria, Canada, Finland, Germany, Ireland, Japan, Netherlands, New Zealand, Norway, Poland, the UK, and the US.[314] It implored WADA to reconsider the Executive Committee's decision and it viewed the reinstatement of RUSADA as a moving of the goal posts and a deviation from the Roadmap of Compliance.[315] The signatories were most concerned about the lack of access to the urine samples stored in the Moscow laboratory.[316] **2–87**

WADA attached the following conditions to the reinstatement: **2–88**

- RUSADA and the Russian Ministry of Sport must procure that the authentic Information Management System (LIMS) data and underlying analytical data of the former Moscow Laboratory set out in the WADA President's letter of 22 June 2018 are received by WADA (via access to the data by an independent expert agreeable to both WADA and the Russian authorities) by no later than 31 December 2018.
- RUSADA and the Russian Ministry of Sport must procure that any re-analysis of samples required by WADA following review of such data is completed by no later than 30 June 2019.[317]

WADA stipulated that 'a successful audit of RUSADA must be carried out within four months to ensure RUSADA continues to meet compliance standards'.[318] It added that these conditions were 'critical requirements under the International Standard for Code Compliance by Signatories (ISCCS)'.[319] If these conditions were not achieved, then the WADA Executive Committee would 'consider proposals from the CRC to address such non-compliance based on the relevant provisions of the ISCCS'.[320] **2–89**

At the end of November 2018, a three-person delegation met with officials in Moscow whereby they visited the laboratory.[321] A technical mission was scheduled to take place before the end of December 2018 **2–90**

---

313 US Anti-Doping Agency, 'Anti-Doping Leaders Urge WADA to Postpone Russian Reinstatement' 18 September 2018 <https://www.usada.org/announcement/anti-doping-leaders-urge-wada-to-postpone-russian-reinstatement/> accessed 2 May 2024.

314 ibid.

315 ibid.

316 ibid.

317 WADA (n 311).

318 ibid.

319 ibid.

320 ibid.

321 World Anti-Doping, 'WADA Meets with Russian Authorities Regarding Moscow Laboratory Access' 28 November 2018 <https://www.sportsintegrityinitiative.com/wada-meets-with-russian-authorities-regarding-moscow-laboratory-access/

which would entail a full inspection of the laboratory and access to the LIMS data.[322] Russia was warned that if WADA was not given access to the requested data, RUSADA would be deemed non-compliant and would be required to adhere to the more stringent ISCCS, which came into force on 1 April 2018.[323] A five-member delegate arrived in Moscow on 17 December 2018, however, it was refused entry into the laboratory on the grounds that the team's equipment was not certified as required under Russian law.[324] In January 2019, the three-person WADA delegate successfully retrieved data from the Moscow laboratory.[325]

2–91 In 2019, the investigations continued with WADA announcing that RUSADA was not WADC compliant and it was unanimously decided by CRC that a four-year sanction be imposed upon RUSADA.[326] The consequences of this were far-reaching and included a ban on the hosting of major events for four years and a ban on Russian government officials attending Winter and Summer Olympics and other major events.[327] Russian athletes could only compete in events where they had not been implicated in the doping scandal and had to compete as neutrals. The Russian flag was banned from being displayed at events for four years. Fines were also levied on RUSADA which had to be paid within the four-year period.[328] As discussed below, the CAS reduced the four-year period to two.[329]

2–92 In late 2018, the IAAF refused to reinstate Russia until the two conditions, public acknowledgment and access to samples and data,

---

> accessed 2 May 2024. The original media release from the WADA website is no longer available.

322 ibid.

323 World Anti-Doping Agency, 'WADA's New Compliance Standard and Code Revisions Enter into Force on 1 April 2018' 28 March 2018 <https://www.wada-ama.org/en/media/news/2018-03/wadas-new-compliance-standard-and-code-revisions-enter-into-force-on–1-april–2018> accessed 2 May 2024.

324 World Anti-Doping Agency, 'WADA's "Operation LIMS" Investigation Reaches Important Milestone with More than 200 Sanctions' 18 May 2023 <https://www.wada-ama.org/en/news/wadas-operation-lims-investigation-reaches-important-milestone-more–200-sanctions> accessed 2 May 2024. A total of 203 Russian athletes were sanctioned by 17 ADOs with an additional 73 charged, as well as another 182 cases that were under investigation as of 18 May 2023.

325 World Anti-Doping Agency, 'WADA Successfully Retrieves Data from Moscow Laboratory' 17 January 2019 < https://www.wada-ama.org/en/news/wada-successfully-retrieves-data-moscow-laboratory> accessed 2 May 2024.

326 World Anti-Doping Agency, 'WADA Executive Committee Unanimously Endorses Four-Year Period of Non-compliance for the Russian Anti-Doping Agency' 9 December 2019 <https://www.wada-ama.org/en/news/wada-executive-committee-unanimously-endorses-four-year-period-non-compliance-russian-anti > accessed 1 July 2024.

327 ibid.

328 ibid.

329 CAS 2020/O/6689 *World Anti-Doping Agency v Russian Anti-Doping Agency* award of 17 December 2020 <https://www.tas-cas.org/fileadmin/user_upload/CAS_Award_6689.pdf> accessed 2 May 2024.

were fulfilled.[330] It also sought costs, including legal costs, from RusAF.[331] In September 2019, the ban was again extended by the IAAF. In June 2019 it was announced that the IAAF was being rebranded as World Athletics, and following the Doha Games which took place between 27 September and 6 October 2019, the new name was adopted.[332] The name change may have been conceived as way of the IAAF distancing itself from the Russian doping scandal. Cognisance is given to the fact that the IAAF had been in existence for 100 years and was due a name change. IAAF CEO Jon Ridgeon noted that IAAF name had 'little understanding or relevance to those outside of athletics' and the 'new identity creates a symbol that can stand alone and work with partners and events'.[333]

Russia continued to be banned from taking part in the Olympics and **2–93**
from hosting any major sporting events for two years. The ban ended on 16 December 2022. Athletes who were not implicated in the scandal were permitted to compete as 'neutral athletes' during the two years. In a 186-page arbitral award, the CAS reduced WADA's four-year ban to two.[334] The CAS Panel recognised that the reduction could be viewed as a 'validation of the conduct of RUSADA or the Russian authorities', however, it stated that this was not case.[335] It referred to the limitations placed on the CAS Panel 'by the powers granted under the applicable law'.[336] The case was heard under the 2018 WADC, Swiss Law and the ISSCCS.[337] It was the ISSCCS and the WADC that the CAS Panel specifically cited as imposing limitations on it.[338] The CAS Panel reasoned that it had 'considered matters of proportionality and, in particular, the need to effect cultural change and encourage the next generation of Russian athletes to participate in clean international sport'.[339] The CAS Panel added its 'hope that this Award will mark a new path towards reconciliation and allow Russian athletes a fresh start to contribute to their otherwise proud sporting history'.[340]

---

330 'IAAF Extends Ban on Russia to Put World Athletics Championships Participation in Doubt' *The Independent* (London, 4 December 2018) <https://www.independent.co.uk/sport/general/athletics/iaaf-russia-ban-drugs-doping-world-athletics-championships-qatar–2019-a8666786.html> accessed 1 July 2024.

331 ibid.

332 The name change was approved by the IAAF's 217th Council Meeting in Monaco June 2019: see World Athletics, 'IAAF Unveils New Name and Logo' 9 June 2019 <https://www.worldathletics.org/news/press-release/iaaf-unveils-new-name-and-logo> accessed 2 May 2024.

333 ibid.

334 CAS 2020/O/6689 (n 329). There were 50 intervening parties, including the International Olympic Committee (IOC), the International Paralympic Committee (IPC) and the International Ice Hockey Federation (IIHF).

335 ibid [861].

336 ibid.

337 ibid [545].

338 ibid [861].

339 ibid [861].

340 ibid [862].

2–94 The decision was not met with universal welcome as it meant that neutral athletes could compete in 2021 in red jerseys with the word Russia and neutral on it.[341] In a Statement from the USADA CEO Travis T Tygart, the reduction of the ban was referred to a 'devastating decision' which 'hands WADA and clean athletes a significant loss'.[342] Tygart continued:

> At this stage in this sordid Russian state-sponsored doping affair, now spanning close to a decade, there is no consolation in this weak, watered-down outcome. To once again escape a meaningful consequence proportional to the crimes, much less a real ban, is a catastrophic blow to clean athletes, the integrity of sport, and the rule of law.[343]

2–95 WADA did not appeal the CAS Panel decision to the SFT as it cited the limited procedural circumstances in which a decision of the CAS can be appealed to the Swiss Court.[344] WADA 'strongly believes an appeal would have served no useful purpose and decided to refrain from doing so'.[345] WADA published a Q&A on the lengthy CAS decision in order to explain the decision of the CAS to ADOs, the media and other stakeholders.[346]

2–96 Following Russia's invasion of Ukraine, the IOC placed a ban on the ROC and athletes with a Russian or Belarusian passport must compete only as Individual Neutral Athletes.[347] Russian and Belarusian athletes were permitted to compete in the 2024 Games so long as they had not supported Russia in the war against Ukraine.[348]

---

341 Sean Ingle, 'Decision to Halve Russia's Wada Doping Ban Met with Disbelief and Anger' *The Guardian* (London, 17 December 2020) <https://www.theguardian.com/sport/2020/dec/17/russia-doping-ban-halved-but-name-and-flag-barred-from-next-two-olympics-court-of-arbitration-for-sport-world-anti-doping-agency> accessed 1 July 2024.

342 US Anti-Doping Agency, 'Statement from USADA CEO Travis T Tygart on Russia CAS Appeal and Ruling' 17 December 2020 <https://www.usada.org/statement/usada-ceo-statement-russia-cas-appeal-ruling/> accessed 2 May 2024.

343 ibid.

344 World Anti-Doping Agency, 'WADA Does Not Appeal CAS Decision Regarding Russian Anti-Doping Agency to Swiss Federal Tribunal' 2 February 2021 <https://www.wada-ama.org/en/media/news/2021-02/wada-does-not-appeal-cas-decision-regarding-russian-anti-doping-agency-to-swiss> accessed 2 May 2024.

345 ibid.

346 World Anti-Doping Agency, 'RUSADA Compliance, Court of Arbitration for Sport Decision of 17 December 2020: Questions and Answers' 4 February 2021 <https://www.wada-ama.org/sites/default/files/resources/files/2021-02-04_rusadacompliance_qa.pdf> accessed 2 May 2024.

347 International Olympic Committee, 'Q&A Regarding the Participation of Athletes with a Russian or Belarusian Passport in International Competitions' 25 October 2023 <https://olympics.com/ioc/media/q-a-on-solidarity-with-ukraine-sanctions-against-russia-and-belarus-and-the-status-of-athletes-from-these-countries> accessed 1 July 2024. Individual Neutral Athletes were not permitted to use the Russian or Belarusian flags or national anthems.

348 See Sean Ingle, 'Russian and Belarusian Athletes Allowed to Compete at Paris 2024 Olympics' *The Guardian* (London, 8 December 2023 <https://www.theguardian.

The Russia doping scandal unearthed a toxic and complex system of governance.[349] The ensuing investigation and resulting reports such as the McLaren Reports could 'prove to be a catalyst for fundamental change'.[350] However, this must be considered in light of previous 'tipping points', Ben Johnson being a case in point.[351] These tipping points did not result in fundamental change.[352] As King asserts: 2–97

> Ostensibly, for doping in sport to be addressed, organisations are required to investigate themselves, ensure safeguards for whistleblowers, provide a more robust voice for athletes as key stakeholders, and develop a culture of trust and information-sharing. Further, governing bodies would have to address problematic relationships with the media, government and regulatory agencies to ensure a negotiated level of scrutiny and compliance.[353]

In looking to the future, King foresees increased state-led intervention in sport governance which will result in 'further legislation, regulation and criminalisation', however, a '"war on drugs" is highly unlikely to be successful'.[354] 2–98

Fédération Internationale de Football Association: FIFA

In 2015, the world governing body of football, FIFA, faced allegations of bribery, racketeering, wire fraud, money laundering and corruption which spanned two decades. In May of that year the Swiss police, at the behest of US prosecutors, carried out a dawn raid on several senior officials staying at a hotel in Zurich.[355] The officials were in Zurich for FIFA's annual congress and faced extradition to the US.[356] The Federal Bureau of Investigators (FBI) had been investigating FIFA for 2–99

---

com/sport/2023/dec/08/athletes-who-have-not-supported-ukraine-war-to-compete-at-paris–2024> accessed 2 May 2024.

349 Neil King, 'Governance and Corruption in Sport with Respect to Doping' in David R Mottram and Neil Chester (eds), *Drugs in Sport* (7th edn) (Routledge 2018) 391.

350 ibid.

351 ibid. See ch 6 para 6-08.

352 ibid.

353 ibid.

354 ibid.

355 For a discussion on Switzerland as a base for a number of world sporting bodies and recent changes to its anti-corruption laws, see Lucien W Valloni and Eric P Neuenschwander, 'Chapter 6.4: The Role of Switzerland as Host: Moves to Hold Sports Organisations More Accountable, and Wider Implications' <https://valloni.ch/wp-content/uploads/2021/06/SwitzerlandAsHost_Valloni_Neuenschwander_GCRSport.pdf> accessed 2 May 2024. See also Martine Brocard, 'Why Switzerland Remains at the Heart of Corruption in Sport' 1 March 2022 <https://www.swissinfo.ch/eng/business/why-switzerland-remains-at-the-heart-of-corruption-in-sport/47372632> accessed 3 May 2024.

356 Owen Gibson and Damien Gayle, 'FIFA Officials Arrested on Corruption Charges as World Cup Inquiry Launched' *The Guardian* (London, 27 May 2015) <https://www.theguardian.com/football/2015/may/27/several-top-fifa-officials-arrested> accessed 1 July 2024

the previous three years. Attorney General Loretta Lynch announced at a press conference in New York that a number of events had come under investigation, including the awarding of the 2010 World Cup to South Africa and the 2011 FIFA presidential election.[357] Lynch listed the allegations, including selling rights downstream to sports marketing executives in lucrative agreements which began in 1991 and involved two generations of the Confederation of North, Central American and Caribbean Association Football (CONCACAF) and the South American Football Confederation (CONMEBOL).[358] Both regional confederations 'used their positions of trust' by soliciting bribes from sports marketers in exchange for commercial rights for their tournaments.[359] One such tournament was the centennial COPA America in 2016 which took place in the US, the first time since its inception in 1916 that the tournament was played outside of South America.[360] Attorney General Lynch stated that the tournament was 'used as a vehicle in this broader scheme' with bribes amounting to $110m, which was one-third of the legitimate cost of hosting the COPA America.[361] Similarly, bribes were paid for the 2010 World Cup to be held in South Africa, the first time it was held on the continent of Africa.[362] Nike was implicated in the payment of bribes to secure the sponsorship of the Brazilian football team.[363] Attorney General Lynch noted that two corporate defendants, a US sports marketing company and Brazilian sports marketing company, and four individuals had already pleaded guilty and had forfeited over $150m.[364]

Blatter and Platini

2–100 The FIFA President at the time, Sepp Blatter, and the then Vice-President and member of the Executive of FIFA and the then UEFA (Union des Associations Européennes de Football) President, Michel Platini, were banned for eight years by the adjudicatory chamber of the FIFA Ethics

---

[357] Loretta Lynch, 'FIFA Corruption Charges' (YouTube, 27 May 2015) <https://www.youtube.com/watch?v=YXO0_CZNTvc> accessed 2 May 2024.

[358] ibid.

[359] ibid.

[360] Graham Parker, 'Centenary Copa América to Be Played in US in 2016' *The Guardian* (London, 1 May 2024) <https://www.theguardian.com/football/2014/may/01/centenary-copa-america-to-be-played-in-usa-in–2016> accessed 3 May 2024.

[361] Loretta Lynch (n 357).

[362] Luke Brown and Nicholas Randall, 'FIFA Corruption: "Morocco won 2010 World Cup Vote – not South Africa" – as it Happened', *The Telegraph* (London, 7 June 2015) <https://www.telegraph.co.uk/sport/football/fifa/11657595/Fifa-corruption-Morocco–2010-World-Cup-vote-live.html> accessed 3 May 2024.

[363] Initially referred to as Company A, Nike paid $40m to a Swiss bank account of an affiliate of the Brazilian marketing company, Traffic. This was in addition to the $160m paid to secure the sponsorship. Jamie Doward, 'Nike Fights on Two Fronts as Brand Is Linked to Bribery and Doping Allegations' *The Guardian* (London, 6 June 2015) <https://www.theguardian.com/sport/2015/jun/06/nike-fifa-salazar-brazil-football-athletics-doping-allegations> accessed 3 May 2024.

[364] Loretta Lynch (n 357).

Committee.[365] While cleared of bribery, the men were found to have acted in a manner that constituted a conflict of interest and a breach of dereliction of duty over the payment of 2 million Swiss Francs from Blatter to Platini in 2011.[366] FIFA's Appeal Committee reduced Blatter and Platini's suspensions to six years in February 2016.[367] Platini appealed the six-year suspension to the CAS, which subsequently reduced his ban from six years to four and the fine from 80,000 Swiss Francs to 60,000.[368] After an unsuccessful appeal to the SFT, Platini applied to the European Court of Human Rights (ECtHR) alleging that his rights under the European Convention (ECHR) had been infringed.[369] Platini based his claim on Article 6 (right to a fair hearing), Article 7 (no punishment without law) and Article 8 (right to respect for private and family life) of the ECHR.[370] In regard to Article 6, Platini contended that the proceedings in the CAS were incompatible with the right to a fair hearing. Under Article 7, he argued that the prohibition on the retrospective application of law had been impugned, given that the FIFA rules in force at the relevant time, those between 2007 and 2011, had not been applied.[371] In reference to Article 8, Platini proffered that the four-year suspension was 'incompatible with his freedom to exercise a

365 The Ethics Committee is one of FIFA's judicial bodies, the two others being the Appeal Committee and the Disciplinary Committee. Since 2012 it has been divided into two separate chambers: the investigatory chamber and the adjudicatory chamber. For details on the judicial and other committees, see FIFA, 'Committees' <https://inside.fifa.com/about-fifa/organisation/committees> accessed 3 May 2024.

366 Owen Gibson, 'Sepp Blatter and Michel Platini Banned from Football for Eight Years by FIFA' *The Guardian* (London, 21 December 2015) <https://www.theguardian.com/football/2015/dec/21/sepp-blatter-michel-platini-banned-from-football-fifa> accessed 3 May 2024.

367 FIFA, 'FIFA Appeal Committee Dismisses Appeals from Investigatory Chamber, Joseph S Blatter and Michel Platini; Grants a Reduction on Sentences' 24 February 2016 <https://www.fifa.com/about-fifa/who-we-are/news/fifa-appeal-committee-dismisses-appeals-from-investigatory-chamber-jos–2766869> accessed 3 May 2024.

368 CAS 2016/A/4474 *Michel Platini v Fédération Internationale de Football Association*, award of 16 May 2016 <https://www.tas-cas.org/fileadmin/user_upload/Media_release_4474_final_eng.pdf> accessed 1 July 2024. The CAS referred to the severity of the suspension of six years and reduced it to four, which equated with a presidential term within FIFA.

369 *Platini v Switzerland* App no 526/18. The judgment is available only in French: see 'DÉCISION Requête no 526/18 Michel PLATINI contre la Suisse, La Cour européenne des droits de l'homme (troisième section), siégeant le 11 février 2020' <https://hudoc.echr.coe.int/eng#{%22itemid%22:[%22001-201734%22]}> accessed 3 May 2024.

370 Press Release of the European Court of Human Rights, 'Michel Platini: Suspension from Football-Related Professional Activity Was Justified' ECHR 085 (5 March 2020) <https://www.google.com/url?sa=t&source=web&rct=j&opi=89978449&url=https://hudoc.echr.coe.int/app/conversion/pdf/%3Flibrary%3DECHR%26id%3D003665786488494 94%26filename%3DDecision%2520Platini%2520v.%2520Switzerland%2520%2520suspension%2520from%2520footballrelated%2520professional%2520activity%2520was%2520justified.pdf&ved=2ahUKEwjh0c6UuPGFAxUGSkEAHQ4fAaQQFnoECA4QAw&usg=AOvVaw1MTxpwsiSnl-–2E3NjCIYx> accessed 3 May 2024.

371 ibid 2.

professional activity'.[372] The ECtHR rejected Platini's complaint under Article 6(1) and deemed inadmissible his complaint under Article 7.[373] While acknowledging the broad and non-exhaustive nature of Article 8, the ECtHR found that it could not be extended to cover the applicant's professional life.[374] While the stigmatisation and negative repercussions would impinge on his private life, the ECtHR found that sufficient institutional and procedural safeguards had been afforded to Platini, thus it deemed the Article 8 complaint as manifestly unfounded.[375]

2–101 In July 2022, Blatter and Platini were acquitted of allegations of fraud and bribery by judges of the Federal Criminal Court in Switzerland.[376] Prosecutors sought the return of 2.23 million Swiss Francs to FIFA and the imposition of a suspended sentence of 20 months.[377] Platini maintained that the 2.23 million related to back-dated salary for consultancy work carried out between 1998 and 2002.[378] Both men were awarded legal costs, 80,000 Swiss Francs for Blatter and 140,000 Swiss Francs for Platini.[379] Blatter also received moral damages of 20,000 Swiss Francs, while Platini refused such compensation. The decision meant that he could now access the frozen 2 million Swiss Francs back-dated pay.[380]

FIFA Code of Ethics

2–102 FIFA revised its 2012 Code of Ethics with an updated Code of Ethics 2018 that came into force on 12 August 2018.[381] The Associated Press criticised the changes as it pointed to the omission of the word 'corruption' in Article 27 which refers only to 'bribery'.[382] The 2012 edition, Article 21, referred to 'Bribery and corruption'.[383] The 2012 Code, Article 12(2) stated: 'Prosecution for bribery and corruption is not subject to such a limitation period.'[384] However, under the revised 2018 Code, Article

---

372 ibid.
373 ibid.
374 ibid 3.
375 ibid.
376 'Swiss Court Throws Out Blatter and Platini Charges' 8 July 2022 <https://www.swissinfo.ch/eng/politics/court-throws-out-blatter-and-platini-corruption-charges/47736762> accessed 3 May 2024.
377 ibid.
378 ibid.
379 ibid.
380 ibid.
381 FIFA, 'FIFA Code of Ethics 2018 Edition' <https://digitalhub.fifa.com/m/302ad028a0bf7784/original/dhkhat135uw887piqha0-pdf.pdf> accessed 3 May 2024.
382 Rob Harris, 'FIFA Quietly Drops "Corruption" as Code of Ethics Offence' *Global News* (Vancouver, 14 August 2018) <https://globalnews.ca/news/4386347/fifa-drops-corruption-code-of-ethics/> accessed 3 May 2024.
383 FIFA, 'FIFA Code of Ethics 2012 Edition' <https://www.safa.net/wp-content/uploads/2017/03/codeofethics_v211015_e_neutral.pdf> accessed 3 May 2024.
384 ibid. The general time limit under the 2012 Code was 10 years. Under the 2018

12(2) provided: 'Bribery, misappropriation of funds and manipulation of football matches or competitions may no longer be prosecuted after a lapse of ten years.'[385] The 2018 Code introduced, under Article 22(2), a prohibition on persons bound by the Code 'from making any public statements of a defamatory nature towards FIFA and/or towards any other person bound by this Code in the context of FIFA events'. There was no such provision on defamation in the 2012 Code.

The Associated Press article resulted in FIFA issuing a statement clarifying the issues raised.[386] It stated that the article contained 'several inaccurate statements, despite the fact that comprehensive background information was provided to the journalist'.[387] In relation to the omission of the word 'corruption', the statement countenanced this by explaining that it was for clarity in the English, German and Spanish versions.[388] The French version never included the word 'corruption'.[389] The substance of Article 12, it contended, remained the same and the revised Code was **2–103**

> actually more stringent regarding bribery, by dint of having minimum sanctions to punish any instance of bribery, which did not exist under the previous code. Thus, any bribery offence will be sanctioned with a minimum ban from all football-related activity of five years, as well as a minimum fine of CHF 100,000.[390]

In response to the inclusion of defamation, FIFA defended this on the grounds that it needed to protect the reputation of not only FIFA but 'also to protect any other person covered by the code who may be subjected to discriminatory or defamatory statements in the context of FIFA events'.[391] With regard to the introduction of a time limitation on the prosecution of bribery cases, the statement referred to the purpose of this as bringing about 'more legal certainty to the world of football by ensuring that potential infringements to the code are dealt with in a **2–104**

Code the general time limit for prosecution was reduced to five years under art 12(1).

385 FIFA Code 2018 (n 381) 13.

386 FIFA, 'Clarification Concerning the Revised FIFA Code of Ethics' 14 August 2018 <https://www.fifa.com/about-fifa/who-we-are/news/clarification-concerning-the-revised-fifa-code-of-ethics> accessed 3 May 2024.

387 ibid.

388 ibid.

389 ibid.

390 ibid. CHF refers to the Swiss Franc.

391 ibid. It was claimed that Sepp Blatter planned to sue the current president of FIFA, Gianni Infantino, for defamation, unpaid pension contributions and the return of his valuable watch collection: see Tom Morgan, 'Disgraced Former FIFA President Sepp Blatter Suing His Successor Gianni Infantino for Alleged Defamation', *Telegraph* (London, 8 May 2019) <https://www.telegraph.co.uk/football/2019/05/08/disgraced-former-fifa-president-sepp-blatter-suing-successor/> accessed 1 July 2024.

swift manner'.[392] It added that statutes of limitation are general principles of law in civil and common law jurisdictions.[393]

2–105 The omission of the word corruption in the 2018 Code of Ethics in the view of FIFA is simply a matter of semantics. In *Murdoch's Dictionary of Irish Law*, bribery and corruption are contained in the one entry.[394] By omitting corruption under Article 12(2), FIFA attracted criticism and if it were simply a matter of semantics then it could have been left as bribery and corruption. The 2018 Code presented FIFA with an opportunity to demonstrate that it was taking a more robust position regarding its governance. The Code was launched in August 2018; prior to this an IPSOS survey found that six out of 10 people trusted FIFA to do its best in the interest of football and its spectators.[395] The survey took place from 20 April 2018 to 4 May 2018 and involved 27 countries, including China, with 87% of respondents; Russia, with 65% of respondents; Australia, with 50% of respondents; and Britain, with 32% of respondents agreeing with the statement.[396] Britain recorded the lowest rate of trust in FIFA. In June 2019 it was reported that the former UEFA president and member of the FIFA Executive Platini had been detained in France by the Anti-Corruption Office of the Judicial Police (OCLCIFF) over his vote in the award of the 2022 World Cup in Qatar, a development which will not have aided FIFA in its endeavours to improve its public image.[397] Platini's four-year ban expired in March 2019. The arrest came five years after the *Daily Telegraph* reported that Platini had numerous meetings with the former Asian Football Confederation President Mohammed Bin Hammam before the Qatar vote. [398] Bin Hammam was banned from all football-related activity for life by the FIFA Ethics Committee in December 2012 following repeated violations of Article 19 (conflict of interest) under the 2012 Code of Ethics.[399] Platini responded to media reports relating to his alleged arrest by stating that he was not arrested but detained in order

392 ibid.

393 ibid.

394 Brian Hunt, *Murdoch's Dictionary of Irish Law* (5th edn, Tottel Publishing 2007) 129. Corruption is entered on its own on page 283.

395 IPSOS Global Advisor, 'Attitudes Towards the FIFA World Cup 2018 in Russia' (2018) 24 <https://www.ipsos.com/sites/default/files/ct/news/documents/201806/ipsos_globaladvisor_fifa_worldcup_2018-final_draft.pptx_us.pdf> accessed 3 May 2024. The survey was answered by 12,207 adults aged between 16 and 64, who were aware of the upcoming FIFA World Cup 2018.

396 ibid.

397 Tom Morgan, 'Former UEFA President Michel Platini Detained by Police Over Awarding of 2022 World Cup to Qatar' *Telegraph* (London, 18 June 2019) <https://www.telegraph.co.uk/football/2019/06/18/former-uefa-president-michel-platini-arrested-awarding–2022/?li_source=LI&li_medium=li-recommendation-widget/> accessed 3 May 2024.

398 ibid.

399 Press Association, 'FIFA Issues New Life Ban to Ex-Co Member Mohamed bin Hammam' *The Guardian* (London, 17 December 2012) <https://www.theguardian.com/football/2012/dec/17/fifa-life-ban-mohamed-bin-hammam> accessed 3 May 2024.

to preserve the confidentiality of the police interview.[400] In 2022, Blatter acknowledged that Qatar was 'a mistake'.[401] It was alleged that Platini was under pressure from the then French President Nicolas Sarkozy to vote for Qatar a week before FIFA's Executive Committee meeting on 2 December 2010.[402]

The Code of Ethics was updated in 2019 to include 'corruption' in the article on bribery,[403] and provide for sterner sanctions for sexual abuse. Under the 2018 Code, Article 23, titled Protection of Physical and Mental Integrity, subsection 4, stated that sexual harassment was forbidden.[404] The sanction for a violation under Article 23(5) was that of **2–106**

> an appropriate fine of at least CHF 10,000 as well as a ban on taking part in any football-related activity for a maximum of two years. In serious cases and/or in the case of repetition, a ban on taking part in any football-related activity may be pronounced for a maximum of five years.[405]

The 2019 Code of Ethics increased the ban on taking part in any football-related activity in serious cases or cases of repetition to a maximum of 10 years.[406] It also amended the wording of Article 23(5) to include 'cases of sexual exploitation or abuse' before 'in serious cases and/or in the case of repetition'. The 2023 Code of Ethics Article 24 covers Protection of Physical and Mental Integrity.[407] Article 24(5) replicates the text of Article 23(5) of the 2019 edition and adds subsection 6, which provides for recourse to the CAS to those who may have been the victim of **2–107**

---

400 David Conn, 'Michel Platini Detained Over Award of 2022 World Cup to Qatar' *The Guardian* (London, 18 June 2019) <https://www.theguardian.com/football/2019/jun/18/michel-platini-arrested-over-award-of–2022-world-cup-to-qatar> accessed 3 May 2024. There are no follow-ups to this, and it is not clear if legal proceedings ensued in France.

401 Paul MacInnes, 'Sepp Blatter Says Choosing Qatar to Host World Cup Was "a Mistake"' *The Guardian* (London, 8 November 2022) <https://www.theguardian.com/football/2022/nov/08/sepp-blatter-qatar-hosting-world-cup-mistake > accessed 3 May 2024. He was not talking about the human rights aspect, but that Qatar was a small country.

402 ibid. For background on the link between Sarkozy, Platini and Qatar, see Tariq Panja, 'France to Investigate How Qatar Got the World Cup' *The New York Times* (New York, 1 December 2019, updated 20 October 2021) <https://www.nytimes.com/2019/12/11/sports/soccer/qatar-world-cup-michel-platini.html> accessed 3 May 2024. It was claimed that Sarkozy wanted the Qataris to purchase the club he supports, Paris St-Germain, see David Conn, 'A Sarkozy lunch, PSG and beIN sports: questions for Platini over Qatar 2022' *The Guardian* (London, 18 June 2019) <https://www.theguardian.com/football/2019/jun/18/sarkozy-psg-bein-sports-questions-michel-platini-qatar-2022-world-cup> accessed 1 July 2024.

403 Article 27 of the FIFA, 'Code of Ethics Edition 2019' <https://digitalhub.fifa.com/m/1c429d1b627be00c/original/la3f5yqsox5cns9oypkg-pdf.pdf> accessed 3 May 2024.

404 FIFA Code 2018 (n 381) 20.

405 ibid 21.

406 FIFA Code 2019 (n 403) Art 23(5).

407 FIFA, 'Code of Ethics Edition 2023' <https://digitalhub.fifa.com/m/4f048486c1f7293c/original/FIFA-Code-of-Ethics–2023.pdf> accessed 3 May 2024.

potential sexual abuse or harassment. It provides increased procedural rights for victims as it allows them to appeal the decision rendered by the adjudicatory chamber. If they decide to appeal to the CAS, subsection 6 states that the victim must be furnished with the following:

> the decision, the final report of the investigatory chamber, as well as with any document or evidence produced by the parties before the adjudicatory chamber. Their deadline to appeal the relevant decision before CAS shall commence on the day of notification of those documents.[408]

2–108 The 2023 Code of Ethics provides that the limitation period for prosecution does not apply to Article 24; this is a change from the 2019 Code of Ethics.[409] Generally, the limitation period is five years, apart from Articles 28 and 29, which may no longer be prosecuted after 10 years have elapsed.[410]

2–109 Following on from the Code of Ethics 2019, Article 28 of the 2023 Code of Ethics refers to both bribery and corruption. A breach of this article under Article 28(3) will result in a fine of at least 100,000 Swiss Francs as well as a ban on taking part in any football-related activity for a minimum of five years. Article 28(3) adds:

> Any amount unduly received shall be included in the calculation of the fine. The sanction shall be increased accordingly where the person holds a high position in football, as well as in relation to the relevance and amount of the advantage received.[411]

2–110 Article 29 covers misappropriation and misuse of funds. The sanctions outlined in Article 29(3) mirror those of Article 28(3).[412]

Football Association of Ireland: Governance and Reform

2–111 The FAI was one of a few national federations that featured in the FIFA scandal. In 2009, Ireland missed out on a place at the 2010 World Cup Finals in South Africa after losing to France following a handball goal by Thierry Henri. It later emerged that FIFA had paid the FAI €5m, which it claimed was a loan to help finance the refurbishment of the Aviva Stadium.[413] However, the FAI accounts did not document the €5m

---

408 ibid 20. Article 24(7) is a new subsection, and it provides: 'Confederations and associations shall immediately notify FIFA of any decision taken by their respective bodies sanctioning a person for conduct described in this article.'

409 ibid art 13(3).

410 ibid art 13(1) and (2).

411 ibid 21–22. Article 30 refers to manipulation of football matches or competitions.

412 The 2023 Code refers to independent integrity experts and match-fixing under art 61(2). The Disciplinary Code 2023 Edition explains the role of integrity experts under Art 36: see FIFA, 'The Disciplinary Code 2023 Edition' <https://digitalhub.fifa.com/m/59dca8ae619101cf/original/FIFA-Disciplinary-Code–2023.pdf> accessed 3 May 2024.

413 Emmet Malone, 'FAI's €5m FIFA Payment Not Apparent in Published

and it was subsequently written off after Ireland failed to make it to the 2014 World Cup Finals in Brazil.[414] It was described as constituting a 'legitimate agreement', however, it was questioned how a refereeing decision could result in a pay-out of €5m.[415] FIFA feared that the FAI would take legal action and the €5m was given to 'avoid a long, costly and protracted legal case'.[416]

The internal governance of the FAI came under scrutiny in 2019 as the chief executive, John Delaney, was placed on 'gardening leave' and subsequently resigned amid a flurry of allegations, including the payment of a €100,000 bridging loan to the FAI in 2017 and the FAI payment of benefit-in-kind worth €3,000 per month towards the rental of a house for Delaney and his partner.[417] This was in addition to his annual salary of €360,000. **2–112**

Governance Review Group Report for the FAI Board and Sport Ireland

In response to the actions of Delaney, the FAI reviewed and subsequently revised its governance structures. The *Governance Review Group Report for the FAI Board and Sport Ireland* was published on 21 June 2019. The Governance Review Group used the following working definition of governance: **2–113**

> Governance comprises the arrangements put in place to ensure that the Football Association of Ireland fulfils its overall purpose and achieves its intended outcome for all its stakeholders. Governance is concerned with leadership and direction, structures and authority levels, processes for decision making, accountability arrangements, risk management, internal controls, culture and related behaviours within the organisation.[418]

In embracing the working definition above, the Governance Review Group promulgated six principles of governance for the FAI, in accordance with best practice in general and the principles imbued by UEFA: **2–114**

Accounts' *The Irish Times* (Dublin, 4 June 2015) <https://www.irishtimes.com/sport/soccer/international/fai-s–5m-fifa-payment-not-apparent-in-published-accounts–1.2238001> accessed 4 May 2024.

414 ibid.

415 ibid.

416 Football Association of Ireland, 'FAI Statement on €5m Settlement Agreement with FIFA' 4 June 2015. The statement is no longer available on the FAI website; however, it is reproduced in the Malone article (n 413).

417 'FAI Silent on Reports John Delaney Is Still Being Paid €360k CEO Salary' *Irish Independent* (Dublin, 13 June 2019) <https://www.independent.ie/sport/soccer/international-soccer/fai-silent-on-reports-john-delaney-is-still-being-paid–360k-ceo-salary–38216419.html> accessed 4 May 2024. For an interesting discussion of Delaney's activities, see Emmet Malone, 'Excesses of the John Delaney FAI Years Laid Bare Again' *The Irish Times* (Dublin, 5 December 2019) <https://www.irishtimes.com/sport/soccer/international/excesses-of-the-john-delaney-fai-years-laid-bare-again–1.4106302> accessed 4 May 2024.

418 (21 June 2019) 7.

1. Good governance
2. Effective leadership
3. Accountability and transparency
4. Ethical behaviour and integrity
5. Stakeholder engagement
6. Professionalism.[419]

2–115 The Review concluded with 78 recommendations.[420] Recommendation 54 outlined the creation of a new 12-person Board consisting of four independent Directors, which included a chair, six members from the football community, a President and Vice-President.[421] The final recommendation noted the process of 'rebuilding trust, faith and confidence' in the FAI and thus an interim board should be appointed pending the FAI's annual general meeting (AGM) in July 2020.

2–116 To ensure the recommendations of the Governance Review Group were followed, an Implementation Oversight Group was created. By 18 December 2019, John Treacy, the CEO of Sport Ireland, announced that '40% of the recommendations had been implemented, including 11 priority actions'.[422] Sport Ireland acknowledged its limitations when it came to its investigatory and enforcement powers in relation to the governance of funded bodies. As the statutory body for the development of sport in Ireland, it is not a regulatory body that is empowered to inspect or audit the financial accounts of bodies in receipt of funding.[423] There is no section of the Sport Ireland Act 2015 that endows Sport Ireland with such powers. Sports governing bodies in receipt of Sport Ireland funding must adhere to Sport Ireland's Terms and Conditions of Grant Approval, which provides that funded bodies can consent to being audited.[424] However, the Board of Sport Ireland approved more stringent provisions in the Terms and Conditions of Grant Approval that 'explicitly confer full audit, inspection and investigative rights on Sport Ireland for every funded body'.[425] This applied from 2020. In a further augmentation of its supervisory powers, the Board of Sport Ireland mandated that by the end of 2021, each governing body, subject to independent verification, would be fully compliant with the Code of Practice for Good Governance of Community, Voluntary and Charitable Organisations in Ireland.[426] Any funded body that fails to 'cooperate

---

419 ibid 23.
420 ibid 118–28.
421 ibid 125.
422 Dáil Éireann: Joint Committee on Transport, Tourism & Sport, 'Governance and Funding of Football Association of Ireland: Discussion' (18 December 2019) 12 <https://data.oireachtas.ie/ie/oireachtas/debateRecord/joint_committee_on_transport_tourism_and_sport/2019-12-18/debate/mul@/main.pdf> accessed 4 May 2024.
423 ibid 12.
424 ibid 11.
425 ibid. This includes the power to investigate and audit in situations where the concern does not involve Sport Ireland funding.
426 ibid.

fully with any audit, inspection and/or investigation on a timely basis will entitle Sport Ireland to suspend/withhold grant funding and/or claim repayment of any grants previously advanced by Sport Ireland'.[427]

Clause 4.3 of the Terms and Conditions of Grant Approval places an **2–117**
obligation on funded bodies to inform Sport Ireland

> in writing without delay in the event of any material deterioration in its financial position or of any other matter which may jeopardise the organisation's overall financial viability and/or its ability to comply with its commitments in the Approved Submission, and thereafter to provide Sport Ireland with such information and documentation as Sport Ireland may request in connection with the relevant matter and any steps being taken to rectify it.[428]

In accordance with Clause 1.1 of the Terms and Conditions of Grant **2–118**
Approval, the allocation of funds to the FAI was withheld.[429]

KOSI Audit

Prior to the FAI's *Governance Review Group Report for the FAI Board and* **2–119**
Sport Ireland, Sport Ireland appointed KOSI Corporation Ltd, a Northern Irish company, to carry out an 'extensive and independent' audit of the FAI accounts.[430] Consisting of senior auditors and a forensic accountant, the then Minister for Transport, Tourism and Sport Shane Ross

> received the Final Report of the Independent Audit of the FAI, conducted by KOSI Corporation Ltd, on behalf of Sport Ireland. The Minister said that Sport Ireland has today referred the report to An Garda Síochána. The Minister will not be [in] a position to publish the report or make any comment on its findings at this time.[431]

Memorandum of Understanding

On 30 January 2020, the FAI and the government signed a Memorandum **2–120**
of Understanding (MOU).[432] Under the terms of the MOU, funding for the period of 2020 to 2023 would be restored as well as the provision

---

427 ibid.

428 Sport Ireland, 'Sport Ireland Statement on Funding to the Football Association of Ireland' 9 April 2019 <https://www.sportireland.ie/news/sport-ireland-statement-on-funding-to-the-football-association-of-ireland> accessed 4 May 2024.

429 ibid.

430 Sport Ireland, 'Sport Ireland Appoints KOSI to Audit Football Association of Ireland' 10 May 2019 <https://www.sportireland.ie/news/sport-ireland-appoints-kosi-to-audit-football-association-of-ireland> accessed 4 May 2024.

431 Department of Tourism, Culture, Arts, Gaeltacht, Sport and Media, 'Independent Audit of the FAI' 27 November 2019 <https://www.gov.ie/en/press-release/3616ae-independent-audit-of-the-fai/> accessed 4 May 2024.

432 Department of Tourism, Culture, Arts, Gaeltacht, Sport and Media, 'Memorandum of Understanding between Minister for Transport, Tourism and Sport and Football Association of Ireland' 30 January 2020 <https://www.

of additional funding.[433] Several conditions were imposed on the FAI, including Constitutional and Council reforms,[434] corporate governance and the establishment of a new Governance Oversight Group,[435] Financial and Internal Controls,[436] Human Resources,[437] the Development of Irish Soccer,[438] and the acknowledgement of the support of Sport Ireland and the one-off nature of the funding commitment under the MOU, which expired on 31 December 2023.[439]

Report on the FAI's Progress and Implementation of the MOU

2–121 A Report to the Department of Tourism, Culture, Arts, Gaeltacht, Sport and Media on FAI's progress on the implementation of MOU reforms was published on 30 January 2024.[440] In reference to the 163 recommendations provided for under the 2019 Governance Review Group Report, the 2019 KOSI audit, and the 2020 MOU, 159 (98%) were identified as either completed or Phase 1 complete.[441] The four recommendations that were not delivered within the agreed timeframes related to gender balance of 33.3% on the FAI Board within one year (deadline: June 2020), gender balance of 33.3% at Council, Committee and annual general meeting (AGM) level within three years (deadline: June 2023), the MOU mandate that all the Governance Review Group Report be fully implemented

---

gov.ie/pdf/?file=https://assets.gov.ie/49784/30b467b4a638458fa456032709b5f445.pdf#page=null> accessed 4 May 2024.

433 ibid 1.

434 ibid 2. The conditions included the retirement of Council members who had served a term greater than 10 years. This was also a requirement of the Governance Review Group. The FAI had to amend the Rulebook of the Association to provide that past Board Members were ineligible for membership of FAI Board Committees.

435 ibid 2–3. All the conditions of the Governance Review Group had to be implemented by the end of 2020.

436 ibid 3–4. One condition was that the FAI implement the high-risk recommendations set out by the KOSI Report by 30 June 2020 at the latest. The KOSI Report was not published as there was an ongoing criminal investigation.

437 ibid 4–5. Details of all renumeration of FAI staff including High Performance coaches to Sport Ireland, low- and middle-earners employed by the FAI could not be made redundant for 18 months save in exceptional circumstances such as restructuring.

438 ibid 5. The FAI had to develop a new strategic plan for a period of between three and five years that complied with the principles of good governance practice and which aligned to the National Sports Policy 2018–2027.

439 ibid 5.

440 The report is available at <https://www.gov.ie/pdf/?file=https://assets.gov.ie/282284/6cfbc760–562e–4fe0-b69c–6d2acc34c716.pdf#page=null> accessed 4 May 2024.

441 ibid 3. The report relied on two Assurance Processes: Phase 1 and Phase 2. Phase 1 was described as the set-up. This related to developing organisation infrastructures and internal control systems. Phase 2 was explained as completion and embedding. It was defined as '[e]vidence that the recommendations and new policies were being implemented as part of normal management, and were not viewed as something extra that needed to be done to "comply" with MOU requirements'. Pages 2 and 3 of the report provide more detail.

(deadline: end of 2020) and the MOU requirement that the FAI fully implement all KOSI audit recommendations (deadline: end of 2020).[442]

The report concluded:

> Since 2020 the FAI have been on a pathway toward best practice corporate governance in line with the requirements of the MOU. A robust monitoring and oversight system was in operation via Sport Ireland and the Governance Oversight Group during this period. Whilst the FAI's journey of reform and change was not without its challenges and setbacks, the FAI demonstrated that significant and solid progress was made on its transition to a better governance structure and improved practices. This transition will require ongoing work, resourcing and nurturing to ensure that good governance is at the heart of how the FAI operates and does its business into 2024 and beyond.[443]

On 22 February 2024, the FAI was before the Public Accounts Committee (PAC) to debate oversight regarding governance and funding received by Sport Ireland and Department of Tourism, Culture, Arts, Gaeltacht, Sport and Media in 2022.[444] An issue arose in relation to Recommendation 35 of the MOU concerning the salary of the CEO would not exceed that of officers in the grade of General Secretary. However, Jonathan Hill, the FAI CEO, received pay for unused holidays.[445] The extra €12,500 payment and a benefit in kind payment resulted in Sport Ireland commissioning KOSI to investigate the matter.[446] In November 2023, the state withheld €6.8m in funding.[447] At the PAC, Sport Ireland confirmed that it **2–122**

---

[442] ibid 2–3. 33.3% of the Board amounts to four female members. Here is a tracker report on the MOU: Summary Update on Overall MOU Position (22 December 2023) <https://www.gov.ie/pdf/?file=https://assets.gov.ie/282282/26fe373c-eb7c–4d45–970e-ff94b7614de5.pdf#page=null> accessed 4 May 2024.

[443] Report (n 440) 5.

[444] Committee of Public Accounts debate – Thursday, 22 Feb 2024, FAI: Matters Relating to Governance and Funding <https://www.oireachtas.ie/en/debates/debate/committee_of_public_accounts/2024-02–22/5/> accessed 4 May 2024. For more details on the documentation submitted by the FAI to the PAC, see Jonathan Hill, 'Correspondence' R2399 (iii) PAC33 <https://data.oireachtas.ie/ie/oireachtas/committee/dail/33/committee_of_public_accounts/submissions/2024/2024-02–26_correspondence-jonathan-hill-ceo-football-association-of-ireland-r2399-pac33_en.pdf> accessed 4 May 2024.

[445] Committee of Public Accounts (n 444) Mr Feargal Ó Coigligh <https://www.oireachtas.ie/en/debates/debate/committee_of_public_accounts/2024-02–22/speech/4/> accessed 4 May 2024.

[446] Hill also received €8,500 in benefit in kind to facilitate his commute from London to Ireland: see Mark Tighe, 'FAI Funding Suspended as CEO Jonathan Hill Told to Repay €20,000 He Received' *Irish Independent* (Dublin, 10 November 2023) <https://www.independent.ie/irish-news/fai-funding-suspended-as-ceo-jonathan-hill-told-to-repay–20000-he-received/a424192290.html> accessed 4 May 2024.

[447] Daniel McDonnell, 'Minister for Sport Confirms €6.8m in State Funding to FAI Has Been Suspended' *Irish Independent* (Dublin, 21 November 2023) <https://www.independent.ie/sport/soccer/minister-for-sport-confirms–68m-in-state-funding-to-fai-has-been-suspended/a104788468.html> accessed 4 May 2024.

> was adequately assured that MOU condition no. 35 is now fully implemented in the FAI and the associated KOSI audit findings and recommendations have been satisfactorily implemented by the FAI. On this basis, on 30 November 2023, the Department informed Sport Ireland it could release the 2022 and 2023 funding to the FAI, which had previously been delayed.[448]

2–123 Hill resigned as CEO, with his term ending on 30 April 2024. The Chief Operating Officer (COO) David Courell was appointed interim CEO. While the FAI will be under pressure to ensure that the final conditions of the MOU are fulfilled and hopefully equilibrium will be restored by the confirmation of Courell as the new CEO on 4 October 2024, the legal issues of John Delaney have been the subject of litigation in the Superior Courts.

Delaney and Legal Professional Privilege

2–124 The Office Director of Corporate Enforcement (ODCE) applied to the High Court to determine whether certain documents seized under a search warrant from the offices of the FAI were subject to legal professional privilege.[449] Section 795(1) of the Companies Act 2014 defines information as 'information contained in a document, a computer or otherwise', privileged legal material 'means information which, in the opinion of the court, a person is entitled to refuse to produce on the grounds of legal professional privilege'. Legal professional privilege 'is the rule of evidence that entitles a party to withhold certain confidential documents from inspection in a discovery process or for use in evidence even if they are relevant'.[450] Delaney was claiming legal professional privilege over 1,123 digital documents.[451] The onus of establishing the burden of proof fell on Delaney.[452] In referring to relevant authority Reynolds J stated:

> it is evident that what is required to be produced by a party asserting privilege must be of sufficient detail as to allow the court to make a finding regarding the intention behind the generation of the documents and explaining 'the nature, genesis and purpose of the documents in issue'.[453]

---

[448] Committee of Public Accounts (n 444) Mr Feargal Ó Coigligh.

[449] *In the Matter of the Companies Act, 2014; Director of Corporate Enforcement v Cumann Peile Na H—Eireann Football Association of Ireland & Delaney* [2022] IEHC 593. For more context of the background to the case, see two previous decisions by Reynolds J in the *Director of Corporate Enforcement v Cumann Peile Na H-Eireann & Delaney* [2021] IEHC 141 and [2021] IEHC 651. The ODCE is now the Corporate Enforcement Authority, CEA). The CEA was created under Companies (Corporate Enforcement Authority) Act 2021.

[450] William Fry, 'Legal Professional Privilege' 1 <https://www.williamfry.com/docs/default-source/practice-area-industry-sector-brochures/william-fry—-legal-professional-privilege.pdf?sfvrsn=720315f_2> accessed 4 May 2024.

[451] [2022] IEHC 593 (n 449) [9].

[452] ibid [57].

[453] ibid [60].

In finding that Delaney had not discharged the requisite burden of proof, the judge rejected his claim of privilege.[454] Reynolds J found that Delaney had 'been afforded every opportunity to furnish the necessary information to substantiate his claim but has resolutely failed to do so' and she directed that all documents, 'both soft and hard copies, be disclosed to the Director'.[455] **2–125**

Delaney appealed the decision of the High Court judgment along with a subsequent judgment relating to costs.[456] In dismissing the appeal, the Court of Appeal decided not to interfere with the order of costs made in the High Court, which was 'within the range open to that court'.[457] The Court of Appeal rejected the contention that the material over which Delaney was claiming legal professional privilege related to 'family' proceedings. Noonan J found it 'remarkable that Mr. Delaney has entirely failed in any instance to give details of those proceedings or how they could be regarded as still extant'.[458] **2–126**

In invoking Article 34.5.3° of the Constitution, Delaney sought leave to appeal to the Supreme Court.[459] Article 34.5.3° states: **2–127**

> The Supreme Court shall, subject to such regulations as may be prescribed by law, have appellate jurisdiction from a decision of the Court of Appeal if the Supreme Court is satisfied that—
>
> i. the decision involves a matter of general public importance, or
>
> ii. in the interests of justice it is necessary that there be an appeal to the Supreme Court.

In considering that the decision did not involve a matter of general public importance and the interests of justice did not necessitate an appeal, the leave to appeal was not granted by the Supreme Court. **2–128**

Governance and Amateur Sport

Sports governance is an important facet of both professional and amateur sport. In 2023, the GAA had a consolidated revenue of €112m with a consolidated surplus of €6.5m.[460] In the past, it has been proffered that the GAA could be run more efficiently and even though it is an **2–129**

---

[454] ibid [122].

[455] ibid [121]–[122].

[456] *In the Matter of the Companies Act, 2014; Director of Corporate Enforcement v Cumann Peile Na H—Eireann Football Association of Ireland & Delaney* [2023] IECA 226.

[457] ibid [120], [126].

[458] ibid [103].

[459] *In the Matter of the Companies Act, 2014; Director of Corporate Enforcement v Cumann Peile Na H—Eireann Football Association of Ireland & Delaney* [2024] IESC 7.

[460] John Harrington, 'GAA Invested €13.2M in Coaching and Games Development in 2023' 8 February 2024 <https://www.gaa.ie/article/gaa-invested–13–2m-in-coaching-and-games-development-in–2023> accessed 4 May 2024.

amateur organisation, good governance is nevertheless essential.[461] After the removal of the ban on foreign games in 1971, the McNamee Commission produced a 90,000-word report.[462] It recommended a number of reforms to the structure and governance of the GAA and amendments to the rules and administration of the games.[463] The report was the result of a motion in 1969 by Antrim at the Annual Congress.[464] In 2002, there was a strategic review, however, this review centred on the division of Dublin into two county units.[465] Aside from annual reports and various strategic plans, the McNamee Report remains the most substantial report on the GAA.[466]

2–130 The GAA commissioned a report 'Towards 2034 – The 150th Anniversary of the GAA', however, it remains unpublished and there is much speculation as to whether it will ever be published.[467] The report consists of 18,000 words and was finalised in January 2018.[468] One of the reasons

[461] David Hassan, 'Governance and the Gaelic Athletic Association: Time to Move Beyond the Amateur Ideal?' (July 2010) 11(4) Soccer and Society 414. Hassan's article is centred on the 2002 strategic review. Hassan was one of the 12 members of the committee convened to make recommendations in the commissioned report titled Towards 2034 – the 150th anniversary of the GAA.

[462] Paddy Downey, 'New Approach to Varied Problems: Report Recommends Changes in Many Aspects of Association Activities' *The Irish Times* (Dublin, 2 December 1971). It recommended the creation of a management committee, the acceptance of commercial sponsorship, and the establishment of full time Public Relations and Development Officers.

[463] ibid. The report recommended the reduction from 15 to 13 aside in hurling teams. The report also looked at the issue of discipline, which the report stressed was about education and training and that the referee should not be expected to instil good behaviour and sportsmanship: that should be the preserve of the officials of the Association who know the players and can lead by example. The report also recommended that the All-Ireland semi-finals and provincial finals should be no longer be televised. Instead, it was proffered, the matches could be recorded and shown on television after the match. A decline in attendance at matches was identified in the report.

[464] ibid.

[465] Seán Moran, 'Tale of Two City Teams Dominates GAA Review' *The Irish Times* (Dublin, 22 January 2002) <https://www.irishtimes.com/sport/tale-of-two-city-teams-dominates-gaa-review–1.1047385> accessed 4 May 2024. Dublin remains a one county unit.

[466] Seán Moran, 'Reluctance to Publish "Towards 2034" Report Seems Odd' *The Irish Times* (Dublin, 4 April 2018) <https://www.irishtimes.com/sport/gaelic-games/sean-moran-reluctance-to-publish-towards–2034-report-seems-odd–1.3449587> accessed 4 May 2024.

[467] Martin Breheny, 'Pay Proposal for Players and Managers Ill-Advised but Other Ideas from 2034 Committee Have Merit' *Irish Independent* (Dublin, 28 April 2018) <https://www.independent.ie/sport/gaelic-games/gaelic-football/pay-proposal-for-players-and-managers-ill-advised-but-other-ideas-from–2034-committee-have-merit/36852934.html> accessed 4 May 2024. The report was leaked to *The Irish Times*. According to a newspaper article in December 2021, its publication was 'shortly expected': John Fogerty, 'How Much Will the GAA Change Before it Turns 150?' *Irish Examiner* (Cork, 30 December 2021) <https://www.irishexaminer.com/sport/gaa/arid–40775094.html> accessed 4 May 2024.

[468] It was commissioned by a previous president of the GAA, Aogán Ó Fearghaíl, whose term ended in February 2018.

cited for the reluctance on the part of the GAA to officially publish the report is the recommendation that senior inter-county players and managers be paid 'an agreed allowance' which would be in line with 'their enormous contribution to their sport'.[469] Managers and players at club level would not receive any payment. By labelling it an 'agreed allowance' and not payment renders the recommendation oblique and conceals what some view as an erosion of the amateur ethos of the GAA and a move towards professionalism.[470] The recommendation lacks detail and many questions remain unanswered, including whether the allowance would be taxable and would the allowance increase as the teams remain in the championship.[471] The above development is highly unlikely given that the newly appointed President Jarlath Burns has created an Amateur Review Status Committee to protect the GAA's amateur status.[472] It has been referred to a 'pillar' of Burns' presidency.[473] The remit of the Amateur Review Status Committee will be extensive, with the committee 'looking to curb the amount of training sessions done by county teams'.[474] Burns has also proposed a licencing system as part of a move towards enhanced financial stability, as '[e]ach county will have to apply for a licence and that will come into good governance, audit and risk, and [make] sure that the money is being spent wisely'.[475]

The 'Towards 2034' Report 'envisages that the GAA will become, as part of its mission, a beacon of best practice in gender equality in terms of clear pathways for progression, participation levels, official status, administration arrangements, management positions and Board **2–131**

---

469 Breheny (n 467). Moran (n 466) does not believe that the reason for the non-publication of the report is due to the payment issue. He asserts that it is 'a disservice to the T150 report to hang the entirety of its deliberations' on that proposal. The full text from the leaked report is as follows: 'By 2034, the GAA will have developed a model to recognise the time and effort contributed by senior inter-county players and their respective managers. This will facilitate effective budgeting where senior inter-county players and managers will retain their existing amateur status but have their value to the Association, and their enormous commitment to their sport, recognised by a defined and agreed allowance': 'Leaked GAA Report Recommends Payment for Inter-county Players' 30 March 2018 <https://m.hoganstand.com/Article/Index/283194?county=Ladies> accessed 4 May 2024.

470 ibid.

471 ibid.

472 Damian Lawlor, 'New Committee Will Aim to Protect GAA's Amateur Status' 26 February 2024 <https://www.rte.ie/sport/football/2024/0226/1434523-new-committee-will-aim-to-protect-gaas-amateur-status/> accessed 4 May 2024.

473 Colm Keys, 'Brian Cody Signs Up to Croke Park's Hurling Development Committee for Three Years' *Irish Independent* (Dublin, 25 March 2024) <https://www.independent.ie/sport/gaelic-games/brian-cody-signs-up-to-croke-parks-hurling-development-committee-for-three-years/a1102523133.html> accessed 4 May 2024.

474 John Fogerty, 'What Will GAA Financial Fair Play Entail?' *Irish Examiner* (Cork, 28 February 2024) <https://www.irishexaminer.com/sport/gaa/arid–41341379.html> accessed 4 May 2024.

475 ibid.

membership'.[476] Women will be more involved in the decision-making and organisational structures of the GAA by 2034.[477] There have been some developments with regard to gender equality, as there is a move towards creating one association for Gaelic games: the GAA, the Camogie Association and the Ladies Gaelic Football Association (LGFA).[478] This was a recommendation of the 'Towards 2034' report. The female players' Charter is slated to be finalised before the end of 2024.[479] As part of the integration, players in all three associations will receive a 50-cent-per-mile travel expense rate, players will be provided with a weekly nutrition allowance, the presence of a physiotherapist at male and female games and training sessions, and the access to sports facilities and other services.[480]

2–132 The 'Towards 2034' report acknowledges the increased multiculturalism of Ireland. In adopting a more holistic approach both at home and in an international context, the report provides:

> The GAA has the opportunity to engage with significant groups, communities and individuals, both in Ireland and abroad, whose national identity is decidedly non-Irish and with those whose familiarity with the GAA may be fleeting … Without identifying, prioritising and resourcing engagement with such groups and communities the GAA could miss a significant opportunity to develop its games both at home and abroad … The aim of enlisting a broad a spectrum of people in the creation and development of more inclusive, multicultural and diverse communities suggests that the GAA must be active in catering for the needs of both men and women, people with disabilities, those who identify themselves as other than Irish and those with little or no engagement with the GAA within Ireland and abroad.[481]

2–133 While some of the proposals may seem radical, the 'Towards 2034' report should be viewed as a starting point in discussions. The report merely makes recommendations that should stimulate debate among members.[482]

2–134 According to the GAA, governance is 'the system of rules, practices and processes by which the Association and all of its Units are directed and

---

476 Seán Moran, 'Radical GAA Report Proposes Payment of Allowance to County Players' *The Irish Times* (Dublin, 30 March 2018) <https://www.irishtimes.com/sport/gaelic-games/gaa-report-envisages-reduced-focus-on-intercounty-schedules–1.3445030> accessed 4 May 2024.

477 ibid.

478 Damian Lawler, 'Female GAA Players' Charter in Final Stages of Completion' (RTÉ Sport, 27 February 2024) <https://www.rte.ie/sport/womens-football/2024/0227/1434708-female-players-charter-in-final-stages-of-completion/> accessed 4 May 2024.

479 ibid. The Steering Committee responsible for the integration of male and female associations has been chaired by Mary McAleese, the former Irish President.

480 Lawler (n 478).

481 Moran (n 476).

482 ibid.

controlled'.[483] As part of its governance, the GAA Governance Guide enumerates a number of core principles of good governance including leadership, control, transparency and accountability, effective operation and integrity.[484] There is a checklist that accompanies each principle; for example, in relation to leadership, the checklist includes the delineation of various roles within the organisation.[485]

There have been governance issues within the GAA, however, early detection is paramount.[486] The use of technology in ticket sales and increased regulation of cash collections means that opportunities for mismanagement have been reduced.[487] Former GAA Public Relations Officer (PRO) Danny Lynch stated that the 'secret to good governance is being pro-active rather than reactive'.[488] **2–135**

Sports Governance at Domestic and International Level

In a domestic setting, sports are governed by their national governing body or federation. For example, football in Ireland is regulated by the FAI.[489] The regional body for football in Europe is UEFA.[490] FIFA is the international governing body for football.[491] The FAI is affiliated with UEFA and FIFA, thus it is bound by the rules and regulations of both organisations. National Governing Bodies (NGBs) must keep up-to-date with any changes in the rules or regulations of their affiliates. At international level, sporting bodies are governed by IFs, and the IOC. **2–136**

---

483 GAA, 'Governance' 22 April 2024 <https://www.gaa.ie/article/governance> accessed 4 May 2024.

484 GAA, 'Governance Guide' <https://learning.gaa.ie/sites/default/files/2024-04/GAA%20Governance%20Guide.pdf> accessed 4 May 2024.

485 ibid 10. The National Audit Committee (NAC) was tasked with drafting and publishing the Governance Code. The NAC, established by the GAA, is referred to as an 'on-site watchdog': see Dermot Crowe, 'Dermot Crowe on GAA governance: 'It's Not Our Money, That's the Culture' *Irish Independent* (Dublin, 21 April 2019) <https://www.independent.ie/sport/gaelic-games/dermot-crowe-on-gaa-governance-its-not-our-money-thats-the-culture–38034979.html> accessed 4 May 2024.

486 Crowe (n 485).

487 ibid.

488 ibid.

489 The FAI was originally known as the Football Association of the Irish Free State (FAIFS), which was established in 1921. Until 1950, a player could play for the FAIFS and for the Northern Ireland association, the Irish Football Association (IFA). In 1946, the IFA re-joined FIFA as Northern Ireland. Subsequently, the FAIFS became known as the FAI. Until 1985, Derry FC played in Northern Ireland but joined the League of Ireland. For more details, see Conor Moore, *The Irish Soccer Split* (Attic Press 2021).

490 Established in 1954 in Basle, Switzerland. UEFA comprises 55 national football associations. It is recognised by FIFA as one of the six continental federations. The FAI joined in 1954. For a full list of the national associations see UEFA, 'National Associations' <https://www.uefa.com/nationalassociations/> accessed 4 May 2024.

491 Established in 1904, governed by Swiss law and based in Zurich. It has 211 member associations. The FAI joined in 1923.

2–137 The status of domestic sports bodies differs among sports organisations in Ireland. Some are created by way of legislation. These are called statutory bodies. The Irish Greyhound Board (IGB) or Rásaíocht Con Éireann (RCÉ) is one such statutory body which was established by the Greyhound Industry Act 1958.[492] Other governing bodies are established as private limited companies and are regulated by the Companies Act 2014. Some sports bodies may benefit from certain exemptions when it comes to income tax and corporation tax.[493] The requirements under the Charities Act 2009 excludes sports bodies. A guide prepared by the Charities Regulator refers to sport being excluded under the Act.[494] Section 235(1)(a) of the Taxes Consolidation Act 1997 applies to an 'approved body of persons', which is defined as 'any body of persons established for and existing for the sole purpose of promoting athletic or amateur games or sports'. To apply for the Sports Body Tax Exemptions, the body must comply with several formalities, including being registered with Revenue; being legally established, managed and controlled within the State; be member-controlled and -owned; and have at least three officers or directors, the majority of which must be unrelated and independent.[495]

State Involvement in Sport in Ireland

2–138 In Ireland, the regulation of sport falls under the auspices of the Department of Tourism, Culture, Arts, Gaeltacht, Sport and Media. It was originally established in 1959 and has undergone numerous name changes over the years. The Department has several important functions in relation to sport. Its primary function is the formulation, development and evaluation of sport policy (the implementation of which in the main is a matter for Sport Ireland) and overseeing major sports projects, including the National Aquatic Centre at Abbotstown, developing proposals for the provision of a national stadium and

[492] The board has wide powers ranging from issuing licences to use certain tracks to issuing permits to officials, bookmakers, and trainers. It controls nine of the 15 licensed tracks in the Republic of Ireland, Greyhound Racing Ireland, 'About GRI' <https://www.grireland.ie/About-GRI/about-gri/> accessed 5 May 2024. It was renamed under the Greyhound Racing Act 2019. Its former Irish name was Bord na gCon.

[493] To qualify for tax exemptions, the sports body must show the Revenue that all income has been or will be used for the sole purpose of promoting that amateur game or sport. The body must be a not-for-profit, member-controlled and -owned organisation. For more information see Revenue, 'Sports Bodies Tax Exemption' <https://www.revenue.ie/en/companies-and-charities/charities-and-sports-bodies/sports-bodies-tax-exemption/apply-sports-body-tax-exemption.aspx> accessed 5 May 2024.

[494] Charities Regulator, 'What Is a Charity?' (Dublin 2023) 10 <https://www.charitiesregulator.ie/media/eqvh32ky/what-is-a-charity-rev-001.pdf> accessed 5 May 2024.

[495] Revenue, 'Sports Bodies Tax Exemption' <https://www.revenue.ie/en/companies-and-charities/charities-and-sports-bodies/sports-bodies-tax-exemption/apply-sports-body-tax-exemption.aspx> accessed 5 May 2024.

the administration of the Sports Capital and Equipment Programme (SCEP) and the Large Scale Sport Infrastructure Fund (LSSIF).[496] Since 1998, 13,000 projects amounting to €1.15bn have been funded under the sports capital programme.[497] The SCEP is described as 'the Government's primary vehicle for providing support to sports clubs and communities to develop sustainable sports infrastructure and increase active participation in sport around the country'.[498] The LSSIF programme funds large-scale projects ranging from €600,000 to €30m.[499]

There is a heavy state involvement in the regulation of sport in Ireland. **2–139**
The state's involvement can be characterised as both direct and indirect control. The Department exercises direct governmental regulation, while Sport Ireland, a body created by statute, exercises quasi-governmental regulation. The individual NGBs, while recipients of funding from the Department and Sport Ireland, are categorised as autonomous and private associations.[500] Sport Ireland was established under the Sport Ireland Act 2015 which dissolved the Irish Sports Council (ISC) and the National Sports Campus Development Authority (NSCDA) and formed a new body, Sport Ireland.

In addition to the Department and quasi-governmental agencies, there **2–140**
is also the OFI, which has been in existence since 1922.[501] As with all NOCs, the OFI's role is to promote the Olympics in accordance with the Olympic Charter. Other NGBs include Swim Ireland, the FAI, the Irish

[496] Dáil Deb 15 February 2024 (Sports Funding) <https://www.oireachtas.ie/en/debates/question/2024-02–15/41/speech/467/> accessed 5 May 2024.

[497] ibid.

[498] Department of Tourism, Culture, Arts, Gaeltacht, Sport and Media, 'Sports Capital & Equipment Programme 2023 Receives Record Number of Applications' 17 January 2024 <https://www.gov.ie/en/press-release/747f6-sports-capital-equipment-programme–2023-receives-record-number-of-applications/> accessed 5 May 2024. It is part funded by the National Lottery: see Department of Tourism, Culture, Arts, Gaeltacht, Sport and Media, 'Sports Capital Programme' <https://www.sportscapitalprogramme.ie/> accessed 5 May 2024.

[499] These are the figures for 2024, Department of Tourism, Culture, Arts, Gaeltacht, Sport and Media, 'Large Scale Sport Infrastructure Fund (LSSIF) 2024' 25 April 2024 <https://www.gov.ie/en/service/6f3f3-large-scale-sport-infrastructure-fund-lssif–2024/> accessed 5 May 2024. In total, there is €120m available under the scheme.

[500] The NSCDA was created under the National Sports Campus Development Authority Act 2006. A Public Service Reform Plan was published by the Irish Government on 17 November 2011. Under the Plan, it was decided that several state agencies would be rationalised and reduced. In short, it was determined that the Irish Sports Council and the National Sports Campus Development Authority (NSCDA) would be merged to create one body, called Sport Ireland. On 21 January 2014, the Government approved the draft bill, Sport Ireland Bill 2014. The Sport Ireland Act 2015 was enacted in May 2015 and commenced on 1 October 2015.

[501] The OFI is a company limited by guarantee and not having a share capital. It has been registered since 21 April 1981 with the Companies Registration Office (CRO) in Dublin. Until September 2018, it was called the Olympic Council of Ireland, however, it was then rebranded and renamed the OFI.

Rugby Football Union (IRFU), Cricket Ireland, Deaf Sports Ireland, the GAA, Tug of War Ireland and Weightlifting Ireland

2–141 Although most sports in Ireland are regulated directly or indirectly by the state, the intervention of the State is a more recent development with public spending on sports emerging in the 1990s.[502] The late 1980s and early 1990s was a period of great success among Irish sports people. Irish cyclist Stephen Roche won the Tour de France in 1987; Barry McGuigan won the world featherweight title in boxing in 1985; the Republic of Ireland football team reached the quarter finals of the 1990 World Cup; and Michael Carruth won a gold medal in boxing, and Wayne McCullough silver, at the 1992 Olympics.[503] While the state basked in the reflective glory of its sporting heroes, this did not translate 'into financial support from the government, which until 1992 managed to escape without really major provision being made'.[504] The National Lottery was established in 1987 and was to fund arts, sport and culture. In 1993, with a turnover of almost €381 million, only 8% was allocated to sport.[505] The government was instead using the money to fund the health service.[506] The figures in 2024 demonstrate a very different picture, as Sport Ireland's budget is €106.7 million.[507]

2–142 As part of the Programme for Government in 2020, the establishment of a gambling regulator focused on public safety and wellbeing, covering gambling online and in person, and the powers to regulate advertising, gambling websites and applications (apps) was proposed.[508] In December 2022, the Bill was published.[509] The Bill has, at the time of writing, been passed by both Houses of the Oireachtas.[510] While

---

502 Liam Delaney and Tony Fahey, 'Social and Economic Value of Sport' (Econ & Soc Research Inst 2005) 11 <https://www.esri.ie/system/files/media/file-uploads/2015-08/BKMNINT180.pdf> accessed 23 April 2024.

503 Gemma Hussey, *Ireland Today: Anatomy of a Changing State* (Townhouse 1993) 445.

504 ibid 446. Houlihan makes the point that the GAA was so successful at promoting Gaelic Games that the state was not under pressure to intervene: see Barrie Houlihan, *Sport, Policy and Politics: A Comparative Analysis* (Routledge 1997) 42.

505 Hussey (n 503) 446.

506 ibid.

507 Department of Tourism, Culture, Arts, Gaeltacht, Sport and Media, 'Statement by Minister of State Thomas Byrne at the Budget 2024 Debate in Dáil Éireann' 13 October 2023 <https://www.gov.ie/en/publication/15465-statement-by-minister-of-state-thomas-byrne-at-the-budget–2024-debate-in-dail-eireann/> accessed 5 May 2024.

508 Department of the Taoiseach, 'Programme for Government: Our Shared Future' (June 2020) 86 <https://www.gov.ie/en/publication/7e05d-programme-for-government-our-shared-future/> accessed 5 May 2024.

509 For more detail, see the Gambling Bill 2022, Explanatory Memorandum (December 2022) <https://data.oireachtas.ie/ie/oireachtas/bill/2022/114/eng/memo/b11422d-memo.pdf> accessed 5 May 2024.

510 Houses of the Oireachtas, 'Gambling Regulation Bill 2022 (Bill 114 of 2022)' 14 May 2024 <www.oireachtas.ie/en/bills/bill/2022/114/?tab=bill-text> accessed 16 October 2024.

not specific to sport, the Bill establishes a body called the Gambling Regulatory Authority of Ireland 'for the purposes of licensing and regulating betting, gaming, certain lotteries and the sale or supply of products or services related to gambling'.[511] It aims to create a register of licence-holders, to eliminate or reduce compulsive and excessive gambling and to impose obligations on licensees.[512] The Bill places 'obligations relating to advertising, promotion and sponsorship for the purposes of safeguarding persons participating in gambling'.[513] This provision has resulted in questions being raised as to whether it would block the broadcasting of sports events, including the 'Premier League, horse racing and other live sporting events in the State'.[514] However, the Minister of State at the Department of Justice (Deputy James Browne) stated, 'This is not the case. It is not accurate.'[515]

Sport Ireland

Sport Ireland was established under s 7(1) of the Sport Ireland Act 2015. It is a body corporate with perpetual succession. It is an overarching structure that encompasses the following: the Sport Ireland Institute and Sport Ireland Coaching. A notable feature of the 2015 Act is the updating of anti-doping provisions.[516] The main of aim of Sport Ireland is to encourage participation in sport from people of all ages and abilities, from recreational to high performance level. Sport Ireland's functions are detailed in s 8 of the 2015 Act with s 8(a) providing for the development of strategies for increasing participation in recreational sport and for the promotion of recreational sport and the provision of recreational facilities by public authorities.[517] **2–143**

The Sport Ireland Institute's mission is to 'Drive Excellence, Create Solutions and Impact Performance'.[518] Athletes are placed at the forefront of the Institute's services, which include top-class equipment and **2–144**

---

511 ibid.
512 ibid.
513 ibid.
514 Dáil Deb 1 May 2024, vol 1053, col 3 <https://www.oireachtas.ie/en/debates/debate/dail/2024-05-01/speech/313/> accessed 5 May 2024.
515 ibid.
516 This is discussed in ch 6.
517 The Act defines public authority as: (a) a Minister of the Government, (b) a local authority for the purposes of the Local Government Act 2001, (c) an education and training board, or (d) a person established— (i) by or under any enactment (other than the Companies Acts), (ii) by any scheme administered by the Government, or (iii) under the Companies Acts, in pursuance of powers conferred by or under another enactment, and financed wholly or partly, whether directly or indirectly, by means of moneys provided, or loans made or guaranteed, by a Minister of the Government or by subscription for shares held by or on behalf of a Minister of the Government, or (e) a company (within the meaning of the Companies Acts), a majority of the shares in which are held by or on behalf of a Minister of the Government.
518 Sport Ireland, 'Sport Ireland Institute' <https://www.sportireland.ie/institute> accessed 6 May 2024.

experienced staff to assist athletes in their quests to achieve medals at international competitions. The Sport Ireland Institute is responsible for the Carding scheme, a role previously carried out by Coaching Ireland (or, as it was known, National Coaching and Training Centre, NCTC). The Carding Scheme was introduced in 1998 and most recently it has been revised to provide 'equal funding at the maximum award levels to both a para-athlete and their pilot or guide'.[519] Under the scheme, direct financial support is given to elite athletes. In 2023, the International Carding Scheme received funding in the amount of €3,829,625.[520] In 2024, Sport Ireland will invest €4,400,000 in the scheme.[521] Under the 2024 scheme, 33 athletes have been awarded the top category of Podium funding, €40,000–€80,000.[522] There are 31 athletes in receipt of €25,000 under World Class funding, and 59 athletes have been awarded International funding of €18,000. The current carding scheme covers elite athletes for two years as previously funding was only available on an annual basis.

2–145 Sport Ireland Coaching is responsible for the development of coaching on the entire Island of Ireland. Its main objective is to raise the standard, status, and profile of coaching in Ireland and provide sportspeople with the best quality of coaching in their sport.[523] Sport Ireland Coaching works in partnership with 60 governing bodies.[524]

Olympic Level

2–146 The Olympic movement encompasses three constituent parts: the IOC, the IFs[525] and NOCs.[526] The Olympics is a worldwide movement which governs 40 sports, thus not all sports are recognised by the IOC.[527] Sportspersons who participate in a sport governed by an IF that is not recognised by the IOC are not permitted to compete in the Olympics. The IOC may seem remote to those taking part in particular sports at

---

[519] Sport Ireland, Sport Ireland, 'High Performance Investment 2024' 3 <https://www.sportireland.ie/sites/default/files/media/document/2024-02/hp_invest_final_0.pdf> accessed 6 May 2024.

[520] ibid 4. Of the 123 athletes, 65 (53%) are male and 58 (47%) are female.

[521] ibid 7.

[522] ibid 7–11.

[523] Sport Ireland Coaching, 'Sport Ireland Coaching Plan 2020–2025' <https://www.sportireland.ie/sites/default/files/media/document/202206/SI%20Coaching%20Plan%20Final%20%2815.02.21%29.pdf> accessed 6 May 2024.

[524] ibid 10.

[525] International federations require athletes to adhere to their rules and regulations, ranging from on-field conduct (ie violence) to off-field conduct (ie bringing the sport into disrepute), doping and player eligibility.

[526] Rule 1.2 of the Olympic Charter. Rule 28 of the Charter provides that the role of the NOCs is to 'develop and protect the Olympic Movement in their respective countries, in accordance with the Olympic Charter'.

[527] There are 32 Summer sports and eight Winter sports: see International Olympic Committee, 'Sports' <https://olympics.com/en/sports/summer-olympics> accessed 6 May 2024.

national level. However, the matrix of affiliations makes it necessary for the sport to comply with IOC rules at all levels. Taking the example of the FAI, a player in the League of Ireland, although not part of the Olympics, is bound by the rules of the FAI, the FAI in turn is bound by the rules of the IF, FIFA. Thus, the rules of the IOC can pervade through many levels of sport.[528]

Olympic Federation of Ireland

Each country has an NOC.[529] In Ireland, the OFI promotes the Olympics **2–147**
in accordance with the Olympic Charter. The OFI has been in existence since 1922, when it was called the Irish Olympic Council.[530] In 1951 it became known as the Olympic Council of Ireland.[531] In 2018 it became known as the OFI.

The 2018 rebranding was due to a change in the governance structures **2–148**
of the OFI due to the allegations that arose in relation to the touting of Irish allocation tickets at the 2016 Summer Olympics in Rio. It resulted in the incarceration of the President of the OCI, Pat Hickey, in a Brazilian prison.[532] It was alleged that the touting of Irish tickets went back to the

---

[528] Antonio Buti and Saul Fridman, *Drugs, Sport and the Law* (Scribblers Publishing 2001) 17: 'one can therefore see how the rules established by the IOC find their expression at all levels of sport, even in events that are not officially part of the Olympic Games'.

[529] There are currently 206 NOCs. For more information, see International Olympic Committee, 'National Olympic Committees' <https://olympics.com/ioc/national-olympic-committees> accessed 6 May 2024.

[530] The Irish Olympic Committee received full recognition on 9 June 1922 at the IOC's Annual Session in Paris: Matthew P Llewellyn, *Rule Britannia: Nationalism, Identity and the Modern Olympic Games* (Taylor & Francis 2014) 160.

[531] In 1952 the OCI amended its Constitution to define a national association as one which 'controls its sports for the 32 counties and is affiliated as such to its international federation': see Tony Hunt, 'Ireland's Footballers at the 1924 and 1948 Olympic Games: Compromised by the Politics of Sport' in Conor Curran (ed), *The League of Ireland: An Historical and Contemporary Assessment* (Routledge 2022) 100.

[532] The scandal erupted on 5 August 2016 as an Irish citizen, Kevin Mallon, was arrested and OCI allocation tickets were seized. Mallon was the finance director of THG in Ireland, an unauthorised ticket seller. THG (The Hospitality Group) was a British ticket agency owned by the Marcus Evans Group, which is now based in Bermuda. The authorities in Rio found correspondence between Hickey and Evans. The OCI wanted THG to be the official ticket seller, however, the organisers of the Rio Olympics rejected THG as the OCI authorised seller. A company called Pro10 was approved as an authorised seller: see Tom Hennigan, 'Pat Hickey and Marcus Evans Had Email, Text Contact – Rio Police' *The Irish Times* (Dublin, 23 August 2016) <http://www.irishtimes.com/news/ireland/irish-news/pat-hickey-and-marcus-evans-had-email-text-contact-rio-police–1.2766197> accessed 6 May 2024. Pro10 was alleged to have connections with THG: see Daniel McConnell and Fiachra Ó Cionnaith, 'Close Ties Between Firms at Heart of Olympics Ticket Touting Scandal Revealed' *Irish Examiner* (Cork, 17 August 2016) <http://www.irishexaminer.com/ireland/close-ties-between-firms-at-heart-of-olympics-ticket-touting-scandal-revealed–416245.html> accessed 6 May 2024. See also Conor Pope, 'What Is the Story with the Olympics Ticketing Controversy?' *The Irish Times*

London Olympics in 2012. The OCI received state funding of €1.7m from 2012–16 and the then Minister Shane Ross acknowledged the autonomy of sports governing bodies, however, he expressed his concern over the effect the allegations would have on Irish sport. Minister Ross stated:

> I don't want to interfere with the autonomy of Irish sport but I want to make absolutely certain that the funding is properly used and that there is proper governance because they are representing Ireland overseas and that is something we have got to protect.[533]

2–149 In response to the allegations, Ross met with the Attorney General to discuss the options available in relation to the type of inquiry needed to investigate the allegation of ticket touting. Retired judge Carroll Moran was appointed to lead the non-statutory inquiry and was tasked with reporting his findings to Minister Ross and Minister Patrick O'Donovan, Minister of State with responsibility for Tourism and Sport. Judge Moran's terms of reference included the 2014 Winter Olympics, the 2016 and 2012 Olympics, and any other games the judge wished to investigate.[534] The Report of the Moran Inquiry was presented to the Minister on 9 June 2017.[535] The lengthy report consisting of 235 pages made a number of recommendations and endorsed the Deloitte Report, which was commissioned by the Crisis Management Committee of the OCI.[536] The Deloitte Report made 25 recommendations which were presented to OCI members at an extraordinary general meeting (EGM) in January 2017. The Deloitte Report acknowledged its limitations as 'ultimately effective governance depends on people and fundamentally the right behaviours and culture, an assessment of which are outside the scope of this Review'.[537] The Moran Report noted the lack of limitation on the length of time served by office-holders; at the time of the Deloitte Report Pat Hickey had been president of the OCI for 28 years.[538] It

---

(Dublin, 16 August 2016) <http://www.irishtimes.com/news/ireland/irish-news/what-is-the-story-with-the-olympics-ticketing-controversy–1.2757968> accessed 6 May 2024.

533 Sarah Bardon and Keith Duggan, 'OCI Ticket Touting Inquiry Could Cover 2012 Olympics – Ross' *The Irish Times* (Dublin, 19 August 2016) <http://www.irishtimes.com/news/ireland/irish-news/oci-ticket-touting-inquiry-could-cover–2012-olympics-ross–1.2761113> accessed 6 May 2024.

534 The Hon Mr Justice Carroll Moran, 'Inquiry into the Receipt, Distribution and Sale of Tickets to Olympic Games and Ancillary Matters' (9 June 2017) 3–4 <https://www.gov.ie/pdf/?file=https://assets.gov.ie/19173/eac78697a98745408b527571f79330b6.pdf#page=null> accessed 6 May 2024.

535 ibid.

536 ibid 196. The report was confined to reviewing the OCI's Articles and Memorandum of Association/Constitution. It examined other NOCs in order to make recommendations to the OCI. It engaged in discussions with the relevant stakeholders including the Executive Committee of the OCI, OCI Member Federations, Sport Ireland, the European Olympic Committees (EOC) and IOC: the Terms of Reference are outlined ibid 197.

537 ibid 198.

538 Peter Murtagh, 'OCI Fails on Basic Requirements, Deloitte Report Suggests' *The Irish Times* (Dublin, 28 October 2016) <https://www.irishtimes.com/news/ireland/irish-news/oci-fails-on-basic-requirements-deloitte-report-suggests–1.2846078>

highlighted the lack of transparency, the lack of demarcation between the roles of office-holders, and that little cognisance was given to conflicts of interest and ethics.[539] According to the report, 96% of stakeholders surveyed favoured the introduction of specified lengths for terms of office.[540] The Deloitte Report recommended that period of office be limited to two four-year terms, with a third term permitted only in exceptional circumstances.[541] It further advised that the Memorandum and Articles of Association be amended to clearly define the differing roles of the council and the executive, thus there should be no 'double hatting'.[542] The absence of a Strategic Plan and the need to implement one was recommended, a role for the CEO and committee executive.[543] It also recommended the appointment of two independent members 'chosen for their independence, skill, expertise and knowledge' and the removal of honorary life membership.[544] It called for proper compliance with the Companies Act 2014 in relation to meetings and the removal of underperforming executive committee members.[545] The Moran Report recommended the weighting of votes for the sports federations in the OCI, as all federations had one vote irrespective of size and whether the particular sport sent participants to the Olympic Games.[546]

The Moran Report acknowledged its two main limitations: it was a non-statutory inquiry, meaning that it could not compel relevant parties to appear before the Inquiry or to furnish documents or statements, and the invocation of a number of individuals of the right against self-incrimination.[547] With the lack of relevant documentation and statements, no criminality on the part of Hickey could be established.[548] While Hickey was facing trial in Brazil, the ticket touting charges were suspended, as one of the other parties involved, Kevin Mallon, obtained an injunction with the Supreme Court in Brazil stating that the injunction extended 'to all of the accused in this process'.[549] It was reported in early **2–150**

accessed 6 May 2024. Deloitte examined seven NOCs and found that four of them limited the length of tenure. The Deloitte Report is not available online and thus secondary sources are being relied upon.

539 ibid.

540 ibid.

541 ibid.

542 ibid. Several stakeholders surveyed felt that the president had too much power.

543 ibid.

544 ibid.

545 ibid.

546 Moran Inquiry (n 534) 222.

547 ibid 204–05.

548 Hickey was critical of what he perceived as inaccuracies in the Report; however, he was pleased to see his 'reputation and good name' had been cleared: see Ian O'Riordan, 'Pat Hickey: "Significant Inaccuracies" in Moran Report' *The Irish Times* (Dublin, 14 August 2017) <https://www.irishtimes.com/sport/other-sports/pat-hickey-significant-inaccuracies-in-moran-report-1.3186195> accessed 6 May 2024.

549 Ian O'Riordan, 'Pat Hickey Trial Over Olympic Games Ticket Touting Suspended' *The Irish Times* (Dublin, 1 November 2017) <https://www.irishtimes.com/

2022 that three charges against Hickey and two others, including Mallon, had been dropped on the grounds of 'extinction of punishability'.[550]

2–151 On foot of the Moran Report and Deloitte Reports, several changes to the governance of the OCI were made. The position of Team Ireland chef de mission was created: although previously in existence, the role was recruited internally and done on a voluntary basis.[551] The OFI has a new Constitution and has in place a Strategic Plan 2018–2024.[552] Sarah Keane, the chief executive of Swim Ireland, became the President following an election at an EGM on 9 February 2017.[553]

2–152 In a statement to the Joint Oireachtas Committee on Transport, Tourism and Sport, Keane outlined the OCI/OFI's commitment to transparency and apologised to Irish Olympians, support personnel and member federations for the issues that arose in Rio.[554] She acknowledged the newly created Athletes' Commission which was established on 14 June 2017 and held its inaugural meeting on 27 June 2017.[555] Its role is to 'advise the OCI Executive Committee on all athlete related matters

---

news/crime-and-law/pat-hickey-trial-over-olympic-games-ticket-touting-suspended–1.3287686> accessed 6 May 2024.

550 'Brazilian Court Drops Three Charges Against Pat Hickey' (*Breaking News*, 5 January 2022) <https://www.breakingnews.ie/ireland/brazilian-court-drops-three-charges-against-pat-hickey–1238028.html> accessed 6 May 2024. The remaining charges have not yet been the subject of a court hearing. Hickey resigned from the OFI on 5 December 2022 following six years of 'self-suspension'. See also International Olympic Committee, 'IOC Statement on Mr Patrick Hickey' 5 December 2022 <https://olympics.com/ioc/news/ioc-statement-on-mr-patrick-hickey> accessed 6 May 2024. The statement noted that in 'accordance with Rule 16.3.1 of the Olympic Charter, the IOC EB accepted the resignation of Mr Hickey for health reasons following the advice of his doctor'.

551 Sport Ireland, 'Olympic Federation of Ireland Announce Ground-Breaking Athlete-Centred Partnership with Sport Ireland Institute' 11 December 2018 <https://www.sportireland.ie/institute/news/olympic-federation-of-ireland-announce-ground-breaking-athlete-centred-partnership> accessed 6 May 2024.

552 The Constitution was amended by a special resolution on 5 December 2017 <http://www.olympics.ie/wp-content/uploads/2018/01/OCI-Constitution-Final-post-January–2018-EGM.pdf> accessed 6 May 2024. OFI, 'Vision, Mission, What We Value, Strategic Pillars, Strategic Plan 2018 – 2024' <https://olympics.ie/wp-content/uploads/2017/12/Strategic-Plan-Booklet.pdf> accessed 6 May 2024.

553 Keane is planning to step down as President at the end of 2024; her name was put forward as a possible CEO of the FAI due to the 'transformative roles she performed as CEO of Swim Ireland and then president of the Olympic Federation of Ireland': Shane McGrath, 'FAI Needs Expertise, Competency and Integrity – and They Have the Woman for the Job' 28 April 2024 <https://extra.ie/2024/04/28/sport/soccernews/fai-sarah-keane-pick-for-job> accessed 6 May 2024.

554 Joint Oireachtas Committee on Transport, Tourism and Sport, 'Statement by Sarah Keane, President of the OCI' 17 August 2017 <https://data.oireachtas.ie/ie/oireachtas/committee/dail/32/joint_committee_on_transport_tourism_and_sport/submissions/2017/2017-08–18_opening-statement-olympic-council-of-ireland-oci-re-the-judge-moran-inquiry-report_en.pdf> accessed 6 May 2024.

555 Olympic Federation of Ireland, 'Olympic Council of Ireland Announce Details of New Athletes Commission' 14 June 2017 <https://olympics.ie/olympic-council-of-ireland-announce-details-of-new-athletes-commission/> accessed 6 May 2024.

and to ensure that the voice of Irish athletes is heard in all future OCI decision making'.[556] Keane referred to the OCI/OFI Board's 'strong and positive working relationship with Sport Ireland and the Department'.[557] She alluded to the Deloitte Report and the significant changes in the OFI Constitution including the introduction of limits to terms of office.[558]

The Athletes' Commission Strategy is based on the principle that puts athletes first 'to ensure that being an Olympian is the pinnacle of their sporting career'.[559] Its Strategic Plan 2023–2025 focuses on athlete welfare, the athlete voice, athlete impact and athlete spirit.[560] Its eight members are former Olympians including Annalise Murphy, sailor, who competed in London 2012, Rio 2016, and Tokyo 2020.[561] **2–153**

The OFI in December 2018 announced an 'athlete-centred' partnership with the Sport Ireland Institute that would focus 'on performance support delivery for 2018–2022'.[562] Keane referred to the partnership as 'a major step forward in placing the athlete first and comes at a crucial time as preparations for Tokyo gather pace'.[563] This partnership has continued: from 2021 to 2024, €3,195,000 in funding from Sport Ireland has been granted to the OFI.[564] Paralympics Ireland has received €2,813,000 in funding from Sport Ireland during the same period.[565] **2–154**

Since the arrival of Keane, good governance has been prioritised and 'is one of the five strategic pillars' of the OFI.[566] Constitutional reforms and the drafting and implementation of 23 policy documents have followed **2–155**

---

[556] ibid.
[557] Statement (n 554) 2.
[558] ibid 2–3.
[559] Olympic Federation of Ireland, 'Athletes' Commission' <https://olympics.ie/about/athlete-commission/> accessed 6 May 2024.
[560] ibid.
[561] ibid. Murphy won silver in the Women's Laser Radial at the Rio Olympics.
[562] Association of National Olympic Committees, 'Olympic Federation of Ireland Announce Partnership with Sport Ireland Institute' 19 December 2018 <http://www.anocolympic.org/nocs-highlights/olympic-federation-of-ireland-announce-partnership-with-sport-ireland-institute/> accessed 6 May 2024.
[563] Sport Ireland (n 551). The partnership provided for the delivery 'of a comprehensive performance support programme for Team Ireland, covering athlete life-skills, sports science and medicine as well as various Games readiness activities before, during and after Games time'.
[564] Sport Ireland, 'Record Investment of €25m in High Performance Sport for 2024' 13 February 2024 <https://www.sportireland.ie/high-performance/news/record-investment-of-eu25m-in-high-performance-sport-for–2024> accessed 6 May 2024. Out of the total funding, €850,000 was allocated 'to support the costs associated with the 2024 Olympic Games in Paris'. Paralympics' funding included €800,000 to support athletes going to the Paralympic Games 2024.
[565] ibid. Along with Sport Northern Ireland, the OFI and Paralympics Ireland are listed as High Performance partners of Sport Ireland, 'Our Partners' <https://www.sportireland.ie/high-performance/about-us/our-partners> accessed 6 May 2024.
[566] Olympic Federation of Ireland, 'Governance' <https://olympics.ie/about/governance/> accessed 6 May 2024.

the appointment of a new executive committee 'appointed for the Tokyo Olympic cycle'.[567] The creation of standing committees that 'provide oversight and direction' as well as 'a 40% minimum gender balance on the Executive Committee' are examples of good governance within the OFI.[568] The overhaul of the OFI is summed up as follows:

> Much of the work from 2019 onwards, was to put the final actions in place to ensure compliance with the Code of Good Governance, having already taken steps in 2017 and 2018 to bring our constitution into line with the 25 recommendations of the Deloitte report and the IOC's Governance requirements based on the Olympic Charter. The Olympic Federation of Ireland is now fully compliant with the Governance Code for the Community, Voluntary and Charitable Sector in Ireland.[569]

International Olympic Committee

2–156 The IOC is based in Lausanne, and operates under Swiss law. It falls under the jurisdiction of the international legal system and operates within a framework like that of the United Nations (UN). The IOC 'plays a key role in determining the international legal norms which govern sport'.[570] It has fostered close relations with a number of UN agencies, including the United Nations Education and Scientific and Cultural Organisation (UNESCO). The IOC and UNESCO forged links in 1984 and in 2004 a new bilateral agreement was signed to reinforce the commitment of both organisations, in particular the fight against doping.[571] The IOC and UNESCO work together to promote common interests in the areas of physical education and sport.[572] Most recently, UNESCO and the IOC partnered to create guidelines on improving physical education in schools.[573] Given the importance of sport in promoting well-being and health, the IOC also works closely with the World Health Organisation (WHO). However, in the lead-up to the Rio Olympics in 2016, the IOC and WHO were criticised over the

---

[567] ibid.

[568] ibid.

[569] ibid.

[570] Buti and Fridman (n 528) 14.

[571] International Olympic Committee, 'The IOC Signs a Cooperation Agreement with UNESCO' 19 January 2004 <https://olympics.com/ioc/news/the-ioc-signs-a-cooperation-agreement-with-unesco> accessed 6 May 2024.

[572] ibid. In 2005, UNESCO adopted the International Convention against Doping in Sport. It came into force on 1 February 2007. The Convention presents formalised global anti-doping rules and regulations with the aim of eradicating prohibited substances from sport. The Convention also endeavours to enforce the WADC in international law by placing obligations on nations to ensure compliance with the Code. For more details, see UNESCO, 'International Convention against Doping in Sport' <https://www.unesco.org/en/legal-affairs/international-convention-against-doping-sport#item-0> accessed 6 May 2024.

[573] International Olympic Committee, '"Getting the Couch Potatoes Off the Couch"': IOC Joins Forces with UNESCO to Improve Physical Education in Schools' 29 January 2015 <https://olympics.com/ioc/news/getting-the-couch-potatoes-off-the-couch-ioc-joins-forces-with-unesco-to-improve-physical-education-in-schools> accessed 6 May 2024.

WHO's failure to call for the cancellation or postponement of the Games following an outbreak of the Zika virus.[574] However, the COVID–19 pandemic saw the two organisations align in 'promoting vaccine equity and healthy lifestyles'.[575]

The legal status of the IOC is somewhat vague. Rule 15(1) of its Charter describes it as 'an international non-governmental not-for-profit organisation, of unlimited duration, in the form of an association with the status of a legal person, recognised by the Swiss Federal Council in accordance with an agreement entered into on 1 November 2000'.[576] While it is recognised as a legal entity, it is not 'incorporated in the usual sense of the word'.[577] The Olympic Charter is the constitutional document of the Olympic movement. It is a codification of all the principles of Olympism,[578] the rules and bye-laws adopted by the IOC. Rule 1.1 of the Charter recognises the IOC as the supreme authority of the Olympic movement.[579] The IOC establishes rules governing eligibility to participate in the Olympic Summer and Winter Games and have some input into the rules governing each Olympic sport, as all Olympic sports must be in compliance with the rules and spirit of the Olympics. Rule 27.1 provides that it is the mission and role of the NOCs to 'develop, promote and protect the Olympic Movement in their respective countries, in accordance with the Olympic Charter'.[580] Under Rule 27.3 NOCs must establish eligibility criteria for participation in the Olympics that are in conformity with the Olympic Charter.[581] **2–157**

Each IF comprises of the affiliate national federations (NFs) of the relevant sport under Rule 28.1.2.[582] This rule is augmented by the Bye-law to Rules 27 and 28, which provides that at least five national **2–158**

574 Patrick Sawer, 'WHO and IOC Accused of "Conflict of Interest" over Zika Virus Threat to Rio Olympics Athletes and Fans' *Telegraph* (London, 26 May 2016) <https://www.telegraph.co.uk/news/2016/05/28/who-and-ioc-accused-of-cover-up-over-zika-virus-threat-to-rio-ol/> accessed 6 May 2024.

575 World Health Organisation, 'IOC and WHO Reaffirm Collaboration to Promote Vaccine Equity and Healthy Lifestyles' 6 February 2022 <https://www.who.int/news/item/06-02–2022-ioc-and-who-reaffirm-collaboration-to-promote-vaccine-equity-and-healthy-lifestyles> accessed 6 May 2024.

576 International Olympic Committee, *Olympic Charter* (In force as from 15 October 2023) 30 <https://stillmed.olympics.com/media/Document%20Library/OlympicOrg/General/EN-Olympic-Charter.pdf> accessed 6 May 2024.

577 Buti and Fridman (n 528) 14.

578 The Charter defines Olympism as 'a philosophy of life, exalting and combining in a balanced whole the qualities of body, will and mind. Blending sport with culture and education, Olympism seeks to create a way of life based on the joy of effort, the educational value of good example, social responsibility and respect for internationally recognised human rights and universal fundamental ethical principles within the remit of the Olympic Movement', Charter (n 576) 8.

579 ibid.

580 ibid 60.

581 ibid 61.

582 ibid 63.

federations must be affiliated with the IFs governing sports included in the programme of the Olympic Games.[583]

The Federation of Irish Sport

2–159 The Federation of Irish Sport was established in 2002 due to several reasons. At the time there was a need for NGBs to have representation, a forum for advice and consultation – there was an increase in funding opportunities and it was felt that NGBs were lacking a voice.[584] The Federation of Irish Sport consists of 81 NGBs and 29 Local Sports Partnerships (LSPs), which translates into the Federation representing over 13,000 sports clubs nationwide. Among the NGBs that are affiliated with the Federation are the GAA, FAI, IRFU, Swim Ireland and Athletics Ireland.[585]

2–160 The Federation offers a number of services to its members: dispute resolution[586] and Garda vetting.[587] Dispute resolution will be discussed in Chapter 12; however, at this juncture it should be noted that Sport Dispute Solutions Ireland (SDSI) was created by the Federation of Irish Sport in response to the increase in litigation and disputes that were going before the courts. It offers mediation and arbitration services to the 64 NGBs that provide for recourse to the SDSI.[588]

The European Union and Sports Governance

2–161 The European Union (EU) adopts a soft law approach when it comes to the regulation of sport. Soft law measures in the context of the EU include declarations, resolutions, communications, and reports. As will be discussed in Chapter 13, prior to the entry into force of the Treaty on the Functioning of the European Union (TFEU) on 1 December 2009, the EU lacked an explicit competency when it came to sports policy.[589] Article 26(2) of the TFEU provides that the aim of the EU is to establish an area where goods, persons, services, and capital can freely circulate and where competition is not distorted. Accordingly, sport is an area of commercial importance and thus sports bodies must not engage in activities that would breach these treaty provisions. Articles 6 and 165

---

[583] ibid 64. Bye-law 1.2.

[584] Federation of Irish Sport, 'Background' <https://www.irishsport.ie/about/> accessed 6 May 2024.

[585] Federation of Irish Sport, 'About Us' <https://www.irishsport.ie/about/> accessed 6 May 2024.

[586] Federation of Irish Sport, 'Dispute Resolution' <https://www.irishsport.ie/dispute-resolution/> accessed 6 May 2024.

[587] Federation of Irish Sport, 'Garda Vetting' <https://www.irishsport.ie/garda-vetting/> accessed 6 May 2024.

[588] Federation of Irish Sport, 'Dispute Resolution' <https://www.irishsport.ie/dispute-resolution/> accessed 6 May 2024.

[589] Consolidated version of the Treaty on the Functioning of the European Union [2012] OJ C 326.

of the TFEU emphasise the importance of sport in the EU and give the European Commission a formal competence on sport.[590] Article 165 gives the EU a 'soft' competence on sport, meaning that the European Commission is empowered to develop a specific EU sports programme, which is supported by a budget. The competence also allows for better promotion of sport in other EU policy areas and programmes, including health and education.

It remains to be seen if Article 165 TFEU will have much impact on sports policy within the EU. The European Commission's role is limited to coordinating and supplementing the actions of the Member States. In the main, it is the Member States that 'retain the primary authority'.[591] Over the years the EU has become increasingly involved in sport. More recently it has adopted the Erasmus+ sports programme which provides support to grassroots organisations to become involved in partnerships with grassroots organisations in other Member States.[592] 2–162

Recent Developments

There have been recent developments effected by sports governing bodies that demonstrate a willingness to promote principles of good governance. World Athletics established an independent integrity unit, disciplinary tribunal, and vetting panel. In football, UEFA has refined the Financial Fair Play Regulations, now known as the UEFA Club Licensing and Financial Sustainability Regulations, which are discussed in more detail in Chapter 13. 2–163

Athletics Integrity Unit, Disciplinary Tribunal and Vetting Panel

In April 2017, the then IAAF created an independent Athletics Integrity Unit (AIU). It deals with both doping and non-doping matters: for example, betting, corruption and bribery and competition results and age manipulation.[593] Cases brought before the AIU are processed under World Athletics Anti-Doping Rules, the World Athletics Manipulation of Sports Competition Rules, and the World Athletics Integrity Code of 2–164

---

590 Art 6: 'The Union shall have competence to carry out actions to support, coordinate or supplement the actions of the Member States. The areas of such action shall, at European level, be: (a) protection and improvement of human health; (b) industry; (c) culture; (d) tourism; (e) education, vocational training, youth and sport; (f) civil protection; (g) administrative cooperation'.

591 Danish Institute for Sports Studies, 'Action for Good Governance in International Sports Organisations Final Report' edited by Jens Alm (Copenhagen 2013) 25 <https://www.playthegame.org/media/rc2g510y/aggis_final_report.pdf> accessed 6 May 2024.

592 European Commission, 'Sport Action' <https://erasmus-plus.ec.europa.eu/opportunities/opportunities-for-organisations/sport-actions> accessed 6 May 2024.

593 Athletics Integrity Unit, 'Know Us' <https://www.athleticsintegrity.org/know-us> accessed 6 May 2024.

Conduct.[594] World Athletics is the first sport's organisation operating at an international level that has delegated the management of its integrity programmes to an independent body.[595] The AIU reports through its own Board and is 'fully separated' from World Athletics.[596] It uses state of the art testing methods and provides education and prevention programmes.[597] It publishes on its website the names of all individuals (athletes, support persons and officials) who are ineligible to compete in athletics.[598]

2–165 According to its 2022 Annual Report, 349 doping and seven non-doping disciplinary cases were brought before AIU.[599] This figure includes 87 international-level doping cases and 262 national-level doping cases.[600] Of the 87 international-level doping cases, eight were found to have atypical findings, 40 were sanctioned and 32 were pending.[601] There were seven non-doping cases, two involved participation while ineligible; one a breach of integrity standards of honesty, dignity and protection of reputation; three cases involved competition manipulation; and one concerned age manipulation.[602]

2–166 On 21 November 2019, the AIU announced that it was charging RusAF with failing to cooperate with and obstructing an investigation.[603] The charges related to allegations concerning senior RusAF officials and 'whereabouts' violations committed by Danil Lysenko, a Russian high jumper.[604] The AIU carried out a 15-month investigation and found that RusAF officials had provided false explanations and forged documents in relation to Lysenko's failure to be in the location he was supposed to be under the whereabouts rules.[605] In 2021, the CAS partially upheld

---

594 World Athletics, 'Understand the Rules of Governance' <https://www.athleticsintegrity.org/know-the-rules/understand-the-rules-of-governance> accessed 6 May 2024.

595 Know us (n 593).

596 ibid.

597 Details of the disciplinary process are explained at: World Athletics, 'Athletics Integrity Unit Disciplinary Process' <https://www.athleticsintegrity.org/disciplinary-process> accessed 6 May 2024.

598 Athletics Integrity Unit, 'Global List of Ineligible Persons' <https://www.athleticsintegrity.org/disciplinary-process/global-list-of-ineligible-persons> accessed 6 May 2024. The list is updated every month.

599 Athletics Integrity Unit, '2022 Annual Report' (2023) 11 <https://www.athleticsintegrity.org/downloads/pdfs/know-us/en/Annual-Report–2022-ENGLISH.pdf> accessed 6 May 2024.

600 ibid. The doping cases involved 66 countries. Three CAS appeal decisions were handed down in 2022.

601 ibid.

602 ibid 11. Six cases resulted in a sanction, while one was pending.

603 Athletes Integrity Unit, 'Athletes Integrity Unit Charges Russian Athletics Federation with Obstructing an Investigation and Provisionally Suspends Several Senior Federation Officials for Tampering and Complicity' 21 November 2019 <https://www.athleticsintegrity.org/downloads/pdfs/know-us/en/AIU-Press-Release-RUSSIAN-ATHLETICS-FEDERATI.pdf> accessed 6 May 2024.

604 ibid.

605 The whereabouts rules are explained in ch 6 paras 6–66—6–69.

the decision of the AIU and imposed a six-year ban on Lysenko, with two years suspended.[606]

Article 76(1) of the World Athletics Constitution established the Disciplinary and Appeals Tribunal.[607] Operational since 3 April 2017, the Disciplinary Tribunal is mandated to hear and determine, at first instance, breaches of the World Athletics Integrity Code of Conduct and its Anti-Doping Rules.[608] The Disciplinary Tribunal has a chair and a panel of tribunal members who serve a four-year term which is renewable.[609] Sport Resolutions, an independent dispute resolution service domiciled in London, acts as the secretariat for the Disciplinary Tribunal.[610] Decisions of the Disciplinary Tribunal may be appealed to the CAS.[611] **2–167**

In February 2017, the then IAAF announced the inaugural Vetting Panel, a panel consisting of three independent persons who check on the eligibility of World Athletics' members.[612] Rules relating to the vetting panel are contained in Articles 65–69 of the 2019 Constitution (as amended in 2023) and its 2022 Vetting Rules.[613] **2–168**

Conclusion

This chapter has explained the importance of governance and the need for sports governing bodies to be held accountable for their actions. Sports bodies that are in receipt of state funding are under a fiduciary **2–169**

[606] CAS 2021/0/7668 *World Athletics v Danil Lysenko* award of 21 May 2021 <https://www.athleticsintegrity.org/downloads/pdfs/disciplinary-process/en/CAS-award-operative–1.pdf> accessed 6 May 2024. The appeal was partially upheld as the CAS recognised the Substantial Assistance provided by Lysenko pursuant to art 10.7.1 of World Athletics' Anti-Doping Rules 2021, which allowed for the suspension of two years of the six-year period of ineligibility.

[607] World Athletics, '2019 Constitution as Amended and Approved by Congress, on 18 August 2023, effective 01 September 2023' (Book A-A1) <https://worldathletics.org/about-iaaf/documents/book-of-rules> accessed 6 May 2024.

[608] Athletics Integrity Unit, 'Pending First Instance Cases' <https://www.athleticsintegrity.org/disciplinary-process/pending-first-instance-cases> accessed 6 May 2024. The Disciplinary Tribunal Rules can be downloaded from Book D – D5.1 <https://worldathletics.org/about-iaaf/documents/book-of-rules> accessed 6 May 2024.

[609] World Athletics, 'Disciplinary Tribunal' <https://worldathletics.org/about-iaaf/structure/independent-bodies/disciplinary-tribunal> accessed 6 May 2024.

[610] ibid. Sport Resolutions will act as secretariat until 31 December 2025.

[611] Disciplinary Tribunal Rules (n 608) r 13.2.

[612] World Athletics, 'Vetting Panel' <https://worldathletics.org/about-iaaf/structure/independent-bodies/vetting-panel> accessed 6 May 2024. Decisions of the Vetting Panel may be appealed to the CAS: see Art 69(1) of the 2019 Constitution (n 607).

[613] World Athletics, '2019 Constitution' (n 607) and 'Vetting Rules, approved by Council on 13 July 2022 and in force from 15 August 2022' (Book B – B3.2) <https://worldathletics.org/about-iaaf/documents/book-of-rules> accessed 6 May 2024. Decisions of the Vetting Panel may be appealed to the CAS: see art 69(1) of the 2019 Constitution (n 607).

duty to act in a manner akin to a corporation and should incorporate and embrace principles such as accountability, responsibility, and transparency. Sport is an industry, and its organisational structure needs to reflect the modern commercial realities. This chapter has documented examples of poor governance at both domestic and international level. Equally, it has shown the changes that sports governing bodies have made to improve their governance structures. Instead of being reactionary, it would be more prudent for sports governing bodies to have more robust structures in place and not just incorporate them following an unmasking of their weaknesses. The chapter has demonstrated that corruption in sport can reach state levels, Russia as the case in point. The role of the CAS and the contribution of the European Union to sports policy will be discussed in more detail in Chapters 12 and 13, respectively.

CHAPTER 3

SPORTS LAW OR SPORT AND THE LAW?

Introduction

Before deciding whether the appropriate term is Sports Law or Sport and the Law, it is necessary to define what exactly is Sports Law/Sport and Law. The terms Sports Law/Sport and the Law have been further broken into sub-categories: for example, *lex sportiva*, *lex Olympica*, global sports law, European Union (EU) sports law and domestic sports law. The confusion surrounding the definition of Sports Law/Sport and the Law is compounded by the fact that there is no legal definition of a sport. **3–01**

This chapter purports to define a sport and will examine whether the definition includes esports (Electronic Sports). It then discusses whether there is a branch of law that pertains to sport. To define the parameters of Sports Law/Sport and the Law, the initial reluctance of the courts to become involved in the determinations of sports governing bodies will be discussed. The chapter will examine critical junctures in the intervention of the courts. It explores recent developments, including the juridification of sport, the emergence of a global sports law and the reluctance of the courts to become involved in sports disputes as exemplified by recent cases, in what has been described as a 're-privatisation' of sport. The sources of law to which sports lawyers consult are discussed. The chapter debates whether the appropriate term, in an Irish context, is Sports Law or Sport and the Law. **3–02**

What Is a Sport?

There is no legal definition of a sport; it is defined from a sociological perspective. There are many reasons why a sports body or individual would want a particular activity to be defined as a sport. A sporting body may receive tax relief or state funding, as discussed in Chapter 2. Certain contact sports, including boxing and rugby, may result in injury that would ordinarily be defined as an assault but if it occurs in the context of a sport, it immunises the sport from the intervention of the law to a large extent. **3–03**

Section 2 of the Sport Ireland Act 2015 defines recreational sport as 'all forms of physical activity, which through casual or organised participation, aim at expressing or improving physical fitness and mental well-being and at forming social relationships'. The same **3–04** section defines competitive sport as 'all forms of physical activity which, through organised participation, aim at expressing or improving physical fitness and at obtaining improved results in competition at all levels'. This definition tells us very little about what constitutes a sport. However, it is clear from the definitions that there must be a physical element. An activity which lacks a physical component and relies heavily on mental agility is not enough for an activity to be classified as a sport, as the English Bridge Union discovered in the case of *The English Bridge Union Limited v Commissioners for Her Majesty's Revenue & Customs*.[1]

Is Bridge a Sport?

3–05 The English Bridge Union (EBU) is the governing body for contract bridge in England and is membership-funded and affiliated to the European Bridge League and the World Bridge Federation.[2] In the domestic tribunal, the EBU argued that it was entitled to the repayment of Value Added Tax (VAT) in relation to bridge competition entry fees from 30 June 2008 to 31 December 2011. Her Majesty's Revenue and Customs (HMRC) refuted the claim on the grounds that it did not consider that bridge constituted a sport for the purposes of an exemption under domestic law, the VAT Act 1994, and under EU law, the VAT Directive.[3] The domestic tribunal acknowledged that 'sport normally connotes a game with an athletic element rather than simply a game'; however, it was concerned that by using physical activity as a defining element of a sport, it would exclude older people. The case was sent by the domestic tribunal to the Court of Justice of the European Union (CJEU) under the preliminary reference procedure provided for by Article 267 of the Treaty on the Functioning of the European Union (TFEU) which allows a Member State court or tribunal refer a case to the CJEU when it is unsure of how to apply or interpret EU law. Before the CJEU gave its judgment, Advocate General (AG) Szpunar delivered a non-binding Opinion on 15 June 2017.[4] The AG opined that bridge constituted a sport for the purposes of the VAT Directive. However, AG Szpunar was careful to confine the definition of sport to the VAT Directive as he did not wish to apply a universal definition. By drawing parallels with recognised sports that do not imbue a physical element including archery, the AG put forward strong arguments in favour of

---

1 Case C–90/16 *The English Bridge Union Limited v Commissioners for Her Majesty's Revenue & Customs* [2017] ECLI:EU:C: 2017:814.

2 English Bridge Union, 'About the English Bridge Union (EBU)' <https://www.ebu.co.uk/information-resources/about-ebu> accessed 6 May 2024.

3 Council Directive 2006/112/EC of 28 November 2006 on the common system of value added tax, [2006] OJ L 347. This directive was amended in December 2020 and the consolidated version is available at <https://eur-lex.europa.eu/legal-content/EN/TXT/?uri=CELEX%3A02006L0112-20201212> accessed 6 May 2024.

4 Opinion of Advocate General Szpunar delivered on 15 June 2017, Case C–90/16 *The English Bridge Union Limited v Commissioners for Her Majesty's Revenue & Customs* ECLI: EU: C:2017: 464.

recognising bridge as a sport.[5] The AG also referred to the regional nature of a number of sports such as hurling in Ireland.[6] He opined that bridge had a significantly broader appeal in some Member States such as the United Kingdom (UK), Ireland and northern EU countries, thus cognisance needed to be given to 'regional perceptions' when defining sport at an EU level.[7] The AG explicitly excluded from the definition of sport games of chance 'as there is no relation between the effort invested and the outcome, and the tasks involved do not require any mental or physical skill'.[8]

The CJEU, as it is entitled to do so, did not follow the Opinion of AG Szpunar. On 26 October 2017, the CJEU handed down its judgment and held that bridge was not a sport for the purposes of the VAT Directive as 'sport' in the context of the VAT Directive 'is limited to activities satisfying the ordinary meaning of the term "sport", characterised by a not negligible physical element, but not covering all activities that may, in one way or another, be associated with that concept'.[9] **3–06**

While bridge is an activity that promotes mental health and well-being, that was not sufficient for it to be classified as a sport for the purposes of the VAT Directive. The CJEU did, however, recognise that bridge could fall under 'cultural services', a section of the VAT Directive which provides for exemptions on the grounds of public interest.[10] The CJEU held that bridge could be considered a cultural service 'if the activity, in the light of the way in which it is practised, its history and the traditions to which it belongs, in a given Member State, holds such a place in the social and cultural heritage of that country that it may be regarded as forming part of its culture'.[11] **3–07**

Although not recognising bridge as a sport, the CJEU by suggesting that bridge could fall under cultural services for the purposes of the VAT Directive recognised that it is a popular activity in several Member States. While the case concerned the definition of a sport for the purposes of an exemption from VAT, arguably had the CJEU held that bridge was a sport for the purposes of the VAT Directive then it might only be a matter of time before it was considered as a sport in general. If there were an EU-wide definition of sport it would have consequences for sports councils in all the Member States when it would come to the allocation of funding and the recognition of sports governing bodies of non-physical activities. The decision reflects a cautious approach by the CJEU on one hand, but on the other it quelled much disquiet that **3–08**

---

[5] ibid [26].
[6] ibid [43].
[7] ibid.
[8] ibid [44].
[9] Case C–90/16 (n 1) [22].
[10] ibid [28].
[11] ibid.

arose after the AG's Opinion as there was a concern among several of the Member States that the recognition of bridge for the purposes of the VAT Directive could be refined in a future decision to include sport in general, outside the confines of the VAT Directive.

Characteristics of Sport

3–09 It is worth noting the work of Allan Guttmann, who identified seven interrelated characteristics of modern sport:

1. Secularism: there are no religious connections. [12]
2. Equality: participation is in theory based on athletic ability and not restricted on grounds of gender, ethnicity, class, or religion which premodern sport often exemplified.[13]
3. Specialisation: the development of specialised roles and positions in sports.
4. Bureaucratisation/bureaucratic organisation: sports are administered at local, regional, municipal, and international level.
5. Rationalisation: Guttmann compares this characteristic to Weber's *Zweckrationalität* (instrumental rationality) whereby sporting contests 'take place in built-to-purpose facilities where scientifically trained athletes compete with standardised equipment on the basis of constantly revised rules and regulations that are looked upon as a means to an end'.[14]
6. Quantification: modern sport is measured in numbers, from distances to times.
7. Obsession with records: which Guttmann describes as the 'unsurpassed quantified achievement'.[15]

3–10 If the seven criteria are applied, then contract bridge is a sport. Guttmann's theoretical framework is influenced by Max Weber and Norbert Elias as he identifies three principles that distinguish premodern and modern sport:

1. The formal-structural characteristics of modern sport are very different to those of pre-modern sport.
2. Premodern sports have either adopted the formal-structures of modern sport or in the absence of absorbing formal-structures have continued to survive on the fringes and
3. The evolution of premodern sports to modern sports is an example of the civilising process, which Guttmann aptly describes as: 'in the course of which the members of a society internalise values that reduce the level of expressive (but not instrumental) interpersonal violence'.[16]

---

12 *Sports: The First Five Millennia* (University of Massachusetts Press 2004) 4–6. Guttmann identified the seven characteristics in his seminal book *From Ritual to Record: The Nature of Modern Sports* (Columbia University Press 1978). An updated edition was released in 2012.

13 *Sports: The First Five Millennia* (n 12) 5.

14 ibid.

15 ibid.

16 ibid 4. Norbert Elias, *The Civilising Process Sociogenetic and Psychogenetic*

Notwithstanding Guttmann's criteria, bridge is not considered a sport. There are other considerations when it comes to defining a sport. Not only must a sport have a physical element, but there are also policy reasons why an activity is not classified as a sport, as demonstrated by the decision of the House of Lords in *R v Brown*.[17] *R v Brown* concerned a group of homosexual men who engaged in violent activities, including genital torture, for the purposes of sexual gratification. All the participants were consenting adults, with the acts taking place in private and no participant ever suffered permanent injury. Video cameras recorded the activities; however, these recordings were intended for private use only among the men involved and were not commercially produced. On interception of the tapes by the police, the men were charged with assault occasioning actual bodily harm under s 47 of the Offences Against the Person Act 1861.[18] The men argued that there could be no offence if the parties involved consented. The trial court rejected this contention, and the decision was appealed by five of the men to the Court of Appeal (Criminal Division).[19] The case was sent to the House of Lords, which upheld the illegality of the acts. The House of Lords, in adopting a paternalistic approach, held that the activities of the men were unlawful irrespective of consent. The House of Lords referred to contact sports as being lawful as there is a public interest in the continued practice of contact sports, including boxing. Contact sports are deemed to be socially acceptable whereas the acts of the men in *Brown* were perceived as being deviant and contrary to public policy. The House of Lords held that it was in the interest of the men involved and also for society to prevent a 'cult of violence' which had the possible danger 'of proselytisation and corruption of young men'.[20] None of the men involved ever required hospital treatment nor did any of the men suffer permanent injuries: 'these players were true professionals'.[21] The activities took place in private chambers, code words were used when the pain inflicted had gone beyond an accepted level and all the equipment was sterilised. Lord Jauncey noted that the activities of the men were unlike a situation in sport where there is a 'referee present, such as there would be in boxing or a football match'.[22] Lord Jauncey reiterated that there was a public interest in allowing for reasonable surgeries and parental chastisement.[23] **3–11**

Investigations (Revised Edition) (edited by Eric Dunning, Johan Goudsblom, and Stephen Mennell) (Blackwell Publishing 2000).

17 [1993] 2 All ER 75.

18 For a more detailed discussion of the case, see Laura Donnellan, 'Consent and the Common Law Exceptions: *R v Brown* Still Good Law' (2020) 30(3) Irish Criminal Law Journal 62. The case is also discussed in ch 4 paras 4–46, 4–112—4–115 and 4–117.

19 [1992] QBD 491.

20 *Brown* (n 17) 237 G, 246 C.

21 David McArdle, *From Boot Money to Bosman* (Cavendish Publishing Ltd 2000) 146.

22 *Brown* (n 17) 238 G.

23 ibid 245 A.

3–12 In December 2018, the Irish Supreme Court handed down its judgment in the case of the *Director of Public Prosecutions (DPP) v Brown*.[24] While not involving sport, the case could have consequences for sports such as Mixed Martial Arts (MMA).[25] It dismissed the appeal and held that ss 2 and 3 assault under the Non-Fatal Offences Against the Person Act 1997 were separate offences. This case concerned a former Garda, Stephen Cooper, who was attacked by a fellow prisoner, Gerard Brown. The accused/appellant claimed that he had been asked to attack Cooper so that Cooper would be transferred to an open prison. Cooper denied that he had instructed Brown to hit him. Brown was found guilty of assault causing harm under s 3 of the Non-Fatal Offences Against the Person Act 1997. The trial judge would not permit the defence of consent to be put to the jury and added three years on to Brown's sentence. The Supreme Court held that consent is immaterial if the act is illegal.

3–13 McKechnie J, dissenting, made an interesting observation in relation to the exceptions and the subjectivity of public policy. He stated:

> Picking up on boxing as an example, it seems that the reasons most commonly cited in support of its lawful status are the fact that it is properly regulated; that the combatants are properly trained; that it has clear rules of engagement and that the safety of the fighters and probity of the combat is overseen by a referee; and that medical assistance will be on hand, if required. It is these factors that differentiate it from prize-fighting, street-fighting and the like. In such circumstances, with the risks minimised insofar as it is possible to do so, the law will tolerate the deliberate infliction of personal injury. With respect I do not find those reasons compelling. Such a sport is not engaged in for recreation or personal improvement: it is for the money and the attendant glory that fame and success bring. So causing a brain injury, rendering one's opponent unconscious, damaging a vital organ or fracturing this or that bone, even the risk of death itself, are all overlooked. So on what legal basis is it tolerated? Social value seems intuitively objectionable. The factors mentioned as justification seem to offer little else and certainly do not permit the deduction of a general theory that can carry through to the other exceptions. Perhaps Lord Mustill is right: he simply posits that boxing is by now so well-entrenched in our sporting and cultural psyche as to occupy an anomalous position in law.[26]

3–14 In following the rationale of *R v Brown* and, by extension, the *DPP v Brown*, the case law suggests that for a sport to be classified as such it needs to be regulated by a governing body and be deemed socially acceptable. There are limits to what can be defined as a sport. The Law Commission of England and Wales' Consultation Paper on Consent in the Criminal Law provides some guidance on what constitutes a legal

[24] [2018] IESC 67. The case is discussed in more detail in ch 4 paras 4–30—4–33.

[25] Conor Gallagher, 'Top Court to Hear Arguments on Consent to Being Assaulted' *The Irish Times* (Dublin, 28 August 2017) <https://www.irishtimes.com/news/crime-and-law/courts/supreme-court/top-court-to-hear-arguments-on-consent-to-being-assaulted-1.3200246> accessed 6 May 2024.

[26] *Brown* (n 24) [83].

definition of sport.[27] It referred to criteria devised by the then British Sports Council (now known as UK Sport). The British Sports Council identified the following criteria used by it in determining whether an activity was recognised as a sport:

- Physical skill
- Physical effort
- Accessibility
- Rules and organisation
- Essential purpose
- Physical challenge
- Risk
- Uniqueness
- Strategies and tactics
- Level of participation
- Martial arts
- Other considerations

This final point is of relevance to the activities practised in *R v Brown*.[28] The guidelines ask if there any political, moral, or other ethical considerations which might prohibit UK Sport from recognising the activity? Otherwise, most of the criteria could be applied to sadomasochism. **3–15**

The Law Commission, in reference to on-field violence, proposed that sports participants should not be held criminally liable for injury caused if the injury in question is inflicted in the 'course of playing or practising a recognised sport in accordance with its rules'.[29] Thus, liability should only attach if the injury inflicted is done so outside the rules of the sport. The Law Commission recognised the need to define what constitutes a lawful sport.[30] It acknowledged that the rules and regulations, and what would be acceptable, differ between sports. In boxing, for example, it is within the rules to hit an opponent from the waist up, yet in a non-contact sport such as tennis, any form of physical contact would be outside the rules of the sport. To provide a legal definition of sport, the rules and regulations of a particular sport need to be verified for it to be recognised as a lawfully constituted sport. **3–16**

In 2017, the UK Sports Councils' Recognition Policy was published.[31] It outlines two stages of recognition for sports governing bodies, one **3–17**

---

[27] Law Commission, *Criminal Law: Consent in the Criminal Law: A Consultation Paper* (Paper No 139–1995) para 1.11 <https://cloud-platform-e218f50a4812967ba1215eaecede923f.s3.amazonaws.com/uploads/sites/30/2016/08/No.139-Criminal-Law-Consent-in-the-Criminal-Law-A-Consultation-Paper.pdf> accessed 6 May 2024.

[28] *Brown* (n 17).

[29] Law Commission (n 27) para 13.11.

[30] ibid para 13.1.

[31] The full document is available at Sport England, 'Sports Councils' Recognition Policy 2017' <https://sportengland-production-files.s3.eu-west-2.amazonaws.com/s3fs-public/uk-recognition-policy-2017.pdf> accessed 6 May 2024. The

that is required for pre-application and one that is required for full application.[32] The criterion used in assessing the purposed recognition in the pre-application includes sporting activity. Sporting activity is primarily based on 'physical activity', which is in line with the Council of Europe's Sports Charter.[33] The Sports Councils in the UK are advised to place emphasis 'on the human physical activity involved when the sporting activity takes place and not activity in preparation for the sporting activity, or on its conclusion'.[34] The recognition policy adds that the 'purpose of the activity must be solely for sport … and not a means to another end'.[35] While an activity like gardening is physically demanding, it would not constitute a sport under this policy.[36]

3–18 Reference may also be made to sports that are recognised by the International Olympic Committee (IOC). However, some anomalies may denigrate the effectiveness of using the IOC as a guide. Until 2016, golf and rugby sevens were not recognised as Olympic sports, both of which are very popular participant and spectator sports. It was not until October 2009 that the IOC decided to allow both sports to be included in the 2016 Olympics.[37] The 2024 Summer Olympics included one new sport, breaking (or break dancing, an urban dance style).[38] Following their debut at the Tokyo Olympics in 2021, sport climbing,[39] skateboarding,[40] and surfing returned to Paris 2024.[41]

---

recognition is operated by all five Sports Councils, UK Sport, Sport Scotland, Sport England, Sport Wales, and Sport Northern Ireland.

32 ibid 6.

33 Council of Europe, 'Committee of Ministers, Recommendation No R (92) 13 REV of the Committee of Ministers to Member States on the Revised European Sports Charter' (16 May 2001) <https://www.coe.int/t/dg4/epas/resources/texts/Rec(92)13rev_en.pdf> accessed 6 May 2024. The Charter was again revised in 2021: see Council of Europe, 'Enlarged Partial Agreement on Sport, Revised European Sports Charter' Recommendation CM/Rec (2021) 5 Adopted by the Committee of Ministers on 13 October 2021 at the 1414th meeting of the Ministers' Deputies <https://rm.coe.int/revised-european-sports-charter-web-a6/1680a7534b> accessed 7 May 2024. The definition of sport remains the same under the 2021 revision: see art 1.

34 UK Sport Councils (n 31) 12.

35 ibid.

36 ibid. Other criteria include the Organisational History, the Constitutional Structure, Affiliation, Influence and Membership Numbers, ibid 13–14.

37 International Olympic Committee, 'Golf and Rugby – New Kids on the Block' 16 March 2016, <https://www.olympic.org/news/golf-and-rugby-new-kids-on-the-block> accessed 7 May 2024.

38 International Olympic Committee, 'Breaking' <https://olympics.com/en/paris-2024/sports/breaking> accessed 7 May 2024.

39 International Olympic Committee, 'Sport Climbing' <https://olympics.com/en/paris-2024/sports/sport-climbing> accessed 7 May 2024.

40 International Olympic Committee, 'Skateboarding' <https://olympics.com/en/paris-2024/sports/skateboarding> accessed 7 May 2024.

41 International Olympic Committee, 'Surfing' <https://olympics.com/en/paris-2024/sports/surfing> accessed 7 May 2024.

Esports

The main criterion in recognising a sport is that of physical activity; secondary to that, the activity must be socially acceptable. Esports present an interesting development. Esports refers to competitive video gaming between individuals or teams. One writer explains the level of organisation and skill required to become an esports athlete: 3–19

> Of course, dedicating hours to playing these games on its own does not make someone an esports athlete. While tossing a ball around the yard with friends can be considered 'playing football', it takes organisation, dedication, discipline and training to be 'a football player'. And there's a similar difference between casual gaming and esports.[42]

In general, games are broadcast on the live-streaming platform, Twitch.[43] The first game was invented in a laboratory in Massachusetts Institute of Technology (MIT) by Steve Russell and a group of other hackers in 1962.[44] *Spacewar!* was created by Russell and others as part of a demonstration program for the Programmed Data Processor–1 (PDP–1) minicomputer by the Digital Equipment Corporation (DEC), a company established by two MIT employees in 1957.[45] *Spacewar!* provided the template for the first commercial arcade game, *Computer Space!*, which was created in 1971.[46] 3–20

Esports has come a long way since 1971. In July 2019, the Fortnite World Cup took place in the Arthur Ashe Stadium in New York and had a total prize pool of $15.1m.[47] The event was organised by Epic Games, a video game and software development company based in North Carolina. The location of the Fortnite World Cup is noteworthy. The Arthur Ashe Stadium, with a spectator capacity of 23,000, is one of the main stadia used in the US Tennis Open.[48] 3–21

In 2017, the League of Legends World Championship took place in 3–22

---

[42] James O'Hagan, 'More than a Game: The Unstoppable Growth of Esports' (*RTÉ Brainstorm*, Dublin, 11 September 2019) <https://www.rte.ie/brainstorm/2019/0909/1074856-more-than-a-game-the-unstoppable-growth-of-esports/> accessed 7 May 2024.

[43] The site can be accessed at <https://www.twitch.tv/> accessed 7 May 2024.

[44] Devin Monnens and Martin Goldberg, 'Space Odyssey: The Long Journey of Spacewar! From MIT to Computer Labs around the World' (June 2015) Kinephanos, Cultural History of Video Games Special Issue 124, 124, <https://www.kinephanos.ca/Revue_files/2015_Monnens_Goldberg.pdf> accessed 7 May 2024.

[45] ibid. DEC ceased trading in 1998.

[46] Monnens and Goldberg (n 44) 124.

[47] Fortnite, 'Fortnite World Cup 2019/Finals' <https://fortnite-esports.gamepedia.com/Fortnite_World_Cup_2019/Finals> accessed 7 May 2024.

[48] Steve Flink, '50 Moments that Mattered: Arthur Ashe Stadium Makes its Debut' 11 July 2018 <https://www.usopen.org/en_US/news/articles/2018-07-11/2018-07 11_50_moments_that_mattered_arthur_ashe_stadium_makes_its_debut.html> accessed 7 May 2024.

various cities in China from September to November. Twenty-four teams took part and peak viewership reached 2,102,206.[49] The 2019 tournament had a peak viewership of 3,985,787, with 24 teams taking part between 2 October and 10 November in Paris, Berlin, and Madrid.[50] Esports tournaments include live commentary, player and team statistics, instant replay analysis and interviews with players/teams following a game.[51]

3–23 In the run-up to the Tokyo 2020 Olympics, Intel, one of the main sponsors of the Summer Games, had organised an esports tournament. This followed on from the inaugural Intel® Extreme Masters that took place at the Winter Olympics in PyeongChang.[52] Qualifying rounds began in December 2019 and players competed online to get on a national team. In light of the COVID–19 pandemic and the postponing of the Olympics to 2021, a decision was made to postpone the Intel Esports Tournament to July 2021.[53] The involvement of Intel was significant as it brought a number of technical advancements to the 2021 Summer Games including facial recognition, artificial intelligence (AI) and 5G platforms. The IOC expressed its excitement about the Intel Esports Tournament, with Kit McConnell, the IOC's Sports Director, announcing: 'As we explore the engagement between esports and the Olympic Movement, we are looking forward to learning from this event and continuing to engage with the passionate esports community from around the world.'[54]

3–24 A forum on esports took place on 21 July 2018 at the Olympic Museum in Lausanne, Switzerland.[55] It was hosted by the IOC and the Global Association of International Sports Federations (GAISF) with attendees including representatives from international federations (IFs), sponsors, media, event organisers and athletes from Olympic sports and the

[49] Esports Charts, '2017 World Championship' <https://escharts.com/tournaments/lol/2017-world-championship> accessed 7 May 2024.
[50] Esports Charts, '2019 World Championship' <https://escharts.com/tournaments/lol/2019-world-championship> accessed 7 May 2024.
[51] Daniel Railsback and Nicholas Caporusso, 'Investigating the Human Factors in eSports Performance' in Tareq Z Ahram (ed), *Advances in Human Factors in Wearable Technologies and Game Design* (Proceedings of the AHFE 2018 International Conferences on Human Factors and Wearable Technologies, and Human Factors in Game Design and Virtual Environments, Held on 21–25 July 2018, in Loews Sapphire Falls Resort at Universal Studios, Orlando, Florida, USA (Springer International Publishing 2019).
[52] International Olympic Committee, 'Intel Technology Set to Deliver Several Innovations During Tokyo 2020' 12 September 2019 <https://www.olympic.org/news/intel-technology-set-to-deliver-several-innovations-during-tokyo-2020> accessed 7 May 2024.
[53] ibid. See Trent Murray, 'Intel Confirms World Open Esports Event Will Take Place Alongside Tokyo Olympics' (*The Esports Observer*, 5 May 2021) <https://archive.esportsobserver.com/intel-world-open-tokyo-olympics/> accessed 7 May 2024.
[54] ibid.
[55] International Olympic Committee, 'Olympic Movement, Esports and Gaming Communities Meet at the Esports Forum' 21 July 2018 <https://www.olympic.org/news/olympic-movement-esports-and-gaming-communities-meet-at-the-esports-forum> accessed 7 May 2024.

esports community.[56] In dispelling rumours that esports would become an Olympic sport, Kit McConnell referred to the forum as

> a unique opportunity to hear from a wide variety of stakeholders ... There was a consensus that future collaboration will be based on ensuring that any activity supports and promotes the Olympic values; and while the goal was not to develop a pathway towards the inclusion of esports on the Olympic programme, we have a strong plan for ongoing dialogue and engagement, and are in a strong position to coordinate and support the wider engagement of the Olympic Movement with esports.[57]

In 2023, the IOC, in collaboration with IFs and game publishers, established the Olympic Esports Series 2023.[58] It was described as 'a global virtual and simulated sports competition' involving ten sports: 3–25

- Archery (Tic Tac Bow)
- Baseball (WBSC eBASEBALL™: POWER PROS)
- Chess (Chess.com)
- Cycling (Zwift)
- Dance (Just Dance)
- Motor sport (Gran Turismo)
- Sailing (Virtual Regatta)
- Shooting (ISSF Challenge featuring Fortnite)
- Tennis (Tennis Clash)
- Taekwondo (Virtual Taekwondo)[59]

The Olympic Esports Series 2023 involved qualifying rounds and the finals took place in person in Singapore during the inaugural Olympic Esports Week 2023 from 22 to 25 June.[60] While esports are not part of the Summer or Winter Olympic programmes, the IOC seems open to developing an Esports Olympic Games which would run alongside the traditional games. In referring to the Intel Esports Tournament 2021 and the Olympic Esports Series 2023, the IOC stated: 3–26

> in line with the Olympic Agenda 2020 + 5, ... supporting and promoting the development of virtual sports throughout the Olympic Movement and further connecting with gaming communities are goals. We look forward to welcoming some of the world's best to compete on the global stage, as well as explore together shared opportunities and lessons – across health and wellbeing, training and innovation.[61]

In operating as a distinct event, the President of the IOC Thomas Bach was quoted as saying that the inaugural Olympic Esports Games could 3–27

---

[56] ibid.
[57] ibid.
[58] International Olympic Committee, 'Esports FAQ' <https://olympics.com/ioc/esports-faq> accessed 7 May 2024.
[59] ibid.
[60] ibid. This was in conjunction with the Ministry of Culture, Community and Youth, Sport Singapore and the Singapore National Olympic Committee (SNOC).
[61] ibid.

possibly take place in 2025 or 2026.[62] Bach referred to AI and how it 'will play a major role and a very important role not only for sports and the Olympic Games, but for all our lives'.[63]

3–28 For the foreseeable future, esports will not form part of the Winter or Summer Olympics, but rather will be a distinct and separate tournament. If it were to be considered a Summer or Winter Olympic sport it would need to satisfy the definition of physical activity. The ten esports that featured in the Olympic Esports Series 2023 all entailed physical activity, albeit not in the traditional sense of physically playing those sports. If a broad definition of physical activity is applied, for example, the American Heart Association's definition as 'anything that moves your body and burns calories', esports could constitute physical activity.[64] If a narrower definition is applied, where physical activity is measured in metabolic equivalent of task (MET), then the threshold for physical activity is higher than mere movement of the body. An individual sitting quietly should have a resting metabolic rate that amounts to one MET, a healthy adult walking around five to six kilometres per hour is equivalent to three to six METs.[65] While esports require hand-eye coordination and swift response levels, they do not possess the physical activity that is required for an activity to be classified as a sport.[66] Aside from the physical element, esports are devoid of organisational structures in the form of a governing body or federation. Another important factor that influences the acceptance of an activity as a sport is the media and whether the activity is covered in the news or in the sport section of a newspaper.[67] Currently, 'eSports is close to but not yet equivalent to sports'.[68] However, as it gains more mainstream acceptance and is placed under the control of a governing body, it may become an Olympic sport. The list of Olympic sports is continually under review. If there is an Olympic Esports Games in 2025 or 2026, it could pave the way for its acceptance in the Summer or Winter Games in the next decade or so. Or it may remain a separate event much like the Youth Olympic Games (YOG), which began in 2010.[69]

---

62 Xinhua, 'Inaugural Olympic Esports Games to Take Place No Later than 2026: IOC President Bach' 29 January 2024 < https://english.news.cn/20240129/caef828f2b754d11b9ec1a774a2f90c8/c.html> accessed 7 May 2024.

63 ibid.

64 American Heart Association, 'American Heart Association Recommendations for Physical Activity in Adults and Kids' 19 January 2024 <https://www.heart.org/en/healthy-living/fitness/fitness-basics/aha-recs-for-physical-activity-in-adults> accessed 7 May 2024.

65 Kirstin Hallmann and Thomas Giel, 'eSports: Competitive Sports or Recreational Activity?' (2018) 21 Sport Management Review 14, 15.

66 ibid 17.

67 ibid 16.

68 ibid 17.

69 The YOG is an event for elite athletes aged 15 to 18. The first games took place in Summer 2010 and its Winter Games took place in 2012. The next Summer YOG takes place in 2026 in Dakar, Senegal. For more information, see International

The Application of Private and Public Law to Sport

Traditionally, sport was viewed as a private activity that was regulated by private law. The public law was very reluctant to become involved in sporting matters. However, as sport became increasingly commercialised and professionalised, the public law began to intervene. However, in what has been referred to as the 're-privatisation' of sport, the courts have returned to their supervisory role, preferring to leave the resolving of disputes to the autonomous sports governing body. The case law, as the discussion below demonstrates, suggests that the courts will only get involved when the internal disciplinary mechanisms of the sport have been exhausted. **3–29**

Private law governs the legal rights and relationships of individuals both natural (humans) and legal persons (companies and associations). Examples of private law include contract law, tort law, and family law. Public law, on the other hand, governs legal rights and relationships between individuals and the state. Criminal law, constitutional law and administrative law are branches of public law. Most sporting bodies are categorised as private and voluntary associations and, as discussed below, it is the private nature of sport that has resulted in it being largely immunised from intervention of the courts. An association is defined as 'a self-governing body whose members are in an ongoing contractual relationship defined by rules, agreements and customs of the fellowship'.[70] Due to sporting bodies' private structure, the public law has, in the past, been loath to interfere with the determinations of these organisations. However, from the mid-1980s, sports organisations found it increasingly difficult to evade to intervention of the public law. The involvement of the public law can be attributed to the increased commercialisation of sport; the stakes are higher for sports bodies and persons. Increased professionalisation and commercialisation of sport has meant sporting bodies and persons have more to lose if their rights have been unduly compromised. Governing bodies have also assumed greater power within their sports. They must adhere to their own rules and regulations as failure to do so may result in litigation. Society has become more litigious and sport, as an important social activity, has been unable to remain unsusceptible from such developments. In recent years sportspersons have seen an increase in earning potential. If an athlete suffers a career-ending injury, a contract or sponsorship dispute, or a doping allegation, they will be more likely to seek redress in the courts. **3–30**

The public law will especially intervene in situations where there is an allegation of a breach of natural justice. A sportsperson who is aggrieved by a decision of their governing body may initially view the courts as the most appropriate forum to resolve their dispute. There **3–31**

Olympic Committee, 'Youth Olympic Games' <https://olympics.com/ioc/youth-olympic-games> accessed 7 May 2024.

[70] John Barnes, *The Law of Hockey* (LexisNexis 2010) 97.

are merits to seeking redress in the courts. As Little and Morris note, judicial intervention embodies a 'copper bottomed guarantee of ultimate justice for individual sportsmen embroiled in stormy long running (invariably disciplinary) disputes with their governing bodies'.[71] In other situations, it is much more beneficial for the sportsperson and the sporting organisation to seek to resolve their dispute without recourse to the courts.

3–32 In light of the increased commercialisation and professionalisation of sport, sportspersons are demanding higher standards of justice. As a result of these sporting cases, a cohesive body of law has developed, namely Sport and the Law, or Sports Law. The application of both public and private law to sport is not confined to a domestic level; it is transnational and global in nature, as Foster refers to it as 'law without a state and so outside the governance of national laws, that is immune from state regulation and a legal order in its own right, and that is legitimised by its subjects'.[72] In 2009, the IOC was granted observer status by the United Nations (UN) in order to 'promote sport at a new level'.[73] Sport transcends national boundaries and in effect, world governing bodies or agencies such as the World Anti-Doping Agency (WADA) and the IOC along with the body of principles created by the Court of Arbitration for Sport (CAS) have been instrumental in creating a *lex sportiva*. In adopting a broad definition, de Oliveira notes that 'lex sportiva is not solely made of the CAS jurisprudence but the rules and regulations imposed by the SGBs and their interpretation by CAS'.[74]

3–33 Irish sport is largely amateur and thus much of the discussion in this book relates to other jurisdictions: namely England and Wales, Canada, and Australia. However, the developments in these other jurisdictions will be of importance to Ireland in the future. The nature of Irish sport has changed over the years. Rugby, for example, was professionalised in 1995 and professionalism brought with it a plethora of legal issues. Ireland has produced several high-profile professional and amateur boxers, including Katie Taylor and Kellie Harrington. As more and more sports become professionalised in Ireland, the issues raised in this book will become increasingly pertinent. In addition, although sport may be classified as a past-time or recreational activity does not mean that it is immune from judicial scrutiny. On-field violence should be equally dissuaded in a local Gaelic Athletic Association (GAA) match as much as it is in a professional match. While Ireland has limited case law and

---

[71] Philip Morris and Gavin Little, 'Challenging Sports Bodies' Determinations' (1998) 17 Civil Justice Quarterly 128, 129.

[72] Ken Foster, 'Global Sports Law Revisited' (2019) 17(1) The Entertainment and Sports Law Journal 1, 2.

[73] International Olympic Committee, 'IOC Becomes UN Observer' 19 October 2009 <https://www.olympic.org/news/ioc-becomes-un-observer> accessed 7 May 2024.

[74] Leonardo VP de Oliveira, 'Lex Sportiva as the Contractual Governing Law' (2017) 17(1–2) The International Sports Law Journal 101, 102. SGBs stands for Sports Governing Bodies.

material on sport and the law, the comparative analysis will provide a template from which Irish sporting bodies and the courts can develop a body of sporting jurisprudence.

Sources of Law: National and Transnational

Domestic Sources of Law

Apart from the Sport Ireland Act 2015, which repealed and replaced the Irish Sports Council Act 1999 and the National Sports Campus Development Authority Act 2006, there is no other general legislation pertaining to sport in Ireland. There is legislation regulating animal sports, for example, the Horse Racing Ireland Act 2016 and the Greyhound Racing Act 2019. The 2019 Act renamed Bord na gCon; it is now named Rásaíocht Con Éireann. The Act also provides for greyhound welfare, controlled and prohibited substances, and restrictions on the use of artificial insemination. These acts are examples of national sports law, laws which have been created by the Oireachtas and are applied and interpreted by the judiciary. 3–34

Domestic sports law is defined as 'the body of internally applicable legal norms created and adhered to by national governing bodies of sport'.[75] Taking the GAA as an example, it is bound by the *Official Guide – Part 1* and *Official Guide – Part 2*.[76] Within the GAA there is the Dispute Resolution Authority (DRA), which was established in 2005 and is independent of the GAA.[77] According to Rule 2.1 (e) of Appendix 5, disputes can only be referred to the DRA on '[c]onfirmation that available avenues of Appeal under the Rules of the Association have been exhausted'.[78] The only disputes the DRA is precluded from hearing are those involving doping as the GAA has its own hearing committee, the Anti-Doping Hearings Committee, as provided for under Rule 1.13 of Chapter 1 on Aims and Ethos.[79] 3–35

Transnational Sources of Law

Academic commentators have advanced several sources that relate to the regulation of sport, for example, *lex sportiva*, *lex Olympica* (the law of the Olympic Movement), EU sports law, international sports law, and global sports law. *Lex sportiva*, as noted above, is often defined as 3–36

---

[75] Mark James, *Sports Law* (3rd edn, Palgrave 2017) 3.

[76] Gaelic Athletic Association, *Official Guide – Part 1* (Central Council of the Association 2024). This part contains the Constitution and Rules of the GAA. The *Official Guide – Part 2* (Central Council of the Association 2024) which contains the Playing Rules of Hurling and Football. The guides are available for download at <https://www.gaa.ie/article/gaa-official-guides-codes> accessed 24 April 2024. Both Guides were approved by Central Council on 23 March 2024.

[77] ibid Appendix 5 of the *Official Guide – Part 1* (2024) 90–95.

[78] ibid 90.

[79] ibid 5.

the jurisprudence of the CAS. However, some authors disagree with such a narrow definition and contend that *lex sportiva* is a much broader concept. Much debate surrounds the 'terminological knot' that is *lex sportiva*.[80] The English translation of *lex sportiva* is the laws of sport, however, using a Latin term means that it is understood universally.[81] *Lex sportiva* can be understood to mean global sports law wherein international sports federations and the CAS have created a corpus of sports-related laws that transcend national boundaries and have garnered acceptance from the national law courts. EU sports law refers to the soft law measures created by the EU Institutions, particularly the European Commission, as briefly discussed in Chapter 2, and the case law of the CJEU, which is examined in detail in Chapter 13. International sports law has been succinctly described as 'the general or universal principles of law which are part of international customary law, or the *jus commune*, that are applied to sports disputes'.[82] *Lex Olympia* means Olympic law and it refers to the creation of national law to support the holding of the Olympics and Paralympics in the host country.[83] Legislation will be introduced by the host country to enable it to exploit its association with the Olympic Games and thus advance its commercial interests; this can range from legislation protecting its logos and symbols to legislation suspending Sunday trading laws.[84] The British Parliament enacted the London Olympic and Paralympic Games Act 2006 (LOPGA 2006) in order to regulate the holding of the Games in accordance with the Olympic Charter.[85] In 1995, the first piece of Olympic legislation was enacted, Olympic Symbol etc (Protection) Act 1995.[86] This Act endowed the British Olympic Association (BOA) an Olympic association right which granted the BOA exclusive rights to use the Olympic symbol, the Olympic motto, and the protected words.[87] A private company limited by guarantee was created by the BOA, the Mayor of London and the then Secretary of State for Culture, Media and Sport in 2005 and was given the responsibility of 'organising, publicising and staging the London 2012 Olympic and Paralympic Games of 2012'.[88] As it was

80 Robert CR Siekmann, *Introduction to International and European Sports Law: Capita Selecta* (Springer Science & Business Media 2012) 23.

81 ibid.

82 James (n 75) 3.

83 ibid. See also Alexandre Miguel Mestre, *The Law of the Olympic Games* (TMC Asser Press 2009) and Dimitrios P Panagiōtopoulos, *Sports Law: Lex Sportiva & Lex Olympica: Theory and Praxis* (Ant N Sakkoulas 2011).

84 For example, the Sunday Trading (London Olympic Games and Paralympic Games) Act 2012, c 12. There are several Statutory Instruments that introduced restrictions on flying over certain areas of London: for example, The Air Navigation (Restriction of Flying) (London 2012 Olympic and Paralympic Games, Road Cycle Event, Leatherhead, Surrey) (Amendment) Regulations 2012, UK Statutory Instruments 2012 No 1972.

85 UK Public General Act 2006, c 12.

86 UK Public General Acts 1995, c 3.

87 ibid s 2.

88 The National Archives, 'Records of the London 2012 Organising Committee of the Olympic and Paralympic Games (LOCOG)' <http://discovery.nationalarchives.gov.uk/details/r/C13273031> accessed 8 May 2024.

a limited company and unable to discharge the functions required under the IOC's Host City contract, the LOPGA 2006 was introduced to provide a legislative framework.[89] It created the Olympic Delivery Authority (ODA), a body corporate whose general functions under s 4 included preparing for the London Olympics, the management of the games, the acquisition of property, the disposal of property and to make arrangements for the construction, adaptation or provision of systems or facilities for transport. The ODA was dissolved by way of a statutory instrument in 2014.[90]

Juridification of Sport

The term juridification is often used to explain the increased intervention of the law into private spheres. Foster notes that very few areas of life are not regulated by law, he asserts that '[l]aw in liberal democracies is increasingly invasive'.[91] The term was first used in the early 1980s in reference to the increased regulation of industrial relations in Britain.[92] The commodification of sport has paved the way for the increased legal regulation of sport, a development that some academic commentators question. In situations involving on-field violence in sports where physical contact is an integral part, Gardiner and Felix contend that there should be specific situations where the law, both civil and criminal, becomes involved.[93] In relation to the infliction of deliberate harm, the writers contend that if the 'internal disciplinary mechanisms fail to deter such conduct, the criminal law may be an appropriate though limited tool'.[94] In other situations, the use of arbitration or the imposition of vicariously liability on the club for the actions of the player may be a better option than invoking the law.[95] Foster raises an interesting argument. He contends that the juridification of sport is a form of domestication and not colonialisation.[96] Sporting bodies have voluntarily adopted legal norms, including principles of fairness.[97] Although juridification has placed limits on the autonomy of governing **3–37**

89 Mark James and Guy Osborn, 'London 2012 and the Impact of the UK's Olympic and Paralympic Legislation: Protecting Commerce or Preserving Culture?' (2011) 74(3) The Modern Law Review 410. This article offers an interesting critique on the national Olympic legislation.

90 The Olympic Delivery Authority (Dissolution) Order 2014, UK Statutory Instruments 2014 No 3184.

91 Ken Foster, 'The Juridification of Sport' in Steven Greenfield and Guy Osborn (eds), *Readings in Law and Popular Culture* (Routledge 2007) 155. Foster refers to the juridification of military law at 157.

92 ibid 156.

93 Simon Gardiner and Alexandra Felix, 'Juridification of the Football Field: Strategies for Giving Law the Elbow' (1995) 5 Marquette Sports Law Journal 189.

94 ibid 201.

95 ibid 208.

96 Foster (n 91) 158.

97 ibid.

bodies, social and cultural developments have caused governing bodies to be more amenable to the imposition of external norms.[98]

3–38 One of the characteristics of juridification is the influence of lawyers on the rules of the game and the prevalence of lawyers in sports disciplinary tribunals. Rulebooks are often shrouded in legalise and, in most cases, they are drafted by lawyers.[99] Some sports refer to their codes as laws; for example, the Laws of Cricket and the Laws of Rugby. Rules have become increasingly codified, particularly the rules that relate to the disciplinary powers of the sport.[100] In an Irish context, the DRA is an example of the juridification of sport. The DRA has a panel of solicitors, barristers, arbitrators (Group 1, no fewer than 15) and persons 'who, by virtue of their experience and expertise in the affairs of the Association, are properly qualified to resolve disputes relating to the Rules of the Association' (Group 2, no fewer than 15).[101] The current secretary, Rory Hanniffy, was appointed for a three-year term in 2017 and is serving a second term from 2021–2024.[102]

3–39 The DRA hears cases including player transfers, player eligibility, on-field violence and challenging suspensions. In 2015, a case involving the transfer of an underage player within the county of Armagh came before the DRA.[103] In coming to a decision, the DRA looked at the UK Supreme Court decision of *Kennedy v Charity Commission*.[104] In *Peadar O'Flionn*, a 14-year-old player requested a transfer to another club within the county after his family relocated, which necessitated a 20-mile round trip for his father.[105] Antrim CCC refused to approve the transfer on grounds that the transfer did not comply with Bye-law 15.1(c) in that it had not been signed by the Parent Club Secretary. The player's father challenged the refusal before the Antrim Hearings Committee, who dismissed the appeal on the grounds that there was no clear infringement or misapplication of the rule by Antrim CCC and that there was no breach of the right to a fair hearing pursuant to Rules 7.3 and 7.11 of the Official Guide 2014. In the aftermath of this decision, an application for arbitration to the DRA was filed. St Patrick's Lisburn justified the refusal on the grounds of 'talent drain' as over half a dozen transfers had been requested in recent years while Antrim contended

---

98 ibid.

99 ibid 160.

100 ibid 161.

101 Appendix 5 of the *Official Guide – Part 1* (2024) (n 76) 90.

102 Hanniffy is a barrister who played hurling for Offaly.

103 *In the matter of the arbitration under the Disputes Resolution Code and under the Arbitration Act 2010, O'Flionn v Coiste Comórtas na gCluchí Aintroim (Antrim CCC) agus Naomh Pádraig GLC Lios na gCearrbhach (St Patrick's GAC Lisburn)* DRA 06 of 2015 <http://www.sportsdra.ie/wp-content/uploads/2014/03/DRA-6-2015.pdf> accessed 8 May 2024.

104 (2014) UKSC 20.

105 This case is discussed in Laura Donnellan, 'Dispute Resolution in Irish Sport: The Courts as Reluctant Interlopers' (2016) 14 Entertainment and Sports Law Journal 1.

that the restriction was in compliance of the rules and that it was under no obligation to take into account 'exceptional circumstances'.[106] The DRA referred to how inflexibility of interpretation of the rules 'have an obvious potential for injustice'.[107] Antrim CCC was deemed not to have given any consideration to the 'unique factual circumstances' of the player and his family.[108] The DRA deemed the refusal to be unreasonable and in doing so applied the test devised by the UK Supreme Court in *Kennedy v Charity Commission*:

The court involved in the review will take the following steps: **3–40**

> (a) The identification of the legitimate objective(s) to be pursued by the restrictions;
> (b) Establishing a rational connection between the restriction and the achievement of one or more of those legitimate objectives; and
> (c) A proportionality test, namely that the restrictions must be a proportionate response, and must be no more than necessary to accomplish the legitimate purpose in question.[109]

The DRA, in finding the refusal to allow the player transfer to be unlawful, quashed the decision made by Antrim CCC. In relation to the wording of Bye-Law 15(1)(c), the DRA suggested an amendment be made to the wording to allow for more flexibility.[110] This case highlights the increased legalise employed by a disciplinary body. The UK Supreme Court case was of persuasive authority; however, it is the use of legal norms in the Tribunal hearing that is noteworthy. It highlights that the juridification applies in an amateur sport setting and not just professional sports. **3–41**

Re-Privatisation of Sport

Foster refers to *R v Barnes* as an example of the re-privatisation of sport.[111] Following a four- day trial in the Crown Court in Canterbury, Barnes was convicted of one count of unlawfully and maliciously inflicting grievous bodily harm under s 20 of the Offences of Person Act 1861.[112] Barnes was handed down a Community Punishment Order of 240 hours and was ordered to pay the victim, Bygraves, compensation amounting to £2,609, which would be paid over a period of time in weekly payments of £20.[113] The prosecution arose from a leg injury sustained by Bygraves, which was inflicted by Barnes at an amateur football game in December 2002. The prosecution successfully argued that it was a 'crushing tackle, **3–42**

---

[106] *O'Flionn* (n 103) [8] and [12].
[107] ibid [19].
[108] ibid [20].
[109] ibid [21].
[110] ibid [22].
[111] Foster (n 72) 7.
[112] [2004] EWCA Crim 3246.
[113] ibid [1].

which was late, unnecessary, reckless and high up the legs'.[114] Barnes appealed his conviction to the Court of Appeal (Criminal Division) and centred his appeal on seven grounds.[115] The Court of Appeal upheld the appeal and set aside Barnes' conviction. Foster describes the decision to overturn the conviction as signifying 'a strong statement of sporting autonomy'.[116] The Lord Chief Justice (LCJ) held:

> In determining what the approach of the courts should be, the starting point is the fact that most organised sports have their own disciplinary procedures for enforcing their particular rules and standards of conduct. As a result, in the majority of situations there is not only no need for criminal proceedings, it is undesirable that there should be any criminal proceedings. Further, in addition to a criminal prosecution, there is the possibility of an injured player obtaining damages in a civil action from another player, if that other player caused him injuries through negligence or an assault. The circumstances in which criminal and civil remedies are available can and do overlap. However, a criminal prosecution should be reserved for those situations where the conduct is sufficiently grave to be properly categorised as criminal.[117]

3–43 In an Irish context, the case of *Dundalk Racing* illustrates the reluctance of the Irish courts to intervene in sporting disputes and in doing so impliedly endorses the attitude of the English authorities in relation to the re-privatisation of sport.[118] Hogan J in the High Court established that the courts should only intervene in sporting matters that are 'exceptional involving something akin to fraud or manifest irrationality'.[119] The judge expanded on this by asserting that if the courts were to intervene in matters that fell below this threshold it would mean that

> the courts would have assumed a strange new jurisdiction which would test the traditional boundaries of justiciability, and, indeed, raise questions as to the appropriate judicial role in relation to such matters. Could, for example, the courts be expected to adjudicate on questions such as the handicapping of horses, competitor seedings, team selection or on-field disciplinary or refereeing decisions? Could it mean that the courts might subsequently be called upon to rule on questions such as whether a penalty ought to have been given or whether a player was properly sent off or even whether a point, goal or try (as the case may be) ought to have been awarded?[120]

3–44 Similarly, McGovern J in *O'Connell & Another v The Turf Club and Another*, noted that '[t]he courts in this jurisdiction and elsewhere have taken the view that the regulation of sporting activities should not, as a general

---

114 ibid [2].
115 This case is discussed in more detail in ch 4 paras 4–48, 4–49, 4–56, 4–57 and 4–60.
116 Foster (n 72) 7.
117 *Barnes* (n 112) [5].
118 *Hyland v Dundalk Racing (1999) Ltd t/a Dundalk Stadium* [2014] IEHC 60.
119 ibid [39].
120 ibid [40].

rule, come within the remit of judicial scrutiny but is best left to those organisations themselves'.[121]

On the one hand there has been an increase in the application of the law in relation to sport; however, on the other, the courts have exhibited a reluctance to intervene in matters which could be better resolved by the internal disciplinary mechanisms of that sport or by recourse to arbitration or mediation. In the words of Cox and others, the law 'should only intervene where it can be certain that it will be effective in doing so'.[122] The next part of the chapter considers whether the appropriate term is Sports Law or Sport and the Law and why sport is treated differently to other activities. **3–45**

Sports Law or Sport and the Law

At this juncture, it has been established that the law has a role to play in sporting disputes. However, the extent of that involvement is one that has attracted diverse academic opinions. In most situations the internal disciplinary mechanisms should be exhausted before the parties seek redress in the courts. Thus, it follows that the law should only intervene in the most exceptional of circumstances, as stated by Hogan J in *Dundalk Racing*, discussed above.[123] **3–46**

Before examining the differing views, it is important to distinguish Sports Law from Sport and the Law. In an Irish context, the most appropriate term is 'Sport and the Law'. The term 'Sport and the Law' reflects a more interdisciplinary approach. By using the term 'Sport and the Law', it contends that there is no separate identifiable body of law that currently relates to sport; however, it equally acknowledges that recent developments suggest that in the near future there will be a more substantive corpus of law pertaining to sport.[124] As the public law has intervened more in sporting matters, it has resulted in cases going before the courts. However, as discussed above, while the Irish courts have accepted jurisdiction for these cases, sports bodies and persons have been reminded that recourse to the courts is not always the most appropriate method of redress. For the foreseeable future, the term 'Sport and the Law' more appropriately reflects the situation in Ireland. **3–47**

Sports Law implies that there is a unique body of law that applies specifically to sport whereas Sport and the Law suggests an inter- **3–48**

---

121 The Supreme Court in *O'Connell & Lambe v Turf Club* [2015] IESC 57 upheld the decision of McGovern J. Of significance is O'Donnell J's discussion of the history of sport and the importance of the rules of sport, see [1]-[10].

122 Neville Cox and Alex Schuster (with Cathryn Costello), *Sport and the Law* (First Law 2004) 1.

123 *Hyland* (n 118).

124 See Timothy Davis, 'What is Sports Law?' (2001) 11 Marquette Sports Law Review 211.

disciplinary relationship between the law and sport. A situation may arise in a sporting context that requires reference to contract law, the law of torts, employment law, the criminal law, or EU law. In this situation, a recognised branch of law is being applied to a particular industry, that industry being sport. Some academic commentators have argued that 'sports law' is a 'misleading term' and 'in reality, sports law is nothing more or less than law as applied to the sports industry'.[125]

3–49 Beloff, Kerr and Demetriou in the first edition of their book, emphasised the need to define 'Sports Law' and contended that 'one must delineate its scope, however blurred its edges and however indistinct its outline'.[126] They cautiously defined Sports Law as

> a loose but increasingly cohesive body of rules governing the practice of sport and the resolution of disputes in law. That body of rules straddles the boundaries between many well-known branches of our law but has at its centre an unusual form of international constitutional principle prescribing the limited autonomy of non-governmental decision-making bodies in sport.[127]

3–50 Beloff, Kerr and Demetriou argued that sport should not be treated any differently to any other field of human activity and that legal rules and regulations should be applied without exception.[128] In the second edition of the book, Beloff and his co-authors offer a more authoritative definition and state that 'it is a body of rules governing the practice of sport and the resolution of disputes in law'.[129] They note that Sports Law is 'not a hermitically sealed, self-contained body of law' as '[i]t crosses boundaries'.[130]

3–51 Morris and Little, in contrast, see sport as having its own 'micro legal systems' due to its special characteristics, which validates the restraint of the legislature and judiciary from devising legal doctrines and procedures which may be employed to examine the determinations of sport governing bodies, thus interfering with their inherent functions.[131]

3–52 The Sport and the Law/Sports Law debate can be divided into three arguments.[132] The first position holds that there is no separate identifiable body of law that relates exclusively to sport and the possibility that

---

[125] Michael J Cozzillio and Mark S Levinstein, *Sports Law Cases and Materials* (Carolina Academic Press 1997) 5.
[126] Michael Beloff, Tim Kerr and Marie Demetriou, *Sports Law* (Hart Publishing 1999) para 1.5.
[127] ibid para 1.12.
[128] ibid para 1.8.
[129] Michael Beloff and others, *Sports Law* (2nd edn, Bloomsbury Publishing 2012) para 1.19.
[130] ibid para 1.18.
[131] Morris and Little (n 71) 129.
[132] Davis (n 124).

such a corpus of law will emerge in the future is extremely remote.[133] The second position contends that there is no separate identifiable body of law that currently relates to sport; however, as the public law has begun to intervene and this has resulted in cases being brought before the courts, it is predicted that in the near future a substantive corpus of law pertaining to sport will emerge.[134] The third position asserts that there is a body of law that can be referred to as Sports Law.[135]

The first approach reflects the traditional view that there is no specific branch of law that applies exclusively to sport.[136] Traditionalists argue that the term Sports Law is misleading as sport as an activity and form of entertainment is governed by the overarching legal system.[137] It is superfluous to contend that there is a body of law that can be designated as Sports Law. Sports Law is seen as the application of basic legal rules to a particular industry, the industry being sport. 3–53

The second approach encapsulates a more moderate view. Academic commentators including Professor Kenneth Shropshire see Sports Law as developing into a field of law in the future.[138] Shropshire refers to state and federal legislation in the US which has impacted on sport, from the regulation of sports agents to anti-discrimination under Title IX of the Education Amendments Act 1972.[139] Shropshire considers the term Sport and the Law as the appropriate term as he posits that there is a 'growing sports-only corpus of law'.[140] The moderates see Sports Law as an emerging field of law which will develop into its own substantive branch of law in the future. Weisart and Lowell support the view that Sports Law is a field of study. They point to the anomalies that exist, ie in some situations a specific provision may apply to sport and nowhere else.[141] For example, baseball in the United States (US) is exempt from anti-trust legislation.[142] Sport permits peculiarities, including the 3–54

133 ibid 211.
134 ibid.
135 ibid.
136 ibid 212.
137 ibid.
138 'Introduction: Sports Law?' (1998) 35 American Business Law Journal 181, 182.
139 Title 20 USC Sections 1681–1688. This Act banned sex discrimination in schools. The prohibition applies to education and athletics.
140 Shropshire (n 138) 182. See also Hayden Opie, who contends that '"Sports law" is one of those fields of law which is applied law as opposed to pure or theoretical law. Rather than being a discipline with a common legal theme such as criminal law, equity or contract law, sports law is concerned with how law in general interacts with the activity known as sport. Hence, the label "applied law". Yet there is an increasing body of law which is specific to sport', see 'Sport and the law implications for the nonprofit corporation' (1993) Queensland University of Technology, Brisbane, Qld [Working Paper No 29] 2-3 <https://eprints.qut.edu.au/53166/1/29_Opie.pdf> accessed 30 September 2024.
141 Cym H Weistart and John C Lowell, *The Law of Sports* (Bobbs-Merrill 1979) xviii.
142 Under the Sherman Act 1890 and the Clayton Act 1914 any business that operates across state borders and participates in interstate commerce is subject to anti-trust legislation. In 1922, an exemption was given to baseball. The Supreme Court

segregation of men and women in competitions, which would ordinarily constitute sex discrimination, and consequently these peculiarities require the unique application of legal principles.[143]

3–55 The third approach sees Sports Law as a separate field of law. Proponents argue that sport is being marginalised and is not being treated like other forms of business.[144] Sport is viewed more as entertainment and this perception has resulted in it being considered less serious than other forms of business. There is a great reluctance among the traditionalists to recognise sport as being the subject matter of legal relationships.[145] Given its peculiarities, its uniqueness, the growing body of cases and commentary, proponents of the third category hold that Sports Law has become a separate body of law.

3–56 Lewis and Taylor contend that the distinction between Sports Law and Sport and the Law 'is an issue of academic rather than practical interest'.[146] However, the authors concede that they 'share the belief of many writers in the field that in at least some areas, for example where international institutions such as the CAS review the decisions of sports governing bodies, a separate and distinct body of law inspired by general principles of law common to all states is in the process of development'.[147]

3–57 Barnes asserts that 'the proliferation of sports legislation, litigation and arbitral decisions has led to some special doctrine'.[148] This is true in respect to countries such as Australia, England and Wales, and Canada; however, in an Irish context, Sports Law is still in embryonic form. Thus, as noted, the more appropriate term here is Sport and the Law. The current situation in Ireland would fall under the second category, the moderate view wherein it is a developing area and in the future a corpus of case law and legislation may well be created and in turn, a special doctrine emerge. The development of Sports Law has been aided by the EU and its involvement in sport. In referring to the situation in England and Wales, Gardiner and others proclaim: 'As an area of academic study and extensive practitioner involvement, the time

---

held that baseball was exempt from the Sherman and Clayton Acts in the case of *Federal Baseball Club of Baltimore, Inc v National Baseball Clubs* 259 US 200 (1922) 259 US 200. The Supreme Court ruled that even though there was scheduling of games across state lines, those games were intrastate events, as the travel from one state to another was 'not the essential thing'. See John W Neville, 'Baseball and the Antitrust Laws' (1947) 16 Fordham Law Review 208.

143 Cozzillio and Levinstein (n 125) 214 and Weistart and Lowell (n 141) xviii–xix.

144 Davis (n 124) 215.

145 ibid. Similarly, marriage is a social relationship, yet it is governed by legal rules.

146 Adam Lewis and Jonathan Taylor (eds), *Sport: Law and Practice* (Butterworths 2003) preface.

147 Adam Lewis and Jonathan Taylor (eds), *Sport: Law and Practice* (2nd edn, Bloomsbury 2008) vii.

148 John Barnes, *Sports and the Law in Canada* (Butterworths 1996) 2.

is right to accept that a new legal area has been born and is thriving in the "bloom of its youth" – *viva* sports law.'[149]

When Should the Law Intervene into Sporting Matters?

Cox and others see sport and law as 'natural enemies' as sport is 'idealistic and ethereal' and thus 'above the crude machinations of the law'.[150] The authors are realistic and admit that there are times when the law should get involved in sporting disputes; however, the question is not when the law should intervene but to what extent should the law involve itself in sporting matters.[151] In most cases, decisions should be left to the sports governing bodies. Consequently, sports bodies should not be subjected 'to the dogmatic formalities associated with the law'.[152] Sport is a multi-billion-euro industry and, like other industries, it needs to be regulated by the law as it is just as prone to irresponsible business decisions and corruption as any other industry.[153] Thus, the law 'should only intervene where it can be certain that it will be effective in doing so' – for example, if there is a reckless tackle and serious injury ensues and the internal disciplinary mechanisms of the sport are ill-equipped to deal with the gravity of the situation, this may constitute an assault and warrant the application of the criminal law.[154] **3–58**

Lord Denning, the Master of the Rolls (MR), in the case of *Enderby Town Football Club Ltd v Football Association Ltd* highlighted the reticence of the law to intervene in the determinations of sporting bodies.[155] He remarked, in relation to domestic tribunals that operate informally and lack legal representation, that **3–59**

> justice can often be done in them better by a good layman than a bad lawyer. This is especially so in activities like football and other sports, where no points of law are likely to arise, and it is all part of the proper regulation of the game.[156]

---

149 Simon Gardiner and others, *Sports Law* (4th edn, Routledge 2012) 86.
150 Cox and others (n 122) 1.
151 ibid.
152 ibid.
153 ibid.
154 ibid 3.
155 [1971] 1 Ch 591. See also the comments of Vice-Chancellor Megarry in *McInnes v Onslow-Fane* [1978] 1 WLR 1520, 1535 where he held the sports governing body to be 'far better fitted to judge than courts'.
156 [1971] 1 Ch 591, 605. Enderby Town was fined and censured by its county association, which was affiliated to the English Football Association (FA). It appealed the decision to the FA; however, at the FA hearing, the club was told that it could not have legal representation at the hearing as provided for under r 38(b) unless the chairman or secretary of the club was a lawyer. Enderby Town sought an injunction restraining the FA from holding the appeal without the club having a lawyer present, however, Foster J refused to grant the injunction and the matter was appealed to the Court of Appeal. The Court of Appeal dismissed the appeal and held that r 38(b) was not in contravention of natural justice. An organisation

3–60 However, Lord Denning cautioned that he 'would emphasise that the discretion must be properly exercised. The tribunal must not fetter its discretion by rigid bonds.'[157]

3–61 In the case of the *Australian Football League v Carlton Football Club Limited*, Tadgell J of the Supreme Court of Victoria recognised that there are some situations where the courts should not intervene in the decisions of sports governing bodies.[158] However, he continued that governing bodies are not above the law and, if the justice of the case so demands, the courts should be willing to intervene:

> Statutes aside, the courts have been disposed to interfere in a limited way with decisions of private or domestic tribunals in order to protect private rights that have been adjudged to deserve protection, including rights in property. The concept of property has been broadly interpreted for this purpose and, in cases within that category, I believe that there is no decision of a private or domestic tribunal with which the courts will refuse to interfere if interference be considered necessary for the attainment of justice.[159]

3–62 These cases demonstrate the willingness of the courts to hear sports disputes; however, the courts are at times reluctant to intervene in the decisions of domestic tribunals. The domestic tribunal has been created with the sport in mind and those who run the sport have been entrusted with the power to adjudicate disputes. In most disputes, the internal disciplinary procedures should be used and exhausted and only in the most exceptional of circumstances should recourse be made to the courts. As Chapter 12 discusses, an increasing number of sportspersons and bodies are seeking redress through the CAS, a sport-centric arbitral body.

3–63 It is generally accepted that the law should be involved in sport; however, the extent of its involvement has resulted in academic discourse. There are varying opinions on when the law should intervene and when decisions should be left to the internal disciplinary mechanisms of the sport. It is to the views of Grayson, Cox and others and Gardiner and others that the chapter now turns.

3–64 Gardiner and others and Grayson have very different views on the role of law in sport. Gardiner and others proffer that the law should only become involved in the most exceptional of circumstances. Grayson

---

could set up a domestic tribunal that did not allow for legal representation. Lord Justice (LJ) Cairns added that the use of lawyers would protract the proceedings and would be costly and he did not think that it would yield a fairer decision.

157 (n 155) 605.

158 [1998] VR 546. This case concerned an application for judicial review by a player who was suspended for nine matches by the Australian Football League (AFL) Tribunal.

159 ibid 549–50.

contends that the intervention of the law into the sport realm was a positive development and Cox and others occupy a midway position in that they assert that the law has a role in sport but should only become involved when it is certain that it will be effective in doing so.

Grayson, a barrister who specialised in sports litigation, is often referred to as the inventor of sport and the law.[160] He viewed the intervention of the law in the regulation of sport as a positive thing. Grayson wrote: **3–65**

> the law can and should come to the help of sport; and indeed, ... sport with its high profile and image can come to the help of the law. For sport without rules and their control creates chaos. Society without laws and their enforcement means anarchy.[161]

Grayson was inspired by the old Corinthian ideal of fair play, where sportspersons excelled through their own endeavours and where the rules of the sport were respected.[162] He argued that **3–66**

> if sport and its rulers cannot or will not try to preserve that Corinthian tradition ... then the courts can and will do it for them, through the law of the land at both criminal and civil levels and certainly if adequate compensation is required.[163]

Grayson refers to sporting history and the sportsmanship that epitomised amateur sport in the mid-1950s.[164] The genesis of Sport and the Law can be traced back to the early post-War period when the Corinthian ideals of fair play, self-discipline, health and education were espoused by members of the Association of Football Players' and Trainers' Union (now the Professional Footballers' Association).[165] Modern sport is, according to Grayson, beset by violence and ungentlemanly behaviour. Grayson refers to several sportspersons, including Gary Lineker, David Gower, and Lawrence Dallaglio, as examples of post-War sportspersons who embody the Corinthian ideal. Gardiner and others are not persuaded by Grayson's arguments. Gardiner and others see the Corinthian ideal as being intertwined with class. The sportspersons that emerged in the 1900s and personified the Corinthian ideal were all from upper-class backgrounds who received their education in public schools.[166] Their background and subsequent entry into the professions, including law, education and medicine, instilled in them a respect for the **3–67**

---

160 Grayson published the first edition of his book in 1988: see *Sport and the Law* (Butterworths 1988).

161 Edward Grayson, *Sport and the Law* (2nd edn, Butterworths 1994) vii.

162 Edward Grayson, 'Sport and the Law: A Return to Corinthian Values' (1998) 6(1) Sport and the Law Journal 5; Edward Grayson, *Sport and the Law* (3rd edn, Butterworths 2000).

163 Grayson (n 161) xxxvi.

164 Grayson 2000 (n 162) 65.

165 ibid.

166 Gardiner and others (n 149) 70.

laws and spirit of sport.[167] The writer and academic CB Fry, best known for his career as a cricketer, in reference to the cricketer RE ('Tip') Foster, remarked that 'his feet had, as it were, the Oxford accent'.[168] In support of the nexus between the Corinthian ideal and class, Porter observes:

> It is not easy to discern exactly what contemporary references to the Corinthian spirit implied beyond playing the game for its own sake in a manner which reflected creditably on gentlemen who had enjoyed the benefits of a good school and one or other of the ancient universities.[169]

3–68 It would seem that Grayson's utopian view is at variance with historical accounts of sport. Violence and competitiveness are not only synonymous with today's sports. Gardiner and others note that in the past sports were rife with violence, secularism, partisanism and competitiveness and thus they question whether the Corinthian ideal ever existed in the manner Grayson suggests.[170] The Corinthian values of fair play and the love of participation are still relevant in modern sports, but these values are largely confined to amateur and recreational sports.[171] Fair play and the joy of participation in competitive sport, while noble virtues, are not the instigating factors for involvement in modern competitive and elite sports.[172] The professionalisation and commercialisation of sport has resulted in the nature of sport becoming increasingly complicated and beset by legal rules and regulations. In short, Grayson believes that the intervention of the law is necessary, given the increased commercialisation of sport. In 1993, Grayson co-wrote a response to an article written by Gardiner, both of which were published in the *Solicitors Journal*.[173] Gardiner proffered that the criminal law should not intervene in alleged assaults on the playing field.[174] Grayson and Bond's rebuttal centred on their belief that the law should not stop at the touchline. While the article specifically referred to the involvement of the criminal law in sport, Grayson believed that both the private and public law should apply to sport.

3–69 The state has been involved in the regulation of sport for centuries and its involvement varied from preserving men for the King's army, to preventing drinking and gambling at Sunday sports, to preventing the lower-classes from hunting on royal land. Thus, the intervention of the state in sporting matters is not a recent development. However, in

---

[167] ibid.

[168] Charles Burgess Fry, *Life Worth Living: Some Phases of an Englishman* (Ian Allen 1957) 27. See also Adrian Smith and Dilwyn Porter (eds), *Amateurs and Professionals in Post-War British Sport* (Routledge 2014).

[169] Dilwyn Porter, 'Amateur Football in England, 1948–1963: The Pegasus Phenomenon' (2000) 14(2) Contemporary British History 1, 1–2.

[170] Gardiner and others (n 149) 71.

[171] ibid.

[172] ibid.

[173] Edward Grayson and Catherine Bond, 'Making Foul Play a Crime' (1993) 137(27) Solicitors Journal 693.

[174] 'Not Playing the Game: Is It a Crime?' (1993) 137(25) Solicitors Journal 628.

more recent times the law is becoming more involved in the regulation of all aspects of sport[175]; testament to this is the growing academic commentary,[176] specific legislation,[177] cases, and law firms specialising in sport and the law. Gardiner and others recognise that the law has a role to play; however, it should only intervene in the most exceptional circumstances. The writers contend that sport should be largely self-regulated and there should be what they refer to as a 'sporting autonomy' whereby 'outside regulation and law should not intrude'.[178] There are situations when the law should be involved: for example, in a situation where an athlete had been unfairly treated by their governing body. In this situation, recourse to the law should be a last resort. All the internal disciplinary mechanisms of the sport should first be exhausted before an individual or governing body seeks the invention of the law.[179] There are situations where the governing body is best equipped to deal with a problem. Ben Flower is an example where a lengthy suspension was imposed on a rugby player for a violent outburst during a match. Flower played for Wigan and two minutes into the final of the Super League, he double punched his opponent Lance Hohaia of St Helens. An independent disciplinary tribunal fined Flower £300 and banned him for six months or 13 matches for Grade F violent and aggressive punching.[180] The Rugby Football League issued the following statement:

> At the tribunal the player acknowledged that his actions were unacceptable and expressed shame for the effect the incident had had on everybody. The tribunal panel accepted that Flower had been provoked by a challenge from his opponent but took the view that his actions were malicious, intentional and had the potential for serious injury.[181]

Flower had a relatively clean disciplinary record and spoke of his shame over the incident.[182] This is an example where the intervention of the law may well have been a blunt instrument. In this situation, the 3–70

---

175 Laws regulating football agents, media rights, personal injuries, liability of stadium owners, liability of equipment manufacturers, liability of referees, assault cases, for example.

176 Numerous books and specific journals: for example, the *Journal of Sport and the Law, Sports Law Administration and Practice*, the *Marquette Sports Law Review*, to name but a few.

177 For example, the Sport Ireland Act 2015.

178 Gardiner and others (n 149) 73.

179 The internal disciplinary procedures do not require involvement of the courts, solicitors, or barristers. It is less costly and more expeditious.

180 James Riach, 'Wigan's Ben Flower Banned for Six Months after Grand Final Punches' *The Guardian* (London, 14 October 2014) <https://www.theguardian.com/sport/2014/oct/14/ben-flower-wigan-st-helens-six-month-ban> accessed 8 May 2024.

181 ibid.

182 Jonathan Liew, 'Ben Flower Could Face Life Ban from Rugby for Vicious Assault on Lance Hohaia in Super League Grand Final' *The Telegraph* (London, 13 October 2014) <https://www.telegraph.co.uk/sport/rugbyleague/11160241/Ben-Flower-could-face-life-ban-from-rugby-for-vicious-assault-on-Lance-Hohaia-in-Super-League-Grand-Final.html> accessed 1 July 2024.

imposition of a lengthy suspension by an independent tribunal has more of a deterrent on violent play than a criminal case wherein the player is fined a week's wages and receives a suspended sentence. An interesting comment was made by the Chairman of St Helen's, Eamonn McManus, about the role of the sport in supporting players in the aftermath of a ban:

> These matters have to be dealt with by the appropriate body within the game and it has so been ... Whilst serving his ban it is critical that Ben is now provided all due personal and professional support. His rehabilitation is now paramount. During the period of his ban he will be no more than a 25-year-old boy who will be extremely vulnerable emotionally. We must assist him in any way that we can and accept him back into the sport. There is a person behind the player, and I am reliably informed by all that it is a good one. He must know that from all. Lance Hohaia certainly feels that way towards him also ... The sport of Rugby League should not be judged by this event, but by how it deals with it.[183]

3–71 Cox and others highlight the flaws in the arguments raised by Grayson and Gardiner and others. The debate centres on whether the law of self-regulation will improve a sport (Gardiner and others) or whether some form of external control would be more beneficial (Grayson).[184] Cox and others note that there are also public policy considerations. While the interests of sport are important, it is also in the public interest that violence on the field is dissuaded, that an injured athlete has in interest in seeking redress if the injury sustained ends their career, and that anti-competitive practices are prohibited.

What makes sport different to other human-led activities?

3–72 Beloff and others add an interesting dimension to the debate. They make the point that some areas of life are regulated by the law, while others are not.[185] For example, air travel and sea travel are regulated by aviation and shipping law, respectively. However, gardening, flower arranging and cooking are all human activities not governed by any legal principles.[186] The writers argue that something more than the existence of law is needed to justify the term 'sports law'.[187] In support of this argument, the writers note that other areas of human life are regulated by law, for example the law of trusts and tort law.[188] Both the law of trusts and tort law contain legal rules that encapsulate rights and obligations 'which apply irrespective of the subject matter of the particular case in which they are relevant'.[189] The law of trusts and

183 News, 'Saints Issue Statement' 14 October 2014 <https://www.saintsrlfc.com/2014/10/14/saints-issue-statement/> accessed 1 July 2024.
184 Cox and others (n 122) 3.
185 Beloff and others (n 129) xxvii.
186 ibid.
187 ibid.
188 ibid.
189 ibid.

tort can be termed 'horizontal law' (rule-led law), whereas categories of law that are defined by reference to human activity can be termed 'vertical law'.[190] In using this distinction, we can place the relationship between sport and law as a human-led activity under the category of vertical law. Activities under this category are not distinct areas of law but borrow their content from rule-led branches of law such as tort, contract, criminal, and trusts.[191] If a sportsperson breaches a term of a contract, the applicable law is contract law, as there is no specific Sports Law that would apply here.

Sport is different to other industries or businesses. Sport has existed since antiquity and its importance has survived. Sport is an important leisure activity and, as Beloff and others note, sport 'is a primary and atavistic form of self-expression'.[192] Sport is also international in nature. The commercialisation of sport has resulted in international competition. There is a huge international public interest in sport. A form of international law relating to sport has emerged.[193] The relationship between sport and the law is also non-governmental, which again distinguishes it from other areas of life that are subject to law. Sport enjoys certain privileges that would not be permitted in other industries, such as the segregation male and female athletes in events. 3–73

As discussed in Chapter 4, when it comes to contact sports and on-field violence, the criminal law is reluctant to intervene. The courts have broadened the definition of consent to include the playing culture. Sportspersons do not just consent to injuries that may result from playing the game by the rules but also what is deemed to be incidental to the playing of the game by the rules. The standard of proof 'to the comfortable satisfaction of the panel' is often used by disciplinary bodies and the CAS. This standard is also used by the WADA in the World Anti-Doping Code (WADC). The standard lies above the balance of probabilities but below beyond reasonable doubt. 3–74

These peculiarities differentiate sport from other sectors and thus justify its special treatment. However, such peculiarities do not seem to embody the professionalisation of sport. Cox and others issue a word of caution: 'as long as the consequences of professionalisation are *not* fully appreciated, the law will find sport to be a fertile ground for *its* business'.[194] 3–75

---

190 ibid.
191 ibid.
192 ibid xxviii.
193 For example, see James Nafziger (ed), *Transnational Law of Sports* (Edward Elgar 2013); James Nafziger, *International Sports Law* (2nd edn, Transnational Publishers 2004).
194 Cox and others (n 122) 5.

Conclusion

3–76 This chapter has shown that sport, although considered an industry, is treated differently from other industries as sport occupies a very special position in society. As described by Haynes, 'Sport is a microcosm of society.'[195] The intervention of the law into the sporting realm has caused much debate. Some academic commentators favour the interference of the law and see such intervention as a positive step; others are of the view that sport is a private matter that should be exempt from the intrusion of the law except in the most exceptional of circumstances. It is not just the application of the law of the land to sport that has caused much debate, the actual term for such a branch of law has caused a rift between academic writers. Some purist lawyers argue that there is no such area as Sport and the Law or Sports Law; others argue that Sport and the Law or Sports Law is not a discrete area of law but rather borrows its content from the more established areas of law, including contract, tort, and criminal law. Sports Law implies that there is a distinct body of law that pertains to sport. Sport and the Law is a more moderate term, while recognising the application of the law to sport, it posits that there is no distinct body of law relating to sport now but with time it could develop into a specific branch of law. In an Irish context, Sport and the Law is the more appropriate term as it recognises the cultural, political, and social importance of sport but also recognises that the law has a role to play. The matter of the appropriate terminology aside, the law should intervene in the sporting realm, albeit in exceptional circumstances.

3–77 While the courts have been willing to encroach upon the determinations of sports governing bodies, they have highlighted the need for the internal disciplinary mechanisms of the sport to be exhausted before coming before the courts. Indeed, what the discussion has demonstrated is that there has been a re-privatisation of sport as seen in decisions from the courts in England and Wales and Ireland.

3–78 The law and its application to sport transcends boundaries. It is global and international in nature. There are specific laws that relate to the country that hosts the Olympics, *lex Olympica*, and the CAS has developed its own corpus of law that is referred to as *lex sportiva*. There is also the regulation of sport at EU level and the creation of sports-specific legislation, for example, the Sport Ireland Act 2015.

3–79 There is no legal definition of a sport: however, what can be gleaned from the discussion is that a sport must have a physical element and be socially acceptable. While esports encompass a physical element, it is not currently considered a Summer or Winter Olympic sport. However, current trends, such as the Olympic Esports Series 2023, suggest that it might be in the future.

---

[195] Jason Haynes, 'Sport, Sexual Violence and the Law: A Feminist Critique and Call to Action' (2023) 23 The International Sports Law Journal 99, 99.

Recourse to the law should be seen as a last resort and should only be used when all the internal mechanisms of the sport have been exhausted and it can be sure that the dispute will be effectively dealt with by the courts. The following chapters will demonstrate the law's involvement in sporting disputes, from violence in sport to the constitutional and human rights issues arising from drug testing and the involvement of the EU. The legal relationship between sport and the law is both complex and sometimes unclear. Beginning with a discussion on violence in sport, Chapter 4 will examine the role of the criminal law in dealing with participator violence on the field of play. **3–80**

CHAPTER 4

CRIMINAL LAW AND SPORT

Introduction

This chapter will examine the application of the criminal law to sport, in particular on-field violence. Violence in sport can attract either criminal or civil liability, or indeed both. The evidentiary requirements differ under the criminal and civil law, with the standard of proof under the criminal law being beyond reasonable doubt, the lower standard of the balance of probabilities applying in civil cases. If a sportsperson is injured by reason of an intentional, deliberate, or reckless infliction of harm, the offender may be charged under the criminal law. There may also be a civil suit whereby the injured sportsperson seeks monetary compensation for the injury sustained. **4–01**

It is accepted that in contact sports there will be a significant degree of contact between participants; equally, cognisance is given to the fact that this will vary from contact sport to contact sport. The nature of the sport is a crucial factor: for example, what is acceptable in boxing would not be permitted in rugby. In most cases where a participant is injured, even seriously injured, criminal liability will not attach due to the defence of consent. However, a sportsperson does not consent to the intentional, deliberate, or reckless infliction of harm. As will be discussed in this chapter, the parameters of the defence of consent have evolved over the years to include what is referred to as the 'playing culture'. Sportspersons consent not only to injuries that may be sustained by playing the sport by the rules but also what is incidental to the playing of the game by the rules of the sport. This has effectively broadened the definition of consent. **4–02**

Most infractions of the rules of the game or sport are dealt with by the internal disciplinary mechanisms of the sport or league. The case law suggests that only incidents of excessive violence will be subject to the criminal law. For more trivial infringements of the rules, self-regulation by the sporting bodies will continue to be the more popular and effective method of dealing with on-field violence. **4–03**

This chapter will examine how the criminal law has been applied to on-field violence and the distinction between lawful and unlawful assaults. It will look at the Non-Fatal Offences Against the Person Act 1997 and the definition of assault. The defence of consent, including the playing culture and other defences, will be discussed. It will proceed to evaluate how the Irish courts have addressed the issue of on-field violence by **4–04** reflecting on a number of cases involving the Gaelic Athletic Association (GAA). The chapter will proceed to discuss the approach of the English courts to on-field violence. The chapter will conclude with a discussion on the legality of boxing and Mixed Martial Arts (MMA).

Criminal Liability and the Standard of Proof

4–05 This chapter will focus on criminal liability and the next chapter will examine civil liability. At this juncture, it is important to briefly distinguish a crime from a tort. A tort is a civil wrong that arises from a breach of a private duty. In contrast, a crime is defined as a wrong arising from a violation of a public duty. In a criminal case, it is the Director of Public Prosecutions (DPP) in Ireland or the Crown (Rex or Regina) in England and Wales that brings the case against the defendant, the victim is a mere witness in the proceedings.[1] In a tort case, the injured party (the plaintiff) brings the action against the tortfeasor (the person who has committed a tort). The primary remedy under tort is monetary compensation or damages. In a criminal case, the offender faces a conviction and a custodial or non-custodial sentence. In a criminal case, the standard of proof is beyond reasonable doubt and if in doubt, the defendant must be acquitted. In a civil case, the standard is on the balance of probabilities. At the start of the case, the scales of justice are balanced as each party is level. However, as the cases progresses, the left and right side of the scales are no longer aligned and begin to tip in favour of one side. Given that the defendant in a criminal case may lose their liberty, the standard is much higher than the tort standard.

When Will the Criminal Law Intervene in Sporting Assaults?

4–06 In most instances of on-field violence, violent play is usually dealt with by the referee. In other situations, the club or league may discipline the player in the form of a suspension or fine. A player consents to injuries which are reasonably foreseeable hazards of the sport.[2] In fast-

---

1 In Ireland when a crime is reported to An Garda Siochana, the gardaí will investigate the alleged crime and, depending on the investigation and evidence gathered, a decision will be made whether to arrest the suspect. If the allegation relates to a serious crime, the gardaí will send on the file to the DPP and the DPP will decide whether to prosecute or not. If the crime is less serious, it is the gardaí that make the decision to prosecute or not; however, the case is still taken in the name of the DPP. In this situation the gardaí are guided by the DPP and the DPP retains 'the right to tell the Gardaí how to deal with the case': Director of Public Prosecutions, 'Investigation' <https://www.dppireland.ie/criminal-justice-system/investigation/> accessed 8 May 2024.

2 Although not a criminal case, this case is interesting as the judge referred to inherent dangers involved in sport. In the case of *Baldwin v Foy and Forest Way Riding Holidays Ltd* [1997] IEHC 111 (1st July 1997), the plaintiff was awarded damages for injuries sustained at an equestrian centre. Laffoy J acknowledged that horse riding is a risky sport and 'the Plaintiff in participating in this sport accepted the normal hazards and dangers inherent in it' [16]. The High Court had

paced and robust contact sports, it is very difficult to ascribe intent to the conduct of a player. Criminal prosecutions in sporting assaults are rare due to the issue of consent and because injuries can occur in the 'heat of the moment'.[3] In the United States (US), for example, there is a marked reluctance to bring criminal cases, as the encroachment of the criminal law can be seen as curbing the vigour of certain contact sports due to participators fearing prosecution.[4] The US courts have demonstrated a reluctance to convict athletes and in response, legislatures endeavoured to introduce specific legislation on sports violence, including the federal Sports Violence Act 1980 – however, this act and others have never become law.[5] The Sports Violence Act 1980 purported to amend the

> Federal criminal code to establish a maximum penalty of one year's imprisonment and/or a $5,000 fine for any player in a professional sports event who knowingly uses excessive physical force and causes risk of significant bodily injury to another person involved in such event.[6]

Most sportspersons are reluctant to have the authorities initiate charges against an opponent as to do so may be considered unsportspersonlike or may be deemed to be letting the team down. Sports cases present evidentiary problems as it is difficult to prove the *mens rea* (the mental element) or intent on the part of the defendant.[7] Also, the issue of consent is an important factor. When an individual joins a sports club, they agree to be bound by the rules of that club. Typically, disputes are submitted to the internal disciplinary mechanisms of the sport. When an individual plays a contact sport, it is reasonably foreseeable that they will sustain an injury, as contact sports by their very nature involve contact between the players. Individuals consent to inherent risks that are associated with the sport. However, there are limits to what an individual can consent to, as will be discussed in this chapter.[8] **4–07**

---

to determine whether the defendants had exposed Ms Baldwin to a reasonably foreseeable risk 'but which is not normally inherent in undergoing instruction in cross-country riding in an equestrian centre' [16]. The judge found the defendants had failed in their duty of care owed to the plaintiff and were negligent.

3 This chapter focuses on criminal liability in relation to on-field violence. The criminal law can apply in other ways, including match fixing, illegal gambling pertaining to a match and the use of illegal drugs by sportspersons.

4 Jeff Yates and William Gillespie, 'The Problem of Sports Violence and the Criminal Prosecution Problem' (2002–2003) 12 Cornell Journal of Law & Public Policy 145. The authors note that, while prosecutions and civil litigation are low, nevertheless 'society is willing to hold sports participants accountable for their actions': 146. Some critics refer to violence in sport and its societal effects, including the influence on children and spectators: see 150–51.

5 Jeffrey Standen, 'The Manly Sports: The Problematic Use of Criminal Law to Regulate Sports Violence' (2009) 99 (3) Journal of Criminal Law and Criminology 619, 638.

6 HR 7903 – Sports Violence Act of 1980, 96th Congress (1979–1980) <https://www.congress.gov/bill/96th-congress/house-bill/7903?s=1&r=4> accessed 8 May 2024.

7 As many incidents arise in the heat of the moment in a fast-paced contact sport, it may be an arduous task to prove that the opponent deliberately or recklessly intended to injure the victim.

8 Paul McCutcheon, 'Sports Violence and Consent and the Criminal Law' (1994)

4–08 The case law demonstrates that the criminal law will intervene if a player intentionally or recklessly injures an opponent, and the violent act is beyond that which is ordinarily incidental to the playing of the game.[9] In *R v Leclerc*, the accused was charged with aggravated assault after cross-checking his opponent in a non-contact game of hockey.[10] The opponent collided with the boards and suffered a spinal injury resulting in permanent paralysis. The accused was acquitted by the trial court and the Attorney General appealed to the Court of Appeal for Ontario. Lacourciere J, in delivering the judgment, held:

> The weight of judicial authority appears to be that a player, by participating in a sport such as hockey, impliedly consents to some bodily contact necessarily incidental to the game, but not to overly violent attacks, all of which should be determined according to objective criteria.[11]

4–09 The referee described the incident as 'vicious' and 'deliberate'. However, the Court of Appeal viewed the actions of Leclerc as 'an instinctive reflex reaction' that was employed in order 'to avoid a more dreaded contact'.[12] While acknowledging that Leclerc's action violated the rules of the Canadian Amateur Hockey Association (CAHA), 'it lacked malicious design'.[13] The courts have adopted a broad definition of what constitutes ordinarily incidental to the playing of the game 'to include gratuitous fighting', which according to White 'makes a mockery of the entire test'.[14] Implied consent and the broad definition given to 'incidental' has meant that to a large extent, sport is immunised from the intervention of the criminal law so long as the actions of the defendant are not reckless, intentional, deliberate or malicious.

4–10 The latitude given to sport when it comes to on-field violence should not be seen as 'a licence for thuggery'.[15] Anderson notes that the criminal law will intervene in certain situations as 'no particular segment of society, even one adjudged to have a high social value such as sport, should be

---

45(3) Northern Ireland Legal Quarterly 267, 267 notes: 'there is a point beyond which the consent of the participation in sport is considered immaterial and the conduct is treated as unlawful'.

9 Diane V White, 'Sports Violence as Criminal Assault: Development of the Doctrine by Canadian Courts' (1986) 6 Duke Law Journal 1030, 1054.

10 *R v Leclerc*, 1991 CanLII 7389 (ON CA) <https://canlii.ca/t/g129w> accessed 8 May 2024. The rules of the Canadian Amateur Hockey Association (CAHA) precluded bodily contact.

11 ibid.

12 ibid. It is interesting to note that the Court held: 'While the "no contact" rule is relevant in determining the scope of implied consent, it is not by itself determinative of the issue.'

13 ibid. *Leclerc* was more recently cited in the case of *R v Bugayong* [2018] ONCJ 707 (CanLII) <https://canlii.ca/t/hvjzr> accessed 8 May 2024.

14 White (n 9) 1040. The author gives the example of *R v Henderson* [1976] 5 WWR, 119, 123 (BC Co Ct 1976), where the judge held that 'fighting is part of the game of hockey'.

15 Jack Anderson, 'No Licence for Thuggery: Violence, Sport and the Criminal Law' (2008) 10(10) Criminal Law Review 751.

permitted to commit crime with impunity'.[16] In a similar vein, Hechter contends that 'criminal liability for an athlete's actions should not stop as a player leaves the realm of ordinary citizen and enters the realm of athletic competition'.[17]

The law is more likely to intervene if the sport's governing body or league seems passive when it comes to on-field violence. In 1985 Leigh Matthews was captaining his team, the Hawthorns, in a Victorian Football League (VFL) match against Geelong.[18] He broke his opponent's jaw in an off-the ball incident. There was no incident report as the assault took place out of the view of the match officials.[19] As a result, Matthews was not sanctioned by the VFL. Due to television replays showing the incident, the VFL was pressurised into disciplining Matthews and charging him with 'conduct unbecoming'.[20] Matthews was brought before the VFL Commission and was de-registered for four matches. A few days later, he was charged with grievous bodily harm. At the Melbourne Magistrates Court, Matthews was convicted of assault causing harm and fined $1,000.[21] On appeal, his conviction was overturned, and he was granted a 12-month good-behaviour bond.[22] In 2018, there was much public outcry following the actions of Andrew Gaff who punched his opponent in the face, fracturing his jaw. The Australian Football League (AFL) Tribunal suspended Gaff for eight matches.[23] Anderson asserts that while the 'criminal law should always be the last resort for on-field violence', he is nevertheless critical of the inaction by the police, which gave the impression that contact sports **4–11**

---

16 Jack Anderson, 'Law and a New Order' *The Sunday Tribune* (Dublin, 16 November 2008).

17 William Hechter, 'The Criminal Law and Violence in Sports' (1979) 19(3–4) Criminal Law Quarterly 425, 425.

18 Jon Pierik, 'Matthews Charge "Still Mystery"' *The Age* (Melbourne, 30 July 2013 <https://www.theage.com.au/sport/afl/matthews-charge-still-mystery-20130729-2quxt.html> accessed 8 May 2024.

19 James J Paterson, 'Discipling Athletes for Off-Field Discretions: A Comparative Review of the Australian Football League and the National Football League's Personal Conduct Policies' (2009) 4(1) Australian and New Zealand Sports Law Journal 105, 118.

20 Pierik (n 18). For a brief history and explanation of 'conduct unbecoming', see Peter Ryan, 'Rule-Breakers: A Short History of "Conduct Unbecoming"' 13 August 2013 <https://www.afl.com.au/news/450386/rule-breakers-a-short-history-of-conduct-unbecoming> accessed 8 May 2024.

21 In 2015 the Supreme Court of South Australia overturned a conviction for assault causing harm imposed on an Australian Rules football player. The appellant argued that he had not deliberately struck his opponent but had used his arm to block the player, which was within the rules of the game and had accidentally hit his opponent in the face. The opponent suffered a broken jaw which required surgery. McKenzie was not sentenced pending the decision of the appeal. A retrial before a different magistrate was ordered: see *McKenzie v Police* [2015] SASC 78.

22 Pierik (n 18).

23 Kate O'Halloran, 'Andrew Gaff Deserves His Ban, but the AFL Has a Bigger Problem with Off-Field Violence' *The Guardian* (London, 8 August 2018) <https://www.theguardian.com/sport/2018/aug/08/andrew-gaff-deserves-his-ban-but-the-afl-has-a-bigger-problem-with-off-field-violence> accessed 8 May 2024.

in Australia 'have an immunity from the law'.[24] Anderson sums up the attitude of the Australian authorities:

> In the Gaff incident, the fact the incident happened beyond the touchline seems to have acted symbolically to protect him from criminal charges and deter the police. It ought not to have, but it did. Once the touchline is cleared and the players are off the field, there can be no doubt about the criminal law's reach.[25]

4–12 Public policy was an instigating factor in the conviction of footballer Lee Boyer, who pleaded guilty to an offence under s 5 of the Public Order Act 1985 after a brawl erupted between him and his teammate Keiron Dyer when Dyer failed to pass him the ball during a soccer game.[26] The fact that the brawl took place between two players from the same team would have made it very difficult to argue that the incident was part of the game.[27] The Northumbria Police Deputy Chief Constable David Warcup explained that the reason behind his decision to prosecute was based on public policy, as a number of complaints were received from the public. Deputy Chief Warcup stated:

> policing at football matches is to ensure the effective safety of the public, and any incidents of violence, whether they be on the pitch or in the stands, can affect the safety of people attending the event. Therefore, it's not only the spectators who have a responsibility to behave themselves, but also the players on the pitch.[28]

4–13 It is clear from the above discussion that on-field violence is largely immunised from the intervention of the criminal law. However, it is not a licence for thuggery and there are limits. The above cases establish that the criminal law will intervene if a sportsperson intentionally or recklessly injures an opponent, and the violent act is beyond that which is ordinarily incidental to the playing of the game. A factor to consider is whether the incident occurred on- or off-the-ball. With off-the-ball incidences, there is often very little difference between the violent act on the field of play and that of a violent act in the street or in the terraces. On-the-ball injuries, on the other hand, can often be explained as resulting from the 'heat of the moment'. There are times when the internal disciplinary mechanisms of the sport are better suited to deal with on-field violence. However, some commentators are critical of the

---

24 Jack Anderson, 'When Does a Pitch Assault Cross the Line between Sport and Crime?' *The Examiner* (Cork, 23 August 2018) <https://www.irishexaminer.com/opinion/columnists/arid-20473168.html> accessed 8 May 2024.

25 ibid.

26 The incident took place in front of 52,000 fans in St James's Park during a match against Aston Villa in April 2005.

27 Deborah Healey, *Sport and the Law* (4th edn, University of New South Wales Press 2009) 198.

28 As quoted by Martin Wainright, 'Court Fines Bowyer for Punching Team-Mate' *The Guardian* (London, 6 July 2006) <https://www.theguardian.com/uk/2006/jul/06/football.martinwainwright> accessed 8 May 2024.

use of the governing body to deal with on-field violence or indiscipline. Flakne and Caplan equate the use of the governing body determining the appropriate sanction with

> granting the board of directors of General Motors jurisdiction over the determination of guilt or innocence and the appropriate punishment for one of their employees who, while on the job, killed his foreman. It would seem that if violence in sports is to be curtailed, the only effective remedy lies with the state, where the capability of meting out effective deterrent sanctions exists.[29]

There is a conflict of interest and in some situations the use of the criminal law is the more appropriate route. If the club or league do not take on-field violence seriously and appropriately sanction players, public policy may necessitate the intervention of the police and subsequently the courts. If an activity is unlawful, the situation is more clear-cut as there is no discretion regarding the intervention of the criminal law, as the next section demonstrates. **4–14**

Lawful and Unlawful Sports

As discussed in Chapter 3, an activity that is classified as a sport enjoys certain privileges. A recognised sport may be given fiscal benefits in the form of funding and tax exemptions. Certain activities that would be rendered illegal in a situation outside the sporting sphere are deemed acceptable within the confines of a recognised and legitimate sport. **4–15**

If a sport is recognised as lawful, this does not mean that the law will never intervene. For example, the criminal law will become involved if a sportsperson deliberately and recklessly disregards the rules of the sport and intentionally goes beyond the limits of that sport. Even in a contact sport like boxing, there are limits, and a boxer must adhere to the rules of the sport. For example, a boxer may not hit below the belt or hold, trip, kick or butt their opponent with the foot or knee.[30] A boxer is **4–16**

---

[29] Gary W Flakne and Allen H Caplan, 'Sports Violence and the Prosecution" (1977) 13 Trial 33, 33–34.

[30] The British Boxing Board of Control, 'Rules of Boxing' <https://bbbofc.com/boxing-rules> accessed 8 May 2024. Rule 3.38 states: 'The following acts shall not be permitted during a Contest: –

> (a) hitting below the belt: (b) using the "pivot blow": (c) hitting on the back of the head or neck: (d) kidney punching; (e) hitting with the open glove, the inside, or the butt or the back of the hand, or with the wrist or elbow; (f) holding, butting, or careless use of the head, shouldering, wrestling or roughing: (g) not trying; (h) persistently ducking below the waistline; (i) intentional falling without receiving a blow; (j) failing to break when so ordered, or striking or attempting to strike an opponent on the break; (k) deliberately striking an opponent when they are dropping to the floor or when they are down; (l) hitting an opponent after the termination of a round; (m) unsporting conduct; (n) any other conduct which a Referee may deem foul; (o) boxing whilst under the influence of a prohibited substance'.

precluded from striking their opponent with the open side of the glove or the inside of the glove.[31]

4–17 Similarly, in rugby, there are many instances in which violent conduct is permitted. While a tackle may not be within the rules of the sport, some have become part of what is known as the playing culture, as discussed below. This has caused a blurring of the distinction between breaches of the rules of the game and those which are breaches but are deemed to be acceptable. As Cox and others note:

> in simple terms then, the rules of most contact sports seem to permit and encourage uncivilised behaviour, and remarkably the law of the land allows them to do so, provided only that the sport in question is recognised as lawfully constituted.[32]

4–18 Some sports are illegal irrespective of consent, the use of rules or the presence of a referee. The following sports are illegal in Ireland and in most countries: prize fighting, gladiatorial fights to death, cockfighting, cock throwing, and bearbaiting. These so-called blood sports were banned due to the rioting and drinking that often accompanied them and not necessarily on grounds of animal welfare as discussed in Chapter 15.

4–19 Until October 2009, it was an offence in New South Wales (NSW) in Australia for women to take part in boxing contests by virtue of ss 8(1) and 62D of the Boxing and Wresting Control Act 1986 (NSW). Section 8(1) provided: 'A male person of or above the age of 18 years may make an application to the Authority to be registered as a boxer of a prescribed class.' Section 62D expressly excluded amateur female boxers with the following text:

> Prohibition on female boxing contests
> (1) A female person of any age shall not take part in any amateur boxing contest
> (2) A person shall not hold or promote an amateur boxing contest in which a female person is a contestant.

---

31 A boxer may not bite the ear of an opponent, as the incident involving Mike Tyson and Evander Holyfield in 1997 demonstrated. At a World Boxing Association (WBA) title fight at the MGM Hotel in Las Vegas, Tyson bit a chunk out of Holyfield's ear. Tyson had his boxing licence revoked for one year by the Nevada State Athletic Commission and was fined $3m plus costs: see Ellis Cashmore and Ernest Cashmore, *Tyson: Nurture of the Beast* (Polity 2005) 81. Criminal proceedings were not brought against Tyson. For a detailed discussion on the incident, see George Willis, *The Bite Fight: Tyson, Holyfield and the Night that Changed Boxing Forever* (Triumph Books 2013).

32 Neville Cox, Alex Schuster (with Cathryn Costello), *Sport and the Law* (First Law 2004) 165.

Maximum penalty: 20 penalty units.

The ban on female boxers was removed by the Combat Sports Act 2008 (NSW) by virtue of s 75, which repealed the Boxing and Wresting Control Act 1986. The 2008 Act was subsequently repealed by Combat Sports Act 2013.[33] It is interesting to note that female involvement in fighting sports is not a recent development as women's prize fighting can be traced to the 18th and 19th centuries.[34] However: 'Although women have been competitively boxing since the eighteenth century, the centrality of the paternalistic legal system which characterises most Western and developing countries has prohibited women from fully participating in amateur boxing.'[35] It was not until 2000 that Queensland removed the ban on female boxers.[36] **4–20**

Australia was not alone in prohibiting female boxers competing. In 1998 the refusal of the British Boxing Board of Control (BBBC) to provide female boxers with a licence to box professionally was deemed to be a form of sex discrimination. In a landmark decision by a London South industrial tribunal, *Couch v British Board of Boxing Control Ltd*, the BBBC was found to have unlawfully discriminated against a female boxer on grounds of sex.[37] Jane Couch was forced to fight outside the United Kingdom (UK) and challenged the decision of the BBBC to refuse to grant her a licence.[38] Counsel for the BBBC defended the policy of the governing body not to grant licences to female boxers on the grounds that 'many women suffer from premenstrual tension which makes them more emotional and more labile and accident-prone. They are too fragile to box and they bruise easily.'[39] Hargreaves observes that **4–21**

---

[33] Combat Sports Act 2013 No 96. The full title is: An Act to regulate the conduct of combat sports and combat sport contests; to constitute the Combat Sports Authority of New South Wales; to repeal the Combat Sports Act 2008; and for other purposes. The full text of the Act can be accessed here: <https://legislation.nsw.gov.au/view/html/inforce/current/act-2013-096#frnt-lt> accessed 8 May 2024.

[34] Jennifer Hargreaves, 'Women's Boxing and Related Activities: Introducing Images and Meanings' in Thomas A Green and Joseph R Svinth (eds), *Martial Arts in the Modern World* (Greenwood Publishing Group 2003) 212. Hargreaves refers to fights between working class women that took place in London from the 1720s.

[35] Amy Godoy-Pressland, 'Moral Guardians, Miniskirts and Nicola Adams: The Changing Media Discourse on Women's Boxing' in Christopher R Matthews and Alex Channon (eds), *Global Perspectives on Women in Combat Sports: Women Warriors around the World* (Springer 2016) 26.

[36] Malissa Smith, *A History of Women's Boxing* (Rowman & Littlefield 2014) 236. See also LA Jennings, *She's a Knockout!: A History of Women in Fighting Sports* (Rowman & Littlefield 2014).

[37] [1997] unreported, IT No 2304231/97.

[38] Couch discusses her legal battle and career in her autobiography: Jane Couch and Abi Smith, *The Final Round: The Autobiography of Jane Couch* (Pitch Publishing 2019).

[39] Donald McRae and Jane Couch: 'I wish I hadn't been the first in boxing … I'm damaged' *The Guardian* (London, 19 September 2019) <https://www.theguardian.com/sport/2019/sep/25/jane-couch-britains-first-licenced-female-boxer-interview> accessed 8 May 2024.

the 'blood, bruises, cuts and concussion, which accompany boxing's intrinsic aggression, violence and danger, are popularly considered to be legitimate and even "natural" for men but at odds with the essence of femininity'.[40]

4–22 The industrial tribunal disagreed with Counsel for the BBBC and thus paved the way for the licencing of professional female boxers in Britain. Following the decision, the BBBC amended its rules to allow for the licencing of female boxers.[41] The incremental dismantling of impediments to professional female boxers culminated in the inclusion of female boxing into the Summer Olympics in 2012. Women's boxing was part of the 1904 Olympics in St. Louis; however, it was an exhibition sport only. On 13 August 2009, the International Olympic Committee (IOC) announced that three weight categories of women's boxing would be added to the London Olympics 2012.[42] As a consequence, the number of men's events was reduced from 11 to 10 so that the total number of boxers would remain at 286.[43] As men's boxing was already part of the Olympics programme, the decision to add women's boxing did not require a more formal approval process at an IOC session.[44]

Origins of the Intervention of the Criminal Law

4–23 The intersection between on-field violence and the criminal law dates to the late Victorian period. There is a trilogy of cases that demonstrate the judicial recognition of the application of the criminal law to sport. In *R v Bradshaw*, during a football match the accused jumped in the air and struck an opponent in the stomach with his knee.[45] The injury caused the death of the victim. Lord Justice (LJ) Bramwell, in his direction to the jury, outlined the criminal law's involvement in sport. The judge directed the jury to find the accused guilty of manslaughter if they were satisfied that the accused intentionally or recklessly caused serious harm to the deceased.[46] The accused was acquitted after testimony from the

---

40 Hargreaves (n 34) 212.

41 'Women Boxers Win UK Licence' (*BBC*, 14 August 1998) <http://news.bbc.co.uk/2/hi/sport/150908.stm> accessed 8 May 2024. Couch was awarded £15,000 in damages.

42 The three categories are: flyweight (48–51kg), lightweight (56–60kg) and middleweight (69–75kg): see Reuters, 'Women's Boxing Confirmed for 2012 Games' (*ABC News*, 13 August 2009) <https://www.abc.net.au/news/2009-08-14/womens-boxing-confirmed-for-2012-games/1390174> accessed 2 July 2024.

43 Women's Boxing Confirmed for 2012 Games (n 42).

44 ibid. In 2010, the International Boxing Association (AIBA, now IBA) requested female boxers to wear a skirt as part of their uniform at the 5th Women's Boxing World Championships in Barbados. Several national federations refused and in March 2012 the AIBA announced that skirts would not be mandatory. For an interesting discussion, see Elise Paradis, 'Skirting the Issue: Women Boxers, Liminality and Change' in Lisa Hunter, Wayne Smith, and Elke Emerald (eds), *Pierre Bourdieu and Physical Culture* (Routledge 2014) ch 8.

45 (1878) 14 Cox CC83.

46 ibid 85.

referee showed that there had been no unfair play. Twenty years later, in *R v Moore*, the accused was found guilty of manslaughter after a violent tackle in a football match resulted in the death of the victim.[47] Similar to the LJ in *Bradshaw*, Hawkins J directed the following to the jury: 'no one has the right to use force which is likely to injure another and if the prisoner used such force and death resulted, he was guilty of manslaughter'.[48] As will be discussed at the end of the chapter, in *R v Coney*, the Court held that prize fighting was an unlawful sport as it amounted to a breach of the peace.[49]

The late 1970s witnessed an escalation of on-field violence of sports resulting in cases coming before the courts. In *R v Billinghurst*, the defendant punched an opponent, breaking his jaw, during an amateur rugby match in South Wales.[50] The Court, in handing down a nine-month sentence (which was suspended for two years given the previous good character of the accused), held that rugby was a physical game which involved the use of force and, as such, players were deemed to consent to force that was reasonably foreseeable. However, it was not a licence for thuggery and participants were not deemed to have consented to the intentional or reckless infliction of harm. In the 1980s, in *R v Bishop*, the Welsh international rugby player David Bishop punched an opponent who lay on the ground during an off-the-ball incident in a club rugby match in Wales.[51] Bishop was initially given a one-month sentence, but this was changed by the Court of Appeal to a 12-month suspended sentence.[52] In the 1990s there were more high-profile cases, including *R v Rees* where the defendant, Gary Rees, a Nottingham and England rugby player, was charged and subsequently acquitted of inflicting grievous bodily harm on his opponent.[53] In *R v Hardy*, a row between opponents in a rugby match caused the death of a player.[54] Following a punch to the jaw, the victim fell to the ground, and the ground was still hard with frost. He died days later in hospital. Hardy defended his **4–24**

---

47 (1898) 14 TLR 229.

48 ibid 230.

49 (1882) 8 QBD 534.

50 (1978) Crim LR 553.

51 (1986) *The Times*, London (12 October 1986). See also *R v Shervall* (1989) 11 Cr App R 284; *R v Davies* (1990) 12 Cr App *R* (S) 308.

52 See McCutcheon (n 8) 270 for further case examples. See also Jack Anderson, 'Citius, Altius, Fortius? A Study of Criminal Violence in Sport' (2000–2001) 11 Marquette Sports Law Review 87, 98–99; and Mark James, 'The Trouble with Roy Keane' (2002) 1(3) Entertainment Law 72.

53 *R v Rees* (1992) All ER Rev 365. Rees argued that his opponent had been obstructing him throughout the match and the incident had resulted from an attempt by Rees to drag the opponent out of his way.

54 *The Independent*, 27 July 1994 <https://www.independent.co.uk/news/uk/rugby-player-cleared-of-manslaughter-on-the-pitch-punch-thrown-in-illtempered-match-1416446.html> accessed 2 July 2024. Hardy 'was the first player in the game's 171-year history to be prosecuted for manslaughter in relation to a death on the field'.

actions on the ground that he was simply protecting himself as he was being hit from behind. The defendant was acquitted of manslaughter.

4–25 In *R v Devereux*, the defendant, a rugby player, punched his opponent, fracturing his jaw in three places.[55] Devereux was convicted of grievous bodily harm and was sentenced to nine months in prison. However, following an unsuccessful appeal to overturn his conviction, he served only four months.

4–26 As will be discussed under the defence of consent, the intervention of the criminal law continued into the 2000s with the cases of *R v Barnes* and *R v Chapman*.[56] These cases demonstrate that the authorities in England and Wales are willing to prosecute players for on-field violence. Admittedly, such cases are rare and in many cases the defendants were acquitted. Illustrative of such acquittals are the cases of *R v Evans*[57] and *R v Chester*,[58] as cited by Pendlebury.[59] In *Evans*, the accused was charged with assault occasioning actual bodily harm and common assault after he stomped on the victim in a rugby union match. Bolton J ordered the jury to acquit Evans of both charges. The judge said she was 'flabbergasted' that the Crown Prosecution Services (CPS) had proceeded with the case. In *Chester*, an amateur player was acquitted of maliciously causing grievous bodily harm to his opponent. Pendlebury concludes that 'Evans and Chester both convey that an act of foul play is ultimately not determinate of criminality.'[60]

Range of Offences

4–27 When it comes to the application of the criminal law to on-field violence, the cases range from assault to manslaughter.[61] It is highly improbable

---

55 *The Independent*, 23 February 1996 <https://www.independent.co.uk/news/player-jailed-1320447.html> accessed 2 July 2024. For more detailed discussion on the case see Anderson (n 15) 761.

56 *R v Barnes* [2004] EWCA Crim 3246; *R v Chapman* (unreported) Crown Court (Warwick), 3 March 2010.

57 (Unreported), Crown Court, (Newcastle), 15 June 2010.

58 (Unreported), Crown Court, (York), 16 August 2010.

59 Adam Pendlebury, 'The Regulation of On-the-Ball Offences: Challenges in Court' (2012) 10(1) Entertainment and Sports Law Journal 1.

60 ibid 5.

61 Under Irish law, homicide relates to two offences: murder and manslaughter. Manslaughter is divided into involuntary and voluntary manslaughter. Voluntary manslaughter was defined by the Law Reform Commission's Report on *Homicide: Murder and Involuntary Manslaughter* as satisfying the requirements of a murder charge but where the accused was acting under provocation, (IRC 87 – 2008) ch 4, s 4.04(i)(a). In this situation there is a mitigating factor. Involuntary manslaughter was defined in s 4.04(ii)(b) as 'Manslaughter by unlawful and dangerous act ie the act must be a criminal offence, carrying with it the risk of bodily harm to another – a tort will not suffice (dangerousness is judged objectively); (b) Manslaughter by gross negligence involving a high risk that substantial personal injury will follow the accused's negligent act or

that a case involving murder would ever occur on the field of play.[62] Prosecutions for criminal sporting assaults are rare; however, a number have been recorded in ice hockey in Canada. In England and Wales, there have been a few cases involving rugby and football players that have resulted in the intervention of the criminal law. As discussed above, in criminal cases, the standard of proof required is 'beyond reasonable doubt'. If in doubt, the judge or jury must acquit. As sports cases raise evidentiary problems (given the fact, for example, that the incident in question can arise in the 'heat of the moment'), the court may find the accused guilty of reckless or intentional disregard for the safety of an opponent.

Non-Fatal Offences Against the Person Act 1997

In Ireland, the Non-Fatal Offences Against the Person Act 1997 governs assault and other offences against the person. Prior to this Act, assault and battery were two separate offences. Assault was the term used to describe the situation where a person was in fear of immediate danger and the battery was the carrying out of the threat. Section 28(1) of the 1997 Act abolished a number of common law offences, including assault and battery, and assault occasioning actual bodily harm. It merged the offences of assault and battery; however, they remain separate offences under the law of tort where they are referred to as intentional torts. **4–28**

Sections 2 to 4 of the 1997 Act relate to assault. Section 2 of the Act defines assault as the actual carrying out or threat of reckless or intentional, direct, or indirect force or as causing impact to the body of another without the consent of that person. According to Stevenson: **4–29**

> What is notable is that section 2 is unequivocal, providing for lack of consent to be part of the actus reus (the act) of assault. But section 3 is much more opaque. Although lack of consent is not explicitly set out within this section, for a number of years following the enactment of the 1997 Act, it was assumed that section 2 must be carried into section 3.[63]

Section 3 concerns 'assault causing harm'; however, there is no mention of consent.[64] A recent Supreme Court decision has clarified that consent may be a defence under s 3 in limited circumstances, including legitimate **4–30**

omission'. If a manslaughter charge against a sportsperson ensued, it would most likely fall under involuntary manslaughter.

62 David Thorpe and others, *Sports Law* (2nd edn, Oxford University Press 2013) 96 note that a murder charge, in theory under Australian law, could be brought in a situation where the opponent intentionally inflicts grievous bodily harm and as a result the victim dies. For example, if a player deliberately strikes an opponent with the intention of fracturing their jaw, but the victim dies because of the blow.

63 Michelle-Thérèse Stevenson, 'Is Consent Ever a Defence to Assault?' (28 January 2020) Garda Review 28, 28–29.

64 The Act defines harm as 'harm to body or mind and includes pain and unconsciousness'.

sporting activity.[65] In the *Director of Public Prosecutions (DPP) v Brown*, a former Garda, Stephen Cooper, was attacked by a fellow prisoner, Gerard Brown.[66] Counsel for Brown contended that s 3 assault was predicated upon s 2 assault and s 2 assault provides for the defence of consent. As noted, s 3 is silent on the defence of consent. The DPP contended that s 3 was a standalone offence and to view it as an extension of s 2 where consent as a defence would be contrary to public policy. The trial judge agreed with the DPP and held that if consent were to be permitted under s 3 then the legislature would have provided for it in the statute. The Court of Appeal held that ss 2 and 3 were separate and distinct provisions and that

> proof of an absence of consent is therefore not a necessary ingredient in a s.3 assault. Consent may however provide a defence to a s.3 assault charge in limited circumstances such as, for example, legitimate sporting activity and appropriate medical treatment.[67]

4–31 The case was appealed to the Supreme Court and the issue for the Supreme Court was whether consent was a defence under s 3 and whether the alleged consent was unlawful on the grounds that there was 'no effectual consent' as the conduct of the appellant was illegal. In referring to *R v Coney*, a prize fighting case, the Supreme Court stated that 'the illegal aspect of the conduct involved meant that one could not give an effectual consent'.[68] In further support of this contention, the Supreme Court alluded to sexual offences where 'absence of consent is an ingredient of the offence concerned'.[69] The majority of Supreme Court disagreed with the holding of the Court of Appeal that proof of an absence of consent was not a necessary ingredient in a s 3 assault.

4–32 Dunne J, in delivering the majority decision, held:

> It seems to me that the alleged consent in this case could not be relied on by Mr. Brown to negate the absence of consent in respect of a charge contrary to s. 3 of the Act of 1997. In short, consent to an assault causing harm for an unlawful purpose is no consent.[70]

4–33 The Supreme Court examined the 1997 Act in light of its predecessor, the Offences Against the Person Act 1861, in order to clarify the definition of assault and the absence of consent in s 2 of the 1997 Act. The Supreme Court accepted 'the proposition' that ss 2 and 3 of the Act of 1997 created separate and distinct offences.[71] Dunne J pointed to the different

---

65 *DPP v Brown* [2018] IESC 67.

66 See ch 3 para 3–12 for details on the facts of the case.

67 *DPP v Brown* [2016] IECA 405 [38].

68 ibid. [57].

69 ibid.

70 ibid [56]. For a more detailed discussion of this case, see Laura Donnellan, 'Consent and the Common Law Exceptions: *R v Brown* Still Good Law' (2020) 30(3) Irish Journal of Criminal Law 62.

71 *Brown* (n 65) [37].

penalties under ss 2 and 3, with s 2 incurring a lesser penalty than that of s 3. However, in departing from its earlier decision of *Minister for Justice, Equality and Law Reform v Dolny*,[72] the Supreme Court in *DPP v Brown* held 'the definition of assault in section 2 carries over to the word "assaults" in section 3'.[73]

The Court of Appeal in December 2015 overturned a sentence imposed on a GAA player by a Circuit Court judge. This case concerned s 3 assault. In the *Director of Public Prosecutions (DPP) v Prendergast*, the three-judge Court of Appeal found in favour of the appellant who had been sentenced to two years in prison by McCabe J in the Circuit Court in Castlebar with the final 12 months suspended.[74] Prendergast pleaded guilty to assault causing harm under the Non-Fatal Offences Against the Person Act 1997. The victim alleged that he was punched in the left eye as he attempted to retrieve the ball. The victim, according to his victim impact statement, contended that he fell to the ground due to the impact of the punch. The victim asserted that he had no altercation with Prendergast nor was Prendergast marking him. It seemed to be an unprovoked attack according to the victim. In addition, the victim's team was losing and was 'playing for pride' at the time the incident occurred.[75] Prendergast appealed his sentence on three grounds: **4–34**

1. The severity of the sentence which was in the higher end of the scale of penalties under s 3 (on summary conviction: 12 months and/or a fine and on indictment: a maximum of five years and/or a fine);
2. The failure of the trial judge to consider mitigating factors; and
3. The trial judge erred in considering the offence so serious that it required Prendergast to be immediately incarcerated.[76]

Sheehan J delivered the judgment of the Court of the Appeal. He referred to the very different account given by the referee in his match report in which he described the incident involving a tussle for the ball from both players as Prendergast 'swung out and struck the injured party in the face and the injured party clearly fell to the ground'.[77] Sheehan J found that the trial judge placed too much credence on the victim impact statement and not on the referee's report. The judge acknowledged that neither version of events justified the actions of the appellant, **4–35**

[72] [2009] IESC 48. The Supreme Court upheld the High Court decision which held that the two offences were separate and distinct and as such the definition of assault in s 2 did not carry over to the definition of assault under s 3. In s 2, the word 'assault' is used as a noun ('offence of assault), whereas in s 3 the verb 'assaults' is used ('A person who assaults another causing him or her harm shall be guilty of an offence').

[73] *Brown* (n 65) [40].

[74] [2015] IECA 318.

[75] ibid [4].

[76] ibid [3]. The five years has been increased to 10 years by s 20 of Criminal Justice (Miscellaneous Provisions) Act 2023 <https://www.irishstatutebook.ie/eli/2023/act/24/section/20/enacted/en/html#sec20> accessed 2 July 2024.

[77] ibid [5].

however, the appellant's culpability was somewhat diminished as it was an on-the-ball incident and not an unprovoked attack as claimed by the victim. McCabe J in the Circuit Court had made no distinction between incidences of on-field violence and that of anti-social behaviour on the streets: he asserted 'what happened on the pitch that day was no different in principle to a street assault at night'.[78] The Court of Appeal did not wish to criticise the decision of the trial court judge, however, it held that the judge should have referred to the referee's report when it came to deciding on the appropriate sentence. Instead, McCabe J felt obliged to base his decision on the victim's statement.[79] The victim stated that he was 95% blind in one eye and that he considered himself to be physically impaired. The Court of Appeal noted the importance of the distinction between injuries that result from on-the-ball incidents and those injuries that arise from off-the-ball instances. The Court of Appeal held that the facts of this case required that it be 'treated in a different way to someone involved in an unprovoked off the ball violent attack'.[80]

4–36 Section 4 relates to assault 'causing serious harm'. Serious harm is defined as

> injury which creates a substantial risk of death or which causes serious disfigurement or substantial loss or impairment of the mobility of the body as a whole or of the function of any particular bodily member or organ.[81]

4–37 This section is silent as to the absence of consent. However, it is extremely doubtful that the defence of consent could be invoked under s 4 as the offender, if found guilty of the offence, could face life imprisonment. Section 22 retains the basic common law rule that consent cannot be an absolute defence to all forms of assault.[82]

The Law Reform Commission Report on Non-Fatal Offences and its Application to Sport

4–38 The 1997 Act was largely based on the recommendations of a Law Reform Commission (LRC) Report.[83] The report examined the position

[78] ibid [8].
[79] ibid [9].
[80] ibid [13]. In considering the mitigating factors and the fact that the appellant had paid compensation to the injured player, he was unlikely to reoffend and had character references that portrayed him in a favourable light, the Court of Appeal quashed the original sentence of two years. It instead imposed a one-year sentence that was backdated to 16 October 2015 with the remainder suspended and an order that the appellant carry out 100 hours' community service within a 12-month period: [16].
[81] Non-Fatal Offences Against the Person Act 1997, s 1.
[82] Finbarr McAuley and Paul McCutcheon, *Criminal Liability* (Round Hall Sweet & Maxwell 2000) 533.
[83] Law Reform Commission, *Report on Non-Fatal Offences Against the Person* (LRC–45–1994) <https://www.lawreform.ie/_fileupload/Reports/rNonFatalOffences.htm> accessed 2 July 2024

of contact sport in Chapter 9 on Discussion and Proposals for Reform in paragraphs 9.148–9.160. It acknowledged that contact sports, by their very nature, entail violent conduct. Quoting from the Canadian Law Reform Commission's Working Paper on Assault from 1984, the LRC proposed that the criminal law should be used as a 'policeman' of last resort or as an 'enforcer'.[84] The LRC recommended that no general exemption should be given to contact sports where the victim does not expressly or impliedly consent to the infliction of injury.[85] In referring to the Canadian Working Paper on Assault, the LRC recommended the need for a more long-term strategy.[86] In order to dissuade on-field violence in the long term, a series of administrative and educational measures were needed which would involve local governments, sporting bodies, coaches and parents.[87]

The LRC summarised the situations in which a person is said to have consented in a contact sport. A sportsperson is said to have consented: **4–39**

1. to any contact within the rules of the game;
2. to any contact of an accidental nature arising from incidentally in the course of it; and
3. to incidental pain to the risk of hurt or injury from such contact.[88]

For example, 'a footballer impliedly consents to be tackled, to being kicked accidentally and to the risk of being thereby injured, but does not consent to being punched or kicked'.[89] As most sports do not authorise intentional or reckless tackles or injury, there should be no exemption given to contact sports.[90] If a player does not have the requisite intent **4–40**

---

[84] Law Reform Commission of Canada, *Criminal Law: Assault* (Working Paper No 38) para 9.148. The Working Paper is available at <http://www.lareau-law.ca/LRCWP38.pdf> accessed 8 May 2024. The Working Paper added that 'occasional sanctioning under the criminal law will not solve the wider problem. A careful combination of social and educational measures is needed involving governments, leagues and associations, parents, sports officials and the press.'

[85] LRC Report (n 83) para 9.149. The LRC noted that while the occasional prosecution will have some deterrent in the short term, it will not solve the wider problem of violence in sport.

[86] ibid para 9.150.

[87] The LRC also suggested that those who aid or abet in the commission of on-field violence could be subject to the criminal law: see para 9.151. This would include coaches or managers who encourage players to injure a key player from an opposing team. See *Pinkerton* v *United States* 328 US 640 (1946). See also John H Kerr, *Motivation and Emotion in Sport: Reversal Theory* (Psychology Press 1997) 115–16 where the writer states: 'In general, aggression is seen as an unprovoked hostility or attacks on another person which are not sanctioned by society. However, in the sports context, the aggression is provoked in the sense that two opposing teams have willingly agreed to compete against each other. Aggression in team contact sports is intrinsic and sanctioned, provided that plays remain permissible within the boundaries of certain rules, which act as a kind of contract in the pursuit of aggression (and violence) between consenting adults.'

[88] LRC Report (n 83) para 9.152.

[89] ibid para 9.153.

[90] ibid.

or recklessness and the contact is within the rules of the sport, it is irrelevant that the force used was likely to cause injury.[91]

4–41 The LRC acknowledged that it is very difficult if not impossible to ascertain whether a contact is intentional or reckless. The courts, when faced with a sporting case, often refer to the standards of the particular sport in deciding whether or not the conduct is acceptable.[92] Such an approach is understandable given that 'sports produce valuable social benefits through the practice and example of fair play within an agreed set of rules'.[93] This approach has attracted criticism as it is contended that 'the participants' right to bodily integrity is no longer adequately protected by the standards of professional sports in which the stakes are high and violence is a not uncommon occurrence'.[94] The Canadian Law Reform Commission suggested that the criminal law should apply irrespective of the rules (with the exemption of boxing) of the sport and thus treat on-field and off-field violence uniformly.[95]

4–42 In reference to the amateur nature of Irish sport, the LRC noted that rules of most sports place reasonable limits on the degree of violence to which one may consent. Consequently, the LRC concluded that no specific penalties should be devised for sporting violence.[96] It was also concluded that boxing should not be signalled out for exemption. Any proposed changes to the rules of the sport are a matter for the relevant regulatory sports body in accordance with public debate and medical evidence.[97]

4–43 In the absence of any statutory intervention, the LRC concluded that the criminal law would continue to apply in situations where the rules of the sport are breached. It did, however, note its limitations.[98] In some martial arts, a serious injury may result from a kick which is within the rules of the sport. Failure to prosecute and attempts to prosecute would both attract public debate. It would seem unjust to hold the opponent criminally liable for conduct that is part of the rules of the sport. The victim would have also consented to the risk. Public opinion may call for sports that can cause serious injury, including professional boxing, to be declared unlawful. The LRC recommended that a specific provision be made for consent to injuries inflicted in the course of, and in accordance with, the rules of a lawful sporting activity. It summed up its position as follows:

---

[91] ibid.
[92] ibid para 9.154.
[93] ibid.
[94] ibid para 9.155.
[95] Canadian Law Reform Commission (n 84) 32. It subsequently dispensed with the suggestion and instead favoured an exemption of a general nature.
[96] LRC Report (n 83) para 9.157.
[97] ibid.
[98] ibid para 9.158.

> Every person is protected from criminal responsibility for causing harm or serious harm to another where such harm is inflicted during the course of, and in accordance with the rules of any bona fide sporting activity.[99]

The 1997 Act did not incorporate the findings of the LRC report in relation to sport. However, s 22(1) on the general defences implies that the sporting exemption is retained as it provides that '[t]he provisions of this Act have effect subject to any enactment or rule of law providing a defence, or providing lawful authority, justification or excuse for an act or omission'. At the Second Stage of the Non-Fatal Offences Against the Person Bill 1997, Minister Durkan in the Seanad stated that 'the common law rules concerning bodily harm arising in the course of sports, dangerous exhibitions or medical treatments will apply, where appropriate, to exempt the action from criminal liability'.[100] **4–44**

Defences

When a sportsperson is faced with a criminal charge, several defences are available to them, depending on the circumstances. These defences include consent, self-defence, involuntary reflex, provocation, and diminished capacity. Each defence will be considered in turn. **4–45**

Consent

As discussed in Chapter 3, in the case of *R v Brown* the House of Lords recognised, depending on the circumstances in which they are committed, that assaults can be lawful or unlawful.[101] Lawful assaults including injuries sustained in contact sport, reasonable surgeries and parental chastisement are permitted as they constitute good reason. There are overriding public policy concerns that immunise such assaults from the intervention of the criminal law. There is a public interest or benefit derived from the playing of contact sports. Equally, the state has an interest in the well-being of its citizens. It follows that the defence of consent can only be raised where the activity in question constitutes good reason, it is legal, and the degree of harm inflicted does not involve actual bodily harm or more serious harm. The general exceptions that the common law courts have developed over the years are exhaustive and thus cannot be added to as the Irish case of *DPP v Brown* and the Court of Appeal of England and Wales in the case of *R v BM* demonstrate.[102] The courts in Ireland, and England and Wales, are reluctant to create more exceptions and instead have deferred the matter to the legislature. **4–46**

---

99 ibid para 9.159.

100 Seanad Deb 7 May 1997, vol 151 col 8, Non-Fatal Offences Against the Person Bill 1997: Second Stage <https://www.oireachtas.ie/ga/debates/debate/seanad/1997-05-07/speech/239/> accessed 8 May 2024.

101 [1994] 1 AC 212.

102 [2018] IESC 67; *Brown* (n 65); [2018] EWCA Crim 560.

4–47 As sport falls under one of the general exceptions, the defence of consent is often raised by sportspersons in on-field violence cases. Sportspersons consent to the reasonably foreseeable hazards of the sport, and consent to harm that is within the rules of the game or incidental to the playing of the game. However, sportspersons do not consent to harm that is intentional, deliberate, or reckless. In the words of Thorpe and others: 'The consent of the victim operates through the *actus reus*: there is no unlawful act upon which to base a criminal charge.'[103]

4–48 Consent can be implied or expressed. With regard to express consent, a sportsperson consents to play the game by the rules of the game. The rules of the game will have been clearly stated, thus is there is little room for any ambiguity. The case of *R v Barnes* is illustrative of this principle as the Court referred to play that is within the 'rules and practice of the game and does not go beyond it'; in this situation it 'will be a firm indication that what has happened is not criminal'.[104] Players impliedly consent to injuries that may occur during the game that are not within the rules of the particular sport but have become the 'norm'. Again, *R v Barnes* provides guidance on implied consent. The Court held:

> In making a judgment as to whether conduct is criminal or not, it has to be borne in mind that, in highly competitive sports, conduct outside the rules can be expected to occur in the heat of the moment, and even if the conduct justifies not only being penalised but also a warning or even a sending off, it still may not reach the threshold level required for it to be criminal. That level is an objective one and does not depend upon the views of individual players. The type of the sport, the level at which it is played, the nature of the act, the degree of force used, the extent of the risk of injury, the state of mind of the defendant are all likely to be relevant in determining whether the defendant's actions go beyond the threshold.[105]

4–49 The extent or the degree of the consent depends on objective criteria that surrounds 'the incident rather than on a determination of the subjective willingness of the victim'.[106] The courts will consider whether the incident occurred during official play or during time-out or at end of play and if it is an off-the-ball or on-the-ball incident. The Canadian Case of *R v Cey* was cited with approval in *R v Barnes*.[107] In *Cey*, the accused body checked an opponent into the boards surrounding the ice rink, resulting in the infliction of facial injuries and concussion on the opponent. The trial court acquitted Cey on the grounds that he had not intended to injure his opponent more than what was customary for the game. Cey argued that the opponent had consented to incidents of this nature. The Saskatchewan Court of Appeal overturned the acquittal, and a re-trial was ordered. The Court of Appeal agreed that the consent given in sport

---

103 (n 62) 97.
104 *Barnes* (n 56) [15].
105 ibid.
106 Yates and Gillespie (n 4) 161.
107 (1989) 48 CCC (3d) 480 (Sask CA)

was an exception to the general rule that consent to force, which is likely to result in bodily harm, was not normally a defence. However, the Court qualified this by asking whether the force used (body checking in close proximity to the boards) by the accused was 'so violent and inherently dangerous as to have been excluded from the implied consent'.[108] The Court held that egregious acts of violence which went beyond that which was incidental to the game would negate the victim's consent. The Court also noted that the state of mind of the accused was not the only consideration. It identified a number of objective criteria in order to determine the scope of the participant's implied consent, including the setting of the game, whether the game was part of a league and the nature of such a league, the age of the players, conditions under which the game was played, the extent of the force used, the degree of risk and the probability of serious harm occurring.[109]

The case was welcomed as it created a set of principles which a court can consider in contrast to the vague tests that earlier cases suggested.[110] Any acts of violence that go beyond what is customary to the playing of the game will be deemed to exceed the implied consent. The Court clearly found that conduct which carried a high risk of injury would be rendered unlawful regardless of consent or the frequency with which it occurs in the sport.[111] The level of force permitted would depend on the circumstances of the game. **4–50**

Anderson succinctly summarises the *Cey* case as follows: **4–51**

> the court attempted to clarify the vagueness of the earlier approach by providing that in future the consent of sports participants should be recognised by reference to a number of specific factors such as the nature and standard of the game played, the nature of the act from the point of view of the degree of force and harm inflicted and the state of mind of the accused.[112]

In the case of *State of Iowa v Floyd*, the violent act occurred during a time-out in a four-on-four game of basketball. [113] The defendant was found guilty of two counts of assault without intent to inflict serious injury but causing bodily injury, a serious misdemeanour under s 708.2(2) of the Iowa Code.[114] The Court held that there was 'no nexus between the **4–52**

---

[108] ibid [491]–[492].
[109] ibid [490]–[491].
[110] McCutcheon (n 8) 276.
[111] ibid.
[112] Jack Anderson, 'Mens Sana in Corpore Sano? Violence in Sport and the Criminal Law' (1998) 6(1) Irish Student Law Review 64, 76.
[113] (Iowa App 1990), 466 NW 2d 919.
[114] ibid 920. The Code has been amended over the years. Title XVI Criminal Law and Procedure, ch 708 deals with assault. The latest version of ch 708 from the Iowa Code 2024 can be accessed here: <https://www.legis.iowa.gov/law/iowaCode/sections?codeChapter=708&year=2024> accessed 8 May 2024.

defendant's acts and playing the game of basketball'.[115] The altercation had broken out after the game had finished and the defendant and some of his victims had been on the side line and the victims had not participated in the game, therefore the Court reasoned the victims were not 'voluntary participants in a sport'.[116] The Court reiterated the point that the violent act was not a reasonably foreseeable incident. It created an unreasonable risk of serious injury or breach of the peace.[117]

4–53 In another American case involving a game of 'pick up' basketball, the Court of Appeals in the *State of Washington v Shelley* agreed that consent may be a defence to assault in a sporting context, however, there are limits.[118] Shelley was convicted of assaulting another player after he struck and broke his victim's jaw in three places. The Court of Appeals dismissed the appeal, holding

> that a defendant is entitled to argue that another player may legally consent to conduct that causes or threatens bodily harm if the conduct and the harm are reasonably foreseeable hazards of joint participation in a lawful, athletic contest or competitive sport cures any problem with vagueness. With this defence, an ordinary person should understand that intentionally punching a person in an athletic competition may result in criminal prosecution.[119]

4–54 Generally, it is accepted that sportspersons consent to risks that are permitted by the rules of the game. The rules of the sport serve a dual purpose. They provide for the protection of the player and provide that the game is played uniformly, thus ensuring a better game. However, the Canadian court in *R v Green* disagreed with this hypothesis.[120] It held that contact in violation of the rules may also be consented to: for

---

115 *Floyd* (n 113) [922].

116 ibid. Section 708.1(2) defines an 'assault' as occurring when 'without justification, a person carries out any act which is intended to cause pain or injury to, or which is intended to result in physical contact which will be insulting or offensive to another, coupled with apparent ability to execute the act'. Section 708.1 (3) (a) provides that the act described in sub-s 2 does not constitute an assault in situations 'where the person doing any of the above enumerated acts, and such other person, are voluntary participants in a sport, social or other activity, not in itself criminal, and such act is a reasonably foreseeable incident of such sport or activity, and does not create an unreasonable risk of serious injury or breach of peace'.

117 *Floyd* (n 113) [923].

118 929 P.2d 489, 85 Wn.App. 24. The majority determined that the case lacked precedential value and thus it was not published in the Washington Appellate Reports. It was filed for public record. The judgment can be accessed here <https://caselaw.findlaw.com/wa-court-of-appeals/1485551.html> accessed 8 May 2024. Pick-up games do not have a referee and instead the players call their own fouls. Gonzalez, the victim, had fouled Shelley a few times during the game and had scratched Shelley's face resulting in Shelley leaving and subsequently returning to the game. The assault occurred after playing resumed. By all accounts, Gonzalez was known to engage in aggressive play.

119 ibid.

120 [1971] 1 O R 591; 2 CCC (2d) 442; 16 DLR (3d) 137.

example, there are situations where the conduct is a common occurrence (outside the rules of the game, but within the playing culture) and does not create a high risk of injury.

The Playing Culture

The courts traditionally confined consent to incidents that fell within the rules of the game. The courts in both *R v Bradshaw* and *R v Billinghurst* implied that consent could be interpreted in a broader context.[121] In *Bradshaw*, the Court referred to the 'rules and practices of the game', while in *Billinghurst*, the Court referred to players consenting to force that could be 'reasonably expected to happen during a game'. In the case of *R v Blissett* the doctrine of playing culture received tacit recognition.[122] However, the English courts, unlike their Canadian counterparts, remained reluctant to expressly recognise that consent could include the playing culture of the sport. Playing culture has been defined to include codes of conduct, tactics and commonly occurring incidents of foul play.[123] **4–55**

The case of *R v Barnes* is an important development as for the first time an English court, the Court of Appeal of England and Wales, considered a wider definition of consent to include the playing culture.[124] It stated that consent could be a defence in the case of a legitimate sport if the use of force by the defendant was of the kind that could be expected during the game. The Court of Appeal relied heavily on Canadian jurisprudence; it held that a number of factors as listed above should be considered by the jury. **4–56**

While the case presented the Court of Appeal with an opportunity to expressly adopt the concept of playing culture, its analysis is somewhat flawed. Pendlebury notes that the Court of Appeal did not properly apply the criteria to the case – if it had, then Barnes' conviction would have been upheld.[125] Evidence from the match officials showed that the tackle was a two-foot lunge and the force used was not of a degree to which the victim would have consented.[126] The decision is disappointing in this respect and until a future case provides a clearer definition of playing culture or the governing bodies are entrusted to develop more precise guidelines, 'sportspersons will still struggle to compete within **4–57**

---

[121] *Bradshaw* (n 47); *Billinghurst* (n 50).

[122] *The Independent*, London (4 December 1992) <https://www.independent.co.uk/sport/football-blissett-s-case-causes-confusion-the-blissettuzzell-case-has-brought-a-range-of-reactions-within-the-football-world-1561769.html> accessed 2 July 2024.

[123] Adam Pendlebury, 'Perceptions of Playing Culture in Sport: The Problem of Diverse Opinion in the Light of *Barnes*' (2006) 4(2) Entertainment and Sports Law Journal 5.

[124] *Barnes* (n 56).

[125] Pendlebury (n 123) para 14.

[126] ibid.

the boundaries of the law'.[127] Since the Pendlebury article, the CPS published the *Agreement on the Handling of Incidents Falling under both Criminal and Football Regulatory Jurisdiction* in 2015.[128] The Agreement endorses the decision of the Court of Appeal in *Barnes* as it footnotes the case in relation to the following statement: 'In respect of incidents on the field of play which cause injury, prosecutions should be reserved for situations where the conduct is considered sufficiently grave to be properly categorised as criminal.'[129] It provides two examples, one relating to an on-the-ball incident and the other relating of an off-the-ball incident:

> a. An alleged incident which takes place in or around the action in the game (an 'on the ball' incident) is more likely to be dealt with adequately by the FA. However, where it is apparent that the player involved in an 'on the ball' incident clearly intended to harm or injure another player, and serious harm or injury is caused, a criminal investigation may be required.
>
> b. An alleged incident which does not take place in or around the action in the game (an 'off the ball' incident), especially where it takes place some distance from the action, whether there is a clear intention to harm or injure or whether the result of a reckless action, and serious harm or injury is caused, may require a criminal investigation.[130]

4–58 This Agreement has in some way countenanced the criticisms made by Pendlebury. As seen in the discussion on the handful of cases that have gone before the courts, the approach in England and Wales is generally one of non-intervention on the part of the authorities.[131] This is reflected in the 2020 Working Practices document, which updates the 2015 Agreement and provides:

> It is generally desirable for the FA/FAW to deal exclusively with all football regulatory matters and sanction their Participants appropriately

---

127 ibid para 40. Pendlebury concedes that the governing bodies may be the more appropriate body to devise rules in relation to the playing culture as 'they act responsibly, and they certainly have the expertise to set an appropriate boundary for sportspersons'.

128 *Agreement between the Crown Prosecution Service, Association of Chief Police Officers, the Football Association and the Football Association of Wales on the Handling of Incidents Falling under Both Criminal and Football Regulatory Jurisdiction* (2 September 2015). It is no longer available on the CPS website but the 2013 version, *Protocol on the Handling of Incidents Falling under both Criminal and Football Regulatory Jurisdiction* (23 December 2013) can be sourced at <https://www.google.com/url?sa=t&source=web&rct=j&opi=89978449&url=https://www.thefa.com/~/media/files/pdf/the-fa-2013-14/governance/crown-prosecution-fa-faw.ashx&ved=2ahUKEwiQnY-Ckf-FAxV0WkEAHSzKCRIQFnoECBQQAQ&usg=AOvVaw15m2ItuJnKKrAWm-z0DC07> accessed 8 May 2024.

129 Agreement on the Handling of Incidents (n 128) 4.

130 ibid 4–5.

131 Edge Hill University, 'The Criminal Law and Sport' (*Sports Law Insights*, 18 March 2020) <https://www.edgehill.ac.uk/law/research/centre-for-sports-law-research/sports-law-insights-two-faces-sports-law/criminal-law-sport/> accessed 8 May 2024.

> for breaches of their Rules and Regulations. There will, however, be instances where the breach is so serious that it will also be appropriate for a criminal investigation or prosecution to take place. Each case must be considered on its own facts.[132]

For the most part, it is the disciplinary mechanisms of the sports **4–59**
governing bodies that deal with on-field violence. The prosecutions have been limited to the more egregious cases. One such example is *R v Chapman*, which concerned a violent altercation during a rugby match.[133] As the game was nearing to an end, the ball had gone out of play and Chapman struck his opponent, Johnson, with his boot studs. He stomped on Johnson's leg, resulting in it being broken in two places.[134] The victim suffered serious injuries which required reconstructive surgery and skin grafts on his right leg. One of the match officials testified that it was a 'callous deliberate act with intent to cause injury to the player'.[135] The matter was dealt with initially by the internal disciplinary mechanism of the English Football Association (FA) who imposed an 84-day suspension on Chapman. Unhappy with the internal handling and arguably lenient sanction, Johnson brought it to the attention of the police, who investigated the incident. On foot of this investigation, the file was sent to the CPS, who decided to prosecute Chapman for unlawfully and maliciously inflicting grievous bodily harm contrary to s 20 of the Offences against the Person Act 1861.[136] At the Warwick Crown Court, Chapman was sentenced to six months in prison. Orme J set out the parameters of the criminal law's involvement in sport and stated:

> This is a deliberate act, a premeditated act. A football match gives no-one any excuse to carry out wanton violence … The result of what you did was that Mr Johnson suffered a badly broken leg – it horrified those who saw it. I accept you showed very early remorse and there is substantial mitigation which can be put forward for you. But I have also had to consider the position of the victim and your very deliberate criminal act.[137]

---

132 Crown Prosecution Services, *Working Practices on the Handling of Incidents Falling under both Criminal and Football Regulatory Jurisdiction* (18 August 2020) 1 <https://www.cps.gov.uk/sites/default/files/documents/publications/Working-Practice-football-incidents-July-2020.pdf> accessed 8 May 2024. However, the 2020 iteration does not refer to *Barnes*. In the 2013, 2015 and 2020 documents, they all state the following: 'If an alleged offence is aggravated by factors that would potentially make it a "hate crime", it is more likely that a criminal investigation will be required': 3.

133 *Chapman* (n 56).

134 'Warwickshire Sunday League Footballer Jailed for Breaking Opponent's Leg' *Business Live* (Liverpool, 4 March 2010) <https://www.business-live.co.uk/economic-development/warwickshire-sunday-league-footballer-jailed-3932916> accessed 8 May 2024.

135 ibid.

136 Offences against the Person Act 1861, UK Public General Acts 1861 c 100 (Regnal. 24_and_25_Vict) <https://www.legislation.gov.uk/ukpga/Vict/24-25/100/section/20> accessed 2 July 2024. The section has been amended over the years. Initially the penalty was penal servitude.

137 Quoted by Pendlebury (n 59) 2.

4–60 The *Chapman* decision was criticised by Pendlebury.[138] He called for 'dialogue' between law enforcement and the key stakeholders at all levels of sport.[139] He views the *Chapman* decision as taking away on-the-ball offences from the remit of sports governing bodies as advocated by the judgment in *Barnes* to the increased involvement of criminal law enforcement agencies. His article predates the CPS 2015 Agreement and 2013 Protocol.[140] There is no reference to *R v Chapman* in the 2015 Agreement; the only case cited is *R v Barnes*. The Agreement explicitly states that the criminal law will only become involved in situations which are 'sufficiently grave to be properly categorised as criminal'.[141] Arguably, *R v Barnes* is still good law, and the criminal law will only interfere in the decisions of sports governing bodies where there is the deliberate or intentional infliction of harm. *R v Chapman*, although not referenced in the Protocol, would fall under the on-the-ball incident described by the 2015 Agreement (a) above.[142]

Self-Defence

4–61 For self-defence to be raised, the defendant's force must be proved to be proportionate to the perceived or actual infliction of harm. A player could not invoke this defence if there was an element of vindictiveness. Self-defence is only available to players who reacted honestly and in good faith.[143] Self-defence was successfully raised in the case of *R v Maki*.[144] This is a Canadian case that arose from an altercation that occurred in 1969 in an ice hockey match between the Boston Bruins and the St Louis Blues. It was an exhibition match between a US team and a Canadian team that took place in Ottawa. Ted Green, of the Boston Bruins, swung and hit Wayne Maki of St Louis Blues on the face with his glove. Maki then turned and speared Green in the abdomen with his hockey stick. Green retaliated by swinging the stick at Maki's shoulder. Maki ended the altercation by striking his opponent's head with his hockey stick, resulting in Green suffering from a fractured skull which required the insertion of a steel plate in his head. The incident took place over a ten-second period. The two players were tried in two separate actions, *R v Green* and *R v Maki*.[145]

4–62 In *Maki*, the accused was charged with assault causing bodily harm under the Canadian Criminal Code.[146] The Court acknowledged that

138 ibid.
139 ibid 9.
140 Protocol on the Handling of Incidents (n 128).
141 ibid 4.
142 ibid.
143 Hechter (n 17) 451.
144 [1970] 3 OR 780, 1 CCC (2d) 333, 14 DLR (3d) 164 (Prov Ct).
145 *Green* (n 120); *Maki* ibid.
146 Bodily harm is defined as 'any hurt or injury to a person that interferes with the health or comfort of the person and that is more than merely transient or trifling in nature'. It was s 230 at the time of the case. It is now s 267(b), Criminal

players assume certain risks and hazards when they step on the rink, however, 'no sports league, no matter how well organized or self-policed it may be, should thereby render the players in that league immune from criminal prosecution ... no athlete should be presumed to accept malicious, unprovoked, or overly violent attacks'.[147] The judge reiterated that an important factor in sporting assaults was the degree of force used, which depends on the circumstances, including the nature of the sport. Maki successfully pleaded self-defence and was acquitted of all charges. Carter J held that the Crown had failed to prove beyond reasonable doubt that the accused did not feel that he was under reasonable apprehension of bodily harm or that he had used excessive force in the circumstances.[148] In *R* v *Green*, the accused was charged with common assault.[149] Fitzpatrick J adopted a different approach to Carter J and held that 'no hockey player enters onto the ice of the National Hockey League without consenting to and without knowledge of the possibility that he is going to be hit in one of many ways once he is on that ice'.[150] Kitchen J concluded that the hitting on the face with a glove was something that occurred hundreds of times; it was the spearing of Green by Maki that 'was the real cause of the altercation'.[151] In acquitting Green, the judge held that 'Mr. Green's action was instinctive, and I find it was more protective in his own interests than anything else of his own safety'.[152]

Involuntary Reflex

For an injury to be the result of an involuntary reflex, the requisite *mens rea* must have been absent. The defence is based on the premise that the action of the defendant is instinctive as opposed to premeditated.[153] Baxter notes that the defence negates the *mens rea* requirement and the prosecution is thus limited in proving its case beyond a reasonable 4–63

Code, RSC 1985, c C–46, s 267, <https://canlii.ca/t/7vf2#sec267> accessed 9 May 2024. Section 267(a) concerns the carrying of or the use of or threat of a weapon. Most hockey cases come within the ambit of s 267(b), and not s 267(a). Arguably s 267(b) is deemed more appropriate in these cases as they involve sports stars and assault with a weapon attracts far more negative press: see Anna Husa and Stephen Thiele, 'In the Name of the Game: Hockey Violence and the Criminal Justice System' (2001–2002) 45 Criminal Law Quarterly 509, 513. One notable exception is the case of *R v McSorley* [2000] BCPC 116 (BC Prov Ct). Kitchen J took a stern view of the use of the hockey stick as a weapon. He stated: 'Every time a player uses a stick to apply force to another player, the stick is being used as a weapon and not to direct the puck as it was designed to do': [105].

147 1 CCC (2d) 333, 336.

148 Up to the point of Maki's blow, Green had been the aggressor.

149 [1971] 1 OR 591 (n 120).

150 ibid 594.

151 ibid 597.

152 ibid.

153 Don Eugene-Nolan Gibson, 'Violence in Professional Sports: A Proposal for Self-Regulation' (1981) 3(3) Hastings Communications and Entertainment Law Journal 425, 438.

doubt.[154] In *R v Green*, the defendant's 'half chop' to Maki's shoulder was not an assault but rather an 'instinctive' reaction to a prior blow from Maki.[155] Sports agent Bob Woolf disagrees with the defence.[156] He argues that the 'heat of the game has always been a kind of moral defence in sports to excuse bad manners and irrational acts'.[157] However, Kitchen J in *R v Green* recognised that playing a high-level game of hockey was not the same as 'the ordinary facts of life', and this was an important consideration in the acquittal of Green:

> We must remember that we are dealing with a hockey game. We are dealing with two competent hockey players at the peak of their form. We are not now dealing with the ordinary facts of life, the ordinary going and coming. We must remember that when we discuss the action of these men we are examining it within that forum and we are discussing it within the context in which the game is played, at high speed and obviously with people keenly on edge.[158]

4–64 In support of the conclusion reached by Kitchen J, Gibson asserts that a sportsperson's actions are 'the result of attitudes instilled in him at an early age, combined with the high level of pressure and emotion associated with sports'.[159]

4–65 The defence was also successful in the case of *R v Leyte*, which involved a play-off game of handball.[160] Perkins J outlined the limitations of the defence. It cannot be invoked if there is a 'significant time interval' between the end of play and the blows struck.[161] If this occurs, the actions can no longer be labelled as instinctive and players 'cannot be deemed to consent to assaults at that stage'.[162]

Provocation

4–66 Under Irish law, provocation provides a partial defence in a situation 'only where a person is charged with murder, and it operates to reduce murder to the lesser charge of manslaughter'.[163] It follows that provocation would unlikely provide a sportsperson with a defence unless the charge against them is murder and the accused can demonstrate that they lost self-control due to the provocation of the victim.

---

154 Angela Baxter, 'Hockey Violence: The Canadian Criminal Code and Professional Hockey' (2005–2006) 32(2) Manitoba Law Journal 281, 294.

155 *Green* (n 120). Maki had struck Green in the testicles. See also R v *Wolfe* (1974) 20 CCC (2d) 333, 10 CRNS 268, [1970] 3 OR 780, 14 DLR.

156 *Behind Closed Doors* (Atheneum 1976) 141.

157 ibid.

158 *Green* (n 120) 142.

159 Gibson (n 153) 438–39.

160 13 CCC (2d) 458.

161 ibid 459.

162 ibid.

163 Law Reform Commission Report, *Defences in Criminal Law* (LRC 95–2009) 7–8, para 24.

The defence has been criticised as continuing to 'polarise common law jurisdictions'.[164] While the defence only applies to someone charged with murder, it can be considered in lesser crimes, for example assault, when it comes to sentencing. In 2000, the New Zealand Law Commission noted that the defence is a difficult one which requires the juxtaposition of an objective test and a subjective test.[165] In applying a subjective test, the individual characteristics of the accused are considered: what made them more susceptible to losing control in comparison to someone else.[166] In utilising an objective test, the defence assumes that people should be able to keep their emotions in check.[167] New Zealand abolished the defence by way of the Crimes (Provocation Repeal) Amendment Act 2009.[168] In England and Wales, the partial defence of provocation was abolished under the Coroners and Justice Act 2009.[169] Section 54 of the 2009 Act, which commenced on 4 October 2010, created the partial defence to murder of a loss of control.[170] **4–67**

In the Canadian tort case of *Agar v Canning*, Bastin J of the Manitoba Court of Queen's Bench observed that the defence of provocation had not been raised by the defendant and Canning denied that he had been provoked.[171] The judge held that '[a]lthough provocation is not a defence, the law is clear that in assessing damages evidence of provocation should be considered in mitigation'.[172] The case arose from an altercation at an ice hockey game involving Agar, who was aged 17½ at the time of the game, and the defendant, Canning, was 23.[173] In a scramble for the puck, the plaintiff attempted to thwart the defendant's efforts to reach the goal after the defendant had body checked the plaintiff and **4–68**

---

164 Michelle-Thérèse Stevenson, 'Provocation in Ireland: Is There Still a Defence for the Defence?' (*Criminal Justice in Ireland Blog*, 20 November 2019) <https://criminaljusticeinireland.wordpress.com/2019/11/20/provocation-in-ireland-is-there-still-a-defence-for-the-defence/> accessed 9 May 2024.

165 New Zealand Law Commission, *Battered Defendants: Victims of Domestic Violence Who Offend: A Discussion Paper* (Te Aka Matua o te Ture, Preliminary Paper 41, 7 August 2000) ch 6: Provocation, para 83. The chapter is available here: <http://www.nzlii.org/nz/other/nzlc/pp/PP41/PP41-6_.html> accessed 9 May 2024.

166 ibid.

167 ibid.

168 Public Act 2009 No 64, s 5 provides: 'The partial defence of provocation in cases of culpable homicide, in so far as it has any effect as a rule or principle of common law in New Zealand, is abolished.' The text of the Act is available at <https://www.legislation.govt.nz/act/public/2009/0064/latest/DLM2258102.html> accessed 9 May 2024.

169 UK Public General Acts 2009 c 25.

170 The text of s 54 can be accessed at <https://www.legislation.gov.uk/ukpga/2009/25/section/54> accessed 2 July 2024. For a detailed discussion on the defence, see Kate Fitz-Gibbon, 'Replacing Provocation in England and Wales: Examining the Partial Defence of Loss of Control' (2013) 40(2) Journal of Law and Society 280.

171 (1965) 54 WWR 302 (Man QB). The decision contains only 13 paragraphs. It was appealed to the Manitoba Court of Appeal who unanimously upheld Bastin J's decision: see *Agar v Canning* (1965) 55 WWR 384 (Man CA).

172 (1965) 54 WWR 302 [9].

173 ibid [1].

in doing so retrieved the puck.[174] The plaintiff used the stick to block the defendant resulting in the defendant suffering from a painful injury on the back of his neck.[175] Canning stopped and hit Agar with the blade of the stick in his face between the nose and right eye. Agar was rendered unconscious and fell to the ice and at that stage the game was terminated.[176] In referring to the latitude generally granted to a lawfully constituted sport, the judge noted its limits:

> The conduct of a player in the heat of the game is instinctive and unpremeditated and should not be judged by standards suited to polite social intercourse. But a little reflection will establish that some limit must be placed on a player's immunity from liability. Each case must be decided on its own facts so it is difficult, if not impossible, to decide how the line is to be drawn in every circumstance. But injuries inflicted in circumstances which show a definite resolve to cause serious injury to another, even when there is provocation and in the heat of the game, should not fall within the scope of the implied consent. I have come to the conclusion that the act of the defendant in striking plaintiff in the face with a hockey stick, in retaliation for the blow he received, goes beyond the limit marking exemption from liability.[177]

4–69 While not a criminal case, *Agar v Canning* is an example of a sports case where the defence of provocation was discussed. It may act as a mitigating factor when it comes to damages. Healey notes that a murder charge would only ensure if a sportsperson pulled a knife on an opponent and stabbed them to death.[178] Thus, for a charge of murder to succeed, proof of premeditation on the part of the defendant is required.

Diminished Capacity

4–70 The defence of diminished capacity, like provocation, is a partial defence that can only be used in a case of murder.[179] The defence was introduced into Irish law by way of s 6 of the Criminal Law (Insanity)

---

[174] ibid [2].

[175] ibid. Bastin stated J: 'I find that he did this in retaliation for the blow he had received.'

[176] ibid.

[177] ibid [7] and [8]

[178] Healey (n 27) 194.

[179] A recent study shows that the defence in Ireland is used 23 times more often than in England: see Conor Gallagher, 'Insanity Pleas During Homicide Trials Rise Threefold' *The Irish Times* (Dublin, 25 May 2021) <https://www.irishtimes.com/news/crime-and-law/insanity-pleas-during-homicide-trials-rise-threefold-1.4574049> accessed 9 May 2024.

Act 2006.[180] The defence has never been invoked by a sportsperson.[181] Standen remarks that it is surprising that no athlete has endeavoured to rely on this defence given the volume of sociological research that supports the view that sportspersons' 'conditioned behaviour tends to produce violent conduct off of the playing field'.[182]

On Field-Violence and the Gaelic Athletic Association

Given the largely amateur nature of Irish sport, there are very few **4–71**
cases where a sportsperson has been prosecuted. The fact that a sport is amateur does not mean that the criminal law will not intervene. The Irish courts have traditionally taken a 'soft' approach to on-field violence in sport.[183] There is a marked reluctance on the part of the players, sports bodies and indeed the public to invoke the criminal law in on-field disputes. The Irish courts tend to be lenient on sportspersons in situations where they have paid compensation to the victim in advance of the trial, or a donation has been made to a charity. In the case of the *Director of Public Prosecutions (DPP) v McCartan*, McCartan, a Down footballer, was found guilty of s 3 assault after breaking the jaw of an opponent, Larkin, during a match between Down and Westmeath.[184] Early J decided to postpone sentencing and stated that his final determination would be influenced by any offer of compensation to the victim.[185] Early J decided against a prison sentence as McCartan had made a generous donation to a charity.[186] McCartan was ordered to pay €1,243 in legal costs.[187]

---

180 Number 11 of 2006 <http://www.irishstatutebook.ie/eli/2006/act/11/enacted/en/print#sec6> accessed 2 July 2024. Section 6(1) provides: 'Where a person is tried for murder and the jury or, as the case may be, the Special Criminal Court finds that the person—(a) did the act alleged, (b) was at the time suffering from a mental disorder, and (c) the mental disorder was not such as to justify finding him or her not guilty by reason of insanity, but was such as to diminish substantially his or her responsibility for the act, the jury or court, as the case may be, shall find the person not guilty of that offence but guilty of manslaughter on the ground of diminished responsibility.

181 Standen (n 5) 619–20.

182 ibid.

183 Jerome Reilly, 'Courts Soft on Violent Tackles on Sports Field' *Irish Independent* (Dublin, 1 April 2007) <https://www.independent.ie/irish-news/courts-soft-on-violent-tackles-on-sports-field-26286476.html> accessed 9 May 2024.

184 Unreported, 1 November 2004, District Court.

185 The case was first heard on 1 November 2004 at Dublin District Court.

186 McCartan made a €10,000 donation to the Lions Club in Portlaoise at the behest of Larkin, who was stationed there as a Garda. See 'GAA Man in Assault Donates €10,000' *The Irish Times* (Dublin, 11 January 2005) <https://www.irishtimes.com/news/gaa-man-in-assault-donates-10-000-1.405187?mode=sample&auth-failed=1&pw-origin=https%3A%2F%2Fwww.irishtimes.com%2Fnews%2Fgaa-man-in-assault-donates-10-000-1.405187> accessed 9 May.

187 'McCartan to Pay €10,000 to Charity of Victim's Choice' *The Irish Times* (Dublin, 6 November 2004) <https://www.irishtimes.com/news/mccartan-to-pay-10-000-to-charity-of-victim-s-choice-1.1167580?mode=sample&auth-failed=1&pw-

4–72 The judge recognised that Larkin's marking of McCartan would have caused much irritation. However, he held: 'to strike someone without legal justification is a crime, whether it takes place in the street, in the family home, or the football pitch or elsewhere'.[188] There is nothing new in this sentiment. Similar comments have been made in English cases. What is interesting from the case is the attitude of GAA's Games Administration Committee (GAC). The GAC had convened an inquiry into the matter but decided to drop it.[189] The matter had gone before the GAC and subsequently to an Appeals Management Committee (AMC) and, after a 17-month inquiry, it was dropped on procedural grounds.[190] The GAC attracted much criticism as this case involved a very serious injury and it seemed to be making light of serious incidents of on-field violence. Perhaps the criticism was somewhat harsh given that the GAA has made concerted efforts to deal with ill-discipline in sport.[191] Anderson concludes: 'in sum, the GAC/AMC's handling of the investigation is a classic example, from a sports administration point of view, of how not to deal with such incidents'.[192] The GAA showed a great reluctance to involve the authorities and was reported to have criticised the gardaí as they attempted to question McCartan after he left a hearing at Croke Park.[193]

4–73 In October 2008, Keane, a hurler from Fethard GAA club, was found guilty of assault at Clonmel Circuit Court. Ryan, the victim, was bitten on both ears and required reconstructive surgery. Keane was sentenced to 12 months in Limerick Prison, with nine suspended. Keane was also ordered to pay €12,000 in compensation to Ryan. This was the first time, in recent years, that a GAA player was imprisoned for on-field violence.[194] There have been other instances where players have been given suspended sentences and one player was ordered to enter a

---

origin=https%3A%2F%2Fwww.irishtimes.com%2Fnews%2Fmccartan-to-pay-10-000-to-charity-of-victim-s-choice-1.1167580> accessed 2 July 2024.

[188] Frank McNally, 'McCartan Found Guilty of Assaulting Westmeath Player' *The Irish Times* (Dublin, 2 November 2004 <https://www.irishtimes.com/news/gaa-footballer-guilty-of-assaulting-opponent-1.1164535?mode=sample&auth-failed=1&pw-origin=https%3A%2F%2Fwww.irishtimes.com%2Fnews%2Fgaa-footballer-guilty-of-assaulting-opponent-1.1164535> accessed 9 May 2024.

[189] Down had appealed the decision of the GAC to the Management Committee.

[190] Jack Anderson, 'Policing the Sports Field: The Role of the Criminal Law' (2006) 5(2) International Sports Law Review 25, 26.

[191] Jack Anderson, 'Ignorance of the Law Is No Defence' *The Irish Times* (Dublin, 18 December 2004) <https://www.irishtimes.com/sport/ignorance-of-the-law-is-no-defence-1.1170547?mode=sample&auth-failed=1&pw-origin=https%3A%2F%2Fwww.irishtimes.com%2Fsport%2Fignorance-of-the-law-is-no-defence-1.1170547> accessed 9 May 2024. Anderson adds that 'its mooted independent appeals tribunal is to be welcomed, and if given precise terms of reference and adequate resources will enhance the GAA'.

[192] Anderson (n 190) 26. Anderson adds that Westmeath may have been frustrated with the delay in proceedings and decided to go to the courts to seek redress.

[193] McNally (n 188).

[194] In the early days of the GAA, several players were imprisoned for on-field violence and the occasional unlawful killing. See Anderson (n 16).

peace bond for five years, which means he was prohibited from playing football for five years.[195]

Not surprisingly, the decision was unwelcomed by the GAA. The player had been suspended for 96 games and compensation had been paid to the victim under the GAA's player injury scheme. A spokesman for Fethard GAA was quoted as saying, 'the GAA would not have survived a century-and-a-half if people went running to the courts'.[196] 4–74

The case of *DPP v Prendergast* is an example of a superior court dealing with on-field violence in the GAA.[197] As it was an appeal case, the decision did not offer much in the way of a discussion of the substantive issues including consent. In line with the lenient approach taken in previous cases in relation to on-field violence, the Court of Appeal overturned the sentence imposed by a Circuit Court judge. 4–75

In the *Director of Public Prosecutions (DPP) v Friel*, a three-month custodial sentence was suspended for twelve months.[198] During the course of a Gaelic football match, Friel was accused of ripping his opponent's scrotum resulting in a 7cm laceration. Friel was charged with assault causing harm and tried summarily in the Letterkenny District Court. Cunningham J, on reviewing video footage of the altercation, stated that the grabbing of an opponent's testicles was not 'within the rules or culture' of Gaelic football.[199] On the issue of consent, Cunningham J acknowledged that in a contact sport 'certain conduct is admissible and consented to' and there is a 'certain degree of assumed risk', however, the actions of the defendant fell outside the explicit consent of the victim.[200] Given the seriousness of the s 3 assault, the judge placed it at the upper end of the District Court's jurisdiction.[201] 4–76

---

195 ibid. The case of the *Director of Public Prosecutions v Kelly*, Unreported, 2 November 2005 was heard by Neilan J at Tullamore District Court. The defendant kicked his opponent in the head during a club game. The victim spent 13 days in hospital and made a full recovery. The defendant was given a suspended 11-month sentence and paid €15,000 in compensation. The judge also instructed Kelly to enter a peace bond for five years, a condition of which required him not to play football for the duration of the bond. This amounted to a type of 'banning order' which was a novel form of punishment in the circumstances. Kelly's solicitor sought to save the defendant's playing career as he had recently been selected to play for Offaly. However, the Neilan J refused, saying that he was unimpressed with the GAA's apparent tolerance of on-field violence.

196 Anderson (n 16).

197 (n 74).

198 Unreported, 13 March 2023. See Chris McNulty, 'Suspended sentence for GAA player who ripped opponent's scrotum' *The Irish Examiner* (Cork, 13 March 2023) <https://www.irishexaminer.com/news/courtandcrime/arid-41092420.html> accessed 3 July 2024.

199 McNulty ibid. The defendant maintained that it was an accident and unintentional.

200 ibid.

201 ibid. The judge applied s 99 of the Criminal Justice Act 2006 which relates to a bond. If Friel is brought before the court within 12 months, his three-month sentence will be imposed.

4–77 On 5 June 2024, a Wicklow GAA player was found guilty of s 3 assault by a jury in the Bray Circuit Court.[202] During a Wicklow Division 1 match on 9 June 2019, Cullen punched his opponent, Rodgers, in the face. Cullen had pleaded not guilty to the charge of assault and argued self-defence following an alleged foul by the victim.[203] Cullen had informed the gardaí that the victim had sustained his injury after he collided with the back of the head of one of his teammates as 'a general melee' ensued following the alleged foul by Rodgers.[204] The incident occurred in the second half of the match when the victim's team was ahead, with his team winning the game against the defendant's team. Video evidence was presented to the court which showed that the incident occurred after play continued even though the referee had blown the whistle following a foul committed by other players. Rodgers asserted that he shouldered and tripped the defendant, Cullen fell to the ground and after getting back on his feet, he threw the ball at Rodgers, and punched him in the face.[205] The victim described blood pouring down his face and noted that his gum guard had been split in two. The referee gave Cullen a red card, and Rodgers attempted to keep his loosened teeth in place with the gum guard, however, he required emergency dental treatment.[206] Counsel for the DPP rejected Cullen's contention that Rodgers had attempted to stop the defendant with a 'clothes line' tackle, however, it was accepted that Rodgers had tripped Cullen. There was a time lapse between the tripping and the punch inflicted by the defendant, and thus was a form of retribution.[207] The defence counsel accepted that the defendant could not legitimately contend that he was acting in self-defence if he had just been tripped or shouldered or 'clothes line' tackled. However, in looking at the cumulative effect of the single incidences, counsel for Cullen conjectured that his client did not know if Rodgers was 'going to stop'.[208] O'Sullivan J explained to the jury that they needed to be satisfied that Cullen had thrown a punch at Rodgers. With respect to the defence of self-defence, the judge advised the jury about the parameters of the defence. As discussed above, for self-defence to be raised, the defendant's force must be proved to be proportionate to the perceived or actual infliction of harm. The jury did not accept the defence and found the defendant guilty of s 3 assault. A date for sentencing has not yet been fixed. It remains to be seen if Cullen

[202] WWDP0010/2020 *Director of Public Prosecutions v Cullen*, unreported, 5 June 2024. The case was heard over two days, 4 and 5 June 2024. For more details of the case see Séan McCárthaigh, 'GAA player (39) found guilty of assault after punch in club match left victim with several damaged teeth' *Irish Independent* (Dublin, 5 June 2024) <https://www.independent.ie/irish-news/courts/gaa-player-39-found-guilty-of-assault-after-punch-in-club-match-left-victim-with-several-damaged-teeth/a813597261.html> accessed 4 July 2024.

[203] ibid.

[204] ibid.

[205] ibid.

[206] ibid. The victim lost one tooth and required surgery on the other loosened teeth, his treatment is ongoing.

[207] ibid.

[208] ibid.

will receive a custodial sentence. Given the lenient sentences handed down in previous cases, it is probable that the defendant will receive a suspended sentence.

On 27 June 2024, a Westmeath GAA player was convicted of assault causing harm and had his two years and six months sentence suspended upon agreeing to pay the victim €20,000.[209] The victim suffered a fracture to his eye socket which left him visually impaired following an off-the-ball incident during a Gaelic football match which took place on 19 February 2019.[210] The defendant admitted that he had used excessive force, however, he claimed that his actions were due to an earlier incident that occurred during the match.[211] The judge set a headline sentence of four years as it was at the upper end of the offence but reduced it to 30 months due to mitigating circumstances. Johnson J suspended the sentence for four years and ordered that the defendant pay the victim within one year. In acknowledgment of the egregious nature of the assault and the fact that it was an off-the-ball incident, the defendant was sanctioned by way of a 24-match ban under the GAA discipline process. Johnson J seemed to be alluding to the recent surge in on-field violence as he stated, 'I think the competitive element of the GAA and its growth in the last number of years has reduced considerably the degree of sportsmanship that one should have and should be a cornerstone of sporting engagement'.[212] The judge stressed that the payment of €20,000 to the victim was 'not a case of Mr Molloy buying his way out of trouble, but him suffering the pain of having to earn €20,000, which will be of some assistance to Mr Reilly in his recovery'.[213] Of significance, the judge recognised that the assault occurred 'during a heightened GAA event where a competitive element overtook the sporting motivation'.[214] **4–78**

The above cases illustrate that, although on-field violence can attract the attention of the criminal law in Ireland, the punishments imposed tend to be lenient, with suspended sentences and compensation seeming to be the primary punishments imposed. Thus, although charges are brought for on-field violence and offenders are convicted of assault, the penalties imposed reflect the fact that on-field violence is treated differently to assaults which occur outside the sporting context. **4–79**

The use of the criminal law in sport in Ireland is quite rare and for the **4–80**

---

209 *Director of Public Prosecutions v Molloy*, Unreported, 27 June 2024. The facts of the case are reported here: 'Westmeath footballer who escaped jail for 'off the ball' match assault must pay €20,000 compensation' *The Irish Times* (Dublin, 28 June 2024) <https://www.irishtimes.com/crime-law/courts/2024/06/28/westmeath-footballer-who-escaped-jail-for-off-the-ball-match-assault-must-pay-20000-compensation/> accessed 4 July 2024.

210 ibid.

211 ibid.

212 ibid.

213 ibid.

214 ibid.

most part infractions of the rules are dealt with by the officials on the field of play or in a subsequent internal disciplinary hearing. In response to on-field violence, the GAA in 2013 introduced a black card for 'cynical behaviour fouls', the rules came into force on 1 January 2014.[215] The most recent rules provide for a Sin-Bin in place of the black card. As provided for in the *GAA Official Guide 2024 – Part 1*, Rule 7.2, under Category II Cynical Behaviour Infraction (in Football) is defined as:

> (i) Deliberately pulling down an opponent.
> (ii) Deliberately tripping an opponent with the hand(s), arm, leg, or foot.
> (iii) Deliberately body colliding with an opponent after he has played the ball away or for the purposes of taking him out of a movement of play.
> (iv) Threatening or the use of abusive or provocative language or gestures to an opponent or a teammate.
> (v) Remonstrating in an aggressive manner with a Match Official.[216]

4–81 The penalties for a first infraction provide that the offender must spend 10 minutes in the 'Sin-Bin'.[217] An exception to this is if the offender received a Yellow Card previously in the game for committing a Cautionable Infraction, the player in this situation is prevented from playing in the remainder of the game including any extra time. There is a fixed penalty for a player that resumes playing after spending 10 minutes in the Sin-Bin and commits a further Cynical Behaviour or a Cautionable Infraction; the player is precluded from playing for rest of the game including extra time.[218]

4–82 The rules distinguish between an accidental (within the rules) and a deliberate tackle (outside the rules) in football:

> The tackle is a skill by which one or more players may dispossess an opponent or frustrate his objective within the Rules of Fair Play. A tackle is aimed at the ball, not the player. A tackler may use his body to confront the opponent but deliberate bodily contact such as punching, slapping, arm holding, pushing, tripping, jersey pulling or a full frontal charge is forbidden. The only deliberate physical contact allowed is

---

[215] Gaelic Athletic Association, 'GAA Football Rule Changes 2014' <https://learning.gaa.ie/Rule_changes> accessed 9 May 2024.

[216] Gaelic Athletic Association, *Official Guide – Part 1* (Central Council of the Association 2024) 57 <https://www.gaa.ie/article/gaa-official-guides-codes> accessed 9 May 2024.

[217] ibid.

[218] ibid. The rules provide for 'Fixed Penalty for the accumulation of three ordering-offs for Cynical Behaviour or Second Cautionable infractions committed in the same year in the National Football League, the Inter-County Senior Football Championship or in a combination of both Competitions: A One Match Suspension applicable to the next game in the combination of the National Football League/Inter-County Senior Football Championship, even if that game occurs in the following year. The Penalty of serving the ten minutes in the Sin-Bin shall not count as an "ordering off" under this provision of Rule.'

> that in the course of a Fair Charge one player only with at least one foot on the ground, makes a shoulder to shoulder charge on the player in possession.[219]

In hurling under Rule 5 on Aggressive Fouls, a player will be ordered off if found to have committed any of the following Category IV infractions: **4–83**

> 5.24 To strike or attempt to strike with arm, elbow, hand or knee either with force or causing injury.
>
> 5.25 To strike or attempt to strike an opponent with the head.
>
> 5.26 To strike an opponent with a hurley, either with force or causing injury.
>
> 5.27 To attempt to strike an opponent with a hurley, with force.
>
> 5.28 To kick an opponent either with force or causing injury.
>
> 5.29 To attempt to kick an opponent with force.
>
> 5.30 To stamp on an opponent.
>
> 5.31 To inflict an injury recklessly on an opponent by means other than those stated above.
>
> 5.32 To use abusive language to a Referee, Score Umpire, Line Umpire or Sideline Official.
>
> 5.33 To assault an opposing Team Official.
>
> 5.34 To commit any of the fouls listed in 5.24 to 5.31 (inclusive) against a team-mate.[220]
>
> To act by deed, word or gesture of a racist, sectarian or anti-inclusion / diversity nature against an opponent or match official.

In February 2021 at the Annual Congress the GAA approved Motion 20, which introduced new penalties for aggressive and cynical behaviour in both codes.[221] In hurling, the rules provide for the Sin-Bin to deter **4–84**

[219] Gaelic Athletic Association, *Official Guide-Part 2* (Central Council of the Association 2024) 59–60 <https://www.gaa.ie/article/gaa-official-guides-codes> accessed 9 May 2024. It is explained under the section titled 'Important Terms and Definitions – Football and Hurling'.

[220] ibid 32. At the Annual Council in 2021, the GAA approved several Motions, including Motion 24, which extended the scope of the rule dealing with abuse of a racist, sectarian, or anti-inclusion nature against an opponent to also include such abuse against a match official. It is provided for under r 1.10 of the *Official Guide – Part 1* (n 216).

[221] The rules were initially introduced on a trial basis. See r 5 of *Official Guide – Part*

aggressive play.[222] In 2018 the GAA President highlighted the need to adopt 'zero tolerance' towards on-field violence. In encapsulating the dicta from the courts regarding violence on the pitch, the President reiterated that the GAA:

> cannot allow people to believe that they can behave differently than they would on the street just because they are wearing a jersey or a team tracksuit top or are attending a game. The perpetrators of these incidents are not above the law.[223]

4–85 The black card was introduced to deter cynical and aggressive play in both codes. It 'has been the subject of debate, discussion ... and a whole lot of derision ever since congress gave it the green light in Derry in March 2013'.[224] In the past decade it 'has become a familiar part of Gaelic football, less so hurling' and consequently the controversy surrounding it has dissipated.[225] While black cards 'have improved Gaelic football', it has at times been used for 'honest mistakes instead of truly cynical behaviour'. [226]

4–86 It shows that the GAA is taking on-field violence seriously and that it acknowledges that some incidents of violence will require the intervention of the criminal law. Another form of redress for an injured player may be the civil route of damages. For a GAA player that is injured during a match, their amateur status means that they may be unable to work for a period of time and consequently may be more likely to bring a civil action in order to claim compensation. The GAA operates a wholly self-funded Injury Benefit Fund, however, the fund does not provide full compensation for injuries as it is there to supplement the player's own health insurance or personal accident insurance.[227] It is a limited pool and only provides cover for unrecoverable losses.[228]

---

2 (n 219) 50–56 in relation to football, and r 5.45 of *Official Guide – Part 2* (n 219) 34 in relation to hurling.

222 It was introduced in 2021. See *Official Guide – Part 2* ibid 34.

223 Eoin Ryan, 'President John Horan Warns GAA Brawlers They Are "Not Above the Law"' (*RTÉ Sport*, 26 October 2018) <https://www.rte.ie/sport/gaa/2018/1026/1006798-horan-warns-gaa-brawlers-they-are-not-above-the-law/> accessed 9 May 2024.

224 Niall McCoy, 'The GAA's Black Card – A Decade of Debate' (1 January 2024) <https://www.rte.ie/sport/football/2023/1221/1423288-the-gaas-black-card-a-decade-of-debate/> accessed 9 May 2024.

225 ibid.

226 Malachy Clerkin, 'Black Cards Have Improved Gaelic Football. But We Should Not Forget their Original Purpose' *The Irish Times* (Dublin, 26 February 2024) <https://www.irishtimes.com/sport/gaelic-games/2024/02/26/black-cards-have-improved-gaelic-football-but-we-should-not-forget-their-original-purpose/> accessed 9 May 2024.

227 Gaelic Athletic Association 'GAA Injury Benefit Fund' <https://www.gaa.ie/my-gaa/administrators/gaa-injury-benefit-fund> accessed 9 May 2024.

228 ibid.

The Legal Position of Boxing and Mixed Martial Arts

As already discussed, sportspersons can consent to harm that is within the rules of the game, incidental to the playing of the game or within the playing culture. However, sportspersons do not consent to harm, which is intentional, deliberate, or reckless. The sport of boxing presents an anomaly. The primary objective of boxing is to inflict harm on one's opponent. In the words of Anderson: **4–87**

> boxing presents a level of physicality that is unparalleled in most contact sports. To this day, the most efficient means of victory in a boxing match is to render one's opponent unconscious. That the object of a sport is so crude (and dangerous) is problematic.[229]

Boxing is a legal and recognised sport.[230] As a recognised sport, the law provides it with significant protection. As previously noted, assaults, depending on the circumstances in which they are committed, can be classified as lawful or unlawful. Lawful assaults include injuries sustained in contact sport, reasonable surgeries and parental chastisement and such assaults are permitted as they constitute good reason. There are overriding public policy concerns that immunise such assaults from the intervention of the criminal law. It follows that the defence of consent can only be raised where the activity in question constitutes good reason, it is legal, and the degree of harm inflicted does not involve actual bodily harm or more serious harm. However, applying the common law general exceptions to boxing seems incongruous as it can expose fighters to serious harm. It leads to the question why fighting sports such as boxing remain legal. In order to understand contemporary society's tolerance of boxing and, by extension, MMA, it is necessary to examine the legality of boxing through the paradigm of seminal judgments in the 19th century in which the courts began to distinguish between sparring or boxing and prize fighting. Gunn and Ormerod refer to the legal recognition of boxing as being by 'default rather than design'.[231] In the 19th century, prize fighting became increasingly associated with breaches of the peace and, in explaining the position of the courts up until the 1840s in relation to prize fighting, Anderson states that **4–88**

> the law on prize fighting can be said to be clear; they were illegal primarily on the grounds that they were riotous, unlawful assemblies ... as the nineteenth century progressed, increased policing ... resulted in the

---

[229] Jack Anderson, *The Legality of Boxing: A Punch Drunk Love?* (Birkbeck Law Press 2007) 1.

[230] It is a recognised Olympic sport along with other fighting sports, fencing, judo, taekwondo, and wrestling. The national governing body for boxing in Ireland is the Irish Athletic Boxing Association (IABA). See ch 2 paras 2–21 and 2–22 on governance issues with the International Boxing Association (IBA).

[231] Michael Gunn and David Ormerod, 'The Legality of Boxing' in Steven Greenfield and Guy Osborn (eds), *Law and Sport in Contemporary Society* (Frank Cas 2000) 23.

emphasis in prize fighting prosecutions switching away from unlawful assembly and riot towards assault.[232]

4–89 A number of cases came before the courts in the 19th century, which presented the courts with an opportunity to outlaw prize fighting. While prize fighting was banned, a tamer version of the sport, namely boxing, gained judicial acceptance. It is important to note that prize fighting and bare-knuckle fighting were not devoid of rules but lacked a uniform set of principles.[233] Prize fighting, as the name suggests, involved a financial reward for the fighter that had physically overcome their opponent. In 1743 the Broughton Rules were introduced, which became the sport's first uniform set of rules.[234] Jack Broughton was an English bare-knuckle heavyweight champion and the rules he devised 'defined how the fight should begin and how it should end'.[235] Gloves or mufflers, which were also called 'broughtons', were introduced under the rules.[236] The rules did not define legal or illegal blows, nor did they refer to 'wrestling holds, clinching, head butts, gouging out eyes, biting, kicking or scratching'.[237] The Broughton Rules presented the first attempt to regulate boxing since the Ancient Olympics.[238] While welcomed at first, the Broughton Rules proved to be inadequate; however, they remained in force for almost a century.[239] Brailsford observes that by the 1830s the Broughton Rules' influence had waned:

> The unreliability of the result of appeals to any higher authority meant that much was allowed to pass that in earlier days would have meant disqualification – head butting, hitting a man down on one knee, falling on an opponent with knees in throat or groin and even the equivalent of rugby tackles and blows to the genitals.[240]

4–90 In 1838 the London Prize Ring Rules were introduced, and the rules proved to be more detailed and extensive, including the standardised ring size of 24 feet.[241] The London Prize Ring Rules were revised in 1853

---

232 Anderson (n 229) 44.

233 According to Anderson (ibid 15), a formal roped-off section was rarely used, often the ground would be marked with chalk, there was no such thing as rounds and there was no limit on the duration of the fight.

234 ibid 14. For a historical discussion of boxing, see Rudolph Brasch, *How did Sport Begin? A Look into the Origins of Man at Play* (Longman 1972) 39–43.

235 Arly Allen, *The Beginning of Boxing in Britain, 1300–1700* (McFarland 2020) 126.

236 David HT Scott, *The Art and Aesthetics of Boxing* (U of Nebraska Press 2008) 20.

237 Allen (n 235) 126.

238 Robert G Rodriguez, *The Regulation of Boxing: A History and Comparative Analysis of Policies Among American States* (McFarland 2009) 24.

239 Anderson (n 229) 25.

240 Dennis Brailsford, *Bareknuckles: A Social History of Prize-fighting* (Lutterworth 1988) 89.

241 Rodriguez (n 238) 26. The London Prize Ring Rules were devised by the Pugilists' Protective Association. W Russel Gray, 'For Whom the Bell Tolled: The Decline of British Prize-fighting in the Victorian Era' (1987) 21(2) Journal of Popular Culture 53, 57 states that the London Prize Ring Rules were introduced to 'make the sport more "scientific" or artful'.

and were superseded by the Queensbury Rules. In 1865 the Queensberry Rules were drafted by the eighth Marquis of Queensberry.[242] They came into force in 1867. Under these 12 rules no wresting or hugging was permitted, rounds were three minutes in length, and one minute's time between rounds, gloves of the best quality were worn and if a glove burst or came off it had to be replaced to the referee's satisfaction.[243] Rule XII provided: 'The contest in all other respects is to be governed by the revised rules of the London Prize Ring.'[244]

While the Broughton Rules were replaced by the London Prize Ring Rules, the significance of the rules – in particular, the introduction of mufflers – needs to be highlighted. Scott contends that the introduction of mufflers should not be underestimated as it made the sport relatively safe and opened it up to schools, colleges, and gentleman in the later part of the 18th and early 19th centuries.[245] Among the gentleman pugilists were the poets John Keats and Lord Byron.[246] Perhaps more importantly, the mufflers opened up the regulated sport of boxing to the prize fighters.[247] As the discussion on the attitude of the Victorian era courts will show, the distinction between prizefighters and boxers became increasingly blurred. **4–91**

The Courts and Prize fighting

As prizefighters began to wear gloves, the distinction between boxing (sparring) and prize fighting became less clear. The courts distinguished between sparring matches and prize fighting based on the likelihood of one of the fighters suffering serious injury.[248] The courts, finding it difficult to distinguish the two, decided to leave the issue to the jury. In *R v Young*, a boxer faced charges for the manslaughter of an opponent during an indoor sparring match.[249] Bramwell J instructed the jury as follows: **4–92**

> If a death ensued from a fight, independently of it taking place for money, it would be manslaughter, because a fight was a dangerous thing and likely to kill; but the medical witness here stated that this sparring was not dangerous, and not a thing likely to kill.[250]

---

242 Jack Anderson, 'Pugilistic Prosecutions: Prize fighting and the Courts in Nineteenth Century Britain' (2001) 21(2) The Sports Historian 37, 45 notes that changes introduced by the Queensbury rules were superficial and may even have intensified the physicality of the sport.
243 Anderson (n 229) 28.
244 Cited by Anderson: ibid 29.
245 Scott (n 236) 20.
246 ibid.
247 ibid.
248 Gunn and Ormerod (n 231) 24.
249 (1866) 10 Cox CC 371.
250 ibid 373.

4–93 In the course of a bout in a private house, the victim fell and hit his head against a post and died. As it took place in a private dwelling, the bout did not give rise to a charge of a breach of the peace.[251] Young was acquitted on the grounds that the bout was an exhibition of skill and not a prize fight. In contrast, in the case of *R v Orton* the Court reasoned that if a fight were a mere exhibition of skill in sparring it was lawful, however, if the combatants had met intending to fight until one gave into exhaustion or injury he had received it was a breach of the peace and thus unlawful irrespective of whether the fighters wore gloves.[252] Although the pugilists wore gloves, the level of violence was above that of a sparring match and was thus deemed to be a prize fight and consequently a breach of the peace.[253] The consent of the fighters was irrelevant.

4–94 In the leading case of *R v Coney*, the Court established that prize fighting was illegal as it caused a breach of peace.[254] The Court did not hold boxing or sparring legal but declared prize fighting illegal. While the case considered a charge of aiding and abetting at a prize fight, it 'provides an ideal starting point in contemporary legal attitudes to violence in sport'.[255] The *Coney* case is important for a number of reasons. On a micro level, it represents an attempt by the judges to curb inter-male violence.[256] On a macro level, the intention of the Court for Crown Cases Reserved (CCCR)

> was the eradication of prize fighting, not only to prevent the combatants trading blows, but also to bring an end to the sometimes vast, often unruly and largely male crowds who were drawn to watch such contests. However, only the three minority judges went as far to seek to achieve this by criminalising even those who were merely present at a contest.[257]

4–95 Accounts vary as to the reason why the three defendants came upon the fight. One account claims that the men were labourers who had finished work in a nearby field and as they made their way home a fight was taking place in a privately owned field.[258] While spectators were said to have made bets, there was no evidence that the pugilists had entered the contest for money nor was it clear if the fighters were wearing gloves or not.[259] At the trial court, the defence contended that

---

251 Roy G Beran and Joshua R Beran, 'The Law(s) of the Rings: Boxing and the Law' (2009) 16(4) Journal of Law and Medicine 684, 693.

252 (1878) 39 LT 293, 294.

253 Cave J in *Coney* referred to 'the ferocity and severe punishment to the boxers deposed to in *Reg v Orton*', *Coney* (n 49) 539.

254 ibid.

255 Anderson (n 52) 87.

256 Lois S Bibbings, *Binding Men: Stories About Violence and Law in Late Victorian England* (Routledge 2014) 48.

257 ibid.

258 ibid 49.

259 ibid. There was no evidence that Coney, Gilliam, and Tully were 'fight followers' and there was nothing to suggest that they had planned to attend the fight.

the three men should be acquitted as there was no proof that the contest was a prize fight and thus illegal.

The defendants argued that their attendance at the fight was merely passive in nature as they were not involved in the management or organisation of the fight. In the trial court, the Chairman left it to the jury to decide whether this was a prize fight and, if so, it was illegal and an assault. He also directed that all persons who attend a prize fight to watch the combatants strike each other and who are present when they do so are also guilty of an assault. The Chairman added the words of Littledale J from *R v Murphy* to his direction: 'if they were not casually passing by, but stayed at the place, they encouraged it by their presence, although they did not say or do anything'.[260] The jury, in following the direction of the Chairman, found the defendants Gilliam, Tully and Coney guilty of assault. Burke and Mitchell, as the two fighters, were found to be guilty of an assault. Similarly, Parker and Symonds, the organisers of the fight, were also found guilty. The case was appealed to the CCCR as the trial judge sought confirmation regarding his direction to the jury in relation to Coney, Gilliam, and Tully.[261] In an 8–3 majority, the convictions of the three men were quashed. The majority held that mere voluntary presence at such an event could not be equated with aiding and abetting a criminal activity. The issue of passive and active presence was not an issue for the CCCR, what is most interesting from this case is the Court's attitude to prize fighting.[262] The Court unanimously held prize fighting to be illegal as it caused a breach of the peace. Cave J held: 4–96

> The true view is, I think, that a blow struck in anger, or which is likely or is intended to do corporal hurt, is an assault, but that a blow struck in sport, and not likely, nor intended to cause bodily harm, is not an assault, and that an assault being a breach of the peace and unlawful, the consent of the person struck is immaterial.[263]

The judgments of Cave and Hawkins JJ are instructive regarding the issue of consent.[264] Hawkins J reaffirmed the 4–97

[260] 172 Eng Rep 1164, 1165 (1833). Bibbings (n 256) 51 argues that the direction from Littledale J set a very low threshold so that 'any degree of lingering to see what was going on would amount to assisting the fight and therefore, would constitute aiding and abetting any offences committed in the course of competition'.

[261] The Court for Crown Cases Reserved was created in 1848 under the Crown Cases Act 1848 (11 & 12 Vict c 78). It was an appellate court for criminal cases. It had jurisdiction only to hear cases that had resulted in a conviction and were referred to it by the trial judge. In 1907 it was replaced by the Court of the Appeal. For an interesting discussion on the CCCR, see Phil Handler, 'The Court for Crown Cases Reserved, 1848–1908' (2011) 29(1) Law and History Review 259.

[262] Anderson (n 52) 89.

[263] (n 49) 539.

[264] Justices Stephens, Lopes, North, and Huddleston all agreed with Cave J that the trial judge had erred in relying on *Littledale* in *R v Murphy* (n 260). Like Cave J, the judges distinguished between active presence and mere casual attendance.

> general proposition ... that there can be no assault unless the act charged as such be done without the consent of the person alleged to be assaulted, for want of consent is an essential element in every assault, and that which is done by consent is no assault at all.[265]

4–98 Cave J continued to hold that a blow struck in anger, or which is intended to do corporal harm, constitutes an assault.[266] However, a blow struck in sport which is not likely or intended to cause bodily harm is not an assault.[267] Assaults that result in a breach of peace are unlawful, irrespective of the consent of the parties.[268] In applying this to sport, Cave J held prize fighting was illegal as it amounted to a breach of the peace, but playing with single-sticks or wrestling did not amount to an assault; 'nor does boxing with gloves in the ordinary way'.[269] Matthew J, in a similar vein, referred to the 'trained fists of pugilists are dangerous weapons, which they are not at liberty to use against each other'.[270]

4–99 The CCCR declared prize fighting illegal as it encouraged a breach of the peace and gambling. The dangerous nature of the sport seemed to be a secondary consideration.[271] Stephen and Matthew JJ were the only judges that seemed concerned about the degree of harm inflicted on a combatant during a fight. Stephen J held prize fighting to be not only injurious to the public but also to the fighters themselves.[272] A fighter's health may be endangered by blows and because prize fights are disorderly exhibitions, they are 'mischievous on many obvious grounds'.[273]

4–100 In short, the CCCR held prize fighting to be unlawful due to its tendency to draw riotous crowds. The Court made a distinction between prize fighting and sparring. Prize fighting satisfied the *mens rea* requirement of assault, whereas sparring involved a test of skill with an absence of intent to cause harm.[274] Anderson comments:

> ... on this dubious thread of policy does the legality of boxing hang. The legality of this sport is defined in entirely negative terms, i.e., it is not

Except for Cave and Hawkins JJ, the other judges did not discuss the issue of consent at length. See Anderson (n 52) 91.

265 (n 49) 553.
266 ibid 539.
267 ibid.
268 ibid.
269 ibid.
270 ibid 547.
271 Gardiner criticises the reasoning of the Court. If they had adopted a paternalistic approach, they should have declared prize fighting illegal on the grounds of the safety and health of the fighters. Instead, the Court held prize fighting to be illegal due to its 'potential for crowd disorder': see Simon Gardiner, *Sports Law* (3rd edn, Cavendish 2006) 622.
272 (n 49) 549.
273 ibid.
274 Gardiner (n 271) 622.

prize fighting which is illegal because it disturbs the peace and may incite rioting and social disorder.[275]

The Queensberry Rules did not preclude the victor being awarded a monetary prize nor did they ban betting.[276] The distinction between boxing/sparring and prize fighting became even more diluted. Parpworth also questions the CCCR's rationale in distinguishing between two very similar activities on the basis of intent.[277] Parpworth asserts that 'both prize fighter and boxers seek the same end; to hurt the opponent more than he is hurt himself'.[278] The Court upheld sparring, wrestling, and fighting with single-sticks, yet held prize fighting to be an unlawful activity. The distinction is even more difficult to understand when one considers modern-day professional boxing. Professional boxers are paid to fight, and fighters often knock each other out. The aim of the fight is to score more points than your opponent and one way to ensure your opponent does not score any points is to knock them out.[279] Gardiner argues that modern boxing may place 'an unnecessary premium on the knock-out punch at the expense of more skilful fighting'.[280] Sparring was held to be legal as there was an absence of intent to inflict injury and there was less of a likelihood of causing harm.[281] However, 'modern day boxing appears strikingly similar to the prize fights that the House was intent on banning'.[282] **4–101**

The case *People v Fitzsimmons* shows the American approach.[283] A sparring match resulted in the death of an opponent. The fight was held in public, and the defendant argued that it was lawful. The New York Supreme Court found in favour of the defendant, holding that rules and practices of the fight were reasonable and thus criminal liability could not attached. Had *Fitzsimons* been heard by an English court, and the sparring had been defined as a prize fight, the rules and practices of the fight would have been deemed to be unreasonable and thus criminal liability would attach. James views the American approach as a 'much simpler approach to the determination of legality of an activity and would have allowed English law to have developed incrementally in a **4–102**

---

275 Anderson (n 52) 93.
276 Bibbings (n 256) 59.
277 Neil Parpworth, 'Boxing and Prize fighting: The Indistinguishable Distinguished?' (1994) 2 Sport and the Law Journal 5, 8.
278 ibid.
279 Gardiner (n 271) 622.
280 ibid.
281 ibid. Mark James, *Sports Law* (Palgrave MacMillan 2017) 149 defines sparring 'as being an exercise of pugilistic skill, a demonstration of the ability to attack and defend oneself, that promotes strength and agility, and where violence was not the aim of the participants who would fight wearing padded gloves for a pre-determined number of rounds', whereas prize fighting was characterised 'by violence and personal danger', a breach of the peace, and the fight would go on to until one of the fighters became incapacitated.
282 Gardiner (n 271) 622.
283 34 NYS 1102 (1895).

more structured manner than it has when confronted by mixed martial arts events'.[284]

4–103 While *Coney* is a seminal case, it is important to note that there were earlier authorities where the courts declared prize fighting to be illegal. According to East's 1803 *Pleas of the Crown*, if death ensued from a sporting activity and it was 'innocent and allowable', that would fall under 'excusable homicide'.[285] However, 'if the sport be unlawful in itself, or productive of danger, riot or disorder, from the occasion, to as to endanger the peace, and death ensue; the party killing is guilty of manslaughter'.[286] The decision of the CCCR in *Coney* can be distinguished from earlier cases as such cases were heard by a single judge in a trial court and not a judicial panel.[287] Bibbings refers to *Coney* as a test case on the illegality of prize fighting and the attempt to attribute criminal liability to those who attended a fight.[288]

Should Boxing Be Banned?

4–104 There have been legislative attempts to ban professional boxing in England and Wales. In 1960, Dr Edith Summerskill endeavoured to introduce a Bill to prohibit professional boxing.[289] As a physician, Dr Summerskill discussed the effects of boxing on the brain:

> These injuries do not heal and the destruction of the brain cells is permanent. The frontal lobes which are damaged in this way are those parts which control man's highest functions, namely, his power to co-ordinate his movements, to restrain his impulses and to exercise his power of self-control.[290]

4–105 Dr Summerskill countenanced objections in the House of Commons. Lieutenant-Colonel WH Bromley referred to Dr Summerskill 'living in the past' and said she was referring to conditions that existed 40 years previously, before the establishment of the BBBC.[291] Her motion for leave to introduce the Bill was rejected by 120, with only 17 in favour of the measure.[292]

---

284 James (n 281) 153.

285 Edward Hyde East, *A Treatise of the Pleas of the Crown, Volume 1* (A Strahan 1803) 268.

286 ibid.

287 Bibbings (n 256) 61. These single pronouncements were still important and relied upon in *Coney*. Coleridge J made this point when he stated that 'the criminal law is built up of the dicta of single judges': (1882) 8 QBD 534, 569.

288 Bibbings (n 256) 65.

289 HC Deb, 21 December 1960, vol 632, cols 1307–3014 <https://hansard.parliament.uk/Commons/1960-12-21/debates/6ee77ad0-90df-42fa-a35b-48e866f5150a/Boxing> accessed 9 May 2024.

290 ibid.

291 ibid col 1309.

292 ibid cols 1312–13.

In 1962, Dr Summerskill, now known as Baroness Summerskill, **4–106**
introduced another Bill to ban professional boxing. During the second reading in the House of Lords, Baroness Summerskill spoke of the 'attitude of the public … hardening against this so-called sport'.[293] She referred to advances in scientific knowledge that demonstrated the effect of repeated blows to the head.[294] Baroness Summerskill contended that sensibilities had changed and '[f]urthermore, the sight of a human being seeking to punch another unconscious becomes repugnant to people who during the last half-century have raised their standard of living and achieved a vastly improved code of behaviour'.[295] The motion for the Bill to be read a second time in the House of Lords was defeated by 27 to 22 votes.[296]

In 1981, Lord Taylor of Gryfe requested that the House of Lords move **4–107**
to read the Boxing Bill for a second reading.[297] He based the Bill on three propositions. First, he proffered that 'anything that perpetrates violence is an evil and anything that glamorises violence damages the fabric of a civilised society'.[298] Second, he pointed to evidence of the British Medical Association (BMA) on the dangers of boxing and, third, there were moral and ethical considerations that supported the ban of professional boxing.[299] The Bill did not move to a second reading as it was defeated by 77 to 47 votes at first reading.[300]

Lord Taylor of Gryfe introduced another bill on 4 December 1991.[301] **4–108**
The Earl of Balfour could not support the legislation as he argued that it was beneficial for children to learn about the art of boxing and self-defence.[302] He referred to the case of *Coney* and expressed concerns about the use of the word 'profit', which, in his view, could render any boxing fight illegal where there was a charge for ringside seating.[303] The Earl of Shrewsbury argued that banning professional boxing would drive the sport underground.[304] Unlike in Scandinavia, where professional boxing had been banned but had not been driven underground, the Earl of Shrewsbury contended:

---

293 HL Deb, 10 May 1962, vol 240, cols 347–409, col 348 <https://api.parliament.uk/historic-hansard/lords/1962/may/10/boxing-bill-hl-1> accessed 9 May 2024.
294 ibid col 349.
295 ibid.
296 ibid cols 408–09. After Baroness Summerskill's two failed attempts to introduce legislation to ban boxing, there were subsequent attempts, however, these bills never got past a first reading.
297 HL Deb, 26 November 1981, vol 425, cols 875–94 <https://api.parliament.uk/historic-hansard/lords/1981/nov/26/boxing-bill-hl> accessed 9 May 2024.
298 ibid col 875.
299 ibid.
300 ibid cols 893–94.
301 HL Deb, 4 December 1991, vol 533, cols 290–320 <https://api.parliament.uk/historic-hansard/lords/1991/dec/04/boxing-bill-hl> accessed 9 May 2024.
302 ibid col 293.
303 ibid.
304 ibid col 303.

> It will happen in this country. I know it is illegal but there is a growing movement for underground bare knuckle fighting and it happens whether we like it or not. This in itself will produce illegal betting, which is something that none of us wants. It will produce much less supervision and control.[305]

4–109 The motion to move to a second reading was defeated by three votes.[306] Lord Taylor of Gryfe introduced another Bill to ban boxing in 1995.[307] The bill did not progress to a second reading in the House of Lords. In 1994, the Law Commission published a Consultation Paper.[308] The Consultation Paper did not review the legality of professional boxing. However, it concluded that boxing would remain legal so long as public policy supported its continued legality. In 1995 the Commission stated that 'the continuing legality of boxing, amateur or professional, is a matter for Parliament to decide'.[309]

4–110 In Ireland, legislation to ban professional boxing has never been introduced. In 1995, Dr Bill Toomey, a consultant chemical pathologist at Beaumont Hospital in Dublin, called for a ban on boxing which he referred to as 'legalised savagery'.[310] His comments came after the death of Scottish boxer Jim Murray, who had passed away the previous year due to a bleed on the brain.[311] In April 1995, the Irish Medical Organisation (IMO) passed a motion demanding a ban on professional boxing.[312] Outside of this, the legality of professional boxing in Ireland has not been challenged.

Arguments in Favour of Boxing

4–111 Those in favour of the continued legality of boxing note that boxing provides an outlet for young people in disadvantaged areas. It demands

---

305 ibid col 304.

306 ibid cols 319–20.

307 HL Deb, 5 April 1995, vol 563, cols 288–310 <https://api.parliament.uk/historic-hansard/lords/1995/apr/05/boxing-bill-hl> accessed 9 May 2024.

308 Law Commission, *Consent and Offences Against the Person* (Law Com CP No 134, 1994) <https://cloud-platform e218f50a4812967ba1215eaecede923f.s3.amazonaws.com/uploads/sites/30/2016/08/No.134-Criminal-Law-Consent-and-Offences-Against-the-Person-A-Consultation-Paper.pdf> accessed 9 May 2024.

309 Law Commission, *Consent in the Criminal Law* (Law Com CP No 139, 1995) para 12.38 <https://cloud-platform e218f50a4812967ba1215eaecede923f.s3.amazonaws.com/uploads/sites/30/2016/08/No.139-Criminal-Law-Consent-in-the-Criminal-Law-A-Consultation-Paper.pdf> accessed 9 May 2024. Professional boxing has been banned in Sweden, Norway, and Iceland.

310 Gareth O'Connor, 'Doctor Wants Boxing Ban' (*RTÉ Archives*, 16 October 1995) <https://www.rte.ie/archives/2020/1006/1169794-call-to-ban-boxing/> accessed 9 May 2024.

311 ibid.

312 ibid. This is referred to on page 22 of Irish Medical Organisation, *Policy Handbook of the Irish Medical Organisation 2010* <https://www.imo.ie/policy-international-affair/documents/policy-archive/imo-motions-and-policy-handbook/IMO-Policy-Handbook-2010.pdf> accessed 9 May 2024.

skill, strength, and courage on behalf of the participants. Boxing instils discipline; it offers a chance for self-advancement for young people from poorer backgrounds.[313] If boxing were banned it could drive the sport underground and it would develop into an unregulated sport similar to prize fighting. In applying liberal principles, boxing should remain legal on the grounds of civil liberties.[314]

R v Brown

The case of *R v Brown* provides a contemporary discussion on the legality of boxing.[315] As detailed in Chapter 3, the *Brown* case involved a group of sadomasochist homosexual men who engaged in violent activities, including genital torture for the purposes of pleasure. All the men were consenting adults, the acts took place in private, and no one suffered permanent injury. Video cameras recorded the activities; however, these recordings were not for public viewing but for the group of men involved. The Court, in adopting a paternalistic approach, held that the activities of the men were unlawful irrespective of consent. The Court referred to contact sports as being lawful as there is a public interest in the continued practice of contact sports, including boxing. Contact sports are deemed to be socially acceptable whereas the acts of the men in *Brown* were perceived as being deviant and contrary to public policy. The House of Lords held that it was in the interest of the men involved and also for society to prevent a 'cult of violence'.[316] None of the men involved ever required hospital treatment nor did any of the men suffer permanent injuries: 'these players were true professionals'.[317] The activities took place in private chambers, code words were used when the pain inflicted had gone beyond an accepted level, and all the equipment was sterilised. Lord Jauncey noted that the activities of the men were unlike a situation in sport where there is a 'referee present, such as there would be in boxing or a football match'.[318] The absence of a referee meant that the sado-masochistic activities were unregulated.[319] **4–112**

In his dissenting judgment, Lord Mustill exhibited a more liberal approach. He reasoned that the Offences Against the Person Act 1861 was not appropriate in a case involving the private sexual acts of consenting adults. Lord Mustill argued that the case should be about the 'criminal law of private sexual relations, if about anything at all'.[320] The 1861 Act was devised to deal with behaviour which **4–113**

---

313 Gunn and Ormerod (231) 32–34.
314 ibid 21–22 and Anderson (n 229) 135–70.
315 (n 101).
316 ibid 237.
317 David McArdle, *From Boot Money to Bosman: Football, Society and the Law* (Cavendish 2000) 146.
318 (n 315) 238.
319 McArdle (n 317) 147.
320 (n 101) 256.

> involves brutality, aggression and violence, of a kind far removed from the appellants' behaviour which, however worthy of censure, involved no animosity, no aggression, no personal rancour on the part of the person inflicting the hurt towards the recipient and no protest by the recipient.[321]

4–114 Lord Mustill recognised that the case presented a new challenge to the courts. His discussion of boxing, prize fighting and sparring and contact sports is of importance.[322] In reference to boxing, Lord Mustill stated: 'it is in my judgment best to regard this as another special situation which for the time being stands outside the ordinary law of violence because society chooses to tolerate it'.[323]

4–115 Cox and others make a compelling argument in relation to the *Brown* case.[324] Boxing takes place in public, unlike the activities of the men in *Brown*. A boxer may be considered a social role model. Arguably, the intentional infliction of harm that takes place in a boxing match has greater potential to cause social problems than the private sexual acts of the men in *Brown*.[325]

4–116 Those who favour the abolition of boxing highlight the health dangers associated with boxing.[326] As the head is the primary target, safety precautions are of little benefit. The BMA has long called for the banning of boxing. While there may be fewer fatalities in comparison to other sports, boxers can suffer more long-term brain injury. It may take years for the injuries to manifest. It has been suggested that doctors could withdraw their support and refuse to attend bouts. If there were no medical cover, it would mean that the sport would become illegal. However, given that doctors are under a legal duty to provide medical cover at bouts, this suggestion is not feasible and could expose doctors to civil liability.

Continued Legal Recognition of Fighting Sports

4–117 While *R v Brown* provides a more recent discussion on the continued legal recognition of fighting sports, there are two other important authorities.[327] In *R v Donovan*, the defendant caned a 17-year-old girl

---

321 ibid 258.

322 Lord Mustill also looked at surgery, parental chastisement, dangerous pastimes, and rough horse play: (n 101) 266-67.

323 ibid 265.

324 (n 32) 171.

325 ibid.

326 Anderson (n 229) 117–33. See also Hugh Brayne, Lincoln Sargeant, and Carol Brayne, 'Could Boxing Be Banned? A Legal and Epidemiological Perspective' (1998) 316(7147) British Medical Journal 1813; Ken Jones, 'A Key Moral Issue: Should Boxing be Banned?' (2001) 4(1) Culture, Sport, Society 63.

327 *Brown, Coney, Donovan*, and the *AG's Reference* were recently cited with approval in the case of *R v BM* [2018] EWCA Crim 560: for a discussion on this case, see Donnellan (n 70).

for purposes of sexual gratification.[328] The girl was left with red marks on her body. Although the girl had consented, Swift J held that to be immaterial. Swift J held that consent would only be considered in situations where the blows struck were neither likely nor intended to do bodily harm. The judge, in referring to the exemption given to sport, held: 'another exception to the general rule is to be found in cases of rough and undisciplined sport or play, where there is no anger and no intention to cause bodily harm'.[329]

Similarly, in the *Attorney General's Reference (No 6 of 1980)*, Lord Lane held: **4–118**

> It is not in the public interest that people should try to cause, or should cause, each other bodily harm for no good reason ... This means that most fights will be unlawful regardless of consent. Nothing we have said is intended to cast doubt upon the accepted legality of properly conducted games and sports, lawful chastisement or correction, reasonable surgical interference, dangerous exhibitions etc. These apparent exceptions can be justified as involving the exercise of a legal right, in the case of chastisement or correction, or as needed in the public interest, in the other cases.[330]

The judgment of McInerney J of the Supreme Court of Victoria, Australia, in the civil case of *Pallante v Stadiums Pty (No 1)* is often cited in discussions surrounding the legality of boxing.[331] The plaintiff, a semi-professional boxer, suffered serious injuries to his eyes and brought a claim for damages against the organisers of the fight, the promoter, the trainer and the referee. The plaintiff argued, *inter alia,* that the defendants' negligence was due to there being a mismatch between him and his much stronger opponent.[332] The defendants contended that the fight was a prize fight and as an illegal activity, damages could not be ordered against them. McInerney J contrasted boxing with assault. Assault differs from the sport of boxing as in an assault there is no consent, and the infliction of harm is done in a hostile or angry manner. McInerney J's distinction between assault and boxing has been criticised, as an assault need not take place in a hostile or angry manner.[333] Some assaults are permissible where the parties involved consent to intentional harm and the harm does not exceed the limits in law. Such a narrow construction did not consider that sporting contests often invoke hostility and anger, particularly contact sports.[334] McInerney J, aware of the inconsistency in his argument, qualified his comments and stated **4–119**

328 [1934] 2 KB 498.
329 ibid 507.
330 [1981] QBD 715, 719.
331 [1976] VR 331.
332 The plaintiff did not enjoin his opponent in the action.
333 Thorpe and others (n 62) 125.
334 ibid.

that consent would only be negated in situations where the mind of the accused boxer was predominated by either hostility or anger.[335]

The Legality of Mixed Martial Arts

4–120 MMA is a hybrid sport in that it combines traditional martial arts sports with non-traditional ones. MMA is a form of ancient sport, however, its modern inception dates back to 1993 when the Ultimate Fighting Championship (UFC) was founded. MMA has few rules and permit wrestling holds, punching, marital arts throws, and kicking.[336] MMA has posed a number of difficulties as it appears to have little regulation and a lack of universally accepted, standardised rules.[337] In 2012, there were two bodies established that sought to develop the sport of MMA: the International Mixed Martial Arts Federation (IMMAF) and the World Mixed Martial Arts Association (WMMAA).[338] The two bodies were created independently, however, they merged in 2019 to create a 'unified governing body'.[339]

4–121 In an Irish context, the Irish Mixed Martial Arts Association (IMMAA) is the conduit through which promoters can seek advice on the organisation of MMA events in Ireland.[340] It is one of the listed national federations recognised by the IMMAF.[341] The IMMAA refers to itself as the governing body for MMA in Ireland, however, Sport Ireland does not as of yet recognise the IMMAA as a national sports governing body. The creation of the IMMAA is a step in the right direction with regard to the regulation of the sport, but it lacks the legitimacy that other sports governing bodies possess. The IMMAF website offers the following definition:

> A national federation is a non-profit, democratic organization that deals with the overall development and structure for MMA in a country. Our stated ambition is for each national federation to be approved by the ministry of sports (or the equivalent) and the Olympic committee in

---

335 (n 331) 332.
336 James (n 281) 165.
337 ibid.
338 International Mixed Martial Arts Federation, 'History' <https://immaf.org/about/history/> accessed 9 May 2024.
339 ibid.
340 For more detail, see Irish Mixed Martial Arts Association, 'Welcome' <https://mmaireland.ie/> accessed 9 May 2024. Established in 2016, IMMAA was the result of a restructuring of the Irish Amateur Pankration Association (IAPA), a body established in 2014, which was affiliated to the IMMAF. The IAPA was an associated body of the Irish Amateur Wrestling Association (IAWA) <https://www.irishwrestling.ie/> accessed 9 May 2024. However, the IAWA is a recognised sports governing body and receives direct and indirect state funding through the auspices of Sport Ireland.
341 International Mixed Martial Arts Federation, 'National Federations' <https://immaf.org/about/national-federations/> accessed May 2024.

> their respective country. The responsibilities and activities of a national federation for MMA is much like those of any other sport.[342]

In 2018, Sport Ireland's Mixed Martial Arts Working Group published a report. There were a number of key findings regarding the governance of the IMMAA: **4–122**

> The Irish Mixed Martial Arts Association (IMMAA) is not yet fully established as an organisation ... The IMMAA membership is in very early stages of development and governance ... The governance and status of the club membership structure within the IMMAA needs to be clarified.[343]

The report acknowledged that obtaining recognition as a national governing body is 'a challenging process' and **4–123**

> gaining recognition does not confer accreditation in terms of health and safety standards for events and other processes. The leaders and members of sport have, currently, serious responsibilities to self-regulate and to adhere to relevant standards and are ultimately responsible for how their sport operates ... Ultimately the safety and welfare of amateur and professional participants is at stake and it is paramount that whatever route taken by the IMMAA serious and onerous issues and duty of care are at stake. They can learn much from members of IMAC and other sporting codes who have had to make tough choices in prioritising the needs of athletes.[344]

In short, the IMMAA did not meet the criteria required to be recognised as a national governing body of Sport Ireland. One option is for the IMMAA to acquire recognition through the Irish Martial Arts Commission (IMAC).[345] The IMAC was asked if it would bring MMA within its remit. It refused to do so, outlining its reasons in a position paper to Sport Ireland, the contents of which were secured by way of a Freedom of Information request.[346] In response, the IMMAA said that 'guided by medical professionals, we have voluntarily instated medical standards at events that exceed those in place for the vast majority of sporting events in Ireland'.[347] **4–124**

---

342 International Mixed Martial Arts Federation, 'What Is a National Federation?' <https://immaf.org/about/national-federations/#national-federations> accessed 9 May 2024.

343 Sport Ireland, Mixed Martial Arts Working Group, 'Final Report' (May 2017) 2 <https://www.sportireland.ie/sites/default/files/media/document/2021-01/final-report-mma-report.pdf> accessed 9 May 2024.

344 ibid 4. IMAC is the Irish Martial Arts Commission, a Sport Ireland recognised governing body.

345 IMAC recognises several martial arts including Aikido, Kickboxing, Tae Kwon Do, Karate, Sumo, Kung Fu, Jiu Jitsu, Tai Chi, Muaythai, Ninjitsu and Bujitsu. For more detail, see <https://www.imac.ie/> accessed 4 July 2024.

346 'Irish Martial Arts Body Opposes Recognition of MMA' (*RTÉ News*, 1 June 2017) <https://www.rte.ie/news/2016/0808/807658-mma/> accessed 9 May 2024.

347 ibid.

4–125 The legality of MMA has been questioned. Anderson asserts that 'no exemption, implied or otherwise, exists for MMA in Irish law and thus in the absence of clarity on its recognition, the nearest legal definition we have for the sport in Ireland is that of a prize fight'.[348] In applying the rule established in *R v Coney*, Anderson proffers:

> Theoretically … the Gardaí could move to shut down Bellator 217 on Saturday night. This is unlikely to happen considering the licencing, medical and other safety measures that Bellator and the host venue will have in place on the night … The issue of whether MMA is an illegal, criminal act is, as has been discussed in countries such as Canada, one for parliamentary debate and not night-time policing.[349]

4–126 In 2021, the Council of Europe published a Recommendation calling on its member states to take action to improve the safety of those who practice extreme martial arts and combat activities.[350] In 1999, following an informal meeting of the European Ministers responsible for Sport, a Recommendation on banning of free-fighting contests, such as cage rage, was adopted.[351] The Recommendation was not advocating 'a straight ban … which would not be respected, governments were therefore invited to consider more elaborate measures to encourage a better framework and mitigate the risks'.[352] At the time of the 1999 Recommendation MMA was largely unregulated, however, in the early 2000s, the position had changed.[353]

4–127 The Enlarged Partial Agreement on Sport (EPAS), at a round table discussion on 12 November 2014, recognised the evolution of combat sports since the Recommendation in 1999.[354] Further discussions ensued, culminating in the 2021 Recommendation which replaces the 1999 Recommendation. The 2021 Recommendation

> focuses on those aspects which can significantly help to prevent risks to the health of the practitioners, so that these activities are in keeping with

---

[348] Jack Anderson, 'It's Time to Recognise MMA Is Here to Stay' *The Irish Examiner* (Cork, 21 February 2019) <https://www.irishexaminer.com/opinion/columnists/arid-30906005.html> accessed 9 May 2024.

[349] ibid.

[350] Committee of Ministers of the Council of Europe, 1400th Meeting, 31 March 2021, Recommendation CM/Rec (2021)3 of the Committee of Ministers to Member States on Extreme Martial Arts and Combat Activities <https://rm.coe.int/0900001680a1f4e7> accessed 9 May 2024.

[351] Committee of Ministers of the Council of Europe, 669th Meeting, 22 April 1999, Recommendation No R (99) 11 of the Committee of Ministers to Member States on the Prohibition of Free Fighting Contests such as Cage Fighting <https://rm.coe.int/09000016804d07be> accessed 9 May 2024.

[352] Explanatory memorandum to Recommendation CM/Rec (2021) 3 of the Committee of Ministers to Member States on Extreme Martial Arts and Combat Activities <https://search.coe.int/cm/Pages/result_details.aspx?ObjectId=0900001680a189fa> accessed 9 May 2024.

[353] ibid.

[354] Anderson (n 348).

> the requirements of existing norms with regard to the values of sport, the prevention of doping and the manipulation of sports competitions, fair competition and the training of coaches and referees.[355]

MMA is considered a properly constituted sport so long as the rules **4–128** and regulations are adhered to, there are appropriate safety procedures, the rules are enforced by independent referees, and it is appropriately administered.[356] If these criteria are followed, then MMA will be 'at least as safe as boxing as it places so much less emphasis on blows to the head that so concern the BMA'.[357]

Conclusion

The application of the criminal law to sporting assaults is quite rare. It **4–129** follows that the criminal law will only intervene in situations where there is an intentional, deliberate, or reckless infliction of harm. Sportspersons consent to harm that is within the rules of the game or incidental to the playing of the game, or within the playing culture. For more minor infractions of rules, the governing body of the particular sport is best suited to deal with the matter. Only acts of egregious violence should attract criminal prosecution. In general, a person may not consent to infliction of actual bodily harm or serious harm. However, contact sport is given an exemption. There is a public interest or benefit derived from the playing of contact sports.

Boxing presents an anomaly as by its very nature it involves the **4–130** intentional infliction of harm. Boxing remains legal because society continues to tolerate it. There are many advantages connected with the sport: it is popular, it instils discipline, it promotes fitness, and it offers young people in disadvantaged areas an outlet. The arguments against boxing have centred on the health implications and dangers for the boxers, the promotion of a cult of violence, the accompaniment of gambling and riotous crowds. While boxing for profit has been banned in some countries, both professional and amateur boxing are legal in Ireland. There has been little debate on its continued legality in Ireland. It is one sport where Ireland has excelled at the Olympics and, in the professional realm, Ireland has produced a number of world-class fighters.

MMA is legal due to its association with boxing and other lawfully **4–131** recognised fighting sports. It is becoming more accepted as a mainstream sport. The IMMAA is the governing body for the sport in Ireland, however, it is not recognised by Sport Ireland. The more barbaric

---

355 Council of Europe, 'Extreme Martial Arts and Combat Activities' <https://www.coe.int/en/web/sport/mixed-martial-arts-and-combat-practices> accessed 9 May 2024.

356 James (n 281) 166.

357 ibid.

elements of the sport have caused the IMAC to refuse to bring it within its remit. MMA seems to occupy a similar position to prize fighting and under the *Coney* rules, it could be declared unlawful. However, given its popularity and the discussions that have taken place around its position within Irish sport, the IMMAA may well become recognised by Sport Ireland in its own right. The creation of rules and regulations by the IMMAA has given the sport an air of legitimacy that was perhaps henceforth missing.

Chapter 5

CIVIL LIABILITY IN SPORT

Introduction

The law of tort covers a wide range of areas, including personal injuries, defective products, defamation, and nuisance both public and private. Participants, referees, coaches, instructors, and governing bodies may be sued under the law of tort. With regard to participants, a player is under a duty to take all reasonable care taking account of the circumstances. The standard is objective; it is based on the reasonable person rather than the individual defendant. Liability will not attach in situations where there is an error or lapse of judgement. Something more serious is required for the defendant to be held liable. The threshold for liability is high and thus very difficult to reach. Consequently, there have been very few cases involving civil liability and sportspersons and sports bodies. 5–01

This chapter discusses the application of the law of tort to participants, referees, governing bodies, and coaches and instructors. The civil liability cases relating to sport are based on the tort of negligence. Like with a criminal case, a tort case may be brought on the grounds of assault and battery. However, given the evidentiary requirements of assault and battery in tort, most sports cases are based on negligence. The application of the tort of negligence to sport is examined through the lens of a few seminal cases. The issue of concussion in rugby and legal implications will be assessed in relation to provisional clubs and world governing bodies. 5–02

Torts and Sports

A tort is a civil wrong, other than a breach of contract, that arises from a breach of a private duty. The word tort comes from 'the Latin *tortus*, meaning twisted or crooked'.[1] The law of tort falls under the branch of law referred to as private law. Private law regulates relationships between natural (human) and legal (companies and associations) persons. In the words of Quill, tort 'serves multiple purposes' and endeavours 'to provide an impartial set of rules for resolving private disputes over claims of improper interference with individual rights'.[2] Tort involves wrongful acts or omissions on the part of the tortfeasor which cause physical, economic, or psychological injury to the claimant. An individual will bring a case in tort primarily to obtain compensation. 5–03

[1] John G Fleming, *The Law of Torts* (5th edn, Law Book Company 1977) 1.
[2] Eoin Quill, *Torts in Ireland* (4th edn, Gill & Macmillan 2014) 2.

Lord Bingham of Cornhill in *Fairchild v Glenhaven Funeral Services Ltd and Others* explained that the 'overall object of tort law is to define cases in which the law may justly hold one party liable to compensate another'.[3]

5–04 The law of tort can be invoked in situations involving personal injuries, defamation,[4] passing off (where the customer is misled as to the origin of goods or services of another), nervous shock (psychological damage or post-traumatic stress disorder), private and public nuisance[5] and vicarious liability (where the employer is held liable for the torts of an employee committed during the course of their employment).

5–05 Participation in sport may give rise to civil liability. A sports participant may be injured due to the negligence of an opponent and thus unable to play for a few weeks or months, or the injury may be career-ending.[6] The injured participant may consequently seek damages in the form of compensation for the loss of earnings, future earnings, medical expenses and for pain and suffering caused by the injury.[7] A sports participant may also suffer harm due to the negligence of a coach, a referee, a league manager, an association official or medical personnel. A spectator may bring proceedings against the operator of a facility, the occupiers or owners of the ground, the security, or the policing and stewarding personnel. A sportsperson may be injured due to defective equipment and consequently bring an action against the manufacturer of the equipment.[8] A governing body may be sued for changes in the rules or administration of the sport. If the sporting body does not have

---

3 [2002] UKHL 22 (20 June 2002) [9].

4 See Chapter 10 on 'Commercial Issues in Sport' for a discussion on defamation.

5 Public nuisance concerns interference with the rights of the general public, rather than a particular individual. Civil proceedings may only be brought by the Attorney General, as the representative of the public interest in Ireland. An individual may bring an action if they suffer special or peculiar damage above that suffered by the general public. For an incident to be considered a nuisance, it must be ongoing and not just a once-off event. The following cases concern nuisance and sport: *Bolton v Stone* [1949] 1 All ER 237 and the Court of Appeal's decision in [1951] AC 850, [1951] 1 All ER 1078; and *Miller v Jackson* [1977] 3 WLR 20. In the case of *Dewar v City and Suburban Racecourse* [1899] 1 IR 345, an injunction was granted to prohibit the operation of a racecourse on Sundays.

6 Most sports entail some inherent risk. In many situations the party is injured, and no one is to blame.

7 Quill (n 2) 528–62.

8 See *McCormick v Lowe & Campbell Athletic Goods Co* 144 SW 2d 866 (Mo Ct App 1940). In this case a high school pole vaulter was seriously injured after the vaulting pole broke while in use. The Kansas City Court of Appeals held that the defendant manufacturer owed a duty of care to exercise ordinary care to test the product and to determine whether it was fit for the purpose intended. As the plaintiff was using the pole in the ordinary and usual manner, failure to inspect the pole rendered the defendant liable. For a discussion on injuries sustained from football helmets, see Raymond L Yasser, *Torts and Sports Legal Liability in Professional and Amateur Athletics* (Quorum Books 1985) 78–82. See also Andrew T Pittman, John O Spengler, and Sarah J Young, *Case Studies in Sport Law* (3rd edn, Human Kinetics 2021) ch 2 'Tort Law and Products Liability'.

an adequate insurance scheme, the injured player is more likely to go through the courts to obtain damages.

Within the law of torts there is a category referred to as intentional torts and, as the name suggests, it involves the alleged tortfeasor or wrongdoer intentionally causing harm or damage to another person. Intentional torts are divided into trespass to the person, trespass to land and trespass to chattels. Under trespass to the person, there are three separate torts: namely assault, battery, and false imprisonment.[9] The burden of proof in trespass to the person cases is placed on the plaintiff to demonstrate that the defendant intended to cause them harm and if this is proved then the burden is placed on the defendant to show that their actions were neither intentional nor negligent.[10] Given these evidentiary requirements in assault and battery in tort, the majority of sports cases are based on negligence.[11] It is important to note that battery cases in sport are very rare as most insurance policies expressly exclude cover for deliberately inflicted injuries.[12] This means that the defendant will be held personally liable and not the club.[13] **5–06**

The Rules of the Sport and the Nature of the Sport

The rules of the sport or the game are but one consideration for the court when it comes to deciding whether a breach of the duty of care has occurred. The rules of sports vary and what is permitted in one sport may not be permitted in another. In the Australian case of *Sibley v Milutinovic*, the plaintiff and defendant were playing in an unrefereed training soccer match.[14] During the course of the game, Sibley made several low-sliding tackles on the defendant from behind, resulting in **5–07**

---

9 Quill (n 2) 171.

10 ibid 169.

11 There is an interesting American case on the intentional infliction of emotional distress and false imprisonment involving a coach and a high school dance team: *Achcar-Winkels v Lake Oswego School District*, No 3:15–cv–00385–YY (D Or 25 May 2017). See Anne L DeMartini, 'Coaches' Surprising Tort Liability' (2017) 88(9) Journal of Physical Education, Recreation & Dance 57.

12 See *Elliott v Saunders and Liverpool FC* (HC, 10 June 1994). The trespass case was dropped as Liverpool FC's insurance would not pay out on a battery claim. Elliott proceeded with a negligence claim. See also Mark James, 'The Trouble with Roy Keane' (2002) 1(3) Entertainment Law 72, 81; and Mark James and David McArdle, 'Player Violence or Violent Players? Vicarious Liability for Sports Participants' (2004) 12(3) The Tort Law Review 1, 11.

13 See Simon Gardiner and others, *Sports Law* (4th edn, Routledge 2012) 501. Battery has been successfully pleaded in some Australian cases: see *McNamara v Duncan* (1971) 26 ALR 584. While there are very few sporting cases involving intentional torts, there are some examples from Australia: see *Canterbury Bankstown Rugby League v Rogers* (1993) Aust Tort Reports 81–246; and *McCracken v Melbourne Storm Rugby League Club* [2005] NSWSC 107. See also David Thorpe and others, *Sports Law* (2nd end, Oxford University Press 2013) 176–77.

14 [1990] ACTSC 6 (9 February 1990). The judgment is available here: <http://www6.austlii.edu.au/cgi-bin/viewdoc/au/cases/act/ACTSC/1990/6.html> accessed 11 May 2024.

both players falling over. The defendant chastised the plaintiff and told him to watch out. Following this exchange of words and a subsequent sliding tackle, the defendant punched Sibley in the jaw with a closed fist. Sibley brought an action to sue Milutinovic, while Milutinovic counter-sued, alleging that Sibley had kicked him on his right ankle. The plaintiff and the defendant both raised the defence of voluntary assumption of risk.[15] The judge contended that the defence of voluntary assumption of risk was appropriate in a negligence case, however, as this case involved an intentional tort (assault), the defence should be that of consent. The Chief Justice (CJ) Miles of the Supreme Court of the Australian Capital Territory proceeded on the basis that the parties meant to raise the defence of consent.[16]

5–08 There were no rules pertaining to friendly games to guide the Court; the judge instead relied on judicial knowledge.[17] In using this judicial knowledge, Miles CJ stated that, while soccer was mainly a non-contact sport, some contact was inevitable.[18] However, the intentional application of force was outside the rules of the game whenever the degree of force used was likely to result in injury.[19] The actions of Milutinovic were clearly outside the rules of the game, and thus outside the scope of Sibley's consent. As it was a training match, Miles CJ held:

> The game being played was not a competition match and the extent to which players were entitled to adopt tactics likely to result in physical injury to an opposing player is, in my view, to be distinguished from conduct justifiable during the course of a competition match.[20]

5–09 The Chief Justice referred to the evidence presented that the actions of Sibley in a competitive match would have resulted in him being sent off.[21] Miles CJ held that he was 'not satisfied that the action of the plaintiff was within the ambit of the rules which the players on that evening expected to be observed'.[22] The judge was also not satisfied that the plaintiff had discharged the onus of proving that the defendant had consented to the sliding tackle. He found in favour of the defendant in the counterclaim. As the injuries of the defendant were minor and had not resulted in persisting disability or loss of earnings, he awarded Milutinovic damages of $1,187.[23] This was to be offset from the damages of $9,344.61 awarded to the plaintiff.[24] The final award to the plaintiff

---

15 ibid [6].
16 ibid.
17 ibid [8].
18 ibid.
19 ibid. The judge stated: 'but soccer is basically a non-contact sport in that the intentional application of force by one player to the body of another player is outside the rules at least where the degree of force is likely to cause injury'.
20 ibid [9].
21 ibid [10].
22 ibid.
23 ibid [20].
24 ibid [14]–[18]. The plaintiff was off work for several weeks. His jaws had to be

was damages of $8,157.61 and the defendant was ordered to pay the plaintiff's costs.[25]

This case is important for two reasons. First, it demonstrates the importance of having written or express rules for a sport and, second, it shows the potential complications that can arise in a situation where there is no referee or other match official.[26] The case centred on the lack of express rules; however, it does not mean that the rules of the sport or the game are the only determining factor. In the High Court of Australia case of *Rootes v Shelton*, Barwick CJ acknowledged that a breach of the rules is but one factor for the court to consider when it comes to assessing the duty of care in a sport or game, in this case a sport with an inherent risk, water-skiing. [27] The Chief Justice held that 'the rules of the sport or game ... are neither definitive of the existence nor of the extent of the duty; nor does their breach or non-observance necessarily constitute a breach of any duty found to exist'.[28] Kitto J concurred: 5–10

> even though he infringed the 'rules of the game', non-compliance with such rules, conventions or customs (where they exist) is necessarily one consideration to be attended to upon the question of reasonableness; but it is only one, and it may be of much or little or even no weight in the circumstances.[29]

The case *Hargreaves v Hancock* illustrates the consideration given to the nature of the sport and the rules of the sport.[30] The parties to the case collided in a harness racing event. The defendant admitted a breach of Rule 265 of New South Wales Harness Racing.[31] However, Simpson J of the New South Wales Supreme Court did not consider the defendant's breach of Rule 265 or his subsequent admission of a breach as 'conclusive'.[32] The judge accepted the defendant owed a duty of care to the plaintiff and that harness racing involved inherent risks and that the speed at which the horses race increases such risks.[33] For Simpson J, 5–11

wired and he was unable to eat solid food for a few weeks. He was also advised not to play for the remainder of the season.

25 ibid [20].

26 Thorpe and others (n 13) 200.

27 [1967] 116 CLR 383. 'The breaking of any rules of the activity in question of course is not necessarily indicative of negligence': Peter Charlish, 'Sports: Ordinary Negligence in the Final Furlong' (2005) 4 Journal of Personal Injury Law 308, 311.

28 116 CLR 383, 385.

29 ibid 389.

30 1997 NSW Lexis 685.

31 The Rules of Harness Racing of the Harness Racing Authority of NSW have updated over the years. The most recent version of the rules can be accessed at <https://www.hrnsw.com.au/racing-information/hrnsw-local-rules> accessed 11 May 2024. Rule 265 provided: 'Any driver who, in the opinion of the Stewards, caused or contributed to any crossing, jostling or interference by foul, careless or incompetent driving shall be deemed guilty of an offence against these Rules and may be dealt with accordingly.'

32 (n 30) [5].

33 ibid.

the increased risks created a 'significantly' higher duty of care than the duty that would arise from partaking in a less riskier activity.[34]

5–12 The Queensland Law Handbook best explains the role that rules play in sports cases:

> The rules of the sport are a good starting point for determining what is acceptable conduct, and what is not. It must be stressed, however, that the rules of any sport or game are not going to exhaustively determine the level or existence of a legal duty owed by one player to another.[35]

5–13 There is one Irish case that illustrates the weight the court will give to the nature of the sport, *McComiskey v McDermott*.[36] McComiskey was acting as a navigator for the defendant in a car rally. On the dashboard there was a sign which stated that passengers travelled at their own risk. The car crashed and McComiskey issued civil proceedings against McDermott. The Court was faced with two important factors: namely, what was the effect of the sign and was the defendant guilty of a breach of duty? Regarding the first question, the Supreme Court held that the plaintiff had not waived his right to sue the defendant for negligence. The sign was deemed to be ineffective unless the plaintiff expressly assented to its terms. On the second question, the Supreme Court held that the defendant was not in breach of his duty owed to the plaintiff. It held that 'the duty of care owed by the defendant to the plaintiff was to drive as carefully as a reasonably careful, competitive rally-driver would be expected to drive in the prevailing circumstances'.[37]

5–14 The case of *McComiskey* sets out the approach of the Irish courts and what can be gleaned from it is that a sports participant has a duty to behave reasonably in the context of the sport in which they participate. In this respect, the Supreme Court seems to view the duty of care and standard of care as being interchangeable. The reference to driving as carefully as a reasonably careful, competitive rally driver would seem more appropriate in the context of the standard of care. However, the case is evidence to both that sports participants owe a duty of care to those who they may foresee could be harmed by their actions, and that this duty will be breached where the participant fails to behave in a manner which is reasonable in the circumstances.

5–15 As will be seen in the discussion below, the English courts have more experience of sport-related cases than their Irish counterparts. Seminal English civil liability cases, including *Condon v Basi*, although

---

[34] ibid.

[35] The Queensland Law Handbook, 'Sport and Duty of Care', last updated 25 October 2021, <https://queenslandlawhandbook.org.au/the-queensland-law-handbook/health-and-wellbeing/sport/sport-and-duty-of-care/> accessed 11 May 2024.

[36] [1974] IR 75.

[37] ibid 89.

of persuasive authority, are instructive to an Irish court.[38] Most civil liability cases and sport are grounded in negligence, and it is to the tort of negligence that the chapter now turns.

Negligence

The seminal case of *Donoghue v Stevenson* is the starting point in the discussion on negligence.[39] The plaintiff, Donoghue, drank from a bottle of ginger beer that contained the remains of a decomposed snail. Donoghue later complained of stomach pains and was diagnosed by her doctor as having gastroenteritis. The plaintiff argued that the manufacturer owed her a duty of care not to produce the beer in a negligent manner, especially in a situation where the product left the manufacturer (in a sealed bottle) in the form in which it was intended to reach the ultimate customer. The House of Lords allowed Donoghue to sue for negligence with Lord Atkin developing the seminal neighbour principle, which is like the Christian concept of loving your neighbour. Lord Atkin's 'neighbour principle' is explained as follows: **5–16**

> The rule that you are to love your neighbour becomes in law you must not injure your neighbour; and the lawyer's question: Who is my neighbour? receives a restricted reply. You must take reasonable care to avoid acts or omissions which you can reasonably foresee would be likely to injure your neighbour. Who, then, in law, is my neighbour? The answer seems to be persons who are so closely and directly affected by my act that I ought reasonably to have them in contemplation as being so affected when I am directing my mind to the acts or omissions that are called in question.[40]

The case of *Donoghue v Stevenson* is important in a number of respects. The case established that the existence of a contract between the parties was not required to establish liability in negligence.[41] The neighbour principle established a general test for liability in negligence. A person owes a duty of care not to cause injury to those who they can reasonably foresee could be injured by their act or omission. When it comes to reasonable foreseeability, it is based on the actions of a reasonable person and how they would act in the particular circumstances and is not based on the actions of the defendant. The neighbour principle limits the duty of care to only those that one could reasonable foresee would be affected by the act or omission. It follows that a person does **5–17**

38 [1985] 2 All ER 453. This case was recently cited by the High Court in *Begadon v Laois Hunt Club Ltd & Anor* [2019] IEHC 343.

39 [1932] AC 562.

40 ibid 580. The principles of *Donoghue v Stevenson* were adopted by the Irish courts in *Kirby v Burke & Holloway* [1944] IR 207.

41 It was Donoghue's friend that had purchased the ginger beer and, under privity of contract, Donoghue was not a party to the contract between her friend and the café owner. Her friend could not sue the café owner as she was not the one whose beverage had the decomposed remains of the snail nor was the friend the person who became ill.

not owe a duty to the world at large. There must be proximity between the parties, thus a relationship between the parties is required. Proximity can relate to 'closeness in distance, time, relationship, or some other connecting factor'.[42]

5–18 The neighbour principle has developed to include situations outside of defective products. In assessing whether a defendant is liable in negligence several factors must be considered:

1. Duty of care – did the defendant reasonably foresee that by their act or omission that the plaintiff would suffer an injury? Once it has been established that a duty of care exists, the next issue to be determined is the extent of this duty, namely, the standard of care.
2. Standard of care – the standard of care depends on the circumstances. The test employed by the courts is that of how a reasonable person would have acted in the prevailing circumstances. It is an objective test which looks at the general standard of behaviour and not that of the particular individual.[43]
3. Damage – because of the defendant's conduct, the plaintiff has suffered a personal injury or damage to their property. Damage may be a combination of physical injury, consequential economic loss, pure economic loss, and psychological damage.[44]
4. Causation – is there a causal link between the injury suffered by the plaintiff and the defendant's conduct? If there is no causal link, then liability will not attach even though the defendant may have acted negligently. Remoteness of damage provides a cut-off point after which the defendant will not be held liable.[45]
5. Lack of defence – *volenti non fit injuria* (voluntary assumption of risk) – means that an individual assumes risk. The defence will argue that the plaintiff by their conduct or agreement assumed the risk that they would be injured. In a sporting situation, participants assume that contact sports carry an inherent risk. If an injury is sustained within the rules of the game, and there was no intention on the part

---

[42] Quill (n 2) 21. A proximate relationship includes the following: doctor–patient, solicitor–client, priest–parishioner, and driver–pedestrian.

[43] ibid 68.

[44] ibid 45. Consequential economic loss refers to the financial loss that occurs due to physical damage. Pure economic loss relates to financial loss without property loss or personal injury. Quill (n 2) 47 observes that most jurisdictions adopt a cautious approach when a case is based purely on economic loss. The Irish Supreme Court decision in *Glencar Exploration plc v Mayo County Council* (2002) 1 IR 84 demonstrates the 'hostility', in the words of Quill, for financial losses that are not accompanied by physical injury or damage to property.

[45] Quill (n 2) 401–38. See *Overseas Tankship (UK) Ltd v Morts Dock & Engineering Co* (The Wagon Mound) [1961] AC 388. In this case the defendant's employees spilt a large quantity of oil into Sydney Harbour. The oil spread to another part of the harbour where the plaintiff was welding. He stopped welding and resumed on receipt of expert advice that oil would not ignite on water. The oil ignited as some sparks from the welding fell on cotton waste. The wharf was damaged. The Court held that harm to the wharf by the oil spill was foreseeable; however, the harm caused by the fire was not foreseeable as oil does not usually ignite on water. The claim for damages for harm caused by the fire was rejected by the Court. The Wagon Mound case was adopted in Ireland: see *Burke v John Paul & Co Ltd* [1967] IR 277.

of the defendant to injure their opponent deliberately or recklessly, the defendant will not be held liable. In the case *Begadon v Laois Hunt Club Ltd & Anor*, an experienced rider was injured during a fox hunt after her horse got caught in brambles at a jump and rolled over the plaintiff. The plaintiff was left with a severe back injury.[46] The plaintiff contended that she should have been warned not to jump that particular obstacle, which she argued was a foreseeable hazard. In dismissing the action, O'Hanlon J held that the plaintiff had

> voluntarily assumed the risk of a mare which had only hunted once before, even though the plaintiff was an accomplished horse person she was an inexperienced hunter on an inexperienced horse taking part in an entirely unpredictable sport with the fox at its centre.[47]

An important consideration for O'Hanlon J was the nature of the sport. There was an inherent risk in fox hunting and the plaintiff did not have due regard for her own safety.[48] The defence of voluntary assumption of risk, originally a common law defence, was given a statutory footing under s 34(1)(b) of the Civil Liability Act 1961. A defendant may also raise the partial defence of contributory negligence, also provided for under s 34 of the Civil Liability Act 1961. Under the defence of contributory negligence, a plaintiff is deemed partially responsible for the injury suffered due to their lack of care and a defendant's negligent conduct have contributed to the injury. The court will apportion damages and damages will be reduced as the plaintiff has contributed to their own injury. For example, the defence could be used in a case where a crash helmet was not worn, or a player did not wear shin guards or other protective clothing or equipment. **5–19**

The Duty of Care: Participants

As mentioned above, it must be established that the defendant owes a duty of care to the plaintiff, which depends on the circumstances of the case. The duty of care is succinctly defined by Fleming as 'an obligation recognised by law, to avoid conduct fraught with unreasonable risk of danger to others'.[49] The plaintiff must establish that there is a relationship between them and the defendant and that relationship required the defendant to take reasonable care not to cause injury to the plaintiff. In the case of *Condon v Basi*, the Court of Appeal of England and Wales held that ordinary principles of negligence applied in a sporting context.[50] The plaintiff, Condon, was playing for Whittle Wanderers and the defendant, Basi, for the Khalsa Football Club; both teams were in a local league. A foul tackle by the defendant caused the plaintiff to break his **5–20**

---

46 *Condon* (n 38).
47 *Begadon* (n 38) [44].
48 ibid [45].
49 John G Fleming, *The Law of Torts* (8th edn, Law Book Company 1992) 149.
50 *Condon* (n 38).

leg. In the Warwick County Court, the defendant was found to have been negligent and £4,900 in damages was awarded to the plaintiff. The Warwick County Court judge held:

> It is not for me in this court to attempt to define exhaustively the duty of care between players in a soccer football game. Nor, in my judgment, is there any need because there was here such an obvious breach of the defendant's duty of care towards the plaintiff. He was clearly guilty, as I find the facts, of serious and dangerous foul play which showed a reckless disregard of the plaintiff's safety and which fell far below the standards which might reasonably be expected in anyone pursuing the game.[51]

5–21 The trial judge accepted that there was no malicious intent to cause harm but that the defendant had acted in a manner that was reckless and dangerous.[52] The referee had considered the tackle to be 'reckless and dangerous' and that it amounted to 'serious foul play'.[53]

5–22 The defendant appealed on two grounds. On the first ground, Basi argued that the County Court judge made no finding at all of the defence of consent to risk of injury and if he had, it would not have been established that Basi owed a duty of care to Condon. On the second ground, it was contended that the Court had erroneously found the defendant negligent on the grounds of that he was grossly negligent or very careless whether he consciously took a risk or not. Basi asserted that a duty of care should only have been imposed if it were shown that he had acted recklessly and was aware of the risk of injury to Condon and was cognisant that it was unreasonable for him to take such a risk. In short, Basi contended that a subjective test of recklessness more akin to the criminal standard was the more appropriate test to be applied.

5–23 In dismissing the appeal, the Court of Appeal held that a player owed a duty to exercise the degree of care that was reasonable in the circumstances, which in a game of football was different from going for a walk in the countryside.[54] The Court of Appeal agreed with the findings of the County Court judge but instead of using the standard of reckless disregard, the Court of Appeal used ordinary negligence principles.[55]

5–24 The Court of Appeal was heavily influenced by the High Court of Australia's judgment in the case of *Rootes v Shelton*, specifically the

---

51 ibid 869D.

52 Opie remarks in his case note that it is not clear whether the trial judge meant that the defendant did not mean to make contact with Condon or that the defendant did not mean to cause the plaintiff any physical harm. See Hayden Opie, '*Condon v Basi*' (1986) 15(4) Melbourne University Law Review 756, 756.

53 *Condon* (n 38) 869B.

54 ibid 868.

55 ibid. Simon Gardiner, *Sports Law* (Cavendish Publishing 2006) 631 is critical of the Court of Appeal's approach. He argues that Sir Donaldson MR did little to clarify the legal position. However, Opie (n 52) 756 applauds the Court of Appeal for not using the cumbersome and confusing standard of reckless disregard.

judgments of Kitto J and Barwick CJ.[56] *Rootes* involved a water-skiing accident whereby the plaintiff suffered serious injuries and subsequently sued the respondent for negligence for failing to take care in the control of the towboat and in failing to warn of the presence of a stationary boat.[57] Barwick CJ accepted that there are risks inherent in the sport of water-skiing; however, failure by the driver of the towboat to warn of the presence of a stationary boat and to drive so close to a stationary boat were not inherent risks.[58] The Chief Justice held:

> By engaging in a sport or pastime the participants may be held to have accepted risks which are inherent in that sport or pastime: the tribunal of fact can make its own assessment of what the accepted risks are: but this does not eliminate all duty of care of the one participant to the other.[59]

Lord Donaldson, the Master of the Rolls (MR), in *Condon v Basi* contended that this was 'a more generalised duty of care which was modified to reflect the fact that participants in the sport or pastime impliedly consent to taking risks which otherwise would be a breach of the duty of care'.[60] Kitto J's judgment, Lord Donaldson MR deduced, was that in sport there is a general standard of care that is akin to Lord Atkin's neighbour principle in *Donoghue v Stevenson*.[61] Lord Donaldson MR favoured the approach of Kitto J, although he contended that, while both judges had different approaches, the end result was the same.[62] Lord Donaldson MR summarised Kitto J's judgment as follows: **5–25**

> you are under a duty to take all reasonable care taking into account of the circumstances in which you are placed; which in a game of football, are quite different from those which affect you when you are going for a walk on the countryside.[63]

Lord Donaldson MR rejected the contention by the defendant's counsel that the standard of care was subjective; this would mean that if the defendant 'was a wholly incompetent football player, he could do things without risk of liability which a competent football player could not do'.[64] Instead, Lord Donaldson MR held that the standard is objective but objective in a different set of circumstances.[65] In applying the objective standard, controversially, Lord Donaldson MR added that a higher **5–26**

---

56 *Rootes* (n 27) 383.
57 ibid 384.
58 ibid 386.
59 ibid 384.
60 *Condon* (n 38) 868C. Gardiner (n 55) 634 is critical of the approach of Barwick CJ. He notes that players do not consent to risks but rather they consent to contacts that are inherent in the sport, and they run the risk of being injured due to such contacts.
61 *Condon* (n 38) 868C.
62 ibid 868E.
63 ibid 868D.
64 ibid 868F.
65 ibid 868F.

duty of care would be required from a first division player than from a player in a local league game.[66] However, such an assertion would seem improbable. For example, in the Football Association Challenge Cup (more commonly referred to as the FA Cup), teams from different league levels play each other and if Lord Donaldson's comments were taken to its logical conclusion it would mean that in a match involving a premier league side and a lower division team, the premier side would owe a higher duty of care than their opponents in the same match.[67] Admittedly, there is a different standard of play expected from a professional player than that of an amateur player. However, the same standard of care in the circumstances is expected.

5–27 Lord Donaldson MR dismissed the appeal. In his concluding remarks, he referred to the trial judge's conclusion:

> It is not for me in this court to attempt to define exhaustively the duty of care between players in a soccer football game. Nor, in my judgment, is there any need because there was here such an obvious breach of the defendant's duty of care towards the plaintiff. He was clearly guilty, as I find the facts, of serious and dangerous foul play which showed a reckless disregard of the plaintiff's safety and which fell far below the standards which might reasonably be expected in anyone pursuing the game.[68]

5–28 The case is disappointing in several respects.[69] The Court of Appeal had the opportunity to clarify the standard of care in sports cases, however, it caused confusion. In referring to a different set of circumstances, it seems to infer a subjective element. The standard is objective; however, by considering the circumstances of the particular case, that suggests a subjective element.[70] The reference to reckless disregard compounded

---

66 ibid 868F.

67 Sir Donaldson's comments conflict with the earlier case of *Nettleship v Weston* [1976] 2 QB 691. In this case, the Court of Appeal held that the standard of care for a learner driver was that which is expected of the ordinary, reasonably careful, and prudent qualified driver. The standard is an objective one. However, the driving analogy has its limitations when applied to sport. Every driver owes every other driver the same duty of care, irrespective of the individual skill of the particular motorist. As Gardiner (n 55) 636 asserts: 'In sport, the analogy only stretches as far as each individual game or at most each individual competition, not each entire sport … however, that does not mean that those at the higher levels of play owe a higher duty of care. A higher degree of skill may still be expected but also would a higher degree of risk taking and the acceptance by all involved of those risks.' See Craig Moore, *Sports Law and Litigation* (2nd edn, CLT Professional Publishing 2000) 145. Moore notes that varying standards have been accepted in other fields, for example, medicine.

68 *Condon* (n 38) 869C and D.

69 However, it is evident from the case that the Court of Appeal clearly accepted that a breach of the rules of the game would be needed for liability to attach. The Court of Appeal seemed to be suggesting that a breach of the rules is 'virtually a necessary, albeit not a sufficient, requirement for liability to attach. Again, there is nothing special about sports cases in this regard': see Michael Beloff and others, *Sports Law* (2nd edn, Bloomsbury Publishing 2012) 39.

70 Objective means that the standard is based on the reasonable person rather than

the confusion and, as will be discussed in the next part of the chapter, it was left to subsequent cases to clarify the appropriate standard of care.[71]

Participants and the Standard of Care

The standard of care has posed some problems for the courts. The debate has centred on whether the standard of care should be the standard associated with ordinary negligence or whether a higher threshold for liability is required. The Australian case of *Frazer v Johnston* provides an example of the two standards.[72] The case centred on a collision between two jockeys in a flat race. The defendant's horse had veered in too close to the plaintiff's horse in a situation where there was no room to do so. The plaintiff suffered severe injuries due to the collision. The plaintiff argued that the standard owed was that of ordinary negligence, citing the cases of *Rootes v Shelton*[73] and *Condon v Basi*.[74] The defendant, on the other hand, argued that the appropriate test was that of reckless disregard, as held in *Wooldridge v Sumner*[75] and *Turcotte v Fell*.[76] The Court applied the case of *Rootes*, and in doing so rejected the standard of reckless disregard proposed by the defendant. The Court held that Johnston owed Frazer a duty of care and awarded damages of $121,490. On appeal, Johnston argued that the duty in sporting cases differed from other activities. However, the Court of Appeal rejected this and held that sporting cases should be treated the same as all other negligence cases.[77] **5–29**

The Court of Appeal in *Condon v Basi* established that the ordinary principles of negligence applied to sport.[78] Some earlier cases suggested that the more appropriate standard in a sporting context was that of reckless disregard. In *Wooldridge v Sumner*, the claimant was a professional photographer who was employed by the directors of a company who wished to make a film; however, at the time of the accident, Wooldridge had run out of film and was not taking any photographs.[79] The photographer was situated within the ring of the horse show and not behind barriers where the spectators were located. **5–30**

the individual defendant.

71 For criticisms of the case, see Mark James, 'Liability for Professional Athletes' Injuries: A Comparative Analysis of Where the Risk Lies' (2006) 1 Web Journal of Current Legal Issues <https://www.bailii.org/uk/other/journals/WebJCLI/2006/issue1/james1.html> accessed 11 May 2024.

72 (1989) Aust Tort Reports 80–248.

73 *Rootes* (n 27).

74 *Condon* (n 38).

75 [1963] 2 QB 43.

76 510 NYS 2d 49 (Ct App) (1986). Turcotte was a professional jockey and during a race the defendant's horse clipped off his horse, causing him to be thrown. The New York Supreme Court, in dismissing the appeal, held that there were risks inherent in the sport and that the plaintiff consented to the race but did not consent to intentional or reckless acts.

77 *Johnston v Frazer* (1990) 21 NSWLR 89.

78 *Condon* (n 38).

79 *Wooldridge* (n 75).

Wooldridge, it seemed, had no experience of or interest in horses. Holladay was a highly experienced and skilled competitor who rode Work of Art, owned by Sumner. Wooldridge and one of the directors were seated on a bench and as Work of Art came galloping towards the bench, the photographer attempted to move and ended up being knocked over by Work of Art. In the High Court, liability was imposed on Sumner and the matter was referred to the Court of Appeal.[80] In reversing the decision of Barry J of the High Court, the Court of Appeal held that Holladay did not owe Wooldridge a duty of care. Lord Justice (LJ) Danckwerts held:

5–31 Mr. Holladay's duty to his employer was to utilise the qualities of the horse so as to show it to the best advantage. This involved the horse going at a fast gallop. Decisions have to be taken in a split second and it is impossible for a rider, as it seems to me, in such circumstances to calculate every possible result in his mind. He could not possibly be expected to foresee that someone would jump out from the line of the bench into the track of the horse. Persons who stand so close to the scene of such events must take the risk of something going wrong in the ordinary course of the sport, and which is a risk incidental to it.[81]

5–32 Sellars LJ distinguished the actions of Holladay from those of someone who deliberately intended to injure a person whose presence is known or had acted in reckless disregard of the safety of others.[82] In this situation, liability may attach as there is a deviation from the standards which might reasonably be expected of a competitor. Sellars LJ provided the following example:

> There would, I think, be a difference, for instance, in assessing blame which is actionable between an injury caused by a tennis ball hit or a racket accidentally thrown in the course of play into the spectators at Wimbledon and a ball hit or a racket thrown into the stands in temper or annoyance when play was not in progress.[83]

5–33 Diplock LJ also referred to the standard of reckless disregard. He acknowledged that a spectator assumes the risk of damage and in a situation where the participant has made an error of judgement or a lapse of skill, this is not tantamount to negligence. The participant should not be found liable 'unless the participant's conduct is such as to evince a reckless disregard of the spectator's safety'.[84] As will be discussed below, the standard of reckless disregard creates a very high threshold, one that is not easily breached. The English courts apply the ordinary principles of negligence to sports cases, with consideration given to the prevailing circumstances. The case of *Elliott v Saunders*

---

[80] [1961] 1 WLUK 22.
[81] *Wooldridge* (n 75) 60.
[82] ibid 57.
[83] ibid.
[84] ibid 68.

is illustrative of this approach.[85] This was the first time the court was given the opportunity to assess the standard of care owed from one professional footballer to another.

Drake J in *Elliott v Saunders* made an interesting observation at the outset of his judgment. An incident that lasted less than one second and had devastating consequences for Elliott required a nine-day hearing which included numerous witnesses and two high-profile professional football players.[86] Saunders, a striker, was playing for Liverpool and had played at international level for Wales. Elliott, a central defender, played for Chelsea and was considered a 'rising star' and it was envisaged that he would play international football for England.[87] In what was described as a 50–50 ball, Saunders jumped and landed on Elliott's outstretched leg. The resulting collision caused a career-ending injury for Elliott. Elliott contended that Saunders had not intended to cause him serious injury, however, he asserted that the defendant deliberately broke the rules of the game by going for his (the plaintiff's) legs and not the ball. Elliott further claimed that Saunders had jumped with the deliberate intention of landing on his legs or had done so recklessly without any care that by jumping he would land on Elliott's legs.[88] The plaintiff contended that Saunders had failed to exercise the duty of care that was owed to him in the particular circumstances.[89] **5–34**

The extent of the duty of care owed by the defendant to the plaintiff was disputed by the parties. Elliott contended that Saunders was reckless or did not care that his actions would result in injury. Counsel for Elliott cited several cases to elucidate the duty of care, including *Wooldridge v Summer*,[90] *Rootes v Shelton*[91] and *Condon v Basi*.[92] Drake J stated that it was 'really unnecessary to look beyond the decision in *Condon v Basi*'.[93] **5–35**

In line with the comments of Lord Donaldson MR in *Condon v Basi*, Elliott endeavoured to argue that a different standard of care applied in a professional game. Elliott proposed that Saunders owed him, a fellow professional, a higher standard of care in line with that expected of a highly trained and skilled participant. However, Drake J disagreed and held: **5–36**

> The fact that players are top professionals with very great skills, is no

---

85 *Elliott* (n 12).
86 The judgment was downloaded from LexisNexis with the citation of *Elliott v Saunders and Another* [1994] Lexis Citation 3968. Drake J's observation can be found on page 1 of a 14-page judgment.
87 ibid 1.
88 ibid.
89 ibid.
90 *Wooldridge* (n 75).
91 *Rootes* (n 27).
92 *Condon* (n 38)
93 *Elliott* (n 86) 3.

> doubt one of the circumstances to be considered, but in my judgment, the fact that the game is in the Premier League rather than at a lower level does not necessarily mean that the standard of care is different; liability on the part of a defendant depends on the facts and circumstances of each individual case.[94]

5–37 Saunders stated that he was going for the ball and when he saw that Elliott's legs had left the ground, he instinctively raised his legs to avoid injury to himself.[95] The Court agreed with Saunders and held that he had not acted in a reckless and deliberate manner as suggested by Elliott.[96] Drake J was heavily influenced by the testimonies of the match officials, namely the referee, linesmen and the football league's assessor who was watching from the main stand between the director's box and the press box.[97] Drake J dismissed video and photographic evidence as being two-dimensional and, with modern technology, it was easy to edit and manipulate.[98]

5–38 The lack of success for Elliott did not mean that other footballers were dissuaded from bringing tort actions. In a similar case in 1994, Northern Ireland international and Norwich player O'Neill received a reported £70,000 in damages from John Fashanu of Wimbledon in an out-of-court settlement.[99] McCord, the former Stockport County player, successfully sued Swansea City and its captain, Cornford, after his career was ended by a tackle during a match.[100] McCord was the first professional footballer to succeed in a negligence case.

5–39 In *Watson v Gray*, the defendant and his club, Huddersfield Town, were found liable for injuries suffered by the plaintiff in a match involving Bradford City and Huddersfield Town.[101] Hooper J, sitting in the Bradford District registry of the Queen's Bench Division, held that a professional footballer is at risk of being proved negligent if he is shown to have caused injury with an act which a reasonable professional player

---

94 ibid 4.

95 ibid 6.

96 As the case was dismissed, there was no hearing in relation to damages; however, Elliott was seeking £1 million. He had moved from Celtic to Chelsea on 1 July 1991 for a transfer fee of £1.53 million: see <https://www.transfermarkt.co.uk/paul-elliott/transfers/spieler/222499> accessed 11 May 2024. According to Nick Harris, the average weekly wage of a top division player in 1994 was £2,738: see 'From £20 to £33,868 per Week: A Quick History of English Football's Top-Flight Wages' *Sporting Intelligence* (Helensburgh, 20 January 2011) <https://www.sportingintelligence.com/2011/01/20/from-20-to-33868-per-week-a-quick-history-of-english-footballs-top-flight-wages-200101/> accessed 11 May 2024.

97 *Elliott* (n 86) 13.

98 ibid 5.

99 O'Neill's legal fees amounted to £150,000 and he never played football again: Daniel Taylor, 'Stakes Raised in Football's Grudge Match' *The Guardian* (London, 17 August 2002) <https://www.theguardian.com/football/2002/aug/17/newsstory.sport11> accessed 11 May 2024.

100 *McCord v Swansea City AFC Ltd* [1996] 12 WLUK 409.

101 [1998] 10 WLUK 559.

would know to carry a significant risk of causing serious injury. The tackle in question was considered late, forceful, and high. Watson had been chasing a loose ball while Gray was around two to three yards away from him at a right angle, Watson kicked the ball and a split second later his leg had been clipped by Gray's boot. Watson suffered a double fracture to his leg. Hopper J was influenced by video evidence which he watched on several occasions in slow motion.[102]

In *Pitcher v Huddersfield Town Football Club Ltd*, the claimant was a professional footballer who was injured in a match by his opponent, Reid.[103] The claimant argued that the defendant was liable in negligence as he had failed to exercise reasonable skill and care and that his standard of football fell below that expected of a professional footballer. Damages was a crucial factor as the injury was career-ending. Hallett J dismissed the claim and held on the balance of probabilities that a lapse in judgement or a mistimed tackle could not be equated with negligence, especially in a fast-paced game such as football. Expert witnesses testified that tackles of this nature, although outside of the rules, occurred on Saturday up and down the country in the First Division. **5–40**

Hallett J held that the claimant had not shown that the challenge crossed 'the high threshold to take this case from a simple late tackle, albeit one with tragic consequences, to one of negligence'.[104] In applying the ordinary principles of negligence, the judge noted that certain sports carried inherent risks and the standard of care depended on the circumstances of the case. Pitcher was required to show on the balance of probabilities that Reid's actions had fallen below the standard required of a professional footballer. The judge found that the lack of supporting evidence and Pitcher's inability to establish liability on the balance of probabilities required her to find against the claimant. **5–41**

Caldwell v Maguire and Fitzgerald – The Standard of Care Clarified

Shortly before the *Pitcher* decision, the Court of Appeal heard a similar civil liability case involving professional jockeys.[105] It is an important judgment as the Court clarified the standard of care in sporting cases. The incident involved four horses and occurred at the two-mile novice hurdle race at Hexham on 30 September 1994. At a subsequent Steward's Inquiry, Maguire and Fitzgerald were found to have engaged in careless riding as they had not given enough room for another rider (Byrne) to come around the inside rail and as a result, Caldwell was unseated from his horse. Caldwell suffered a serious injury. The two riders were suspended for three days. In the trial court, liability was not imposed on **5–42**

[102] James (n 12) 82.
[103] [2001] 7 WLUK 390.
[104] ibid.
[105] *Caldwell v Maguire and Fitzgerald* [2001] EWCA 1054.

Maguire and Fitzgerald as Holland J did not consider the actions of the riders to be negligent. Holland J held that a lapse or error of judgement was not tantamount to negligence. Caldwell appealed the decision to the Court of Appeal on the grounds that Holland J had applied a standard of care that

> was too low; that he effectively required proof of deliberate or reckless disregard for safety. If he had applied the correct standard, in any event, he would or should have found that the Respondents were negligent.[106]

5–43 Holland J set out five propositions that should be considered when deciding liability. These five propositions were approved by the Court of Appeal:

> (1) Each Contestant in a lawful sporting contest (and in particular a race) owes a duty of care to each and all other contestants.
>
> (2) That duty is to exercise in the course of the contest all care that is objectively reasonable in the prevailing circumstances for the avoidance of infliction of injury to such fellow contestants.
>
> (3) The prevailing circumstances are all such properly attendant upon the contest and include its object, the demands inevitably made upon its contestants, its inherent dangers (if any), its rules, conventions and customs, and the standards, skills, and judgment reasonably to be expected of a contestant. Thus, in the particular case of a horse race the prevailing circumstances will include the contestant's obligation to ride a horse over a given course competing with the remaining contestants for the best possible placing, if not for a win. Such must further include the Rules of Racing and the standards, skills, and judgment of a professional jockey, all as expected by fellow contestants.
>
> (4) Given the nature of such prevailing circumstances the threshold for liability is in practice inevitably high; the proof of a breach of duty will not flow from proof of no more than an error of judgment or from mere proof of a momentary lapse in skill (and thus care) respectively when subject to the stresses of a race. Such are no more than incidents inherent in the nature of the sport.
>
> (5) In practice it may therefore be difficult to prove any such breach of duty absent proof of conduct that in point of fact amounts to reckless disregard for the fellow contestant's safety. I emphasise the distinction between the expression of legal principle and the practicalities of the evidential burden.[107]

5–44 In dismissing the appeal, the Court of Appeal reiterated the point that an error of judgement, an oversight, or a lapse of which any participant might be guilty in the context of a race of that kind could not be equated with negligence. Something more serious is required to attribute

---

[106] ibid [3].
[107] ibid [11].

negligence to the actions of the defendants. Incidents of this nature happened often and were part of what is termed the 'playing culture of the sport'.[108] James and Deeley note that the Court of Appeal, in dismissing the standard of reckless disregard, 'has ensured that sports participants are judged by the same legal standard as everyone else'.[109]

The Duty of Care and the Standard of Reckless Disregard

The High Court in *Begadon v Laois Hunt Club Ltd & Anor* cited the five conditions developed by Holland J in *Caldwell v Maguire and Fitzgerald*.[110] *Rootes v Shelton* and *Condon v Basi* were also cited by O'Hanlon J.[111] The Irish and English courts endorse a generalised duty of care, which is derived from Lord Atkin's neighbour principle. A participant is under a duty to take all reasonable care, taking account of the prevailing circumstances. The threshold for liability is high and a lapse or error of judgement is not tantamount to negligence. **5–45**

Reckless disregard has caused some confusion among academic commentators and the courts alike. Most of the cases above provide that the ordinary negligence principles should apply to sport. Sport should not be treated differently to other activities. Others argue that reckless disregard seems to be more suitable to professional sportspersons as the standard of care is higher since professional players should be taken to have understood and assumed the inherent risks relevant in the sport.[112] As reckless disregard is a very high standard, it is more difficult for a participant to breach it. It means that participants can engage in the sport in their usual manner without fear of litigation. However, reckless disregard would grant almost total immunity to sports participants.[113] **5–46**

---

108 For a detailed discussion of the playing culture, see Gardiner (n 55) 637–38. Mark James and Fiona Deeley, 'The Standard of Care in Negligence Cases: *Caldwell v Maguire and Fitzgerald* [2001] EWCA 1054' (2002) 1(1) Entertainment Law 104, 106–07, in support of the playing culture, note that 'it concentrates on the playing of the game and its inherent dangers rather than allowing the defendant to show a greater degree of negligence to the claimant before liability is imposed'.

109 James and Deeley (n 108) 106. Some academic commentators welcomed the decision as, in the words of Gardiner (n 55) 632, the case 'has come closest to defining the true scope of negligence in this area'. Similar comments are made by James (n 12) 82. However, Charlish (n 27) 324 is most critical of the decision and argues that the decision has led to more uncertainty and 'stripped away the relative clarity that had been present since *Condon v Basi* and replaced it with an unsatisfactory compromise that is going to need further judicial intervention to settle the appropriate *standard* of care for sports in England and Wales'.

110 *Begadon* (n 38) [31]–[35]; *Caldwell* (n 105).

111 *Rootes* (n 27); *Condon* (n 38).

112 Simon Gardiner and Alexandra Felix, 'Juridification of the Football Field: Strategies for Giving the Law the Elbow' (1994–1995) 5 Marquette Sports Law Journal 189, 208. The writers argue that the better course of action is to hold the clubs vicariously liable for the actions of their players. However, as Drake J pointed out in *Elliott* (n 86) 2, the clubs would in turn go after the player to recover the compensation paid out, so the dispute would still end up in the court.

113 Charlish (n 27) 323. Charlish adds that if such a standard was used it would mean

5–47 In interpreting conditions 4 and 5 as developed by Holland J in *Caldwell,* James best explains the status of reckless disregard in the following statement:

> The Court in Caldwell made it clear that there is no separate test, or new tort, of acting with reckless disregard towards another person. Instead, by linking this statement to the fourth point they are again highlighting that behaviour in sport is based on a different understanding of normative behaviour and that courts should not be recompensing the unfortunate accidents that can occur in fast, physically combative, dynamic sports. What the Caldwell restatement of the law does clarify is that it is only behaviour that goes beyond the norm, beyond the playing culture of a sport, that should be found to be negligent ... Errors, misjudgements and mistimings are an integral part of all sports.[114]

5–48 The courts apply the ordinary principles of negligence in a sporting context and there is not a new tort called reckless disregard in Irish or English law. Liability will not attach for lapses or errors of judgement; it should be reserved for situations where the actions of the defendant go beyond the accepted norms of the sport. The High Court of England and Wales, in a judgment handed down on 18 May 2022, applied the *Caldwell* and *Condon* decisions in the case of *Fulham Football Club v Jones*.[115] This was an appeal from Recorder Craven sitting in Swansea Civil Justice Centre. In a match between two under-18 teams in December 2016, Jones was playing for Swansea and Harris, a midfielder, was playing for Fulham. As the first half was ending, Harris tackled Jones, with Jones suffering a career-ending injury. In December 2019, Jones initiated proceedings against Harris and Fulham. Jones contended that the tackle constituted an assault or in the alternative Harris was negligent.[116] In October 2021, Recorder Craven handed down his decision. He dismissed the assault action against Harris, however, found Fulham vicariously liable for the negligent act committed by Harris on Jones.[117] Fulham sought leave to the appeal the decision, however, the recorder refused to grant permission.[118] Permission to appeal was subsequently granted by Eady J on four grounds that were raised by Fulham.[119]

5–49 Ground 1 contended 'that the recorder erred in failing to apply the test set out in the authorities concerning the standard for liability for personal injury claims in the professional sports context'.[120] In referring to the case of *Caldwell,*[121] counsel for Fulham argued that the court

that claimants would find it almost impossible to obtain compensation.

114 James (n 71).

115 [2022] EWHC 1108 (QB).

116 ibid [3].

117 ibid [5].

118 ibid.

119 ibid.

120 ibid [50].

121 (n 105).

should apply a two-stage analysis.[122] The first stage required that the court must determine whether the defendant breached the Laws of the Game, and the second stage required the determination whether there was negligence 'which is set at a materially higher standard than the Laws of the Game'.[123]

Lane J stated the recorder: **5–50**

> by closely aligning serious foul play in the Laws of the Game with actionable negligence, he wrongly reduced the ambit of the inquiry required in order to answer the question of whether, in all the circumstances, Mr Harris's tackle was not only a breach of the Rules of Game but negligent.[124]

Ground 2 contended that the recorder failed to give any reasons why he rejected the evidence of Fulham's expert, Canning, 'an eminent former referee' and co-author of the Laws of the Game.[125] The recorder rejected Canning's evidence, as his view in relation to the video evidence conflicted with that of the expert.[126] In finding the recorder's rejection of the expert 'legally flawed', Lane J allowed this ground to succeed. **5–51**

Ground 3 was based on the contention that 'the recorder erred in law' in his explicit refusal to consider the situation in which the tackle took place and his failure to recognise 'the realities of the playing culture of professional football, which is a fast-paced, competitive game necessarily involving physical contact'.[127] Counsel for Fulham proffered that the recorder 'analysed the tackle in a vacuum, with the benefit of hindsight, thereby imposing a counsel of perfection on Fulham and Mr Harris'.[128] In referring to a material error in paragraph 65 of the recorder's decision, Lane J stated that it purported 'to set a standard for reckless or quasi-reckless behaviour in the context of professional football, which is far below what is needed to establish such liability'.[129] **5–52**

Ground 4 centred on the submission 'that the recorder erred in law by failing to take into account all the contemporaneous evidence'.[130] This ground related to the failure of the recorder to give any weight to the fact that the referee did not sanction the tackle; he did not issue either a red or yellow card.[131] Lane J acknowledged that the failure of the match official not to take action or 'relatively minor action' was 'of course, **5–53**

---

[122] *Fulham* (n 115) [50].
[123] ibid.
[124] ibid [64].
[125] ibid [68]–[77].
[126] ibid [76] and [77].
[127] ibid [78].
[128] ibid.
[129] ibid [85].
[130] ibid [87].
[131] ibid.

not determinative'.[132] In support of this contention, Lane J cited with approval the case of *Tylicki v Gibbons*.[133] In *Tylicki*, a flat race jockey had ridden with reckless disregard of the safety of another jockey.[134] The defendant had steered his horse in the path of the claimant's horse, resulting in three horses and four riders falling. Convening immediately after the race, a Stewards' Enquiry was held without Tylicki, who was being attended to on the track.[135] The Stewards concluded that the actions of Gibbons were accidental and did not constitute dangerous or careless riding.[136]

5–54 In holding that the Stewards' Enquiry was not binding on the Court, the judge in *Tylicki* acknowledged the highly skilled and experienced nature of the Stewards.[137] While 'their determination after a short hearing is an important part of the matrix', however, 'it would be wrong to give that finding a greater weight than it deserves, particularly given the significant limitations with respect to the evidence they received'.[138] In finding for the claimant, the judge referred to the actions of the defendant as not amounting to 'mere lapses of concentration or inattentiveness'.[139] The judge, although finding in favour of Tylicki, stressed

> that the threshold of liability for negligence is a high one and has been determined as made out in this case, on its own particular facts. The finding does not set a precedent either within horse-racing or in sport general.[140]

5–55 Of importance to Lane J in *Fulham v Jones*, the Stewards' Enquiry in *Tylicki* was deemed not to be determinative.[141] However, the evidence of the referee Lane J found 'to matter to be engaged with by the court, in determining whether actionable negligence has occurred'.[142]

5–56 In allowing the appeal on the four grounds, Lane J ordered a new trial. In his analysis on the case, Thorpe makes two observations:

> Recorder Craven's judgment of negligently inflicted 'sports violence' was flawed in two main respects: One, a failure to differentiate between a breach of the rules of football and the law applicable to negligence, in effect finding that a breach of football's rules was sufficient to ground

---

132 ibid [89].
133 [2021] EWHC 3470 (QB) [89].
134 It was a maiden race for fillies aged three years or older: ibid [34].
135 ibid [49]. Tylicki required four months of hospital treatment. The judge explained that Tylicki sustained T4 AIS complete paraplegia and, as a result, he will be wheelchair-bound for the rest of his life: ibid [1].
136 ibid [15]. This was disputed by McGrath, a presenter for Sky Sport who viewed the actions of the defendant as not just careless but dangerous.
137 ibid [55].
138 ibid.
139 ibid [93].
140 ibid [95].
141 *Fulham* (n 115) [89].
142 ibid.

> liability in negligence. Two, a failure to appreciate that errors of judgment, inadvertence, fatigue, poor timing and the like are inherent in high-speed sport and are circumstances to which athletes are deemed to have consented, along with any consequential physical contact and resultant harm.[143]

Fulham v Jones reiterates the approach of the English courts to civil liability in sport. The courts need to adopt a two-pronged test. First, it must be determined whether the rules of the game or Laws of the Game have been breached; second, it must be ascertained whether there was negligence, 'which is set at a materially higher standard than the Laws of the Game'.[144] The threshold for liability is high and one that is not easily reached. The incident should not be viewed in isolation or in a vacuum, the wider context of the playing culture and realities of a fast-paced competitive contact sport must be considered. The evidence of match officials is not determinative; however, it should be considered by the court in deciding whether actionable negligence has occurred. **5–57**

Damages

Collett v Smith, Middlesbrough Football and Athletics Company (1986) Ltd concerns the assessment of damages for a career-ending injury.[145] Collett was aged 18 and playing for the Manchester United Reserves' team when he suffered a fracture of the tibia and fibula in his right leg following a high and 'over the ball' tackle by his opponent, Smith, who played for Middlesbrough Reserves' Team. Collett returned to football but never reached his pre-injury standard and retired at the age of 21. While he never played a first team match for Manchester United, in the High Court of England and Wales, Collett was awarded just under £4 million. Swift J assessed damages as follows[146]: **5–58**

General damages for pain and suffering, loss of amenity and loss of congenial employment (agreed)	=£ 35,000.00
Interest thereon (agreed)	=£ 1,515.00

143 David Thorpe, 'Consent and the Rules of Play in Sports Violence' (2022) 38(4) Professional Negligence 239, 244.

144 *Fulham* (n 115) [50]. There are other more recent cases that endorse approach of the earlier cases of *Condon* and *Caldwell*, for example: *Elbanna v Clarke* [2024] EWHC 627 (KB) and *Czernuszka v King* [2023] EWHC 380 (KB). In referring to *Elbanna v Clarke*, one writer asserts that '[a]lthough the law is now well settled that recklessness is not a necessary element of holding sports players liable for injuries caused during play, the judge did conclude that the Defendant had been reckless by running full speed towards the Claimant and by colliding with him in the manner that he did', see Carin Hunt, 'Tackling liability: Lessons from Elbanna v Clark on negligence in sports injuries' (*Law In Sport*, 8 May 2024) <https://www.lawinsport.com/topics/item/tackling-liability-lessons-from-elbanna-v-clark-on-negligence-in-sports-injuries> accessed 4 July 2024.

145 [2008] EWHC 1962 (QB).

146 ibid [145].

Value of past gratuitous care (agreed)	=£ 2,469.00
Interest thereon (agreed)	=£ 740.00
Past loss of earnings	=£ 456,095
Interest thereon	=£ To be determined
Future loss of earnings	=£ 3,854,328.00
Future loss of pension	=£ To be determined

5–59 In total, Collett was awarded damages in the amount of £3,894,508.[147] Future damages were based on the salaries that Collett's contemporaries playing at Championship level would be earning, as Swift J explained:

> Once again, the defendants invited me to apply a statistical approach which would have involved my finding that the claimant had only a 40% chance of playing at Championship level throughout his career. Such a finding would fly in the face of the evidence. That evidence showed that the claimant had the character and ability to play professional football at the highest level. Those of his contemporaries with similar, or even slightly lesser, abilities have already established themselves at Championship level or above. I find that, barring injury or some unforeseen contingency, the claimant would have played professional football, at the least at Championship level throughout his career.[148]

5–60 Smith and Middlesbrough appealed the High Court decision, the main grounds for the appeal being the calculation of loss of future earnings.[149] Carnworth LJ of the Court of Appeal, in dismissing the appeal, could not fault Swift J's calculation of damages and he along with the two other judges were 'satisfied that her conclusion is supportable on the very special facts of this case. As Smith LJ has made clear, the evidence in support of the claim was exceptionally strong, and hardly disputed.'[150]

5–61 Given the financial implications of a career-ending injury for a professional sportsperson, it is interesting to note that it is quite rare for a sportsperson to initiate civil proceedings against the opponent that caused the injury and the opponent's club. Clubs are often enjoined in proceedings as clubs will have 'deeper pockets' and as the player has caused the injury in the course of their employment, the principle of vicarious liability applies.[151] Most clubs, the wealthier and top division clubs, will have adequate insurance to cover the costs of personal injury cases. However, as seen in the case of *Welsh v Ossett Town Football Club*, for lower division or semi-professional and amateur clubs, the costs of litigation and inadequate insurance policies will have drastic effects on

[147] ibid [146]: the judge stated that interest and pension loss had yet to be determined.
[148] ibid [120].
[149] *Smith & Anr v Collett* [2009] EWCA Civ 583.
[150] ibid [51].
[151] For a discussion on vicarious liability and sport, see Phillip Morgan, 'Vicarious Liability and the Beautiful Game – Liability for Professional and Amateur Footballers?' (2018) 38(2) Legal Studies 242.

the viability of a club if the matter goes before the courts.[152] Welsh broke his ankle in an amateur match and was awarded £19,297.38 in damages by a Manchester court.[153] In total, the cost of the case to Ossett Town Football Club amounted to £135,000. Ossett Town's insurance did not cover the pay-out; it only covered the costs of defending the case. The club feared it would have to sell the stadium to cover the costs; however, a party closely associated with the club re-mortgaged their house so that the club could meet the costs of the case.[154]

Participants are not the only ones who have been the subject of negligence cases: referees, governing bodies, coaches, and instructors can also be sued if they fail in their duty of care, as the next part of the chapter discusses. **5–62**

The Liability of Referees

Referees have been held to owe a duty of care to participants. The role of the referee is not just to enforce the rules of the game to ensure fair play but also to ensure that the sport is played according to the rules for the safety of the participants. The seminal case on the liability of referees is *Smoldon v Whitworth and Nolan*.[155] Smoldon successfully sued the referee for injuries sustained because of a collapsed scrum in a game involving underage rugby players. Smoldon was playing in the position of hooker and when a scrum collapsed, he broke his neck and was left with life-altering injuries. The case against Whitworth, the opposing player, was dismissed and proceeded only against Nolan, the referee. **5–63**

In the trial court, the referee admitted that he owed a duty of care to the players; however, he argued that the relevant standard of care was that of reckless disregard. The Court, however, disagreed and followed the approach of *Condon*, holding that the duty was to exercise such degree of care as was appropriate in all the circumstances.[156] An important factor for the Court was the fact that the players were underage. It held that the referee had not enforced safety requirements set out in the Laws of the Game, which contained special provisions relating to players aged under 19. **5–64**

The decision to impose liability was appealed by the referee and went **5–65**

[152] Ben Ransom, 'Footballer Rees Welsh Wins Landmark Injury Claim' (*Sky Sports*, 19 November 2019) <https://www.skysports.com/football/news/11095/11859672/footballer-reece-welsh-wins-landmark-injury-claim> accessed 11 May 2024.

[153] ibid.

[154] Ben McKenna, 'Putting his House on Non-League Club's Survival' *Yorkshire Post* (Leeds, 13 May 2020) <https://www.yorkshirepost.co.uk/sport/football/putting-his-house-non-league-clubs-survival-2851973> accessed 11 May 2024.

[155] [1997] PIQR 133. The game was a colts' game, meaning all the players were under 19 years of age. There was a paternalistic element in the case.

[156] *Condon* (n 38).

before the Court of Appeal. Nolan argued that the Court should have used the standard of reckless disregard. He endeavoured to rely on the dicta of Lord Diplock and Sellers LJ in *Wooldridge v Sumner*.[157] The referee argued that the standard of reckless disregard should apply to protect match officials from litigation. Many referees are volunteers and fear of litigation would mean that such referees would be less likely to offer their services. The Court of Appeal disagreed and held that the appropriate standard of care was to be expressed as follows:

> The level of care required is that which is appropriate in all the circumstances, and the circumstances are of crucial importance. Full account must be taken of the factual context in which a referee exercises his functions, and he could not be held liable for errors of judgment, oversights or lapses of which any referee might be guilty in the context of a fast- moving and vigorous contest. The threshold for liability is a high one. It will not be easily crossed.[158]

5–66 The Court of Appeal imposed liability on the referee, holding that his inability to control the scrummage effectively was a breach of the duty owed to Smoldon. Caddell highlights the 'clear distinction' the Court of Appeal made

> between the match official's obligations regarding the scrummage, when he has paused the game and has taken control over the players, and during passages of fast-moving open play, in which the referee has only the bare minimum of control over the players.[159]

5–67 If an injury is sustained during passages of robust open play, then the referee cannot be held liable. In contrast, if the referee has blown the whistle and has time to consider their options and has made the safety instructions clear to the players, failure on the part of the referee to properly enforce the rules may result in the imposition of liability.

5–68 It was feared that the decision in *Smoldon* would open the floodgates of litigation. The trial judge in the case expressed such concerns and in the words of the Lord Bingham CJ, the judge had reached his decision 'on the very special facts of this case', namely the fact that the match involved players aged under 19 and there were specific rules in relation to scrums for such players and the excessive number of collapsed scrums that occurred during the game.[160] The decision to impose liability on the referee was not based on the intention 'to open the door to a plethora of

---

[157] (n 75) 57, Sellers LJ stated: 'If the conduct is deliberately intended to injure someone whose presence is known, or is reckless and in disregard of all safety of others so that it is a departure from the standards which might reasonably be expected in anyone pursuing the competition or game, then the performer might well be held liable for any injury his act caused.'

[158] *Smoldon* (n 155) 139.

[159] Richard Caddell, 'The Referee's Liability for Catastrophic Sports Injuries – A UK Perspective' (2005) 15(2) Marquette Sports Law Review 415, 420.

[160] *Smoldon* (n 155) 147.

claims by players against referees'.[161] The Court of Appeal stressed how difficult it would be for 'any plaintiff to establish that a referee failed to exercise such care and skill as was reasonably to be expected in the circumstances of a hotly-contested game of rugby football'.[162]

It was to transpire that the fear of a plethora of claims was unfounded as there is only one other reported English and Welsh case where a referee was sued, *Vowles v Evans and the Welsh Rugby Union*.[163] Vowles suffered a severe spinal cord injury and was rendered wheelchair-bound following an incident in an amateur rugby match in Wales. The Court of Appeal upheld the decision of the trial court and held that an amateur referee in an amateur match owed a duty of care to the participants.[164] Ironically, Evans was a solicitor who specialised in personal injuries and the Court noted that he had provided very detailed notes in his referee's report. Lord Philips MR made an important point in relation to volunteer referees.[165] He noted that at times a referee may not turn up to an amateur match or the referee may be injured during the game and a volunteer steps in. In this situation, the volunteer cannot reasonably be expected to show the skill of one who holds themselves out as a referee or to be fully conversant with the laws of the game. However, this did not apply to Evans as he had played rugby for many years and had attended a Welsh Rugby Union (WRU) refereeing course and had been refereeing ever since. **5–69**

The element of control was a deciding factor for the Court of Appeal.[166] The referee's role is to take control over the players in situations involving scrums. Had the incident occurred in an ordinary passage of play, then the referee would not be held liable as he would have minimum control over the players.[167] **5–70**

---

161 ibid.

162 ibid. The Court of Appeal suggested that players could be 'insured not against negligence but against risk of catastrophic injury'. However, the Court acknowledged that it was a matter for those responsible for the administration of rugby to consider.

163 [2003] EWCA Civ 318. The Welsh Rugby Union was held to be vicariously liable as it had appointed Evans as a referee.

164 Their first team had a game on the same day and had availed of the specialist front forward from the second team. This meant that the second team did not have a specialist front forward to sit on the bench. The specialist front forward was injured during the game and Vowles offered to come on from the bench in the position of specialist front forward. The referee was aware of the lack of a specialist front forward. The pitch was boggy after much rain.

165 *Vowles* (n 163) [28].

166 ibid [27]. Lord Philips MR referred to *Smoldon* where it was suggested that the level of skill to be expected of a referee depended upon the grade of the referee, or upon the grade of match they were refereeing. The discussion was inconclusive in the case as the answer to that question did not matter in *Smoldon*. The issue did not apply in the case of *Vowles*.

167 This would be the position in rugby. However, in sports such as football, players have sustained serious injuries due to tackles which take place in open play. Caddell (n 159) 423 notes that in cases where there is an undercurrent of violence

5–71 The Court of Appeal refused to grant leave to appeal to the House of Lords. Liability was imposed on Evans as he had failed to observe the Laws of the Game, laws which are designed to minimise the risk 'of just the kind of accident which subsequently occurred'.[168] The Court of Appeal did not expect the decision to impose liability to dissuade volunteer referees taking part in games due to the fact that a failure to observe the Laws was a rare occurrence.[169]

The Liability of Governing Bodies

5–72 Governing bodies may also be liable for injuries sustained on the field of play. In the joined cases of *Agar v Hyde* and *Worsley v Australian Rugby Football Union*, an action brought against the International Rugby Football Board (IRFB) was dismissed on the grounds that the board could not be held liable for injuries sustained as a result of rule changes due to the minimalist control each member of the IRFB had over the creation of new rules for rugby.[170] Initially, the claimants were successful but this was overturned by the High Court of Australia. Had the decision been upheld by the High Court it would have exposed the members of the IRFB to thousands of claims.

5–73 In *Watson v British Boxing Board of Control*, the defendant was held liable for the injuries sustained by a boxer.[171] The referee had to stop the fight in the final round when Watson appeared to be unable to defend himself.[172] Watson had sustained a brain haemorrhage and lapsed into unconsciousness. It took seven minutes for the doctor to get to the ring and a further 25–30 minutes before Watson arrived at the hospital. By the time he arrived at St Bartholomew's Hospital, he had already sustained serious brain damage.[173]

5–74 The Court of Appeal noted that the British Boxing Board of Control (BBBC) was the sole controlling body that regulated boxing in the United Kingdom (UK).[174] All fighters, clubs, agents, match-makers and any

---

and the referee fails to assert their authority to prevent certain incidents, a player could take an action against the opponent who caused the injury and the referee for failing to exert adequate control over the match.

168 *Vowles* (n 163) [49].

169 ibid.

170 (2000) 201 CLR 552; (2000) 74 ALJR 1219; (2000) ATR 81–569. Hyde was 19 at the time of the accident and he suffered a severe spinal injury and was left with incomplete quadriplegia. Worsley was aged 18 and he too suffered a severe spinal injury resulting in quadriplegia.

171 [2000] EWCA Civ 2116.

172 ibid [1]. The fight was against Chris Eubank. The fight was for the World Boxing Organisation Super-Middleweight title at Tottenham Hotspur Football Club in London. In the High Court, Watson was successful in his claim; however, the BBBC appealed the decision.

173 (n 171) [1].

174 The BBBC is not a statutory body. Counsel for the BBBC argued that liability should not be imposed as the BBBC was not a profit-making organisation and

person involved in the sport of boxing must obtain a licence from the BBBC.[175] The BBBC argued that it did not owe Watson a duty of care. The BBBC further argued that, had the necessary medical equipment and personnel been there on time, it would not have made any difference given the nature of the injuries sustained. Although the BBBC was not directly involved in the fight (there was no contractual involvement), it was held to be negligent in not providing immediate resuscitation at the ringside. As the BBBC had sanctioned the fight, the High Court held that to constitute sufficient proximity between Watson and the BBBC, and the Court of Appeal concurred.[176] Lord Philips MR made a distinction between 'making Rules and giving advice'.[177] If the role of the BBBC were just to give advice, there would be insufficient proximity between it and individual boxers to give rise to a duty of care.[178] However, the role of the BBBC

> went far beyond this. It made provision in its Rules for the medical precautions to be employed and made compliance with these Rules mandatory ... by reason of its control over boxing the Board was in a position to determine, and did in fact determine, the measures that were taken in boxing to protect and promote the health and safety of boxers.[179]

In referring to the 'unprecedented decision' as liability was imposed on a regulatory body, George observes that the case was 5–75

> apparently the first reported case in which the English courts have had to consider whether a regulatory body can be held liable in negligence for failing to make adequate rules. Claims against regulators in respect of inadequate enforcement and supervision have generally failed on the ground that no duty of care was owed to any particular member of the public or to any regulated person.[180]

Concussion

The *Watson* case may well have set the precedent for recent concussion claims in rugby. Lord Philips MR in his judgment referred to the arguments made by Counsel (Walker) for the BBBC in relation to the Court finding in favour of Watson: 5–76

> Mr Walker also suggested that a finding in favour of Mr Watson in this case would involve postulating that other sporting regulatory bodies,

---

did not carry insurance. However, Lord Philips MR rejected this contention and said it was irrelevant.

175 *Watson* (n 171) [13].

176 *Watson v British Boxing Board of Control* [1999] 9 WLUK 369.

177 *Watson* (n 171) [82].

178 ibid.

179 ibid.

180 James George, '*Watson v British Boxing Board of Control*: Negligent Rule-Making in the Court of Appeal' (2002) 65(1) The Modern Law Review 106, 106.

> such as the Rugby Football Union, owed duties of care to the participants in their sports in relation to their rules and regulations.
>
> It does not follow that the decision in this case is the thin end of a wedge. The facts of this case are not common to other sports. In any event it would be quite wrong to determine the result of the individual facts of this case by formulating a principle of general policy that sporting regulatory bodies should owe no duty of care in respect of the formulation of their rules and regulations. I conclude that the Judge correctly found that the Board owed Mr Watson a duty of care.[181]

5–77 Lord Philips MR held that the decision in *Watson* was confined to the facts and that he was not proposing a 'general policy' of the duty of care owed by regulatory bodies to participants. In December 2020, Rylands' Law, a law firm representing nine rugby players, sent pre-action letters of claim to World Rugby, the Rugby Football Union (RFU), and the WRU.[182] The players have all been diagnosed with long-term brain injuries which they assert are a result of concussions sustained during their playing careers. They contend that World Rugby failed to minimise the risks associated with the long-term health issues resulting from concussion.

5–78 Cisneros asserts that the position of the BBBC and World Rugby may be 'somewhat analogous' and 'the rugby litigation will require a small "incremental" extension of the duty of care to rugby's governing bodies'.[183] World Rugby is the international federation for rugby. It is based in Dublin and its membership consists of 132 national member federations, which are grouped into six regional associations.[184] Of significance to the class action, the 'Laws of the game are maintained by World Rugby'.[185] The role of the World Rugby and that of another international federation, the Federation Internationale de l'Automobile (FIA) may be distinguished as the case of *Wattleworth v Goodwood and Ors* demonstrates.[186] Wattleworth was driving his Austin Healey on the Goodwood motor racing circuit and, as he came out of the second

181 *Watson* (n 171) [90] and [91].

182 'Six More Former Rugby Players Join Concussion Lawsuit' (*RTÉ Sport*, 17 December 2020) <https://www.rte.ie/sport/rugby/2020/1217/1185062-six-more-former-rugby-players-join-concussion-lawsuit/> accessed 12 May 2024.

183 Ben Cisneros, 'Concussion Litigation in Rugby – Part I: Duty of Care' (*Rugby and the Law*, 9 February 2021) <http://rugbyandthelaw.com/2021/02/09/concussion-litigation-rugby-union-part-i-duty-of-care-negligence-world-rugby-rfu-wru/#_ftnref13> accessed 12 May 2024.

184 World Rugby, 'About World Rugby' <https://www.world.rugby/organisation/about-us/overview> accessed 11 May 2024. The six regional associations that are affiliated to World Rugby are: Asia Rugby, Rugby Africa, Rugby Europe, Oceania Rugby, Rugby Americas North, and Sudamérica Rugby.

185 It further states, 'Sometimes World Rugby trials changes to the laws, before deciding whether those changes should be implemented on a global basis and accepted into full law': World Rugby, 'Governance' <https://www.world.rugby/organisation/about-us/governance> accessed 12 May 2024.

186 [2004] EWHC 140 (QB).

part of a bend (called the Lavant Bend), he lost control of his car. He collided with a tyre-fronted earth bank on the inside of the track and died. His widow brought the action against the defendants, Goodwood Road Racing Company Limited, the Royal Automobile Club Motor Sports Association Limited (MSA) and the Federation Internationale de l'Automobile (FIA). Davis J dismissed the action, holding that Goodwood owed Wattleworth a duty of care but had not breached that duty.[187] Similarly, the MSA owed a duty of care but had not breached it. However, the FIA did not owe a duty of care to Wattleworth and if the Court found otherwise (that a duty of care was owed), it had not been breached. The reason that the FIA was found not to owe a duty of care is due to the lack of proximity in the relationship between it and the deceased. Davis J explained his decision as follows:

> the fact remains that the relationship of the MSA to Goodwood was far closer than that of the FIA: and I am, I think, entitled to bear in mind the (relative) lack of proximity on the part of the FIA, as compared to the MSA, with regard to Goodwood in deciding whether or not the FIA owed a duty of care to users of the circuit such as Mr Wattleworth. It is also not unreasonable, I think, to indicate that a line should be drawn somewhere, in terms of liability: the more so when, by reason of its involvement in international events, the FIA has to concern itself with many scores of countries other than the UK and essentially primarily entrusts circuit safety matters to national sporting authorities.[188]

In a similar vein as Lord Philips MR in *Watson* and his distinction between a governing body that merely gives advice and one that makes the rules, the roles of the FIA and World Rugby are quite different. **5–79**

The first reported reference to concussion dates back to 1927 when an article was published in the *Archives of Neurology and Psychiatry*.[189] The literature from the 1950s to early 1970s focused on Chronic Traumatic Encephalopathy (CTE) 'being diagnosed posthumously in boxers'.[190] It **5–80**

[187] ibid [179].

[188] ibid [138].

[189] Michael Osnato and Vincent Giliberti, 'Postconcussion Neurosis-Traumatic Encephalitis – A Conception of Postconcussion Phenomena' (1927) 18 Archives of Neurology and Psychiatry 181. For a detailed discussion of the response of governing bodies, see Ben Cisneros, 'Concussion in Sport: What Did, or Should, Governing Bodies Have Known?' (*Morgan Sports Law*, 19 January 2021) <https://morgansl.com/en/latest/concussion-sport-what-did-or-should-governing-bodies-have-known/> accessed 13 May 2024. This blog includes a very useful timeline on important developments between 1927 and 2020.

[190] Cisneros (n 189). CTE is defined by Headway as 'a progressive disease of the brain found in athletes and other people with a history of repeated head injury, including concussions. The symptoms include memory loss, confusion, impaired judgment, impulse control problems, aggression, depression, and, eventually, progressive dementia. CTE historically has been most associated with boxing and American Football, but more recent studies have identified other sports which present risk of CTE, including Rugby, Football, Hockey, Wresting, Equestrian sports and others': Headway, 'Concussion (Mild Traumatic Brain Injury, mTBI)' <https://headway.ie/about-brain-injury/concussion/> accessed 13 May 2024.

was not until 1975 that a study looked at the effects of concussion on athletes in general.[191] While there were studies published by medics in the following decades, it was not until the 1990s that the long-term effects of concussion became an issue of concern for governing bodies.[192] In 1994 that the National Football League (NFL) in the United States (US) commissioned a study into brain injury caused by playing-related brain injuries. The NFL established the Mild Traumatic Brain Injury (MTBI) Committee with Dr Elliot Pellman as Chair.[193] Cisneros contends that rugby was aware of the effects of concussion from the early 1980s and perhaps even before that as the Laws of the Game at that time provided for a mandatory three-week stand-down period for players who were concussed, which was in line with the approach taken by the BBBC.[194]

5–81 It seems that sports governing bodies were aware of the long-term implications of concussion since the mid-1970s; however, the concussion protocols were not robust enough, as the class action against World Rugby demonstrates. In October 2021 several England, Wales and Scotland international rugby league players were reported to have initiated proceedings against the Rugby Football League (RFL). The former players contend that the RFL did not protect them from the risks associated with concussion.[195] The class action came at a time when the RLF carried out a pilot study on concussion in all levels of rugby. To the former players involved in the litigation, this is of little or no benefit to them. In April 2021, the RFL announced that a pilot study had been launched in partnership with Leeds Beckett University.[196] The research

---

[191] Dorothy Gronwall and Philip Wrightson, 'Cumulative Effect of Concussion' (1975) 306(7943) The Lancet 995. The study focussed on 20 young adults who had suffered a second concussion.

[192] Cisneros (n 189) notes that it 'is arguable, therefore, that from 1975 onwards, sports governing bodies knew, or should have known, of the risks of long-term damage from repeated concussions and/or head trauma. Certainly, from 1997, this seems to be an inevitable conclusion.'

[193] Elliot Pellman and David C Viano, 'Concussion in Professional Football: Summary of the Research Conducted by the National Football League's Committee on Mild Traumatic Brain Injury' (2006) 21(4) Neurological Focus 15.

[194] Cisneros (n 189). The author states that the three-week stand down was introduced in 1977 by the International Rugby Board (now World Rugby) in the aftermath of the Gronwall and Wrightson study.

[195] 'Former Rugby League Players to Sue Over Head Injuries' (*RTÉ Sport*, 27 October 2021) <https://www.rte.ie/sport/rugby/2021/1027/1256078-former-rugby-league-players-to-sue-over-head-injuries/> accessed 13 May 2024.

[196] Leeds Beckett University, 'Leeds Beckett University Links with Rugby League on Head Impact Research Project' (16 April 2021) <https://www.leedsbeckett.ac.uk/news/2021/04/leeds-beckett-university-links-with-rugby-league-on-head-impact-research-project/> accessed 13 May 2024. A three-year study was commissioned by the RFL in association with Leeds Beckett University in 2022: Rugby Football League, 'RFL Confirms Launch of Extensive Research Project in 2022 Season' (8 January 2024) <https://www.rugby-league.com/article/36417/rfl-confirms-launch-of-extensive-research-project-in-2022-season> accessed 13 May 2024. As part of the three-year study, RFL trialled two law modifications from June 15 to July 30 in 2023. The modifications were described as follows: 'the legal tackle height will be reduced to below the armpit at initial contact, with penalisation for contact on

project involved quantifying 'the risk of head impact in the sport with the aim of increasing understanding and reducing future risk'.[197] The pilots ran from May to August 2021 and covered over '1,200 players across 50 teams at various levels of the game, also including Academy players, the Betfred Women's Super League … and a number of different age groups at Community clubs'.[198]

World Rugby updated its player welfare measures to include the Head Injury Assessment (HIA) Protocol. The HIA Protocol is based on a four-stage test 'for elite adult teams to assist with the identification, diagnosis and management of head impact events with the potential for a concussion'.[199] The four stages are: **5–82**

- Stage 1 – game day assessment using the HIA1 Form
- Stage 2 – post-game, same day assessment using HIA2 Form
- Stage 3 – 36–48-hour post-injury assessment using HIA3 Form
- Stage 4 – clearance to return to full play following competition of individualised rehabilitation which includes use of the HIA4 form.[200]

A detailed description of each stage and the role of relevant personnel is detailed in the Protocol.[201] World Rugby stresses that '[c]oncussion and suspected concussion must be taken extremely seriously by all those involved in the Game in order to protect the safety, health and welfare of Players'.[202] The HIA Protocol is not a diagnostic tool, but it is there to help medics identify if the player is suspected of being concussed.[203] **5–83**

---

the head and neck at any point; while kick-offs will now be taken from 10 metres further forward – on the opposition's 40-metre line, rather than the halfway line at present – to reduce the impact of ensuing collisions': see Rugby Football League, 'Reduction of Head Contact and Head Accelerations – Law Trials 2023' (21 April 2023) <https://www.rugby-league.com/article/61651/reduction-of-head-contact-and-head-accelerations-%E2%80%93-law-trials-2023> accessed 13 May 2024.

197 Leeds Beckett University 2021 Pilot Study (n 196).

198 ibid.

199 World Rugby, 'Head Injury Assessment Protocol' (2024) 1 <https://resources.worldrugby-rims.pulselive.com/worldrugby/document/2024/01/17/7cf72fa9-eb2e-4046-a5a8-1d3068d4503f/HIA-protocol-2024.pdf> accessed 13 May 2024.

200 ibid.

201 ibid 2–6.

202 World Rugby, 'Regulation 10. Medical' <https://www.world.rugby/organisation/governance/regulations/reg-10> accessed 13 May 2024. The HIA Protocol applies only to elite players. For Community rugby and aged-grade Rugby the approach is 'recognise and remove'. This is explained here: World Rugby, 'Recognise and Remove Process' <https://www.world.rugby/the-game/player-welfare/medical/concussion/recognise-and-remove> accessed 13 May 2024.

203 Kevin Beirne and Paul Clarke, 'What Is a HIA and What Is the Protocol at the Rugby World Cup 2019?' (*Wales Online*, 29 September 2019) <https://www.walesonline.co.uk/sport/rugby/rugby-news/what-hia-what-protocol-rugby-16952675> accessed 13 May 2024.

5–84 A Joint Committee on Health and Children Report on Concussion in Sport was published in December 2014.[204] The 41-page report made a number of recommendations, including the establishment of a Taskforce on Sport and Concussion, which would develop uniform guidelines to ensure consistency.[205] The Taskforce, the Joint Committee recommended, would include representatives from the medical community; the National Rehabilitation Hospital, Acquired Brain Injury Ireland and Headway Ireland; the Departments of Health, Children and Youth Affairs, Education and Skills; representatives from key sporting codes and nominees from Comhairle na n-Óg.[206] The report identified a lack of education and awareness as well as a lack of data and research.[207] It strongly recommended the acceleration of research on sports and concussion in Ireland.[208] It suggested accelerated research could be aided by '[i]nternational co-operation, involving the pooling of data, may be the best way forward and could add a valuable insight into the condition'.[209]

5–85 The report pointed to professional sport and the increased risks to player safety, in particular the increased size of rugby players. The report concluded:

> Generally, the pace of games has quickened, training regimes have radically intensified, and there has been a noticeable increase in the physical stature of players in field sports. For example, in elite rugby, players are much bigger, and the number and intensity of collisions has increased over time.[210]

5–86 A Taskforce has yet to be established, thus it has been left to the governing bodies to devise their own concussion guidelines and protocols. A number of Irish sports governing bodies have guidelines on concussion, including the Gaelic Athletic Association (GAA),[211]

---

[204] Houses of the Oireachtas Joint Committee on Health and Children Report on Concussion in Sport December 2014 <https://data.oireachtas.ie/ie/oireachtas/committee/dail/31/joint_committee_on_education_and_social_protection/reports/2014/2014-12-17_report-on-concussion-in-sport_en.pdf> accessed 13 May 2024.

[205] ibid. The report highlighted the lack of consistency between governing bodies. For example, it noted that the IRFU Return to Play guidelines differ markedly from GAA guidelines. To address such issues, the Committee recommended the creation of the Taskforce on page 11, para 6.

[206] ibid 11.

[207] ibid 10.

[208] ibid 11.

[209] ibid.

[210] ibid 7.

[211] Gaelic Athletic Association, 'Concussion in Gaelic Games' <https://learning.gaa.ie/concussion> accessed 13 May 2024.

the Football Association of Ireland (FAI),[212] Hockey Ireland[213] and the Irish Rugby Football Union (IRFU).[214] Academics, on foot of the Joint Committee Report, have recommended that a Sports Related Concussion (SRC) Taskforce should be established.[215] The proposed SRC would act as a regulatory body which would 'oversee the management of concussion and RTP guidelines among schools and sporting bodies'.[216]

In 2017, New Zealand Rugby introduced the Blue Card. Like the HIA **5–87** Protocols, it is not a diagnostic tool, but it allows referees to remove a player from the match if the referee suspects that the player is concussed.[217] Once removed, the player cannot return to play. New Zealand Rugby will reimburse a blue-carded player for their medical clearance examinations.[218] The Blue Card is but one method of protecting a player, however, it 'is not a fail-safe process as concussion symptoms might not appear for 24–48 hours. Coaches, players, and family must keep an eye out for any of the signs and symptoms.'[219]

The former players involved in the class actions against World Rugby, **5–88** the WRU, the RFU and the RFL, are facing, in the words of Anderson, 'substantive legal issues' if the cases go to court.[220] Professor Jack Anderson identifies several issues:

> [r]elated to breach of duty and causation; to statute of limitations and access to medical records; and even to applicable defences ... At the same time, having very popular former players up the steps of court, giving direct evidence about their medical status, is probably something that is

[212] Football Association of Ireland, 'FAI Concussion Guidelines' <https://www.fai.ie/about/library/> accessed 13 May 2024. The guidelines can be downloaded from the tab titled Medical Resources.

[213] Hockey Ireland, 'Concussion Guidelines' <https://hockey.ie/concussion-policy/> accessed 13 May 2024.

[214] Irish Rugby Football Union, 'IRFU Concussion Protocols' <https://www.irishrugby.ie/playing-the-game/medical/irfu-concussion-protocols/> accessed 13 May 2024.

[215] Mark Beakey and others, 'Are Irish Sporting Organisations Neglecting the Safety of their Athletes? A Narrative Review on Concussion Return-to-Play Protocols' (2016) 3(2) European Journal of Sports Medicine 41, 50.

[216] ibid. RTP is Return to Play.

[217] New Zealand Rugby, 'Blue Card' <https://www.nzrugby.co.nz/about-nzr/policies-regulations-and-rules/safety-and-welfare/concussion/blue-card> accessed 13 May 2024.

[218] ibid.

[219] ibid. The Blue Card has also been adopted by the Equestrian Sports New Zealand: see 'Concussion and Serious Injury Blue Card FAQs for Riders' <https://www.nzequestrian.org.nz/wp-content/uploads/21029-ESNZ-Concussion-FAQ-Booklet-WEB.pdf> accessed 13 May 2024.

[220] Sean Ingle, 'Rugby Players' Claim for Brain Injury Has "Less than 50/50" Chance, Say Experts' *The Guardian* (London, 13 December 2020) <https://www.theguardian.com/sport/2020/dec/13/rugby-union-players-claim-for-brain-injury-dementia-world-rugby> accessed 13 May 2024.

> in the best interest of the authorities to avoid. That is why a settlement makes sense for all sides.[221]

5–89 Anderson points to *Agar v Hyde* and *Worsley v Australian Rugby Football Union*, as discussed above, where the international governing board was not held liable for injuries suffered by players as a result of rule changes.[222] The Court found that there was a lack of causation between the actions of the IRFB and the injuries sustained by the two players. O'Connor adds:

> There will also be a big debate about where the responsibility lies in all this between the doctors, clubs, countries and World Rugby. But also remember that in the early years of professional rugby the culture was often about players beasting themselves. There is going to be an element of voluntary assumption of risk among the players, too.[223]

5–90 In April 2024 it was reported that 60 more players were part of a class action against World Rugby, the RFU and the WRU.[224] This brings the number to 328 players who are alleging that the governing bodies failed to take reasonable care in protecting the players from early onset dementia and motor neurone disease, which they claim is a direct result of repetitive concussion.[225]

5–91 It may well be that the cases are settled out of court and if they are to go before the court, it will take several years for the case to be heard. Medical reports showing the long-term effects will have to be produced. If the matter reaches the court, it will be interesting to see whether the court will apply *Watson* or *Agar*.[226]

The Liability of Coaches and Instructors

5–92 Like referees, governing bodies and participants, coaches can be held civilly liable. Coaches owe a duty of care to those they coach, manage, or instruct, and if it is found that they have fallen below the standard of care required, liability may well be imposed. As with participants and referees, the extent of the duty varies from case to case. In most situations, a coach cannot be deemed to guarantee playing success or

---

221 ibid.

222 *Agar* (n 170).

223 Ingle (n 220). Ingle was citing barrister Tim O'Connor.

224 'Sixty New Claimants Added to Legal Action against Rugby Union Governing Bodies' (3 April 2024) <https://www.rte.ie/sport/rugby/2024/0403/1441414-sixty-join-legal-action-against-rugby-governing-bodies/> accessed 13 May 2024.

225 ibid.

226 This article pre-dates the class action; however, it offers an interesting discussion on the role of World Rugby and the author contends that actions against World Rugby would likely fail: see Richard Bunworth, 'Egg-Shell Skulls or Institutional Negligence? The Liability of World Rugby for Incidents of Concussion Suffered by Professional Players in England and Ireland (2016) 16 International Sports Law Journal 82.

the safety of the sportsperson under their pupillage, save in situations where it is reasonable to have such an expectation. For example, in some sports that carry inherent dangers, the coach is required to teach the techniques necessary to play the sport safely and to demonstrate how the game should be played to minimise injury.

There is a higher duty of care owed to children as the coach is said to be *in loco parentis*, which means 'in the place of the parent'. It refers to the legal responsibility placed on an adult who is not the parent of the child but assumes a duty, given the relationship between them and the child. Whitlam contends that '*specialists* in a particular area, or adults leading higher risk activities, are deemed to have a higher duty of care (ie, a higher level of responsibility) for those in their care'.[227] Partington proffers that volunteer coaches 'would likely be judged at the same standard as more experienced colleagues' – this could expose a non-specialist coach who exhibits 'inadequate' instruction to liability.[228] **5–93**

Similarly, coaches and organisers may owe a higher duty of care to athletes with disabilities according to the *obiter* comments of Mitchell J in *Morrell v Owen and Ors*.[229] Morrell, a disabled archer, was struck by a discus on the temple, which caused permanent brain damage. Both events (archery and the discus-throwing event) were taking place in the same hall and were separated by a curtain. The plaintiff successfully sued the organisers and coaches.[230] **5–94**

Legal Duties of a Coach

Figone lists seven major duties of a coach: **5–95**

1. Adequate general and specific supervision.
2. Sound planning.
3. Clear warnings of the risk of the activity.
4. Safe environment for practice and play.
5. Evaluation of players for injuries and incapacities and determination of any limitations caused by injuries or incapacities.
6. Fairly matching or equating players for practice and competitive conditions.
7. Use of appropriate first aid and emergency medical procedures that can be implemented immediately.[231]

---

227 Peter Whitlam, *Case Law in Physical Education and School Sport: A Guide to Good Practice* (Coachwise 1st4sport 2005) 24.

228 Neil Partington, 'Legal Liability of Coaches: A UK Perspective' (2014) 14(3) The International Sports Law Journal 332, 238.

229 [1993] 12 WLUK 6.

230 The defendants contended that the plaintiff had contributed to her injury; however, the Court rejected the defence of contributory negligence.

231 Albert J Figone, 'Seven Major Legal Duties of a Coach' (1989) 60(7) Journal of Physical Education, Recreation & Dance 71, 71.

5–96 Other legal duties include the

- Use of current knowledge of proper skills and methods of instruction.
- Use of safe and appropriate equipment.
- Provision of adequate supervision of athletes.
- Sensitivity to the health and well-being of athletes under a coach's care.[232]

5–97 In *Brady v Sunderland Football Club,* former Irish international football player Kieron Brady brought an action in contract and negligence against his club on the grounds that the coach and the physiotherapist had failed to diagnose and take seriously his complaint of serious leg pains.[233] Buckley J dismissed the claim, finding that the club was not in breach of contract, nor had it breached its duty of care owed to the player. The judge acknowledged that the coach's attitude in instructing the player to continue with the training session was 'robust' but that 'does not begin to amount to negligence'. Brady appealed the decision of Buckley J to the Court of Appeal; however, the appeal was dismissed.[234]

Instructors and Guides

5–98 The case of *Woodroffe-Hedley v Cuthbertson* is the leading authority on the duty of care owed by professional instructors to their clients.[235] Cuthbertson was a qualified guide and experienced mountaineer who had recently acquired his International Guide badge. He was paid £500 by Hedley to escort Hedley on a climb on the Mont Blanc Massif. During their ascent, Cuthbertson feared that the ice would melt as there had been some sun so he decided it would be prudent to move towards an area in the shade in case the ice melted and caused rocks to dislodge and fall.

---

[232] This list is taken directly from Rich Engelhorn, 'Legal and Ethical Responsibilities of a Coach' <https://ihsaa-static.s3.amazonaws.com/RichEngelhorn.html> accessed 11 May 2024. Engelhorn adopted the list from R Stratton, *The Legal Duties of a Coach* (CYS Coach Newsletter 1999). Engelhorn also includes preventing harassment and discrimination by coaching staff and athletes; reporting suspected child abuse to proper authorities; respecting and protecting the confidentiality of student personal records; and reporting breaches of ethical behaviour by colleagues.

[233] *Brady v Sunderland Association Football Club Limited and Others* [1998] EWCA Civ 1780. Brady alleged that his complaints were not taken seriously and instead it was viewed as an attitude problem. According to the judgment: 'It is alleged that complaints and apparent difficulties in training were attributed to an attitude problem and proper investigation which should have included taking a careful history from the plaintiff would have revealed, if the Club did not otherwise appreciate, that he suffered pain in his right leg, in particular the calf, associated with exercise as opposed to trauma.'

[234] ibid.

[235] [1997] 6 WLUK 603.

According to established mountain-climbing practice, when two climbers are connected two screws are inserted into the ice as an anchor and an intermediary point between the two climbers should be created (called a running belay) to lessen the strain. Cuthbertson only inserted one screw and did not set up the running belay. A large sheet of ice broke away causing Cuthbertson to slip and, as the lead climber, he dragged Hedley, who was connected to him. The sole screw could not hold the weight of both men. Hedley fell and was killed. Cuthbertson suffered minor injuries. Dyson J held that Cuthbertson was negligent and that he breached the standard expected of a reasonably competent and careful Alpine guide.[236] The judge concluded that **5–99**

> in deciding to dispense with the second screw, Mr Cuthbertson fell below the standard to be expected of a reasonably competent and careful alpine guide. He was also negligent when he compounded that error by his decision not to use a running belay ... Objectively viewed, this was not a situation of emergency. Mr Cuthbertson had time to reflect. He reached a decision which, even without the benefit of hindsight, could not reasonably have been justified.[237]

Conclusion

Participants, referees, governing bodies, and coaches may be held liable in negligence if their actions fall below the requisite standard of care. The case law demonstrates that the ordinary principles of negligence apply, with cognisance given to the prevailing circumstances. The standard is objective; it is based on the reasonable person rather than the individual defendant. However, by considering the individual circumstances of the case, there is a subjective element. Some judges have referred to the standard of reckless disregard, however, the Irish and English courts have applied the ordinary principles of negligence. A new tort of reckless disregard has not been created. Liability will not attach for lapses or errors of judgement; it should be reserved for situations where the actions of the defendant go beyond the accepted norms of the sport. **5–100**

The rules of the sport or the game are but one consideration for the court when it comes to deciding whether a breach of the duty of care has occurred. The rules differ from sport to sport and what is permissible in one sport may not be permitted in another sport. A sport's participant has a duty to behave reasonably in the context of the sport in which they are participating. The court will look at the nature and rules of the sport, but a failure to observe the rules does not necessarily mean that it **5–101**

---

[236] For a more detailed discussion on this case, see Julian Fulbrook, *Outdoor Activities, Negligence and the Law* Ashgate 2005) 132–34. See also *Affiong Day v High Performance Sports Ltd* [2003] EWHC 197 (QBD). Here liability was not attached as the plaintiff, an experienced climber, had not tied her ropes properly. Her father brought the case against the manager of the leisure centre but lost. The Court held that the actions of the defendant were reasonable.

[237] (n 235).

will find that there has been breach of the duty of care. The courts need to adopt a two-pronged test. First, it must be determined whether the rules of the game or Laws of the Game have been breached; second, it must be ascertained whether there was negligence, 'which is set at a materially higher standard than the Laws of the Game'.[238]

5–102 Referees may be found to have acted in a manner that falls below the standard of a reasonably competent referee. The threshold for liability is high and one that is not easily reached. Similarly, coaches may be subject to litigation. Coaches have several legal and ethical duties. They must keep up to date with developments and ensure that players or athletes do not compete while injured. The coach must not encourage an athlete to take prohibited substances or be aggressive on the field of play. Guides and instructors owe a duty of care to a client and the relevant standard of care is that of a reasonably competent and careful instructor or guide. Sports such as mountain climbing carry inherent risks (normal hazards), but climbers are not said to assume the risk of their instructor acting negligently. A client is entitled to rely on the expertise of a guide, and it is the role of the guide to minimise the risk of injury or death.

5–103 The position of governing bodies and the duty of care owed to participants depends on the role of the governing body and the control it exerts over the sport. The case law suggests that if a governing body has a mere advisory role, then the court may well find that there is a lack of proximity in the relationship between it and the participants. The recent class actions against the governing bodies of rugby have yet to come before the courts. It may well be that they are settled out of court as the former players face an arduous task in establishing a breach of the duty of care as the court will consider the elements of negligence, namely proximity, causation, and the defence of voluntary assumption of risk.

5–104 The above discussion shows that civil litigation in sport is quite rare. For the most part, sports bodies deal with personal injuries through their insurance schemes. Other cases do not make it to the court as they are settled before they come before a judge. Most governing bodies do not want to go to court due to the adverse publicity that often surrounds a high-profile case involving a sportsperson. Developments in technology, including Video Assistant Referees (VAR), means that if the on-field officials miss a 'serious foul', the VAR can review such incidents and the player may be issued a red card.[239] In the words of Gardiner and Felix, 'better a man with a whistle regulating the game than a man with a wig'.[240]

---

238 *Fulham* (n 115) [50].

239 Jan Zglinski, 'Rules, Standards, and the Video Assistant Referee in Football' (2020) Sport, Ethics and Philosophy 1–1.

240 (n 112) 216.

CHAPTER 6

DRUGS IN SPORT

Introduction

The use of performance-enhancing drugs is not a recent phenomenon, 6–01
however, the prohibition of drugs and the testing of prohibited substances did not take hold until the 1960s when the International Olympic Committee (IOC) established a Medical Commission in 1967. The Medical Commission was tasked with devising a list of prohibited substances and methods.[1] The International Amateur Athletic Federation (IAAF) was the first International Federation (IF) to ban doping in 1928.[2] However, the ban was largely ineffective as no tests were carried out on athletes.[3] It was at the IOC's 108th Extraordinary Session that the proposed establishment of the World Anti-Doping Agency (WADA) was accepted.

Drug testing, in particular, the testing of urine and blood, is considered 6–02
by some to be highly invasive. Questions have been raised as to the creation of other viable alternatives, as well as the proportionality of WADA's rules.[4] Equally, participation in sport is viewed as a privilege and not a right. Sports governing bodies are private organisations that create their own rules and regulations. Elite athletes accept that certain rules and regulations, while being somewhat invasive, are a basic part of their profession. Drug testing has become an integral part of both amateur and professional sport since the late 1960s. It is viewed as a fundamental component of maintaining the element of fairness in sport. Drug testing also serves to protect the athlete's health and endeavours

1 Albert D Fraser, 'Doping Control from a Global and National Perspective' (2004) 26(2) Therapeutic Drug Monitoring 171, 171.

2 World Athletics, 'Chapter 15, Drugs in Sports/Doping Control' (2015) <https://worldathletics.org/download/download?filename=c3ec4cd7-c80f-4062-85d2-efaf8c26afce.pdf&urlslug=Chapter%2015%3A%20Drugs%20in%20sport%20%2F%20Doping%20control%20> accessed 13 May 2024. It defined doping in its Handbook as 'the use of any stimulant not normally employed to increase the poser of action in athletic competition above the average. Any person knowingly acting or assisting as explained above shall be excluded from any place where these rules are in force or, if he is a competitor, be suspended for a time or otherwise from further participation in amateur athletics under the jurisdiction of this Federation.'

3 Fraser (n 1).

4 Bart van der Sloot, 'Looking at the Anti-Doping Regime Through a Human Rights Lens' in Bart van der Sloot, Mara Paun, and Ronald Leenes (eds), *Athletes' Human Rights and the Fight Against Doping: A Study of the European Legal Framework* (TMC Asser Press 2020) 189–243.

to ensure that the image of the sport is not undermined by allegations of drug use.

6–03 This chapter begins with a brief discussion of the history of drugs. It details the Irish Sport Anti-Doping Rules and will examine some decisions made by the Irish Sport Anti-Doping Disciplinary Panel (ISADDP). It will proceed to look at the methods of testing and the sanctions for Anti-Doping Rule Violations (ADRV). References are also made to arbitral awards of the Court of Arbitration for Sport (CAS) and case law from domestic courts where athletes have challenged the anti-doping rules on the right to earn livelihood, the right to fair procedures, and the presumption of innocence. The chapter ends with a discussion on the fundamental rights of athletes when it comes to drug testing with a focus on the right to privacy and the right to fair trial under the European Convention on Human Rights (ECHR).

A Brief History of Drugs in Sport

6–04 The use of drugs in sport is not a recent phenomenon but rather the 'modern manifestation of an old, perhaps even ancient, difficulty'.[5] In the Ancient Olympics the use of performance-enhancing drugs was not considered cheating.[6] There is no evidence to suggest that the ingestion of performance-enhancing substances were 'discouraged' and branded as cheating.[7] The use of drugs in sport can be traced back to the third century, where athletes in Ancient Greece were reported to have taken substances to enhance their performance.[8] At the Olympic Games of 668 BC it was claimed that the winner of the 200m sprint, Charnis of Sparta, had been on a special diet of dried figs and water to enhance his performance.[9]

6–05 In the mid-to-late 19th century, cocaine and opium were considered to have medicinal properties. These drugs were commonly used in America and Britain.[10] In the late 19th and early 20th centuries, doping was not viewed in the same light as it is today. The use of performance-enhancing drugs that would increase the capacity of athletes to excel

---

5 Charles L Dubin, *Commission of Inquiry into the Use of Drugs and Banned Substances Intended to Increase Athletic Performance* (Ottawa: Canadian Government Publishing Centre 1990) 69 <https://www.doping.nl/media/kb/3636/Dubin-report-1990-eng%20(S).pdf> accessed 2 May 2024.

6 Charles E Yesalis and Michael S Bahrke, 'History of Doping in Sport' (2002) 24(1) International Sports Studies 42, 43.

7 ibid. To Ancient Olympians, cheating constituted taking bribes and other types of fraud.

8 Michele Verroken, 'Drug Use and Abuse in Sport' in David R Mottram (ed), *Drugs in Sport* (2nd end, E & FN Spon 1996) 18.

9 Patrick Lenehan, *Anabolic Steroids* (CRC Press 2003) 61. Lenehan adds that Charnis' long-distance colleagues claimed that sesame seeds improved stamina.

10 David F Musto, 'Opium, Cocaine and Marijuana in American History' (1991) 265(1) Scientific American 40.

in their sports was considered a positive development by many people who viewed 'medicine and science ... as ways to improve life, and for athletes, that meant doing better in competition'.[11]

By the early 20th century, the dangers of cocaine and opium became **6–06**
apparent, with the the Parliament of the United Kingdom (UK) enacting the Dangerous Drugs Act in 1920.[12] This Act limited the availability of cocaine and opium to prescription only.[13] The IAAF, now World Athletics, in 1928 became the first IF to ban the use of stimulating substances. Scientists in the 1930s were able to isolate the male hormone, testosterone.[14] By the late 1940s, bodybuilders in the United States (US) were using hormones in their endeavours to increase stamina and strength. The Soviet Union weightlifting team resorted to similar measures in the 1950s. Amphetamines were developed to combat fatigue among the soldiers during World War II. After the War, amphetamines found a new use among cyclists. It was not until the 1960s that drugs became associated with modern sport. Danish cyclist Knud Jensen collapsed during a race and died shortly after in a hospital in Rome in August 1960.[15] Tests revealed the presence of amphetamines in Jensen's body.[16] In the aftermath of Jensen's death, drug use in sport became highly topical.[17] There were rumours of drug use and gender fraud among athletes.[18] In response, the IOC became the first sporting organisation to establish a Medical Commission (1967) that was entrusted with the task of policing the use of banned substances and

[11] Daniel M Rosen, *A History of Performance Enhancement in Sports from the Nineteenth Century to Today* (ABC–CLIO 2008) 1.

[12] 10 and 11 GEO 5, O 46.

[13] In the United States, the Harrison Narcotic Act 1914 was enacted to regulate the production, importation, and distribution of opiates and cocaine as well as the imposition of a special tax 'on the produce, import, manufacture, compound, deal in, dispense, sell, distribute, or give away opium or coca leaves, their salts, derivatives, or preparations, and for other purposes'. The Act was introduced to comply with the Hague International Opium Convention 1912. Each signatory state had to incorporate into national law restrictions on opium: see EM Brecher, 'Drug Laws and Drug Law Enforcement – A Review and Evaluation Based on 111 Years of Experience' (1986) 1(1) Drugs and Society 1 <https://www.ojp.gov/ncjrs/virtual-library/abstracts/drug-laws-and-drug-law-enforcement-review-and-evaluation-based-111> accessed 2 May 2024.

[14] Edward J Bird and Gert G Wagner, 'Sport as a Common Property Resource: A Solution to the Dilemmas of Doping' (1997) 41(6) Journal of Conflict Resolution 749, 750.

[15] Rosen (n 11) 2: 'a culture of doping – or an assumed culture of doping – has existed for some time' and sports including swimming, cycling, and running had athletes taking drugs from the second half of the 19th century.

[16] It was announced that Jensen had died of sunstroke. Two of his teammates were also brought to hospital.

[17] In 1886 Arthur Linton, a Welch cyclist, died from allegedly ingesting strychnine. It was reported that he died from typhoid fever. His coach was banned from sport after it was claimed that he had administered the strychnine. This is disputed by Paul Dimeo, *A History of Drug Use in Sport: 1876–1976: Beyond Good and Evil* (Taylor & Francis 2008) 7–8.

[18] This is discussed in ch 7.

of verifying gender. In 1968 the IOC carried out drug and gender tests at the Olympic Games in Mexico City.

6–07 During the 1970s, allegations of drug use among athletes were rife. Dr Robert Voy, a former chief medical officer with the US Olympic Committee, wrote of his experience at the Olympic Games.[19] He concluded that 'instead of being a competition and celebration for the human, the Olympics have in some ways become a mere proving ground for scientists, chemists, and unethical physicians'.[20] During the 1970s, there were concerns about the change in appearance of some of the female athletes. As discussed in Chapter 7, doubt was cast upon the femininity of some of the elite female athletes.

6–08 Throughout the 1980s and 1990s performance-enhancing drugs continued to infiltrate sport.[21] In the 1988 Olympic Games in Seoul, the Canadian athlete Ben Johnson broke the world 100 metre record in a time of 9.79 seconds and won the Olympic title. Johnson tested positive for the banned substance stanozolol and was stripped of his medal. The positive result and subsequent ban shocked the world as it was (mistakenly) believed that doping was a problem associated with Eastern European countries. As a direct result of Johnson's positive test, the Dubin Commission was established to investigate the use of drugs in sport.[22] The Commission, headed by Charles L. Dubin, was convened in Canada in 1988–89 to discuss the widespread use of drugs in sport and the methods employed in detecting prohibited substances. Evidence was heard from 122 witnesses with 48 athletes including Johnson admitting that they had used prohibited substances. The Commission found that doping was omnipresent in the higher levels of sport. Cox and others note that the time following the report saw the beginnings of the first period of intense anti-doping practices within sport and at government level.[23]

6–09 The Tour de France 1998, as discussed in more detail below, was mired in controversy following the Festina Affair (l'Affaire Festina). The physiotherapist for the French Festina team, Voet, was arrested in France

---

19 Robert O Voy and Kirk D Deeter, *Drugs, Sport and Politics* (Leisure Press 1991).

20 ibid XV. Voy refers to the 1976 Games in Montreal where the head of the East German swimming team was asked about the deep voices of the female swimmers. The official sardonically replied: 'we have come here to swim, not to sing'. Shirley Babashoff, an American swimmer, remarked, 'They had tremendous muscular developments and deep, masculine voices. They didn't look or sound like women at all': see Ellen Galford, *XXIV Olympiad: Seoul 1988, Albertville 1992 (The Olympic Century Book 22)* (Warwick Press Incorporated 2015) eBook.

21 The Council of Europe Convention on Doping is an international convention on doping, which was opened for signatories in November 1989. It has been ratified by 50 states, including Ireland. For more detail see: <http://www.coe.int/t/dg4/sport/Doping/convention_en.asp#TopOfPage> accessed 2 May 2024.

22 Dubin (n 5).

23 Neville Cox and Alex Schuster (with Cathryn Costello), *Sport and the Law* (Firstlaw 2004) 83.

as he was attempting to cross into Belgium. Customs officials found large quantities of Erythropoietin (EPO) and other controlled substances along with syringes in Voet's car.[24] The team's sporting director admitted that the riders were taking prohibited substances under medical supervision which he had personally organised.[25] The entire team was suspended from the race. A parliamentary Commission published a report in July 2013 in which it revealed the names of those found to have used EPO at the 1998 Tour de France.[26] The Commission interviewed 84 witnesses under oath, including sportspersons, organisers, and anti-doping experts. While cycling was the focus, the Commission also looked at rugby, tennis, and football.[27]

In 2004, several high-profile scandals emerged as some elite athletes were found to have links with a Californian laboratory, BALCO (Bay Area Laboratory Cooperative), after a syringe containing a mysterious substance was sent to the US Anti-doping Agency (USADA). The substance was identified as the designer drug Tetrahydrogestrinone (THG) that had been hereto undetectable. Following an investigation, several Olympic champions were found to have taken testosterone, human growth hormones (HGH) and THG.[28] Dwain Chambers and Linford Christie were among those who admitted to having used these designer drugs. Marion Jones, the American athlete, who had won five medals at the Sydney Olympics, was found to have lied to a Grand Jury during the investigation and was sentenced to six months in prison in 2008.[29] In imposing a custodial sentence, US District Judge Karas remarked that '[a]thletes in society have an elevated status, they entertain, they inspire, and perhaps, most important, they serve as role models'.[30] Jones was forced to return the five Olympic medals she had **6–10**

---

24 It was reported that there were '500 doses of doping products, including EPO and growth hormone': Patrick Mignon, 'The Tour de France and the Doping Issue' (2003) 20(2) International Journal of the History of Sport 227, 234.

25 ibid. Mignon describes the reasoning of Russel, the sporting director, as 'following a strategy of risk reduction'.

26 The Local, 'Top Riders Named in Tour de France Doping Report' 24 July 2013 <https://www.thelocal.fr/20130724/top-cyclists-named-in-tour-de-france-doping-report> accessed 2 May 2024.

27 ibid.

28 Jason Giambi, the New York Yankees star batter, initially denied using performance-enhancing drugs. He was also implicated in the BALCO scandal. Fraud charges were brought against him, with Giambi admitting to a federal grand jury that he injected HGH and used steroids. See Mark Fainaru-Wada and Lance Williams, *Game of Shadows: Barry Bonds, BALCO, and the Steroids Scandal that Rocked Professional Sports* (Penguin Publishing Group 2007).

29 Jones was also charged with cheque fraud: see Clayton Bolton and Samantha Roberts, 'The World Anti-Doping Agency and Ethics in Sport' in Eric MacIntosh, Gonzalo Bravo, and Ming Li (eds), *International Sport Management* (Human Kinetics 2019) 195, 204.

30 Cited by Delia D Douglas, 'Forget Me … Not: Marion Jones and the Politics of Punishment' (2014) 38(1) Journal of Sport and Social 3, 9. Douglas contends that the judge's references to Jones as a persistent liar could be perceived 'as a continuation of America's preoccupation, fascination, and fear of Black bodies'.

previously won, going back to the 2000 Olympics. The IOC banned Jones for two years from competing in track and field athletics.[31]

6–11 The Athens Olympics in 2004 was not without controversy. Two Greek athletes, Kostas Kenteris and Katerina Thanou, had evaded testing before the Games and it was claimed that a motorbike accident had prevented them from providing a sample. The two athletes did not compete in the Olympics and the IAAF provisionally banned them for two years pending disciplinary proceedings. The athletes eventually admitted the offence and were banned for two years. The IAAF had sent the case to the CAS, on both parties reaching a settlement, the CAS allowed for the case to be withdrawn in November 2006.

6–12 At Beijing in 2008, six athletes were found to have committed doping infractions. However, a few other positive tests were recorded after 948 samples were re-tested after new testing technologies were developed by the French Anti-Doping Agency. Five athletes were found to have Continuous Erythropoietin Receptor Activator (CERA) in their B sample.[32] The new technology was used also to detect the use of insulin by non-diabetic athletes.[33]

6–13 Going back to the 2004 Olympics, the IOC extended its anti-doping programme by having samples re-analysed by the International Testing Agency (ITA) after the event.[34] Before the 2016 Rio Olympics, 2,727 samples collected at London 2012 were re-analysed.[35] The selection of samples was based on several variables including doping risks in

Douglas acknowledges that Jones should be held accountable; however, she argues that the judge was endeavouring to make an example of Jones.

31 'It's Official: Marion Jones Is No Olympian' (*CBS News*, 12 December 2007) <https://www.cbsnews.com/news/its-official-marion-jones-is-no-olympian/> accessed 13 May 2024. Jones retired from athletics and had a short-lived career playing for Tulsa Shock in the Women's National Basketball Association (WNBA): see Lynn Zinser, 'Jones, Disgraced Sprinter, Is Joining the WNBA' *New York Times* (New York, 10 March 2010) <https://www.nytimes.com/2010/03/11/sports/basketball/11jones.html> accessed 13 May 2024.

32 International Olympic Committee, 'Beijing 2008: IOC Completes Further Analysis of Beijing Samples' 28 April 2009 <https://olympics.com/ioc/news/beijing-2008-ioc-completes-further-analysis-of-beijing-samples> accessed 13 May 2024. CERA is a newer version of EPO, which enables the blood to carry more oxygen, which means the athlete has greater endurance.

33 ibid.

34 International Testing Agency, 'The ITA Concludes the Sample Re-analysis Program for the Olympic Games London 2012' 5 December 2022 <https://ita.sport/news/the-ita-concludes-the-sample-re-analysis-program-for-the-olympic-games-london-2012/> accessed 13 May 2024. The ITA is a not-for-profit, independent international organisation based in Lausanne, Switzerland. For more detail see <https://ita.sport/about-us/> accessed 13 May 2024.

35 International Testing Agency, *Report on the Re-analysis Program Olympic Games London 2012* <https://ita.sport/resource/ita-london-2012-sample-re-analysis-report/> accessed 5 July 2024

certain sports and certain countries.[36] The re-analysation resulted in 73 ADRVs with the IOC withdrawing 31 and re-allocating 46 medals.[37] The re-analysis focused on anabolic steroids as a new analytical method not available at the time of the 2012 Games, the 'long-term metabolite (LTM) test', was developed.[38] In 2012, under the World Anti-Doping Code (WADC) Article 17 on the Statute of Limitations, samples could be re-analysed for up to eight years, hence the re-testing concluding in 2020. Since 2015, the WADC extended the statute of limitations to 10 years. Irish walker Rob Heffernan was re-allocated an Olympic Bronze Medal in 2016 following a decision of the CAS in *International Association of Athletics Federations (IAAF) v All Russia Athletics Federation (ARAF), Sergey Kirdyapkin & Russian Anti-Doping Agency (RUSADA)*.[39] Kirdyapkin had been 'selectively' disqualified for a period that excluded the 2012 Olympics by Disciplinary Anti-Doping Committee of the RUSADA. The CAS's arbitral award determined that all competitive results obtained by Kirdyapkin from 20 August 2009 to 15 October 2012 were disqualified.

Anti-Doping and Sport Ireland: The Legislative Framework and International Conventions

Athletes are subject to the anti-doping rules of their sports council or federation/governing bodies. In the Irish context, Sport Ireland has incorporated the WADC and recognised governing bodies adhere to the Sport Ireland Anti-Doping Rules 2021 (as amended in 2023).[40] **6–14**

Part 4, ss 40–45 of the Sport Ireland Act 2015 place anti-doping in Irish sport on a statutory level.[41] The Irish Sport Council Act 1999 placed drug testing in sport on a statutory basis for the first time under Irish law. However, the 2015 Act repealed the 1999 Act and one important feature of this Act has been the enhancement of the anti-doping provisions. The 1999 Act provided for the creation of the Irish Sports Council (ISC) and one of the immediate functions placed on the newly created body was to establish an Anti-Doping Committee of the Irish Sports Council.[42] In conjunction with s 6(1)(d), the Anti-Doping Committee would 'take **6–15**

[36] ibid. With Russia accounting for 21 of the 73 ADRVs, Belarus next with 11 ADRVs.

[37] ibid.

[38] ibid.

[39] CAS 2015/A/4005 award of 25 April 2016 (operative award of 24 March 2016) <https://jurisprudence.tas-cas.org/Shared%20Documents/4005.pdf> accessed 2 May 2024.

[40] Sport Ireland, 'The Irish Sport Anti-Doping Rules 2021' <https://www.sportireland.ie/sites/default/files/media/document/2023-01/2021%20Irish%20Anti-Doping%20Rules%20January%202023.pdf> accessed 2 May 2024.

[41] Section 43 relates to the requirement of Sport Ireland to comply with the Data Protection Acts 1988 to 2018. Section 45 refers to the continuance of the previous Anti-Doping Rules in the form of the Irish Anti-Doping Rules made by Sport Ireland pursuant to Article 42.

[42] s 18(1)(3). The newly formed Sports Council was mandated to establish an anti-doping committee '[a]s soon as practicable after the establishment day'.

such action as it considers appropriate, including testing, to combat doping in sport'. In devising more robust anti-doping provisions, s 41 of the 2015 Act designates Sport Ireland 'as the national anti-doping organisation for the State'. As the designated anti-doping organisation (ADO), Sport Ireland is required to perform the functions and obligations of such an organisation referred to in the WADC, the United Nations Educational, Scientific and Cultural Organization (UNESCO) Anti-Doping Convention and the Irish Anti-Doping Rules.[43]

6–16 Section 42 details the Sport Ireland Anti-Doping Rules. Under s 42(1), Sport Ireland is empowered to implement such measures as it deems appropriate for the delivery of a 'comprehensive, co-ordinated and effective response to doping' and the provision of anti-doping facilities, such as testing and education, to national governing bodies (NGBs) that follow the WADC. According to s 42(2), Sport Ireland is required to develop Anti-Doping Rules which must include rules and arrangements in relation to the following:

a. Application of rules;
b. Violations of rules;
c. Prohibited substances and methods;
d. Therapeutic use of substances and methods;
e. Testing of sportspersons;
f. Intelligence relating to doping in sport;
g. Disqualifications;
h. Disciplinary procedures;
i. Sanctions;
j. Implementation, reporting and publication of decisions.

6–17 Subsection 3 provides that Sport Ireland can amend the anti-doping rules, while s 42(4) states that Sport Ireland may provide or obtain information (including personal data) from several agencies, both state and other anti-doping organisations:

a. The Health Products Regulatory Authority;
b. The Garda Síochána;
c. The Revenue Commissioners;
d. Other anti-doping organisations that are code-compliant with the code mentioned;
e. Any other public body, considered necessary by the Minister.

6–18 Section 44 outlines the sanctions for those that contravene the Irish Sport Anti-Doping Rules. A person who fails to comply with the Rules will be deemed ineligible to receive funding from Sport Ireland or represent Ireland in sport.

6–19 The WADC is enforced by Sport Ireland. All NGBs in receipt of public funding in Ireland are bound by the WADC and the Council of Europe

[43] s 41(a), (b) and (c).

Anti-Doping Convention. Sport Ireland carries out drug testing in all Irish sport, both recreational and competitive. All NGBs are bound by Sport Ireland's Anti-Doping Rules, which have been adapted from the WADC. As many governments cannot be legally bound by a non-governmental document, the WADC was implemented by way of international treaty, the International Convention Against Doping in Sport, which was drafted by the UNESCO.[44]

Ireland initially followed the Council of Europe's Anti-Doping Convention, which was adopted in 1989 and entered into force in 1990. The Anti-Doping Convention was augmented by an Additional Protocol in 2002.[45] The protocol is significant as it was 'the first instrument of international public law, which recognises the competence of the World Anti-Doping Agency to conduct out of competition controls'.[46] 6–20

Its aim is to standardise and harmonise the doping rules of sports organisations as well as reducing and eliminating doping from sport.[47] 6–21

---

[44] The International Convention Against Doping in Sport was the first global convention on doping in sport. It was adopted at the 33rd session of the UNESCO General Conference on 19 October 2005 and entered into force on 1 February 2007. It has 191 States Parties. A state party is defined as 'a country that has ratified, accepted, approved or acceded to this international instrument, and is therefore legally bound by its provisions', United Nations Educational, Scientific and Cultural Organization, 'States Parties' <https://en.unesco.org/themes/sport-and-anti-doping/convention/states-parties> accessed 2 May 2024. Ireland's instrument of ratification was deposited with the Director-General of UNESCO on 18 July 2008. The Convention is available as part of the Irish Treaty Series: No 9 of 2009, and is titled International Convention against Doping in Sport, adopted in Paris on 19 October 2005. It entered into force in Ireland on 1 September 2008. It can be viewed at <https://www.gov.ie/pdf/?file=https://assets.gov.ie/262917/4d9ca4d9-ea1f-4c0c-93ed-98aabdc70b74.pdf#page=null> accessed 2 May 2024. Article 4 outlines the relationship of the Convention and the WADC as follows: 'In order to coordinate the implementation, at the national and international levels, of the fight against doping in sport, States Parties commit themselves to the principles of the Code as the basis for the measures provided for in Article 5 of this Convention. Nothing in this Convention prevents States Parties from adopting additional measures complementary to the Code.'

[45] Council of Europe, 'The Anti-Doping Convention: An Instrument of International Co-operation' <https://www.coe.int/en/web/sport/anti-doping-convention> accessed 2 May 2024. For more information on the Protocol, see Additional Protocol to the Anti-Doping Convention (European Treaty Series No 188) <https://rm.coe.int/1680081569> accessed 2 May 2024. The Protocol, as explained in art 1, called on the parties 'to mutually recognise the competence of sports or national anti-doping organisations to conduct doping controls on their territory, in compliance with the national regulations of the host country, on sportsmen and women coming from other Parties to the Convention'. This would reduce the need for state parties to conclude multiple bilateral agreements and increase the effectiveness of anti-doping controls.

[46] Council of Europe, 'Details of Treaty No 188' <https://www.coe.int/en/web/conventions/full-list?module=treaty-detail&treatynum=188> accessed 13 May 2024. See art 1(3) of the Protocol.

[47] Article 1 of the Anti-Doping Convention, Strasbourg, 16.XI.1989 (European Treaty Series No 135) <https://rm.coe.int/168007b0e0> accessed 13 May 2024.

The most recent amendments to the Anti-Doping Convention took place in November 2023 when, in line with the WADC, the prohibited list was updated and came into effect on 1 January 2024.[48] On the establishment of the ISC, the Irish Sport Anti-Doping Programme aligned with that of the Anti-Doping Convention, due to the commitment of the Irish government.[49] However, following the government's ratification in 2009 of the UNESCO Convention against Doping in Sport, the additional requirements under this Convention ensured that the Irish government was committed to ensuring 'full compliance with the World Anti-Doping Code'.[50]

6–22 Ireland is one of 193 signatories to the Copenhagen Declaration on Anti-Doping in Sport.[51] The Copenhagen Declaration was the result of the 2nd World Conference on Doping in Sport held in Copenhagen, Denmark in 2003. Its scope is described in Article 1:

> In pursuing all paragraphs of this Declaration, Participants act within the limits of their respective constitutional and other legal provisions and acknowledge the diversity in constitutional and legal systems between governments, combined with diverse approaches to the fight against doping in sport.[52]

6–23 The Copenhagen Declaration uses words including 'recognises', 'seeks', 'encourages', 'coordinates and 'supports'. The signatories have all agreed to recognise the role of WADA under Article 4. Before governments ratify the UNESCO Convention against Doping in Sport, they must first become signatories to the Copenhagen Declaration.[53] The then Minister for Arts, Sports and Tourism signed the Copenhagen Declaration in April 2003, which meant that Ireland recognised the WADA and the WADC.[54] Consequently, Ireland introduced new anti-doping rules in 2004.

---

48 Council of Europe, 'Amendments to the Appendix (approved by the Monitoring Group at its 57th meeting) (Strasbourg, 10 November 2023) <https://rm.coe.int/1680adadec> accessed 13 May 2024.

49 Sport Ireland, 'The National Anti-Doping Programme' 5 August 2010 <https://www.sportireland.ie/news/the-national-anti-doping-programme> accessed 13 May 2024.

50 ibid.

51 The Declaration is available on the WADA site <https://www.wada-ama.org/sites/default/files/resources/files/WADA_Copenhagen_Declaration_EN.pdf> accessed 5 July 2024. It came into force on 2 January 2003. The list of signatories is available at <https://www.wada-ama.org/en/copenhagen-declaration-list-of-signatories> accessed 5 July 2024. The signatories are divided in regions: Africa, Americas, Europe, Oceania, and Asia.

52 ibid.

53 World Anti-Doping Agency, 'Copenhagen Declaration' <https://www.wada-ama.org/en/resources/copenhagen-declaration> accessed 13 May 2024.

54 'Minister Launches New Irish Anti-Doping Rules' *The Irish Times* (Dublin, 21 April 2004) <https://www.irishtimes.com/news/minister-launches-new-irish-anti-doping-rules-1.977117> accessed 13 May 2024.

Article 9 of the Council of Europe's Anti-Doping Convention requires that 6–24
States Parties complete an annual questionnaire on the implementation of their anti-doping policies. The most recent reports published on the Council of Europe website are from 2022.[55] Ireland's submission in 2022 indicates that the WADA definition of doping is used by Sport Ireland.[56] The list of banned pharmacological classes of doping agents and doping methods in Ireland is that of WADA's Prohibited List.[57] The legal status of Sport Ireland is described as a public authority.[58] With the exception of the coordination of the fight against trafficking, which is the preserve of the Health Products Regulatory Authority (HPRA), Sport Ireland is responsible for: coordinating the actions of all stakeholders, carrying out risk assessment and test distribution planning (TDP), maintaining the registered testing pool (RTP) and/or whereabouts pools management, collecting and transporting samples to a laboratory, providing training for sample collection personnel training, obtaining accreditation and re-accreditation, results, Therapeutic Use Exemptions (TUEs) and intelligence management, carrying out investigations and research, and providing education for athletes and support personnel.[59] In 2022, Sport Ireland's annual budget for its anti-doping programme amounted to €2,051,706, of which 100% was provided for by the government.[60] Sport Ireland withholds funding to governing bodies who are in breach of the anti-doping programme as well as athletes and athlete support personnel who are suspended due to a doping infraction.[61] Sport Ireland uses WADA-accredited laboratories based in Cologne, Lausanne, London, and Sydney.[62] With regard to in-competition testing, Sport Ireland collected 346 urine samples, however, it collected 647 urine and 422 blood out-of-competition samples in 2022.[63] Ireland has signed international agreements with the Union Cycliste Internationale (UCI) and UK Anti-Doping (UKAD) in order to share information pertaining to doping.[64]

Bodies that Assist Sport Ireland in its Anti-Doping Functions

Section 8(1)(d), (e), (f) and (g) of the 2015 Act sets out the functions of 6–25

55 Council of Europe, 'Anti-Doping Questionnaire (ADQ): Annual Reports' <https://www.coe.int/en/web/sport/adq-reports# {%22101769298%22:[1]}> accessed 13 May 2024.

56 Council of Europe, 'Implementation of Anti-Doping Policies in 2022 – Ireland' 2 <https://rm.coe.int/adq-report-2022-ireland/1680ae8117> accessed 13 May 2024.

57 ibid 2.

58 ibid 3.

59 ibid 3–4.

60 ibid 4.

61 ibid 5.

62 ibid 6.

63 ibid 6–7. There were zero blood samples collected in-competition.

64 ibid 12. UKAD is a public body that performs the functions of a National Anti-Doping Organisation in the United Kingdom. For more information, see <https://www.ukad.org.uk/> accessed 13 May 2024.

Sport Ireland in relation to anti-doping. Under s 8(1)(d), Sport Ireland is required 'to facilitate, through the promulgation of guidelines and codes of practice, standards of good conduct, fair play and the elimination of doping in sport'. Section 8(1)(e) provides that Sport Ireland should take such action as it considers appropriate, including testing, to combat doping in sport. According to s 8(1)(e), Sport Ireland is required 'to plan, implement, evaluate and monitor education and information programmes for good conduct, fair play and the elimination of doping in sport', and under s 8(1)(g), Sport Ireland is mandated 'in its capacity as the national anti-doping organisation in the State, to direct the collection of samples, to manage the testing and test results of samples and attend hearings, as required'.

6–26 As discussed above, s 42(2) of the 2015 Act provides Sport Ireland with the power to create the Irish Sport Anti-Doping Rules. As the National Anti-Doping Organisation (NADO), Sport Ireland is responsible for carrying out testing, issuing sanctions and overseeing the disciplinary process. Each year, the WADA updates its list of prohibited substances which requires Sport Ireland to reflect the changes in its prohibited list.[65] Coming into force on 1 January 2024, Tramadol was removed from the WADA Monitoring Programme and is now prohibited in-competition.[66]

Anti-Doping Committee

6–27 There are several bodies that aid Sport Ireland in its anti-doping endeavours. Section 6(3)(a) of the 2015 Act required Sport Ireland to create the Anti-Doping Committee to assist and advise it in relation to performance of its functions under s 8(1)(d)–(g), as outlined above. Section 6(3)(b) states that the Anti-Doping Committee must 'exercise such powers and carry out such duties relating to that function as Sport Ireland may from time-to-time delegate to the committee'.[67] The 2022 Annual Review describes the Anti-Doping Committee as an advisory body to the Board of Sport Ireland which provides

---

65 Sport Ireland, 'Prohibited List 2024' <https://www.sportireland.ie/anti-doping/athlete-zone/athlete-zone/2023-Prohibited-List> accessed 13 May 2024.

66 The list of changes can be accessed at World Anti-Doping Agency, 'Summary of Major Modifications and Explanatory Notes' <https://www.wada-ama.org/sites/default/files/2023-09/2024list_explanatory_list_en_final_22_september_2023.pdf> accessed 13 May 2024. The WADC 2021 includes a universally accepted definition of 'In-Competition'. In Appendix 1, p 76 of the Irish Sport Anti-Doping Rules, 'In Competition' is defined as the 'period commencing at 11:59 p.m. on the day before a Competition in which the Athlete is scheduled to participate through the end of such Competition and the Sample collection process related to such Competition. Provided, however, WADA may approve, for a particular sport, an alternative definition if an International Federation provides a compelling justification that a different definition is necessary for its sport; upon such approval by WADA, the alternative definition shall be followed by all Major Event Organisations for that particular sport': Irish Anti-Doping Doping Rules 2021 (n 40).

67 According to s 6(6), the Minister, following consultation with the chairperson of Sport Ireland, shall appoint chairpersons of the committees.

guidance to Sport Ireland.[68] The committee comprises of members from medical, business administration, sports administration, and scientific backgrounds and an athlete representative.[69] Given the wide range of expertise, the committee supports the Anti-Doping Unit (ADU).[70] The ADU carries out the testing of athletes and represents Sport Ireland at NADO and WADA meetings.[71]

Irish Sport Anti-Doping Disciplinary Panel

The Irish Sport Anti-Doping Disciplinary Panel (ISADDP) was established in 2004. There was a separate panel of experts who heard appeal cases, the Irish Sport Anti-Doping Appeal Panel. In January 2009, the ISADDP and the Irish Sport Anti-Doping Appeal Panel merged to form one entity, the ISADDP. The ISADDP Procedures are made under s 42(2) of the 2015 Act.[72] The ISADDP is empowered to hear and determine the consequences of any ADRV that falls under the Irish Anti-Doping 2021 Rules (as amended) in line with changes introduced by WADA.[73] It also has the power to hear and determine a Provisional Hearing by an Athlete or other Person as provided for under Article 7.5.3 of the 2021 Rules.[74] The 2021 Rules constitute an agreement to arbitrate and a hearing before the ISADDP will be considered arbitration proceedings and, as such, the Arbitration Act 2010 applies.[75] An independent nominations committee, appointed by Sport Ireland, review applications and appoint the members to the ISADDP, which comprises of a chair and up to nine vice-chairs who are chosen based on their legal expertise.[76] It also comprises of up to 10 members each of whom is appointed due to their medical or scientific expertise and up to 10 members who are appointed for their sports experience.[77] Sport Ireland must ensure that members appointed to the ISADDP are 'Operationally Independent'.[78] 6–28

68 Sport Ireland, 'Sport Ireland Anti-Doping Annual Review 2022' (22 December 2023) 10 <https://www.sportireland.ie/news/sport-ireland-publish-2022-anti-doping-report> accessed 21 August 2024.

69 ibid.

70 ibid.

71 Sport Ireland, 'Sport Ireland Annual Report 2022' (February 2024) 17 <https://www.sportireland.ie/sites/default/files/media/document/2024-02/report_updated.pdf> accessed 13 May 2024.

72 See Sport Ireland, 'Irish Sport Anti-Doping Disciplinary Panel Procedures' (January 2023) <https://www.sportireland.ie/sites/default/files/media/document/2023-01/Irish%20Sport%20Anti-Doping%20Disciplinary%20Procedures%20January%202023.pdf> accessed 13 May 2024.

73 Irish Anti-Doping Rules 2021 (n 40).

74 ibid. Article 7.5.3 provides that Provisional Hearings are heard by a single arbitrator who will be either the Chair or a Vice-Chair of the ISADDP. See Panel Procedures (n 72) rr 2.1.1. and 2.12 for the jurisdiction of the ISADDP.

75 Panel Procedures (n 72) r 2.2. See also art 16.4.2 of the Irish Anti-Doping Rules 2021 (n 40).

76 Panel Procedures (n 72) rr 3.1 and 3.1.1.

77 ibid rr 3.1.2. and 3.1.3.

78 ibid r 3.2. Irish Anti-Doping Rules 2021 (n 40) Appendix 1, p 78 defines Operational

6–29 It is a four-year term which may be renewed by the independent nominations committee.[79] A panel hearing consists of three experts each from a legal, medical and sports (administration/former athlete) background.[80] The role of the Panel is to hear cases fairly and impartially.[81] When an athlete or 'other Person' is alleged to have committed an ADRV, Sport Ireland or the NGB refers the matter to the ISADDP.[82] The reference to 'other Person' includes natural persons (for example a coach, a manager or an agent) and legal persons (such as NGBs). The athlete or other person may waive a hearing and admit liability and, in that case, Sport Ireland will outline the consequences in a Results Management Agreement.[83] A recent example of a reasoned decision of the ISADDP where the athlete did not dispute the findings of an ADRV is that of Sport Ireland and Aidan Byrne.[84] Byrne initially contended that his positive test for cocaine metabolite benzoylecgonine was the result of antibiotics and steroids he ingested via an IV drip while attending the accident and emergency department of a hospital.[85] In an

Independence as follows: 'This means that (1) board members, staff members, commission members, consultants and officials of Sport Ireland or its affiliates (e.g. Member federation or confederation), as well as any Person involved in the investigation and pre-adjudication of the matter cannot be appointed as members and/or clerks (to the extent that such clerk is involved in the deliberation process and/or drafting of any decision) of the Hearing Panel or appeal panel and (2) the Hearing Panel and appeal panel shall be in a position to conduct the hearing and decision-making process without interference from Sport Ireland or any third party. The objective is to ensure that members of the Hearing Panel and appeal panel or individuals otherwise involved in the decision of the Hearing Panel or appeal panel, are not involved in the investigation of, or decisions to proceed with, the case'.

79 ibid r 3.3.1. According to r 3.3.2, the members should not be removed from their positions before the expiry of the term unless there is 'an objective and/ or overriding legal reason'; it lists legal incapacity, involvement in doping or criminal activities, violation of their duties such as a breach of confidentiality or intentional non-disclosure of a conflict of interest. Sport Ireland provides a sample template relating to the terms of reference for Nomination Committees that reflects the principles of the Governance Code for Sport. For more detail, see <https://www.sportireland.ie/sites/default/files/media/document/2021-11/nominations-committee-terms-of-reference.docx> accessed 13 May 2024. For more details on the Code, see *The Governance Code for Sport: A Code of Practice for Good Governance of Sport Organisations in Ireland* (Sport Ireland 2019) <https://www.sportireland.ie/sites/default/files/media/document/2020-12/the-governance-code-for-sport-a-guide.pdf> accessed 13 May 2024.

80 Panel Procedures (n 72) Rule 4.1.

81 Irish Anti-Doping Rules 2021 (n 40) art 8.2.3.

82 ibid art 8.1.

83 Results Management Agreements are explained under art 10.7 of the Irish Anti-Doping Rules 2021 (n 40).

84 Sport Ireland, 'Sport Ireland Reasoned Decision – Aidan Byrne' 20 December 2023 <https://www.sportireland.ie/sites/default/files/media/document/2024-01/reasoned-decision.pdf> accessed 13 May 2024. Byrne was found to have committed a doping infraction under art 2.1 – 'the presence of a Prohibited Substance or its Metabolites or Markers in an Athletes Sample'; and art 2.2 – 'Use or Attempted Use by an Athlete of a Prohibited Substance or a Prohibited Method', Irish Anti-Doping Rules 2021 (n 40).

85 Sport Ireland Reasoned Decision- Aidan Byrne (n 84) [1.4] and [1.5].

email to Sport Ireland, the Tug of War Ireland athlete admitted he had taken cocaine recreationally on 30 June 2023.[86] Sport Ireland followed up with the athlete, requesting more information, however, the athlete never responded. Had he furnished 'corroborating evidence', including witness statements, that could attest that he had taken cocaine out-of-competition and recreationally, he would only face a three-month ban.[87] The athlete was sanctioned with a four-year period of ineligibility, beginning on 3 August 2023, the date of the imposition of the provisional ban.[88] Byrne was also sanctioned by the disqualification of his results from 2 July 2023 until the date of his Provisional Suspension on 3 August 2023.[89]

If the athlete or other person does not admit liability, the ISADDP will determine whether a violation has occurred, or where an athlete has not contested the positive test but makes a submission for an elimination or reduction of the sanction.[90] None of members of the Panel and Registrar are permitted to have had any prior involvement in the case.[91] At the hearing Sport Ireland presents the case against the athlete or other person.[92] If it is agreed in advance between the athlete's or other person's NGB and Sport Ireland, the NGB is permitted to present the case.[93] In this situation, Sport Ireland can join and attend the hearing as a party to the case.[94] If Sport Ireland is not a party to the proceedings, WADA, the **6–30**

---

86 ibid [1.7].

87 ibid [1.6] and [1.8]. Article 10.1.4.1 of Irish Anti-Doping Rules 2021 (n 40) refers to the three-month period of ineligibility for a Substance of Abuse, discussed in more detail further on in this chapter.

88 Sport Ireland Reasoned Decision – Aidan Byrne (n 84) [2.1].

89 ibid [2.2.1].

90 Irish Sport Anti-Doping Rules (n 40): art 10.4 (Elimination of the Period of Ineligibility based on No Fault or Negligence); art 10.5 (Reduction of the Period of Ineligibility based on No Significant Fault or Negligence); and art 10.6 (Elimination, Reduction, or Suspension of Period of Ineligibility or other Consequences for Reasons other than Fault). A new provision was introduced by the WADC in 2021 and is explained in art 10.3 and it relates to Aggravating Circumstances which may Increase the Period of Ineligibility. It applies to an ADRV other than other than violations under art 2.7 (Trafficking or Attempted Trafficking), 2.8 (Administration or Attempted Administration), 2.9 (Complicity or Attempted Complicity), or 2.11 (Acts by an Athlete or Other Person to Discourage or Retaliate Against Reporting). The athlete may, depending on the seriousness of the doping violation and the aggravating circumstances, have an additional two years added to their period of ineligibility. However, the additional sanction will not apply if the Athlete or other Person can establish that they did not knowingly commit the anti-doping rule violation. The reason for the exclusion of arts 2.7, 2.8, 2.9, and 2.11 is that such offences can result in a lifetime ban, thus aggravating circumstances are factored into the sanction.

91 Panel Procedures (n 72) r 4.4. The role of the Registrar is explained in r 6. Sport Ireland is responsible for appointing a Registrar. The Registrar provides administrative assistance to the ISADDP and contacts the relevant parties and devises a timetable for proceedings.

92 Irish Anti-Doping Rules 2021 (n 40) art 8.5.2.

93 ibid art 8.5.3.

94 ibid.

IF and NGB may attend as observers.[95] Sport Ireland keeps the relevant bodies apprised of pending cases and the result of all hearings.[96]

6–31 The burden of proof is placed on Sport Ireland (or the NGB if applicable) to prove that there has been an ADRV.[97] The standard of proof placed on Sport Ireland or the NGB is to establish that an anti-doping violation has occurred to the comfortable satisfaction of the ISADDP, bearing in mind the seriousness of the allegation that is made.[98] This standard of proof in all cases is greater than a mere balance of probability but less than proof beyond a reasonable doubt.[99] In rebutting the charges, the burden of proof placed on the athlete or other person is on the balance of probabilities.[100] There is a presumption that the sample was analysed properly in the WADA-accredited laboratory and in accordance with the International Standard for Laboratories (ISL), however, the athlete or other person may rebut and argue that there was a deviation from the accepted standards and practices that caused an Adverse Analytical Finding (AAF).[101] In this situation, the burden is placed on Sport Ireland or the NGB to establish that such departure from the accepted standards did not cause the AAF.[102] The ISADDP may draw adverse inferences in the situation where the athlete, who has been given reasonable notice, does not appear at the hearing, either in person or telephonically or by other electronic means.[103]

6–32 Hearings are held in private and are confidential unless the Panel otherwise decides. The Panel may conduct the hearing in person, by teleconference or thereby any other electronic means as directed by the ISADDP.[104] Each party has the right to avail of the services of an interpreter.[105] The Panel may request that documentation and other evidence be made available to the other party. If the party does not comply with the request, the Panel will take this into account when making its decision. The hearing will still go ahead in the absence of one of the parties. It may be adjoined or postponed, and the Panel may appoint an expert to advise them on any matter pertaining to the case.

6–33 The NGB, with the agreement of Sport Ireland, may use its own disciplinary panel to determine the case.[106] However, the NGB is

---

95 ibid art 8.5.4.
96 ibid.
97 ibid art 8.6.1.
98 ibid.
99 ibid.
100 ibid art 8.6.2.
101 ibid art 8.6.6.
102 ibid.
103 ibid art 8.6.10.
104 ibid art 8.4.9.
105 Decision issued by the Irish Sport Anti-Doping Disciplinary Panel (Chair: David Casserly, Barrister) in the disciplinary proceedings between Athletics Ireland and Tomas Rauktys, dated 23 October 2013.
106 Irish Anti-Doping Rules 2021 (n 40) art 8.8.1.

bound by the rules and conditions imposed by Sport Ireland, all references to the ISADDP and/or the Hearing Panel are construed as the rules of the NGB's disciplinary panel, with the exception of the definition in Appendix 1 relating to the Disciplinary Procedures, which refers explicitly to the ISADDP.[107] If Sport Ireland is of the opinion that the NGB's disciplinary panel is not adhering to the rules and regulations, the agreement is rescinded and the matter is referred to the ISADDP.[108] The Gaelic Athletic Association (GAA) has adopted the Irish Anti-Doping Rules as the Anti-Doping Rules of the GAA, and it has its own anti-doping disciplinary panel, the Anti-Doping Hearings Committee.[109] Carlow GAA player Raymond Walker tested positive for meldonium, a non-specified substance which is prohibited at all times.[110] The Prohibited List refers to specified substances and non-specified substances. To broaden the scope of the list of banned substances, the Prohibited List includes 'other substances with a similar chemical structure or similar biological effect(s)'.[111] As explained by the UKAD, 'Specified substances are those that, if found to be present in an athlete's bodily sample, may be more likely to have a credible, non-doping explanation,' while 'Non-specified substances are those where there is no non-doping explanation for having these substances in an athlete's system.'[112] Walker was selected for out-of-competition testing following a training session.[113] The sample divided into A and B was analysed at a WADA-accredited laboratory in Cologne.[114] Following an AAF, the laboratory contacted Sport Ireland. Walker was contacted and informed that he had committed a violation of Article 2.1 relating to 'the presence of a Prohibited Substance or its Metabolites or Markers in your Sample'.[115] The player was facing a four-year period of ineligibility for the presence of a non-specified substance under Article 10.1.1. The period of ineligibility could be reduced to two years if Walker could establish that the violation was unintentional, as provided for under Article 10.1.2. Sport Ireland informed Walker of three options regarding his response to the AAF:

---

107 ibid.

108 ibid art 8.8.3.

109 See r 1.13 of Gaelic Athletic Association, *Official Guide – Part 1* (Central Council of the Association 2024) <https://www.gaa.ie/article/gaa-official-guides-codes> accessed 24 April 2024.

110 Sport Ireland, 'Sport Ireland Reasoned Decision – Raymond Walker' (8 April 2020) <https://www.sportireland.ie/sites/default/files/media/document/2020-04/reasoned-decision-mr-raymond-walker-published-april-2020.pdf> accessed 13 May 2024.

111 World Anti-Doping Agency, 'The 2024 Prohibited List, World Anti-Doping Code' (Valid 1 January 2024) <https://www.wada-ama.org/sites/default/files/2023-09/2024list_en_final_22_september_2023.pdf> accessed 13 May 2024.

112 UK Anti-Doping, 'What's Banned in Sport – The Prohibited List' <https://www.ukad.org.uk/athletes/whats-banned-sport-prohibited-list> accessed 13 May 2024.

113 Sport Ireland Reasoned Decision – Raymond Walker (n 110) [1.3].

114 ibid [1.4].

115 Irish Anti-Doping Rules 2021 (n 40).

1. Admit to the violation, accept the consequences imposed by Sport Ireland, in the absence of furnishing corroborative evidence to support the assertion that he had unintentionally ingested meldonium, accept a period of ineligibility of four years[116];
2. Admit the violation, but elect for a hearing before the GAA Hearings Committee seeking a ban of less than four years[117]; or
3. Deny the violation, and to have the matter and the ban and other sanctions (if any) determined at a hearing of the GAA Hearings Committee.[118]

6–34 The player chose to admit the violation and waive the requirement for a ISADDP hearing. Due to his prompt acceptance of the terms of the sanction, Sport Ireland backdated his period of ineligibility to the date of the sample collection, 18 February 2020.[119] Until midnight on 18 February 2024, Walker was eligible for testing, could 'not participate in any capacity in Inter-County or Club Gaelic Football (or indeed in other organised sport)' including playing, training, and coaching.[120]

6–35 Rule 8.9 provides that the ISADDP may offer an athlete or other person a public hearing.[121] Sport Ireland may also request a public hearing, however, the athlete or other person must provide written consent.[122] A request for a public hearing:

> may be denied in the interests of morals, public order, national security, where the interests of Minors or the protection of the private life of the Parties so require, where publicity would prejudice the interests of justice or where the proceedings are exclusively related to question of law.[123]

6–36 With the exception of Rule 8.9, the deliberations of the ISADDP are held in private and are confidential.[124] At the hearing, each party has the right to be legally represented at a hearing of which they bear their own expenses.[125] They are entitled to present evidence, make submissions, call witnesses, and cross-examine the witnesses of the other parties.[126] There are no dissenting decisions, thus one single decision is given.[127]

---

116 Sport Ireland Reasoned Decision – Raymond Walker (n 110) [1.7.1].
117 ibid [1.7.2].
118 ibid [1.7.3].
119 ibid [2.3].
120 ibid [2.4]. According to [2.5], the player could return to training 'with a team or to use the facilities of a club or other member organisation of a Signatory's member organisation or a National Governing Body, during the last 2 months of his period of Ineligibility'.
121 Panel Procedures (n 72) r 8.9.
122 ibid.
123 ibid.
124 ibid.
125 ibid r 8.2.
126 ibid.
127 There is just one ISADDP decision available online: it relates to the 2015 Code and involved a Motor Sport Ireland go-kart racing driver's failure to provide a urine sample. The athlete was banned for four years: Summary of ISADDP Ruling – Kenneth Daly (30 June 2020) <https://www.sportireland.ie/sites/default/files/

No member of the ISADDP may abstain from making a decision. The decision is in writing and dated, and reasons for the decision are stated. If Sport Ireland or WADA are not party to the proceedings, they are notified of the decision as soon as practicable. Decisions of the ISADDP are final and binding; however, decisions may be appealed to the CAS.[128] If the ISADDP or the disciplinary panel of the NGB fail to render a decision within a reasonable deadline set by WADA, WADA may make a direct appeal to the CAS as if the ISADDP or the NGB's disciplinary panel have found that no anti-doping violation has occurred.[129] If the CAS Panel holds that an anti-doping violation has been committed and it finds that WADA acted reasonably in the circumstances, the expenses incurred will be reimbursed by the ISADDP or the NGB's disciplinary panel.[130]

The Rules also stipulate that an athlete may not initiate court proceedings or any other forum 'that are inconsistent with the foregoing submission to the jurisdiction of the Irish Sport Anti-Doping Disciplinary Panel and CAS'. [131] It would be illegal and unconstitutional to oust the jurisdiction of the court in all circumstances. However, athletes should exhaust all the internal disciplinary mechanisms within the sport before seeking redress in the courts. **6–37**

Therapeutic Use Exemption Committee

The Therapeutic Use Exemption Committee (TUEC) consists of a panel of physicians who evaluate applications for a TUE.[132] An athlete may have an illness or condition that requires medication or requires the athlete to undergo procedures. However, the medication or procedure **6–38**

media/document/2020-08/kenneth-daly-isaddp-summary-decision.pdf> accessed 13 May 2024.

128 Panel Procedures (n 72) r 10.1. The decision that is subject to an appeal to the CAS remains in full force, pending a decision of the CAS, unless the CAS orders otherwise. This is affirmed in art 13.1 of Irish Anti-Doping Rules 2021 (n 40). Article 13.1.2 provides: 'Where WADA has a right to appeal under Article 13 and no other party has appealed a final decision within Sport Ireland's process, WADA may appeal such decision directly to CAS without having to exhaust other remedies in Sport Ireland's process.'

129 Irish Anti-Doping Rules 2021 (n 40) art 13.3.

130 ibid. Footnote 85 on p 63 of the 2021 Rules adds: 'Given the different circumstances of each anti-doping rule violation investigation, Results Management and hearing process, it is not feasible to establish a fixed time period for the Irish Sport Anti-Doping Disciplinary Panel to render a decision before WADA may intervene by appealing directly to CAS. Before taking such action, however, WADA will consult with the Irish Sport Anti-Doping Disciplinary Panel and give the Irish Sport Anti-Doping Disciplinary Panel an opportunity to explain why it has not yet rendered a decision.'

131 Irish Anti-Doping Rules 2021 (n 40) art 1.3.4.5.

132 ibid art 4.2.1 outlines the composition. It must consist of not less than three members, one of whom will act as Chair. Article 4.2.2 provides that the physicians must have 'experience in the care and treatment of Athletes and a sound knowledge of clinical, sports and exercise medicine'.

may be in breach of WADA's Prohibited List. If a TUE is granted, it means that the

> presence of a Prohibited Substance or its Metabolites or Markers, and/or the Use or Attempted Use, Possession or Administration or Attempted Administration of a Prohibited Substance or a Prohibited Method, shall not be considered an anti-doping rule violation if it is consistent with the provisions of a TUE granted in accordance with these Rules and the International Standard for Therapeutic Use Exemptions.[133]

6–39 The application is made under Article 6 of the International Standard for Therapeutic Use Exemptions (ISTUE).[134] A TUE granted by the TUEC of Sport Ireland applies only to national events. If the athlete is competing internationally or at a major international event, the national exemption must be recognised by the IF or the Major Event Organisation (MEO).[135] A retrospective TUE may be granted by Sport Ireland to a non-International-Level or a non-National-Level Athlete in certain circumstances, including an emergency or urgent treatment.[136] International-Level and National-Level athletes may also request retroactive approval for a TUE 'if considering the purpose of the Code, it would be manifestly unfair not to grant a retroactive TUE'.[137] It requires the prior approval of WADA, and WADA may reject or accept Sport Ireland's decision.[138]

Sport Ireland Anti-Doping Rules

6–40 The Irish Sport Anti-Doping Rules were revised in 2021 as the fourth version of the WADC came into force on 1 January 2021.[139] Article 2 details the following acts or omissions which constitute anti-doping violations:

- Article 2.2.1: Presence of a Prohibited Substance in an Athlete's Sample
- Article 2.2: Use or Attempted Use by an Athlete of a Prohibited Substance or a Prohibited Method

---

[133] ibid art 13.3.

[134] World Anti-Doping Agency, 'International Standard for Therapeutic Use Exemptions 2023' <https://www.wada-ama.org/sites/default/files/2022-09/international_standard_for_therapeutic_use_exemptions_istue_2023.pdf> accessed 13 May 2024.

[135] Irish Anti-Doping Rules 2021 (n 40) art 4.1.4.

[136] ibid arts 4.4.1 and 4.4.2. This would arise if Sport Ireland was collecting a sample from the athlete.

[137] ibid art 4.4.4.

[138] ibid.

[139] The WADC was previously amended in 2015 and 2009. The Code was first published in 2003. The prohibited list is updated annually, with changes coming in force on 1 January each year. The 2027 Code is currently being drafted: World Anti-Doping Agency, 'WADA Launches First Phase of 2027 World Anti-Doping Code and International Standards Update Process' 26 September 2023 <https://www.wada-ama.org/en/news/wada-launches-first-phase-2027-world-anti-doping-code-and-international-standards-update> accessed 13 May 2024.

- Article 2.3: Evading, Refusing or Failing to Submit to Sample Collection by an Athlete
- Article 2.4: Whereabouts Failures by an Athlete[140]
- Article 2.6: Tampering or Attempted Tampering with any Part of Doping Control by an Athlete or Other Person
- Article 2.7: Possession of a Prohibited Substance or a Prohibited Method by an Athlete or Athlete Support Person[141]
- Article 2.8: Administration or Attempted Administration by an Athlete or Other Person to any Athlete In-Competition of any Prohibited Substance or Prohibited Method, or Administration or Attempted Administration to any Athlete Out-of-Competition of any Prohibited Substance or any Prohibited Method that is Prohibited Out-of-Competition
- Article 2.9: Complicity or Attempted Complicity by an Athlete or Other Person[142]
- Article 2.10: Prohibited Association by an Athlete or Other Person[143]
- Article 2.11: Acts by an Athlete or Other Person to Discourage or Retaliate Against Reporting to Authorities

Article 2.11 is a new offence which was introduced under the 2021 WADC.[144] While not explicitly referring to whistleblowers, it provides protection for those who may be threatened or discouraged from providing, in good faith, information alleging an anti-doping violation or alleged non-compliance with the WADC.[145] The 2021 Code also reintroduced an additional period of ineligibility due to aggravating circumstances.[146] If aggravating circumstances are present, apart from violations under Articles 2.7, 2.8, 2.9, and 2.11, Sport Ireland or the NGB where applicable can impose an additional period of ineligibility of up to two years, depending on the 'seriousness of the violation and the nature of the Aggravating Circumstances'.[147] However, the additional **6–41**

[140] Irish Anti-Doping Rules 2021 (n 40) art 2.4.1. This requires the athlete to commit three Whereabouts Failures, either due to Filing Failures or Missed Tests, in a 12-month period by an Athlete in a RTP. The RTP is defined by Sport Ireland as 'a list of elite athletes, agreed between the NGB and Sport Ireland, who meet certain criteria'. The criteria include athletes on the carding scheme in the Contract, World Class and International categories, Olympic or Paralympic Qualifiers, athletes who are included in an International Federation RTP and any athlete currently serving a period of ineligibility: Sport Ireland, 'Registered Testing Pool' <https://www.sportireland.ie/anti-doping/athlete-zone/athlete-zone/registered-testing-pool> accessed 13 May 2024.

[141] Doping methods are discussed further on in this chapter.

[142] Complicity and attempted complicity include physical and psychological assistance. It refers to aiding and abetting or covering up an anti-doping violation.

[143] Irish Anti-Doping Rules 2021 (n 40) explains this as follows: 'Associating with a person such as a coach, doctor or physio who has been found guilty of an ADRV or equivalent offence to a doping violation will be sanctioned with a ban of up to 2 years'.

[144] The relevant article of the WADC is also art 2.11: see World Anti-Doping Agency, 'World Anti-Doping Code 2021' <https://www.wada-ama.org/sites/default/files/resources/files/2021_wada_code.pdf> accessed 13 May 2024.

[145] Those found to have committed such an ADRV face a ban of two years to a lifetime ban, depending on the seriousness of the violation.

[146] Article 10.4 of the WADC and art 10.3 of the Irish Anti-Doping Rules 2021 (n 40).

[147] ibid. Comment 64 on p 69 of the WADC explains that arts 2.7, 2.8, 2.9 and 2.11

period of ineligibility does not apply in situations where the athlete or other person can demonstrate that they unknowingly committed the ADRV.[148] Aggravating circumstances include an athlete taking numerous prohibited substances concurrently or where an athlete or other is involved in a plan or scheme to commit an ADRV or engaged in 'a conspiracy or common enterprise' either individually or with others to commit an anti-doping violation.[149]

6–42 The 2021 Code reduced the period of ineligibility for 'substance of abuse', as provided for under Article 10.1.4 of the Irish Sport Anti-Doping Rules and Article 10.2.4 of the WADC. This refers to recreational drugs whose use is unrelated to sports performance. It signifies that WADA is more concerned with the use of performance-enhancing substances and sanctioning those who are cheating as opposed to substances that are 'frequently abused in society outside of the context of sport'.[150] According to Article 10.2.4.1 of the WADC and Article 10.1.4.1 of the Irish Anti-Doping Rules, if the athlete can establish that any ingestion or use occurred out-of-competition and was unrelated to sport performance, then a period of ineligibility of three months may be imposed. This can be further reduced to one month if the athlete satisfactorily completes a 'Substance of Abuse treatment programme approved by Sport Ireland'.[151] The decision rendered by Sport Ireland in relation to Aidan Byrne, as discussed above, is an example of the use of a substance of abuse.[152] However, as Byrne did not furnish evidence that the use of cocaine was recreational, unrelated to sports performance and out-of-competition, he received a four-year period of ineligibility.

6–43 Appendix 1 of the 2021 Code introduced the concept of institutional independence, as noted above under the discussion on the ISADDP.[153] This means that appeal panels must be wholly independent institutionally from the ADO for results management. An appeal from a decision of ISADDP will automatically be referred to the CAS.

---

are excluded as those violations allow for the discretion to impose a lifetime ban.

148 ibid.

149 See *CAS 2016/O/4463 International Association of Athletics Federations (IAAF) v All Russia Athletics Federation (ARAF) & Kristina Ugarova* award of 29 November 2016 [118] <https://jurisprudence.tas-cas.org/Shared%20Documents/4463.pdf> accessed 13 May 2024.

150 Irish Sport Anti-Doping Rules (n 40) art 3.4.

151 ibid art 10.1.4.1. The wording in the WADC is 'if the Athlete or other Person satisfactorily completes a Substance of Abuse treatment program approved by the Anti-Doping Organization with Results Management responsibility'. Comment 60 on p 66 of the World Anti-Doping Code 2021 (n 144) refers to the discretion of the relevant anti-doping organisation in identifying and using the services of a reputable treatment programme as opposed to 'sham' programmes.

152 Sport Ireland Reasoned Decision – Aidan Byrne (n 84).

153 WADC Appendix 1: Definitions (n 144) 170.

Types of Doping

6–44 Doping is not only the use of a pharmacological or chemical substance or physical manipulation, there are other methods, including blood doping and gene doping.[154] In basic terms, blood doping involves the taking of blood out of the athlete's body; re-oxygenating it and pumping it back into the athlete's body. Scientists define blood doping as 'the misuse of certain techniques and/or substances to increase one's red blood cell (RBC) mass, which enables the body to transport more O2 to muscles and therefore increase performance'.[155] The CAS Panel in *El Mahjoub Dazza v World Athletics* stated:

> Three widely known substances or methods are used for blood doping, namely (i) administering recombinant human erythropoietin ('rEPO') (by injection to trigger erythropoiesis, the stimulation of red blood cells); (ii) the use of synthetic oxygen carriers (i.e., infusing blood substitutes such as haemoglobin-based oxygen carrier or perfluorocarbons to increase haemoglobin ('HGB') concentration well above normal levels); and (iii) blood transfusions (i.e., infusing a matching donor's or an athlete's own (previously extracted) red blood cells to increase the HGB well above normal.[156]

6–45 The CAS recently partially upheld an appeal by a tennis player who had been banned for four years for alleged blood doping.[157] Simona Halep appealed the decision of the International Tennis Integrity Agency (ITIA) in relation to two separate charges. One charge related to the presence of the prohibited substance Roxadustat in a urine sample, and the second related to a change in Halep's Athlete Biological Passport (ABP) found in a blood sample.[158] Roxadustat, a blood-boosting drug, has been on the banned list since 2017.[159] The CAS Panel accepted Halep's

---

154 Stephen R Bird and others, 'Doping in Sport and Exercise: Anabolic, Ergogenic, Health and Clinical Issues' (2016) 53(2) Annals of Clinical Biochemistry 196.

155 Andreas Breenfeldt Andersen and others, 'Contemporary Blood Doping – Performance, Mechanism, and Detection' (2024) 34(1) Scandinavian Journal of Medicine & Science 1, 2.

156 CAS 2020/A/7377 *El Mahjoub Dazza v World Athletics* award of 23 April 2021 [8] <https://www.athleticsintegrity.org/downloads/pdfs/disciplinary-process/en/CAS-EMD.pdf> accessed 13 May 2024. For a user-friendly explanation on blood doping, see United States Anti-Doping Agency, 'Blood Doping and EPO: An Anti-Doping FAQ' <https://www.usada.org/spirit-of-sport/education/blood-doping-epo-faq/> accessed 13 May 2024.

157 CAS 2023/A/10025 *Simona Halep v International Tennis Integrity Agency (ITIA)* and CAS 2023/A/10227 *International Tennis Integrity Agency (ITIA) v Simona Halep* award of 5 March 2024 <https://www.tas-cas.org/fileadmin/user_upload/CAS_Award_10025___10227__for_publication_.pdf> accessed 30 September 2024.

158 The ABP will be discussed in more detail under indirect detection, paras 6–54 and 6-55. The ITIA filed a separate appeal, CAS 2023/A/10227 (n 157). The ITIA asked the CAS to consider Halep's two ADRVs as one single violation, which would place the infraction as a more serious breach carrying a period of ineligibility from four to six years.

159 As explained by the *New York Times*, Roxadustat 'artificially stimulates haemoglobin and red blood cell production, which is a technique for players to gain more endurance. The drug does this by getting the body to produce more

explanation of ingesting a contaminated supplement. It found that Halep had established, on the balance of probabilities, that her ingestion of Roxadustat was unintentional. Consequently, she did not bear significant fault or negligence, although she should have exercised sufficient care in using the supplement. The ITIA had to prove to the comfortable satisfaction of the CAS Panel that the one blood sample obtained as part of her APB demonstrated the presence of a prohibited substance. The ITIA was unable to discharge this burden to the comfortable satisfaction of the CAS Panel. Her appeal was partially successful as her period of ineligibility was reduced from four years to nine months; however, her request to backdate the start of her suspension to 29 August 2022, the date of the collection of the urine sample, was denied.[160]

6–46 Gene doping involves the non-therapeutic use of genes to enhance athletic performance. Since 2003, it has been banned under the WADC list of prohibited substances and methods of doping.[161] There is a 'fine line' between gene doping and the therapeutic use of genes for legitimate medical purposes.[162] According to Clark and Pazdernik, 'It is a fact that some people are born with superior genetics for athletic performance.'[163] This leads to the question whether athletes who are less 'genetically gifted' should be permitted to engage in gene doping in order 'to level the playing field'.[164] Similarly, 'mechanical enhancements' can give an unfair advantage.[165] Although not technically a form of doping, a recent development has been technological doping. Swimming provides an illuminating example.[166] For several years swimmers have worn very high-tech swimming suits. A second-generation suit

---

of the hormone erythropoietin, commonly referred to as "EPO," which plays an important role in red blood cell production': Matthew Futterman, 'Halep Gets 4-Year Suspension for Doping Violation' *New York Times* (New York, 12 September 2023) <https://www.nytimes.com/2023/09/12/sports/tennis/halep-suspended-doping.html> accessed 13 May 2024.

160 The blood sample was collected on 22 September 2022.

161 Gene doping can be generally 'grouped into three different types: gene transfer, gene silencing and gene editing' according to Teruaki Tozaki and Natasha A Hamilton, 'Control of Gene Doping in Human and Horse Sports' (2022) 29 Gene Therapy 107, 107. One of the authors, Hamilton, is a member of WADA's Gene and Cell Doping Expert Advisory Group, which is overseen by the Health, Medical and Research (HM&R) Committee, a WADA Standing Committee. For more detail, see <https://www.wada-ama.org/en/gene-and-cell-doping-expert-advisory-group> and <https://www.wada-ama.org/en/health-medical-research-committee> accessed 13 May 2024.

162 Blair H Moses, 'Comment, Eligibility of Athletes Receiving Necessary Gene Therapy: The Oscar Pistorius Case as Procedural Precedent (2009) 49 Jurimetrics 343, 344.

163 David P Clark and Nanette J Pazdernik, *Biotechnology* (2nd edn, Elsevier Science 2015) 766. eBook.

164 ibid.

165 ibid.

166 It is interesting to note that the use goggles was introduced in 1976 – after this rule change most Olympic records were set: see Denrie Perez, 'The Technology Behind Speedo's High-Tech Swimsuits that Challenged the Olympics' (*Engineering.com*, 2 December 2020) <https://www.engineering.com/story/the-technology-behind-

was launched in February 2008. The LZR Racer swimsuit, designed by Speedo scientists and engineers, was made of 100% polyurethane panels and had 'no stitched seams'.[167] Within six weeks of the launch of the LZR, 13 world records were set, and a further 25 world records were achieved by athletes wearing the Speedo swimsuit at the Beijing Summer Olympics.[168] The suit compressed muscle and added buoyancy, which meant that swimmers could 'more easily go over the water, rather than through it'.[169] The suit was revolutionary and '[g]iven that air is more than 750 times less dense than water, the resulting friction was exceedingly important'.[170]

On 24 July 2009 the world governing body for swimming, FINA (Fédération Internationale de Natation, now World Aquatics), banned the LZR swimsuit. FINA tried to ban the LZR swimsuit prior to the World Championships in Rome in 2009. However, fearing legal action from some swimmers, it was decided to make the ban effective from January 2010. World Aquatics updates the list of approved swimwear on 1 September every year, in accordance with section 1.7 of World Aquatics Competitions Regulations.[171] **6–47**

World Aquatic rules provide only suits made from 'textiles' are permitted, including woven material. The swimsuit may not have any fastening devices such as a zipper (drawstrings on male jammers are permitted). The Regulations permit the use of LZR Racer jammers and kneeskins, however, it prohibits the full swimsuit.[172] The ban on LZR Racer applies only to World Championships and Olympic Games. The record-breaking abilities of the LZR were deemed to be performance-enhancing, a benefit that was initially only conferred on elite teams who were endorsed by Speedo, and the cost of $550 was prohibitive to competitors from poorer countries and thus created 'an unlevel playing field between the haves and have-nots'.[173] **6–48**

---

speedos-high-tech-swimsuits-that-challenged-the-olympics> accessed 13 May 2024.

167 Peter Merton McGinnis, *Biomechanics of Sport and Exercise* (Human Kinetics 2020) 7.

168 ibid. More than 90% of the gold medals were won by swimmers wearing the LZR.

169 Todd A McFall, Amanda L Griffith and Kurt W Rotthoff, 'The Impact of Technology and Rule Changes on Elite Swimming Performance' in Jill Harris (ed), *The Economics of Aquatic Sports* (Springer International Publishing 2020) 79. Speedo worked with NASA and university scientists in its quest to create the record-breaking swimsuit. To demonstrate the effectiveness of the LZR, the authors note that 14 records were set at the 2000 Olympics and eight at the 2004 Games.

170 ibid.

171 World Aquatics, 'World Aquatics Approved Swimwear' <https://www.worldaquatics.com/swimming/approved-swimwear> accessed 13 May 2024.

172 A list of the LZR jammers and kneeskins can be searched at <https://approved.swimwear.fina.org/> accessed 13 May 2024.

173 Meg Maher, 'The Impact of Invention on Sport' *Smithsonian Institution* (9 September 2019) <https://invention.si.edu/impact-invention-sport> accessed

6–49 In 2008, South African athlete Oscar Pistorius was prevented from competing in able-bodied events by the IAAF due to his 'Cheetah Flex-Foot' prosthetic legs which constituted technical devices and gave him an advantage over able-bodied athletes in breach of IAAF Competition Rule 144.2(e).[174] Pistorius, a double amputee since the age of 11 months who competed in the 100-, 200- and 400-metre sprint, challenged the ban before the CAS. A scientific study commissioned by the IAAF with the approval and participation of Pistorius found that 'the double transtibial amputee received significant biomechanical advantages by the prosthesis in comparison to sprinting with natural human legs'.[175] In confining its decision to the eligibility of Pistorius and his specific protheses, the CAS Panel asserted that the IAAF had not proven on the balance of probabilities that the athlete's 'passive device' provided him with 'an overall net advantage over other athletes'. The CAS Panel decision made him eligible to compete in the 2008 Olympics, however, he failed to qualify for the South African Olympic team. The athlete won three gold medals in the 100, 200 and 400 metre events at the Paralympics in September 2008.[176] Pistorius competed in both the able-bodied Olympics and Paralympics at the London Olympics in 2012. While he did not secure a medal, he was the first double amputee to compete in the able-bodied Olympics. He won two gold and one silver medal in the 2012 Paralympics.

6–50 In a more recent case involving protheses, American athlete Blake Leeper, a bilateral transtibial amputee sprinter who runs in the 400-metre event, challenged before the CAS a decision of the IAAF not to let him compete in the 2020 Olympic Games due to his passive-elastic carbon-fibre running-specific prostheses (RSPs).[177] The IAAF held that Leeper, on the balance of probabilities, had not demonstrated that his RSPs 'would not provide him with an overall competitive advantage over an athlete not using such prostheses'.[178] The RSPs gave Leeper an overall standing height of 189.2 cm, making his height 15cm over the International Paralympic Committee (IPC) and World Para Athletics'

13 May 2024. The author notes that, surprisingly, FINA allowed the records to remain. Since the 2010 ban, records continue to be broken, however, 'at a more moderate pace'.

174 CAS 2008/A/1480 *Pistorius v/ IAAF* award of 16 May 2008 <https://jurisprudence.tas-cas.org/Shared%20Documents/1480.pdf> accessed 13 May 2024.

175 World Athletics, 'Oscar Pistorius – Independent Scientific Study Concludes that Cheetah Prosthetics Offer Clear Mechanical Advantages' (14 January 2008) <https://worldathletics.org/news/news/oscar-pistorius-independent-scientific-stud-1> accessed 13 May 2024.

176 International Paralympic Committee, 'Oscar Pistorius' <https://www.paralympic.org/oscar-pistorius> accessed 13 May 2024.

177 CAS 2020/A/6807 *Blake Leeper v International Association of Athletics Federations* award of 23 October 2020 [1] and [3] <https://www.tas-cas.org/fileadmin/user_upload/Award__6807___for_publication_.pdf> accessed 13 May 2024.

178 ibid [5].

Maximum Allowable Standing Height (MASH) rule.[179] In dismissing the appeal, the CAS Panel found that the IAAF had

> established on a balance of probabilities that the particular running specific prostheses used by Mr. Blake Leeper give him an overall competitive advantage over an athlete not using such a mechanical aid. Accordingly, Blake Leeper may not use his particular running specific prostheses in the Olympic Games or World Athletics Series competitions.[180]

Leeper unsuccessfully tried to appeal the CAS award to the Swiss Federal Tribunal (SFT). In a second appeal to the CAS, Lepper challenged the decision of World Athletics' Mechanical Aids Review Panel.[181] On 24 December 2020, Leeper applied to the Mechanical Aids Review Panel to allow him use particular RSPs: **6–51**

> in the same competition as able-bodied athletes in World Athletics sanctioned 400 metre events, including (if selected) the 2021 Tokyo Olympic Games, and any qualification events leading up to the Olympic Games. Subsequent to that application, by arrangements between Mr Leeper and World Athletics, an extensive testing regime was undertaken by Mr Leeper at the Southern Methodist University in Texas, USA, over several weeks in February and March 2021.[182]

On 26 April 2021, the Mechanical Aids Review Panel found that the RSPs gave Leeper a competitive advantage and he was not permitted to use them at any World Athletics-sanctioned events as they were in contravention of Technical Rule 6.3.4.[183] The CAS Panel in *Leeper v World Athletics (WA)* considered the proportionality and reasonableness of the decision Mechanical Aids Review Panel along with the possibility of **6–52**

---

179 ibid [378]. For the most recent MASH rules, see World Para Athletics Rules and Regulations (March 2024) Appendix 3, 270–87 <https://www.paralympic.org/sites/default/files/2024-03/World%20Para%20Athletics%20Rules%20and%20Regulations_March%202024_0.pdf> accessed 13 May 2024.

180 ibid [391].

181 For more detail, see World Athletics, 'Mechanical Aids Regulations (Approved by Council on 10 March 2022 and effective from 25 March 2022) < https://www.worldathletics.org/download/download?filename=66b24876-a6d2-46a0-9f33-c311ab921b18.pdf&urlslug=C2.1B%20-%20Mechanical%20Aids%20Regulations> accessed 13 May 2024.

182 Decision of World Athletics Mechanical Aids Review Panel, In the matter of an Application by Blake Leeper dated 21 April 2021 [3] <https://www.worldathletics.org/download/download?filename=3a466903-081c-4f64-95d2-b4d6512c0730.pdf&urlslug=Decision&_gl=1*esmulw*_ga*MTUzOTc0MzE0NS4xNjg5MDg1MjEy*_ga_7FE9YV46NW*MTcxMjQ0NjgyMy45LjEuMTcxMjQ0NzE1OS4wLjAuMA> accessed 13 May 2024.

183 ibid [58]. A summary of the decision is available here <https://worldathletics.org/news/press-releases/world-athletics-panel-decision-application-from-blake-leeper?_gl=1*onnbi8*_ga*MTUzOTc0MzE0NS4xNjg5MDg1MjEy*_ga_7FE9YV46NW*MTcxMjQ0NjgyMy45LjEuMTcxMjQ0NzE1MS4wLjAuMA> accessed 13 May 2024.

other practical, workable alternatives.[184] In dismissing the appeal and upholding the decision of the Mechanical Aids Review Panel, the CAS Panel found that Leeper had not explained 'to the Panel why, as he contended, Rule 6.3.4 was not a necessary, reasonable or proportionate way of achieving WA's legitimate objective of ensuring the fairness and integrity of competition'.[185] In the absence of workable alternatives, the CAS Panel could not 'adopt a novel alternative to the requirement that, in order to compete in WA-sanctioned events, Mr Leeper must run at his MASH height'.[186] Furthermore, the CAS Panel could not establish, due to lack of medical evidence, that running at his MASH height that Leeper was exposed to any risks.[187] The CAS Panel acknowledged that Leeper did not have sufficient time to acclimatise himself to MASH-compliant RSPs for the US trials for the Tokyo Olympics; however, he would have time to acclimatise for the 2022 Indoor and Outdoor World Championships.[188]

Detection and Testing Procedures

6–53 Sport Ireland conducts both direct and indirect detection. Direct detection refers to urine and blood analysis. In 2023, Sport Ireland began using a new method, Dried Blood Spot (DBS) Testing.[189] DBS involves the collection of a few drops of blood from the athlete's fingertips or upper arm. It is considered minimally invasive, quick, cost-effective, and requires only a few droplets of blood.[190] DBS, while innovative, will be used in addition to rather than replace the traditional testing methods of urine and blood.[191]

6–54 Indirect detection refers to the ABP which entails testing over a period of time in order to analyse biological parameters.[192] As explained in

[184] CAS 2021/A/7930 award of 4 November 2021 <https://jurisprudence.tas-cas.org/Shared%20Documents/7930.pdf> accessed 13 May 2024.

[185] ibid [164].

[186] ibid [166].

[187] ibid [167].

[188] ibid.

[189] Sport Ireland, 'Dried Blood Spots' < https://www.sportireland.ie/dried-blood-spots> accessed 13 May 2024.

[190] Sport Ireland, 'Dried Blood Spot (DBS) Testing' <https://www.sportireland.ie/sites/default/files/media/document/2023-05/DBS%20Factsheet.pdf> accessed 13 May 2024.

[191] DBS was approved by WADA in 2021: see World Anti-Doping Agency, 'With Dried Blood Spot Analysis, Anti-Doping Science Is Pushing the Boundaries at Beijing 2022 and Beyond' 15 February 2022 <https://www.wada-ama.org/en/news/dried-blood-spot-analysis-anti-doping-science-pushing-boundaries-beijing-2022-and-beyond> accessed 13 May 2024.

[192] For more details, see Sport Ireland, 'Sample Collection Procedures – Urine & Blood' (April 2020) 2 <https://www.sportireland.ie/sites/default/files/media/document/2020-05/scp-procedures-leaflet.pdf> accessed 13 May 2024. The CAS upheld the ABP in TAS 2010/A/2308 *Franco Pellizotti c Comitato Olimpico Nazionale Italiano (CONI) & Union Cycliste Internationale (UCI)* et *TAS 2011/A/2335 UCI c*

Sport Ireland's 2022 Anti-Doping Report, it 'is a longitudinal profile of a number of samples collected from individual athletes that can indirectly reveal the effects of doping rather than direct detection of doping'.[193] In 2009, WADA's Executive Committee approved the Athlete Biological Passport Operating Guidelines (ABP Guidelines), which came into effect on 1 December 2009.[194] The term ABP was 'coined in the early 2000s by anti-doping's scientific community when monitoring selected haematological variables over time in order to uncover blood doping'.[195] The first module was introduced in December 2009, the Haematological Module, which 'considers a panel of biomarkers of blood doping that are measured in an athlete's blood sample'.[196] The second module, the Steroidal Module, introduced in January 2014, 'considers a panel of biomarkers of steroid doping measured in an athlete's urine sample'.[197] *Pechstein* discussed below and *Halep* above both concern the ABP.[198]

In theory, every national-level Irish athlete and every sport, in accordance with the Irish Anti-Doping Rules, may be subject to indirect detection. However, Sport Ireland has limited the ABP to endurance sports and power sports. According to the 2022 Annual Report, 313 ABP blood samples were collected by Sport Ireland. There were 87 samples collected from athletics, four in boxing, six in canoeing, 44 in cycling, five in modern pentathlon, three in Paralympics athletics, 29 in Paralympics cycling, 61 in rowing, 45 in swimming, and 29 in triathlon.[199] **6–55**

Testing can take place either in-competition or out-of-competition.[200] If the event is taking place at national level and in-competition, Sport **6–56**

Franco Pellizotti, Federazione Ciclistica Italiana (FCI) & CONI award of 14 June 2011 <https://jurisprudence.tas-cas.org/Shared%20Documents/2308,%202335.pdf> accessed 13 May 2024. The decision is available only in French.

193 Annual Anti-Doping Report 2022 (n 71) 20.

194 World Anti-Doping Agency, 'Athlete Biological Passport' <https://www.wada-ama.org/en/athlete-biological-passport> accessed 13 May 2024.

195 World Anti-Doping Agency, 'WADA's Athlete Biological Passport: An Important Tool for Protecting Clean Sport' (19 August 2021) <https://www.wada-ama.org/en/news/wadas-athlete-biological-passport-important-tool-protecting-clean-sport> accessed 13 May 2024.

196 ibid.

197 ibid.

198 CAS 2009/A/1912 *Claudia Pechstein v International Skating Union and CAS 2009/A/1913 Deutsche Eisschnelllauf Gemeinshaft eV v International Skating Union* award of 25 November 2009 <https://jurisprudence.tas-cas.org/Shared%20Documents/1912,%201913.pdf> accessed 13 May 2024.

199 Annual Anti-Doping Report 2022 (n 71) 20. The Athlete Passport Management Unit (APMU) is a dedicated unit that is responsible for the ABP programme. An APMU must be hosted independently in a WADA-accredited laboratory. Sport Ireland uses a laboratory in Oslo for the management of blood passports and Cologne for the management of steroidal passports: see Annual Anti-Doping Report 2022 (n 71) 21. The total figure provided states 299, however, on calculation of the individual numbers, it adds up to 313.

200 See (n 66) for the definition of 'In-Competition'. Out-of-Competition is simply defined as '[a]ny period which is not In-Competition'.

Ireland initiates and directs the collection of samples.[201] If it is an international event and in-competition, the international organisation which is the ruling body for the event initiates and directs the collection of the samples, subject to the right of Sport Ireland to initiate and conduct the testing.[202] The following organisations are permitted to initiate out-of-competition testing: WADA, Sport Ireland, the IF, the IOC or International Paralympics Games in connection with the Olympic or Paralympic Games, and any other anti-doping organisation that has jurisdiction over the athlete.[203] Athletes who are part of the RTP must provide information about their whereabouts and can be tested at home, at the training ground, any other relevant location, and overseas.[204] National teams and squads are usually tested at their training ground, however, they can be tested at their homes.[205] There is a User Pays Programme, whereby governing bodies can request extra testing, for which Sport Ireland is paid to carry out these tests. In 2022, there were 196 User Pays tests, consisting of 172 urine tests and 24 blood tests.[206]

6–57 Minors (under 18) may be tested with the consent of their parents or guardians.[207] The testing of minors is carried out in line with Annex B of the International Standard for Testing and Investigations (ISTI).[208] The ISTI has several requirements, including the right of a minor athlete to request that an athlete representative is present in the area where the urine sample is being provided.[209] If the minor athlete does not wish for the athlete representative to be present, they may liaise with the Chaperone/Doping Control Officer (DCO) to organise another appropriate person to be present when the testing is taking place.[210]

6–58 An athlete, if selected for testing, is required to sign the Doping Control Form, and must inform the DCO if they are taking any medications or have a TUE.[211] The athlete will be asked to provide a urine or blood sample. Before providing the urine sample, the athlete must put on gloves. They then choose a sealed Sample Collection Vessel from a choice

---

201 ibid art 5.4.1.

202 ibid art 5.4.2.

203 There should be coordination between the various bodies so that athletes are not tested repeatedly.

204 Sample Collection Procedures-Urine & Blood (n 192) 3.

205 ibid.

206 Annual Anti-Doping Report 2022 (n 71) 17.

207 Irish Sport Anti-Doping Rules (n 40) art 5.6.2. A minor may not compete in a sport unless the parent or guardian consents to the testing of the minor.

208 ibid art 5.6.1. For more information, see World Anti-Doping Code, 'The International Standard for Testing and Investigations 2023' 63–64 <https://www.wada-ama.org/sites/default/files/2022-12/isti_2023_w_annex_k_final_clean.pdf> accessed 13 May 2024.

209 The International Standard for Testing and Investigations (n 208).

210 ibid B.4.3. If an athlete representative cannot be located, then two Sample Collection Personnel must always accompany the minor athlete until their Sample Collection Session is completed.

211 Sample Collection Procedures-Urine & Blood (n 192) 4.

of vessels, which the athlete must check to ensure that the seal has not been tampered with and is intact, before going to the toilet area with the DCO/Chaperone of the same gender.[212] The DCO/Chaperone must have an unobstructed view of the urine leaving the athlete's body and going into the Sample Collection Vessel.[213] A sample of 9mls is required, if below this, the Partial Sample Procedure applies. The athlete holds on to the Sample Collection Vessel, which is sealed and secured with partial sample equipment, until further urine is collected.[214]

Once the collection of the urine sample is complete, the athlete chooses a kit containing a pair of bottles marked A and B, on confirming that the seals have not been broken or tampered with, the athlete ensures that the sample code numbers match.[215] The athlete divides the samples between bottles A and B and tightly seals on the lids. **6–59**

Regarding providing a blood test, the athlete is asked to present their non-dominant arm and a tourniquet is used by a certified and experienced phlebotomist, referred to as the Blood Collection Officer (BCO).[216] After choosing a kit, the athlete's blood sample is collected in two to four tubes of blood, each containing 3–5mls.[217] The samples are divided in two vacutainer blood test tubes, labelled A and B.[218] The athlete tightly seals the two test tubes which are placed in transport containers.[219] An athlete must disclose if they recently had a blood transfusion and if they are currently taking any medications or supplements.[220] **6–60**

The blood and urine samples are sent to a WADA-accredited laboratory and no personal information is recorded on the copy of Doping Control Form furnished.[221] Following security checks to ensure the integrity of the samples, the A sample is tested while the B sample is safely stored.[222] On completion of the analysis of the samples, the laboratory informs Sport Ireland of the result who forwards it on to the NGB, who must inform the athlete in writing of the result.[223] Blood tested as part of the ABP is not furnished to the athlete; it is recorded on the ABP and the NGB is informed. If the athlete wishes to see the results, they must request it directly from Sport Ireland.[224] Sport Ireland informs WADA and other relevant anti-doping organisations of 'a potential anti-doping **6–61**

[212] ibid 6.
[213] ibid.
[214] ibid 7.
[215] ibid 6. The sample code number is noted on the Doping Control Form.
[216] ibid 7.
[217] ibid.
[218] ibid.
[219] ibid.
[220] ibid 8.
[221] ibid.
[222] ibid.
[223] ibid 9. A copy is also sent to WADA by the laboratory.
[224] ibid 9.

violation' prior to informing the athlete and their NGB, using the Anti-Doping Administration & Management System (ADAMS).[225] ADAMS acts as a central database and will show if an athlete has a prior ADRV.

6–62 On being informed of a ADRV or an Adverse Passport Finding, Sport Ireland will impose a mandatory Provisional Suspension where it does not involve a Specified Substance or a Specified Method.[226] The mandatory Provisional Suspension will not apply, however, if the athlete or other person can establish that the violation is likely due to a contaminated product, or it relates to a Substance of Abuse (as discussed above).[227] Sport Ireland may impose an Optional Provisional Suspension where there is an AAF for Specified Substances, Specified Methods, Contaminated Products or other ADRVs.[228] Before the Provisional Suspension may be imposed, the athlete or other person has the right to attend a Provisional Heading, or in situations where the Provisional Suspension has been invoked, the hearing takes place on a 'timely basis' after its imposition.[229] Provisional Hearings are heard by a single arbitrator who is either the Chair or a Vice-Chair of the ISADDP. An athlete may voluntarily accept the Provisional Suspension on the expiration of 10 days from the report of the B sample or the waiver of the B sample. [230] Where 'the B sample analysis (if requested by the Athlete or Sport Ireland) does not confirm the A Sample analysis, then the Athlete shall not be subject to any further Provisional Suspension on account of a violation of Article 2.1'. [231] As discussed above, the athlete may contest the findings of the AAF at an ISADDP hearing.

6–63 If an athlete fails an in-competition test, any results, titles, medals or points from the competition or event are forfeited.[232] If the athlete establishes that the doping violation was due to no fault or negligence on their part, the results of other competitions are not forfeited unless it was likely that the results were affected by the doping violation.[233]

---

[225] Irish Sport Anti-Doping Rules (n 40) art 7.3. See also World Anti-Doping Agency, 'ADAMS' <https://www.wada-ama.org/en/what-we-do/adams> accessed 13 May 2024.

[226] Irish Sport Anti-Doping Rules (n 40) art 7.5.1.

[227] ibid arts 7.5.1.1 and 7.5.1.2.

[228] ibid art 7.5.2.

[229] ibid art 7.5.3.

[230] ibid art 7.5.4.1. Article 7.5.4.2 refers to 'Other Persons' voluntarily accepting a Provisional Suspension within 10 days of the notification of the ADRV.

[231] ibid art 7.5.5. If an athlete has been removed from a team competing at an Event, and the B sample does not confirm the findings of the A sample, 'it is still possible for the Athlete or team to be reinserted, the Athlete or team may continue to take part in the Event'.

[232] ibid art 9.1.

[233] ibid art 9.2.2.

Periods of Ineligibility

The periods of ineligibility vary depending on the seriousness of the anti-doping violation and whether there is no significant fault or negligence or whether the doping infraction was unintentional. Article 10 categorises ineligibility into the following: **6–64**

1. Ineligibility for the Presence, Use or Attempted Use, or Possession of a Prohibited Substance or Prohibited Method under Article 10.1 – this carries a four-year ineligibility sanction with a potential reduction under Articles 10.3 (Evading, Refusing or Failing to Submit to Sample Collection), 10.4 (Whereabouts Failures by an Athlete) and 10.5 (Tampering or Attempted Tampering with any Part of Doping Control). The four-year ban applies in situations where Sport Ireland can establish that the violation of the rules is intentional and involves a specified prohibited substance.[234] If it can be shown that the breach of the rules was unintentional, the period of ineligibility may be reduced to two years, as per Article 10.1.2.
2. Ineligibility for Other Anti-Doping Rule Violations under Article 10.2 – this applies to Article 2.3 and Article 2.5. This carries a four-year ban, unless in relation to Article 2.3 it can be shown that it was unintentional, then the suspension is reduced to two years.[235] An athlete who commits three whereabouts failures in 12 months, as provided for under Article 2.4, faces a two-year period of ineligibility, however, this may be reduced to one year depending on the degree of fault.[236] It will not be possible to get the reduction of one year if the athlete often changes their whereabouts at the last minute or their conduct raises suspicions that they are trying to evade testing.[237] A four-year ban or a lifetime ban may be imposed in the case of Trafficking or Attempted Trafficking in any Prohibited Substance or Prohibited Method (Article 2.7) and the Administration or Attempted Administration to any Athlete In-Competition and Out-of-Competition of any Prohibited Substance or Prohibited Method (Article 2.8).[238] A lifetime ban will be applied to support personnel in situations where the athlete is a Protected Person.[239] These infractions may also come within the remit of the criminal justice system and expose those involved to criminal prosecution. Under Article 2.9, anyone who aids, abets, conspires, covers up or any other type of intentional complicity or attempted complicity, the commission of a doping infraction may face a four-year or two-year period of ineligibility, depending on the seriousness of the violation.
3. Aggravating Circumstances which may Increase the Period of

---

234 ibid art 10.2.1.
235 ibid art 10.2.1.
236 ibid art 10.1.1.2.
237 ibid art 10.2.2.
238 ibid art 10.2.3.
239 ibid Appendix 1: Definitions, p 79 defines a Protected Person as '[a]n Athlete or other natural Person who at the time of the anti-doping rule violation: (i) has not reached the age of sixteen years; (ii) has not reached the age of eighteen years and is not included in any Registered Testing Pool and has never competed in any International Event in an open category; or (iii) for reasons other than age has been determined to lack legal capacity under applicable national legislation'.

Ineligibility under Article 10.3 – if aggravating circumstances are present, apart from violations under Articles 2.7, 2.8, 2.9, and 2.11, Sport Ireland or the NGB where applicable can impose an additional period of ineligibility of up to two years, depending on the 'seriousness of the violation and the nature of the Aggravating Circumstances'.

4. Elimination of the Period of Ineligibility where there is No Fault or Negligence under Article 10.4 – this applies only in the most exceptional of circumstances as explained by a footnote in the Irish Sport Anti-Doping Rules.[240] Article 10.4 could be invoked 'where an Athlete could prove that, despite all due care, he or she was sabotaged by a competitor'.[241]
5. Reduction of the Period of Ineligibility based on No Significant Fault or Negligence under Article 10.5 – this relates to specified substances (Article 10.5.1.1.) and contaminated products (Article 10.5.1.2). In this situation, the athlete must establish how the prohibited substance entered their system. At a minimum the athlete will be reprimanded, and no period of ineligibility will be imposed; the maximum sanction is two years of ineligibility depending on the degree of fault. Regarding contaminated products, the sanctions under Article 10.5.1.1 apply. As with specified substances, the athlete must demonstrate no significant fault or negligence.[242]
6. Elimination, Reduction, or Suspension of Period of Ineligibility or other Consequences for Reasons other than Fault under Article 10.6 – the period of ineligibility may be reduced if the athlete or other person has provided substantial assistance in discovering or establishing a violation of the anti-doping rules.[243] If there is admission of an infringement of the rules in the absence of other evidence,[244] the period of ineligibility may be reduced 'but not below one-half of the period of *Ineligibility* otherwise applicable'.[245] If an athlete can establish 'multiple grounds for a reduction of a sanction', the ban may be reduced to a quarter of the period of ineligibility.[246]
7. Results Management Agreements under Article 2.7 – if an athlete or other person are facing a four year or more period of ineligibility, they may receive a reduction of one year for certain ADRVs due to early admission and the acceptance of a sanction. They have 20 days after the notification of the ADRV to admit the violation and accept the sanction. The consequences which the athlete or other person agrees to will be those that Sport Ireland and WADA deem acceptable, as provided for under Article 10.7.2.
8. Multiple Violations under Article 10.8 – a second doping violation will result in a period of ineligibility over six months, one half of the period of ineligibility of the first violation or twice the period of

---

240 ibid 47, fn 63.

241 ibid. The footnote adds that there are several situations where No Fault or Negligence would apply: for example, where a positive test results from a mislabelled or contaminated vitamin or nutritional supplement. This is because the athlete is responsible for what they ingest, as provided for under art 2.1.1, 'and have been warned against the possibility of supplement contamination'.

242 The same sanction applies to Protected Person and Recreational Athletes, with the exception of a Substance of Abuse, see art 10.5.1.3.

243 ibid art 10.6.1.1.

244 ibid art 10.6.2.

245 ibid.

246 ibid art 10.6.3.

> ineligibility.[247] A third anti-doping violation will result in a lifetime ban, unless the third violation fulfils the criteria for a reduced period of ineligibility, or the athlete has a third violation of Article 2.4 or 2.5, in which case the period of ineligibility may be reduced from a lifetime ban to eight years.[248] If an athlete or other person has established no fault or negligence in a previous case, this is not considered a prior violation for the purpose of Article 10.8.[249]

Any athlete who is suspended may not take part in any competitions or events during the currency of their suspension. If the athlete participates in a competition or event, the period of ineligibility starts over again from the date of the violation.[250] Article 11 details the testing and sanctions for team sports where more than one member has been found to have committed a doping infraction. Article 12 provides for sanctions for NGBs, which may result in Sport Ireland withdrawing financial and non-financial support. Article 13 details the appeal process. Article 14 outlines the role of Sport Ireland in reporting to WADA, the applicable NGB and any other relevant anti-doping agency of whereabouts failures, reporting of all tests carried out in- and out-of-competition on athletes in the RTP to WADA, reporting information concerning AAFs and other alleged ADRVs; reporting compliance with the WADA code; and the publishing of statistics.[251] Sport Ireland is required, after 20 days of the final appeal hearing or where an appeal has been waived, to publish the name of the athlete who has been found to have committed a doping offence.[252] If the athlete is found not to have committed an offence, they may request that their name is not published; a summary of the decision may be published after Sport Ireland has used reasonable efforts to obtain the consent of the athlete. If consent is obtained, a redacted version of the decision may be published as approved by the athlete or other person.[253] **6–65**

Whereabouts Rule

In 2003, the WADC introduced the whereabouts rule under Article 2.4, which was titled 'Violation of applicable requirements regarding Athlete availability for Out-of-Competition Testing including failure to provide required whereabouts information and missed tests which are declared based on reasonable rules'.[254] Halt refers to the article as defining 'vague **6–66**

---

[247] ibid art 10.8.1.1 (a) and (b).

[248] ibid art 10.8.1.2.

[249] ibid art 10.8.2. See also art 10.8.3 relating to Additional Rules for Certain Potential Multiple Violations and art 10.8.4 concerning Multiple Anti-Doping Rule Violations During Ten Year Period.

[250] ibid art 10.10.3. The decision may be appealed under art 13.

[251] ibid art 14.2 provides for confidentiality and art 14.3 refers to privacy.

[252] ibid arts 15.3 and 15.4. However, art 15.5 provides that mandatory reporting does not apply where the athlete is a Minor, Protected Person, or Recreational Athlete.

[253] ibid arts 15.3 and 15.6.

[254] World Anti-Doping Agency, 'World Anti-Doping Code 2003' <https://www.

and loose requirements' with much discretion given to the IF and the NADO. [255] Until 2009 athletes were required to select one hour per day, five days a week to be available for unannounced drug tests. These tests could take place at home or at the training ground. However, on 1 January 2009, changes were introduced that requires athletes to be available seven days a week and, unlike the previous system, athletes have to be available for the full hour.[256] In Belgium, 65 athletes challenged the 2009 whereabouts rules, with the case against the Flemish regional government as it was responsible for anti-doping in the Dutch-speaking region of Flanders.[257] The challenge was based on the protection of the right to privacy under the Belgian Constitution and under Article 8 (right to privacy) of the ECHR.[258] Questions were raised as to the compatibility of the whereabouts rule and the Working Time Directive, which limits the average working time for each seven-day period that must not exceed 48 hours, including overtime.[259] In conjunction with the WADA's Canadian-based ADAMS wherein athletes submit their whereabouts information, the issue of surveillance and privacy have, in the words of Duval, represent a 'Foucauldian turn of the anti-doping fight. In practice it is looking more and more like a panopticon, devised to optimize the surveillance of athletes, while irremediably failing to do so.' [260] The Article 29 Data Protection Working Party[261] established under Article

wadaama.org/sites/default/files/resources/files/wada_code_2003_en.pdf> accessed 13 May 2024.

255 James Halt, 'Where Is the Privacy in WADA's "Whereabouts" Rule?' (2009) 20(1) Marquette Sports Law Review 267, 269–70 <http://scholarship.law.marquette.edu/sportslaw/vol20/iss1/12> accessed 13 May 2024.

256 WADA includes a questions-and-answer section on the website regarding the whereabouts system: <http://www.wada-ama.org/en/Resources1/Q-and-A/Whereabouts/> accessed 13 May 2024.

257 Matt Slater, 'Legal Threat to Anti-Doping Code" (*BBC Sport*, 22 January 2009) <http://news.bbc.co.uk/sport2/hi/front_page/7844918.stm> accessed 13 May 2024.

258 ibid. There is no information on what happened with the case; however, as the whereabouts rule is still in force, it would seem that the case did not progress or was dismissed by the Flemish court.

259 Directive 2003/88/EC of the European Parliament and of the Council of 4 November 2003 concerning certain aspects of the organisation of working time, OJ L 299. Article 1(1) states, 'This Directive lays down minimum safety and health requirements for the organisation of working time. 2. This Directive applies to: (a) minimum periods of daily rest, weekly rest and annual leave, to breaks and maximum weekly working time; and (b) certain aspects of night work, shift work and patterns of work.'

260 Antoine Duval, 'Right to Privacy 1:0 Whereabouts Requirement – A Case Note on a Recent Decision by the Spanish Audiencia Nacional' (*Asser International Sports Law Bog*, 29 July 2014) <https://www.asser.nl/SportsLaw/Blog/post/right-to-privacy-1-whereabouts-requirement-0-a-case-note-on-a-recent-decision-by-the-spanish-audiencia-nacional#_ftn12> accessed 13 May 2024. See also Dag Vidar Hanstad and Sigmund Loland, 'Elite Athletes' Duty to Provide Information on their Whereabouts: Justifiable Anti-Doping Work or an Indefensible Surveillance Regime?' (2009) 9(1) European Journal of Sport Science 3. The writers discuss the principles of autonomy and the right to self-determination.

261 'Second opinion 4/2009 on the World Anti-Doping Agency (WADA) International Standard for the Protection of Privacy and Personal Information, on related provisions of the WADA Code and on other privacy issues in the context of the

29 of Directive 95/46/EC[262] reiterated its support for WADA, however, it insisted on 'pursuing this fight with respect for the fundamental rights of athletes and their entourage, particularly for the right to protection of their privacy and personal data'.[263]

The whereabouts rule was challenged by the Fédération Nationale des Syndicats Sportifs (FNASS) and Others against France before the European Court of Human Rights (ECtHR).[264] FNASS, a syndicate comprising football, rugby, handball and basketball players, and one cyclist, challenged the whereabouts rule under Article 8(1) of the ECHR ,which provides for the respect for family and private life.[265] The ECtHR found that there was no violation of Article 8(1) as the whereabouts rule served a legitimate aim under Article 8(2) in that it concerned the protection of health and ensured fairness of sports competitions, which provided 'protection of the rights and freedoms of others'. The ECtHR stated: **6–67**

> Indeed, the use of prohibited substances to gain an advantage over other

fight against doping in sport by WADA and (national) anti-doping organizations' adopted 6 April 2009, 0 746/09/EN WP 162 <https://ec.europa.eu/justice/article-29/documentation/opinion-recommendation/files/2009/wp162_en.pdf> accessed 13 May 2024.

[262] Directive 95/46/EC of the European Parliament and of the Council of 24 October 1995 on the protection of individuals with regard to the processing of personal data and on the free movement of such data, OJ L 281. This Directive was repealed by Regulation (EU) 2016/679 of the European Parliament and of the Council of 27 April 2016 on the protection of natural persons with regard to the processing of personal data and on the free movement of such data, and repealing Directive 95/46/EC (General Data Protection Regulation) OJ L 119.

[263] Second opinion (n 261) 18. The opinion expressed concerns over the transfer of data under ADAMS and concluded: 'in the light of the proportionality principle ... the Working Party invites WADA and anti-doping organisations to reassess the collection of Whereabouts as it is conceived today, and more in general, the current retention period of processed data'.

[264] *National Federation of Sportspersons' Associations and Unions (FNASS) and Others v France* – 48151/11 and 77769/13, Judgment 18 January 2018 <https://hudoc.echr.coe.int/eng#{%22itemid%22:[%22002-11815%22]}> accessed 13 May 2024. For information on how the EtCHR operates and the applicants that bring cases, see van der Sloot (n 4) 190–92. See also European Court of Human Rights, 'Questions and Answers' <https://www.echr.coe.int/documents/d/echr/questions_answers_eng> accessed 5 July 2024.

[265] Article 8 ECHR states: '1. Everyone has the right to respect for his private and family life, his home and his correspondence. 2. There shall be no interference by a public authority with the exercise of this right except such as is in accordance with the law and is necessary in a democratic society in the interests of national security, public safety or the economic wellbeing of the country, for the prevention of disorder or crime, for the protection of health or morals, or for the protection of the rights and freedoms of others.' They also challenged it under art 2 of Protocol No 4 on the right to freedom of movement, which they contended was infringed by virtue of the whereabouts rule. Article 2 of Protocol 4 was deemed inapplicable as the whereabouts rule did not impede their leaving their country of residence, they just had to provide information on where they would be residing. A detailed guide on Article 2 of Protocol 4 is available at <https://www.echr.coe.int/documents/d/echr/Guide_Art_2_Protocol_4_ENG> accessed 13 May 2024.

> athletes unfairly eliminated competitors of the same level who did not have recourse to them, dangerously encouraging amateurs and especially young people to follow suit in order to enhance their performance, and thus deprived spectators of the fair competition which they legitimately expected.[266]

6–68 In ascertaining the necessity of such an interference in a democratic society under Article 8(2), it required a balancing of the rights of the member state (France) and the applicants. In examining the dangers of doping and the common consensus of 'European and international views on the need for unannounced testing, which was made possible partly through the whereabouts mechanism, as shown in various international instruments, which reflected a continuous development of the applicable norms and principles', the ECtHR unanimously found there was no violation of Article 8(1).

6–69 Under the current whereabouts rule, athletes that are part of RTP which includes elite athletes, those who have qualified for the Olympics and Paralympics, must furnish on quarterly basis (every three months) the following information to their anti-doping agency: 'home address, email address and phone number, an address for overnight accommodation, regular activities, such as training, work, and school, the locations and the times of these activities, competition schedules and locations'.[267] They must provide a 60-minute time slot for each day where they will be available and accessible for testing. As discussed above, an athlete who commits three whereabouts failures in 12 months as provided for under Article 2.4 faces a two-year period of ineligibility, however, this may be reduced to one year depending on the degree of fault.[268] However, it will not be possible to get the reduction of one year if the athlete often changes their whereabouts at the last minute or their conduct raises suspicions that they are trying to evade testing.[269]

Human Rights and Anti-Doping Procedures

6–70 WADA recently announced that it has instigated an Initial Human Rights Impact Assessment (IHRIA) to examine the intersection between the anti-doping rules and the human rights of athletes.[270] Its practical

---

266 *FNASS* (n 264).

267 World Anti-Doping Agency, 'Provide Whereabouts' <https://www.wada-ama.org/en/athletes-support-personnel/provide-whereabouts> accessed 13 May 2024. There is a useful guide provided by WADA titled 'Athlete Whereabouts at a Glance' <https://www.wada-ama.org/sites/default/files/2022-03/At_a_Glance_Whereabouts_English_Live_2021.pdf> accessed 13 May 2024.

268 Irish Sport Anti-Doping Rules (n 40) art 10.1.1.2. Aside from ADAMS, athletes may submit and upload their whereabouts details on an app called 'Athlete Central'.

269 Irish Sport Anti-Doping Rules (n 40) art 10.2.2.

270 World Anti-Doping Agency, 'WADA Initiates Assessment to Ensure that the Human Rights of Athletes Are Respected under the World Anti-Doping Program' 7 March 2023 <https://www.wada-ama.org/en/news/wada-initiates-assessment-

significance remains to be seen. For many years it has been argued that urine and blood testing are invasive as blood testing requires the use of a needle to puncture the skin and urine testing involves a DCO closely watching the athlete's genitalia.[271] Less invasive alternatives 'such as saliva or hair have not been identified'.[272] The introduction of DBS Testing as discussed above is considered less invasive, however, it still involves the extraction of blood, albeit in lesser amounts. It has never been explained by WADA why other alternatives have not been explored.[273] The whereabouts rule, as discussed above, has been unsuccessfully challenged under the right to privacy. The ABP has raised concerns among those who view the longitudinal profiling as an invasion of privacy. The ABP does not detect doping but 'changes in biological markers collated over an athlete's career'.[274] As athletes store their confidential information on databases, a data breach could have significant consequences for an athlete.[275] While the CAS decision in *WADA v Sun Yang and FINA* did not reference Article 8 of the ECHR, the issue of privacy was raised by the athlete.[276] Sun Yang, a swimmer, tested positive for a prohibited substance. It was his second doping violation. FINA contended that the swimmer's test had not been properly conducted and therefore did not impose a period of ineligibility on Yang. WADA objected to the leniency and appealed the decision of FINA to the CAS. WADA was seeking a period of ineligibility ranging from two years at a minimum to eight years at a maximum. On 28 February 2020, the CAS Panel published its decision and declared a period of ineligibility of eight years for the AAF.[277] The swimmer referred the matter to the SFT, where he sought an annulment of the CAS decision on the grounds of alleged biased comments that had been expressed on social media

---

ensure-human-rights-athletes-are-respected-under-world-anti-doping> accessed 13 May 2024.

[271] van der Sloot (n 4) 200. The issue of privacy and urine testing has been raised in some cases involving high school and college athletes from the US, including *Earls v Board of Education* F 3rd 1264, 1276 (10th Cir 2001); *Todd* v *Rush County Schools and Ed Lyskowinski* 133 F 3d 984 (7th Cir 1998); *Vernonia School Dist 47J v Wayne Acton* 115 S Ct 2386 (1995). In *University of Colorado v Derdeyn* 863 P 2d 929 (Colo 1993) the university drug testing policy was challenged as it not only tested student athletes but also the cheerleaders, student trainers and managers. See Laura Donnellan, 'The Right to Privacy and Drug Testing: An Irish Perspective' (2002) 10(5) Sports Law Administration and Practice 11.

[272] van der Sloot (n 4) 200.

[273] ibid.

[274] Dhruv Mahendru and others, 'Athlete Biological Passport: Need and Challenges' (2020) 54 Indian Journal of Orthopaedics 264, 264.

[275] ibid 268.

[276] CAS 2019/A/6148 *World Anti-Doping Agency v Mr Sun Yang & Fédération Internationale de Natation (FINA)* award of 22 June 2021 <https://www.tas-cas.org/fileadmin/user_upload/Award_6148__FINAL_.pdf> accessed 13 May 2024.

[277] Court of Arbitration for Sport Media Release, 'Sun Yang Is Found Guilty of a Doping Offense and Sanctioned with an 8-year Period of Ineligibility' (28 February 2020) <https://www.tas-cas.org/fileadmin/user_upload/CAS_Media_Release_6148_decision.pdf> accessed 13 May 2024.

by the Chair of the CAS Panel.[278] The Swiss court annulled the award and sent the matter back to the CAS to convene a second Panel. The eight-year period of ineligibility was lifted pending the decision of the second CAS hearing. The appeal filed by WADA was partially upheld as the period of ineligibility was reduced from eight years to four year and three months, beginning on 28 February 2020.[279]

6–71 In relation to the issue of privacy, the swimmer claimed that the Doping Control Assistant (DCA) had taken numerous photographs and videos on their phone without his consent. The DCA contended that pictures were of where the test was taking place to prove that the testing team had arrived at the location as they waited one hour for Yang.[280] The swimmer also alleged that the Sample Collection fell short of ISTI requirements.[281] He also raised the argument

> that sample collection entails an infringement of athletes' fundamental human rights to physical integrity, privacy and dignity. The severity of the infringement is also evident in the system's use of a regime of 'strict liability' for athletes found guilty of an anti-doping rule violation.[282]

6–72 The CAS Panel found that the swimmer's refusal to allow the blood samples to leave with the Sample Collection Officer constituted Evading, Refusing or Failing to Submit to Sample Collection by an Athlete, a doping violation. Rigozzi refers to the *Yang* case and writes that

> there was an interesting debate on the requirements that need to be followed in order to collect blood from an athlete, in particular as to the notification formalities and the qualifications of doping control personnel. A careful reading of the CAS award suggests that there is room for an argument that the way in which the doping control was conducted in the circumstances and the severity of the sanction imposed (an 8 year ban) would allow for scrutiny under Article 8 ECHR. Still with respect to anti-doping controls, Article 8 ECHR is certainly also relevant with regard to night-time testing.[283]

6–73 The WADA Code defines doping as a strict liability offence. Article 2.1.1 states:

> It is the Athletes' personal duty to ensure that no Prohibited Substance enters their bodies. Athletes are responsible for any Prohibited Substance or its Metabolites or Markers found to be present in their Samples. Accordingly, it is not necessary that intent, Fault, Negligence or knowing

[278] CAS 2019/A/6148 (n 276) [10].
[279] ibid. FINA's decision was set aside.
[280] ibid [34]. See also [35].
[281] ibid [214]–[261].
[282] ibid [214].
[283] Antonio Rigozzi, 'Sports Arbitration and the European Convention of Human Rights – Pechstein and Beyond' in Antonio Rigozzi, Christoph Müller, and Sébastien Besson (eds), *New Developments in International Commercial Arbitration 2020* (Stämpfli 2020) 123.

> Use on the Athlete's part be demonstrated in order to establish an anti-doping rule violation under Article 2.1.

Once an athlete is found to have an AAF, they are automatically deemed to have committed a doping violation. However, the principle of strict liability seems to be at variance with the right to the presumption of innocence. Since the 2009 WADC, there has been more flexibility when it comes to sanctions. If an athlete can demonstrate to the satisfaction of the disciplinary panel that the substance was ingested through no fault of the individual, the sanction may be reduced. The burden of proof is on the athlete. The CAS has upheld the strict liability in the interest of fair competition. In *Hansen* v *FEI* the CAS acknowledged that the principle is consistent with Article 6(2) of the ECHR on the right to a fair trial.[284] **6–74**

Article 6(1) of the ECHR provides: **6–75**

> In the determination of his civil rights and obligations or of any criminal charge against him, everyone is entitled to a fair and public hearing within a reasonable time by an independent and impartial tribunal established by law. Judgment shall be pronounced publicly but the press and public may be excluded from all or part of the trial in the interests of morals, public order or national security in a democratic society, where the interests of juveniles or the protection of the private life of the parties so require, or to the extent strictly necessary in the opinion of the court in special circumstances where publicity would prejudice the interests of justice.[285]

Article 6(2) provides: 'Everyone charged with a criminal offence shall be presumed innocent until proved guilty according to law.' Article 6 has been raised in several doping cases, including *Bakker v Switzerland*[286] and *Mutu and Pechstein v Switzerland*.[287] Article 6 has been described as having two limbs: a civil limb and a criminal limb.[288] Article 6(1) includes both limbs, criminal and civil, while Article 6(2) only applies to criminal charges. In a doping case, unless it is a criminal offence under national law, the ECtHR would not apply the criminal limb of Article 6(2).[289] **6–76**

---

[284] CAS 2009/A/1768 *Hansen v Fédération Equestre Internationale (FEI)* award of 4 December 2009. The CAS referred to the cases of *Salabiaku v France* App no 10519/83 [28]–[29]; *Janovic v Sweden* App no 346/9/92 [101]. As discussed in detail in ch 9 paras 9-15—9-16 and 9-91. Swiss athlete Sandra Gasser challenged the IAAF anti-doping rules on the grounds of strict liability and restraint of trade.

[285] For a useful guide on art 6, see <https://www.echr.coe.int/documents/d/echr/guide_Art_6_eng> accessed 13 May 2024.

[286] *Erwin Bakker v Switzerland* App no 7198/07 (3 September 2019).

[287] *Case of Mutu and Pechstein v Switzerland* App nos 40575/10 and 67474/10 (Strasbourg, 2 October 2018) <https://hudoc.echr.coe.int/fre#{%22itemid%22:[%22001-186828%22]}> accessed 13 May 2024.

[288] van der Sloot (n 4) 213.

[289] van der Sloot (n 4) 224. On 10 December 2015, Germany's Anti-Doping in Sport Act (AntiDopG) came into force. It is a criminal offence under German law to engage in doping. It was amended in 2020 and 2021: see National Anti-Doping Agency of Germany, 'Anti-Doping Law' <https://www.nada.de/en/legal-matters/anti-doping-law> accessed 13 May 2024.

Kornbeck, in referring to the European Union (EU), contends that the presumption of innocence (or *in dubio pro reo*) 'must be applied in penal law, there is nothing barring [Member States] from applying it in other areas also, whenever this seems warranted in order to ensure fairness and avoid gross injustice, in particular on account of the severity of the sanctions imposed'.[290] Pechstein raised the issue of the presumption of innocence before the CAS in relation to Article 6(2).[291] However, the ECtHR found it 'more appropriate' in the joined case with Mutu to confine itself to Article 6(1).[292] The standard of proof used by the CAS is 'the comfortable satisfaction' of the Panel, a standard that is beyond the balance of probabilities but less than beyond reasonable doubt. Van der Sloot questions the inequality of arms in cases involving the ABP as in *Pechstein*, where the accusations were based on 'indirect evidence, although she denied having used any substances or methods, and the fluctuation was due to a disease'.[293] According to the CAS in *B v International Judo Federation*, 'Every athlete enjoys the presumption of innocence until such time as the presence of a banned substance in his body is established. It is a matter for the sports organization to prove that presence.'[294]

6–77 All signatories to the WADC recognise the jurisdiction of the CAS. Athletes are said to have consented to this jurisdiction based on an ad-hoc contract or a standard clause within the statutes and regulations of the NGB or the IF that should a dispute arise between them and the governing body, then it will be resolved exclusively by reference to arbitration before the CAS. A clause that ousts the jurisdiction of the courts would arguably be unconstitutional, however, as seen in Chapter 12, domestic courts are reluctant to intervene in decisions made by the CAS.[295] In relation to Pechstein, the ECtHR gave cognisance to the fact that athletes were compelled to agree to arbitration clauses, however, the Court held that the CAS was an independent and impartial tribunal established by law.[296] Pechstein also disagreed with the method in which the arbitrators were selected and argued that there was an 'imbalance between federations and athletes in the mechanism for appointing arbitrators'.[297] However, the ECtHR rejected this claim on the grounds that it was too vague and hypothetical.[298] Article 6(1) of the ECHR

---

[290] Jacob Kornbeck, 'The EU, the Revision of the World Anti-Doping Code and the Presumption of Innocence' (2016) 15 International Sports Law Journal 172, 175.

[291] *Mutu and Pechstein v Switzerland* (n 287) [52]. The case of *Mutu and Pechstein v Switzerland* is also discussed in ch 12 paras 12-72–12-77.

[292] ibid [53].

[293] van der Sloot (n 4) 227.

[294] CAS 98/214 *B v International Judo Federation* award of 17 March 1999, CAS Digest II, 308.

[295] See *Raguz v Sullivan* [2000] NSWCA 240 where the New South Wales Court of Appeal 'confirmed' the 'exclusivity' of the CAS.

[296] See also CAS 2002/A/370 *Lazutina v IOC* award of 29 November 2002, discussed in ch 12.

[297] *Mutu and Pechstein* (n 287) [152].

[298] ibid [151].

provides for the right to a fair and public hearing within a reasonable time by an independent and impartial tribunal established by law. Pechstein had requested a public hearing before the CAS in 2009 and her request had been denied. The ECtHR agreed with Pechstein on this ground, and she was awarded €8,000 in damages for a violation of her rights under Article 6(1). Mutu lodged an application to the ECtHR arguing that his right to a fair trial under Article 6(1) of the ECHR had been breached. However, the ECtHR dismissed the application, finding that his rights had not been violated.

In *Bakker* v *Switzerland*, a Dutch cyclist applied to the ECtHR following an unsuccessful appeal to the SFT.[299] Bakker was found by the Royal Dutch Cycling Union (RDCU) to have committed an ADRV in relation to testosterone and was sanctioned by way of a two-year period of ineligibility. In the first of two appeals to the CAS, the CAS Panel on 20 April 2006 issued its arbitral award and upheld the two-year suspension.[300] A second violation occurred following an injection given by Bakker's doctor, which he admitted was a 'risky product' on 20 June 2005.[301] He was already involved in anti-doping proceedings and had a few days prior to the injection requested the testing of his B Sample. The CAS Panel's arbitral award dated 5 May 2006 found that Bakker had committed a second ADRV and imposed lifetime ineligibility.[302] In an appeal to the SFT to set aside the CAS decisions, the case was dismissed.[303] On 3 September 2019, the ECtHR held that Bakker's application was inadmissible.[304] Bakker argued that his right to a fair hearing under Article 6(1) was violated as the SFT decision was 'arbitrary and insufficiently reasoned'.[305] The cyclist further contended that the SFT had a limited review function as provided for under Article 190(2) of the Swiss Private Law International Act (PILA).[306] However, the ECtHR **6–78**

299 *Bakker v Switzerland* (n 286).

300 CAS 2005/A/936 *Bakker v Koninklijke Nederlandsche Wielren Unie (KNWU) & Union Cycliste Internationale (UCI)* award of 20 April 2006.

301 CAS 2005/A/969 *Bakker v Koninklijke Nederlandsche Wielren Unie (KNWU) & Union Cycliste Internationale (UCI)* award of 5 May 2006 [69] <https://jurisprudence.tas-cas.org/Shared%20Documents/969.pdf> accessed 13 May 2024.

302 ibid [70]. In referring to possible reductions in the sanction, the Panel held 'that the sole sanction that is applicable is lifetime ineligibility'.

303 *Bakker v UCI*, 4P.176/2006 of 14 August 2006. Bakker filed a second appeal to the SFT, Decision of the Swiss Federal Tribunal 4A_237/2010 – 6 Oct 2010 <https://jusmundi.com/en/document/decision/en-erwin-bakker-v-koninklijke-nederlandsche-wielren-unie-knwu-union-cycliste-internationale-uci-decision-of-the-swiss-federal-tribunal-wednesday-6th-october-2010#decision_46901> accessed 13 May 2024. The second appeal was a request for a revision and the annulment of the two CAS arbitral awards.

304 Requête no 7198/07 *Bakker contre la Suisse* <http://hudoc.echr.coe.int/eng#{%22itemid%22:[%22001-196440%22]}> accessed 13 May 2024. The judgment is available only in French.

305 Despina Mavromati, 'CAS through the Lens of the European Court of Human Rights and Other Tribunals' in James AR Nafziger and Ryan Gauthier (eds), *Handbook on International Sports Law* (2nd edn, Elgar 2022) 215.

306 The PILA is discussed in more detail in Chapter 12.

rejected this contention 'to the extent that the CAS appeal mechanism provides for a *de novo review* (of both the facts and law) and the athlete did not argue that the SFT did not review the matter on the merits'.[307] As discussed in Chapter 12, the CAS hears cases 'de novo', in line with the decisions of the ECtHR.[308] It has stated that procedural errors of sports disciplinary tribunals/committees can be cured with the appeal *de novo* before the CAS.[309]

6–79 Article 14 of the ECHR concerns the prohibition of discrimination. It provides:

> The enjoyment of the rights and freedoms set forth in [the] Convention shall be secured without discrimination on any ground such as sex, race, colour, language, religion, political or other opinion, national or social origin, association with a national minority, property, birth or other status.[310]

6–80 Although Article 14 has not been raised in doping cases, it has been raised in other contexts, including the case of *Semeyna v Switzerland* relating to the Athletes with Differences of Sex Development Regulations, as discussed in Chapter 7.[311] Article 14 can only be invoked in conjunction with another Article of the ECHR, it is a secondary right. Theoretically, it could be used in conjunction with Articles 6 and/or 8 in doping cases.[312]

Domestic Courts and Doping Cases

6–81 In Chapter 8, the doctrine of restraint of trade and doping is examined. When an athlete is sanctioned by way of a period of ineligibility, it affects their right to earn a livelihood. In *Gasser v Stinson,* the plaintiff argued that the IAAF policy of strict liability and its imposition of a mandatory suspension constituted an unreasonable restraint of trade.[313] Restraint of trade and doping was also raised by Dwain Chambers, the British sprinter, who challenged the controversial Byelaw 25.[314] The right to fair

---

307 Mavromati (n 305) 216.

308 Court of Arbitration, 'Sport and Human Rights: Overview from a CAS Perspective' 20 June 2022, <https://www.tas-cas.org/fileadmin/user_upload/2022.06.20_Human_Rights_in_sport__20_June_2022_.pdf> accessed 13 May 2024.

309 See CAS 2009/A/1957 *Fédération Française de Natation (FFN) v Ligue Européenne de Natation (LEN)* award of 5 July 2010 [1] and [14] <https://jurisprudence.tas-cas.org/Shared%20Documents/1957.pdf> accessed 13 May 2024.

310 For more details, see European Court of Human Rights, 'Guide on Article 14 of the European Convention on Human Rights and on Article 1 of Protocol No 12 to the Convention' <https://www.echr.coe.int/documents/d/echr/Guide_Art_14_Art_1_Protocol_12_ENG> accessed 13 May 2024.

311 *Semenya v Switzerland* App no 10934/21 (11 July 2023). See Laura Donnellan and Jacob Kornbeck, 'Droit de L'Homme: Athlétisme et Hyperandrogénie' (2024) 249 Jurisport 33.

312 van der Sloot (n 4) 232.

313 *Gasser v Stinson & Anor* [1988] 6 WLUK 333.

314 *Chambers v British Olympic Association* [2008] EWHC 2028 (QBD).

procedures was raised in the case of *Quirke v Bord Luthchleas na hÉireann (BLÉ),* discussed in Chapter 11.[315]

Conclusion

The creation of the WADA in 1999 and the WADC in 2003 resulted in the global harmonisation of anti-doping rules. The WADC acts as a blueprint for anti-doping agencies all over the world. Over the years, the WADC has evolved in line with scientific developments. It has responded to challenges and has adapted the rules to introduce protections for whistleblowers and redoubling its efforts to sanction those that are using performance-enhancing drugs or methods while modifying the rules in relation to substances of abuse, those unrelated to enhancing performance. The 2009 WADC introduced lesser sanctions for those found to have unintentionally or without fault or negligence committed an ADRV, and in doing so it relaxed the principle of strict liability. However, strict liability remains a cornerstone of the WADC. **6–82**

Developments have occurred at domestic level as Part 4, ss 40–45 of the Sport Ireland Act 2015 introduced more robust anti-doping provisions into Irish sport. Sport Ireland has wide-ranging powers under the 2015 Act. As the NADO, Sport Ireland is responsible for carrying out testing, issuing sanctions and overseeing the disciplinary process. **6–83**

Anti-doping agencies, IFs, WADA, NGBs and other relevant bodies must ensure that the rules are adhered to and that the appropriate sanctions are imposed. As discussed in Chapter 12, the Anti-Doping Division (ADD) was established by the CAS in 2016. Its role is to hear and decide anti-doping cases at first instance, and the authority to do so is pursuant to the delegation of powers from the IOC, the Olympic IFs and any other signatories to the WADC. The ADD acts as a disciplinary tribunal in lieu of the anti-doping panel of the IF or other signatories to the WADC. A decision made by the ADD may be appealed to the CAS's Appeals Arbitration Division and subsequently to the SFT. The CAS has created a body of law, *lex sportiva,* much of which relates to anti-doping. It has been recognised by the ECtHR as an impartial and independent tribunal. It hears cases *de novo,* and in limited circumstances, the decision may be appealed to the SFT. Athletes have an extra layer of protection as the ECtHR has recognised that the ECHR, in particular, Articles 6 and 8 can be invoked by athletes. **6–84**

The relationship between the athlete and the governing body is one of contract and the prohibition of banned substances is an implied term of that contract. By taking a banned substance or engaging in a prohibited method the athlete is in breach of the rules of the sport. However, their rights must be respected, and the relevant bodies must ensure that **6–85**

---

[315] [1988] IR 83.

proper procedures are followed. The integrity of the sport, the principle of fair play and the health of the athletes all command that anti-doping continues to occupy a central role in sport. Less-invasive methods of testing would be welcome, however, if the anti-doping processes and procedures continue to serve a legitimate purpose and are proportionate, the traditional testing methods will remain.

Chapter 7

ATHLETES WITH DIFFERENCES OF SEXUAL DEVELOPMENT AND TRANSGENDER ATHLETES

Introduction

7–01 World Athletics introduced the Hyperandrogenism Regulations in 2011. The regulations were challenged by Dutee Chand and were provisionally suspended by the Court of Arbitration for Sport (CAS).[1] Following the publication of a study that linked athletic performance and higher levels of testosterone in female athletes, the regulations were modified and were challenged by Caster Semenya with the Swiss Federal Supreme Court upholding the decision of the CAS.[2] Semenya successfully lodged a case against Switzerland in the European Court of Human Rights (ECtHR).[3] On 23 March 2023, the Council of World Athletics agreed to update the eligibility regulations for transgender and Athletics with Differences of Sexual Development (DSD) to compete in the female category.

7–02 The International Olympic Committee (IOC) relaxed the rules to allow female-to-male transgender athletes to compete without any restriction and male-to-female transgender athletes to compete subject to certain restrictions regarding testosterone levels that had to be below a cut-off level one year prior to participation. Previous rules (from 2004) had requirements in relation to pre-pubescent gender reassignment and post-pubescent gender reassignment. A change to the rules in 2015 removed the requirement of surgery and permitted female transgender athletes to compete in female events once their testosterone levels were reduced to what was considered within the average female range. However, since March 2022, the IOC has permitted each sport to determine its own policies regarding transgender athletes. Examples of the rules in relation to eligibility of transgender athletes of a few sports are discussed

---

1 CAS 2014/A/3759 *Chand v AFI & IAAF* award of 24 July 2015 <https://jurisprudence.tas-cas.org/Shared%20Documents/3759-PA.pdf > accessed 13 May 2024.

2 CAS 2018/O/5794 *Mokgadi Caster Semenya v International Association of Athletics Federations*; CAS 2018/O/5798 *Athletics South Africa v International Association of Athletics Federations* award of 18 June 2018 <https://jurisprudence.tas-cas.org/Shared%20Documents/5794,%205798.pdf> accessed 13 May 2024. The Swiss Federal Supreme Court is often referred to as the Swiss Federal Tribunal, SFT. This is discussed in Chapter 12.

3 *Semenya v Switzerland* App no 10934/21 (ECtHR, 17 May 2021) <https://hudoc.echr.coe.int/eng#{%22appno%22:[%2210934/21%22],%22itemid%22:[%22001-226011%22]}> accessed 15 May 2024.

including the British Triathlon Federation, World Rugby, World Athletics, World Aquatics, and the Gaelic Athletic Association (GAA).

7–03 To place recent developments in context, it is necessary to examine the history of gender testing and its evolution from the nude parades to more scientific methods. While no longer mandatory, the IOC and World Athletics retain the right to gender test athletes in situations where there are suspicions raised to the athlete's femininity.

History of Gender Testing

7–04 Most sporting events, with equestrian and motor sports being the outliers, are segregated into male and female events. The CAS Panel observed in its Interim Arbitral Award in the case of *Chand* that all the parties agreed that dividing athletes into male and female events was 'reasonable and appropriate'.[4] In the interests of ensuring fairness, the CAS Panel found that it was 'legitimate and necessary to divide athletes into male and female categories'.[5] Male elite athletes are generally faster and more powerful than female athletes.[6] Male athletes have greater lean body mass (LBM) and more testosterone than women and this is attributable to the male advantage in athletics.[7] It accepted that division according to sex is appropriate, however, it was not appropriate

> to subject athletes to gender verification; or to mere examination of external genitalia; or to chromosomal testing in order to determine eligibility to compete as women or for the purpose of making a determination about their sex or gender status.[8]

7–05 It has been argued that the segregation of sport into male and female events provides an incentive for an individual to commit gender fraud.[9] However, there are only a handful of documented cases of where an alleged male athlete competed as a woman in a female event.[10] One notable example is Dora or Heinrich Ratjen. The 1936 Berlin Olympics

---

4 *Chand* (n 1) [510].
5 ibid [230].
6 ibid [35 (c)].
7 ibid [35 (h)] and [35 (i)].
8 ibid [35 (g)].
9 JC Reeser, 'Gender Identity and Sport: Is the Playing Field Level?' (2005) 39 British Journal of Sports Medicine 695, 695.
10 Barry D Dickinson and others, 'Gender Verification of Female Olympic Athletes' (2002) 34(10) Medicine and Science in Sport and Exercise 1539. There are a couple of other documented cases, as discussed by Dickinson and others: for example, Stanislawa Walasiewicz, a Polish sprinter, competed in the 1932 and 1936 Olympics. She moved to the United States and changed her name to Stella Walsh. In 1980 she was accidentally shot during an armed robbery and her autopsy revealed that she had male genitalia. She was found to have had both male and female chromosomes, a genetic condition known as mosaicism. Mosaicism is said to occur in 0.018% live births and, as Walsh had never undergone gender reassignment surgery, she was not considered transgender: see Sheldon

witnessed Heinrich Ratjen bind up his genitals and compete as a female high jumper called Dora. Ratjen came fourth in the final and his alleged 'deception' was not discovered until 1957. Ratjen contended that he was forced by the Nazi Youth Movement to pose as a woman in the hope of winning the gold medal for Germany and in turn preventing a Jewish athlete from competing. Ratjen's depiction of the events has recently been challenged. It is now claimed that Ratjen had 'ambiguous genitalia' and was raised female, however, he later identified as male and after retiring from sport lived as a man.[11] Thus, 'There is no good evidence that he competed fraudulently or was recruited by the Nazis in an act of deception.'[12] From the available literature, it seems that athletes whose gender raised suspicions were not masquerading as women but had chromosomal abnormalities.

Polish sprinter and Olympic champion Ewa Klobukowska was gender tested using the Barr test, also known as the sex-chromatin test, which was introduced by the International Amateur Athletic Federation (IAAF, now World Athletics) at the European Athletics Cup in Kiev in 1967.[13] The 21-year-old athlete was the first female athlete to fail the Barr test.[14] She was stripped of her Olympic and other medals after she was found to have 'one chromosome too many to be declared a woman for the purposes of athletic competition'.[15] Klobukowska had successfully passed the nude parade the previous year. Klobukowska received a lifetime ban from the sport. Medical experts differ in their conclusions regarding Klobukowska. Alan Ryan, a British gynaecologist and obstetrician, argues that one too many chromosomes could mean that Klobukowska had three X chromosomes.[16] Some contend that she had male genitalia; others argue that Klobukowska had a genetic defect that made her neither XX nor XY but XX/XXY.[17] While there is no definite **7–06**

Anderson, *The Forgotten Legacy of Stella Walsh: The Greatest Female Athlete of Her Time* (Rowman & Littlefield 2017) 174.

11 Haley Shapley, *Strong Like Her: A Celebration of Rule Breakers, History Makers, and Unstoppable Athletes* (Simon and Schuster 2020) 96.

12 ibid.

13 Robyn Ryle, *Throw Like a Girl, Cheer Like a Boy: The Evolution of Gender, Identity, and Race in Sports* (Rowman & Littlefield 2020), 19. It was known as the International Amateur Athletic Federation until 2001 when the word 'amateur' was replaced and it became known as the International Association of Athletic Federations. It became known as World Athletics in 2019.

14 Claire F Sullivan, 'Gender Verification and Gender Policies in Elite Sport: Eligibility and "Fair Play"' (2011) 34(4) Journal of Sport and Social Issues 400, 405.

15 Cited by Alison Turnbull, 'Woman Enough for the Games' (15 September 1988) New Scientist 61, 64.

16 Cheryl L Cole, 'One Chromosome Too Many' in Kay Schaffer and Sidonie Smith (eds), *The Olympics at the Millennium: Power, Politics, and the Games* (Rutgers University Press 2000) 129.

17 ibid. At the Paris 2024 Olympics two boxers who had previously been deemed ineligible by the International Boxing Association (IBA) were permitted by the IOC to compete in the female category. For a discussion of Imane Khelif, the Algerian Olympic gold-medal winner in the women's welterweight competition,

answer as to her condition, most agree that Klobukowska had a rare genetic condition that gave her no competitive advantage over her fellow competitors. Ironically, Klobukowska gave birth to a child a couple of years after receiving her lifetime ban.[18] The regulatory bodies, namely the IOC and IAAF, used the above case examples to justify their decisions to introduce mandatory gender testing in the late 1960s.[19] As will be seen in the discussion below, gender testing did not expose any male athletes competing as women 'but instead had unfairly disqualified numerous women with disorders of sex development (DSD)'.[20] DSD 'is defined by congenital conditions in which development of chromosomal, gonadal, or anatomic sex is atypical'.[21]

7–07 Political tension between the United States (US) and the former Soviet Union seemed to have provided an impetus for the IOC to introduce gender testing.[22] Improved training and sociological changes have been cited as the reasons behind 'striking improvement in athletic achievement by women'.[23] As women's sport became increasingly popular and accepted in the 1960s, it caused some to question the femininity of these women. Of particular importance was the competition between the US and former Soviet Union during the Cold War period. The US placed pressure on the IOC to introduce mandatory gender testing as Soviet athletes were dominating the Games.[24] Several Soviet athletes and

---

see Antonio Pequeño IV, 'What To Know About Olympics Gender Debate As Imane Khelif Wins Women's Boxing Final' *Forbes* (Jersey City, 9 August 2024) <https://www.forbes.com/sites/antoniopequenoiv/2024/08/09/what-to-know-about-olympics-gender-debate-as-imane-khelif-faces-off-in-womens-boxing-final/> accessed 22 August 2024. For information about the Taiwanese boxer, Lin Yu-ting, who won gold in the featherweight division, see Sofia Bettiza, 'What does science tell us about boxing's gender row?' (*BBC World Service*, 9 August 2024) <https://www.bbc.com/news/articles/crlr8gp813ko> accessed 22 August 2024.

18 Sullivan (n 14) 405.

19 The IAAF and IOC were not the first sports bodies to introduce gender testing. Some 20 years earlier, the British Women's Amateur Athletic Association required certification from a doctor to attest the athlete's gender before being permitted to compete in women's events. This method was subsequently abandoned as letters from doctors could be falsified: see Kathryn Henne, 'The "Science" of Fair Play in Sport: Gender and the Politics of Testing' (2014) 39(3) Signs: The Journal of Women in Culture and Society 787, 797.

20 Shari L Dworkin and others, 'Hurdling Over Sex? Sport, Science, and Equity' (2014) 43 Archives of Sexual Behaviour 1035, 1036.

21 This definition is taken from Peter A Lee and others in collaboration with the participants in the International Consensus Conference on Intersex organised by the Lawson Wilkins Pediatric Endocrine Society and the European Society for Paediatric Endocrinology, 'Consensus, Statement on Management of Intersex Disorders (2006) 118(2) Pediatrics e488.

22 Sullivan (n 14) 403.

23 Myron Genel, 'Gender Verification No More?' (2000) 5(3) Medscape Women's Health <https://www.medscape.com/viewarticle/408918/> accessed 5 July 2024.

24 For a discussion on the impact on the Cold War and the western norms of femininity, see Lindsay Parks Pieper, 'Sex Testing and the Maintenance of Western Femininity in International Sport' (2014) 31(13) The International Journal of the History of Sport 1557.

former East German athletes were rumoured to be intersexed owing to their masculine physiques. It is estimated that 0.018% of people are intersexed and it is defined as 'the atypical appearance of the external genitalia at birth where they differ from the usual development of either sex and create difficulty in sex assignment'.[25] It was later discovered that a number of these athletes were using steroids. A notable example is that of Heidi Krieger, the former East German shot putter, now known as Andreas. His coach put him on steroids and the contraceptive pill at the age of 17. With the combination of the pill and steroids, Krieger's weight increased as did his muscle mass. At the age of 19, Krieger began to question the gender he was ascribed at birth.[26] In 1997, Krieger had gender reassignment and is quoted as saying that the combination of the drugs and his own confusion regarding gender were factors in his decision to undergo surgery.[27]

Introduction of Mandatory Gender Testing by the IAAF and IOC

The mandatory gender testing of all female athletes was introduced in 1966 by the IAAF and in 1968 by the IOC.[28] In 1966, the IAAF introduced gender testing in the European Athletic Championships in Budapest as an increasing number of female athletes began to compete.[29] All 243 female athletes were required to take part in 'nude parades' where female doctors inspected to see if the competitors were biologically female. All 243 athletes were certified as female. This highly invasive method was deemed both humiliating and degrading. Around this time a few female athletes who had been competing until 1966 failed to appear for examination, citing illness and retirement as reasons.[30] Two Russian sisters, Irina and Tamara Press, who between them had set 26 world records and had won five gold medals, unexpectedly retired at this time. The idea that a female athlete could possess such **7–08**

25 Robert Ritchie, John Reynard, and Tom Lewis, 'Intersex and the Olympic Games' (2008) 101 Journal of the Royal Society of Medicine 395, 395. The writers contend that if other conditions are added, including Turner's syndrome and Klinefelter's syndrome, then the percentage increases to 1.7%.

26 Ellis Cashmore, *Sports Psychology: The Key Concepts* (Routledge 2002) 262.

27 Emine Saner, 'The Gender Trap' *The Guardian* (London, 30 July 2008) <https://www.theguardian.com/sport/2008/jul/30/olympicgames2008.gender> accessed 13 May 2024.

28 Women competed in the Olympics for the first time in 1900. Out of the 1225 participants, 19 were women. Women competed in tennis, yachting, and golf. In 1910 the IOC added gymnastics and swimming for women for the 1912 Olympics. In 1960, 611 women competed in Rome. This figure represented only 11.5% of the total participation. By 1980, 20% of the participants were women and by 2000, 4,069 women competed out of a total participation of 10,651 (38%). This information is taken from Olympic Review, *Focus: Women in Sport* (Official Publication of the Olympic Movement, February 2004) <https://stillmed.olympic.org/AssetsDocs/importednews/documents/en_report_792.pdf> accessed 13 May 2024.

29 Louis J Elsas and others, 'Gender Verification of Female Athletes' (2000) 2(4) Genetics in Medicine 249, 250.

30 Reeser (n 9) cites six athletes whose careers ended at this time.

superiority over her competitors caused much disquiet.[31] To some, the nexus between 'athleticism and masculinity becomes institutionalized through the gender verification policies of international and national governing bodies (NGBs) of sport, given that sex testing is only carried out on female athletes'.[32] Culturally and socially, women had traditionally been viewed as being 'athletically inferior' to men and, by excelling in their sport, it cast doubt on Irina and Tamara's femininity. Both sisters presumably were intersexed and were not male impostors.[33] After Budapest, female athletes were subjected once again to physical examination by a gynaecologist in the Commonwealth Games in Kingston, Jamaica, in 1967.

IOC Medical Commission

7–09 In 1962, the IOC Executive Board established the Medical Commission as part of its endeavours to combat the use of drugs in sport.[34] The Medical Commission did not meet during the years of 1962–66; however, at the IOC's 66th Session in Tehran in 1967 the Medical Commission was revived under new leadership in the form of a Belgium member, Alexandre de Merode.[35] This new IOC Medical Commission became the first sporting organisation, along with the International Cycling Union (UCI), to establish a Medical Commission.[36] Drug testing became an important issue for the IOC in the 1960s. The IOC Medical Commission was entrusted with the task of policing the use of banned substances and of verifying gender. Once a female athlete was certified as female, she would be furnished with a gender-verification certificate, which was signed by the Chair and another member, and it was valid for all competitions recognised by the IOC.[37]

7–10 In viewing doping and gender fraud as moral equivalents, the IOC carried out drug and gender tests at the 1968 Olympic Games in Mexico City. Female athletes resented the use of physical examination. As stated above, in 1967 the IAAF introduced the sex-chromatin test

31 Joyce Duncan, *Sport in American Culture From Ali to X Games* (ABC–CLIO 2004) 150–51.

32 Shari L Dworkin, Amanda Lock Swarr and Cheryl Cooky, '(In) Justice in Sport: The Treatment of South African Track Star Caster Semenya' (2013) 39(1) Feminist Studies 40–69, 43.

33 David McArdle, 'Swallows and Amazons, or the Sporting Exception to the Gender Recognition Act' (2008) 17(1) Social and Legal Studies 39, 41.

34 Olympic Studies Centre, 'Overview of the Content of the Archives Concerning the History, Missions and Activities of the IOC Medical Commission from 1936 to 1995' (July 2015) <https://www.google.com/url?sa=t&source=web&rct=j&opi=89978449&url=https://library.olympics.com/Default/basicfilesdownload.ashx%3FitemGuid%3DA601C930-F7EA-4BA7-A65C-99FDED2540FE&ved=2ahUKEwiW2s3z1YuGAxXtSPEDHdUAAU0QFnoECBsQAQ&usg=AOvVaw0Smw6SlPr0vyf6hSQ80mKm> accessed 13 May 2024.

35 ibid 2.

36 ibid.

37 ibid 3.

at the European Athletics Cup in Kiev. This 'femininity control' test marked a turning point in gender testing.[38] The criteria for assessing a female athlete's gender changed from one of physical examination to a more radical, though less invasive, test.[39] Gender testing assumed a more sinister role. It was no longer concerned with men posing as women athletes but with athletes that externally appeared as women but whose genetic properties claimed otherwise. An abnormality in an individual's chromosomes could render a person who has the outward appearance of one sex to be that of the other sex. The sex chromatin involves the collection of cells (a buccal smear) from inside the cheek to determine the chromosome properties. Normally, men and women have 46 chromosomes; men have one X and one Y chromosome, while women have two X chromosomes. Only those who were found to have to two X chromosomes were deemed to be eligible to compete in women's events. It is estimated that 1 in 500 people have abnormalities when chromatin tested.[40] Some women have what is known as androgen insensitivity and as a result have a Y chromosome.

Attitudes to Gender Testing

Gender testing has attracted much criticism from the medical profession as gender is not simply determined by chromosome properties: other factors must be considered, including the environment in which the person was raised; the gender identity that the individual presumes themselves to have; the external genitalia; and the gender of the individual presumed by others.[41] Thus, there is no definitive test for determining gender. Leading medical academics and practitioners **7–11**

---

[38] Simon Jenkins, *Sports Science Handbook: The Essential Guide to Kinesiology, Sports and Exercise Science* (Multi-Science Publishing 2000) 318.

[39] It was a cheaper and quicker method: see Cole (n 16) 129.

[40] See Gail Vines, 'Last Olympics for the sex test? The world's biggest sports body has just banned sex tests, branding them unfair and unnecessary. But the old guard at this year's Olympics still insists the practice must go on' *New Scientist* (4 July 1992) <https://www.newscientist.com/article/mg13518284-900-last-olympics-for-the-sex-test/> accessed 13 May 2024. Vines notes that genes can swap from one chromosome to another. A woman with an XY complement may physically be feminine but may have conditions known as an androgen insensitivity or testicular feminisation. These women produce more testosterone than an average woman. Saner (n 27) estimates that 1 in 1000 people are intersexed. For a scientific article that explains DSD and the statistics, see Mary García-Acero and others, 'Disorders of Sexual Development: Current Status and Progress in the Diagnostic Approach' (2019) 13 Current Urology 169.

[41] Arne Ljungqvist, 'Gender Verification' in Barbara L Drinkwater (ed), *Women in Sport: Volume VIII of The Encyclopaedia of Sports Medicine* (Blackwell Science 2000) 188. Ljungqvist lists eight criteria that are used to determine gender and argues that for some individuals one or two of the criteria may be vague and question the assumed sex of the individual. Most governing bodies use only one of the eight criteria, the chromosome pattern. This calls into question the real reason behind gender testing if the objective is simply to catch men masquerading as women.

have long called for the abolition of gender testing.[42] The test has been referred to as 'unscientific', 'nonsense', 'morally destitute'.[43] Questioning a person's gender can have serious repercussions. The Tamil Nadu middle-distance runner Santhi Soundarajan failed a gender-verification test after coming second in the 800-metre final at the 2006 Asian Games. Soundarajan had placed first and second in several international events prior to the gender test.[44] Soundarajan was examined by four IAAF doctors who took blood tests and carried out a physical examination, which required the athlete to be naked.[45] None of the officials spoke her native Tamil language, and no one informed Soundarajan of the purpose of the medical examination.[46] However, a few days later when Soundarajan had returned home, it was broadcast on the evening news that the athlete had failed a gender-verification test.[47] The IAAF stripped her of the silver medal she had won in Qatar at the Asian Games and placed a ban on her competing in future events. Soundarajan was diagnosed with androgen insensitivity and never had her medals returned and never competed again.[48] Soundarajan is believed to have attempted suicide because of the public humiliation she suffered. As a small token, the state government of Tamil Nadu supported her and awarded her 1.5 million rupees (approximately €25,650) for her performance in the Asian Games.[49]

7–12 Most female athletes diagnosed with androgen insensitivity are not aware they have the condition. Sullivan remarks:

> Due to the complex nature of intersexual bodies, some competitors would be unaware that there would be a problem in determining their sex for the purpose of sports competitions. Therefore, the rationale of using testing to uncover acts of deception and cheating could not justifiably be used.[50]

7–13 María José Martínez-Patiño illustrates this point. Martínez-Patiño, a Spanish hurdler, had passed a sex test in 1983 and was issued with a Certificate of Femininity.[51] In 1985 while competing at the World University Games in Japan, she realised that she had forgotten to bring

---

42 Vines (n 40).

43 ibid.

44 Parks Pieper (n 24) 1568.

45 ibid.

46 ibid.

47 ibid.

48 Kathryn Henne, 'The "Science" of Fair Play in Sport: Gender and the Politics of Testing' (2014) 39(3) Signs: The Journal of Women in Culture and Society 787, 803.

49 Colm O'Connor, '"Failed Sex Test" Deposes India's Track Queen' *Irish Examiner* (Cork, 19 December 2006) <https://www.irishexaminer.com/sport/arid-20021104.html> accessed 13 May 2024.

50 Sullivan (n 14) 405.

51 Laura Donnellan, 'Gender Testing at the Beijing Olympics' (2008) 16(1) Sport and the Law Journal 20, 23–24. See also María José Martínez-Patiño, 'Personal Account: A Woman Tried and Tested' (December 2005) 366 The Lancet S38.

her verification-certificate with her. Martínez-Patiño was retested and was informed by the team doctor that there were problems with her result. As further tests were required, Martínez-Patiño was told that this could take months and that she should feign an injury and not compete the next day in her scheduled event. Martínez-Patiño followed the advice of the doctor and two months later her results arrived. She was diagnosed with androgen insensitivity. In 1986 she was about to enter the national championships in Spain, when her doctor once again advised her to feign an injury but this time Martínez-Patiño refused. On crossing the line, her story was leaked to the press. Her records were erased; her scholarship was revoked; and she was expelled from her athlete's residence. For two years she challenged the results of her test. With the help of an American coach and journalist, Alison Carlson, and a Spanish professor, Martínez-Patiño gathered enough medical evidence to support her claim, namely that she was a woman and that she had in no way cheated. In 1988 she was re-instated but failed to qualify for the 1992 Olympics. Her case was instrumental in ending the chromatin test, although by the time she was re-instated she had lost her momentum and never returned to form.

Developments in the 1990s

Up until the early 1990s, when an athlete was chosen for a gender test, she would be tested using the chromatin test. If the results were inconclusive, she would be asked to provide a blood sample. If the blood sample were inconclusive, the athlete would be examined physically. Where a female athlete identified as female and had the physical appearance of a woman but was found to have a Y chromosome it would result in a failed test. Evidence suggests that the buccal smear does not always present a clear picture.[52] The Barr body test/buccal smear test was used until the 1980s; however, its unreliability was noted as it resulted in some female athletes 'with genetic difference affording no physical advantage for sports' being excluded from their sport.[53] In a recent Human Rights Watch report titled '"They're Chasing Us Away from Sport": Human Rights Violations in Sex Testing of Elite Women Athletes', the authors contend that the use of the Barr body test was of itself **7–14**

> insufficient as a proxy for sex, and because this technique only assesses whether someone has more than one X chromosome it ruled some women ineligible to compete in the female category while, theoretically at least as there were no analogous regulations for men, rendering some men eligible.[54]

---

52 Ljungqvist (n 41) 186. It is estimated that 30% of the cells will be positive and accordingly judged as female.

53 Louis J Elsas and others, 'Gender Verification of Female Athletes' (2000) 2(4) Genetics in Medicine 249, 250.

54 Human Rights Watch, '"They're Chasing Us Away from Sport": Human Rights Violations in Sex Testing of Elite Women Athletes' 4 December 2020, 20 <https://

Testing Methods Reconsidered

7–15 In the late 1980s and early 1990s, the IOC and IAAF convened several workshops.[55] At these workshops it was stressed that the objective of gender testing was not to stigmatise women but to prevent male athletes masquerading as women. It was on this tenuous hook the continued use of the chromatin test rested. Under current drug testing methods, officials observe the athlete urinating so it would seem highly improbable that a male could masquerade as a woman. Despite its stated objectives, the IOC continued to exclude intersexed athletes and those suffering from androgen insensitivity in situations where there was a perceived competitive advantage.[56] A group of international professionals convened a 'milestone' IAAF Workshop on Methods of Femininity Verification held in Monaco in the later part of 1990.[57] They recommended the discontinuation of gender testing. In 1991 the IAAF duly followed the recommendation and introduced medical examinations for the purposes of checking the health of the athlete, both male and female.[58] In 1992 a conference was held in London, and at this conference the IAAF discussed the feasibility of continuing with medical examinations. The IAAF decided to dispense with the requirement of medical examinations and opted not to replace it with any other form of screening or examination.

7–16 The IOC remained committed to gender testing and introduced a DNA-based method called polymerase chain reaction (PRC) to detect Y chromosomal properties.[59] PRC allows scientists to produce unlimited copies of a DNA strand in a very short space of time. This new method replaced the chromatin test and was first used at the 1992 Winter Games in Albertville.[60] If the results were found to be abnormal, the athlete would be required undergo a gynaecological examination.

7–17 The PRC method was not without its critics. The supposedly sophisticated method excluded as many female competitors as its chromatin predecessor. Initially, although the PRC method was supposed to 'identify uniquely male DNA sequences, further investigation revealed that at least one of the DNA sequences used to prime the PCR was in

---

www.hrw.org/sites/default/files/media_2020/12/lgbt_athletes1120_web.pdf> accessed 14 May 2024.

55 Myron Genel and Arne Ljungqvist, 'Essay Gender Verification of Female Athletes' (December 2005) 366 The Lancet S41.

56 Joe Leigh Simpson and others, 'Gender Verification in the Olympics' (2000) 284(12) The Journal of the American Medical Association 1568.

57 Genel and Ljungqvist (n 55) S41.

58 ibid. All but five of the 34 Olympic sport federations abandoned mandatory gender testing: four of them did so soon after the IOC announced it would dispense with testing in 1999. Myron and Ljungqvist note that the International Volleyball Federation was the last IOC federation to discontinue gender testing in 2004.

59 ibid.

60 Genel and Ljungqvist (n 55) S41.

fact not specific to males and may have contributed to an unfortunate number of false positive test results'.[61] At the Atlanta Olympics in 1996, out of the 3,387 female athletes gender tested, only eight tested positive under the PCR test, seven of whom had either full or partial androgen insensitivity.[62] The cost in administering the test and counselling that had to be provided for athletes who failed the test brought to the fore the 'limited return' of PCR testing.[63] The IOC's Athletes' Commission called for the test to be discontinued and their Executive Board agreed in June 1999 to dispense with mandatory gender testing in advance of the 2000 Sydney Olympics.[64]

In the aftermath of the 1996 Games, an increasing number of medical organisations were calling for the abolition of gender testing.[65] The organisations included the American Medical Association, the American College of Physicians, and the American Society of Human Genetics.[66] As mentioned above, the organisations reasoned that the direct supervision of officials in observing urination for doping purposes made it impossible for men to compete in women's events.[67] **7–18**

At its 109th Session in 1999, the IOC decided to abandon its policy of mandatory gender testing. At the 2008 Olympic Games in Beijing, a gender-verification laboratory was set up at the Peking Union Medical College Hospital. The laboratory was like those established for the Atlanta Games. The laboratory examined the outward appearance, genes and hormones of suspect female athletes using a series of four tests, including blood, gene, and chromosome tests. While the establishment of a specific gender laboratory was quite surprising as the IOC had suspended gender testing in 1999, the IOC reserves the right to examine individual athletes if there are suspicions raised as to the gender of the athlete. In the words of Cole: 'Gender verification tests can be seen as one element in a matrix of surveillance and policing practices of the boundaries around gendered bodies.'[68] **7–19**

While the IOC reserves the right to gender test if suspicions are raised, World Athletics no longer uses gender testing. Instead it uses its DSD **7–20**

---

[61] Reeser (n 9) 696.
[62] Genel and Ljungqvist (n 55) S41. All eight were permitted to compete: Reeser ibid.
[63] Genel and Ljungqvist (n 55) S41.
[64] ibid.
[65] Dickinson and others (n 10) 1539.
[66] ibid.
[67] Arne Ljungqvist and Joe Leigh Simpson, 'Medical Examination for Health of All Athletes Replacing the Need for Gender Verification in International Sports: The International Amateur Athletic Federation Plan' (1992) 267(6) Journal of the American Medical Association 850, 852.
[68] Cheryl L Cole, 'Resisting the Canon: Feminist Cultural Studies, Sport, and Technologies of the Body' (1993) 17(2) Journal of Sport and Social Issues 77, 90.

Regulations, formerly, the Hyperandrogenism Regulations. It is to the evolution of these Regulations that the chapter now turns.

Hyperandrogenism Regulations

7–21 In August 2009 at the Berlin World Championships, Caster Semenya, the South African 800m world champion, was gender tested. Questions were raised as to her femininity and Semenya was subjected to a gender test. The IAAF never disclosed the results of her gender verification test; however, it is believed she is intersexed. Semenya went on to win the gold medal in the 800m at the Summer Olympics in London 2012 and Rio 2016. The General Secretary of the IAAF was quoted as saying: 'It is clear that she is a woman, but maybe not 100 per cent. We have to see if she has an advantage from her possibly being between two sexes compared to the others.'[69]

7–22 In response to Semenya, the IAAF introduced the Hyperandrogenism Regulations in 2011 following consultation with the IOC Medical Commission.[70] The IOC adopted its own regulations, the IOC Regulations on Female Hyperandrogenism, in advance of the London Olympics in 2012. The IOC stressed that the Regulations were not a form of gender testing:

> Nothing in these Regulations is intended to make any determination of sex. Instead, these Regulations are designed to identify circumstances in which a particular athlete will not be eligible (by reason of hormonal characteristics) to participate in 2012 OG Competitions in the female category. In the event that the athlete has been declared ineligible to compete in the female category, the athlete may be eligible to compete as a male athlete, if the athlete qualifies for the male event of the sport.[71]

7–23 The IAAF Hyperandrogenism Regulations provided the rules for the testing of the levels of testosterone in female athletes. Under the Regulations, an upper limit on testosterone was introduced and provided that female athletes with 10 nanomole per litre of blood

---

69 Shinohara Tsubasa, *Paving the Way for the Protection of Human Rights in Sports: The Case of Intersex and Transgender Female Athletes* (Stämpfli Verlag 2024) 10.

70 The 2011 Regulations are no longer available online; however, a summary may be found here: World Athletics, 'IAAF to Introduce Eligibility Rules for Females with Hyperandrogenism' 12 April 2011 <https://www.worldathletics.org/news/iaaf-news/iaaf-to-introduce-eligibility-rules-for-femal-1> accessed 5 July 2024. See also Jaime Schultz, 'New Standards, Same Refrain: The IAAF's Regulations on Hyperandrogenism' (2012) 12(7) The American Journal of Bioethics 32. Semenya was only permitted to compete in 2010 on condition that she take medication to lower her testosterone levels, and this prompted the introduction of the Regulations.

71 IOC Regulations on Female Hyperandrogenism Games of the XXX Olympiad in London, 2012 (Lausanne, 22 June 2012) <https://stillmed.olympic.org/Documents/Commissions_PDFfiles/Medical_commission/2012-06-22-IOC-Regulations-on-Female-Hyperandrogenism-eng.pdf> accessed 14 May 2024.

(nmol/L) would be permitted to compete without any surgical or pharmacological intervention. The lower range of testosterone for men is reported to be 6.9 nmol/L.[72] At 10 nmol/L, the upper limit is 'more than 10 standard deviations above the mean for women, making this a highly improbable threshold to cross'.[73]

The Hyperandrogenism Regulations, which came into effect on 1 May 2011, provided: **7–24**

> A female with hyperandrogenism who is recognised as a female in law shall be eligible to compete in women's competition in athletics provided that she has androgen levels below the male range (measured by reference to testosterone levels in serum) or, if she has androgen levels within the male range, she also has an androgen resistance which means that she derives no competitive advantage from such levels.[74]

The Case of Dutee Chand

Chand, an Indian sprinter, challenged the validity of the IAAF Hyperandrogenism Regulations before the CAS.[75] The Athletics Federation of India (AFI), an affiliated federation of World Athletics, suspended Chand pending the reduction of her testosterone levels by either taking medication or having surgery. Chand based her challenge on four grounds. The first ground was that the IAAF Hyperandrogenism Regulations unlawfully discriminated against female athletes and against athletes who possess a particular natural physical characteristic. Secondly, she contended that the IAAF Hyperandrogenism Regulations were based on flawed and unscientific assumption regarding the nexus between testosterone and athletic performance. Thirdly, Chand argued that the IAAF Hyperandrogenism Regulations were disproportionate to any legitimate objective and, lastly, it was an unauthorised form of doping control. Professor Bruce Kidd, the Vice-President of the University of Toronto and former athlete, was cited by the CAS Panel as stating 'to date, it has only been used against women from developing countries'.[76] He was concerned that athletes were being forced to undergo medical procedures and drug treatments.[77] **7–25**

The CAS Panel accepted that Chand was a woman, she had never taken a banned substance and her testosterone levels exceeded the upper limit for a female athlete.[78] Equally, it accepted that the exact levels of **7–26**

---

72 Francisco J Sánchez, María José Martínez-Patiño, and Eric Vilain, 'The New Policy on Hyperandrogenism in Elite Female Athletes is not about "Sex Testing"' (2013) 50(2) Journal of Sex Research 112, 113.
73 ibid.
74 World Athletics (n 70).
75 *Chand* (n 1).
76 ibid [22].
77 ibid.
78 ibid [36].

Chand's testosterone levels had not been established as the three-stage assessment method of the Initial Clinical Examination, Preliminary Endocrine Assessment and Full Examination and Diagnosis had not been carried out.[79] It was presumed that Chand had exceeded the limit of 10 nmol/L.[80] The CAS Panel acknowledged that there was no bad faith on the part of the IAAF in drafting the Hyperandrogenism Regulations.[81]

7–27 The CAS Panel consulted the relevant regulations, namely the Olympic Charter, the IAAF Constitution, the World Anti-Doping Code (WADC) and the IAAF Regulations on Hyperandrogenism. Chand was seeking an interim measure as she was being pressurised by a sponsor to undergo a medical procedure. Decisions of the Appeal Arbitration Division of the CAS are usually publicly available unless the parties decide otherwise. Chand agreed for the decision to be made public subject to her personal medical records remaining private. Chand stated that the case 'raises important issues of public interest and general application'.[82]

7–28 It is interesting to note that Professor Martínez-Patiño was one of the experts who provided the CAS Panel with a report on the Hyperandrogenism Regulations. As discussed above, she had failed a gender test in 1985; however, she opined that the IAAF Hyperandrogenism Regulations were necessary to ensure fairness and she agreed with their 'spirit and approach'.[83] In highlighting the lack of privacy afforded to Chand by the AFI, Martínez-Patiño highlighted the importance of preserving confidentiality.[84]

7–29 The burden of proof was placed on Chand to prove on the balance of probabilities that the IAAF Hyperandrogenism Regulations were *prima facie* discriminatory.[85] The CAS Panel asserted that the standard of proof for each issue was the balance of probabilities and it did not accept that the IAAF had to justify that the Regulations were proportionate and appropriate using the standard of 'the comfortable satisfaction of the Panel'.[86] However, if Chand could not prove that the Hyperandrogenism Regulations were discriminatory, then the burden would be placed on the IAAF to justify the discrimination which would be a higher level than that of the balance of probabilities.[87]

7–30 The CAS Panel found that the Hyperandrogenism Regulations were discriminatory as they only applied to female athletes. The onus was on the IAAF to establish that the Hyperandrogenism Regulations were

---

79 ibid.
80 ibid.
81 ibid [37].
82 ibid.
83 ibid [321].
84 ibid.
85 ibid [441].
86 ibid [447].
87 ibid [443].

'necessary, reasonable and proportionate for the purposes of ensuring a level playing field for female athletes'.[88]

On the second issue, the scientific basis for the Hyperandrogenism Regulations, the CAS Panel relied on expert witnesses from both sides and concluded 'that no single study has established, to an appropriate level of certainty, a scientific basis to come to a definitive conclusion one way or the other'.[89] The onus was on Chand to demonstrate that the Hyperandrogenism Regulations were unsupported by scientific data and the CAS Panel determined that Chand had failed to meet the onus.[90] 7–31

On the third issue regarding proportionality, the CAS Panel found this ground to be difficult. The burden was placed on the IAAF on the balance of probabilities.[91] Unless the IAAF could justify the Hyperandrogenism Regulations, then they would be deemed contrary to the Olympic Charter, the IAAF Rules, and the Laws of Monaco.[92] The CAS Panel accepted that the Hyperandrogenism Regulations were 'intended to pursue a legitimate objective'.[93] The CAS Panel reiterated that the categorisation of men and women in sport was necessary in order to the ensure the element of fairness as it recognised the biological differences between men and women.[94] However, the CAS Panel recognised the need to look at this from 'a legal perspective'.[95] It reasoned that gender testing was not an appropriate criterion as athletes may still be female but have high levels of testosterone and thereby have an increased LBM, which creates a competitive advantage.[96] It asserted that whether a person is a female is a matter of law and there was no evidence that the legal recognition of gender varied in most countries except for a small number where it is 'determined exclusively by a process of self-identification'.[97] For the CAS Panel, the level of testosterone was an appropriate criterion and it acknowledged that there are women with high levels of testosterone relative to other women and these women are sensitive to testosterone and consequently remain females.[98] There is no separate category for intersexed athletes and the Hyperandrogenism Regulations only apply to women. If the female athlete is precluded from competing in women's events, she cannot compete in men's 7–32

---

88 ibid [450].
89 ibid [474].
90 ibid [488].
91 ibid [500].
92 In all cases involving the IAAF/World Athletics the applicable law in the CAS is Monegasque Law as World Athletics is based in Monaco. Chand was in support of Monegasque Law being used as it provided for the elimination of discrimination against women: ibid [115].
93 ibid [508].
94 ibid [510].
95 ibid [509].
96 ibid [510].
97 ibid [510].
98 ibid.

events.[99] The CAS Panel observed that the Regulations 'do not police the male/female divide but establish a female/female divide within the female category'.[100] The CAS Panel surmised that the level of accepted testosterone (10 nmol/L) was based on best available science. However, it was unable to conclude

> on the balance of probabilities that androgen-sensitive hyperandrogenic female athletes enjoy such a substantial performance advantage over non-hyperandrogenic female athletes that excluding them from competing in the female category, and thereby excluding them from competing at all unless they take medication or undergo treatment, is a necessary and proportionate means of preserving fairness in athletics competition and/or policing the binary male/female classification.[101]

7–33 IAAF could not discharge the burden that the Hyperandrogenism Regulations were necessary and proportionate.[102]

7–34 The fourth and final ground of the Hyperandrogenism Regulations being an impermissible doping sanction was refuted by the IAAF; it was deemed to the be weakest ground by Chand's own counsel.[103] The burden of proof was on placed on Chand using the balance of probabilities – she would have to prove that the Hyperandrogenism Regulations were a disguised doping sanction and thus incompatible with the WADC. The CAS Panel distinguished doping from the Hyperandrogenism Regulations.[104] If an athlete is found to have committed a doping infraction, they face a punishment. The use of the words 'violation' and 'sanctions' are used, and a ban is imposed as a deterrent. In contrast, the Hyperandrogenism Regulations relate to an eligibility rule. There is no reprimand or censure and, while the athlete may be disqualified, they may resume once they lower their testosterone levels by either surgery or medication. The CAS Panel duly rejected this fourth ground.

7–35 The Hyperandrogenism Regulations were deemed invalid and suspended for two years subject to the following conditions:

- The IAAF provide further written evidence in support of the claim that Hyperandrogenism in female athletes creates a competitive advantage.[105]
- Or, if the IAAF writes to the CAS to inform it that it does not intend to file such evidence, then the Hyperandrogenism Regulations would be deemed void.[106]

---

99 ibid.
100 ibid.
101 ibid [532].
102 ibid.
103 ibid [540].
104 ibid [542]–[546].
105 ibid [548].
106 ibid.

The CAS Panel would revisit Chand's case if written evidence and expert reports were furnished by the IAAF and would determine whether the Regulations were valid if new evidence were put forward in support of the contention. In the interim period, Chand was permitted to compete both nationally and internationally.[107] 7–36

The CAS Panel adopted a very balanced approach. The Interim Arbitral Award is very detailed and almost resembles a judgment of a court. As discussed in Chapter 12, the CAS was established to provide an athlete-centric tribunal for the resolution of sporting disputes. Given the scientific evidence and the sensitive issues involved, the decision is quite verbose and requires a thorough reading. One notable aspect of the decision was the CAS Panel's emphasis on gender testing not being an appropriate criterion. Any attempt by World Athletics and the IOC to re-introduce mandatory gender testing, if challenged, would arguably be deemed void by the CAS. 7–37

Aftermath of the Interim Arbitral Award

The final decision of the CAS was expected by the summer of 2017. However, the IAAF was granted an extension until September 2017 pending the publication in the *British Journal of Sports Medicine* of an article that supported the link between hyperandrogenism and athletic performance. The article, 'Serum Androgen Levels and their Relation to Performance in Track and Field: Mass Spectrometry Results from 2127 Observations in Male and Female Elite Athletes' by Stéphane Bermon and Pierre-Yves Garnier, found that female athletes with higher testosterone levels had a 'significant competitive advantage over those with low' testosterone levels in the following events: the 400m, the 400m hurdles, 800m, hammer throw and pole vault.[108] 7–38

In commenting on their findings, Bermon noted: 7–39

> Our starting position is to defend, protect and promote fair female competition. If, as the study shows, in certain events female athletes with higher testosterone levels can have a competitive advantage of between 1.8–4.5% over female athletes with lower testosterone levels, imagine the magnitude of the advantage for female athletes with testosterone levels in the normal male range. This study is one part of the evidence the IAAF will be submitting to CAS regarding the degree of performance

---

[107] ibid 160 [2].

[108] (2017) 51(17) British Journal of Sports Medicine 1309, 1309. Both authors have links with World Athletics and the IOC, and the study was funded by the IAAF/World Athletics and WADA. Dr Bermon was on the working groups of the IAAF and IOC on athletes with hyperandrogenism and transgender athletes, while Dr Garnier is the Director of World Athletics' Health and Science Department: see World Athletics, 'Levelling the Playing Field in Female Sport: New Research Published in the *British Journal of Sports Medicine*' 3 July 2017 <https://www.worldathletics.org/news/press-release/hyperandrogenism-research> accessed 14 May 2024.

> advantage that hyperandrogenic female athletes enjoy over female athletes with normal testosterone levels. We continue to gather more data and research on our journey to providing a fair and level playing field for females in our sport.[109]

7–40 On 29 September, the IAAF submitted the journal article and other supporting documentation to the CAS, and it included draft revised regulations that would only apply to female track events over distances of between 400 metres and one mile.[110]

7–41 In a response on 6 October 2017, Chand contended that the IAAF had not complied with the Interim Award in that it had furnished supporting documentation for the revised Hyperandrogenism Regulations and the not the 2011 Hyperandrogenism Regulations on which her challenge was based.[111] She submitted that the 2011 Hyperandrogenism Regulations should be declared invalid. She further argued that she did not fall within the distances of the revised Hyperandrogenism Regulations and thus they did not apply to her.[112]

7–42 The CAS Panel did not issue a determination at this point; instead it suspended the 2011 Hyperandrogenism Regulations for another six months. If the IAAF were continuing with the 2011 Hyperandrogenism Regulation then the proceedings would resume with the same panel of arbitrators; however, if the IAAF were replacing the 2011 Hyperandrogenism Regulations with the revised ones, then the proceedings would be terminated.[113]

Correction of the Bermon and Garnier Article

7–43 The Bermon and Garnier article was subject to a correction in 2021.[114] The writers acknowledged that ethical and methodological criticisms were directed at the article. In a trio of articles published by the *British*

---

109 World Athletics (n 108). It is worth noting that the article was criticised by three academics (Roger Pielke Jr, University of Colorado Boulder; Ross Tucker, University of Cape Town; and Erik Boye, Oslo University Hospital) who, in a letter, called for the *British Journal of Sports Medicine* to retract the article: see Roger Pielke Jr, 'A Call for Bermon and Garnier (2017) to be Retracted' (*Sports Integrity Initiative*, 13 July 2018) <https://www.sportsintegrityinitiative.com/call-bermon-garnier-2017-retracted/> accessed 14 May 2024.

110 Court of Arbitration for Sport, 'Dutee Chand Case: The Application of the IAAF Hyperandrogenism Regulations Remain Suspended' (Lausanne, 19 January 2018) <https://www.tas-cas.org/fileadmin/user_upload/Media_Release_3759_Jan_2018.pdf> accessed 14 May 2024.

111 ibid.

112 ibid.

113 ibid.

114 Stéphane Bermon and Pierre-Yves Garnier, 'Correction: Serum Androgen Levels and their Relation to Performance in Track and Field: Mass Spectrometer Results from 2127 Observations in Male and Female Elite Athletes' (2021) 55(17) British Journal of Sports Medicine 7e.

Journal of Sports Medicine in 2017 and 2018, including the Bermon and Garnier article, the link between elevated testosterone levels and athletic performance was explored.[115] The writers contended that many of the criticisms were addressed in a 2018 article that included Bermon as one of the co-authors.[116] The second article published in 2017 was also subject to a correction in 2021.[117] In the correction to their 2017 article, Bermon and Garnier highlighted the exploratory nature of their findings, which were 'not confirmatory or evidence for a causal relationship' between athletic performance and testosterone levels.[118]

They concluded: **7–44**

> Even though exploratory findings between enhanced testosterone levels in females and high athletic performance levels are on a lower level of evidence, they are important for Athletics in the absence of more robust evidence and when considering eligibility criteria to compete in the women's category.[119]

In responding to criticisms, Bermon and Garnier acknowledged that 'an independent, prospectively designed, randomly controlled trial is needed to establish confirmatory scientific evidence for the causal relationships between the variables analysed'.[120] The correction raises questions about the findings of the original article as it recommends that further research is needed, research that is not exploratory and more concrete findings based on scientific evidence. **7–45**

Eligibility Regulations for Female Classification (Athlete with Differences of Sexual Development)

In April 2018, the IAAF announced its new Regulations, the 'Eligibility Regulations for Female Classification (DSD)' for events from 400m to the mile, including 400m, hurdles races, 800m, 1500m, one-mile races and combined events over the same distances ('Restricted Events').[121] Under the DSD Regulations: **7–46**

---

115 Emma Eklund and others, 'Serum Androgen Profile and Physical Performance in Women Olympic Athletes' (2017) 51(17) British Journal of Sports Medicine 1301; and Stéphane Bermon and others, 'Serum Androgen Levels Are Positively Correlated with Athletic Performance and Competition Results in Elite Female Athletes (2018) 52 British Journal of Sports Medicine 1531.

116 Bermon and others (n 115).

117 Emma Eklund and others, 'Correction: Serum Androgen Profile and Physical Performance in Women Olympic Athletes' (2021) 55(19) British Journal of Sports Medicine 8e.

118 Bermon and Garnier (n 114) 7e.

119 ibid.

120 ibid.

121 World Athletics, 'IAAF Introduces New Eligibility Regulations for Female Classification' 26 April 2018 <https://www.worldathletics.org/news/press-release/eligibility-regulations-for-female-classifica> accessed 14 May 2024.

> Any athlete who has a Difference of Sexual Development (DSD) (i.e., her levels of circulating testosterone (in serum) are five (5) nmol/L or above and who is androgen-sensitive) must meet the following criteria to be eligible to compete in Restricted Events in an International Competition (or set a world record in a Restricted Event at competition that is not an International Competition):
>
> (a) she must be recognised at law either as female or as intersex (or equivalent).
>
> (b) she must reduce her blood testosterone level to below five (5) nmol/L for a continuous period of at least six months (e.g., by use of hormonal contraceptives); and
>
> (c) thereafter she must maintain her blood testosterone level below five (5) nmol/L continuously (i.e.: whether she is in competition or out of competition) for so long as she wishes to remain eligible.[122]

Caster Semenya: The CAS to the European Court of Human Rights

7–47 The DSD Regulations were to come into force on 1 November 2018 and thus would replace the 2011 Hyperandrogenism Regulations, effectively terminating the *Chand* proceedings. However, these revised DSD Regulations were challenged by Caster Semenya, who sought a decision by the CAS that the 2018 DSD Regulations were unlawful and in doing so prevent them coming into force.[123] In dismissing her request for arbitration, the CAS Panel concluded:

> the majority of the Panel finds that the DSD Regulations are discriminatory but that on the evidence currently before the Panel such discrimination is a necessary, reasonable and proportionate means of achieving the aim of what is described as the integrity of female athletics and the upholding of the 'protected class' of female athletes in certain events.[124]

7–48 In upholding the DSD Regulations, the CAS Panel agreed with the condition that female athletes with 5 nmol/L or more would be required to take medication to reduce their testosterone levels or face being ineligible to compete.

7–49 In July 2019, Semenya appealed the decision of the CAS to the Swiss Federal Supreme Court, with the Swiss Court temporarily suspending the DSD Regulations with immediate effect.[125] This was pending the appeal being heard by the Swiss Federal Supreme Court. The decision was handed down on 25 August 2020 and published on 8 September

---

122 ibid.

123 *Semenya* (n 2).

124 ibid [626].

125 This was the Super-Provisional Order dated 31 May 2019: see Swiss Info, 'Swiss Federal Court: Semenya Free to Run without Medication until Appeal Heard' (4 June 2019) <https://www.swissinfo.ch/eng/society/athletics-case_swiss-federal-court—semenya-free-to-run-without-medication-until-appeal-heard/45007906> accessed 14 May 2024. See (n 2) for an explanation of the SFT/Swiss Federal Supreme Court.

2020.[126] It dismissed both actions: the action brought by Semenya and the action brought by Athletics South Africa.[127] The Swiss Federal Supreme Court stated that 'as far as possible, fair sport is a perfectly legitimate interest'.[128] It referred to the ECtHR and the importance it attaches to fair competition.[129] In finding that 46 XY DSD athletes had an advantage, albeit a natural one, over other female athletes who do not have DSD, the Court asserted that such athletes 'are disadvantaged and deprived of a chance of success when they have to face athletes 46 XY DSD'.[130] XY DSD athletes have an advantage 'of such magnitude that it allows them, over distances between 400 metres and the mile, to systematically beat female athletes without DSD'.[131]

Semenya argued that her right to human dignity had been infringed; **7–50** however, the Swiss Federal Supreme Court disagreed and held:

> In some contexts as particular as that of competitive sport, it may be accepted that biological characteristics may, exceptionally and for the purposes of equity and equal opportunities, eclipse a person's legal sex or gender identity. Otherwise, the very idea of a binary male/female division, present in the vast majority of sports, would lose its raison d'être. Under these conditions, restricting the access of female athletes 46 XY DSD, who naturally have an insurmountable advantage over other women, to certain competitions, does not appear to be contrary to the human dignity of these athletes.

It found that Semenya's appeal 'did not appear with high probability **7–51** to be well founded'.[132]

[126] For the English translation of the judgment, see Swiss Federal Supreme Court, 4A–248/2019 and 4A–398/2019, judgment of 25 August 2020 <https://www.bger.ch/ext/eurospider/live/fr/php/aza/http/index.php?highlight_docid=aza%3A%2F%2Faza://25-08-2020-4A_248-2019&lang=de&zoom=&type=show_document> accessed 14 May 2024. See also Press Release of the Swiss Federal Supreme Court, judgment of 25 August 2020 (4A_248/2019, 4A_398/2019) 'DSD Regulations: Caster Semenya's Appeal against the Decision' (Lausanne, 8 September 2020) <https://www.bger.ch/files/live/sites/bger/files/pdf/en/4A_248_2019_yyyy_mm_dd_T_e_18_18_10.pdf> accessed 14 May 2024.

[127] Press Release of the Swiss Federal Supreme Court (n 126) 2 summarises the main points as follows: 'Fairness in sport is a legitimate concern and forms a central principle of sporting competition. It is one of the pillars on which competition is based. The European Court of Human Rights also attaches particular importance to the aspect of fair competition. In addition to this significant public interest, the CAS rightly considered the other relevant interests, namely the private interests of the female athletes running in the "women" category.'

[128] Swiss Federal Supreme Court (n 126) [9.8.3.3].

[129] ibid. The Swiss Court was referring to the case of *National Federation of Sportspersons' Associations and Unions (FNASS) and Others v France – 48151/11 and 77769/13*, judgment of 18 January 2018 <https://hudoc.echr.coe.int/eng#{%22itemid%22:[%22002-11815%22]}> accessed 13 May 2024. This case is discussed in detail in ch 6 paras 6-67—6-68.

[130] ibid [9.8.3.4].

[131] ibid [9.8.3.3].

[132] Press Release of the Swiss Federal Supreme Court (n 126) 2.

7–52 Semenya lodged an application against Switzerland at the ECtHR alleging that the decision of the Swiss Federal Supreme Court was in breach of her human rights protected by the European Convention of Human Rights (ECHR).[133] She based her claim on the following articles of the ECHR:

- Article 3 (prohibition of inhuman or degrading treatment)
- Article 8 (right to respect for private life), taken alone and in conjunction with Article 14 (prohibition of discrimination)
- Article 6 (right to a fair hearing)
- Article 13 (right to an effective remedy)

7–53 On 11 July 2023, the ECtHR handed down its decision in *Semenya v Switzerland*.[134] By a 4–3 majority, it found there to be a violation of Article 14 taken together with Article 8 and a violation of Article 13 in relation to Article 14 taken together with Article 8 of the ECHR.[135] The ECtHR found:

> that the applicant was not afforded sufficient institutional and procedural safeguards in Switzerland to allow her to have her complaints examined effectively, especially since they concerned substantiated and credible claims of discrimination as a result of her increased testosterone level caused by DSD … The high stakes of the case for the applicant and the narrow margin of appreciation afforded to the respondent State should have led to an in-depth institutional and procedural review, but such a review was not available to the applicant in the present case. As a result, the Court is unable to find that the application of the DSD Regulations to the applicant's case could be considered a measure that was objective and proportionate to the aim pursued.[136]

7–54 The ECtHR was critical of the way both the CAS and Swiss court did not apply the provisions of the ECHR and

> left open serious questions as to the validity of the DSD Regulations, in particular as regards: the side-effects of the hormone treatment; the potential inability of athletes to remain in compliance with the DSD

---

133 *Semenya* (n 3).

134 ibid.

135 The dissenting judges were Grozev, Roosma and Ktistakis. In a joint dissenting opinion, the judges did not agree with the majority in 'that there was nothing arbitrary or manifestly unreasonable in the judgment of the Federal Supreme Court. It is primarily for the national authorities, in particular the courts, to interpret, and assess compliance with, domestic law.' In relation to Article 14, the judges argued that 'the alleged violation requires a particularly careful and balanced analysis of the rights of two protected groups under the Article 14 case-law of the Court, women on the one hand and intersex people on the other. And this, in the context of a novel issue, fairness in sport, on which there is precious little general guidance and/or agreement.' The short dissenting opinion is included at the end of the majority decision.

136 *Semenya* (n 3) [201].

> Regulations; and the lack of evidence of 46 XY DSD athletes having an actual significant athletic advantage in the 1,500 and 1 mile races.[137]

It was also critical of the review carried out by the Swiss Federal Supreme Court of the CAS decision, which is referred to as being 'very limited' as it was confined to determining whether the CAS arbitral award was compatible with public policy.[138] The Swiss Court, the ECtHR held, 'failed ... to respond to the serious concerns expressed by the CAS in a manner compatible with the requirements of Article 14 of the Convention'.[139] **7–55**

Articles 43 and 44 of the ECHR provide that a chamber decision is not final. Any of the parties have three months to request that a case is referred to the Grand Chamber.[140] The request is considered by a five-judge panel, who decide whether the case requires further deliberation.[141] Switzerland referred the decision to the Grand Chamber on 6 November 2023. The hearing before the Grand Chamber took place on 15 May 2024.[142] **7–56**

DSD Regulations Amended

On 23 March 2023, World Athletics announced changes to its DSD regulations and rules relating to transgender athletes.[143] For DSD athletes, the new regulations mandate that athletes must reduce their testosterone levels below a limit of 2.5 nmol/L for a minimum of 24 months to compete internationally in any female category event. Thus, it has removed 'restricted events' from the DSD Regulations. The new regulations came into effect on 31 March 2023.[144] Until then, Semenya **7–57**

---

137 ibid [200].

138 ibid.

139 ibid. World Athletics responded to the judgment of the 'deeply divided Chamber' and insisted that the DSD Regulations are necessary, reasonable, and proportionate. It stated it would liaise with the Swiss government and encourage a referral to the Grand Chamber given the dissenting views of three of the judges: World Athletics, 'World Athletics Responds to European Court of Human Rights Decision' 11 July 2023 <https://worldathletics.org/news/press-releases/response-european-court-human-rights-decision-2023> accessed 15 May 2024.

140 This flowchart provides a simple explanation of the process: <https://www.echr.coe.int/documents/d/echr/Case_processing_Court_ENG> accessed 15 May 2024.

141 European Court of Human Rights, 'The Grand Chamber' <https://www.echr.coe.int/documents/d/echr/faq_gc_eng> accessed 15 May 2024. The ECHR is available at <https://70.coe.int/pdf/convention_eng.pdf> accessed 15 May 2024.

142 European Court of Human Rights, '*Semenya v Switzerland*' (ECHR, 15 May 2024). The judges go into private deliberations after the hearing and the judgment will be published in due course: see European Court of Human Rights, 'Grand Chamber Hearing Concerning Switzerland' (15 May 2024) <https://www.echr.coe.int/w/grand-chamber-hearing-concerning-switzerland-2> accessed 15 May 2024.

143 World Athletics, 'World Athletics Council Decides on Russia, Belarus and Female Eligibility' 23 March 2023 <https://worldathletics.org/news/press-releases/council-meeting-march-2023-russia-belarus-female-eligibility> accessed 15 May 2024.

144 World Athletics, 'Eligibility Regulations for Female Classification (Athletes

had switched to competing at the 200m distance, which was outside the scope of the pre-March 2023 DSD Regulations and thus she was not required to reduce her testosterone levels. World Athletics did provide for interim provisions for athletes who were competing in unrestricted events. Female athletes or intersexed athletes affected by the Regulations 'must have continuously maintained the concentration of testosterone in their serum below 2.5 nmol/L3 for a period of at least 24 months'.[145] Athletes must suppress their testosterone levels below 2.5 nmol/L for a minimum of six months before they were eligible to compete again.[146] The six-month period is consistent with the previous regulations, which required six months of testosterone suppression (below 5nmol/L) for DSD athletes to compete in the restricted events.

7–58 Affected athletes:

> must continue to maintain the concentration of testosterone in their serum below 2.5 nmol/L at all times (i.e., whether they are in competition or out of competition) for so long as they wish to retain eligibility to compete in the female classification at World Rankings Competitions and/or to have recognised any World Record performance in the female classification at a competition that is not a World Rankings Competition.[147]

7–59 The implications of the decision of the ECtHR on the DSD Regulations remain uncertain. The regulations are a creation of World Athletics and thus the ECtHR was limited to examining 'whether the review carried out by the CAS and the Swiss Court satisfied the requirements of the Convention'.[148] The 2023 DSD Regulations could be subject to challenge again before CAS and on appeal to the Swiss Federal Supreme Court if the 17-judge Grand Chamber were to hold that they violate Semenya's human rights under the ECHR.

7–60 In an open letter to the IAAF, Human Rights Watch argue that '[w]omen with intersex variations have the same rights to dignity and bodily integrity as all women', and the DSD Regulations are a form of discrimination against women. They further contend that the *British Journal of Sports Medicine* article is based on 'bad science'.[149] The Women's Sport Foundation has blamed the DSD Regulations for 'exacerbating discrimination against women in sport who are perceived as not prescribing to normative ideas about femininity'.[150] World Athletics

---

with Differences of Sex Development) (Version 3.0, approved by Council on 23 March 2023, and coming into effect on 31 March 2023) Book C – C3.6 <https://worldathletics.org/about-iaaf/documents/book-of-rules> accessed15 May 2024.

145 ibid Regulation 3.2.1.

146 ibid Regulation 3.2.2.

147 ibid Regulation 3.2.3.

148 *Semenya* (n 3) [80].

149 Human Rights Watch, 'Revoke Discriminatory Athletics Gender Regulations' (26 July 2018) <https://www.hrw.org/node/320925/printable/print> accessed 15 May 2024.

150 'Human Rights Watch: Testosterone Limit for Female Athletes Is Discrimination'

has defended the DSD Regulations, citing the need to ensure fairness and stating that the DSD Regulations are akin to the age/weight divisions in a number of sports and make 'no judgment about gender or sexual identity' and, further, are based on the premise of maintaining 'a fair and meaningful category for women to compete in athletics'.[151]

An interesting point is raised in an article in the *New York Times*: 'If 7–61
elevated testosterone provided an overriding competitive advantage ... why did Chand, the Indian sprinter, not advance beyond the first round of the Olympic 100 meters?'[152] Equally, World Athletics 'does not investigate further if atypically high levels of testosterone in men are determined to occur naturally'. [153] In an editorial in *American Scientific*, the editors contend, 'Fairness and science both dictate that women should be treated exactly the same.'[154] It has also been argued that elite athletes are at risk of 'a broken bone, a torn ligament, a concussion'.[155] Athletes should thus not be expected to take on 'additional risk caused by unnecessary medical interventions ... Caster Semenya is being forced to undertake the risk associated with this intervention to be able to compete'.[156]

The use of high levels of testosterone in female athletes as a biological 7–62
marker is both a complex and highly contentious issue. For those female athletes that have naturally occurring high levels of testosterone, it is an inherent characteristic. Parallels can be drawn between athletes that are naturally very tall and who may have a competitive advantage in certain sports.

The DSD Regulations, while discriminatory to women, have been 7–63
justified as being proportionate, necessary, and reasonable to ensure that there is a level playing field for female athletes. In addition to the amended DSD Regulations, World Athletics' Council agreed to

The Guardian (London, 26 July 2018) <https://www.theguardian.com/sport/2018/jul/26/human-rights-watch-iaaf-testosterone-limit-discrimination> accessed 15 May 2024.

151 World Athletics, 'IAAF Response to Open Letter from the Women's Sports Foundation and Athlete Ally' 17 July 2018 <https://www.worldathletics.org/news/press-release/iaaf-response-to-womens-sports-foundation-and> accessed 15 May 2024.

152 Jeré Longman, 'Understanding the Controversy Over Caster Semenya' *New York Times* (New York, 18 August 2016) <https://www.nytimes.com/2016/08/20/sports/caster-semenya-800-meters.html> accessed 15 May 2024.

153 ibid.

154 The Editors, 'Naturally Occurring High Testosterone Shouldn't Keep Female Athletes Out of Competition' *American Scientific* (New York, 1 August 2016) <https://www.scientificamerican.com/article/naturally-occurring-high-testosterone-shouldn-t-keep-female-athletes-out-of-competition/> accessed 15 May 2024.

155 Hilary Bowman-Smart and others, 'World Athletics Regulations Unfairly Affect Female Athletes with Differences in Sex Development' (2024) 51(1) Journal of the Philosophy of Sport 29, 47.

156 ibid.

exclude male-to-female transgender athletes who have been through male puberty from female World Rankings competition from 31 March 2023. The next part of the chapter will discuss the rules surrounding transgender athletes.

Transgender Athletes: International Olympic Committee

7–64 In 2004 the IOC introduced provisions allowing transgender athletes to compete subject to certain criteria[157] and these rules were amended in November 2015.[158] Under the 2004 guidelines, transgender athletes were permitted to compete once they had undergone gender reassignment surgery. If the athlete had gender reassignment prior to puberty, they could compete immediately as their assigned gender. However, for post-puberty gender reassignment, there were several conditions, including the requirement of a gonadectomy; their assigned gender had to be legally recognised by the relevant authorities; and hormonal therapy had to be completed for at least two years before the athlete could compete.[159] In 2015, the IOC Medical Commission recommended that the guidelines be revised and the requirement for gender reassignment was removed as a condition for eligibility to compete. The IOC Consensus Meeting on Sex Reassignment and Hyperandrogenism concluded that the autonomy of gender identity should be recognised and that requirement of 'surgical anatomical changes as a pre-condition to participation is not necessary to preserve fair competition and may be inconsistent with developing legislation and notions of human rights'.[160] The 2015 guidelines were referred to as a 'living document', one that would evolve in line with scientific and medical developments.[161] For females who identify as male, there were no restrictions. For males who transition to female, there were a few conditions which had to be met under Clause 2.1 and 2.2 of the Guidelines, provided

> 2.1 The athlete has declared that her gender identity is female. The declaration cannot be changed, for sporting purposes, for a minimum of four years.
>
> 2.2. The athlete must demonstrate that her total testosterone level in serum has been below 10 nmol/L for at least 12 months prior to her first competition (with the requirement for any longer period to be based

---

157 International Olympic Committee, 'IOC Approves Consensus with Regard to Athletes Who Have Changed Sex' 18 May 2004 <https://www.olympic.org/news/ioc-approves-consensus-with-regard-to-athletes-who-have-changed-sex-1> accessed 15 May 2024.

158 International Olympic Committee, 'IOC Consensus Meeting on Sex Reassignment and Hyperandrogenism November 2015' <https://stillmed.olympic.org/Documents/Commissions_PDFfiles/Medical_commission/2015-11_ioc_consensus_meeting_on_sex_reassignment_and_hyperandrogenism-en.pdf> accessed 15 May 2024.

159 ibid.

160 ibid 1(a), (b) and (e).

161 ibid 1(g).

> on a confidential case-by-case evaluation, considering whether or not 12 months is a sufficient length of time to minimize any advantage in women's competition).[162]

There were plans to halve the permissible testosterone level to 5nmol/L in the lead-up to the 2020 Tokyo Olympics. However, there was a lack of consensus from the scientific experts. Some saw the reduction to 5 nmol/L as a compromise; others contend that transgender women still retain some of the physical advantages after transitioning, especially after they have gone through puberty as men.[163] Due to COVID–19, the Tokyo Olympics did not go ahead until 2021; however, the IOC decided in March 2020 that the 2015 Guidelines would remain, and any amendments would be formulated after the Olympics.[164] **7–65**

An article published in late 2020/early 2021 questioned the fairness of the IOC Regulations on Transgender Athletes. The research was conducted on 29 transmen and 46 transwomen in the US Air Force using a combination of fitness tests and medical records.[165] The researchers summarised their findings: **7–66**

> The 15–31% athletic advantage that transwomen displayed over their female counterparts prior to starting gender affirming hormones declined with feminising therapy. However, transwomen still had a 9% faster mean run speed after the 1-year period of testosterone suppression that is recommended by World Athletics for inclusion in women's events.[166]

In 2022, a new policy emerged and signified a change of approach. In November 2021, the IOC published the *IOC Framework on Fairness, Inclusion and Non-Discrimination on the Basis of Gender Identity and Sex Variations*.[167] The Framework was the result of two years of consultation with over 250 athletes and stakeholders. The Framework provides that it is up to each sport to decide the eligibility requirements for transgender athletes, taking to consideration a 10-principle approach: **7–67**

---

162 ibid 2.

163 Sean Ingle, 'IOC Unable to Agree on Guidelines for Transgender Athletes' *The Irish Times* (Dublin, 25 September 2019) <https://www.irishtimes.com/sport/other-sports/ioc-unable-to-agree-on-guidelines-for-transgender-athletes-1.4029778> accessed 15 May 2024.

164 Graham Dunbar, 'Olympic Guidelines on Transgender Athletes to Come after 2020 Games' (*CBC*, 4 March 2020) <https://www.cbc.ca/sports/olympics/summer/olympics-tokyo-2020-transgender-guidelines-1.5485290> accessed 15 May 2024. It was estimated that there could be up to three transgender athletes competing in the Tokyo Games.

165 Timothy A Roberts, Joshua Smalley, and Dale Ahrendt, 'Effect of Gender Affirming Hormones on Athletic Performance in Transwomen and Transmen: Implications for Sporting Organisations and Legislators' (2020) 55(11) British Journal of Sports Medicine 577.

166 ibid 577.

167 The six-page document is available at <https://stillmed.olympics.com/media/Documents/Beyond-the-Games/Human-Rights/IOC-Framework-Fairness-Inclusion-Non-discrimination-2021.pdf> accessed 15 May 2024.

1. Inclusion
2. Prevention of harm
3. Non-discrimination
4. Fairness
5. No presumption of advantage
6. Evidence-based approach
7. Primacy of health and bodily integrity
8. Stakeholder-centred approach
9. Right to privacy
10. Periodic reviews.

7–68 The new approach reflects 'this evolving policy landscape[;] the IOC has moved from one-size-fits-all guidance toward a principled approach to be undertaken on a sport-by-sport basis'.[168] The IOC Framework does not endorse or prohibit 'the use of testosterone levels as part of eligibility criteria for trans athletes'.

> The IOC acknowledges that testosterone may be an important factor shaping performance in elite athletes in certain sports, events and disciplines. It also acknowledges that, where established as relevant, testosterone levels could be investigated as a means to mitigate performance and offer some trans athletes a pathway to inclusion in elite sport. However, a robust and evidence-based approach to eligibility criteria starts with an assessment of unfair and disproportionate advantage that is informed by the specificities of a given sport/discipline/event, is supported by appropriate data and is consistent with the Framework as a whole.[169]

World Athletics

7–69 The IAAF Regulations Governing Eligibility of Athletes who have undergone Sex Reassignment to compete in Women's Competition came into force on 1 May 2011.[170] These Regulations expressly excluded from its remit female athletes who had transitioned.[171] Chapter 2 on Notification of Cases of Sex Reassignment to the IAAF provided that a male-to-female transgender athlete had to notify the IAAF of her gender reassignment at least three months in advance of an international competition. If the athlete competed without giving the prior notification, she would be deemed to have breached the IAAF Rules and accordingly be sanctioned by being declared ineligible to compete.[172] Under Clause

---

168 Magali Martowicz and others, 'Position Statement: IOC Framework on Fairness, Inclusion and Non-Discrimination on the Basis of Gender Identity and Sex Variations' (2022) 57(1) British Journal of Sports Medicine 26, 31. This article, from IOC medical experts and scientists from various universities, hospitals and one author from World Archery, explains each principle.

169 ibid 29.

170 The 2011 Regulations are no longer available on the World Athletics website.

171 ibid ch 1 Scope of Regulations, para 1.4. The only requirement for transgender male athletes was to have an identity card or certificate that attested that they were male.

172 ibid para 2.1.

2.3 the athlete was required to furnish the IAAF with a sex-recognition certificate, details of the medical procedures carried out, post-surgery monitoring and details of dosage and periodicity of medication. The Expert Medical Panel would gather all the necessary medical data and would make a recommendation on eligibility to the IAAF.[173] On foot of the recommendation from the Expert Medical Panel, the IAAF would decide on eligibility and the athlete would be required to submit to ongoing monitoring during competition by the Expert Medical Panel with conditions decided by the Panel.[174] Failure to agree to this meant that the athlete would be declared non-compliant and would face a minimum of two weeks ineligibility to compete, which would not be lifted until the athlete was compliant with the conditions laid down by the Expert Medical Panel.[175]

On 1 October 2019, the 2011 IAAF Regulations were replaced by the World Athletics' Eligibility Regulations for Transgender Athletes.[176] In aligning the DSD Regulations with the Eligibility Regulations for Transgender Athletes, the 2019 Regulations provided that the athlete's new gender identity did not need to be recognised by law; however, the athlete was required to sign a declaration that her gender was female. The eligibility criteria were provided for under Clause 3.2: **7–70**

> 3.2.1 she must provide a written and signed declaration, in a form satisfactory to the Medical Manager, that her gender identity is female;
>
> 3.2.2 she must demonstrate to the satisfaction of the Expert Panel (on the balance of probabilities), in accordance with clause 4, that the concentration of testosterone in her serum has been less than 5 nmol/L3 continuously for a period of at least 12 months; and
>
> 3.2.3 she must keep her serum testosterone concentration below 5 nmol/L for so long as she wishes to maintain her eligibility to compete in the female category of competition.[177]

As COVID–19 saw the cancellation of sport both nationally and internationally and the postponement of the Tokyo Olympics, the debate surrounding the eligibility of transgender athletes was somewhat shelved. World Rugby announced in October 2020 the publication of its new guidelines on the participation of transgender players, which **7–71**

---

[173] ibid ch 8 Recommendation of Expert Medical Panel on Athlete's Eligibility, paras 8.1–8.6.

[174] ibid ch 9 IAAF decision on Eligibility, para 9.7.

[175] ibid para 9.8.

[176] World Athletics, 'Eligibility Regulations For Transgender Athletes (Effective as from 1 October 2019)' <https://www.iaaf.org/download/download?filename=63067c17-1ab4-4a08-a132-5e36bda5fc61.pdf&urlslug=Eligibility%20Regulations%20for%20Transgender%20Athletes%2C%20in%20force%20from%201%20October%202019> accessed 15 May 2024.

[177] Clause 4 refers to the Assessment by the Expert Panel.

continues the ban on transgender women playing against women at international level:

> ... it was concluded that safety and fairness cannot presently be assured for women competing against transwomen in contact rugby. As a result, the new guidelines do not recommend that transwomen play women's contact rugby on safety grounds at the international level of the game where size, strength, power and speed are crucial for both risk and performance, but do not preclude national unions from flexibility in their application of the guidelines at the domestic/community level of the game. Transmen are permitted to participate in men's contact rugby.[178]

7–72 World Athletics voted to ban transgender women from competition on 23 March 2023.[179] In advance of the World Athletics' Council meeting, it was reported that the 'preferred option' was 'to tighten the sport's eligibility rules, but still use testosterone limits as the basis for inclusion'.[180] A consultation process, which took place in January and February 2023, involved several stakeholders, including Member Federations, the Global Athletics Coaches Academy, Athletes' Commission, the IOC as well as representative transgender and human rights groups.[181] The general consensus following the consultation process was

> that there was little support within the sport for the option that was first presented to stakeholders, which required transgender athletes to maintain their testosterone levels below 2.5 nmol/L for 24 months to be eligible to compete internationally in the female category.[182]

7–73 The President of World Athletics, Sebastian Coe, acknowledged the difficulty of balancing the rights and needs of different groups, but maintaining 'fairness for female athletes' was placed 'above all other considerations'.[183] Coe asserted that World Athletics would be

> guided in this by the science around physical performance and male advantage which will inevitably develop over the coming years. As more evidence becomes available, we will review our position, but we believe the integrity of the female category in athletics is paramount.[184]

---

178 World Rugby, 'World Rugby Approves Updated Transgender Participation Guidelines' 9 October 2020 <https://www.world.rugby/news/591776/world-rugby-approves-updated-transgender-participation-guidelines?lang=en> accessed 15 May 2024. The revised Transgender Women Guidelines are available at <https://www.world.rugby/the-game/player-welfare/guidelines/transgender/women> accessed 15 May 2024.

179 'World Athletics Council Decides on Russia, Belarus and Female Eligibility' (n 143).

180 Dan Roan, 'World Athletics Proposes New Transgender Eligibility Rules' (*BBC Sport*, 23 January 2023) <https://www.bbc.com/sport/athletics/64373487> accessed 15 May 2024.

181 'World Athletics Council Decides on Russia, Belarus and Female Eligibility' (n 143).

182 ibid.

183 ibid.

184 ibid.

World Aquatics

World Aquatics (formerly Fédération Internationale de Natation, FINA) does not permit transgender females to compete. Its Policy on Eligibility for Women's and Men's Competition Category came into force on 24 March 2023.[185] The objective of the Policy is 'to maintain the separation of Aquatic sports into men's and women's categories according to scientifically grounded, sex-based criteria'.[186] Equally, the Policy recognises the opportunity for transgender and 46 XY DSD athletes to compete in open categories.[187] Lia Thomas, an American swimmer, challenged World Aquatics' Eligibility Policy and commenced ordinary arbitration proceedings in the CAS.[188] As it was an ordinary arbitration proceeding, the default position is that decision is confidential unless the parties otherwise agree.[189] However, the parties waived the right to confidentiality and the decision was published on 12 June 2024.[190] Thomas challenged the Policy under the Olympic Charter, the World Aquatics Constitution, Swiss law, the ECHR and the United Nations (UN) Convention on the Elimination of All Forms of Discrimination against Women on the grounds that it was unlawful and invalid.[191] She contended that the policy was discriminatory, unnecessary, unreasonable and disproportionate in achieving a legitimate sporting objective.[192] In dismissing the challenge, the CAS Panel found that Thomas lacked standing. The Panel noted that the Policy and Operational Requirements, which implemented the Policy, did not specify who had a 'substantive right to challenge their rights', thus the Panel looked to Swiss law.[193] It followed under Swiss law 'for a claimant to have standing to sue under Swiss law, it shall demonstrate that he/she has a substantive right of its own in the matter at stake'.[194] It acknowledged that as it was an ordinary **7–74**

---

185 World Aquatics, 'Policy on Eligibility for Women's and Men's Competition Category' (both approved by the FINA Bureau and ratified by the FINA Congress on 19 June 2022) <https://resources.fina.org/fina/document/2023/03/27/dbc3381c-91e9-4ea4-a743-84c8b06debef/Policy-on-Eligibility-for-the-Men-s-and-Women-s-Competiition-Categrories-Version-on-2023.03.24.pdf> accessed 16 May 2024.

186 ibid.

187 For the Swimming World Cup which took place between 6 and 8 October 2023, no applications were received for the open category: see World Update on the Open Category competitions at the World Aquatics Swimming World Cup – Berlin 2023 Aquatics (3 October 2023) <https://www.worldaquatics.com/news/3715191/update-on-the-open-category-competitions-at-the-world-aquatics-swimming-world-cup-berlin-2023> accessed 16 May 2024.

188 Court of Arbitration for Sport, 'The Procedure *Thomas v World Aquatics* Is the 10,000th Case Registered by CAS since its Creation in 1984' (26 January 2024) <https://www.tas-cas.org/fileadmin/user_upload/CAS_Media_Release_10kprocedures_L._Thomas.pdf> accessed 16 May 2024.

189 See Chapter 12 para 12–55.

190 CAS 2023/O/10000 *Thomas v World Aquatics* award of 10 June 2024 <https://www.tas-cas.org/fileadmin/user_upload/10000_Arbitral_Award__for_publ._.pdf > accessed 5 July 2024.

191 *Thomas* (n 188).

192 ibid.

193 *Thomas* (n 190) [74].

194 ibid [76].

division procedure, the athlete was not challenging a decision made by World Athletics, rather she was challenging the Policy and Operational Requirements.[195] As Thomas was not a member of USA Swimming at the time the proceedings in the CAS were initiated, her link to World Athletics was as an indirect member.[196] The CAS Panel asserted that indirect membership was 'not sufficient to demonstrate standing in the present matter because in the present matter there is no decision personally affecting the Athlete's membership rights'.[197] The CAS Panel, in examining the Policy, stated that it did not govern eligibility for World Athletics events or events recognised by World Athletics and 'unless and until an athlete is registered for a WA Competition by a member federation, the Policy and Operational Requirements of WA have no impact on that athlete, and they are simply not triggered'.[198]

7–75 World Aquatics welcomed the decision and referred to as 'a major step forward in our efforts to protect women's sport'.[199] However, the CAS Panel award did not affirm the Policy on Eligibility for Women's and Men's Competition Category, it merely found that Thomas did not have legal standing to challenge the Policy.

British Triathlon Federation

7–76 Under the rules of the British Triathlon Federation, for athletes over the age of 12, competitive women's events are reserved 'for those who are female sex at birth'.[200] In January 2023, an open category was created for transgender males and females, males, and non-binary athletes who were male sex at birth.[201] The open category applies to all events and all levels, both elite and grassroots, where there are prizes, times or rankings at stake.[202]

Union Cycliste Internationale

7–77 Prior to 17 July 2023, the Union Cycliste Internationale (UCI) permitted transgender female athletes who had a plasma testosterone concentration

---

195 ibid [80].
196 ibid [82].
197 ibid [83].
198 ibid [89].
199 Quoted by Rohith Nair, 'Transgender swimmer Lia Thomas loses case to overturn World Aquatics ban' *The Independent* (London, 12 June 2024) <https://www.independent.co.uk/sport/olympics/lia-thomas-transgender-world-aquatics-ban-b2561525.html> accessed 5 July 2024.
200 British Triathlon Transgender Policy Implementation Guidance (2023) para 5.2 <https://www.britishtriathlon.org/britain/documents/about/edi/british-triathlon-transgender-guidance.pdf> accessed 16 May 2024.
201 Dan Roan, 'British Triathlon Becomes First UK Sport to Create "Open" Category for Transgender Athletes' (*BBC Sport*, 6 July 2022) <https://www.bbc.com/sport/triathlon/62063359> accessed 16 May 2024.
202 ibid.

of 2.5 nmol/L or less for a 24-month period.[203] However, it found that transgender female athletes that had gone through male puberty had not sufficiently eliminated the 'benefits of testosterone during puberty in men'.[204] On 17 July 2023, the UCI Management Committee approved changes to its Eligibility Regulations, which prohibits female transgender athletes from competing in women's events if they transitioned after male puberty.[205]

The UCI Management Committee referred to 'considerable inter- **7–78**
individual variability in response to gender-confirming hormone therapy'.[206] It concluded:

> Given the current state of scientific knowledge, it is also impossible to rule out the possibility that biomechanical factors such as the shape and arrangement of the bones in their limbs may constitute a lasting advantage for female transgender athletes.[207]

Gaelic Athletic Association

In 2022, the Gaelic Games Transgender Working Group was established, **7–79**
and its role was to produce 'a white paper designed to inform policy regarding the participation in Gaelic Games by persons from the transgender/non-binary community'.[208] According to a submission to the Joint Committee on Tourism, Culture, Arts, Sport and Media, the White paper, now completed, has been forwarded to the Safeguarding, Player Welfare and Sport Science committees for consideration.[209]

Renee Richards and the Supreme Court of New York

The Supreme Court of New York decided the legal status of a transgender **7–80**
athlete in 1977.[210] The ECtHR briefly discussed *Richards* in *Semenya v*

---

203 Union Cycliste Internationale, 'The UCI Adapts its Rules on the Participation of Transgender Athletes in International Competitions' 14 July 2023 <https://www.uci.org/pressrelease/the-uci-adapts-its-rules-on-the-participation-of-transgender-athletes-in/6FnXDIzvzxtWFOvbOEnKbC> accessed 16 May 2024.

204 ibid.

205 ibid.

206 ibid.

207 ibid. For more details see, Union Cycliste International, 'Part 13 – Medical Rules, Chapter V Eligibility Regulations for Transgender Athletes' (2023) <https://assets.ctfassets.net/76117gh5x5an/5Qwu5ycbagkT3ApUSZg9N9/c7b5fea8d1d49aab3b0375d95769b721/20230714_Modification_Transgender_Regulation_Juillet_2023_ENG_red.pdf> accessed 16 May 2024.

208 Gaelic Athletic Association, 'Inclusion in Sport Submission' (27 February 2024) 7 <https://data.oireachtas.ie/ie/oireachtas/committee/dail/33/joint_committee_on_tourism_culture_arts_sport_and_media/submissions/2024/2024-02-27_submission-gaelic-athletic-association-gaa_en.pdf> accessed 16 May 2024.

209 ibid.

210 *Richards* v *US Tennis Assn*, 93 Misc 2d, 713, 400 NYS 2d 267 (Sup Ct NY, 1977).

Switzerland.[211] In 1934 Renee Richards was born male and called Richard Raskind. In 1975 Raskind had a gender re-assignment operation and changed her name to Renee Richards. Richards had a successful career as a tennis player and in 1976 was refused entry as a female competitor into the US Open by the US Tennis Association (USTA). Richards refused to be physically examined to verify her biological gender. She successfully challenged the decision of the USTA with the Supreme Court of New York, holding that there was overwhelming medical evidence that supported the contention that Richards was in fact female. The USTA compared the position of transgender athletes to 'drug cheats' and 'female impersonators' and 'impostors'.[212] The Court rejected this comparison and held 'there to be very few biological males, who are accomplished tennis players, who are also either preoperative or postoperative transsexual'.[213]

World Anti-Doping Code and Transgender Athletes

7–81 The most recent version of the WADC came into force on 1 January 2021. In Comment 115 to Article 23.2.2 on the Implementation of the Code, there is a reference to transgender athletes. It states: 'an International Federation could use data from a Doping Control test to monitor eligibility relating to transgender and other eligibility rules'.[214] In its December 2020 Report, Human Rights Watch requested that WADA 'rescind the provision in the World Anti-Doping Code that allows data from doping tests to be used for the purposes of sex testing'.[215] This is a new provision – it was not included in the 2015 version of the Code. In the third draft of the revised Code, it was not included and yet appeared in the final version of the Code, leading one commentator to conclude it 'would therefore appear that the text was inserted without full consultation with WADA's stakeholders'.[216] In defending the inclusion of Comment 115, one of the drafters of 2021 Code was cited as saying that there had 'always been a provision in the Code – and you can find it in the 2015 Code – that you can use anti-doping samples for disciplinary and health purposes'.[217] The inclusion of a specific provision is a precarious development as it could be used 'to target

211 *Semenya* (n 3) [74]–[76].
212 Richards (n 210) 269.
213 ibid.
214 World Anti-Doping Agency, 'World Anti-Doping Code 2021' <https://www.wada-ama.org/sites/default/files/resources/files/2021_wada_code.pdf> accessed 16 May 2024.
215 Human Rights Watch (n 54) 14.
216 Andy Brown, 'Doping Samples Can Be Used for Gender Verification under 2021 Code' (*Sports Integrity Initiative*, 17 June 2020) <https://www.sportsintegrityinitiative.com/doping-samples-can-be-used-for-gender-verification-under-2021-code/> accessed 16 May 2024.
217 ibid.

athletes with high testosterone competing in the female category for medical intervention'.[218]

It remains to be seen if the provision will be included in the 2027 Code. It is highly probable that it will. If used improperly it could be challenged before the CAS. The way in which it was nonchalantly inserted by way of a footnote is perhaps a more worrying development. The lack of discourse surrounding its inclusion suggests that the drafters knew that it would be a contentious provision and perhaps thought it would go unnoticed. **7–82**

Conclusion

It is established that the categorisation of most sports into female and male events is appropriate. It gives cognisance to the biological differences between men and women. Gender testing proved to be a humiliating and devasting experience for many female athletes. Questioning a person's gender can have serious ramifications for their mental well-being, not to mention the media intrusion into their private lives. The decision to end mandatory gender testing by the IAAF and the IOC was welcomed. While accepting that the Hyperandrogenism Regulations and its successor, the DSD Regulations, are discriminatory against women, they can be justified in the interests of preserving the element of fairness in sport. **7–83**

The 2022 IOC Policy leaves it up to the relevant IFs to decide eligibility. As discussed, several IFs prohibit transgender female athletes who went through male puberty from competing in female events. The introduction of open categories is an interesting development; however, World Aquatics did not receive a single entry for its open category at its Swimming World Cup in Berlin in October 2023. The decision of the Grand Chamber of the ECtHR in the case of *Semenya v Switzerland* may not be published for many months given the complexities, not to mention the considerations and deliberations of 17 judges. **7–84**

The scientific discourse on the nexus between higher testosterone levels and athletic performance is still in embryonic form. The reliance of the IAAF on one *British Journal of Sports Medicine* article, which was subsequently corrected and whose authors had affiliations with both the IOC and IAAF, is questionable. For the findings to be validated, more independent studies will need to be carried out. Similarly, studies on transgender female athletes and the effect of residual testosterone need to be explored. It is an evolving area and one that requires a multidisciplinary approach from the various stakeholders. **7–85**

---

[218] ibid.

CHAPTER 8

THE LAW OF CONTRACT AND SPORT

Introduction

A contract is a legally binding agreement between two or more parties. Contract law falls under the branch of law called private law, which regulates relationships between individuals. Every day individuals make contracts, often without realising it – the purchase of goods in the supermarket involves a contractual agreement. A person buying a house will enter a contract of sale. An employee who works for a regular wage or salary will have a contract of employment.[1] The role of the law of contract is to identify binding agreements, interpret and enforce them. Not all agreements are legally binding as favours, gifts and moral obligations can never be the subject of a contract. Contracts to defraud the Revenue or commit a crime are illegal and can never be enforced. **8–01**

Sports contracts can be used to regulate and govern the relationships between a sportsperson and a club, namely a professional services contract (also known as a standard professional contract), endorsement/sponsorship contracts, intermediary contracts (a contract between a player and an agent), a contract between a club and a manager, participation contracts (contracts for competing at a particular event: for example, the Paralympic or Olympic Games), transfer contracts (an agreement between a player and clubs to change the player's registration from one club to another whether for a short period or permanently) and the sale of media rights of an event or competition. At the outset it is important to distinguish judicial review of statutory bodies (such as those established in Ireland in the horse racing and greyhound industries) and the judicial scrutiny of sports bodies, which is often done on a private law (contractual) basis. The law of contract can also be used by a sportsperson against a private sports body when a decision of the sports body is challenged on the grounds of procedural unfairness, the implication being that there has been a breach of the contractual obligation to act fairly.[2] **8–02**

1 The Terms of Employment (Information) Acts 1994–2014 provide that an employer is obliged to provide an employee with a written statement of terms of employment within the first two months of the commencement of employment. Chapter 9 'Employment Law and Sport' will discuss this in detail.

2 Jack Anderson, *Modern Sports Law: A Textbook* (Hart 2010) 28. This will be discussed in Chapter 11 'Judicial Review and Sporting Bodies'.

8–03 The focus of this chapter will be on how the law of contract applies to sport. It will provide the basis for the subsequent chapters: Chapter 9 will examine 'Employment Issues in Sport', including contracts of employment and, more specifically, standard professional contracts; Chapter 10 will address 'Commercial Issues in Sport'; and Chapter 11 'Judicial Review and Sports Bodies' discusses the role of contract law and private sports bodies.[3]

8–04 This chapter begins by discussing the elements of a contract, contractual relationships in sport and capacity to contract. It examines the limits of capacity and minors by looking at a few seminal cases. The chapter proceeds to discuss how governing bodies have augmented the legal protections by introducing restrictions on underage players contracting to an international transfer, namely Article 19 of the Fédération Internationale de Football Association's (FIFA) Regulations on the Status and Transfer of Players (RSTP). It briefly discusses the protection of underage players in relation to agents. The terms used in contracts are examined, as are the ways in which a contract can be discharged and the remedies that are available for breach of contract.

The Elements of a Contract

8–05 Every contract has four essential elements:

1) offer;
2) acceptance;
3) consideration; and
4) intention to create legal relations.

Offer

8–06 An offer can be oral, written or inferred by conduct.[4] An offer must be clear and unambiguous so that an interested party must be able to understand exactly to what the contract relates. An example of an unclear and ambiguous offer would involve a seller, for example, stating that they will sell their car for around €5,000.[5] However, if the seller says they will sell the car for €5,500, there is no ambiguity and this is thus clear enough to constitute an offer for the purposes of a contract. In the case of *Guthing v Lynn*, the terms of the agreement were that the plaintiff would purchase the defendant's horse for £63; however, if the horse were lucky, the plaintiff would pay an additional £5 or purchase another

3 Chapter 10 will discuss agency, image, and media rights. This chapter does not discuss every aspect of contract law; however, a number of leading Irish books on contract law are cited throughout for the reader to consult.

4 For example, the consumer picks up a bar of chocolate and goes to the checkout and hands the appropriate money to the cashier.

5 See Raymond J Friel, *The Law of Contract* (Round Hall 1995) 23–24.

horse.[6] The Chief Justice (CJ) Lord Tenterden held the 'substantial and operative part' of the payment of £63 to be acceptable; however, the £5 extra if the horse proved to be lucky was considered 'too loose and vague to be considered in a Court of Law'.[7] Lord Tenterden added: 'Who is to say under what circumstances a horse shall be said to have proved "lucky"?'[8]

It is important to distinguish an offer from an invitation to treat. An invitation to treat is something that invites the potential purchaser to treat themselves by buying the goods or services. The goods could be advertised in a catalogue or brochure, newspaper, magazine, online, a shop shelf or part of a window display. It could be a kitchen in showroom that is arranged in a particular manner but does not mean that it would look that way in the buyer's home. The display is not usually for sale and is instead indicative of how the kitchen could look.[9] The case of *Carlill v Carbolic Smoke Ball Co* makes a distinction between an offer and an invitation to treat.[10] The Carbolic Smoke Ball Co had advertised its medical preparation called 'The Carbolic Smoke Ball' in the *Pall Mall Gazette* on 13 November 1891 and in other newspapers with the announcement that a reward of £100 would be paid to any person who contracted influenza after using the Smoke Ball three times daily for two weeks. The money was deposited, according to the advertisement, with the Alliance Bank, Regent Street, to demonstrate their 'sincerity in the matter'.[11] In the Queen's Bench Division, Hawkins J found in favour of the plaintiff, who in good faith had purchased the smoke ball and used it as directed yet still caught the flu.[12] The defendants appealed to the Court of Appeal, with counsel arguing that the terms of the advertisement were so vague that it could not form the basis of a contract as there was no deadline as to when claims should be made nor was there any way of checking whether the customer had properly used the smoke ball as per the instructions.[13] The Court of Appeal dismissed the appeal and held that although the advertisement was made to the public at large, once Carlill had acted upon it (had used the smoke ball three times a day for three weeks) there was a contract between the defendant company and the plaintiff. A newspaper advertisement would usually constitute an invitation to treat; however, in this case the lodging of £100 in the Alliance Bank showed that the defendant had offered consideration and thus the essential elements of a contract were present.[14] 8–07

6 (1831) 2 B & Ad 232.

7 ibid 234.

8 ibid 234–35.

9 Friel (n 5) 23–24.

10 [1893] 1 QB 256.

11 ibid 257.

12 [1892] 2 QB 484.

13 (n 10) 257–58.

14 The Court of Appeal discussed the lack of notification of acceptance of the offer; however, it held that once the plaintiff 'performed the condition' then 'the condition notification is dispensed with (Lord Justice (LJ) Bowen, ibid 270). As will

Acceptance

8–08 Acceptance is a response to the offer. Only the offeree (the person to whom the offer was made) can accept the offer. The offer can be accepted expressly (orally or in writing) or inferred by conduct. There are two types of contracts: bilateral and unilateral. The distinction is important as 'they yield different consequences' when it comes to acceptance.[15] With a bilateral contract, the 'offeror is requesting a promise or undertaking as distinct from the thing itself'.[16] The bilateral contract is addressed to a specific individual and a contract is created once it is accepted 'even though the object of that contract has not been performed'.[17] In contrast, a unilateral contract can be addressed to the world at large and acceptance takes place 'by performing a stipulated or requested action'.[18] A unilateral contract is one-sided, as the case of *Carlill* demonstrates above. Bilateral contracts are more common: as Simpson explains, they are 'two-sided in the sense that the parties enter into reciprocal obligations to each other'.[19]

8–09 In *Billings v Arnott & Co Ltd*, an example of a unilateral contract, the High Court held in favour of the plaintiff who sought £366 from his employer, the defendant company.[20] The company posted the following announcement:

> During the present emergency as stated by the Government, the directors have agreed to facilitate any employee joining the Defence Forces by guaranteeing his reinstatement and half his salary up to £2 per week.

8–10 On foot of this announcement, Billings informed his employer that he would be joining the Defence Forces but was told that another employee from his department had enlisted and he could not be spared.[21] In meeting with a director of the company Billings was told that the offer had been revoked; he nonetheless applied to join the Defence Forces and was accepted. The plaintiff sought three-and-a-half years' pay from the defendant company and, when he was refused, an action was brought before Maguire J in the High Court. In finding in favour of the plaintiff, the judge referred to the notice as 'an inducement to the employees to

---

be explained in the discussion on acceptance, the contract in *Carlill* is an example of a unilateral contract. Simpson suggests that a factor for the Court in finding in favour of Carlill was due to the increase in the later part of the 19th century of 'quackery' and 'extravagant claims made for medicines and appliances', AWB Simpson, 'Quackery and Contract Law: The Case of the Carbolic Smoke Ball' (June 1985) 14(2) The Journal of Legal Studies 345, 382.

15 Friel (n 5) 41.

16 Robert Clark, *Contract Law in Ireland* (8th edn, Round Hall 2016) ch 1, s 4, para 1.37.

17 Friel (n 5) 41.

18 Clark (n 16) para 1.36.

19 Simpson (n 14) 377.

20 [1946] 80 ILTR 50.

21 ibid.

join the Defence forces' which was 'unconditional, with no reservation to allow a refusal to any employee'.[22] The judge did not accept 'that it was a mere declaration of intention' – once the plaintiff joined the Defence Forces acceptance was completed.[23]

If the offeree makes a counteroffer, this in effect is a rejection of the original offer, as it varies the terms of the offer.[24] In a sporting context, a sportsperson has several options when it comes to accepting or not accepting the offer. They can accept it, reject it, make a counteroffer or neither reject or accept and the offer then lapses after a reasonable amount of time. **8–11**

Consideration

Consideration is the price paid under a contract. It distinguishes a contract from a promise.[25] Something of value must be exchanged, either money or money's worth.[26] Consideration must be sufficient, that means that it is regarded by the law as being good or acceptable. However, consideration need not be adequate, in that it does not need to represent the full economic value of the good or service.[27] **8–12**

Intention to Create Legal Relations

By entering into the contract, it can be inferred (or is implied) that the parties intend to create legal relations. In *Blue v Ashley*, Leggatt J of the High Court of England and Wales held that a conversation between Jeffrey Blue and Mike Ashley in a public house in London on 23 January 2013 did not give rise to a valid contract.[28] Blue had a background in investment banking and began working with Sports Direct in 2012, and Ashley was the founder and majority shareholder of Sports Direct and then owner of Newcastle United.[29] Blue contended that he was owed **8–13**

---

22 ibid.

23 ibid.

24 For example: a seller offers to sell her car for €10,000 and the buyer says he will give her €8,500; this counteroffer is effectively a no to the original offer and thus terminates the original offer.

25 The only instance when an agreement without consideration can be binding is if it is a deed under seal, which must be in writing and clearly state that it is intended to be legally binding.

26 An undertaking to confer a benefit on the other party or to suffer a detriment can amount to consideration.

27 For example, an agreement to sell a Porsche for €10 is a valid contract. In this situation the consideration is sufficient and thus satisfies the legal requirement. However, the €10 is not adequate, but that is of no concern to the law. Note, however, that inadequacy might be evidence of fraud, duress or undue influence that would justify setting the contract aside.

28 [2017] EWHC 1928 (Comm).

29 Ashley owned the club between 2007 and 2021 and sold it in October 2021 for £305m to the Saudi Public Investment Fund: Joe Moore, 'Newcastle Takeover CONFIRMED as Saudi-Led Group Finally Purchase Premier League Club from Mike Ashley, with Steve Bruce Expected to Depart as Manager' (*Talksport*,

£14m under a contract he contended was formed during the conversation in the Horse and Groom public house. The claimant and the defendant were discussing share prices and how much they might rise to if Sports Direct continued to do well. At the time of the meeting in the Horse and Groom, the share price was about £4.[30] Blue contended that Ashley said that if the share price of Sports Direct doubled to £8 over a three-year period, then he would pay the claimant £15m.[31] Ashley did not recall their being such an agreement, although he admitted that there had been a conversation about share prices.[32]

8–14 In May 2014, Ashley paid the claimant £1m so as to reward him for his work on obtaining shareholder approval for Ashley to be included in Sports Direct employee bonus scheme.[33] The claimant proffered that this was evidence of the defendant's acceptance that the conversation in the public house had given rise to a valid contract.[34]

8–15 In dismissing the action on the grounds that there was no intention to create legal relations, Leggatt J concluded:

> In the course of a jocular conversation with three investment bankers in a pub on the evening of 24 January 2013, Mr Ashley said that he would pay Mr Blue £15 million if Mr Blue could get the price of Sports Direct shares (then trading at around £4 per share) to £8. Mr Blue expressed his agreement to that proposal, and everyone laughed. Thirteen months later the Sports Direct share price did reach £8. But no reasonable person present in the Horse & Groom on 24 January 2013 would have thought that the offer to pay Mr Blue £15 million was serious and was intended to create a contract, and no one who was actually present in the Horse & Groom that evening – including Mr Blue – did in fact think so at the time. They all thought it was a joke. The fact that Mr Blue has since convinced himself that the offer was a serious one, and that a legally binding agreement was made, shows only that the human capacity for wishful thinking knows few bounds.[35]

8–16 In short, a contract is formed when an offer made by one party (the offeror) has been accepted by the other and is supported by consideration. The parties must intend to create legal relations, and, in some instances, evidentiary formalities are required (for example, a contract must be in writing).[36] Under the doctrine of privity, only

---

7 October 2021) <https://talksport.com/football/958066/newcastle-takeover-confirmed-saudi-arabia-mike-ashley-steve-bruce-premier-league/> accessed 16 May 2024.

30 *Blue* (n 28) [12].

31 ibid [14].

32 ibid [15].

33 ibid [36].

34 ibid [34].

35 ibid [142].

36 In general, contracts may be either written oral or a combination of both. The Statute of Frauds (Ireland) 1695 provided that certain contracts were enforceable only if they are evidenced in writing, ie the principal terms of the agreement must

those party to a contract can have rights and obligations arising from that contract. The parties must be regarded by the law as having the capacity to contract, as discussed below.[37]

The Role of Contract in Sport

8–17 In discussing the role contract law plays in sport, Beloff, Kerr and Demetriou remark that the law of contract 'is the legal tool with which the stage designers of sport create the scene; and it contains the script used by the sporting actors to play to the public'.[38] In the sporting realm, contracts are entered into by a player and a club, a sportsperson and a sponsor, a sportsperson and an agent or a manager. If a coach is hired to train a team, there will be a contract between the club and the coach to give legal effect to the relationship. A contract may be used in situations involving the right of access to sporting competitions.[39] The rules of a sporting body, once accepted by the club or individual, form the basis of a contract between the body and the club or individual. A referee is contractually bound to enforce the rules of the sport as set by the governing body. A contract will also form the basis of an agreement to grant media rights. For an event manager or a governing body to secure exclusive broadcast rights over a sporting event, a contractual agreement must be negotiated with the owner of the venue.[40] This agreement will provide that only the official broadcaster can gain access to the venue for the purpose of broadcasting the footage of the event in question.

Contractual Relationships in Sport

8–18 For those that are a member of a club or association that is unincorporated, once the membership form is signed (either expressly by signing a form or impliedly by conduct) a contractual relationship has been entered

be noted and signed by both parties. The following had to be in writing: contracts for the sale of land, contracts for the sale of goods worth over £10 (Sale of Goods Act 1893, s 4), contracts of guarantee and contracts which are to be performed more than 12 months after the date of the agreement. Section 2 of the Statute of Frauds has been replaced by s 51 of the Land and Conveyancing Reform Act 2009. Section 4 of the Sale of Goods Act 1893 was repealed by the Consumer Rights Act 2022, s 8(1) and sch 1 part 1 ref 1, SI No 596 of 2022.

37 See Clark (n 16) ch 16.

38 Michael Beloff and Tim Kerr and Marie Demetriou, *Sports Law* (Bloomsbury 1999) para 2.18.

39 ibid paras 3.25–26 gives the example of a third-division team that wins the third-division championship. The team have a contractual right to compete in the second division the next season on the basis of a pre-existing contract between an individual or club and a sporting body. The club has a contract of membership with the league and the league has terms, including the automatic promotion to the higher league. If the league tried to stop the promotion it would be a breach of contract unless there was some rule entitling them to prevent the winning team from being promoted to the higher division.

40 Neville Cox and Alex Schuster (with Cathryn Costello), *Sport and the Law* (Firstlaw 2004) 364. Media rights are discussed in ch 10.

into and the member has accepted the rules and regulations of the club. Often clubs will amend their rules and such rule changes are permitted so long as the club follows the proper constitutional procedures. Any changes validly introduced are binding on the members and there is no need for the club to contact each member to inform them of the changes.

8–19 An unincorporated club or association is one that is voluntary and non-trading. It involves the coming together of individuals (members) who have a common purpose. Unincorporated clubs are relatively simple to set up and there is no requirement to make public or file the accounts or returns of the club.[41] An unincorporated club does not have to comply with the formalities that an incorporated company has under the Companies Act 2014. Most local clubs who have little property or staff are unincorporated. The main drawback for these organisations is that they do not enjoy the principle of separate legal personality. Separate legal personality means that the company and the human agents are separate. The company has legal personality similar to that of a natural (or human) person. When an incorporated company with limited liability is being wound up, each member is only liable for the amount unpaid on their shares.[42] If their shares are fully paid up, then is there no further liability. However, with an unincorporated club or association, in the event of the club/association being wound up, the members can be held jointly and severally accountable for all of its debts and obligations without any limitation. Most local sports clubs in Ireland are unincorporated. However, many large sports clubs and governing bodies are limited liability companies: for example, Munster Rugby is a Company Limited by Guarantee (GLC).[43]

---

41 The Citizen's Information website provides a detailed guide to creating an unincorporated club: 'How to Set Up a New Club' 17 January 2023 <https://www.citizensinformation.ie/en/travel-and-recreation/sport-and-leisure/setting-up-a-new-club/> accessed 16 May 2024.

42 *Salomon v Salomon & Co* [1897] AC 22.

43 A CLG is defined in under s 1172 of the Companies Act 2014, Part 18, ch 1 as 'a company which does not have a share capital and which, as provided under section 1176(2)(e), has the liability of its members limited by the constitution to such amount as the members may respectively thereby undertake to contribute to the assets of the company in the event of its being wound up'. Section 1176(2)(e) provides its Memorandum of Association shall state that each member undertakes that, if the company is wound up while they are a member, or within one year after the date on which they cease to be a member, they will contribute to the assets of the company such amount as may be required for: (i) payment of the debts and liabilities of the company contracted before they cease to be a member; (ii) payment of the costs, charges, and expenses of winding up; and (iii) adjustment of the rights of contributories among themselves, not exceeding an amount specified in the memorandum. The format of the CLG's Constitution is provided for under Schedule 10 of the 2014 Act <https://www.irishstatutebook.ie/eli/2014/act/38/schedule/10/enacted/en/html#sched10> accessed 16 May 2024. The Constitution of the CLG includes the Memorandum of Association (which sets out the objects of the company) and Articles of Association (which sets out the internal management and regulation of the company).

If an individual is a member of an unincorporated club or association, there is a contractual relationship between each member. Each member is in a contractual relationship with every other member. There is what Beloff, Kerr and Demetriou refer to as 'a horizontal matrix of contracts binding each member to all other members'.[44] As the unincorporated club has no legal existence, there is no contract which binds the members to the club. **8–20**

An individual may attend a local sports centre – for example, a gym or swimming pool. These organisations are set up as commercial entities and are usually companies with limited liability. The individual pays a causal user fee or has a subscription in return for the use of the facilities. While there is a contract between the individual and the club or gym (a vertical contract), there is no contract between the various members save as to the extent that the rules so provide. **8–21**

Capacity

In order to enter into a contract, a person must have capacity.[45] In Ireland, minors or infants are generally deemed to lack the capacity to contract. A minor or infant is the legal term used to refer to persons under the age of the 18.[46] In general, contracts involving minors are voidable, which means that they can be repudiated by the minor. However, there is an exception in situations where the contract is for *necessaries*. Necessaries constitute goods and services which are essential or beneficial to the minor's condition in life: for example, food, clothing, shelter, medical assistance, transport, educational services, and apprenticeship.[47] As the minor athlete or player may be required to sign a contract, the issue has **8–22**

---

44 (n 38) para 2.21.

45 Under s 8 of the Forfeiture Act 1870, a convicted person could not enter into a contract. The entire Act was repealed by the Third Schedule of the Criminal Law Act 1997. A person may also lack capacity if they are intoxicated or if they are mentally incapacitated: see Clark (n 16) ch 16, paras 16–46–16–52.

46 Section 2 of the Age of Majority Act 1985 reduced the age from 21 to 18. The reason why the age of majority in several jurisdictions was 21 was that 'it was only then that a young knight would have the physical strength, necessitated by the very heavy and bulky armour then in vogue, required to enable him to discharge his military duties': John W Carter and David J Harland, *Contract Law in Australia* (Butterworths 1996) 272.

47 Section 2 of the Sale of Goods Act 1893 states: 'Capacity to buy and sell is regulated by the general law concerning capacity to contract, and to transfer and acquire property. Provided that where necessaries are sold and delivered to an infant, or minor, or to a person, who by reason of mental incapacity or drunkenness is incompetent to contract, he must pay a reasonable price therefor. Necessaries in this section mean goods suitable to the condition in life of such infant or minor or other person, and to his actual requirements at the time of the sale and delivery.' The reference to 'mental incapacity' in this section was repealed by s 137(2) of the Assisted Decision-Making (Capacity) Act 2015. Section 137 commenced on 26 April 2023, see Assisted Decision-Making (Capacity) Act 2015 (Commencement) Order 2023, art 4(k), SI No 193 of 2023.

arisen whether the contract is voidable or should be upheld by the court. In breach of contract cases, the matter is decided by a judge and not a jury. The judge will consider if the particular good or service constitutes a necessary. The definition is not immutable and changes in line with societal developments. The court will look to see if the contract benefits the minor – it 'is a question of fact' which requires the court to adopt a holistic approach 'to strike a balance between the beneficial and onerous elements of the agreement'.[48]

8–23 There are some early case examples involving minor athletes and beneficial contracts of service. In *Roberts v Gray*, a contract to enable a minor to receive instruction and earn a living as a professional billiard player was upheld as valid.[49] The contract between John Roberts and Joseph George (JG) Gray (then nine years of age) was signed on 10 May 1910.[50] According to the contract, the tour would begin on 2 April 1911 and the duration of tour was 18 months with an end date of 1 October 1912.[51] Roberts agreed to pay all travel and hotel expenses of JG Gray and his father, Harry William (HW) Gray, accompanying him.[52] However, the contract further stipulated the travelling and accommodation expenses would be covered initially by Roberts but would be borne equally by Roberts and JG Gray from profits made on the tour.[53] If the costs associated with travel and accommodation exceeded the earnings and gifts received by the younger Gray then neither Gray nor his father would be personally liable or responsible.[54] Roberts made a number of payments to the Grays for their expenses in April 1911.[55] A disagreement over the types of billiard balls to be used between the parties resulted in JG Gray, on 20 April 1911, repudiating the contract.[56] The plaintiff brought an action for damages in May 1911 and, in response, JG Gray counterclaimed, contending that the contract should be rescinded.[57] The plaintiff was successful in the trial court; however, the defendant appealed to the Court of Appeal. Counsel for the appellant argued that JG Gray was not bound by the contract as it was not for a necessary and

---

48 Meaghan Mahadeo, 'Minor Matters: Ensuring the Enforceability of Contracts with Minors in the Entertainment Industry' (2015) 93(1) The Canadian Bar Review 277, 282 <https://canlii.ca/t/76x> accessed 16 May 2024.

49 [1913] 1 KB 520.

50 ibid 520. The contract provided that Gray's father would accompany him on the tour.

51 ibid 521.

52 ibid.

53 ibid.

54 ibid.

55 ibid 521–22.

56 ibid 522.

57 ibid 522. Recission is an equitable doctrine that places the parties in the position they were pre-contract. The doctrine may only be invoked prior to the execution of the contract. However, in a situation involving fraud, the doctrine may be used even when the contract has been executed. If a contract is rescinded it means that it is deemed void: see Friel (n 5) 225.

not beneficial, thus the contract was voidable at the option of the minor.[58] The Master of the Rolls (MR) Cozen-Hardy asserted that necessaries included 'education and instruction' and not just 'bread and cheese and clothes', and the Court must look at the contract as a whole in order to determine whether or not it was beneficial to the minor.[59] In a unanimous judgment, the Court of Appeal dismissed the appeal and upheld the award of damages to Roberts for the appellant's breach of contract.

In the case *Doyle v White City* Stadium, the plaintiff minor was a heavyweight boxer.[60] Doyle was under the age of 21 when he applied to the British Boxing Board of Control (BBBC) for a licence to box with the following words in his application: **8–24**

> I hereby apply for a licence as a boxer and, if the licence is granted to me, I declare to adhere strictly to the rules of the British Boxing Board (1929) as printed and abide by any further rules or alterations to existing rules as may be passed.[61]

He made the application in March 1932, which was duly granted and renewed for another year in 1933. The plaintiff was provided with a copy of the rules, which included Regulation 20, paragraph 16, which stated that a boxer may be precluded from receiving money if he were disqualified 'for committing a deliberate foul, for not trying, or retiring without sufficient cause, or if the referee gives a no contest decision'.[62] Paragraph 16 was amended on 17 June 1932 – however, the plaintiff was not informed of the change in rules which provided, 'Boxers in case of disqualification are only entitled to receive bare travelling expenses, pending the decision of the board … when the board … may deal with the money as it thinks fit.'[63] **8–25**

An oral agreement was concluded by Doyle's manager on his behalf with White City Stadium on 29 June 1933 that he would box with Jack Petersen on 12 July 1933 in the heavyweight championship of Great Britain.[64] During negotiations it was agreed that the plaintiff would be paid if he won, lost or drew.[65] In the second round of the fight, the plaintiff was disqualified for hitting below the belt and Petersen was declared the winner. At an inquiry convened by the BBBC, a decision was made to ban Doyle from fighting for six months and to withhold the prize money. The Lord Justice (LJ) Slesser made an important **8–26**

[58] *Roberts* (n 49) 522–25.
[59] ibid 525–26.
[60] [1935] 1 KB 110. It is interesting to note that *Roberts* (n 49) was not cited in this case.
[61] ibid 110.
[62] ibid.
[63] ibid.
[64] ibid 112.
[65] ibid 112.

observation in relation to the contractual relationship between a member and a club as he stated:

> it would appear that this plaintiff had agreed, first, by his application, which was accepted, and secondly, by the actual provisions of the rules themselves, to be a member of this society and to be bound by its rules and regulations. It would follow that the rules and regulations would authorize the society dealing with the money which was to be his prize or reward for taking part in this contest in the way in which they have dealt with it.[66]

8–27 In the trial court, the judge found in favour of Doyle who had argued that, under the terms of the contract, he was entitled to be paid the prize money. However, the Court of Appeal reversed the decision and held that as the term was for his general benefit, in encouraging clean and fair fighting, he was bound by it although it operated in this case against him. The Court of Appeal cited with approval the judgment of Smith LJ in *Clements v London & North Western Railway Company*.[67] Smith LJ held that 'the agreement, instead of being detrimental to the infant, is, on the whole, manifestly to his advantage'.[68]

8–28 In both *Roberts* and *Doyle*, the Court of Appeal upheld the validity of the contracts. Fry LJ in the Chancery Division in the case of *de Francesco v Barnum* found that the terms of the contract involving two young stage dancers were unreasonable and could not be enforced.[69] The judge could not find any benefit to the minors under the terms of the contract. De Francesco ran a dance stage school and concluded an agreement with the mother of the two girls, Helen Maude Parnell, aged 14, and her sister, Ada, aged 12.[70] The contract provided that the apprenticeship would be for a period of seven years; the dancers could not accept professional engagements; and they could not get married during the said term without the consent of the master, de Francesco. Under the terms of the agreement, de Francesco 'would properly instruct' the minor dancers and 'make certain payments' for all their 'dancing engagements' in America, London and its suburbs, and in foreign or colonial countries.[71] The apprentice dancers' services would be entirely at the disposal of de Francesco and, during the tenure of the seven years, the dancers were precluded from entering into any professional engagements without the permission, in writing, of the plaintiff.[72] During periods of unemployment, there was no provision in the contract that placed

---

66 ibid 130.
67 [1894] 2 QB 482; *Doyle* (n 60) 125–26.
68 *Clements* (n 67) 495.
69 (1890) 45 Ch D 430.
70 ibid 431.
71 ibid 432.
72 ibid.

an obligation on de Francesco to provide renumeration nor to provide engagements for the two apprentice dancers.[73] Fry LJ stated:

> The matter, therefore, rests with Signor *De Francesco* as to how far those children shall take any wages at all. Nor can it be entirely put out of consideration that he has a right to send these apprentices for performances to any foreign state or foreign country, a power which, if exercised, would remove the infants, or probably would remove the infants from maternal care.[74]

Enjoined in the proceedings against the mother of the dancers were two other defendants, Barnum and Parravicini. Parravicini, as an agent of Barnum, had contracted the two girls to perform at Barnum's hit show, *Olympia*, for 21 shillings a week.[75] The plaintiff sought an injunction against Barnum and Parravicini on the ground that they had enticed the two apprentice dancers to breach their contract with him.[76] 8–29

Fry LJ dismissed the action for damages on the grounds that the dancers were not bound by the contract. As the contract was deemed invalid, no action could be taken against Barnum on the grounds of enticing the dancers to breach the contract with de Francesco as the contract was not binding on Helen Maude and Ava Parnell.[77] 8–30

These three cases were cited more recently in the case of *Proform Sports Management Ltd v Proactive Sports Management Ltd*.[78] Proform Sports had contracted with Wayne Rooney when he was 15 years old. The plaintiff alleged that Proactive Sports had induced Rooney to breach his contract with Proform. Proactive Sports argued that a contract between a minor footballer and an agent was voidable as it was not a necessary and thus the Court was not required to consider if the contract was for the benefit of the minor. As the contract was voidable, there could be no liability imposed on a third party for inducing a breach of that contract. In distinguishing the case of *Doyle v White City*, where the plaintiff had to sign a contract in order to earn a living as a professional boxer, 8–31

---

73 ibid 440.

74 ibid 440–41.

75 ibid 434. The contract with de Francesco was signed on 6 December 1886 and the agreement with Barnum was concluded in August 1889. Both Barnum and his agent contended that they were not aware that the two dancers were contracted to de Francesco.

76 Chitty J, in the motion hearing for the injunction, dismissed the action on the grounds that the repressive nature of the agreement could not be enforced neither at law nor in equity. Counsel for de Francesco explained that they could not disagree with the findings of Chitty J in relation to the denial of injunctive relief; however, they contended that damages were owed to the plaintiff as Barnum became aware of the contract between the two dancers and de Francesco after employing them, yet he continued to keep them in the show: *De Francesco* (n 69) 435.

77 ibid 443. The case was dismissed against all the defendants and the plaintiff was ordered to pay all costs.

78 [2006] EWHC 2903 (Ch); [2007] Bus LR 93.

Hodge J held that a contract between a footballer and an agent was not a necessary.[79] Rooney was already contracted to Everton so there was no need of a contract with an agent to represent him as a professional footballer. Once Rooney reached the age of 17, he would be in a position to earn his living via a contract with Everton or any other club. He would not need an agent for two years.[80] Hodge J held that a football management and agency agreement between a minor footballer and a company was not a contract for necessaries or analogous to a contract of apprenticeship, education or service. Judgment was given in favour of the defendants.[81]

8–32 Clark is critical of the archaic and 'extremely irrational distinctions' in contracts involving minors.[82] He proffers that the better approach for courts would be to examine such cases under the equitable doctrine of unconscionability. He cites the Ontario Court of Appeal in *Toronto Marlboro Major Junior A Hockey Club et al v Tonelli et al* in support of this contention.[83] The Court dismissed an appeal by the appellate hockey club after the High Court of Justice held that the contract between the club and a minor player was voidable at the option of the player.[84] The bargaining acumen of the club was much greater than that of the young player and as such there was imbalance of the bargaining power between the parties. In the High Court, Lerner J dismissed an action for damages and conspiracy to induce a breach of contract.[85] Tonelli at the age of 17 signed a contract with the Marlboro Major Junior A Hockey Club, an amateur club. The duration of the contract was for a period of three years, or four years at the option of the plaintiff club. The player received minimal pay and on securing a professional contract he would have to pay 20% of his earnings for three years. The club could terminate and assign the contract at any time. On reaching the age of 18, Tonelli repudiated the contract by signing for a professional club. Lerner J held that the contract was not wholly beneficial to the defendant player and was thus voidable at his option. Even if conspiracy to induce a breach of contract could be shown, as the contract was voidable, the defendants (Tonelli, his agent and the new club) could not be sued. The Ontario Court of Appeal dismissed the appeal and upheld Lerner J's judgment.[86]

---

79 [2007] Bus LR 93, 105.

80 ibid 105.

81 ibid 109.

82 Clark (n 16) ch 16, s 8, para 16–42.

83 96 DLR (3d) 135 – 23 OR (2d) 193; 1979 CanLII 1969 (ON CA) <https://canlii.ca/t/g16t2> accessed 16 May 2024.

84 ibid.

85 *Toronto Marlboro Major Junior A Hockey Club et al v Tonelli et al* 1977 CanLII 1385 (ON SC) [21] <https://canlii.ca/t/g133c> accessed 16 May 2024.

86 Not all commentators agree with this. Tarantino, in reference to *Tonelli*, asserts that for 'reasons of analytical and doctrinal clarity, adhesion, unconscionability and restraint of trade should be pleaded and considered in the alternative, not as adjuncts to the discrete question of whether a contract against a minor is enforceable': Bob Tarantino, 'A Minor Conundrum: Contracting with Minors in

Protection of Minor Football Players and International Transfers

The above discussion examined capacity from the point of view of the legal framework; individual sports will have their own regulations on minor athletes that add an extra layer of protection. Taking the example of FIFA's RSTP, it contains protective measures for players under the age of 18 in relation to international transfers.[87] Article 19(1) of the Regulations states that international transfers of players are only permitted if the player is over the age of 18.[88] However, Article 19(2) allows for five exceptions to this rule.[89] The first exception, Article 19(2)(a), relates to the relocation of the minor player's parents to the country where the new club is based, and the move is unconnected to football. The second exception, Article 19(2)(b), provides that the player must be aged between 16 and 18 and the transfer takes place within the European Union (EU) or the European Economic Area (EEA),[90] or the transfer takes place between two Associations in the same country.[91] In continuing with the second rule, the new club must fulfil a number of minimum obligations, namely it 'shall provide' the player with an 8–33

Canada for Film and Television Producers' (2006) 29(1) Hastings Communications and Entertainment Law Journal 45, 59.

87 FIFA, 'Regulations on the Status and Transfer of Players' (February 2024) <https://digitalhub.fifa.com/m/6a0797ec77cbc02c/original/Regulations-on-the-Status-and-Transfer-of-Players-February-2024-edition.pdf> accessed 16 May 2024. The regulations were introduced in 2001 following discussions and negotiations between FIFA and the European Commission. Advocate General (AG) Szpunar in an Opinion delivered on 30 April 2024 in Case C-650/22 *Fédération internationale de football association (FIFA) v BZ, Interveners: Union Royale Belge des Sociétés de Football-Association ASBL (URBSFA), SA Sporting du Pays de Charleroi, Fédération Internationale des Footballeurs Professionnels, Union Nationale des Footballeurs Professionnels, Fédération Internationale des Footballeurs Professionnels, Division Europe* questioned the compatibility of the RSTP and the termination of a contract without just cause under art 45 of the Treaty on the Functioning of the European Union (TFEU) on the free movement of persons as well as under EU competition law. The judgment of the Court of Justice of the European Union (CJEU) was handed down on 4 October 2024. The Opinion ECLI:EU:C:2024:375 is available at <https://eur-lex.europa.eu/legal-content/EN/TXT/?uri=CELEX%3A62022CC0650&qid=1715864555575> accessed 16 May 2024. For information on the CJEU decision, see para 13-36, fn 114.

88 RSTP (n 87) 39.

89 The original rules were introduced by FIFA in 2001 under art 12, which provided for two exceptions. There were amendments made in 2005 and 2009. For an overview of the development of the RSTP and underage players see Enric Ripoll González, 'A Review of FIFA's Minor Application Guide for U18 International Transfers' (*Law in Sport*, 8 January 2021) <https://www.lawinsport.com/topics/item/a-review-of-fifa-s-minor-application-guide-for-u18-international-transfers#_ftn4> accessed 16 May 2024.

90 RSTP (n 87) art 19(2)(b)(i). The EEA comprises of the 27 EU Member States along with three members of the European Free Trade Area (EFTA) – Iceland, Liechtenstein and Norway, with the exclusion of Switzerland. See Eurostat, 'Glossary: European Economic Area (EEA)' <https://ec.europa.eu/eurostat/statistics-explained/index.php?title=Glossary:European_Economic_Area_(EEA)> accessed 16 May 2024.

91 RSTP ibid art 19(2)(b)(ii). An example would be a minor player moving from England to play in Scotland.

adequate football education and/or training in line with the highest national standards.[92] In addition to the player's football education, the club 'shall guarantee' an academic and/or school and/or vocational education and/or training to facilitate the player following a career other than football should they cease to play professional football.[93] The club 'shall make all necessary arrangements to ensure that the player is looked after in the best possible' way with regard to 'optimum living standards with a host family or in club accommodation, appointment of a mentor at the club'.[94] On registration of the minor player, the club is mandated to provide the relevant association with proof that it is complying with the above obligations.[95]

8–34 The third exception, Article 19(2)(c), provides that the minor player who resides less than 50km from a national border and the club which they wish to register within the neighbouring association is also within 50km of that border, is permitted to do so with a maximum distance of 100km between where the player is domiciled and the club's headquarters. In this situation, the player is required to continue to reside at home and the two associations concerned must give their explicit consent.

8–35 Article 19(2)(d) refers to a player fleeing their home country for humanitarian reasons, the restriction on transfer of players under the age of 18 is permitted in the following situations:

> The player is at least temporarily permitted to reside in the country of arrival and/or is recognised by the competent state authorities as vulnerable and requiring state protection by the country of arrival after fleeing their country of origin (or previous country of domicile) for humanitarian reasons, without their parents, due to either of the following:
>
> i. their life or freedom being threatened on account of race, religion, nationality, belonging to a particular social group, or political opinion; or
>
> ii. any other circumstances where their survival is seriously threatened.[96]

---

[92] ibid art 19(2)(b)(iii). This needs to be read in conjunction with Annexe 4 (Training Compensation), art 4. Article 4 provides a formula for associations to use in order to calculate the compensation associated with education and training costs. Associations are required to divide their clubs into a maximum of four categories which factors in the clubs' financial investment in training players: see RSTP ibid 85–87.

[93] ibid art 19(2)(b)(iv).

[94] ibid art 19(2)(b)(v).

[95] ibid art 19(2)(b)(vi).

[96] The article further provides: 'If the minor has been formally recognised as a refugee or a protected person, they may be registered with a professional club or purely amateur club. There are no restrictions on any subsequent national transfer of the minor prior to their turning 18. If the minor has been formally recognised as [an] asylum seeker or has been recognised by the competent state authorities as vulnerable in accordance with article 19 paragraph d) above, they may only be registered with a purely amateur club. They may be the subject of a subsequent national transfer, but are not permitted to register with a professional club until they turn 18.'

Annexe 7, Article 6 explicitly refers to Ukraine. It provides for automatic 8–36
acceptance of the requirements of Article 19(2)(d) in relation to minor players residing in the territory of Ukraine who wish to register with a new club.[97]

The fifth and final exception, Article 19(2)(e), relates to a minor player 8–37
who is a student and moves temporarily to another country without their parents for academic purposes to take part in an exchange programme. The player's registration for the new club will last until they turn 18 years of age or until the end of the academic or school programme, which cannot exceed one year. The new club 'may only be a purely amateur club without a professional team or without a legal, financial or de facto link to a professional club'.[98]

All applications relating to the international transfer of underage players 8–38
go before the Players' Status Chamber (PSC), one of three chambers that fall within the ambit of the Football Tribunal.[99] The PSC reviews applications to ensure that they fall within one of the exceptions under Article 19(2).[100] The Court of Arbitration for Sport (CAS) found that

> Article 19 RSTP sets key principles designed to protect the interests of minor players. Therefore, it must be applied in strict, rigorous and consistent manner. This means that there can be no other exceptions to the principle of Article 19 RSTP than those carefully drafted in paragraph 2 of said provision.[101]

The rules relating to international transfers and players under the 8–39
age of 18 are quite clear – however, some clubs have been sanctioned for breaches of the rules. An Italian club was sanctioned by the FIFA

---

[97] RSTP (n 87) 100.

[98] ibid art 19(2)(e). Article 19(4) provides for the approval of the international transfer by the Players' Status Chamber where the player is at least 10 years old; art 19(6) outlines the obligations and responsibilities of associations and affiliated clubs when it comes to international transfers and minor players under the age of 10; and Article 19(7) explains the procedure for a Limited Minor Exemption (LME).

[99] See art 54(1)(b) of the FIFA Statutes: Regulations Governing the Application of the Statutes, Standing Orders of the Congress (May 2022 edition) <https://digitalhub.fifa.com/m/3815fa68bd9f4ad8/original/FIFA_Statutes_2022-EN.pdf> accessed 16 May 2024. The three chambers are the Dispute Resolution Chamber; the PSC; and the Agents Chamber. For more information on the role of these chambers see FIFA, 'Football Tribunal' <https://www.fifa.com/legal/football-tribunal> accessed 16 May 2024. Amendments to the Regulations Governing the Application of the Statutes, Standing Orders of the Congress, formed part of the FIFA Congress 2024 Agenda, which took place on 17 May 2024. For more details see FIFA Congress 2024 <https://inside.fifa.com/en/about-fifa/congress> accessed 27 August 2024.

[100] For a description of the PSC see Frans de Weger, *The Jurisprudence of the FIFA Dispute Resolution Chamber* (Springer 2016) 35–39, fn 46 cites several CAS cases which have upheld the validity of art 19.

[101] CAS 2013/A/3140 *A v Club Atlético de Madrid SAD & Real Federación Española de Fútbol (RFEF) & Fédération Internationale de Football Association (FIFA)* award of 10 October 2013 [4] <https://jurisprudence.tas-cas.org/Shared%20Documents/3140.pdf> accessed 16 May 2024.

Disciplinary Committee following an investigation by the FIFA Regulatory Enforcement Department.[102] Spezia Calcio brought several Nigerian minors to Italy in breach of Article 19 of the RSTP as well as breaching national law, the Italian Legislative Decree no 286/98 on immigration.[103] The minor players were brought to Italy on tourist visas. The scheme was known as the 'Nigerian System' whereby top talent from a Nigerian club, Football College Abuja, were sent to Italy. A named coach from Football College Abuja accompanied the minors to Italy, and he received payments from Spezia Calcio. The players were assigned a tutor guardian who would enrol them in a local school, however, a police investigation found that they were not attending school and had instead been 'parked' with either Spezia Calcio's youth side, the amateur club USD Lavagnese 1919 or Valdivara 5Terre who received a payment from Spezia Calcio.[104] The idea behind the scheme was to sell the players when they reached 18 and make a profit.[105] The Disciplinary Committee referred to the scheme as a form of 'child trafficking' and, given the seriousness of the offence, imposed a fine of 4,000 Swiss Francs on USD Lavagnese 1919 and Valdivara 5Terre and a registration ban at both national and international level for four registration periods. Spezia Calcio was fined 500,000 Swiss Francs and a registration ban at both national and international level for four registration periods.[106]

---

102 The Regulatory Enforcement Department is responsible for ensuring compliance with the transfer regulations and investigating alleged breaches: FIFA, 'Football Regulatory' <https://www.fifa.com/legal/football-regulatory> accessed 16 May 2024. The Football Disciplinary Committee is one of three independent committees that make up FIFA's Judicial Bodies along with the Appeal Committee and Ethics Committee. The roles of these judicial bodies are explained in arts 50–53, Part VII: Independent Committees, Regulations Governing the Application of the Statutes, Standing Orders of the Congress (n 99). The independence of these committees is also stated in the FIFA Governance Regulations (FGR), reg 34, which references art 48 of the Statutes and provides that 'the independent committees as well as their individual members shall conduct their activities and perform their duties entirely independently but always in the interests of FIFA and in accordance with the Statutes and regulations of FIFA' (December 2022 edition) <https://digitalhub.fifa.com/m/381ee2ffb41f05ad/original/FIFA-Governance-Regulations-2022.pdf> accessed 16 May 2024.

103 Decision of the FIFA Disciplinary Committee passed on 30 June 2021, Valdivara 5Terre, FDD–8070, <https://sennferrero.com/wp-content/uploads/2021/10/Decision-FDD-8070.pdf> accessed 16 May 2024; and Decision of the FIFA Disciplinary Committee passed on 30 June 2021, USD Lavagnese 1919, FDD–8069, <https://sennferrero.com/wp-content/uploads/2021/10/Decision-FDD-8069.pdf> accessed 16 May 2024.

104 Valdivara (n 103) 1.

105 ibid. The onus of proof was placed on FIFA to prove that there was a breach of art 19. The standard used by the Discipline Committee is that of the comfortable satisfaction of the judging body, a standard which is higher than the civil standard of the balance of probabilities but lower than the criminal standard of beyond reasonable doubt: see Valdivara (n 103)[28]–[32]. Decisions of the Discipline Committee may be appealed to the FIFA Appeal Committee.

106 FIFA, 'FIFA sanctions for Spezia Calcio, USD Lavagnese 1919 and Valdivara 5 Terre for Breaches of the Rules Governing the International Transfer of Minors' 16 July 2021 <https://www.fifa.com/legal/media-releases/fifa-sanctions-for-spezia-calcio-usd-lavagnese-1919-and-valdivara-5-terre> accessed 16 May 2024.

8–40 In August 2019, the Disciplinary Committee fined Manchester City 370,000 Swiss Francs for a breach of Article 19 of the RSTP, but the club did not receive a registration ban.[107] Article 19 is there to protect underage players and its validity has been upheld by the CAS. In *FC Midtjylland A/S v FIFA*, the CAS noted that it could be argued that Article 19 constituted a restriction of fundamental rights; however, it could be justified given that it was based on a legitimate objective and was proportionate.[108] In citing with approval earlier CAS decisions on the legality of the rules, the CAS Panel found rules limiting the international transfer of underage players was not in breach of any provision of public policy nor were they in conflict with any provision of EU law.[109]

Football Agent Regulations and Minor Athletes

8–41 Chapter 10 will include an outline of the role of agents and intermediaries and the regulations that pertain to their activities. On 1 April 2015 the FIFA licencing system for agents ceased and was replaced by the Working with Intermediaries Regulations.[110] In 2023, FIFA introduced new regulations, the FIFA Football Agent Regulations.[111] Of significance to minor athletes, the 2023 Regulations have enhanced protections for minor athletes. Article 11(1) states that an agent can only contact the minor athlete, or their legal guardian, at least six months before the minor athlete signs their first professional contract, which is subject to the law of the relevant country. The agent must first receive the written consent of the guardian before they approach the minor player. Article 11(2) provides that an agent who wishes to represent a minor

[107] FIFA, 'Manchester City Football Club Sanctioned for International Transfers of Minors' (13 August 2019) <https://www.fifa.com/legal/football-regulatory/news/manchester-city-football-club-sanctioned-for-international-transfers-of-minors> accessed 16 May 2024.

[108] CAS 2008/A/1485 *FC Midtjylland A/S* v *Fédération Internationale de Football Association (FIFA)* award of 6 March 2009 [45] <https://jurisprudence.tas-cas.org/Shared%20Documents/1485.pdf> accessed 16 May 2024.

[109] ibid [46]. The CAS affirmed that art 19 applied to amateur and professional minor players at [4].

[110] FIFA, 'Working with Intermediaries Regulations' <https://resources.fifa.com/image/upload/fifa-regulations-on-working-with-intermediaries.pdf?cloudid=bntdqpzf9y8ntewsosb1> accessed 16 May 2024.

[111] The Regulations are available here: <https://digitalhub.fifa.com/m/1e7b741fa0fae779/original/FIFA-Football-Agent-Regulations.pdf> accessed 16 May 2024. The Regulations partially entered into force on 1 January 2023 with full enforcement on 1 October 2023. There is an interim injunction against the new Regulations in Germany due to a decision by the Dortmund Regional Court in Germany. The interim measure was imposed by the Court on 24 May 2023. FIFA has instructed its member associations to suspend certain provisions, see ch 10, paras 10–102—10–104. It is expected that the new Agent Regulations will be subject to a preliminary reference to the CJEU: see Björn Christian Becker, 'Oral Hearing in the Preliminary Injunction Proceedings Concerning the FIFA Football Agents Regulations (FFAR)' (*Kluwer Competition Law Blog*, 29 February 2024 <https://competitionlawblog.kluwercompetitionlaw.com/2024/02/29/oral-hearing-in-the-preliminary-injunction-proceedings-concerning-the-fifa-football-agents-regulations-ffar/> accessed 16 May 2024.

player or represent a club in a transaction involving a minor must first successfully complete a Continuing Professional Development (CPD) course. An agent who is in breach of Article 11(1) will be 'sanctioned, at a minimum, with a fine and a suspension of a Football Agent licence of up to two years'.[112]

Terms in Contracts and their Interpretation

8–42 When it comes to construing a contract, a term may be expressed, or it may be implied. An express term is one that is explicitly stipulated by the parties: for example, the salary and the duration of the contract. Implied terms refer to terms which have not been explicitly stipulated but are read into the contract by necessary implication. A contract might not state that a player is confined to playing for just one club; however, the courts would imply such a term.[113] The court uses the *officious bystander* test and centres its decision on whether its inclusion is necessary for the efficacy of the contract. The role of the court in disputes of this nature is to determine whether a term is to be implied or not.

8–43 In situations where the contract is in writing, the express terms are confined to those set out in the document. The parol evidence rule provides that where there are express terms in a contract, oral or implied terms should not be used to add or contradict the written terms. However, Friel adds that the parol evidence rule has been 'virtually' abolished by the courts given the 'considerable injustice'.[114] In cases involving a contract dispute, oral evidence would often need to be admitted as 'the written agreement might not contain the full scope of the contract'.[115] An implied term was read into the contract in the case of *Bournemouth and Boscombe AFC v Manchester United*.[116] Bournemouth concluded a transfer agreement on 27 September 1972 with Manchester United. The terms of the agreement provided that the transfer fee paid for the player, Edward John MacDougall, amounting to £194,445 would be paid. An additional £27,777 would be paid to Bournemouth if MacDougall 'scored 20 goals in first team competitive football for Manchester United'.[117] Manchester United requested the inclusion of this special clause to be sure of the ability of the player.[118] Between October and December of 1972, as a striker MacDougall scored four goals in

[112] The 2023 Regulations will be discussed in more detail in ch 10 paras 10-89—10-104.
[113] The courts are reluctant to imply terms on the grounds that a contract represents a consensus reached by the parties. It is up to the parties to agree on the terms, and the role of the court is merely as an enforcer of those terms.
[114] Friel (n 5) 153.
[115] ibid.
[116] *The Times* (London, 22 May 1980) 6.
[117] ibid. In his 166 appearances for Bournemouth, MacDougall had scored 126 goals. Lord Denning MR remarked that MacDougall had been a 'first class player for Bournemouth'.
[118] ibid.

11 matches. The manager was dismissed by Manchester United, and the new manager played MacDougall for three games; however, the player was subsequently dropped and did not get an opportunity to play again. On 29 December 1972, there was a telephone call between the new manager and Sheffield United about a possible transfer of MacDougall. At the end of February 1973, MacDougall had been transferred to West Ham United for a fee of £170,000. Lord Denning MR remarked that the new manager had no place for MacDougall 'in his scheme of things for Manchester United'.[119] Although MacDougall had not scored 20 goals, Bournemouth sought the additional payment of £27,777. The question for the Court of Appeal was whether there was an implied term in the contract. If this were answered in the affirmative, there would be no requirement for the implied term to be reasonable, it just had to be necessary.[120] In dismissing the appeal and upholding the judgment of the trial judge, Talbot J, the Court of Appeal held that Manchester United was in breach of an implied term that the player would be given reasonable opportunity in a sufficient number of games to score the 20 goals.[121]

Similarly, in *Madison Square Garden Boxing Inc v Shavers*, Earnie Shavers, a heavyweight fighter, entered into a contract to fight Muhammed Ali in a championship bout.[122] The contract did not contain a clause which specifically prohibited him from engaging in other fights during the eight-week period between the signing of the contract and the scheduled fight. Madison Square Garden Boxing sought an injunction restraining Shavers from participating in another fight prior to the Ali clash. The Court, by granting the injunction, implied a 'non-competition' covenant into the contract based on the practice of the industry and on the fact that an eight-week training period was necessary preparation for a championship contest. Also influential to Owen J in the District Court, Southern District of New York, was the consideration that if Shavers lost the pre-Ali fight, then the value of the Ali fight (to Madison Square Garden) 'would diminish considerably'.[123] The granting of negative injunctive relief in personal service contracts is a discretionary matter for the courts, and Owen J stated that the Court must be satisfied that it will not be 'unduly harsh or one-sided'.[124] He held that Shavers would not be 'injured by the granting of the preliminary injunction', whereas Madison Square Garden would to 'a measurable extent' be **8–44**

> irreparably injured as a viable promoter of major boxing matches were Shavers with impunity able to simply disavow a prior agreement with

[119] ibid.
[120] ibid.
[121] ibid. Lord Brightman dissented. The Court of Appeal agreed with the trial judge's decision to award £22,221 in damages, a 20% deduction on £27,777 to factor in the chance of the player getting injured.
[122] 562 F2d 141, 144 (2d Cir 1977).
[123] ibid, fn 3.
[124] ibid 452.

> the Garden to take advantage of a later-made more attractive offer. The Garden's credibility could be destroyed in the eyes of boxing managers, as well as various media representatives, such as television producers, or others, who, in reliance, enter into further contracts that in fact may well represent the major source of income from the event being promoted, possibly being the difference between profit and loss for the promoter. In any event, it is beyond question that the balance of hardships is in the Garden's favour.[125]

Conditions, Warranties and Innominate Terms

8–45 Express and implied terms can be further broken down into conditions, warranties, and innominate terms.[126] A condition is considered to be an integral or vital term in a contract. If a condition is breached, the injured party may have the contract rescinded and sue for damages or have terms of the contract fulfilled and sue for damages. If the parties intend that a breach of a term will result in the contract being set aside, then the term is a condition. McDermott and McDermott note that the 'issue of whether an express term is a condition or a warranty is not a matter of law but one of interpretation of the contract'.[127] According to the Sale of Goods Act 1893, s 11(1)(b), as substituted by s 10 of the Sale of Goods and Supply of Services Act 1980, whether a term is a condition or warranty 'depends in each case on the construction of the contract. A stipulation may be a condition, though called a warranty in the contract.'[128]

8–46 A condition can be classified as a condition precedent or condition subsequent. In a sporting context, a condition precedent would be a requirement for an athlete to have successfully passed a medical examination before the contract is valid. In theory, the athlete should undergo the medical assessment before the contract is signed and this is the approach taken by FIFA. Under special provisions relating to contracts between professionals and clubs, Article 18(4) of the RSTP provides that the 'validity of a contract may not be made subject to a successful medical examination and/or the grant of a work permit'.[129] In the Commentary on the latest version of the RSTP, the rationale for the regulation is explained as follows:

> Clubs have a specific obligation to organise a medical examination before signing a contract with a player. If a club fails to abide by this fundamental

---

[125] ibid.

[126] Innominate terms are also referred to as intermediate terms: see Paul S Davies, *JC Smith's the Law of Contract* (OUP 2018) 358.

[127] Paul A McDermott and James McDermott, *Contract Law* (2nd edn, Bloomsbury Professional 2017) para 20.02.

[128] 1893 Act, s 11(1)(b) can be found at <https://www.irishstatutebook.ie/eli/1893/act/71/section/11/enacted/en/html>; and 1980 Act, s 10 at <https://www.irishstatutebook.ie/eli/1980/act/16/section/10/enacted/en/html#sec10>. Section 10 of the 1980 Act renumbered s 11(1)(b) as s 11(2).

[129] (n 87) 31.

> principle, and instead decides to sign the contract before it receives confirmation that the player is fit and healthy, it does so at its own risk. A contract signed under these circumstances will be considered valid and binding, and the club will not be permitted to terminate it unilaterally if the player goes on to fail a medical. A contract terminated in this way is considered to have been terminated without just cause.[130]

FIFA's Dispute Resolution Chamber (DRC) has consistently held that a condition precedent relating to a medical examination will be deemed null and void.[131] The remaining contract will still stand, as the Commentary on the RSTP explains that the effect of Article 18(4) 'is to render any condition precedent regarding the medical examination invalid, rather than the entire contract in which that condition is included'.[132] This reflects the jurisprudence of the CAS in *Hakan Calhanoglu v Trabzonspor FC & FIFA* and *Trabzonspor FC v Hakan Calhanoglu* whereby it stated that '[o]nly the clause containing the medical check condition precedent is to be disregarded'.[133] The CAS has recognised that there are situations where a club may rescind the contract due to an unsuccessful medical test. In *FC Aris Limassol v Jiří Mašek*, the CAS Panel referred to the medical status of the player being **8–47**

> so essential to the employment relationship that it cannot be expected from the employer to execute the contract and is clear that if it had known about it before signing the employment agreement it would have never signed it.[134]

The new club can only rescind the contract if it can establish all the factual elements. However, this does not apply if the new club was fully aware of the player's medical condition and the player did not act in bad faith nor did they hide any relevant medical information from the new club.[135] It is envisaged that a club will exercise due diligence when it comes to assessing the health status of a player, thus 'the onus is quite high' on the new club.[136] **8–48**

---

130 FIFA, 'Commentary on the Regulations on the Status and Transfer of Players' (2023) 235 <https://digitalhub.fifa.com/m/40da0f707efdd011/original/FIFA-Commentary-on-the-FIFA-Regulations-for-the-Status-and-Transfer-of-Players-2023-edition.pdf> accessed 16 May 2024.

131 See Boaz Sity, 'Can Player Contracts Be Made Conditional on Passing a Medical Examination? Comparing the Approaches in Football and Basketball' (*Law in Sport*, 21 January 2020) <https://www.lawinsport.com/topics/item/can-player-contracts-be-made-conditional-on-passing-a-medical-examination-comparing-the-approaches-in-football-and-basketball#_ftnref8> accessed 16 May 2024.

132 Commentary (n 130) 236.

133 CAS 2016/A/4495 *Hakan Calhanoglu v Trabzonspor FC & FIFA*; and CAS 2016/A/4535 *Trabzonspor FC v Hakan Calhanoglu* award of 2 February 2017 [2] <https://jurisprudence.tas-cas.org/Shared%20Documents/4495,%204535.pdf> accessed 16 May 2024.

134 CAS 2013/A/3261 *FC Aris Limassol v Jiří Mašek* award of 27 August 2014 [3] <https://jurisprudence.tas-cas.org/Shared%20Documents/3261.pdf> accessed 16 May 2024.

135 ibid.

136 CAS 2008/A/1589 *MKE Ankaragücü Spor Külübü v J* award of 20 February 2009 [2] <https://arbitrationlaw.com/sites/default/files/free_pdfs/CAS%202008-A-1589%20

8–49 Friel explains that a condition subsequent 'arises after a contract has come into existence but full performance is subject to some condition; failure to perform brings the contract to an end: rights will still exist arising from the contract that once was'.[137] A 'morals clause' is an example of a condition subsequent. It is common practice for a sponsor to protect its reputation in the event of an individual sportsperson becoming embroiled in a controversy. The misconduct on the part of the sponsee may cause embarrassment or the stigmatisation of the product or service of the sponsor or endorser.[138]

8–50 A warranty is a term of minor importance, a breach of which does not entitle the party to set aside the contract. However, the injured party would be entitled to damages in the event of a breach. If the parties intend that a breach will result in damages only, then the term is a warranty.

8–51 An intermediate or innominate term is one that cannot be classified as a condition or a warranty. If there is a breach of an innominate term the injured party is entitled to compensation. The contract will not automatically be voidable at the option of the injured party. It depends on the gravity of the breach – for example, a fundamental breach would entitle the innocent party to have the contract set aside. The role of the court is to assess how serious the consequences of the breach are for the injured party. If it is a fundamental breach, the court may order that the contract be terminated.

Exclusion Clauses and Waivers

8–52 Exclusion (or exemption) clauses attempt to exclude or restrict the liability of one party in a specified circumstance. It protects the party (usually the one who has drafted the contract) from being sued by the other party for a breach of contract, damages, loss, or negligence, or it may limit the party's liability. For example, a term of the contract may stipulate that liability is restricted to a fixed sum or it may require that the injured party bring an action within a stipulated time, or it may state that the party is not liable for any damage howsoever caused. The courts do not favour exclusion clauses and if there is any ambiguity,

---

MKEASK%20v%20J%20Award.pdf> accessed 16 May 2024. The club endeavoured to terminate the contract on grounds that the player had acted in bad faith by not disclosing that he suffered from asthma. The Panel did not accept that the player had acted in bad faith.

137 Friel (n 5) 76.

138 See Stuart Benzie and Timothy Killen, 'Contractual Remedies for Damage to Reputation in Sport Sponsorship' (*Law in Sport*, 22 November 2013) <https://www.lawinsport.com/topics/contract-law/item/contractual-remedies-for-damage-to-reputation-in-sport-sponsorship> accessed 17 May 2024. Sponsorship contracts and moral clauses will be discussed in more detail in ch 9.

the clause is read *contra proferentem* – it is read in favour of the party against whom the clause operates.[139]

Discharge of the Contract

Discharge of contract is the process whereby the 'primary obligations' of the contract have been carried out by the parties and as such the contract comes to an end.[140] A contract can be discharged in several ways: for example by performance, by agreement, by frustration or by breach. **8–53**

Performance

Generally, a contract is discharged by performance when the contracting parties fulfil all their obligations, both express and implied, as required by the terms of the contract. This is referred to as entire performance. There are two exceptions to this general rule, namely substantial performance and partial performance. Substantial performance refers to a party substantially but not fully and exactly performing their contractual obligations. Substantial performance is not possible if it relates to a condition; however, it may be invoked if the term in question is a warranty. Partial performance can be applied to contracts that have several parts; it may be possible to recover payment for the parts that have been completed. However, this is only possible if it was the intention of the contracting parties that the agreement was capable of being completed in parts or instalments. It follows that if the parties intended the contract to be viewed as whole, partial performance will not be possible.[141] **8–54**

Agreement

Regarding discharge by agreement, the parties may vary or terminate the contract by agreement. In essence, the discharge by agreement involves the parties agreeing 'to forego the implementation of the contract'; it requires another contract to nullify the original contract.[142] As it is a new contract, consideration is required to ensure that the discharge by agreement can be enforced.[143] However, the requirement of consideration is not necessary if there is a discharge by deed and **8–55**

---

[139] Exclusion clauses in consumer contracts are common. However, such a clause is only valid if it is specifically brought to the consumer's attention and only if it is fair and reasonable.

[140] Mairead Enright, *Principles of Irish Contract Law* (Clarus 2007) 383. Discharge differs from termination of contract. In ch 9 termination of contract will be examined by looking at the rules under the FIFA RSTP.

[141] Áine Keenan, *Essentials of Irish Business Law* (6th edn, Gill and MacMillan 2012) 160.

[142] Friel (n 5) 284.

[143] ibid.

under seal.[144] This involves a deed being executed that is sealed by way of authentication through the use of an imprint (a wax seal) or the embossing of the paper on which the agreement has been drafted.[145]

8–56 Keenan lists four ways in which discharge by agreement can be achieved:

1. conditions contained in the contract: a contract containing a condition precedent or condition subsequent 'are means by which the contract may include provisions for its own discharge'.[146]
2. waiver of the contract: the parties by way of a waiver may decide to cancel the contract where it remains wholly unperformed by either party. As it is a new contract and consideration is required, this is satisfied by the parties waiving their rights and obligations.[147]
3. release of one of the parties: one of the parties who has fully or partially performed their obligations can unilaterally discharge the contract by relieving the other party of their obligations. Consideration is required which can take the form of a cancellation fee.[148]
4. novation of the old contract: where the obligations of the parties under the contract remain unperformed and it is replaced by a new contract with sufficient consideration. Novation involves a third party taking over the obligations of one of parties of the original contract.[149]

Frustration

8–57 A contract may be terminated due to the incapability of one of the parties to fulfil their contractual obligations due to circumstances outside their control. This would arise in cases where one party is ill and, through no fault of the ailing individual, it is impossible to perform their contractual obligations. Frustration due to illness or injury would be an important consideration for a sportsperson. In deciding whether the contract has been frustrated, the court will look at the terms of the contract and the surrounding circumstances, including the nature of the job and the nature of the illness as well as the terms of the contract.[150] In contact sports, physical injury would be an occupational hazard and would arguably not lead to the frustration of the contract; however, an unrelated illness may well be grounds for frustration. There is no case law in Ireland to support this assertion; the English case of *Condor v Barron Knights* may

[144] ibid. Friel adds that 'few discharges by way of agreement are made with the foresight that sealing calls for'.
[145] For a historical discussion of the use of seals, see Lon L Fuller, 'Consideration and Form' (1941) 41(5) Columbia Law Review 799.
[146] Keenan (n 141) 162.
[147] ibid 162. This is an example of a bilateral discharge.
[148] ibid. Keenan explains that this is referred to as 'accord and satisfaction of the foregone obligations'. For a historical discussion see Samuel Williston, 'Accord and Satisfaction' (1903–04) 17(7) Harvard Law Review 459.
[149] Kennan (n 141) 162.
[150] Brenda Daly and Michael Doherty, *Principles of Irish Employment Law* (Clarus Press 2010) 272.

provide some instruction.[151] This case concerned a 16-year-old drummer who entered into an agreement with the defendants whereby it was agreed that Condor would be employed by the band for a period of five years, and he would devote all of his time and attention to the band. The contract could be terminated by either party by giving six months' notice in writing. The contract also provided that the plaintiff could be dismissed without notice if he breached any of his obligations under the contract. The plaintiff was required to work seven nights a week and up to twice a night depending on the band's engagements. The young drummer was required to reside away from home and travel to and from where the band was performing. In addition to performing as a band, the Barron Knights also gave acting and comic performances, and the drummer was instrumental in the timing of the various acting and comedy performances. In January 1963, Condor collapsed and was admitted to a mental health facility following his arrival at a local hospital. In the month preceding this, Condor had been living alone in a caravan and had not been eating properly. The doctor informed the band that if the drummer continued to perform seven nights a week, he would become seriously ill.[152] The doctor recommended that Condor play no more than four nights a week. The defendants contended that obtaining the services of a substitute drummer for three nights a week would be difficult, not to mention finding one with the requisite reputation, and they decided to dismiss Condor.[153] In holding against the plaintiff, Thompson J found that the drummer had not been wrongfully dismissed and that his inability to play for seven nights a week 'made it impossible for him to continue to perform or for the defendants have him perform the terms of the contract as a member of their group'.[154]

Breach

Discharge by breach occurs where one of the parties either fails to fulfil a condition of the contract (actual breach) or fulfils their obligations but does so defectively under the contract.[155] If the breach relates to a condition, the injured party may choose to repudiate the contract and seek damages. If the breach relates to a warranty, then the injured party is only entitled to damages and may not seek to have the contract set aside. If one party informs the other of their intention in advance of their inability or unwillingness to fulfil their obligations, this is referred to as an anticipatory breach. In this situation, the injured party can sue the defaulting party immediately and does not have to wait until performance of the contract is due. However, the injured party may 8–58

---

151 [1966] 1 WLR 87.

152 The doctor was worried that the plaintiff would develop schizophrenic symptoms if under strain again: ibid 89.

153 Arranging rehearsals with a substitute drummer was also an issue for the band.

154 *Condor* (n 151) 91.

155 As in performs their obligations differently to what they were required to do under the terms of the contract.

decide to continue with the contract and ignore the anticipatory breach in the hope that the other party changes their mind and decides to fulfil their obligations.[156] Chapter 9 discusses in detail the RSTP provisions in relation to breach of contract by footballers and how FIFA's DRC and the CAS have dealt with such cases.

Remedies for Breach of Contract

8–59 The court has several remedies at its disposal when it comes to a case involving a breach of contract, namely damages, specific performance, injunctive relief and recission.

Damages

8–60 At common law, the primary remedy for a breach of contract is damages. Damages relate to monetary compensation.[157] The idea behind the award of damages is to place the injured party in the place they would have been had the obligations of the contract been performed. Damages may not always be the appropriate or adequate remedy and thus the court can decide that an equitable remedy is more suitable in the particular circumstances.

Specific Performance

8–61 Under the equitable remedy of specific performance, the court will order that the parties perform their respective obligations under the contract. Specific performance is often used in contracts involving the sale of land. As the next chapter will examine, in the context of an employment contract, the use of specific performance and injunctions may not be appropriate given the personal nature of the relationship between an employer and employee.

Injunctions

8–62 The court has the discretion to grant an injunction to either order that the obligations under the contract are fulfilled or that one of the parties agrees not do something. In the case of *Madison Square Garden Boxing Inc v Shavers* as discussed above, the court granted an injunction that prevented the boxer from engaging in another fight for the eight weeks in the lead up to the Mohammed Ali fight.[158]

---

[156] Keenan (n 141) 166.

[157] For a succinct description of the remedies available for breach of contract under Irish law see Cliona Kelly, *Contracts Law in Ireland* (Kluwer Law International 2021) ch 6.

[158] (n 122). This is an example of a negative covenant (obligation to refrain from doing something). Under the doctrine of specific performance only positive covenants (an obligation to do something) may be enforced, whereas with injunctions the court can enforce both positive and negative covenants.

Recission

Recission, another equitable doctrine, aims to return the parties to the position they were in prior to entering into a contractual relationship.[159] The Latin term of *restitutio in integrum* is used to denote the restoration of the injured party to their pre-contractual position. The court in exercising its discretionary powers can grant recission in a number of situations where there has been misrepresentation,[160] duress,[161] undue influence or unconscionability.[162] Duress is a common law doctrine, while undue influence and unconscionable bargain are creations of the law of equity.[163] While all three doctrines can result in the contract being deemed voidable, the 'distinction between the three doctrines is not always clear and attempts have been made to formulate a single general principle of inequality of bargaining power'.[164] Nevertheless, under Irish law they remain separate doctrines.[165] **8–63**

If it can be shown that the contract is 'tainted' by misrepresentation, duress, undue influence or unconscionability, the court may order that the agreement be rescinded.[166] There are, however, limits to the court granting recission. It must be possible to return the parties to their original position. The contract remains voidable and not void unless ordered by the court.[167] Once the court grants an order of recission the contract is void *ab initio*, which means that it applies retrospectively.[168] **8–64**

Conclusion

It is imperative that any sportsperson who is preparing to sign a contract with a club, an agent or sponsor is aware of the elements of a contract **8–65**

159 Enright (n 140) 236.
160 Misrepresentation refers to pre-contractual statements that are subsequently found to be untrue. The misrepresentation may be fraudulent, negligent, or innocent. The statement could pertain to facts, opinions, or law. The misrepresentation must have induced the injured party into entering into the contract. If the misrepresentation forms the basis of the contract, then Friel (n 5) 219 notes that the appropriate action is to sue for breach of contract. For a recent Supreme Court case that set out the law regarding misrepresentation, see *Harlequin Property (SVG) Ltd v O'Halloran* [2019] IESC 76 [19] and [20].
161 For a detailed discussion on duress, undue influence and unconscionable bargain, see Enright (n 140) ch 18; and McDermott and McDermott (n 127) ch 15. See the case of *Tonelli* as discussed above under capacity for an example of unconscionable bargain. Duress concerns the removal of free will and threats made to a party to enter a contract when the person does not want to, and undue influence, in the words of Friel (n 5) 231 is 'a case of constructive duress' in which the person's free will has been removed not due to violent threats but 'subtlety and guile'.
162 Friel (n 5) 313.
163 McDermott and McDermott (n 127) para 15.01.
164 ibid.
165 ibid.
166 Friel (n 5) 313.
167 ibid.
168 ibid 314.

and the consequences that flow from the contractual relationship. The contract sets out the rights and obligations of the parties. It is a legally binding agreement that needs to adhere to certain formalities. The law will become involved when a dispute arises as to the nature of the terms of the contract or when one of the parties has not fulfilled their obligations. The courts have several remedies, both common law and equitable, at their disposal.

8–66 The next chapter will focus on employment issues and, in using a standard professional contract as a case study, it will delve deeper into the employment relationships that exist in sport, including those with players, coaches, managers, agents and sponsors.

CHAPTER 9

EMPLOYMENT ISSUES AND SPORT

Introduction

A sportsperson can be classified as amateur, semi-professional or professional. For professional and semi-professional sportspersons, cognisance of employment law and its role in protecting the rights of workers is imperative. In general, athletes who play for a team are considered employees while those who participate in solo sports, for example, tennis or golf, would be considered self-employed or independent contractors. 9–01

This chapter explores how employment law applies to sportspersons. In building on the previous chapter, it examines standard professional contracts and the main terms that are included. It discusses how an employment contract is terminated. The doctrine of restraint of trade is assessed by tracing the 'retain-and-transfer system' in football to challenges by sportspersons who are serving a period of ineligibility due to a ban arising from a doping violation. The chapter will discuss the Fédération Internationale de Football Association's (FIFA) Regulations on the Status and Transfer of Players (RSTP) in relation to breach of contract by footballers and how Court of Arbitration for Sport (CAS) has dealt with such cases. The final part of the chapter will look at morals clauses in sponsorship contracts. 9–02

Sportspersons as Employees

In a sporting context, the distinction between a 'contract of service' and a 'contract for service' is important for several reasons. A contract of service forms the basis of the relationship between an employee and their employer. The employee provides a service in return for remuneration under the control of the employer. A contract for service relates to independent contractors or self-employed persons who operate outside a relationship of subordination.[1] An employee enjoys statutory protection under employment legislation whereas an independent 9–03

[1] In relation to boxers, this view of the self-employed as operating outside a relationship of subordination is not entirely true. As Neville Cox and Alex Schuster (with Cathryn Costello), *Sport and the Law* (First Law 2004) 309 observe, 'The boxer – who is technically under the de facto control of his manager – is "self-employed" in a narrow, legalistic sense of the term.'

contractor does not.[2] Self-employed persons and employees are treated differently when it comes to taxation and social security. The distinction between a contract of service and a contract for service may not always be clear cut and in response to this the courts have developed a few tests, as discussed below.

9–04 Employment law in Ireland is regulated by ordinary principles of contract law and specific employment legislation, including equality and health and safety legislation.[3] If classified as an employee, the person benefits from statutory protection under, for example, the Unfair Dismissal Acts 1977–2021. However, under the Health, Safety and Welfare at Work Act 2005 as amended, employers, employees and self-employed persons are all under a duty to adhere to the requirements of the Act.[4]

9–05 In general, athletes in team sports are deemed to be employees. The authority for this contention goes back to 1910 and the case of *Walker v Crystal Palace Football Club Limited*.[5] Walker was a footballer who contracted with Crystal Palace for one year from 1 May 1908 to 30 April 1909.[6] He was paid a weekly wage and under the terms of the contract he was precluded from running a public house or any business connected with a public house, he could not reside in a public house or licensed premises and could not engage in professional running or any other sport without the written consent of the club.[7] Walker agreed not to play for another other club during the currency of the contract with Crystal Palace and on expiration of his contract the club could offer him another contract 'upon such terms as he would be willing to enter into with any other club or person'.[8] In return for his weekly wage, Walker was contracted to play in all matches as required by the club, attend training and follow training and general instructions, keep himself fit, sober and temperate.[9]

---

2 The following acts form the main sources of employment law in Ireland: Unfair Dismissals Acts 1977–2021; Employment Equality Acts 1998–2015; Parental Leave and Benefit Act 2016; Payment of Wages Act 1991 and the Payment of Wages (Amendment) (Tips and Gratuities) Act 2022; Terms of Employment (Information) Acts 1994–2014; Employment (Miscellaneous Provisions) Act 2018; European Union (Transparent and Predictable Working Conditions) Regulations 2022; Organization of Working Time Act 1997 and European Communities (Protection of Employees on Transfer of Undertakings) Regulations 2003.

3 Employees are also considered preferential creditors when their employer is being wound up: see s 621(2)(a)(iii) of the Companies Act 2014. Independent contractors would, if they have not taken security, rank with other unsecured creditors.

4 To see recent amendments and Statutory Instruments created under the Act, see <https://www.irishstatutebook.ie/eli/isbc/2005_10.html> accessed 17 May 2024.

5 [1910] 1 KB 87. *Walker v Crystal Palace FC* was cited in the Irish case of *Hughes v Quinn* [1918] 52 ILTR 21.

6 Walker (n 5).

7 ibid 87–88.

8 ibid 88.

9 ibid.

During a match Walker injured his knee and the club agreed to pay his wages until 30 April 1909. However, Crystal Palace did not re-engage him as Walker was left permanently incapacitated.[10] Walker applied for compensation under the Workmen's Compensation Act 1906 for permanent incapacity. In the Croydon County Court, the judge held Walker to be a worker and thus awarded him compensation under the Act. The club appealed and the matter came before Cozens-Hardy Master of the Rolls (MR) in the Court of Appeal. **9–06**

In upholding the decision of the Croydon County Court, Cozens-Hardy MR held the respondent to be a worker for the purposes of the Workmen's Compensation Act 1906 as Walker was **9–07**

> bound according to the express terms of his contract to obey all general directions of the club, and I think in any particular game in which he was engaged he would also be bound to obey the particular instructions of the captain or whoever it might be who was the delegate of the authority of the club for the purpose of giving those instructions.[11]

The judge added that an individual could not be excluded from the Act 'simply because in doing a particular kind of work which he is employed to do, and in doing which he obeys general instructions, he also exercises his own judgment uncontrolled by anybody'.[12] An individual would be considered to be an employee if it could be shown that the employer had the right to control not only what was done but also how it was done by the worker. It was argued that skilled workers (including professional athletes) were not under the control of the employer; however, Cozens-Hardy MR rejected this contention and held that a football player was an employee and thus came within the ambit of the Workmen's Compensation Act 1906. **9–08**

Individual athletes such as boxers, golfers, tennis players, and track and field competitors are not considered employees but rather independent contractors. Such individuals are usually contracted for a particular event or competition. In most cases, there is a standardised agreement between the individual and the tour or event.[13] **9–09**

Control and Mixed Tests

At the time of *Walker*, the test employed was the control test, one of the first tests to be developed by the courts. The test was established in the 19th century when the terms 'master and servant' were used. In *Roche v Kelly*, Walsh J explained the control test as follows: **9–10**

---

[10] ibid 89.
[11] ibid 92.
[12] ibid.
[13] The International Olympic Committee has a section on its websites whereby it explains athletes' agreements, IOC, 'Athletes' Agreements FAQ' <https://olympics.com/athlete365/faq-athletes-agreements/> accessed 17 May 2024.

> While many ingredients may be present in the relationship of master and servant, it is undoubtedly true that the principal one and almost invariably the determining one, is the fact of the master's right to direct the servant not merely as to what is to be done but as to how it is to be done.[14]

9–11 The control test is not appropriate in the context of skilled workers as the employer may exercise little control over the work carried out by the employee: for example, journalists, doctors, and university lecturers. Such workers have discretion in how they carry out their work. A similar discretion and responsibility would apply to sportspersons: for example, football and rugby players.

9–12 Carroll J in the case of In *Re Sunday Tribune* highlighted the inherent flaws of the control test when he stated that 'the control test is no longer of universal application. In the present day when senior staff with professional qualifications [are] employed, the nature of their employment cannot be determined in such a simplistic way'.[15] Thus, in the context of Irish employment law, the control test is rarely used as a stand-alone test.[16] Nowadays, other tests are used: mixed test, integration and economic reality/enterprise test.[17] The mixed test looks to see if the individual receives a wage, is tax-deducted at source by the employer, if the employer provides tools and equipment, and if the employer has the exclusive service of the individual. If the answer is yes to these questions, the individual will be deemed to be an employee.

9–13 Although it is important to note that tax not being deducted at source or even a contract term stating that the individual is an independent contractor does not preclude the finding that the person is employed under a contract of service, as the case of *Henry Denny & Sons (Ireland) Ltd T/A Kerry Foods v Minister for Social Welfare* demonstrates.[18] In this case, the Supreme Court held that Mahon was an employee even though her contract stated that she was an independent contractor. Mahon was a supermarket food demonstrator with Denny (trading as Kerry Foods) and under the terms of the contract, she was paid on a daily basis plus mileage. She was provided with all the necessary food and equipment. Mahon would be given 24 hours' notice and if on arrival at the supermarket, the demonstration was cancelled, Mahon would have to be available for an alternative demonstration. If there was no alternative, Mahon was entitled only to her mileage. Mahon was responsible for her own tax affairs and was not insured for any damage or injury she might sustain or cause while working for Denny/Kerry Foods. Her contract was renewed annually. The Supreme Court held that Mahon was an employee as she was supplied with the equipment,

---

14 [1969] IR 100, 108.
15 *In Re Sunday Tribune* [1984] IR 505, 508.
16 Brenda Daly and Michael Doherty, *Principles of Irish Employment Law* (Clarus Press 2010) 44.
17 The integration and economic reality tests are discussed further on in this chapter.
18 [1997] IESC 9.

she had no independent input into the job, and she had no opportunity to benefit financially or be exposed to loss.

The Chief Justice (CJ) made an interesting observation in relation to domestic tribunals.[19] Hamilton CJ, in upholding the decision made by the deciding officer and chief appeals officer of the Department of Social Protection, held that bodies that have statutory powers entrusted to it to perform and exercise statutory tasks do so usually 'with a high degree of expertise and provide coherent and balanced judgments on the evidence and arguments heard by them'.[20] He cautioned such decisions being subject to judicial review.[21] As discussed in Chapter 11, 'Judicial Review and Sporting Bodies', a similar reticence to intervene in the decisions of sports governing bodies has been expressed by the Irish courts. **9–14**

Categories of Sportspersons

Those who participate in sport fall under three categories: amateur, self-employed, and employed professionals.[22] The focus of this chapter is on employed and self-employed sports professionals. At this juncture, the following observations may be made in regard to the Gaelic Athletic Association (GAA), which prides itself on being the 'largest amateur sporting organisation in the world'.[23] Although classified as amateur, the GAA has acknowledged that some of the managers/management teams at club and Inter-County level have received irregular payments, contrary to the amateur ethos and voluntary commitment of the organisation.[24] Coaches and team trainers at the GAA may be considered 'internal' in that they are volunteers who have an interest in the GAA and want to help in the development of the playing standards at their **9–15**

---

19 This case was sent to the High Court by way of judicial review following the decision of the deciding officer and chief appeals officer of the Department of Social Welfare, in the circumstances that Mahon was an employee with a contract of employment pursuant to the Social Welfare (Consolidation) Act 1981. The High Court agreed with this finding and the appellants appealed the matter to the Supreme Court.

20 *Henry Denny & Sons (Ireland) Ltd trading as Kerry Foods (appellants) v Minister for Social Welfare (respondent)* [1998] 9 Employment Law Report 36, 51.

21 ibid.

22 Cox and others (n 1) 307.

23 Croke Park, 'The Games Gallery' <https://crokepark.ie/stadium/about/experience-match-day/the-games-gallery> accessed 17 May 2024. See also Gaelic Athletic Association, 'GAA Amateur Status and Payment to Team Managers' (January 2012) 5. This discussion paper is no longer available online. As discussed in ch 1 para 2-135 the recently appointed president, Jarlath Burns, has created an Amateur Review Status Committee to protect the GAA's amateur status. The amateur status of the GAA is enshrined in r 1.8 of Gaelic Athletic Association, *Official Guide – Part 1* (Central Council of the Association 2024) <https://www.gaa.ie/article/gaa-official-guides-codes> accessed 17 May 2024. Rule 1.8 'shall not prohibit the payment of salaries or wages to employees of the Association'. A breach of r 1.8 may result in a suspension of 24 weeks or expulsion.

24 GAA Amateur Status and Payment to Team Managers (n 23).

clubs.[25] Other coaches and team trainers provide professional services and are recruited from outside the GAA; they are paid on foot of an invoice for professional services rendered.[26] For example, there are a number of coaches and team trainers who acquired their expertise by way of volunteering in the GAA and are now providing coaching and training on a fee basis and have a service contract with the GAA.[27] The amateur status can become somewhat diluted. The English case of *Gasser v Stinson* provides a useful analogy for the Irish position.[28] Gasser, a Swiss 800m and 1500m runner, came third in the 1500m at the World Championships held in Rome in August and September 1987. Gasser was selected for a drug test and an anabolic steroid was detected in her urine sample.[29] The International Amateur Athletic Federation (IAAF) announced on 29 September 1987 that Gasser had received a two-year ban for testing positive for a prohibited substance.[30] Gasser challenged the ban under the doctrine of restraint of trade and on the principle of strict liability. The IAAF defended the ban on grounds that the athletes were 'amateurs' and that they 'did not and could not under IAAF rules, earn their daily bread as athletes'.[31] Pollack, counsel for the IAAF, accepted that athletes had the ability to earn substantial sums due to their activities as athletes; however, such contracts were between the athletes' national federations and third parties (such as sponsors), and the athletes were not privy to these contracts. Pollack proffered that the ability to earn money was not immediate but lay in the future.[32] Scott J rejected this argument; however, he acknowledged that restraint of trade was not applicable to activities that did not yield financial reward.[33] He gave the example of school sport:

> If a headmaster chooses to ban boxing at his school, he may be inhibiting the future careers of some of his pugilistically inclined pupils, but restraint of trade rules are not in point … But, in a sport which allows competitors to exploit their ability in the sport for financial gain, which allows that gain to be a direct consequence of participation in competition, a ban on competition is, in my judgment, a restraint of trade.[34]

9–16 On holding that restraint of trade could apply to amateur athletes, Scott

---

25 ibid 8.
26 ibid.
27 ibid.
28 *Gasser v Stinson & Anor* [1988] 6 WLUK 333; [1988] Lexis Citation 2320.
29 The test took place on 5 September 1987. Gasser had difficulty in supplying a sample and managed only 30ml and not the required 70ml. The 30ml was divided into two samples, A and B.
30 At the time of the case, the IAAF had its headquarters in London (from 1946 to 1993). Its name was changed to the International Association of Athletic Federations in 2001 and it was rebranded as World Athletics in 2019. Monaco has been its headquarters since 1993. As it was domiciled in London, the case came before an English court.
31 [1988] Lexis Citation 2320, 20.
32 ibid.
33 ibid.
34 ibid.

J had to decide if the two-year period of ineligibility was reasonable or unreasonable. He held it to be reasonable and, in doing so, dismissed the action.[35]

9–17 In relation to the GAA, players would not have a written contract between them and the GAA. The GAA players receive only expenses and are not employed under a contract of service or a contract for service. Unlike the situation in *Gasser*, GAA players (or teams or officials) cannot enter into sponsorship agreements to wear any brand of playing gear or equipment or accessories that do not comply with the *Official Guide – Part 1*: Chapter 1 Aims and Ethos, paragraph 1.14.[36]

Defining an Employee

9–18 There is no definition of an employee under Irish employment law. The employment status of an individual is generally determined by the Revenue or the Department of Social Protection. The *Code of Practice for Determining Employment or Self-Employment Status of Individuals* was prepared by the Employment Status Group in association with the Department of Social Protection, the Office of the Revenue Commissioners, and the Workplace Relations Commission (WRC).[37] The Code lists several factors that are indicative of an individual being considered an employee.[38] However, there are several important caveats that must be read in conjunction with the list.[39] The Code provides the following as typical characteristics of an employee:

- Is under the control of another person who directs them as to how, when and where the work is to be carried out,[40]
- Supplies labour only,
- Receives a fixed hourly/weekly/monthly wage,[41]
- Cannot subcontract the work,[42]
- Does not supply materials for the job,

---

35 ibid 21.
36 (n 23).
37 Department of Social Protection, the Office of the Revenue Commissioners, and the Workplace Relations Commission, *Code of Practice for Determining Employment or Self-Employment Status of Individuals* (July 2021) <https://www.gov.ie/pdf/?file=https://assets.gov.ie/34185/fcfac49276914907b939f64fad110ae8.pdf#page=null> accessed 17 May 2024.
38 ibid 6.
39 ibid 7.
40 With the caveat: an individual could have considerable freedom and independence in carrying out work and still be an employee, and an employee with specialist knowledge might not be directed as to how the work is to be carried out.
41 With the caveat: an individual who is paid by commission, by share, or by piecework, or in some other atypical fashion may still be regarded as an employee.
42 With the caveat: if the work can be subcontracted and 'paid on' by the person subcontracting the work, it is possible the employer/employee relationship may simply be transferred on.

- Does not provide equipment other than the small tools of the trade,[43]
- Is not exposed to personal financial risk in carrying out the work,
- Does not assume any responsibility for investment and management in the business,
- Does not have the opportunity to profit from sound management in the scheduling of engagements or in the performance of tasks arising from the engagements,
- Works set hours or a given number of hours per week or month,[44]
- Works for one person or for one business,[45]
- Receives expense payments to cover subsistence and/or travel expenses,
- Is entitled to sick pay or extra pay for overtime,
- Is obliged to perform work on a regular basis that the employer is obliged to offer to them (this is known as 'mutuality of obligation'),
- Has their tax deducted from their wages through the Pay As You Earn (PAYE) system.[46]

---

[43] With the caveat: it is possible that the provision of tools or equipment will not have a significant bearing on reaching a conclusion about which employment status is appropriate, having regard to all the circumstances of a particular case.

[44] With the caveat: the hours of work or remuneration of an employee may be uncertain, employees may work in a range of ways, including, but not limited to, part-time work, temporary work, seasonal work or occasional work, and some employees are paid by reference to contracted hours, while others may be paid by reference to the amount of work actually done.

[45] With the caveat: some employees work for more than one employer at the same time and some employees may also be self-employed in respect of other work being done by them.

[46] With the caveat: if tax is not deducted from the individual's earnings through the PAYE system, this does not mean a person with the other 'employee' characteristics is self-employed. In a Supreme Court judgment delivered on 20 October 2023, Murray J in *Revenue Commissioner v Karshan (Midlands) Ltd t/a Domino's Pizza* [2023] IESC 2 devised five factors that need to be considered in deciphering for purposes of Schedules D and E of the Taxes Consolidation Act 1997 whether a delivery person was an independent contractor (a contract for service under Schedule D) or an employee (a contract of service under Schedule E). The five factors are:

1. Does the contract involve the exchange of wage or other remuneration for work? [219]–[223]
2. If the answer to 1 is yes, has the worker agreed to provide their services to the employer personally? [224]–[226]
3. If the answer to 2 is yes, 'does the employer exercise sufficient control over the putative employee to render the agreement one that is capable of being an employment agreement?' [253], for more detail see [227]–[234]
4. All the circumstances of the employment [235]–[250]. At [253] Murray J summarised this as follows: 'If these three requirements are met the decision maker must then determine whether the terms of the contract between employer and worker interpreted in the light of the admissible factual matrix and having regard to the working arrangements between the parties as disclosed by the evidence, are consistent with a contract of employment, or with some other form of contract having regard, in particular, to whether the arrangements point to the putative employee working for themselves or for the putative employer'.
5. The legislative context [251]–[252]. Murray J concluded: 'Finally, it should be determined whether there is anything in the particular legislative regime

To reflect the changes in work practices introduced in light of the COVID-19 pandemic, one of the caveats included relates to remote working and an individual still being considered an employee when they work away from the employer's premises.[47] The Code alludes to statements in contracts which purport to define an individual as not being an employee, however, 'the courts have found that they are of minimal value in coming to a conclusion as to the actual employment status of the person concerned and may be overruled'.[48] **9–19**

If a person is classified as a worker, it means the employer may be vicariously liable for the acts or omissions of the employee which occur during the employee's employment. At common law there is no vicarious liability for the acts and omissions of an independent contractor save in exceptional circumstances. In the case of *Phelan v Coillte Teoranta and Others*, an employer was held vicariously liable for the negligent actions of an independent contractor.[49] The independent contract (Carwood) was a welder/fitter who carried out work for Coillte (the Irish Forestry Board), a state-owned company which operates and manages all state forests on behalf of the Minister for Agriculture, Food and the Marine. Carwood did not receive a weekly wage or holiday pay and had no pension entitlements. He provided his own tools and equipment and was paid an hourly rate along with a mileage rate for his own vehicle. Carwood was under the control of his superiors at Coillte, who would instruct him on what to do and, if necessary, how to do it. While repairing a heavy vehicle, Carwood asked Phelan to assist him by lifting part of the vehicle. Phelan was an employee of Coillte and thus was under a contract of service. In lifting the part of the vehicle, a substantial section of the frame fell on Phelan and as a result he suffered a personal injury. Coillte, although recognising the negligent act of Carwood, did not accept it was vicariously liable as Carwood was not an employee but an independent contractor. Barr J held: **9–20**

> Although control is not invariably a crucial factor (e.g., it is not so where the employee is a specialist having professional qualifications such as

under consideration that requires the court to adjust or supplement any of the foregoing' [253].

In applying the five-limb test, the Supreme Court held that the driver was an employee for the purposes of tax.

The Supreme Court referred to the Denny case, as discussed in paras 9–13 and 9–14, as continuing 'to provide a reliable structure for the identification of a contract of employment' [253].

47 *Code of Practice on Determining Employment Status* (n 37) 7.

48 ibid. The Code gives a list of typical characteristics of self-employed persons, which includes: owns their own business, is exposed to financial risk by having to bear the cost of making good faulty or substandard work carried out under the contract, assumes responsibility for investment and management in the enterprise, has the opportunity to profit from sound management in the scheduling and performance of engagements and tasks and has control over what is done, how it is done and whether they do it personally. Page 9 lists three important caveats.

49 [1993] 1 IR 1; [1993] ELR 56.

> a surgeon or physician on the staff of a hospital), in cases where the employer's right to direct the worker as to how he shall perform his task is the norm, it is of major consequence.[50]

9–21 The judge added that the 'raison d'etre' of the distinction between contracts of service and contracts for service was that there 'is no justification in law for holding an employer vicariously liable for the negligence of a person over whom he has no control'.[51] Barr J found that Carwood was employed under a contract of service for several reasons. Carwood was employed full time by Coillte; he occasionally received specific instructions from an engineer on site in relation to specific jobs; and he received a mileage allowance for the use of his own vehicle. The fact that Carwood provided his own tools and equipment did not preclude the finding of a contract of service as Barr J noted that many tradespersons, including carpenters and mechanics, traditionally provided their own tools. [52] The judge held that the proper course was to examine the work aspect of the employment in question in a more holistic manner and decide whether it was indicative of a contract of service or a contract for service. It was irrelevant, in Barr J's view, whether the nature of particular contract of employment was one for or of services; what was relevant, on the balance of probabilities, was that the employer's right of control over the employee's work would have been the same, irrespective of the nature of the contract of employment.[53] In finding that the employment fell with the former, Coillte was held to be vicariously liable for the plaintiff's personal injury caused by Carwood's negligence.

Economic Reality/Enterprise Test

9–22 In deciding whether an individual is an employee, the courts and employment tribunals have used a variety of tests, from the traditional control test to the mixed test and the integration test. Under the integration test, the court looks at the extent to which the person employed is an integral (or vital) part of the business. [54] In more recent

---

50 [1993] ELR 56, 59.

51 ibid.

52 ibid 60.

53 ibid.

54 The integration test was considered in the case of *Kelly v Irish Press Ltd* (UD 23/1985) and Circuit Court, 19 November 1985. The applicant had been a sports columnist with the newspaper on a part-time basis for more than 30 years. He was also a civil servant. During the soccer season, Kelly would submit weekly material to the sports editor, who in turn had ultimate control over the content of the submission and copyright was vested in the newspaper. Kelly was held not to be an employee because he did not work all year round and the newspaper could not prevent him working elsewhere. This decision highlights the inadequacies of the integration test as Kelly had worked with the paper since 1952 and his work was calculated at 24 hours per week during the season. Arguably Kelly was an integral and vital part of the business. Daly and Doherty (n 16) 45 argue 'that the courts have not spelt out clearly what is meant by "integration"' and, while the

times, a more practical test – the economic reality or the enterprise test – has emerged. This test was used by the Employment Appeals Tribunal (EAT) in *Kirwan v Dart Industries and Leahy*.[55] The EAT held that the proper approach was to 'consider the reality of the situation, consider all the aspects, no single one is decisive'. Dart Industries were the manufacturers of Tupperware, and Leahy was the distributor for part of Ireland. Kirwan was a sales representative for Leahy who in turn provided her with a taxed and insured car so that she could travel to sell Tupperware. Kirwan paid the running costs of the car out of the commission she earned from selling the Tupperware. The EAT acknowledged that the applicant had some freedom as to her work; however, the ultimate control rested with Leahy. The EAT took account of the fact that the Kirwan was an integral part of the company's distribution system.[56]

The attributes of the economic reality/enterprise test were recently summarised by the WRC Adjudicator in *Hanley v PBR Restaurants Limited* as follows: **9–23**

> It is evident that the complainant and his co-directors were in business on their own account. This is the basis of the enterprise test; if the business had done well, the directors were on course to profit; however, as they expanded their enterprise, they increased their exposure to financial risk, ending eventually in examinership. The burden of financial risk is not carried by employees and employees do not make decisions about opening new outlets and taking leases on buildings. These and other commercial decisions including who to employ and how much to pay them were made by the complainant and his co-directors. This 'economic reality' (*U.S. v Silk* [1946] 331 U.S. 704) points to the complainant's role as the head of an enterprise, and not as an employee shielded from the vicissitudes of commercial life.[57]

Daly and Doherty refer to the economic reality test as more of an approach than a 'conceptional categorisation'.[58] It allows the courts **9–24**

---

integration test would seem to benefit professionals over whom the employer does not exercise direct control, it may not cover those who are outworkers or sub-contractors who may be integral to the business but are not deemed to be employees. For a detailed discussion of the case see Declan Madden and Tony Kerr, *Unfair Dismissal: Cases and Commentary* (2nd edn, Irish Business & Employers' Confederation 1996) 5.

55 *Kirwan v Dart Industries Ltd & Leahy and Anor* (UD 1/1980).

56 The economic reality test was approved and applied by Barr J in *O'Coindealbhain v Mooney* [1990] IR 422. In a recent case, *Maunsel v Glenpatrick Spring Water Company Limited*, in using the economic reality test, the Adjudicator found that the complainant was not a worker but an independent contractor. Of significance to the Adjudicator was that 'the Complainant took on others to assist him in the work', Ref no: ADJ–00031208 (25 March 2022) <https://www.workplacerelations.ie/en/cases/2022/march/adj-00031208.html> accessed 17 May 2024.

57 Ref no: ADJ–00030290 (22 June 2021) <https://www.workplacerelations.ie/en/cases/2021/june/adj-00030290.html> accessed 17 May 2024.

58 Doherty and Daly (n 16) 45.

to examine the particular circumstances of the individual more panoramically.

Employment Contracts: Statutory Requirements

9–25 In Chapter 8, the formation and terms of a contract were discussed. The following section examines the law governing employment contracts and maternity leave in Ireland. Under s 3(1) of the Terms of Employment (Information) Act 1994 (as amended) an employer must provide an employee with a written statement of the terms of employment within the first two months of the commencement of employment.[59] Section 3(1)(a)–(m) prescribes a list of information which must be included in the statement.[60] The 1994 Act is one of a group of Acts that are collectively known as the Terms of Employment (Information) Acts 1994–2014.[61]

9–26 Prior to the 1994 Act, s 9 of the Minimum Notice and Terms of Employment Act 1973 provided that an employee was entitled to a written statement of terms, but only if the employee requested it.[62] Although the Terms of Employment (Information) Acts 1994–2014 state that a written statement of terms of employment must be furnished, a breach of this statutory requirement may result in an employee presenting a complaint to the WRC. Under s 7 of the Terms of Employment (Information) Act 1994, the recommended penalty for the employer is no more than four weeks' wages compensation to the employee. Given the lack of financial deterrence, oral contracts may well be in existence, in contravention of the statutory requirement.

---

[59] For details on the information that should be furnished as well as recent developments in relation to the five-day statement, see the Workplace Relations Commission, 'Terms of Employment' <https://www.workplacerelations.ie/en/what_you_should_know/employer-obligations/terms-of employment/> accessed 17 May 2024.

[60] Including the following: (a) The full name of the employee and employer; (d) Job title or nature of work; (e) Date of commencement of work; (f) Expected duration of employment, if contract is temporary and if the contract of employment is for a fixed term, the date on which the contract expires; (h) Pay intervals (weekly, monthly, or otherwise); (i) Details of hours of work and overtime; and (m) Details of any collective agreements which affect the terms of employment.

[61] The other Acts are the Protection of Employees (Part-Time Work) Act 2001, insofar as it relates to the Terms of Employment (Information) Act 1994, the Industrial Relations (Amendment) Act 2012 and Local Government Reform Act 2014. A revised and consolidated version of the Terms of Employment (Information) Acts 1994 and 2014 was updated to 16 December 2022 <https://revisedacts.lawreform.ie/eli/1994/act/5/revised/en/html> accessed 17 May 2024.

[62] The Law Reform Commission has a revised version of the 1973 Act updated to 14 October 2020 <https://revisedacts.lawreform.ie/eli/1994/act/5/revised/en/html> accessed 17 May 2024.

Maternity Leave for Athletes

9–27 In 2019, Sport Ireland announced its Maternity Policy for elite athletes.[63] High Performance athletes, those that are part of the International Carding scheme, will continue to receive their funding for 12 months if they become pregnant as well as 'a comprehensive system of supports available to female athletes'.[64] International carded athletes are not employees of Sport Ireland or their national governing bodies (NGBs).[65] The Policy is divided into two stages. Under stage 1, the athlete will continue to receive funding as normal up until the birth of the child. The athlete is required to notify those involved in the high-performance programme of her pregnancy at the end of the first trimester or earlier if she chooses.[66] Stage 2 relates to the period following the birth of the child. The athlete is guaranteed to receive Carding for six consecutive months, regardless of the award period.[67]

9–28 Coming into force on 1 January 2021, FIFA's Women's Football Minimum Labour Conditions for Players amended the RSTP.[68] Article 18(7) helps to ensure the continuity and stability of the contract, as it states:

> Female players are entitled to maternity leave during the term of their contract, paid at the equivalent of two thirds of their contracted salary. Where more beneficial conditions are provided in the applicable national law in the country of their club's domicile or an applicable collective bargaining agreement, these beneficial conditions shall prevail.[69]

9–29 Maternity leave is defined as a minimum period of 14 weeks' paid leave with a minimum of eight weeks taken after the birth of the child.[70] Article 18quarter of the RSTP details its special provisions relating to female players, which includes returning to work after maternity leave (18(4)(d)), the opportunity to breastfeed while providing services to the club (18(5)), the calculation of compensation owed to a pregnant player whose contract has been unilaterally terminated due to her being pregnant

63 Sport Ireland, 'Maternity Policy Announced for Carded Athletes' 19 December 2019 <https://www.sportireland.ie/women-in-sport/news/maternity-policy-announced-for-carded-athletes> accessed 17 May 2024

64 ibid.

65 Sport Ireland, 'Sport Ireland Maternity Policy International Carding Scheme' (2020) 4 <https://www.sportireland.ie/sites/default/files/2020-01/maternity-policy_final.pdf> accessed 17 May 2024.

66 ibid.

67 ibid. The Policy explains this as meaning if the six months overlaps two years.

68 The most recent version of the Regulations is from 2024. FIFA, 'Regulations on the Status and Transfer of Players' (February 2024) <htps://digitalhub.fifa.com/m/6a0797ec77cbc02c/original/Regulations-on-the-Status-and-Transfer-of-Players-February-2024-edition.pdf> accessed 16 May 2024. There is a two-page document explaining the changes to the RSTP: FIFA, 'Women's Football: Minimum Labour Conditions for Players' <https://digitalhub.fifa.com/m/033101649cc3c480/original/f9cc8eex7qligvxfznbf-pdf.pdf> accessed 17 May 2024.

69 Women's Football: Minimum Labour Conditions for Players (n 68).

70 ibid 10.

or being on maternity leave (18(3)(i)–(iv)) and the right to continue to provide a service to her club while pregnant subject to medical approval (18(4)(a)) or to provide services to her club in an alternative manner where her medical practitioner has deemed it unsafe for the pregnant player to provide a sporting service (18(4)(b)).[71]

9–30 In Ireland, maternity leave is governed by the principal act, the Maternity Protection Act 1994, the Maternity Protection (Amendment) Act 2004 and the Maternity Protection, Employment Equality and Preservation of Certain Records Act 2024. Section 8(1) (as amended) entitles a pregnant worker to up to 26 weeks of consecutive maternity leave.[72] An additional 16 weeks of unpaid leave may be taken. A pregnant employee is required to give her employer at least four weeks' notice (in writing) of the commencement of the maternity leave and furnish the employer with relevant medical certification and the expected week of confinement.[73] Maternity leave must be taken at least two weeks before the birth and at least four weeks from the date of the birth.[74] A sportsperson who is an employee would be entitled to the above leave and subject to the same notification requirements as any other pregnant employee. A self-employed pregnant woman is entitled to the same period of leave, however, the requirements relating to Maternity Benefit differ from that of pregnant women who are employees. Employees are required to apply for Maternity Benefit at least six weeks before they plan taking maternity leave, whereas for self-employed pregnant workers, they must apply 12 weeks in advance of their intended leave. There are different Pay Related Social Insurance (PRSI) requirements for pregnant employees and pregnant self-employed persons.[75]

Standard Professional Contracts/Professional Services Contract

9–31 Standard form contracts are used in many professions including professional sport. A standard form contract will have blank spaces which will later be filled in by the parties to the contract. Standard professional contracts are often abbreviated to SPK, with K denoting

---

71 ibid 36–37.

72 Section 2 of the 2004 Act inserted an amendment into s 8(1) of the 1994 Act.

73 1994 Act, s 9. The section states that the pregnant employee should inform the employer as soon as practicable but no later than four weeks in advance of the leave.

74 1994 Act, s 10(1) as amended by the 2004 Act, s 3. The 1994 Act was recently amended by the Maternity Protection, Employment Equality and Preservation of Certain Records Act 2024. Section 3 (a) of 2024 Act inserts s 14C into s 14 of the 1994 Act, which was inserted by the 2004 Act. Section 14C has been inserted after s 14B and provides for the postponement of maternity leave in event of a serious health condition of the pregnant employee.

75 For more detail on maternity benefit, see Department of Social Protection, 'Maternity Benefit' 4 January 2024 <https://www.gov.ie/en/service/apply-for-maternity-benefit/#how-to-qualify> accessed 17 May 2024.

contract.[76] They are referred to as 'boilerplate' agreements as 'they are mass-produced and all the same, for the most part'.[77] The contract will contain provisions relating to the salary, the duration, the club's obligations – for example, the provision of medical treatment and the payment of the player's basic wage while they are injured, the provision of transport and accommodation when the player is on club business, the provision of training and professional coaching and services. The standard professional contract will also outline the player's obligations to the club, which will include not playing for another club[78] during the currency of the contract, attending all training sessions and matches as required, maintaining their physical fitness and health, not to take part in another profession or sport that would be likely to affect their fitness or ability to play for the club without the club's permission, the wearing of appropriate safety equipment (such as shin guards or mouth guards), player secondment or loan, termination, incapacity (due to illness or injury), disciplinary rules and grievance procedure and hours of work and holidays. Given the nature of the player's employment as a professional player, there are no set hours of work. The contract would require the player to make themselves available (subject to advance notification) to play and train on any day of the week, including Sundays and bank holidays. The player would be entitled to at least one day of rest per week and would be entitled to several days of annual leave.

Using the English Premier League Contract as an example, the first page is where the personal information regarding the player is entered on the top half in tabular form and bottom of the page begins with 'An Agreement made … day of … Between'.[79] The next few pages (315–18) provide a list of abbreviations and definitions: for example, holiday year 'shall mean a period of twelve months from 1st July in one year to 30th June in the next year'.[80] In reference to the 'Laws of the Game', the section defines these as 'the laws from time to time in force governing the game of association football as laid down by the International Football Association Board (as defined in the statutes of FIFA)'.[81] There are 21 clauses and two schedules.[82] The final page of the agreement includes 9–32

[76] Adam Epstein, *Sports Law* (Cengage Learning 2012) 55.

[77] ibid. The athlete's name, date of birth, postal address, phone number, salary and bonuses will not be the same, but the rest of the contract will be generic.

[78] This term is implied to prevent physical burnout for the player, who may have been bought by the club for a huge amount of money and who is in receipt of a salary and for the club it prevents the player lining up for a rival team.

[79] Football Association, 'Premier League Contract: Form 20' 314–41<https://static1.squarespace.com/static/579f1eef2c69cf81541f5565/t/57bc6605e58c62993057c155/1471964677468/standard%2Bpl%2Bcontract.pdf> accessed 22 July 2024.

[80] ibid 317.

[81] ibid.

[82] Schedule 1 contains two parts. Part 1 deals with the Disciplinary Procedure and Penalties, while Part 2 outlines the Grievance Procedures, 334–36. Schedule 2 requires more personal information on the player, including the insertion of their name, and there is a heading titled Supplemental Provisions and Employment Rights Act 1996, 337–40. 7. Under this second schedule, there is information on

spaces for signatures and witnesses on behalf of both the club and the player.[83] If the player is under the age of 18, their parents/guardians must also sign the contract. If an agent was used by either the club or the player or both, the agents must sign the contract.[84]

9–33 Clause 3 details the duties and obligations of the player.[85] The player is required to attend matches when selected (3.1.1.2); attend training (3.1.1.2); play to the best of their ability and skills (3.1.2); except when prevented by injuring or illness, the player must maintain a high level of fitness at all times and should avoid any activities including other sports that may impair their physical and mental ability to practice or train (3.1.3); to observe the Laws of the Game when playing football (3.1.8) and to submit promptly to medical and dental examinations at no cost to the player when required to do so by medical advisors and dentists of the club or the club's insurers (3.1.10). Clause 3.2 outlines what a player 'shall' not do: for example, they should not engage in an activity or practice which would exclude them from the club's insurance cover (3.2.1), they must refrain from wearing anything dangerous, including jewellery, when playing or training (3.2.2).

Bringing the Sport into Disrepute

9–34 In the context of a professional playing contract, of particular importance is Clause 3.2.5, under which a player may not

> knowingly or recklessly do, write or say anything or omit to do anything which is likely to bring the Club or the game of football into disrepute, cause the Player or the Club to be in breach of the Rules or cause damage to the Club or its officers or employees or any match official. Whenever circumstances permit the Player shall give to the Club reasonable notice of his intention to make any contributions to the public media in order to allow representations to be made to him on behalf of the Club if it so desires.[86]

9–35 This clause pertains to bringing the sport into disrepute. This may include extramarital affairs, the taking of recreational drugs, and off-field violence. It could also be extended to include cruelty to animals.[87] It is also possible for the sportsperson to bring themselves into disrepute. In *D'Arcy v Australian Olympic Committee,* the CAS defined bringing

'The Professional Footballers' Pension Scheme' (337) and 'Remuneration' (339–40). Under 'Renumeration' s 11, it states that the 'Player's normal retirement age is 35 years' (340).

[83] ibid 341.

[84] ibid 341.

[85] ibid 319–21.

[86] ibid 320.

[87] Laura Donnellan, 'The Zouma Cat Video and Bringing the Sport into Disrepute' (*RTÉ Brainstorm*, 10 February 2022) <https://www.rte.ie/brainstorm/2022/0210/1278939-law-kurt-zouma-cat-video-animal-cruelty-morals-clauses-contracts-sponsors/> accessed 17 May 2024.

a person into disrepute as 'to lower the reputation of the person in the eyes of ordinary members of the public to a significant extent'.[88] D'Arcy had his membership with the Australian Olympic Committee (AOC) terminated after he struck a fellow swimmer in the face with his elbow causing a serious facial injury. The incident took place in a bar and D'Arcy was found to have consumed a large amount of alcohol and was intoxicated. The New South Wales Police issued a statement stating that a 20-year-old man had been interviewed and charged with assault occasioning grievous bodily harm.[89] D'Arcy issued a statement to the media where he apologised to the complainant, the Australian Olympic Swimming Team, and his family.[90] His statement became highly publicised by the Australian media. In a letter to D'Arcy, the President of the AOC wrote of the swimmer's actions bringing him into disrepute and the likelihood of the swimmer bringing the AOC and the Swimming Team into disrepute if he remained a member.[91]

On 28 February 2008, just a month prior to the incident, D'Arcy entered into an agreement, the Membership Agreement, with the AOC which governed his participation, if he were selected as part of the Swimming Team to represent Australia at the Beijing Summer Olympics. The Membership Agreement incorporated the AOC Ethical Behaviour By-Law.[92] According to Clause 2.2(6) of the Membership Agreement: 'All Relevant Persons must not, by their acts or omissions, engage or participate in: conduct which, if publicly known, would be likely to bring person, the person's sport or the AOC into disrepute or censure.'[93] **9–36**

In his appeal to the CAS, D'Arcy was seeking relief in the form of the setting aside of the decision to terminate his membership and a declaration that he be reinstated as a member of the 2008 Australian Olympic Team.[94] The CAS Panel was satisfied that the actions of the appellant brought him into disrepute; however, 'whether the conduct of the Appellant would be likely to bring the sport of swimming or the AOC into disrepute or censure is a more difficult issue that [they did] not need to resolve for present purposes'.[95] **9–37**

In relation to D'Arcy's behaviour bringing himself into disrepute, the CAS Panel opined: **9–38**

---

88 CAS 2008/A/1539 award of 27 May 2008 [8] <https://jurisprudence.tas-cas.org/Shared%20Documents/1539.pdf> accessed 17 May 2024.
89 ibid 3.
90 ibid.
91 ibid 3–4.
92 ibid 5. It also incorporated the Olympic Charter, the AOC Constitution, the AOC 2008 Australian Olympic Team Selection By-Law, the AOC 2008 Australian Olympic Team Selection Criteria – Swimming, and the AOC 2008 Australian Olympic Team Swimming Australia Ltd Nomination Criteria, ibid 5–6.
93 ibid 7.
94 ibid 1–2.
95 ibid 8 [9].

> … the conduct of the Appellant was such that, when reported by the public media, it could not help but be likely to bring him into disrepute. Members of the public would learn that a member of the Olympic Team had been out at a public bar in the early hours of the morning, intoxicated and had become involved in a fracas with another former athlete, which led to that person being very seriously injured and taken to hospital. Members of the public were also told that the conduct of the Appellant was such as to cause members of the New South Wales Police to reasonably believe that he was guilty of a serious criminal charge arising out of the incident.[96]

9–39 On 10 April 2019 Israel Folau, a Tongan Australian rugby player, posted on Instagram that 'hell awaits drunks, homosexuals, adulterers, liars, fornicators, thieves, atheists and idolators'.[97] In the wake of the comments and taking into account that the player had previously been warned, Rugby Australia announced that Folau had breached the Code of Conduct.[98] There was no express or implied clause in the player's contract in regard to making such comments on social media.[99] However, an express term of the contract required players to adhere to the Code of Conduct.[100] Under the Code of Conduct at the time of the Folau incident, Clause 1.3 provided that players and other relevant persons and organisations were expected to 'treat everyone equally, fairly and with dignity regardless of gender or gender identity, sexual orientation, ethnicity, cultural or religious background, age or disability. Any form of bullying, harassment or discrimination has no place in Rugby.'[101] As was his right to do so under the Code of Conduct, Folau requested a full Code of Conduct Committee Hearing, which began on 4 May 2019.[102] After three days of hearing evidence from both sides, the three-member

---

[96] ibid 8 [8].

[97] 'Israel Folau: Rugby Star's Hearing Date Set over Homophobic Instagram Post' (*Sky News*, 22 April 2019) <https://news.sky.com/story/israel-folau-rugby-stars-hearing-date-set-over-homophobic-instagram-post-11700660> accessed 17 May 2024.

[98] Jack Anderson, 'Israel Folau and Rugby Australia's Code of Conduct Hearing – The Likely Legal Arguments' (*Law in Sport*, 29 April 2019) <https://www.lawinsport.com/topics/employment-law/item/israel-folau-and-rugby-australia-s-code-of-conduct-hearing-the-likely-legal-arguments?category_id=113> accessed 17 May 2024.

[99] Georgina Robinson, 'Folau Ignored my Warning, Says Rugby Australia Chief Castle' *Sydney Morning Herald* (Sydney, 15 April 2019) <https://www.smh.com.au/sport/rugby-union/folau-ignored-my-warning-says-rugby-australia-chief-castle-20190415-p51ee3.html> accessed 17 May 2024. The player had made similar comments a year previously and no extra terms had been added to his contract. Raelene Castle, the chief executive of Rugby Australia, was quoted as saying: 'Not within the contract, but there was a number of meetings, documented meetings, that were put … verbally and in writing to Israel about our expectations.'

[100] Anderson (n 98).

[101] The code has since been revised and Clauses 4.1(n)(iii) and (s) expressly forbids the use of social media and other forms of electronic means to engage in sexist, homophobic/transphobic and racist behaviour. The most recent version of the Code from September 2022, see Australian Rugby, 'Code of Conduct' <https://d26phqdbpt0w91.cloudfront.net/NonVideo/999e923c-f9ce-4396-431c-08d96222fb24.pdf> accessed 17 May 2024.

[102] Anderson (n 98).

panel found that Folau had committed a high-level breach of the Code which allowed Rugby Australia to terminate his contract.[103] Before the hearing, commentators described the case as 'complex' and a 'perfect storm of conflicting religious, corporate sponsorship and moral issues'.[104] The legal implications were far-reaching with employment law, contract law and anti-discrimination law as possible avenues for Folau.[105]

Folau argued that his employment had been terminated due to his religious beliefs and commenced proceedings against Rugby Australia in the Fair Work Commission, where he was seeking $10m in damages for loss of income and opportunities.[106] However, no settlement between the parties could be reached and the matter was referred for mediation by Folau's legal representatives to the Federal Circuit Court of Australia.[107] In a 26-page submission to the Court, Folau contended that the termination of his employment was unlawful and amounted to an unreasonable restraint of trade.[108] On 4 December 2019, a confidential settlement between Folau and Rugby Australia was reached.[109] Folau was not reinstated by Rugby Australia; however, he was not banned from playing in Australia. It was doubtful that any Australian club would sign him. There was much speculation at the time that his only option would be to play overseas.[110] In January 2020, he signed a one-year contract with Catalans Dragons, a French club that is part of **9–40**

---

[103] Beth Newman, 'Folau Found Guilty of Breach, Contract Termination Still an Option as Hearing Concludes' (*Rugby.com.au*, 7 May 2019) <https://www.rugby.com.au/news/2019/05/03/israel-folau-hearing> accessed 17 May 2024. Had the panel found that Folau had committed a mid- or lower-level breach, termination would not be a possible sanction.

[104] Giuseppe Carabetta, an employment law expert at the University of Sydney Business School, as quoted by ESPN, 'Israel Folau Case Could Take Years' (3 May 2019) <https://www.espn.com/rugby/story/_/id/26659221/israel-folau-case-take-years> accessed 17 May 2024. Anderson (n 98) also discussed the possible legal ramifications.

[105] Carabetta (n 104).

[106] Sally Rawsthorne, 'Israel Folau Fronts Fair Work Commission for Rugby Australia Mediation' *The Sydney Morning Herald* (Sydney, 28 June 2019) <https://www.smh.com.au/national/nsw/israel-folau-fronts-fair-work-commission-for-rugby-australia-mediation-20190628-p5225w.html> accessed 17 May 2024. If an agreement could not be reached, Folau said he would take the matter to the High Court.

[107] Assisted Dispute Resolution filed by Folau, Isileli 'Israel' (A) on 2 October 2019, Commonwealth Courts' Portal <https://www.comcourts.gov.au/file/Federal/P/MLG2486/2019/actions> accessed 17 May 2024.

[108] Tom Decent, 'Folau Lodges Statement of Claim in Federal Circuit Court' *The Sydney Morning Herald* (Sydney, 29 October 2019) <https://www.smh.com.au/sport/rugby-union/folau-lodges-statement-of-claim-in-federal-circuit-court-20190829-p52lxx.html> accessed 17 May 2024.

[109] The other respondent, Waratahs Rugby Pty Ltd (New South Wales Rugby), was also party to the settlement.

[110] Iain Payton, 'Ugly Folau Saga Finally Ends after Sacked Star Settles with Rugby Australia and NSW Rugby' (*Rugby.com.au*, 4 December 2019) <https://www.rugby.com.au/news/2019/12/04/israel-folau-mediation> accessed 17 May 2024.

the Super League Europe.[111] There were numerous dissenting voices in the Super League and Rugby Football League on Folau's signing, with the Super League chief executive chairman Robert Elstone stating that 'strict guidelines are in place' to prevent a repeat of the player's actions on Twitter and in the event of Folau making such comments again, his contract would be 'terminated immediately'.[112] Folau signed a contract extending his stay with the French club until the end of 2021. However, in early 2021, Folau was granted compassionate leave to return to Australia due to a family member being seriously ill.[113] While still contracted to Catalan Dragons, Folau signed with the Queensland Rugby League (QRL) amateur team, Southport Tigers. As Folau was still contracted to Catalan Dragons and he had not furnished the QRL with documentation that proved otherwise, the QRL refused to register the player until he had clearance from the Catalans Dragons.[114] Folau sought an injunction in the Queensland Supreme Court to compel the QRL to register him as a player for the Southport Tigers to allow him to compete in the Gold Coast club competition.[115] His lawyer argued that it was an unreasonable restraint of trade for the QRL to refuse registration. Catalan Dragons released Folau from his contract, which paved the way for his registration by the QRL, thus the injunction hearing scheduled for 12 July 2021 did not go ahead.[116]

9–41 In February 2014, Nicholas Anelka was banned for five games and fined by West Bromwich Albion (West Brom) for making an anti-Semitic ('quenelle') gesture after scoring a goal in a match played on 28 December 2013. In describing the quenelle gesture in reference to Anelka, Clavane explains how 'the French striker celebrated the first of his two

---

[111] 'Israel Folau: Catalans Dragons Sign ex-Australia Full-Back in Cross-Code Switch' (*BBC Sport*, 8 January 2020) <https://www.bbc.com/sport/rugby-league/51282586> accessed 17 May 2024.

[112] ibid. The team would also be fined substantially.

[113] 'Israel Folau: Catalans Dragons Consider Legal Action after He Agrees to Join Amateur Team' (*BBC Sport*, 21 May 2021) <https://www.bbc.com/sport/rugby-league/57198280> accessed 23 July 2024.

[114] Reuters, 'Israel Folau's Return Hits Hitch as QRL Refuses Registration Over Contract Issue' *The Guardian* (London, 26 May 2021) <https://www.theguardian.com/sport/2021/may/26/israel-folaus-return-hits-hitch-as-qrl-refuses-registration-over-contract-issue> accessed 17 May 2024.

[115] 'Israel Folau Takes Out Supreme Court Injunction against Queensland Rugby League' (*ABC News*, 3 June 2021) <https://www.abc.net.au/news/2021-06-03/israel-folau-takes-out-supreme-court-injunction-against-qrl/100189398?utm_campaign=abc_news_web&utm_content=link&utm_medium=content_shared&utm_source=abc_news_web> accessed 17 May 2024.

[116] Mike Hytner, 'Israel Folau to Return with Gold Coast Amateur Team after Securing Catalans Release' *The Guardian* (London, 29 June 2021) <https://www.theguardian.com/sport/2021/jun/29/israel-folau-on-brink-of-rugby-league-return-after-securing-catalans-release> accessed 17 May 2024. Very shortly after being registered to play in the QRL, Folau was signed by Japanese club the Shining Arcs: see Ben Church, 'Israel Folau Makes Shock Rugby Union Return after Signing for Japanese Side Shining Arcs' (*CNN*, 5 July 2021) <https://edition.cnn.com/2021/07/05/sport/israel-folau-rugby-union-shining-arcs-return-spt-intl/index.html> accessed 17 May 2024.

West Brom goals with his right arm extended towards the ground, palm opened, and the other one bent across his chest touching his right upper arm'.[117] Anelka denied it was the Nazi salute, he asserted that it was a tribute to his comedian friend, Dieudonné.[118] Dieudonné, however, is a controversial figure who 'argues that he is anti-Zionist or anti-system rather than anti-Semitic'.[119] Despite Dieudonné's attempts to distance himself from accusations of antisemitism he 'has been found guilty of inciting hatred on several occasions'.[120] The Football Association (FA) charged Anelka with a breach of Rule E3[1], which provides:

> A Participant shall at all times act in the best interests of the game and shall not act in any manner which is improper or brings the game into disrepute or use any one or a combination of, violent conduct, serious foul play, threatening, abusive, indecent or insulting words or behaviour.[121]

The FA further alleged a breach of Rule E3[2] relating to an aggravated breach of Rule E3[1] 'where it includes a reference, whether express or implied, to any one or more of the following: ethnic origin, colour, race, nationality, religion or belief, gender, gender reassignment, sexual orientation or disability'.[122] **9–42**

The FA Independent Regulatory Commission (the Regulatory Commission) convened for two days on 25 and 26 February 2014 and issued its decision on the second day of the hearing, with the written reasons published on 6 March.[123] The Regulatory Commission found that Anelka had breached both Rule E3[1] and Rule E3[2]. It was satisfied that the player had performed the quenelle salute which was 'strongly associated with anti-Semitism'.[124] However, in reference to the evidence presented on the part of the FA, the Regulatory Commission was 'not satisfied (to the requisite standard)' that Anelka 'was or is an anti-Semite or that he intended to express or promote anti-Semitism by his use of the quenelle'.[125] Thus, once it was accepted that the player had breached both rules, it was not necessary to examine his 'state of mind'.[126] The sanction reflected this factor. Aggravating factors noted by the Regulatory **9–43**

---

117 Anthony Clavane, 'The Beautiful Game?' (2014) 43(1) Index on Censorship 145, 145.

118 Jonathan Ervine, 'Nicolas Anelka and the Quenelle Gesture: A Study of the Complexities of Protest in Contemporary Football' (2017) 34(3–4) International Journal of the History of Sport 236, 241.

119 ibid 241.

120 ibid.

121 FA Handbook 2023–24 <https://www.thefa.com/football-rules-governance/lawsandrules/fa-handbook> accessed 17 May 2024.

122 ibid 141.

123 The FA, 'West Bromwich Albion's Nicolas Anelka: Written Reasons' 6 March 2014 <https://www.thefa.com/news/2014/mar/06/nicolas-anelka-written-reasons> accessed 17 May 2024.

124 ibid para 86.

125 ibid para 97.

126 ibid.

Commission included Anelka's status as a high-profile player, the endeavours of the FA to be an inclusive and diverse organisation, and the global damage to the reputation of English football.[127] Among the mitigating factors were the player's clean disciplinary record, that the gesture was not made to anyone in particular, and the inability of the Regulatory Commission to find that Anelka was an anti-Semite or that he intended to use the salute to promote or express anti-Semitic views.[128] The Regulatory Commission fined him £80,000, imposed a five-match suspension, ordered him to pay costs and to complete a compulsory education course.[129]

9–44 Shortly after the publication of the written reasons underpinning the Regulatory Commission's decision, Anelka announced on Twitter that he had resigned from West Brom.[130] However, he had not directly informed the club, which had placed conditions on the player, including an apology to the supporters. In labelling the actions of Anelka 'highly unprofessional' and as 'gross misconduct', West Brom gave the player 14 days' notice termination, as required by the terms of his contract.[131]

9–45 It is not just sanction from the club a player may face in bringing the sport into disrepute; they may also be penalised by their sponsor. Zouma, a West Ham player, was videoed on Snapchat kicking and slapping one of his cats.[132] The video was widely shared on social media, prompting calls from animal welfare groups that the player be sanctioned under animal welfare legislation in England and Wales, the Animal Welfare Act 2006.[133] The Royal Society for the Prevention of Cruelty to Animals (RSPCA) took the two cats into its care. The club fined the player £250,000 and Adidas, Zouma's sponsor, severed ties with him.[134] The life insurance company Vitality suspended its sponsorship deal with the club.[135] As will be discussed in more detail in this chapter, sponsors will often include morals clauses in contracts with individual athletes and clubs. If the actions of the athlete or club do not align with the values of the sponsor, the sponsorship deal may be terminated.

---

[127] ibid para 101.
[128] ibid para 104.
[129] ibid para 113.
[130] Stuart James, 'Nicolas Anelka Sacked by West Brom for "Gross Misconduct"' *The Guardian* (London, 15 March 2014 <https://www.theguardian.com/football/2014/mar/14/nicolas-anelka-terminate-west-brom-contract> accessed 17 May 2024.
[131] ibid.
[132] Donnellan (n 87).
[133] UK Public General Acts 2006, c 45.
[134] Jim Van Wijk, 'Adidas Cut Ties with Kurt Zouma as West Ham Fine Defender "Maximum Amount" and RSPCA Take His Cats into Care' *Irish Independent* (Dublin, 9 February 2022 <https://www.independent.ie/sport/soccer/premier-league/adidas-cut-ties-with-kurt-zouma-as-west-ham-fine-defender-maximum-amount-and-rspca-take-his-cats-into-care-41329900.html> accessed 17 May 2024.
[135] Jessie Sale, 'Vitality Suspends West Ham Deal Following Zouma Scandal' (*Insider Sport*, 11 February 2022) <https://insidersport.com/2022/02/11/vitality-suspends-west-ham-deal-following-zouma-scandal/> accessed 17 May 2024.

Standard form contracts are often criticised as there is a lack of negotiation on the part of the player. However, there can be some advantages. If the contract is drawn up by the governing body, this contract will have the interests of the player and the club in mind.[136] A standard form contract eliminates the need to negotiate every minor detail and thus leaves more time to negotiate the more important terms.[137] **9–46**

Collective Bargaining Agreements (CBAs)

As the name suggests, collective bargaining relates to the voluntary coming together of employers and employee representatives such as trade unions to agree on terms or working conditions. Thorpe and others point to collective bargaining as 'an effective way of overcoming the power of inequalities inherent in the employment relationship'.[138] In Ireland, there is a lack of legal protection when it comes to collective bargaining. The approach in Ireland has been characterised as encompassing elements of both 'adversarial' and 'voluntarism'.[139] Adversarial is the term used to describe the 'them and us' relationship, with employers described as them and employees as us and each vying for their respective interests. Voluntarism, on the other hand, refers to the lack of state involvement and a preference for joint trade union and employer regulation of employment relations.[140] The state's primary role is seen as providing a 'support framework' for collective bargaining.[141] Unlike the position in other countries – for example, the United States (US) – Irish sport is not associated with trade unionism. Most professional sports will have player associations: for example, Rugby Players Ireland (RPI), which was established in 2001. It offers advice on tax, insurance, and medical issues.[142] GAA players are represented by the Gaelic Players Association (GPA). Founded in 1999 by players, it merged with the Women's Gaelic Players Association in 2020.[143] It is the representative body for high-performance inter-county players.[144] The Irish Rugby Football Union (IRFU) and RPI negotiated **9–47**

---

136 Deborah Healey, *Sport and the Law* (4th edn, University of New South Wales Press 2009) 70.

137 ibid.

138 David Thorpe and others, *Sports Law* (2nd edn, OUP 2013) 84.

139 Daly and Doherty (n 16) 2.

140 ibid 3.

141 ibid 172. The Report of the Commission of Inquiry on Industrial Relations defined voluntarism as meaning that 'employers and employees are free to agree or not to agree on the substantive principles which are to govern their mutual rights and obligations and to regulate their behaviour without the intervention of the State': Commission of Inquiry on Industrial Relations, 'Report of the Commission of Inquiry on Industrial Relations' (Stationery Office 1981) 10.

142 Rugby Players Ireland, 'We Represent' <https://www.rugbyplayersireland.ie/represent/> accessed 17 May 2024.

143 Gaelic Players Association, 'About the Gaelic Players Association' <https://www.gaelicplayers.com/about-us/> accessed 17 May 2024.

144 ibid.

a CBA in 2019, 'the first of its kind in the northern hemisphere'.[145] The CBA was revised in 2023 to include all contracted players as the first professional contracts in women's rugby were introduced in 2022.[146]

9–48 The use of CBAs in American sports dates back to 1968 when a group of baseball players, with the help of a well-known economist, Marvin Miller, negotiated the first CBA in professional sport.[147] The CBA resulted in the increase of player wages from $6,000 to $10,000 per year.[148] In adopting an incremental approach, in 1970 Miller helped the 'players negotiate the right to arbitration to resolve grievances – an achievement Miller considered the most significant of the union's early years because the process paved the way for future gains'.[149] Nowadays, most major sports leagues in America have created unions that negotiate and draft CBAs: for example, the National Hockey League (NHL) and the National Football League (NFL).

9–49 There are many reasons why CBAs are used. In the main, they support sportspeople in obtaining better pay and working conditions, which is for the benefit of the team as a whole.[150] A CBA is the result of negotiations between player associations or unions and the clubs.[151] The CBA is a legally binding contract which regulates the relations between the players and the club.[152] A CBA usually includes provisions relating to club discipline, non-injury grievances, injury grievances, base salaries, access to personal files, medical rights and retirement.[153]

9–50 As discussed above, the standard professional contract gives players more time to negotiate the more important terms as the basics have already been covered by the contract.[154] It leaves the player with more time to discuss the more personal terms of the contract with the club, including salary and bonuses.

---

145 Irish Rugby Football Union, 'IRFU And Rugby Players Ireland Agree New Collective Bargaining Agreement' 24 November 2023 <https://www.irishrugby.ie/2023/11/24/irfu-and-rugby-players-ireland-agree-new-collective-bargaining-agreement/> accessed 17 May 2024.

146 ibid.

147 Major League Baseball Players, 'History' <https://www.mlbplayers.com/history> accessed 17 May 2024.

148 ibid. The players had not received an increase in pay in over two decades.

149 ibid.

150 Nicola Laver, 'What Are Collective Bargaining Agreements and How Are They Used in Sport?' <https://www.claims.co.uk/knowledge-base/sports-law/collective-bargaining-agreements-in-sport> accessed 17 May 2024.

151 'Collective Bargaining Agreements in Sports Leagues' (*Justia*, July 2023) <https://www.justia.com/sports-law/collective-bargaining-agreements-in-sports-leagues/> accessed 17 May 2024.

152 Laver (n 150).

153 ibid. See Irish Rugby Football Union (n 145) for a list that includes college relocation costs and clear maternity and paternity policies.

154 Laver (n 150).

A CBA is not static and will be renewed and reviewed over time. In 2020, the National Hockey League Players' Association (NHLPA) and the NHL agreed on a four-year extension to the CBA which will continue up until the end of the 2025/26 season.[155] The prior agreement was entered into on 15 February 2015 and was to expire on 15 September 2022.[156] The NHL and NHLPA agreed to extend the CBA, albeit with modifications, for four years, which will cease on 15 September 2026. This CBA is 71 pages in length, including appendices, and covers economic issues, including pay, player-benefit issues (including insurance and disability benefits), medical-legal issues (including expenses for post-career medical treatment for hockey-related injuries), player contracting issues (including minimum salary), working-conditions issues (including days off and other issues, including commitment to play in the 2022 and 2026 Winter Olympics).[157] **9–51**

Employment Contract Disputes in Sport

Contract disputes are not specific to players; they can also involve managers and coaches. Managers and coaches are employees of the club and owe several duties to the club, including the duty to carry out any reasonable instruction connected with the responsibilities of the job. *Macari v Celtic*, a Scottish case, concerned a former professional player who became a manager.[158] Macari entered a contract of service with Celtic FC in October 1993 and one the terms of the contract provided that the **9–52**

> period of notice required to be given, by either party, to terminate the employment of the Manager shall be not less than two years, such notice not to be given during the first year of the employment of the Manager. The Company may elect to make payment in lieu of notice.

Macari was dismissed less than a year into his contract in June 1994 and did not receive the required notice, nor did he receive any payment in lieu of notice. Macari contended that the club was in breach of contract and consequently sought damages. Celtic outlined the reasons for the dismissal. The club viewed the actions of Macari as constituting a flagrant breach of the contract. Celtic had employed a new management team, including a new managing director who had invested money into the club. The new management had a greater involvement in overseeing the role of the team manager than their predecessors who had hired Macari. Macari's autonomy at Celtic began to decrease as the new **9–53**

---

155 NHLPA, 'Collective Bargaining Agreement' <https://www.nhlpa.com/the-pa/cba> accessed 17 May 2024.

156 National Hockey League/National Hockey League Players' Association Memorandum of Understanding <https://cdn.nhlpa.com/img/assets/file/NHLPA_NHL_MOU.pdf> accessed 17 May 2024.

157 ibid 1–33.

158 *Macari v Celtic Football and Athletic Co Ltd* [1999] SC 628.

managing director contended that he had a directory and supervisory role over the manager. Of significance was Clause 3.3 of the contract, which stated that the 'Manager, during the duration of this Contract, shall not, without the written permission of the Board, reside at an address which is outwith the radius of 45 miles from George Square, Glasgow'.[159] Macari was living with his wife and family in rented accommodation in Stoke-on-Trent. After being appointed to Celtic, Macari resided in the Hilton Hotel in Glasgow and, subsequently, he secured rented accommodation. Macari's family remained in Stoke-on-Trent while the manager would return home immediately after the match on Saturdays and would often not return to Celtic Park until the following Wednesday. McCann, the managing director, was anxious to replace Macari and this was supported by the club's investors. A 'warning letter' was sent to Macari wherein he was asked to move to Glasgow in conformity with the residence clause. His frequent absences from matches were referenced in the warning along with a request from McCann that Macari should report to him on a weekly basis. Macari refuted the claims, contending that the club wanted him gone and he had not done anything that justified his dismissal. In finding against the pursuer and reclaimer, Macari, Lord Marnoch held that the actions of Macari constituted material breaches of the contract:

> The defenders' managing director gave him instructions about residence, attendance and reporting, all of which were lawful and legitimate and related to his work under the contract. For the reasons which I have given, the pursuer was obliged to comply with those instructions and his persistent failures to do so were not only breaches but material breaches of his contract with the defenders.[160]

9–54 While mutual trust and confidence is an implied term, its breach was considered to be fundamental in the case of *McBride v Falkirk Athletic*.[161] McBride was a football coach who was employed by the defendant/respondent club from June 2007 to December 2009. He resigned and brought a claim for constructive dismissal. The Employment Tribunal (ET) in Glasgow dismissed the claim and McBride appealed to the Employment Appeal Tribunal (EAT). McBride was the coach to the first team and the reserves. There was also an under-19 team that was coached by another member of staff, May. The under-19 team prepared players for the first team, coached by McBride. May was also the Director of Falkirk's Youth Academy and his role included deciding on set pieces, conducting the team talks before, during and after matches, and deciding on team formation.[162] McBride was an experienced coach who had previously worked with Youth Academies for other Scottish

159 ibid 631.
160 ibid 642.
161 Appeal No UKEATS/0058/10/BI, Employment Appeal Tribunal 2011 WL 2649444. See the case of *Hearn and Matchroom Boxing Limited v Stephen Collins* [1998] IEHC 187 for an interesting Irish High Court case on fundamental breaches of contract.
162 *McBride* (n 161) [7].

clubs. May was appointed as the overall manager of Falkirk Football Club and made what the EAT referred to as 'two decisions that were of particular significance for the Claimant'.[163]

In or around June 2008, May disbanded the reserve team and appointed McBride as the manager/head coach of the under-19 team. May assured McBride, at the time of his appointment, that he would oversee the under-19 team without impinging on McBride's role.[164] McBride's role with the under-19 team included daily training, coaching, development and picking the team for matches.[165] As far as McBride was concerned that was his role and it would not change in the foreseeable future. McBride was not informed whether the appointment of a Director of Falkirk's Youth Academy would impact upon his role with the under-19 team.[166] The under-19 team was successful and at the top of the league when McBride resigned.[167] The respondent appointed a Director of Youth Academy, McPherson, who had no experience and in order to get an overview of the club he attended the under-19 training sessions which were coached by McBride and another coach.[168] Following a defeat against Hibernian in the fourth round of the Scottish FA Youth Cup, May expressed his anger at McBride, who had permitted a few of the under-19 players to attend the Academy late that day and the players had not picked up cones from the pitch after the game.[169] The other coach telephoned McBride to inform him of his May's anger as the claimant was not present on that day. May decided that the Academy coach, McPherson, would pick the under-19 team.[170] While Falkirk contended that this was always the plan, which was hastened by May's anger, McBride stated that he was not aware of this and it had not been communicated to him at the time he was appointed to the under-19 team.[171] The decision meant that McPherson would take over a number of McBride's duties and 'he would have primary responsibility for shaping the team'.[172] **9–55**

McBride could not work under such conditions and was advised by an assistant coach to write a letter of resignation.[173] In his letter, he made several claims, including that there was a fundamental breach of contract and he had been the subject of unfair constructive dismissal. He was seeking compensation for loss of earnings and other benefits, and he **9–56**

[163] ibid.
[164] ibid [9].
[165] ibid.
[166] ibid [9].
[167] ibid [11].
[168] ibid [13].
[169] ibid [14].
[170] ibid [15].
[171] ibid [16].
[172] ibid [17].
[173] ibid [18].

wanted a reference that would help him secure future employment.[174] At the end of the letter, McBride stated that he would give the club two weeks to respond and if he did not hear anything, he would seek legal advice with a view to initiating legal proceedings.[175]

9–57 The ET dismissed the action on the grounds that there was no breach of contract, 'the real intention' was that when new Academy Director was appointed they would have final say. The implied term of mutual trust and confidence had to be both obvious and precise which, according to the ET, it was not.[176] The ET viewed the lack of prior consultation with McBride not to amount to a breach of mutual trust and confidence as it had 'heard evidence that this style of communication is not unusual within football, an autocratic style of management being the norm'.[177]

9–58 McBride appealed the ET decision on two grounds. First, that it had erred in law in accepting that future interference was an implied term. It was, according to counsel for McBride, 'entirely contradictory' to find 'that it was implied that there could be interference at a future date by Mr May or someone else who had not even been appointed as at the date of the contract'.[178] The ET had erred in law in failing to find that there was no breach of mutual duty of trust and confidence as McBride had resigned due to that breach.[179] The claimant disagreed with the contention that football was different and being treated badly was common. Counsel argued that the 'standard of conduct to be expected of an employer in terms of the duty was an objective one and was not confined to the particular industry in question'.[180] The second ground of the appeal was based on unfair constructive dismissal.

9–59 The EAT cited with approval the case of *Malik v Bank of Credit and Commerce International SA*.[181] Lord Steyn held that the implied term of mutual trust and confidence can be defined as a

> general obligation not to engage in conduct likely to undermine the trust and confidence required if the employment relationship is to continue in the manner the employment contract implicitly envisages ... The conduct must, of course, impinge on the relationship in the sense that looked at objectively, it is likely to destroy or seriously damage the degree of trust and confidence the employee is reasonably entitled to have in his employer.[182]

---

[174] ibid [19].
[175] ibid.
[176] ibid [20] and [21].
[177] ibid [24] citing the ET [7.8].
[178] ibid [29].
[179] ibid [36].
[180] ibid. In support of this contention, Jones, counsel for McBride, cited *Morrow v Safeway Stores* UKEAT/0275/00.
[181] [1998] AC 20.
[182] ibid 35.

The EAT upheld the appeal. It found that McBride had been unfairly dismissed and that there was a breach of the implied term of mutual trust and confidence in the way May's decision to install McPherson was communicated to McBride.[183] However, the EAT could not make a finding of fact that there was a causative link between the breach of mutual trust and confidence and McBride's resignation.[184] The case was returned to a 'freshly constituted' ET to determine the appropriate remedy for the unfairly dismissed McBride.[185] **9–60**

Commenting on the case, Clare Gregory, an employment law partner with the law firm DLA Piper, stressed the importance of 'good management': **9–61**

> The employer will not be excused from its duty of care simply because a workplace has an autocratic, brusque or even insensitive character. It also serves as a reminder that terms will be implied only where absolutely necessary, or where they reflect the understanding of both parties, and highlights the importance of well-drafted contracts.[186]

The decision of the Premier League Manager's Arbitration Tribunal in *Keegan v Newcastle United Football Co Ltd* was cited in the *McBride* case.[187] Keegan was appointed as the club manager for Newcastle United and his contract included a term which provided that he would have 'final say' (unless otherwise agreed) on transfers of players into the club.[188] A Uruguayan player, Ignacio Gonzalez, was transferred to Newcastle United without Keegan's consent. Keegan resigned, arguing that the club was in breach of contract and seeking £25m in damages. He sought £8,607,534 for loss of salary and other benefits; however, he also sought 'stigma damages' on the ground that ability to secure work again as a topflight manager would be difficult if not impossible and, consequently, he would accrue further losses amounting to £16.5m.[189] The Premier League Arbitration Panel found that Keegan had been constructively dismissed and awarded him £2m plus interest in damages.[190] The Premier League Arbitration Panel had **9–62**

> no difficulty in understanding how, in a case where he has been given the final say, a Manager's position, for example, his authority over the

[183] *McBride* (n 161) [64].
[184] ibid [65].
[185] ibid [66].
[186] Case of the Week: *McBride v Falkirk Football and Athletic Club*' (*Personnel Today*, 9 August 2011) <https://www.personneltoday.com/hr/case-of-the-week-mcbride-v-falkirk-football-athletic-club/> accessed 17 May 2024.
[187] [2009] 10 WLUK 539.
[188] ibid [1].
[189] ibid.
[190] ibid [36]. His contract was worth £3m for the first year, £3.2m for year two and £3.4m for year three plus benefits: ibid [34].

> players...would be undermined if a player whom he did not want was brought in by the club over his head.[191]

9–63 In finding that there was a fundamental breach of an express term in the contract, the Premier League Arbitration Panel noted that Keegan was vocal in his opposition of the transfer of the player. Newcastle defended its decision on the grounds that it was a loan, no fee was paid, and the transfer 'for the purposes of cementing commercial ties with agents was not a repudiatory breach'.[192] The Premier League Arbitration Panel dismissed this contention; the club had breached a fundamental term of Keegan's contract.

9–64 In *Manchester City Football Club PLC v Royle* a former manager challenged the amount of compensation given to him on the termination of his contract with the club.[193] Royle's contract was for a period of four years (beginning on 1 June 2000) and at the time the contract was signed, Manchester City had just been promoted to the Premier League. The season finished on 19 May 2001 and Royle was dismissed two days later. Royle contended that under the terms of the contract he was entitled to compensation based on club performance. His salary would be increased if the team were promoted from the First Division of the League to the Premier Division. A term of the contract further stipulated that if Royle were dismissed before the end of his contract and the team were playing in the Premier League, he should be paid one year of the higher salary or six months of the lower salary if he were dismissed while Manchester City were in the First Division. At the end of the 2000/2001 season, Manchester City was relegated to the First Division after finishing in the bottom three. Royle argued that he should receive the higher salary as on 21 May; the team was still in the Premier League as the share transfer that would bring membership to an end had not yet taken place. Kershaw J of the Mercantile Court of Manchester held in favour of Royle; however, on appeal, the Court of Appeal disagreed and set aside the judge's order.[194] The Court of Appeal held that as the team would be playing in the lower division the next season, Royle was only entitled to compensation based on the lower salary.[195]

Restraint of Trade

9–65 Restraint of trade relates to a term of a contract which restricts a legal person (a business or a company) or a natural person (an individual) carrying out their trade. Restraint of trade is a common law doctrine developed by the courts to protect individuals from being restricted in their ability to earn a livelihood. A sportsperson could be restricted in

---

191 ibid [36].
192 ibid [38].
193 [2005] EWCA Civ 195.
194 ibid [1].
195 ibid [22] and [26].

their ability to earn a livelihood in several ways: for example, it could take the guise of a salary cap, a restriction on player movement,[196] or the draft system that operates in some North American, Australian, and Canadian sports. The doctrine of restraint of trade can also be invoked when there is a rule or practice of a sports governing body that impedes a sportsperson's ability to ply their trade, as will be seen in a number of the seminal cases including *Eastham*[197] and *Nagle*.[198] Part-time sportspersons[199] fall within the ambit of the doctrine as do cases involving athletes who have been sanctioned with a period of ineligibility for a doping offence.[200]

Initially, the doctrine of restraint of trade operated to invalidate contract terms which unduly restricted the parties' freedom to contract.[201] Over time the courts extended the doctrine to non-contractual cases whether imposed voluntarily or involuntarily.[202] Any agreement which restricts trade is *prima facie* void. However, if it is considered reasonable and in the interests of the parties as a whole, the court may uphold the agreement. **9–66**

In *Ryanair DAC v Bellow*, the High Court held that a 12-month restriction on the former chief operating officer being employed 'in any capacity in any business wholly or partly in competition with the Company for air passenger services in any market' was an unreasonable restraint of trade.[203] While the 12-month period was not considered excessive, it was the fact that the defendant would be restrained from being employed in the airline industry in any capacity, including being engaged as a pilot or air steward.[204] Allen J found 'that the covenant in this case, properly construed, would prevent the defendant from taking up employment with any European airline, including the legacy carriers, and so goes beyond what the plaintiff has shown to be justified'.[205] **9–67**

The burden is placed is on the party supporting the restrictive clause to prove that it is reasonable. For the party arguing that it is an unreasonable restraint of trade, it will be argued that the clause cannot be justified in the public interest. The role of the courts in restraint of **9–68**

196 Case C–415/93 *Union Royal Belge des Societies de Football Association ASBL & Others v Jean-Marc Bosman* [1995] ECR I–4921; this case will be discussed in detail in ch 13.

197 *Eastham v Newcastle United FC* [1964] ch 413.

198 *Nagle v Feilden* [1966] 2 QB 633.

199 *Johnston v Cliftonville* [1984] 1 WLUK 304, [1984] 2 NIJB; and *Gasser* (n 28).

200 *Gasser* (n 28); and *Wilander and Novacek v Tobin & Anor* [1997] 2 CMLR 346.

201 In Ireland, the doctrine was acknowledged by the Court in *Murtagh Properties v Cleary* [1972] IR 330 where Kenny J relied on art 40.3.i°. See also *Landers v Attorney General* [1973] 109 ILTR 1 where Finlay J dismissed the plaintiff's claims, although he acknowledged that 'to prepare and follow a chosen career' was an unenumerated right.

202 Thorpe and others (n 138) 410.

203 *Ryanair DAC v Bellew* [2019] IEHC 907 [22].

204 ibid [195].

205 ibid [209].

trade cases is to decide if the restraint is reasonable and enforceable or unreasonable and thus void.

9–69 The common law doctrine of restraint of trade is supplemented by statutory provisions that are found in the Competition Act 2002 as amended by the Competition (Amendment) Act 2022 under Irish law and by European Union (EU) law under Articles 101 and 102 of the Treaty on the Functioning of the European Union (TFEU).

Reasons Behind Anti-Competitive Agreements

9–70 Clubs and governing bodies will justify anti-competitive agreements on the grounds that they protect and enhance the sport. Taking salary caps as an example, the argument is that if maximum levels are set in the particular sport it will mean that richer clubs cannot monopolise the playing talent by offering more attractive wages.[206] Prior to the *Bosman* case, a quota system operated in European football.[207] The quota system which restricted the number of foreign players in domestic and European club games was justified by the Union des Associations Européennes de Football (UEFA) and the clubs on the grounds that the 3+2 rule ensured the top clubs could not employ all the leading players and that there was a bond between club and country which preserved national identity in European competition. In the *Bosman* case, the quota system was struck down by the European Court of Justice (ECJ).

Evolution of the Doctrine of Restraint of Trade

9–71 The origins of the doctrine can be traced back to the 1894 case of *Nordenfelt v Maxim Nordenfelt Guns and Ammunition Co Ltd*.[208] The Court of Appeal held that there were three elements to be satisfied for a restraining agreement to be justified:

> If the restriction is reasonable … reasonable that is in the interests of the public, so framed and so guarded as to afford adequate protection to the party in whose favour it is imposed, while at the same time it is no way injurious to the public.[209]

9–72 Nordenfelt was a Swedish national who had established a business in England and Sweden which manufactured quick-firing guns. Nordenfelt held the patent and manufactured the gun and ammunition for the purposes of warfare. His customers were states and governments. Although his customer base was limited, he had worldwide sales.[210] The business was sold in 1886 to a limited company that was established

---

206 *Johnston* (199); and *Adamson v New South Wales Rugby League Ltd* (1991) 103 ALR 319.
207 *Bosman* (n 196).
208 [1894] AC 535.
209 ibid 565.
210 ibid 559.

to facilitate the purchase of Nordenfelt's company. Nordenfelt entered into a restrictive covenant with the purchasers. In 1888, the purchasers sold the company to the respondent company, Maxim Nordenfelt Guns and Ammunition Co Ltd, who combined the Nordenfelt business with a similar business founded by Maxim. The amalgamation resulted in the creation of a much larger company. In the words of Lord MacNaughton, 'The transfer was made with the concurrence of Mr. Nordenfelt. Without his concurrence and co-operation it is plain that it would not have been made at all.'[211] Nordenfelt entered into a restrictive covenant with the respondents, one which was broader in some respects and narrower in other aspects than the one entered into by the appellant in 1886.[212] Had he not accepted the transfer in 1888, then the original restrictive covenant would have remained in effect.[213] The restrictive covenant provided that Nordenfelt could not either directly or indirectly trade in the manufacturing of guns for a period of 25 years. In dismissing the appeal, the House of Lords held that the clause was enforceable given the specialist nature of the business.[214]

When faced with a restraint of trade case, the court is required to perform a balancing act. The court must reconcile the interests of both parties and consider the effect on the public interest. In *Nordenfelt*, the restrictive covenant was deemed to be reasonable and was not injurious to the public interest.[215] **9–73**

A more modern interpretation of the doctrine can be found in *Esso Petroleum v Harpers Garage (Stourport) Ltd* where the Court set out three criteria in determining whether a restrictive covenant is reasonable or unreasonable: **9–74**

1. Does the restraint go further than necessary to afford adequate protection to the party in whose favour it is granted?
2. Can it be justified in the interests of the party who is restrained?
3. Can it be justified in the public interest?[216]

---

211 ibid 559–60.
212 ibid 560.
213 ibid.
214 In citing *Nordenfelt* and offering a more expansive view of the doctrine of restraint of trade, Thorpe argues 'that the personal qualities of athletes sought after for purposes of endorsement marketing are a form of "subjective knowledge" recognised under the restraint of trade doctrine as private property to be utilised as the athlete sees fit and are not subject to control by sporting organisations in the absence of direct compensation': see David Thorpe, 'Athlete Persona as Subjective Knowledge under the Common Law Restraint of Trade Doctrine' (2013) 13 International Sports Law Journal 211, 211.
215 *Nordenfelt* (n 208) 575.
216 [1968] AC 269. The UK Supreme Court recently departed from the decision of *Esso* in *Peninsula Securities Ltd v Dunnes Stores (Bangor) Ltd* [2020] UKSC 36. For a discussion on the Supreme Court decision, see David Capper, 'Restrictive Covenants, Use of Land and the Restraint of Trade Doctrine' (2021) 72(1) Northern Ireland Legal Quarterly 132.

9–75 In the Irish case of *Murgitroyd and Company Limited v Purdy*, Clarke J in the High Court provided a succinct definition of restraint of trade as he held that

> [a] restraint on a person working or being engaged in one or more lines of business is by definition a restraint of trade. It is well settled that such a term will not be enforced by the courts unless it meets a two-fold test: —
> (a) it is reasonable as between the parties; and
> (b) it is consistent with the interests of the public.[217]

9–76 While the above cases relate to situations outside the sporting sphere, the doctrine has been used by sportspersons and sports bodies to challenge restrictions that impede the ability to earn a livelihood or ply a trade. Gummow J of the Federal Court of Australia in the case of *Adamson v New South Wales Rugby League* explained:

> The principle on which the restraint of trade doctrine rests is that in the public interest the citizen should be free of any unreasonable restraint upon the exercise of his capacity to be gainfully employed or to engage in trade or commerce.[218]

9–77 It is important to note that the courts were not always receptive to restraint of trade cases involving sporting organisations. In *McInnes v Onslow Fane*, the Court showed its reluctance for intervening in the decisions of sporting bodies and held that such reluctance applied in situations 'even where those bodies are concerned with the means of livelihood of those who take part in those activities'.[219] As the next part of the chapter demonstrates, the courts have been willing to apply the doctrine of restraint of trade to sport.

Retain-and-Transfer System

9–78 The retain-and-transfer system operated for seven decades in English football.[220] Under the rules of the FA, a player had to be registered with the association for the club and the league. While registered with one club, a player could not play for another club. Players were furnished with a written contract for a period of 12 months. At the end of season, there were two possible outcomes, namely retain or transfer. The player

---

[217] [2005] 3 IR 12 [15]. The judgment was recently cited with approval in *Ryanair DAC* (n 203) [133].

[218] (n 206) 359.

[219] [1978] 3 All ER 211, 223.

[220] The player registration system was introduced in 1885 by the FA and the retain-and-transfer system came into force for the 1893-94 season. The English football league was established in 1888. A maximum wage of £4 was introduced in 1901. There was also a ban on the payment of bonuses. For a more detailed discussion, see David McArdle, 'One Hundred Years of Servitude: Contractual Conflict in English Professional Football before Bosman' (2000) 2 *Web Journal of Contemporary Issues* <https://www.bailii.org/uk/other/journals/WebJCLI/2000/issue2/mcardle2.html> accessed 17 May 2024.

could be retained by the club at a reasonable wage; however, the FA could prevent this if it considered that the wage was too low. If the player was retained by the club, he continued to be a registered player for his club and consequently he was prevented from playing for any other association club. Until the player was re-signed by his club, he did not have a contract, nor was he re-employed by the club. There was no maximum period of retention. The second outcome for a player at the end of the season was a transfer to another club. Wilberforce J in *Eastham* noted the 'player might be transferred to another club for a transfer fee, sometimes as large as £120,000, only a trivial part of which went to him'.[221]

Each club furnished the league with its retain-and-transfer list on the last day of the season. The transfer fee was included, and the league would circulate the lists to all its clubs.[222] The league did not possess any control over the transfer fee, that fell within the remit of the clubs.[223] However, the league could not register a player until the transfer fee had been paid or secured.[224] Even though the player was out of contract, the club he had been registered with could effectively prevent him from moving and earning a livelihood with a new club. While it had a far more draconian effect on the player, it also affected clubs as they were restricted from signing out-of-contract players. Players could appeal to the League Management Committee if they were dissatisfied with the terms offered for their retention or if they were unhappy with the transfer fee or their inability to secure a transfer.[225] **9–79**

In essence, the system inhibited the free labour market in professional players. As discussed above, *Walker v Crystal Palace Football Club Limited* established that footballers are employees.[226] If a similar system operated in any other labour market it would have been deemed unlawful. However, the practice existed for several years in professional football. The 1912 case of *Kingaby* was a missed opportunity for the court to rule on the restrictive nature of the retain-and-transfer system, owing to the plaintiff's counsel's focus on Aston Villa's alleged malicious intent and failure to raise the issue of restraint of trade.[227] On 7 March 1906, Kingaby transferred to Aston Villa from Clapton Orient for a transfer fee of £300 and a maximum wage of £4 per week with a bonus of £10 on transfer.[228] The contract provided that Kingaby would play for Aston Villa on Saturdays and holidays until 30 April 1906, the final date of the season. On 26 April 1906, Aston Villa contacted Kingaby's former club, Clapton Orient, to offer to transfer him for £150. Kingaby had played **9–80**

221 *Eastham* (n 197) 414.
222 ibid.
223 ibid.
224 ibid.
225 ibid.
226 *Walker* (n 5).
227 *Kingaby v Aston Villa, The Times* (London, 28 March 1912).
228 ibid. The case was reported over a two-day period.

for only eight weeks; however, according to Aston Villa, his time at the club had been unsuccessful.[229] Clapton Orient was not interested in re-engaging the services of Kingaby. As a result, Kingaby was placed on the retain list and unless another club in the league paid a transfer fee, the player could remain on the retain list indefinitely without pay. Kingaby decided to play for Fulham, a team in the Southern League. The Southern League was not bound by the retain-and-transfer regulations of the English League.[230] In 1910, Kingaby joined Leyton Orient, an English League team, and soon after the transfer, the Southern League and English League concluded an agreement whereby the Southern League would recognise the English League's regulations. This resulted in Kingaby being re-registered with Aston Villa, who sought a transfer fee of £350. This was way beyond the budget of Leyton Orient and 'far in excess of any objective valuation of this ageing player's worth'.[231] Kingaby sought redress in the courts on the ground that the actions of Aston Villa amounted to an unreasonable restraint of trade. He sought an injunction and damages. The approach of counsel for Kingaby before Lawrence J was highly questionable and undermined the merits of the case. Instead of arguing the case under the doctrine of restraint of trade, counsel contended that the actions of Aston Villa constituted a malicious use of the retain-and-transfer system. In his judgment, Lawrence J stated that there were two aspects to the case.[232] The first related to the plaintiff's counsel's argument that it was a tort to charge an excessive fee for a transfer. The judge replied that it was up to the club to set a *bona fide* price for the transfer of the player; there was no cause of action because that fee was too high. In any case, the transfer fee could be appealed to the League Management Committee and the Board of Appeal. On the allegation of malice, the judge rejected this contention. There was no evidence to suggest a malicious intent and the amalgamation of the Southern League and English League was based on the justified interests of both leagues. While the judge acknowledged that the retain-and-transfer system operated harshly against the plaintiff, there was no evidence of malice. Judgment was given to the defendants, with costs.[233]

9–81 Not only did the decision operate harshly against Kingaby, it would also continue to impinge on the free movement of players as the clubs took this case as authority that the retain-and-transfer system was lawful. McArdle explains that

> counsel had failed to challenge the fundamental legality of the retain-and-transfer system, the case proceeded on the presumption that the transfer

---

[229] ibid.

[230] David McArdle, *From Boot Money to Bosman: Football, Society and The Law* (Routledge 2013) 22.

[231] ibid.

[232] *Kingaby* (n 227).

[233] Kingaby was aided financially by the players' union, which was left almost bankrupt after the case.

> system was lawful and the club had acted lawfully in seeking a transfer fee for the player. Under those circumstances, Aston Villa's motives were irrelevant because even the most malicious or capricious of motives could not render a lawful act unlawful. The club had no case to answer.[234]

It was not until the challenge by Eastham that the court declared the retain-and-transfer system an unreasonable restraint of trade.[235] Eastham was employed as a professional footballer and had a yearly contract. At the end of the 1961 season, Eastham requested a move to another club but was refused by Newcastle and told that he would be retained for another year on his existing wage. Eastham refused to re-sign and was informed by the club that he was being retained as provided by the FA regulations. He appealed the decision to the League Management Committee; however, his request was declined.[236] Eastham decided to challenge the decision in the courts and sought a declaration that the agreement was an unreasonable restraint of trade and/or illegal and/or ultra vires.[237] Eastham also sought damages. Wilberforce J declared the system to be an unreasonable restraint of trade; however, he dismissed the action for damages.[238] In relation to the retain system, Wilberforce J contended that it was 'more of a restraint than is necessary to prevent richer clubs from buying all the best players'.[239] It led the judge to conclude 'that the legitimate interests of the association, the league and the employing club cannot justify it in its present form'.[240] Wilberforce J viewed the transfer system as less objectionable: while he acknowledged it was a restraint, 'it would not require so much to justify it'.[241] The issue for the judge was the combination of the transfer system with the retain system: **9–82**

> that is, when a man is retained and it is made known that his club is open to offer, or when a man is put on both the transfer and the retain list – he cannot escape outside the league, all he can do is (in the latter case) to apply to have the transfer fee reduced. But even if it is reduced, no club in the league may pay it, and yet he cannot go outside.[242]

The useful purpose and effectiveness of the declaration was raised by Wilberforce J in the case. He asserted that a declaration in this case was effective and the 'court does not grant declarations of purely academia interest, and this declaration would be of that character'.[243] The judge **9–83**

---

234 McArdle (n 230) 23.

235 (n 197). In *Aldershot FC v Banks* (unreported, 4 November 1955) restraint of trade was raised in the case, but the case was not ruled on this ground.

236 The League Management Committee had disciplinary powers and powers to adjudicate on disputes: *Eastham* (n 197) 417.

237 ibid 415.

238 ibid 453.

239 ibid 434.

240 ibid 437.

241 ibid.

242 ibid 438.

243 ibid 449–50.

held that the league, association, and constituent clubs could not legitimately justify the system, and granted a declaration to the effect

> that the rules of the Football Association and the regulations of the Football League relating to retention and transfer of players of professional football, including the plaintiff, are not binding on the plaintiff and are in unreasonable restraint of trade and ultra vires.[244]

9–84 While Wilberforce J declared the combined retain-and-transfer system to be an unreasonable restraint of trade, the transfer system continued, albeit in modified form. The club could offer the player a new contract with the terms as favourable as the expired contract to retain his registration. If the club decided not to renew the contract, the player was deemed a free agent. However, transfers were still at the discretion of the selling club. If a club was willing to maintain the player at the previous wage, he was obliged to stay with that club.[245] Wages inflated because of *Eastham*. Johnny Haynes, who captained England and played for Fulham, saw his wages inflate by 400% when his wages were increased to £100.[246] In response, the clubs began to employ fewer players and by the 1967 season there were 2,700 fewer professional players employed.[247]

9–85 The implications of the *Eastham* case have been described as representing 'a turning point for labour relations in professional football'.[248] Following a number of years of negotiations, changes were made to the transfer system in English football in 1978.[249] Players were deemed to have freedom of contract but there were still restrictions.[250] If a club offered a player a new contract that was as favourable as his expired contract and he refused it, the new club would be required to pay a transfer fee. The fee was to be decided by the two clubs, but if a compensation fee could not be decided, it would be decided by an FA tribunal. An out-of-contract player faced several obstacles. He would have to find a club that was either willing to agree on a compensation fee with the old club and if an agreement was not reached would be willing to have the fee decided by an FA tribunal.[251]

9–86 It was not until the *Bosman* case that the UEFA transfer system and its restriction on foreign players were deemed to be a breach of the free movement of persons provisions of the then European Community (EC)

---

[244] ibid 453. For an interesting discussion of the case a year after the judgment, see MP Furmston, 'Retain and Transfer System Offside' (1964) 27(2) The Modern Law Review 210.

[245] Stephen Dobson and John A Goddard, *The Economics of Football* (2nd edn, Cambridge University Press 2001) 91–92.

[246] ibid 92.

[247] ibid.

[248] Leanne O'Leary, *Employment and Labour Relations Law in the Premier League, NBA and International Rugby Union* (Springer 2017) 29.

[249] ibid 29–32.

[250] Dobson and Goddard (n 245) 93.

[251] ibid 93.

Treaty.[252] However, the practical effects of the judgment are questionable as O'Leary contends that the decision in *Bosman* did not seem to 'affect substantially the collective relationship in the Football League'.[253] While it 'strengthened the bargaining power' for some players during contract negotiations and it made some minor changes to the Football League Transfer System so that it was in conformity with EU law, O'Leary posits that not much has changed, apart from changes in the playing rules, in English professional football since the founding of the Football League in 1888.[254]

In a High Court of Australia case, *Buckley v Tutty*, the retain-and-transfer system in rugby was challenged.[255] Tutty was a professional rugby player whose club, Balmain District Rugby League Football Club, played matches organised by the New South Wales Rugby League (NSWRL) and Buckley was the president of the League. Tutty argued that the retain-and-transfer rules of the NSWRL was an unreasonable restraint of trade. The Supreme Court of New South Wales did not agree with Tutty and the case was appealed to the High Court of Australia. In reiterating that restraint of trade applies to non-contractual agreements and relationships, the Court observed that '[t]here is both ancient and modern authority for the proposition that the rules as to restraint of trade apply to all restraints, howsoever imposed, and whether voluntary or involuntary'.[256] The High Court adopted Lord Atkin's broad definition of trade from the case of *Hepworth Manufacturing Co Ltd v Ryott*, who stated: 9–87

> It is a misapprehension to suggest that this doctrine is confined merely to restraint of trade in any ordinary meaning of the word 'trade'; it extends further than trade, it undoubtedly extends to the exercise of a man's profession or calling.[257]

The High Court of Australia overruled the Supreme Court of New South Wales, labelling its decision erroneous. It cited with approval the decision in *Eastham*, and held: 9–88

> This is plainly a fetter on the right of a player to seek and engage in employment. It is not to the point to say that the player may resign from the League. If he does resign, he may perhaps obtain employment as a labourer or as a cricketer, but he will not be able to obtain employment as a professional Rugby League footballer, either in New South Wales or in a number of other places. The rules in our opinion operate as a restraint of trade.[258]

The High Court held that both the retain-and-transfer system constituted 9–89

---

[252] *Bosman* (n 196).
[253] O'Leary (n 248) 33.
[254] ibid.
[255] (1971) 125 CLR 353.
[256] ibid 373.
[257] (1920) 1 ch 1, 26, cited ibid 372.
[258] *Buckley* (n 255) 373.

an unlawful restraint of trade, and that the restraint went further than necessary to protect the reasonable interests of the League.[259] In effect, the High Court of Australia in *Buckley* went further than its English counterparts in *Eastham*.

Restraint of Trade and Doping Cases

9–90 The above cases involved league regulations on the retain-and-transfer system. The courts had no reservations about declaring the rules to be unreasonable restraints of trade. However, reconciling an athlete's right to earn a livelihood after being suspended following a doping infraction has not always met with universal approval. Suspensions can range from three months to lifetime ban depending on the prohibited substance and the number of offences committed. As discussed earlier in this chapter, in the case of *Gasser v Stinson* the plaintiff argued that the IAAF (now World Athletics) policy of strict liability and its imposition of a mandatory suspension constituted an unreasonable restraint of trade.[260] Scott J had to establish if the restraint was reasonable or unreasonable with Scott J holding it to be the former. He agreed with the IAAF that the rules on drug testing were in both the interest of the sport and of the public. Gasser's action was dismissed, with Scott J concurring with a quote from the judgment of Sir Robert Megarry Vice-Chancellor (V-C) in *McInnes v Onslow-Fane*:

> I think that the courts must be slow to allow an implied obligation to be fair to be used as a means of bringing before the courts for review honest decisions of bodies exercising jurisdiction over sporting and other activities which those bodies are far better fitted to judge than the courts. This is even so where those bodies are concerned with the means of livelihood of those who take part in those activities. The concepts of natural justice and the duty to be fair must not be allowed to discredit themselves by making unreasonable requirements and imposing undue burdens.[261]

9–91 The Court of Appeal of England and Wales in *Wilander and Novacek v Tobin* rejected claims by tennis players that the International Tennis Federation (ITF) rules on doping were contrary to the EC Treaty.[262] The players, who had tested positive for a banned substance at the 1995 French Open and as a result had been eliminated from competition, claimed, *inter alia*, that the doping rules of the IFT and their subsequent suspension was an unreasonable restraint of trade.[263] The applicants also

---

[259] ibid 378.
[260] *Gasser* (n 28).
[261] [1978] 1 WLR 1520, 1535. This argument was raised by Denning LJ in *Lee v The Showmen's Guild of Great Britain* [1952] 2 QB 329; [1952] 2 ALL ER 1175.
[262] [1997] 2 CMLR 346.
[263] The case came before courts in England and Wales as the IFT's headquarters is in London.

challenged the fact that the burden of proof had been placed on them, in reverse of the situation that usually applies.

The case centred around Rule 53 of the IFT, which provided that where a sample yielded a positive result, the IFT's Review Board would consider whether there had been a breach of the doping rules. If the Review Board decided in the affirmative, the second sample which had been taken at the same time as the first sample would be tested. While the second sample was being tested, the player was permitted to attend in person or to be represented. If the player or a representative did not attend, a third party would attend on behalf of the player. If the second sample also showed the presence of a prohibited substance, mandatory penalties would be imposed on the player. The player had a right of appeal to the IFT's Appeals Committee. At the Appeals Committee, the burden of proof was placed on the player to prove their innocence. If the Appeals Committee found against the player, the player automatically received a period of ineligibility and forfeited any prize money or ranking points attained. Following positive results in sample A and sample B, Wilander and Novacek availed of their right of appeal to the Appeals Committee. However, before the hearing took place, the two players initiated legal proceedings against the IFT, alleging that Rule 53 was a breach of their rights under EC law. They contended that Rule 53 was a breach of the following provisions: Article 48 on the free movement of workers (now 45 of the TFEU), Article 59 (now 49 of the TFEU) on the freedom of establishment, Article 60 (now 56 of the TFEU) on the freedom to provide a service, Article 85 (now 101 of the TFEU) on restrictive agreements, and Article 86 (now 102 of the TFEU) on an abuse of a dominant position. In the trial court, Master Moncaster dismissed the action and struck out the claim based on EC law. Master Moncaster also held that Rule 53 did not constitute an unreasonable restraint of trade. The players appealed on both grounds, namely the EC provisions and the common law doctrine of restraint of trade. Lightman J of the Chancery Division held that there was 'a serious question' whether Rule 53 was in breach of Article 7 (Co-operation with sports organisations on measures to be taken by them) of the Council of Europe's Anti-Doping Convention.[264] Article 7 relates to governing bodies and the harmonisation of their obligations with regard to anti-doping regulations including disciplinary procedures. Article 7(2)(d) provides that governing bodies must apply 'agreed international principles of natural justice and ensuring respect for the 9–92

[264] (n 262) 353. The Council of Europe Anti-Doping Convention was adopted in 1989 and a protocol was added in 2002. Its aim was to standardise and harmonise the doping rules. It has been signed by the 46 Members of Council of Europe and four other states. It was signed by Ireland on 25/06/1992, ratified by Ireland on 29/01/2003 and came into force on 01/03/2003. This is discussed in ch 6 paras 6-20 and 6-21. The Convention can be accessed at <https://www.coe.int/en/web/conventions/cets-translations-by-number/-/asset_publisher/3qwZSGaOwtSE/content/council-of-europe-anti-doping-convention-ets-no-135-translations?_101_INSTANCE_3qwZSGaOwtSE_viewMode=view/> accessed 17 May 2024.

fundamental rights of suspected sportsmen and sportswomen'.[265] Of significance to the case, was Article 7(2)(d)(iii) which requires governing bodies to have 'clear and enforceable provisions for appealing against any judgment made'. Lightman J held that Rule 53 conflicted with Article 7 and thus constituted an unreasonable restraint of trade. He allowed the complainants to amend their statement of claim to include Article 53 being a possible breach of Article 59 EC. The IFT appealed the decision with the Court of Appeal upholding the appeal and restoring the Order of Master Moncaster. Leave to appeal to the House of Lords was refused.[266] While the Appeals Committee was not a public body for the purposes of judicial review, it did not mean that its decisions could not be scrutinised by the High Court.[267] The Court of Appeal held that the jurisdiction of the Appeals Committee was based on contract, with an implied requirement that the procedure outlined in Article 53 would be 'conducted fairly'.[268] Lord Woolf MR looked at the issue of proportionality and Rule 53. In finding that proportionality, while not identical to reasonableness and natural justice, was related to both concepts, Lord Woolf MR held that the 'combination here of the Review Body, Appeal Committee and the Courts provide ample protection for players in the position of the plaintiff, and it would be totally unreasonable to require yet further procedures for their protection'.[269] Lord Woolf MR cautioned sportspersons about using the courts to circumvent domestic disciplinary proceedings:

> While the courts must be vigilant to protect the genuine rights of sportsmen in the position of the plaintiffs, they must be equally vigilant in preventing the courts' procedures being used unjustifiably to render perfectly sensible and fair procedures inoperable.[270]

9–93 The issue of restraint of trade was also raised by Chambers, the British sprinter.[271] Chambers won the 100m at Olympic trials hosted by UK Athletics in July 2008. His 10-second win made him the fastest man in Britain.[272] UK Athletics was required to submit three nominees in the 100m and, as the winner at the Olympic trial, Chambers should have been deemed eligible to compete as part of Team GB at the Beijing Olympics. The nominees were to be sent to the British Olympic Association (BOA), who in turn was to notify the International Olympic Committee (IOC). The BOA refused to deem Chambers eligible for the Beijing Olympics on the ground that he had previously been suspended for a serious doping infraction. The BOA based its decision on the controversial

---

[265] Anti-Doping Convention (n 264) 4.
[266] *Wilander and Novacek* (n 262) 359.
[267] ibid 355.
[268] ibid 356.
[269] ibid 358.
[270] ibid 358.
[271] *Chambers v British Olympic Association* [2008] EWHC 2028 (QBD).
[272] ibid [1].

Bye-law 25, a provision which was introduced in 1992.[273] Bye-law 25(1) provided that the BOA was empowered to preclude athletes who had been found to have committed a doping offence from being considered eligible to compete as part of Team GB in any Olympic games.[274] The appeal mechanism was outlined in Bye-law 25(2), which provided for a three-person Appeals Panel to 'consider any appeal by a person made ineligible' by virtue of Bye-law 25(1).[275]

Chambers, 'at the eleventh hour', applied to the High Court to obtain an interlocutory injunction.[276] He argued that the Bye-law constituted an unreasonable restraint of trade under common law and a breach of EC competition provisions of Article 81 and Article 82. He also argued that the Court had the right to set aside the Bye-law as part of its supervisory jurisdiction. The High Court did not pursue the case under Articles 81 and 82.[277] **9–94**

On the issue of restraint of trade, Mackay J held that it would be difficult for Chambers to prove that his ability to earn a livelihood had been affected as the Olympic Games was only one competition and those who qualify for the Olympics and win medals are not rewarded financially; it was 'an indirect financial benefit' and his prospects of success were 'at best speculative'.[278] The judge considered whether Bye-law 25 was proportionate or went beyond what was reasonable or necessary to achieve the legitimate aims of the BOA.[279] Mackay J could not find, on the evidence presented by the claimant, that Bye-law 25 was in conflict with the principle of proportionality.[280] **9–95**

On the issue that the Court had the power to set aside the rule as part of its supervisory jurisdiction, Mackay J cited with approval the case of *Stevenage Borough v Football League Ltd*.[281] In *Stevenage*, the plaintiffs delayed in bringing the action and as a result Carnwath J dismissed the action, holding that even if it were an unreasonable restraint of trade, **9–96**

---

273 Up until 2011, there had been 25 appeals in relation to the Bye-law with only one successful appeal: CAS 2011/A/2658 *British Olympic Association (BOA) v World Anti-Doping Agency (WADA)* award of 30 April 2012 [2.7] <https://jurisprudence.tas-cas.org/Shared%20Documents/2658.pdf> accessed 17 May 2024.

274 *Chambers* (n 271) [6].

275 ibid.

276 ibid [9]. Mackay J contended that it was a mandatory order that was being sought as the likelihood of there being a full trial was remote: see [14]–[16].

277 ibid [29].

278 ibid [46].

279 ibid [48]–[53].

280 ibid [54].

281 [1996] 7 WLUK 369; *The Times* (London, 1 August 1996). Carnwath J held that the onus of proof was on Stevenage to prove that the League rules constituted an unreasonable restraint of trade. The League had requirements relating to stadium capacity and accounts that had to be met by a specified date for the team to be promoted to the third division. While it had finished top of the League, the criteria precluded Stevenage from being promoted.

it was immaterial as the plaintiffs delayed in issuing proceedings. Stevenage knew of the rules of the competition from the start of the season and by waiting until the end of the season to challenge the rules it was prejudicial to another team, Torquay United, who had been promoted in the meantime.[282] Similarly, Chambers knew of the Bye-law when he returned from his suspension and by leaving it until 72 hours before the BOA sent its team selection to the IOC, Chambers had delayed in bringing an action and such action justified Mackay J in not granting the relief sought.[283] Two other athletes were affected by Bye-law 25, a shot-putter and a cyclist, neither of whom sought to challenge their exclusion before the Court, although one was considering it and was waiting for the decision in *Chambers*. Mackay J observed that changes to the team as such a late stage would bring disharmony to Team GB and would undermine the administration of the BOA.[284]

9–97 In 2011, the Bye-law was deemed incompatible with the World Anti-Doping Code (WADC) by way of an arbitral award issued by the CAS in *British Olympic Association v WADA*.[285] The World Anti-Doping Agency (WADA) challenged the Bye-law in the aftermath of a CAS decision on 4 October 2011 in the case of *US Olympic Committee v International Olympic Committee*.[286] In the US Olympic Committee (OC) award, the CAS examined a similar restriction placed on US athletes who had been sanctioned with a suspension of more than six months. In the USOC award the CAS found that it contravened Article 23.2.2 of the WADC, which provided that Signatories to the Code must implement enumerated articles of the Code 'without substantive change' and '[n]o additional provision may be added to a Signatory's rules which change[d] the effect' of the enumerated articles.[287]

9–98 Following the USOC award, WADA contacted the BOA via a letter dated 21 November 2011, stating that it was non-complaint with the WADC as the selection rule for the Olympic Games constituted 'an extra sanction, and non-compliant for the same reason the IOC eligibility rule was deemed non-compliant by the Court of Arbitration for Sport'.[288] This resulted in the BOA challenging WADA before the CAS. The CAS

---

[282] The decision of Carnwath J was appealed to the Court of Appeal, who dismissed the appeal: *Stevenage Borough Football Club Limited v The Football League Limited* [1996] 8 WLUK 30; (1997) 9 Admin LR 109; *The Times* (9 August 1996); [1996] CLY 3933.

[283] *Chambers* (n 271) [58], [59], and [67].

[284] ibid [65].

[285] CAS 2011/A/2658 (n 273).

[286] CAS 2011/O/2422 award of 4 October 2011 <https://jurisprudence.tas-cas.org/Shared%20Documents/2422.pdf> accessed 17 May 2024.

[287] World Anti-Doping Agency, 'World Anti-Doping Code' (1 January 2021) 145–46 <https://www.wada-ama.org/sites/default/files/resources/files/2021_wada_code.pdf> accessed 17 May 2024.

[288] CAS 2011/A/2658 (n 273) [2.4].

concluded that Bye-law 25 was a doping sanction and thus in breach of the WADC.[289]

Restraint of Trade: Wage Restrictions and Salary Caps

Wage ceilings restrict the amount an individual player can earn while salary caps set a limit on the earnings of the players collectively.[290] The issue of a wage ceiling was considered in *Johnston v Cliftonville*.[291] Johnston was a part-time footballer who was given a signing-on fee in excess of that permitted by the league rules.[292] The Northern Irish League regulations specified maximum payments for wages, sign-on bonuses and match bonuses in League competition. Clubs were obliged to adhere to these maxima as a failure do so could result in a fine and a deduction of points. The plaintiff challenged these rules on the grounds that they were an unreasonable restraint of trade. The Chancery Court (Northern Ireland) accepted that the rules were a restraint, and that the restraint was unreasonable. The Court found that the League had failed in its attempts to justify the restraint as being reasonable. The restriction was defended on the grounds that the wealthier clubs would monopolise the playing talent and it would threaten the financial viability of some of the smaller clubs. The Court rejected both arguments and held that the restrictions were an unreasonable restraint of trade. **9–99**

Salary caps operate in several North American sports, including the NFL, the NBA, the Canadian Football League, and Women's National Basketball Association (WNBA).[293] In England, both Premiership Rugby (officially known as Gallagher Premiership Rugby) in rugby union and the Super League in rugby league operate salary caps.[294] Some Australian major league sports use salary caps, including the Australian Football League (AFL), the National Rugby League (NRL), and the National Basketball League (NBL).[295] As discussed in Chapter 13, UEFA's Club Licensing and Financial Sustainability Regulations restrict European clubs from spending more than they have earned to ensure the long-term viability of clubs. **9–100**

---

[289] ibid [9.1].

[290] Thorpe and others (n 138) 84.

[291] (n 199).

[292] Johnston was paid a signing-on bonus of £120, £12 per week as wages, and more than £12 as a match bonus for a win or £6 for a draw.

[293] Salary caps can be hard or soft caps. For a glossary of terms, see Sam Quinn, 'NBA Salary Cap Explained: Glossary for the Terms You Need to Know Ahead of Basketball Free Agency' (*CBS Sports*, 30 June 2022) <https://www.cbssports.com/nba/news/nba-salary-cap-explained-glossary-for-the-terms-you-need-to-know-ahead-of-basketball-free-agency/> accessed 17 May 2024.

[294] For information on the Premiership Rugby Salary Regulations for the 2023/24 season see <https://media-cdn.incrowdsports.com/a4f08b9e-8f9a-427a-ba6d-e32b23c2b2c5.pdf> accessed 17 May 2024.

[295] For information on the NBL, see Olgun Uluc, 'NBL Salary Cap Rises for 2024–25 Season' (*ESPN*, 9 April 2024) <https://www.espn.com.au/nbl/story/_/id/39903010/nbl-salary-cap-rises-maximum-amount-2024-25-season> accessed 17 May 2024.

9–101 The purpose of a salary cap is to ensure economic viability of clubs and to ensure parity between clubs so that the richer clubs cannot buy all the best players and thus dominate competition.[296]

Restraint of Trade and Player Drafts

9–102 Player drafts (entry drafts) are used in a number of sports in the US, Canada, and Australia. The draft provides that the last placed team from the previous season is given the first choice of available players from a pool. The draft works in reverse order with the top team being the last to pick available players. The process is repeated for a second round, third round and so on.[297] The draft system remains legal as it is deemed to be in the interests of sport (and in the public interest) that the richer teams do not monopolise the player talent. It is difficult to see many benefits for the players as '[s]tudies have shown that the draft does depress salaries' and there is 'a clear benefit to the league's owners'.[298]

9–103 To prevent teams purposely losing, there is a lottery mechanism built into the draft system. While it would seem that a player picked in the first round rather than the final round has more potential, this is not always the case.[299] For example, Tom Brady, one of the most well-known NFL quarterbacks 'was chosen in the 6th round, as the 199th pick' of the draft in 2000.[300]

Restraint of Trade and Exclusionary Rules

9–104 It was not until the seminal case of *Nagle v Feilden* that a female trainer was permitted to obtain a horse trainer's licence in her own name and not under the name of the 'head lad'.[301] Nagle challenged the Jockey Club's refusal to grant her a licence based on her sex under s 1 of the Sex Disqualification (Removal) Act 1919.[302] Section 1 provided that:

> A person shall not be disqualified by sex or marriage from the exercise of any public function, or from being appointed to or holding any civil or judicial office or post, or from entering or assuming or carrying on any civil profession or vocation, or for admission to any incorporated

[296] See Andrew Caiger and Simon Gardiner, *Professional Sport in the European Union: Regulation and Re-Regulation* (Cambridge University Press 2000) 8.

[297] Chris Davis, 'The Draft System in Professional Team Sports and the Restraint of Trade Doctrine: Is the AFL Draft Distinguishable from the NSWRL Draft?' (2006) 1(1) Australian and New Zealand Sports Law Journal 80, 81.

[298] David J Berri and Rob Simmons, 'Catching a Draft: On the Process of Selecting Quarterbacks in the National Football League Amateur Draft' (2011) 35 Journal of Productivity Analysis 37, 37.

[299] Kathryn Johnston and others, 'To Draft or Not to Draft? A Systematic Review of North American Sports Entry Draft' (2022) 32(1) Scandinavian Journal of Medical and Science in Sports 4, 5.

[300] ibid.

[301] (n 198).

[302] [9 & 10 Geo V, c 71].

> society (whether incorporated by Royal Charter or otherwise), and a person shall not be exempted by sex or marriage from the liability to serve as a juror …[303]

The Court of the Appeal allowed the appeal on the grounds that the Jockey Club's practice of not granting trainers' licences to women was against public policy and an unreasonable restraint of trade. While there was nothing within the Rules of Racing that prohibited women from obtaining licences, the practice of the stewards was to refuse trainers' licences to women solely based on their sex. Nagle required a licence for her horses to compete in races organised by the Jockey Club. The Jockey Club had no issue with Nagle's experience or character; thus, the Court of Appeal held the refusal to be capricious. In addition, the subterfuge involving the 'head lad' obtaining the licence served to undermine the practice of the stewards even further. With all three Court of Appeal judges concurring, the appellant had a *prima facie* case, and the appeal was thus allowed.[304] **9–105**

Restraint of Trade and Agents

A tennis player contended that his contract with an agent constituted an unreasonable restraint of trade in the case of *Zverev v Ace Group International Ltd*.[305] A highly ranked tennis player signed a contract with an agent at the age of 15 on 6 December 2012. Zverev challenged the duration of the contract, which was to expire in 2023, on the grounds that it constituted an unreasonable restraint of trade. At a hearing in November 2020, the Court did not deal with the restraint of trade issue; the issue concerned the disclosure of documents. It was a matter of urgency as the civil trial was taking place on 9 December 2020. The case was settled in December 2020 on the second day of a nine-day trial with non-confidential terms.[306] Zverev was relieved of his contractual relationship with Ace and was not required to pay any costs.[307] **9–106**

Restraint of Trade and Governing Body Rules

In *Greig v Insole*, the International Cricket Conference (ICC) placed **9–107**

---

303 The 1919 Act was repealed by the Sex Discrimination Act 1975, c 65, which in turn was repealed by the Equality Act 2010, c 15.

304 The Court of Appeal found that there was an arguable case that at common law there is a right to work at one's profession without being arbitrarily or unreasonably excluded by anyone having governance of it; to exclude a woman from being a horse trainer by reason of her sex would be capricious and unreasonable and therefore the practice of the defendants was contrary to public policy.

305 [2020] EWHC 3513 (ch).

306 '11KBW in Restraint of Trade Case for Tennis Star' (11 December 2020) <https://www.11kbw.com/knowledge-events/case/11kbw-in-restraint-of-trade-case-for-tennis-star/> accessed 17 May 2024.

307 ibid.

restrictions on cricketers playing in competitions not sanctioned by it.[308] The ICC placed a retrospective ban on cricketers who agreed to join the Kerry Packer World Series Cricket. Packer was a private promoter who organised for several test cricketers to play in an autumn and winter series in Australia. The ICC, as the controlling body of test cricket, had the exclusive power to regulate the qualification rules for cricketers to play in test matches. The ICC, in response to the Packer agreement, retrospectively changed the qualification rules for test cricketers so that no player could play in a match not approved by the ICC unless the ICC gave express permission. The Test and County Cricket Board (TCCB) (now the England and Wales Cricket Board (ECB)) planned a meeting, and it was believed that a similar ban would be introduced. Before this meeting took place, three of the cricketers brought proceedings against the TCCB and ICC seeking a declaration that the rules were in restraint of trade. The promoter also sued the defendants for unlawful inducement in breach of contract. Both claims were heard in the same case by Slade J. In holding in favour of both sets of plaintiffs, Slade J held that the rule changes by the ICC and proposed change by the TCCB were *ultra vires* and void as being an unreasonable restraint of trade.[309] While the Court accepted that the rule changes were introduced to protect the sport and were in the public interest, they were unjustifiable.

9–108 Exclusionary rules imposed by a governing body were challenged in the case of *Hughes v Western Australian Cricket Association and Ors*.[310] The applicant was banned from professional cricket for his part in a rebel tour to South Africa. The boycott of players was based on the premise of putting pressure on South Africa to end its policy of Apartheid.[311] The respondents introduced rules that disqualified players if they participated in non-sanctioned matches, including the South African tours. The applicant argued that the decision to disqualify him and other cricketeers from playing was exclusionary and in breach of the Trade Practices Act 1974. The Federal Court found that the disqualification of Hughes constituted an unreasonable restraint of trade under s 45(2)(a)(i) of the Trade Practices Act.[312]

9–109 In *Watson v Prager*, the plaintiff, a professional boxer, entered into an agreement with the defendant to act as his manager/promoter for a three-year period.[313] The agreement involved a conflict of interest as the roles of manager and promoter seek different aims. A manager has a

---

[308] [1978] 1 WLR 302.

[309] ibid 354–55 G and 355 B–356 D.

[310] (1986) 69 ALR 660.

[311] ibid [206]. Toohey J referred to the Gleneagles Agreement and the policy of the present and previous Government, the policy of the Australian Cricket Board and the Western Australian Cricket Association to not associate with South Africa due to its racist policies.

[312] The case fell on other grounds, including conspiracy and bad faith and bias. Damages of $250 were awarded to Hughes.

[313] [1991] 1 WLR 726.

duty to organise events and negotiate on behalf of the boxer. A manager should act in the best interests of the boxer. However, as a promoter, the individual has a personal and financial interest in events they are promoting. Scott J stated that:

> Whatever criticism there may be of the conflict of interest that afflicts the manager-promoters such as the first defendant, it is fair to say that the plaintiff was from the beginning well aware that the first defendant was a leading promoter, and that was one of the first defendant's main attractions as a manager.[314]

The agreement replicated the standard form prescribed by the British Boxing Board of Control (BBBC). Professional boxers and managers would only be licensed if they signed the standard form contracts and the only term left open to negotiation was the duration. The contract contained an option to extend the length of the contract if the boxer won one of several championships. Watson won the Commonwealth title and the defendant purported to extend the contract for a further three years. Scott J held that the agreement constituted an unreasonable restraint of trade because it tied the boxer to fighting on promotions in which the manager had a direct financial interest and on terms unilaterally imposed by the manager.[315] It meant that Watson could not negotiate his own fight terms. Scott J considered that a manager's duty to the boxer is both contractual and fiduciary, and 'a contract which permits such a conflict of interest is to my mind a very strange animal indeed'.[316] **9–110**

In *Newport AFC v Football Association of Wales*, the plaintiff clubs sought a declaration that a resolution passed by the Football Association of Wales (FAW) to prevent Welsh clubs playing in a league organised by the English FA was an unreasonable restraint of trade.[317] The FAW on 30 November 1991 passed the resolution which would apply from the 1992/93 season. The object of this prohibition was to promote the League of Wales and to enable Welsh teams to play in European competitions. The three plaintiff clubs resigned from the FAW and joined the English FA. The FAW objected to the clubs playing home matches in Wales and the FA honoured that objection by insisting that the clubs play home matches within the territory of England. The plaintiffs suffered a decrease in revenue from their home games and sponsorship also decreased. Their survival was threatened by the decision of the FAW. After appealing to the FAW to reconsider the resolution and availing of arbitration, the plaintiff clubs sought an urgent injunction to have the Court declare that the ban on playing their home games in Wales was an unreasonable restraint of trade and an interlocutory injunction that would enable the teams to continue playing in England the **9–111**

314 ibid 737 G.
315 ibid 747 E.
316 ibid 747 F. Scott J did not find the three-year duration to be unreasonable; however, the extension of another three years was 'of dubious reasonableness', 748 H.
317 [1995] 2 All ER 87.

following season. It was hoped that a full trial would be heard before the subsequent season began.

9–112 The Court granted the interlocutory injunction on the basis that the clubs had shown that there was a serious issue to be tried in that there was a strong case to be made that the plaintiff clubs were subject to an unreasonable restraint of trade.[318] The FAW failed to establish that its rule was no more than was necessary to protect the legitimate interests of the Welsh FA.

Restraint of Trade and Irish Sport

9–113 There is one Irish case on restraint of trade in sport. In *Macken v O'Reilly*, Macken, the international show jumper, challenged the rules of the Equestrian Federation of Ireland (EFI) (now Horse Sport Ireland).[319] The EFI, the NGB, was affiliated to the Fédération Équestre Internationale (FEI). Consequently, the FEI rules were binding on the EFI. Article 100, Rule 1 of the FEI General Regulations provided that the Regulations were established so that competitors would compete on fair and equal conditions. The EFI passed a resolution that required Irish competitors in international competitions to ride Irish-bred horses.

9–114 Macken challenged the resolution on two grounds. In the first instance, he contended that the resolution constituted an unlawful restraint of trade and, secondly, it prevented Irish competitors from competing under fair and equal conditions, in accordance with Article 100. O'Higgins CJ reiterated the common law position regarding restraint of trade:

> All interference with an individual's freedom of action in trading is per se contrary to public policy and, therefore, void. The general prohibition is subject to the exception that certain restraints may be justified. Restraints, restrictions or interferences are permitted if they are, in the circumstances obtaining, fair and reasonable. Whether what is complained of can be justified on this basis involves a careful examination of all the circumstances – the need for restraint, the object sought to be attained, the interests sought to be protected and the general interest of the public. What is done or sought to be done must be established as being reasonable and necessary and on balance to serve the public interest.[320]

9–115 The Supreme Court ruled in favour of the defendants and upheld the validity of the resolution. It was considered to be reasonable, necessary and fair; it was needed to assist building the Irish horse-breeding industry in the interests of equestrian sport generally in the country.

---

318 *American Cyanamid Co v Ethicon Ltd* [1975] 1 All ER 504, [1975] AC 396, [1975] 2 WLR 316, HL.
319 [1979] ILRM 79.
320 ibid 90.

Termination of a Sportsperson's Employment Contract

An employment contract may be terminated at common law and under statute. As discussed in Chapter 8, a contract may be terminated under the common law by agreement, performance, frustration, and breach. There are other grounds on which an employment contract may be terminated, including the death of the employer or employee, resignation, dismissal, retirement, and insolvency.[321] **9–116**

Resignation occurs when the employee decides to end the employment relationship. There are number of statutory requirements that the employee must adhere to as provided for under the Minimum Notice and Terms of Employment Acts 1973–2005. Section 4(2)(a)–(e) of the 1973 Act provides that an employee in continuous service must give the following notice periods: **9–117**

(a) Less than two years, one week's notice.
(b) Two years or more but less than five, two weeks' notice.
(c) Five years or more but less than ten years, four weeks' notice.
(d) Ten years or more but less than fifteen years, six weeks' notice,
(e) Fifteen years or more, eight weeks' notice.[322]

In situations where there is no express provision in the contract in relation to notice, the court may have to imply a term which is 'reasonable', and what is deemed reasonable depends on the circumstances.[323] An employee may be dismissed without notice under s 8 of the Minimum Notice and Terms of Employment Act 1973 if there is misconduct.[324] A contract may be terminated if the sportsperson commits a criminal offence which results in a custodial sentence. A sportsperson's contract may also be terminated if they are found to have committed a doping violation or failed to provide a sample when requested. A sports body may terminate a contract if a player is unable to play due to excessive alcohol or drugs or has brought the game or club into disrepute. The contract may also be terminated if the player seriously breaches one of the terms of the contract.[325] **9–118**

---

[321] The Protection of Employees (Employers' Insolvency) Acts 1984–2012 protect certain unpaid entitlements relating to the remuneration of employees in the event of their employers becoming insolvent as defined in the Acts. Remuneration owed to employees in a range of situations may be paid by the Department of Social Protection out of the Social Insurance Fund (SIF).

[322] Continuous service is defined as 52 consecutive weeks and the continuous is not broken if the employee is dismissed and immediately re-employed by the employer. This is provided for in sch 1 of the Minimum Notice and Terms of Employment Act 1973 on the Computation of Continuous Service. The Unfair Dismissals (Amendment) Act 1993 amended the 1977 Act by inserting sub-s 5 into s 2 of the 1977 Act.

[323] See *Lyons v MF Kent & Co International Ltd* [1996] ELR 103; and *Cahill v DCU* [2007] IEHC 20.

[324] Dismissal without notice is referred to as summary dismissal: see *Carvill v Irish Industrial Bank Ltd* [1968] IR 325.

[325] As will be discussed in the next part of the chapter on the RSTP provisions relating

9–119 The death of either the employee or employee will usually result in the termination of the contract in the absence of an express or implied term to the contrary. If the employer is a company, termination will not ensue as companies usually have perpetual succession. Death of either party does not negate any liabilities: for example, if the employee dies and money was owed, it should be paid into the deceased's estate.[326]

9–120 An employment relationship may be terminated due to the conduct of either the employee or the employer. An employer would repudiate the contract if the agreed salary was not paid – according to the Commentary on the RSTP, '[t]his is the most common reason for a professional player to terminate a contract with a club'.[327] An employee would be repudiating the contract if they refused to do the work agreed or by leaving the job.[328] If the employee resigns on foot of the repudiatory conduct of the employer, there may be a claim for wrongful dismissal at common law or for constructive dismissal under the Unfair Dismissals Acts 1977–2015.[329] If the employee repudiates the contract, the contract comes to an end as the employee is dismissed.[330]

9–121 Wrongful dismissal, as the name suggests, refers to dismissal in breach of the employment contract. It may be invoked by the employee where there is inadequate notice of the termination of a contract or where the employer has repudiated one of the core tenets of the contract.[331] The primary remedy is damages, which may include damages for loss of reputation.

9–122 The Unfair Dismissals Act 1977 Act is underpinned by two main principles, the first being that there must be substantial grounds to justify the termination of a contract of employment (s 6(1)) and, second, the employer is under an obligation to adhere to the principle of fair procedures when terminating the contract of employment.[332] Unfair dismissal can be divided into three categories: (a) the termination of the

---

to serious breaches.

326 Áine Keenan, *Essentials of Irish Business Law* (6th edn, Gill and MacMillan 2012) 331.

327 FIFA, 'Commentary on the Regulations on the Status and Transfer of Players' (2023) 134 <https://digitalhub.fifa.com/m/40da0f707efdd011/original/FIFA-Commentary-on-the-FIFA-Regulations-for-the-Status-and-Transfer-of-Players-2023-edition.pdf> accessed 16 May 2024.

328 Daly and Doherty (n 16) 273.

329 ibid. Section 8 of the 1977 Act was amended by s 9 of the Workplace Relations (Miscellaneous Provisions) Act 2021. This relates to the proceedings of the adjudication officer being held in public unless there are 'special circumstances' that require it to be held in private.

330 See Daly and Doherty (n 16) 273 for a detailed decision of what constitutes 'repudiatory conduct'.

331 ibid 275–84 for a more detailed discussion of wrongful dismissal and the breach of implied and express terms of the employment contract, along with the constitutional protection of fair procedures.

332 Cox and others (n 1) 312.

contract of employment with or without notice; (b) the resignation of the employee owing to the conduct of the employer, such as constructive dismissal; and (c) the expiration and non-renewal of a fixed-term or specified-purpose contract. The three main forms of dismissal are explained in the definition section of the 1977 Act. Since the 1977 Act, legislation has been introduced to protect employees with fixed-term contracts, the Protection of Employees (Fixed-Term Work) Act 2003. In general, employees under fixed-term contracts (contracts which are for a specific purpose and end once that purpose is completed or end at a specific date) have the same rights as other employees. Cox and others note that most fixed-term contracts in Ireland which are concluded between players and clubs will contain a clause that excludes the Unfair Dismissals Acts 1977–2015.[333]

For a sportsperson to fall within the ambit of the Unfair Dismissals Acts 1977–2015, they must meet the following conditions: **9–123**

- Be under a contract of service.
- Have one year of continuous service (subject to certain exceptions) with the employer.
- Have been dismissed.

It is important to note that the Acts do not protect an employee from dismissal. Instead, it provides a system of appeal whereby the employee is given the opportunity to question the fairness of the decision of dismissal. The appeal may only be initiated after the dismissal has taken place. It is up to the employer to prove that the dismissal was not unfair. Thus, the burden of proof rests on the employer; however, the WRC ultimately makes the decision on whether the dismissal was fair or unfair. **9–124**

Section 6(4)(a)–(d) of the 1977 Act refers to specific grounds where the dismissal of the employee is deemed fair. These grounds are (a) capability, competence, or qualifications; (b) the conduct of the employee; (c) the redundancy of the employee; and (d) an employee rendered unable to work due to a restriction imposed by statute. In situations where a dismissal is fair, it is prudent for the employer to give reasons and in doing so apply the principle of fair procedures as failure to do so may result in the employer losing the protection of s 4(2) and rendering the dismissal unfair. **9–125**

The dismissal will be deemed unfair if the employee is dismissed under s 6(2) of the 1977 Act for one or more of the following: trade union membership,[334] religious or political opinions, race, pregnancy-related **9–126**

[333] ibid 313.

[334] The one-year continuous service requirement is not applicable in the case of dismissal for membership of a trade union. The legislation provides for proposed membership and not just actual membership. If the activity takes place outside

issues, litigation against the employer (criminal or civil proceedings), sexual orientation, age or membership of the Travelling community, or unfair selection for redundancy.

9–127 Section 6(2)(f) relates to unfair dismissal and pregnancy. A pregnant employee cannot be dismissed on grounds of pregnancy unless the employee is unable, by reason of the pregnancy, to adequately do the work for which she was employed or if her continuing to work will result in a breach of the legislation by her employer. It will not be deemed unfair dismissal if the employer does not have a suitable vacancy to provide her with alternative work at the time of the dismissal; equally it will not be a breach of the legislation if the pregnant employee refuses an offer of alternative employment with terms and conditions corresponding to the position at issue when this offer is made to enable her to be retained by the employer. A pregnant sportsperson will invariably have their career suspended, albeit temporarily, and their employer will not be required to keep the contract open, unless there is an express term which provides otherwise.[335] A ban on sports bodies employing pregnant sportspeople would arguably be an unreasonable restraint of trade. It would be very difficult to justify it in the interests of the parties or in the public interest.[336] As discussed at the beginning of this chapter, FIFA's RSTP provide protections for pregnant footballers and those on maternity leave.

Remedies for Unfair Dismissal

9–128 Section 7 of the 1977 Act as amended provides for the following remedies for unfair dismissal: reinstatement, re-engagement and compensation (with a maximum of 104 weeks' remuneration). Regarding reinstatement, the employee is reinstated into the position that they held before the unfair dismissal. The employee is entitled to any arrears of salary from the date of the dismissal to the date of the reinstatement, and there is no break in the continuity of service during this time. Any improvements or benefits that have been granted to comparable employees will also be given to the reinstated employee. Re-engagement provides for the employee to be redeployed into the same position or a different job but with such terms and conditions that are reasonable, having regard to all the circumstances. The re-engaged employee does not have an automatic right to the payment of arrears of salary nor is there a guarantee of unbroken continuity of service.[337] Daly and Doherty explain the distinction between reinstatement and re-

work time or at permitted times during work, trade union activities are not grounds for dismissal.

[335] Cox and others (n 1) 313.

[336] As Lord Reid in *Esso Petroleum* (n 216) 300 stated: 'Surely it can never be in the interest of a person to agree to suffer a restraint of trade unless he gets some compensating advantage, direct or indirect.'

[337] Daly and Doherty (n 16) 383.

engagement, as a reinstated employee is rendered 'blameless', while the re-engaged employee 'has not been totally blameless'.[338] The WRC has complete discretion when it comes to deciding which one applies to the particular situation. In some situations, where the trust and confidence between the parties has been damaged, reinstatement or re-engagement may not be the appropriate remedies. Compensation may be the most appropriate remedy in these situations.

An employment injunction may also be granted; however, the Irish courts are reluctant to grant such injunctions given the personal nature of the relationship.[339] It seems incongruous to the employment relationship to compel the worker to remain with the employer through the granting of an injunction, especially in situations where the mutual trust between the employer and employee has been damaged. In a sporting context, the case of *Evans v IRFB* is an example of an employment injunction involving the Head of Rugby Development in the International Rugby Football Board (IRFB, now World Rugby).[340] Evans was employed as the Head of Rugby Development in 2001. He was a former Welsh international rugby player and was asked to apply for the job of 'game developmental manager' with the IRFB by the then chairman Vernon Pugh Queen's Counsel (QC). Evans was employed as a head of Department of Applied Science in the South Bank University in London. His post in the university was both permanent and pensionable, and he had a remuneration of £55,000 per annum. In a letter to the plaintiff dated 17 June 2001, Pugh notified Evans of his appointment along with details of his appointment, including a section on responsibilities, which stated 'as per attached job description'. In 2004, it was proposed that there would be an amalgamation of the plaintiff's department with another department to form a new rugby unit. Evans had a five-year fixed-term contract commencing on 1 September 2001 and contended that he was entitled to carry out the duties like those outlined in his initial job description for the remainder of his contract. The plaintiff sought an interlocutory injunction to prevent the appointment of anybody to the proposed new position. In granting the interlocutory injunction, Clarke J held that a: **9–129**

> basic job description constitutes a condition of service so that it was at least arguable that a sufficiently radical alteration in the duties and responsibilities of an employee might amount to breach of contract. The plaintiff had established an arguable case that what was proposed

[338] ibid.

[339] Peter Charleton, 'Employment Injunctions: An Over-Loose Discretion' (2009) 2 Irish Judicial Studies Journal 1. See also Paul McCutcheon, 'Negative Enforcement of Employment Contracts in the Sports Industries' (1997) 17 (1) Legal Studies 65–100; and Hilary Delany, 'Employment Injunctions: The Role of Mutual Trust and Confidence' (2006) 28 Dublin University Law Journal 363. In most unfair dismissal cases, the appropriate remedy is damages and only in the most limited of circumstances should injunctive relief be granted.

[340] [2005] 2 ILRM 358.

amounted to a sufficiently radical alteration to render it a breach of his contract.[341]

9–130 Clarke J emphasised the reluctance of the courts to grant injunctions in the employment context where it would in effect result in indirect specific performance. However, the issue did not arise here as the new appointment might have the effect of breaching an existing employee's contract; also, no question arose to the Court having to supervise the specific performance of the contract of employment.[342]

Regulations and the Status and Transfer of Players and Breach of Contract

9–131 As discussed earlier on in this chapter, standard professional contracts are used in many professional sports. FIFA's RSTP provides a template for national football associations, which may be amended to reflect provisions of domestic employment law.[343] Under Chapter IV on the Maintenance of Contractual Stability between Professionals and Clubs there are six articles: Articles 13, 14, 15, 16, 17 and 18. The RSTP were introduced in 2001; it is important to note that it augments domestic laws in that 'many of the further rules contained in the Regulations in the chapter concerning contractual stability simply reflect generally accepted principles of contract and employment law'.[344] Article 13 provides for respect of contract and states that a 'contract between a professional and a club may only be terminated upon expiry of the term of the contract or by mutual agreement'.[345] Article 14(1) outlines the provisions relating to termination of contract with just cause. This permits either the club or the player to terminate the contract without incurring a penalty of any kind, namely compensation or sporting sanction.[346] Article 17(1) enumerates the principle that compensation should be paid whenever a contract is terminated without just cause. There are a number of rules under Chapter IV 'that are specific and unique to football', including the termination of a contract with sporting just cause (Article 15)[347]; a contract cannot be unilaterally terminated

---

341 ibid 359.

342 ibid.

343 (n 68).

344 Commentary (n 327) 122. From pages 122 to 245 the Commentary augments the RSTP by giving the background, providing explanations, and referring to the jurisprudence of the CAS and FIFA's Dispute Resolution Chamber regarding Chapter IV.

345 RSTP (n 68) 28.

346 ibid 19. Article 14bis refers to arrears of salary as constituting good cause and abusive conduct under Article 14(2).

347 Article 15 pertains to an established player who, during the season appeared in less than 10% of the official matches in which the club has been involved, may terminate the contract on the ground of sporting just cause. This ground is considered on a case-by-case basis and the player's circumstances will be an important factor. Sporting sanctions will not apply; however, compensation may payable. The player can only terminate the contract in a specified timeframe:

during the course of a season (Article 16)[348]; a professional and their new club should be held jointly and severally liable for compensation payable by the player to their former club (Article 17(2))[349]; sporting sanctions may be imposed for terminating a contract without just cause (Article 17(3) and (4)); and the imposition of sporting sanctions on a club if it induces a player to terminate a contract without just cause (Article 17 (4)). The RSTP Commentary provides:

> The contractual relationship between a professional and a club they join on loan is governed by the same rules and principles that apply to professionals engaged on a permanent basis, in particular the provisions of the Regulations on the maintenance of contractual stability.[350]

There is no definition of just cause in the Regulations; however, the CAS **9–132** considers just cause to constitute a material breach of a contract.[351] In using Swiss law to fill in the gaps, the CAS Panel in its arbitral award in *Békéscsaba* cited Article 337 paragraph 2 of the Swiss Code of Obligations (CO), which provides: 'Any circumstances which, according to the rules of good faith, mean that the party who has given notice of termination cannot be required to continue the employment relationship, shall be deemed good reason.'[352] The CAS equates just cause with good reason. In following the jurisprudence of the Swiss Federal Supreme Court in relation to 'good reason', the CAS Panel determined that an 'employment contract may be terminated immediately when the main terms and conditions (either general/objective or specific/personal), under which it was entered into are no longer respected'.[353]

---

they have 15 days following the last official match of the season of the club with which he was registered. Sporting sanctions include a suspension or a restriction on playing.

348 Unilateral contracts are discussed in ch 8.

349 Article 17(2) states: 'Entitlement to compensation cannot be assigned to a third party. If a professional is required to pay compensation, the professional and his new club shall be jointly and severally liable for its payment. The amount may be stipulated in the contract or agreed between the parties.' See CAS 2018/A/6017 *FC Lugano SA v FC Internazionale Milano SpA* award of 9 September 2019 <https://jurisprudence.tas-cas.org/Shared%20Documents/6017.pdf> accessed 17 May 2024.

350 Commentary (n 327) 99. For more information on recent developments and termination without just cause and joint and several liability, see ch 13 para 13.36, n 114. There is a rebuttable presumption that the new club induced the player to terminate the contract with the former club.

351 CAS 2017/A/5465 *Békéscsaba 1912 Futball v George Koroudjiev* award of 20 September 2018 [4] <https://jurisprudence.tas-cas.org/Shared%20Documents/5465.pdf> accessed 17 May 2024. See also CAS 2006/A/1180 *Galatasaray SK v Frank Ribéry & Olympique de Marseille* award of 24 April 2007 <https://jurisprudence.tas-cas.org/Shared%20Documents/1180.pdf> accessed 17 May 2024; CAS 2014/A/3706 *Christophe Grondin v Al-Faisaly Football Club* award of 17 April 2015 <https://jurisprudence.tas-cas.org/Shared%20Documents/3706.pdf> accessed 17 May 2024; and CAS 2018/A/6017 *FC Lugano SA v FC Internazionale Milano SpA* award of 9 September 2019 <https://jurisprudence.tas-cas.org/Shared%20Documents/6017.pdf> accessed 17 May 2024, where the CAS refers to a serious breach of confidence.

352 CAS 2017/A/5465 (n 351) [90].

353 ibid [91].

9–133 In awarding damages against the appellant club, the CAS Panel upheld the decision of FIFA's Dispute Resolution Chamber (DRC) who had found in favour of the player. The CAS Panel deemed forcing a player to train alone and his subsequent termination of the contract constituted just cause. It concluded:

> Not allowing a professional football player to train with his/her teammates can indeed be – absent specific circumstances such as injury recovery – equivalent to a severe breach of said player's personality rights by the club which employs him/her (and implicitly of the employment agreement concluded between the two).[354]

9–134 Article 17 outlines the consequences of terminating a contract without just cause. Article 17(1) provides that damages will be awarded in all cases where it is found that a contract has been terminated without just cause. Article 17(1) also refers to other factors that must be considered, including the law of the country concerned, the specificity of sport and any other objective criteria which includes renumeration due to the player and other benefits due, the time remaining on the contract up to a maximum of five years, and fees and expenses incurred by the club. Article 17(3) states that sporting sanctions, in addition to damages, will be imposed on a player that has breached the contract during the protected period.[355] The player will be precluded from playing for six months if there are aggravating factors. Examples of terminating a contract without just cause include a player failing a medical after being signed; this constitutes a condition precedent as discussed in Chapter 8. Article 18(4) of the RSTP provides that the 'validity of a contract may not be made subject to a successful medical examination and/or the grant of a work permit'.[356]

Morals Clauses in Sponsorship Contracts

9–135 This section will briefly discuss morals clauses in sponsorship contracts. As the next chapter on commercial issues will discuss in more detail, sponsorship contracts can involve a sportsperson, a club, or a league, who are referred to as the sponsee. They enter into an agreement with a sponsor. Sponsorship contracts are atypical as there no standard contract that can be used for all types of sponsorship agreements. As discussed earlier on in this chapter, a sportsperson can be sanctioned by the sporting organisation for bringing the sport into disrepute, a term included in professional playing contracts. Similarly, a sponsor

---

354 ibid [6].

355 RSTP (n 68) 7 defines protected period as 'a period of three entire seasons or three years, whichever comes first, following the entry into force of a contract, where such contract is concluded prior to the 28th birthday of the professional, or two entire seasons or two years, whichever comes first, following the entry into force of a contract, where such contract is concluded after the 28th birthday of the professional'.

356 ibid 31. This is discussed in ch 8 paras 8–46–8-48.

may a include a morals clause in the agreement with a sportsperson to protect themselves. When drafting a contract, the sponsor may ask that a term be included that terminates the contract in the event of the sportsperson engaging in behaviour that is detrimental to the sponsor.[357] Misconduct on the part of the sponsee may cause embarrassment or the stigmatisation of the product or service of the sponsor or endorser.[358]

When the sponsor is endeavouring to include such a term in relation to a particular sportsperson, the situation is more straightforward; however, it becomes complicated when a sponsor requires such a clause in relation to a team or a club. In that situation, most sponsees would take issue with the sponsor exercising such a large degree of control.[359] **9–136**

In general, the sponsor would not be entitled to damages, but would be permitted to terminate the contract.[360] In using the example of Tom Brady and the aftermath of 'Deflategate', Under Armour, the sporting goods company, did not terminate the contract.[361] This is largely believed to be due to the fact that is not a family centred company, and more latitude seems to be given to sportspersons and teams by luxury and fashion companies.[362] **9–137**

If a contract does not include a morals clause, it leads to the question whether the court would imply such a term. The court may be more willing to do so in situations where the sportsperson has breached the contract by engaging in conduct that is associated with the sport (for example, testing positive for a banned substance).[363] However, conduct **9–138**

---

357 Donnellan (n 87).

358 Stuart Benzie and Timothy Killen, 'Contractual Remedies for Damage to Reputation in Sport Sponsorship' (*Law in Sport*, 22 November 2013) <https://www.lawinsport.com/topics/contract-law/item/contractual-remedies-for-damage-to-reputation-in-sport-sponsorship> accessed 17 May 2024.

359 See Christopher Evans, 'Negotiating Sponsorship Deals Using the Moral High Ground' (*Law in Sport*, 7 March 2013) <https://www.lawinsport.com/topics/commercial-law/item/negotiating-sponsorship-deals-using-the-moral-high-ground> accessed 17 May 2024.

360 Unless the contract stipulates otherwise.

361 Cari Grieb, 'Tom Brady's Endorsement Value Takes Significant Hit from Deflategate' (*Sporting News*, 12 August 2015) <https://www.sportingnews.com/us/nfl/news/tom-brady-deflategate-endorsements-moral-clauses-arod-alex-rodriguez-yankees-biogenesis/1m78gewlg80j812njakpm24dhg> accessed 17 May 2024. For an account of 'deflategate', see Jill Martin and Steve Almasy, 'NFL Deflategate: Brady Timeline' (*CNN Sports*, 12 May 2015) <https://edition.cnn.com/2015/05/09/us/nfl-deflategate-timeline/index.html> accessed 17 May 2024. See also Laura Donnellan, 'Godolphin and Under Armour: Historic Sports Marketing Partnership' (*Sports and Taxation*, 16 April 2016) <https://sportslawandtaxation.com/news/553-godolphin-and-under-armour-historic-sports-marketing-partnership> accessed 17 September 2024.

362 Grieb (n 361).

363 Benzie and Killen (n 358). The writers contend that a well-drafted morals clause could entitle the sponsor to recover damages for breach of contract. The term of the contract could stipulate a fixed amount or include the words 'consequential loss caused by breach'.

that is not associated with the sport – such as extramarital affairs or abuse of animals – is a more complex situation. In this situation, 'the question will be answered by the scope of the term which it is said has been breached'.[364]

9–139 A sponsor would be advised not to use terms such as 'bad', 'immoral' or 'moral turpitude'.[365] Extensive lists of offending behaviour should also be avoided. Sponsors should be mindful of the fact that morals differ from person to person, so a less emotive phrase might be more acceptable to the parties, for example: 'whether the commercial value of the team has been substantially reduced by acts or omissions of a named list of parties', using a 'mixed subjective and objective test', or including the words 'in the reasonable opinion of the sponsor'.[366] The issue of control and the extent of such control which is acceptable to the sponsee is an important factor to consider.[367]

Conclusion

9–140 This chapter built on Chapter 8 as it examined the application of employment law to contracts entered into by sportspersons. Sportspeople are entitled to be protected by employment law; however, cognisance is given to the fact that sport occupies a special position. As noted in the discussion on the FIFA RSTP, the provisions generally reflect accepted principles of contract and employment law. The RSTP often refer to the more favourable domestic law being applied; that means that at times the Regulations establish a minimum level of protection, which are augmented by national law, a notable example being the maternity rights of pregnant football players.

9–141 Disputes concerning the terms of contracts of employment have resulted in litigation in the courts. The courts have countenanced cases involving a matrix of contractual relationships, namely, player and club, manager and club, player and agent, and player and governing body. The doctrine of restraint of trade demonstrated how a sportsperson's right to earn a livelihood can be curtailed. The doctrine applies the same way to sport as it would in a non-sporting context. What emerged from the discussion was the courts' willingness to apply the doctrine to several situations, including wage ceilings, the rules of governing bodies and doping cases. The courts will consider whether the restraint is unreasonable or whether it can be justified. The public interest is an important consideration for the courts as well as the effect the restraint has on the parties.

---

364 ibid.
365 Evans (n 359).
366 ibid.
367 ibid.

The ways in which an employment contract can be terminated highlight both the uniqueness of sport and how ordinary principles of employment and contract law apply to sportspersons in the same way as they would to non-sportspersons. Certain provisions, including sporting sanctions and the termination of a contract with sporting just cause, only apply in a sporting context. **9–142**

Morals clauses in sponsorship contracts underscore the importance of brand protection and the commercial value attached to endorsements. Adverse publicity generated by a sponsee can result in damage to the sponsor's reputation. The next chapter will examine commercial issues, with a focus on sponsorship, broadcasting rights, image rights, merchandising and the law of agency. **9–143**

CHAPTER 10

COMMERCIAL ISSUES IN SPORT

Introduction

Modern sport is a multibillion-dollar global industry. The global sports market is very broad as it encompasses 'sales of sports services and related goods by entities (organizations, sole traders and partnerships) that offer spectator sports and participatory sports'.[1] Due to COVID-19 restrictions, including social distancing, there was a decrease in the market from $458.8bn in 2019 to $388.3bn in 2020.[2] However, the future projections are far more optimistic with the global sports market expected to reach $599.9bn by 2025, and by 2030 the figure is estimated to reach $826bn.[3] **10–01**

As discussed in Chapter 9, the decision in the *Eastham* case brought about a change in English football.[4] While the commercialisation of sport is not a recent development, the ways in which sport became commodified changed. The traditional medium of gate receipts and prize money was no longer the main source of revenue, instead it was coming from sponsorship and broadcasting deals.[5] With the increased professionalisation and commercialisation of sport, the issue of sponsorship contracts, agents, image rights, merchandising and media rights have assumed an even greater importance. As society has become more litigious, individuals, both natural and legal, have become more aware of their rights and if they feel their rights have been unduly compromised, they will seek redress in the courts. Sport has been unable to remain immune from such developments. As the law has a role to play in sport, the nature of relationships between those involved in sport has changed and this is reflected in the selected areas of commercial law and its impact on sport. This chapter will provide an overview of sponsorship contracts, image rights, intellectual property (IP), media rights, merchandising and the law of agency. **10–02**

---

1 Mukul Kumar and Sandeep Bhalla, 'Global Sports Market Today: An Overview' (2021) 8(4) International Journal of Physical Education, Sports and Health 223, 223. The writers add that spectator sports 'includes teams or clubs and independent athletes that present sporting events before a paying audience'.

2 ibid.

3 ibid.

4 *Eastham v Newcastle United FC* [1964] ch 413.

5 Neville Cox and Alex Schuster (with Cathryn Costello), *Sport and the Law* (Firstlaw 2004) 304. See also Caroline Connolly, 'The Sponsorship Contract as a Mechanism of Safeguarding and Influencing the Level of Return on Investment in Sport Sponsorship' (2005) 12(8) Commercial Law Practitioner 199.

Sponsorship Contracts

10–03 A sponsorship contract or agreement is considered an atypical contract as there is no standard contract that can be used for all types of sponsorship agreements. There are no formalities prescribed for a sponsorship contract; however, in entering into such an agreement a sportsperson needs to consider the impact that it may have on their sporting commitments, their image rights, any effects it may have on third parties and the renewal rights contained in the agreement.[6]

10–04 The duration of the agreement is an important factor, as it may be for a particular event, or pertain to a particular team, league, governing body, or individual. The sponsorship agreement could involve a sports product such as footwear, equipment such as a golf ball, tennis racket or an energy drink. A team may enter into a sponsorship agreement with a global brand including its name on the jersey or any agreement with a sports clothing company to produce and sell replica football kits. Usually, the duration will be fixed and there may be the option to extend or renew; for example, renewal may be subject to the sponsee (the sportsperson/team/club) attaining a particular success such as winning the league. Some sponsor agreements will include a term that allows the sponsor to extend or renew the contract if it can match the offer made by another brand. A specific date should be set and after that date if the sponsor has not opted to renew the contract, the sponsee is free to contact other possible sponsors. This gives the sponsee time to have an alternative sponsor in place so there is no gap in sponsorship after the expiration of the contract. Sportspersons and teams are advised not to include an automatic renewal term as it may restrict their ability to enter into negotiations with prospective sponsors.

Matching Rights

10–05 There are two recent 'matching rights' cases from the superior courts of England and Wales, namely *New Balance Athletics Inc v Liverpool Football Club and Athletic Ground Ltd*[7] and *SDI Retail Services Limited v The Rangers Football Club Limited*.[8] In the former, the High Court of England and Wales held against the claimant, New Balance, which had entered into a sponsorship agreement with Liverpool FC to manufacture and sell replica shirts. The agreement was to end in 2020; however, a term of the contract provided that Liverpool had to inform New Balance of any third-party offers and within 30 days of receipt of the submission New Balance would decide whether it would offer Liverpool an extension on

---

6 Joe Tompkins, 'Key Points for Athletes to Consider Before Signing a Sponsorship Agreement' (*Law in Sport*, 23 May 2018) <https://www.lawinsport.com/topics/item/key-points-for-athletes-to-consider-before-signing-a-sponsorship-agreement/> accessed 17 May 2024.

7 [2019] EWHC 2837 (Comm).

8 [2019] EWHC 1929 (Comm).

the agreement on no less favourable terms offered by the third party.[9] Nike was the third party who offered Liverpool a new sponsorship deal with more favourable terms, including distribution and marketing initiatives in which the Liverpool replica jerseys would be sold globally in over 6,000 stores, 500 of which would be owned and controlled by Nike.[10] Nike included a term whereby the jersey would be marketed by internationally renowned people from the world of sport and music 'of the calibre of Lebron James, Serena Williams, Drake, etc'.[11] New Balance endeavoured to offer similar distribution and marketing initiatives, which Liverpool did not believe were offered in good faith, which was an implied term in the contract.[12] Liverpool contended that New Balance had neither the distribution nor marketing capacity to match the offer made by Nike. The High Court, in finding against the claimant, held that New Balance failed to show that it had matched the terms of Nike's offer.

The facts of the *Rangers* case are slightly different but at the core is the issue of matching rights. The agreement between SDI Retail Services Limited (SDIR/Sports Direct) and Rangers was to end on 31 July 2018. Under Schedule 3, paragraph 5, the terms of the agreement provided that six months prior to the expiry of the agreement, Rangers was permitted to enter discussions and negotiations with third parties in relation to the offered rights. The offered rights were all the rights granted to SDIR in the initial agreement and included the following: the right to operate and manage the operations; the right to perform permitted activities regarding branded products and/or additional products; and the right to perform the 'permitted activities' in relation to the official kit and/or replica kit.[13] 10–06

The agreement stipulated that if Rangers received an offer from a third party it was to contact SDIR in writing with details made by the third party and SDIR had the right to match the offer, referred to as the 'Notice of Offer'.[14] The offer could relate to any, all or a combination of the offered rights and any connected commercial arrangement, as provided by Schedule 3, paragraph 5(3). Within 10 business days of receiving the Offer of Notice, SDIR was entitled to invoke the matching rights, whether any, all or a combination of offered rights. It could also request more information or clarification. If the matching rights were invoked, a further agreement on the same terms as the existing agreement would be concluded, save for any variations required to 10–07

9 *New Balance Athletics Inc* (n 7) [3].
10 ibid [26].
11 ibid [7].
12 ibid [14].
13 *SDI Retail Services Limited* (n 8) [16].
14 ibid [38]. The Notice of Offer was required to include the following information: any payments to be made by the third party to Rangers; any revenue share or royalties to be paid between Rangers and the third party; and the duration of the agreement between Rangers and the third party (together, the material terms).

affect the material terms in the third-party offer and to state to what the matched rights referred to: any, all, or a combination of rights and 'any connected commercial arrangement'.

10–08 SDIR was never given the opportunity to match the Elite/Hummel agreement. Rangers concluded the agreement with Elite/Hummel. SDIR issued proceedings against Rangers seeking an injunction on grounds that Rangers had breached the contract. SDIR contended that it had the right to match each of the rights or benefits that made up 'the whole bargain, and not only those elements that are offered rights'.[15] Under the SDIR agreement, the inclusion of the provision of 'any connected commercial arrangement' meant that the ambit of the agreement was widened. Had the agreement concluded with Elite/Hummel related only to manufacturing rights then SDIR would have had no matching rights.[16] However, under the Elite/Hummel agreement, by offering the right of manufacturing as part of a package, 'the right to manufacture became a connected commercial arrangement. It was part of the commercial deal.'[17] This information should have been included in the Notice of Offer. Persey J, Queen's Counsel (QC), sitting as a judge of the Commercial Court, stated that if it had been included, he was sure SDIR would have been able to match it.

10–09 The judge reiterated the fundamentals of English contract law, namely that the subjective intentions of the parties and their previous negotiations are not admissible as an aid to interpreting the terms of a contract/agreement.[18] It is the role of the court to examine the agreement as a whole and give words an objective meaning; in looking at the agreement in a wider context the court will adduce the objective meaning of the parties' language. SDIR argued that Rangers did not set out the material terms for each of its offered rights. Thus, a dispute arose as to what requirements were needed for compliance with the Offer of Notice. The High Court granted injunctive relief to the claimant to prevent the performance of the Elite/Hummel agreement for the 2020/21 football season.[19] Rangers was also ordered to inform Elite and Hummel that the agreement between them was the subject of an injunction and thus the agreement between them could not be performed.[20] In the words of Teare J, SDIR and Rangers 'are keen on litigation'.[21]

---

15 ibid [55].

16 ibid [76].

17 ibid.

18 ibid [45]–[47].

19 There was another High Court case in which SDIR sought an order for the disclosure of certain documents pertaining to the third-party agreement. McDonald QC, sitting as a deputy judge of the High Court, granted the order for disclosure: *SDI Retail Services Ltd v The Rangers Football Club Ltd* [2021] EWHC 3364 (Comm).

20 *SDI Retail Services Ltd v The Rangers Football Club Ltd* [2020] EWHC 136 (Comm).

21 *SDI Retail Services Ltd v The Rangers Football Club Ltd* [2018] EWHC 2772 (Comm) [1]. Teare J granted three injunctions to SDIR: [54]–[65].

In his 2019 decision, Persey J 'contemplated that Rangers would continue to receive (and, therefore, be entitled to receive) revenues and royalties due from Elite under the Elite/Hummel Agreement for both the 2018/2019 season and also the 2019/2020 season'.[22] As alluded to by the Court of Appeal, Persey J acknowledged that there had been no provision to deal with the situation of Elite defaulting on its obligations; however, the judge referred to the 'unattractive consequence' that would arise if Elite were permitted to breach with impunity its agreement with Rangers.[23] Rangers subsequently sought a declaration that the injunction did not preclude it from pursuing a claim against Elite.[24] It was also seeking to recover sums it said were owed to it by Elite and it also wished to pursue Elite through the Scottish courts.[25] On 29 January 2020, the judge handed down a reserved judgment and granted the declaration sought by Rangers.[26] SDIR appealed that decision, with permission granted by Lord Justice (LJ) Flaux, on 27 May 2020.[27] The Court of Appeal reversed the January 2020 declaration granted by Persey J.[28] In a decision dated 27 May 2021, by a 2–1 majority, the Court of Appeal upheld the appeal. Phillips LJ was critical of Persey J's decision, as in his view: **10–10**

> the Judge did not give sufficient, if any, consideration or weight to this broader context and purpose of the Injunction in considering its interpretation. Permitting Rangers to sue on the Elite/Hummel Agreement, whether to enforce a payment obligation or any other obligation, would not be enforcing the terms of the Agreement 'as far as possible' (the Judge's own contemporaneous explanation of the purpose of the Injunction) but would be allowing Rangers to rely upon and enforce the very contract it had entered with Elite in unlawful breach of the Agreement and was expressly required to repudiate. What is more, it would be permitting the use of the court process to do so, entailing that the court would be enforcing an agreement which it had held should not have been made and had required, in so far as possible, not to be performed and to be terminated.[29]

The injunction granted on 27 January 2020 prohibited Rangers from performing or assisting in the performance of the Elite/Hummel agreement and included an order that in effect required Rangers to 'undo' that agreement 'as far as possible'.[30] However, Persey J in his construction of the word 'assist' as provided for under paragraph 6(2) of **10–11**

---

[22] (n 8) [95].

[23] *SDI Retail Services Ltd v The Rangers Football Club Ltd* [2021] EWCA Civ 790 [45].

[24] *SDI Retail Services Limited v Rangers* (n 8).

[25] *SDI Retail Services Limited* (n 23) [50] and [51] refer to the litigation in Scotland. On foot of the declaration granted by Persey J on 29 January 2020, Rangers issued a summons in the Court of Session in Scotland. When Flaux LJ granted permission to SDIR to appeal, he also ordered a stay on the declaration granted by Persey J pending the outcome of the Court of Appeal.

[26] *SDI Retail Services Ltd* (n 23) [4].

[27] ibid.

[28] ibid.

[29] ibid [63].

[30] ibid [39].

the injunction, determined that it did not apply to the paying of monies owed to Rangers by Elite.[31] Persey J construed the word 'assist' in its ordinary meaning as signifying 'to help'.[32] He contended, 'Coercive action in the sense of requiring someone to perform cannot, in my view, sensibly be regarded as assisting that person to perform.'[33] The Court of Appeal disagreed and defined the word 'assist' in broader terms to mean that Rangers was prohibited 'from taking any steps to cause or contribute to Elite's performance of the agreement'.[34] It rejected the contention that it would amount to a coercive action if Rangers were precluded from recovering monies from Elite. If the analysis of Persey J was correct then it would mean that Rangers could sue Elite for damages for failure to perform its obligations in relation to the 2020/2021 season which, in the words of Phillips LJ, 'would drive a coach and horses through the Injunction'.[35] Phillips LJ adopted a restrictive approach with regard to the injunction and held that if Rangers sought to enforce the payment of monies owed under the Elite/Hummel Agreement that it would be a breach of paragraph 6(2) and amount to contempt of court.[36] Baker LJ concurred with Philips LJ. Baker LJ echoed the words of Philips LJ when he observed that for Rangers to vary the terms of the injunction, there would need to be 'strong reasons' to permit the respondent 'to benefit from their wrongful act'.[37]

10–12 The cases above highlight the issues that can arise when there is a lack of definition as to what the matching right pertains. It is imperative that the parties to the agreement clearly set out the terms. For example, do matching rights apply solely to the material terms, such as the price or duration of the agreement or just to the financial offer? Are other factors considered, as in the *Liverpool* case where Liverpool contended that Nike had a superior distribution network and promotional opportunities? It all depends on the terms of the contract and, while a club may contend that it was its subjective intention that these factors – for example, a superior distribution by a global brand, be applied – in the absence of a clause in the agreement that provides explicitly for this or where there is a clause which denotes a broader definition of matching rights, the court will arguably ascribe an objective definition and it will be difficult to read such factors into the agreement based on an implied term.

---

31 ibid [4].
32 *SDI Retail Services Ltd* (n 8) [10].
33 ibid.
34 *SDI Retail Services Ltd* (n 23) [62].
35 ibid [69].
36 ibid [72].
37 ibid [81]. Baker LJ added that the Court was not able to ascertain whether such reasons existed. Uphill LJ dissented and contended that the appeal should not be allowed: [82]–[99].

Image Rights

Arden J of the Court of Appeal in *Proactive Sports Management v Rooney* simply defined the term 'image rights' to denote 'rights that individuals have in their personality, which enables them to control the exploitation of their name or picture'.[38] In the High Court decision, Hegarty J deemed the image rights representative agreement (IRRA) concluded between Proactive, a company providing management and agency services to the former professional footballer, Wayne Rooney, as constituting an unreasonable restraint of trade.[39] The IRRA, as cited by Hegarty J, was expansive and provided the following description: **10–13**

> Image Rights means the right for any commercial or promotional purpose to use the Player's name, nickname, slogan and signatures developed from time to time, image, likeness, voice, logos, get-ups, initials, team or squad number (as may be allocated to the Player from time to time), reputation, video or film portrayal, biographical information, graphical representation, electronic, animated or computer-generated representation and/or any other representation and/or right of association and/or any other right or quasi-right anywhere in the World of the Player in relation to his name, reputation, image, promotional services, and/or his performances together with the right to apply for registration of any such rights.[40]

The IRRA turned out to be lucrative for all parties involved with Proactive employing a group of specialists who worked solely for Rooney; this group was referred to as Team Rooney. However, relations between Rooney and Proactive began to deteriorate and Rooney endeavoured to terminate the contract. For Proactive, this was a repudiatory breach of the contract. No further commissions were paid to Proactive and consequently the case came before Hegarty J in the High Court and was subsequently appealed to the Court of Appeal. The Court of Appeal allowed the appeal in part; however, it found that image rights were ancillary as Rooney's primary occupation was that of a professional footballer. Although ancillary, the doctrine of restraint of trade could still apply to Rooney's image rights, as it would with any other occupation.[41] Public policy was an important consideration for the Court of Appeal as it **10–14**

> is concerned with the manner in which a person may properly realise his potential, not only for the good of that individual but for the economic benefit of society generally. It cannot logically matter whether the realisation is a person's primary activity or not. The protection for the other party to the contract is that the restriction is not a bar to enforcement of a contract if it is capable of justification as being reasonable. Moreover,

---

38 *Proactive Sports Management Limited v Wayne Rooney, Coleen Rooney (Formerly McLoughlin), Stoneygate 48 Limited, Speed 9849 Limited* [2011] EWCA Civ 1444 [1].

39 *Proactive Sports Management Limited v Wayne Rooney, Coleen Rooney (Formerly McLoughlin), Stoneygate 48 Limited, Speed 9849 Limited* [2010] EWHC 1807 (QB).

40 ibid [187].

41 *Proactive Sports Management Limited* (n 38) [93].

> the endorsement of goods encourages the purchase and consumption of goods, and the court is entitled to assume that it is in the interests of the public that image rights should be fully realisable for this economic purpose.[42]

10–15 A sportsperson's proprietary right in their personality allows them to exploit those rights, promote their 'brand' in return for financial gain. Sportspersons have a commercial interest in their brand and associated goodwill which they may accrue for a product by endorsing it. Equally, if there is unauthorised use of their image it can lead to a dilution of their brand. In Ireland, there is no legislation that pertains to image rights. A sportsperson pursuing a claim against an unauthorised third party who has used, for example, their image, likeness, autograph, voice, or photograph, will need to rely on both common and statutory protections, including IP rights, passing-off and the right to privacy. The Island of Guernsey, a British Crown dependency located off the coast of Normandy, France, introduced the Image Rights (Bailiwick of Guernsey) Ordinance in 2012, which was amended in 2017.[43] The 2012 Ordinance established an image rights' register and it sets out *inter alia* the grounds for the refusal of registration, the application process, the infringement of image rights and limitations to image rights.[44]

Defamation

10–16 The absence of image rights legislation in many jurisdictions has not precluded litigants from pursuing their claims on other grounds. It is not a recent issue, as the case of *Tolley v Fry* demonstrates.[45] A caricature of a well-known amateur golfer appeared in advertisements in the *Daily Sketch* and the *Daily Mail*. The defendants manufactured chocolate and, in the caricature, Tolley appeared in his golfing clothes with a bar of chocolate protruding from his pocket, accompanied by his caddie who held up a few bars of chocolate to the golfer. Underneath the caricature the following rhyme was included:

> The caddie to Tolley said, Oh, Sir,
> Good shot, Sir! That ball, see it go, Sir,
> My word how it flies,

---

42 ibid.

43 No XLVII of 2012; as amended by the Organisation of States' Affairs (Transfer of Functions) Ordinance 2016 (No IX of 2016); the Image Rights (Bailiwick of Guernsey) (Amendment) Ordinance 2017 (No XI of 2017); the Image Rights (Bailiwick of Guernsey) Regulations 2012 (GSI No 55 of 2012). For more detail on the legislation and regulations, see Intellectual Property Office, 'Image Rights Legislation & Regulations', <http://ipo.guernseyregistry.com/article/158676/Image-Rights-Legislation—Regulations> accessed 17 May 2024.

44 The Image Rights (Bailiwick of Guernsey) Ordinance, 2012, No. XLVII of 2012; as amended by the Organisation of States' Affairs <https://www.guernseylegalresources.gg/CHttpHandler.ashx?documentid=58332> accessed 17 May 2024.

45 [1931] AC 333.

> Like a cartet of Frys,
> They're handy, they're good, and priced low, Sir.[46]

Tolley had not consented for his image to be used in this manner and had no knowledge of the advertising campaign prior to its launch. In the trial court, the plaintiff sought damages for the innuendo that the advertisement gave rise to as Tolley was not complaining about the image and words, but that the actions of the defendant gave rise to the assumption that he 'had prostituted his reputation as an amateur golf player for advertising purposes'.[47] Damages were awarded in the trial court; Frys appealed the decision to the Court of Appeal on the grounds that the amount was excessive.[48] The Court of Appeal held that the trial judge should have removed the case from the jury as the actions of the respondent could not be reasonably be deemed libellous, thus judgment in favour of the respondent was ordered. The Court of Appeal also found that the damages awarded were excessive, which necessitated a new trial.[49] Tolley appealed only on the first ground and on appeal to the House of Lords, the Court of Appeal judgment was reversed, and judgment given in favour of the appellant. The House of Lords held that the trial judge was correct in determining the caricature to be capable of being defamatory and it was up to the jury to decide if it was in fact defamatory.[50] Lord Blanesburgh highlighted how professional sportspeople viewed amateurs endorsing products as a form of subterfuge: **10–17**

> There is a widespread belief, well or ill founded, that amongst some gentlemen cricketers, amateur lawn tennis players, and other amateur athletes, including golfers, a practice obtains to utilize and exploit their amateur status for reward by, for example, assisting advertisement campaigns or pushing by the use of their name and personality the sale of proprietary articles, and that the respondents' caricature was such as falsely to represent to the public that the appellant was one of these athletes whose amateur status is believed to be a mere masquerade.[51]

The Lords accepted that the caricature had defamed Tolley – it was a wrongful act on the part of the respondent. It held that the matter of damages was to be decided in a new trial. **10–18**

In the Australian case of *Ettingshausen v Australian Consolidated Press*, a **10–19**

---

[46] ibid 337.

[47] ibid.

[48] In the trial court other golfers gave evidence and the point was made the advertisement could give rise to an assumption that Tolley was no long amateur, and this could affect his club membership in that he might be forced to resign. Correspondence between Frys and the advertising agency showed that this concern had been considered: [1931] AC 333, 333.

[49] *Tolley v JS Fry & Sons Ltd* [1930] 1 KB 467.

[50] *Tolley* (n 45) 350.

[51] ibid 348.

footballer was pictured without his consent in the shower after a match.[52] He successfully sued the Australian Consolidated Press on the grounds that the publication of the picture suggested that he was the type of person who would consent to a picture of this nature being published.

10–20 The tort of defamation concerns the protection of an individual's right to their reputation against false allegations. The Defamation Act 2009 codified the law in Ireland.[53] Defamation, prior to the Defamation Act 2009, encompassed two constituent torts: slander and libel. Slander was defined as defamation by way of an oral comment or gesture – for example, a comment made on radio. Libel was a more permanent form of defamation – for example, an allegation in a newspaper. The 2009 Act, Part 2, ss 6(1)(a) and (b) collectively refer to slander and libel as the tort of defamation.[54] The Act defines a defamatory statement as 'a statement that tends to injure a person's reputation in the eyes of reasonable members of society'.[55] Statement is given a broad definition. It refers to a statement made orally or in writing; visual images, sounds, gestures and any other method of signifying meaning; a statement broadcast on the radio or television, or published on the internet; and an electronic communication.[56]

10–21 The defences available to a defendant include truth (s 16), absolute privilege (s 17), qualified privilege (s 18), and honest opinion (s 20).[57] Truth provides the defendant with a complete defence. Absolute privilege protects, for example, statements made by a judge, or other person, performing a judicial function, statements made in the European Parliament by a member of that Parliament and statements made in either the Dáil or the Seanad by a member of either House of the Oireachtas.[58] Qualified privilege offers protection to those who have made a statement in the honest belief that it is true and it is communicated on the basis of the defendant having a legal, social and moral duty and those that had the statement communicated to them had a corresponding legal, social and moral interest. The defence of qualified privilege will be lost if it is proved that the defendant acted with malice.[59] The defence of honest opinion requires the defendant to prove that the opinion was honestly held. Section 21(3)(a)(i) states

---

52 (1991) 23 NSWSC 443.

53 It repealed the Defamation Act 1961.

54 For a discussion of the law relating to defamation, see Eoin Quill, *Torts in Ireland* (4th edn, Gill & Macmillan 2014) 309–55.

55 2009 Act, s 2.

56 ibid.

57 There are other defences: see ss 22 and 23 relating to the offer to make amends, which is a partial defence. It may go towards mitigation of damages. Section 24 details the defence of apology, s 25 consent to publish, s 26 fair and reasonable publication on a matter of public interest, and s 27 relating to innocent publication. Section 21 of the Act aids the court in deciphering fact from opinion.

58 See ss 17(2)(a)–(w) for the full list.

59 2009 Act, s 19.

that the defence will fail unless the defendant proves the truth of those allegations. This defence replaced the fair comment defence. The Report of the Review of the Defamation Act 2009 was published on 1 March 2022.[60] It made recommendations, including the amendment of s 21 'to remove the condition that the speaker must have believed the opinion to be "true". The opinion would still have to be "honestly held".'[61] It further recommended the return to the previous common law defence of fair comment.[62]

The remedies available in a defamation action include an application **10–22**
to the Circuit Court for a declaratory order that the statement made by the defendant is false and defamatory (s 28), lodgement of money in settlement of the action without the defendant admitting liability (s 29), a correction order (s 30), and damages (s 31).[63] Under s 32, the defendant may be ordered to pay punitive and aggravated damages as well as general and special damages. Section 33 provides that the plaintiff may seek an order prohibiting the publication or further publication of the statement – the order can be interim, interlocutory, or permanent.[64] This section was recently the subject of litigation in a defamation action involving Conor McGregor and Artem Lobov, Mixed Martial Arts (MMA) fighters.[65] The plaintiff alleged that McGregor had referred to him as a 'rat' on several occasions on Twitter (now X) since 26 November 2022.[66] Lobov contended that the word 'rat' referred to 'a person who has betrayed somebody; a person who reveals confidential information; and a person who double crosses'.[67] The alleged defamatory statements stemmed from a contractual dispute between the parties.[68] Section 33(1) of the Defamation Act 2009 states:

> The High Court, or where a defamation action has been brought, the court in which it was brought, may, upon the application of the plaintiff,

---

60 Department of Justice, 'Report of the Review of the Defamation Act 2009' (1 March 2022) <https://www.gov.ie/pdf/?file=https://assets.gov.ie/217314/724d9faf-6793-4f2b-9438-cf1e381c0e4d.pdf#page=null> accessed 17 May 2024.

61 ibid 28.

62 ibid 23. The report also recommended that when it comes to an offer of amends under s 22, in the absence of an agreement made by the parties, damages should be fixed by a judge and not a jury. This recommendation was based on the Supreme Court case of *Higgins v The Irish Aviation Authority* [2022] IESC 13.

63 Report of the Review of the Defamation Act 2009 (n 60) 26 recommended the abolition of juries in High Court defamation cases. A judge would sit alone and decide the appropriate level of damages as well as deciding whether a defamatory statement has been made. The benefits include more transparency, reducing delays, and reducing the incidences of excessive damages being awarded.

64 2009 Act, ss 33(3)(a), (b) and (c).

65 *Lobov v McGregor* [2022] IEHC 724.

66 The judgment was handed down by Simons J on 23 December 2022.

67 *Lobov* (n 65) [1].

68 Lobov claimed that he and McGregor had entered an oral contract whereby the plaintiff would receive 5% of the proceeds from the sale of McGregor's whiskey brand, Proper 12. Lobov issued specific performance proceedings in the High Court on 22 November 2022.

> make an order prohibiting the publication or further publication of the statement in respect of which the application was made if in its opinion – (a) the statement is defamatory, and (b) the defendant has no defence to the action that is reasonably likely to succeed.

10–23 Once the two requirements of (a) and (b) are satisfied, the court in using its discretionary jurisdiction may grant an interlocutory injunction. However, courts are reluctant to grant an interlocutory injunction in such cases as cognisance must be given to the constitutional right of freedom of expression.[69] Thus courts tend to wait until the full trial.[70] Simons J cited Cox and McCullough, who advise

> that if there is any realistic dispute on meaning, then the matter should be sent for trial and interlocutory relief not be granted. Once again, it is important to highlight the consistent judicial acceptance that difficult issues of fact (including meaning) simply cannot properly be resolved on the basis of affidavit evidence alone.[71]

10–24 Simons J, in line with the United Kingdom (UK) Supreme Court's decision in *Stocker v Stocker*, endorsed the view that social media posts are a more casual medium than a newspaper or television.[72] The judge observed the importance of the context in which 'rat' was used and '[i]t is far more likely that the hypothetical reasonable reader would view the tweets as part of a rant by a "trash talking" MMA fighter'.[73] Simons J acknowledged that the term 'used in isolation … is no more than a term of vulgar abuse'; however, to succeed in a defamation action, '[m]ore is required'.[74] The term did not satisfy the first limb of the test under s 33(1)(a). The application for an interlocutory injunction was refused by Simons J.

10–25 The Report of the Review of the Defamation Act 2009 advised that the legislation be amended to expressly provide for 'Norwich Pharmacal' orders, which requires an internet service provider (ISP) to identify an anonymous poster when compelled by both the High Court and Circuit courts.[75] As new technologies emerge, the report also recommended that 'Take-down' orders be included in amended legislation. This entails a court ordering an ISP to remove a post that has been held to be

69 *Lobov* (n 65) [9].
70 ibid.
71 Neville Cox and Eoin McCullough, *Defamation: Law and Practice* (2nd edn, Clarus Press 2022) para 12.57.
72 [2019] UKSC 17; [2020] AC 593.
73 *Lobov* (n 65) [28].
74 ibid 31.
75 (n 60) 20–21 and 272. For an interesting discussion on Norwich Pharmacal orders, see David Culleton, 'The Law Relating to Norwich Pharmacal Orders' (2021) 5(1) Irish Judicial Studies Journal 20.

defamatory.[76] The report also recommended that a statutory obligation be included in the Act for parties to consider mediation.[77]

In December 2022, the Court of Appeal in *Gordon v The Irish Racehorse Trainers Association* upheld the High Court decision wherein the plaintiff, the head of security of the Turf Club, was awarded €300,000 in damages.[78] Gordon claimed that he had been defamed in seven different publications which related to his duties as the head of security.[79] Gordon carried out inspections at yards and around this time performance-enhancing drugs had been found on the properties of persons connected with the Irish horseracing industry. The Turf Club did not have any power to enter a premises in search of prohibited substances; it could only do so if permission was given by the trainer and the trainer was present at the time of the inspection.[80] It was claimed that Gordon knowingly fabricated a document to entrap an individual into admitting some wrongdoing. Costello J in the Court of Appeal dismissed the appeal taken by the Irish Racehorse Trainers Association, who had challenged the significant damages awarded by the jury in the High Court case. She stated that the 'defendant was indeed acting in furtherance of an orchestrated campaign to disable [Gordon] in the discharge of his functions as head of security of the Turf Club and to stop the joint inspections' with the Department of Agriculture.[81] **10–26**

Whilst defamation was used in *Tolley* and *Ettingshausen*, in recent times it is not seen as the most appropriate route to redress in situations involving misappropriation of an individual's image. Rather, it has recently been accepted that the tort of passing-off is the appropriate avenue for a remedy for individuals whose image has been used without their consent. Alternatively, for individuals who wish to be proactive and take preventative measures to protect their image, they may seek to register their name as a trademark, as discussed below. **10–27**

---

[76] Report of the Review of the Defamation Act 2009 (n 60) 20–21.

[77] ibid 272.

[78] [2022] IECA 303. The Turf Club ceased on 31 December 2017 and was replaced on 1 January 2018 by the Irish Horseracing Regulatory Board (IHRB). The €300,000 included €50,000 in aggravated and €50,000 in exemplary damages, as well as €200,000 in general damages. The High Court citation for the case is *Gordon v The Irish Racehorse Trainers Association* [2020] IEHC 425.

[79] The Court of Appeal judgment referred to these publications as follows: 1. Statements and instructions from two trainers, 2. A letter, 3. Newspaper article in the Irish Field, 4. A petition to have Gordon removed from his position, 5. Meeting at a hotel, 6. Defamatory comments made by way of relaying a complaint, and 7. Inspection of a premises owned by a trainer based in Wicklow. He was successful on five of the seven publications: the first, second, third, fifth, and sixth.

[80] *Gordon* (n 78) [6]. The Department of Agriculture, Food and the Marine (DAFM) has statutory powers to enter premises to investigate breaches of and to enforce the law relating to animal remedies. However, it is expressly prohibited from entering a dwelling home.

[81] ibid [155].

Passing-Off

10–28 There are three elements to the tort of passing-off: namely, goodwill, misrepresentation, and damage.[82] In *Reckitt and Colman v Borden*, also known as the *Jif Lemon* case, Lord Oliver in the House of Lords explained passing-off in the simplest of terms: 'the principle that no man is entitled to steal another's trade by deceit'.[83] McMahon and Binchy explain that passing-off occurs when one trader represents its goods or services as those of another, so as to be likely to mislead the public and involve an appreciable risk of detriment to the plaintiff.[84] In the *Jif Lemon* case, the House of Lords had to establish whether Reckitt Colman had exclusive reputation in the get-up of the product, the yellow plastic bottle in the shape of a lemon, which had been on the market since 1956. The squeezable bottle contained 55mls of lemon juice and had the word Jif embossed on the front and green paper leaves around the nozzle. In 1985, the defendant company introduced a similar product, a yellow plastic bottle in the shape of a lemon containing 75mls. The House of Lords had to determine whether the defendant's product was likely to cause confusion and deceive the public. It upheld the injunction granted by the trial judge finding that the get-up of the defendant's product constituted misrepresentation.

10–29 The Court of Appeal in Ireland recently clarified the law in relation to passing-off in this jurisdiction in the case of *Galway Free Range Eggs Limited v O'Brien and Hillsbrook Eggs Limited*.[85] The case centred on the use of the word 'Galway' in the marketing of free-range eggs. Galway Free Range Eggs sought injunctive relief against a competitor who began to market their eggs as O'Brien's of Galway Free Range Eggs.[86] In the High Court, O'Connor J endorsed the triple test of reputation or goodwill, misrepresentation and damages and cited McMenamin J in *McCambridge v Brennan Bakeries*, who set out the majority judgment of the Supreme Court.[87] In relation to the get-up of the product and the application of the triple test, McMenamin J held in order to meet the threshold:

> it is sufficient that the defendant represents its goods in such a way that it is a reasonably foreseeable consequence that the claimant's business or goodwill will be damaged … proof of intention to deceive is not required. A claimant may prove misrepresentation by calling evidence that the

---

82 *Reckitt & Colman Products Ltd v Borden Inc and Others* (No 3) [1990] 1 All ER 873], [1990] 1 WLR 491. For a detailed discussion of the history of passing-off, see Christopher Wadlow, *The Law of Passing-off: Unfair Competition by Misrepresentation* (Sweet & Maxwell 2011) 21–40.

83 [1990] 1 WLR 491, 509.

84 Bryan ME McMahon and William Binchy, *Law of Torts* (4th edn, Bloomsbury Professional 2013) 1123.

85 [2019] IECA 8.

86 *Galway Free Range Eggs Limited v Kevin O'Brien, Carmel O'Brien and Hillsbrook Eggs Limited* [2016] IEHC 249.

87 ibid [25].

> relevant public were in fact confused but may also succeed in the case where there was no such evidence. The overall impact of the get up is the litmus test, as well as the length of the time the conduct complained of has gone on. It will not be an answer to a complaint of misrepresentation to contend that an observant person who made a careful examination, or who compared both products side by side, would not be misled. The test is, rather, the impression likely to be produced, on the likely customer, taking into account customer perception and imperfect recollection … dependent on the transaction in contemplation.[88]

There have been no cases involving passing-off and sportspersons in Ireland, but English case law is instructive, and it is likely that Irish courts would adopt a similar approach.[89] The seminal case on passing-off a sports star's image is *Irvine v Talksport*, which involved the use of a photo of the then Formula 1 driver Eddie Irvine. [90] The picture was lawfully obtained but was altered so that the phone which Irvine was using in the picture was replaced with a radio with the defendant's logo on it. Irvine brought an action in passing-off alleging that the use of the picture in promotional materials for the radio station constituted unauthorised endorsement of the radio station. Laddie J confirmed that the tort of passing-off can be used to tackle unauthorised endorsements. Originally, the tort had been confined to situations where one individual was 'passing-off' their goods as the goods of another, thereby exploiting the reputation and goodwill of the latter. Interpreted in this way, passing-off would not be applicable in unauthorised endorsements. However, Laddie J noted that the tort must develop with modern practices (such as the tendency for famous people to exploit their name and reputation to endorse goods in return for financial gain), and that it was logical that the tort should be applicable in unauthorised endorsement cases. According to Laddie J: **10–30**

> Manufacturers and retailers recognise the realities of the market place when they pay for well-known personalities to endorse their goods. The law of passing off should do likewise. There appears to be no good reason why the law of passing off in its modern form and in modern trade circumstances should not apply to cases of false endorsement.[91]

To initiate an action for passing-off in this context, Laddie J held that it is necessary to prove two things: **10–31**

---

[88] [2013] 1 ILRM 369 [33].

[89] A passing-off case involving Mary Peters, an Olympic gold-medal winner, was settled out of court in 2001. Thus, there was no judgment assessing the application of the tort of passing-off in this context. For a discussion of the *Mary Peters* case, see Eoin MacNeill and Tom Heerey, 'Ireland' in Ian S Blackshaw & Robert CR Siekmann (eds), *Sports Image Rights in Europe* (TMC Asser Press 2005) 168–69. There are two cases involving O'Neill's, the sportswear company: see *O'Neill's Irish International Sports Co v O'Neill's Footwear Drying Co* [1997] IEHC 75 (Barron J); and the Supreme Court case of *Adidas Sportschuhfabriken Adi Dassler KA v Charles O'Neill & Co Ltd* [1983] ILRM 112.

[90] [2002] 1 WLR 2355.

[91] ibid 2369.

1. That at the time of the acts complained of he had a significant reputation or goodwill.[92]
2. That the actions of the defendant gave rise to a false message which would be understood by a not insignificant section of his market that his goods have been endorsed, recommended, or approved of by the claimant.[93]

10–32 With regard to the latter requirement, Laddie J emphasised that the pertinent issue was the likely effect of the material in question and not the intention of the defendant (ie whether they intended to portray a false message or not).[94] So in this instance if the photo was likely to have the effect of conveying to a significant number of the recipients that Irvine was endorsing Talksport, then it did not matter whether or not that was the radio station's intention.[95] Irvine proved both that he had significant reputation in Formula 1 racing and that this in turn generated significant goodwill, which could benefit products he endorsed, and that the Talksport material portrayed a false message that he was endorsing their radio station. Consequently, he was held entitled to succeed in his action. This case shows that the tort of passing-off can provide a remedy where a sports personality has an endorsement falsely attributed to them. However, commentators have pointed out that while the tort is a useful remedy in cases like *Irvine*, it is by no means a panacea for problems which sports personalities may encounter in relation to false attribution of endorsement. Cox and others point out that the damages payable to Irvine were assessed by reference to what would be a reasonable fee for the endorsement.[96] Thus, Irvine was awarded £25,000, which is the fee he would demand for such an endorsement. Cox and others note that

> the logic from this case seems to be that if a celebrity declines to endorse a product, then the relevant company might just as well use his image anyway, content that it will merely have to pay the relevant image fee, should the action be challenged in court.[97]

10–33 In *Fenty v Arcadia Group Brands Ltd*, the Court of Appeal in England and Wales found that Topshop had used singer Rihanna's image on a t-shirt without her permission and that the activities of Topshop amounted to passing-off.[98] The Court of Appeal reiterated the point that under English Law there is no such right as an image right or character right, in that there is no law that allows a celebrity to control the licencing of their name or likeness.[99] This is also the situation in Ireland. The Court

---

92 ibid.
93 ibid 2370.
94 ibid 2376.
95 ibid.
96 Cox and others (n 5) 334.
97 ibid.
98 [2015] EWCA Civ 3.
99 ibid [29].

of Appeal in *Fenty* cited with approval the case of *Douglas v Hello!*[100] This case concerned actors Michael Douglas and Catherine Zeta-Jones, who sought to prevent *Hello!* magazine from publishing unauthorised photographs taken surreptitiously at their wedding. Lord Hoffmann, with Baroness Hale of Richmond and Lord Brown of Eaton-under-Heywood concurring, stated:

> There is in my opinion no question of creating an 'image right' or any other unorthodox form of intellectual property. The information in this case was capable of being protected, not because it concerned the Douglases' image any more than because it concerned their private life, but simply because it was information of commercial value over which the Douglases' had sufficient control to enable them to impose an obligation of confidence.[101]

In distinguishing the case of *Irvine v Talksport*, Lord Nicholls of Birkenhead explained: **10–34**

> Publication of wedding photographs in 'Hello!' was not, of itself, improper exploitation of the reputation, name or likeness of the Douglases such as may be protected in some circumstances in the US ... Nor did 'Hello!'s publication of pictures of this event constitute 'character merchandising' or, still less, a case of 'false endorsement' as discussed by Laddie J in *Irvine v Talksport*.[102]

In highlighting the difficulties faced by litigants in a passing-off case, MacNeill and Heerey point to situations where there is an absence of goodwill and damage.[103] This might be a problem for more minor sports personalities in an Irish context, such as amateur Gaelic Athletic Association (GAA) stars. MacNeill and Heerey also contend that 'the passing-off action does not provide "positive" rights of privacy or rights to control publicity. Rather it is a negative right, which, in certain circumstances, may be used to prevent certain action or to seek damages.'[104] **10–35**

The use of passing-off as a basis for an action is very much a reactive one. For this reason, sports personalities who wish to protect their image or brand may wish to take proactive or preventative measures to prevent false attribution. In the absence of legislation protecting image rights in Ireland, the primary means of achieving this is using trademark law, as will be discussed below. There is another route a sportsperson can take in protecting their image: they may argue that their right to privacy has been violated. **10–36**

---

[100] *OBG Ltd and another v Allan and others, Douglas and others v Hello! Ltd and others (No 3) Mainstream Properties Ltd v Young* [2007] UKHL 21, [2008] 1 AC 1.

[101] [2008] 1 AC 1 [124].

[102] ibid [253]. The case of *Irvine* was more recently mentioned in *Shazam Productions Ltd v Only Fools The Dining Experience Ltd* [2022] EWHC 1379 (Intellectual Property Enterprise Court) 2022 WL 02067748.

[103] (n 89) 172.

[104] ibid 167.

Right to Privacy

10–37 The right to privacy is protected under both the Irish Constitution and the European Convention on Human Rights (ECHR). The right to privacy is an unenumerated right under the Irish Constitution. This means that the right is not expressly included in the text of the Constitution but is an implied right which has been recognised by the Irish courts as being protected as one of the personal rights guaranteed to the individual in Article 40.3.1°. Article 40.3.1° provides that the 'State guarantees in its laws to respect, and, as far as practicable, by its laws to defend and vindicate the personal rights of the citizen'.

10–38 The first recognition of an unenumerated right to privacy in the Irish Constitution was in *McGee v Attorney General*, where the right to marital privacy was recognised.[105] This was extended to include an individual right to privacy in *Norris v Attorney General*[106] and *Kennedy v Ireland*.[107] Thus, a sportsperson in Ireland has a constitutional right to privacy which they are entitled to assert against anyone who may infringe it by, for example, publishing unauthorised pictures or stories about that individual in a newspaper. In this context, it is important to note that the right to privacy is not absolute and must be balanced against the rights of other individuals, as well as the general or public good. There may be cases where although an individual's right to privacy has been intruded upon, and this may be seen as legitimate when balanced against, for example, the right of the public to be aware of certain information about them. The right to privacy is also protected by Article 8 of the ECHR.[108] The ECHR Act 2003 requires the Irish courts to interpret and apply any statutory provision or rule of law in a manner which is compatible with the state's obligations under the ECHR. As with the constitutional protection of the right, the right to privacy under Article 8 of the ECHR is not absolute and must be balanced against other competing interests.

10–39 The case of *Herrity v Associated Newspapers (Ireland) Ltd* is noteworthy as it confirmed that an individual may take legal action for breach of their right to privacy against a private individual or entity (such as a newspaper) and that such actions are not confined to actions against the state.[109] There has only been one privacy case involving a sportsperson

---

105 [1974] IR 284.
106 [1984] IR 36.
107 [1987] IR 587.
108 Article 8 of the ECHR on the right to respect for private and family life provides: '1. Everyone has the right to respect for his private and family life, his home and his correspondence. 2. There shall be no interference by a public authority with the exercise of this right except such as is in accordance with the law and is necessary in a democratic society in the interests of national security, public safety or the economic wellbeing of the country, for the prevention of disorder or crime, for the protection of health or morals, or for the protection of the rights and freedoms of others.' For other situations where art 8 has been invoked by sportspersons see paras 2–100, 6–66—6–68, 6–70—6–72 and 7–52—7–53.
109 [2009] 1 IR 316, 337. In this case, the plaintiff received damages for breach of

in Ireland. In *Sinnott v Carlow Nationalist*, a GAA player received €11,000 in damages to compensate him for the publication of a photograph in which his genitals were exposed.[110] The pictures were taken while he was playing in a GAA match. There is no written judgment available but, as Slattery notes, reports of the case seem to indicate that the grant of damages was on the basis that the player's right to privacy had been infringed.[111] Given the increasing celebrity status of Irish sports personalities, it is possible that further actions for breach of privacy could occur in the future. However, thus far, *Sinnott* remains the only case in the area.

Intellectual Property: Trademarks and Copyright

The Intellectual Property Office of Ireland (IPOI) explains that IP 'is **10–40**
the product of someone's mental efforts'.[112] White defines IP: 'property which is intellectual property is so classified because it can in some way be attributed to the creative mind'.[113] Copyright, patents, designs, and trademarks are regulated by statute. As discussed above, there is also the tort of passing-off, a common law principle. In a sporting context, copyright and trademark protection are the most common avenues for a sportsperson or organisation and will thus be the focus of this section.[114] However, patents and design could also apply in a sporting context: for example, a running shoe's 'look' would be the subject of design

---

privacy in relation to the publication of newspaper articles about her alleged affair with a Roman Catholic priest. The articles contained transcripts of phone conversations which had been obtained illegally by her husband tapping her phone-line.

110 (High Court, 26 January 2007). The Circuit Court had originally awarded €6,500 damages, but this was increased to €11,000 by the High Court.

111 Robbie Slattery, 'The Law on Privacy' (2009) 14(4) *The Bar Review* 74, 77.

112 Intellectual Property Office of Ireland, 'What Is IP?' <https://www.ipoi.gov.ie/en/understanding-ip/getting-started-with-intellectual-property/what-is-ip-/> accessed 17 May 2024.

113 Fidelma White, *Commercial Law* (Thomson Round Hall 2012) 638.

114 According to the Intellectual Property Office of Ireland, 'Patents protect technological advances.' It is a form of 'industrial property' which can be licensed, assigned, transferred, and used by the owner. The territorial scope in limited, thus a patent obtained in Ireland is protected only in Ireland. The relevant legislation in Ireland is the Patent Acts 1992–2006. For more information, see Intellectual Property Office of Ireland, 'Patents Explained' <https://www.ipoi.gov.ie/en/types-of-ip/patents/understanding-patents/patents-explained/> accessed 17 May 2024. Designs are governed by the Industrial Property Act 2001 (as amended) and more information can be accessed from the Intellectual Property Office of Ireland, 'Patents Explained' <https://www.ipoi.gov.ie/en/types-of-ip/designs/understanding-designs/designs-explained/> accessed 17 May 2024. There is no case law on patents relating to sport in Ireland. As such, patents are quite rare due to the need for three criteria to be met under the 1992 Act: 1. Novelty – must be new and form part of the state of the art (s 11), 2. Inventive step – must not be obvious to someone skilled in the particular area (s 13), and 3. Industrial applicability – must have some use in all types of industry, including agriculture (s 14).

protection and a patent would be obtained to protect the technology used in the shoe.[115]

10–41 IP can be traded like goods are traded.[116] The rights can be fully assigned in return for a cash payment, or the rights holder can permit others to exploit the rights in the form of a licence.[117] A licence may give exclusive rights of exploitation to one party or can give non-exclusive rights and have several people exploiting the rights under licence. To protect its IP, the rights holder will generally restrict the licensee from obtaining trademark registration in relation to the rights as the licensee has a mere licence.[118] While the licence grants specified rights, it does not transfer ownership to the licensee. Protections of this nature will be included in the merchandising contract, as discussed further on in this chapter.

Trademarks

10–42 To take proactive action to protect their name and image, a sports personality in Ireland could register their name, a nickname or an image associated with them as a trademark. Trademarks have been sought for goods, services, and even a sportsperson's method of posing, as in the case of Usain Bolt. Bolt filed to trademark an illustration. According to the trademark application filed on 17 August 2022, the 'mark consists of the silhouette of a man in a distinctive pose, with one arm bent and pointing to the head, and the other arm raised and pointing upward'.[119]

10–43 Trademark registration in Ireland is governed by the Trade Marks Act 1996 (as amended). For the purposes of the Act, a trademark is defined 'as any sign capable of being represented graphically which is capable of distinguishing goods or services of one undertaking from those of other undertakings'.[120] The Act permits words, including names, to be registered as trademarks, as well as designs, letters, or numerals.[121]

---

[115] World Intellectual Property Organization, 'Sports and Intellectual Property' <https://www.wipo.int/sports/en/> accessed 17 May 2024.

[116] White (n 113) 637.

[117] ibid.

[118] Christopher Evans and Katie Ellis, 'Best Practice Provisions and Considerations for Sports Merchandising and Agreements' (*Law in Sport*, 27 March 2014) <https://www.lawinsport.com/topics/features/item/best-practice-provisions-and-considerations-for-sports-merchandising-agreements> accessed 17 May 2024. The writers note that if the licensee becomes aware that an unauthorised third party is exploiting the rights holder's brand then it should notify the rights holder immediately.

[119] Gerben Trademark Library, 'Usain Bolt Trademarks' (updated 15 May 2024) <https://www.gerbenlaw.com/trademarks/athletes/usain bolt/#97556602> accessed 17 May 2024.

[120] Trade Marks Act 1996, s 6(1). The grounds on which the Controller may refuse to register a trademark are listed in ss 8–11.

[121] Section 6(2) provides that a trademark 'may … consist of words (including personal names), designs, letters, numerals or the shape of goods or their packaging'.

Thus an Irish sportsperson could register their name or an image as a trademark. An application for registration of a trademark is made to the IPOI and a fee must be paid for registration.[122] Trademark registration is also important for sports organisations such as football clubs who wish to protect their ability to profit from the sale of their merchandise and do not want this to be diluted by the sale of counterfeit or replica merchandise. In a preliminary reference from the High Court of England and Wales, the European Court of Justice (ECJ) in *Arsenal FC v Reed* concluded that the unauthorised sale of merchandise bearing a registered trademark may constitute trademark infringement.[123]

Trademark registration subsists for a period of 10 years from the date of registration and may be renewed for further periods of 10 years.[124] Once a trademark is registered, it gives the holder a property right which they can assert against those who may try to use the mark without authorisation.[125] The proprietor of a registered trademark has exclusive rights in it, and these rights will be infringed where the trademark is used in the state[126] without the proprietor's consent.[127] In this respect, it is important to note that where an individual wishes to permit someone to use their trademark, they can grant the latter a licence to do so.[128] In this way, the individual controls the use of the trademark and can earn a fee for its use, if applicable. Both civil and criminal remedies are available for trademark infringement. Civil remedies are likely to be the most appropriate in the case of infringement of an individual's trademark in their name or image. [129] The available remedies include damages or an account for profits or an injunction.[130] White notes that usually a plaintiff will seek an injunction to prevent the defendant from continuing to use the trademark, and damages for any losses caused **10–44**

---

[122] The fee is currently €70: Intellectual Property Office of Ireland, 'Statutory Trade Mark Fees' <https://www.ipoi.gov.ie/en/types-of-ip/trade-marks/statutory-trade-mark-fees/> accessed 17 May 2024.

[123] Case C–206/01 *Arsenal Football Club plc v Matthew Reed* (2002) ECLI:EU:C: 2002:651. See MacNeill and Heerey (n 89) 165.

[124] Trade Mark Act 1996, s 47. The procedure for renewal of registration is provided for in s 48.

[125] Trade Mark Act 1996, s 7(1).

[126] For sports persons who want to protect their name and image outside of the jurisdiction as well, they could register a Union trademark which would apply throughout the European Union: Trade Mark Act, ss 56 and 57.

[127] Trade Mark Act 1996, s 13(1).

[128] Trade Mark Act 1996, ss 32–36.

[129] Criminal remedies are found in Part VI of the 1996 Act and punish activities such as counterfeiting.

[130] Section 18(2) provides that in an action for infringement all remedies such as damages, accounts or otherwise will be available in the same way that they are available for infringement of any other property right. It is also possible to obtain an order to have the sign that infringes the plaintiff's trademark erased from any infringing goods or materials or for the infringing goods or materials to be delivered up and dealt with as the Court may direct: Trade Mark Act 1996, ss 18–23.

by such use.[131] Trademark registration creates an 'official record' of the rights of the owner and makes it easier to prevent unauthorised use by third parties.[132] White also notes that the benefit of a trademark is that the owner can prevent others using the mark without having to show that the trademark owner has a reputation or that they have suffered damage.[133] For an individual such as a sports personality, this is significant as it short-circuits the process of proof and thus renders it more expeditious and straightforward to get relief than perhaps would be the case in an action for passing-off.

Copyright

10–45 As the name suggests, copyright refers to the right to copy. According to the IPOI, 'Copyright is an intellectual property right which features mainly in, but is not exclusive to the cultural, arts and information technology sectors.'[134] The principal act governing copyright in Ireland is the Copyright and Related Rights Act 2000 (as amended). Copyright can be distinguished from other IP rights, such as patents and trademarks, as it 'arises automatically and is not dependent upon registration'.[135] In addition, copyright does not protect ideas per se 'but the expression or embodiment of ideas in some permanent form'.[136] Section 17(1) of the Copyright Act 2000 states that copyright is a property right in which the owner can undertake or authorise its use by third parties and similarly restrict its use. Furthermore, copyright has been held to be a property right under the Irish Constitution. Keane J in *Phonographic Performance (Ireland) Ltd v William Cody and Princes Investments Ltd* held:

> The right of the creator of a literary, dramatic, musical or artistic work not to have his or her creation stolen or plagiarised is a right of private property within the meaning of Articles 40.3.2 and 43.1 of the Constitution.[137]

10–46 Section 17(2) of the 2000 Act provides that copyright subsists in:

---

131 White (n 113) 715 notes that a successful party will also normally be awarded costs against the other party.

132 Intellectual Property Office of Ireland, 'Benefits of Trade Mark Registration' <https://www.ipoi.gov.ie/en/types-of-ip/trade-marks/understanding-trade-marks/benefits-of-trade-mark-registration/> accessed 17 May 2024.

133 White (n 113) 692.

134 Intellectual Property Office of Ireland, 'Understanding Copyright' <https://www.ipoi.gov.ie/en/types-of-ip/copyright1/understanding-copyright/> accessed 17 May 2024.

135 White (n 113) 643. Forde asserts that once the work comes into being, copyright automatically arises: see Michael Forde, *Commercial Law* (3rd edn, Tottel Publishing 2005) para 10.183.

136 Forde (n 135) para 10.183. For a useful guide on copyright, see the Intellectual Property Office of Ireland, 'General Information Concerning Copyright and Related Rights' <https://www.ipoi.gov.ie/en/understanding-ip/help-guidance/ip-information-booklets/copyright-and-related-rights.pdf> accessed 17 May 2024.

137 [1994] 2 ILRM 241, 247.

(a) original literary, dramatic, musical or artistic works,
(b) sound recordings, films, broadcasts or cable programmes,
(c) the typographical arrangement of published editions, and
(d) original databases.

The emphasis is on 'original', meaning that it must be the result of the creative endeavours of the individual who has created the work. A leading case on originality is *Gormley v EMI Records (Ireland) Ltd.*[138] Part I, s 2 of the 2000 Act defines 'literary' as 'a work, including a computer program, but does not include a dramatic or musical work or an original database, which is written, spoken or sung'. 'Work' is defined under s 2 as **10–47**

> a literary, dramatic, musical or artistic work, sound recording, film, broadcast, cable programme, typographical arrangement of a published edition or an original database and includes a computer program except in Part II, Chapter 7 where 'work' means 'literary, dramatic, musical or artistic film or work'.

In the Chancery Division of the High Court of England and Wales, a case involving the copyright of a chronological list of football fixtures came before Upjohn J in *Football League Ltd v Littlewoods Pools Ltd.*[139] The plaintiff was seeking a declaration that it owned the copyright of the Football League fixture lists and sought an injunction restraining the defendant from infringing the copyright. The plaintiff had to arrange fixtures for four divisions. It would compile a list of fixtures for the year, with copyright in such fixtures vested in the Football League. Each team in the division played each other once at home and once away. Once the list was sent to the clubs and the scheduling was confirmed, the Football League would pass on the schedule to a third party who would finalise the schedule. Much work went into compiling the list of fixtures, which 'required a high degree of skill and ingenuity'.[140] **10–48**

Upjohn J came to the **10–49**

> conclusion that this systematic pirating by the defendants week by week throughout the season of that part of the League's list which is relevant to that week deliberately and (by their defence of this action) under a claim of right amounts in the end to a reproduction of the plaintiffs' compilation and infringes accordingly.[141]

Upjohn J granted the declaration that the Football League was entitled to copyright in the chronological fixture list, as it constituted an 'original literary work'. However, he did not grant an injunction as the 1958–59 **10–50**

---

[138] [1999] 1 ILRM 178. This was an appeal from the High Court to the Supreme Court.
[139] [1959] ch 637.
[140] ibid 638.
[141] ibid 658.

season had ended, nor did he grant an injunction for the next season as the document, while likely in production, was not in existence.[142]

10–51 The ECJ in the *Football Dataco and Others v Yahoo UK Ltd and Others* held that a football fixture list cannot be protected by copyright in situations where its compilation is 'dictated by technical considerations, rules or constraints which left no room for creative freedom'.[143] This applies even in situations where the creator has used significant judgment, labour, and skill.[144]

10–52 Part I, s 2 of the 2000 Act provides that an 'artistic work' includes a work of any of the following descriptions, irrespective of their artistic quality:

> (a) photographs, paintings, drawings, diagrams, maps, charts, plans, engravings, etchings, lithographs, woodcuts, prints or similar works, collages, or sculptures (including any cast or model made for the purposes of a sculpture);
> (b) works of architecture, being either buildings or models for buildings; and
> (c) works of artistic craftsmanship.

10–53 Part II, s 21 of the 2000 Act defines 'author' as the person who creates the work and it provides a list of such persons, including a photographer being the author of a photograph.[145] In a sporting context, photographs of sportspersons and events would constitute artistic works and be protected by copyright. Equally, works of architecture including stadia would fall under the definition of artistic work as per s 2(b).

10–54 Over the years, the length of protection given to copyright holders has been extended due to the increase in the average lifespan. According to s 24(1) the copyright in a literary, dramatic, musical, or artistic work, or an original database ends 70 years after the death of the author, irrespective of the date on which the work is first lawfully made available to the public. The duration of copyright in sound recordings, broadcasts, cable programmes, and typographical arrangements is 50 years.[146]

10–55 There are situations where an infringement of copyright may be permitted by way of an exemption.[147] Sections 50 and 51 of the Act

---

142 [1959] ch 637, 658–59.

143 Case C–604/10 *Football Dataco Ltd and Others v Yahoo! UK Ltd and Others* [2012] ECLI:EU:C: 2012:115 [39].

144 The ECJ held that football fixtures fell within the meaning of 'databases' under art 1(2) of European Parliament and Council Directive 96/9/EC of 11 March 1996 on the legal protection of databases [1996] OJ L 77. However, copyright protection under the Directive related to the structure of the database and not the actual contents.

145 Copyright and Related Rights Act 2000, s 21(h).

146 Copyright and Related Rights Act 2000, ss 26, 27, 28, and 29. The duration for computer-generated works is 70 years: s 30.

147 Copyright and Related Rights Act 2000, s 49.

relate to fair dealing, which allows extracts from the copyrighted material to be used in general news programmes and in sporting news. The fair-dealing exemption also arises where the work is used for private study or research, for the purpose of criticism or review, and is accompanied by sufficient acknowledgement. According to s 51(3) 'sufficient acknowledgement' means an acknowledgement identifying the work concerned by its title or other description and identifying the author. This requirement is waived in the case of a work which has been lawfully made available to the public, if it was so made available anonymously; and if the work has not been made available to the public, if it is not possible for a person without previous knowledge of the facts to ascertain the identity of the author of the work by reasonable enquiry. The defence was upheld in the case of *British Broadcasting Corporation v British Satellite Broadcasting Ltd*, where the British Broadcasting Corporation (BBC) had obtained the rights to transmit live coverage of the World Cup in 1990.[148] The defendant broadcasting company used short extracts consisting of 14- to 37-second snippets from the BBC live broadcasts to show highlights of the matches on Sky News. The Court acknowledged that the snippets consisted mainly of the goals and held that the defendant could rely on the defence of fair dealing as it acknowledged the BBC as the source for each snippet that was transmitted.[149]

Apart from fair dealing, there are further exemptions detailed in the Act, namely, education (ss 53–58), prescribed libraries and archives (ss 59–68 and 70), public administration (ss 71–77), designs (ss 78–79), computer programs (ss 80–82), original databases (s 83), and typefaces (ss 84–85). **10–56**

Section 52 of the 2000 Act provides for the inclusion in an incidental manner in another work. In this situation, copyright is not infringed, provided the interests of the owner of the copyright are not unreasonably prejudiced. 'Incidental' and 'transient' are defined in Part II, s 87 on Miscellaneous Matters Relating to Copyright. **10–57**

Part II, Chapter 8 on Dealings with Rights in Copyright Works, s 120(1) of the 2000 Act states that copyright in a work is transmissible by assignment, by testamentary disposition or by operation of law, as personal or movable property. An assignment may be whole or partial as stated in s 120(2). Section 120(3) provides that an assignment of the copyright in a work, whether in whole or in part, is not effective unless it is in writing and signed by or on behalf of the assignor. Section 121 provides for the prospective ownership of copyright, which is defined **10–58**

---

[148] [1992] ch 141.

[149] The case was considered more recently in *England and Wales Cricket Board Ltd and Another v Tixdaq Ltd and Another* [2016] EWHC 575 (Ch). However, the defence of fair dealing was not available to the defendants as Arnold J considered 'that the Defendants' objective was purely commercial rather than genuinely informatory' [129].

as copyright which will or may come into existence in respect of a future work or class of works or on the occurrence of a future event.

10–59 A breach of copyright may result in either civil or criminal sanctions. Civil remedies available for breach of copyright include damages, an account of profits, injunctions, or an order for delivery up and destruction of the infringed material.[150]

Media Rights

10–60 The first sporting event that was televised was the Berlin Olympics in 1936. Its broadcast was due to political machinations as Hitler wanted to show off Germany's technological advances as well as the success of its athletes.[151] With the motivations aside, it did prove to be a technological feat and, while the coverage was limited to Germany, it heralded the beginning of sports broadcasting.[152] Over time, the mediums through which sport is watched have changed. While radio broadcasts are still used and television broadcasting has evolved to cable and pay-per-view, the use of the internet to watch sports has opened small broadcasting outlets to a larger audience.[153] Live-streaming applications (apps) offer sports fans an array of sporting events, some for free while others are subscription based. Recent trends include the increasing use of digital platforms as well as long-term broadcasting contracts with streaming media companies such as Paramount+ and Amazon (Prime Video).[154] In 2017, Amazon secured the non-exclusive rights to broadcast 10 televised National Football League (NFL) games, 'Thursday Night Football'. The deal was reported to have cost Amazon $50m with an estimated extra $30m for the marketing and promotion of the NFL.[155] Amazon renewed the deal with the NFL for the 2018 and 2019 seasons for a reported $65m per year.[156] It simulcasted 11 'Thursday Night Football' games on Prime Video, which were broadcast on television by Fox.[157] The Amazon-owned Twitch app live-streamed the games for free. Beginning with

---

150 The remedies are set out in Part II, ch 9, 'Remedies: Copyright Owner', ss 127–34. See also ch 10, 'Rights and Remedies: Exclusive Licensee', ss 135 and 136; and ch 11, 'Remedies: Moral Rights', ss 137 and 138.

151 Kevin Hull, *Sports Broadcasting* (Human Kinetics 2021) 5.

152 ibid 6.

153 ibid 14.

154 Brad Adgate, 'More Live Sports Are Joining the Streaming Wars' *Forbes* (Jersey City, 7 June 2021) <https://www.forbes.com/sites/bradadgate/2021/06/07/more-sports-are-joining-the-streaming-wars/?sh=4ca2256a52bc/> accessed 17 May 2024..

155 Scott Soshnick, 'Amazon's NFL Deal Includes $30 Million in Free Marketing' (*Bloomberg*, 17 April 2017) <https://www.bloomberg.com/news/articles/2017-04-17/amazon-s-nfl-deal-said-to-include-30-million-in-free-marketing?leadSource=uverify%20wall> accessed 17 May 2024.

156 Todd Spangler, 'NFL Renews Amazon Streaming Deal for "Thursday Night Football" for 2018–19 Seasons' (*Variety*, 26 April 2018) <https://variety.com/2018/digital/news/nfl-renews-amazon-thursday-night-football-1202789145/> accessed 17 May 2024.

157 ibid.

the 2023 season and up until 2033, Amazon secured exclusive rights to 15 'Thursday Night Football' games.[158] As Amazon Prime Video is the only 'destination for Thursday games as opposed to one option among many', the deal is slated to be valued at $1bn per year, $10bn in total.[159] In the words of the New England Patriots owner and chairperson of the NFL's media committee, Robert Kraft, 'Streaming is truly the future.'[160]

The GAA's nine-year relationship with Sky Sports began in April 2014 and ended with 'mutual consent' in October 2022.[161] Beginning with a three-year deal, Raidió Teilifís Éireann (RTÉ), the national broadcaster in Ireland, secured exclusive rights to 25 (+6) games while Sky Sports secured exclusive rights to 14 (+6) games.[162] Both broadcasters secured the rights to six other games, namely the All-Ireland semi-finals and finals in football and hurling.[163] A second agreement was concluded between 2017 and 2022.[164] RTÉ retained the rights to 31 (25 exclusive +6) games while Sky Sports retained rights to 20 (14 exclusive +6). As under the previous agreement, Sky Sports retained the right to broadcast the All-Ireland hurling and football semi-finals and finals on a simulcast basis with RTÉ. BBC Northern Ireland continued to broadcast live television coverage from the Ulster senior football championship.[165] The amount paid by Sky has never been publicly released; however, one commentator proffered that the GAA may have earned €0.5m more in 2014 than it had in 2013.[166] This information was gleaned from comparing the media income in the 2014 annual financial report with that of the 2013 report.[167] There was much criticism about Sky acquiring exclusive 10–61

158 Alison Herman, 'Live Sports Are the Next Great Battle of the Streaming' (*The Ringer*, 14 April 2021) <https://www.theringer.com/sports/2021/4/15/22385705/live-sports-streaming-wars-future-industry> accessed 17 May 2024.

159 ibid.

160 Dylan Byers, 'Are You Ready to Stream Some Football? NFL Has $100 billion that Says You Are' (*NBC News*, 18 March 2021) <https://www.nbcnews.com/media/nfl-tv-amazon-rights-deal-rcna447> accessed 17 May 2024. Other companies have rights: for example, Disney. ESPN and ABC are owned by Disney and 'will pay around $2.7 billion annually to keep Monday Night Football while also getting rights to additional regular season and playoff games'.

161 Gordon Manning, 'Sky Sports and GAA End Nine-Year Broadcasting Deal' *The Irish Times* (Dublin, 24 October 2022) <https://www.irishtimes.com/sport/gaelic-games/2022/10/24/sky-sports-and-gaa-end-nine-year-broadcasting-deal/> accessed 17 May 2024.

162 'RTÉ & Sky Secure GAA Rights, RTÉ in Worldwide Deal' (*RTÉ Sport*, 2 April 2014) <https://www.rte.ie/sport/gaa/2014/0401/606028-gaa-rights-deal/> accessed 17 May 2024.

163 ibid.

164 Gaelic Athletic Association, 'December 2016 Nuachtlitir' (December 2016) 13 <https://www.gaa.ie/api/pdfs/image/upload/upmp4pk0utzzhwmwhaac.pdf> accessed 17 May 2024.

165 ibid.

166 Paul Rouse, 'Sports Rights Commercialization Revisited: Sky and the GAA' (2015) 6 History and Policy Opinion 1, 3 < http://historyhub.ie/wp-content/files_mf/1424337651HH_OP6_Rouse_Sky_and_the_GAA.pdf> accessed 17 May 2024.

167 Ibid.

rights to games.[168] It was defended on the grounds that it would open the game up to an international audience and would appeal to Irish emigrants living in the UK.

10–62 In October 2022, it was announced that RTÉ and BBC Northern Ireland had secured the media rights in a four-year deal for 2023–27.[169] BBC Northern Ireland continues to broadcast live the All-Ireland semi-finals and the Ulster championship, however, the possibility that an All-Ireland final could be shown on BBC 2, which would 'extend the GAA's reach across the UK for its showpiece game' was mentioned in 2022.[170] The All-Ireland Football Final was televised on BBC 2 and BBC iPlayer for the first time in July 2023.[171]

10–63 The securing of media rights, whether exclusive or non-exclusive, is a lucrative business for most sports. Emerging digital platforms will shape the way spectators view sport. However, the agreement between the GAA and RTÉ/BBC Northern Ireland demonstrates that the traditional medium of television is still a viable option for sports and one that recognises the importance of fans having free access to important cultural events. The GAA and its entrenched position within Irish society is difficult to reconcile with the approach by the NFL. While Amazon Prime Video works for the NFL, it is doubtful that a similar development will occur with the GAA in the foreseeable future.

Proprietary Rights and Sports Events

10–64 Irish law does not recognise a property right in a sports event itself or in the news emanating from the event.[172] Although of persuasive authority in Ireland, the Australian case of *Victoria Park Racing and Recreational Grounds Co Ltd v Taylor & Others* is instructive as it confirmed that a property right does not arise in the event itself or news emanating from it, as Chief Justice (CJ) Latham held that a 'spectacle' cannot be 'owned'

[168] Cormac Byrne, 'RTÉ Pundit Michael Duignan Passionately Criticises the GAA's Deal with Sky' *Irish Independent* (Dublin, 9 July 2017) <https://www.independent.ie/sport/gaelic-games/hurling/rte-pundit-michael-duignan-passionately-criticises-the-gaas-deal-with-sky-35911772.html> accessed 17 May 2024.

[169] Colm Keys, 'GAA Detail Broadcast Rights for Next Five Years Following End of Deal with Sky' *Irish Independent* (Dublin, 25 October 2022) <https://www.independent.ie/sport/gaelic-games/gaa-detail-broadcast-rights-for-next-five-years-following-end-of-deal-with-sky-42093756.html> accessed 17 May 2024.

[170] ibid.

[171] 'GAA All-Ireland Football Final: How to Watch and Follow Dublin vs Kerry on BBC TV, iPlayer and Online' (*BBC Sport*, 26 July 2023) <https://www.bbc.com/sport/gaelic-games/66299662> accessed 17 May 2024. The All-Ireland Hurling Final between Clare and Cork was televised for the first time on BBC 2 and BBC iPlayer on 21 July 2024.

[172] See Laura Donnellan, 'TV Rights in Irish Football' in Ian Blackshaw, Steve Cornelius, and Robert Siekmann (eds), *TV Rights in Europe Legal Aspects* (TMC Asser Press 2009) 373–387.

in any ordinary sense of that word.[173] This case was an appeal to the High Court of Australia from a judgment for the defendants handed down by the Supreme Court of New South Wales. One of the defendants, Taylor, owned land near the racecourse. He erected a 16-foot high scaffolding, which created an elevated observational platform on his land. From this platform, he was able to see what took place on the racecourse and was able to read the information which appeared on notice boards on the course as to the starters and the winners of the races. The other defendant, the Commonwealth Broadcasting Corporation, placed a wooden structure on the platform in Taylor's land and through a telephone proceeded to comment and give results from the racecourse. The Commonwealth Broadcasting Corporation held a broadcasting licence under the regulations made under the Wireless Telegraphy Acts 1905–1936. Victoria Park Racing argued that the activities of the defendants dissuaded people from going to the races and paying for admission.[174] This was based on evidence that some spectators preferred hearing the races from the adjoining land than attending the racecourse. Victoria Park Racing brought an action against the defendants for nuisance and an unnatural use of the platform on Taylor's land. By a 3–2 majority, the High Court of Australia rejected the appeal and upheld the decision of the Supreme Court of New South Wales.

For an event manager or a governing body to secure exclusive broadcast rights over a sporting event, a contractual agreement must be negotiated with the owner of the venue that the only broadcaster that can gain access is the official broadcaster.[175] When the proprietary right in question concerns a private individual who privately owns a sports ground, the situation is quite straightforward. The matter becomes more complicated when an event takes place outside the confines of an enclosed venue: for example, a marathon, motor rally or ocean yacht race.[176] In this situation, an event owner may find it difficult to invoke proprietary rights against a broadcaster who sets up in the vicinity of the event (such as a neighbouring property) and whose actions do not give rise to an actionable obstruction.[177] **10–65**

A more problematic situation arises where there is a series of events that all occur in different locations and are owned by different bodies or individuals, most notably a league, a championship or a related competition.[178] Accordingly, if matches are to be played in different locations involving different participants, then the question of proprietary rights should be addressed at the time the league or **10–66**

173 (1937) 58 CLR 479, 496.
174 Victoria Park Racing was a limited liability company which held around 13 race meetings per year: ibid 480.
175 Cox and others (n 5) 363–64.
176 David Griffith-Jones and Adrian Barr-Smith, *Law and Business of Sport* (Butterworths 1997) 304.
177 ibid.
178 ibid.

competition in question is being set up.[179] Identifying and delineating proprietary rights by those involved at the outset will arguably prevent future strife and most importantly maximise the overall value of any grant of broadcasting rights.[180]

10–67 While Irish law does not recognise broadcasting rights per se in a sporting event, a broadcaster will own a copyright in any broadcasts that are produced.[181] There are, however, two limitations to this right: namely, the principle of 'fair dealing' and 'off-tube' coverage. There are no case examples of 'off-tube' coverage under Irish law, nor are there any statutory provisions. The defence of fair dealing, as discussed above, is recognised under the Copyright and Related Acts 2000–2007 by virtue of ss 50 and 51.

10–68 Off-tube coverage involves a radio commentator sitting in front of a television screen and watching footage of an event that is being transmitted by the broadcaster. The commentator describes the action and communicates this to the listener. Often the off-tube coverage will lack the ambiance associated with a sporting event and in response noises will often be simulated by the broadcaster, such as crowd noises that have been obtained from a different match, a case example being *British Broadcasting Corporation v Talksport (No 1)*.[182] The BBC had exclusive broadcast rights to transmit live radio coverage of the European Football Championships (Euro 2000) in 2000. Talksport, a licensed UK radio broadcaster that allots much of its airspace to sporting matters and events, broadcast coverage of Euro 2000 'off-tube'. The commentators were watching the matches from hotel rooms in Belgium and, to entice listeners, the commentators advertised the matches as 'live' and included simulated crowd noises to add ambiance and authenticity to the matches. The BBC sought injunctive relief, as it argued that Talksport was incorrectly representing the nature of the coverage it was providing, and incorrectly representing itself to be the holder of live broadcasting rights.[183] While sympathetic to the BBC's claims, Blackburne J dismissed the action for an interlocutory injunction, holding that the balance of convenience did not favour its granting. The event was going to be over in two weeks and Blackburne J felt that the disadvantages of granting the interlocutory injunction outweighed the advantages such as loss of ambient sound. He contended that an injunction would cause Talksport to end altogether its further off-tube broadcasting of Euro 2000; this would threaten Talksport's commercial well-being and revenue.[184] The BBC argued that the actions of Talksport constituted passing-off; however, Blackburne J, while finding 'it

179 ibid.
180 ibid.
181 Cox and others (n 5) 364.
182 [2001] FRS 6.
183 ibid [12].
184 ibid [39] and [40].

deceptive and therefore wrong', did not consider that it gave the BBC a cause of action under the tort of passing-off.[185]

Traditionally, broadcast rights involved the sale of the exclusive rights to a single company. With developments in modern technology, rights can now be divided into 'sub packages', consequently giving rise to the possibility of 'a far more sophisticated exploitation of the potential in an event'.[186] The owner of the event will want to obtain the highest revenue possible from all the 'sub packages' while setting out the rights and obligations of all parties involved in the broadcasting contract.[187] The broadcasting contract will include standard contractual clauses, including payment, the term and termination of the agreement,[188] and options to renew.[189] More importantly, the contract will deal with issues of ownership of the rights; exclusivity; the nature and extent of the coverage[190]; quality of the coverage; promotional and advertising obligations; obligations to event sponsors; the timetabling and content of advertising breaks in the coverage of the event; issues relating to copyright and future use of the broadcast material; statutory and regulatory requirements; territorial rights[191]; capacity to sub-license; resolution of disputes[192]; insurance against the event being cancelled; and measures to be taken to prevent ambush marketing.[193] Broadcasting rights for major sporting events such as the Olympics or the Fédération Internationale de Football Association (FIFA) World Cup will often be concluded between the rights holder and a third-party production company, or a subsidiary company will be established to act as host broadcaster.[194] It is also possible for broadcasters from several countries **10–69**

185 ibid 38.

186 Cox and others (n 5) 365.

187 ibid.

188 The event may be a one-off event; thus, the broadcasting contract will be for the duration of that specific event. For ongoing or continuing events, the contract may be for a fixed term or at term for an indeterminate term terminable by notice: see Griffith-Jones and Barr-Smith (n 176) 312–13.

189 Cox and others (n 5) 365.

190 Is the match live, is it deferred, highlights or other?

191 This is an important consideration for international matches.

192 The contract should outline the ways of resolving disputes. For example, the contract may provide for arbitration, including referral to the Court of Arbitration for Sport (CAS).

193 Ambush marketing is defined as Sandler and Shani as 'a planned effort by an organization to associate itself indirectly with an event in order to gain at least some of the recognition and benefits that are associated with being an official sponsor': Dennis M Sandler and David Shani, 'Olympic Sponsorship vs "Ambush" Marketing: Who Gets the Gold?' (1989) 29 Journal of Advertising Research 9, 11. For more information on ambush marketing, see Gerd Nufer, *Ambush Marketing in Sports* (Routledge 2013); Andrew M Louw, *Ambush Marketing & the Mega-Event Monopoly: How Laws are Abused to Protect Commercial Rights to Major Sporting Events* (TMC Asser Press 2012) and Philip Johnson, *Ambush Marketing and Brand Protection* (3rd edn, Oxford University Press 2021).

194 Dennis Deninger, *Live Sports Media: The What, How and Why of Sports Broadcasting* (Routledge 2022) 139–50.

to come together as a consortium to secure the broadcast rights for a particular event.[195]

Audiovisual Media Services Directive

10–70 The Television without Frontiers (TVWF) Directive was introduced in 1989 and was first amended in 1997.[196] In 2007, the TVWF Directive was amended by the Audiovisual Media Services Without Frontiers Directive to reflect technological developments since the original Directive.[197] The TVWF Directive provided that where practicable and by appropriate means, broadcasters would reserve a large proportion of their transmission time to European audiovisual programmes. In 2010, the TVWF Directive was repealed and replaced by the Audiovisual Media Services Directive. The most recent update to the Audiovisual Media Services Directive was in 2018.[198] Five Member States including Ireland were referred to the Court of Justice of the European Union (CJEU) by the European Commission under Article 258 of the Treaty on the Functioning of the European Union (TFEU).[199] The European Commission initiated infringement proceedings against the Member States for failing to incorporate the Directive into their national legal systems. The 2010 Directive was amended to reflect the changing market realities. In the action brought by the European Commission against Ireland in November 2022, the European Commission explains:

> Both the 2010 and 2018 Directives harmonise national legislation concerning audiovisual media – traditional TV broadcasts and on-demand services. The 2018 Directive provides rules to shape technological

---

195 ibid.

196 Directive 97/36/EC of the European Parliament and of the Council of 30 June 1997 amending Council Directive 89/552/EEC on the coordination of certain provisions laid down by law, regulation or administrative action in Member States concerning the pursuit of television broadcasting activities [1989] OJ L 202.

197 Directive 2007/65/EC of the European Parliament and of the Council of 11 December 2007 amending Council Directive 89/552/EEC on the coordination of certain provisions laid down by law, regulation or administrative action in Member States concerning the pursuit of television broadcasting activities [2007] OJ L 332. The 2007 directive was amended by Directive 2010/13/EU of the European Parliament and of the Council of 10 March 2010 on the coordination of certain provisions laid down by law, regulation or administrative action in Member States concerning the provision of audiovisual media services (Audiovisual Media Services Directive) (Codified version) [2010] OJ L 95.

198 Directive (EU) 2018/1808 of the European Parliament and of the Council of 14 November 2018 amending Directive 2010/13/EU on the coordination of certain provisions laid down by law, regulation or administrative action in Member States concerning the provision of audiovisual media services (Audiovisual Media Services Directive) in view of changing market realities [2018] OJ L 303.

199 European Commission, 'Audiovisual Media Services Directive: Commission Refers Ireland to the Court of Justice of the EU' 19 May 2022 <https://ireland.representation.ec.europa.eu/news-and-events/news/audiovisual-media-services-directive-commission-refers-ireland-court-justice-eu-2022-05-19_en> accessed 18 May 2024.

> developments and creates a level playing field for emerging audiovisual media.[200]

In December 2022, the President signed into law the Online Safety and Media Regulation (OSMR) Act 2022, which implements the 2010 Directive as amended by the 2018 Directive. This Act partially fulfils Ireland's requirements under the Directive. In a decision handed down on 29 February 2024, the CJEU found Ireland in breach of its obligations under European Union (EU) law and ordered the state to pay a fine of €2.5m and daily penalties of €10,000 should Ireland continue to infringe EU law. A statement released after the judgment referred to the OSMR as **10–71**

> a landmark piece of legislation which Minister Catherine Martin brought to enactment and which established Coimisiún na Meán, the new online safety and media regulator with significant and robust powers. Ireland is completely committed to implementing the Directive into Irish law. Full transposition will be achieved once Coimisiún na Meán adopts online safety and media services codes.[201]

Of relevance to sporting events, the TVWF Directive was transposed into Irish law by way of the Broadcasting (Major Events Television Coverage) Act 1999, which was amended by the Broadcasting (Major Events Television Coverage) (Amendment) Act 2003. The 2003 Act provided that 'a portion of the public is not deprived of the possibility of following events live or on a deferred basis on free television services which are regarded by the Minister … as being of major importance to society'.[202] The 1999 and 2003 Acts were repealed by the Broadcasting Act 2009. Part II, ss 160–73 of the 2009 Act deal with Major Events Television Coverage. The Minister of the Environment, Climate and Communications is tasked with creating a list every three years of 'events of major importance to society for which the right of a qualifying broadcaster to provide coverage on free television services should be provided in the public interest'.[203] The Minister mandates whether the free television coverage events of major importance are live, deferred, in whole or in part.[204] Under s 162(2), the Minister must consider the following: **10–72**

> (a) the extent to which the event has a special general resonance for the people of Ireland, and

---

200 Case C–679/22 *European Commission v Ireland* [2024] ECLI:EU:C: 2024:178.

201 Department of Tourism, Culture, Arts, Gaeltacht, Sport and Media, 'Statement in Relation to Fines Imposed by the Court of Justice of the European Union' 29 February 2024 <https://www.gov.ie/en/press-release/0bbdb-statement-in-relation-to-fines-imposed-by-the-court-of-justice-of-the-european-union/> accessed 18 May 2024. Coimisiún na Meán is Ireland's media regulator: <https://www.cnam.ie/> accessed 18 May 2024.

202 This was stated in the long title of the Act.

203 Broadcasting Act 2009, s 162(1)(a). The 2009 Act refers to the Minister for Communications, Energy and Natural Resources.

204 ibid s 162 (1)(b)(i) and (ii).

(b) the extent to which the event has a generally recognised distinct cultural importance for the people of Ireland.

10–73 There are two important considerations for the Minister in that they must determine 'whether the event involves participation by a national or non-national team or by Irish persons' and 'past practice or experience with regard to television coverage of the event or similar events'.[205] Under s 162(5), the Minister is required to liaise with the Minister for Arts, Sport and Tourism 'before making, revoking or amending an order under this section'.[206]

10–74 Section 168 gives a pivotal role to the High Court in ensuring the proper implementation of the Act. A qualifying broadcaster may apply to the High Court for an order to allow them to provide coverage of a designated event on free television services upon terms fixed by the High Court. A qualifying broadcaster is defined as a broadcaster who provides 'near universal coverage' which refers to free television services that are available to at least 95% of the population of the State, of a designated event.[207] If there are less than three broadcasters able to provide the 95% coverage, the figure is reduced to 'at least 90 per cent of the population of the State'.[208]

10–75 If the qualifying broadcaster and event organiser cannot agree on the amount to be paid for the rights of the event, either party may appoint an arbitrator to determine reasonable market rates for the acquisition of the rights.[209] Reasonable market rates are determined either by the arbitrator or by the High Court in relation to the following: previous fees (if any) for the event or similar events, time of day for live coverage of the event, the period for which rights are offered, the revenue potential associated with the live or deferred coverage of the event and such other matters as may appear to be relevant.[210]

10–76 The most recent list of designated events dates to 2017.[211] The Broadcasting Act 2009 (Designation of Major Events) Order 2017

---

[205] Broadcasting Act 2009, ss 162(3)(a) and (b). Section 162(4) provides that the Minister must consider (a) the nature of the event, (b) the time within the State at which the event takes place, and (c) practical broadcasting considerations.

[206] Section 162(5) of the Broadcasting Act 2009 was amended by s 17 of the Planning and Development, Heritage and Broadcasting (Amendment) Act 2021 to substitute 'such Minister or Ministers of the Government as he or she considers appropriate' and replace with 'the Minister for Arts, Sport and Tourism'. The current name for the Department is the Department for Tourism, Culture, Arts, Gaeltacht, Sport and Media.

[207] Broadcasting Act 2009, s 160(1)(a).

[208] ibid s 160(1)(b).

[209] ibid ss 168(a) and (b), and s 169.

[210] ibid s 170.

[211] Broadcasting Act 2009 (Designation of Major Events) Order 2017, SI No 465 of 2017.

provides the following events are available on free television, live and in whole in the public interest:

- The Summer Olympics
- The All-Ireland Senior Inter-County Football and Hurling Finals
- Ireland's home and away qualifying games in the European Football Championship and the FIFA World Cup Tournaments
- Ireland's games in the European Football Championship Finals Tournament and the FIFA World Cup Finals Tournament
- The opening games, the semi-finals and final of the European Football Championship Finals and the FIFA World Cup Finals Tournament
- Ireland's games in the Rugby World Cup Finals Tournament
- The Irish Grand National and the Irish Derby
- The Nations Cup at the Dublin Horse Show
- The All-Ireland Ladies Gaelic Football Final
- The All-Ireland Ladies Camogie Final

Deferred coverage in whole and on free television services was granted to each of Ireland's games in the Six Nations Rugby Football Championship. **10–77**

Merchandising

Merchandising refers to the selling of rights by a sporting organisation or a sporting individual (a licensor) to a third party (a licensee) and granting the licensee the right to use its branding or imagery in return for payment. It covers a range of products, including replica kits, sports equipment that has been endorsed by a sportsperson, and souvenirs.[212] A sports organisation may create its own line of merchandised or branded goods or may have the goods produced by a manufacturer using the sports organisation's own specifications.[213] **10–78**

The rights holders will generally licence a third party to exploit the rights under licence. A licence grants defined rights without transferring ownership to the licensee. However, it is prudent for the parties to the agreement to carefully construct the agreement to provide protection against exploitation by unauthorised third parties (ie counterfeiting). This is where IP rights are important. **10–79**

As discussed in relation to sponsorship contracts, merchandising contracts will follow a similar format and should include the details about the parties: for example, is the contract between the rights holder (such as the governing body, the league, the club, the individual sportsperson) and a third party who wants to exploit the rights?[214] The **10–80**

---

212 Clive Lawrence, 'Merchandising and Licensing' in Adam Lewis and Jonathan Taylor (eds), *Sport: Law and Practice* (LexisNexis Butterworths 2003) 734.

213 ibid.

214 This list has been adapted from Simon Gardiner, *International Encyclopedia of*

agreement should expressly state the parameters of the licence, which will be negotiated between the rights holder(s) and the third party. For example, if the rights pertain to a football club, do they extend to the right to use images of the club's players? [215] Whether or not the third party has secured exclusivity to the rights should be stipulated in the agreement. If exclusivity is secured, the licensee will need to pay appropriately for this.[216] Another important consideration is the territorial reach of the agreement. Will it apply nationally, regionally, or internationally? The effect of competition law will need to be considered when deciding on the geographical scope of the agreement.[217] The parties must decide on the duration of the agreement and the payment. Generally, the licensor will be entitled to a percentage of the royalties arising from the sales of the licenced product. The quality of the merchandise is an important consideration. The agreement should set out the extent, if any, the licensor is liable for attesting to the quality of the merchandise. The agreement should expressly provide for the termination of the agreement and detail the type of conduct on the part of the licensee that would result in the setting aside of the merchandising agreement. An unsafe product may be grounds for termination or the failure of the licensee to pay royalties.[218] With regard to royalties, 'A royalty rate can vary significantly between the brand being licensed, the product category and the territory, but as a rule of thumb can be expected to be between 10 and 15%.'[219]

Agents and Intermediaries

10–81 The use of a sports agent is not a recent development, however, '[w]hat is comparatively new are the high finances and intense competition that pervade the profession'.[220] Agency is a common law creation and was used for practical and commercial considerations to allow a party to act through an agent.[221] The law of agency is based on the following maxim: *qui facit per alium facit per se* which means that they who act for another is deemed to act in person: in other words, a principal is liable for the acts of their agent. There is a subtle difference between an agent and an intermediary. An agent is a person employed to bring the principal into contractual relations with a third party. Therefore, the agent is in a fiduciary relationship with the principal. The central feature of the relationship is that the agent has power to make a binding contract

---

Sports Law (Kluwer 2008) [15].

215 Evans and Ellis (n 118).

216 ibid.

217 ibid.

218 ibid.

219 ibid.

220 Kenneth L Shropshire, Timothy Davis, and N Jeremi Duru, *The Business of Sports Agents* (University of Pennsylvania Press 2016) 11.

221 See Laura Donnellan, 'The Regulation of Football Agents in Ireland' in Robert Siekmann and others (eds), *Players' Agents Worldwide: Legal Aspects* (TMC Asser Press, 2007) 295–308.

between the principal and a third party without the agent becoming a party to the contract. Once the agent has performed the contracted task, the agent departs, and the principal and third party continue with the contract. Generally, the law does not require any formalities to be observed in the appointment of an agent.[222] The appointment may be made orally, in writing,[223] by deed[224] or by conduct.[225]

An intermediary tends to have a less formal relationship in that 'they mainly carry out material actions (establishing contact, arranging meetings, etc) in order to bring the contracting parties together'.[226] While that is the 'strict legal position', the words 'agent' and 'intermediaries' are often used interchangeably, most notably by the media, thus the legal dichotomy between the two has becoming increasingly conflated.[227] The most recent version of FIFA Football Agent Regulations (FFARs) were approved in December 2022 and member associations had until 30 September 2023 'to implement and enforce national football regulations'.[228] As discussed at the end of the chapter, some of provisions of the FFARs have been suspended pending a decision of the CJEU, which is not expected until mid-2025.[229] **10–82**

Duties of an Agent

Most of the law pertaining to agency is judge-made.[230] The focus is on the actions of an agent which bind the principal to the third parties and in this area the following are of importance: actual, usual, and ostensible authority.[231] Actual authority can be express or implied and is explained by Lord Denning Master of the Rolls (MR) in *Hely-Hutchinson v Brayhead Ltd*: **10–83**

> It is express when it is given by express words, such as when a board of directors pass a resolution which authorises two of their number to sign cheques. It is implied when it is inferred from the conduct of the parties and the circumstances of the case, such as when the board of directors

---

222 Henry Ellis, *Modern Irish Commercial and Consumer Law* (Jordans 2004) para 38.3.

223 ibid. If the agency agreement is in writing, the agent is usually appointed by way of a written document or letter of appointment. Ellis notes that this is not always necessary unless required by statute.

224 This would be used in the appointment of a universal agent who is appointed under a power of attorney.

225 Here an agency appointment is implied from the conduct of the parties involved.

226 Giambattista Rossi, Anna Semens, and Jean Francois Brocard, *Sports Agents and Labour Markets: Evidence from World Football* (Routledge 2016) 1.

227 ibid 1–2.

228 The Regulations are available here <https://digitalhub.fifa.com/m/1e7b741fa0fae779/original/FIFA-Football-Agent-Regulations.pdf> accessed 16 May 2024. See art 3(1) of the FFAR.

229 William Sternheimer and others, 'The FIFA Football Agent Regulations: Latest Developments' (*Morgan Sports Law*, 30 April 2024) <https://morgansl.com/en/latest/fifa-football-agent-regulations-latest-developments> accessed 18 May 2024.

230 Michael Forde, *Commercial Law* (3rd edn, Tottel Publishing 2005) para 1.069.

231 ibid.

appoint one of their number to be managing director. They thereby impliedly authorise him to do all such things as fall within the usual scope of that office. Actual authority, express or implied, is binding as between the company and the agent, and also as between the company and others, whether they are within the company or outside it.[232]

10–84 Usual authority pertains to the express authority of the principal which is 'supplemented by an implied authority, which the principal by implication consented that the agent should' have so that 'every agent has implied authority to whatever is necessary for, or incidental to, the effective execution of his express authority in the usual way'.[233] Ostensible authority is also known as apparent authority and is based on the assumption of the third party that the principal has 'held out' the agent as having such authority.[234] There are three elements to apparent/ostensible authority beginning with a representation made by the agent which has been relied upon by the third party who altered their position as a result of the representation.[235]

10–85 The agent must carry out the instructions given by the principal. In the case of *Turpin v Bilton*, the defendant was an insurance broker who was employed to arrange insurance on the plaintiff's ship.[236] However, the agent failed to insure the ship, which was subsequently lost at sea. The agent was held liable in damages. The agent must also exercise a certain standard of care and skill; the level depends on whether the agent is getting paid. In *Chariot Inns v Assicurazioni Generali SPA and Coyle Hamilton Phillips*, the plaintiff company employed insurance brokers as agents who advised them not to disclose relevant information on the proposal form relating to a previous fire claim.[237] A serious fire occurred at the premises in Ranelagh and the insurance company repudiated liability on the grounds of the non-disclosure of the claim in respect of the Leeson Street property. The Court held the agents liable in negligence. An agent is also under a duty to perform the task personally and not to delegate without authority from the principal[238]; the agent must avoid a conflict of interests[239]; and may not make a secret profit.[240]

Principal's Duties

10–86 An agent may receive remuneration, commission, or a lien.[241] An agent

---

[232] [1968] 1 QB 549, 583.
[233] JA Hornby, 'The Usual Authority of an Agent' (1961) 19(2) Cambridge Law Journal 239, 239.
[234] ibid.
[235] Roderick Munday, *Agency: Law and Principles* (OUP 2010) 65.
[236] (1843) 5 Man & G 455.
[237] [1981] IR 199; [1981] ILRM 173.
[238] Unless they obtain the implied or expressed consent of the principal. See *De Bussche v Alt* (1878) 8 Ch D 286 (CA).
[239] *Aberdeen Rly Co v Blaikie Bros* (1854) 1 Marq 461.
[240] *Lamb v Evans* [1893] 1 ch 218.
[241] An agent may hold on to the principal's property to secure payment of any money

may only claim remuneration where there is an express or implied term to that effect contained in the contract. The amount depends on the terms of the contract. If there is no agreed sum, a reasonable sum is payable. Where an agent carries out extra work in addition to those outlined in their contract, the principal is under an implied duty to pay the agent for this extra work.[242] In a situation where the agent is a professional person and there is no express agreement as to remuneration, there is a presumption that they are entitled to receive reasonable remuneration for their services.[243] Reasonable may be assessed as what is customary in the business.[244]

Commission

In general, an agent will only be entitled to commission if they bring about the desired result. An agent will not be entitled to commission where they act outside the scope of their actual authority, or act in a manner that they know, or ought to have known, is unlawful or dishonest, or commit a serious breach of their duties.[245] **10–87**

Termination of Agency

Agency may be terminated by acts of the parties or by operation of law. The relationship may be terminated as the contract has been performed; it may be ended by agreement between the parties; or there may be a fundamental breach of a condition which renders the contract void. In this instance the principal may also sue for damages. Agency is automatically terminated on the bankruptcy, liquidation, death or insanity of the agent or principal, or the agency may have simply been created for a limited period and that time has now lapsed. **10–88**

FIFA Agent Regulations

The above discussion sets out the common law approach to the agency. At EU level, commercial agents are subject to a Directive, however, this relates to the sale or purchase of goods and does not apply to sports agents.[246] FIFA's initial involvement in the regulation of football agents occurred in the early 1990s with the introduction of the Players' Agents Regulations (PAR) in 1994.[247] There was in an increase in cross-border transfers and, as a corollary, there was an increase in the use of player **10–89**

owed to them by the principal.

242 Ellis (n 222) [38.29].

243 ibid.

244 ibid.

245 ibid.

246 Council Directive 86/653/EEC of 18 December 1986 on the coordination of the laws of the Member States relating to self-employed commercial agents [1986] OJ L 382.

247 Richard Parrish and others, *Promoting and Supporting Good Governance in the European Football Agents Industry-Final Report* (European Commission 2019) 27

agents.[248] The 1994 PAR provided that a natural person could obtain a licence from the national association in the country in which they were a national or legally domiciled.[249] The PAR expressly excluded legal persons, namely companies and organisations, from acting as player agents.[250] The PAR applied to the use of an agent in transfers between national associations, and national associations were permitted to draft their own regulations for transfers within their association subject to approval by FIFA.[251] The requirement of a licenced agent did not apply if the agent was a close relative of the player or the player/club employed a registered solicitor in the country of or place of residence of the player.[252]

10–90 In order to obtain a licence, the applicant had to furnish either a police report that they did not have a criminal record or similar documentation attesting to their good reputation.[253] Clubs and players were not to employ the services of unlicenced agents.[254] Applicants with criminal records or bad reputations were not to be granted licences from the national association, save as in exceptional circumstances where FIFA's Players' Status Committee considered there to be mitigating circumstances.[255] The national association would decide whether an applicant was admissible and, if so, a personal interview would be organised. If the national association deemed the applicant to be non-admissible, the FIFA's Players' Status Committee would hear the appeal and its decision would be final.[256] At the interview, the national association would ascertain the applicant's knowledge of football regulations and statutes of FIFA and the national association, basic legal

---

<https://ec.europa.eu/programmes/erasmus-plus/project-result-content/c9408418-3ba4-4636-9020-df0ad78293e0/On-line_book-final.pdf> accessed 18 May 2024.

248 ibid 57.

249 FIFA, 'Regulations Governing Players' Agents and Match Agents' (1994) art 2(1) <https://digitalhub.fifa.com/m/90f772e9b57f30f/original/e1cw5jajdufoqasn1cja-pdf.pdf> accessed 18 September 2024. The agent had to be legally resident in that country for a period of at least five years. The Regulations were adopted on 20 May 1994, amended on 11 December 1995, and entered into force on 1 January 1996: see T–193/02 *Laurent Piau v Commission of the European Communities* 2005 II-00209 [5]. The decision of the then Court of First Instance (now General Court) was appealed to the ECJ, Case C–171/05 P *Laurent Piau v Commission of the European Communities* [2006] ECR I–37.

250 PAR (n 249) art 2(3).

251 ibid Preamble and art 22.

252 ibid art 1(3). If the agent is a solicitor, they may act as an agent in the course of their work as a solicitor. A solicitor who acts as football agent is not only bound by the terms of the agency contract but also by the lawyer–client relationship. Under Irish law, solicitors are governed by their professional body, the Law Society of Ireland. Solicitors are regulated by several Acts and statutory instruments: see the Solicitors Acts 1954–2011 and the Legal Service Regulation Act 2015. There is also the Law Society Guide to Professional Conduct 2022, which is available at <https://www.lawsociety.ie/globalassets/documents/committees/conduct-guide.pdf> accessed 18 May 2024.

253 PAR (n 249) art 2(2).

254 ibid arts 16 and 18.

255 ibid art 3(2). The decision of the Players' Status Committee would be final.

256 ibid art 5.

principles and whether the interviewee 'generally appears capable of advising a player or a club who calls on his services'.[257] At the end of the interview, the official would inform the applicant if they had been successful or not and, if not successful, the applicant could request a second personal interview.[258] If the applicant was unsuccessful after the second interview, the licence application was rejected and the applicant was precluded from re-applying for one year.[259] If on the expiry of a year, the applicant was unsuccessful for a third time, the Players' Status Committee would make a final determination.[260] The successful applicant's details would be sent to FIFA and the relevant confederation, either of whom could reject the national association's decision to grant a licence.[261] The final decision would rest with FIFA. The licenced agent was required to deposit 200,000 Swiss Francs which was issued by a Swiss bank and irrevocable.[262] The PAR stated that a written contract between the club or player with the agent was limited to a period of two years; however, this could be renewed with the express agreement of both parties.[263] An agent who abused their rights or failed to comply with the PAR would be subject to the following sanctions outlined under Article 15:

(a) reprimand, censure, or caution
(b) a fine
(c) suspension of the licence
(d) withdrawal of the licence.

Players who obtained the services of an unlicensed agent could be fined 50,000 Swiss Francs, or be reprimanded, censured, or cautioned and receive a disciplinary sanction of up to 12 months.[264] Clubs also faced sanctions in the form of reprimand, censure or caution, the suspension of all or part of its management bodies, a fine of up to 100,000 Swiss Francs, a prohibition on national and/or international transfers and a ban on all national and/or international footballing activity.[265] **10–91**

The stringent nature of the PAR resulted in complaints being made to the European Commission.[266] Following an investigation, the European Commission issued a statement of objections on 19 October 1999 to FIFA wherein it stated that the PAR constituted a decision by an association of undertakings within the meaning of then Article 81 EC Treaty (now Article 101 of the TFEU).[267] It questioned the compatibility **10–92**

---

257 ibid art 6(1).
258 ibid arts 7(1) and (2).
259 ibid art 7(3).
260 ibid art 7(4).
261 ibid arts 8(1) and (2).
262 ibid art 9(1).
263 ibid arts 13(1) and (2).
264 ibid art 17.
265 ibid art 19(1)(a)–(e).
266 See T-193/02 *Piau* (n 249) [8,] [9], and [10].
267 Article 101 TFEU refers to restrictive agreements.

of Article 81 EC with the requirement of a licenced agent, the exclusion of legal persons, the prohibition placed on clubs and players using unlicenced agents, the bank guarantee and the sanctions for breaches of the PAR.[268] In response, FIFA introduced new PAR in 2001, which were acceptable to the European Commission: 'As the most significant restrictive provisions have been removed, the need for a licence can be justified by the need to raise moral standards within the profession of players' agents.'[269] The 2001 PAR came into force on 1 March 2001 and were amended on 3 April 2002. Under the 2001 PAR as amended, the bank guarantee was replaced by liability insurance. The applicant was required to satisfy the national association that they had an impeccable reputation. On fulfilling this requirement, they had to sit a written examination consisting of 20 multiple choice questions. Once the applicant had passed the examination and had obtained professional liability insurance, they received their licence from the national association. The national association would draw up a list of its licensed agents and return it to FIFA after every examination date. Once the agent had passed the examination and had satisfied the minimum criteria required by FIFA, they were permitted to offer their services throughout the EU and European Economic Area (EEA). The agent had to keep accounts and sign a Code of Professional Conduct 'containing the principles of professional integrity, transparency, honesty and the fair management of interests'.[270] The revised PAR still excluded legal persons from becoming agents.[271]

10–93 The European Commission further announced that if it were possible for Member States to regulate player agents or if a high level of professionalism could be achieved within a self-regulated system in place of the PAR, the European Commission was open to reviewing such rules.[272] At the time of the press release, two complaints had been received by the European Commission, one from Multiplayers International Denmark, a company, and one from a French agent, Laurent Piau. Piau argued that the PAR were in breach of European Community (now EU) competition law and the freedom to provide a service. Piau also questioned the lack of legal remedies against decisions and sanctions. The European Commission dismissed the complaint and Piau challenged this before the then Court of First Instance (CFI,

---

268 See T-193/02 *Piau* (n 249) [10].

269 European Commission, 'Commission Closes Investigations into FIFA Rules on Players' Agents' (IP/02/585) (18 April 2002) <https://ec.europa.eu/commission/presscorner/detail/en/IP_02_585> accessed 18 May 2024. The quote is from the then Competition Commissioner Mario Monti.

270 ibid.

271 Gregory Ioannidis, 'Football Intermediaries and Self-Regulation: The Need for Greater Transparency through Disciplinary Law, Sanctioning and Qualifying Criteria' (2019) 19 The International Sports Law Journal 154, 157.

272 European Commission (n 269).

now the General Court).[273] The CFI dismissed the action and Piau was ordered to pay his own costs and those of the European Commission.

The PAR were revised again in 2007 and came into force in 2008.[274] The PAR continued to apply only to natural persons, they provided for financial penalties and sanctions for violations of the PAR on players (Article 34), clubs (Article 35), and associations (Article 36). The financial penalties were significantly lower than those under the 2001 PAR: for example, a player faced a fine of at least 5,000 Swiss Francs, a club at least 10,000 Swiss Francs and an association at least 30,000 Swiss Francs. The non-financial penalties were less draconian than previous versions of the PAR as a player could be sanctioned with a match suspension, a reprimand or warning or ban in taking part in any football-related activity. Clubs could have a transfer ban imposed, points deducted and demotion to a lower level. An association could be excluded from competition if found to have breached the PAR. Sanctions for agents found to have violated the PAR were outlined under Article 33 and included a reprimand or a warning, a fine of at least 5,000 Swiss Francs, a suspension of licence for up to 12 months, a licence withdrawal, and a ban on taking part in any football-related activity. Article 22 precluded an agent from approaching a player in contract with a view to inducing the player to terminate the contract prematurely or persuading a player to breach a term of their contract.[275] Annex 1 detailed the Code of Professional Conduct and paragraph 7 ousted the jurisdiction of the courts, arguably an illegal clause. It stated, 'The players' agent is prohibited from taking a dispute to ordinary courts of law as stipulated in the FIFA Statutes and is required to submit any claim to the jurisdiction of the association or FIFA.' The Players' Status Committee continued to occupy an important role in the operation of the PAR. **10–94**

The PAR proved to be complex and made it very difficult for an individual to become a licenced agent.[276] FIFA introduced the Regulations on Working with Intermediaries in 2015. These new Regulations effectively deregulated agents.[277] Intermediary was defined as **10–95**

> A natural or legal person who, for a fee or free of charge, represents players

[273] See Case C-171/05 *Piau* (n 249) for details of appeal to ECJ, which was dismissed. For more details, see Pablo Ibáñez Colomo and Denis Waelbroeck, 'Case C–171/05 P, Laurent Piau, Order of the Court of Justice (Third Chamber) of 23 February 2006, [2006] ECR I–37' (2006) 43(6) Common Market Law Review 1743.

[274] FIFA, 'Player Agent Regulations' (2008) <https://digitalhub.fifa.com/m/31193b5991418bff/original/umrmelh3zftzj9yme11q-pdf.pdf> accessed 18 May 2024.

[275] For a more detailed discussion on the 2008 PAR, see Parrish and others (n 247) 32–35.

[276] Santiago Barroso Torres, 'FIFA's New Agents' Regulations' (*Lex Sportiva Blog*, 13 July 2019) <https://lexsportiva.blog/2019/07/13/fifas-new-agents-regulations/> accessed 18 May 2024.

[277] ibid.

and/or clubs in negotiations with a view to concluding an employment contract or represents clubs in negotiations with a view to concluding a transfer agreement.[278]

10–96 FIFA explained in the Preamble that the Intermediaries Regulations prescribed minimum standards/requirements and it fell to the national associations to implement them.[279] Article 1(3) provided that national associations could go beyond these minimum provisions. National associations were tasked with creating an intermediary register, which had to be made publicly available at the end of March of every year on their official website.[280] National associations were also required to publish the total amount of all remunerations or payments made to the intermediaries by players and their affiliated clubs.[281] Natural persons were required to have an impeccable reputation.[282] Legal persons were also required to have an impeccable reputation, which was assessed through the medium of the individuals representing such entities.[283]

10–97 Article 7 outlined the requirements in relation to the payment of intermediaries. Article 9 provided for sanctions with the responsibility to impose penalties devolved to the national associations. National associations were 'obliged to punish accordingly' and inform FIFA of any disciplinary sanctions taken against any intermediary. The FIFA Disciplinary Committee would then decide if the sanction should be extended to have worldwide effect in accordance with the FIFA Disciplinary Code.

10–98 Of significance was the exclusion of the FIFA Players' Status Committee, which had featured predominantly in the PAR. The deregulation of agents had taken the Players' Status Committee 'out of the football ecosystem'.[284] The Regulations on Working with Intermediaries decentralised the regulation of agents, resulting in several issues. There was a lack of consistency between the approaches of the national associations and 'a perceived lack of quality control'.[285] The Intermediaries Regulations were characterised by an 'inability to impose appropriate sanctions at an international level, such as fines, suspensions and termination of agent registrations, thereby perpetuating unethical

278 FIFA, 'Regulations on Working with Intermediaries' (2015) 5 <https://digitalhub.fifa.com/m/352df54820ee1a59/original/cr6dquxm2adupv8q3ply-pdf.pdf> accessed 18 May 2024.

279 ibid.

280 ibid arts 3(1) and 6(3).

281 ibid art 6(3).

282 ibid art 4(1).

283 ibid art 4(2).

284 Barroso Torres (n 276).

285 Carol Couse, Rustam Sethna, and Mark Dennis, 'A Guide to the New FIFA Agent Regulations for Football Agents & Clubs' (*Law In Sport*, 12 January 2023) <https://www.lawinsport.com/topics/item/a-guide-to-the-new-fifa-football-agent-regulations-the-deregulation-regulation-full-circle> accessed 18 May 2024.

and unfair practices'.[286] There were some positive aspects: for example, the deregulated rules reduced the barriers to entry for many individuals who wished to become agents.[287] In 2017, the Football Stakeholders Committee (FSC) was created and in September 2019 it proposed a second reform package focused on three areas: training rewards, loans, and agents.[288] It recommended 'the reintroduction of a FIFA football-agent licensing system, incorporating a mandatory licensing system, further educational requirements, a cap on commissions, the prohibition of conflicts of interest, and the establishment of an effective dispute resolution system'.[289] FIFA approved the FFAR in December 2022 and, while some provisions came into force on 9 January 2023, the remaining were to come into force on 1 October 2023.[290] The Intermediaries Regulations ceased on 1 October 2023.

Article 1 of the FFAR state the objectives of the Regulations and provide that FIFA has a statutory obligation to regulate all matters relating to the football transfer system. The core objectives of the football transfer system are to: **10–99**

> a) protect the contractual stability between professional players and clubs,
> b) encourage the training of young players,
> c) promote a spirit of solidarity between elite and grassroots football,
> d) protect minors,
> e) maintain competitive balance, and
> f) ensure the regularity of sporting competitions.

An agent is defined as a natural person licensed by FIFA to perform Football Agent Services. In contrast to the 2015 Intermediary Regulations, legal persons are not permitted to provide the services of a football agent. Part II, Articles 4–10 govern the requirements for becoming an agent.[291] Part III, Articles 11–17 pertain to the regulatory requirements of an agent.[292] Of significance is Article 16(1)–(b), which states that an agent **10–100**

---

[286] ibid.

[287] ibid.

[288] FIFA, 'Historical Record and Achievements: Football Stakeholders Committee' (2017–2021) 3 <https://digitalhub.fifa.com/m/f6c4450d706291da/original/vbykzozs9uhtlgzvfsaa-pdf.pdf> accessed 18 May 2024.

[289] ibid. See also FIFA, 'FIFA and Football Stakeholders Recommend Cap on Agents' Commissions and Limit on Loans' (25 September 2019) <https://www.fifa.com/legal/media-releases/fifa-and-football-stakeholders-recommend-cap-on-agents-commissions-and-limit-on-> accessed 18 May 2024.

[290] FFAR (n 228) art 28 enforcement: (a) On 9 January 2023: arts 1–10 and arts 22–27, which generally relate to the processes for obtaining a licence, (b) On 1 October 2023: the remaining articles, which generally relate to acting as a football agent and the obligations of football agents and clients.

[291] ibid, including art 5 eligibility requirements; art 6 exam procedure; art 7 licence fee; art 8 issue of licence; art 9 continuing professional development; art 10 request for a suspension or termination of licence.

[292] ibid, including art 12, which details the representation agreement, which must be in writing and not exceed two years but may be renewed; art 13 representation of minors; art 14 service fee; and art 15 service fee cap.

may not approach a client that is bound by an exclusive Representation Agreement with another Football Agent, except in the final two months of that exclusive Representation Agreement.

10–101 Part IV contains a single article, Article 18 on the Rights and Obligations of Clients. Part V, Article 19 is on the disclosure and publication by FIFA of certain information, including names and details of all football agents. Part VI, Article 20 on disputes, recommends the use of the Agents Chamber of the Football Tribunal where there is an international dimension and, where there is no international dimension, disputes relating to the Representation Agreement are subject to the decision-making body in the national association.[293] Unlike the Intermediaries Regulations, there is no attempt to prevent parties seeking redress in ordinary courts of law. Disciplinary Matters are explained in Part VII, Article 21; there is no reference to the Players' Status Committee and instead the FIFA Disciplinary Committee and, where relevant, the independent Ethics Committee, are empowered to impose sanctions on any football agent or client. If the violation relates to national regulations, that is the preserve of the relevant national association. Part VIII, Articles 22–28 deal with the final provisions.[294]

10–102 As mentioned above, FIFA temporarily suspended certain provisions of the FFAR in December 2023.[295] The suspension was in response to an interim injunction granted by the District Court of Dortmund in Germany on 24 May 2023.[296] The injunction requested FIFA 'to suspend the application and enforcement of the certain provisions of the FFAR', namely:

- The service fee cap (Article 15, paras 1–4)
- The rules concerning service fee payments (Article 14, paras 6, 8 and 11)
- The client pays rule (Article 14, paras 2 and 10)
- The rules regarding the timing of service fee payments (Article 14, paras 7 and 12)
- The prohibition of double representation (Article 12, paras 8–10)

[293] More information on the Agents Chamber can be found here <https://www.fifa.com/legal/football-regulatory/agents/agents-chamber> accessed 25 July 2024.

[294] Including art 22 transitory provisions, and art 24 recognition of national law licensing systems.

[295] FIFA Circular no 1873, 'FIFA Football Agent Regulations: Update on Implementation' 30 December 2023 <https://digitalhub.fifa.com/m/76b4cdc63e42e03f/original/1873_FIFA-Football-Agent-Regulations-update-on-implementation.pdf> accessed 18 May 2024.

[296] ibid. *LG Dortmund, judgment of 24.05.2023 – 8 O 1/23 (Kart)* is available at <https://openjur.de/u/2470417.html> accessed 18 May 2024. For more details on the appeal hearing in the Higher Regional Court of Düsseldorf, see Björn Christian Becker, 'Oral Hearing in the Preliminary Injunction Proceedings Concerning the FIFA Football Agents Regulations (FFAR)' (*Kluwer Competition Law Blog*, 29 February 2024) <https://competitionlawblog.kluwercompetitionlaw.com/2024/02/29/oral-hearing-in-the-preliminary-injunction-proceedings-concerning-the-fifa-football-agents-regulations-ffar/> accessed 18 May 2024.

- The reporting obligations (Article 16, paras 2h), j), and k) and para 4)
- The rules regarding disclosure and publication (Article 19, para 2)
- The submission rule (Article 4, para 2; Article 16, para 2b); Article 3, paras 2c) and d); Article 20; and Article 21)
- The rule that service fee payments must be made via the FIFA Clearing House (Article 14, para 13).[297]

On 29 September 2023, a FIFA Press Release referred to the CAS affirming the legality of the FFAR and that the Regulations would fully come into effect on 1 October 2023 except for Germany where the listed provisions above would not apply.[298] Agents have challenged the FFAR on the grounds of the capping of 'an agent's commission at three per cent on all player salaries over £161,000, limiting payments to agents for brokering transfers to ten per cent of the fee and the necessity for agents to pass an exam if they are to continue to operate'.[299] The suspension applies worldwide and not just the EU, as FIFA explained the need for consistency and equality: **10–103**

> In order to comply with the Injunction, FIFA will suspend the implementation of the FFAR for any transfer which has a link to the European Union. Implementing the Injunction only for transfers linked to the European Union would create a situation of unequal legal standards within the international transfer system, in particular between Europe and the rest of the world. As the world governing body of football and a prudent and responsible regulator, FIFA has a duty to prevent such uncertainty and inequality and protect competitive balance at a worldwide level.[300]

All FIFA member associations have been instructed to suspend the above-listed provisions or equivalent from their national football agent regulations, 'unless they conflict with mandatory provisions of the law applicable in their territory'.[301] Sternheimer and others contend that **10–104**

[297] FIFA Circular (n 295) 2–3.

[298] FIFA, 'FIFA Football Agent Regulations to Fully Enter into Force as of 1 October' 29 September 2023 <https://inside.fifa.com/legal/football-regulatory/agents/media-releases/fifa-football-agent-regulations-to-fully-enter-into-force-as-of-1-october> accessed 18 May 2024. See CAS 2023/O/9370 *Professional Football Agents Association (PROFAA) v FIFA* award of 24 July 2023 <https://www.tas-cas.org/fileadmin/user_upload/CAS_Award_9370.pdf> accessed 18 May 2024. The CAS dismissed the claims filed in their entirety. The lengthy decision refers to Swiss competition law and personality rights under Swiss law, the EU's Charter of Fundamental Rights, EU competition law, art 16 of EU Directive 2006/123/EC on Services in the Internal Market (the 'EU Services Directive'), French law and Italian law.

[299] David Ornstein, 'FIFA Suspends Introduction of New Agent Regulations' *New York Times* (New York, 30 December 2023) <https://www.nytimes.com/athletic/5169636/2023/12/30/fifa-agent-regulations-suspend/> accessed 18 May 2024.

[300] FIFA Circular (n 295) 2.

[301] ibid. See Sternheimer and others (n 229), who summarise the 'current state of play' in England, Germany, Spain, France, Italy, Switzerland, and the Netherlands.

the decision of FIFA to suspend the contested provisions of the FFAR pending the decision of the CJEU, which is expected around mid-2025,

> was necessary to avoid the risk of regulatory conditions for football agents differing considerably between national markets. Such a situation would inevitably have resulted in obvious competitive advantages for agents operating in markets where the FFAR are not, or not fully, applied and would run contrary to one of FIFA's core objectives in enacting the FFAR, that being harmonising the regulatory landscape for football agents worldwide.[302]

Conclusion

10–105 Sport is multibillion-dollar global industry. In juxtaposition to the increased commercialisation of sport is the increased involvement of the law, in particular private law. Sponsorship, merchandising, image rights, IP, the law of agency and media rights have assumed a greater importance in the life of a sportsperson, club, league, or event. As the stakes are higher, there is more of a need to protect one's brand and control its exploitation. Increased regulation, whether it relates to agents, media rights or IP, is to be welcomed as it helps curb and dissuade unethical and unfair practices.

10–106 The FFAR represent a return to the orthodoxy: the centralised regulation of football agents. The new Regulations provide a good balance between the stringent requirements of the original PAR and the *laissez-faire* approach adopted by the 2015 Intermediaries Regulations. It will be interesting to see if the CJEU will uphold the FFAR as being compatible with EU law or if the contested provisions will be deemed a breach of EU law. If it is the latter, FIFA will be forced to redraft the Regulations, which may well see the reintroduction of the Regulations on Working with Intermediaries.

[302] Sternheimer and others (n 229).

CHAPTER 11

JUDICIAL REVIEW AND SPORTING BODIES

Introduction

11–01 In the last 20 years, there have been several judicial review cases involving sports governing bodies in Ireland. What is evident from these cases is that the Irish courts are willing to hear such cases; however, judges have often highlighted that judicial intervention in the decisions of sporting organisations should not occur lightly and recourse to the courts should only happen in the most exceptional of circumstances. The Irish courts have referred to the need for sports bodies to submit their dispute to arbitration or mediation. In Ireland, there are two domestic bodies offering alternative dispute resolution in the sporting context, namely Sport Dispute Solutions Ireland (SDSI, formerly Just Sport Ireland) and the Disputes Resolution Authority (DRA) of the Gaelic Athletic Association (GAA). The availability of alternative forms of dispute resolution in Ireland provides a welcome alternative to the expensive, often divisive, option of judicial review proceedings. Given the benefits of the resolution of disputes through the DRA or SDSI and considering the Irish courts' general reluctance to become involved in sporting disputes, it is likely that these processes will become increasingly availed of: most pertinently, in 2016 Sport Ireland announced that it would require governing bodies to insert a dispute-resolution mechanism within their Constitutions. By 2019, all governing bodies were compliant and any future governing body seeking recognition by Sport Ireland will be required to have a clause referring to dispute resolution in its rules.[1]

11–02 This chapter will examine the approach of the Irish courts to judicial review and sports governing bodies through the lens of seminal cases. It will demonstrate that the courts are not always best-placed to deal with such cases and the use of alternative methods of dispute resolution is often the better course of action. This will lead into the next chapter on Alternative Dispute Resolution, which will focus on the Court of Arbitration for Sport (CAS), the DRA and SDSI.

---

1 Sport Ireland, 'Annual Report 2019' 16 <https://www.sportireland.ie/sites/default/files/media/document/2021-03/sport-ireland-annual-report-2019-english.pdf> accessed 18 May 2024. Annual Reports from 2015 to 2022 are available at <https://www.sportireland.ie/about-us/publications/annual-reports> accessed 18 May 2024.

Judicial Review in Ireland

11–03 Judicial review is a means whereby the High Court can oversee the administrative decisions of public bodies.[2] The aim of this oversight is not to act as an appeal process which reassesses the merits of such decisions but rather to make sure that such decisions are made in accordance with fair procedures and the principle of natural justice. While the courts in some sports-related cases have discouraged the use of judicial review, sometimes recourse to the courts can be a positive thing, as Coffey notes:

> The benefits of having an independent system for review of wrongful administrative decisions includes encouraging higher quality decision making, which serves to enhance public confidence in government and public administration.[3]

11–04 An individual will have grounds for judicial review where the procedures involved in an administrative action were unfair, where the person contends that they have not been given a fair opportunity to be heard (*audi alteram partem*) or where those adjudicating were biased in some way (*nemo judex in causa sua*). The procedure for seeking judicial review is set out in Order 84 of the Rules of the Superior Courts.[4] Rule 18(1) of Order 84 provides that the orders available in judicial review proceedings include the public law remedies of mandamus (compel the performance of a duty),[5] certiorari (quash a decision),[6] prohibition (prevent the action being taken),[7] or quo warranto.[8] With regard to quo warranto, Coffey notes that this order is seldom used.[9] Historically, it was invoked to determine whether someone who claimed an office, franchise or liberty had a right to such a prerogative.[10] The private

---

2 See Laura Donnellan and Susan Leahy, *Sports Law in Ireland* (Kluwer 2014) 57–68.

3 Ger Coffey, *Administrative Law* (2nd edn, Round Hall 2010) 15.

4 Superior Court Rules, 'Order 84 Judicial Review and Orders Affecting Personal Liberty' <https://www.courts.ie/rules/judicial-review-and-orders-affecting-personal-liberty> accessed 18 May 2024. Order 84 was recently amended by SI No 163/2024 - Rules of the Superior Courts (Order 84) 2024. The explanatory note explains: 'These rules amend Order 84 of the Rules of the Superior Courts to provide that the three-month time period within which an application for judicial review must be made stops when the notice and affidavit required by rule 20(2)(a) and (b) are filed.'

5 Mandamus is an order to secure the performance of a public duty imposed on a public body, either by statute or by common law: Gerard Hogan and David Gwynn Morgan, *Administrative Law in Ireland* (Thomson Reuters 2010) 829.

6 ibid. Hogan and Gwynn Morgan define certiorari as an order quashing the decision of a public body which has been arrived at in excess of jurisdiction or where an error appears on the face of the record.

7 ibid. Prohibition is an order restraining a public body from doing something which would be in excess of its jurisdiction.

8 According to the Legal Information Institute, quo warranto is Latin for 'by what warrant (or authority) <https://www.law.cornell.edu/wex/quo_warranto> accessed 18 May 2024.

9 Coffey (n 3) 312.

10 ibid 339. Coffey gives the example of quo warranto being used to ensure that

law remedies of injunctions,[11] declarations,[12] and damages[13] are also available. To be eligible to apply for judicial review, the applicant must show that they have 'a sufficient interest in the matter to which the application relates.'[14] The time limit for applications is three months from the time when the grounds for the application first arose.[15] Applications for judicial review in Ireland involve a two-stage process. First, the applicant must make an *ex parte* application for leave to seek judicial review.[16] The necessity for the leave stage is explained by Kelly J in *O'Leary v Minister for Transport, Energy and Communications* as follows:

> The judicial review procedure is designed so as to ensure that cases which are frivolous, vexatious or of no substance cannot be begun, hence the necessity for judicial screening at the stage where leave is sought. The procedure is also designed to ensure that a fair and expeditious trial takes place and that such trial is focused upon the issues, in respect of which the judge, at the leave stage, felt ought to be argued, and those alone.[17]

The court hearing an application for leave has discretion to direct that the application be heard on notice.[18] It is also possible for the court hearing the application for leave to treat that application as if it were the hearing **11–05**

'a judge had fulfilled the statutory requirements for appointment'. This could be that the proposed judge has the required length of service. Section 5 of the Courts (Supplemental Provisions) Act 1961, as amended by s 4 of the Courts and Court Officers Act 2002, and s 11 of the Court of Appeal Act 2014, provide that 'a person shall be qualified for appointment as a judge of the Supreme Court or the Court of Appeal or the High Court if the person is for the time being a practising barrister or practising solicitor of not less than 12 years standing who has practised as a barrister or a solicitor for a continuous period of not less than two years immediately before such appointment'.

11 Order 84 (n 4) Rule 18(2) An injunction is sought to either prevent an action or compel someone to do something.

12 ibid. Declarations and injunctions are remedies that fall under the law of equity. Declarations are, according to the Law Reform Commission, a 'modern remedy' which originated in section 155 of the Chancery (Ireland) Act 1867, Working Paper No. 8-1979, 'Judicial Review of Administrative Action: The Problem of Remedies', (December 1979) [2.23] <https://www.lawreform.ie/_fileupload/consultation%20 papers/wpjudicialreviewadminaction.html> accessed 18 May 2024. A declaration is where the parties to the action seek a judge's declaration on the rights of the parties involved in the case.

13 Ord 84 (n 4), r 25(1).

14 Ord 84 (n 4), r 20(5).

15 Ord 84 (n 4), r 21(1). Rule 21(3) provides that extensions of this time limit are available but only where the Court is satisfied that (a) there is good and sufficient reason for doing so and (b) the circumstances that resulted in the failure to make the application for leave within the period mentioned either (i) were outside the control of, or (ii) could not reasonably have been anticipated by the applicant.

16 Ord 84 (n 4), r 20(1). The Citizen's Information website provides the following definition of ex parte: 'A Latin term meaning "by or for one party". An ex parte court application is one where only one party is present. Often the other side will have a right to apply to have the ruling set aside', see 'Legal terms explained' <https://www.citizensinformation.ie/en/justice/legal-terms-explained/#l7422d> accessed 18 May 2024.

17 [2000] 1 ILRM 391, 397.

18 Ord 84 (n 4), r 24(1).

of the application itself, thereby short-circuiting the two-stage process. This may be done with the consent of all parties on the application of one of the parties where 'there is good and sufficient reason for so doing and it is just and equitable in all the circumstances'.[19]

Judicial Review and Sports Governing Bodies in Ireland

11–06 Typically, sport is considered to be a private activity and, as such, is regulated by private law. However, the public law will intervene in situations especially where there is an allegation of a breach of natural justice. A sportsperson who is aggrieved by a decision of their governing body may initially view the courts as the most appropriate forum to resolve their dispute. There are merits to seeking redress in the courts. As Little and Morris note, judicial intervention embodies a 'copper bottomed guarantee of ultimate justice for individual sportsmen embroiled in stormy long running (invariably disciplinary) disputes with their governing bodies'.[20] In other situations, it is much more beneficial for the sportsperson and the sporting organisation to seek to resolve their dispute without recourse to the courts, as discussed in detail in Chapter 12. As this chapter will discuss, several sports-related cases have come before the Irish courts in the last two decades.[21] While these cases have resulted in judicial intervention into decisions of sports governing bodies, the judges have often alluded to alternative methods of dispute resolution. Judges have recommended that sports governing bodies should exhaust the relevant internal disciplinary mechanisms of the sport and instead of seeking redress in the courts, the matter should be resolved using arbitration or mediation.

The Contractual Relationship Between Sports Governing Bodies and Sportspersons

11–07 At the outset it is important to distinguish judicial review of statutory bodies (such as those established in Ireland in the horseracing and greyhound industries) and the judicial scrutiny of sports bodies, which is often done on a private law (contractual) basis by way of a plenary summons.[22] In invoking the law of contract, the sportsperson will argue that the decision reached by the governing body is tainted

---

19 Ord 84 (n 4), r 24(2).

20 Philip Morris and Gavin Little, 'Challenging Sports Bodies' Determinations' (1998) 17 Civil Justice Quarterly 128, 129.

21 The Supreme Court in *O'Connell & Lambe v Turf Club* [2015] IESC 57 upheld the decision of McGovern J. Of significance is O'Donnell J's discussion of the history of sport and the importance of the rules of sport, see [1]-[10].

22 'The plenary summons is intended to be followed by exchange of pleadings and a trial on oral evidence, and the summons is endorsed only with the relief claimed': McCann Fitzgerald, 'A Guide to Litigation in Ireland' (2016) 6 <https://www.mccannfitzgerald.com/uploads/Litigation_in_Ireland_-_An_Overview.pdf> accessed 18 May 2024.

with procedural unfairness 'such that the implication of a contractual duty to act fairly has been breached'.[23] There are a number of English decisions that illustrate the contractual relationship between athletes/ trainers and sports governing bodies and the need for decisions to be fair and reasonable. In *Law v National Greyhound Racing Club Ltd*, the Court of Appeal held that the rules of the sporting organisation applied provided that those who participated were deemed to have submitted to the rules and jurisdiction of that sport.[24] Law was a trainer who had his licence suspended by the Stewards of the National Greyhound Racing Club. The trainer contended that the actions of the Stewards constituted 'a breach of the implied term of the agreement between the plaintiff and the defendants [such] that all actions taken by the Stewards which could deprive the plaintiff of his licence, would be reasonable and fair and made on reasonable grounds'.[25]

In agreeing that the appeal should be dismissed, Lord Justice (LJ) Fox asserted: **11–08**

> Accordingly, in my view, the authority of the Stewards to suspend the licence of the plaintiff derives wholly from a contract between him and the defendants. I see nothing to suggest that the defendants have rights or duties relating to members of the public as such. What the defendants do in relation to the control of greyhound racing may affect the public, or a section of it, but the defendants' powers in relation to the matters with which this case is concerned are contractual.[26]

Similarly, in *Korda v International Tennis Federation* (ITF), a tennis player was held to be in a contractual relationship with the governing body in relation to its disciplinary jurisdiction.[27] Korda tested positive for the prohibited substance nandrolone and was banned for one year by the Independent Anti-Doping Review Board, who found that Korda was in breach of the ITF's anti-doping rules. Korda appealed his ban and forfeiture of prize money and ranking points achieved at Wimbledon to the ITF's Appeals Committee. The Appeals Committee concurred with Korda, who had claimed that he had unknowingly ingested the prohibited substance and it overturned the one-year suspension **11–09**

---

[23] Jack Anderson, *Modern Sports Law: A Textbook* (2010 Hart) 28.

[24] [1983] 3 All ER 300. In this case, the defendants, the National Greyhound Racing Club, appealed the decision of Walton J of the Chancery Division. Walton J had refused to strike out the plaintiff's action for want of jurisdiction. Law sought to have the suspension declared void on grounds that the Stewards had acted *ultra vires* their powers.

[25] ibid [1].

[26] ibid.

[27] *Korda v ITF Ltd* (t/a The International Tennis Federation) [1999] APP LR 03/25. This was an appeal from the High Court, *Korda v ITF Ltd* [1999] 3 WLUK 452. In the High Court, Lightman J made a declaration that the ITF was not entitled to appeal the decision of the Appeals Committee to the CAS; however, he granted the ITF leave to appeal. As a declaration was granted, the injunction sought by Korda was not granted. The Court of Appeal allowed the ITF to appeal.

on grounds that there were exceptional circumstances. The rules provided that the Appeals Committee could reduce the sanction if the player could show that on the balance of probabilities, there were exceptional circumstances. The rules defined exceptional circumstances 'as circumstances where the player did not know that he had taken or been administered the relevant substance provided that he had acted reasonably in all the relevant circumstances'.[28] The ITF lodged an appeal to the CAS on the grounds that the Appeals Committee had erroneously applied 'exceptional circumstances'. Korda sought an injunction from the High Court to prevent the ITF lodging the appeal to the CAS. He contended that he was not contractually bound by the rules of the ITF and, if he were, the rules did not provide for an appeal to the CAS on these grounds. The High Court acknowledged that there was no written or oral agreement between Korda and the IFT; however, it was inferred from the conduct of the parties, including the player submitting a urine sample.[29]

11–10 According to Lord Denning in *Lee v The Showman's Guild of Britain*, the jurisdiction of 'domestic tribunals' was based in contract and such tribunals must comply with the rules of fairness.[30] While not a sports case, the situation is analogous to the contractual relationship between a sportsperson and their governing body. Lee, a travelling showman, was a member of the Showman's Guild of Britain and he had been offered a place at a fairground for his roundabout show. However, it was subsequently re-allocated to another member of the Guild who had occupied the spot prior to World War II.[31] Both men turned up to the fairground and an argument ensued. The Guild imposed a fine on Lee. Lee refused to pay the fine and was expelled from the Guild. He sought an injunction against the Guild on the grounds that his right to earn a livelihood was restricted. In the trial court, the injunction was granted by Ormerod J. The Court of Appeal upheld the decision of Ormerod J. Lord Denning held:

> The jurisdiction of a domestic tribunal, such as the committee of the Showmen's Guild, must be founded on a contract, express or implied. Outside the regular courts of this country, no set of men can sit in judgment on their fellows except so far as Parliament authorizes it or the parties agree to it. The jurisdiction of the committee of the Showmen's Guild is contained in a written set of rules to which all the members subscribe.

---

[28] ibid [10].

[29] For an interesting discussion on fair procedures and the ITF, see Ben Livings and Karolina Wlodarczak, 'Procedural Fairness in the International Tennis Federation's Disciplinary Regime' (2020) 18(1) Entertainment and Sports Law Journal 1.

[30] [1952] 2 QB 329; [1952] 1 All ER 1175.

[31] The re-allocation was based on a provision of a war-emergency rule. Rule 26 provided that '(i) All members of the Guild shall have the option of again taking up their pre-war positions at all fairs at the termination of the present war, or before, providing that the section committees are satisfied that such claim is justifiable': [1952] 2 QB 329, 330.

> This set of rules contains the contract between the members and is just as much subject to the jurisdiction of these courts as any other contract.[32]

Anderson adds that the 'legal nexus is crucial, both in a procedural and substantive sense' and, using *Modahl v British Athletic Federation (No 2)*[33] as an example, it is imperative to consider the nature of the contractual relationship between the sportsperson and their club and the relevant national and international governing body.[34] In the absence of a contract, the claimant will be unable to claim for damages.[35] If there is no contractual relationship between the parties, judicial review 'may be the *only* procedure available to the applicant'.[36] 11–11

Public Body

For judicial review of a decision of a sports governing body to be possible, it must be a public body. If it is not a public body, any dispute about a decision made by such a body would need to proceed on the basis of a private action, as discussed above. The case of *Murphy v The Turf Club* is an example where the Court held that the sport's regulatory body was not a public body.[37] Barr J held that judicial review was not possible due to the consensual contractual relationship of the respondent and the applicant and 'in purporting to revoke the applicant's licence, the respondent was not executing a public law function'.[38] However, in a more recent case, *O'Connell & Lambe v The Turf Club*, the Turf Club was found to be a public body as it had been placed on a statutory footing by way of the Irish Horseracing Industry Act 1994.[39] McGovern J, in the High Court, held that the Turf Club was now amenable to judicial review as its decisions could no longer be seen as arising only from a private law contract.[40] Thus, it would seem that if an organisation has its origins in statute, it will be held to be a public body. In the Irish context, judicial review may be available to private bodies that operate in the public domain and occupy a monopolistic position rather there being 11–12

---

32 ibid 341.
33 [2001] EWCA Civ 1447; [2002] 1 WLR 1192.
34 Anderson (n 23) 29.
35 ibid.
36 Neville Cox and Alex Schuster (with Cathryn Costello), *Sport and the Law* (Firstlaw 2004) 30.
37 [1989] IR 171.
38 ibid 173–74.
39 See [2014] IEHC 175 (n 21). The Turf Club was the racing regulatory body in Ireland until it was replaced by the Irish Horseracing Regulatory Board (IHRB). The IHRB was established by the Turf Club and Irish National Hunt Steeplechase Committee (INHSC). It has been in operation since 1 January 2018. The IHRB is the Irish equivalent of the British Horseracing Authority (BHA). Section 10 of the Horse Racing Ireland Act 2016 amended s 36 of the Irish Horseracing Industry Act 1994 to empower the Turf Club and the INHSC to set up limited companies to carry out regulatory functions.
40 ibid [19].

consensual relationships with their members.[41] In such situations, the organisation's decisions 'may be judicially reviewed even where the source of its power is non-statutory'.[42]

11–13 There seems to be a lack of clarity in Irish law as the courts 'have intervened to ensure fair procedure, but there appears to have been no systematic analysis on which this has been done'.[43] O'Connor, in reference to a number of cases, contends that the Irish courts seem to have assumed an implied power to intervene on the basis of the type of decision involved without assessing fully whether the organisation and the decision qualify as ones which should be amenable to judicial review.[44]

11–14 Apart from sports bodies which are created by way of statute, most sporting organisations in Ireland are private and voluntary associations. Traditionally the approach in Ireland was that only decisions made by public bodies (which include sports bodies created by statute) were challengeable by way of judicial review.[45] However, in the case of *Beirne v Commissioner* of *An Garda Síochána*, Flood J held that where the duty being carried out by a decision-making authority is of a nature which might ordinarily be seen as coming within the public domain then judicial review is applicable.[46] However, the inverse is that judicial review is not possible in situations when the decision is 'solely and exclusively derived from an individual contract made in private law'.[47] This was cited with approval in *O'Connell & Lambe v The Turf Club*:

> Since the Respondent is incorporated in the Racing Regulatory Body, it would seem to follow that it must be amenable to judicial review because its decisions can no longer be considered as '... solely and exclusively derived from an individual contract made in private law'.[48]

11–15 The question has risen whether private bodies should be subject to

---

41 Cox and others (n 36) 32.

42 ibid. Cox and others add that in the case of a public body making a decision that is private in nature, the appropriate action will be a private action by way of plenary summons.

43 Tim O'Connor, 'Rugby Discipline and the Courts: Going Through the Phases?' (2013) 4 Bar Review 75, 78–79.

44 ibid 79–80. O'Connor gives the following case examples: *Clancy v Irish Rugby Football Union (IRFU) and Dawson* [1995] 1 ILRM 195; *Barry v Rogers & Allen & Others* [2005] 4 JIC 1301; *Moloney v Bolger* [2009] 9 JIC 0601; *JRM Sports t/a Limerick Football Club* (n 21); *Conway v Irish Tug of War Association and Others* [2011] IEHC 245.

45 Cox and others (n 36) 31.

46 [1993] ILRM 1, 2. The applicant sought judicial review after his employment as a trainee Garda was terminated. Beirne was deemed to have engaged in behaviour that amounted to misconduct on a bus that was travelling from Dublin to Templemore, the Garda Training College. Flood J found that the applicant had not been afforded fair procedures and awarded the relief sought.

47 ibid 2.

48 [2014] IEHC 175 (n 21) [19].

judicial scrutiny in the absence of government control.[49] One response to the question in England and Wales has been: 'If they did not exist, the government might have to invent them.'[50] Beloff and Kerr contend that the 'correct question is whether government would intervene and regulate *if no one else did*'.[51] The Master of the Rolls (MR) Bingham in *R v Disciplinary Committee of the Jockey Club, ex parte Aga Khan* referred to the applicant's arguments in relation to the status of Jockey Club in the following manner:

> Its powers are of a nature and scope which affect the public. It matters not that it is a private body: that is an accident of history. What matters is that if it or some other private body did not perform the functions it does the government would be obliged to create a body to perform those functions.[52]

The application for judicial review was denied as the Jockey Club was deemed to be a private body, as Hoffmann LJ held that 'there is no public source for any of its powers. It operates directly or indirectly by consent.'[53] The decision has been criticised as flawed; however, 'English law is settled in its view' that sports governing bodies are 'not amenable' to judicial review.[54] Beloff and others assert that 'it is not clear that the last word has been said on the subject'.[55] Since the 1990s, the increased involvement of the government in sporting matters has imbued a public function in sports governing bodies. In *R v Panel on Take-overs and Mergers, ex parte Datafin PLC*,[56] Lloyd LJ held: 'If the body in question is exercising public law functions, or if the exercise of its functions has public law consequences, then that may … be sufficient to bring the body within the reach of judicial review.'[57] The Panel of Take-overs and Mergers contended that it was a self-regulated private body in which its powers were based on consent of those over whom it exercised its power. However, the Court of Appeal disagreed and found the Panel performed public duties and was under an obligation to act judicially and thus subject to judicial review. **11–16**

As with the position in England and Wales, a sporting body in Ireland may not be public in nature but, given its importance in the lives of its members and taking a more holistic view, ie the impact it has on the **11–17**

49 David Gwynn Morgan, *Hogan and Morgan's Administrative Law* (4th edn, Thomson Reuters 2012) 619.
50 ibid.
51 Michael Beloff and Tim Kerr, 'Why Aga Khan Is Wrong' (1996) 1(1) Judicial Review 30, 31.
52 [1993] 1 WLR 909, 915. For a detailed discussion on the challenging decisions of non-state bodies under English law, see Morgan (n 49).
53 [1993] 1 WLR 909, 931.
54 Ben Cisneros, 'Challenging the Call: Should Sports Governing Bodies Be Subject to Judicial Review?' (2020) 20 The International Sports Law Journal 18, 18.
55 Michael Beloff and others, *Sports Law* (2nd edn, Bloomsbury Publishing 2012) IX.
56 [1987] QB 815, [1987] 1 All ER 564, [1987] 2 WLR 699.
57 [1987] QB 815, 847.

community, it may be subject to judicial scrutiny. Thus, there is a public interest that warrants the intervention of the courts.

Procedures Involved in Making the Decision

11–18 There are three broad areas of activity in which fair procedures should be observed by the sports governing body or club: in the creation of the rules; in the application of the rules; and in the operation of a disciplinary process conducted pursuant to such rules.[58] The Irish courts have made clear that, as with all cases of judicial review, it is the procedures involved in the decision and not the decision itself which should be the subject of the review. Thus, the courts will assess whether the decision is one which the organisation was entitled to make according to its rules and that the applicant was given an appropriate opportunity to be heard without bias. It will not overturn a decision because the judge would have come to a different conclusion based on the facts.[59]

11–19 The fact that judicial review is only available in relation to the procedures employed in making a decision and not its merits was again re-iterated in *Jacob v Irish Amateur Rowing Union Ltd*, a case involving an oarsman who was not selected as part of the team to compete in a competition to qualify for the 2008 Olympics in Beijing.[60] The Court refused to grant the relief sought as there was no evidence of a lack of fairness in the procedures involved in making the decision not to allow him to complete in the qualifying event. The Court noted that the applicant had the benefit of two internal appeals, and there was no evidence to suggest that it would be unjust to refuse the injunction. Laffoy J emphasised that team selection is not an issue for the courts:

> it is pertinent to ask whether it is appropriate at all, in the absence of proof of mala fides, for a court to intervene in a decision of an organisation governing a particular sport as to matters of selection and de-selection for competitive events of team members based on performance and fitness. The court has been referred to cases in which the courts in this jurisdiction and in the United Kingdom have intervened, or been prepared to intervene, to overrule the decision of a sporting organisation, but the focus of such interventions has primarily been concerned with the conduct of disciplinary proceedings, frequently involving drug testing.[61]

11–20 Laffoy J made clear that unless there was bad faith on the part of the organisation 'or some obvious egregious injustice' to the applicant, it would be difficult to justify the intervention of the court.[62] The case

58 Cox and others (n 36) 59.
59 See *JRM Sports Ltd t/a Limerick Football Club v Football Association of Ireland* [2007] IEHC 67. This case concerned the tightening up of licences for clubs in the domestic league to improve the professionalism of Irish soccer.
60 [2008] 4 IR 731 (n 21).
61 ibid 742.
62 ibid.

of *Quirke v Bord Luthchleas na hÉireann* (BLÉ) was cited with approval in *Jacob*.[63] Quirke was a shot-putter who was competing at a national championship meeting. The championship took place on 25–26 July 1987. The BLÉ was the national governing body responsible for the development, promotion, control, and management of amateur athletics in Ireland and it was affiliated to the International Amateur Athletics Federation (IAAF) and thus bound by the rules and regulations of the international federation (IF).[64]

In accordance with the rules of the IAAF, the BLÉ carried out drug testing at the championship. Quirke competed internationally and was selected to provide a urine sample. He asked if he could return to the track to collect his belongings, which he was permitted to do; however, he did not return to the doping control centre. A few days later he contacted the BLÉ to explain his absence and he was advised to write a letter outlining the reasons for his failure to provide the sample. Quirke wrote the letter and a few weeks later received a letter from the BLÉ informing him that he was being suspended for 18 months. The applicant complained that had he been told of the consequences of not providing the sample, he would have returned, and that this information should have been provided. Accordingly, he was alleging that there was a breach of fair procedures in how his case was handled by the BLÉ and requested an order of certiorari by way of judicial review. Barr J granted the relief sought by Quirke. The judge emphasised the 'substantial penalty' involved in the case, the suspension of an international athlete from all major competitions for 18 months resulting in Quirke being unable to compete in the Olympics, as well as the 'moral implications of its imposition' which would remain even after the penalty expired.[65] Barr J found that the applicant should have been allowed to put forward a defence before the sanction was imposed. Therefore, there was a breach of fair procedures, and the suspension was overturned. However, Barr J noted that this did not preclude the BLÉ from re-opening the matter as long as the applicant was given the opportunity to put his side of the case in any future disciplinary procedure.[66] **11–21**

There are no minimum requirements for what constitutes fair procedures. It will vary from case to case and must be judged on a contextual analysis of the situation. It would seem that the level of fair procedures to which an individual is entitled will primarily depend on the severity of the consequences of such decision for them, as **11–22**

---

63 [1988] IR 83.

64 The BLÉ is now known as Athletics Ireland and the IAAF is now known as World Athletics.

65 [1988] IR 83, 88.

66 The case of *Quirke* was distinguished in the case of *Gould v McSweeney and Others* [2007] IEHC 5 as *Quirke* was deemed to be a case of public rights and the issue of the athlete's livelihood was an important consideration for the Court. *Gould* was held not to be a case of judicial review.

demonstrated in *Quirke*.[67] In a case involving a plagiarism by a student, *Flanagan v UCD*, Barron J held:

> Matters to be considered are the form in which the complaint should be made, the time to be allowed for the person to prepare a defence, and the nature of the hearing at which the complaint may be presented. In addition, depending upon the gravity of the matter, the person concerned may be entitled to be represented and may also be entitled to be informed of their rights. Clearly matters of a criminal nature must be treated more seriously than matters of a civil nature, but ultimately the criterion must be the consequences for the person concerned of an adverse verdict.[68]

11–23 As well as adhering to fair procedures, it is also important that sports organisations apply the rules of that organisation strictly and do not make decisions that are *ultra vires*. The importance of a sporting organisation adhering closely to its internal rules and procedures is evident in *Clancy v Irish Rugby Football Union (IRFU) and Dawson*, where the IRFU introduced eligibility rules which applied retrospectively.[69] McCutcheon notes that this decision makes clear that sports associations 'must implement their rules to the letter, especially where a player's interests are potentially affected by the implementation of the rule in question'.[70]

11–24 Another case which demonstrates the importance of a sporting organisation following its rules and internal processes is *Dundalk AFC Interim Co Ltd v FAI National League*.[71] This case concerned the potential relegation of Dundalk AFC from the premier division of the Football Association of Ireland (FAI) National League to the first division and the allegation of fielding of an ineligible player by the third-placed team. Ultimately, it was held that the player had been properly registered and hence no breach had been committed by the third-placed team. Accordingly, the problem relating to the failure to adhere to the internal procedures was rendered moot. However, the case provides an important reminder that 'a governing body and by extension a club, once it has created its rules must follow them'.[72]

11–25 A more recent case involving a claim of *ultra vires* action on the part of a sports organisation is *Byrne v Irish Sports Council*.[73] The applicant was a member of the Irish Sports Council (ISC), now known as Sport Ireland. Allegations of a breach of the Code of Conduct in relation to conflict of interest and inappropriate interference with funding decisions were made against him. After a meeting of ISC members of which the

---

67 Cox and others (n 36) 74.
68 [1988] ILRM 724 [19].
69 [1995] 1 ILRM 193 (n 44).
70 Paul McCutcheon, 'Judicial Scrutiny of Sports Administration' (1995) 13 Irish Law Times 171, 175.
71 [2001] 1 IR 434.
72 Cox and others (n 36) 64.
73 [2013] IEHC 438.

applicant was not permitted to attend, a unanimous decision was taken to launch an independent investigation into the allegations and to obtain a report on the findings. The applicant alleged that the action of calling an independent investigation was *ultra vires*. After examining the Irish Sports Council Act 1999, Peart J concluded that the ISC did not have the power to take such action and that the launch of such an investigation and that the decision to remove a ISC member could only be taken by the Minister by virtue of s 13(2) of Irish Sports Council Act 1999. Thus, the decision to appoint an independent investigator was quashed. The applicant also alleged a breach of fair procedures as he was not given access to material relating to the allegations against him. Since the Court found in favour of the applicant on the *ultra vires* issue, it was unnecessary to assess the fair procedures point. However, the judge noted that the material should have been provided to him, and that he should have been given an opportunity to make representations to the ISC meeting where the decision to appoint the independent investigator was taken.

Although judicial review is typically not available in relation to the merits of the decision, it is possible to challenge a decision of a sporting body through judicial review on the basis that it was irrational. However, whilst this is analogous to a review on the merits, the threshold of proof is very high on this ground and, in reality, what an applicant must show in this instance is that the decision is so perverse that it suggests that fair procedures could not have been adhered to in reaching it.[74] In the case of *Matthews v The Irish Coursing Club & Hogan* it was held that in order to prove that a decision is so unreasonable as to warrant being overturned, 'the test of unreasonableness lies in whether the impugned decision flies in the face of common sense or is so unreasonable as to be perverse'.[75] This case concerned a greyhound that tested positive for banned substances contrary to Rule 88 of the Rules of the Irish Coursing Club. The notice party, Hogan, was the owner of the greyhound that was found to have been drugged. Matthews' greyhound was the runner up. The Irish Coursing Club did not disqualify Hogan's dog, nor did it declare Matthews's dog the winner.[76] Matthews had entered two dogs, with an entry fee of £100 per dog, into the Irish Cup meeting. The winner of the race would win a trophy and £8,000 in prize money. The winning dog would also be in demand for breeding, given that it was the most important race in the Coursing Club's calendar.[77] 11–26

74 [1993] 1 IR 346.

75 ibid 347.

76 ibid 352. The Executive Committee of the Irish Coursing Club imposed a 50% reduction in the prize money, subject to a minimum of a fine of £1,000. Penalties were not imposed on the greyhound who had tested positive. Initially, in the hearing before the sub-committee, the greyhound was suspended 'from racing, coursing and stud' for a few months (until 1 January 1991) but Hogan appealed the penalties and received only a financial sanction.

77 ibid 356.

11–27 The Court established that the Irish Coursing Club was a statutory body exercising important public duties.[78] O'Hanlon J accepted that the Executive Committee in its endeavours to show leniency to Hogan, 'was manifestly unjust in relation to the applicant's rights in the matter'.[79] The judge referred to the principal act that governed activities of the Irish Coursing Club, the Greyhound Industry Act 1958. He cited the long title of the act to demonstrate its role and obligations: 'An Act to provide for the improvement and development of the greyhound industry, greyhound racing and coursing, and for the better control of greyhound racetracks and coursing grounds'. Hence, in permitting 'a "doped" dog to retain the premier award of the year in the coursing calendar', appeared to O'Hanlon J, 'to be so completely at variance with those objectives as to be unsustainable'.[80]

11–28 As discussed, judicial review typically deals with the procedures involved in the decision-making process and not the merits of the decision. O'Hanlon J held that this case was 'one of the infrequent cases where the intervention of the court may legitimately be invoked to challenge the validity of a decision made by an administrative tribunal'.[81] For an applicant arguing that a decision is irrational, it requires a very high threshold of proof and, as such, it is a ground that is not usually invoked in judicial review cases.

11–29 The above cases demonstrate that whilst the courts will not review a decision of a sporting body lightly, there is still space for intervention where the principle of natural justice has been breached. Therefore, sporting organisations should be very careful to ensure that rules are fairly created and adhered to, particularly where significant decisions such as those relating to discipline are concerned. Similarly, although it will be a very rare case where a decision will be held to be so unreasonable or irrational as to warrant being rendered invalid in judicial review proceedings, sporting organisations should take care to ensure that any decisions reached are fully justifiable.

Judicial Review: Only in the Most Exceptional of Circumstances

11–30 It is evident from the case law on judicial review that judicial intervention in the decisions of sporting organisations should only occur in the most exceptional of situations and should be seen as a measure of last resort. For the most part, decisions made by governing bodies are immune from judicial scrutiny. However, there are situations where the courts

[78] ibid 354.
[79] ibid 358.
[80] ibid 358.
[81] ibid 358. There have been recent developments in judicial review and the limits of the executive power: see Oran Doyle, 'Executive Power and its Limits: *Burke v Minister for Education* [2022] IESC 1' in Sarah Hamill (ed), *Irish Supreme Court Review*, vol 5 (Clarus Press 2023).

will become involved and as a result the determination of the sports governing body will be subject to judicial review.

In the same vein as the Irish approach, Popplewell J in *Modahl v British Athletic Federation (No 1)* held that 11–31

> generally a court will not interfere with the findings of fact by an independent tribunal, because an independent tribunal is somebody who has the experience of matter. But it does have a right to interfere where a point of law is involved, or where there is alleged to be a breach of natural justice.[82]

The Court of Appeal of England and Wales decision in *Modahl v British Athletic Federation (No 2)*[83] was cited in the case of *Conway v Irish Tug of War Association and Others*.[84] The *Conway* case concerned an allegation of the wearing of non-compliant shoes by a team at the International Indoor Championship in February 2006. Disciplinary sanctions were levied against St Pat's, resulting in the IF banning the club for two years, with the second year suspended, and a fine of €1,000. An important issue that arose in the case was that of the contractual relationship between Conway, the club secretary, and the IF. Conway did not raise the contract issue; her claim was based on tort, although her Statement of Claim did not identify how the actions of the respondents constituted a tort as recognised under Irish law. It was contended that the IF was comprised of the national associations and not of individual clubs or individuals. This was provided for in Constitution of the IF. Consequently, the 11–32

[82] [1996] Lexis Citation 5737, page 8 of a 15-page judgment. Popplewell J's decision was appealed to the Court of Appeal (Civil Division) where Modahl's appeal was dismissed, see *Modahl v British Athletic Federation (No 1)* [1997] 7 WLUK 561. For the House of Lords' judgment, see *Modahl v British Athletic Federation (No 1)* [1999] 7 WLUK.

[83] [2001] EWCA Civ 1447. Modahl was drug tested after an event in Lisbon and her urine sample showed high levels of testosterone. She was banned for four years by the Disciplinary Committee of the British Athletic Federation (BAF). The members of the Disciplinary Committee were chosen by an independent Drugs Advisory Committee. Modahl appealed this decision and furnished evidence that was not presented in the initial hearing. Her suspension was lifted. Modahl sued the BAF for breach of contract and sought damages for loss of earnings for the period she was under suspension. She contended that the BAF was in breach of contract as there was an implied contract between her and the BAF, including the conditions that the BAF's 'Drugs Advisory Committee would take all reasonable steps to ensure that those who sat as members of the Disciplinary Committee were free from bias, and that the appellant would have a fair and impartial hearing before the Disciplinary Committee', [4]. The BAF denied there was such a contract, and that the Disciplinary Committee hearing was conducted without bias and was fair. While the Court of Appeal held that there was a contractual relationship between Modahl and the BAF, it had not been breached. In dismissing her claim for damages, the Court of Appeal distinguished between 'a loss of chance' and a real and substantial loss: [135]. The losses Modahl may have suffered due to her period of ineligibility were speculative. The Court of Appeal also rejected the claim that the Disciplinary Committee was biased.

[84] [2011] IEHC 245 (n 44).

respondents argued that Conway enjoyed neither a contractual nexus with the IF as individual participant nor as a Club representative.

11–33 Counsel for the respondents endeavoured to rely on the judgment of Mance LJ in *Modahl v British Athletic Federation Ltd (No 2)*.[85] The respondents referred to the part of the judgment where Mance LJ contended that there was no contractual agreement between Modahl and the IAAF. The relevant paragraph cited by counsel for the respondents is as follows:

> I do not consider that it is necessary to seek to determine what relationship was between the appellant and the IAAF, and whether that was in any respect contractual. The appellants' relationship with her own national federation was, on any view, much closer than any with the IAAF. The IAAF rules can, it seems to me, be viewed as directed primarily at national federations. Any relationship which the appellant had with the IAAF is even more sparsely evidenced than that which she had with the respondents. Making the assumption, which I am for the present purposes quite prepared to do, that she had no contractual relationship with the IAAF, that does not preclude or change my conclusion that a contract came into existence with the respondents. An absence of complete contractual protection, if that be the right analysis, is no reason for refusing to recognise the existence of limited contractual protection, if the circumstances indicate that conclusion. As the facts of the present case show, the handling of any alleged incident of doping, wherever it occurred, would devolve upon the respondents.[86]

11–34 The Court of Appeal held that Modahl had a contractual relationship with the IF, the IAAF. Although there was no express contract with Modahl, the national governing body, the British Athletic Federation (BAF), was contractually obliged to appoint unbiased members of a disciplinary hearing. Laffoy J held that *Modahl* was of limited assistance to the present case; however, she did refer to the observations of Mance LJ as '*obiter*'.[87] Had the *Modahl* case been of more relevance to Conway, Laffoy J would have found there to be a contractual relationship between the IF and Conway. The claim was struck out as the proceedings against the respondents were deemed to an abuse of process. Laffoy J emphasised the need for sportspersons and bodies to exhaust the internal disciplinary mechanisms of their sport before going before the courts as she observed that it was 'usual for a court to lean in favour of disputes involving sporting bodies and members being resolved by the relevant internal mechanisms'.[88]

11–35 Echoing the sentiments of Laffoy J, Scott Baker LJ in the case of *Flaherty v National Greyhound Racing Club Limited* made a very valid point as to the use of the internal disciplinary mechanisms when he stated:

---

85 ibid [7.5].
86 (n 83) [95].
87 (n 84) [7.5].
88 ibid [7.8].

> It seems to me inherently unsatisfactory that a hearing before a sporting tribunal lasting between 1 and 2 hours should be followed by a High Court hearing lasting 10 days and an appeal taking up a further day and a half.[89]

Similarly, McGovern J in *O'Connell & Lambe v The Turf Club & Another* stated: **11–36**

> The courts in this jurisdiction and elsewhere have taken the view that the regulation of sporting activities should not, as a general rule, come within the remit of judicial scrutiny but is best left to those organisations themselves.[90]

This case arose from an inquiry of the Turf Club in relation to a jockey and a racehorse trainer – both of whom were licenced by the Turf Club – who were accused of engaging in suspicious betting practices and the jockey was deemed to have failed to ride the horse in such a manner as to allow it to run to its maximum ability in the race, contrary to the Rules of Racing.[91] The Turf Club informed the applicants that the Referrals Committee would consider the matter. On foot of this, the applicants sought judicial review on the following grounds: **11–37**

1. The Turf Club was a public body and thus amenable to judicial review.[92]
2. The Rules of Racing were made *ultra vires* by the Turf Club and/or without jurisdiction and/or otherwise than in accordance with law.[93]
3. That sections 39[94] and/or 45[95] and/or 62[96] of the Irish Horseracing Industry Act 1994, as amended, were unconstitutional in light of Article 15.2.1° of the Constitution.[97]

---

89 [2005] EWCA Civ 117 [19]. For a detailed discussion on judicial review and governing bodies in the English courts, see Jack Anderson, 'An Accident of History: Why the Decisions of Sports Governing Bodies are not Amenable to Judicial Review' (2006) 35(3) Common Law World Review 173.

90 [2014] IEHC 175 (n 21) [36].

91 r 273(ix) of the Rules of Racing and Irish National Hunt Steeplechase Rules 2014 (Office of the Governing Bodies, The Curragh, Co Kildare, 2014).

92 The Irish Horseracing Industry Act 1994 placed it on a statutory footing; prior to this the Turf Club was a voluntary association governed by contract law. The respondents argued that it was a private body and thus not amenable to judicial review.

93 It was contended that the Rules of Racing did not advance principles or policies contained in the legislative scheme and that the Rules of Racing were in breach of the statutory provisions governing horse racing in Ireland, the Irish Horseracing Industry Act 1994, as amended by the Horse and Greyhound Racing Act 2001.

94 This section outlines the functions of the Racing Regulatory Body

95 This section relates to appeals against sanctions of Racing Regulatory Body – s 45(2) states that the Racing Regulatory Body shall provide an appeals procedure and ensure appeals are heard in a fair and impartial manner.

96 This section refers to the exclusion of certain persons from racecourses.

97 'The sole and exclusive power of making laws for the State is hereby vested in the Oireachtas: no other legislative authority has power to make laws for the State.' Section 39 of the 1994 Act, the applicants contended, had failed to impose sufficient limitations upon the purported ability of the Turf Club to issue

4. That sections 39 and/or 45 and/or 62 of the Irish Horseracing Industry Act 1994, as amended, were unconstitutional in light of Articles 34.1[98] and 37[99] of the Constitution.[100]

11–38 McGovern J remarked that 'the application brings into focus the extent to which it is permissible (or desirable) for the courts to intervene in sporting matters'.[101] In first deciding whether or not the Turf Club was a public body, the judge proffered that the respondent was legally 'in a somewhat unusual position'.[102] The Turf Club was founded in 1790 and the Irish National Hunt Steeplechase Committee (INHSC) was established in 1869, both of which are voluntary members' organisations. The Turf Club was responsible for all-Ireland flat, national hunt and point-to-point racing.[103] The 1994 Act did not create either the Turf Club or the INHSC. The 1994 Act created the Racing Regulatory Body, which incorporated the Turf Club and the INHSC; it had jurisdiction over the entire island of Ireland. In referring to the contractual relationship between the respondent and the applicant, McGovern J noted that such a relationship meant that the parties were bound by the Rules of Racing and the rules of INHSC from time to time. However, no such contract existed between members of the public and the respondent and the INHSC, although members of the public could be excluded from certain racing events under the Rules of Racing and under s 32 of the 1994 Act. In addition, the Racing Regulatory Body was empowered to enforce the Rules of Racing and regulate horseracing, thus the regulation of horseracing was placed on a statutory footing in 1994. This was the case at the time even though the pre-1994 Rules which operated based on contract continued to apply.

---

secondary instruments, which resulted in an impermissible derogation of the functions of the legislature.

98 'Justice shall be administered in courts established by law by judges appointed in the manner provided by this Constitution and save in such special and limited cases as may be prescribed by law, shall be administered in public.'

99 arts 37.1 and 2: '1. Nothing in this Constitution shall operate to invalidate the exercise of limited functions and powers of a judicial nature, in matters other than criminal matters, by any person or body of persons duly authorised by law to exercise such functions and powers, notwithstanding that such person or such body of persons is not a judge, or a court appointed or established as such under this Constitution. 2. No adoption of a person taking effect or expressed to take effect at any time after the coming into operation of this Constitution under laws enacted by the Oireachtas and being an adoption pursuant to an order made or an authorisation given by any person or body of persons designated by those laws to exercise such functions and powers was or shall be invalid by reason only of the fact that such person or body of persons was not a judge or a court appointed or established as such under this Constitution.'

100 The applicants argued that these sections of the 1994 Act violated both articles of the Constitution on the grounds that it allowed the Turf Club to exercise judicial functions without apparent limitations.

101 [2014] IEHC 175 (n 21) [6].

102 ibid [13].

103 The Turf Club was the racing regulatory body in Ireland until it was replaced by the Irish Horseracing Regulatory Board (IHRB). See (n 39) for more detail.

In deeming that the applicants had *locus standi* to bring the application for judicial review, the judge examined the delegated legislative functions of the respondent. The judge, in juxtaposing the Rules of Racing and the legislative provisions, observed that the purpose of the 1994 Act (as amended) is 'to promote integrity and fair play in horseracing. Each of the impugned Rules is consistent with and serves that purpose'.[104] In holding that the respondent's powers did not amount to an administration of justice, nor did it exercise a judicial function, the judge dismissed the application for judicial review. McGovern J highlighted the fact that the applicants did not contend there was a lack of fair procedures or a breach of natural justice.[105] In a cautionary tone, the judge reiterated the fact that the applicants had voluntarily submitted themselves to the jurisdiction of the respondent. They had agreed to be bound by the rules and regulations of the sporting organisation. McGovern J, in demonstrating the Court's reluctance to intervene in the decisions of sports bodies, concluded: 'it is difficult to see how this is something which comes within the ambit [of] public law'.[106] **11–39**

The most recent statement on this issue is perhaps the most vehement. In *Hyland v Dundalk Racing (1999) Ltd t/a Dundalk Stadium*, Hogan J noted that the instances where the courts intervene in sporting disputes are 'exceptional involving something akin to fraud or manifest irrationality'.[107] He held: **11–40**

> If it were otherwise, the courts would have assumed a strange new jurisdiction which would test the traditional boundaries of justiciability, and, indeed, raise questions as to the appropriate judicial role in relation to such matters. Could, for example, the courts be expected to adjudicate on questions such as the handicapping of horses, competitor seedings, team selection or on-field disciplinary or refereeing decisions? Could it mean that the courts might subsequently be called upon to rule on questions such as whether a penalty ought to have been given or whether a player was properly sent off or even whether a point, goal or try (as the case may be) ought to have been awarded?[108]

What emerges from these recent judicial review cases is the reluctance of the courts to intervene in the decisions of sports governing bodies. The case law demonstrates that the courts will only become involved in the most exceptional of circumstances. For the most part, the internal disciplinary mechanisms of the sport are best equipped to deal with disputes, and redress to the courts should only occur after the internal processes have been exhausted. The final part of this chapter will discuss a trio of test cases wherein Hogan J highlighted the importance of alternative dispute resolution (ADR). **11–41**

---

[104] [2014] IEHC 175 (n 21) [34].
[105] [2014] IEHC 175 (n 21) [39].
[106] ibid [41].
[107] *Hyland v Dundalk Racing (1999) Ltd t/a Dundalk Stadium* [2014] IEHC 60.
[108] ibid [40].

Trio of Test Cases

11–42 *Hyland* is one of three test cases involving three bookmakers and a racecourse operator.[109] The test cases were heard over a 14-day period as there was overlap with witnesses. The dispute arose from the requirement of a capital contribution of €8,000 from each bookmaker holding a pitch at Dundalk Racecourse. The three applicants all held established seniorities to trade at particular bookmaking pitches at Dundalk Racecourse. Seniority refers to a right of priority that a bookmaker acquires at a particular racecourse. In 2001 the racecourse closed and was refurbished and reopened in August 2007 as Ireland's first all-weather racecourse.[110] On reopening the racecourse, the bookmakers were informed that they were mandated to pay €8,000 each in order for the racecourse to recoup some of the investment amounting to €35m. The bookmakers refused on the grounds that the requirement of €8,000 was in breach of the then Racecourse Executives' Seniority and Pitch Rules (Pitch Rules), resulting in a breach of contract, as the applicants contended that the Pitch Rules constituted a contract between them and the racecourse.[111] The matter was referred to the Pitch Tribunal, which according the Pitch Rules 'shall determine its own procedures provided that same shall comply with the principles of natural justice'.[112] The central issue to be decided was whether the re-furbished Dundalk Racecourse was a new course and if it were considered to be a new course then the Pitch Rules would not apply.[113] The inverse being that if it were considered an existing course then the Pitch Rules would apply, and thus

[109] *Hyland* (n 107); *Hyland v Dundalk Racing (1999) Ltd t/a Dundalk Stadium (No 2)* [2015] IEHC 57; and *O'Hare & Another v Dundalk Racing (1999) Ltd t/a Dundalk Stadium* [2015] IEHC 198. The three test cases refer to three bookmakers: Hyland, the Chairman of the Irish National Bookmakers' Association (INBA), O'Hare and Hughes. The *O'Hare & Another* case also dealt with mitigation of loss and quantum of damages arising from the breach of contract findings in the first *Hyland* case. The cases were brought on behalf of over 30 bookmakers.

[110] All-weather courses attract the best and highest-ranked horses as the fast grass course is safe for such valuable horses and as most tracks abroad are all-weather it would mean that Irish horses would be prepared for these tracks. The traditional turf course limits the number of meetings that can take place, whereas with all-weather there is, in principle, no limitation (with the exception of economic reasons, including TV rights and an insufficient number of horses): see *Hyland* (n 107) [21] and [22].

[111] The Rules were revised in 2011. See *Hyland* (n 107) [7]–[15] for a detailed discussion of the seniority rules.

[112] Paragraph 21(b) of Racecourse Executives' Seniority and Pitch Rules. The rules are available here <https://www.hri.ie/HRI/media/HRI/Racing/Documents/PDFs/levyoffice/Pitch-Rules-effective-from-05-12-2018.pdf> accessed 19 May 2024.

[113] This case dealt with a number of other issues, including: the legality of protests outside the stadium [73]–[91], held to be constitutionally protected under free speech and free assembly); whether the Pitch Rules were anti-competitive and a breach of the Competition Act 2002 [92]–[112], held not to be a restrictive agreement under s 4(1) of the Competition Act 2002) and whether there was a collective trade boycott [113]–[140], held that there was an unlawful boycott and breach of s 4(1) of the Competition Act 2002; Hogan J held it must stop immediately or it would expose the perpetrators to criminal or civil liability and an injunction would be granted by the Court to compel the relevant individuals

the requirement of a financial contribution would amount to a breach of contract. The Pitch Tribunal decided that a financial contribution was required in the event of a new racecourse. However, the Pitch Tribunal did not determine whether Dundalk Racecourse was a new course or not. The decision of the Pitch Tribunal lacked clarity, which resulted in uncertainty for the applicants. In essence, a theoretical question was put to the Pitch Tribunal, one that was not specific to Dundalk Racecourse. The Pitch Tribunal wrote out to the relevant parties recommending that they meet face to face to discuss the matter, which they did; however, the issue could not be resolved. Hogan J held that the Pitch Rules constituted a legally binding contract and that Dundalk Racing had breached the contract by requiring a financial contribution.[114] Hogan J, perhaps more crucially, held that the reopened all-weather racecourse was the same course as it was in 2001 – albeit unrecognisable – and thus the €8,000 could not be lawfully extracted from the bookmakers who held an established seniority at Dundalk Racecourse.

The second *Hyland* case dealt solely with the questions of mitigation of loss and quantum of damages arising from the first judgment.[115] Hogan J emphasised the need for sports governing bodies to seek redress in the form of arbitration or mediation even in cases as complex and exceptional as these. His observations are worth citing in full: **11–43**

> this case – which is, admittedly, in many ways, a very exceptional one – nonetheless illustrates the desirability, where possible, of having complex sporting disputes of this kind resolved either by mediation, or, should such fail, by expert binding adjudication involving the appropriate mix of sporting and legal expertise.
>
> In this jurisdiction, the Disputes Resolution Authority of the Gaelic Athletic Association has led the way with an established corpus of published formal decisions on matters such as the construction of rules, player eligibility, player transfers, fair procedures and penalties for disciplinary infringements. These decisions are nearly always accompanied by extensive legal and quasi-legal reasoning, thus providing for an open and objective method of adjudication of these invariably complex problems.

---

to end the boycott). Hughes had his award of damages reduced by 20% due to his involvement in the illegal boycott.

114 Hogan J held that the Pitch Rules not only regulated the relationship between the individual bookmakers and individual racecourses, but also regulated aspects of the relationship of bookmakers *inter se*. In effect Hogan J held that there was, in the words of Beloff, 'a horizontal matrix of contracts binding each member to all other members': Michael Beloff, Tim Kerr, and Marie Demetriou, *Sports Law* (Hart Publishing 1999) para 2.21.

115 Hyland was awarded €23,929 in damages, [2015] IEHC 57 (n 109) [74]. In *O'Hare* (n 109), Hogan J held that O'Hare was entitled to recover 100% of the losses he suffered in the period from August 2007 to August 2008. However, for the subsequent years, the damages were reduced to 20% owing to the plaintiff's failure to mitigate his own losses. Hogan J noted 'that there was continuing fault on both sides' (see [8] and [9]). The judge awarded €48,376 in damages to O'Hare [77] and €41,484 to Hughes [85].

> All parties to this present dispute might well wish to give consideration to this suggestion and it may be that the Dispute Resolution Authority might yet serve in this regard as a model which might yet guide the Pitch Tribunal for future complex cases of this kind were they ever to arise.[116]

11–44 The significance of the three test cases is twofold. The internal disciplinary procedure showed itself to be inadequate. Had the Pitch Tribunal indicated whether Dundalk Racecourse was a new course or an existing one, the issue would most likely never have come before the Court. Hogan J was most vociferous in his appeal for sportspersons to avail of arbitration or mediation. He explicitly referred to the DRA as a template that other governing bodies could use. The *Hyland* and *O'Hare* cases demonstrate that at times the internal dispute mechanisms are not always equipped to deal with more complex problems; there are times when the courts will be called upon to give an impartial judgment.

Conclusion

11–45 Judicial review can be availed of by sportspersons and sports governing bodies; however, it should only be used in the most exceptional of circumstances. It is evident from the case law that the Irish courts are reluctant to intervene in the decisions of sports governing bodies. Judicial review is a mechanism whereby the decision-making process is scrutinised by the court. The court is not reviewing the merits of the decision made. However, if there is an allegation of irrationality in the decision made by the decision-making body, the court will review the decision. Such cases are quite rare and the threshold of proof that the applicant is required to meet is very high.

11–46 In judicial review cases involving a sports body, there several limitations. The body must either be a public body or a statutory body who exercises public duties. If it is not a public body, any dispute about a decision made by such a body would need to proceed based on a private action. In this situation, the applicant would argue that there is contractual relationship between them and the respondent and that there has been a breach of that contract. Judicial review may be available to private bodies which operate in the public domain, whose powers are not derived under statute and the relationship between them and their members is monopolistic.

11–47 For the most part, the courts do not intervene in the decisions of sporting organisations. Sports governing bodies in Ireland can be primarily confident that their decision-making process will not be subject to judicial scrutiny. Nonetheless, the Irish courts will intervene in the decisions of sports governing bodies where there is an allegation of a breach of natural justice or on a point of law. In several of the cases

[116] [2015] IEHC 57 (n 109) [30] and [31].

discussed, including *Conway*, *Hyland* and *O'Connell*, the judges have highlighted the need for governing bodies to exhaust the internal disciplinary mechanisms within their sports and if that fails, to avail of mediation or arbitration. Mediation and arbitration are alternative forms of dispute resolution. As the next chapter will demonstrate, Irish sports governing bodies who receive funding from Sport Ireland are required to include a mediation and arbitration rule in their rules. As these alternative methods of redress become more engrained in sports governing bodies, this will hopefully result in only the most exceptional cases seeking judicial review.

CHAPTER 12

ALTERNATIVE DISPUTE RESOLUTION

Introduction

Alternative dispute resolution or ADR, as the name suggests, provides an alternative method of resolving disputes, the traditional method being that of litigation through the courts. While the intervention of the courts into the realm of sport has been a welcoming development in some respects, there are limitations and disadvantages. Litigation in the courts is expensive; it may take months for the case to come before the court; and the parties may face adverse publicity. Sports governing bodies have become more amenable to the use of ADR. Instead of seeking redress in the courts, an increasing number of sports have embraced arbitration,[1] negotiation[2] and mediation.[3] Consequently, the use of specialised sports-focused tribunals has assumed greater importance.[4] In Ireland, there are two domestic bodies offering ADR in the sporting context. The first is the Dispute Resolution Authority (DRA), established in 2005 at the Gaelic Athletic Association's (GAA) Congress. The DRA is independent of the GAA. The second body offering mediation and arbitration is Sport Dispute Solutions Ireland (SDSI). It is an independent not-for-profit dispute resolution service that was established by the Federation of Irish Sport. **12–01**

This chapter begins with a discussion on the advantages and disadvantages of sportspersons and bodies seeking redress in the courts. It proceeds to examine the merits and demerits of using alternative methods of dispute resolution. The functions of the DRA and SDSI are detailed, and the chapter concludes with an in-depth look at the history, **12–02**

---

1 Arbitration involves a third party who is given the power impose a decision upon two or more parties who are seeking agreement in relation to an issue that affects the parties involved. For a discussion of the use of arbitration in sport, see Laura Donnellan, 'Player Eligibility and Club Sanctions – The Position in Ireland' (2007) 14(2) Sports Law Administration and Practice 12.

2 Negotiation involves two or more parties seeking to reach an agreement concerning an issue affecting them both. The parties involved have direct control over what is discussed.

3 Mediation is a type of negotiation between two or more parties whereby a mediator facilitates and coordinates the discussion. The mediator may introduce issues for discussion.

4 Arbitration is not appropriate in all situations; it is usually appropriate where there is a dispute between an individual sportsperson and a sports governing body. See Neville Cox and Alex Schuster (with Cathryn Costello) *Sport and the Law* (First Law 2004) 20.

evolution, and role of the Court of Arbitration for Sport (CAS). Some seminal CAS arbitral awards will provide a paradigm through which its *lex sportiva* can be evaluated.

The Benefits of Litigation in the Courts

12–03 Under the Irish Constitution, there is a separation of powers. The legislature drafts legislation, the executive implements legislation, and the judiciary interprets and applies the law. Each institution has a delineated role and must adhere to its limits as provided by the Constitution. In a system of separation of powers, no institution holds all the power. By dividing the power between the three institutions, there is an element of checks and balances.

12–04 However, there is no such separation of powers in sports governing bodies, both national and international. While the governing body may be deemed to be in the best position to regulate its own sport, several sports cases have come before the courts, as documented throughout this book. In 1997, Ebsworth J of the Queen's Bench Division of the High Court delivered her judgment in the case of *Jones and Ebbw Vale Rugby Football Club v The Welsh Rugby Union*.[5] During the match between Ebbw Vale and Swansea, Evans of Swansea stamped on one of Jones' teammates who was on the ground. A fight broke out amongst some of the players and Jones asserted that he became involved to restrain players; however, another Swansea player or players punched Jones. Shortly after the melee, Jones and Evans became engaged in a confrontation involving repeated punches. The referee blew the whistle; however, Jones claimed that the noise of the crowd prevented him from hearing the repeated blows of the whistle. The referee sent Jones off for punching and sent Evans off for stamping and punching. At a subsequent hearing of the Disciplinary Committee of the Welsh Rugby Union (WRU), the plaintiff was sanctioned, *inter alia*, by way of a four-match suspension. Jones challenged the sanction on the ground that he was denied the right to fair procedures in breach of natural justice, namely a refusal to allow him legal representation and the opportunity to present his case at the hearing.[6] The plaintiff's action was based on contract given the private nature of the relationship between the club and the WRU.[7] The plaintiff sought an interlocutory injunction to lift the suspension imposed on him by the WRU pending the conclusion of the disciplinary process. In finding that the balance of convenience favoured the granting of the interim relief, Ebsworth J lifted the suspension. It is

---

5 1997 WL 1103802.

6 The grounds are listed in the appeal decision: *Jones and Ebbw Vale Rugby Football Club v The Welsh Rugby Union* [1997] EWCA Civ 3066.

7 Thus, judicial review was not an option; however, the judge noted that the case was of great public interest.

worth quoting at length the observation of Ebsworth J in relation to the use of the courts to settle sporting disputes. She held:

> There are likely to be many people who take the view that the processes of the law have no place in sport and the bodies which run sport should be able to conduct their own affairs as they see fit and that by and large they have done so successfully and fairly over the years. It is a tempting and attractive view in many ways, particularly to those (and I almost said those of us) who grew up on windy and often half-deserted touchlines. However, sport today is big business. Many people earn their living from it in one way or another. It would, I fear, be naive to pretend that the modern world of sport can be conducted as it used to be not very many years ago.[8]

The WRU appealed Ebsworth J's order; however, the Court of Appeal dismissed the action and disagreed that the judge was erroneous in her decision to find that the relationship between the parties was based on contract.[9] **12–05**

The business of and professionalisation of sport was recognised in *Jones*.[10] What emerges from the case law and *lex sportiva* are principles which the governing bodies must adhere to, as failure to do so may result in litigation. Sports governing bodies must respect the concept of natural justice, including the right to fair procedures and due process, as observed in the *Jones* case.[11] Sports governing bodies are bound by the general principles of fairness and good faith.[12] Governing bodies must not reach a decision that is biased – justice must not only be done but be seen to be done as demonstrated in *Modahl* v *British Athletic Federation (No 2)*.[13] British athlete Diane Modahl tested positive for the banned substance testosterone. The Disciplinary Committee of the British Athletic Federation (BAF) unanimously found that Modahl had committed a doping infraction and banned her for four years. The **12–06**

---

8 *Jones* (n 5).

9 *Jones* (n 6). The subsequent order of Potts J was also appealed; however, the Court upheld that appeal. A second hearing took place under revised discipline regulations and, following the imposition of a 28-day suspension on Jones, the first- and second-named plaintiffs applied *ex parte* for an order which requested that there be no further suspension imposed on Jones until trial or a further order. It also required that the defendant pay costs under this order. Potts J granted the order.

10 *Jones* (n 5).

11 ibid.

12 CAS 2014/A/3828 *Indian Hockey Federation (IHF) v International Hockey Federation (FIH) & Hockey India* award of 17 September 2015 <https://jurisprudence.tas-cas.org/Shared%20Documents/3828.pdf> accessed 19 May 2024. This dispute centred on the autonomy of private associations and membership. The CAS Panel dismissed the action and concluded, 'If the principles of fairness and good faith (among others) are not breached, if (by way of example) no issue of legitimate expectation arises …, if the decision in issue does not appear to have been made arbitrarily, then there are no grounds on which to infringe upon an association's right to autonomy': [154].

13 [2001] EWCA Civ 1447; [2002] 1 WLR 1192.

Discipline Committee consisted of five members who were all members of the defendant's Drugs Advisory Committee. Modahl appealed the decision to an independent appeal panel, who reasoned that there was a possibility that bacterial contamination could have affected the accuracy of the tests. The panel lifted the ban and allowed Modahl to appeal. The case was litigated in the courts, culminating in the decision of the Court of Appeal of England and Wales.[14] Modahl sought compensation on the grounds that she was unable to earn a livelihood from the time of her ban to the acquittal and that members of the Discipline Committee had been biased against her, which constituted a breach of contract on the part of the BAF. There was no written contract, but the Court held that there was an implied contract, and a term of that contract was that the BAF should operate a fair disciplinary process.[15] On the issue of bias, the Court rejected the claim, holding that any bias which allegedly existed at the time of the panel hearing would have been rendered irrelevant by the hearing of the independent appeal panel.[16] Lord Justice (LJ) Latham contended:

> In a case such as the present, where the danger of bias can be evaluated and excluded, I consider that taken together with a wholly untainted appellate process a fair result has been achieved. Any apparent bias on the part of Dr Lucking did not amount to a breach of the obligation on the disciplining body to provide a fair hearing overall.[17]

12–07 Governing bodies must not act unreasonably, capriciously, or arbitrarily, as held in the case of *Nagle v Feilden* where the Court of the Appeal allowed the appeal on the grounds that the Jockey Club's practice of not granting trainers' licences to women was against public policy and an unreasonable restraint of trade.[18]

12–08 Governing bodies must not decide a disciplinary case and issue a sanction without giving the defendant an opportunity to be heard, as demonstrated in the case of *Quirke v Bord Lúthchleas na hÉireann*.[19] An 18-month ban imposed on an Irish athlete for a doping violation was

---

[14] ibid.

[15] The *Modahl* decision relating to implied contracts was recently cited with approval in *Bony v Kacou and Others*, a case involving a premiership football player and his claim to recover an alleged £8m in secret commissions earned by his agents during contract negotiations with Swansea City: see *Wilfried Guemiand Bony v Gilbert Francis Kacou, Gilbert Francis Kacou Promotion SARL, Dalibor Lacina, International Football Marketing & Management SRO, Swansea City Association Football Club Limited* [2017] EWHC 2146 (Ch). It was also cited with approval in *Bradley v Jockey Club* [2004] EWHC 2164 (QB).

[16] [2001] EWCA Civ 1447, 1213 [67]. This was an appeal from the judgment of Douglas Brown J in *Modahl v British Athletic Federation Ltd (No 2)* [2000] 12 WLUK 424.

[17] [2001] EWCA Civ 1447 [67].

[18] [1966] 2 QB 633. See paras 9–105—9–106 of Chapter 9, 'Employment Issues and Sport', for a more detailed discussion on the case.

[19] (1988) IR 83; (1989) ILRM 129. See ch 11 paras 11–20—11–21 for more details on the case.

challenged by way of judicial review in the High Court. The absence of an opportunity afforded to the applicant to present his case before the governing body led Barr J to hold that 'no man shall be condemned unheard', and those who have a duty to act judicially must observe this principle. The suspension was overturned, and Quirke was permitted to return to competition.[20]

The general principles of the right to legitimate expectation and equality of treatment were recognised by the CAS in an arbitral decision involving nine figure skaters at the 2022 Winter Olympics in Beijing.[21] The skaters sought a decision from the Ad Hoc Division (AHD) that the International Olympic Committee (IOC) be compelled to hold a public medal ceremony for the silver winning team before the conclusion of the Winter Olympics. The AHD dismissed the application and upheld the decision of the IOC Executive Board of 14 February 2022, which decided not to hold the medal ceremony for the figure skating team event during the Olympic Games 2022. On 2 February 2022, the figure skaters placed second in the event, with the Russian Olympic Committee (ROC) finishing third and Japan placing first. The medal ceremony was to take place the same day; however, it was decided to hold the ceremony the next day to facilitate all members of the teams attending. On 8 February 2022, the IOC announced that a 'legal issue' prevented the holding of the ceremony. However, it subsequently transpired that one of the ROC team had tested positive for a banned substance, the heart drug trimetazidine, from a sample obtained on 25 December 2021. The athlete's temporary suspension was lifted at their behest by the Russian Anti-Doping Agency (RUSADA) Disciplinary Anti-Doping Committee (DADC). Both the World Anti-Doping Agency (WADA) and the International Skating Union (ISU) appealed the DADC decision **12–09**

---

[20] The CAS has recognised the need for governing bodies to respect the right to fair procedures: for example, see CAS 2011/A/2403 *World Anti-Doping Agency (WADA) v Fédération Internationale de Gymnastique (FIG) & Anastasiya Melnychenko* award of 25 August 2011 <https://jurisprudence.tas-cas.org/Shared%20Documents/2403.pdf> accessed 19 May 2024. The CAS Panel imposed a four-month suspension on a 15-year-old gymnast who tested positive for a prohibited substance. The athlete had been prescribed a three-day course of medication for a furuncle on her nose. While accepting that the athlete bore a high level of responsibility for ensuring that a prohibited substance is not ingested, it must be looked at in a wider context when dealing with an under-age athlete. At [14], the CAS Panel stated that it 'expects that much of the responsibility normally accorded to an athlete must be expected of the athlete's coaches and the Ukrainian National Federation. The particular circumstances of this case mean that a decision relating to the health and welfare of the athlete was required to be taken quickly by the athlete's father.' WADA requested a two-year period of ineligibility but, in light of the 'exceptional circumstances', the CAS Panel considered four months to be an appropriate sanction.

[21] CAS Ad Hoc Division (OG Beijing) 22/011 *Evan Bates, Karen Chen, Nathan Chen, Madison Chock, Zachary Donohue, Brandon Frazier, Madison Hubbell, Alexa Knierim & Vincent Zhou v International Olympic Committee (IOC)* award of 30 March 2022 (operative part of 19 February 2022) <https://jurisprudence.tas-cas.org/Shared%20Documents/OG%2022-011.pdf> accessed 19 May 2024.

to the AHD, requesting that it be set aside. The AHD dismissed the application; however, it stated that the award:

> did not decide whether or not the Athlete, with the status of a Protected Person, committed an anti-doping rule violation ('ADRV'), but whether or not the provisional suspension imposed on the Athlete by RUSADA was to be reinstated.[22]

12–10 Kamila Valieva, the athlete, was 15 years old at the time. The IOC released a statement reiterating the decision of the AHD and as the principle of due process required further investigation, the ceremony would not take place 'in the interests of all athletes' and the National Olympic Committees (NOCs) concerned as it had not yet been established whether the athlete had committed a doping infraction.[23] While sympathetic to the figure skaters in what it described as an 'unfortunate situation', the CAS Panel dismissed the application.[24] It referred to the unprecedented nature of the situation and, as such, the CAS Panel could not find there was a sufficient legal basis to the contention that their right to legitimate expectations meant that the appealed decision should be set aside, nor did it consider the appealed decision to amount to a sanction on the applicants.[25] It came to the same conclusion with regard to the argument based on the principle of equal treatment of the figure skaters.[26] In January 2023, RUSADA found that Valieva had committed a doping infraction; however, she bore 'no fault or negligence' and therefore a four-year period of ineligibility as sought by WADA was not imposed.[27] It only ordered the disqualification of her results on the date of the sample collection, which was 25 December 2021. Three appeals were lodged with the CAS under the appeals arbitration procedure, which involved hearing appeals from WADA, RUSADA and the ISU simultaneously. On 29 January 2024, the CAS decision in *CAS 2023/A/9451 Association Russian Anti-Doping Agency (RUSADA) v Kamila Valieva, CAS 2023/A/9455 International Skating Union (ISU) v Kamila Valieva, Association Russian Anti-Doping Agency (RUSADA), and CAS 2023/A/9456 World Anti-Doping Agency (WADA) v Association Russian Anti-Doping Agency (RUSADA) & Kamila Valieva)* was published.[28] Valieva was found to have committed an anti-doping rule violation (ADRV) and was banned for four years commencing on 25 December 2021.

---

22 ibid [9].
23 ibid [10].
24 ibid [78].
25 ibid [75].
26 ibid [76].
27 World Anti-Doping Agency, 'WADA Statement on Russian Anti-Doping Agency Finding of "No Fault or Negligence" in Case of ROC Figure Skater' (13 January 2023) <https://www.wada-ama.org/en/news/wada-statement-russian-anti-doping-agency-finding-no-fault-or-negligence-case-roc-figure> accessed 19 May 2024.
28 Award of 29 January 2024 <https://www.tas-cas.org/fileadmin/user_upload/9451-9455-9456_Arbitral_Award__publ._.pdf> accessed 19 May 2024.

Sports governing bodies, in applying the doctrine of fair procedures, must consider an appeal *de novo* (anew) and not by way of review of a decision of another body.[29] In *Clancy v Irish Rugby Football Union (IRFU) and Dawson*, the plaintiff sought an injunction to restrain the defendants from declaring him ineligible for playing for his club, Blackrock College Rugby Football Club.[30] The changes were applied retrospectively, meaning that Clancy was prevented from moving to a new club in the next season. He appealed the rule change – however, the appeal tribunal simply reviewed the decision of the disciplinary panel. Morris J was of the view that 'fair procedures would require that the Committee consider the applications de novo and not deal with them on the basis of approving or disapproving the decision of another body'.[31] **12–11**

Disadvantages of Recourse to the Courts

There are a number of disadvantages in seeking redress in the courts. A court case can be very expensive and time-consuming. This point was made by Scott Baker LJ in *Flaherty v National Greyhound Racing Club Limited*: 'it seems to me inherently unsatisfactory that a hearing before a sporting tribunal lasting between 1 and 2 hours should be followed by a High Court hearing lasting 10 days and an appeal taking up a further day and a half'.[32] **12–12**

Often sportspersons can use the courts to evade a ban by seeking injunctive relief, in particular, an interlocutory injunction. An interlocutory injunction is a prohibitory injunction and is a temporary measure that is granted pending the final hearing. The court must consider several criteria, including whether there is a fair question to be tried and whether the balance of convenience (balance of justice) favours the granting of the injunction.[33] In one sporting case, Westmeath GAA player Rory O'Connell applied to the High Court for an interlocutory injunction in order to resume playing for his county, even though he had been suspended following an alleged stamping incident involving an opponent.[34] The incident had been witnessed by the linesman and not the referee, with the referee sending O'Connell off. The interlocutory injunction was granted which allowed O'Connell to be reinstated on the Westmeath team. O'Connell claimed that he had unintentionally injured his opponent after they and a third player had collided. The **12–13**

---

29 For a detailed discussion on the case, see Paul McCutcheon, 'Judicial Scrutiny of Sports Administration' (1995) 13 Irish Law Times 171.

30 [1995] 1 ILRM 193.

31 ibid.

32 [2005] EWCA Civ 111 [19].

33 For more detail on interlocutory injunctions and the principles used by the Irish courts in recent cases, see *Merck Sharp & Dohme Corporation v Clonmel Healthcare Ltd* [2019] IESC 65, [2020] 2 IR 1; and *Bristol-Myers Squibb Holdings Ireland Unlimited Company v Norton (Waterford) Limited T/A Teva Pharmaceuticals Ireland* [2023] IECA 173.

34 *O'Connell v GAA* (2004) Record 2004 105 34 P.

judge emphasised the point that this was an interlocutory hearing and he was not adjudicating on how O'Connell would succeed at the final hearing. However, the case was never heard at full hearing as O'Connell was reinstated and eligible to play for Westmeath in the Leinster Football Final, thus eliminating the need for a full hearing. Similarly, the High Court granted an interlocutory injunction in a case involving David Bardon, a Longford player. Bardon had been banned for six months by the Games Administration Committee (GAC) of the GAA. The injunction allowed Bardon to be reinstated on the team.[35] Anderson refers to the use of interlocutory injunctions in this way as 'ambush injunctions' used as an 'opportunistic legal tactic'.[36]

12–14 The decision of the Court in *O'Connell* to grant the injunction attracted sharp criticism from members of the GAA. Liam Mulvihill, the then director general of the GAA, contended that O'Connell had no right to take the action before the High Court as it created a right of appeal that is not permitted under the GAA rules. He added that players are voluntary members of the GAA and they agree to be bound by the rules of the organisation.[37] However, an attempt to oust the jurisdiction of the court would be deemed unconstitutional. Sportspersons have the right to seek redress in the courts; however, the use of ambush injunctions in situations such as this have been restricted in the United States (US) by way of the Olympic and Amateur Sports Act of 1998.[38] The Act restrains a court from granting injunctive relief against the US Olympic Committee (USOC) pertaining to an athlete's eligibility to compete 21 days in advance of the Olympic Games, the Paralympic Games and the Pan American Games.[39] This amendment in 1998 was a consequence of the Tonya Harding litigation.[40]

---

35 See Laura Donnellan, 'The GAA Disciplinary Procedures and Player Reinstatement?' (2004) 11(6) Sports Law: Administration and Practice 14.

36 Jack Anderson, 'Rushing to Judgment: The Evolution of Sports Disciplinary and Arbitral Bodies in Ireland' (2007) 4(3) Entertainment and Sports Law Journal 1.

37 Donnellan (n 35).

38 Ted Stevens Olympic and Amateur Sports Act, Pub L No 105–225, 112 Stat 1253, 1466–78 (1998) (codified as amended at 36 USC ss 220501–29 (2012). The 1998 Act amended the Amateur Sports Act of 1978, Pub L No 95–606, s 105, 92 Stat 3045, 3047 (1978). The Act was amended more recently: see 36 USC Ch 2205: United States Olympic and Paralympic Committee <https://www.usef.org/forms-pubs/wBWt_Wsuaxc/ted-stevens-olympic-amateur-sports> accessed 19 May 2024. For a discussion on the evolution of the Act, see Dionne L Koller, 'A Twenty-First-Century Olympic and Amateur Sports Act' (2018) 20(4) Vanderbilt Journal of Entertainment & Technology Law 1027 <https://scholarworks.law.ubalt.edu/all_fac/1078> accessed 19 May 2024.

39 36 USC s 220509 (2018) <https://uscode.house.gov/view.xhtml?req=granuleid:USC-prelim-title36-section220522&num=0&edition=prelim> accessed 19 May 2024. The long title of the 1998 Act explains its remit: 'To amend the Amateur Sports Act to strengthen provisions protecting the right of athletes to compete, recognize the Paralympics and growth of disabled sports, improve the U.S. Olympic Committee's ability to resolve certain disputes, and for other purposes.'

40 Anderson (n 36).

US figure skater Tonya Harding availed of an injunction so that she could compete in the 1994 Winter Olympics in Lillehammer, Norway. Harding was accused of being involved in the assault of fellow skater Nancy Kerrigan, with the incident taking place shortly before the 1994 Winter Olympic Games. The US Figure Skating Association (USFA, now US Figure Skating) was of the opinion that Harding, due to her suspected involvement in the assault, had breached the Olympic code of fair play. The USOC decided that a disciplinary hearing would take place in Norway. Harding sought an injunction in an American court to prevent the hearing taking place.[41] The Court granted the injunction and Harding was allowed compete in the Games. Panner J in the Oregon District Court highlighted that recourse to the courts should only occur in the most exceptional of circumstances: **12–15**

> The courts should rightly hesitate before intervening in disciplinary hearings held by private associations, including the defendant United States Figure Skating Association. Intervention is appropriate only in the most extraordinary circumstances, where the association has clearly breached its own rules, that breach will imminently result in serious and irreparable harm to the plaintiff, and the plaintiff has exhausted all internal remedies. Even then, injunctive relief is limited to correcting the breach of the rules. The court should not intervene in the merits of the underlying dispute.[42]

However, the judge considered Harding's case to be 'one of those rare cases where judicial intervention was appropriate' given the irreparable harm that Harding could suffer as she: **12–16**

> would have been obliged to appear before the panel and prematurely present her defence without having adequate time to prepare for that hearing. If the Hearing Panel found her guilty as charged, the resultant publicity could have severely prejudiced her chances for a fair trial in any future criminal case.[43]

Harding was included in the US Olympic Team with her event beginning on 23 February, 10 days after the court hearing.[44] The decision of Panner J meant that Harding's hearing was deferred until after the Games. **12–17**

---

41 *Harding v United States Olympic Committee* 1477–81 (Clackamas Country Cir Or, 13 February 1994) <https://law.justia.com/cases/federal/district-courts/FSupp/851/1476/1622192/> accessed 19 May 2024.

42 ibid 1479.

43 ibid. Harding was seeking $20m in damages from the USOC: Serge Kovaleski, 'Harding Files $20M Lawsuit Against the USOC' *Washington Post* (Washington DC, 10 February 1994) D1 <https://www.washingtonpost.com/wpsrv/sports/longterm/olympics1998/history/timeline/articles/time_021094.htm> accessed 19 May 2024.

44 Kerrigan recovered in time to compete at the Lillehammer games, and narrowly missed out on the gold medal: International Olympic Committee, 'Kerrigan Defies Rival to Land Figure Skating Silver' (updated on 27 June 2023) <https://olympics.com/en/news/kerrigan-defies-rival-to-land-figure-skating-silver> accessed 19 May 2024.

In accepting a plea agreement, Harding pleaded guilty to the felony charge of 'hindering prosecution' and received 500 hours of community service, a fine of $100,000, a contribution of $50,000 to set up a fund for the Special Olympics in Oregon, pay the county 'special costs' of $10,000 and resign immediately from the USFA.[45] In June 1994, the USFA held a two-day hearing and found that Harding had prior knowledge of the attack and imposed a lifetime ban and stripped her of the 1994 national championship title.[46]

12–18 The use of the courts in settling disputes involving sports governing bodies and sportspersons has both positive and negative aspects, as noted above. As discussed in detail in Chapter 11, redress to the courts should be reserved for the more serious and contentious cases.[47]

12–19 In *Hyland v Dundalk Racing (1999) Ltd t/a Dundalk Stadium*, Hogan J asserted that the instances where the courts intervene in sporting disputes should be limited to those that are 'exceptional involving something akin to fraud or manifest irrationality'.[48] He cautioned against the use of the courts outside these exceptional circumstances.[49]

12–20 The next section of the chapter will examine how sports disputes can be resolved without the intervention of the courts. The focus will be on the GAA's DRA, SDSI and the CAS, beginning with a discussion of the merits and demerits of ADR.

The Merits and Demerits of Alternative Dispute Resolution

12–21 There are many benefits to using ADR in a sporting context. It offers sportspersons and sports bodies an informal, less costly and quicker method of resolving disputes in comparison to the courts. The legal system and its oftentimes verboseness can be intimidating to people. While attempts have been made to make the law more user-friendly, the legalese can be off-putting for many. Individuals can avail of ADR without having to instruct legal counsel.

12–22 While sports bodies prefer to be self-regulating and by using sports-specific ADR, 'specialist expertise' can be availed of, benefits of recourse

45 John Balzar, 'Harding Pleads Guilty to Obstructing Justice: Sentence: Olympian Resigns from Skating Team. Plea Bargain Includes Probation, Fine, Community Service' *Los Angeles Times* (Los Angeles, 17 March 1994) <https://www.latimes.com/archives/la-xpm-1994-03-17-mn-35216-story.html> accessed 19 May 2024.

46 Christine Brennan, 'Harding Stripped of Title; Banned for Life' *Washington Post* (Washington DC, 1 July 1994) C1 <https://www.washingtonpost.com/wpsrv/sports/longterm/olympics1998/history/timeline/articles/time_070194.htm > accessed 19 May 2024.

47 See *O'Connell & Lambe v The Turf Club & Another* [2014] IEHC 175 [36]. This case is discussed in ch 11 paras 11–36—11–39.

48 *Hyland v Dundalk Racing (1999) Ltd t/a Dundalk Stadium* [2014] IEHC 60 [39].

49 ibid [40]. See ch 11 para 11–40 for more detail.

to the courts should not be 'overlooked'.[50] As the courts have showed a willingness to intervene in the decisions of sports governing bodies, it has resulted in them becoming increasingly conscious of the impact of judicial scrutiny and need to rethink

> their decision-making procedures in the discipline sphere ... in order that they meet ideals of fairness, independence and openness which suffuse the judge-made principles of natural justice.[51]

There are situations when 'recourse to the court for a determination of legal rights represents a "copper bottomed" guarantee of ultimate justice for individual sportsmen embroiled in stormy, long running (invariably disciplinary) disputes with their governing bodies'.[52] **12–23**

While redress to the courts can offer such protections, it is important to note that bodies offering dispute resolution to sports have become increasingly aware of procedural and human rights. As will be discussed, legal experts with a knowledge of and interest in sport are members of the DRA and CAS, which has resulted in narrowing the gulf between the protections offered by the courts and those offered by ADR. Cognisance should be given to the detailed arbitral awards that have been handed down by CAS Panels. In many respects, these CAS decisions resemble that of a judgment. The CAS has recognised a catalogue of human rights from the legal principles it has adopted on a case-by-case basis: for example, from the legal systems of the parties to a case, Swiss law and international conventions, including the European Convention on Human Rights (ECHR) and the United Nations Guiding Principles on Business and Human Rights.[53] It has recognised numerous rights, including the right to freedom from discrimination, the right to freedom of expression, the right against self-incrimination, the right to due process, the right to personality rights, the right to privacy, and the right to professional and economic freedom.[54] It recognises the principle of proportionality with regard to sanctions. The CAS hears cases *de novo*, in line with the decisions of the European Court of Human Rights (ECtHR).[55] It has stated that procedural errors of sports disciplinary tribunals/committees can be cured with the appeal *de novo* before the CAS.[56] The AHD of the CAS reiterated this more recently in its decision in *Henry v International Bobsleigh & Skeleton Federation (IBSF)* when it **12–24**

---

50 Philip Morris and Gavin Little, 'Challenging Sports Bodies' Determinations' (1998) 17 Civil Justice Quarterly 128, 129.

51 ibid.

52 ibid.

53 Court of Arbitration, 'Sport and Human Rights: Overview from a CAS Perspective' (as at 20 June 2022) <https://www.tas-cas.org/fileadmin/user_upload/2022.06.20_Human_Rights_in_sport__20_June_2022_.pdf> accessed 19 May 2024.

54 ibid.

55 ibid 11, fn 6.

56 See CAS 2009/A/1957 *Fédération Française de Natation (FFN) v Ligue Européenne de Natation (LEN)* award of 5 July 2010 [1] and [14] <https://jurisprudence.tas-cas.org/Shared%20Documents/1957.pdf> accessed 19 May 2024.

stated that 'any issues with regard to due process in that tribunal are cured by this hearing before the Panel, which is conducted de novo'.[57] The CAS and its recognition of human rights is evolving and will require institutional reform so as to provide 'an effective check on the transnational power of SGBs in CAS proceedings'.[58] Duval contends that recent appeals of CAS decisions to the ECtHR in the form of *Mutu* and *Pechstein* provide 'an external check exercised by the ECtHR, the SFT [Swiss Federal Tribunal] and potentially other national courts on the basis of the ECHR' which 'remains crucial to ensure that the CAS operates in a manner that is compatible with fundamental due process rights'.[59]

Dispute Resolution Authority

12–25 At its Annual Congress in 2005, the GAA adopted an Arbitration Rule and a Disputes Resolution Code.[60] It is a 'last resort' appeals body that hears disputes when the internal appeal mechanisms have been exhausted.[61] Initially, its jurisdiction was challenged in *Vaughan* concerning player eligibility; however, the DRA asserted that it was 'an arbitral body with jurisdiction co-extensive with those of a Court dealing with a contractual dispute'.[62]

12–26 Rule 7.7 of the 2024 *GAA Official Guide – Part 1* refers to arbitration.[63] The DRA must conduct hearings in compliance with the Disputes Resolution Code, the rules of the GAA, the Arbitration Acts 1954 and 1980 or any statutory modification or re-enactment thereof, and the law of Ireland.[64] Rule 7.7(c) precludes members from issuing court proceedings in any

57 Arbitration CAS Ad Hoc Division (OG Beijing) 22/003 *Henry v International Bobsleigh & Skeleton Federation (IBSF)* award of 1 February 2022 [8.13] <https://www.tas-cas.org/fileadmin/user_upload/Award_OG_22_03_Final__Publication_.pdf> accessed 19 May 2024.

58 Antoine Duval, 'Lost in Translation? The European Convention on Human Rights at the Court of Arbitration for Sport' (2022) 22 International Sports Law Journal 132, 132. SGBs refers to sports governing bodies.

59 ibid 149.

60 Disputes Resolution Authority, 'Welcome to the Disputes Resolution Authority' <http://www.sportsdra.ie/> accessed 19 May 2024.

61 Cliona Foley, 'New Disputes Authority Set for Legal Challenge' *Irish Independent* (Dublin, 1 July 2005) <https://www.independent.ie/sport/gaelic-games/gaelic-football/new-disputes-authority-set-for-legal challenge/25973462.html> accessed 19 May 2024.

62 DRA09/2005 *Vaughan v Leinster Council & Central Appeals Committee* (2005) [16] <http://www.sportsdra.ie/wp-content/uploads/2015/10/01-DRA-1-2005.pdf> accessed 19 May 2024. For a discussion of the decision see Seán Moran, 'Finer Points of Vaughan Ruling Explained' *Irish Times* (Dublin, 21 September 2005) <https://www.irishtimes.com/sport/finer-points-of-vaughan-ruling-explained-1.495283> accessed 19 May 2024.

63 Gaelic Athletic Association, *Official Guide – Part 1* (Central Council of the Association 2024) ch 7 <https://www.gaa.ie/article/gaa-official-guides-codes> accessed 19 May 2024.

64 ibid r 7.7(a).

jurisdiction regarding the dispute in question. Disputes can be referred to the DRA once 'all available avenues of Appeal under the Rules of the Association have been exhausted'.[65] Rule 7.7(f) states that only disputes raised by members or units from Ireland or Britain may avail of arbitration.[66] The DRA does not hear cases involving doping.[67] The Disputes Resolution Code is located in Appendix 5 of the 2024 *Official Guide - Part 1*.[68] The DRA consists of a Secretary who is appointed for a term of three years and a panel of a minimum of 30 people.[69] This group is divided into two sub-groups, Group 1 and Group 2. Group 1 consists of qualified solicitors, barristers or arbitrators, while Group 2 comprises of 'persons without such qualification who, by virtue of their experience in the affairs of the Association, are properly qualified to resolve disputes relating to the Rules of the Association'.[70] Each group must have at least 15 persons. In order to apply to the DRA for arbitration, the claimant must complete a written request for dispute-resolution proceedings and deposit €1,000 towards the expenses of the DRA.[71] Rule 3 outlines the procedure for the respondent to reply to the complaint with either an admission or a denial.[72] Where practical, the Secretary of the DRA will encourage mediation and negotiation. If the parties avail of this, it 'shall be without prejudice to the dispute resolution proceedings and may take place and continue at any time during the dispute resolution proceedings'.[73]

Disputes are heard by a tribunal of three individuals selected from the panel and will include at least one member from Group 1 and one from Group 2.[74] If the parties to the dispute agree, the tribunal may consist of just one person nominated from the DRA panel.[75] Interim temporary **12–27**

---

[65] ibid r 7.7(d).

[66] An example of a dispute involving British-based parties is that of DRA26/2022 *St Finbarr's GAC v Central Appeals Committee and British Provincial Council Hearings Committee and British Provincial Council and Warwickshire CCC* <http://www.sportsdra.ie/wp-content/uploads/2022/11/22.11.18-Interim-Decision.pdf> accessed 19 May 2024. This dispute centred on the fielding of an illegal player.

[67] *Official Guide – Part 1* (n 63) r 7.7(e). See r 1.13; and also the Anti-Doping section on its website: 'GAA Anti-Doping Information' <https://www.gaa.ie/my-gaa/players/anti-doping> accessed 19 May 2024.

[68] (n 63) 90. Template forms are included in Appendix 5.

[69] ibid Appendix 5, r 1.1.

[70] ibid.

[71] ibid rr 2.1(a)–(f) list the information that must be furnished, including the names and addresses of the parties, a brief description of the dispute and the remedy sought, the applicable rules, bye-laws, and relevant legal authorities to support the claim. The claim must be made in accordance with the template provided. Under r 2.2, the completed form should be furnished to the Secretary of the Disputes Resolution within seven days of the final decision; however, this can be extended if the Secretary is satisfied that there is good reason. Rule 2.3 provides for the €1,000 deposit.

[72] ibid rr 3(a)–(e).

[73] ibid rr 4.1 and 4.2.

[74] ibid r 5.1.

[75] ibid r 5.4.

remedies are detailed in Rule 8.[76] Rule 9 explains the procedure for hearings, and Rule 10 provides information on the identification and calling of witnesses. The decision of the tribunal must be in writing and accompanied by the reasons on which it is based.[77] Decisions of the DRA are published on its website.[78] Anderson comments that the DRA 'is an excellent example of the benefits of ADR for a sports organisation', denoting it as 'a trustworthy, inexpensive, quick and expert-led alternative to the courts'.[79]

12–28 The DRA hears cases involving player transfers, player eligibility, on-field violence and cases wherein suspensions are challenged. A decision that perhaps best encapsulates Anderson's assertion above is that of *O'Flionn (Flynn)*.[80] The dispute centred on the transfer of an underage player within the county of Antrim. In coming to a decision, the Tribunal cited the Supreme Court of the United Kingdom (UK) decision of *Kennedy v Charity Commission*.[81] The Tribunal referred to the inflexibility of the rules and how inflexibility of interpretation or of the rules 'have an obvious potential for injustice'.[82] Antrim CCC was deemed not to have given any consideration to the 'unique factual circumstances' of the player and his family.[83] The Tribunal deemed the refusal to be unreasonable and in doing so applied the test devised by the Supreme Court in *Kennedy v Charity Commission*:

> The court involved in the review will take the following steps:
> (a) The identification of the legitimate objective(s) to be pursued by the restrictions;

---

[76] ibid r 8.1 provides that where an interim ruling is required, it must be stated on the claim form. The rule explains that the claimant may apply for an interim temporary remedy 'where necessary in order to preserve the status quo ante pending the Hearing'. Status quo ante denotes the state of affairs that existed previously or the way things were before. DRA06/2023 *Patrician Academy Mallow v Munster Council and Munster Council Hearings Committee and Abbey CBS Tipperary Town* is a recent example where an application for interim relief was denied: see <http://www.sportsdra.ie/wp-content/uploads/2023/02/23.02.15-Decision-Interim-Relief.pdf> accessed 19 May 2024. See also *St Finbarr's GAC* (n 66) where interim relief was denied as the Tribunal at [30] could not find 'a serious/fair issue to be tried such as to merit the granting of the interim relief'.

[77] *Official Guide – Part 1* (n 63) r 11.2. Rule 11.4 provides that in situations where a decision or procedure is quashed, with the agreement of the parties, the Tribunal may conduct a full hearing 'as if it were an appellate body of last resort'.

[78] Dispute Resolution Authority, 'Statements and Decisions' <http://www.sportsdra.ie/statements-decisions/#> accessed 19 May 2024.

[79] Jack Anderson, 'Keeping Sports Out of the Courts: The Use of Alternative Dispute Resolution in Irish Sport' (2010) 76(4) Arbitration 647, 653.

[80] DRA06/2015, *O'Flionn v Coiste Comórtas na gCluchí Aintroim (Antrim CCC) agus Naomh Pádraig GLC Lios na gCearrbhach (St Patrick's GAC Lisburn)* <http://www.sportsdra.ie/wp-content/uploads/2014/03/DRA-6-2015.pdf> accessed 19 May 2024. For more details on this decision see ch 3 paras 3–39—3–41.

[81] (2014) UKSC 20. This was an appeal from *Kennedy v Charity Commission* [2011] EWCA Civ 367; *Kennedy v Charity Commission* [2012] EWCA Civ 317.

[82] (2014) UKSC 20 (n 51) [19].

[83] ibid [20].

(b) Establishing a rational connection between the restriction and the achievement of one or more of those legitimate objectives; and
(c) A proportionality test, namely that the restrictions must be a proportionate response, and must be no more than necessary to accomplish the legitimate purpose in question.[84]

The Tribunal, in finding the refusal to allow the player transfer unlawful, quashed the decision made by Antrim CCC. In relation to the wording of Bye Law 15(1)(c), the Tribunal suggested an amendment be made to the wording to allow for more flexibility.[85] **12–29**

Parallels can be drawn between the approach of the DRA and judicial review. The DRA at paragraph 24 in the case of *Breathnach and O'Baoil (Walsh and O'Boyle)* expressly stated that it is not an appellate body nor does it hear cases *de novo* but 'rather the DRA is akin to a review body which considers the decisions made by the authorities at first instance and on appeal with a view to pronouncing on the correctness of those decisions'.[86] Interestingly, the applicants endeavoured to rely on the ECHR and contended that they had a 'vested right' in regard to the retrospective application of the rules.[87] The Tribunal was quick to point out the distinction between public law nature of rights granted under statute and those found in the rules of a private organisation such as the GAA.[88] The claim was dismissed and both claimants were ordered to pay costs out of the deposits lodged at the outset.[89] **12–30**

In general, the DRA will not interfere with a decision unless it is unreasonable or irrational.[90] The DRA will not intervene even in situations where the Tribunal may espouse a different opinion on the **12–31**

---

[84] ibid [21].
[85] ibid [22].
[86] DRA 10/2012 *Breathnach & O'Baoill v Comhairle Ardoideachais* (2012) [24] <http://www.sportsdra.ie/wp-content/uploads/2015/10/DRA-10-2012.pdf> accessed 19 May 2024. The Panel added: 'In this context, it is particularly important, therefore, that claimants avail of the opportunities to canvass any and all points and evidence of relevance and adduce all before the appellate decision-maker, which can hear cases de novo and, consequently, all the more important that the appellate body is formally named as a respondent to any referral to the DRA, in addition to the decision-maker at first instance.' This case concerned two players who sought special permission to participate in third-level competitions with Dublin City University (DCU).
[87] ibid [38]. The Tribunal referred to this claim at 'unmeritorious': [46].
[88] ibid [44].
[89] ibid [49].
[90] *Vaughan* (n 62) [39]. See also DRA05/2015 *McCoindlis (GLG Seamroga Baile) v Coiste* Éisteachta *Uladh (CEU) agus Coiste* Éisteachta *Dhoire (CED)* (5) [11] where the Tribunal referred to Finlay CJ and the test of unreasonableness in *O'Keefe v An Board Pleanala* [1993] IR 39 <http://www.sportsdra.ie/wp-content/uploads/2014/03/DRA-5-2015.pdf> accessed 19 May 2024. There have been recent developments in judicial review and reasonableness: see Oran Doyle, 'Executive Power and its Limits: *Burke v Minister for Education* [2022] IESC 1' in Sarah Hamill (ed), *Irish Supreme Court Review*, vol 5 (Clarus 2023).

merits of the decision. In setting out its general principles in its first case of *Vaughan*, the Tribunal stated at paragraph 40 that where the issue relates to the interpretation of a statute or a contract, 'the Court (and consequently the DRA) will review the decision without restraint, because it is in excess of jurisdiction to make an error of law'.[91]

12–32 The DRA provides detailed and well-thought-out decisions; it refers to Irish case law and case law from other jurisdictions. The claimants and respondents are given the opportunity to present their arguments and accompanying evidence. In effect, it offers a court-like approach yet in a much more informal and cost-effective setting.

Sport Dispute Solutions Ireland

12–33 The other avenue for alternative dispute resolution in the sporting context outside of the GAA is SDSI.[92] SDSI was originally known as Just Sport Ireland (JSI) and was established by the Federation of Irish Sport in 2007.[93] SDSI, a not-for-profit dispute resolution service, was established to offer mediation and arbitration services to sportspersons in order to provide an alternative to protracted and expensive litigation in the courts.

12–34 SDSI is a company limited by guarantee without a share capital and it offers

> a fair, inexpensive and expeditious method of resolving disputes that remain unresolved after all the procedures owed for within the sport have been exhausted. In particular, the SDSI mediation procedure assists in avoiding more confrontational or costly methods of resolution for disagreements, conflicts or disputes with sport.[94]

12–35 In 2014, Sport Ireland made it a condition that funded bodies agree to submit to dispute resolution and many expressly refer to SDSI in their rules. By 2019, all governing bodies were compliant and any future governing body seeking recognition by Sport Ireland will be required to have a clause referring to dispute resolution in its rules.[95]

---

91 *Vaughan* (n 62).

92 For more details, see its website <http://sportdisputesolutions.ie/> accessed 19 May 2024.

93 The Federation of Irish Sport was established in 2002 by the national governing bodies. It refers to itself as the 'voice of Irish sport' and as such it is the representative organisation for the National Governing Bodies (NGBs) and Local Sports Partnerships (LSPs) in Ireland. Its membership consists of 81 NGBs and 29 LSPs including the GAA, FAI, IRFU, Swim Ireland and Athletics Ireland: see Federation of Irish Sport, 'About us' <https://www.irishsport.ie/about/> accessed 19 May 2024.

94 Sports Dispute Solutions Ireland, 'About' <http://sportdisputesolutions.ie/about/> accessed 19 May 2024.

95 Sport Ireland, 'Annual Report 2019' 16 <https://www.sportireland.ie/sites/default/files/media/document/2021-03/sport-ireland-annual-report-2019-english.pdf>

12–36 SDSI offers two types of arbitration, similar to the CAS's Ordinary Arbitration Division (OAD) and the Appeals Arbitration Division (AAD), as discussed below. For disputes at first instance, SDSI has the Standard Arbitration Procedure under Rule 15.[96] For an appeal of a decision, there is the Appeal Arbitration Procedure as detailed under Rule 14.[97] SDSI has jurisdiction to offer its services where an ADR clause has been inserted into the governing documents or policies of the relevant sporting organisation. Rule 14.1(b) provides that disputes involving doping are not within the SDSI's jurisdiction. It can hear cases involving selection disputes; registration disputes; international governing body disputes; branch or club disputes; disputes about sponsorship; and disputes relating to disciplinary procedures. Part 4, Rules 33–45 outline the procedure for mediation. [98] SDSI mediation is based on an agreement between the parties concerned to submit their dispute to mediation, which is facilitated by an independent third party. Rule 59 states that all proceedings with SDSI are confidential except for generic information relating to decisions being published on the SDSI website.[99] Details of the costs can be found in an FAQ document.[100] The cost to initiate mediation with SDSI is €100 (non-refundable) and for the actual mediation the cost is €1,500, with both parties contributing €750.

12–37 The Appeal Arbitration Procedure is used when a party is challenging or appealing a disciplinary or other decision of a sports governing body where the regulations of the relevant body provide for recourse to SDSI, or where there is a specific written agreement that allows for SDSI's arbitration service.[101] This procedure can only be used after the parties have exhausted the internal disciplinary procedures of the governing body in question. The parties can be represented or assisted by individuals of their choosing.[102] Where the parties agree, arbitrations are decided by a single arbitrator or by a panel of three.[103]

---

accessed 18 May 2024. Annual Reports from 2015 to 2022 are available at <https://www.sportireland.ie/about-us/publications/annual-reports> accessed 18 May 2024.

96 Sport Dispute Solutions Ireland, 'SDSI Rules Including Arbitration and Mediation Rules' (2024) 13 <https://sportdisputesolutions.ie/wp-content/uploads/2024/02/SDSI_Rules.pdf> accessed 19 September 2024.

97 ibid 14.

98 ibid 24–28.

99 ibid 32. Short case studies are published: see <http://sportdisputesolutions.ie/cases/> accessed 19 May 2024.

100 Sport Dispute Solutions Ireland, 'FAQ: How much does it cost?' (2021) 3 <http://sportdisputesolutions.ie/wp-content/uploads/2021/07/SDSI-FAQ-July-2021.pdf> accessed 19 May 2024.

101 SDSI Rules (n 96) rr 14.1(i) and (ii).

102 ibid r 58(1).

103 ibid r 19(1). See rr 19.2–19.9 for more details, including situations where the Secretariat intervenes due to lack of agreement between the parties and decides the number of the arbitrators depending on the circumstances of the case. Where the parties agree that the dispute is to be heard by a three-person panel, each party appoints one arbitrator with the third person, the Chairperson, appointed by the SDSI Registrar.

The decision of the panel is in writing and will state the reasons for the decision given.[104] Rule 59(1) expressly provides for the confidentiality of arbitration outcomes.[105] SDSI may publish non-identifying information which it refers to as case studies.[106] The details on the cases are very scant and only three case studies are published on its website.[107] As it stands, the current practice is not conducive to creating a body of sports-related jurisprudence in Ireland. SDSI is not affiliated with Sport Resolutions, a UK-based global not-for-profit dispute resolution service that offers arbitration, mediation, tribunal and investigative services.[108] Sports Resolutions operates the International Hearing Panel (IHP),[109] the National Anti-Doping Panel (NADP),[110] and the National Safeguarding Panel (NSP).[111] Sport Resolutions publishes summaries of decisions as well as the full decision, which includes the parties' names on its website.[112] Unlike its Irish counterpart, it offers arbitration in anti-doping disputes. In 2021, it administered the Independent Review into Child Sex Abuse Allegations in Football, which examined child sex-abuse allegations in football between the years of 1970 to 2005.[113] SDSI operates on a much smaller scale, both in terms of the types of

---

[104] ibid r 30(1).

[105] However, the confidentiality clause will be waived in certain circumstances: for example, 'where disclosure of the information may be required by law, to pursue or protect a legal right, to enforce or challenge an award in bona fide legal proceedings or where such documents may already be in the public domain (otherwise than in breach of this undertaking)'.

[106] SDSI Rules (n 96) r 59(2)(i).

[107] Case Studies (n 99). The SDSI's Strategic Report 2019–2022 does not add much in the way of information about the types of disputes it hears. For more detail, see <http://sportdisputesolutions.ie/wp-content/uploads/2019/01/A5_Strategic_report_ONLINE.pdf> accessed 19 May 2024.

[108] Sports Resolutions, 'About Sports Resolutions' <https://www.sportresolutions.com/about/sport-resolutions> accessed 19 May 2024.

[109] <https://www.sportresolutions.com/services/independent-hearing-panel> accessed 19 May 2024.

[110] <https://www.sportresolutions.com/services/national-anti-doping-panel> accessed 19 May 2024.

[111] <https://www.sportresolutions.com/services/national-safeguarding-panel> accessed 19 May 2024.

[112] A recent example can here found here: *UK Anti-Doping Limited (UKAD) v Dr Richard Freeman* (20 July 2023) <https://www.sportresolutions.com/assets/documents/230720_-_UKAD_v_Dr_Richard_Freeman__Decision.pdf> accessed 19 May 2024.

[113] Football Association, 'Clive Sheldon QC's Report into Non-Recent Child Sexual Abuse Allegations in Football' (28 May 2021) <https://www.thefa.com/news/2021/mar/17/clive-sheldon-qc-independent-commission-report-released-20210317> accessed 19 May 2024. Three annexes to the report were kept confidential pending the criminal case involving Geoffrey Broome who was convicted of eight counts of indecent assault against minors. After his conviction and following a General Data Protection Regulation (GDPR) review, Annex C was published. The GDPR's full title and citation is Regulation (EU) 2016/679 of the European Parliament and of the Council of 27 April 2016 on the protection of natural persons with regard to the processing of personal data and on the free movement of such data, and repealing Directive 95/46/EC (General Data Protection Regulation) (Text with EEA relevance) (2016) OJ L 119.

disputes and geographically, and thus cannot be compared to Sport Resolutions. However, it could consider publishing more case studies and expanding its website.

The cost of SDSI arbitration is determined at the end of the proceedings and must be borne by the parties. It costs €2,000 for a single arbitrator and €3,000 for the panel of three.[114] In the absence of agreement between the parties, the award may stipulate which party bears the costs or whether the costs are to be apportioned between the two parties.[115] Unless the decision provides, the parties are responsible for their own expenses (ie legal fees, witness expenses, etc). An advance on the costs must be provided by the parties equally.[116] A decision may be appealed to the CAS if the sport in question recognises the jurisdiction of the CAS; if not, the decision of the SDSI panel or arbitrator is final and cannot be appealed.[117] **12–38**

SDSI also offers a Referral Facility which provides that a sports body can contact it and request it to make available personnel, including a legally qualified person, to that sports body in situations where it needs such suitably qualified person(s) to be appointed to the sports body's internal disciplinary and/or complaints committees, inquiries or investigations.[118] **12–39**

The availability of alternative forms of dispute resolution in Ireland provides a welcome alternative to the expensive, often divisive, option of judicial review proceedings. Given the benefits of resolution of disputes through the DRA or SDSI and in light of the Irish courts' general reluctance to become involved in sporting disputes, it is likely that these processes will become increasingly popular going forward. **12–40**

At present, all governing bodies seeking recognition from Sport Ireland must have 'an Internal Appeal process consistent with established principles of due process and natural justice and containing a provision that allows disputes to be referred to the alternate dispute resolution services of Just Sport Ireland' (now SDSI).[119] The inclusion of an ADR clause is important from the point of view of government funding. As sport is funded directly by the state and indirectly by Sport Ireland, money used to pay for legal bills arising from litigation comes from taxes paid by the public. Thus, ADR offers a more cost-effective method of resolving disputes. **12–41**

---

114 SDSI FAQ (n 100).
115 SDSI Rules (n 96) r 50.
116 ibid r 51(1).
117 ibid r 31.
118 ibid Part 5, rr 46–49.
119 Sport Ireland, 'Recognition Criteria for National Governing Bodies of Sport' (2018) <https://www.sportireland.ie/sites/default/files/2020-02/sport-ireland-recognition-criteria_0.pdf> accessed 19 May 2024.

The Court of Arbitration for Sport

12–42 The CAS is an independent body that resolves sports-related disputes through arbitration or mediation. It is not a court in the strict sense of the word, but rather an arbitral body that hears disputes that are directly or indirectly related to sport. It hears cases brought by natural persons (individuals) and legal persons (governing bodies and associations). The CAS has approximately 300 arbitrators from 87 countries.[120] All arbitrators are persons with specialist knowledge of arbitration and sport and are appointed by the International Council for Arbitration for Sport (ICAS). Arbitrators are appointed for a renewable term of four years and must sign a letter of independence on appointment. The CAS has a permanent President who is also President of the ICAS, as explained below.

12–43 The CAS is based in Lausanne, Switzerland, and has two permanent outposts (decentralised offices) in Sydney (Oceania) and New York (North America).[121] Hearings in the CAS are held in private and, depending on the nature of the case, decisions may be confidential. Statistics published in 2022 demonstrate the evolution of the CAS in terms of case numbers and case types.[122] In 1986, two procedures were commenced, one ordinary and one consultation procedure.[123] As will be discussed in more detail further on in the chapter, before the entry into force of the Code of Sports-Related Arbitration on 22 November 1994, the CAS only provided the ordinary arbitration procedure and advisory opinions.[124] By 1996, 21 cases commenced, consisting of four ordinary procedures, 10 appeal procedures, six ad hoc and one consultation procedure.[125] By 2006, the case commencement load had greatly expanded with 207 applications, which included 17 ordinary procedures, 125 appeal procedures, 12 ad hoc and three mediations.[126] In 2016, 609 cases commenced consisting of 100 ordinary procedures, 458 appeal procedures, 28 ad hoc, 13 anti-doping procedures and

[120] Court of Arbitration for Sport, 'Frequently Asked Questions' <https://www.tas-cas.org/en/general-information/frequently-asked-questions.html> accessed 19 May 2024.

[121] ibid. The North American office was previously located in Denver, Colorado. The office was moved to New York in 1999.

[122] Court of Arbitration for Sport, 'Statistics 1986–2022' (2023) <https://www.tas-cas.org/fileadmin/user_upload/CAS_statistics_2022.pdf> accessed 19 May 2024.

[123] The consultation procedure ceased on 1 January 2011. In 2010 no requests for consultations were lodged, and between 1986 and 2009 the CAS dealt with 82 consultation procedures.

[124] Advisory opinions are described as 'non-contentious' and allow parties seek the advice of the CAS.

[125] Statistics (n 122) 1.

[126] ibid. Mediation was introduced into the Code of Sports-Related Arbitration in 1999. Article 1 of the Mediation Rules expressly exclude disciplinary matters, including doping issues, match-fixing and corruption: see CAS Mediation Rules (in force as from 1 September 2013; amended on 1 January 2016) <https://www.tas-cas.org/fileadmin/user_upload/CAS_Mediation_Rules_2016__clean_.pdf> accessed 19 May 2024.

10 mediations.[127] In 2016 the CAS Anti-Doping Division (ADD) was established for the Summer Olympic Games in Rio de Janeiro and the 2018 Winter Olympic Games in Pyeongchang. As will be explained in more detail, the ADD hears cases at first instance and, while initially set up for two specific events, it became a permanent fixture in 2019. In 2022, 830 cases commenced with 151 ordinary procedures, 644 appeal procedures, 12 ad hoc, 15 anti-doping procedures and eight mediations.[128]

History and Evolution of the CAS

In the early 1980s, there was an increase in sports-related disputes going before the courts. The then President of the IOC, Juan Antonio Samaranch, put forward the idea of creating a specialised authority that would hear sports-specific disputes. The process would be inexpensive, speedy and offer both athletes and sporting bodies an alternative form of redress. The IOC ratified the statutes of the CAS in 1983, which came into force in June 1984.[129] Initially, the IOC bore the costs of the CAS except in cases which involved commercial disputes; in these cases both parties would contribute to the costs. At this time, the CAS was very closely associated with the IOC. Of the 60 members, 15 members were appointed by the IOC, 15 by the International Federations (IFs), 15 by the NOCs, and 15 by the IOC President.[130] The IOC President's 15 members were chosen from organisations outside the IOC, IFs and NOCs.[131] **12–44**

The CAS Statute could be modified only by the IOC Session, at the proposal of the IOC Executive Board.[132] Doubt was cast on the independent nature of the CAS in light of its close workings with the IOC. Matters came to a head in the case of *Gundel v FEI/CAS* in 1992.[133] Gundel, a horse rider, was suspended for three months and fined by the Judicial Commission of the Fédération Equestre Internationale (FEI) following the finding of a prohibited substance, iIsoxsuprine, in the horse's urine sample.[134] Both the rider and the horse were disqualified from the show jumping event.[135] Gundel challenged the decision of **12–45**

---

127 Statistics (n 122) 1. Over 10,000 cases had been registered by 26 January 2024: see Court of Arbitration for Sport, 'The Procedure *Thomas v World Aquatics* is the 10,000th Case Registered by CAS Since its Creation in 1984' (26 January 2024) <https://www.tas-cas.org/fileadmin/user_upload/CAS_Media_Release_10kprocedures_L._Thomas.pdf> accessed 16 May 2024.

128 ibid 1.

129 Court of Arbitration for Sport, 'History of the CAS' <https://www.tas-cas.org/en/general-information/history-of-the-cas.html> accessed 19 May 2024. The CAS Statute of 1984 was augmented by several procedural Regulations.

130 ibid.

131 ibid.

132 ibid. The CAS Statute was slightly amended in 1990.

133 Published in the Recueil Officiel des Arrêts du Tribunal Fédéral [Official Digest of Federal Tribunal Judgements] 119 II 271, the Federal Tribunal (FT).

134 The samples were taken at an international event in Aachen.

135 A summary of the *Gundel* case is available from the *Olympic Review: Official*

the FEI (as provided for by the FEI Statutes) before the CAS.[136] The CAS Panel reduced Gundel's suspension from three months to one month; however, the disqualification of both Gundel and his horse was upheld.[137] The CAS Panel, in partially upholding the appeal, accepted that the prohibited substance had been found in the sample, but it was unlikely to have been a deliberate and intentional method to obtain a competitive advantage.[138] Gundel, it asserted, as the person responsible, was negligent in not insuring that the horse did not absorb the banned substance in the weeks preceding the event and the event itself.[139] Gundel was not satisfied with the outcome and appealed the decision of the CAS to the Swiss Federal Supreme Court or, as it is more commonly referred to, the Swiss Federal Tribunal (SFT).[140] The SFT, in dismissing the appeal, held the CAS:

> therefore represents an alternative to state justice, while, of course, respecting certain inalienable fundamental rights. This neutral and independent institution is therefore in a position to pronounce final and enforceable awards which have the force of a judgment.[141]

12–46 While the SFT was endorsing the neutrality and independence of the CAS, it raised concerns as to the close connection, in terms of funding, appointment powers and the power of the IOC to amend the CAS statute, between the CAS and IOC.[142] In the words of Gilbert Schwaar the General Secretary of the CAS, 'With the intent of safeguarding even better the rights of the parties before the CAS, it was decided in June 1993 to create a "Supreme Council of International Sports Arbitration".'[143] The ICAS, it was contended, would ensure that the CAS operated on a wholly independent basis.[144] The control of this 'top level' body would consist of 20 'high-level lawyers', four of whom would be appointed by the

---

Publication of the Olympic Movement, vols 309–10 (July–August 1993) 304. The summary is written by Gilbert Schwaar, the CAS General Secretary. Archives of the *Olympic Review* can be accessed from the Olympic World Library: <https://library.olympics.com/default/olympic-review.aspx?_lg=enGB&_ga=2.29918396.2069827167.1692789707-436923953.1689690254> accessed 19 May 2024.

[136] CAS 92/63 *G v FEI* in Digest of CAS Awards 1986–1998. On the CAS website only the French version is available: Arbitrage TAS 92/63 *G / Fédération Equestre Internationale (FEI)* award of 10 September 1992 <https://jurisprudence.tas-cas.org/Shared%20Documents/63.pdf> accessed 19 May 2024.

[137] The suspension applied to international equestrian competitions. Gundel was fined 1,000 Swiss Francs.

[138] Summary (n 135) 304.

[139] ibid.

[140] It is important to note that judicial recourse to the Swiss Federal Tribunal is permitted only 'on a very limited number of grounds, such as lack of jurisdiction, violation of elementary procedural rules (eg violation of the right to a fair hearing) or incompatibility with public policy': Frequently Asked Questions (n 120).

[141] Summary (n 135) 304. Gundel was ordered to pay 9,000 Swiss Francs in costs.

[142] Ian Blackshaw, 'CAS 92/A/63 *Gundel v FEI*' in Jack Anderson (ed), *Leading Cases in Sports Law* (ASSER International Sports Law Series 2013) 68.

[143] Summary (n 135) 304.

[144] ibid.

IOC, four by the IFs, four by the NOCs, four by athlete representatives, and four by the ICAS. The ICAS would be headed by a President.[145] The jurisdiction of the CAS was expanded to include the Appeals Arbitration Division (AAD) which would hear appeals, including doping cases, from decisions of the governing bodies based on there being an appeals clause included in the statutes of the sports governing bodies. The ICAS was entrusted to perform administrative and financial duties.[146]

The SFT was given the opportunity to comment on the restructured CAS in 2003 in a case involving two Russian cross-country skiers, *Lazutina v IOC* and *Danilova v IOC*.[147] The SFT recognised the independent nature of the CAS and referred to it as a 'perfectible institution'.[148] In a more recent case, in what has been described as a 'sequel' to the *Lazutina* case, *X v FIFA*, the SFT recognised the independence of the CAS from the Fédération Internationale de Football Association (FIFA).[149] The *X* case concerned a disciplinary sanction placed on a third-division Belgian Club, Football Club Seraing, pertaining to a violation of the Third-Party Ownership (TPO) rules under the Regulations on the Status and Transfer of Players (RSTP). The club contended that the CAS was not a genuine arbitral tribunal. This was rejected by the SFT, which held: **12–47**

> From an independence point of view, the Federal Tribunal has therefore always found that the links established by the International Summer Olympic Federations (in casu, the FEI) or the International Winter Olympic Federations (in casu, the FIS) with the CAS less problematic than those between this arbitral tribunal and the IOC. Therefore, prima facie, there is no reason why this should not be the case today.[150]

The SFT noted that the absence of reliance on the *Pechstein* case (discussed later in this chapter) by the appellant was important.[151] The German court in *Pechstein* found the CAS to be a genuine, independent, **12–48**

---

[145] ibid 304–05.

[146] ibid 304–05.

[147] This was an appeal against the CAS decision in CAS 2002/A/370 *Lazutina v IOC* award of 29 November 2002, a doping case which involved a two-year suspension. Lazutina's appeal against the IOC decision was dismissed by the CAS. Lazutina appealed it to the SFT, who published its decision on 27 May 2003. For details of the Danilova CAS decisions, see CAS 2002/A/371 *Danilova v IOC* and CAS 2002/A/398 *Danilova v Fédération Internationale de Ski (FIS)*. See also CAS 2002/A/397 *Lazutina v Fédération Internationale de Ski (FIS)*.

[148] This was quoted by the SFT in *X v Fédération Internationale de Football Associations*, 4A_260/2017 [3.4.2}. The English translation is available here: <https://law.marquette.edu/assets/sports-law/4A_260.2017%20Swiss%20Federal%20Tribunal%20Judgment%20Seraing%20v.%20FIFA.pdf> accessed 19 May 2024.

[149] Despina Mavromati and Charles Poncet, 'CAS Independence from FIFA Confirmed by the Federal Tribunal' *Swiss International Arbitration Decisions* <https://www.swissarbitrationdecisions.com/atf-4a-260-2017> accessed 15 May 2024.

[150] *X* (n 148) [3.4.1].

[151] KZR 6/15 *Pechstein v International Skating Union*, German Bundesgerichtshof, judgment of 7 June 2016. See Bernd Ehle and Ignacio Guaia, 'Bundesgerichtshof, Az KZR 6/15, *Pechstein v International Skating Union* (ISU), 7 June 2016' in Antoine

and impartial arbitral tribunal, with which the SFT concurred, 'Thus, the fact that the said landmark judgment is not even mentioned in the statement of claim may not be just a coincidence.'[152]

12–49 While the Swiss court has endorsed the independence of the CAS, academics have questioned the independence of the ICAS given the overlap between it and the CAS:

> While the ICAS is intended to act as a buffer layer of governance, the incestuous appointment process of ICAS members is questionable. More broadly, ICAS members wield immense power not only to appoint arbitrators in CAS's list of arbitrators, but also to revise the CAS Statutes.[153]

12–50 The President of the CAS is also the President of the ICAS, which raises questions as to the independence of the ICAS. The provision for two separate individuals would easily remedy the situation. As an oversight body, it should have more autonomy from the CAS. While appeals to the SFT are possible (as well as further appeal to the ECtHR), the grounds are limited. However, in adopting a holistic view, a 'central institution' for the resolution of sport-related disputes is to be favoured over the use of domestic courts which 'will only garner inconsistent and unpredictable jurisprudence and the application of general principles'.[154] As stated by the SFT, the CAS is a 'perfectible institution', thus it is not without its faults. However, it is a well-respected institution that continues to refine its processes. The 2023–26 ICAS Board has seen its numbers grow by two. The 22-person panel are all jurists and includes five Olympians.[155] The two extra members reflect the inclusion of 'a larger representation of football stakeholders, considering that football is by far the sport generating the most cases at the CAS'.[156] Members of the ICAS are appointed by the IFs (six, with five chosen by the Association of Summer Olympic IFs (ASOIF) and one by the Association of the Winter Olympic IFs (AIOWF), chosen from within or outside their membership); the Association of National Olympic Committees (ANOCs) (four, chosen from within or outside its membership); and the IOC (four, chosen within or outside its membership):

Duval and Antonio Rigozzi (eds), *Yearbook of International Sports Arbitration 2016* (TMC ASSER Press 2018) 415–27.

152 *X* (n 148) [3.4.1].

153 Chui Ling Goh and Jack Anderson, 'The Credibility of the Court of Arbitration for Sport' (2022) 13(2) Harvard Journal of Sports and Entertainment Law 233, 238.

154 ibid 263.

155 CAS Bulletin 2023/1, 4 <https://www.tas-cas.org/fileadmin/user_upload/Bulletin_TAS_2023-1_4.pdf> accessed 19 May 2024. There are a president and three vice presidents.

156 ibid. For more information about the role and composition of the ICAS, see the Code of Sports-Related Arbitration, in force as from 1 February 2023, ss 4–11 <https://www.tas-cas.org/fileadmin/user_upload/CAS_Code_2023__EN_.pdf> accessed 19 May 2024. See also ICAS Statutes, <https://www.tas-cas.org/en/icas/code-icas-statutes.html> accessed 19 May 2024.

four members are appointed by the fourteen members of ICAS listed above, after appropriate consultation with a view to safeguarding the interests of the athletes; and four members are appointed by the eighteen members of ICAS listed above, chosen from among personalities independent of the bodies designating the other members of the ICAS.[157]

The ICAS exercises its functions through the Board and three permanent commissions: the CAS Membership Commission,[158] the Athletes' Commission,[159] and the Challenge Commission.[160] **12–51**

The ICAS's main function is to promote arbitration in sport.[161] It is also responsible for the administration and financing of the CAS. It adopts and amends the Code of Sports-Related Arbitration.[162] The changes to the CAS structure and the creation of the ICAS in the aftermath of the SFT's decision in *Gundel* were officially approved in Paris on 22 June 1994 with the signing of the 'Agreement concerning the constitution of the International Council of Arbitration for Sport', more commonly referred to as the 'Paris Agreement'. In the aftermath of the signing of the Paris Agreement, the Olympic IFs and several NOCs began to recognise the jurisdiction of the CAS and included in their statutes an arbitration clause referring disputes to the CAS.[163] As discussed in the chapter on anti-doping, the World Anti-Doping Code (WADC) provides that the CAS is the appeals body for all international doping-related disputes. The Code of Sports-Related Arbitration was revamped and came into force on 22 November 1994. Over the years, it has been revised, and the most recent version came into force on 1 February 2023.[164] There are 70 articles which are divided between 26 Statutes (1–26) and 44 Rules (27–70).[165] **12–52**

The Code of Sports-Related Arbitration provides that the CAS comprises **12–53**

---

[157] The International Council of Arbitration for Sport (ICAS) Statutes B, S4 Composition <https://www.tas-cas.org/en/icas/code-icas-statutes.html#c235> accessed 19 May 2024.

[158] Code (n 156) s 7(2)(a). The Membership Commission is responsible for proposing the nomination of new CAS arbitrators and mediators to the ICAS.

[159] ibid s 7(2)(b). The Athletes' Commission rules on requests for legal aid. For more details, see 'Guidelines on Legal Aid before the Court of Arbitration for Sport' as from 1 February 2023 <https://www.tas-cas.org/en/add/legal-aid/> accessed 19 May 2024.

[160] Code (n 156) s 7(2)(c). For more information on the Challenge Commission, see rr 34 and 35.

[161] ICAS Statutes A Joint Dispositions s 2 provides: 'The purpose of ICAS is to facilitate the resolution of sports-related disputes through arbitration or mediation and to safeguard the independence of CAS and the rights of the parties' <https://www.tas-cas.org/en/icas/code-icas-statutes.html> accessed 19 May 2024.

[162] ICAS Statutes B (n 157) s 5.

[163] History of the CAS (n 129).

[164] Code (n 156).

[165] Statutes of the Bodies Working for the Settlement of Sports-Related Disputes and Procedural Rules.

of an OAD, an ADD and an AAD.[166] The CAS maintains a list of mediators and provides for the resolution of sports-related disputes through mediation.[167] According to Rule 27, the CAS has jurisdiction to hear a dispute if there is an arbitration clause included in a contract or in the regulations of the governing body (ordinary arbitration proceedings) or a challenge is made in relation to a decision made by a governing body and the statutes of that body provide for appeal to the CAS or there is a specific agreement that recognises the jurisdiction of the CAS (appeals arbitration proceedings). Rule 27 states:

> Such disputes may involve matters of principle relating to sport or matters of pecuniary or other interests relating to the practice or the development of sport and may include, more generally, any activity or matter related or connected to sport.[168]

12–54 The parties can be represented at the hearing by a person of choice who does not need necessarily to be a lawyer. The panel consists of three arbitrators, one chosen by each side with the two arbitrators selecting a president from the CAS list.[169] Arbitrators must be completely independent and not have been previously involved in the case.[170] The working languages of the CAS are French, English and Spanish.[171] In certain circumstances, another language may be used; however, this is subject to the agreement of CAS Panel and CAS Court Office.[172] The arbitrators apply the relevant rules and procedures of the particular sport. In certain urgent cases, the CAS can grant interim measures or can suspend the execution of a decision being appealed against as part of the appeal arbitration proceedings.[173] Awards are made in the form of a majority decision or, where this is not possible, a decision from the President of the Panel is made.[174] No dissenting opinions are published. The decision is in writing and will state the reasons behind the award. The award is final and binding as soon as it is communicated to the court office of the CAS – as discussed further on in the chapter, appeals are possible but on very limited grounds to the SFT.[175] CAS awards are enforced in accordance with the Convention on the Recognition and Enforcement of Foreign Arbitral Awards or, as it also known, the New York Arbitration Convention, which has been signed by 24 signatories and 172 parties.[176]

---

[166] Code (n 156) s 3.
[167] ibid. See also CAS Mediation Rules (n 126).
[168] Code (n 156).
[169] ibid r 40.2.
[170] ibid r 30.
[171] ibid r 29.
[172] ibid.
[173] ibid rr 48 and 52.
[174] ibid r 46.
[175] ibid r 46.
[176] More information on the New York Arbitration Convention can be found at <https://www.newyorkconvention.org/> accessed 19 May 2024. The contracting states are listed here: <https://www.newyorkconvention.org/countries> accessed

Ordinary Arbitration Division

The OAD hears disputes of first instance. Decisions are confidential unless the parties agree otherwise.[177] The ordinary procedure lasts between six and 12 months. This division hears cases involving contractual disputes, sponsorship deals, the sale of television rights, and other commercial disputes.[178] In the ordinary arbitration procedure, the parties are free to choose the applicable law, but if there is no agreement, Swiss law is applied. A recent example of an OAD decision is that of the *Professional Football Agents Association (PROFAA) v FIFA*.[179] This case involved a claim by the PROFAA that the new FIFA Football Agents Regulations (FFAR), due to come into force on 1 October 2023, were in breach of several laws, including European Union (EU) competition law, namely Article 101 of the Treaty on the Functioning of the European Union (TFEU) on restrictive agreements and Article 102 relating to abuse of a dominant position.[180] The CAS Panel cited the Opinion of Advocate General (AG) Rantos in the Court of Justice of the European Union (CJEU) case, *European Superleague*.[181] In paragraph 176, the CAS Panel reiterated the comments of AG Rantos: 12–55

19 May 2024. For an example of a court enforcing a CAS award, see *Pencil Hill Ltd v US Citta Di Palermo SpA*, Queen's Bench Division (Mercantile Court) (Manchester) [2016] 1 WLUK 262. This case concerned contracts relating to registration rights of a football player. Pencil Hill, a UK-registered company, acquired the registration for Paulo Dybala's rights from a Spanish football club, Cordoba, and sold them on to an Italian football club, Palermo, for €10m. A dispute arose after Palermo did not pay the fee in instalments, which attracted a penalty fee. The matter came before the CAS with the CAS reducing the amount of the penalty. Palermo appealed the decision to the SFT, which upheld the CAS decision. The Court held that it was not contrary to public policy to enforce a New York Convention award which included a penalty. In Ireland, s 24(1) of the Arbitration Act 2010 provides that the New York Convention, among other international conventions, has the force of law in the state.

177 Code (n 156) r 43. If the case involves an issue at first instance, a written request for arbitration is filed in the Court Office of the CAS.

178 ibid rr 38–46.

179 CAS 2023/O/9370 award of 24 July 2023 <https://www.tascas.org/fileadmin/user_upload/CAS_Award_9370.pdf> accessed 19 May 2024.

180 It was also argued by the PROFAA that art 19 FIFA FFAR infringed the General Data Protection Regulation, art 8 of the ECHR relating to the protection of private and family life, and art 7 of the EU Charter of Fundamental Rights, which provides for the right to privacy and by extension, as argued by PROFAA, the protection of business secrets: ibid [59]. Article 19 FFAR refers to Disclosure and Publication. FIFA shall make available the names and details of all agents, the services provided to each client, any sanctions imposed on agents and clients, and all transactions, including service fees paid to agents: see 'FIFA Football Agent Regulations (2023)' 30 <https://digitalhub.fifa.com/m/1e7b741fa0fae779/original/FIFA-Football-Agent-Regulations.pdf> accessed 16 May 2024. See ch 10 paras 10–98—10–104 for recent developments involving the FFAR.

181 Case C–333/21 *European Superleague Company SL v Unión de Federaciones Europeas de Fútbol (UEFA), Fédération Internationale de Football Association (FIFA), interveners: A22 Sports Management SL, Liga Nacional de Fútbol Profesional, Real Federación Española de Fútbol* ECLI:EU:C:2022:993, Opinion of Advocate General Rantos delivered on 15 December 2022 [31] <https://curia.europa.eu/juris/document/document.jsf?text=&docid=268624&pageIndex=0&doclang=EN&mode=lst&dir

> Sports federations [such as FIFA] play a key role in [sports governance], in particular from an organisational perspective, with a view to ensuring compliance with, and the uniform application of, the rules governing the sporting disciplines in question. That role has, moreover, been recognised by the Court, which has held that it falls to the sports federations to lay down appropriate rules for the organisation of a sporting discipline and that the delegation of such a task to sports federations is, in principle, justified by the fact that those federations have the necessary knowledge and experience to perform that task.[182]

12–56 In recognising 'that the activity of agents cannot be properly defined as being only "peripheral" to the world of football and its organization', the CAS Panel highlighted the important role occupied by agents in their representation of clubs and players and consequently:

> FIFA appears to be entitled, in general terms, to adopt rules' governing the activity of agents, in the same way as (and to the extent in which) it is entitled to issue regulations concerning the status and transfer of players.[183]

12–57 The CAS Panel dismissed the claims filed by PROFFA in their entirety. This case is noteworthy for a couple of reasons, one being that the case involved an attempt to prevent the coming into force of the FFAR and whether arbitration is the most appropriate method to resolve disputes involving complicated competition law issues.[184] Recent developments regarding the FFAR are discussed in Chapter 10.

Appeals Arbitration Division

12–58 The AAD hears disputes where the applicant is appealing a decision made by the governing body and the particular sport provides for recourse to the CAS.[185] The decisions are not confidential unless the parties otherwise agree. In appeal arbitration, the applicable law is that of what the parties have decided but in absence of such choice, the applicable law is that of where the governing body or federation is

=&occ=first&part=1&cid=3748250> accessed 19 May 2024. The CJEU decision is discussed in ch 13 paras 13–75—13–81.

182 CAS 2023/O/9370 (n 179).

183 ibid [179].

184 Marcos Araujo Boyd, 'Arbitration to Preventively Determine Competition Law Compliance? The CAS Award in *PROFAA v FIFA*' (*Kluwer Competition Law Blog*, 3 August 2023) <https://competitionlawblog.kluwercompetitionlaw.com/2023/08/03/arbitration-to-preventively-determine-competition-law-compliance-the-cas-award-in-profaa-v-fifa> accessed 19 May 2024. See also Richard Bush and Magnus Wallsten, 'Football Agents *(PROFAA) v FIFA* – CAS's Biggest EU Competition Law Decision Yet?' (*Law In Sport*, 31 August 2023) <https://www.lawinsport.com/topics/item/football-agents-profaa-v-fifa-cass-biggest-eu-competition-law-decision-yet> accessed 19 May 2024.

185 See Code (n 156) rr 47–59. The appellant could be an athlete or WADA, for example, who could question the leniency shown by the athlete's governing body.

domiciled. This division hears mainly disciplinary cases. An applicant must first exhaust all the internal remedies of the sport before seeking redress in the CAS.[186] The appeal must be lodged within 21 days of the communication of the decision from the governing body.[187]

An example of the appeals arbitration proceedings involves Maria Sharapova, a former number-one tennis player who tested positive for a banned substance, meldonium, on 2 March 2016.[188] Sharapova had competed at the Australian Open Tournament in Melbourne on 26 January 2016. At the tournament, the player had undergone a drug test in accordance with the 2016 version of the Tennis Anti-Doping Programme (TADP). She also had an out-of-competition anti-doping test in Moscow on 2 February 2016. Sharapova was informed that she could request the testing of her B Sample; however, she waived this right and through her counsel she informed the International Tennis Federation (IFT) that she had been taking the substance for 10 years because of a family history of diabetes and magnesium deficiency.[189] The drug was manufactured in Latvia and only distributed in Eastern European countries and Russia under the brand name 'Mildronate'.[190] The substance was not authorised by the Food and Drug Administration (FDA) in the US, nor was it authorised in the rest of Europe. WADA added it to its banned list on 16 of September 2015, and that came into effect on 1 January 2016.[191] WADA had spent the previous year **12–59**

[186] ibid r 47.

[187] ibid r 49. If it is an appeal case, a statement of appeal is filed. If the claimant is seeking ordinary arbitration, a brief statement describing the relevant legal issue must be provided and the claimant must set out in detail what is being sought. The claimant must include a copy of the relevant arbitration clause or arbitration agreement. The Court Office will then ascertain if the CAS has jurisdiction to hear the matter. If the CAS is found to have jurisdiction, the office forwards the application to the opposing body setting out the relevant time limits and the procedures for choosing the arbitrators. The respondent will be required to furnish an answer to the questions raised by the claimant. A defence will usually be included in the response. The respondent may question the jurisdiction of the CAS and may also file a counterclaim. After the necessary formalities have been followed, the parties are summoned to a hearing for the taking of evidence and oral pleadings: see rr 47–59 for more detail.

[188] Arbitration CAS 2016/A/4643 *Sharapova v International Tennis Federation* award of 30 September 2016 <https://jurisprudence.tas-cas.org/Shared%20Documents/4643.pdf> accessed 19 May 2024.

[189] ibid [7].

[190] ibid [36 (ii)].

[191] ibid [36 (v)]. See also Court of Arbitration for Sport, 'The Court of Arbitration for Sport (CAS) Reduces the Period of Ineligibility of Oleg Verniaiev to Two Years' (14 March 2023) <https://www.tas-cas.org/fileadmin/user_upload/CAS_Media_Release_8210.pdf> accessed 19 May 2024. The gymnast tested positive for meldonium on 26 August 2020 and was provisionally banned on 5 November 2020. He was banned by the International Gymnastics Federation (FIG) for four years on 12 July 2021, backdated to 5 November 2020. Verniaiev contended that he ingested contaminated meat. On 15 December 2022 there was a hearing via video link and the decision was announced on 14 March 2023. The CAS Panel reduced the period of ineligibility to two years, which ended on 5 November 2022. For

monitoring the substance and the standard ban under the WADC is four years for an anti-doping violation. At a press conference in March 2016, Sharapova announced that she had failed a drug test, and she took full responsibility for taking the substance. The ITF banned her for two years, with Sharapova appealing to the CAS, which reduced her sanction from 24 months to 15. The CAS Panel accepted that there was no significant fault on the part of the player and lessened her period of ineligibility by nine months. Thus, the CAS partially upheld the appeal which it reviewed *de novo*.[192] An important consideration for the CAS Panel was the fact that Sharapova did not hide that she was taking it and had been forthcoming from the time she received the news of her positive test in the A Sample.

12–60 The Chinese swimmer, Sun Yang, tested positive for a banned substance, which was his second anti-doping violation.[193] On 4 September 2018, an attempt was made to obtain blood and urine samples from the swimmer.[194] The Fédération Internationale de Natation (FINA, now World Aquatics), the world governing body for swimming, issued disciplinary proceedings against the athlete alleging that he had violated Articles 2.3 (Refusing or Failing to Submit) and 2.5 (Tampering or Attempted Tampering) of the FINA Doping Control Rules.[195] A FINA Doping Panel heard the case and acquitted the swimmer of any wrong doing.[196] WADA objected to the leniency and appealed the decision of FINA to the CAS. At the end of February 2020, the CAS Panel published its decision and it declared a period of ineligibility of eight years for the adverse analytical finding (AAF). Yang appealed the CAS decision to the SFT. He sought the setting aside of the arbitral award on the grounds that there was evidence of bias in relation to one of the CAS Panel. He referenced earlier alleged anti-Chinese comments the presiding arbitrator had posted on social media.[197] The SFT annulled the decision of the CAS and sent it back to the CAS to be re-heard with three new arbitrators. The newly constituted CAS Panel's decision was announced

---

another case involving an allegation of contaminated meat, see CAS 2011/A/2384 *Union Cycliste Internationale (UCI) v Contador Velasco & Real Federación Española de Ciclismo (RFEC)*; and CAS 2011/A/2386 *World Anti-Doping Agency (WADA) v Contador Velasco & RFEC* award of 6 February 2012 <https://jurisprudence.tas-cas.org/Shared%20Documents/2384,%202386.pdf> accessed 19 May 2024.

192 CAS 2016/A/4643 (n 188) [103]. There is an interesting article on the performance-enhancing properties of meldonium: see Wolfgang Schobersberger and others, 'Story Behind Meldonium – From Pharmacology to Performance Enhancement: A Narrative Review' (2017) 51(1) British Journal of Sports Medicine 22. The writers refer to the benefits of the increasing recovery rate of exercise performance.

193 CAS 2019/A/6148 *World Anti-Doping Agency v Yang & Fédération Internationale de Natation (FINA)* award of 22 June 2021 <https://www.tas-cas.org/fileadmin/user_upload/Award_6148__FINAL_.pdf> accessed 19 May 2024. This case is discussed in ch 6 paras 6–70—6–72.

194 ibid [4].

195 ibid.

196 ibid.

197 ibid [10].

on 22 June 2021. The Panel sanctioned the swimmer with a period of ineligibility of 4 years and 3 months, beginning on 28 February 2020.

A decision of the Football Association of Ireland (FAI) was challenged in the *Labuts* case.[198] Labuts, a Latvian professional football player, was a goalkeeper for Athlone Town AFC. He was accused of engaging in match-fixing in a game between Athlone Town and Longford Town FC, which took place on 29 April 2017. The end result was a 3–1 win to Longford. A report from the Union des Associations Européennes de Football (UEFA) Betting Fraud Detection System considered there to be 'clear and overwhelming betting evidence that the course or result of this match was unduly influenced with a view to gaining corrupt betting profits'.[199] In an interview with the FAI on 8 May 2017, Labuts contended he had no knowledge or involvement of match-fixing at the match in question.[200] Following a hearing, the FAI Disciplinary Committee sanctioned Labuts and banned him for 12 months from all football-related activity.[201] Labuts appealed the decision to the FAI Appeal Committee, who rejected his appeal. The FAI Appeal Committee was 'comfortably satisfied that Mr. Igor Labuts was guilty of deliberate actions designed to influence the result of the match which took place between Longford Town FC and Athlone Town AFC on 29 April 2017'.[202] The FAI argued before the CAS Panel that the requisite standard of proof was to be that of comfortable satisfaction.[203] The burden of proof lay on the regulatory body, the FAI, to prove that the player had engaged in match manipulation.[204] **12–61**

Comfortable Satisfaction

At this juncture it is important to note that CAS arbitral awards often refer to the law of where the governing body is domiciled, EU law, or general principles, as referred to earlier in this chapter. It will also refer to the statutes and regulations of the sports body. The standard of proof used is that of the comfortable satisfaction of the panel. The more serious the case is, the higher degree of satisfaction that is required. For less serious cases there is a corresponding lower threshold. The comfortable satisfaction standard occupies a position between the balance of probabilities but below beyond reasonable doubt. The CAS Panel in *Labuts* accepted the comfortable satisfaction standard; it was satisfied that the evidence proved that there was match manipulation.[205] **12–62**

---

[198] CAS 2018/A/6075 *Labuts v Football Association of Ireland* award of 17 July 2020 <https://jurisprudence.tas-cas.org/Shared%20Documents/6075.pdf> accessed 19 May 2024.
[199] ibid [4] and [5].
[200] ibid [6].
[201] ibid [7].
[202] ibid [9].
[203] ibid [46].
[204] ibid [45].
[205] ibid [65].

However, it was 'not comfortably satisfied by the evidence brought forward by the Respondent that the Appellant was actually involved in manipulating the result of the Match'.[206] The CAS Panel upheld the appeal and set aside the decision of the FAI.

12–63 In *Pechstein*, the CAS reiterated that the comfortable satisfaction test:

> is well-known in CAS practice, as it has been the normal CAS standard in many anti-doping cases even prior to the WADA Code. Several awards have withstood the scrutiny of the Swiss Federal Tribunal, which has stated that anti-doping proceedings are private law and not criminal law matters and that 'the duty of proof and assessment of evidence [are] problems which cannot be regulated, in private law cases, on the basis of concepts specific to criminal law'. The standard of proof beyond reasonable doubt is typically a criminal law standard that finds no application in anti-doping cases.[207]

Ad Hoc Division

12–64 The AHD is set up for a particular event such as the Olympic Games, the World Cup, the European Championships, and the Commonwealth Games. It renders a decision within 24 hours. The languages of the proceedings provided for at the Olympic Games are English, French or Spanish, as determined by the President of the AHD.[208] The AHD rules for the International Basketball Federation (FIBA) Basketball World Cup 2023 provided for only English as the language of the proceedings.[209]

12–65 The AHD was first used at the Olympic Games in Atlanta in 1996.[210] Since Atlanta, the AHD has been used at the Summer and Winter Olympic Games, the Commonwealth Games since 1998, the UEFA European Championships since 2000 and the AHD set up for the first time at the FIFA World Cup in 2006.[211] It hears disputes from the opening to the closing of the event.[212]

---

[206] ibid.

[207] CAS 2009/A/1912 *Claudia Pechstein v International Skating Union*; and CAS 2009/A/1913 *Deutsche Eisschnelllauf Gemeinshaft eV v International Skating Union* award of 25 November 2009 [53] <https://jurisprudence.tas-cas.org/Shared%20 Documents/1912,%201913.pdf> accessed 19 May 2024.

[208] Article 6 of the Arbitration Rules applicable to the CAS AHD for the Olympic Games <https://www.tas-cas.org/en/arbitration/ad-hoc-division.html> accessed 26 July 2024.

[209] Article 6 of the Arbitration Rules for the FIBA Basketball World Cup 2023 <https://www.tas-cas.org/fileadmin/user_upload/CAS_Arbitration_Rules_FIBA_WC_2023__final_.pdf> accessed 19 May 2024. The World Cup took place between 25 August and 10 September 2023: see art 1. It took place in three host countries – the Philippines, Japan, and Indonesia.

[210] For more information on the Ad Hoc Division see Richard H McLaren, 'Introducing the Court of Arbitration for Sport: The Ad Hoc Division at the Olympic Games' (2001) 12(1) Marquette Sports Law Review 515 <http://scholarship.law.marquette.edu/sportslaw/vol12/iss1/20> accessed 19 May 2024.

[211] History of the CAS (n 129).

[212] For examples of AHD decisions see *Bates and others* (n 21) and *Henry* (n 57).

Anti-Doping Division

The ADD is a more recent addition. Established in 2016, its role is to hear and decide anti-doping cases at first instance. The authority to do so is pursuant to the delegation of powers from the IOC, the Olympic IFs and any other signatories to the WADC. WADA explains the role of the ADD as follows: **12–66**

> Code signatories that have delegated their results management responsibilities to CAS ADD, gives them the power to decide whether or not there has been a violation of their anti-doping rules, as well as to decide any sanction, if applicable, in accordance with the Code.[213]

The ADD acts as a disciplinary tribunal in lieu of the anti-doping panel of the particular IF or other signatories to the WADC. One such example involved the International Biathlon Union (IBU).[214] A decision made by the ADD may be appealed to the AAD and subsequently to the SFT. In *A v IBU*, the SFT found that the ADD was 'not a "true" arbitral tribunal but replaces the first instance of the disciplinary tribunal of the federation'.[215] In relation to the alleged lack of independence of the ADD and the AAD raised by A, the athlete, the SFT deemed such arguments inadmissible. As Mavromati points out: **12–67**

> Interestingly, the SFT held that the coexistence of two instances within the same tribunal is not unusual, because several international tribunals have both first instance and appellate divisions (International Criminal Court, ECtHR etc.). The SFT also noted the efforts to guarantee the independence of the CAS ADD vis-à-vis the CAS, through separate and independent lists of arbitrators for each division.[216]

The SFT recognised the legitimacy of the ADD 'to the extent that such instance replaces the internal disciplinary instance of sports federations and is sufficiently independent from the CAS Appeals Division'.[217] **12–68**

---

[213] WADA, 'Court of Arbitration for Sport' <https://www.wada-ama.org/en/anti-doping-partners/court-arbitration-sport> accessed 26 July 2024.

[214] CAS 2020/A/7509 *Ustyugov v International Biathlon Union*; 4A_232/2022 judgment of 22 December 2022; *Ustyugov v International Biathlon Union* (motion to file the CAS Award CAS 2020/A/7509) 12 January 2023 <https://jusmundi.com/en/document/decision/fr-evgeny-ustyugov-v-international-biathlon-union-ibu-decision-du-tribunal-federal-suisse-4a-232-2022-thursday-22nd-december-2022#decision_43247> accessed 19 May 2024.

[215] Despina Mavromati, 'Swiss Federal Tribunal Confirms the Validity of CAS Anti-Doping Division Proceedings as First Instance Tribunal' (*Law In Sport*, 13 January 2023) <https://www.lawinsport.com/topics/item/swiss-federal-tribunal-confirms-the-validity-of-cas-anti-doping-division-proceedings-as-first-instance-tribunal> accessed 19 May 2024.

[216] ibid.

[217] ibid.

Appeals to the Swiss Federal Tribunal and Applications to the European Court of Human Rights

12–69 As mentioned previously, decisions of the CAS can be appealed to the SFT on the narrowest of circumstances as provided for under Article 190(2) of the Swiss Private Law International Act (PILA).[218] These grounds are:

> (a) If a sole arbitrator was designated irregularly or the arbitral tribunal was constituted irregularly;
> (b) If the arbitral tribunal erroneously held that it had or did not have jurisdiction;
> (c) If the arbitral tribunal ruled on matters beyond the claims submitted to it or if it failed to rule on one of the claims;
> (d) If the equality of the parties or their right to be heard in an adversarial proceeding was not respected;
> (e) If the award is incompatible with Swiss public policy (ordre public).[219]

12–70 Bondolfi explains that the SFT's 'decisions on appeals against CAS rulings are by nature purely cassatory, ie they can only lead to the cancellation of the decision that is being appealed'.[220] The number of appeals of CAS awards to the SFT has 'greatly increased' over the years.[221] Examples include *Gundel*, *Semenya*, *Pechstein* and *Mutu*.

12–71 As discussed in Chapter 7 'Athletes with Differences of Sexual Development and Transgender Athletes', Semenya appealed the CAS decision to the SFT, with the Swiss Court temporarily suspending the Differences of Sexual Development (DSD) Regulations with immediate effect pending the appeal being heard.[222] The STF's final decision was handed down on 25 August 2020 and published on 8 September 2020.[223] It dismissed both actions – the action brought by Semenya, and the action

---

[218] For an interesting discussion on sports cases and the SFT, see Marco Vedovatti, 'Key Sports Law Decisions by the Swiss Federal Tribunal Published in First Half of 2023' (*Law In Sport*, 1 September 2023) <https://www.lawinsport.com/topics/item/key-sports-law-decisions-by-the-swiss-federal-tribunal-published-in-first-half-of-2023> accessed 19 May 2024.

[219] See Frequently Asked Questions (n 120). The PILA are available here <https://www.trans-lex.org/602000/_/swiss-private-international-law-act-/#head_91> accessed 19 May 2024.

[220] Sibilla Bondolfi, 'Why Swiss Judges Ruled on the Caster Semenya Case' (*Swissinfo.ch*, 4 June 2019) <https://www.swissinfo.ch/eng/international-sports_why-swiss-judges-ruled-on-caster-semenya-case/45009992> accessed 19 May 2024.

[221] Louise Reilly, 'An Introduction to the Court of Arbitration for Sport (CAS) & the Role of National Courts in International Sports Disputes' (2012) 1 Journal of Dispute Resolution 63, 75.

[222] 'Swiss Federal Court: Semenya Free to Run without Medication until Appeal Heard' (*Swissinfo.ch*, 4 June 2019) <https://www.swissinfo.ch/eng/society/athletics-case_swiss-federal-court—semenya-free-to-run-without-medication-until-appeal-heard/45007906> accessed 19 May 2024.

[223] *Semenya v Switzerland* App no 10934/21 (ECtHR, 17 May 2021) <https://hudoc.echr.coe.int/eng#{%22itemid%22:[%22001-226011%22]}> accessed 3 September 2024.

brought by Athletics South Africa. It found that Semenya's appeal 'did not appear with high probability to be well founded'.[224]

Athletes must consent based on an ad hoc contract or a standard clause within the statutes and regulations of the domestic governing body or the IF that should a dispute arise between them and the governing body, then it will be resolved exclusively by reference to arbitration before the CAS. As mentioned, any clause that endeavours to oust the jurisdiction of the court would most likely be deemed unconstitutional. However, law courts have demonstrated a reluctance to become involved in CAS decisions, as seen in *Raguz v Sullivan* where the New South Wales Court of Appeal 'confirmed' the 'exclusivity' of the CAS.[225] The inclusion of this standard clause was an issue raised by Claudia Pechstein, a German speed skater. In 2009, the ISU banned Pechstein for two years on the ground that there were abnormal blood values discovered during blood tests. This was part of the ISU's longitudinal haematological profiling of the athlete. The ISU took this to mean that Pechstein had engaged in the prohibited method of blood doping. Pechstein countenanced this with the argument that she had an inherited blood disorder and that was the reason for her irregular blood results.[226] She challenged the ISU's decision before the CAS, which rejected her appeal and upheld the decision of the ISU.[227] Pechstein appealed the decision of the CAS to the SFT; however, her appeal was rejected. She also initiated proceedings in the German Courts where she sought damages from the ISU on the grounds that it had abused its monopolistic position in forcing athletes to sign an arbitration clause to submit disputes to the CAS which, Pechstein submitted, lacked independence.[228] As the CAS is based in Switzerland, Pechstein lodged an application against Switzerland under the ECHR.[229] **12–72**

[224] Press Release of the Swiss Federal Supreme Court, judgment of 25 August 2020 (4A_248/2019, 4A_398/2019) 'DSD Regulations: Caster Semenya's Appeal Against the Decision' (Lausanne, 8 September 2020) 2 <https://www.bger.ch/files/live/trash-727c3e30-911c-443a-8a01-fa5cda5f780f/83c04f87-e4fc-433c-a3a5-2009fb001a36> accessed 19 May 2024.

[225] [2000] NSWCA 240. In 2000, Angela Raguz was dropped by the Australian Olympic judo team after Rebecca Sullivan successfully challenged her omission from the team in the CAS. Raguz appealed the CAS decision to the Supreme Court of New South Wales. The proceedings were removed to the New South Wales Court of Appeal. The Court of Appeal held that the Supreme Court did not have jurisdiction and leave to appeal was denied. See Meinrad Vetter, 'The CAS: An Arbitral Institution with its Seat in Switzerland' (2008) Sports Law eJournal 1, 3 <http://www.austlii.edu.au/au/journals/SportsLeJ/2008/4.pdf> accessed 19 May 2024.

[226] Rüdiger Morbach, 'The Pechstein Saga Continues: The German Federal Constitutional Court Grants Another Round on the Rink' (*Kluwer Arbitration Blog*, 27 July 2022) <https://arbitrationblog.kluwerarbitration.com/2022/07/27/the-pechstein-saga-continues-the-german-federal-constitutional-court-grants-another-round-on-the-rink/> accessed 19 May 2024.

[227] *Pechstein* (n 207).

[228] See Morbach (n 226) for a good summary of the Germany litigation.

[229] *Case of Mutu and Pechstein v Switzerland* App nos 40575/10 and 67474/10 <https://hudoc.echr.coe.int/eng#{%22fulltext%22:[%22\%22CASE%20

Before the ECtHR, Pechstein complained about athletes having to sign arbitration clauses in order to compete in competitions and thus being forced to submit to the jurisdiction of the CAS. Pechstein also disagreed with the method in which the arbitrators were selected; she argued that the sports federations had 'a decisive weight' in the composition of the CAS.[230] The ECtHR gave cognisance to the fact that athletes were compelled to agree to arbitration clauses, but held that the CAS was an independent and impartial tribunal established by law. In relation to the method in which arbitrators were chosen, the ECtHR rejected this claim on the grounds that it was too vague and hypothetical.[231] Pechstein also complained about not being granted a public hearing, a point on which the ECtHR agreed. Article 6(1) of the ECHR provides for the right to a fair and public hearing within a reasonable time by an independent and impartial tribunal established by law. Pechstein had requested a public hearing before the CAS in 2009 and her request had been denied. Pechstein was awarded €8,000 in damages for a violation of her rights under Article 6(1).[232]

12–73 Mutu and Pechstein were enjoined as applicants in the case against Switzerland. Mutu, a Romanian football player, entered into a five-year contract with Chelsea on 11 August 2003. Mutu moved from the Italian Club, AC Parma, with Chelsea paying a €22.5m transfer fee. Under the terms of the employment contract, Mutu would receive an annual salary of £2.35m, and an £330,000 sign-on bonus to be paid in five instalments. His contract with Chelsea was terminated without notice after he tested positive for cocaine in October 2004. The Disciplinary Commission of the Football Association (FA) suspended Mutu from playing for seven months, with effect from 24 October 2004, and fined him £20,000.[233] FIFA's Disciplinary Committee extended the seven-month ban to apply worldwide.

12–74 Under FIFA's Regulations, the decision whether the contract had been breached without just cause, the so-called 'triggering elements', could be heard by the Dispute Resolution Chamber (DRC) of the FIFA Players' Status Committee or by written agreement between the parties that a national sports arbitration tribunal could decide the matter.[234]

OF%20MUTU%20AND%20PECHSTEIN%20v.%20SWITZERLAND\%22%22],%22itemid%22:[%22001-186828%22]}> accessed 19 May 2024. These cases are also discussed in ch 6.

[230] ibid [24].

[231] ibid [150].

[232] ibid [195].

[233] The seven months was conditional on Mutu successfully completing a rehabilitation programme. A mitigating factor was Mutu's explanation that personal issues had led him to take cocaine: see 'FA Takes Lenient Mutu Line' *The Guardian* (London, 4 November 2004) <https://www.theguardian.com/football/2004/nov/04/newsstory.sport> accessed 19 May 2024.

[234] CAS 2005/A/876 *Mutu v Chelsea Football Club* award of 15 December 2005 [2] <https://jurisprudence.tas-cas.org/Shared%20Documents/876.pdf> accessed 19 May 2024.

The parties agreed that the domestic tribunal could decide the matter and, the Football Association Premier League Appeals Committee (FAPLAC) was tasked with deciding whether or not the actions of Mutu constituted gross misconduct as argued by Chelsea. If Mutu was found to have engaged in gross misconduct, Chelsea argued that it should be deemed a 'unilateral breach without just cause'. Chelsea also requested that the FAPLAC make a determination that it was entitled to bring a claim before the DRC to obtain sporting sanctions and/or an award of damages to compensate the club for its alleged loss. Mutu claimed that the relevant section, s 21(a) of the FIFA Regulations, only applied if the contract was terminated or renounced by the player, ie where the player wrongfully walks away from their contract to play for another club. The FAPLAC accepted Chelsea's submissions and thus rejected Mutu's claim. Mutu appealed the decision of the FAPLAC to the CAS. The CAS Panel agreed with the FAPLAC's interpretation of s 21(a) and found that the actions of Mutu constituted a unilateral breach without just cause. The CAS Panel agreed

> with the Club that if the draftsmen had intended such an artificial distinction they would have spelled it out in clear terms. Why should a player who walks away from a contract without just cause be treated differently than one who undermines his team's performance by intentionally playing poorly or continually missing training? Secondly, it is plain from the text of the FIFA Regulations that they are designed to further 'contractual stability' and the latter is as much affected by a player's walk-out as by a player breaking the contract through other serious misconduct, e.g. by using substances forbidden in sport.[235]

Following the CAS Panel decision, Chelsea referred the matter to the DRC in relation to compensation sought for the loss it had suffered. However, the DRC contended that it did not have jurisdiction to award damages in a situation where the determination had been made by a domestic tribunal.[236] The CAS Panel upheld Chelsea's appeal and set aside the decision of the DRC. The CAS Panel concluded that the DRC had jurisdiction to determine and impose the appropriate sanction and/ or order that damages are paid. The DRC accepted jurisdiction ordered Mutu to pay €17,173,990 in compensation to Chelsea. Mutu once again appealed the decision to the CAS.[237] The appeal was dismissed, with the CAS ordering the payment of the compensation along with interest.[238] **12–75**

After three CAS appeals, Mutu lodged an appeal to the SFT.[239] Mutu's claim was based on his assertion that the CAS was neither independent **12–76**

---

[235] ibid [24] and [25].

[236] CAS 2006/A/1192 *FC Chelsea v Mutu* award of 21 May 2007 [22] <https://jurisprudence.tas-cas.org/Shared%20Documents/1192.pdf> accessed 19 May 2024.

[237] CAS 2008/A/1644 *Mutu v Chelsea Football Club Ltd* award of 31 July 2009 <https://jurisprudence.tas-cas.org/Shared%20Documents/1644.pdf> accessed 19 May 2024.

[238] ibid.

[239] Decision of the Swiss Federal Tribunal 4A_458/2009, *Adrian Mutu v Chelsea Football Club*, CAS 2008/A/1644 <https://jusmundi.com/en/document/decision/

nor impartial because one of the panel members had been a partner in a law firm that represented the interests of the owner of Chelsea, Roman Abramovich.[240] In dismissing the appeal under Article 190(2)(e) on the grounds of public order, the SFT ordered Mutu to pay costs.

12–77 In an enjoined case with Pechstein, Mutu lodged an application to the ECtHR arguing that his right to a fair trial under Article 6(1) of the ECHR had been breached.[241] The ECtHR dismissed the application, finding that his rights had not been violated. The matter was finally concluded in 2018, 14 years after Mutu's contract with Chelsea had been terminated. His unsuccessful attempts at evading paying damages to Chelsea resulted in Mutu having to pay over €17m plus the costs in the SFT and the ECtHR.

12–78 Semenya lodged an application against Switzerland at the ECtHR, alleging that the decision of the SFT was in breach of her human rights protected by the ECHR.[242] On 11 July 2023, the ECtHR handed down its decision in *Semenya v Switzerland*. By a 4–3 majority, it found there to be a violation of Article 14 taken together with Article 8 and a violation of Article 13 in relation to Article 14 taken together with Article 8 of the ECHR. As discussed in Chapter 7, Switzerland referred the decision to the Grand Chamber on 6 November 2023. The hearing before the Grand Chamber took place on 15 May 2024.[243]

Conclusion

12–79 The increased use of ADR in sport is a welcomed development. There are situations when recourse to the courts will still be necessary. However, ADR offers a more flexible, efficient and cost-effective method of redress. As bodies such as the DRA, SDSI and CAS comprise of legal experts with an inveterate interest and knowledge of sport, a more specialised system has emerged which is of benefit to the sport, sports bodies and competitors.

12–80 The Irish courts and indeed courts in other jurisdictions are reluctant to intervene in the decisions of sports governing bodies and will only do so in the most exceptional circumstances. Law courts have highlighted the need for sportspersons to exhaust the internal disciplinary mechanisms

---

en-adrian-mutu-v-chelsea-football-club-decision-du-tribunal-federal-suisse-4a-458-2009-thursday-10th-june-2010#decision_20422> accessed 19 May 2024.

240 ibid [3.2.1].

241 *Mutu and Pechstein* (n 229).

242 *Semenya v Switzerland* App no 10934/21 (ECHR, 17 May 2021) 148 <https://hudoc.echr.coe.int/eng#{%22appno%22:[%2210934/21%22],%22itemid%22:[%22001-226011%22]}> accessed 15 May 2024.

243 European Court of Human Rights, '*Semenya v Switzerland*' ECHR 115 (2024) 15 May 2024 <https://www.echr.coe.int/w/grand-chamber-hearing-concerning-switzerland-2> accessed 19 May 2024.

within their sports and, if that fails, to avail of mediation or arbitration. As the *lex sportiva* of the CAS has evolved, general principles have developed. Complex cases such as *PROFAA v FIFA* have brought to the fore EU law, the ECHR, and decisions of the ECtHR, and such well-thought-out CAS decisions are to be embraced from an academic point of view.

The CAS has been instrumental in creating an international corpus of sports law. Beloff, Kerr and Demetriou make an important comment in relation to its jurisdiction.[244] There are certain matters that will never go before the CAS: for example, the decisions of referees. However, the issue is not as straightforward as one may think. It is often difficult to distinguish between rules and the rule of law. Beloff, Kerr and Demetriou note that refereeing decisions may not of themselves give rise to the intervention of the CAS; however, 'appeals from them could raise questions of fair procedures and other recognised grounds of interference which might engage the attention of the CAS or other international arbitral bodies'.[245] It is from the complicated cases that the CAS has gained gravitas. The disputes which commingle different areas of law from varying sources have provided it with more legitimacy and made it more akin to a law court, albeit without the cost and formalities. **12–81**

The CAS is a perfectible institution; there has been an incremental refinement of its procedures. It is has made strides in establishing its independence from the IOC, and recourse to the SFT and the ECtHR offers a 'copper bottomed guarantee of ultimate justice'.[246] James asserts that the 'impact' of the CAS 'on sporting justice worldwide cannot be overstated, as almost all major international sports federations (IFs) engage its services as a forum for final appeals and all elite anti-doping cases have a right of appeal to it'.[247] **12–82**

---

[244] Michael Beloff and Tim Kerr and Marie Demetriou, *Sports Law* (Hart Publishing 1999)

[245] ibid.

[246] Morris and Little (n 50).

[247] Mark James, *Sports Law* (3rd edn, Palgrave 2017) 51.

CHAPTER 13

EUROPEAN UNION LAW AND SPORT

Introduction

Prior to the entry into force of the Treaty on the Functioning of the European Union (TFEU) on 1 December 2009, the European Union (EU) did not have an explicit competence for sport and 'therefore an official EU sport policy did not exist'.[1] As will be discussed in this chapter, Articles 6(e) and 165 were included in the TFEU in order to emphasise the importance of sport in the EU and to give the European Commission a formal competence, albeit somewhat limited, on sport. It is important to note that prior to the inclusion of these articles, EU law applied to and continues to apply to sport in situations where sport constitutes an economic activity. The European Court of Justice (ECJ), now known as the Court of the Justice of the European Union (CJEU), played a pivotal role, on a case-by-case basis, in applying then European Community (EC) law to sporting matters of an economic nature, including competition law, media law (as discussed in Chapter 10) and sport-related intellectual property rights (IPR).[2] On the organisation of sport, case law has centred on the free-movement rights of sportspersons, transfers, financial fair play and agents.[3] 13–01

This chapter will begin by tracing Treaty and other developments relating to sport up until the TFEU. It will examine the 'specificity of sport' and situations where the EU courts and the European Commission do not get involved, namely in matters that are of 'purely sporting interest'. The chapter will examine seminal sport-related cases and look at some recent referrals to the CJEU, including a case concerning the General Data Protection Regulation (GDPR) and anti-doping rules[4] 13–02

---

1 European Olympic Committee (EOC) EU Office, 'Guide to EU Sport Policy' (November 2017) 5 <https://www.euoffice.eurolympic.org/wp-content/uploads/2022/12/guide_to_EU_Sport_Policy-paginas-1-13.pdf> accessed 19 May 2024.

2 The ECJ's involvement in sport goes back to 1974 and the case of C–36/74 *Walrave and Koch v Union Cycliste Internationale* [1974] ECR I–1405, ECLI:EU:C:1974:140.

3 Football agents are discussed in ch 10 paras 10–89—10–104.

4 C–115/22 *EN v Nationale Anti-Doping Agentur Austria GmbH (NADA), Österreichischer Leichtathletikverband (ÖLV), Word Anti-Doping Agency (WADA)* ECLI:EU:C:2023:676. Advocate General Ćapeta delivered her Opinion on 14 September 2023 <https://eur-lex.europa.eu/legal-content/EN/TXT/?uri=CELEX:62022CC0115> accessed 19 May 2024. C–115/22 *EN v Nationale Anti-Doping Agentur Austria GmbH (NADA), Österreichischer Leichtathletikverband (ÖLV), Word Anti-Doping Agency (WADA)* ECLI:EU:C:2024:384. The judgment was handed down on 7 May 2024 <https://

and the preliminary ruling in relation to the proposed Superleague in European football.[5]

Treaty Developments and Sport

13–03 The EU did not have a specific competence to develop a sports policy until the TFEU came into effect on 1 December 2009.[6] Article 26(2) of the TFEU provides that the aim of the EU is to establish an area where goods, persons, services, and capital can freely circulate. Accordingly, sport is an area of commercial importance and thus sports bodies must not engage in activities that would breach the treaty provisions. However, it was not until the Treaty of Amsterdam that sport was mentioned in a Treaty.[7] Following the 1995 decision of the ECJ in the *Bosman* case, representatives of the Member States raised the issue of sport at an Intergovernmental Conference (IGC) established to revise the Maastricht Treaty, and this resulted in a Declaration being attached to the Treaty of Amsterdam.[8] The Declaration emphasised the social and cultural significance of sport in its role of integrating the people of Europe.[9] While the Declaration acknowledged the specific character

---

eur-lex.europa.eu/legal-content/EN/TXT/?uri=CELEX%3A62022CJ0115> accessed 29 July 2024.

5 Judgment of 21 December 2023, Case C–333/21 *European Superleague Company v Fédération internationale de football association (FIFA), Union of European Football Associations (UEFA), intervening parties: A22 Sports Management SL, Real Federación Española de Fútbol (RFEF), Liga Nacional de Fútbol Profesional (LNFP),* ECLI:EU:C:2023:1011.

6 The Treaty of Lisbon amended two Treaties: the European Community (EC) Treaty and the Treaty on European Union (TEU, also known as Maastricht). It replaced the EC Treaty with the Treaty on the Functioning of the European Union (TFEU) and replaced the Maastricht Treaty with a revised Treaty on European Union. Collectively, the two Treaties are referred to as the Lisbon Treaty.

7 Its full title was The Treaty of Amsterdam amending the Treaty on European Union and the Treaties Establishing the European Communities. It came into force on 1 May 1999. According to McArdle, the Adonnino Report in 1985 is cited as being the 'first formal engagement with sporting activity': see David McArdle, 'Sports Law, Sports Policy and The Amateur Athlete: Reflections on *Topfit and Biffi v Deutscher Leichtathletikverband*' (2023) 1(1) Sports Law, Policy and Diplomacy Journal 1, 2. Paragraph 5.9.1 of the Adonnino Report called for the promotion of action in the 'encouragement of sporting activities within the Community and the use of Community emblems in such events' and para 5.9.2 discussed the need for combating violence in and around the stadium with a call for closer cooperation between the authorities of the Member States in preventing and stamping out hooliganism: The 'Adonnino Report' – Report to the European Council by the ad hoc committee 'On a People's Europe' (A 10.04 COM 85, SN/2536/3/85) <https://www.ombudsman.europa.eu/en/historical/en/4659> accessed 19 May 2024.

8 Commission Staff Working Paper, 'The Development and Prospects for Community Action in the Field of Sport' (Brussels, 29 September 1998) 3 <https://ec.europa.eu/assets/eac/sport/library/documents/doc252_en.pdf> accessed 19 May 2024.

9 It stated the following: 'The Conference emphasises the social significance of sport, in particular its role in forging identity and bringing people together. The Conference therefore calls on the bodies of the European Union to listen to sports associations when important questions affecting sport are at issue. In this

(specificity) of sport, it was somewhat aspirational. It did not enjoy the force of law and, as Siekmann remarks, the Declaration 'clearly was a general policy statement'.[10] This is noteworthy considering that sport in the EU is a multibillion-euro industry. According to Eurostat figures from 2023, in 2022, '1.51 million people were employed in the sports sector in the EU, representing 0.8% of total employment'.[11]

After the Declaration, the European Commission published the *European* 13–04
Model of Sport, a consultation document.[12] This document sought to determine the essential characteristics of sport in the EU by attaching questionnaires addressed to relevant stakeholders. The document looked for the views of Member States and sports bodies in three important areas: namely, the organisation of sport in Europe, the relationship between sport and television broadcasting, and sport and social policy.[13] The document identified a pyramid model pertaining to the organisation of sport in Europe with the European Sports Federations at the helm, the National Sports Federations next, followed by the Regional Sports Federations with Grassroots Federations/Clubs at the bottom of the pyramid.[14] The conclusions were presented in the *Helsinki Report on Sport* in 1999.[15] The report acknowledged that certain developments in sport, including its commercialisation, were denigrating the important social and educational functions of sport.[16] The violence that erupted at times at sporting events was identified as a concern and one which would need to be tackled by the responsible authorities by stepping up their cooperation.[17] The report recommended that the Member States, the Community institutions and governing bodies work together to

connection, special consideration should be given to the particular characteristics of amateur sport.' At an Intergovernmental Conference (IGC) established to amend the Maastricht Treaty, the social function of sport was identified and, consequently, Amsterdam included the Declaration: see European Commission, 'The European Model of Sport Consultation Paper of DG X Sport Unit' (Brussels, 1998) <https://www.sportaustria.at/fileadmin/Inhalte/Dokumente/Internationales/EU_European_Model_Sport.pdf> accessed 19 May 2024.

[10] Robert CR Siekmann, *Introduction to International and European Sports Law* (ASSER International Sports Law Series) (TMC Asser Press 2012) 70.

[11] Eurostat, '10.9% Increase in Employment in Sport in 2022 in the EU' 28 July 2023 <https://ec.europa.eu/eurostat/web/products-eurostat-news/w/ddn-20230728-1> accessed 19 May 2024.

[12] The European Model of Sport Consultation Paper of DG X Sport Unit (n 9).

[13] This included sport and education, sport as a means of social integration, combating racism and promoting tolerance, sport and the environment, sport and public health, sport and doping, and sport and employment: see ibid 18–21.

[14] ibid 2–3.

[15] European Commission, 'Report from the Commission to the European Council with a View to Safeguarding Current Sports Structures and Maintaining the Social Function of Sport within the Community Framework' (Brussels, 10 December 1999, COM(1999) 644 final) <https://eur-lex.europa.eu/LexUriServ/LexUriServ.do?uri=COM:1999:0644:FIN:EN:PDF> accessed 19 May 2024.

[16] ibid 4.

[17] ibid 5.

eradicate doping in sport: 'Doping and sport are diametrically opposed. There can be no let-up in the fight against doping.'[18]

13–05 In December 2000, the European Council's Conclusions of the Presidency included Annex IV Declaration on the Specific Characteristics of Sport.[19] The European Council convened its summit meetings in December 2000.[20] The Declaration was not attached to the Treaty of Nice, but instead included in the European Council's Conclusions. This was unlike the Amsterdam Declaration, which was included in the Treaty proper. The Declaration on the Specific Characteristics of Sport was more detailed than the Amsterdam Declaration as it contained 17 articles based on six pillars, namely 'Amateur sport and sport for all', 'Role of sports federations', 'Preservation of sports training policies', 'Protection of young sportsmen and -women', 'Economic context of sport and solidarity' and 'Transfers'.[21] As with the Amsterdam Declaration, the Nice Declaration was not binding. It merely reiterated that the Community lacked any direct powers and that 'the conduct of sporting affairs' were primarily the responsibility of sporting organisations and the Member States.[22]

13–06 The Declaration recognised that sport had 'social, educational and cultural functions' which combined to make sport 'special'.[23] The Declaration endorsed the social aspects of sport, including social inclusion, the protection of children in sport, and the promotion of sport among people with disabilities.[24] Under the pillar of 'Economic context of sport and solidarity', the Declaration acknowledged the importance of broadcasting rights and the resulting revenue.[25] In relation to transfers, the Declaration expressed the European Council's desire for dialogue between the football authorities, in particular, and the professional organisations representing sportspeople, the Community and the Member States 'with due regard for the specific requirements of sport, subject to compliance with Community law'.[26]

13–07 The ill-fated Constitutional Treaty provided sport with a treaty basis for the first time under Article III–282, which provided: 'The Union shall contribute to the promotion of European sporting issues, while

---

18 ibid 10.

19 It was also referred to as the Nice Declaration: its full title was the Declaration on the specific characteristics of sport and its social function in Europe, of which account should be taken in implementing common policies <https://www.europarl.europa.eu/summits/nice2_en.htm> accessed 19 May 2024.

20 France held the Presidency of the European Council from 1 July to 31 December 2000. The meetings took place 7–10 December.

21 Nice Declaration (n 19) paras 3–16.

22 ibid para 1.

23 ibid.

24 ibid paras 3–6. It fell under the pillar of 'Amateur sport and sport for all'.

25 ibid 15.

26 ibid 16.

taking account of the specific nature of sport, its structures based on voluntary activity and its social and educational function.'[27] It is clear from the text that the article was reiterating earlier rhetoric. It did not provide for the harmonisation or approximation of sport at EU level. Nevertheless, it acknowledged the importance of sport in the further integration of the EU.

The White Paper on Sport represented the European Commission's first time in 'addressing sport-related issues in a comprehensive manner'.[28] The Pierre de Coubertin Action Plan accompanied the White Paper.[29] The European Commission's Staff Working Document titled 'The EU and Sport: Background and Context' provided more detail as its function was to 'present the background, context and, where necessary, rationale of the proposals presented in the European Commission's White Paper on Sport'.[30] The White Paper contained several proposed actions that were to be implemented or supported by the European Commission. The purpose of the Action Plan was to consolidate the actions laid out in the White Paper and provide guidance to the European Commission in its endeavours to realise these plans, while respecting the principle of subsidiarity and the autonomy of sports governing bodies.[31] Of significance was the inclusion in the European Commission's Staff Working Document of the fight against doping, the prevention of and fight against racism and violence, the application of competition law to sport, the protection of sport-related IPR and the free-movement rights of sportspersons. In relation to football, the Staff Working Document discussed the transfer system, players' agents, the protection of minors, and a licensing system for clubs. More generally, albeit with a reference 13–08

27 Treaty establishing a Constitution for Europe, OJ C 310.

28 White Paper on Sport {SEC(2007) 932} {SEC(2007) 934} {SEC(2007) 935} {SEC(2007) 936} (/* COM/2007/0391 final */) .2 <https://eur-lex.europa.eu/legal-content/EN/TXT/?uri=celex%3A52007DC0391> accessed 19 May 2024.

29 European Commission Staff Working Document – Action Plan 'Pierre de Coubertin' – Accompanying document to the White Paper on Sport {COM(2007) 391 final} {SEC(2007)932} {SEC(2007)935} {SEC(2007)936} (/* SEC/2007/0934 final */) <https://eur-lex.europa.eu/legal-content/EN/TXT/?uri=CELEX%3A52007SC0934> accessed 19 May 2024.

30 European Commission Staff Working Document – The EU and Sport: Background and Context – Accompanying document to the White Paper on Sport {COM(2007) 391 final} {SEC(2007)932} {SEC(2007)934} {SEC(2007)936} (/* SEC/2007/0935 final */) <https://eur-lex.europa.eu/legal-content/EN/TXT/HTML/?uri=CELEX:52007SC0935> accessed 19 May 2024.

31 Article 5(3) of the TEU states: 'Under the principle of subsidiarity, in areas which do not fall within its exclusive competence, the Union shall act only if and in so far as the objectives of the proposed action cannot be sufficiently achieved by the Member States, either at central level or at regional and local level, but can rather, by reason of the scale or effects of the proposed action, be better achieved at Union level.' The principle is based on the premise that decisions are taken at the closest possible level to the citizen. If the EU decides to take action in an area that is not within its exclusive competence, it must justify why the action is not to be taken at national, local or regional level. Closely associated with the principle of subsidiarity is the principle of proportionality. The EU must not go beyond what is necessary to achieve the objectives of the Treaties.

to football, the Staff Working Document referred to corruption, money laundering and other forms of financial crime, and broadcasting rights.

13–09 The White Paper was the result of discussions over a two-year period between the European Commission and stakeholders, including the Member States, the International Olympic Committee (IOC) and other sports federations.[32] The White Paper, while recognising the social and economic importance of sport, emphasised the need for sporting bodies and Member States to respect the requirements of EU law.[33] The White Paper, the European Commission's Staff Working Document and the Action Plan concluded with a section on follow-up, namely, structured dialogue with sports stakeholders, cooperation with the Member States and social dialogue.[34]

13–10 The Constitutional Treaty formed the basis of the Lisbon Treaty, which came into force on 1 December 2009. Articles 6 and 165 of the TFEU emphasise the importance of sport in the EU and gives it a formal competence, namely the competence to carry out actions to support, coordinate or supplement the actions of the Member States with regard to sport.[35] Article 165 gives the EU a 'soft' competence on sport, as it provides that the European Parliament and the Council, acting in accordance with the ordinary legislative procedure, after consulting the Economic and Social Committee and the Committee of the Regions, shall adopt incentive measures, excluding any harmonisation of the laws and regulations of the Member States. The Council, on a proposal from the European Commission, shall adopt recommendations. Given that sport is regulated at national level by the individual Member States, the exclusion of any measures that endeavour to harmonise the laws means that the practical significance of Article 165 is questionable. Weatherill

---

32 The EU and Sport: Background and Context (n 30) Annex III: Consultations with the Stakeholder. The list of federations and other stakeholders are listed in the Annex.

33 This has been emphasised in the case law of the Court of Justice: see Joined Cases of C–51/96 *Deliège v Ligue Francophone de Judo et Disciplines Associées ASBL, Ligue Belge de Judo ASBL, Union Européenne de Judo*; and C–191/97 *Pacquée* [2000] ECR I–2549 where the Court referred to the 'considerable social importance' of sport at [41] and [106] in C–415/93 *Union Royal Belge des Societies de Football Association ASBL & Others* v *Jean-Marc Bosman* [1995] ECR I–4921 where the Court referred to the 'considerable social importance of sporting activities and in particular football'.

34 Social dialogue was defined as 'discussions, consultations, negotiations and joint actions undertaken by the social partner organisations representing the two sides of industry (management and labour). It is a useful means by which the social partners assist in the definition of European employment and social standards, and play an important role in the governance of the Union': The EU and Sport: Background and Context (n 30) para 5.3.

35 Article 6: 'The Union shall have competence to carry out actions to support, coordinate or supplement the actions of the Member States. The areas of such action shall, at European level, be: (a) protection and improvement of human health; (b) industry; (c) culture; (d) tourism; (e) education, vocational training, youth and sport; (f) civil protection; (g) administrative cooperation.'

refers to the explicit reference to sport as being both 'profound and trivial'. It was profound as it was the first time sport was granted a Treaty base and, 'Given the fundamental principle that the EU possesses only the competences conferred upon it by its Member States the novelty achieved by this express attribution in the field of sport counts as immensely constitutionally significant.'[36] However, he posits two reasons why its inclusion is trivial:

> First because the content of the new provisions has been drawn with conspicuous caution, so that the EU's newly acquired powers in fact represent a most modest grant made by the Member States. And second because, notwithstanding the barren text of the pre-Lisbon Treaty, the EU has in fact long exercised a significant influence over the autonomy enjoyed by sports federations operating on its territory. So the Lisbon Treaty reveals a gulf between constitutional principle – where it seems to carry great weight – and law- and policymaking in practice, on which its effect is likely to be considerably less striking.[37]

The recent decision of *TopFit and Biffi v Deutscher Leichtathletikverband* has challenged the triviality of Article 165 TFEU.[38] According to McArdle, the CJEU's 'approach was far more robust'.[39] Similarly, di Marco asserts that the decision can 'be explained in light of the evolving importance attached to sport, and in particular on the basis of "the constitutional objective of integration" of EU citizens in the host Member State'.[40] **13–11**

The EU Institutions, namely the European Commission, the European Parliament, and the Council, have recognised the importance of sport and have responded in different ways, as the next part of the chapter explains. **13–12**

The EU Institutions and Sport

Within the European Commission, sport falls under the Directorate General of Education, Youth, Sport and Culture (DG EAC). The European Commission provides funding for sport through the Erasmus+ programme and pilot projects and preparatory actions (PPPAs).[41] The **13–13**

36 Stephen Weatherill, 'EU Sports Law: The Effect of the Lisbon Treaty' in Andrea Biondi, Piet Eeckhout, and Stefanie Ripley (eds), *EU Law after Lisbon* (Oxford University Press 2012) 403.

37 ibid.

38 Judgment of the Court (Third Chamber) of 13 June 2019, C-22/18, *TopFit eV and Daniele Biffi v Deutscher Leichtathletikverband eV*, ECLI:EU:C: 2019:497.

39 McArdle (n 7) 8.

40 Antonio di Marco, 'Amateur Sport and Union Citizenship in the Biffi Case: Towards a European Sporting Citizenship' (2020) 27(5) Maastricht Journal of European and Comparative Law 598, 609. Di Marco concludes that the '"constitutional objective of integration" of EU citizens would lead sport within the scope of Union citizenship rights, independently of the economic dimension of sporting activities and of the EU sporting competence': 611.

41 For more detail, see European Commission, 'About Funding Opportunities'

Erasmus+ and PPPAs are managed by the European Education and Culture Executive Agency (EACEA).[42] The competence bestowed by Lisbon means that the European Commission can promote sport in other EU policy areas and programmes, including health and education.[43]

13–14 An important role within the European Commission's remit is that of policing and ensuring observance of competition law under Articles 101 (restrictive agreements) and 102 (abuse of a dominant position) of the TFEU. The European Commission has applied both Articles to sporting bodies engaged in a commercial activity, thus constituting 'undertakings' for the purposes of EU competition law.[44] In light of the pre-existing powers exercised by the European Commission in relation to competition law and its application to sport, the explicit Treaty base given to sport highlights its triviality, as explained by Weatherill above. The application of competition law and free-movement provisions has allowed the EU to intervene in matters which are not within its competence but are the preserve of the Member States. Sport is but one example where 'the functionally broad reach of the Treaty provisions on free movement and competition collide with Member States powers to act in realms' in which the EU does lack competence under the Treaty, but such provisions have enabled the EU 'to usurp national regulatory choices by acting as a substitute legislator'.[45] This is evident in the *Meca-Medina* case, which will be discussed in detail further on in the chapter.

13–15 The European Parliament is involved in sport through the Committee on Culture and Education (CULT).[46] While respecting the principle of subsidiarity, the European Parliament has recognised the importance of sport and the need for the EU to be involved.[47] However, its involvement has been confined to 'soft law' measures which are not legally binding. These soft law measures include resolutions on the European Dimension in Sport,[48] the progress on equality between women and men in the EU,[49]

<https://sport.ec.europa.eu/funding/about-funding-opportunities> accessed 19 May 2024.

42 For more information on the EACEA, see <https://www.eacea.ec.europa.eu/about-eacea/about-eacea_en> accessed 19 May 2024.

43 See the European Commission's 'Health Lifestyle 4 All' initiative <https://sport.ec.europa.eu/initiatives/healthylifestyle4all-2021-2023> accessed 19 May 2024.

44 For example, Case C–519/04 P *Meca-Medina and Majcen v Commission* [2006] ECR I–06991 where the International Olympic Committee was deemed to be engaged in an economic activity and thus EU competition law applied.

45 Stephen Weatherill, 'Anti-Doping Revisited: The Demise of the Rule of "Purely Sporting Interest"?' in Stephen Weatherill (ed), *European Sports Law Collected Papers* (2nd edn, TMC Asser Press 2014) 381.

46 More detail on CULT can be found at <https://www.europarl.europa.eu/committees/en/cult/about> accessed 19 May 2024.

47 See (n 31) for a definition of subsidiarity.

48 European dimension in sport European Parliament resolution of 2 February 2012 on the European dimension in sport (2011/2087(INI)) OJ C 239E <https://eur-lex.europa.eu/legal-content/EN/TXT/?uri=celex%3A52012IP0025> accessed 19 May 2024.

49 European Parliament resolution of 10 March 2015 on progress on equality

match-fixing and corruption in sport,[50] and corruption cases in FIFA (Fédération Internationale de Football Association).[51] More recently, the European Parliament's resolution on esports and video games recognised the challenges and opportunities presented by the video game and esports ecosystems.[52]

Sport is presented in the Council through the configuration of the Education, Youth, Culture and Sport (EYCS) Council. As the regulation of sport (and education, culture, and youth) does not fall within the competence of the EU, the Council as a nation-centred institution represents the interests of the Member States. Thus, the role of the EU through the EYCS Council is limited to providing 'a framework for cooperation between member states, for exchange of information and experience on areas of common interest'.[53] The Council can adopt several positions having no legal effect in the form of conclusions, resolutions, or recommendations relating to sport. Conclusions are adopted following a debate during a meeting and it represents a political position or commitment regarding a specific topic. Resolutions establish what future work is required in a specific policy area. While lacking in legal effect, the Council may invite the European Commission to make a proposal or take further action under Article 241 TFEU.[54] A recent resolution on reviewing the EU Member States' representation and **13–16**

between women and men in the European Union in 2013 (2014/2217(INI)) OJ C 316 <https://eur-lex.europa.eu/legal-content/GA/TXT/?uri=CELEX:52015IP0050> accessed 19 May 2024. Paragraph 44 calls for combating gender stereotypes and '[a]sks the Member States, following the adoption of the Council conclusions on gender equality in sport, to make full use of the opportunities offered by sport to promote gender equality, notably by defining specific action plans to combat stereotypes and violence, favour equality among professional sportsmen and sportswomen, and promote sport for women'.

50 European Parliament resolution of 14 March 2013 on match-fixing and corruption in sport (2013/2567(RSP)) OJ C 36 <https://eur-lex.europa.eu/legal-content/EN/TXT/?uri=CELEX%3A52013IP0098> accessed 19 May 2024.

51 European Parliament resolution of 11 June 2015 on recent revelations on high-level corruption cases in FIFA (2015/2730 (RSP)) OJ C 407 <https://eur-lex.europa.eu/legal-content/EN/TXT/?uri=CELEX:52015IP0233> accessed 19 May 2024.

52 European Parliament resolution of 10 November 2022 on esports and video games (2022/2027(INI)) <https://www.europarl.europa.eu/doceo/document/TA-9-2022-0388_EN.pdf> accessed 19 May 2024.

53 Council Configurations, 'Education, Youth, Culture and Sport Council Configuration (EYCS)' <https://www.consilium.europa.eu/en/council-eu/configurations/eycs/> accessed 26 July 2024. The EYCS meets three or four times a year. The membership depends on what is under discussion: for example, if it relates to sport and education the relevant ministers from the Member States attend. However, the full configuration is required to meet twice a year. The full configuration includes the ministers for education, culture, youth, media, communication, and sport. In some Member States there is overlap between ministries.

54 Article 241 TFEU provides: 'The Council, acting by a simple majority, may request the Commission to undertake any studies the Council considers desirable for the attainment of the common objectives, and to submit to it any appropriate proposals. If the Commission does not submit a proposal, it shall inform the Council of the reasons.'

coordination for the World Anti-Doping Agency (WADA) was adopted by the Council (EYCS) at its meeting of 15–16 May 2023.[55] Three seats in WADA's Foundation Board are allocated to the representatives from the EU. The Foundation Board is WADA's highest decision-making body and consists of 42 members representing the Olympic Movement and Public Authorities.[56] The resolution provides that the representatives must be in charge of sport at ministerial level and that one of the representatives will be from one of the Member States forming the incumbent Trio Presidency, one from the Member States forming the future Trio Presidency, and 'one seat will be jointly allocated by the Member States meeting within the Council to a person responsible for sport at ministerial level'.[57]

Sport as an Economic Activity

13–17 Although sport can, depending on the circumstances, be classified as an economic activity, the European Economic Community (EEC) was initially reluctant to become involved in the regulation of sport. It was largely left up to the individual Member States to regulate sport at national level. While the Council, the European Commission and European Parliament were limited to soft-law measures, the ECJ, by applying Treaty provisions to sport, was able to apply EEC law to sport.[58]

13–18 In the 1970s, the ECJ handed down two important judgments in the cases of *Walrave and Koch v Union Cycliste Internationale*[59] and *Doná*

---

55 General Secretariat of the Council, 'Resolution Reviewing the EU Member States' Representation and Coordination for WADA' (Brussels, 25 May 2023) 9136/23 <https://data.consilium.europa.eu/doc/document/ST-9136-2023-INIT/en/pdf> accessed 19 May 2024. During the meeting of the Youth and Sport Council meeting on 15 May 2023, the ministers also discussed the need for ensuring respect for human rights in the organisation of major international sporting events. For more details, see <https://data.consilium.europa.eu/doc/document/ST-8676-2023-INIT/en/pdf> accessed 19 May 2024.

56 World Anti-Doping Agency, 'Foundation Board' <https://www.wada-ama.org/en/who-we-are/governance/foundation-board> accessed 26 July 2024.

57 Resolution Reviewing the EU Member States (n 55). Nine of the 10 Council configurations have a rotating presidency in which three Member States form a trio and, in an 18-month period, each Member State holds the presidency of the Council for six months. More details on the presidencies can be found at <https://www.consilium.europa.eu/en/council-eu/presidency-council-eu/> accessed 19 May 2024. The Foreign Affairs' Council has a permanent president referred to as the High Representative of the Union for Foreign Affairs and Security Policy; the role is explained here: <https://eur-lex.europa.eu/EN/legal-content/glossary/high-representative-of-the-union-for-foreign-affairs-and-security-policy.html> accessed 19 May 2024.

58 The EEC Treaty was also known as the Treaty of Rome. It entered into force on 1 January 1958. The EEC Treaty was renamed the European Community (EC) Treaty by the Treaty on European Union (TEU). The TEU was also known as the Maastricht Treaty and came into force on 1 November 1993.

59 (n 2). The case was referred from the Dutch Court to the ECJ under the preliminary reference procedure. The preliminary reference allows a national court to refer

v Montero.[60] In *Walrave and Koch*, the plaintiffs, two Dutch nationals, challenged a Union Cycliste Internationale (UCI) rule that required the pacemaker (the person who sets the pace in a race) to be the same nationality as the stayer (medium distance motorcyclist). The plaintiffs contended that the rule was in breach of EEC law as it constituted a form of discrimination based on nationality and was also contrary to the free movement of workers and the freedom to provide a service.[61] The ECJ held that sport was subject to EEC law insofar as it constituted an economic activity within the meaning of Article 2 of the EEC Treaty. However, the ECJ noted that the prohibition on discrimination did not apply to the composition of sport teams, in particular national teams, as the formation of such teams was a question of purely sporting interest and, as such, had nothing to do with economic activities.[62] In the *Doná v Montero* case, the ECJ was tasked with reconciling the nationality rules of the Italian Football Federation and the exclusion of non-Italian players.[63] The Italian Football Federation organised and controlled the activities of football clubs in Italy.[64] It was the only body in Italy empowered to control the clubs and, in order to play, the club had to be in possession of a federation membership card. Under the rules of the Federation, such membership was generally only granted to Italian players residing in Italy.[65] The rule effectively excluded non-Italian nationals from acting as professional players in Italian clubs.[66] The chairman of an Italian football club instructed Doná, a sports agent, to seek top foreign professionals to play on the chairman's team. Doná arranged several offers and asked for the payment of his expenses. The club refused to pay the agent as there was a restriction on the number of foreign players that could be fielded on a domestic team. Doná argued that the restriction was discriminatory and contrary to the free movement of workers and the freedom to provide a service.

---

a matter to the CJEU in situations where the national court is unsure as to how to interpret or apply a provision of EU law. While the preliminary reference is being heard, the case in the national court is delayed. The preliminary reference is found under Article 267 TFEU.

60 C–13/76 *Doná v Montero* [1976] ECR 1333.

61 At the time of the case the relevant Treaty articles were arts 48–51 on the free movement of workers and arts 59–66 on the freedom to provide a service. The current articles are arts 45–48 (workers) and arts 56–62 (services) of the TFEU.

62 *Walrave and Koch* (n 2) 1418 [8].

63 *Doná* (n 60).

64 Opinion of Advocate General Trabucchi delivered on 6 July 1976, *Gaetano Donà v Mario Mantero*, ECLI:EU:C:1976:104 <https://eur-lex.europa.eu/legal-content/HR/TXT/?uri=CELEX:61976CC0013> accessed 19 May 2024.

65 ibid. The AG accepted that it was possible to field foreign players if the club was not a member of the Federation; however, he emphasised the fact that membership alone of the Federation 'enables a football club to compete for the championships. If this condition is not satisfied, it is in practice impossible to play as a professional.'

66 The rules provided for one exception: namely, foreign nationals who were never members of a foreign federation and who were resident in Italy could be enrolled as youth players or amateurs for recreational purposes.

13–19 The ECJ, in applying the case of *Walrave and Koch*, held that professional footballers enjoyed the benefits of the treaty provisions on freedom of movement of persons and of the provision of services. However, the ECJ added that in some circumstances the application of nationality restrictions to those who played on national teams would be a 'non-economic' issue and therefore exempt from the EEC Treaty's provisions.[67]

13–20 Advocate General (AG) Trabucchi, in his Opinion, argued that a sporting exception outside of discrimination based on nationality could be justified.[68] The AG was suggesting that more categories of restrictions could be permitted and that the sporting exception could be used to justify restrictions even in situations involving economic activities.[69] The ECJ did not embrace the AG's expansive approach and instead adopted a more narrow construction of the sporting exemption. The ECJ held that restrictions on foreign players could be permitted in 'certain matches'.[70]

The Significance of Walrave and Koch *and* Doná

13–21 The cases of *Walrave and Koch* and *Doná* are significant as the ECJ held that the EEC Treaty applied to sport so long as it constituted an economic activity. As a corollary, the ECJ created a sporting exception to the application of EEC law. If an activity is of 'purely sporting interest' and 'has nothing to do with economic activity', then the EEC Treaty had no application.[71] For example, in *Doná*, the ECJ held that nationality restrictions on foreign players playing for national teams in international competitions would fall within the sporting exception.[72] However, national teams playing in international games 'have direct economic consequences',[73] although this is something the ECJ did not consider in the judgment. The decisions have been the source of much criticism.[74]

---

[67] *Doná* (n 60) para 1.

[68] AG Trabucchi Opinion (n 64) 1345.

[69] ibid. The AG referred to restrictions on players that were not from the locality of a local club. The AG opined: 'While, within those limits, the principle of engaging only local players is, as one of the principles of freedom to manage one's own business, normally accorded unreservedly to sporting clubs, if the restriction means the exclusion only of foreign nationals, its justification as an exception to the full application of the rules on freedom of movement for workers or the freedom to provide services must be based on solid sporting or athletic requirements.'

[70] *Doná* (n 60) [14].

[71] *Walrave and Koch* (n 2) [8].

[72] AG Trabucchi Opinion (n 64) 1344 proffered that restrictions on foreign players in national teams could be justified 'so as to ensure that the winning team will be representative of the State of which it is the champion team'. As Catherine Barnard notes, the Court was '[r]elying on the contentious argument that such national games were not commercial in nature': *The Substantive Law of the EU: The Four Freedoms* (7th edn, Oxford University Press 2022) 249.

[73] Stephen Weatherill, 'Fair Play Please: Recent Developments in the Application of EC Law to Sport' (2003) 40 Common Market Law Review 51, 56.

[74] Richard Parrish and Samuli Miettinen, *The Sport Exception in European Union Law* (The Hague: TMC Asser Press 2008) 85.

13–22 In the aftermath of the *Doná* case, the European Commission 'invited' the Union des Associations Européennes de Football (UEFA) to change the rules and it gave assurances that it would not initiate legal action during this transitionary period.[75] UEFA assured the European Commission that it would remove the restrictions

> on the number of contracts entered into by each club with players from other Member States and would set the number of such players who may participate in any one match at two, that limit not being applicable to players established for over five years in the Member State in question.[76]

13–23 However, the rules remained unaltered.[77] In 1982 the European Commission sent a letter to UEFA and the national football federations as part of an inquiry into the lack of action since 1978.[78] The respondents contended that the transitionary period was indefinite. Following a request by the European Commission to the federations to alter their rules prior to the 1986/87 season, the request was ignored, and the federations introduced binding rules that restricted the fielding of foreign players.[79] The European Parliament passed a Resolution on the freedom of movement of professional footballers in the Community in April 1989, which requested the European Commission to ensure that EEC law was enforced against UEFA.[80] Following discussions with the European Commission in 1990 and 1991, UEFA implemented the 3 + 2 rule whereby each club could field three foreign players and two assimilated players.[81] Assimilated players were defined as players who played in a country for an uninterrupted period of five years, three of which had been spent at youth level. For example, a club like AC Milan could only field three non-Italian players and two assimilated players, leaving places for six domestic players. A transfer fee was also required in respect of out-of-contract players. These agreements had been sanctioned by a gentleman's agreement between the European Commission and UEFA. A gentleman's agreement is an anti-competitive (or restrictive) agreement which falls under Article 101 of the TFEU (or Article 85 at the time of the *Bosman* case). A restrictive agreement is void according to Article 101(2). However, an exemption may be granted under Article 101(3) if it can be shown that the agreement will be of benefit to the consumer, aid economic or technical progress and

---

75 Press Release, 'Professional Football: European Court Rules in the Bosman Case' (IP/95/1411, 15 December 1995) para viii <https://ec.europa.eu/commission/presscorner/detail/en/IP_95_1411> accessed 19 May 2024.

76 *Bosman* (n 33) [27].

77 Press Release (n 75) para viii.

78 ibid para ix.

79 ibid.

80 European Parliament, 'Resolution of the European Parliament on the Freedom of Movement of Professional Football Players in the Community' (1989) Rapporteur: James L Janssen van Raay. OJ C120/1989.

81 Press Release (n 75) paras xi and xii. The 3 + 2 rule was to be implemented by 1 January 1992 and it was decided that a dispute over the level of compensation paid for a player should not preclude that player moving to another club.

the restriction is proportionate to the aims in which it seeks to achieve. The actions of the European Commission are questionable given that the rules seriously impeded the free movement of persons and went against the decision of the ECJ in *Doná*, which clearly narrowed restrictions to foreign players on national teams and did not apply to domestic clubs. The gentleman's agreement meant that clubs were permitted to limit the number of foreign players (including EC citizens) who could play in the domestic league, and in European competitions clubs could limit the number of non-national players. The European Commission received three formal complaints from three professional football players, including Jean Marc Bosman, whose case was referred to as the 'most prominent'.[82] As will be discussed in more detail, both the transfer system and quota system were challenged by Bosman.

Europe and the Football Transfer System: The *Bosman* Case

13–24 Jean Marc Bosman was a Belgian professional football player who played for RC Liège, a Belgian first-division club. Before his contract was about to expire, in April 1990 RC Liège offered Bosman a new one-year contract at a lower salary than his previous contract. Bosman rejected the offer and was placed on the transfer list. A compensation fee was attached to his contract. French club USL Dunkerque expressed an interest in Bosman and was willing to pay the transfer fee. RC Liège and Dunkerque negotiated a transfer for one year, which included the terms that Bosman would play for Dunkerque and, after a year, the club could obtain the services of Bosman in return for an additional fee.

13–25 The transfer fell through as RC Liège had reservations about Dunkerque's solvency and thus would not authorise the Belgian Federation of Sport to forward the necessary documentation to allow for the transfer. RC Liège suspended Bosman, resulting in him being unable to play for the season. Bosman initiated legal action, claiming that the Belgian Football Federation and FIFA–UEFA transfer rules had prevented his transfer to Dunkerque. He brought an action against RC Liège and later against the Belgian Football Federation and UEFA. He sought a declaration from the national court that the transfer rules and nationality clauses were incompatible with the Treaty of Rome rules on competition law and the free movement of workers.[83] The Belgian National Court referred the issue to the ECJ under the preliminary reference procedure.[84]

---

[82] ibid para xv.

[83] Article 45 of the TFEU provides: 'A worker from one member state is free to take up employment in another member state, free from restrictions which do not apply to nationals of the state in which it is sought to work.'

[84] See (n 59) for details on the preliminary reference.

The Transfer System and 3 + 2 Rule

Both UEFA and FIFA maintained that the transfer system merely regulated the business relationship between clubs and did not affect players. However, the ECJ rejected this contention as it was satisfied that the effect of the system was to impede football players' free movement as workers. It was further argued by UEFA and FIFA that the transfer system provided a measure of economic equilibrium within football. In support of this, reference was made to the nursery clubs that received a transfer fee (development fee) in return for training and developing the talent of a young player. The ECJ accepted that there was a legitimate interest in maintaining a sporting and financial balance; however, the use of a transfer system for out-of-contract players was not appropriate to secure that objective, nor was it suitable for maintaining youth development schemes.[85] An important factor for the ECJ was the fact that the transfer fees under the transfer system were not related to the costs of training young players.[86] Often the fee paid was disproportionate to the cost of training the player. The bigger, richer clubs could pay more than a smaller club. **13–26**

On the issue of the 3 + 2 rule, UEFA and FIFA contended that such a requirement ensured that there was a bond between club and country and preserved national identity in European competition.[87] Unconvinced by this argument, the ECJ pointed out that there were no rules which restricted a club to fielding players from its town or district in national competitions. The ECJ held that a restriction on the number of foreign players violated the free movement of workers under Article 48 of the EC Treaty and under Council Regulation 1612/68, which prohibited provisions that restricted the employment of EC nationals in an undertaking or activity by number or percentage.[88] The ECJ also rejected the contention that the 3 + 2 rule prevented the richest clubs from 'securing the services of the best players'.[89] **13–27**

AG Lenz in his Opinion discussed the alleged hypothetical nature of the nationality rules and their impact on Bosman.[90] The CJEU does not **13–28**

---

85 *Bosman* (n 33) [106]–[109].

86 ibid [109].

87 ibid [123] and [124].

88 Article 4(1) of Regulation (EEC) No 1612/68 on freedom of movement for workers within the Community, 15 October 1968. This was repealed and replaced by Regulation (EU) No 492/2011 of the European Parliament and of the Council of 5 April 2011 on freedom of movement for workers within the Union (codification) [2011] OJ L 141.

89 *Bosman* (n 33) [107].

90 Opinion of the Advocate General of the Court of Justice of 20 September 1995, *Union royale belge des sociétés de football association ASBL v Jean-Marc Bosman, Royal club liégeois SA v Jean-Marc Bosman and others and Union des associations européennes de football (UEFA) v Jean-Marc Bosman*, C–415/93 (ECLI:EU:C:1995:293 <https://curia.europa.eu/juris/showPdf.jsf?docid=99458&doclang=EN> accessed 19 May 2024.

accept preliminary references that are hypothetical in nature.[91] However, AG Lenz opined that a 'question is not hypothetical simply because the fact on which it is based has not yet occurred. A preventive action for a declaration is an important means of securing effective protection of legal rights.'[92] It was accepted that 'Bosman's career was at no time hindered by the rules on foreign players'; it could therefore be viewed as purely hypothetical that he would in the future find it difficult to play for a club outside of his Member State.[93] Following a lengthy consideration, the AG concluded that the Belgian national court had deemed the question on the nationality rules to be admissible.[94] In following the case law of the ECJ, AG Lenz contended that the ECJ should depart from the assessment of the domestic court to refer a matter under the preliminary reference procedure 'only in well-founded exceptional cases'.[95] In deeming the question admissible, AG Lenz opined that the question as to the compatibility of Article 48 EC Treaty and the rules on foreign players could not 'reach the Court in any other way'.[96] The European Commission had not used its infringement proceedings power under then Article 169 EC Treaty (now Article 258 TFEU), for which it was criticised, as much uncertainty surrounded the success of such an action due to procedural concerns.[97] In addition, no Member State had sent a preliminary reference to the ECJ concerning the nationality rules since the *Doná* case in 1976.[98] The AG viewed this not as a matter of chance but felt rather that '[t]hose affected [were] either unwilling or unable to have the matter clarified by the courts'.[99]

13–29 The ECJ, in adopting a holistic approach, held that the issues were not hypothetical, and the national court provided the Court 'with a clear statement of the surrounding facts, the rules in question and the grounds on which it believe[d] that a decision on the questions submitted [was] necessary to enable it to give judgment'.[100]

---

91 ibid. Advocate General Lenz ibid [82] quoted from [18] of C–244/80 *Foglia v Novello* [1981] ECR 3045 where the ECJ held: 'It must in fact be emphasized that the duty assigned to the Court by Article 177 is not that of delivering advisory opinions on general or hypothetical questions but of assisting in the administration of justice in the Member States.'

92 ibid [97].

93 ibid [63] and [97].

94 ibid [100].

95 ibid [101]. The AG added: 'That circumstance itself is a reason for not regarding the relevant question in the present case as inadmissible.'

96 ibid [112].

97 ibid [116]. The AG explained this by citing the answer of the European Commission dated 18 December 1991 to a written question posed by a member of the European Parliament, that infringement proceedings against a Member State posed 'special problems' as the possible restriction of freedom of movement was imposed 'by private individuals rather than public authorities': OJ 1992 C 102, 41.

98 AG Lenz Opinion (n 90) [112].

99 ibid.

100 *Bosman* (n 33) [62].

The transfer system for out-of-contract players was also deemed to be a breach of EC law.[101] The ECJ held that Article 48 of the EC Treaty guaranteed the free movement of workers within the Member States and ruled that the requirement that a fee be paid for an out-of-contract player moving from one club in the EC to another EC club was a breach of the treaty. The fact that the transfer fee concerned a business relationship between clubs and not between clubs and players did not preclude the application of Article 48.[102] There was a nexus between the clubs having to pay a transfer fee and the 'players' opportunities for finding employment and the terms under which such employment is offered'.[103] Article 48 applied to rules laid down by UEFA, FIFA and the Belgian FA which determined the terms on which professional sportspersons could engage in gainful employment.[104] 13–30

It is interesting to note that the ECJ did not give judgment on the compatibility of the transfer and quota system with the competition provisions as the Court considered them to contrary to Article 48 and thus it was not necessary to rule on the interpretation of Articles 85 and 86 of the Treaty.[105] However, in his Opinion, AG Lenz did consider in detail Articles 85 and 86 and opined that the transfer rules and quota system were in breach of Article 85.[106] 13–31

Implications of Bosman

The *Bosman* decision was instrumental in transferring the bargaining power from the clubs to the players as they were recognised as workers within the meaning of now Article 45 TFEU. The decision also signalled the end of transfer fees for out-of-contract players. Since *Bosman*, a club in the EU may field as many EU players as it wishes. A transfer fee is still required for players who are still under contract. 13–32

The decision applies only to EU players; there are still restrictions regarding non-EU players.[107] The decision has affected both clubs and players. Clubs began signing players on longer contracts to prevent a player from being able to move to another club on a free transfer, and this resulted in the payment of higher salaries to the players.[108] It was 13–33

---

[101] ibid 5081.
[102] ibid [75].
[103] ibid.
[104] ibid [87].
[105] ibid [138].
[106] AG Lenz Opinion (n 90) [253]–[286]. At [286] the AG concluded that art 86 had not been infringed.
[107] The decision operates at EU level, but includes European Economic Area countries (Norway, Liechtenstein, and Iceland); it also applies to many non-EU states that have association agreements with the EU. This is discussed in more detail further on in this chapter.
[108] Smaller clubs find it difficult to sign players on a longer contract as they do not have the money to pay the higher wages. For a detailed discussion on the English Premier League, see Mihailo Radoman and Marcel C Voia, 'Internal Promotion

suggested that the nursery clubs who had trained a player through the youth ranks were liable to lose that promising talent to a new club for free.[109] However, Norbäck and others use 'a talent development model with a hiring model' to illustrate how the *Bosman* ruling 'changed the incentive for talent development in the European football market'.[110] The ruling resulted in 'a major institutional change in European sports' and 'signalled a shift in the competitive structure and modernization of the game as we know it today'.[111]

13–34 According to Radoman and Voia:

> the English Premier League is considered to be the richest among top European leagues in terms of club turnover and player salaries, especially after the *Bosman* ruling. This ensures a highly competitive environment where top players from around the globe compete for playing time opportunities. The high salaries in the league attract world-class players, and the financial resources available to clubs do not constrain their player recruitment efforts as much as in other European leagues.[112]

13–35 The *Bosman* decision changed the landscape of European football. Before *Bosman*, the free movement of footballers was greatly impeded under the quota system and the transfer rules for out-of-contract players. Pre-*Bosman*, until a transfer fee was agreed between the old club and the new club, the out-of-contract player could be thwarted indefinitely from moving to another club so long as the old club paid the player's wages.[113]

Training Compensation and Solidarity Mechanisms

13–36 The *Bosman* decision had far-reaching implications, including the establishment of the transfer windows. Furthermore, the decision caused clubs to question the viability of training and developing young players. The club would have invested time and money in the development of that player only for them to move to another club who would benefit from such training without compensation (a transfer fee) being paid on the expiration of the player's contract. In response to concerns raised by clubs and associations, FIFA changed its Regulations on the Status and Transfer of Players (RSTP) in 1997; however, the European Commission considered the revised RSTP to be incompatible with EC

---

and the *Bosman* Ruling: Evidence from the English Premier League' (2022) 36(4) Labour 445.

109 For more details, see Mihailo Radoman and Marcel C Voia, 'Youth Training Programs and their Impact on Career and Spell Duration of Professional Soccer Player' (2015) 29(2) Labour 163. See also Pehr-Johan Norbäck, Martin Olsson, and Lars Persson, 'Talent Development and Labour Market Integration in European Football (2021) 44 World Economy 367.

110 Norbäck, Olsson and Persson (n 109) 368.

111 Radoman and Voia (n 109) 164.

112 Radoman and Voia (n 108) 448.

113 Norbäck, Olsson and Persson (n 109) 397.

law.[114] Following discussions between UEFA, FIFA, and the European Commission, revised RSTP were accepted in March 2001. The European Commission announced:

---

[114] On 30 April 2024, AG Szpunar delivered his Opinion in the case of C-650/22 *International Federation of Association Football (FIFA) v BZ, Interveners: Union Royale Belge des Sociétés de Football-Association ASBL (URBSFA), SA Sporting du Pays de Charleroi, International Federation of Professional Footballers, National Union of Professional Footballers, International Federation of Professional Footballers, Europe Division* ECLI:EU:C:2024:375. The RSTP were the subject of a preliminary reference by the Court of Appeal, Mons, Belgium. The preliminary reference concerned the compatibility of arts 9 (1) and 17 (1), (2) and (4) of the 2014 RSTP with art 45 TFEU and art 101 TFEU. The Belgian Court referred the matter to the CJEU on 17 October 2022 and requested that the CJEU clarify if arts 45 and 101 should be interpreted as precluding a player and the new club being held jointly and severally liable in respect of the compensation due to the club whose contract with the player has been terminated without just cause under art 17 (2) in conjunction with the sporting sanctions provided for in art 17 (4) and the financial sanctions provided for in art 17 (1). The second question concerned art 9 (1) and art 8.2.7 of Annex 3 of the RSTP and the International Transfer Certificate (ITC) and whether it was a breach of EU law that the RSTP prohibit the new club from registering a professional footballer who has terminated their previous contract without just cause. The former club is permitted to withhold the ITC required to register the player in situations where there is a contractual dispute between the former club and player. The player identified as BZ sought damages before the Belgian Court for loss of earnings of €6m due to the disputed provisions of the RSTP. BZ refers to Lassana Diarra, a French footballer player, who played for Lokomotiv Moscow. His contract with the Russian club was terminated following a dispute over performance and wages. There were three years remaining on his contract. The matter was referred to FIFA's Dispute Resolution Chamber (DRC) who found against Diarra and imposed a fine on the player. The RSTP relating to termination without just cause prevented Diarra moving to the Belgian club, SA Sporting du Pays de Charleroi. The AG opined that the disputed provisions could be deemed a breach of arts 45 and 101 TFEU. In relation to art 101, the AG contended that the restriction could be justified if it were legitimate and strictly necessary to achieve that objective. AG Szpunar reasoned that the contested provisions could breach art 45, unless it could be shown that the new club was involved in the 'premature and unjustified termination' of the player's contract, [para 88 (1) and (2)]. On 4 October 2024, the CJEU handed down its decision, which is currently only available in French, Danish and Polish, C-650/22 *Federation Internationale de Football Association (FIFA) v BZ, Union Royale Belge des Sociétés de Football Association (URBSFA) and SA Sporting du pays de Charleroi* ECLI:EU:C:2024:824. However, in a Press Release published on 4 October 2024, it was announced that the CJEU found the contested provisions to be in breach of arts 45 and 101. The case will be returned to the referring court, the Belgian Court of Appeal to apply the CJEU's decision. It will be up to the Court of Appeal to decide if the restrictions can be justified, however, the CJEU's direction is clear. In relation to art 101, the CJEU considers that the contested provisions 'do not appear to be indispensable or necessary' and in reference to the compatibility of art 45 and the relevant articles of the RTSP, the CJEU found 'in a number of respects, to go beyond what is necessary to pursue that objective'. See Court of Justice of the European Union, 'Press Release No 172/24' (Luxembourg, 4 October 2024) <https://curia.europa.eu/jcms/upload/docs/application/pdf/2024-10/cp240172en.pdf> accessed 4 October 2024. Unsurprising, the decision has attracted widespread media attention, for example see Paul MacInnes, 'Diarra verdict a landmark day which could alter balance of football power' *The Guardian* (London, 4 October 2024) <https://www.theguardian.com/football/2024/oct/04/lassana-diarra-fifa-verdict-landmark-day-alter-balance-of-power-analysis> accessed 7 October 2024.

> As far as the compatibility with Community law is concerned, it was concluded that the following principles which meet the specific needs of the sport could pave the way to a positive solution on the competition procedure that is open against FIFA provided that these principles are fully reflected in the FIFA Regulations to be amended.[115]

13–37 The main provisions were as follows:

1. The introduction of training compensation for players under 23 to replace transfer fees.
2. The 'creation of one transfer period per season, and a further limited mid-season window, with a limit of one transfer per player per season'.
3. 'A minimum and maximum duration of contracts of respectively 1 and 5 years'.
4. The 'creation of an effective, quick, and objective arbitration body with members chosen in equal numbers by players and clubs and with an independent' chairperson.
5. The 'creation of solidarity mechanisms that would redistribute a significant proportion of income to clubs involved in the training and education of a player, including amateur clubs'.[116]

13–38 The ECJ was given the opportunity to judicially review the RSTP on foot of a preliminary reference from France.[117] On 16 March 2010, the CJEU handed down its decision in *Olympique Lyonnais SASP v Oliver Bernard and Newcastle United*.[118] The Professional Charter of the French Football Federation contained rules relating to the employment of footballers in France, which included specific provisions relating to young players. The term '*joueur espoir*' pertained to a footballer aged between the ages of 16 and 22 on a fixed-term contract. Under the Charter, a footballer was required to sign with the club that first trained him, if the club so required. Bernard had a three-season *joueur espoir* contract with Lyonnais and, on expiration of the contract, he refused to sign with Lyonnais and instead joined Newcastle United. Lyonnais sued Bernard for €53,357.16, amounting to a year's salary had Bernard signed with Lyonnais. The Cour de Cassation sent the matter to the ECJ under the preliminary reference procedure. The question referred to the ECJ was whether the requirement that the young player had to sign with the club that trained him on expiration of his *joueur espoir* contract constituted a breach of the free movement of workers provisions. The CJEU was satisfied that Bernard was in gainful employment and thus engaged in an economic activity for the purposes of EU law. Also, the Charter

---

115 Press Release, 'Outcome of Discussions between the Commission and FIFA/UEFA on FIFA Regulations on International Football Transfers' IP/01/314, 6 March 2001 <https://ec.europa.eu/commission/presscorner/detail/en/IP_01_314> accessed 26 July 2024.

116 ibid.

117 Before this case, the RSTP had been revised in 2005 and 2008.

118 C–325/08 *Olympique Lyonnais SASP v Oliver Bernard and Newcastle United* [ECR 2010 I-02177] ECLI:EU:C: 2010:143. By the time the judgment was delivered, the ECJ was now known as the CJEU.

had the status of a collective bargaining agreement aimed at regulating gainful employment, which also fell within the ambit of EU law. The CJEU held that the obligation on the player to sign with the club that trained him had the effect of discouraging a player from going to another club as he could be sued. The CJEU held this to be a restriction on the free movement of workers. However, the CJEU recognised the social importance of sport and thus the objective of encouraging the recruitment and training of young players had to be acceptable as legitimate. It held that a scheme which guaranteed compensation to a club which has trained a young player, and that young player decides to sign with another club within the EU, is not a breach of the free movement of workers provisions so long as the scheme is suitable to ensure the attainment of that objective and does not go beyond what is necessary to attain it. As the calculation of damages under the scheme was unrelated to the actual costs of the training, the CJEU found that the *joueur espoir* scheme went beyond that which was necessary to encourage the recruitment and training of young players and the corresponding funding of such activities.

In the 2007 White Paper on Sport, the European Commission accepted that 'investment in and promotion of training of young talented sportsmen and sportswomen in proper conditions is crucial for a sustainable development of sport at all levels'.[119] As long as the provisions did not directly discriminate on the grounds of nationality, they could be acceptable under EC law.[120] The European Commission stated that indirect discrimination could be permitted so long it was proportionate to a legitimate objective being pursued 'such as to enhance and protect the training and development of talented young players'.[121] Thus, the training compensation and solidarity mechanism very much fits within this vista.[122] **13–39**

Over the years, the rules have been revised and the current RSTP provide for Training Compensation and Solidarity Mechanisms under Part 8, Articles 20 and 21.[123] Training compensation is payable at the end of the training contract, while the solidarity mechanism pertains to the proportion of compensation payable to any clubs that contributed to the player's education and training when the player transfers before the expiration of the contract. Article 20 states: **13–40**

> Training compensation shall be paid to a player's training club(s): (1) when

---

[119] White Paper (n 28) para 2.3.

[120] ibid.

[121] ibid.

[122] For an interesting discussion, see Jakub Laskowsk, 'Solidarity Compensation Framework in Football Revisited' (2019) 18 The International Sports Law Journal 150.

[123] FIFA, 'Regulations on the Status and Transfer of Players' June 2024, 46 <https://digitalhub.fifa.com/m/69b5c4c7121b58d2/original/Regulations-on-the-Status-and-Transfer-of-Players-June-2024-edition.pdf> accessed 19 September 2024.

> a player is registered for the first time as a professional, and (2) each time a professional is transferred until the end of the calendar year of his 23rd birthday. The obligation to pay training compensation arises whether the transfer takes place during or at the end of the player's contract. The provisions concerning training compensation are set out in Annexe 4 of these regulations. The principles of training compensation shall not apply to women's football.

13–41 Annexe 4, Article 1 provides that a player's training and education takes place between the ages of 12 and 23.[124] As a general rule, training compensation is payable up to the age of 23 for training incurred up until the age of 21. However, if the player terminates the training period before the age of 21

> the training compensation shall be payable until the end of the calendar year in which the player reaches the age of 23, but the calculation of the amount payable shall be based on the years between the age of 12 and the age when it is established that the player actually completed his training.[125]

13–42 The training compensation is paid to the training club or clubs where the player registered for the first time as a professional or a professional is transferred between clubs of two different associations (whether during or at the end of his contract) up until the end of the calendar year of the player's 23rd birthday.[126] FIFA divides clubs for the purposes of training costs into four categories: I, II, III and IV.[127] The only countries to have Category I clubs are: England, France, Germany, Italy, Belgium, the Netherlands, Spain, Argentina and Brazil. The Football Association of Ireland (FAI) submitted three categories to FIFA, with II relating to the SSE Airtricity League Premier Division Clubs, III pertaining to SSE Airtricity League First Division Clubs, and IV covering all other clubs and the 12–15 age group, irrespective of the club's category.[128] Training compensation is not paid if a player transfers to a Category IV club.[129] There are special provisions for players transferring to another association within the EU or European Economic Area (EEA).[130] When it comes to the calculation of compensation in the EU/EEA, the amount is based on the average training costs of the two clubs in situations where the player is moving from a lower to a higher-category club.[131] In situations where the player is moving from a higher to a lower-category

124 ibid 86.
125 ibid.
126 ibid Annexe 4, arts 2(1)(a)–(b).
127 FIFA, 'Circular no 1853: Regulations on the Status and Transfer of Players – Categorisation of Clubs and Registration Periods' (29 July 2023) <https://digitalhub.fifa.com/m/4db9566315c26398/original/Circular-1853_RSTP-categorisation-of-clubs-and-registration-periods_EN.pdf> accessed 19 May 2024.
128 ibid. According to the Circular, Ireland falls under Categories II–IV.
129 RSTP (n 123) Annexe 4, art 2(b).
130 ibid Annexe 4, art 6(1). The EEA consists of the 27 EU Member States and Norway, Iceland, and Liechtenstein.
131 ibid Annexe 4, arts 6(1)(a) and (b).

club, the compensation calculation is based on the training costs of the lower-category club.[132]

Article 21 of Part 8 refers to the solidarity mechanism, which provides: **13–43**

> If a professional is transferred before the expiry of his contract, any club that has contributed to his education and training shall receive a proportion of the compensation paid to his former club (solidarity contribution). The provisions concerning solidarity contributions are set out in Annexe 5 of these regulations.[133]

Article 1 of Annexe 5 details the how the solidarity payments are apportioned, ranging from 5% of 5% to 5% of 10%. Between the calendar year of the player's 12th birthday to his 15th birthday, the club or clubs receive 5% of 5% from the new club.[134] From 16 to 23 years of age, the solidarity payment is 5% of 10% compensation.[135] **13–44**

Transfer Windows

The *Bosman* decision applies only to players that are out-of-contract. Players that are out-of-contract can transfer to a club without the need for a transfer fee to be paid. For players still in contract, they may begin negotiations and enter a pre-contractual relationship with a prospective club six months or less prior to the expiration of the contract. Once the contract has expired, the player is a free agent. As there is no transfer fee involved, the player may be offered a more lucrative salary and bonuses to sign with the new club. The two-yearly transfer windows are available to players who are still under contract.[136] In Europe, there is a winter transfer window and a summer transfer window. The winter transfer window in the English Premier League opened on 1 January 2024 and closed on 1 February 2024 at 23.00 GMT.[137] The Premier League harmonised the closing dates for the Summer 2023 and Winter 2024 windows with other major European leagues, including La Liga in Spain and Italy's Serie A.[138] **13–45**

FIFA 6 + 5 Rule and the UEFA Home-Grown Player Rules

In the aftermath of the *Bosman* decision, the major leagues of England, Spain, Italy, Germany, and France began to encounter 'an influx of **13–46**

---

132 ibid.

133 ibid 88.

134 It is calculated pro-rata if it is less than one year.

135 See RSTP (n 123) Annexe 5, arts 1(a)–(i).

136 The transfer windows are the result of negotiations between the European Commission and FIFA.

137 Premier League, 'Dates for Summer 2023 and Winter 2024 Transfer Windows Confirmed' (24 May 2023) <https://www.premierleague.com/news/3485999> accessed 19 May 2024. The summer window in the Premier League opened on 14 June and closed at 23:00 GMT on 30 August 2024.

138 ibid.

foreign players' and clubs feared that their national identity would be lost.[139] FIFA raised concerns about the dominance of certain English clubs in the national league and European Championships, which was attributed to the fielding of 'high number of foreign players'.[140] In February 2008, FIFA put forward the 6 + 5 rule. Under this rule, at the beginning of each game, each club would field at least six players eligible to play for the national team of the country of the club. However, there was no restriction on the number of non-EU players a club could sign nor on the number of substitutes.[141] The European Commission rejected the rule as it was deemed to be a direct form of discrimination and contrary to the free movement of persons.[142]

13–47 The European Commission accepted UEFA's home-grown player (HGP) rules. On 2 February 2005, UEFA's Executive Committee adopted rules requiring professional football clubs taking part in UEFA's interclub competitions to include on the match sheet a minimum number of HGP in the maximum 25-player team. Nationality is irrelevant; to qualify as an HGP, the player must have been trained by their club or by another club in the same national association for at least three years between the ages of 15 and 21. In April 2005, UEFA's 52 member associations approved the rule change.[143] UEFA introduced the rule in three phases:

1. Season 2006–7: minimum of four home-grown players in 25-player squad.
2. Season 2007–8: minimum of six home-grown players in 25-player squad.
3. Season 2008–9 and onwards: minimum of eight homegrown players in 25-player squad.

---

139 Felix Majani, 'One Step Forward, Two Hops Backwards: Quotas – The Return: An Excavation into the Legal Deficiencies of the FIFA 6+5 Rule and the UEFA Home-Grown Players Rule in the Eyes of European Union Law' (2009) 1(2) International Sports Law Journal 19, 19.

140 ibid.

141 A team would start out with six players but with three substitutions and three players who were eligible to play for the national team could be replaced by three substitutes who were not eligible. That would mean that at the end of the match, instead of it being 6 + 5 it would become 3 + 8. It is interesting to note that the English League introduced its own HGP rules in 2010 and squad lists for the 2023/24 season are available here: <https://www.premierleague.com/news/3681595> accessed 19 May 2024.

142 European Commission, 'Following Today's Informal Sports Ministers' Meeting in Biarritz, Commissioners Ján Figel and Vladimir Špidla Issued the Following Statement' 28 November 2008 <https://ec.europa.eu/social/main.jsp?langId=en&catId=89&newsId=424&furtherNews=yes> accessed 19 May 2024. The Commissioners stated: 'We understand and sympathise with FIFA's – and others' – concerns to bring more balance to the game of football. We just differ about the means to achieve it.'

143 Opinion of Advocate General Szpunar delivered on 9 March 2023, Case C–680/21 UL, *SA Royal Antwerp Football Club v Union royale belge des sociétés de football association ASBL, joined parties: Union des associations européennes de football (UEFA)* ECLI:EU:C:2023:188 [7].

Unlike the 6 + 5 rule, the HGP policy does not restrict players on the grounds of nationality and a club is not obliged to field home-grown players. The rule provides that there must be eight home-grown players in a 25-player squad, with at least four of whom have been trained by the club in question.[144] In a recent preliminary reference to the CJEU, a player with Belgian and third-country nationality challenged the HGP rules on the ground that they were a breach of Article 45 TFEU and Article 101 TFEU. The AG confined his conclusion to Article 45 and opined that 'Article 45 TFEU must be interpreted as precluding the application of rules on home-grown players'.[145] The CJEU handed down its judgment on 21 December 2023.[146] In examining Article 101 TFEU, which prohibits restrictive agreements, decisions and concerted practices which have as their object or effect the distortion of competition, the CJEU held 'that they are both justified by the pursuit of one or more objectives that are legitimate and strictly necessary for that purpose'.[147] In interpreting Article 45 TFEU, the CJEU held that the HGP rules were precluded under the provisions of the free movement of persons: **13–48**

> unless it is established that those rules are suitable for ensuring, in a consistent and systematic manner, the attainment of the objective of encouraging, at local level, the recruitment and training of young professional football players, and that they do not go beyond what is necessary to achieve that objective.[148]

As the matter was sent by the Belgian Court to the CJEU under the preliminary reference, the Brussels Court of First Instance is required to apply the decision. In doing so, the Brussels Court of First Instance will arguably find that while the HGP rules are precluded under Articles 101 and 45 of the TFEU they may be justified on the grounds that they are based on a legitimate objective (encouraging the recruitment and training of young professional players at local level) and they do not go beyond what is necessary to achieve that objective. **13–49**

With the *Bosman* decision providing context, the evolution of the Financial Fair Play (FFP) Regulations, now known as the UEFA Club Licensing and Financial Sustainability Regulations, will be briefly discussed. **13–50**

Financial Fair Play Regulations to the UEFA Club Licensing and Financial Sustainability Regulations

In the 1991/1992 season, UEFA established the Champions League in **13–51**

---

[144] ibid.
[145] ibid [83].
[146] Case C–680/21 *UL, SA Royal Antwerp Football Club v Union royale belge des sociétés de football association ASBL, joined parties : Union des associations européennes de football (UEFA)* ECLI :EU :C:2023:1010.
[147] ibid [151(1)].
[148] ibid [151(3)].

response to 'the increasing commercialisation and mediatisation' of football.[149] While some clubs benefitted from the increase in revenue gained from broadcasting rights, the 'financial gaps' between rich and poor became increasingly evident.[150] In the aftermath of *Bosman*, player salaries greatly increased. A study by the High Pay Centre in 2012 found that since the creation of the Premier League in 1992, top players had seen their earnings increase by 1,508% in 2010, during the same period the average British citizen had an increase of 186%.[151]

13–52 In 2002, UEFA adopted the Club Licensing Regulations, and the first licences were granted in 2004. To compete in UEFA competitions, clubs had to adhere to 39 criteria based on five pillars – sporting, infrastructure, personnel and administrative, legal, and financial.[152] The Club Licensing Regulations set out criteria that clubs had to meet to be eligible to play in UEFA club competitions. It was 'aimed primarily to raise minimum standards in European football governance following a large number of cases of mismanagement'.[153] The scope of the Club Licencing Regulations evolved and expanded over the years, leading to the amalgamation of the Club Licencing Regulations and the FFP Regulations.

13–53 In 2009, UEFA's Executive Committee unanimously approved the FFP Regulations.[154] At the time, European football clubs were facing financial ruin as several leagues incurred operating losses. In 2001–02, Italian football had an operating loss of €22m; this had reduced to €3.3m in 2007–08.[155] In the financial year 2007–08, the average English Premier League team had pre-tax losses of €15.1m and €21.1m in 2006–07.[156] For lower-division English teams, it was reported that between 2000 and 2009, 35 out of 72 teams had undergone insolvency proceedings.[157]

13–54 The FFP Regulations provided that a club was precluded from spending more than it had earned to ensure its long-term viability. The FFP Regulations were introduced in June 2010 and implemented in 2011 through the *Club Licensing and Financial Fair Play Regulations, Edition*

[149] Mathias Schubert and Francisco Javier Lopez Frias, 'Walk the Talk: Financial Fairness in European Club Football' (2019) 13(1) Sport, Ethics and Philosophy 33.

[150] ibid 35.

[151] David Boyle, 'Football Mad: Are We Paying More for Less?' 20 August 2012, 6 <https://highpaycentre.org/football-mad-are-we-paying-more-for-less/> accessed 19 May 2024.

[152] UEFA, 'Club Licensing' <https://www.uefa.com/insideuefa/protecting-the-game/club-licensing/> accessed 19 May 2024.

[153] ibid.

[154] ibid.

[155] Kjetil K Haugen and Harry Arne Solberg, 'The Financial Crisis in European Football – A Game Theoretic Approach' (2010) 10(5) European Sport Management Quarterly 553, 554.

[156] ibid.

[157] ibid.

2012.[158] They were updated in 2015, 2018 and replaced in 2022. The Executive Committee of UEFA approved the reform and overhaul of the Club Licencing and Financial Fair Play Regulations in April 2022 and replaced them with the UEFA Club Licensing and Financial Sustainability Regulations, which came into force on 1 June 2022.[159] There were some minor amendments made with effect from 25 January 2023.[160] More Regulations were approved on 28 June 2023 by the UEFA Executive Committee with the *Club Licensing and Financial Sustainability Regulations, Edition 2023* coming into force on 1 July 2023, the most recent edition was published on 1 June 2024.[161] The Club Licencing and Sustainability Regulations are based on three key pillars – solvency, stability, and cost control. UEFA consulted several stakeholders from European football clubs and national associations to the EU Institutions (the European Commission, the European Parliament) and the Council of Europe.

The FFP Regulations were devised to ensure that clubs were able to discharge their debts, remain solvent and were not relying on club owners to cover losses.[162] Part II of the 2024 Regulations detail the licencing system. It provides that a club will receive a certificate once it is confirmed that it fulfils UEFA's minimum criteria for admission to its club competitions. The licence requirements are checked once a year by the national licensor. The licence is granted for the next season. The licencing system applies to both men's and women's club football. The Sustainability Regulations apply only to UEFA men's club competitions and involve a process of monitoring the adherence of clubs to the financial criteria established by UEFA. Part III of the Regulations explains the process, which is referred to as UEFA Club Monitoring. **13–55**

To enforce the Club Licensing and Financial Sustainability Regulations, the Club Financial Control Body (CFCB) was established as part **13–56**

[158] The 2012 Regulations can be downloaded from <https://www.uefa.com/MultimediaFiles/Download/Tech/uefaorg/General/01/80/54/10/1805410_DOWNLOAD.pdf> accessed 19 May 2024.

[159] The 2022 Regulations can be downloaded from <https://documents.uefa.com/r/UEFA-Club-Licensing-and-Financial-Sustainability-Regulations-2022-Online> accessed 19 May 2024.

[160] For more detail, see <https://documents.uefa.com/r/UEFA-Club-Licensing-and-Financial-Sustainability-Regulations-2023/Article-100-Disciplinary-procedures-Online> accessed 19 May 2024.

[161] The Regulations are available at <https://documents.uefa.com/viewer/bookattachment/iz_lsPmhmTMVqu7Bl5kcCw/6PBeGzuVORb94t3moea8iA> accessed 19 May 2024. The 2024 edition can be downloaded from <https://documents.uefa.com/r/UEFA-Club-Licensing-and-Financial-Sustainability-Regulations-2024/Preamble-Online> accessed 29 July 2024.

[162] Christopher Flanagan, 'The Evolution of UEFA's Financial Fair Play Rules – Part 1: Background and EU Law' (*Asser International Sports Law Blog*, 21 September 2017) <https://www.asser.nl/SportsLaw/Blog/post/the-evolution-of-uefa-s-financial-fair-play-rules-part-1-background-and-eu-law-by-christopher-flanagan> accessed 19 May 2024.

of UEFA's disciplinary mechanisms. This structure remains under the Sustainability Regulations, with the previous two divisions, the Investigatory Chamber and the Adjudicatory Chamber, replaced with the First Chamber and the Appeals Chamber.[163] The chambers are independent of each other and have different chairpersons. Decisions of the CFCB may only be appealed to the Court of Arbitration for Sport (CAS).

13–57 The FFP Regulations and their conformity with EU law have been raised in relation to the free movement of workers (Article 45 TFEU), services (Article 56 TFEU) and capital (Article 63 TFEU) and under EU competition law, namely Articles 101 and 102 TFEU. Derogations from the free-movement provisions are permitted; however, any restriction must be proportionate to the aims it seeks to achieve and must be objectively justified. Traditionally, the prevailing view was the EU would not involve itself in sport if the question raised were of a purely sporting interest and as such has nothing to do with economic activity. However, in a sport such as football, it is difficult to distinguish elite football the sport from elite football the economic entity.[164] Player agent Daniele Striani and Manchester City along with Paris Saint-Germain fan groups challenged the FFP before the Brussels Court of First Instance, which referred the matter to the CJEU under the preliminary reference procedure in the case of *Daniele Striani and Others v UEFA*.[165] Striani was represented by Jean-Louis Dupont, the lawyer who had represented Bosman twenty years earlier.[166] In July 2015, the CJEU deemed the request to be manifestly inadmissible as it cited, *inter alia*, insufficient information relating to the legal and factual context.

Bosman *and Non-EU Players*

13–58 After *Bosman* there were cases involving non-EC/EU players and the payment of transfer fees for out-of-contract players. This issue arose in *Balog v ASBL Charleroi Sporting Club*, where Balog, a Hungarian national, played for Belgian club Charleroi.[167] In a similar situation to Bosman, Balog's contract was about to expire, and he refused a new contract and was placed on the transfer list. The transfer fee was excessive and

---

[163] UEFA, 'Club Financial Control Body' <https://www.uefa.com/running-competitions/integrity/club-financial-control-body/> accessed 19 May 2024.

[164] Flanagan (n 162).

[165] Case C–299/15 *Daniele Striani and Others v Union Européenne des Sociétés de Football Association (UEFA) and Union Royale Belge des Sociétés de Football – Association (URBSFA)*, ECLI :EU:C:2015:519.

[166] Antoine Duval, 'What Happens in Switzerland Stays in Switzerland: The Striani Judgment of the Brussels Court of Appeal' (*Asser International Sports Law Blog*, 30 April 2019) <https://www.asser.nl/SportsLaw/Blog/post/what-happens-in-switzerland-stays-in-switzerland-the-striani-judgment-of-the-brussels-court-of-appeals> accessed 19 May 2024.

[167] Tribunal de Premiere Instance de Charleroi by judgment of the Court of July 1998 in the case of *Tibor Balog v ASBL Royal Charleroi Sporting Club (RCSC)*.

Balog found it impossible to find a club that would pay that amount for an out-of-contract player. A transfer fee was required as he was a non-EC national (Hungary did not become a Member State of the EU until 1 May 2004). Balog argued that he should be treated the same as an EU national and be allowed to transfer without the need for a transfer fee. The matter was settled by FIFA and the Belgian court decreed that it would be pointless to proceed with the preliminary reference to the ECJ as it had been resolved.[168] The AG's Opinion was subsequently withdrawn.[169] While the case 'carries little authority', it is interesting to note that the AG opined that the club was in breach of EC competition law.[170]

The rights of non-EC/EU players were recognised in two further cases, *Kolpak*[171] and *Igor Simutenkov v Spanish Football Federation*.[172] Kolpak, a Slovak national and goalkeeper for a second-division handball team, was resident in Germany and held a valid residence permit. Kolpak was issued with a player's licence, which included the letter 'A'. This identified Kolpak as a non-EC player who did not enjoy the privilege of equal treatment. Under the league rules, a team could only field two players with an 'A'-marked licence. Kolpak requested that he be re-issued with a licence that did not contain the letter 'A', as he had rights akin to an EC national due to an Association Agreement between the EU and Slovakia.[173] The ECJ found that the restriction was a form of discrimination under EC Law. **13–59**

In *Simutenkov v Spanish Football Federation*, Simutenkov, a Russian national who played for Spanish club Deportivo Tenerife, endeavoured to rely on Article 23 of the Association Agreement between Russia and the EU. Like Kolpak, Simutenkov wished to have his licence converted to an EU player's licence; however, his application was rejected. The case was sent to the ECJ under the preliminary reference. The ECJ found that Article 23 of the Association Agreement allowed a professional sportsman of Russian nationality, who was lawfully employed by a club established **13–60**

---

168 Reference for a preliminary ruling from the Tribunal de Premiere Instance de Charleroi by judgment of that court of 2 July 1998 in the case of *Tibor Balog v ASBL Royal Charleroi Sporting Club (RCSC)* (Case C–264/98) (98/C 278/51). The question sent under the preliminary reference related to the compatibility of the requirement of a transfer fee under Article 85 EC Treaty and Article 53 of the Agreement on the European Economic Area.

169 Adam Lewis and Jonathan Taylor, *Sport: Law and Practice* (4th edn, Bloomsbury 2021) para F3.89.

170 ibid.

171 C–438/00, *Deutscher Handballbund eV v Maros Kolpak* (2003/C146/07) ECLI:EU:C:2003:255. Slovakia became a Member State of the EU on 1 May 2004.

172 C–265/03 *Simutenkov v Spanish Football Federation* ECLI:EU:C: 2005:6.

173 Article 38(1) of the Europe Agreement establishing an association between the European communities and their member states, of the one part, and the Slovak Republic, of the other part, approved on behalf of the communities by Decision 94/909/ECSC, EEC, EURATOM of the Council and the Commission of 19 December 1994 [1994] OJ 1994 L 359.

in a state, to play for a domestic club without any restriction.[174] A club or federation could only impose restrictions in situations where the players were not party to an association agreement.[175]

13–61 On 1 May 2004, 10 new Member States joined the EU – Cyprus, Czech Republic (Czechia), Estonia, Hungary, Latvia, Lithuania, Malta, Poland, Slovakia, and Slovenia. On 1 January 2007, Romania and Bulgaria joined the EU. Croatia joined the EU on 1 July 2013. With this enlargement, the effects of *Kolpak* and *Simutenkov* were somewhat diminished as many of the association agreement countries are now Member States of the EU.

Competition Law and the Freedom to Provide a Service

13–62 The case of *Meca-Medina and Majcen v European Commission* involved two professional long-distance swimmers who tested positive for nandrolone at the World Cup on 31 January 1999. The FINA Doping Panel banned the two swimmers for four years. The CAS heard an appeal from the two swimmers, and confirmed the sanction imposed by FINA (now World Aquatics).[176] Nandrolone and its metabolites were prohibited anabolic substances under the doping rules of FINA, however, scientific tests conducted in January 2000 by FINA- and IOC-accredited laboratories showed that nandrolone's metabolites could be produced 'endogenously by the human body at a level which may exceed the accepted limit when certain foods, such as boar meat, have been consumed'.[177] In cases where there was an unintentional or innocent ingestion of nandrolone, it would only constitute a doping offence if its presence in a male athlete's body exceeded a limit of 2 nanogrammes (ng) per millilitre (ml) of urine.[178] On foot of this information FINA, with the consent of the two swimmers, referred the matter to the CAS to reconsider anew.[179] The CAS reduced the sanction from four to two years.[180] The swimmers did not appeal the decision to the Swiss Federal Tribunal (SFT). However, the swimmers made a complaint to the European Commission arguing that the IOC's doping rules which were implemented by FINA were a violation of EC competition law and were in breach of the freedom to provide a service.[181] The swimmers argued, *inter alia*, that 'the fixing of the limit at 2 ng/ml is a concerted

[174] *Simutenkov* (n 172) [41].

[175] ibid.

[176] CAS 99/A/234 & 235 *David Meca-Medina & Igor Majcen v Fédération Internationale de Natation Amateur (FINA)* award of 29 February 2000.

[177] ibid [2(3)] and [11]. For a detailed discussion of the CAS decisions, see Craig Callery and David McArdle, 'Doping, European Law and the Implications of Meca-Medina' (2011) 3(2) International Journal of Sport Policy and Politics 163, 165–66.

[178] *Meca-Medina* (n 176) [2(3)].

[179] ibid.

[180] ibid [12].

[181] The swimmers brought the application under art 3 of EEC Council: Regulation no 17: First Regulation implementing arts 85 and 86 of the Treaty [1962] OJ 13.

practice between the IOC and the 27 laboratories accredited by it'.[182] The swimmers questioned the arbitrary nature of setting such a limit, which could 'lead to the exclusion of innocent or merely negligent athletes', including them, as they contended that they may have eaten boar meat.[183] An interesting argument raised by the swimmers was the IOC's use of strict liability with regards to doping and the creation of the CAS, and entrusting the International Council of Arbitration for Sport (ICAS) with the task of settling sport disputes which because of being 'insufficiently independent of the IOC strengthens the anti-competitive nature of that limit'.[184]

The European Commission rejected the complaint by way of a Decision on 1 August 2002 wherein it stated that Articles 81 and 82 EC (now Articles 101 and 102 TFEU) did not apply to anti-doping rules.[185] The swimmers sought the annulment of the Decision before the Court of First Instance (CFI). The CFI upheld the Decision, holding that the IOC's doping rules did not come within the rubric of either competition law or freedom of services.[186] The CFI reiterated the earlier dicta from the ECJ and held that sport, in so far as it constitutes an economic activity, was subject to the provisions of EC law – for example, rules restricting the number of foreign players or the requirement of a transfer fee for out-of-contract players.[187] However, EC law did not extend to purely sporting rules and matters that have nothing to do with an economic activity – for example, the composition of national teams, rules fixing the length of matches, or the number of players on the field.[188] In relation to anti-doping, the CFI acknowledged that high-level sport had become 'to a great extent, an economic activity', but 'the campaign against doping [did] not pursue any economic objective'.[189] Anti-doping policies were based on the spirit of fair play, and safeguarding the health of athletes.[190] The preservation of fair play constituted a 'purely social objective' which was 'sufficient to justify the campaign against doping'.[191] The prohibition of doping formed part of the 'cardinal rule of sport', giving **13–63**

182 Case T–313/02 *David Meca-Medina & Igor Majcen v Commission* ECR II–3291 [16]. Meca-Medina's test showed 9.7 ng/ml and Majcen 3.9 ng/ml [8].

183 ibid [8].

184 ibid.

185 Case COMP/38158, *Meca-Medina and Majcen v International Olympic Committee* [1 August 2002]. See Lenita Lindström-Rossi, Sandra De Waele, and Dovile Vaigauskaite, Directorate-General Competition, unit D–3, 'Application of EC Antitrust Rules in the Sport Sector: An Update' (Autumn 2005) 72 <https://op.europa.eu/en/publication-detail/-/publication/278985c7-f1b3-4f74-b38f-80f4db664484> accessed 20 May 2024.

186 *Meca-Medina* (n 182) [17]. The swimmers contended that the European Commission made a manifest error in not finding that the IOC was an undertaking within the meaning of Community law: [30]. The European Commission was supported by Finland: [34].

187 ibid [40].

188 ibid [41].

189 ibid [44].

190 ibid.

191 ibid.

expression to the principle of fair play.[192] The CFI stated that even in situations where an athlete is a professional, the prohibition of doping concerned exclusively 'a non-economic aspect' that was 'intimately linked to sport'.[193] It was accepted by the CFI that the anti-doping rules were non-discriminatory in their application; they applied equally to all athletes.[194] However, if they were discriminatory, such rules could infringe the Treaty provisions on economic freedoms and competition law even though the anti-doping rules were of a 'purely sporting' nature.[195]

13–64 The swimmers appealed the CFI judgment to the ECJ on four grounds, including that the CFI's judgment was delivered following flawed proceedings as it was claimed that the rights of the defence were infringed. The first plea was that the CFI erred in law.[196] The ECJ agreed and held that the CFI erred in law in dismissing the application on the ground that the anti-doping rules in question were subject to neither the freedom to provide a service nor competition law.[197] The ECJ proffered that even if were accepted that the IOC's anti-doping rules constituted a decision of an association of undertakings under then Article 81 EC, they would not necessarily constitute an infringement of competition law as they could be justified by a legitimate objective.[198] The ECJ set aside the judgment of the CFI. However, it held that the European Commission Decision was not to be annulled.[199] It found that the sanction imposed on the swimmers was not excessive and it was deemed proportionate.[200]

13–65 Callery and McArdle assert that in the *Medina-Meca* case, 'the Community created an indirect anti-doping policy through the jurisprudence of the European courts'.[201] In a similar vein to Weatherill's contention about

---

192 ibid.
193 ibid [45] and [47].
194 ibid [49]. The swimmers contended that even if the anti-doping rules were considered non-discriminatory, they were excessive and that took them beyond being purely sporting rules. The CFI rejected this contention as the rules were limited to their proper object, namely the campaign against doping and the safeguarding of the health of athletes: [54] and [55]. The swimmers further argued that the IOC had an economic interest in not having sport tarnished by doping scandals. Consequently, the rules went beyond being purely sporting. Again, the CFI rejected this and countered that, while the IOC may have had legitimate concerns about economic considerations, the premise on which the rules were introduced were still purely sporting: [56] and [57].
195 ibid [49].
196 *Meca-Medina* (n 44) [16].
197 ibid [36]. The appellants also argued that the CFI should have found that the IOC was an undertaking for the purposes of competition law. This plea was deemed to be unfounded as the European Commission decision recognised the IOC as an undertaking and the incorrect reading by the CFI was of no consequence: [38] and [39].
198 ibid [45].
199 ibid [59].
200 ibid [54] and [55].
201 Callery and McArdle (n 177) 167.

the EU circumventing its lack of competence with regard to sport, the writers refer to EU competition law being applied 'to the contentious practices of a sporting body that makes full use of its monopoly powers in order to underpin its anti-doping agenda'.[202] The then Community was not interested in inserting itself into the anti-doping policies of governing bodies but rather it became involved as 'a dominant position had been utilised to prevent athletes from participating in their chosen economic activity'.[203]

13–66 The International Skating Union (ISU) was subject to a European Commission Decision relating to Article 101 TFEU.[204] On foot of a complaint by two professional speed skaters relating to the 2014 Eligibility Rules, the European Commission carried out an investigation which lasted two years. It found that the rules which imposed 'severe exclusionary sanctions on athletes participating in international speed skating events not organised or specifically authorised by the ISU, including a lifetime ban' were in breach of EU competition law.[205] As the ISU Eligibility Rules were binding on all members and their affiliated clubs, the European Commission was satisfied that the rules constituted a decision of an association within the meaning of Article 101(1). The European Commission gave the ISU 90 days to end its infringement of EU law and, failing to do so, it would impose daily fines of 5% of the ISU's average daily turnover in the preceding business year.[206] The ISU sought the annulment of the Decision before the General Court.[207] The General Court held that 'the European Commission was right to conclude that the eligibility rules have as their object the restriction of competition. In the light of their content and their objectives, and of the context of the eligibility rules, those rules reveal a sufficient degree of harm to be regarded as restricting competition by object within the

---

[202] ibid.

[203] ibid.

[204] Commission Decision of 8.12.2017 relating to proceedings under art 101 of the Treaty on the Functioning of the European Union (the Treaty) and art 53 of the EEA Agreement Case AT.40208 – International Skating Union's Eligibility Rules <https://ec.europa.eu/competition/antitrust/cases/dec_docs/40208/40208_1579_5.pdf> accessed 20 May 2024. The ISU is the sole regulator of speed skating and figure skating.

[205] ibid Recital 163.

[206] ibid 83, arts 2 and 4.

[207] The CFI was renamed the General Court under the Treaty of Lisbon. Judgment of the General Court, 16 December 2020, Case T–93/18, *International Skating Union v European Commission,* ECLI:EU:T:2020:610. For an interesting discussion on the case, see Andrea Cattaneo, '*International Skating Union v Commission*: Pre-authorisation Rules and Competition Law' (2021) 12(4) Journal of European Competition Law & Practice 318. Cattaneo asserts that the General Court decision in ISU endorsed previous cases wherein the Court found that 'the use of eligibility rules by an entity engaged in commercial activities in the very same sector inherently raises conflicts of interest': 320. For example, see Case C–49/07, *Motosykletistiki Omospondia Ellados NPID (MOTOE) v Elliniko Dimosio* ECLI:EU:C:2008:376.

meaning of Article 101 TFEU'.[208] The General Court largely dismissed the action; however, it did annul part of Article 2 of the Decision relating to the Appeal Arbitration Rules. Under the ISU rules, an arbitration clause provided for appeal to the CAS with the CAS having exclusive jurisdiction.[209] The European Commission contended:

> Arbitration is a generally accepted method of binding dispute resolution and agreeing on an arbitration clause as such does not restrict competition. However, the European Commission takes the view that the Appeals Arbitration rules reinforce the restrictions of competition that are caused by the Eligibility rules.[210]

13–67 The European Commission argued that the Appeals Arbitration Rules made 'it difficult to obtain effective judicial protection against ineligibility decisions of the ISU that violate Article 101 of the Treaty'.[211]

13–68 On an appeal, the CJEU dismissed the appeal and set aside the General Court decision relating to the annulment of part of Article 2 of European Commission's Decision.[212] The CJEU referred to 'the severe and disproportionate penalties' and the

> absence of objective, transparent, non-discriminatory and verifiable authorisation criteria. The applicant's eligibility rules prevent skaters from offering their services to organisers of international speed skating events not authorised by the applicant and, therefore, prevent those organisers from using their services for competing events within or outside the EEA.[213]

13–69 In *Deliège v Ligue de Judo* the ECJ, consistent with its earlier judgments, held that selection criteria did not come within the ambit of EC law.[214] Deliège practised judo at an advanced amateur level and had obtained excellent results in her 52kg category since 1987. She had been declared a national champion on several occasions. She argued that the Belgian Judo Federation had improperly impeded her career by not allowing her to compete in several competitions, including the 1992 and 1996 Olympics. The athlete argued that she was carrying out an economic activity for the purposes of EC law. Eligibility for the Olympics is decided by pre-determined national quotas set by the national federation. The question for the ECJ was whether the selection criteria conflicted with the provisions relating to the provision of services and competition law.

---

208 *International Skating Union* (n 207) [120].
209 Decision (n 204) Recital 269.
210 ibid.
211 ibid Recital 270. For further details, see Recitals 270–77. It also annulled part of art 4 relating to periodic penalty payments as they related to arbitration under art 2.
212 C–124/21 *International Skating Union v European Commission* 2023. ECLI:EU:C:2023:1012. Judgment of the Grand Chamber, 21 December 2023.
213 ibid [129].
214 *Deliège* (n 33).

The ECJ held that such rules did not fall within the ambit of the freedom to provide a service 'as long as it derives from a need inherent in the organisation of such a competition', although the individual concerned may be affected financially.[215] The ECJ gave considerable latitude to the governing body in fixing selection criteria in sporting events. So long as the rules are reasonable, justifiable, and proportionate, such restrictions should not attract the application of EU law.

In the *Lehtonen* case, a professional basketball player from Finland wished to move to a club in Belgium.[216] However, the player was prevented from participating in the remaining games of the season as he registered after a transfer deadline set by the Belgian Basketball Federation. Lehtonen claimed that the restriction was contrary to the free movement of workers. The ECJ accepted that such a rule could be justified to prevent a player leaving one league at the end of the season to join another league when the season was still in progress. While the rules would seem to be precluded under the free movement of workers' provision, they could be justified if 'objective reasons concerning only sport as such or relating to differences between the position of players from a federation in the European zone and that of players from a federation not in that zone justify such different treatment'.[217] Like in *Deliège*, the ECJ accepted that a governing body could justify certain restrictive rules. **13–70**

The Specificity of Sport and the Sporting Exception

Through the case law of the European Courts and decisions of the European Commission, the specificity of sport has been recognised. It is a legal concept that has derived its legitimacy from the jurisprudence of the CJEU, the General Court, and from European Commission Decisions relating to competition law. In simple terms, the specificity of sport 'refers to the inherent characteristics of sport which set it apart from other economic and social activities'.[218] Kornbeck notes that 'this leaves every case subject to a case-by-case assessment'.[219] **13–71**

---

[215] ibid [69].

[216] C–176/96 *Jyri Lehtonen and Castors Canada Dry Namur-Braine ASBL v Fédération royale belge des sociétés de basket-ball ASBL (FRBSB)* [ECR 2000 I-02681], I–2736. ECLI:EU:C: 2000:201.

[217] ibid I–2736.

[218] Ecorys, KEA and Sport and Citizenship, 'Mapping and Analysis of the Specificity of Sport: A Final Report to the DG Education & Culture of the European Commission' (Publications Office of the European Union, June 2016) 3 <https://ec.europa.eu/assets/eac/sport/library/studies/mapping-analysis-specificity-sport_en.pdf> accessed 20 May 2024.

[219] Jacob Kornbeck, 'Specificity, Monopoly and Solidarity in the European Commission's ISU (International Skating Union) Decision: Anything New Under the Sun?' (2019) 10(2) Journal of European Competition Law & Practice 71, 73.

13–72 The 2007 White Paper reiterated that EU law is applicable to sport.[220] It asserted that the specificity of sport could be examined 'through two prisms':

> – The specificity of sporting activities and of sporting rules, such as separate competitions for men and women, limitations on the number of participants in competitions, or the need to ensure uncertainty concerning outcomes and to preserve a competitive balance between clubs taking part in the same competitions;
> – The specificity of the sport structure, including notably the autonomy and diversity of sport organisations, a pyramid structure of competitions from grassroots to elite level and organised solidarity mechanisms between the different levels and operators, the organisation of sport on a national basis, and the principle of a single federation per sport.[221]

13–73 Due to the specificity of sport, there are situations when EU law will not apply to sporting activity. For example, a sporting exception may apply to organisational rules, as discussed above in *Deliège* and *Lehtonen*. Organisational rules including the rules of the game (including fixing the length of matches or the number of players on the field) would unlikely conflict with EU law.[222] In situations where rules of the sporting activity produce anti-competitive effects, the sporting exception will apply if such rules are 'inherent and proportionate to the objectives pursued'.[223] Thus, if the rules are not inherent and not proportionate, the sporting exception may not be permitted.

13–74 The specificity of sport is explicitly referred to in Article 165(1) TFEU, which provides that 'the Union shall contribute to the promotion of European sporting issues, while taking account of the specific nature of sport, its structures based on voluntary activity and its social and educational function'. It was in the *Bernard* case that the CJEU referred for the first time to Article 165 and the specific nature of the sport, in particular football, and its social and educational function.[224]

13–75 In December 2023, the CJEU handed down its decision in the *Superleague* case.[225] FIFA and UEFA rules required prior authorisation of proposed

---

[220] White Paper (n 28) para 4.1.
[221] ibid.
[222] ibid. As previously noted, this is referred to as 'purely sporting rules'. Siekmann contends that the 'purely sporting defence was expunged in *Meca-Medina*': Robert CR Siekmann, *Introduction to International and European Sports Law* (TMC Asser Press 2012) 119. The CJEU stated: 'it is apparent that the mere fact that a rule is purely sporting in nature does not have the effect of removing from the scope of the Treaty the person engaging in the activity governed by that rule or the body which has laid it down': *Meca-Medina* (n 44) [27].
[223] ibid.
[224] *Bernard* (n 118) [40].
[225] Judgment of 21 December 2023, Case C–333/21 *European Superleague Company v Fédération internationale de football association (FIFA), Union of European Football Associations (UEFA), intervening parties: A22 Sports Management SL, Real*

international matches and competitions.[226] The European Super League Company (ESLC) was established in Spain, operating under private law. The company was the result of an initiative by several professional clubs, namely Real Madrid, Barcelona, AC Milan, Inter Milan, Juventus, Arsenal, Chelsea, Liverpool, Manchester City, Manchester United, and Tottenham Hotspur. The plan was to create a new international professional football competition, the 'Super League'. FIFA and UEFA refused to grant authorisation for the establishment of the Super League and threatened that clubs and players would be sanctioned if they proceeded with the creation of the Super League. The rules relating to the approval of competitions and exploitation of media rights arising from such competitions formed the basis of a case brought by the ESLC to the Commercial Court in Madrid. The ESLC contended that the rules were a breach of Articles 101 and 102 TFEU. The matter was sent to the CJEU under the preliminary reference. The CJEU accepted that the organisation of international competitions and exploitation of media rights were economic activities. It held that the rules on authorisation and media rights amounted to an abuse of a dominant position 'where there is no framework for those various powers providing for substantive criteria and detailed procedural rules suitable for ensuring that they are transparent, objective, non-discriminatory and proportionate'.[227] Similarly, the prior approval and the imposition of sanctions were a breach of Article 101(1)

> where there is no framework for those various powers providing for substantive criteria and detailed procedural rules suitable for ensuring that they are transparent, objective, non-discriminatory and proportionate, [this] constitutes a decision by an association of undertakings having as its object the prevention of competition.[228]

On the issue of exploitation of media rights, the CJEU stated that while exemptions may be granted under Article 101(3) and justifications put forward under Article 102, FIFA and UEFA would be required to demonstrate 'through convincing arguments and evidence, that all the conditions [were] required in order for those rules to benefit' from an exemption or justification.[229] **13–76**

The CJEU recognised the specific characteristics of sport as stated in Article 165(1) TFEU, however, it acknowledged its limitations as it held that Article 165 could not: 'be regarded as being a special rule **13–77**

Federación Española de Fútbol (RFEF), Liga Nacional de Fútbol Profesional (LNFP), ECLI:EU:C:2023:1011. It was sent to the CJEU for a preliminary ruling under art 267 TFEU from the Juzgado de lo Mercantil de Madrid (Commercial Court, Madrid, Spain).

226 ibid [3]–[22] set out the FIFA Statutes, FIFA Regulations Governing International Matches and UEFA Statutes.

227 ibid [258 (1)].

228 ibid [258 (2)].

229 ibid [258 (4)]. The CJEU also ruled under art 56 TFEU.

exempting sport from all or some of the other provisions of primary EU law liable to be applied to it or requiring special treatment for sport in the context of that application'.[230] The specific characteristics of sport may be considered 'along with other elements and provided they are relevant in the application' of the free movement of persons, services, establishment, capital, and competition provisions.[231]

13–78 In citing previous case law, including *Bosman*, *Deliège* and *Lehtonen*, the CJEU asserted that when it is argued that a rule constitutes an obstacle or impediment to the free movement of persons or constitutes an anti-competitive agreement, it is imperative that a specific assessment is carried out that applies the rule to the actual context in which it is to be implemented.[232] The CJEU elaborated on what a specific assessment would entail, including

> taking into account, for example, the nature, organisation or functioning of the sport concerned and, more specifically, how professionalised it is, the manner in which it is practised, the manner of interaction between the various participating stakeholders and the role played by the structures and bodies responsible for it at all levels, with which the Union is to foster cooperation, in accordance with Article 165(3) TFEU.[233]

13–79 In response to the criticisms of the CJEU, UEFA and FIFA modified the rules, which led some experts to contend, in advance of the Spanish court's judgment, that

> the Madrid Commercial Court may indeed be able to conclude that the FIFA and UEFA rules – as revised – could satisfy the criteria of being transparent, objectively non-discriminatory, and proportionate. In other words, a 'softer' version of the status quo.[234]

13–80 This 'softer' version was not accepted by the judge, Sofia Gil Garcia. On 27 May 2024 it was reported that the Madrid Commercial Court found that the actions of FIFA and UEFA were a breach of EU competition law. However, UEFA has asserted that the judgment does not 'explicitly support the creation of a Super League'.[235] A22 Sports Management CEO asserted that 'the era of the monopoly is now definitively over' as the decision represented 'an important step towards a truly competitive and

---

230 ibid [101].
231 ibid [104].
232 ibid [105].
233 ibid.
234 Izzet Sinan and others, 'Sports and EU Law: Madrid Commercial Court to Hear Arguments in European Super League Case' (*Morgan Lewis*, 12 March 2024) <https://www.morganlewis.com/pubs/2024/03/sports-and-eu-law-madrid-commercial-court-to-hear-arguments-in-european-super-league-case> accessed 20 May 2024. The hearing in Madrid began on 14 March 2024.
235 'Spanish court orders FIFA, UEFA to halt opposition to Super League' *Reuters* (Toronto, 28 May 2024) <https://www.reuters.com/sports/soccer/spanish-court-orders-fifa-uefa-halt-opposition-super-league-2024-05-27/> accessed 29 July 2024.

sustainable club football landscape in Europe'.[236] Gil Garcia J 'ordered FIFA and UEFA to immediately reverse any anticompetitive actions committed in the past'.[237]

In September 2023, AG Ćapeta in a case involving the publication of personal data relating to a professional athlete who had tested positive for a prohibited substance opined that there was no GDPR breach.[238] In reference to Article 165 TFEU, the AG observed that the EU 'does not have competence to regulate sport' and, furthermore, this had 'not changed with the introduction of supporting competence in sport by Article 165 TFEU'.[239] She opined: 'Anti-doping rules primarily regulate sport as sport. They are concerned with sport's social and educational functions, rather than its economic aspects, even if the former may influence the latter.'[240] While the EU lacks a regulatory competence in sport, 'it could theoretically harmonise national anti-doping rules, if this is justified as being necessary to remove obstacles to cross-border movements'.[241] The CJEU found the request for a preliminary reference to be inadmissible, thus the AG's Opinion did not feature in the judgment.[242] However, her approach was interesting and novel. Apart from the request being inadmissible, the CJEU is not under any obligation to follow the AG's Opinion. **13–81**

Conclusion

Articles 6 and 165 of the TFEU emphasise the importance of sport in the Union and give the EU a formal competence, namely the competence to carry out actions to support, coordinate or supplement the actions of the Member States in sport. At a Treaty level, the EU has a limited involvement in sport. That, however, belies the truth. Through the case law of the European Courts and European Commission Decisions, EU law has been applied to sporting activities ranging from free-movement rights to anti-competitive agreements. The specificity of sport is a legal principle that has evolved on a case-by-case basis. While EU law is applicable to the economic activities of the sporting sector, the European Courts and the European Commission recognise the special place that sport occupies in the lives of its citizens. There has been a move away from referring to 'purely sporting matters' and instead the more recent cases have referred to the 'inherent' characteristics of sport. In deciding **13–82**

---

[236] ibid.

[237] ibid.

[238] *EN* (n 4). Regulation (EU) 2016/679 of the European Parliament and of the Council of 27 April 2016 on the protection of natural persons with regard to the processing of personal data and on the free movement of such data and repealing Directive 95/46/EC (General Data Protection Regulation) [2016] OJ 2016 L 119.

[239] *EN* (n 4) [88].

[240] ibid [89].

[241] ibid. The AG was pragmatic and acknowledged that there were 'no EU rules that relate, even indirectly, to the anti-doping policies of the Member States'.

[242] *EN* (n 4).

whether there has been a breach of EU law, the European Courts will assess the alleged impediment or obstacle or anti-competitive agreement to decipher whether, in the specific context of the case, the measure can be justified or not. It can be difficult to gauge how the European Courts will decide a sporting case as it depends on the facts of the case and whether the measure is proportionate, pursues a legitimate objective, and can be justified. The decision of the Madrid Commercial Court will alter the football landscape in Europe, however, as UEFA refuses to view the decision as an explicit endorsement of the Superleague, the shape of that landscape remains uncertain.

CHAPTER 14

CHILD PROTECTION IN SPORT

Introduction

Sport is an important facet in the lives of many children. Children derive benefits from participating in sport. In the words of Smith and Westerbeek, 'sport is advantageous in that it improves self-esteem, advances good citizenship, fosters the value of mastery and cooperation, and encourages a physically active lifestyle'.[1] In order to encourage more children to be involved in sport, it is imperative that sports governing bodies and clubs have rigorous policies in place that ensure children are protected and safe from harm. There are several statutory and non-statutory obligations placed on clubs and sports governing bodies in Ireland.[2] All national sports governing bodies and clubs are required to have in a prominent place their child safeguarding statements. Sporting bodies should also have a dedicated child protection and safeguarding section on their websites. 14–01

This chapter will examine the background to Garda vetting by looking at developments in the 1990s. It will discuss the main pieces of legislation that provide protection to children participating in sport. The chapter will conclude by discussing the non-statutory methods of child protection, including the *Children First: National Guidance for the Protection and Welfare of Children.* 14–02

Background to the Legislative Protection for Children in Sport

In the 1990s, individuals within the Irish Amateur Swimming Association (IASA) were found to have abused a number of children.[3] In response, 14–03

---

1 The author would like to thank Marcus Naughton for his help with the research for this chapter. Aaron CT Smith and Hans M Westerbeek, 'Sport as a Vehicle for Deploying Corporate Social Responsibility' (2007) 25 Journal of Corporate Citizenship 43, 51. See also Toni M O'Donovan, Ann MacPhail, and David Kirk, 'Active Citizenship through Sport Education' (2010) 38(2) Education 3–13, 203–15.

2 An example of a non-statutory measure is 'Sport Ireland Safeguarding Guidance', a guidance for children and young people <https://www.sportireland.ie/ethics/safeguarding-guidance-for-children-and-young-people-in-sport> accessed 20 May.

3 In 1999 the IASA was renamed as Swim Ireland. The name change was criticised as the same people remained in charge under Swim Ireland: 'Irish Amateur Swimming Association replaced by Swim Ireland' (*RTÉ*, 5 March 1999) <https://www.rte.ie/news/1999/0124/383-swimming/> accessed 20 May 2024.

many parents contacted the then Minister for Tourism and Sport to establish a judicial inquiry into child sex abuse in swimming; however, such an inquiry would mean that victims would be compelled to give evidence.[4] Instead, it was decided that there would be an independent inquiry, as detailed below.

14–04 Before the parliamentary inquiry, an Expert Committee was established by the Minister in 1995. The Committee was tasked with devising a code of conduct for children in sport. Consisting of representatives from sport, child protection, and government departments, the *Code of Ethics and Good Practice for Children's Sport* was launched in June 1996.[5] The Code was referred to as a 'living document', one which would require revisions and additions over time.[6] Chapter 5 examined child abuse, Chapter 6 detailed awareness and identification of child abuse, and Chapter 7 set out the procedures for reporting child abuse. The Code established 'general principles which should underpin the conduct of sport in all areas, including competitive and non-competitive physical recreation'.[7]

14–05 In 1998, the *Report of the Independent Inquiry into Matters relating to Child Sex Abuse in Swimming*, also referred to as the Murphy Report, was published. The interim report was submitted to the then Minister, Dr James McDaid, on 27 May 1998. The two coaches are not named in the report; however, reference is made to the Circuit Criminal Court imposing a 12-year prison sentence on a 'prominent swimming coach'.[8] The charges related to the period between 1 January 1976 and 31 December 1992 where he was a coach at a swimming club which was attached to, but independent of, a school.[9] Chapter 5 of the Murphy

---

4 Dáil Deb 11 Feb 1998, vol 487 <https://www.oireachtas.ie/en/debates/debate/dail/1998-02-11/7/> accessed 20 May 2024.

5 European Commission, *Study on Gender-based Violence in Sport: Final Report*, ed Lut Mergaert, Catarina Arnaut, Tine Vertommen, and Melanie Lang (European Commission 2016) 59 <https://sport.ec.europa.eu/sites/default/files/gender-based-violence-sport-study-2016_en.pdf> accessed 20 May 2024.

6 Government of Ireland, *Code of Ethics and Good Practice for Children's Sport in Ireland* (Government of Ireland June 1996) 4 <https://www.lenus.ie/handle/10147/575231> accessed 20 May 2024.

7 ibid 6. Accordingly, the 'Code should be adopted by all sporting organisations at national, regional and local levels, and individuals working with children should abide by the provisions contained herein. The Code is designed to cover sporting activities involving children and young people up to 18 years of age.'

8 Roderick Murphy, Senior Counsel, *Report of the Independent Inquiry into Matters relating to Child Sex Abuse in Swimming* (Government Publications 1998) ch 1, 'Terms of Reference and Procedures Adopted', 8.

9 ibid 8. This was in reference to Derry O'Rourke. O'Rourke had coached in a school and a club in the west side of Dublin city and was appointed as the national coach in November 1991. He travelled to the 1992 Summer Olympic Games in Barcelona with the Irish Olympic swimming team. When there were reports that he had abused young swimmers, he was suspended from the school but continued as a coach in the club. In 1995 he was charged with child sex abuse; however, he tried to invoke judicial review to prevent him being charged. He

Report focused on the first named coach, and Chapter 6 on the named school, while Chapter 7 detailed the second named coach. The second named coach had succeeded the first named coach as the Irish Olympic swimming coach.[10]

The inquiry could not compel witnesses and instead relied on voluntary cooperation. Evidence was heard over a three-month period, including weekends and evenings to facilitate witnesses who were working or who were reluctant to give evidence.[11] In excess of 50 witnesses gave oral evidence in an informal setting, which was recorded and subsequently **14–06**

contended that the charges relating to the period of 1976 to 1992 were too old and that in any event he would be contesting the charges. His attempts to evade the charges were unsuccessful. In January 1998 he pleaded guilty to 29 charges relating to sex abuse against 11 female swimmers under the age of 15. O'Rourke was sentenced to 12 years in prison; however, he was released in 2007 from Midlands Prison in Portlaoise: see 'Derry O'Rourke Released from Jail' *The Irish Times* (Dublin, 1 March 2007) <https://www.irishtimes.com/news/derry-o-rourke-released-from-jail-1.803898> accessed 20 May 2024. On 18 July 2024, O'Rourke was found guilty and convicted of rape and indecent assault of a teenage girl in a school on numerous dates between October 1989 and June 1990. The judge directed the jury to acquit the defendant on four counts of assault, however, the jury proceeded on the one charge of rape and 11 charges of indecent assault, see Sonya McClean and Claire Henry, 'Former swimming coach Derry O'Rourke convicted of raping teenage girl 35 years ago' *Breaking News* (18 July 2024) <https://www.breakingnews.ie/ireland/former-irish-international-swimming-coach-derry-orourke-convicted-of-rape-and-sexual-assault-1651431.html> accessed 29 July 2024.

10 This was a reference to George Gibney, who had coached the Irish Olympic swimming team for the 1986 and 1990 Summer Games. In 1991 Gibney resigned as Ireland's Olympic coach as rumours surfaced that he had sexually abused young male and female swimmers. In 1993 Gibney left Ireland and four months later charges of indecency and carnal knowledge of girls under the age of 15 were brought against him. There were in total 27 charges made against him. Gibney succeeded in a High Court judicial review in 1994, which prohibited the Director of Public Prosecutions (DPP) from charging him on the grounds that he would be denied a fair hearing due to the time delay since the alleged offences. He fled first to Scotland and then the United States (US), where he currently resides in Florida. He acquired a green card, and this was the subject of litigation in the US. A podcast titled *Where Is George Gibney?* resulted in two more alleged victims coming forward. See Ed O'Loughlin, 'True-Crime Podcast Puts Spotlight on Irish Coach Accused of Abuse' *New York Times* (New York, 17 January 2021) <https://www.nytimes.com/2021/01/17/world/europe/ireland-george-gibney.html> accessed 20 May 2024. There was another High Court case brought by a female swimmer against Gibney, the IASA and the Olympic Council of Ireland; however, Hogan J struck out the case on the grounds that the plaintiff had inordinately delayed the proceedings without explanation against the second- and third-named defendants, both corporate entities. For more detail, see *Doyle v Gibney & Ors* [2011] IEHC 10. The gardaí recently contacted the authorities in the US about extraditing Gibney to Ireland following a file being sent to the DPP concerning historic child sex abuse allegations: Ali Bracken, 'Gardaí Contact US Authorities about Former Swim Coach George Gibney in Latest Investigation' *Irish Independent* (Dublin, 5 November 2023) <https://www.independent.ie/irish-news/gardai-contact-us-authorities-about-former-swim-coach-george-gibney-in-latest-investigation/a250550243.html> accessed 20 May 2024.

11 *Report of the Independent Inquiry* (n 8) 9.

transcribed.[12] Twenty other witnesses provided evidence via conference call or by telephone.[13] The witnesses included 20 swimmers, 12 parents, and nine professionals including lawyers, psychologists, social workers, academics, and officials from the IASA and individual clubs.[14] Some swimmers provided evidence in their capacity as swimmers and as coaches.[15] All evidence, irrespective of the mode of communication, was treated on the basis of strict confidentiality.

14–07 Chapter 2 of the Murphy Report provided details of the IASA and its history, and its association with the Fédération Internationale de Natation (FINA, now World Aquatics), the international federation (IF) for swimming. The Murphy Report observed that the only safety provisions required of FINA related to open water swimming events where a Safety Officer had to be appointed.[16] In addition, a Medical Officer was required for all medical aspects relating to competition and competitors.[17] A number of witnesses contended that 'the opportunity for abuse is greater at international training sessions and at meets than at home'.[18] It thus followed that it was the sole responsibility of the IASA and not FINA to protect young athletes from abuse.

14–08 The Murphy Report was critical of the lack of supervision of coaches and recommended that female and male team managers should be appointed where there are female and male swimmers on an away trip and 'there should be adequate female and male team managers for female and male swimmers'.[19] Coaches should be required to furnish references from past positions, have a written contract of employment setting out their duties, obligations, and the grievance and disciplinary procedures.[20] Furthermore, the Murphy Report recommended that '[a]ll coaches should be members of the Irish Swimming Teachers and Coaches Association or equivalent organisation'.[21] The need for children and parents to be more aware of sexual abuse was also highlighted.[22] The inquiry did not examine what the IASA knew and, consequently, no one was held responsible. It did, however, raise concerns as to the

---

[12] ibid.

[13] ibid.

[14] ibid.

[15] ibid. Written submissions were also received from several public and private bodies, including the Irish Society for the Prevention of Cruelty to Children (ISPCC), An Garda Síochána, Dublin Rape Crisis Centre, the Department of Education and Science, the Department of Children and Health, and the Amateur Swimming Association of England.

[16] ibid 27, para 8.4.

[17] ibid para 8.5.

[18] ibid para 8.7. In the summary of findings, the Murphy Report noted that '[s]ome of the more serious incidents of abuse took place on trips abroad, in the coaches' cars or in the coaches' homes and not at the swimming pool'.

[19] ibid 137, paras 3.15 and 3.16.

[20] ibid 139, paras 4.1 and 4.6.

[21] ibid para. 4.3.

[22] ibid 143, paras 7.1–7.8.

organisation of the IASA.[23] The IASA, which was established in 1893, was dissolved on 1 January 1999 and was replaced with Swim Ireland. In the words of McCarthy, 'The most tangible change effected by the Murphy Inquiry was the restructuring of the Irish Amateur Swimming Association in the immediate aftermath of the publication of the report.'[24]

The creation of a new body was viewed by some as a mere cosmetic exercise with little change to the substance of the organisation. In support of this, they pointed to the appointment of former IASA members to the newly formed Swim Ireland.[25] However, Swim Ireland assumed civil liability for its predecessor and settled out of court with 13 swimmers.[26] It had taken over 10 years to reach the settlement of a reported €1m and one swimmer was said to have received €500,000.[27] **14–09**

While the irreparable damage caused to the young swimmers will never be erased, the Murphy Report was a watershed moment in Irish sport. It highlighted the lack of protection for young people in sport and the need for the state to place obligations on sporting bodies by way of legislative intervention, and it is to the legal framework that the chapter now turns. **14–10**

Legislation Applicable to Children in Sport

There are several Acts that provide protection for children and young people participating in sport. These Acts are not specific to sport and apply to the protection of children in general. There are specific guidelines and other 'soft law' measures that apply to children in sport. **14–11**

---

23 ibid 118, para 1.2: 'Despite the best efforts of its paid employees and its voluntary officers the IASA lacks the resources and the professional administrative backing that an amateur organisation necessarily needs. While the IASA has a modest premises and a small staff since 1989, the Leinster Branch operates, as the IASA used to operate, out of its officers' homes. While the absence of complete records before 1989, other than those relating to registration of members, made it impossible to ascertain the nature of complaints made prior to that date, the evidence of officers, which the Inquiry accepts, is that there were no sexual abuse complaints made prior to that date nor were any such allegations made to the Inquiry'.

24 Justine McCarthy, *The Relentless Investigation to Bring George Gibney, Derry O'Rourke, Ger Doyle and Other Abusers to Justice* (O'Brien Press 2020) eBook.

25 Tim O'Brien, 'Swimming Body Is Dissolved as Stories Are Told of Sex Abuse' *The Irish Times* (Dublin, 25 January 1999) <https://www.irishtimes.com/news/swimming-body-is-dissolved-as-stories-are-told-of-sex-abuse-1.1257644> accessed 20 May 2024.

26 Johnny Watterson, 'Swim Ireland Not Bankrupt' *The Irish Times* (Dublin, 11 February 2008) <https://www.irishtimes.com/sport/swim-ireland-not-bankrupt-1.892898> accessed 20 May 2024.

27 ibid. In 2006 there were 15 complainants: see Johnny Watterson, 'Swimming Body Faces 15 Claims of Child Sex Abuse' *The Irish Times* (Dublin, 21 April 2006) <https://www.irishtimes.com/news/swimming-body-faces-15-claims-of-child-sex-abuse-1.1041136> accessed 20 May 2024.

The main pieces of legislation that apply to children taking part in sport are as follows:

- National Vetting Bureau (Children and Vulnerable Persons) Act 2012–2016
- Criminal Justice (Withholding of Information on Offences against Children and Vulnerable Persons) Act 2012
- Children First Act 2015
- The Protections for Persons Reporting Child Abuse Act 1998
- Criminal Law (Sexual Offences) Act 2006 as amended by the Criminal Law (Sexual Offences) Act 2017 (as amended).[28]

National Vetting Bureau (Children and Vulnerable Persons) Act 2012–2016

14–12 Until the National Vetting Bureau (Children and Vulnerable Persons) Act 2012–2016 came into force, vetting was placed on a very informal setting. On 29 April 2016, the National Vetting Bureau (Children and Vulnerable Persons) Act 2012–2016 came into effect.[29] The Act was introduced in 2012; however, it did not commence until April 2016. Since the Act commenced, the vetting process has been formalised and standardised, thereby offering more protection to children and other vulnerable persons.

14–13 Prior to the Act, vetting was required by the *Children First: National Guidance for the Protection and Welfare of Children,* the national guidelines on children's welfare.[30] The guidelines provided that every organisation, public or private, that was providing services for children or was in regular contact with children should adhere to best practice in the recruitment of staff or volunteers, including Garda vetting. Prior to the statutory requirement of vetting, Irish sporting organisations were advised to follow the national guidelines – however, there was no

---

[28] The 2017 Act was amended by Criminal Law (Sexual Offences) (Amendment Act 2019). The Child Care (Amendment) Act 2024 was signed into law by the President on 8 July 2024. Schedule 1 of the National Vetting Bureau (Children and Vulnerable Persons) Act 2012 is amended in relation to the wording of 'early years services' to 'pre-school services'. Schedule 2 of the Children First Act was similarly amended, neither amendment fundamentally affects either Act. For the text of the entire Act, see <https://www.irishstatutebook.ie/eli/2024/act/19/enacted/en/print> accessed 29 July 2024.

[29] SI No 214/2016 – National Vetting Bureau (Children and Vulnerable Persons) Act 2012 (Commencement) Order 2016. All but one section came into force on 29 April 2016. Section 20 relates to the process of re-vetting. Section 20 does not state the time period; however, according to the Early Years' 'Quality and Regulatory Framework', re-vetting should occur within three years: Tusla, 'Quality and Regulatory Framework: Full Day Care Service and Part-Time Day Care Service' (Early Years Inspectorate, Tusla 2018) 5 <https://www.tusla.ie/uploads/content/4566-TUSLA_QRF_DAY_CARE_LR.pdf> accessed 20 May 2024.

[30] The first edition was published in 1999: see Department of Health and Children, *Children First: National Guidance for the Protection and Welfare of Children* (Stationery Office 1999).

statutory obligation on them to do so. It seems that most governing bodies used the *National Guidance* recommendations on vetting as an example of best practice.

The National Vetting Bureau (Children and Vulnerable Persons) Act 2012–2016 changed vetting procedures as it placed the process on a statutory footing for the first time. The Act makes vetting mandatory for all organisations whose work relates to children or vulnerable people. It applies to employers and organisations, which means that sporting organisations are under a duty to have formalised vetting procedures in place. **14–14**

Vetting is currently carried out by the National Vetting Bureau of An Garda Síochána (formerly the Garda Central Vetting Unit, GCVU).[31] Vetting is not carried out for individuals on a personal basis but rather for the relevant organisation that is registered with the National Vetting Bureau. Each organisation is required to have a contact person who sends applications to the National Vetting Bureau and receives vetting disclosures. Under ss 12(1)(a) and (b) of the Act, relevant organisations should not employ or enter into a contract of services with a person until a vetting disclosure has been received from the National Vetting Bureau.[32] Relevant organisations are not permitted to engage an individual, whether unpaid or not, to undertake relevant work or activities until the vetting disclosure has been furnished, as per s 12(c), and s 12(d) provides that this section also applies to organisations that provide training, education, and internships. Employers or organisations who are involved in work or activities that include children under the age of 18 or vulnerable persons must ensure that a vetting disclosure has been received in respect of the individual(s) concerned before they can be permitted to undertake work or engage in activities in such **14–15**

31 The name change was effected by s 29 of the Act. The GCVU was established in 2005. In the early days of its operation, it processed approximately 1,000 applications per year. In 2015, this had risen to 350,000 per year, or 30,000 per month: An Garda Síochána, 'Official Launch of eVetting – National Vetting Bureau on the 29/4/16' <https://www.garda.ie/en/about-us/our-departments/office-of-corporate-communications/press-releases/2016/april/official-launch-of-evetting-national-vetting-bureau-on-the-29-4-16.html> accessed 20 May 2024. Applications can be processed online via eVetting at <https://vetting.garda.ie/> accessed 20 September 2024.

32 Relevant organisation is defined as 'a person (including a body corporate or an unincorporated body of persons)'. It includes employers, employment agencies, and organisations, including sports governing bodies.

areas.[33] It is an offence for a person to contravene s 12(1).[34] If the matter is tried summarily and the person is convicted, they face a class A fine or imprisonment for a term not exceeding 12 months or both.[35] If the person is convicted on indictment, the penalty is a fine not exceeding €10,000 or imprisonment for a term not exceeding five years or both.[36]

14–16 Of relevance to sport is Schedule 1, s 2, Part 1 of the Act. It provides that vetting must be obtained if the work or activity being carried out by a person involves 'a necessary and regular part of which consists mainly of the person having access to, or contact with, children' including

> the provision of educational, training, cultural, recreational, leisure, social or physical activities (whether or not for commercial or any other consideration) to children unless the provision of educational, training, cultural, recreational, leisure, social or physical activities is merely incidental to the provision of educational, training, cultural, recreational, leisure, social or physical activities to persons who are not children.

14–17 National governing bodies (NGB) must be registered with the Garda National Vetting Bureau.[37] Any person intending to work or volunteer with an NGB that includes children and vulnerable persons must apply via the relevant governing body for vetting. Taking Athletics Ireland as an example, it outlines the steps that must be taken as part of the eVetting process.[38]

---

[33] Vulnerable person is defined as 'a person, other than a child, who—(a) is suffering from a disorder of the mind, whether as a result of mental illness or dementia, (b) has an intellectual disability, (c) is suffering from a physical impairment, whether as a result of injury, illness or age, or (d) has a physical disability, which is of such a nature or degree—(i) as to restrict the capacity of the person to guard himself or herself against harm by another person, or (ii) that results in the person requiring assistance with the activities of daily living including dressing, eating, walking, washing and bathing'.

[34] This is stated in s 12(2). Section 12(3), however, provides that 'it shall be a defence for the accused person to show that the accused person neither knew nor could reasonably be expected to know that the work or activity to which the employment, contract, permission or placement referred to in subsection (1) constituted relevant work or activities'.

[35] s 27(1)(a). Summary conviction is where the case is before a judge in the District Court with no jury. The Fines Act 2010 defines a class A fine as a fine not exceeding €5,000.

[36] Conviction on indictment is where the case goes before a judge and jury in either the Circuit Court or the Central Criminal Court.

[37] Sport Ireland initially vetted NGBs on a phased basis. It notified the Garda Central Vetting Unit once an NGB was in a position to apply for registration. Each NGB had to have a nominated person who would manage the process and liaise with the Garda Central Vetting Bureau: see Sport Ireland, 'Garda Vetting' <https://www.sportireland.ie/ethics/garda-vetting> accessed 20 May 2024.

[38] Athletics Ireland, 'Garda Vetting Policy' <https://www.athleticsireland.ie/juvenile/child-welfare/garda-vetting-policy/> accessed 20 May 2024.

Vetting and Those Aged 16 and 17

14–18 For those under aged under 18 who are involved in a coaching or mentoring role within a sport, vetting is required, and must be accompanied by parental or guardian consent.[39] Persons under the age of 16 are precluded from applying for vetting.[40]

Criminal Justice (Withholding of Information on Offences against Children and Vulnerable Persons) Act 2012

14–19 Section 2 of the Criminal Justice (Withholding of Information on Offences against Children and Vulnerable Persons) Act 2012 makes it an offence for adults to withhold information relating to Schedule 1 offences against children.[41] Schedule 1, s 2, lists 20 offences against children including murder, manslaughter, false imprisonment, rape, sexual assault, incest, defilement of a child under 15 years old, defilement of a child under 17 years of age, child trafficking and child pornography, assault, and female genital mutilation.[42]

14–20 Schedule 1 of the 2012 Act also provides that s 2 applies to reckless endangerment under the Criminal Justice Act 2006. Section 176 of Criminal Justice Act 2006 introduced the criminal charge of reckless endangerment of children. Section 176(2) provides:

> A person, having authority or control over a child or abuser, who intentionally or recklessly endangers a child by—
> (a) causing or permitting any child to be placed or left in a situation which creates a substantial risk to the child of being a victim of serious harm or sexual abuse, or

---

39 National Vetting Bureau (Children and Vulnerable Persons) Act 2012–2016, s 13(6). The parent/guardian must sign a declaration of consent: see Early Childhood Ireland, 'Guidelines for Completing Under 18 Vetting Invitation Form (NVB 1)' (April 2204) <https://www.earlychildhoodireland.ie/wp-content/uploads/2024/04/Under18s-Vetting-Invitation-Form_April2024.pdf> accessed 20 May 2024.The applicant completes the Under 18's Vetting Invitation Form (NVB 1). The parent/guardian fills out the Parent Guardian Consent Form (NVB3) and both forms are submitted along with photo identification and proof of address.

40 For an example of the GAA vetting procedures, see <https://www.gaa.ie/the-gaa/child-safeguarding-and-protection/vetting> accessed 20 May 2024; and the Irish Athletic Boxing Association (IABA) has its procedure outlined at <http://iaba.ie/club-zone/step-by-step-guide-to-garda-vetting-form/> accessed 20 May 2024.

41 The long title of this Act is: An Act to provide, in connection with the protection of children and certain vulnerable adults, for offences of withholding information relating to the commission of certain arrestable offences (including certain sexual offences) against children, or certain arrestable offences (including certain sexual offences) against such adults, in certain circumstances; To provide for the amendment of s 9 of the Offences against the State (Amendment) Act 1998; to amend s 16 of the Criminal Justice (Female Genital Mutilation) Act 2012; and to provide for related matters.

42 The full list can be accessed here <https://www.irishstatutebook.ie/eli/2012/act/24/schedule/1/enacted/en/html#sched1> accessed 29 July 2024.

(b) failing to take reasonable steps to protect a child from such a risk while knowing that the child is in such a situation,

is guilty of an offence.

14–21 According to s 176(4), the penalty for a person found guilty of this offence is a fine and/or imprisonment for a term not exceeding 10 years.

The Protections for Persons Reporting Child Abuse Act 1998

14–22 Section 3 of the Protections for Persons Reporting Child Act 1998 provides for the protection from civil liability of persons who have communicated, in writing or otherwise, child abuse including sexual, physical and neglect, 'reasonably and in good faith' to an appropriate person. An appropriate person is defined as a designated officer or a member of An Garda Síochána.[43] Section 4 provides protection for employees who report child abuse, who should not be penalised by their employer. The protection means that individuals or employees should not be liable in damages if it transpires that the communication of child abuse was unfounded. If a civil case were to be initiated against the person who communicated the alleged abuse which was later found to be untrue, the plaintiff would need to prove that the communication was not made reasonably and in good faith.

14–23 Section 5 of the Act makes it a criminal offence for a person to knowingly make a statement to an appropriate person, as explained below, alleging child abuse when they know it to be false. The penalties are provided for under ss 5(2)(a) and (b). If the person is convicted summarily, they may be subject to a fine not exceeding £1,500 (approximately €1,900) and/or to imprisonment for a term not exceeding 12 months. If convicted on indictment, the person faces a fine not exceeding £15,000 (approximately €19,000) and/or to imprisonment for a term not exceeding 3 years.

Criminal Law (Sexual Offences) Act 2006 as amended by the Criminal Law (Sexual Offences) Act 2017 (as amended)

14–24 The Criminal Law (Sexual Offences) Act 2006 was enacted in the wake of the case of *CC v Ireland and Ors*.[44] The Supreme Court declared s 1(1) of the Criminal Law (Amendment) Act 1935 unconstitutional. This section related to the defilement of a girl under the age of 15 and provided that

> Any person who unlawfully and carnally knows any girl under the age of fifteen years shall be guilty of a felony, and shall be liable on conviction thereof to penal servitude for life or for any term not less than three years or to imprisonment for any term not exceeding two years.

---

[43] Designated officer refers to an officer of a health board appointed under s 2 of this Act by the Minister for Children, Equality, Disability, Integration and Youth. Under the Act, the reference is to the Minister for Health and Children.

[44] [2006] IESC 33.

The respondent contended that s 1(1) of the 1935 Act conflicted with Article 50.1 of the 1937 Constitution, which states: 14–25

> Subject to this Constitution and to the extent to which they are not inconsistent therewith, the laws in force in Saorstát Éireann immediately prior to the date of the coming into operation of this Constitution shall continue to be of full force and effect until the same or any of them shall have been repealed or amended by enactment of the Oireachtas.[45]

The case concerned an adult male who was charged with four offences under s 1(1) of the 1935 Act. The girl was under the age of 15; however, the respondent claimed that the girl had told him that she was 16 years of age. The 1935 Act did not explicitly provide for the defence of reasonable mistake which, according to the respondent's Senior Counsel, rendered s 1(1) unconstitutional as it 'ceased to have force and effect *to the extent* that it precluded an accused from advancing a defence of reasonable mistake as to the age of the victim'.[46] In allowing the appeal, the Supreme Court granted a declaration that s 1(1) of the 1935 Act was inconsistent with the provisions of the Constitution. 14–26

The decision of the Supreme Court necessitated the introduction of legislation to replace ss 1 and 2 of the 1935 Act and to provide a defence of mistake of age.[47] The Criminal Law (Sexual Offences) Act 2006 was subsequently amended by the Criminal Law (Sexual Offences) Act 2017. The reference to 'honest mistake' under the 2006 Act is replaced by 'reasonable mistake' by virtue of s 16(2), subsections 3 and 4 of the 2017 Act. According to O'Malley: 14–27

> Irish law remains more liberal than that of other jurisdictions in the sense that the defence of reasonable mistake as to age is available in respect of any offence of a sexual act with a child under the age of 15 years. In other jurisdictions, including Scotland and New Zealand, there is no defence whatever of mistake as to age where the child is under 12 or 13 years. However, under the new Irish law, it is most improbable that a person could claim that to have been reasonably mistaken that a child under, say, 12 years was over 15 years.[48]

---

45 Constitution of Ireland <https://www.irishstatutebook.ie/eli/cons/en/html#part17> accessed 29 July 2024.

46 (n 44).

47 Under ss 2(3) and (4) the Act provides a defence for honest mistake as to the age of the child: (3) It shall be a defence to proceedings for an offence under this section for the defendant to prove that he or she honestly believed that, at the time of the alleged commission of the offence, the child against whom the offence is alleged to have been committed had attained the age of 15 years. (4) Where, in proceedings for an offence under this section, it falls to the court to consider whether the defendant honestly believed that, at the time of the alleged commission of the offence, the child against whom the offence is alleged to have been committed had attained the age of 15 years, the court shall have regard to the presence or absence of reasonable grounds for the defendant's so believing and all other relevant circumstances.

48 Presentation by Tom O'Malley BL, 18th Annual National Prosecutors' Conference (Dublin Castle Conference Centre, 25 November 2017) 9 <https://www.

14–28 Section 15 of the 2017 Act amended s 1 of the 2006 Act by extending the list of those that are considered as persons in authority, including aunt/s, uncle/s, grandparent/s, current or former foster parent/s or guardian/s, current or former stepparent/s, anyone who is or has been *in loco parentis* to the child.[49] Of significance to sport, any other person who is or has been responsible for the education, supervision, training, care, or welfare of the child is included. Section 17 of the 2017 Act amended s 3 of the 2006 Act. Section 17 provides that a person in authority who is found to have had sexual intercourse with a child under the age of 17 faces, on indictment, a prison term not exceeding 15 years.[50] According to s 17(5), 'The standard of proof required to prove that the defendant was reasonably mistaken that the child had attained the age of 17 years shall be that applicable to civil proceedings.'

14–29 In 2022, Stack J of the High Court in *CW v The Minister for Justice and Equality, Ireland, the Attorney General and the Director of Public Prosecutions* held the requirement under s 17(5) was unconstitutional.[51] The plaintiff argued that his right to a fair trial under Article 38.1 of the Constitution was breached, as implicit in the right to fair trial is that the standard of proof is beyond reasonable doubt and not that of on the balance of probabilities as required by Article 17(5). Stack J summed up the position as follows:

> The question then is whether the presumption of innocence, that is, the requirement that the prosecution prove guilt beyond a reasonable doubt, is a component part of a fair trial which can be legitimately restricted without compromising the overall fairness of the trial or whether it is so essential to that fairness that it cannot be subject to statutory modification.[52]

14–30 Stack J declared s 3(5) of the 2006 Act to be invalid considering Article 38.1. The judge referred to the 'aspect of the fundamental fairness of a criminal trial that an accused should not be liable to conviction where there is a reasonable doubt as to his guilt', thus s 3(5):

> which deals with the core issue of moral culpability of the accused, and which places an obligation on him to prove on the balance of probabilities that he is not so culpable, is contrary to Article 38.1 of the Constitution.[53]

14–31 There was an appeal by the defendants/appellants to the Supreme Court, and the judgment was delivered by Chief Justice (CJ) O'Donnell and

---

dppireland.ie/app/uploads/2017/11/PAPER_-_Tom_OMalley_BL.1.pdf> accessed 20 May 2024.

49 s 15 of the 2017 Act inserted (a)–(f) into s 2 of the 2006 Act.

50 A person who is not in authority faces seven years' imprisonment for the same offence.

51 [2022] IEHC 336. The plaintiff was 19 years of age when he had sex with a girl aged 15 years 10 months. He was sentenced to one year and ten months, which was to run concurrently with another sentence. His release date was 2025: [8].

52 ibid [45].

53 ibid [101] and [102].

O'Malley J on 23 August 2023.[54] The judges stated that in 'an era when young adults are much more sexually active than in the past, a genuine mistake is a realistic rather than a remote possibility, if the parties are not known to each other'.[55] While acknowledging that the objective of the legislation was a legitimate one 'and justifies both the imposition of a burden of proof on the defence and the requirement that the mistake be reasonable',

> the pitching of that burden at the level of proof on the balance of probabilities either impairs the right to be presumed innocent to the point where it must be considered disproportionate and contrary to the constitutional presumption of innocence or fails to guarantee a trial in due course of law as required by Article 38 of the Constitution.[56]

The Supreme Court dismissed the appeal and stressed that the only part of s 3 to be deemed unconstitutional was subsection 5 – the rest of the section remains fully operational.[57] **14–32**

Children First Act 2015

The Children First Act 2015 was enacted on 17 November 2015 and commenced in full on 11 December 2017.[58] The Act placed on a statutory footing the *Children First: National Guidance for the Protection and Welfare of Children*. In the aftermath of the IASA scandal, *Children First* was published in 1999.[59] It was first amended in 2011, and amended and **14–33**

---

[54] [2023] IESC 22. There was a separate concurring judgment of Charleton J: see <https://www.courts.ie/acc/alfresco/d4b89c46-09ed-48e3-9342-38b0b4b6c864/2023_IESC_22_(Charleton%20J).pdf/pdf#view=fitH> accessed 20 May 2024.

[55] ibid [245].

[56] ibid [247].

[57] ibid [249].

[58] SI No 470/2017 – Children First Act 2015 (Commencement) Order 2017. On 11 December 2015, Part 1 Preliminary and General, ss 1–5; and Part 5 Miscellaneous, Abolition of defence of reasonable chastisement, s 28, commenced. The following commenced on 1 May 2016: Part 3 Reporting, s 18. The Child and Family Agency is a specified body for purposes of National Vetting Bureau (Children and Vulnerable persons) Acts 2012–16 and Part 4 Children First Inter-Departmental Implementation Group, ss 20–26. On 11 December 2017, the following sections commenced: Part 1 Preliminary and General, ss 6–7; Part 2 Child Safeguarding Statements, ss 8–13; Part 3 Reporting, ss 14–17 and 19; Part 4 Children First Inter-Departmental Implementation Group and Sectoral Implementation Plans. This timeline is taken from Department of Children, Equality, Disability, Integration and Youth, 'Commencement of the Provisions of the Children First Legislation' (28 August 2019) <https://www.gov.ie/en/policy-information/45a1ae-commencement-of-the-provisions-of-the-children-first-legislation/> accessed 20 May 2024.

[59] See (n 30). Since 1999, it has been in operation in sectors involving children, including schools, hospitals, sporting organisations, childcare facilities, and youth work: Department of Children, Equality, Disability, Integration and Youth, 'Children First' (4 March 2021) <https://www.gov.ie/en/policy-information/d1b594-children-first/> accessed 20 May 2024.

fully revised in 2017.[60] The most recent version is the *Children First Guidance 2017*. In January 2019, the guidance was amended by way of an addendum 'to ensure that online safety is specifically accounted for in child safeguarding statements'.[61]

14–34 Under the Child First Act 2015, the definition of a child is that of the definition provided for in s 2 of the Child Care Act 1991, which refers to any person under the age of 18 other than a person who is or has been married. The Act amended the Non-Fatal Offences Against the Person Act 1997 and abolished the common law defence of reasonable chastisement.[62] The 2015 Act does not specifically apply to sport; however, there are several sections that are binding on sports governing bodies. In applying s 14 to sporting bodies, all governing bodies are statutorily required to appoint and train a mandated person who is responsible for reporting any allegations to the Child and Family Agency, also known as Tusla.[63] Section 14(1) provides that where a mandated person knows, believes, or has reasonable grounds to suspect, on the basis of information that they have received, acquired, or becomes aware of in the course of their employment or profession, that a child has or is being harmed or is at risk of being harmed, the mandated person, once satisfied that the 'threshold of harm' has been met is legally obliged to contact Tusla as soon as practicable.[64] Section 2 of 2015 Act defines harm to a child in physical, emotional, and sexual terms:

> (a) assault, ill-treatment or neglect of the child in a manner that seriously affects or is likely to seriously affect the child's health, development or welfare, or (b) sexual abuse, of the child whether caused by a single act, omission or circumstance or a series or combination of acts, omissions or circumstances, or otherwise.

14–35 Schedule 2, ss 1–8 of the Children First Act 2015 specify those that are considered to be mandated persons, including medical practitioners,

---

[60] Department of Children, Equality, Disability, Integration and Youth, 'Children First: National Guidelines for the Protection and Welfare of Children 2017' (16 August 2019) <https://www.gov.ie/en/publication/114c50-children-first-national-guidelines-for-the-protection-and-welfare-of/> accessed 20 May 2024.

[61] Department of Children, Equality, Disability, Integration and Youth, 'Online Safety' (16 August 2019) <https://www.gov.ie/en/publication/c7ee34-action-plan-for-online-safety/> accessed 20 May 2024.

[62] Section 28 of the 2015 Act inserted s 24A into the Non-Fatal Offences Against the Person Act 1997.

[63] Tusla was formed under the Child and Family Agency Act 2013 and is a body corporate with perpetual succession. The word Tusla has its origins in the Irish language, albeit a new word that combined *tús* (meaning start) and *lá* (meaning day). According to its website, 'Tusla is a completely new word reflecting a shared desire for a new beginning, forging a new identity': <https://www.tusla.ie/about/> accessed 20 May 2024. The Irish name for the Child and the Family Agency is An Ghníomhaireacht um Leanaí agus an Teaghlach.

[64] Tusla, 'How Do I Make a Mandated Report to Tusla?' <https://www.tusla.ie/children-first/mandated-persons/how-do-i-report-a-concern-about-a-child/> accessed 20 May 2024.

nurses, dentists, speech and language therapists, social workers, teachers, and members of An Garda Síochána. Section 15(i) of Schedule 2 expressly refers to sports bodies as it refers to the

> safeguarding officer, child protection officer or other person (howsoever described) who is employed for the purpose of performing the child welfare and protection function of religious, sporting, recreational, cultural, educational and other bodies and organisations offering services to children.

Mandated persons are under a statutory obligation to report concerns to Tusla when they are satisfied that the threshold of harm has been met or exceeded.[65] They are further required to cooperate with Tusla in its investigations if so requested.[66] **14–36**

Section 10 of the Act provides that a provider of a service should, as far as practicable, ensure that children using its services are safe from harm. Section 11(a) requires a service provider within three months of its commencement to have carried out a risk assessment of any potential harm a child could suffer while availing of its services and subsection (b) provides for a written child-safeguarding statement which attests that the principles and procedures contained therein, are as far as practicable, observed to ensure that the child availing of the service is safe from harm. Subsection (c) refers to a relevant person being appointed to ensure that ss 10 and 11 are followed. A 'relevant person' is defined in s 8 of the 2015 Act as a person who is appointed by a provider of a relevant service to be the first point of contact in respect of the provider's child-safeguarding statement. Every sports club is required to appoint a relevant person. Taking the Football Association of Ireland (FAI) as an example, the relevant person is the club/league children's officer[67]: 'Their remit shall be a key component of the Safeguarding Statement and they shall be the Relevant Person for the Child Safeguarding Statement.'[68] **14–37**

According to s 11(7), service providers must review their safeguarding statement every two years.[69] Under s 11(6), governing bodies and **14–38**

---

65 Tusla, 'Child Safeguarding: A Guide for Policy, Procedure and Practice' (2nd edn, Tusla – Child and Family Agency 2019) 21 <https://www.tusla.ie/uploads/content/Tusla_-_Child_Safeguarding_-_A_Guide_for_Policy,_Procedure_and_Practice.pdf> accessed 20 May 2024.

66 ibid. The mandated person is required to submit a mandated report form to Tusla under s 14(6) of the 2015 Act. See also s 16, which details the mandated person assisting with assessments.

67 Football Association of Ireland, 'Child Welfare and Safeguarding Policy' (2nd edn, March 2019) 7 <http://www.faischools.ie/sites/default/files/leinster/page/attachments/FAI%20Child%20Welfare%20Safeguarding%20Policy.pdf> accessed 20 May 2024.

68 ibid 74.

69 This is subject to s 11(8), which provides that a service provider shall review a child-safeguarding statement as soon as practicable after there has been a material change in any matter to which the statement refers.

clubs are required to display a signed child-safeguarding statement 'in a prominent place'.[70] Athletics Ireland gives the example of a notice board or a public area in the club.[71] It recommends that affiliated clubs distribute the signed child-safeguarding statement to parents and club members via email and social media on a yearly basis.[72] If the club does not have a premises, it should provide the full statement on its website or on its social media accounts.[73]

14–39 Sport Ireland, in conjunction with its counterpart in Northern Ireland, Sport Northern Ireland, and the NGBs, published its *Safeguarding Guidance for Children and Young People in Sport*, which was launched in 2019.[74] The aim of the Guidance/Code is to ensure that NGBs and their clubs follow current best practice and that they comply with the obligations of the legislation.[75] It endeavours

> to create a culture of safety that promotes the welfare of children and young people engaged in sporting activities. This guidance document supports National Governing Bodies to meet their child safeguarding and child protection responsibilities which are cognisant of, and in line with, requirements under policy/legislation and with best practice. It does this through the provision of guidance and information in relation to the carrying out of a risk assessment, the development of a Child Safeguarding Statement and the development and implementation of policies and procedures for safeguarding and protection of children and young people.[76]

14–40 The Guidance/Code sets out the roles within safeguarding and in doing so augments the provisions of the 2015 Act. The Guidance defines the following roles:

- National Children's Officer

---

70 Section 12 deals with non-compliance with a request to furnish child-safeguarding statement and s 13 refers to Tusla's non-compliance register. Section 13(5) provides that the register of non-compliance must be available to members of the public to inspect at all reasonable times at Tusla's principal office. The register is updated monthly on the first working day of each month: Tusla, 'Register of Non-Compliance with Child Safeguarding Statement Requirements' <https://www.tusla.ie/children-first/child-safeguarding-statement-compliance-unit-csscu/child-safeguarding-statement-public-register-of-non-compliance/> accessed 20 May 2024.

71 Athletics Ireland, 'Child Safeguarding Statement and Risk Assessment' <https://www.athleticsireland.ie/juvenile/child-welfare/child-safeguarding-statement-and-risk-assessment> accessed 20 May 2024.

72 ibid.

73 ibid.

74 Federation of Irish Sport, 'Sport Ireland Launches New Safeguarding Guidance' 26 February 2019 <https://www.irishsport.ie/sport-ireland-launches-new-safeguarding-guidance/> accessed 20 May 2024.

75 Sport Ireland, 'Safeguarding Guidance for Children and Young People in Sport' (2021) 2 <https://www.sportireland.ie/sites/default/files/media/document/2021-10/safeguarding-guidance_0.pdf> accessed 20 May 2024.

76 ibid 7.

- Club Children's Officer
- Relevant Person (as explained above)
- Designated Liaison Person
- Mandated Person (as explained above)
- Role of Sport Ireland & Sport Northern Ireland.[77]

Every governing body is required to have a National Children's Officer (NCO), who should be a member of the Executive Committee or, if not, have access to the committee and relevant documentation.[78] The NCO is entrusted with ensuring that 'children's interests are kept on, and influence the decisions of, the agenda of the Governing Body'.[79] The Club Children's Officer's (CCO) role is to promote awareness of safeguarding among members of the club including children, young people, and their parents/guardians.[80] This is achieved by the production and/or distribution of information and maintaining regular information meetings. The CCO should either be a member of the club executive or have access to the executive and applicable documentation.[81] The CCO should establish contact with the relevant NCO and ensure that children know how to make their concerns known to appropriate adults and agencies.[82] **14–41**

As already noted above, s 3 of the Protections for Persons Reporting Child Act 1998 protects persons from civil liability who have communicated, in writing or otherwise, child abuse including sexual, physical, and neglect, 'reasonably and in good faith' to an appropriate person. Section 16(3) of the 2015 Act includes the same provision.[83] In the context of a sporting body, the appropriate person could be either the mandated person or the designated liaison person (DLP). All clubs are required to appoint a DLP. The DLP does not need to be a mandated person as defined under Schedule 2 of the 2015 Act. The roles of the DLP and the CCO may be carried out by the same person.[84] The responsibilities of the DLP include reporting any suspected cases of child neglect or abuse to Tusla or An Garda Síochána and they also **14–42**

[77] ibid 14.

[78] ibid 40. The National Children's Officer must attend training, have knowledge of the legislation, liaise with Club Children's Officers, assist in the development of record-keeping while maintaining confidentiality and ensuring that the Governing Body develops an appropriate sport-specific policy, which includes a policy statement, codes of conduct, disciplinary procedures, bullying policy, safety statement, recruitment and selection policy, and reporting procedures.

[79] ibid.

[80] ibid.

[81] ibid.

[82] ibid.

[83] Section 16(3): 'If a mandated person furnishes any information (including a report), document or thing to the Agency pursuant to a request made under subsection (1), the furnishing of that information, document or thing shall not give rise to any civil liability in contract, tort or otherwise and nor shall the information, document or thing be admissible as evidence against that person in any civil or criminal proceedings.'

[84] Sport Ireland (n 75) 41.

act a resource for volunteers/coaches and ensure that the reporting procedures of the club are followed.[85]

14–43 The role of the mandated person was explained above, and it is important to explain the differences between a mandated person and a DLP. The mandated person has a statutory duty to report to Tusla concerns relating to child protection. While the mandated person can make a joint report with the DLP, they are precluded from transferring their statutory responsibilities to the DLP.[86] If an individual is employed in both the roles of mandated person and DLP, the statutory obligations are fulfilled by them in their capacity as a mandated person.[87] If the individual is informed of a child protection issue and is satisfied that the threshold of harm has been reached or exceeded, the report to Tusla must be made by the person (who occupies the dual roles) as the mandated person.[88]

14–44 Sport Ireland and Sport Northern Ireland have adopted an all-Island approach to child protection and safeguarding in sport in order to have consistency in the advice given to clubs, sports leaders, parents/guardians, and children.[89] In particular, the combined approach endeavours to inform NGBs of their responsibilities and obligations as they are 'responsible for the administration of their sports'.[90] One of the underpinning principles on the joint approach is that the provision of support is 'subject to the adoption and implementation of this Safeguarding Code by National Governing Bodies of Sport'.[91] While support is not defined, it can refer to fiscal and non-fiscal supports. An NGB's funding could be affected if it does not comply with the Safeguarding Code.

Soft Law Measures and Child Protection and Safeguarding

14–45 There are a few soft law measures that augment the legislation. While these measures do not enjoy the force of law, many have been elevated to statutory provisions. As noted above, the 2015 Act placed on a statutory footing *Children First: National Guidance for the Protection and Welfare of Children*.[92] This soft law measure is still in existence and was amended by way of addendum in 2019 to include online safety being included in child-safeguarding statements.

---

[85] ibid. For a detailed explanation of the DLP, see ch 5 of the FAI Policy (n 67) 28–30.

[86] Safeguarding Guidance (n 75) 21.

[87] Tusla, 'Appointing a Designated Liaison Person(s)' <https://www.tusla.ie/children-first/organisations/appointing-a-designated-liaison-person/> accessed 20 May 2024.

[88] ibid.

[89] Safeguarding Guidance (n 75) 41.

[90] ibid.

[91] ibid.

[92] Children First (n 30).

Sport Ireland's *The Safeguarding Guidance for Children and Young People in Sport* provides a code for NGBs and their constituent clubs. While not a legal document, non-compliance could have legal implications for NGBs and clubs. *The Safeguarding Guidance for Children and Young People in Sport* is the successor to the *Code of Ethics and Good Practice for Children's Sport*, which was initially published in 2005 and was a joint code between the then Irish Sports Council (now Sport Ireland) and the Northern Ireland Sports Council (now Sport Northern Ireland).[93] Sport Ireland offers numerous training courses for those involved in sport, including the DLP and CCO.[94] **14–46**

In 2015, Sport Ireland launched the Safe Sport application (app).[95] It can be downloaded on Android phones and the iPhone operating system (IOS).[96] There is a 'travel tracker' feature, which allows parents/guardians and coaches who are driving someone else's child/children to give access to the child's parent/guardian to view a portion of the journey for a specific period of time.[97] It also allows the reporting of suspected child abuse.[98] The app can be used by children and young people, parents/guardians, coaches, and clubs.[99] **14–47**

Conclusion

In the past, there was a divide between the child-protection policy of statutory and non-statutory bodies. The accountability of statutory bodies through the legal framework for protecting children in sport, was 'much clearer'.[100] For voluntary bodies, there was a lack of cohesion and such bodies struggled to protect children from sexual abuse, as demonstrated by the IASA. The Murphy Report was a watershed moment in Irish sport as it paved the way for state intervention in the protection of children in sport. **14–48**

The requirements of vetting, the protections for those who report child abuse and the Children First Act 2015 have resulted in a multifaceted approach to protecting children from harm in general and not just in sport. The child-centric approach means that children are made aware of dangers and are taught how to report concerns to an appropriate adult. **14–49**

93 Sport Ireland, 'Archive – Code of Ethics and Good Practice for Children's Sport' (28 July 2008) <https://www.sportireland.ie/news/archive-code-of-ethics-and-good-practice-for-childrens-sport> accessed 20 May 2024.

94 Sport Ireland, 'Safeguarding Training' <https://www.sportireland.ie/ethics/ethics-test> accessed 20 May 2024.

95 Sport Ireland, 'Code of Ethics Safe Sport App' (26 May 2015) <https://www.sportireland.ie/news/code-of-ethics-safe-sport-app> accessed 20 May 2024.

96 ibid.

97 ibid. For example, children being driven home after training.

98 Code of Ethics Safe Sport App (n 95).

99 ibid.

100 Celia H Brackenridge, '"So what …? Attitudes of the Voluntary Sector towards Child Protection in Sports Clubs' (2002) 7 Managing Leisure 103, 103.

The use of technology in the form of the Stay Safe App is a welcomed development, which came about 16 years after the Murphy Report. While Ireland was slow to introduce child-protection and safeguarding measures, the introduction of legislation and codes of conduct embrace international best practice.

CHAPTER 15

ANIMALS IN SPORT

Introduction

As discussed in Chapter 1 of this book, animals have been used for the purposes of sport and entertainment for centuries. Animals amused crowds by performing tricks, while bears and dogs were trained for baiting. Cockfighting and cock throwing were also popular activities. As sensibilities changed, baiting and fighting sports became increasingly difficult to defend. Initially, it was seen as an abasement of the person to be involved in such activities. Coupled with developments in science which found that animals and humans had similar physiology, the 19th century saw the introduction of animal cruelty statutes. Under these statutes, several baiting and fighting sports were banned.[1] **15–01**

This chapter focuses on the current regulation of animal sports in Ireland and other jurisdictions. It examines fox hunting, horseracing, equestrianism, and greyhound racing. Beginning with fox hunting, the chapter looks at its legal status in Ireland, Northern Ireland, England and Wales, and Scotland. Although the word 'sport' (or blood sport) is often used in reference to fox hunting, it is contended that fox hunting does not encapsulate the characteristics of a modern sport as described by Allan Guttman, which were discussed in Chapter 3.[2] It **15–02**

---

1 The first Act was An Act to Prevent the Cruel and Improper Treatment of Cattle 1822 [3 Geo IV c71]. The Cruelty to Animals Act 1835, to give it its full title, An Act to Consolidate and Amend the Several Laws Relating to the Cruel and Improper Treatment of Animals, and the Mischiefs Arising from the Driving of Cattle, and to Make Other Provisions in Regard Thereto: Cruelty to Animals Act 1835 [5 & 6 Will IV c59], extended the 1822 Act. This Act outlawed bull, bear, badger baiting and cockfighting. The 1835 Act was repealed and replaced by the Cruelty to Animals Act 1849, An Act for the More Effectual Prevention of Cruelty to Animals 1849 [12 & 13 Vict c92]. The 1849 Act reiterated the offences of beating, ill-treating, over-driving, abusing and torturing animals with a maximum penalty of £5 and compensation of up to £10. This Act was again amended by An Act to amend the Law relating to Cruelty to Animals: Cruelty to Animals Act 1876 [39 & 40 Vict c7]. More recently, the Animal Welfare Act 2006 was enacted in England and Wales. This Act pertains to animal welfare in general. In Ireland, modern anti-cruelty legislation dates to the reign of King George V when the Protection of Animals Act 1911 (1 & 2 Geo 5, c27) was enacted. The 1911 Act was not repealed until over 100 years later under the Animal Health and Welfare Act 2013. For more detail on Ireland's animal welfare legislation see Laura Donnellan, 'Recent Developments in Animal Welfare Law in Ireland' in Federico Dalpane and Maria Baideldinova (eds), *Animal Law Worldwide* (T.M.C. Asser Press 2024) ch 10.

2 *Sports: The First Five Millennia* (University of Massachusetts Press 2004) 4–6. Guttmann identified the seven characteristics in his seminal book, *From Ritual to Record: The Nature of Modern Sports* (Columbia University Press 1978). It was

will be referred to as an activity. The chapter proceeds to document the legislative framework of horseracing and how horseracing is governed in Ireland. Against the backdrop of an Independent Review, the Irish Horseracing Regulatory Board's (IHRB) equine anti-doping programme is examined. Animal welfare issues, namely jumps racing and the use of the whip, are explored. The roles of Horse Sport Ireland (HSI) and the Fédération Équestre Internationale (FEI) are noted. The regulations relating to doping at national and international level are examined through the lens of the FEI's equine anti-doping programme and by reference to seminal arbitral awards of Court of Arbitration for Sport (CAS). The chapter concludes with a brief discussion of greyhound racing's legislative basis.

Fox Hunting in Ireland

15–03 Fox hunting remains legal in Ireland following a Dáil (Lower House of the Irish Parliament) vote on the Animal Health and Welfare Bill 2012.[3] With an overwhelming majority of 108 to 13 votes, the members rejected the insertion of a provision that would have made it illegal to hunt 'any animals or the use of canines to extract wild animals that have gone to ground'.[4] Part 3 of the Animal Health and Welfare Act 2013, s 12(11) on the prohibition of animal cruelty, expressly excludes fox hunting from its protection 'unless the animal is released in an injured, mutilated or exhausted condition'.

15–04 Section 25 of the 2013 Act provides that the Minister for Agriculture, Food and the Marine may establish a code of practice or adopt a code (in whole or in part) that has been published by another person (whether within the state or otherwise). The Hunting Association of Ireland (HAI) is the national body 'which coordinates and promotes hunting with hounds'.[5] It established a voluntary code of conduct in which it details the expected conduct of those who take part in fox hunting, including a prohibition on the hunting of injured foxes and the 'humane' disposal of the fox when captured.[6] The Irish Masters of Foxhounds Association (IMFHA) places on its members an 'obligation to maintain the highest

updated in 2012: *From Ritual to Record: The Nature of Modern Sports* (Columbia University Press 2012). See also Eric Dunning and Kenneth Sheard, *Barbarians, Gentlemen and Players* (2nd edn, Routledge 2005) 30–31 where the writers identify 15 'structural properties of folk-games and modern sports'.

3 Dáil Deb 27 March 2013, vol 798, col 417 <https://www.oireachtas.ie/en/debates/debate/dail/2013-03-27/33/> accessed 20 May 2024.

4 ibid. The amendment also proposed the banning of hare coursing.

5 Hunting Association of Ireland, 'Home' <http://www.huntingassociation.ie/> accessed 20 May 2024.

6 The Code of Conduct does not appear to be available on the HAI website. This information was found from a Dáil debate when then Minister Michael Creed referred to the Code and the HAI's respect for the welfare of the injured fox, Dáil Deb 9 May 2019, vol 982, col 135 <https://www.oireachtas.ie/en/debates/question/2019-05-09/12/#> accessed 20 May 2024.

standards of sportsmanship and good behaviour at all times'.[7] It defines fox hunting 'as a sport' which involves 'the hunting of the fox in its wild and natural state with a pack of Registered Foxhounds' and its members may not 'hunt a fox in any way that is inconsistent with this precept'.[8] There is no statement as to the welfare of an injured fox on this Code; however, a previous Minister for Agriculture cited the IMFHA's Code ensuring 'the highest standards of animal welfare'.[9]

Regarding penalties, it is not clear from the 2013 Act what sanctions an individual faces if they breach s 12(11). Under s 52(2), the legislation refers to the penalties for breaching several sections including s 12(2). A breach of s 12(2) will result in either a summary conviction or conviction on indictment.[10] Under s 12(1) a person shall not (a) do, or fail to do, anything or cause or permit anything to be done to an animal that causes unnecessary suffering to, or endanger the health or welfare of, an animal; or (b) neglect, or be reckless, regarding the health or welfare of an animal. Section 12(2) provides that a person who contravenes this section commits an offence. Article 12(1) states that nothing in this section applies in relation to anything which occurs in the ordinary course of – (a) fishing; (b) lawfully hunting an animal unless the animal is released in an injured, mutilated, or exhausted condition; and (c) lawfully coursing a hare, unless the hare is hunted or coursed in a space from which it does not have a reasonable chance of escape. In theory, if the fox is injured, mutilated, or exhausted then it constitutes an offence under s 12(2). There has been no case brought before the Irish courts under s 12(11). Thus, the practical effect of s 12(11) is questionable. **15–05**

As it stands in Ireland, fox hunting remains legal.[11] As foxes are not protected species, there is no requirement for a licence.[12] There do **15–06**

---

7 Irish Master of Foxhounds Association, 'Code of Conduct' <http://imfha.ie/about.html#CodeOfConduct> accessed 20 May 2024. The IMFHA website states: 'The objective of foxhunting as it is practiced in Ireland places the emphasis on the art of venery and not the death of a fox. On occasion when hounds catch their fox, death is instantaneous. In foxhunting either the fox is killed, or he gets clean away': 'Hunting & Hounds' <http://imfha.ie/hunting_hounds.html> accessed 20 May 2024.

8 ibid.

9 7 October 2016, Written Answers Nos 104–11, Rural Development Programme Projects <https://www.oireachtas.ie/en/debates/question/2015-10-07/section/137/> accessed 20 May 2024.

10 Section 52 (2) provides that a person who commits an offence under ss 10(6), 11(2), 12(2), 13(5), 14(4), 15(10), 16(3), 17(2), 19(6), 21(2), 23(7), 42(9), 43(7), 46 , 58(8) or 72(4)–(a) is liable to a class A fine or imprisonment for a term not exceeding six months, or to both, or (b) is liable, on conviction on indictment, to a fine not exceeding €250,000 or imprisonment for a term not exceeding five years, or to both.

11 Hunting with hounds is one of the disciplines that falls under the aegis of Horse Sport Ireland (HSI). Its governing body is the HAI. Equestrian sports in general will be discussed in more detail further on in this chapter.

12 The Wildlife Act 1976 (as amended) provides for the protection of wildlife and provides for the licencing of certain activities, including deer hunting.

not seem to be any plans by the executive to revisit the legality of fox hunting. The codes of conduct are soft law measures and do not provide a legislative framework for the protection of foxes. There are no tangible consequences for hunters that act in contravention of the codes of conduct. Section 12(11) presents evidentiary issues, as it would be difficult to prove that a fox was injured or exhausted prior to the killing by the hounds or that the hunters were aware that the fox was in a weakened state. An absolute ban on hunting with hounds in Ireland is the only way to remove any ambiguities. It is very unlikely that will happen any time soon given the prevailing economic, social, and political dimensions that have justified its continued practice.

15–07 At a European Union (EU) level, Article 13 of Title II of the Treaty on the Functioning of the European Union (TFEU) provides the following:

> In formulating and implementing the Union's agriculture, fisheries, transport, internal market, research and technological development and space policies, the Union and the Member States shall, since animals are sentient beings, pay full regard to the welfare requirements of animals, while respecting the legislative or administrative provisions and customs of the Member States relating in particular to religious rites, cultural traditions and regional heritage.[13]

15–08 While a Treaty basis exists for animal welfare in the EU since the TFEU came into force on 1 December 2009, the reference to 'cultural traditions' means that activities such as fox hunting are not regulated at EU level, and it is open to Member States to decide their own cultural traditions.

Fox Hunting in Northern Ireland

15–09 Unlike Scotland and England and Wales, there is no ban on fox hunting in Northern Ireland.[14] Northern Ireland would have banned hunting had the Foster Bill become law. In 1997, the Labour Party was elected to office after an 18-year absence. During the election campaign, Labour promised Members of Parliament (MP) a free vote on hunting. Michael Foster, a newly elected MP for Worchester, a known anti-hunting supporter, was the first MP to present a private member's Bill.[15] Foster was advised not to proceed with such a controversial Bill; however, he ignored the advice and proceeded to present his private member's Bill entitled the Wild Mammals (Hunting with Dogs) Bill. The Bill won the support of 173 MPs and progressed to a second reading. On

---

[13] Consolidated versions of the Treaty on European Union and the Treaty on the Functioning of the European Union 2012/C 326/01.

[14] The Protection of Wild Mammals (Scotland) Act 2002, Acts of the Scottish Parliament 2002 asp; Hunting Act 2004, UK Public General Acts 2004 c37.

[15] Michael Foster introduced the Wild Mammals (Hunting with Dogs) Bill: HC Deb 28 November 1997, vol 301, cols 1199–272 <https://api.parliament.uk/historic-hansard/commons/1997/nov/28/wild-mammals-hunting-with-dogs-bill> accessed 20 May 2024.

the second reading the Bill was carried by 411 votes to 151. Following mass demonstrations by pro-hunting groups, including the newly created Countryside Alliance, the government decided to withdraw support. Foster's Bill collapsed in the House of Commons as it ran out of parliamentary time.[16] Section 7(4) of the Bill provided: 'This Act extends to Northern Ireland.'[17] On 2 December 1999, the United Kingdom (UK) Parliament devolved powers to the Northern Ireland Assembly. The successor to the Foster Bill, the Hunting Act 2004, extended only to England and Wales. There have been calls for the Northern Ireland Assembly to ban hunting with dogs following a poll carried out in late 2019 which found that 76% of the respondents favoured it being made illegal.[18] This call has not translated into action at Assembly level, as members of the Democratic Unionist Party (DUP) have defended fox hunting as an entrenched cultural tradition that is more about 'the pageantry and social aspect'.[19]

Like equivalent legislation in Ireland, Northern Ireland's Welfare of Animals Act (Northern Ireland) 2011, s 53, mirrors s 12(11) of the Animal Health and Welfare Act 2013 as it provides that nothing in the Act applies to anything which occurs in the normal course of hunting or coursing an animal or fishing unless the (a) the animal is released in an injured, mutilated, or exhausted condition; or (b) the animal is hunted or coursed in an enclosed space from which it has no reasonable chance of escape.[20] As with the situation in Ireland, foxes are not protected species under the Wildlife and Natural Environment Act (Northern Ireland) 2011.[21] **15–10**

Fox Hunting in England and Wales

Hunting with hounds had been a bastion of rural life for centuries in Britain. Exemplifying the divide in British politics, the Conservative party had always been a champion of hunting and an exponent of the country life. Fearing alienation of its core voters and with many members of the party being part of the hunting fraternity, while the **15–11**

16 'How Hunting Went to the Dogs' (*BBC*, 3 July 1999) <http://news.bbc.co.uk/2/hi/uk_news/politics/390091.stm> accessed 20 May 2024.

17 <https://publications.parliament.uk/pa/cm199798/cmbills/007/97007—a.htm#7> accessed 20 May 2024.

18 'Calls for future Northern Ireland Assembly to Ban Hunting with Dogs' *The Belfast Telegraph* (Belfast, 31 December 1999) <https://www.belfasttelegraph.co.uk/news/northern-ireland/calls-for-future-northern-ireland-assembly-to-ban-hunting-with-dogs-38824629.html> accessed 20 May 2024.

19 Mark Bain, 'DUP MP Opposes Call to Ban Hunting with Dogs' *The Belfast Telegraph* (Belfast, 26 December 2019) <https://www.belfasttelegraph.co.uk/news/northern-ireland/dup-mp-opposes-call-to-ban-hunting-with-dogs-38812876.html> accessed 20 May 2024.

20 Acts of the Northern Ireland Assembly 2011, c16 <https://www.legislation.gov.uk/nia/2011/16/section/53> accessed 20 May 2024.

21 Acts of the Northern Ireland Assembly 2011, c15 <https://www.legislation.gov.uk/nia/2011/15> accessed 20 May 2024.

Conservatives remained in office the future of fox hunting was secure. The Labour party, on the other hand, had since the 1970s been the most anti-hunting political party. The Labour party in 1978 formally adopted its position on fox hunting and called for all forms of hunting and coursing to be banned. While occupying a position on the fringe of British politics, the Labour party could do little to give its anti-hunting stance any gravitas. The return of the Labour party to power in 1997 was a pivotal development that signalled the beginning of the end for fox hunting with hounds.

Background to Hunting Act 2004

15–12 During the election campaign titled 'New Labour: Because Britain Deserves Better', Labour promised MPs a free vote on hunting. In its manifesto it promised: 'We will ensure greater protection for wildlife. We have advocated new measures to promote animal welfare, including a free vote in Parliament on whether hunting with hounds should be banned'.[22] As noted above, Foster presented a private member's Bill, the Wild Mammals (Hunting with dogs) Bill.[23] However, the Bill collapsed in the Commons as it ran out of parliamentary time.

15–13 In 1999 the Secretary of State for the Home Department, Jack Straw MP, appointed a committee headed by Lord Burns to inquire into hunting with dogs. The *Committee of Inquiry into Hunting with Dogs in England and Wales* was more commonly referred to as the Burns' Inquiry. The Burns' Inquiry was entrusted with the task of investigating:

> the practical aspects of different types of hunting with dogs and its impact on the rural economy, agriculture and pest control, the social and cultural life of the countryside, the management and conservation of wildlife, and animal welfare in particular areas of England and Wales; the consequences for these issues of any ban on hunting with dogs; and how any ban might be implemented.[24]

15–14 The Burns' Inquiry, while not considering animal suffering or the possibility of a complete ban on hunting, should be viewed as an important juncture as it demonstrated the state was investigating whether the alternatives to fox hunting, namely shooting and trapping, were more humane methods of control. Fox hunting, at this time, was not regulated by the state. It was considered a private activity carried out in the countryside that united people from different strata of society.

15–15 As a tentative conclusion, the Burns' Inquiry suggested that lamping

---

22 Labour Party, *New Labour: Because Britain Deserves Better* (1997).

23 HC Deb (n 15).

24 *The Final Report of the Committee of Inquiry into Hunting with Dogs in England and Wales* (Stationery Office 9 June 2000) <https://assets.publishing.service.gov.uk/government/uploads/system/uploads/attachment_data/file/265552/4763.pdf.> accessed 20 May 2024.

with rifles, if carried out properly and appropriate in the circumstances, could have less welfare implications than hunting and digging out. However, in some areas where lamping was not feasible, other legal methods could be used. Shooting as a method did not find favour with the Burns' Inquiry; similarly, the use of snaring was a particular cause for concern.[25] The Burns' Inquiry considered that it was:

> likely that some mixture of all of these methods would be used. In the event of a ban on hunting, it is possible that the welfare of foxes in upland areas could be affected adversely, unless dogs could be used, at least to flush foxes from cover.[26]

Shortly after the Burns' Inquiry, the government decided to give MPs three options regarding hunting: self-supervision, government regulation, and an outright ban.[27] The House of Commons favoured banning hunting; however, the House of Lords favoured self-supervision. By March 2001, the Bill, after being supported by the House of Commons, was defeated by the House of Lords. In June 2001 Labour won the general election and again promised that the issue of hunting would be resolved. Following the public hearings in Portcullis House, Minister for Rural Affairs Alun Michael introduced the Hunting Bill 2002 (also referred to as the Michael Bill).[28] The Bill, while providing for a ban on deer hunting and hare coursing, proposed a system of registration and tribunals for individuals who wished to hunt foxes. Under the Bill, fox hunting could be permitted where it was shown to be necessary for pest control in a particular area and that hunting with dogs caused the least suffering in comparison to other methods of pest control (such as shooting). If it could not be shown that hunting was necessary for pest control, then registration would be refused. Registration would be granted if the applicant demonstrated that pest control was necessary, thus it would be based on subjective evidence submitted by the relevant individual and not based on objective scientific or ecological studies. The Bill advocated a registration system whereby two tests had to be satisfied – the utility test and the least-suffering test under ss 8(1)[29] **15–16**

---

[25] ibid para 6.60.

[26] ibid para 6.61.

[27] Introduced by Jack Straw, Hunting with Dogs, HC Deb 7 July 2000, vol 353 cols 524–97 <https://api.parliament.uk/historic-hansard/commons/2000/jul/07/hunting-with-dogs> accessed 20 May 2024.

[28] These hearings took place on 9, 10 and 11 September 2002. It was chaired by Michael and, using the Burns' Inquiry as its reference point, examined the key principles of preventing cruelty and recognising utility in the management and control of wild mammals: <https://publications.parliament.uk/pa/cm200203/cmbills/010/03010.1-7.html> accessed 20 May 2024.

[29] Section 8(1) provided that 'the applicant for registration must show that the proposed hunting with dogs is likely to make a significant contribution to the prevention or reduction of serious damage which the wild mammals to be hunted would otherwise cause to livestock; game birds; food for livestock; crops; growing timber; fisheries; other property; or the biological diversity of an area': <http://www.publications.parliament.uk/pa/cm200203/cmbills/010/en/03010x—.htm> accessed 20 May 2024.

and (2).[30] After several proposed amendments in the House of Lords, whereby the registration system was effectively reinstated, the Bill was rendered largely ineffective and ran out of parliamentary time.

15–17 The government, facing increased backbencher pressure, introduced a similar Bill, the Hunting Bill 2004, to the House of Commons on 9 September 2004. The Bill proposed to make hunting a wild mammal with hounds a criminal offence, subject to the exemptions contained in Schedule 1, including the flushing (with no more than two dogs) of a wild mammal out of cover, the stalking (with no more than two dogs) of a wild mammal where that stalking or flushing was for the purpose of preventing or reducing serious damage which the wild mammal might otherwise cause to livestock, to game birds or wild birds, food for livestock, to crops (including vegetables and fruit), to growing timber, to fisheries or other property or to the biological diversity of an area as defined by the United Nations Environmental Programme Convention on Biological Diversity of 1992.[31] Hunting would also be exempt if it were for the purposes of obtaining meat for human or animal consumption or for participation in a field trial.[32] Section 2 of Schedule 1 provided for the use of dogs below ground to protect birds for shooting, subject to a number of conditions.

15–18 Minister Michael spoke of the divisive nature of hunting and need for it to be addressed.[33] The Bill was attacked by its opponents on the grounds of democracy, discrimination, oppression of a minority, as a breach of civil liberties, in conflict with the Human Rights Act 1998, and the fact that no compensation was being offered to those affected by the ban.[34]

---

30 ibid. Section 8(2) provided: 'the applicant for registration must show that a contribution to the prevention or reduction of serious damage equivalent to that mentioned for the utility test in subsection (1) could not reasonably be expected to be made (whether by the applicant or by another person) in a manner likely to cause significantly less pain, suffering or distress to the wild mammal being hunted.'

31 Section 1(7)(a) of sch 1 provided that reasonable steps had to be taken for the purposes of ensuring that as soon as possible after being found or flushed out the wild mammal is shot dead by a competent person. To obtain this objective, dogs are to be kept under sufficiently close control: s 1(7)(b). The 2004 Bill is available at <https://publications.parliament.uk/pa/ld200304/ldbills/129/04129.20-26.html> accessed 20 May 2024.

32 Field trial was defined in s 1(3) of sch 1. It means a competition (other than a hare coursing event) in which dogs flush animals out of cover, or retrieve animals that have been shot, or both, and are assessed as to the likely usefulness in connection with shooting.

33 Hunting Bill (Procedure), HC Deb 15 September 2004, vol 424, cols 1326–422 [1330] <https://api.parliament.uk/historic-hansard/commons/2004/sep/15/hunting-bill> accessed 20 May 2024.

34 The Human Rights Act 1998, c42, incorporated the European Convention of Human Rights (ECHR) into domestic law. The following articles/sections were argued in the case of *Whaley v Lord Advocate*, 2004 SC 78: art 8 (Right to respect for private and family life); art 9 (Freedom of thought, conscience, and religion); art 10 (Freedom of expression); art 11 (Freedom of assembly and association); art 14 (Prohibition of discrimination); and art 17 (Prohibition of abuse of rights).

Following protracted debates and voting in the House of Commons and House of Lords, the discord between the two houses resulted in political stalemate. Minister Michael sent the Bill back to the House of Commons by invoking the Parliament Acts 1911 and 1949 and the Bill was sent back to the House Lords.[35] The Bill became law without the approval of the House of Lords later that night, on 18 November 2004.[36]

The Hunting Act and the Courts

The Hunting Act 2004 entered into force on 18 February 2005. In the same month, the Countryside Alliance challenged the validity of the Parliament Act 1949 contending that it was not a lawful statute. In the case of *R (on the Application of Jackson) v Attorney General*, the validity of the 2004 Act was questioned.[37] As the Act had been enacted without the approval of the House of Lords as required under the Parliament Acts of 1911 and 1949, the applicant sought a declaration that the 2004 Act was not an Act of Parliament. It was also argued that the 1949 Act amounted to unlawful delegated legislation. The Court dismissed the application but granted leave to appeal. The case was subsequently appealed with the Court of Appeal upholding the validity of the 2004 Act.[38] In *R (Countryside Alliance) v Attorney General* a unanimous House of Lords upheld the legality of the Hunting Act 2004.[39] The House of Lords was careful to note that the case came before them under their judicial capacity and not legislative capacity and thus personal views had to be set aside.[40] Lord Bingham alluded to the fact that the Hunting Act 2004 was to 'be seen as the latest link in a long chain of statutes devoted to what is seen as social reform'.[41] **15–19**

The House of Lords accepted that, while not expressly stated in the Act, the impetus behind the legislation was to alleviate animal suffering, which was based on the benevolent concerns of the House **15–20**

This was a Scottish judicial review case concerning the Scottish legislation, the Protection of Wild Mammals (Scotland) Act 2002.

35 Prior to 1911, the House of Lords could veto all legislation passed by the Commons. The 1911 Act removed the power of the House of Lords to veto a Bill, except a Bill that intends to expand the lifespan of the Parliament. The House of Lords could delay a Bill up to two years. The 1911 Act also reduced the lifespan of the Parliament from seven years to five years. The 1949 Act reduced the Lords' delaying time to one year. The Parliament Acts are rarely invoked. For more information, see UK Parliament, 'The Parliament Acts' <https://www.parliament.uk/about/how/laws/parliamentacts/> accessed 20 May 2024.

36 Hunting Bill, HL Deb 18 November 2004, vol 666, cols 1644–46 <https://api.parliament.uk/historic-hansard/lords/2004/nov/18/hunting-bill> accessed 20 May 2024.

37 [2005] EWCA Civ 126.

38 [2006] 1 AC 262.

39 [2008] 1 AC 719.

40 Lord Bingham ibid [1].

41 ibid [37]. For a detailed discussion on the case, see Laura Donnellan, '*R v Countryside Alliance*' in Jack Anderson (ed), *Contribution to Landmark Cases and Decisions in Sports Law* (TMC Asser Press 2013) 337–52.

of Commons.[42] In particular, the intention of the legislature was to decrease animal suffering caused by hunting for the purposes of 'sport' and recreation.[43] Lord Bingham recognised that the Act was very selective in that it excluded the hunting of rabbits and rats; however, he disagreed with the appellants' contention that the inconsistency in the Act precluded the House of Lords upholding its legality.[44] While the extent of the suffering had not been scientifically proven, the Lords acknowledged that there was a degree of suffering, albeit unknowable, and that entitled the House of Commons to prohibit hunting on the grounds that it caused suffering to animals and that it was morally repugnant to hunt for the purpose of 'sport'.[45] The fact that the legislation was introduced to prohibit unnecessary suffering of animals for the purpose of recreation and 'sport' was an important consideration for the House of Lords and took precedence over the claimants' arguments in relation to economic and fundamental freedoms under European Community (EC, now Union) law.[46]

15–21 The Countryside Alliance challenged the Act under the European Convention on Human Rights (ECHR) in the case of *Friend and Countryside Alliance v United Kingdom*.[47] The challenge centred on Article 1 of Protocol 1, which concerns the right to peaceful enjoyment of property, and Article 8, which concerns the right of an individual to respect for their family life, their home and correspondence. The legislation was also challenged under the freedom of peaceful assembly, Article 11 of the ECHR. The European Court of Human Rights (ECtHR) noted the importance of the principle of proportionality in the balancing of rights under the ECHR, namely the general interest of society versus the protection of an individual's rights. In dismissing the action, the ECtHR held that the grounds were inadmissible and manifestly unfounded.

15–22 In *R (Countryside Alliance and Others) v Attorney-General and Another* and *R (Derwin and Others) v Same*, the House of Lords handed down a judgment involving two groups.[48] The first group challenged the Hunting Act 2004 under the ECHR with reference to Articles 8, 11 and 14 (prohibition of

---

42 *R (Countryside Alliance)* (n 39) [40].

43 ibid.

44 ibid. See also Lord Hope ibid [64]. Lord Hope noted that the real reason behind the ban lay in the 'nature of the activity and not in personal characteristics of many people of all kinds and social backgrounds who participate in hunting'.

45 Lord Hope ibid [78].

46 For a detailed discussion on the case and its deliberation before the ECtHR, see Donnellan (n 41).

47 [2009] ECHR 2068 (17 December 2009) <https://www.google.com/url?sa=t&source=web&rct=j&opi=89978449&url=https://hudoc.echr.coe.int/app/conversion/pdf/%3Flibrary%3DECHR%26id%3D001-96372%26filename%3D001-96372.pdf%26TID%3Dthkbhnilzk&ved=2ahUKEwj56LqXmZ2GAxVsV0EAHaBKD70QFnoECBoQAQ&usg=AOvVaw2ZqJ0NKyVTZ3qmH3WcgPOZ> accessed 20 May 2024.

48 [2007] UKHL 52.

discrimination) and Article 1 of the First Protocol (the Human Rights or HR claimants). The second group based their challenge on then Article 28 EC Treaty on the free movement of goods (now Article 34 TFEU) and Article 49 EC Treaty (now Article 56 TFEU) on the freedom of services (EC claimants).[49] The House of Lords dismissed the appeal and upheld the finding of the Court of Appeal that the 2004 Act was compatible with the Human Rights Act 1998 and in compliance with EC law.[50]

Recent Developments

In July 2015 the government withdrew its proposal to relax the ban on **15–23**
fox hunting with hounds in England and Wales after it emerged that the Scottish National Party (SNP) would not support the changes. The proposed amendment would have brought the legislation in line with the then Scottish Act, the Protection of Wild Mammals (Scotland) Act 2002, which at the time allowed for the flushing out of foxes with a pack of hounds and not just two hounds as provided for under the 2004 Act applicable in England and Wales.[51] It also emerged that a number of Labour and Conservative MPs were not in favour of the proposed amendments to the 2004 Act.[52] The limitations of the Act and issues with enforceability have led to continued media reports of alleged breaches of the Hunting Act 2004.[53] In January 2023, Scotland introduced a Bill to replace the Protection of Wild Mammals Act 2002.[54] Under the Hunting

---

[49] Article 34 TFEU refers to quantitative restrictions and measures equivalent to quantitative restrictions. Such restrictions are non-fiscal in nature. A quantitative restriction can be an import ban or a restriction on imports by weight or volume. Measures equivalent to quantitative restrictions include requirements relating to the shape of a product and labelling, for example.

[50] [2006] EWCA Civ 817.

[51] Rowena Mason, 'Government Shelves Foxhunting Vote after SNP Opposition' *The Guardian* (London, 14 July 2015) <https://www.theguardian.com/uk-news/2015/jul/14/foxhunting-vote-shelved-by-tories-in-face-of-snp-opposition> accessed 20 May 2024. The SNP had traditionally not voted on matters of concern only to England and Wales, referred to as English Votes for English Laws (Evel). See also Michael Settle, 'Evel: Ministers Admit Scots MPs Could Still Veto England-Only Measures like Fox-Hunting' *The Herald Scotland* (Glasgow, 22 October 2015) <https://www.heraldscotland.com/news/13887197.evel-ministers-admit-scots-mps-still-veto-england-only-measures-like-fox-hunting/> accessed 20 May 2024.

[52] Rob Merrick, 'Theresa May Abandons Vote on Overturning Fox Hunting Ban in Face of Overwhelming Opposition' *Independent* (London, 7 January 2018) <https://www.independent.co.uk/news/uk/politics/theresa-may-fox-hunting-vote-abandon-overturn-ban-latest-animals-andrew-marr-8-57-a8146161.html> accessed 20 May 2024.

[53] Matthew Weaver, 'Police in England Arrest Six Men over Suspected Illegal Fox Hunting' *The Guardian* (London, 22 January 2023) <https://www.theguardian.com/uk-news/2023/jan/22/suspected-fox-hunting> accessed 20 May 2024.

[54] Craig Paton, 'Bill to Close Fox Hunting Loopholes Introduced' *Independent* (London, 25 February 2023) <https://www.independent.co.uk/news/uk/scottish-government-bill-scotland-government-polls-b2023111.html> accessed 20 May 2024.

with Dogs (Scotland) Act 2023, the number of hounds permitted to flush is limited to two. The Act entered into force on 7 March 2023.[55]

15–24 The Hunting with Dogs (Scotland) Act 2023 bans trail hunting under Part 2, s 14. Section 14(2) defines 'trail hunting' as 'the activity in which a dog is directed to find and follow an animal-based scent which has been laid for that purpose'.[56] A person who commits an offence under this section will be liable on summary conviction to imprisonment for a term not exceeding 12 months or a fine not exceeding £40,000, or both. Section 16 provides an exception or defence in the case of training dogs to follow an animal-based scent. Section 15 empowers the Scottish Ministers to modify the meaning of trail hunting.

Commentary on the Hunting Act 2004

15–25 In England and Wales, flushing with two dogs is permitted if it is undertaken to prevent or reduce damage the wild mammal may cause to livestock (Schedule 1, para 1, s (2)(a)(i)), crops (Schedule 1, para 1, s (2)(a)(iv)) and other property (Schedule 1, para 1, s (2)(a)(vii)). It is also possible that several separate groups with two dogs could set out at the same time and in the same area. In this situation the groups can circumvent the rules on flushing. The power of the police is also limited. Under Part 2, s 8 of the 2004 Act, the police can only enter private lands if there is a reasonable suspicion of illegality.

15–26 Those who support fox hunting refer to the need to control the numbers of foxes, which are considered to be vermin or pests, and fox hunting is viewed as part of the natural order. Those who are against fox hunting reject the view that foxes are a major problem in the country and argue that hunting is not the best method to deal with the problem. They argue that there are more humane ways of culling foxes. From an animal rights perspective, the argument is that animals have the right not to be hunted. The Act permits trail-hunting, exercising of hounds, rabbit, and rat hunting. However, there are loopholes. Foxes can still be killed so long as it is accidental and unintentional. For example, a hunt could set out to kill rabbits, which is legal (though it is unlawful to kill hares, Part 1, s 5), and the dogs could pick up the scent of a fox, run off and the fox is accidentally and unintentionally killed. In this situation, it is lawful, and the hunt will not be exposed to any liability.

15–27 A lawful alternative is drag hunting. This involves the planting of an artificial scent. As for many the thrill of hunting is in the chase, the

[55] 2023 asp 1. The full text of the Act is available at <https://www.legislation.gov.uk/asp/2023/1/contents/enacted> accessed 20 May 2024.

[56] Section 14(2) defines animal-based scent as (a) scent, which is derived from a wild mammal, or (b) scent which mimics, replicates, or resembles the scent of a wild mammal (or which is designed to do so), whether or not that scent is derived wholly or in part from artificial ingredients.

continued practice of drag hunting should satisfy the chase element.[57] The League Against Cruel Sports defines drag hunting as the laying of

> an artificial non-animal scent (mostly aniseed) pulled by a drag, laid down over a predetermined route. Because the route is predetermined the hounds can be kept safely away from livestock, vulnerable crops, roads and railway lines. The route can also be organised so that the risk to sensitive and fragile habitats can be minimised and the drag hunts kept away from areas where they are unwelcome and/or can pose a threat to other domestic and farmed animals. The drag is not laid in areas known to have foxes in them, and the location of the trail is known to the huntsman so he can stop the hounds if they accidentally follow a live quarry scent. All these precautions explain why it is very rare for accidental fox kills to happen during drag hunting.[58]

Labour returned to power following a general election on 5 July 2024. In its manifesto, it pledged to improve animal welfare.[59] One of its commitments is to end trail hunting, which in the words of the League Against Cruel Sports, is a '"smokescreen" for old fashioned illegal fox hunting'. The League Against Cruel Sports defines trail hunting as **15–28**

> hunts laying an animal-based scent trail (using fox urine) which has been laid in areas where foxes or hares are likely to be. Crucially, those laying the trail are not meant to tell those controlling the hounds where the scent has been laid, so if the hounds end up following a live animal scent the hunt can claim that they did not know.[60]

Trail hunting not only differs from drag hunting as it uses an animal-based scent, however, but the main issue for opponents is also that trail hunting is illusionary, 'it is simply a false deceit to cover for illegal hunting'.[61] As intention is required under the 2004 Act, in most cases where a wild mammal is chased or killed in a trail hunt, it is recorded as an accident.[62] The Countryside Alliance view the proposed ban as essentially destroying the rural community as many reside in isolated areas and see the hunt as 'a social hub'.[63] **15–29**

---

57 Emma Griffin, *Blood Sport Hunting in Britain Since 1066* (University Press 2007) 229–30.

58 League Against Cruel Sports, 'Drag hunting, 'Clean boot' hunting and Trail hunting' 1 <https://www.league.org.uk/media/filer_public/cf/12/cf123096-be6a-4eac-b943-22dc01c9bb56/drag_hunting_clean_boot_hunting_and_trail_hunting.pdf > accessed 30 July 2024.

59 Labour Party Manifesto, 'Change' (London, 2024) 60 <https://labour.org.uk/wp-content/uploads/2024/06/Change-Labour-Party-Manifesto-2024-large-print.pdf> accessed 30 July 2024.

60 League Against Cruel Sports, 'Standing Against Trail Hunting' <https://www.league.org.uk/what-we-do/hunting/trail-hunting/> accessed 30 July 2024.

61 League Against Cruel Sports (n 58) 2.

62 ibid.

63 Countryside Alliance, 'Labour criticised after pledging to end trail hunting' <https://www.countryside-alliance.org/resources/news/labour-criticised-after-pledging-to-end-trail-hunting> accessed 30 July 2024.

Horse Sports: Horseracing and Equestrianism

15–30 Horse sports can be divided into two main categories, namely horseracing and equestrianism. In the context of horseracing, there are two bodies in Ireland: Horse Racing Ireland (HRI), the national authority for thoroughbred racing; and the Irish Horseracing Regulatory Board (IHRB), the regulatory body for flat and steeplechase racing. HSI is the national governing body for equestrian sport in Ireland, which consists of 16 disciplines, including eventing, dressage and show jumping.[64]

Legislative Framework

15–31 There are three main pieces of legislation that govern the horseracing industry in Ireland: the Irish Horseracing Industry Act 1994, the Horse and Greyhound Racing Act 2001, and the Horse Racing Ireland Act 2016. The Horse and Greyhound Racing Fund was established under Part 3, s 12(1) of the 2001 Act. The Fund is managed and controlled by the Minister for Agriculture, Food and the Marine. The amount allocated to the Fund is

> determined by the Revenue Commissioners, equivalent to the revenue from excise duty on off-course betting paid into the Exchequer in the preceding year or the year 2000 increased by reference to the Consumer Price Index, whichever is the greater.[65]

15–32 Section 12(5) of the 2001 Act provides that the 'total aggregate amount paid into the Fund … shall not exceed £200,000,000 or such other increased amounts as may stand specified in regulations made by the Minister with the consent of the Minister for Finance'. Section 12(6)(a) apportions 80% of the Fund to be allocated to HRI and 20% to Greyhound Racing Ireland (Rásaíocht Con Éireann). Under the Horse and Greyhound Racing Fund Regulations 2023, €1,735,991,713 was paid into the Fund as required by s 12(5).[66]

15–33 Equestrian sport is not subject to specific legislation; however, HSI is one of the recognised governing bodies of Sport Ireland and thus subject to its rules and regulations. As several of the disciplines are Olympic sports, the HSI is affiliated to the national Olympic committee, the Olympic Federation of Ireland (OFI), which is an affiliate of the European Olympic Committee (EOC) described as the 'umbrella body

64 For a list and more information on the disciplines, see Horse Sport Ireland, 'Disciplines' <https://www.horsesportireland.ie/disciplines/> accessed 20 May 2024.

65 Section 12(4) of the 2001 Act. According to the Horse and Greyhound Fund Dáil Deb 3 March 2021, between 2001 and 2020, €1,365,991,713 was paid from the Fund <https://www.oireachtas.ie/en/debates/question/2021-03-03/209/> accessed 20 May 2024.

66 SI no 642 of 2023.

for Europe's 50 National Olympic Committees'[67] and, on a global level, the International Olympic Committee (IOC).

Irish Horseracing Regulatory Board

The IHRB is the regulatory body of horseracing in Ireland.[68] It is a company limited by guarantee (CLG) and was established by the Turf Club and Irish National Hunt Steeplechase Committee (INHSC). It has been in operation since 1 January 2018. The IHRB is the Irish equivalent of the British Horseracing Authority (BHA). Section 10 of the Horse Racing Ireland Act 2016 amended s 36 of the Irish Horseracing Industry Act 1994 to empower the Turf Club and the INHSC to set up limited companies to carry out regulatory functions. The Turf Club was the regulatory body for flat and national hunt racing for 227 years. It ceased operations on 31 December 2017. One issue that faced the Turf Club was its inability to indemnify its members from personal liability.[69] As discussed in Chapter 11 on Judicial Review, prior to 1994, the Turf Club was considered a private and voluntary association. Barr J in *Murphy v The Turf Club* held that the sport's regulatory body, the Turf club, was not a public body.[70] Thus, judicial review was not possible due to the consensual contractual relationship of the respondent and the applicant and 'in purporting to revoke the applicant's licence, the respondent was not executing a public law function'.[71] However, in *O'Connell & Lambe v The Turf Club*, the Turf Club was found to be a public body, as it had been placed on a statutory footing by way of the Irish Horseracing Industry Act 1994.[72] The IHRB's structure as a CLG means that it does not have a share capital and members are only liable for the amount that they have undertaken to contribute to the assets of the company in the event of the company being wound up. Members do not invest in the company through the purchase of shares; however, the company enjoys a separate legal personality from the members and, at the same time, the **15–34**

67 European Olympic Committee, 'Who We Are' <https://www.eurolympic.org/who-we-are/> accessed 30 July 2024.

68 There are three stakeholder bodies in the horseracing industry: HRI, IHRB and the Irish Racehorse Trainers Association (IRTA): see Joint Committee on Agriculture, Food and the Marine, 'Horse Racing in Ireland' (9 November 2021) 6 <https://data.oireachtas.ie/ie/oireachtas/committee/dail/33/joint_committee_on_agriculture_food_and_the_marine/reports/2021/2021-11-09_report-of-the-joint-committee-on-horse-racing-in-ireland_en.pdf> accessed 20 May 2024. For more information on the IRTA, see Irish Racehorse Trainers Association, 'About IRTA' <https://irta.ie/about/> accessed 20 May 2024.

69 Richard Forristal, 'All Change and No Change as Turf Club Transition to Limited Company Looms' *Racing Post* (London, 15 December 2017) <https://web.archive.org/web/20181224104719/https://www.racingpost.com/news/all-change-and-no-change-as-turf-club-transition-to-limited-company-looms/312421> accessed 20 May 2024.

70 [1989] IR 171.

71 ibid 173–74.

72 The Supreme Court in *O'Connell & Lambe v Turf Club* [2015] IESC 57 upheld the decision of McGovern J. Of significance is O'Donnell J's discussion of the history of sport and the importance of the rules of sport, see [1]-[10].

members have limited their liability to what they have guaranteed in the Memorandum of Association.[73] As will be discussed further on in this chapter, HRI, the national authority for horseracing, is a statutory body which was created under the Horse and Greyhound Racing Act 2001.

15–35 Within the IHRB there are disciplinary, non-disciplinary and non-regulatory committees.[74] Decisions of the Stewards at a race meeting, the Referrals Committee, and the Licensing Committee are open to appeal and the procedure is based on the principles of fairness and impartiality.[75] The Referrals Committee members are appointed by the IHRB from the Disciplinary Panel 'from time to time'.[76] The IHRB decides whether the matter referred will be heard by a panel of one, three, or five.[77] Rule 19A(6) of the Rules of Racing and Irish National Hunt Steeplechase Rules 2023 provides that the Referrals Committee:

> shall have the powers necessary for, and incidental to, the performance of its function of hearing and determining all issues referred to it pursuant to these Rules, including, without limitation, the powers of the Stewards, the disciplinary powers of the Directors of IHRB.[78]

15–36 Rule 19A(6)(i)–(xi) outlines additional powers which include imposing fines and suspending licences. Rule 19B provides for the powers and appointment of the Licencing Committee.[79] Subject to an appeal to the Appeals Body, the Licencing Committee can refuse to issue, suspend, or withdraw all licences of jockeys, trainers, and racecourses.[80] It can impose conditions to any licence as it deems fit.[81] The Appeals Body has jurisdiction to hear and determine appeals against decisions of the Stewards, the Referrals Committee and the Licensing Committee.[82] Decisions of the Appeals Body are published on the IHRB website.[83] IHRB has six unremunerated directors, with three nominated by the Turf Club and three by the INHSC.[84] The day-to-day running of the IHRB

73 The Memorandum of Association sets out the aims and objectives of the company.

74 Irish Horseracing Regulatory Board, 'Non-Raceday Role' <https://www.ihrb.ie/our-role> accessed 20 May 2024.

75 ibid.

76 Rule 19A(1) of the Rules of Racing and Irish National Hunt Steeplechase Rules 2023 <https://www.ihrb.ie/pdf.php?f=RuleBook.pdf> accessed 20 May 2024.

77 ibid r 19A(2). There must always be an uneven number and, when there is disagreement, the majority decision prevails.

78 ibid.

79 ibid.

80 ibid r 19B(6)(1).

81 ibid.

82 ibid r 19C(4)(i). Rule 19C(4)(ii) provides that the Appeals Body has absolute discretion to hear and adjudicate on appeals against any decision of HRI, exercising the Registry Office functions referred to in s 10(2)(b) of the Irish Horseracing Industry Act 1994 as substituted by s 5 of the Horse Racing Ireland Act 2016.

83 Irish Horseracing Regulatory Board, 'Referrals and Appeals' <https://www.ihrb.ie/table/press-releases/referrals-appeals/> accessed 20 May 2024.

84 Irish Horseracing Regulatory Board, 'Governance' <https://www.ihrb.ie/

is the responsibility of the Board of Management, which is headed by the Chief Executive Officer (CEO).[85]

In summarising the role of the IHRB as detailed in ss 39(1)(a)–(i) of the 1994 Act (as amended by s 7 of the 2001 Act and s 11 of 2016 Act), its main functions are: **15–37**

- to be solely and independently responsible for making and enforcing the Rules of Racing;
- to provide integrity services for horseracing;
- to ensure the provision of on course integrity services by employing, monitoring and controlling the activities of horseracing officials;
- to licence all participants in horseracing in Ireland;
- to make all decisions relating to doping control, forensic testing, and handicapping in respect of horseracing;
- to be responsible for the representation of Irish horseracing internationally in respect of its functions;
- to develop codes of practice and assurance schemes for matters within its functions under this Act; and
- to maintain the existing nature of point-to-point races and to provide governance and to enforce the Irish National Hunt Steeplechase Regulations for point-to-point steeplechase.

The IHRB liaises with the Investigation Division, a specialist division in the Department of Agriculture, Food and the Marine (DAFM). The Investigation Division was established in 2014 and **15–38**

> is a key element of [the] Department's enforcement capability, underpinning the quality and traceability standards which facilitate trade and provide reassurance in relation to food safety and authenticity to consumers and customers in Ireland and abroad. All such investigations are carried out with a view to meeting the standard of proof required for prosecution through the courts.[86]

IHRB officials are considered Authorised Officers under the Animal Remedies Act 1993.[87] As Authorised Officers, IHRB officials 'can identify and sample any thoroughbred at any time and in any place and they have the authority to seize products, documentation, or other evidence as necessary'.[88] **15–39**

governance> accessed 20 May 2024. Rules 20–27 give a detailed description of the role of the Directors: see Rules of Racing (n 76).

85 Governance (n 84).

86 Veterinary Inspection Service, Dáil Deb 17 February 2021 <https://www.oireachtas.ie/en/debates/question/2021-02-17/1040/> accessed 20 May 2024. Prior to 2014, investigations were carried out by the Special Investigation Unit (SIU).

87 Section 10 of the 1993 Act as amended by ss 17 and 21(2) of the Horse Racing Ireland Act 2016. The 1993 Act is supplemented by SI no 36/2022 – European Union (Veterinary Medicinal Products and Medicated Feed) Regulations 2022 <https://www.irishstatutebook.ie/eli/2022/si/36/made/en/print> accessed 20 May 2024.

88 Joint Committee on Agriculture, Food and the Marine (n 68) 10.

Horse Racing Ireland

15–40 HRI is the national authority for thoroughbred racing in Ireland. It is a commercial state body that falls under the umbrella of the DAFM. The DAFM oversees the role of HRI by way of a Shareholder's Letter of Expectation, HRI Strategic Plan, compliance with the Code of Governance for State bodies, and regular meetings.[89] Its role is, according to s 5(1) of the Horse Racing Act 2016 (which amended s 10(1) of the Irish Horseracing Industry Act 1994 and substituted the following): (a) to provide for the overall administration, governance, development and promotion of the Irish horseracing industry, other than the functions of the Racing Regulatory Body set out in s 39(1), including promoting and increasing attendance at authorised racecourses; and (b) to provide a single structure for the administration and financial management of Irish horseracing.[90] The Regulatory Body under the 1994 Act was the Irish Horseracing Authority.[91] Section 39(1) relates to the establishment of the Racing Regulatory Body and its functions under the 1994 Act. Its functions are: (a) to regulate horseracing; (b) to make and enforce the Rules of Racing and in so doing to promote integrity and fair play in horseracing; (c) to provide adequate integrity services for horseracing; and (d) to license racecourses under the Rules of Racing. The current Regulatory Racing Body is the IHRB.[92] HRI is a body corporate with perpetual succession and consists of a board, a chairperson and 13 ordinary members. Of the 13 members, three are nominees of the IHRB, and four are nominees which the Minister for DAFM deems to be representative of the following: authorised racecourses, racehorse breeders, racehorse owners, and racehorse trainers. Two are nominated by the industry services committee, one is nominated by the betting industry, and three are chosen by the Minister for their specific skill and competencies, with a least one being a representative of the horseracing industry in Northern Ireland.[93] HRI is the representative of Ireland on the following international racing bodies: the International Federation of Horseracing Authorities, European and Mediterranean Federation of Horseracing Authorities, and the European Pattern Committee.[94]

---

89 ibid 11.

90 The 2016 Act repealed s 10(a) of the 1994 Act, which provided that the general functions of the Authority shall be – (a) the overall administration of Irish horseracing other than services operated by the Racing Regulatory Body under this Act.

91 Under the Racing Board and Racecourses Act 1945, the Racing Board was established under s 4. The Act was repealed by the Irish Horseracing Industry Act 1994.

92 For more detail see Governance (n 84).

93 Sections 8(1)(a)–(h) of the 2016 Act which amended the Schedule to the 1994 Act (as amended by the Horse Racing Ireland (Membership) Act 2001). Under the Schedule to the 1994 Act, there were 15 ordinary members, and the nominees were from several now-defunct bodies. The original Schedule is available at <https://www.irishstatutebook.ie/eli/1994/act/18/schedule/enacted/en/html#sched> accessed 20 May 2024. The Horse Racing Ireland (Membership) Act 2001 was repealed by the Horse Racing Ireland Act 2016.

94 Horse Racing Ireland, 'Company Structure' <https://www.hri.ie/corporate/

Service Level Agreement

The relationship between HRI and the IHRB is described as operating **15–41**
under 'a service level agreement in relation to the provision of integrity services'.[95] Integrity of services is referred to in the IHRB's Strategic Plan 2024–2027 and centres on ensuring 'robust and transparent regulatory practices, implemented with uncompromising integrity by a focused and professional team'.[96] Section 11(2) of the Horse Racing Ireland Act 2016 amended s 42 of the 1994 Act.[97] Section 42 refers to costs of integrity services. HRI is mandated to determine the budget for integrity services 'after appropriate deductions for the reasonable requirements of the Racing Regulatory Body to ensure it maintains appropriate independent functions and infrastructure'. In announcing the budget for 2024, HRI invested €17.3m in integrity services.[98]

Integrity Services: Anti-Doping

Under s 11(1)(f) of the Horse Racing Ireland Act 2016, one important **15–42**
general function of the IHRB is 'to make all decisions relating to doping

---

about-us/company-structure> accessed 20 May 2024. For more information on the International Federation of Horseracing Authorities, see <https://www.ifhaonline.org/> accessed 20 May 2024; and on the European and Mediterranean Federation of Horseracing Authorities, see <https://www.euromedracing.eu/> accessed 20 May 2024. The European Pattern Committee does not have its own webpage; however, the International Federation of Horseracing Authorities provides a summary of its history, see <https://www.ifhaonline.org/default.asp?section=About%20IFHA&area=20> accessed 20 May 2024. It is described as 'a living entity and, if it is to continue to fulfil its original purpose, it must of course be adaptable and responsive to changes in horseracing as a whole'.

[95] Joint Oireachtas Committee on Agriculture, Food and the Marine, Session to discuss the Joint Committee's Report on Horse Racing in Ireland, 'Opening Statement by Irish Horseracing Regulatory Board (IHRB)' (1 June 2022) <https://data.oireachtas.ie/ie/oireachtas/committee/dail/33/joint_committee_on_agriculture_food_and_the_marine/submissions/2022/2022-06-01_opening-statement-cliodhna-guy-interim-ceo-and-head-of-legal-licencing-and-compliance-irish-horseracing-regulatory-board-ihrb_en.pdf> accessed 20 May 2024.

[96] Irish Horseracing Regulatory Board, 'Strategic Plan 2024–2027' (15 December 2023) 4. See s 11(1)(c) of the 2016 Act which amended s 39(1) of the 1994 and refers to the responsibilities of the IHRB 'to ensure the provision of on-course integrity services by employing, monitoring and controlling the activities of horseracing officials, including the following—(i) inspectors of courses, (ii) clerks of the courses, (iii) clerks of scales, (iv) handicappers, (v) starters, (vi) judges, (vii) veterinary officers, (viii) medical officers, (ix) security officers, (x) stewards' secretaries, (xi) veterinary assistants, and (xii) senior racing officials'.

[97] Section 42 of the 1994 Act was previously amended by s 7 of the Horse and Greyhound Racing Act 2001.

[98] Horse Racing Ireland, 'Prize Money Increased for 2024 as Horse Racing Ireland Budget Includes Supports for Integrity, Equine Welfare, Industry Education, Breeders, Point-to-Points, Sustainability and Digital initiatives' 18 December 2023 <https://www.hri.ie/corporate/press-office/press-release/prize-money-increased-for-2024-as-horse-racing-ireland-budget-includes-supports-for-integrity,-equin> accessed 20 May 2024. This was an increase from €16.1m in 2023, €15.4m in 2022, and €12.6m in 2019.

control'. The Equine Anti-Doping Programme (EADP) will be discussed in detail below. To provide some context, the IHRB's EADP came under scrutiny following media reports concerning the use of banned substances, resulting in questions being raised about the robustness of the procedures. This prompted the commission of a report on Horseracing in Ireland by the Joint Committee on Agriculture, Food and the Marine, which was published in November 2021.[99] The Committee convened several meetings to discuss the negative 'commentary in the media regarding alleged issues in the horseracing industry in Ireland'.[100] The relevant stakeholders in the racing industry were invited to attend and respond to questions relating to the allegations. In highlighting the need for increased transparency and accountability, the Committee discussed the governance structure of the IHRB.[101] Between 2001 and 2021, €1.46bn of state funding via the Horse and Greyhound Racing Fund was granted to the horse and greyhound racing industries in accordance with s 12(6) of the Horse and Greyhound Racing Act 2001.[102] The Committee Report outlined the testing methods, the chain of custody of the samples, the use of an accredited laboratory, the UK-based LGC Laboratories, closed-circuit television (CCTV) at racecourses, equine traceability, and the IHRB's doping procedures within the international context.[103] The Committee Report concluded with 11 recommendations and observations.[104] A notable recommendation included the re-classification 'of the IHRB as a semi-state body under the aegis of DAFM to ensure complete transparency in its governance'.[105] While the Committee Report was generally favourable in its assessment of the anti-doping measures adopted by the IHRB, it recommended an independent review of the horseracing industry by an outside body to ensure that the IHRB's procedures were in line with international best practice.[106]

15–43 On foot of the Committee Report's recommendation, the IHRB's EADP was subject to an independent review in 2022.[107] The Independent Review concluded that the EADP did

> at least match international best practice in most respects and has

---

99 (n 68).
100 ibid 5.
101 ibid 14–15.
102 ibid 14.
103 ibid 15–21. The report briefly referred to the British Broadcasting Corporation (BBC) Panorama documentary on the treatment of racehorses after retirement. However, as the report was commissioned to examine the anti-doping measures, it was merely acknowledged.
104 ibid 22–24.
105 ibid 22. It also recommended that the IHRB annually publish a full and transparent set of accounts.
106 ibid 22–23.
107 Craig Suann, 'Independent Review of the Irish Horseracing Regulatory Board (IHRB) Equine Anti-Doping Programme' (22 April 2022) <https://www.ihrb.ie/pdf.php?f=EADP_Independent_Review.pdf> accessed 20 May 2024.

> made significant advances in recent years. However, a number of recommendations have been made that, if adopted, are capable of enhancing the robustness of the programme's processes, capabilities and capacities.[108]

The reviewer, Dr Craig Suann, a former chief veterinary officer for Racing New South Wales, made 18 recommendations, seven of which were deemed high priority,[109] nine medium priority,[110] and two low **15–44**

---

[108] ibid 6.

[109] The high priority recommendations were as follows: Recommendation 1 called for the installation of CCTV at all racecourses, the enhanced use of CCTV and the use of CCTV within the individual sample collection stables: ibid 12. Recommendation 6 advised on the overhauling of rules regarding the analysis of the B sample: ibid 19; while Recommendation 8 highlighted the need for the IHRB to keep up to date with emerging methods of doping and the role of the LGC Laboratory in the detection of gene doping and monitoring of biomarkers: ibid 20–21. Recommendation 10 contended that there should be an increase in race-day sampling. Although the IHRB's race-day sampling was comparable with the BHA, it was lower than France and Australia. It was further advised that the IHRB implement a full regulatory pre-race blood sampling; the number of horses to be sampled would depend on the quality of the race meeting as well as the race itself: ibid 22–23. Recommendation 11 advised the IHRB to revise its out-of-competition testing strategies to focus on more high profile/high stake training yards, which would target the top-level horses: ibid 24. Recommendation 12 had at is centre the welfare of horses and supported the working together of the IHRB, Weatherbys and the DAFM to develop systems that enable the full traceability of thoroughbreds through all stages of their lives. Thoroughbred foals born in 2021 were the first to be provided with e-passports. For more information on this see, The Thoroughbred Breeders' Association, 'First Thoroughbred Issued with a Weatherbys E-Passport' (23 July 2021) <https://www.thetba.co.uk/resource/first-thoroughbred-issued-with-a-weatherbys-e-passport.html> accessed 20 May 2024. Recommendation 17 advised the IHRB to investigate its resources and staffing levels and structures to ensure there are timely hearings by the Referrals Committee for cases involving adverse analytical findings (AAFs). The reviewer noted that there had been 24 AAFs documented in the IHRB's Equine Anti-Doping Report Issue 2 (January 2022) and none of these had been before the Referrals Committee.

[110] The medium priorities were as follows: Recommendation 2 concerned the enhancement of cross-referencing of the Sample Testing Box (STB) contents on race day: (n 107) 13–15. Recommendation 3 advised enhancements of the out-of-competition testing kits and operations, including the use of sniffer dogs: (n 107) 16; while Recommendation 4 suggested that the IHRB enhance the security over the chain of custody of STBs and out-of-competition testing kits, including the increase in the use of CCTV, which would provide evidence at hearing: (n 107) 17–18. Recommendation 9 called on the IHRB to continue to make statistics available publicly: (n 107) 22. Recommendation 13 advised that the IHRB 'develop a comprehensive sampling history for each horse': (n 107) 25. Recommendations 14, 15 and 16 concerned integrity assurances: (n 107) 26–27. Recommendation 14 referred to the need for police background checks as part of the recruitment policy – there should be regular declarations of conflict of interests, whether real or perceived – 'the probity of all staff associated with the [EAD] programme should be beyond reproach'. Recommendation 15 called on the IHRB to regularly review and update the EAD programme Standard Operating Procedures (SOPs), which should be easily accessed by staff and regular staff-training seminars should be made available. Recommendation 16 endorsed the execution of a Memorandum of Understanding (MOU) between the IHRB and the Veterinary Council of Ireland

priority.[111] In order to enhance the robustness of the EADP, more funding was needed which would allow the IHRB to employ extra staff for race day and out-of-competition testing and modify the Sampling Units at the racecourses.[112] The Independent Review noted that the IHRB was the first racing authority in the world to take hair samples at race meetings and out-of-competition.[113] Hair samples are useful in the detection of anabolic steroids and historic exposure to certain prohibited substances.[114] However, the reviewer recommended that an adequate number of blood and urine samples be collected on race day to ensure that as many prohibited substances as possible are detected.[115] The Independent Review referred to the appointment of a number of IHRB officials as AO for the purposes of the Animal Remedies Act 1993 as an 'important and ground breaking initiative'.[116] In comparison to other jurisdictions, AOs have, on receipt of a warrant card, 'unprecedented access' to licenced and unlicensed premises at any time.[117] They can seize unauthorised products or prohibited animal remedies, take documents or any other evidence, inspect horse transport vehicles and take samples from horses.[118] While AOs carry out inspections based on a list of criteria, intelligence plays an important part. It could relate to anti-doping, equine welfare concerns, complaints 'or unusual patterns of performance'.[119] The Independent Review recommended, as a medium priority, the use of one or more sniffer dogs who are trained to identify illicit substances and devices.[120]

15–45 A thread that weaves throughout the Independent Review is the integrity of the sample collection both at race meetings and out-of-competition and the need for a secure chain of custody for the samples.

to facilitate 'the prompt referral and hearing of matters relating to the poor professional performance or professional misconduct of practising veterinarians treating racehorses'. In reference to New South Wales and Victoria in Australia, Dr Suann discussed the licensing system that operates in thoroughbred racing. It is to ensure that veterinary surgeons are accountable to the rules, in particular to the control and use of medications and prohibited substances. Cognisance was given to the fact that such a licencing system in Ireland would be unconstitutional; however, the MOU would be useful in ensuring a speedier hearing: (n 107) 27.

111 Recommendation 5 suggested that the IHRB continue to embrace electronic means of the entry and transmission of data relating to the chain of custody of the samples between the IHRB and LCG: ibid 18. Recommendation 7 referred to the long-term storage of selected blood and urine samples as such samples could be retested as new laboratory techniques emerge: ibid 19.

112 ibid 6 and 9.

113 Irish Horseracing Regulatory Board, 'IHRB Statement on Anti-Doping Testing' (20 December 2020) <https://www.ihrb.ie/general-press-releases/ihrb-statement-on-anti-doping-testing> accessed 20 May 2024.

114 Independent Review (n 107) 23.

115 ibid Recommendation 11.

116 ibid 8.

117 ibid 14. 'Unlicenced' includes stud farms and sales consignors' premises.

118 ibid 15. The AOs often work with DAFM officials to carry out these inspections.

119 ibid 15.

120 ibid 16, Recommendation 3. The reviewer mentioned that there is at least one other racing jurisdiction that uses sniffer dogs.

It was within the terms of reference that the reviewer 'appraise the Chain of Custody'.[121] The reviewer observed that the chain of custody process on race day was 'fundamentally sound, but improved surveillance measures could be considered'.[122] As a high priority, it was recommended that CCTV should be installed in the Sampling Units at every racecourse, including the sample collection stables, the sample collection office area, the hosing stalls and cool-down walking area of the sampling unit.[123]

According to the IHRB's EAD Report published in February 2023, the process to implement the recommendations of the Independent Review was ongoing; however, several were already in place.[124] In the first half of 2022, there were 1,702 samples taken on race day involving 1,321 races.[125] Blood samples accounted for 337, urine 1,083, hair 170, pre-race tests 112, and there was just one adverse analytical finding (AAF). During the first six months of 2022, there were 90 premises inspected for out-of-competition testing.[126] Blood accounted for 442 of the samples obtained; there were no urine samples gathered; and 438 hair samples were collected. Out of the 880 samples tested, there was one AAF. In the aftermath of Independent Report being published, the figures for July to December 2022 show an increase in testing and, consequently, an increase in AAFs.[127] In total, 1,847 samples were taken at 1,556 races involving 325 blood samples, 1318 urine samples, 106 hair samples, 98 pre-race tests and four adverse AAFs.[128] There were 107 premises visited for out-of-competition testing: 152 blood samples were obtained; no urine samples were taken; 224 hair samples were taken; and there were three AAFs.[129] In 2022, there were five AAFs at race day and four out-of-competition.[130] Four AAFs were subject to further investigations, with 41 blood samples and 42 urine samples analysed.[131] Of the 5,417 samples **15–46**

[121] ibid 4.

[122] ibid 12. For details on the sample collection, see 10–12.

[123] ibid 13, Recommendation 1. In other jurisdictions, CCTV has been used in disputes to ascertain whether the sample was taken from the tested horse. The review recommended the use of a live feed of the urine and blood sample collection as well as CCTV recording the packaging and sealing of samples in the sampling office.

[124] Irish Horseracing Regulatory Board, 'Equine Anti-Doping Report for the Six Months Ending 31 December 2022' (Issue 4, February 2023) 1 <https://www.ihrb.ie/pdf.php?f=IHRB_EAD_Report_2_22.pdf> accessed 20 May 2024.

[125] Irish Horseracing Regulatory Board, 'Equine Anti-Doping Report for the Six Months Ending 30 June 2022' (Issue 3, July 2022) 4 <https://www.ihrb.ie/pdf.php?f=IHRB_EAD_Report_1_22.pdf> accessed 20 May 2024.

[126] ibid.

[127] EAD Report (n 124).

[128] ibid 4.

[129] ibid 4.

[130] ibid 4.

[131] ibid 4. One from the first six months of the year and three from the second half of the year. There were four hearings before the Referrals Committee.

taken in 2022 (including 598 taken at point-to-point races where only blood is taken for testing, with two AAFs), 11 (0.2%) showed AAFs.[132]

15–47 While the later part of 2022 showed an increase in testing, the IHRB acknowledged that 'the overall number of samples taken was 9% lower than the comparative figure in 2021'.[133] This was explained by using 'more extensive analysis of certain samples in addition to the standard analysis of the full 5,417 samples taken throughout 2022'.[134]

Equine Anti-Doping Programme

15–48 Regulation 7 Appendix C of the Rules of Racing sets out the drug testing procedures for riders.[135] Regulation 14 Appendix C details the 'Regulations Relating to the Taking of Samples from Horses'.[136] The use of prohibited substances and methods and the use of controlled medicines is based on the welfare of the equine athlete as well as upholding the integrity and reputation of the sport. The equine athlete is unable to choose whether they ingest a prohibited substance or use a prohibited method of doping, thus the onus is placed on the 'Responsible Person' (RP).[137] According to paragraphs 1, 2, and 3 of Regulation 14, the RP refers to the trainer or their representative, or the owner or the person in charge of the premises where the horse is located. In paragraphs 4, 5, and 6, the RP means the trainer or the owner. In paragraph 9 relating to the screening sample of total carbon dioxide concentration, the RP denotes the trainer or their representative. The Schedule of Prohibited Substances refers to '[s]ubstances capable at any time of causing an action or effect, or both an action and effect'.[138] This can occur in one

[132] ibid 1. In 2023, the December EAD Report 2023 stated that 5,866 samples were taken from horses in 2023: 'of which 1,501 were taken during Out of Competition Testing, six (0.1%) were confirmed as an Adverse Analytical Finding (AAF) and either have been or shortly will be brought before a Referrals Committee': Irish Horseracing Regulatory Board, 'Equine Anti-Doping Report for the Six Months Ending 30 December 2023' (Issue 6, February 2024) 1 <https://www.ihrb.ie/pdf.php?f=IHRB_EAD_Report_2_23.pdf> accessed 20 May 2024.

[133] EAD Report (n 124) 1.

[134] ibid 1. The IHRB had worked closely with external stakeholders including LGC Laboratories and the International Federation of Horseracing Authorities.

[135] Rules of Racing 2023 (n 76) 167.

[136] ibid 188–90. Regulation 14 is subject to the provisions of r 20(v) which empowers the Directors of the IHRB to 'publish from time to time in such a manner as they deem appropriate: (a) a schedule of prohibited substances including any thresholds therefor and (b) regulations for the taking of Samples'.

[137] ibid 188–90.

[138] This is taken from the 2021 Rules as the 2023 Rules only provide the following: 'Pursuant to Rule 20(v) of the Rules of Racing and the Irish National Hunt Steeplechase Rules, the Directors of the IHRB publish a schedule of Prohibited Substances, threshold levels where applicable, and prohibited methods on the IHRB website and give notice that each item referred to therein is a Prohibited Substance as defined or a prohibited method within these Rules.' There is no such information provided on the website, thus the 2021 Rules provide detailed information: see Irish Racing Ireland, 'Rules of Racing and Irish National Hunt

or more of the following mammalian body systems: the nervous system, cardiovascular, respiratory, digestive, urinary, reproductive, musculoskeletal, blood system, endocrine, and the immune system, with the exception of licenced vaccines against infectious agents and masking agents.[139] Each category is broadened by the words 'including but not limited to', in reference to non-specified substances. Certain substances are permitted so long as they do not exceed threshold levels.[140] Non-approved substances, those that have not received regulatory approval (veterinary or government), are prohibited.[141] Similar to methods applicable to humans, blood doping (as discussed in Chapter 6) is prohibited unless it is needed to save the life of the horse or is used as part of a veterinary treatment of musculoskeletal injury or disease.[142] Blood transfusions and gene doping are also prohibited methods.[143]

Rule 96(a) states that an AAF is a breach of the Rules of Racing. It outlines the applicable sanctions available to the Referrals Committee or Appeals Body, which include the disqualification of the horse from the race, the forfeiture of the stake, a monetary fine of at least €1,000, and/or the withdrawal of the trainer's licence 'for a such period as it may consider appropriate'.[144] However, no further action will be taken in situations where the prohibited substance is 'not prohibited at all times including in training' and 'can be traced to the clinical treatment of the Horse with an Authorised Medicine which has been properly recorded in the Medicines Register maintained by the Trainer and verified in writing by the stable's Veterinary Surgeon (if applicable)'.[145] The standard of proof applied in doping and other disciplinary matters is that of the balance of probabilities as per Rule 271.[146] **15–49**

As equine athletes will sometimes require medications prescribed by a veterinary surgeon, the Rules of Racing require all licenced trainers/handlers to maintain a Medications Register.[147] Failure to keep a **15–50**

Steeplechase Rules 2021' 284–88 <https://www.hri-ras.ie/getmedia/2beecdd0-58df-4a0a-90c6-2b22927aad90/IHRB-Rule-Book-2021.pdf> accessed 21 May 2024.

139 ibid 283–85.

140 ibid 285–86.

141 ibid 287.

142 ibid 288.

143 ibid 288.

144 Rules of Racing 2023 (n 76) 55. For examples of doping cases heard by the Referrals Committee, see Harry Rogers (Trainer) Prohibited Substance Referral – The Curragh 8 October 2022 <https://www.ihrb.ie/referrals-appeals/harry-rogers-trainer-prohibited-substance-referral-the-curragh-8th-october-2022> accessed 21 May 2024; and Caroline McCaldin (Handler) Prohibited Substance Referral – Route (H) Point to Point at Portrush 15th October 2022 <https://www.ihrb.ie/referrals-appeals/caroline-mccaldin-handler-prohibited-substance-referral-route-h-point-to-point-at-portrush-15th-october-2022> accessed 21 May 2024.

145 Rules of Racing 2023 (n 76) 56, rr 96(ii)(a) and (b).

146 ibid 125.

147 Irish Horseracing Regulatory Board, 'Responsible Use of Equine Medicines' <https://www.ihrb.ie/7-horses-equine-anti-doping> accessed 21 May 2024.

register 'of all authorised medicines used for the bona fide' medical treatment of horses, or failure to allow the register to be inspected by an AO, constitutes a breach of Rule 148(iii)(b) and will be sent to the Referrals Committee.[148] The register must conform to the requirements of the 'Animal Remedies Record' outlined in s 42 and Schedule 7 of the European Communities (Animal Remedies) (No 2) Regulations 2007.[149]

15–51 The IHRB has signed up to several sections of the International Federation of Horseracing Authorities (IFHA) International Agreement on Breeding, Racing and Wagering, described as 'a voluntary agreement designed for the guidance of recognised Racing and Breeding authorities'.[150] The Report on 'Horse Racing in Ireland' from November 2021 states that Ireland is a full signatory to Article 6, 'a formal agreement between global horseracing authorities which commits countries to meeting best international standards in drug testing and forensics'.[151] Article 6 comprises of sections A, B, C, D, and E. According to the most recent version of the Agreement from 2023, Ireland is not a full signatory or partial signatory to Article 6A (Racing) Prohibited Substances[152]; Article 6B (Racing) Prohibition of Genetic Therapy, Gene Editing and Genome Editing[153]; and Article 6E (Racing) Out of Competition.[154] It is, however, a full signatory to Article 6C (Racing) Prohibited Practices[155] and Article 6D Medication in Training.[156]

Animal Welfare Considerations in Racing and Equestrian Sports: Doping, Jumps Racing and the Use of the Whip

15–52 The use of prohibited substances in equine sports raises several ethical issues. The Animal Health and Welfare Act 2013 refers to 'unnecessary suffering' and defines it as 'pain, distress or suffering (whether physical or mental) that in its kind or degree, or in its object, or in the circumstances in which it occurs, is unreasonable or unnecessary'. In England and Wales, the Animal Welfare Act 2006 also refers to

---

148 Rules of Racing 2023 (n 76) 73–74.

149 SI no 786 of 2007.

150 International Federation of Horseracing Authorities, 'International Agreement on Breeding, Racing and Wagering and Appendices (2023 edition) <https://www.ifhaonline.org/resources/ifAgreement.pdf> accessed 21 May 2024. The Agreement is updated every year at the IFHA conference.

151 Joint Committee (n 68) 20.

152 International Agreement (n 150) 38–42, latest update April 2022. There is a table at the end of each section that lists countries that are full signatories, partial signatories, and non-signatories. Ireland is not, however, listed as a non-signatory under arts 6A, B and E.

153 ibid 43–45, latest update January 2020.

154 ibid 52–55, latest update January 2020.

155 ibid 47–49, latest update January 2021. According to Appendix 10C (Racing) Prohibited Substances Guideline, Ireland is not a signatory as the IHRB has its own list of banned substances: see 135–36. This was last updated in February 2019.

156 ibid 49–50, latest update January 2019.

'unnecessary suffering'.[157] Applying the legislative definition of suffering from both jurisdictions to animals in sport is difficult. As the use of horses in sport, for example, is not 'necessary', it would seem that any type of suffering, whether it is racing, show jumping or the administration of drugs (whether prohibited or controlled) would be a breach of Animal Welfare legislation.[158] The more appropriate term is 'avoidable suffering', as this term arguably enables humans 'to address the welfare issues associated with sporting use of animals even if one believes … that the use of animals for sport is fundamentally unethical'.[159]

There are two important considerations when it comes to equine doping, whether it applies to equestrian sports or horseracing. First, if a horse is administered a drug to enhance performance, there is an element of cheating, which is against the principles of clean and fair competition. There is also an animal-welfare issue if a substance is given to a horse either to enhance performance or to mask an injury. In the case of masking an injury, the equine athlete should not take part in an event until the injury has fully healed.[160] To further complicate matters, there is the issue of contaminated food and supplements which can easily be ingested by the horse and unwittingly result in a positive test for a banned or controlled substance, as will be discussed further on in this chapter. **15–53**

In Australia, all but one state, Victoria, permits jumps racing. In 2022, Southern Australia introduced the Animal Welfare (Jumps Racing) Amendment Bill 2022, a Bill to amend the Animal Welfare Act 1985.[161] It passed all stages and was signed into law on 14 July 2022.[162] It is interesting to note that there had been no jumps racing in Southern **15–54**

157 c45 <https://www.legislation.gov.uk/ukpga/2006/45/pdfs/ukpga_20060045_en.pdf> accessed 21 May 2024.

158 MLH Campbell, 'When Does Use Become Abuse in Equestrian Sport?' (2013) 25(10) Equine Veterinary Education 489, 490.

159 ibid.

160 The FEI distinguishes between doping (performance enhancing or masking an injury) and the use of bona fide veterinary treatment in the form of medication.

161 The full Bill can be accessed here <https://www.legislation.sa.gov.au/__legislation/lz/b/current/animal%20welfare%20(jumps%20racing)%20amendment%20bill%202022_hon%20tammy%20franks%20mlc/unofficial%20royal%20arms/animal%20racing%20amendment%20bill%202022.un.pdf> accessed 21 May 2024. The Royal Society of Prevention of Cruelty to Animals of Southern Australia made a submission to the Jumps Racing Select Committee in which it strongly advocated for a ban of jumps racing 'primarily due to the inherent and unacceptable risks of injury, distress and death to horses'. It cited statistics in support of the ban: for example, according to a study carried out by the University of Melbourne, 'the risk of injury and death of a horse competing in a jumps race as 18.9 times greater than a horse competing in a flats race': see RSPCA Knowledge Base (updated 18 May 2022) <https://kb.rspca.org.au/knowledge-base/why-do-horses-die-from-competing-in-jumps-racing/> accessed 21 May 2024.

162 The South Australian Government Gazette (no 49, 14 July 2022) 2220 <https://www.governmentgazette.sa.gov.au/2022/July/2022_049.pdf> accessed 21 May 2024.

Australia since October 2021. Racing Southern Australia cited economic reasons for the decision to phase out jumps racing.[163] A spokesperson for South Australian deputy premier stated, 'While jumps races were once an intrinsic part of the racing industry, it has fallen out of favour with the public who find the number of falls and deaths unacceptable.'[164] The introduction of legislation specifically banning jumps racing will ensure that it does not return unless the legislation is amended in the future. The Animal Welfare (Jumps Racing) Amendment Act 2022 defines jumps racing as a steeplechase or hurdle race involving the racing of horses. It inserts s 14AA into the Animal Welfare Act 1985 and expressly states that jumps racing is prohibited and persons are precluded from organising, promoting, participating, or participating in the organisation or promotion of jumps racing. The maximum penalty for a breach of s 14AA will result in a fine of $20,000 or two years' imprisonment. Section 14AA(2)(a) expressly excludes from the prohibition the organisation, participation and promotion of show jumping, eventing or cross-country events.[165]

15–55 Jumps racing remains legal in Victoria; however, there was an attempt to ban steeplechase and hurdle racing there in 2009.[166] In 2008, Racing Victoria Limited (RVL, currently called Racing Victoria) commissioned an Independent Report by His Honour David Jones titled a 'Review of Jumps Racing in Victoria'.[167] The 200-page report recommended that jumps racing continue in 2009, however, subject to the adoption of essential recommendations.[168] In May 2009, three fatalities in two days at Warrnambool's renowned carnival resulted in the suspension of jumps racing by RVL pending a decision of its board a week later.[169] A RVL Situation Review found:

---

[163] Eleanor Jones, 'Australian Racing Ban is a "Salutary Reminder' to the Equestrian Industry' *Horse and Hound* (Bath, 24 July 2022) <https://www.horseandhound.co.uk/news/australian-racing-ban-is-a-salutary-reminder-to-the-equestrian-industry-795708> accessed 21 May 2024.

[164] ibid.

[165] A person who is jumping a horse over an obstacle, or advertising jumps racing in another state, or shows images or audio of a jumps race taking place outside of Southern Australia, will not be in breach of the law, see ss 14AA(2)(b)–(d).

[166] 'Victoria Bans Jumps Racing' (*ABC News*, 27 November 2009) <https://www.abc.net.au/news/2009-11-27/victoria-bans-jumps-racing/1159658> accessed 21 May 2024.

[167] David Jones, 'Review of Jumps Racing in Victoria' (Victoria Racing Limited 2008) <https://www.yumpu.com/en/document/view/4616534/review-of-jumps-racing-in-victoria> accessed 21 May 2024.

[168] For an interesting article on newspaper reporting of equine deaths from jumps racing between February 2008 and December 2009, see Daniel Montoya, Phil McManus, and Glenn Albrecht, 'Jumping to Conclusions? Media Coverage of Jumps Racing Debates in Australia' (2012) 20(3) Society & Animals 273.

[169] AAP, 'Victorian Jumps Races Suspended After More Deaths' *The Sydney Morning Herald* (Sydney, 8 May 2009) <https://www.smh.com.au/sport/racing/victorian-jumps-races-suspended-after-more-deaths-20090508-gdtinr.html> accessed 21 May 2024.

> Despite the implementation of all of the safety recommendations of the Jones Report, the incidence of falls and fatalities increased during the 2009 season to be the worst in many years. It is also noted that the implemented recommendations of six previous Reviews had not delivered any improvement in safety outcomes.[170]

The increase in equine fatalities and falls in 2009 despite all the recommendations of the Jones Report having been implemented, coupled with the decline in the number of starters in races, and a decline in turnover, led RVL to make the decision to phase out jumps racing.[171] The public interest had also waned as the 2009 Review found: 'Customer research data shows 65% of people believe that the incidents that occur in Jumps racing are not an acceptable price to pay for the retention of the sport.'[172] It proposed transitionary measures for riders, clubs and horses.[173] The ban was slated to enter into effect after the end of the 2010 season. Not surprisingly, the decision was not greeted with much enthusiasm by those involved in the industry. It was expected that many of them who opposed the ban would begin competing in South Australia. It was thought at the time that the 2010 three-day Grand Annual Steeplechase carnival in Warrnambool was to be the last after 138 years. RVL committed $1m to a Transition and Marketing Fund to help promote the 2011 carnival, which was to become a flat race event.[174] **15–56**

The ban, however, did not last long, as in September 2010, the Racing Victoria Board (RVB) decided to reinstate jumps racing for the 2011 season.[175] The RVB decided to implement a three-year programme subject to a Key Performance Indicator (KPI) relating to fatalities.[176] According to the statement, a KPI **15–57**

> of not more than 0.65% of fatalities per starters will be measured as a rolling three year average (including the 2010 season) at the end of the 2012 and 2013 seasons for hurdles. The hurdle racing fatality rate in 2010 was 0.41% and the steeplechase racing fatality rate was 0.58%. The fall

[170] Victoria Racing Limited, '2009 Jumps Racing Review' 8 <https://www.thoroughbrednews.com.au/userfiles/file/RVL%20Jumps%20Racing%20Review%202009%20Background.pdf> accessed 21 May 2024. The first report was published in 1991 by the Senate Report Committee. It raised serious concerns about equine welfare in jumps racing. The reports are documented in tabular form on page 2 of the 2009 Review.

[171] ibid 5–7. According to the Review, '2009 provided the highest incidence of falls to starters (5.08%) and fatalities to starters (1.27%)': ibid 7.

[172] ibid 8.

[173] ibid 9.

[174] ibid.

[175] Andrew Eddy, 'Jumps Boss Fumes at Indecision on Steeples' *The Sydney Morning Herald* (Sydney, 3 September 2010) <https://www.smh.com.au/sport/racing/jumps-boss-fumes-at-indecision-on-steeples-20100902-14rmz.html> accessed 21 May 2024.

[176] ibid.

rate KPI used this year to help determine the future of jumps racing will be scrapped with the sport to be judged on fatalities alone.[177]

15–58 At the time of this statement, RVB had decided to leave the issue of steeplechase racing until a future meeting pending further analysis. There had been a higher number of fatalities at steeplechase events and thus the RVB decided that further analysis was necessary. The reason for the change of decision was attributed to improvements in safety and a corresponding decrease in fatalities. Due to the 'dramatic improvements', the RVB felt that the prohibition could be postponed 'to provide certainty to owners investing in horses and for jockeys, trainers and workers who earn their livelihood from the sport'.[178]

15–59 In October 2010, the RVB approved a one-year steeplechase programme.[179] In assessing the number of falls in the 2010 season, RVB contended that several factors were responsible for the higher fall rate, namely the introduction of new obstacles. The fatality rate for steeplechase racing in 2010 was 0.57%.[180] The programme also provided for a few safety measures which were introduced before the 2011 season. These measures included: improving sight lines on obstacles and reviewing the placement of wings; improving schooling and trialling facilities at training venues; reviewing the racing programme; and assessing the suitability of venues to conduct steeplechase races.[181] In 2010, RVL invested $600,000 on 90 new jumps in the hope of reducing equine deaths. However, one animal-welfare advocate argued that the new jumps had little or no safety effect as it is the combination of speed and jumping that exposes the horses to foreseeable risks.[182]

15–60 Since 2012, hurdle and steeplechase racing continue in Victoria. It has been reported that the changes introduced in 2010 have resulted in a 75% decrease in fatalities due to new technology and research.[183] Proponents of jumps racing contend that jumps horses, while engaged in a more

---

[177] ibid.

[178] ibid.

[179] Racing.com Staff, 'One Year Steeplechase Racing Program Approved' (*Racing.com*, 7 October 2010) <https://www.racing.com/news/2010-10-07/one-year-steeplechase-racing-program-approved> accessed 31 July 2024.

[180] ibid. The rate of fatalities in hurdle racing was 0.41%: see Robert Windmill and Xavier La Canna, 'Horse Death Renews Call for Jumps Ban' *The Sydney Morning Herald* (Sydney, 4 April 2011) <http://news.smh.com.au/breaking-news-national/horse-death-renews-call-for-jumps-ban-20110404-1cydm> accessed 21 May 2024.

[181] ibid. While the Board was hopeful that the new programme would result in fewer falls and fatalities, the practicalities of the new programme were to be tested on the first day of the Victoria season. Casa Boy had to be euthanised after he crashed into the Ace Radio Maiden Hurdle on the first day of the races at Warrnambool in April 2011. Two other horses also fell but were uninjured.

[182] ibid.

[183] Damien Ractliffe, 'Only in Victoria: Why Jumps Racing Survives at the 'Bool' *The Sydney Morning Herald* (Sydney, 1 May 2023) <https://www.smh.com.au/sport/racing/banned-everywhere-but-victoria-why-jumps-racing-survives-at-the-bool-20230412-p5czs8.html> accessed 31 July 2024.

inherently dangerous sport than flat racing, have better post-racing careers as equestrian horses due to their stamina, temperament and ability to jump.[184] The use of 'new lightweight jumps, softer racetracks and expanded veterinary checks have contributed to the fatal-incident rate dropping by two-thirds'.[185] Despite the technological advances, the 2023 Warrnambool Festival saw the first fatality on the track since 2021.[186] Animal Justice Party state Member of Parliament Georgie Purcell in her inaugural speech referred to Victoria being the last state 'to continue with this cruel pastime'.[187] Unless jumps racing is banned in Victoria, it will provide a gateway for horses from the other states, in particular, Southern Australia, to compete. It remains to be seen whether the Victorian legislature will intervene and statutorily ban the sport.

The BHA states that the whip may only be used for the purposes of 'safety and encouragement'.[188] Encouragement is defined as 'using the whip as an aid to activate and focus the horse, so the horse realises its potential by giving its best. Use of the whip to coerce is not permitted, and the rules are designed to reflect this.'[189] The current design of foam-padded and air-cushioned is the only whip permitted by the BHA, which involved the Royal Society for the Prevention of Cruelty to Animals (RSPCA) in its development. A review conducted in 2022 places limits on the occasions a whip can be used in a race.[190] In a flat race, the maximum times a whip can be used is six times, and seven times in a jumps race.[191] Another factor for stewards to consider is the **15–61**

---

184 ibid.

185 ibid. The article adds that the mandate 'that jockeys must retire their horse from a race if it is fatigued, not jumping satisfactorily or out of contention has also helped lead to that reduction'.

186 Damien Ractliffe, 'Horse Dies After Fall During Feature Race at Warrnambool' *The Sydney Morning Herald* (Sydney, 2 May 2023) <https://www.smh.com.au/sport/racing/horse-dies-in-fall-during-feature-race-at-warrnambool-20230502-p5d4zc.html> accessed 31 July 2024. There was a fatality on the first day of the 2024 festival: see Andrew Eddy, 'Vale Grand Promenade' (*Racing.com*, 25 March 2024) <https://www.racing.com/news/2024-03-25/news-lth-vale-grand-promenade#> accessed 21 May 2024. See also Danny Russell, 'The Horse that Never Hit the Ground: Mysterious Case of the Disappearing Thoroughbred' *The Sydney Morning Herald* (Sydney, 29 April 2024) <https://www.smh.com.au/sport/racing/why-so-many-secrets-what-jumps-racing-hides-from-the-public-20240429-p5fnam.html> accessed 21 May 2024.

187 Parliament of Victoria, 'Tuesday, 7 February 2023' <https://new.parliament.vic.gov.au/parliamentary-activity/hansard/hansard-details/HANSARD-974425065-20010#wrapper3> accessed 21 May 2024. Purcell's speech begins at the time of 16.22.

188 British Horseracing Authority, 'The whip' <https://www.britishhorseracing.com/regulation/the-whip-2/> accessed 21 May 2024.

189 ibid.

190 British Horseracing Authority, 'Whip Consultation Report' (July 2022) <https://media.britishhorseracing.com/bha/Whip/Whip_consultation_report.pdf> accessed 21 May 2024.

191 British Horseracing Authority, 'Whip Rules 2023' <http://media.britishhorseracing.com/bha/Whip/Whip_Rules_May_2023.pdf> accessed 21 May 2024.

force at which the whip is used.[192] Any alleged breaches of the whip rules go before the Whip Review Committee (WRC), which considers each case individually.[193] Riders face disqualification if they go over three or four times the threshold in addition to suspension.[194]

15–62 The 2022 Review was in response to the Horse Welfare Board's (HWB) 130-page document titled 'A Life Well Lived: New Strategic Plan for the Welfare of Horses Bred for Racing, 2020–2024'.[195] The HWB is an independent body within the BHA.[196] It was tasked with examining the use of the whip and to provide a public position on its use. In Appendix 1: 'Background Information Relating to the Whip' of the strategic plan it provided statistics on the types of offences and public attitudes.[197] It concluded:

> Be clear that misuse of the whip is still too high, particularly in some circumstances, and setting the expectation that, should increases in the penalties continue to prove an insufficient deterrent, further steps will need to be taken consider the question of whip use in racing and to provide a policy position on the whip.[198]

15–63 Norway has strictly curtailed the use of the whip since 1982 and since 2009 whips have not been used in most flat races.[199] While acknowledging that the industry in Norway is much smaller than in Britain, the Norway model demonstrates that the safety of riders and horses has not been compromised.[211] Rule 10 of the Irish Rules of Racing detail whip requirements, which must be air-cushioned, and it outlines the situations that preclude the use of the whip.[200] In 2019, the IHRB introduced limits on the use of the whip. Riders are permitted to use the whip eight times in a race. A rider who exceeds eight will be subject to a steward's inquiry with leave to appeal to the Referrals Committee. The rider must give the horse at least three strides to respond.[201] The rule

---

192 British Horseracing Authority, 'Guidance on the Use of the Whip' <https://rules.britishhorseracing.com/#!/book/34/chapter/s3136-whip-rule-f45/content?section=s3137-guidance-on-use-of-the-whip> accessed 21 May 2024.

193 For examples of recent WRC decisions from 13–15 May and published on 17 May 2024, see <https://media.britishhorseracing.com/bha/Whip/WRC_Decisions_170524.pdf> accessed 21 May 2024.

194 There is an automatic four-day ban for exceeding the limit. A rider who goes two strikes over the limit faces a seven-day ban.

195 The report is available at <http://media.britishhorseracing.com/bha/Welfare/HWB/WELFARE_STRATEGY.pdf> accessed 21 May 2024.

196 British Horseracing Authority, 'Horse Welfare Board' <https://www.britishhorseracing.com/regulation/horse-welfare-board/> accessed 21 May 2024.

197 Appendix 1 of A Life Well Lived: New Strategic Plan for the Welfare of Horses Bred for Racing, 2020–2024 (n 195) 124–30.

198 ibid 130.

199 Bidda Jones and others, 'A Critical Analysis of the British Horseracing Authority's Review of the Use of the Whip in Horseracing' (2015) 5(1) Animals 138, 141.

200 Rules of Racing 2023 (n 76) 177–79.

201 ibid Regulations 10.3 (i). In the decision of Mr JJ Codd (Rider) Appeal – Fairyhouse on 10 April 2023, the Appeals Body dismissed an appeal by the rider who had

changes introduced by the BHA have implications for Irish riders racing in Britain as the IHRB agreed to recognise suspensions imposed by the BHA in Ireland.[202] The IFHA International Agreement on Breeding, Racing and Wagering provides for the reciprocation of suspensions under Article 10.[203]

Equestrian Sports: Horse Sport Ireland

As noted above, HSI is the national governing body for equestrian sport in Ireland, which consists of 16 disciplines, including eventing, dressage, and show jumping.[204] Unlike horseracing, equestrian sport in Ireland is not subject to specific legislation, however, HSI is one of the recognised governing bodies of Sport Ireland and thus subject to its rules and regulations. The FEI is the world governing body of equestrian sports and within HSI there is a high-performance unit, which represents athletes competing for Ireland in the eight FEI disciplines of show jumping, eventing, dressage, para-equestrian, carriage driving, endurance, reining, and vaulting.[205] **15–64**

HSI is a CLG and was established in 2006 by the then Minister for Agriculture and Minister for Tourism and Sport.[206] On 1 January 2008, HSI became the governing body for equestrian sports on the entire island of Ireland.[207] In terms of funding, HSI receives funding from Sport Ireland and the DAFM. In 2023, HSI received €803,333 in high-performance funding from Sport Ireland: over the period of 2021 to 2024 this amounts to a total of €3.1m.[208] As part of the 2023 budget, the DAFM allocated €5.2m to HSI, However, this was deemed to be below what **15–65**

---

been banned for four days by the race stewards due to excessive use of the whip and not giving the horse at least three strides to respond. The Appeals Body disagreed that the ban was disproportionate and increased it to five days. The decision was published on the IHRB website on 3 May 2023 <https://www.ihrb.ie/referrals-appeals/mr-j-j-codd-rider-appeal-fairyhouse-10th-april-2023> accessed 21 May 2024.

202 Daragh Ó Conchúir, 'IHRB Will Reciprocate Whip Bans to Irish Jockeys Under Controversial New British Rules' *Irish Examiner* (Cork, 22 February 2023) <https://www.irishexaminer.com/sport/racing/arid-41077625.html> accessed 21 May 2024.

203 International Agreement (n 150) 65–70, art 10 (Racing) Disqualifications and Suspensions and their International Application.

204 The disciplines are carriage driving, dressage, endurance, eventing, harness racing, hunting, mounted games, para-equestrian, polo, polocrosse, reining/western, showing, show jumping, side saddle, Tourism Related Equestrian Competitions (TREC), and vaulting.

205 Horse Sport Ireland, 'About HSI High Performance' <https://www.horsesportireland.ie/team-ireland/about-team-ireland/> accessed 21 May 2024.

206 Horse Sport Ireland, 'What We Do' <https://www.horsesportireland.ie/about/what-we-do/> accessed 21 May 2024.

207 ibid.

208 Sport Ireland, 'Sport Ireland High Performance Sport Investment 2024' <https://www.sportireland.ie/sites/default/files/media/document/2024-02/hp_invest_final_0.pdf> accessed 21 May 2024.

was expected due to 'spiralling' costs in the industry.[209] It is claimed that the equestrian industry generates over €1bn annually and employs over 14,000 people, thus the current funding structure was viewed as 'underwhelming'.[210] In the 2024 budget, DAFM allocated €5.45m to HSI, an increase of €250,000 on the 2023 funding.[211]

The Fédération Équestre Internationale and Equine Welfare

15–66 The FEI, a not-for-profit organisation, is the international governing body for 136 fully affiliated national federations, including HSI.[212] There are eight regional groups with HSI in Group EEF, the European Equestrian Federation.[213] The FEI is the only international governing body for equestrian sports recognised by the IOC. In 1921, France, Norway, Sweden, Belgium, Italy, Denmark, the United States (US), and Japan founded the FEI in Lausanne, Switzerland. Ireland, through the Equestrian Federation of Ireland (EFI) joined as an affiliate in 1931.[214] The FEI is headed by a president and a secretary general. The role of the FEI is 'to ensure the good governance of the sport'.[215] Governance is broadly defined to include equine and human welfare.[216]

15–67 The FEI Code of Conduct for the Welfare of the Horse imposes several

[209] Horse Sport Ireland, 'Horse Sport Ireland Voices Disappointment with Budget 2023 Allocation to Equestrian Industry' (30 September 2022) <https://www.horsesportireland.ie/horse-sport-ireland-voices-disappointment-with-budget-2023-allocation-to-equestrian-industry/> accessed 31 July 2024.

[210] ibid.

[211] Judith Faherty, 'DAFM Allocate €5.45 million to Sport Horse Sector in Budget 2024' *Irish Field* (11 October 2023) <https://www.theirishfield.ie/sport-horse/sport-horse-news/news-dafm-allocate-5-45-million-to-sport-horse-sector-in-budget-2024-787674> accessed 21 May 2024.

[212] Fédération Équestre Internationale, 'National Federation's Affiliation Process', <https://inside.fei.org/fei/about-fei/structure/affiliation-process> accessed 21 May 2024. There is one Associate Member National Association. The two categories were recognised at FEI General Assembly 2021. Full and associate membership is defined in arts 5.2(i) and (ii) of the FEI Statutes (25th edn, effective 21 November 2023) <https://inside.fei.org/sites/default/files/FEI%20STATUTES%202023_CLEAN.pdf> accessed 21 May 2024. The affiliates are listed at <https://data.fei.org/NFPages/NF/Search> accessed 21 May 2024. On 8 November 2012, associate membership was abolished at the FEI's General Assembly, as it was contended that this type of membership was 'not working effectively as there were no clear criteria for becoming an FEI associate member nor were there established obligations for the FEI to deliver to its associate members': see 'FEI Abolishes Associate Membership' (*Eurodressage*, 10 November 2012) <https://www.eurodressage.com/2012/11/10/fei-abolishes-associate-membership> accessed 21 May 2024.

[213] For more information on this group, see <https://www.euroequestrian.eu/en/Home/Welcome-to-the-European-Equestrian-Federation-website.html> accessed 21 May 2024.

[214] The EFI was established in 1926. A brief history of the EFI was discussed in the case of *Macken v O'Reilly* [1979] ILRM 79, 85. HSI replaced the EFI in 2008.

[215] Fédération Équestre Internationale, 'The FEI Headquarters Flowchart' <https://inside.fei.org/fei/about-fei/structure/fei-headquarters> accessed 21 May 2024.

[216] ibid.

requirements that must be upheld by the human agents, such as general equine welfare considerations: for example, good horse management, training methods, farriery and tack, transport, and transit.[217] Under fitness to compete, s 2(a)–(c), there are guidelines on fitness and competence, health status, and doping and medication. Under s 2(c), it states that '[a]ny action or intent of doping and illicit use of medication constitute a serious welfare issue and will not be tolerated. After any veterinary treatment, sufficient time must be allowed for full recovery before Competition.'[218] The CAS Panel in *Lyle and Blythe v FEI* expressly referred to the first paragraph of the Code, which provides that the

> FEI requires all those involved in international equestrian sport to adhere to the FEI Code of Conduct and to acknowledge and accept that at all times the welfare of the Horse must be paramount. Welfare of the horse must never be subordinated to competitive or commercial influences.[219]

The CAS Panel acknowledged the vulnerability of horses, who 'unlike humans, cannot themselves take care to avoid the ingestion of prohibited substances'.[220] In Chapter 1, 'Purposes and Principles', of the FEI Statutes 2023, Article 1.4 sets out the role of the FEI in the preservation and protection of 'the welfare of the horse and the natural environment by establishing appropriate codes of conduct'.[221] The CAS has recognised the horse's status as an equine athlete: **15–68**

> the central and distinctive feature of equestrian sport is that it involves a partnership between two types of athlete, one human and one equine. One of those partners is unable to speak for itself, and therefore the FEI has assumed responsibility for speaking on its behalf, by taking every necessary step to ensure that, in every aspect of the sport, the welfare of the horse is paramount.[222]

Article 142 (1) of the General Regulations prohibit the abuse of equine athletes during an event or at any other time.[223] It defines abuse as **15–69**

---

[217] Fédération Équestre Internationale, 'FEI Code of Conduct for the Welfare of the Horse' (1 January 2013) <https://inside.fei.org/sites/default/files/Code_of_Conduct_Welfare_Horse_1Jan2013.pdf> accessed 21 May 2024.

[218] ibid.

[219] CAS 2017/A/5114 *Juliano, Owner of Horizon; Haymon, Owner of Don Principe; Lyle and Blythe v Fédération Équestre Internationale (FEI)* award of 19 March 2018 [68] <https://jurisprudence.tas-cas.org/Shared%20Documents/5114.pdf\> accessed 21 May 2024.

[220] ibid [69]. See Laura Donnellan, 'The Fédération Équestre Internationale Speaks for the Horse Who Has No Voice and the Court of Arbitration for Sport Listened: Equine Welfare and Anti-Doping in Equestrianism' (2019) 31 Denning Law Journal 41.

[221] FEI Statutes (n 212).

[222] CAS 2012/A/2807 *Khaled Abdullaziz Al Eid v Fédération Équestre Internationale*/CAS 2012/A/2808 *Abdullah Waleed Sharbatly v Fédération Équestre Internationale* award of 17 July 2012 (operative part of 11 June 2011) [6.24] <https://jurisprudence.tas-cas.org/Shared%20Documents/2807,%202808.pdf> accessed 21 May 2024.

[223] FEI General Regulations (24th edn, 1 January 2020, updates effective 1 January 2024) 28 <https://inside.fei.org/sites/default/files/FEI%20General%20

an action or omission which causes or is likely to cause pain or unnecessary discomfort to a Horse, including, but not limited to:

(i) To whip or beat a Horse excessively.
(ii) To subject a Horse to any kind of electric shock device.
(iii) To use spurs excessively or persistently.
(iv) To jab the Horse in the mouth with the bit or any other device.
(v) To compete using an exhausted, lame, or injured Horse.
(vi) To 'rap' a Horse.
(vii) To abnormally sensitise or desensitise any part of a Horse.
(viii) To leave a Horse without adequate food, drink, or exercise.
(ix) To use any device or equipment which causes excessive pain to the Horse upon knocking down an obstacle.[224]

15–70 Under Article 164.13, the sanctions for offences are listed.[225] In relation to equine abuse, the sanction for a low-end offence is a suspension period of three months and a fine of 1000 to 1500 Swiss Francs. A mid-range form of abuse will result in a suspension period of three months to two years and a fine of between 2000 and 3000 Swiss Francs.[226] A top-end offence carries a suspension of two to five years and a monetary penalty of 5000 to 10000 Swiss Francs. At the maximum end of equine abuse, the offending individual will receive a lifetime suspension and a fine of 15000 Swiss Francs. In deciding on the appropriate penalty, the FEI Tribunal is bound by the principle of proportionality, as highlighted in the decision in *Mr Ahmed Ali Mohammed Allay AL NAQBI*.[227] The FEI Tribunal cited with approval the CAS wherein a CAS Panel stated that 'there must be a reasonable balance between the kind of misconduct

---

Regulations%20-Effective%201January2024-%20clean_0.pdf > accessed 21 May 2024.

[224] ibid. One of the General Regulations (GR) general principles relates to the filing of a protest. Article 161.1 ibid 34 states: 'Protests may be lodged against any person or body involved in any capacity in an International Event or otherwise subject to the jurisdiction of the FEI including for failure to observe the Statutes, GRs or Sport Rules or violation of the common principles of behaviour, fairness, or accepted standards of sportsmanship, whether occurring during or in connection with an International Event or, in the case of Abuse of Horse, at any other time.' Article 161.4 limits the lodging of protests to specified persons including the FEI and officials; however, art 161.5 provides that '[p]rotests concerning an abuse of Horse may be lodged by any person or body': ibid 35.

[225] ibid 41.

[226] An example of a mid-range sanction can be seen in Decision of the FEI Tribunal Alleged Horse Abuse of horse Flogas Sunset dated 6 June 2017: *In the Matter* of *FEI v Thornton* <https://inside.fei.org/system/files/Final%20Tribunal%20Decision%20-%20FEI%20v.%20Kevin%20Thornton%20-%2006%20June%202017.pdf> accessed 21 May 2024. Thornton was found to have used the whip excessively and was suspended for four months and fined 5000 Swiss Francs and ordered to pay 5000 Swiss Francs towards the cost of the hearing.

[227] Decision of the FEI Tribunal dated 22 October 2021, Case 2019/HA14 <https://inside.fei.org/system/files/06.%2020211022_FINAL%20Decision_C21-0038%20AL-NAQBI%20%5B2019_HA14%5D.pdf> accessed 21 May 2024.

and the sanction'[228]; 'To be proportionate, the sanction must not exceed what is reasonably required in the search of a justifiable aim.'[229]

It is clear from Code and Statutes that the FEI operates in a custodian 15–71
type role, as a representative for the equine athlete, with the 'horse first' as one of its core values.[230] There is also the public interest consideration, as observed by the FEI Tribunal in *Ahlmann* when it stated that 'it is vital for the image and progress of the sport to ensure that the horse's welfare is strictly maintained'.[231] Implicit in horse welfare is the FEI's Equine Anti-Doping and Controlled Medication Regulations (EADCMRs), as will be discussed in the next section.

Equine Anti-Doping and Controlled Medication Regulations: Origins and Evolution

The FEI has a section on its website called 'Clean Sport', which contains 15–72
a number of documents in relation to its doping policy.[232] For the human participants, the World Anti-Doping Code (WADC) applies.[233] The Clean Sport for Horses includes the following subsections: the FEI Equine Anti-Doping and Controlled Medication Regulations (the Regulations),[234] Prohibited Substances (Equine Prohibited Substance List, EPSL),[235] Education,[236] How Testing Works,[237] and Testing Results and Positive Cases.[238] The EADCMRs are divided into two: the Equine Anti-Doping

[228] ibid para 7.15, citing from CAS 2005/C/976 *FIFA & WADA*, Advisory Opinion rendered by the Court of Arbitration for Sport (21 April 2006) [138] <https://www.wada-ama.org/sites/default/files/resources/files/CAS_Opinion_FIFA.pdf> accessed 21 May 2024.

[229] ibid para 7.15, citing from CAS 2005/C/976 *FIFA & WADA* [139].

[230] Fédération Équestre Internationale, 'FEI Values' <https://inside.fei.org/fei/about-fei/values> accessed 21 May 2024.

[231] Decision of the FEI Tribunal dated 22 October 2008, Positive Medication Case no 2008/20, *Christian Ahlmann*, para 4.8.3 <https://inside.fei.org/system/files/20%20-%20COSTER%20-%20Tribunal%20Decision%20-%2022%20October%202008.pdf> accessed 21 May 2024. Both samples A and B were tested, and both were positive for capsaicin.

[232] FEI, 'Welcome to FEI Clean Sport' <https://inside.fei.org/fei/cleansport> accessed 21 May 2024.

[233] FEI, 'Clean Sport for Humans' <https://inside.fei.org/fei/cleansport/humans> accessed 21 May 2024.

[234] FEI, 'Equine Anti-Doping and Controlled Medication Regulations' (3rd edn, effective 1 January 2021, updates effective 1 January 2023) <https://inside.fei.org/sites/default/files/EADCMRs-%201%20January%202021-Updates%20effective%201%20January%202023%20-%20Clean_0.pdf> accessed 21 May 2024.

[235] FEI, 'Clean Sport for Horses – FEI Prohibited Substances List' <https://inside.fei.org/fei/cleansport/ad-h/prohibited-list> accessed 21 May 2024. The EPSL is reviewed on an annual basis.

[236] FEI, 'Clean Sport for Horses – Education' <https://inside.fei.org/fei/cleansport/horses/education> accessed 21 May 2024.

[237] FEI, 'Clean Sport for Horses – How Testing Works' <https://inside.fei.org/fei/cleansport/horses/how-testing-works> accessed 21 May 2024.

[238] FEI, 'Test Results & FEI Tribunal' <https://inside.fei.org/fei/cleansport/horses/testing-results> accessed 21 May 2024.

(EAD) Rules and the Equine Controlled Medication (ECM) Rules.[239] The banned substances and controlled medication are collectively referred to as the Prohibited Substances.[240] Banned substances are defined 'as substances that are deemed by the FEI to have no legitimate use in the competition horse and/or have a high potential for abuse. They are not permitted for use in the competition horse at any time.'[241] Controlled medications are defined 'as substances that are deemed by the FEI to have therapeutic value and/or be commonly used in equine medicine. Controlled Medications have the potential to affect performance and/or be a welfare risk to the horse.'[242]

15–73 Article 7.4.1 of the EADCM Regulations provide that once an AAF has been detected, the horse is provisionally suspended pending a full hearing before the FEI Tribunal.[243] However, the only reference to the customary two-month equine suspension is under Article 8.3.3(c) of the EAD relating to Special Procedure for Minors.[244] In situations involving no fault or negligence, a provisional suspension may be lifted with regards to the 'Person Responsible' (PR). However, 'Article 7.4.4(ii) does not apply to an application to lift a Provisional Suspension imposed on a Horse.'[245] This is qualified by Article 7.4.4(iii), which provides that the two-month provisional suspension is not absolute, and it may be lifted if

> exceptional circumstances exist that make it clearly unfair, in all of the circumstances of the case, to impose a Provisional Suspension prior to final hearing of the FEI Tribunal. This ground is to be construed narrowly, and applied only in truly exceptional circumstances. For example, the fact that the Provisional Suspension would prevent the Person or Horse competing in a particular Competition or Event shall not qualify as exceptional circumstances for these purposes.[246]

15–74 A number of concerns emerged from the CAS arbitral award in *Blythe and Lyle*, namely the confusion surrounding the interpretation of the EADCMRs and the lack of a codified rule that sets out the two-month provisional equine suspension.[247] The CAS Panel upheld the FEI's policy of provisionally suspending horses for two months on grounds

---

239 EADCM Regulations (n 234).

240 FEI, 'Clean Sport for Horses – FEI Prohibited Substances List' <https://inside.fei.org/fei/cleansport/ad-h/prohibited-list> accessed 21 May 2024.

241 ibid.

242 ibid.

243 EADCM Regulations (n 234) 61. Article 7.4.1 refers to this as the 'Person Responsible's Horse'. Under the Rules of Racing (n 76) the term used is 'Responsible Person' (RP).

244 ibid 25.

245 ibid 61.

246 ibid 62–63.

247 CAS 2017/A/5114 (n 219). It rejected the argument that the publicity of the rules was insufficient. Had there been a published rule, then its application would still not have adjusted their behaviour in the lead-up to the AAF and they were at all material times aware of their duty to ensure that the horses did not ingest a prohibited substance. The appellants were informed of the two-month equine

of animal welfare and ensuring a level playing field. However, the CAS Panel agreed with the appellants as to the lack of clarity surrounding the provisional suspension.[248]

Further inconsistencies are evidenced by the fact the fact that the EADCMRs are 'modelled' after the 2021 WADC (the anti-doping code for human athletes) as expressly stated in the introduction to the 2023 edition of the Regulations.[249] This approach has been criticised as Merritt contends that the horse should be considered an equine athlete and not an inanimate object that can be viewed in the same way as 'equipment' used in human sports.[250] **15–75**

In reference to controlled medication substances, it is a violation of the EADCMRs if the substance is present at the time of an event in absence of a valid veterinary form (Article 2.1 of the ECM Rules).[251] It should not be given to the horse close to or during an event 'unless the appropriate FEI guidelines for medication authorisation have been followed'.[252] The FEI proffers that the ECM Rules are based on a distinctive and core characteristics of the human/horse partnership that equestrianism imbues, namely that the horse is unable to speak, and it is the role of the FEI to protect the horse: **15–76**

> It is therefore the FEI's responsibility to speak on its behalf, and to ensure that, at every stage of the governance, regulation, administration and practice of the sport, the welfare of the Horse is paramount ... all treatments must be given in the best health and welfare interests of the Horse, and not for any other reasons.[253]

Under the ECM Rules, a controlled medication may be given to a horse, but it must be 'fully justifiable based on the medical condition of the **15–77**

suspension once the AAF was communicated to them; thus it 'provided a target against which they could direct their forensic fire': [71].

248 The two-month provisional suspension for equine athletes is not defined in the EADCM Regulations. There is no information on the FEI website. The CAS Panel in CAS 2017/A/5114 (n 219) [71] referred to a 2012 resolution providing for the two-month equine suspension, which was evidenced by the minutes of a FEI Executive Board meeting dated 5–6 May 2012.

249 EADCM Regulations (n 234) 3.

250 Jonathan Glen Merritt, '"Don't Look a Gift Horse in the Mouth": Regulating for Integrity, What Equestrianism Can Learn from Thoroughbred Racing' (2017) 16 International Sports Law Journal 198, 200.

251 EADCM Regulations (n 234) 49.

252 ibid. 48. The FEI advocates a margin of safety in relation to the detection time of controlled substances and acknowledges that it is up to the relevant veterinary surgeon as each horse is different; however, it stated in the case of a show jumper from Saudi Arabia that the safety margin should be multiplied by two: see Decision of the FEI Tribunal dated 24 March 2017, Positive Controlled Medication Case No 2016/CM04 para 5.2(c) <https://inside.fei.org/system/files/2016-CM04%20-%20AD%20ARGOS%20-%20Final%20Tribunal%20Decision%20-%2024%20March%202017.pdf> accessed 21 May 2024.

253 EADCM Regulations (n 234) 48.

horse'.[254] If a horse is unable to compete due to injury or disease, the horse must be provided with appropriate veterinary treatment and rest (or recovery period).[255] While there is some flexibility with regard to controlled medication (subject to certain conditions), a prohibited substance is a violation of the EAD Rules.

15–78 The burden of proof that an AAF has occurred under the EAD Rules is placed on the FEI under Article 3.1.[256] However, in certain situations where the EAD Rules reverse the burden and place it upon the PR and/or a member of their support personnel 'to rebut a presumption or establish specified facts or circumstances, the standard of proof shall be by a balance of probability, except where a different standard of proof is specifically identified'.[257]

15–79 The standard of proof placed on the FEI is to demonstrate to the comfortable satisfaction of the Hearing Panel, taking into account the seriousness of the alleged doping infraction.[258] In line with the WADC, the standard of proof in all cases is greater than a mere balance of probability, but less than proof beyond a reasonable doubt.[259] In relation to the ECM Rules, Article 3.1 states that the burden of proof is placed on the FEI; however, the standard is that of the balance of probabilities 'except where a different standard of proof is specifically identified'.[260]

Strict Liability

15–80 A violation of the EADCMRs is a strict liability offence, as per Article 2.1.1 of the EAD Rules.[261] There is an irrebuttable presumption that provides that the PR, which includes the rider and support personnel in certain circumstances, is responsible for an AAF under Articles 2.2–2.8.[262] It is not necessary to demonstrate intent, fault, negligence, or a knowing use of a prohibited substance. The inclusion of support personnel was a result of submissions and feedback from the various national federations in the lead-up to the 2010 Regulations. The use or attempted use of a banned substance or a banned method is provided for under Article 2.2. Regarding the use of a banned substance, the PR has a personal duty along with support personnel to ensure than no prohibited substance enters the horse's body or that any banned method is used.

15–81 By applying a strict liability standard, the PR and/or their support personnel are responsible for any unauthorised substance that the

---

[254] ibid.
[255] ibid.
[256] ibid 7.
[257] ibid.
[258] ibid.
[259] ibid 50.
[260] ibid.
[261] ibid 4.
[262] ibid.

horse ingests. Parallels can be drawn with the English case from the High Court of Justice Chancery Division, *Gasser v Stinson*.[263] Gasser was a Swiss athlete who tested positive for a banned substance. She challenged, *inter alia*, the validity of the testing methods and the strict liability standard. Gasser contended that a malicious prankster could interfere with an athlete's food and the athlete could innocently ingest a banned substance. While sympathetic to her plight, Scott J upheld the strict liability standard on the grounds that to hold otherwise would open the floodgates and render ineffective the drug testing policies of sporting bodies.

Over time WADA has relaxed the strict liability standard in relation to **15–82** human athletes. In relation to equine athletes, however, the FEI and the CAS have upheld the strict liability standard in recognition of animal-welfare concerns and custodial role of the PRs. The CAS Panel reiterated the FEI's application of strict liability in *Ahlmann* as it stated

> that the FEI rules put in place a system according to which the mere presence of a prohibited substance in the horse's body constitutes a rule violation regardless of its concentration, its performance-enhancing effects or its origin, and that the PR is responsible for any such prohibited substance found to be present in the horse's bodily samples.[264]

At the FEI Tribunal hearing, Ahlmann could not explain the presence **15–83** of the prohibited substance capsaicin in Coster, his horse.[265] However, under the principle of strict liability, intent is irrelevant. The mere presence of a prohibited substance is all that is required. Ahlmann argued that the FEI strict liability standard was a breach of Article 7 of the Swiss Cartel Law; the CAS Panel rejected this contention and pointed to the lack of evidence or market analysis to demonstrate that the FEI was abusing its dominant position.[266] The CAS Panel found Ahlmann's argument vague and unsupported by economic evidence. The CAS reiterated the compatibility of strict liability with Swiss law:

> the FEI disciplinary system is indeed compatible with the principles and statutes of Swiss law. Importantly, the Swiss Federal Court has recently ruled that this disciplinary system, based on strict liability, is fully justified in equestrian sport by prevailing public interest, as the fight against doping tends to safeguard parity among competitors and fairness of competitions, protect the animals' health, maintain breeding

---

263 *Gasser v Stinson & Anor* [1988] 6 WLUK 333. See ch 9 para 9–15—9–16.

264 CAS 2008/A/1700 *Deutsche Reiterliche Vereinigung eV v FEI & Ahlmann*; and CAS 2008/A/1710 *Ahlmann v FEI* award of 30 April 2009 (operative part communicated on 2 April 2009) [84] <https://arbitrationlaw.com/sites/default/files/free_pdfs/CAS%202008-A 1700%20DRV%20v%20FEI%20%26%20CA%20%26%20CAS%20 2008-A-1710%20CA%20v%20FEI%20Award.pdf> accessed 21 May 2024. For a detailed discussion on the FEI decision, the German Equestrian Federation and the appeal to the CAS, see Donnellan (n 220) 49–51.

265 Decision of the FEI Tribunal dated 22 October 2008 (n 231).

266 CAS 2008/A/1700 (n 264) [86].

> quality, combat the use of dangerous substances, preserve the integrity of the sport, and ensure that a good example is set for young people. These objectives are unanimously recognised by sports organisations and government institutions. (ATF 134 III 193, p. 203, para. 4.6.3.2.2; in the same sense, see CAS 2008/A/1569 Kürten v/FEI paras. 7.6–7.7; CAS 2008/A/1654 B. Alves v/FEI, paras. 5.18–5.23).[267]

15–84 The CAS Panel dismissed Ahlmann's argument that the List of Prohibited Substances was 'unclear, misleading and has not been adapted to scientific and technical progresses'.[268] The fact that the FEI Tribunal erred in finding that capsaicin was a controlled medication and not a prohibited substance is evidence that the regulations were confusing and needed to be clarified. The CAS Panel did not engage in any detailed discussion as to the lack of coherency in the Regulations. Although, following the *Ahlmann* case, the FEI endeavoured to introduce a more cohesive set of anti-doping regulations.[269]

15–85 Another case that arose from the Beijing Olympics is that of *Hansen v Fédération Equestre Internationale (FEI)*.[270] Hansen was part of a Norwegian team that won bronze in the Team jumping event at the 2008 Olympics. Hansen was disqualified from the team and the individual event and received an additional suspension after his horse, Camiro, tested positive for the prohibited substance capsaicin.[271] Hansen was disqualified for 4.5 months (135 days) and fined 3,000 Swiss Francs.[272] The rider challenged the FEI decision and appealed it to the CAS, where he requested the annulment of the FEI Tribunal Decision on several grounds. The applicant argued that at the FEI Tribunal hearing he was denied 'a fair and transparent hearing'.[273] However, this was rejected by the CAS Panel on the grounds that the case was being heard *de novo* and thus 'any procedural defects which occurred in the internal proceedings of a federation are cured by arbitration proceedings before CAS'.[274] Hansen further argued that capsaicin was not expressly stated as a prohibited substance.[275] The FEI admitted that it was not expressly stated in the material at the time; however, the error would be corrected in the near future. Medical evidence provided that capsaicin fell within the definition of a prohibited substance.

---

[267] ibid [85].
[268] ibid.
[269] See Donnellan (n 220) 51–53.
[270] CAS 2009/A/1768 *Hansen v Fédération Équestre Internationale (FEI)* award of 4 December 2009 <https://jurisprudence.tas-cas.org/Shared%20Documents/1768.pdf> accessed 21 May 2024.
[271] FEI Tribunal Decision dated 22 December 2008, Positive Medication Case no 2008/23 <https://inside.fei.org/system/files/23%20-%20CAMIRO%20-%20Tribunal%20Final%20Decision%20-%2022%20dec%2008.pdf> accessed 31 July 2024.
[272] ibid para 91. He was also ordered to pay 8000 Swiss Francs towards costs.
[273] CAS 2009/A/1768 (n 270) [11.1].
[274] ibid.
[275] ibid [12.1].

15–86 The CAS Panel reiterated the principle of strict liability and its importance in maintaining the element of fairness in competition.[276] The issue for the CAS Panel was whether capsaicin had been in Camiro's system before being detected in his urine or whether it had found its way into the urine sample during or after the process of the collection of the sample.[277] There was no evidence to suggest that the sample had been tampered.[278] Both the Sample A and Sample B were found to have capsaicin. The CAS Panel upheld the decision of the FEI Tribunal.

15–87 More recently, the CAS upheld the FEI's application of the principle of strict liability to equine doping cases. In *Sheik Hazza Bin Zayed Al Nahyan v FEI*, counsel for the appellant proposed that

> the EAD Rules should be interpreted in a manner which allowed a rider to rebut a presumption of strict liability arising from a positive test on a horse and be held not to have committed a violation, if he or she could show that he or she had no knowledge or means of knowing of or controlling the conduct that brought about the violation.[279]

15–88 The appellant challenged the strict liability on the grounds that it was 'an affront to morality and public policy'.[280] He accepted that the standard was appropriate for human athletes who, in most situations, have autonomy over their bodies and make conscious decisions as to what they ingest.[281] Riders, he reasoned, 'necessarily have less control over what goes into the horses body'.[282] The appellant submitted that strict liability was disproportionate, unjustified and constituted a breach of his fundamental rights under Swiss law and EU law, including competition law.[283] The CAS Panel referred to a sporting body's 'margin of appreciation in making rules to regulate the conduct of its members'.[284] The sporting body, generally, is in the best position to decide the

---

276 The CAS referred to the earlier decisions of *CAS 94/129 USA Shooting v UIT* [14]–[16] and *CAS 95/41 C v FINA* [137].

277 Hansen argued that Camiro could have ingested the substance by biting wood in a stable impregnated with it, or breathing in airborne particles, or eating feed contaminated with it (all without knowledge of the rider). The Tribunal dismissed this argument as there were five riders whose horses were found to have ingested capsaicin and three confirmed they had used Equi-Block, which contains capsaicin. It was highly improbable that the other two horses ingested it through contamination.

278 There was conflicting evidence whether the tester had worn gloves when taking the urine sample. A blood test was also taken and tested. The blood test showed traces of capsaicin.

279 CAS 2014/A/3591 award of 8 June 2015 [49] <https://inside.fei.org/system/files/Final%20CAS%20Decision%20-%20Sheik%20Hazza%20Al%20Nayan%20vs%20FEI%20-%208%20June%202015_0.pdf> accessed 21 May 2024.

280 ibid [69].

281 ibid.

282 ibid [71].

283 ibid [144].

284 ibid [149].

applicable rules. The CAS Panel found that the strict liability standard 'is justified in the public interest in the fight against doping in sport'.[285]

15–89 It is clear from the jurisprudence of the CAS in equine doping cases that the use of the strict liability is proportionate, can be justified in the public interest, does not breach fundamental rights and is an appropriate standard to ensure that the welfare of the equine athlete is protected. There is a moral and legal duty on the FEI to safeguard its core values. In short, it is within the preserve of the FEI to determine its own rules and regulations. However, these rules and regulations need to clear, unambiguous and not be left open to varying interpretations.

Contaminated Feed

15–90 The FEI and the CAS have consistently upheld the strict liability standard on the grounds of fairness of competition and animal welfare. PRs, on the other hand, have challenged it on the grounds of proportionality and an infringement of fundamental rights. The strict liability approach of the FEI has been criticised on the grounds that 'there is a fine line … between the need to protect the horse and cases where the strict liability is going too far as to be no longer concerned with clean sports'.[286] However, the line is even more pronounced when cognisance is given to the fact that the horse's food could be contaminated or another horse's presence in the stable results in the horse 'picking up' up traces of contaminated medication.[287]

15–91 A study carried out by Swiss-based researchers found that, in samples taken from 28 types of horse feed, 18 tested positive for prohibited and controlled substances.[288] In situations of contamination, the PR must prove, on the balance of probabilities, that the inadvertently ingested substance was the result of contamination and, if this can be proved, the period of ineligibility may be eliminated or reduced under 10.6.1.2 of the EAD Rules[289] and Article 10.6.1.2 of the ECM Rules.[290]

---

285 ibid [158].

286 Ester Herlin-Karnell, 'EU Sports Law and the Equestrian World: A Galloping Area of Increasing Importance' (2013) 13 International Sports Law Journal 168, 174.

287 ibid.

288 The findings were published online in German, with the abstract in English (C Herholz and others, 'Dopingrelevante Substanzen in Futtermitteln für Pferde' (2017) 159(4) Schweiz Arch Tierheilkd 231. The findings were translated into English by Laura Donnellan and a summary of the study can be found at Laura Donnellan, 'Equestrianism: Swiss Researchers Find 64% of Horse Feed Contains Prohibited or Controlled Substances!' (*SportsandTaxtion*, 29 August 2017) <https://sportslawandtaxation.com/news/757-equestrianism-swiss-researchers-find-64-of-horse-feed-contains-prohibited-or-controlled-substances> accessed 21 May 2024.

289 EADCM Regulations (n 234) 30.

290 ibid 74. In the Decision of the FEI Tribunal dated 20 February 2014 Positive Controlled Medication Case no 2013/FT02 Honky Tonk Whiz, the PR could not prove that the positive test for controlled medication was the result of

The Swiss-based research was undertaken in response to three high-profile failed drug tests in 2015, involving three Swiss jumping riders whose horses tested positive for banned and controlled substances. It was contended that the AAFs could have been the result of contamination of the Swissfritz feed. Two of the riders, Guerdat and Bichsel, were subsequently cleared when it was found that the failed tests were attributed to poppy seed contamination of their horses' food. At an event in France in May 2015, Guerdat's mount, Nino des Buisonnets, tested positive for the banned substances of codeine and oripavine, and morphine, a controlled substance. At the same event, Guerdat had ridden Nasa, whose sample yielded an AAF for codeine and morphine. Nasa's sample also contained trace amounts of oripavine; however, the amount found was not of the requisite level for a doping infraction to have been committed. Both riders had their suspensions lifted as the FEI Tribunal was satisfied that the positive tests were the result of contaminated horse feed.[291] However, the two-month suspension placed on the horses was upheld on the grounds of animal welfare. Both riders appealed the two-month suspension of their horses; however, the FEI Tribunal dismissed the appeals. The riders also had the results achieved at the events quashed, including the forfeiture of medals, points, and prizes. In the third case, involving a horse called Charivari, the two-month equine suspension was upheld, but the rider's period of ineligibility was eliminated due to no fault or negligence.[292] According to the laboratory analysis, it was possible that morphine was present due to the ingestion of poppy seeds. **15–92**

The Swiss researchers interestingly found that poppy seeds harvested using machinery had a higher concentration of morphine than poppy seeds processed by hand.[293] The study concluded that, even with the most careful and up-to-date methods of processing, horse feed can be easily contaminated by prohibited and controlled substances. In all the samples analysed, the amount was not of a level that would adversely affect a horse's health. **15–93**

---

contamination, <https://inside.fei.org/system/files/Case_2013_FT02_HONKY_TONK_WHIZ_Final_Tribunal_Decision_20_February_2014.pdf> accessed 21 May 2024.

[291] Decision of the FEI Tribunal dated 18 September 2015, Case 1 Positive Anti-Doping Case no 2015/BS02 (Nasa) and Case 2 Positive Anti-Doping Case no 2015/BS03 (Nino des Buisonnets), <https://inside.fei.org/system/files/Case%202015-BS02%20-%20NASA%20-%202015-BS03%20-%20NINO%20DES%20BUISSONNETS%20-%20Final%20Tribunal%20Decision%20-%2018%20September%202015.pdf> accessed 21 May 2024.

[292] Decision of the FEI Tribunal dated 25 September 2015, Positive Anti-Doping Case no 2015/BS04 (Charivari KG) <https://inside.fei.org/system/files/2015-BS04%20-%20CHARIVARI%20KG%20-%20FEI%20Tribunal%20Decision%20-%2025%20September%202015.pdf> accessed 21 May 2024.

[293] Herholz and others (n 288) 233–34.

FEI Tribunal and Court of Arbitration for Sport Decisions: Irish Competitors

15–94 The 2004 Olympics in Athens was a turning point for the FEI and anti-doping. Four equine athletes tested positive for banned substances, including Cian O'Connor's horse, Waterford Crystal.[294] The FEI's Judicial Committee imposed a three-month ban and disqualification from the 2004 Olympics.[295] O'Connor did not appeal the decision to the CAS.

15–95 At the Beijing Olympics in 2008, four horses tested positive for capsaicin, including Lantinus and Coster (as discussed above), a component of topical ointments for horses and used in 'Deep Heat', which humans use for the treatment of aches and pains.[296] Irish rider Denis Lynch contended that he had used Equi-Block, similar to Deep Heat, for over a year on his horse, Lantinus. Lynch revealed that he used the product to warm up the back muscles to 'loosen up' Lantinus – it was legal, did not have any therapeutic effect, and was widely sold at events and regularly used by riders.[297] Although Lantinus had been tested numerous times, he never tested positive until the 2008 Games. Lynch was informed on 21 August 2008 that a prohibited substance had been detected. He was told of the possible rule violation and was provisionally suspended for three months.[298] On foot of the notification, Lynch requested a preliminary hearing which took place on 21 August. As the PR, Lynch was informed that the provisional suspension would remain until the final decision of the FEI Tribunal, which was 'subject to review depending on the explanations and evidence that might be submitted by the PR'.[299] On 8 September 2008, the FEI Tribunal issued an interim decision that the suspension would remain in force until its final decision.[300] Before the FEI Tribunal had made its final decision, Lynch appealed the

[294] Waterford Crystal tested positive for fluphenazine and zuclopenthixol, human medicines for the treatment of schizophrenia.

[295] The Judicial Committee published its full decision on 23 May 2005; however, it is no longer available on the FEI website. The decision was summarised by Muriel Faienza, 'FEI Legal Update on the Olympic Case of Waterford Crystal and Cian O'Connor' (*US Equestrian*, 26 May 2005) <https://www.usef.org/media/press-releases/574_fei-legal-update-on-the-olympic-case-of-waterford-crystal-and-cian-oconnor> accessed 21 May 2024. The Judicial Committee is now known as the FEI Tribunal: see art 38 of the FEI Statutes (n 212); and the Internal Regulations of the FEI Tribunal (3rd edn, 2 March 2018) <https://inside.fei.org/sites/default/files/New%20Internal%20Regulations%20of%20the%20FEI%20Tribunal-%20Final%20-%202%20March%202018%20-%20Gender%20Neutral%20-%20clean.pdf> accessed 21 May 2024.

[296] John T Wendt, 'The Crisis of Doping in Equestrian Sport' (2009) 27(3) Entertainment and Sports Lawyer 10. For a detailed discussion on the history of doping and anti-doping in equestrian sports, see Donnellan (n 220).

[297] CAS 2008/A/1655 *Denis Lynch v Fédération Équestre Internationale* award of 6 March 2009 [2.7] <https://inside.fei.org/system/files/LANTINUS%20-%20Final%20CAS%20decision%20dated%206%20March%202009.pdf> accessed 21 May 2024.

[298] Decision of the FEI Tribunal dated 17 October 2008, para 6 <https://inside.fei.org/system/files/22%20-%20LANTINUS%203%20-%20Tribunal%20Final%20Decision%20-%2017%20October%2008_0.pdf> accessed 21 May 2024.

[299] ibid para 9.

[300] ibid para 29.

interim decision to the CAS; however, jurisdiction to hear the appeal was denied.[301] On 17 October 2008, the FEI Tribunal disqualified Lynch from the event and ordered that points, prizes, and medals be forfeited.[302] The FEI Tribunal acknowledged that disqualification was an appropriate sanction even in cases where there was no fault on the part of the rider.[303] In deciding on the appropriate sanction, the FEI Tribunal examined a number of factors, including equine welfare, the behaviour of experienced riders at the top of their profession like Lynch,[304] the hardship suffered by Lynch being unable to compete and the duty of care placed on a PR not to administer a prohibited or controlled substance to a horse.[305] Lynch's three-month suspension was upheld, dating back to 21 August 2008, and he was ordered to pay a fine and costs. In its decision, the FEI Tribunal recognised that there are situations where there is no fault on the part of the PR, yet liability will still be imposed. The principle of strict liability is a cornerstone of equine anti-doping cases, as the case of *Ahlmann* discussed above demonstrates.[306]

Cian O'Conner was before the CAS in 2016 following an incident at the European Championships in Aachen, Germany, on 21 August 2015. As O'Connor approached the 11th fence at the show-jumping Olympic qualifier, a steward ran across the field in front of O'Connor and his mount Good Luck.[307] Good Luck hit the fence and incurred a four-point penalty, which put the Irish Show Jumping Team out of contention of a place at the Rio Olympics. The team finished seventh, with Spain securing the sixth and final place at the 2016 Olympics. The FEI Ground Jury dismissed the protest lodged by O'Connor and the Irish Chef d'Équipe and, at a subsequent FEI Appeal Committee, the decision of the FEI Ground Jury was upheld. HSI and O'Connor filed an appeal against the Appeal Committee to the CAS.[308] The CAS Panel dismissed the appeal as the issue concerned a field of play decision. The **15–96**

---

301 CAS 2008/A/1655 (n 297).

302 Decision of the FEI Tribunal dated 17 October 2008 (n 298) paras 73 and 74.

303 ibid para 73.

304 See also CAS 2019/A/6186 *Mohamed Ahmed Al Owais v Fédération Équestre Internationale* award of 12 July 2019 <https://inside.fei.org/system/files/CAS%20Award%202019A6186%20-%20M.%20Al%20Owais%20v.%20FEI%20-%202018-BS09%20TINA%20-%2012%2007%202019.pdf> accessed 21 May 2024. The CAS Panel referred to the PR as an experienced professional who was engaged in an equine-related family business: [1].

305 CAS 2008/A/1655 (n 297) [75]–[85].

306 CAS 2008/A/1700 (n 264). For a detailed discussion of the case, see Mary Zoeller, 'Gray Area: Court of Arbitration for Sport Says Neigh to Reconsidering Strict Liability for Equestrian Sport' (2016) 23(2) Jeffrey S Moorad Sports Law Journal 457.

307 The steward jumped into a nearby flower bed to get out of the way: see John Tynan, '"No regrets" as CAS Rejects Cian O'Connor's Aachen Appeal' *Irish Examiner* (Cork, 5 August 2016) <https://www.irishexaminer.com/sport/arid-20374482.html> accessed 21 May 2024.

308 CAS 2015/A/4208 *Horse Sport Ireland (HSI) & Cian O'Connor v Fédération Équestre Internationale* award of 15 July 2016 (operative part of 4 January 2016) <https://jurisprudence.tas-cas.org/Shared%20Documents/4208.pdf> accessed 21 May 2024.

CAS Panel stated that 'this principle of respecting field of play decisions is one of the defining characteristics of the *lex sportiva*, as a sport specific rule that guides much of sports competition at a fundamental level'.[309] The Ground Jury and Appeal Committee's decisions were akin to the 'referee's bona fide exercise of judgment or discretion' which 'is beyond challenge other than in so far as provided by the rules of the game themselves'.[310] The field of play doctrine is based on:

> Strong sporting-based principles … the need for finality and to ensure the authority of the referee and match officials, the arbitrators' lack of technical expertise, the inevitable element of subjectivity, the need to avoid constant interruption of competitions, the opening of floodgates and the difficulties of rewriting records and results after the fact. Moreover, it is widely recognised that the respective decisions are best left to field officials as they are specifically trained to officiate the particular sport and are best placed, being on-site, to settle any question relating to it.[311]

15–97 While the CAS held the appeal to be inadmissible, it was impliedly upholding the decision of the FEI Appeal Committee.

Greyhound Racing

15–98 Greyhound racing in Ireland is regulated by Greyhound Racing Ireland (GRI) or Rásaíocht Con Éireann, its name in Irish. It is a commercial semi-state body and up until 30 September 2020 it was known as the Irish Greyhound Board/Bord na gCon. Section 8(1) of the Greyhound Racing Act 2019 provided for the name change. The Irish Greyhound Board was established under the Greyhound Industry Act 1958. The principal act has been amended over the years and is now referred to as the Greyhound Acts 1958 to 2019. Under the Acts, GRI has wide-ranging powers, including the licensing of tracks, the issuing of permits to officials, bookmakers, and trainers. GRI ensures that the rules pertaining to the industry are enforced. There are 15 licensed tracks in the Republic, nine of which are owned by GRI. The remaining tracks are run by private enterprises under licence from GRI.[312]

15–99 There are over 100 pieces of legislation pertaining to the greyhound Industry in Ireland. [313] The vast majority are statutory instruments. For example, there are statutory instruments on admission charges, race card charges, greyhound trainers, artificial insemination of greyhounds, betting charges and levies, totalisation (jackpots) and

---

[309] ibid [48].
[310] ibid [2].
[311] ibid.
[312] Greyhound Racing Ireland, 'About GRI' <https://www.grireland.ie/About-GRI/about-gri/> accessed 21 May 2024.
[313] The Law Reform Revised Acts lists the relevant Acts and Statutory Instruments from 1958 to October 2022 <https://revisedacts.lawreform.ie/eli/1958/act/12/front/revised/en/html> accessed 21 May 2024.

various commencement-order regulations.[314] There are six Acts: the 1958 Act; the 1993 amendment Act; the Horses and Greyhound (Betting, Charges and Levies) Act 1999, ss 8–13, the Horse and Greyhound Racing Act 2001, ss 14, 15, 16 and 17 (in so far as they relate to the Board); Horse Racing Ireland Act 2016, s 15; and Greyhound Racing Act 2019, other than Parts 10 and 11.

The above Acts are augmented by two welfare statutes, the Welfare of Greyhounds Act 2011 and the Animal Health and Welfare Act 2013. The 2011 Act provides for the protection of greyhounds, the regulation of the operation of greyhound breeding establishments and the establishment of a greyhound breeder register. There is also a Code of Practice for the Care and Welfare of Greyhounds as required by s 6 of the 2011 Act. The Code was published in November 2021, and it states, 'The principal theme of this Code is that the welfare and care of a greyhound must at all times take precedence over the demands of the stakeholders and all those involved in the greyhound industry.'[315] The Code sets out minimum welfare requirements and endorses the 'five freedoms' that underpin the 2013 Act. The 'five freedoms' are: **15–100**

1. Freedom from Hunger and Thirst – by ready access to fresh water and a diet to maintain full health and vigour.
2. Freedom from Discomfort – by providing an appropriate environment including shelter and a comfortable resting area.
3. Freedom from Pain, Injury or Disease – by prevention or rapid diagnosis and treatment.
4. Freedom to Express Normal Behaviour – by providing sufficient space, proper facilities, and company of the animal's own kind.
5. Freedom from Fear and Distress – by ensuring conditions and treatment which avoid mental suffering.[316]

Like with horseracing and equestrian sports, greyhound racing has anti- **15–101**
doping provisions. The Greyhound Industry (Racing) (Amendment) (No 2) Regulations 2015 (which amended the Greyhound Industry (Racing) Regulations 2007) provides that a greyhound which has an AAF is banned from competing in any further race unless there is a second sample assessed which comes back negative for a prohibited substance.[317] There have been high-profile cases involving prohibited substances: for example, Clonbrien Hero, who tested positive for traces of cocaine on three occasions from June to July 2017.[318] In the 2017 Kerry AgriBusiness Irish St Leger Final in Limerick on 4 November, Clonbrien

[314] ibid.
[315] Greyhound Racing Ireland, 'Code of Practice for the Care and Welfare of Greyhounds' November 2021, 2 <https://www.grireland.ie/globalassets/rescource-centre/rcegricodeofpracticenovember2021.pdf> accessed 21 May 2024.
[316] ibid.
[317] Section (3C)(a).
[318] Eoin English, 'Trainer whose Greyhound Failed Drug Test "No Case to Answer"' *Irish Examiner* (Cork, 11 February 2020) <https://www.irishexaminer.com/news/arid-30981104.html> accessed 21 May 2024.

Hero won €25,000 in prize money.[319] The matter was not concluded until the Control Committee published its decision in February 2020.[320] In reference to the report from a recognised scientific expert, Professor Tobin, it found that traces of cocaine were of a 'sufficiently low concentration that they were, by definition, pharmacologically and forensically insignificant and completely consistent with innocent and unavoidable environmental origins'.[321]

15–102 A decision of the Control Appeal Committee was subject to judicial review in the case of *McKenna v The Control Appeal Committee of the Irish Greyhound Board (Bord na gCon)*.[322] On 24 February 2017, the Control Committee imposed a €1,000 fine and ordered the forfeiture of certain prize money following the finding of an AAF in samples taken from three of the owner's dogs in September 2015.[323] The dogs tested positive for hydrochlorothiazide, a prohibited substance.[324] McKenna accepted that he had continued to feed his dogs Category 2 meat, defined as meat obtained from fallen animals; however, he did not accept that he had been warned by the Control Committee in 2015 to discontinue feeding his dogs such foodstuffs.[325] In the words of the Control Appeal Committee, McKenna had engaged in a 'reckless feeding regime' and

---

[319] Cormac Byrne, 'Champion Greyhound that Tested Positive for Cocaine Claims €25k St Leger in Limerick' *Irish Independent* (Dublin, 6 November 2017) <https://www.independent.ie/sport/other-sports/champion-greyhound-that-tested-positive-for-cocaine-claims-25k-st-leger-in-limerick/36294129.html> accessed 21 May 2024.

[320] The Control Committee and Control Appeal Committee were created under SI no 301/2007 – Greyhound Industry (Control Committee and Control Appeal Committee) Regulations 2007. Section 6(1) outlines the functions of the Control Committee including '(i) investigate and make a decision on any matter notified, reported or otherwise in anyway brought to the attention of the Control Committee by the stewards of a meeting, a control steward, a stipendiary steward or an authorised officer of the Board under the racing regulations'. Section 10 provides for the establishment of the Control Appeal Committee; s 11 details its membership while s 12 explains its functions. It hears appeals from decisions of the Control Committee. It can impose several sanctions, including fines up to €7,500. The 2007 Regulations were amended by SI no 263/2021 – Greyhound Industry (Control Committee and Control Appeal Committee) (Provisional Extension of Term of Office) Regulations, 2021.

[321] Greyhound Racing Ireland, 'Control Committee Report – February 2020' 2 <https://www.grireland.ie/globalassets/rescource-centre/reports/control/february—-2020.pdf> accessed 21 May 2024.

[322] [2018] IEHC 618.

[323] The prize money amounted to €36,500: see Ann O'Loughlin, 'Dog Owner Challenges Irish Greyhound Board for Withholding Race Prize Money Over Doping Allegation' *Irish Examiner* (Cork, 13 November 2017) <https://www.irishexaminer.com/news/arid-30813933.html> accessed 21 May 2024.

[324] The GRI's website includes links to its anti-doping programme: see <https://www.grireland.ie/Resource/anti-doping-and-medication-control/press-media/> accessed 21 May 2024.

[325] (n 322) [13]. See Greyhound Racing Ireland, 'Guidance on Meat Products', <https://www.grireland.ie/talking-dogs/guidance-on-meat-products/> accessed 21 May 2024. There is a danger that such products may contain prohibited substances as the GRI explains that such animal by-products 'may therefore contain residues

had to accept the consequences – hydrochlorothiazide was a prohibited substance within the meaning of the Greyhound Industry (Control Committee and Control Appeal Committee) Regulations 2007. The testing, maintenance and control of the samples in the UK-based laboratory were in compliance with the regulations, and as 'there were no threshold levels for Hydrochlorothiazide any finding of the same was in breach of the regulations'.[326] Thus, the decision of the Control Committee was upheld by the Control Appeal Committee.

McKenna, in seeking an order of certiorari, requested the quashing of the 'impugned' decision in the High Court.[327] The applicant contended that he was denied the right to fair procedures. He contended that the respondents 'failed to determine the appeal in accordance with law, and/or acted contrary to fair procedure and/or natural justice, and/or unreasonably, and/or irrationally'.[328] The applicant proffered 'that the decision was based on serious errors of fact and breached the principles of legitimate expectation and proportionality and was objectively unjustified discrimination against him'.[329] O'Regan J was satisfied that McKenna had not discharged the burden necessary to secure an order of certiorari and thus refused the request to quash the Control Appeal Committee's decision.[330] **15–103**

Conclusion

The use of animals in sport is a divisive topic. Fox hunting remains legal in Ireland; however, whether future governments will decide to ban it remains uncertain. The attempt to impose a legislative ban on it under the Animal Health and Welfare Bill 2012 proved to be fruitless. Currently, there is no tangible pressure being placed on the government to consider alternatives to hunting with hounds. **15–104**

Media reports of equine deaths at race events, especially high-profile events such as Ascot and the Grand National at Aintree, regularly bring to the fore the issue of thoroughbred racehorse welfare. The deaths of equine athletes are a tragic consequence of an inherently dangerous sport. Animal-rights organisations, including Animal Aid, have **15–105**

of certain drugs used for animal treatment which could affect the performance of racing greyhounds or may return adverse analytical findings upon screening'.

326 Control Appeal Committee Publication (October 2017) <https://www.grireland.ie/globalassets/rescource-centre/reports/control-appeal/control-appeal-committee-publication-report-october-2017.pdf> accessed 21 May 2024.

327 For a definition of an order of certiorari, see ch 11 fn 6.

328 (n 322) [4].

329 ibid.

330 ibid [38]. For a useful explanation of the case see Seosamh Gráinséir, 'High Court: Greyhound Owner Fails to Quash Finding that a Prohibited Substance Was Present in his Animals' (*Irish Legal News*, 13 November 2018) <https://www.irishlegal.com/articles/high-court-greyhound-owner-fails-to-quash-finding-that-a-prohibited-substance-was-present-in-his-animals> accessed 21 May 2024.

appealed for the Grand National and other such events to be banned. However, the banning of horseracing and indeed other sports where horses are used in the pursuit of excellence (show jumping and polo) would render the future of many thoroughbred horses uncertain. The discussion on Victoria demonstrated how changes have been made to improve the safety of the races. Improved veterinary care is now available at most events. However, the effect of such medical improvements is questionable considering the catastrophic limb injuries that horses commonly suffer: with the best medical attention available, if a horse breaks its leg, the result is usually euthanasia. Like the sport of boxing, if horseracing were banned it would drive the sport underground and consequently be unregulated. The respective governing bodies, in their endeavours to demonstrate an element of corporate responsibility, have attempted to address the issue of animal welfare within sport, restrictions on the use of the whip being an example. Most governing bodies liaise with animal-welfare organisations and include on their websites information on equine welfare and their commitment to the promotion and improving welfare standards in line with animal-welfare legislation. The banning of jumps racing would perhaps offer a compromise; however, it is recognised that a transitionary period would be needed, and important lessons can be learned from the Australian states that only permit flat racing.

15–106 The doping policies of animal sports highlight the custodial relationship between humans and the need for the strict liability principle to be upheld. The FEI and the racing bodies all endorse the strict liability standard and the *lex sportiva* of the CAS has been instrumental in recognising the importance of the welfare of the equine athlete. Public policy considerations are also important instigators in the increased regulation of animal sports. Public opinion is a key driver of change, and governing bodies must be seen to be respecting the welfare of equine athletes.

INDEX